BOOK PULGAR
VOLUME I

BOOK PULGAR
VOLUME I
by Angelos Gialamas

Graphic Design: Konstantakopoulou Panagiota

Copyright © 2019 by Angelos Gialamas. All rights reserved.

No part of this publication may be reproduced, stored in a retrieval system or transmitted in any form or by any means, electronic, mechanical, photocopying, recording or otherwise, without the prior written permission of the publisher.

Permissions may be sought directly from Angelos Gialamas. Brief quotations embodied in critical articles or reviews are permitted.

Part of this work is protected under USPTO application no. 62/326,830 *(Enhancing Stringed Instrument Learning With A Wearable Device)* and others.

Angelos Gialamas
3 Giannitson Street
Kalamata, 24100
Greece
https://www.guitartecnica.com

Sent feedback to feedback@guitartecnica.com
Visit online store at https://www.guitartecnica.com

Printed in United States of America
10 9 8 7 6 5 4 3 2 1

To place orders through Guitartecnica:
Tel: (0030) 27210 82838
Mob: (0030) 697 722 1180
E-mail: orders@guitartecnica.com

ISBN-10: 1-947596-01-2
ISBN-13: 978-1-947596-01-6

Significant discounts for bulk and educational institutions are available.
Please contact Angelos Gialamas at info@guitartecnica.com or (0030) 697 722 1180

Acknowledgments

This work would not have been possible without the loving support and contribution of many of you which I am very grateful. Your warmth and consistent encouragement throughout the years has truly been a lightning rod of creativity and hope for me and my music.

On this first ever publication endeavor, I would like to offer my sincere gratitude to my graphic designer Giota Konstantakopoulou for years of excellent collaboration and cooperation. Giota has been instrumental in organizing and presenting all graphical book elements since inception.

Special thanks to my dear friend, Niki Sakareli for her laborious translations. Eamonn Clerkin on his mechanical engineering contribution of the accompanied Rasgueados wearable device. Nikos Avraam for content curation. Petros Tsapralis, Christos Katsireas, Dimitra Margariti, Francesco Santini for their musical editorial review and assessment. Maria Baka, Gioula Nikitea and Kostantina Vraka for their positive attribution of book authoring.

A heartfelt thank you to Giorgos Gialamas and Eleni Asproudi for teaching and instilling in me strong music foundations. Early introduced influences by Giorgos and Eleni resonate strongly in me. Their warmth and tenderness, their countless hours of instruction, commitment and dedication to their pupil, have inspired me to produce this volume of work. I am and always be indebted to them, for the love and consideration I have received.

I would like to also thank my loving spouse Amalia, daughters Christina and Fotini. Throughout the years, their discreet presence, patience and tolerance has cultivated an environment of tranquility and serenity for me to exist and work uninterrupted. Their consistent encouragement and attention is a true testament of selfless love.

Angelo Gialamas

Kalamata,
August 1, 2017

PULGAR

A COMPREHENSIVE, METHODICAL, STEP-BY-STEP TEACHING METHOD OF THE PULGAR TECHNIQUE FOR FLAMENCO GUITAR

The pulgar plays a critical role in the flamenco guitar technique space. However, if you try to find a comprehensive bibliographic reference to pulgar you will be vastly disappointed. These references are either fragmented, incomplete or very few exercises are proposed or offered for practice. These small available collections of exercises are not sufficiently large for a student to practice and effectively learn the pulgar techniques.

The present two-volume, book series refer exclusively to pulgar exercises. In these two volumes, I have tried and provided ample material, taking into consideration the particularities of pulgar practice. Particularities, such as the force of the stroke (the simultaneous stroke of more than one strings is necessary), the precision of the stroke (since the pulgar can strike different adjacent or remote strings) or the delicacy of the stroke (the mastering of striking one, two or more strings simultaneously).

In this book, I have tried as much as possible to give sufficient material within different variations, so that boredom and fatigue that emerges from the monotonous repetition of one or few exercises is eliminated.

Basic formulas of exercises are proposed and off these, plenty of variations are described. I believe the greater the number and pool of exercise variations there are, the better the student learns, since it reawakens interest and jolts enthusiasm. The message, I want to convey to the readers is that, "it is better to perform 100 exercises, a single time rather perform one exercise 100 times".

As mentioned, the contents of these book series refer to the pulgar in flamenco guitar space. Many of these exercises can benefit the classical guitar student learning the pulgar techniques. The student is asked to choose those exercises that upwards to downwards (from the 6th to the 1st string).

Also, many of the exercises offered are open to different interpretations with the insertion of fingers **i**, **m** and **a** and the combination of the pulgar exercises with these fingers. In other words, many exercises can be performed with the fingerings **pi, pm, pa**, or **ip, mp, ap**.

In some chapters this is briefly noted. Upcoming work will include these proposed **i**, **m** and **a** finger combinations of pulgar practice exercises.

HOW TO USE THIS BOOK

As mentioned the learner can practice on the exercises of the volume in a different but equally important way with the insertion of index (**i**), middle finger (**m**) and ring finger (**a**).
The way of performance after the insertion of these fingers is the following:

Regarding double strokes: (in combination and on the same string)
pi, pm, pa or **ip, mp, ap**

Regarding triple strokes: (in combination and on the same string)
pip, pmp, pap or **ipi, mpm, apa**

Regarding quad strokes: (in combination and on the same string)
pipi, pmpm, papa or **ipip, mpmp, apap**

Other ways of practice are the following:

For the double strokes:	pipm	ipmp
	pmpa	apmp
	pipa	apip

For the triple strokes:	pip - ipi	ipi - pip
	pmp - mpm	mpm - pmp
	pap - apa	apa - pap

For the quad strokes:	pipm	ipmp
	pmpi	mpip
	pmpa	mpap
	papm	apmp
	pipa	ipap
	papi	apip

SYMBOLS

The comprehension of the exercises is based on the symbols as described below:

1/. The six lines represent the strings of the guitar as follows:

```
——————————————— 1st
——————————————— 2nd
——————————————— 3rd
——————————————— 4th
——————————————— 5th
——————————————— 6th
```

2/. The fingers of the right hand are symbolized with letters as follows:

      p   pulgar
      i   index finger
      m   middle finger
      a   ring finger
      x   little finger

3/. The fingers of the left hand are symbolized with numbers as follows:

      1   index finger
      2   middle finger
      3   ring finger
      4   little finger

4/. The letters or numbers placed on the lines indicate the stroke of the string or strings which the lines represent.

5/. The symbol ($>$) placed on top of a note / notes indicates the intonation of the specific note / notes.

6/. The symbol (G) indicates Golpe.

7/. The symbol (↑) and (↓) shows the direction of the stroke with the corresponding finger / fingers which is / are noted on the top of it.

eg. i (im)   or below it eg. ↑ ↑
     ↑   ↑   p i

More specifically:

The symbol (↑) indicates stroke with direction from the 6th to the 1st string.
The symbol (↓) indicates stroke with direction from the 1st to the 6th string.

8/. The symbol G̵ with the index finger on the top of the arrow and G or the symbol G̵ with the middle finger on the top of the arrow and G shows the direction of the stroke from the 6th to the 1st string with simultaneous Golpe stroke by the index or middle finger.

9/. The symbol of the small circle (○) that encloses one of the following finger combinations ((im) (ia) (ix) (ma) (mx) (ax)) indicates simultaneous stroke with the two fingers shown in the circle.

10/. The symbol (□) indicates that the notes enclosed in it are played without support (tirando), but when they are not enclosed they are played both ways (tirando and apoyando).

Example:

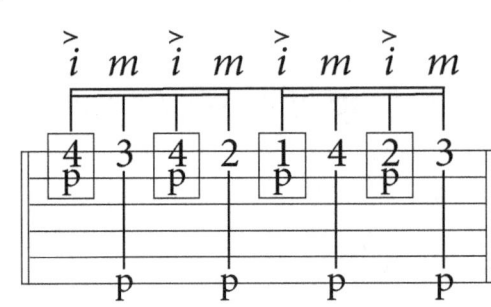

NUMBER SEQUENCES:

Eight numbers in total which represent the fingers of the left hand and are placed on a line that represents the guitar string.
The term chromatic scale of a string or number sequence is used.
Example:

‖ 1 4 2 4 3 4 2 4 ‖

CHROMATIC SCALES of two adjacent strings:

Eight numbers in total are placed in two adjacent strings.
Example:

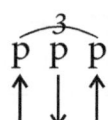

THUMB STROKE:

The double stroke of the pulgar is noted in this book mainly in one way:

p p
↑ ↓

The triple stroke of the pulgar is noted mainly in one way as triplet:

 3
p p p
↑ ↓ ↑

The quad stroke of the pulgar is noted in the book mainly in one way:

p p p p
↑ ↓ ↑ ↓

See variations of the exercises by changing the direction of the pulgar stroke in the double, triple or quad stroke.

VARIATIONS:

A/ In double stroke: p p
                       ↑ ↑

B/ In triple stroke: a/ ³ p p p   b/ ³ p p p
                           ↑ ↑ ↓   ↑ ↑ ↑

C/ In quad stroke: a/ p p p p   b/ p p p p   c/ p p p p   d/ p p p p
                       ↑ ↓ ↑ ↑   ↑ ↑ ↓ ↑   ↑ ↑ ↑ ↓   ↑ ↑ ↑ ↑

Once the learner is familiar with one way of striking the pulgar he / she can change the striking ways contributing the most to his / her practice.

The following formula for example,

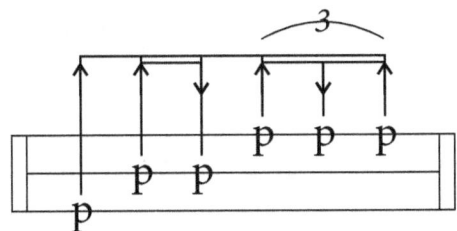

can be also played by changing the direction of the pulgar stroke as follows:

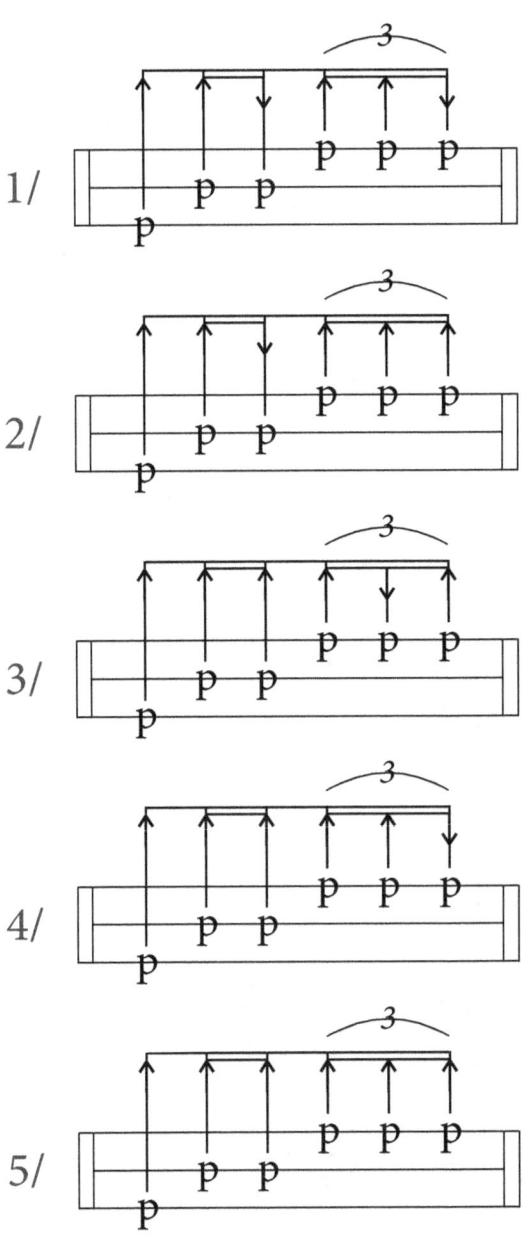

NOTE

The present book contains exercises on the pulgar and only on the pulgar (without the participation of the index, middle and ring finger) on three or four adjacent strings. These exercises can also refer to remote strings as described below. The exercises contain single - double - triple or quad stroke of the pulgar on one string and position. For the direction of the stroke of the pulgar arrows are used.

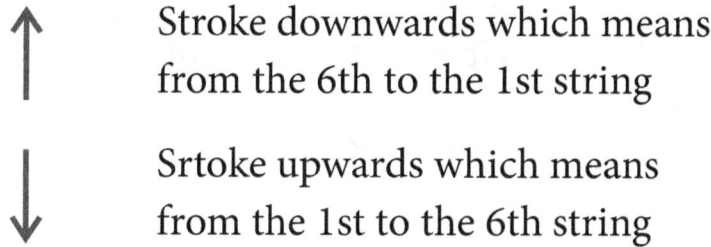

The exercises of the present volume are performed mainly by the pulgar in the following ways:

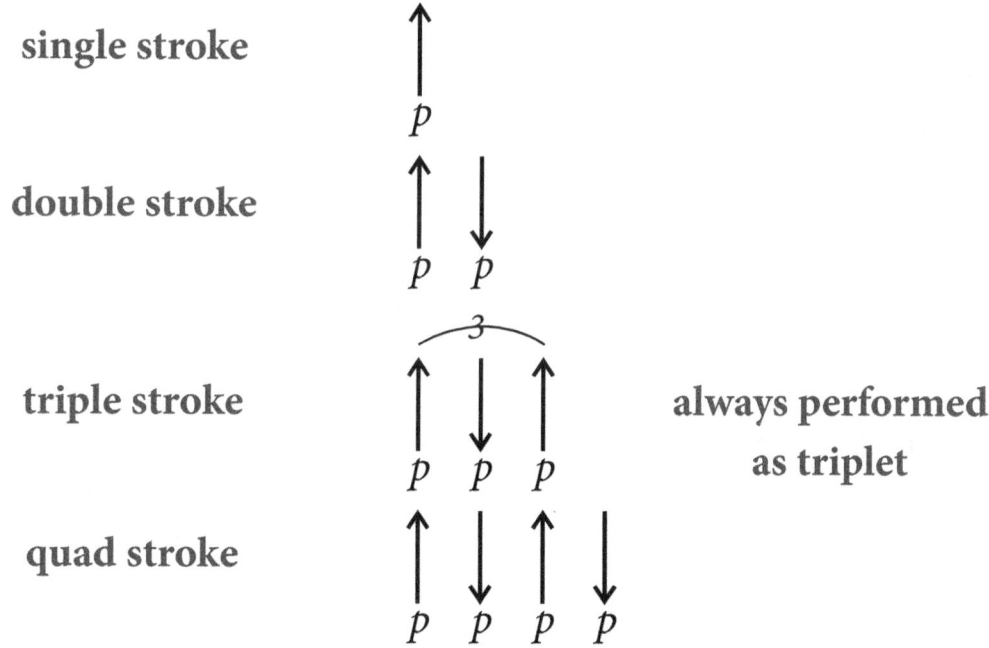

Of course all the exercises can be performed with pulgar stroke towards only one downwards direction (↑). Other ways that can be implemented for the quad stroke of the pulgar are the following as already mentioned.

*Within each formula the single - double - triple and quad strokes have the same duration, they are isochronous.

*The exercises of the present volume are supposed to be performed on adjacent strings. However, they can be also performed on remote strings with the insertion of a string / strings. A description on this follows. The exercises include single - double - triple and quad stroke of the pulgar within each formula. The single, double, triple and quad strokes are isochronous unless described differently.

LEFT HAND POSITIONS

The pulgar exercise in chapters 1 and 2 that follow is carried out on an accord of three notes which the left hand holds and is performed either on three adjacent strings or with the insertion of strings as schematically depicted below:

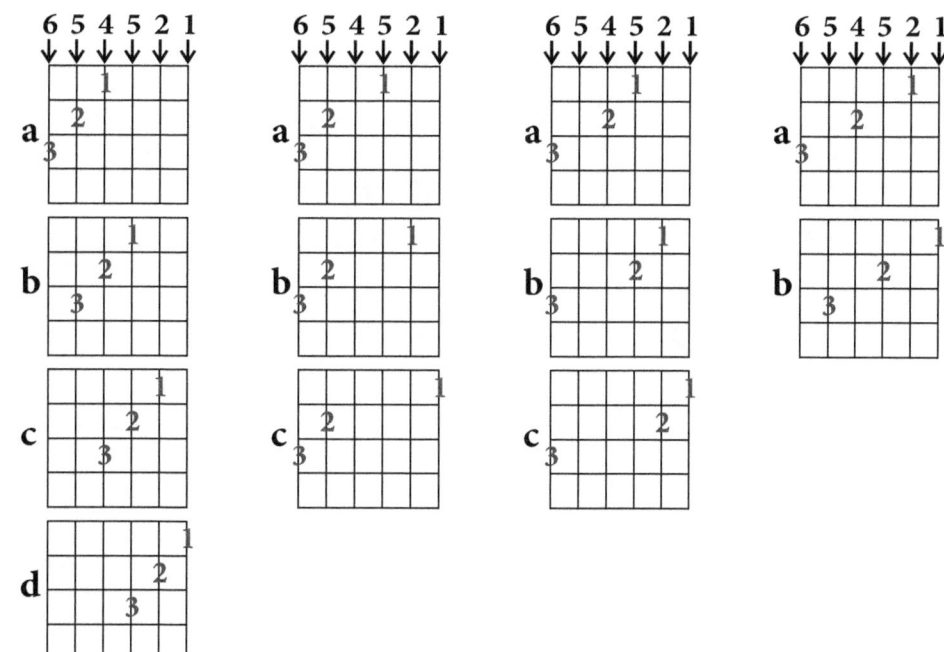

Apart from practicing the pulgar on adjacent strings the exercises can be performed on remote strings too, which means application of the exercises in the 2nd, 3rd and 4th paradigm.

In the 2nd column the 3rd and 2nd finger are stable on the 6th and 5th string and the first finger is remote by 1 string (presses the 3rd string), by 2 strings (presses the 2nd string) and by 3 strings (presses the 1st string).

In the 3rd column the 3rd finger is stable on the 6th string and the 2nd and 1st finger are remote by 1 string (they press the 4th and 3rd string), by 2 strings (they press the 3rd and 2nd string) and by 3 strings (they press the 2nd and 1st string).

In the 4th column the practicing of the pulgar contains 1 string between the 3rd, 2nd and 1st left hand finger (first position on the 6th, 4th and 2nd string and second position on the 5th, 3rd and 1st string.

Different triad (left hand) means different degrees of difficulty. The learner is highly recommended to chose the easiest triplet to start practicing.

TABLE OF CONTENTS

CHAPTER 1 - page 1
UNIT 1 page 3

Exercise on pulgar on three adjacent strings which includes single, double and triple strokes (triplets) in different variations as far as the direction of pulgar stroke and the combinations of strokes within each Formula are concerned.

UNIT 2 page 113

Exercise on pulgar on three adjacent strings which includes one, two or three quad strokes. Different variations as far as the direction of pulgar stroke and the combinations of strokes are concerned (single + double + quad etc).

CHAPTER 2 - page 291

Single - double - triple and quad pulgar stroke on three adjacent strings in various stroke combinations and with changes in the direction of pulgar stroke.

CHAPTER 3 - page 347

Single - double - triple and quad pulgar stroke on four adjacent strings in various stroke combinations and with changes in the direction of pulgar stroke.

CHAPTER 4 - page 397

Single - double - triple and quad pulgar stroke on four adjacent strings within each Formula. Matching of each Formula with its opposite.

CHAPTER 5 - page 417

Exercises for the strengthening of pulgar stroke. Exercises that combine the stroke of one string with two or three strings simultaneously.

CHAPTER 1
EXERCISE ON PULGAR ON THREE ADJACENT STRINGS

UNIT 1

Exercise on pulgar on three adjacent strings
which includes single, double and triple strokes (triplets)
in different variations as far as the direction of pulgar stroke
and the combinations of strokes within each formula are concerned.

§ I

Exercise on pulgar with single stroke on three adjacent strings and towards one direction from the 6th to the 1st string. 6 Formulas in total.

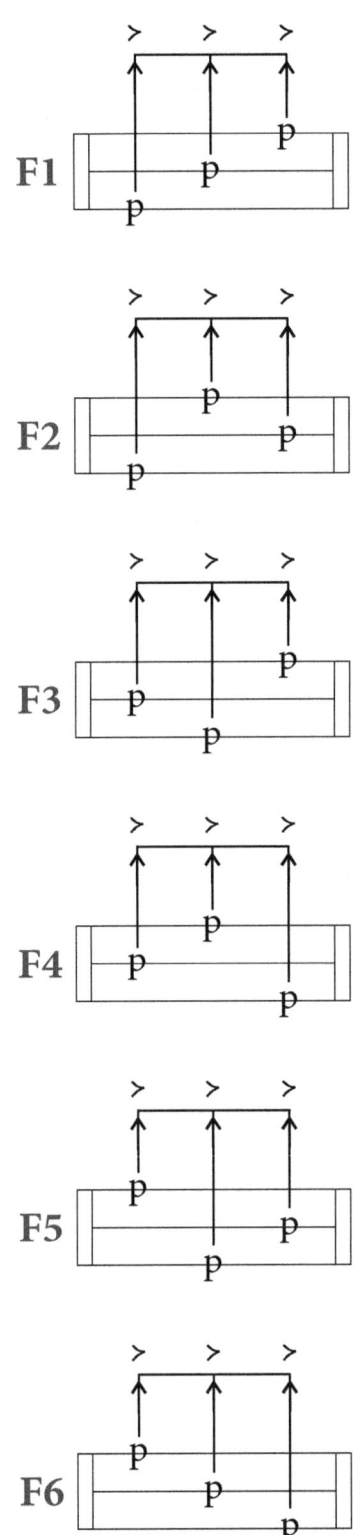

§ II

Exercise on pulgar with two single and one double stroke on three adjacent strings in each Formula. Three variations with 6 Formulas in each one. The first Formula of each variation is cited below. Isochronous playing of single and double stroke within each Formula.

VARIATION I

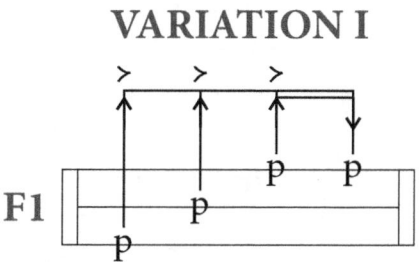

VARIATION II

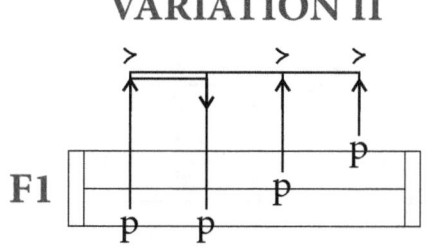

VARIATION III

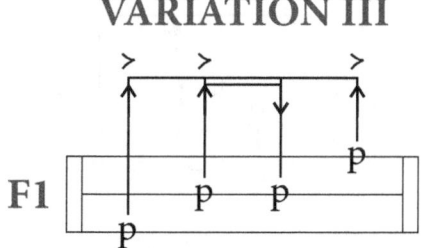

You can also practice beyond the described way with stroke of the pulgar towards one direction.

Example: VARIATION I

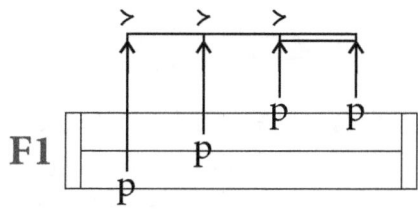

| VARIATION I | VARIATION II | VARIATION III |

§ III

Exercise on pulgar on three adjacent strings with one single and two double strokes. The single and double strokes are isochronous. The exercise includes three variations depending on the sequence of single and double strokes within the Formula. The first Formula on the three variations is cited below.

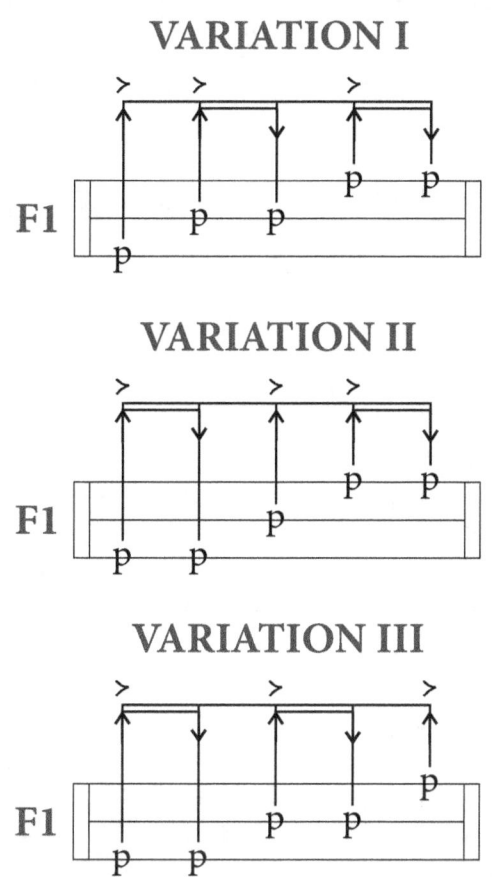

Each variation depending on the pulgar stroke can be carried out in four different ways which are cited in detail.

Practice on all variations and in all performance ways not only on three adjacent strings but also on inserted strings as described in the beginning of the book.

We should note at this point that the following exercises it was considered appropriate to cite all the variations with all the ways of pulgar striking as the procedure would visually facilitate their perception. Practice in all ways initially on three adjacent strings. Experiment also with inserted strings paying special attention to the 5th, 3rd and 1st string.

VARIATION I
WAYS OF PERFORMANCE
1st   2nd

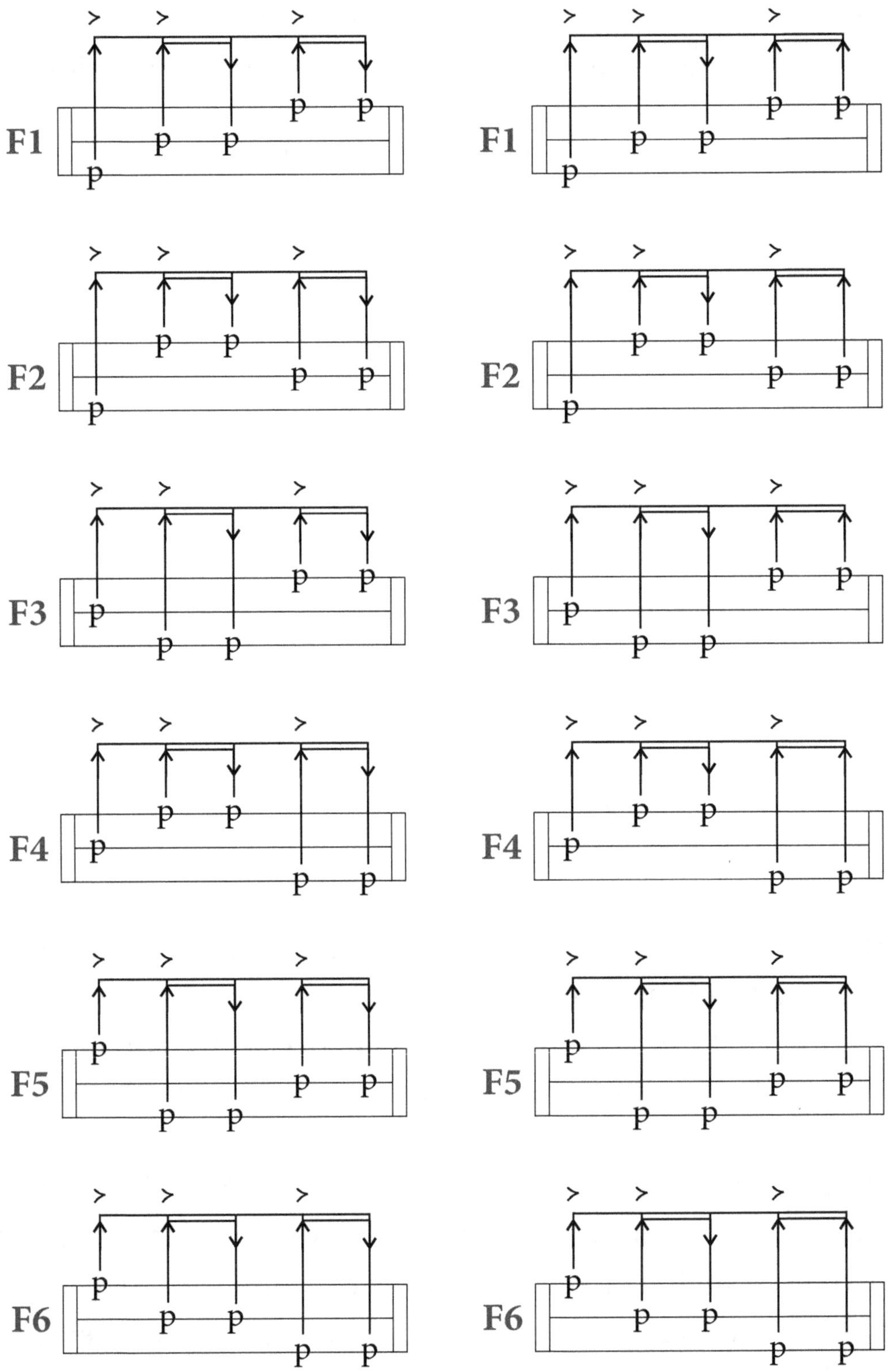

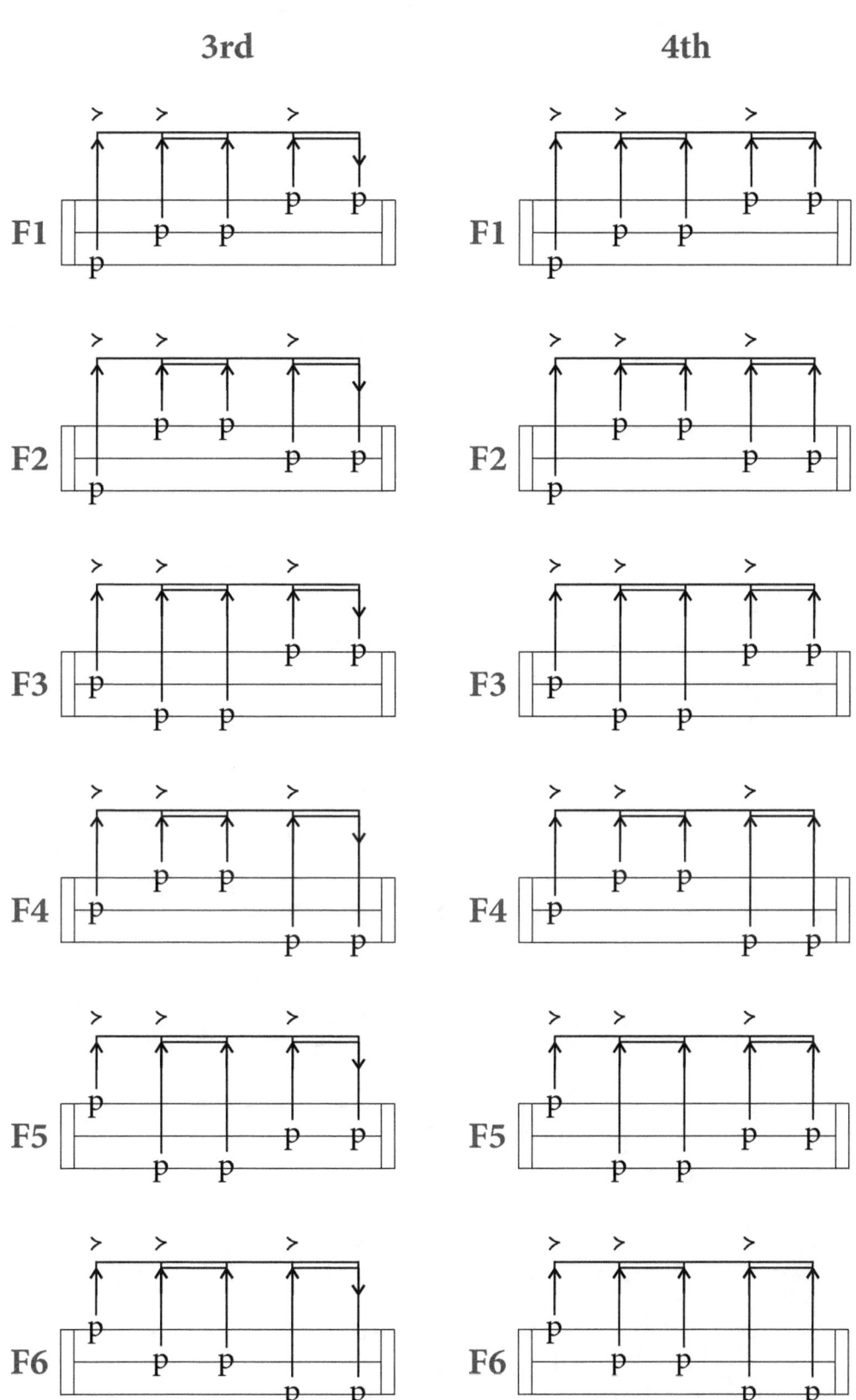

VARIATION II
WAYS OF PERFORMANCE
1st   2nd

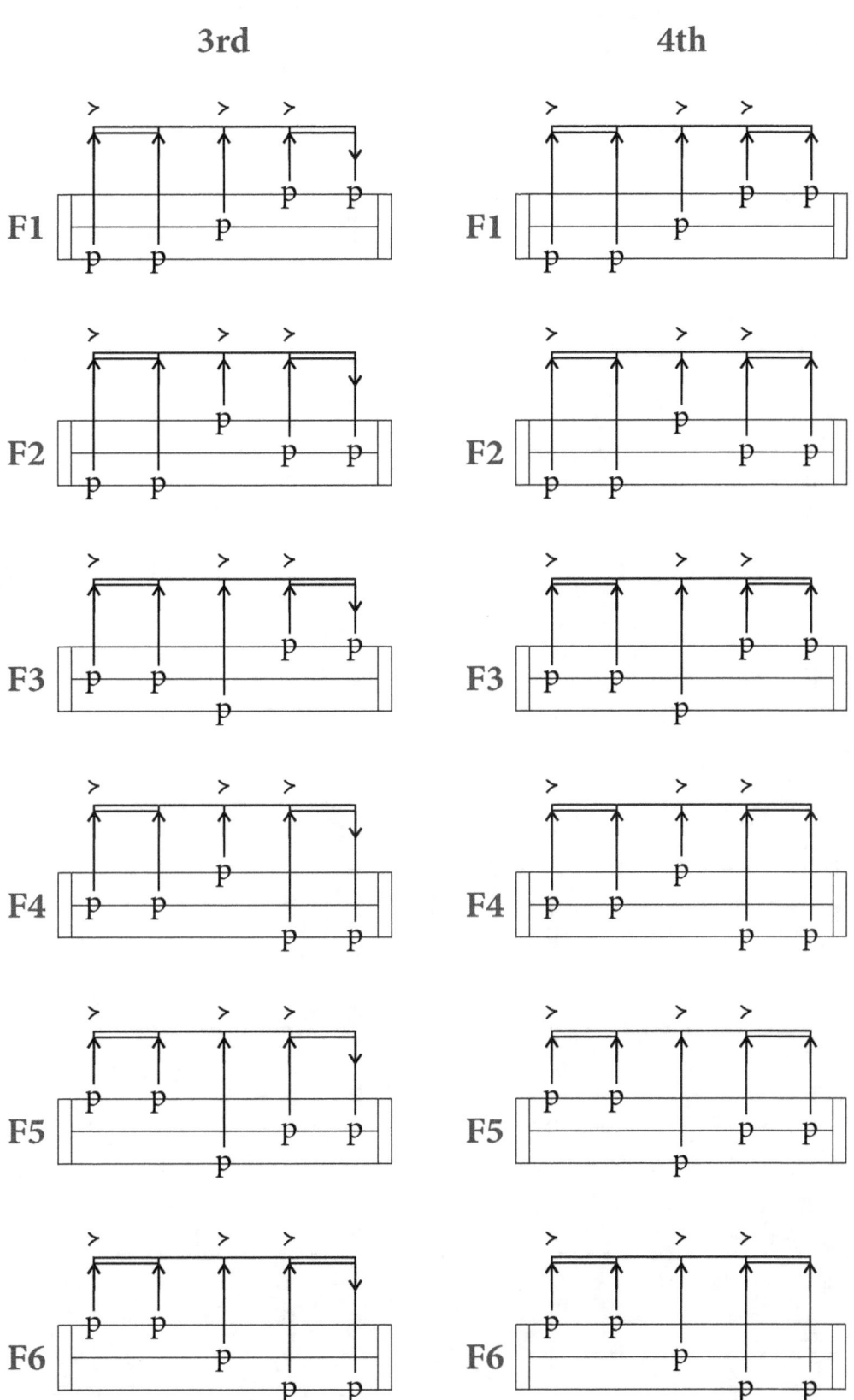

VARIATION III
WAYS OF PERFORMANCE
1st   2nd

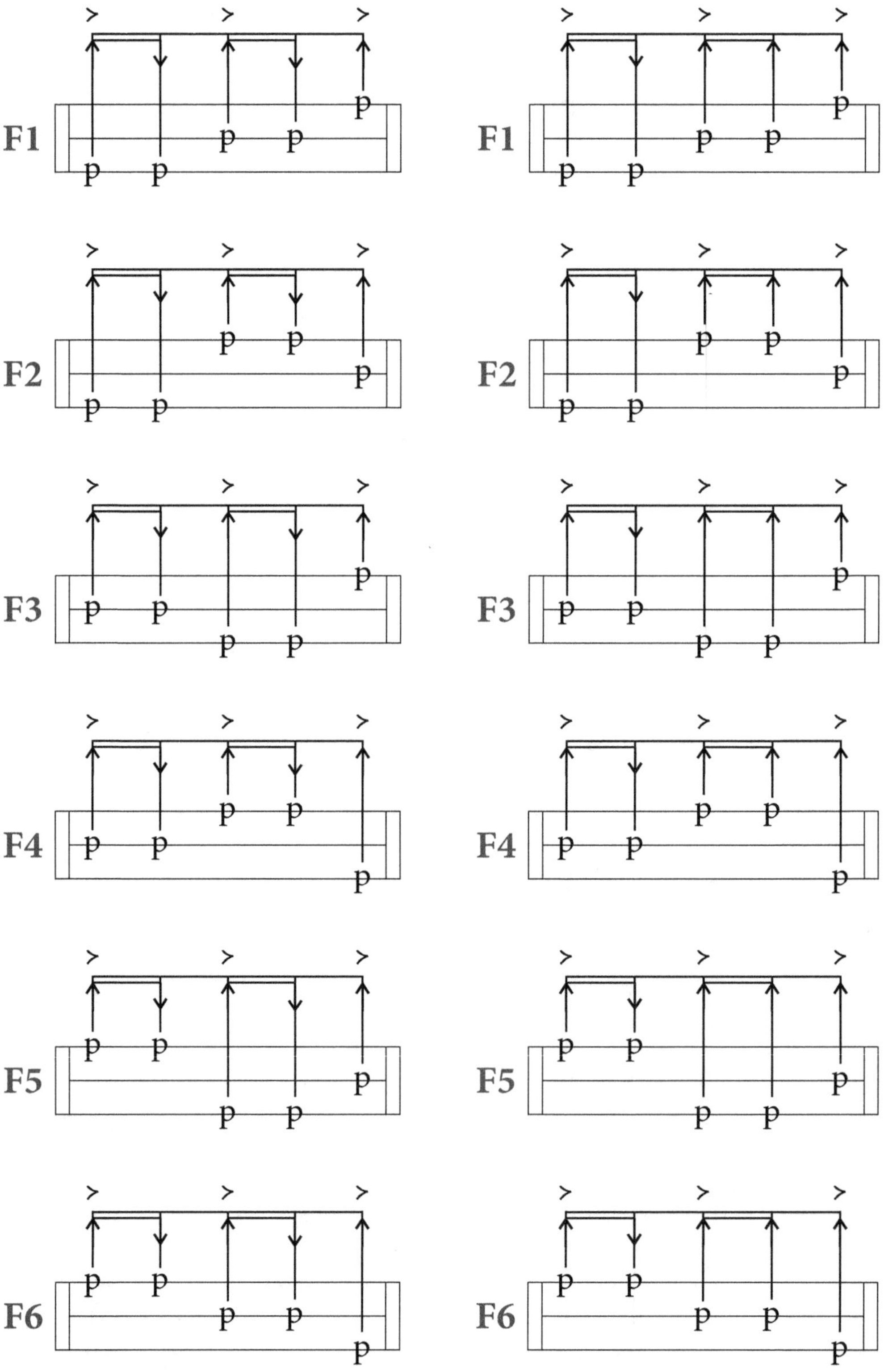

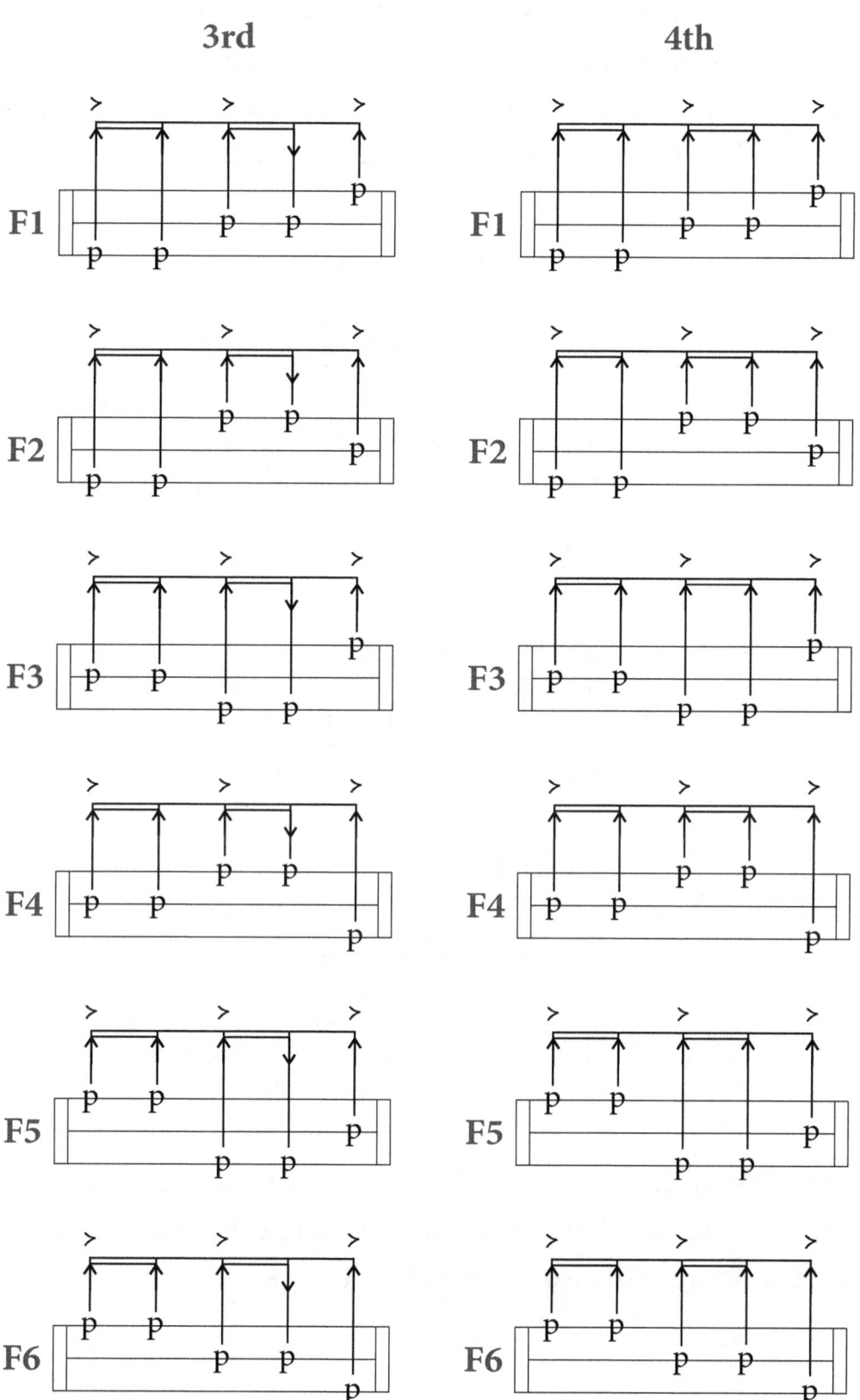

§ IV

Exercise on pulgar on three adjacent strings with one triple (triplet) and two single strokes. The single and triple strokes are isochronous. The exercise contains three variations depending on the sequence of the triple and single strokes within the Formula. The first Formula of the three variations is cited below.

VARIATION I

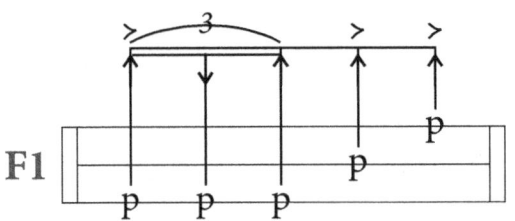

VARIATION II

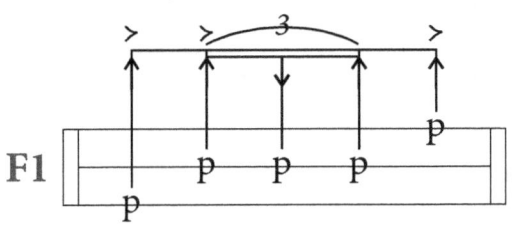

VARIATION III

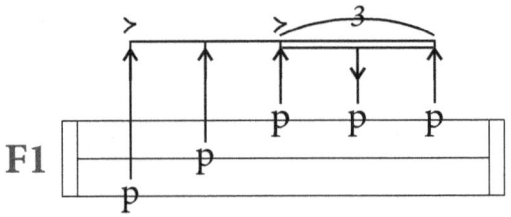

Each variation depending on the pulgar stroke can be carried out in three different ways. Practice on all variations and in all performance ways not only on three adjacent strings but also on inserted strings.

VARIATION I
WAYS OF PERFORMANCE

1st | 2nd | 3rd

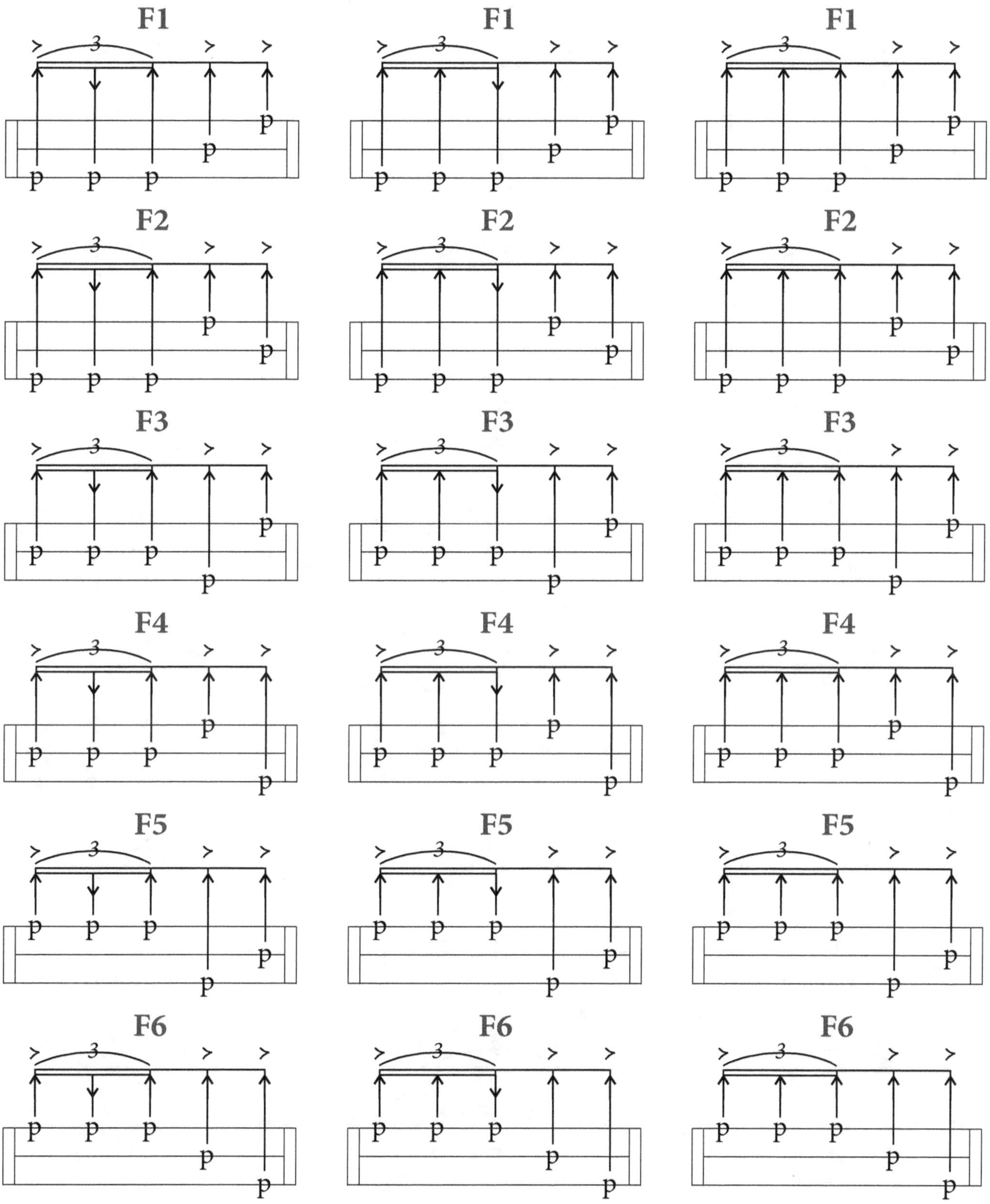

VARIATION II
WAYS OF PERFORMANCE

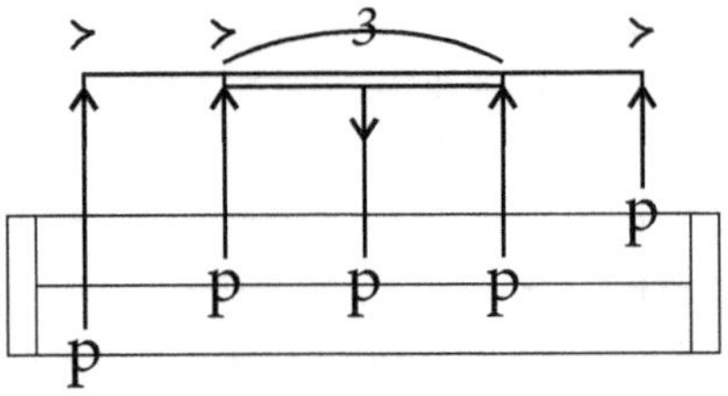

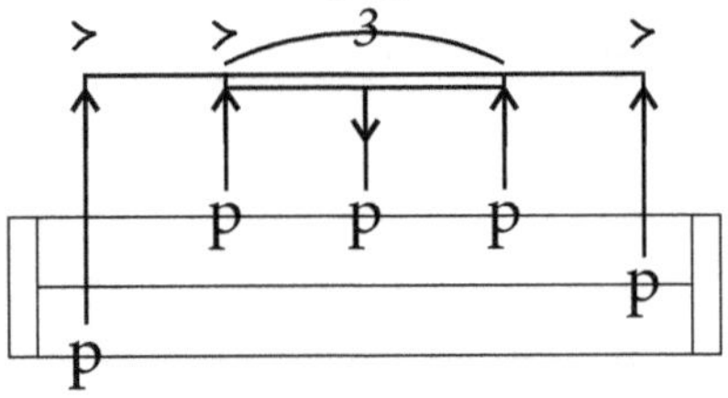

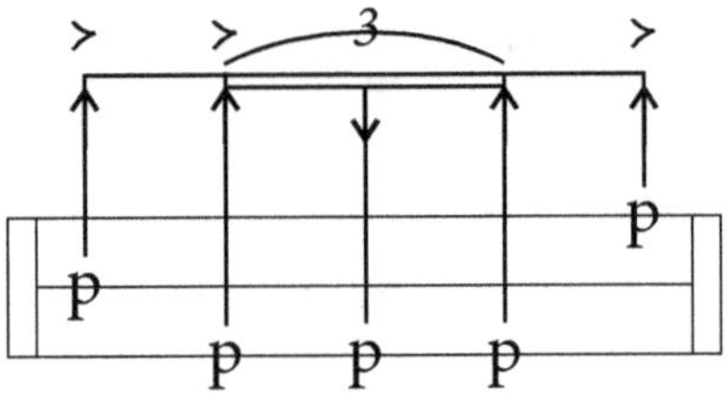

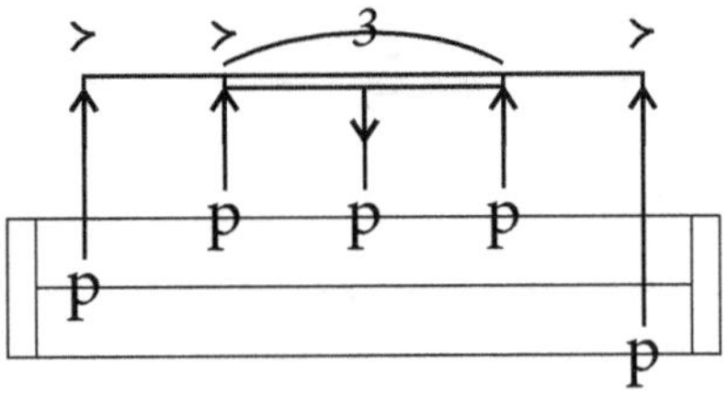

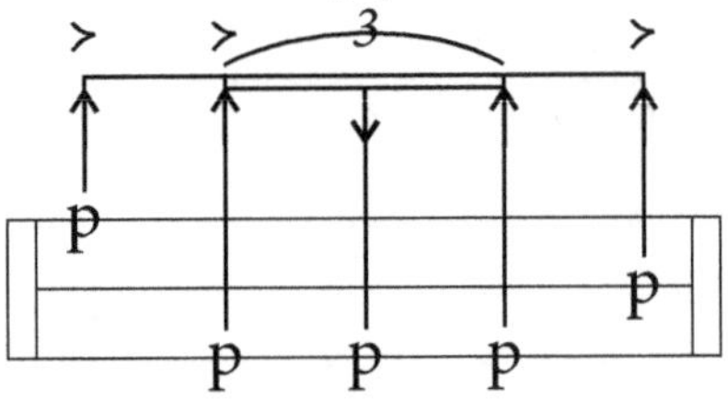

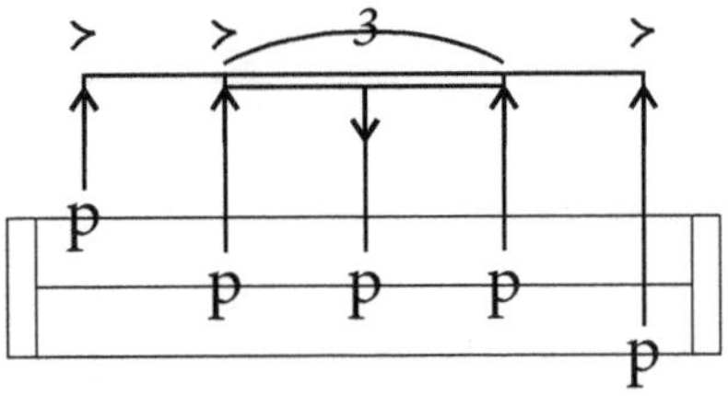

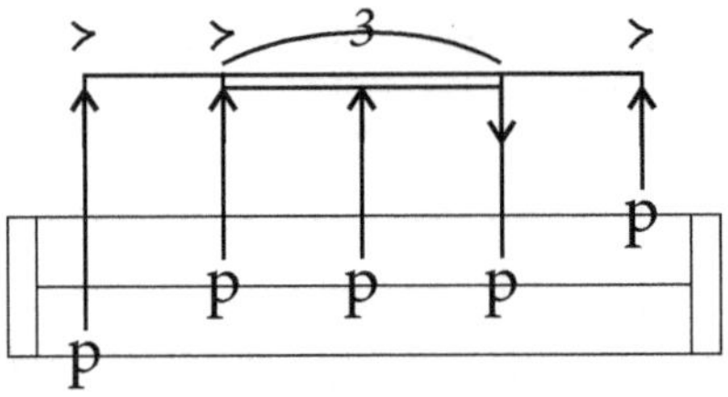

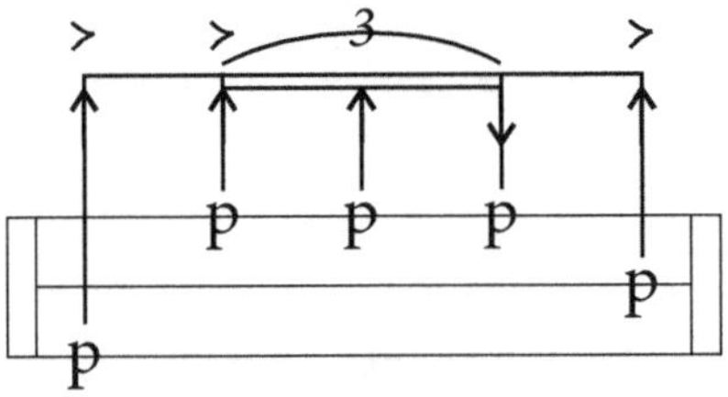

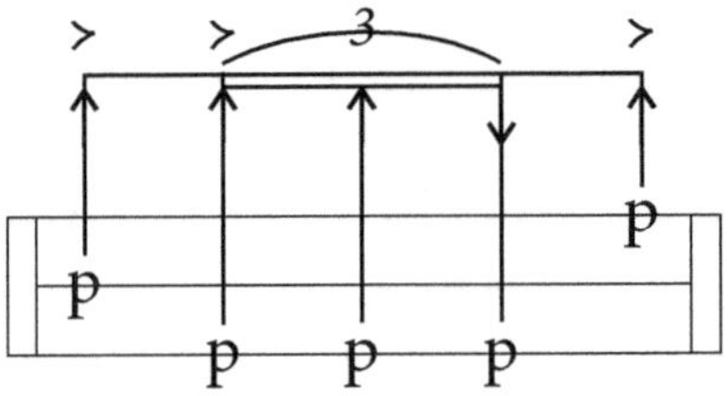

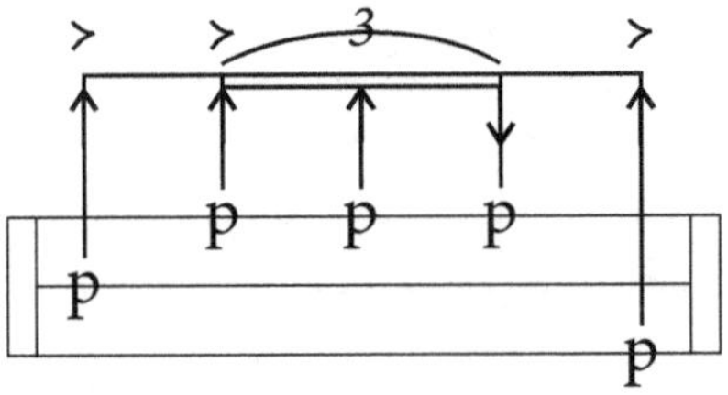

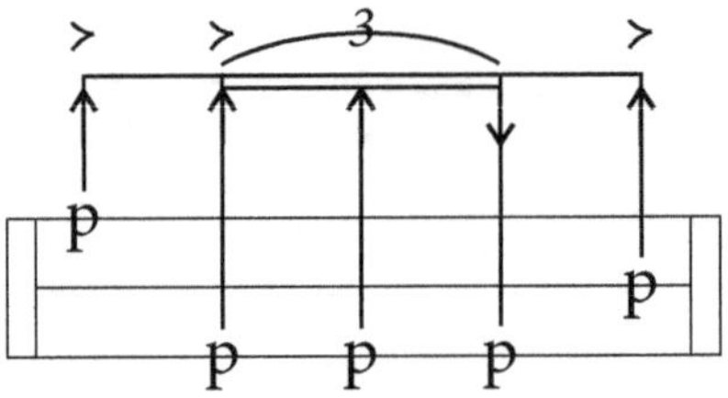

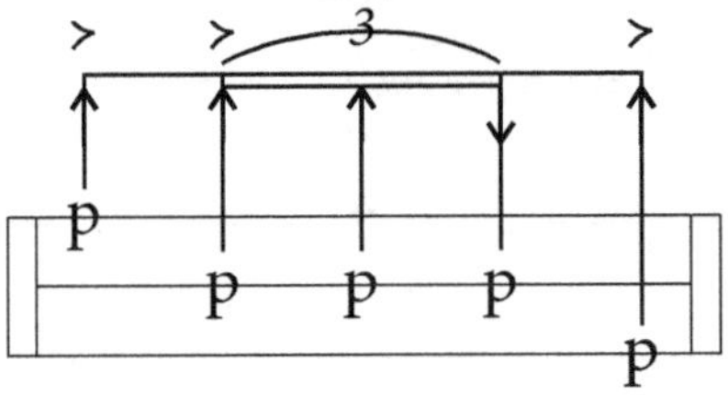

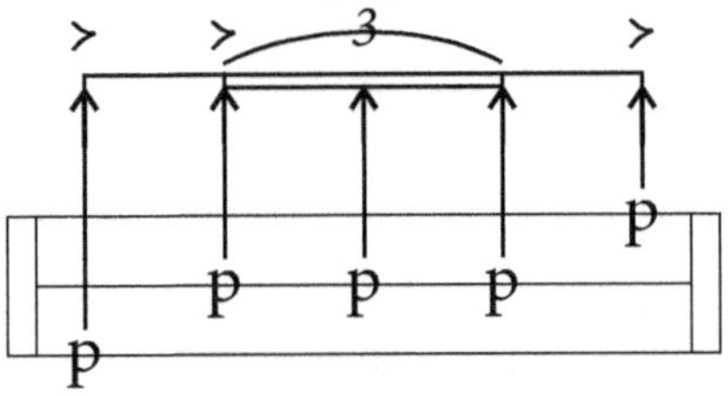

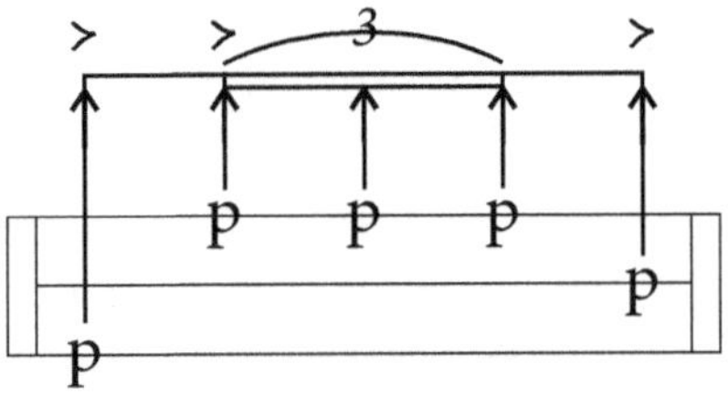

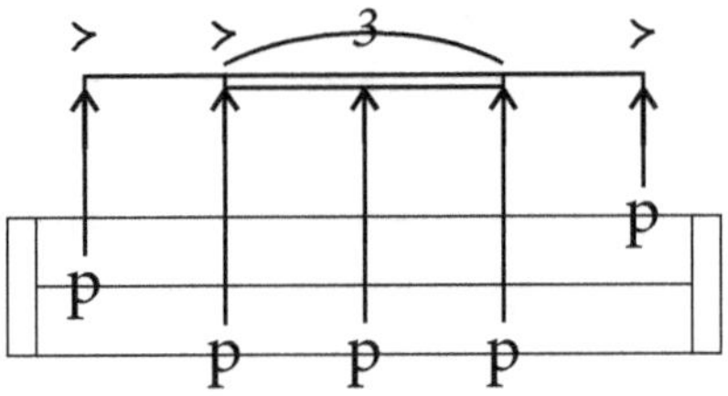

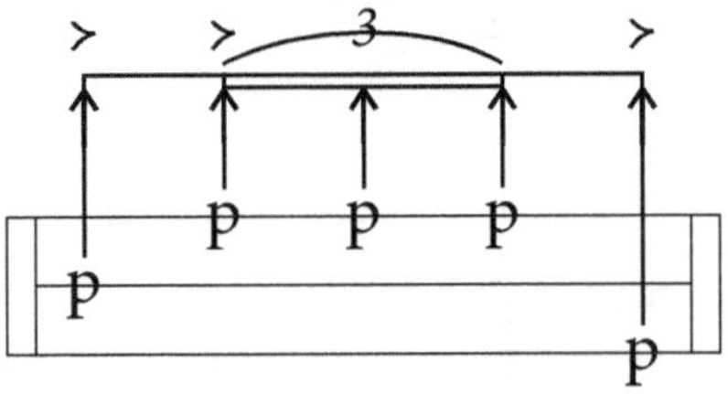

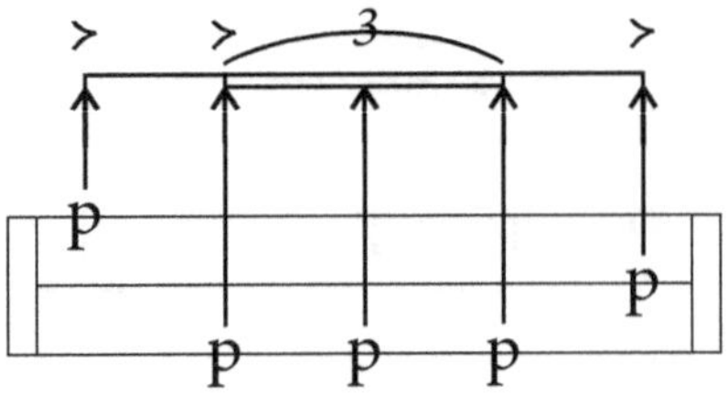

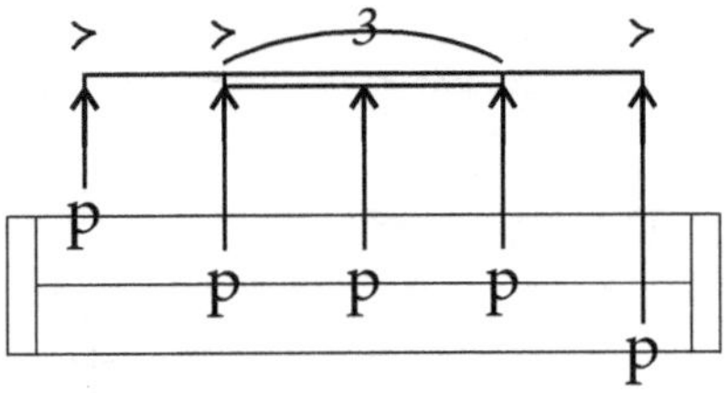

VARIATION III
WAYS OF PERFORMANCE

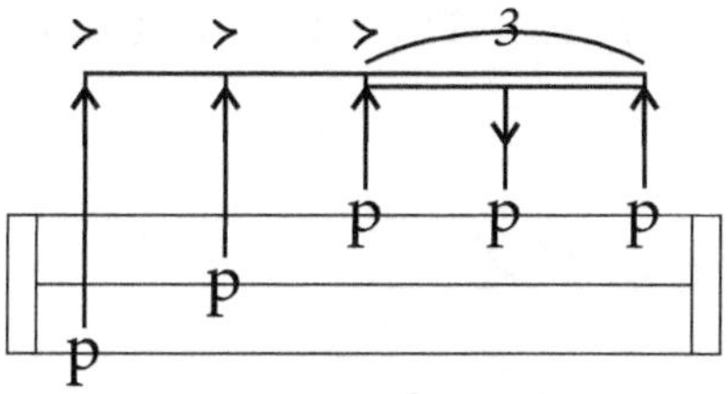

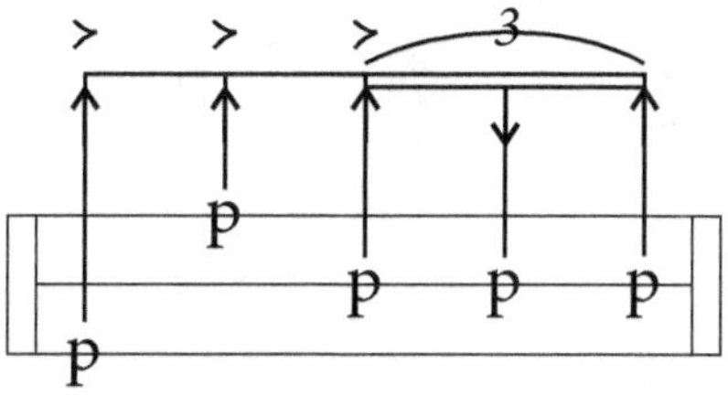

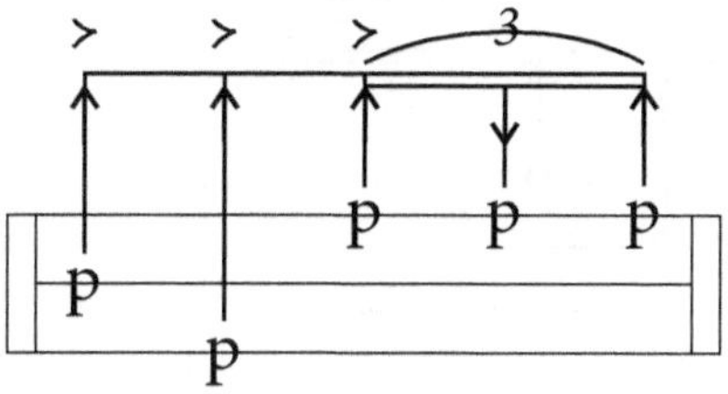

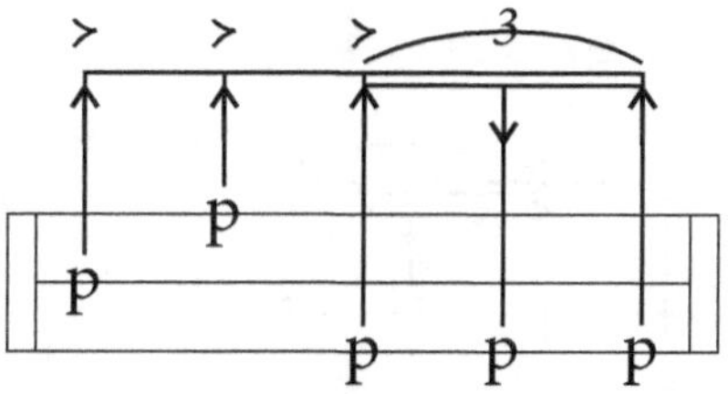

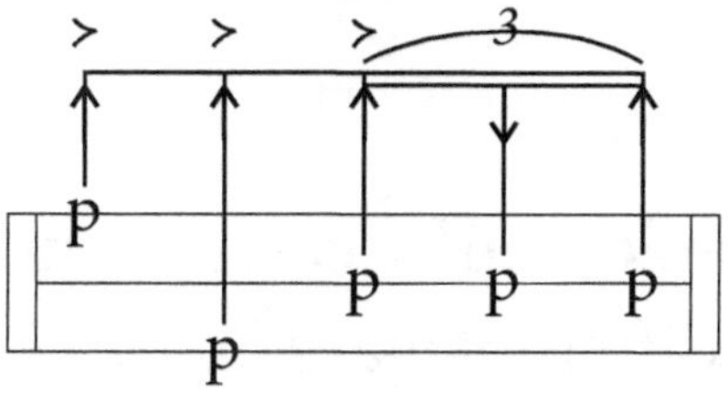

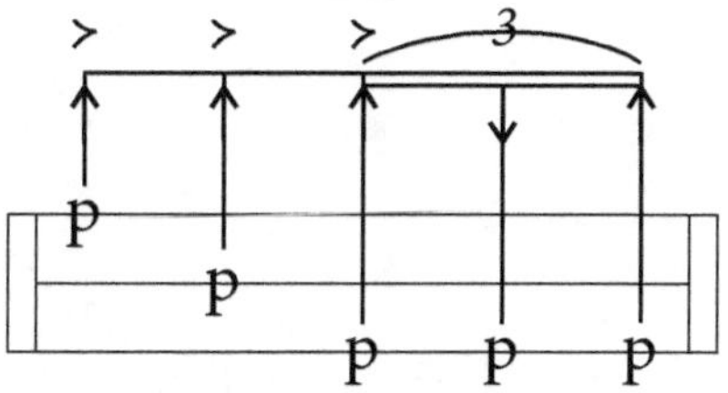

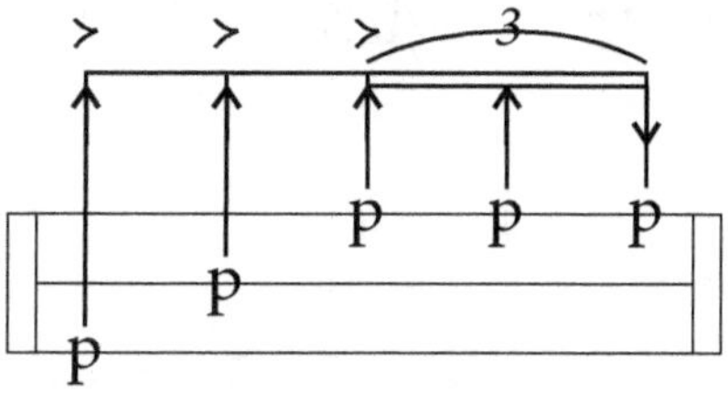

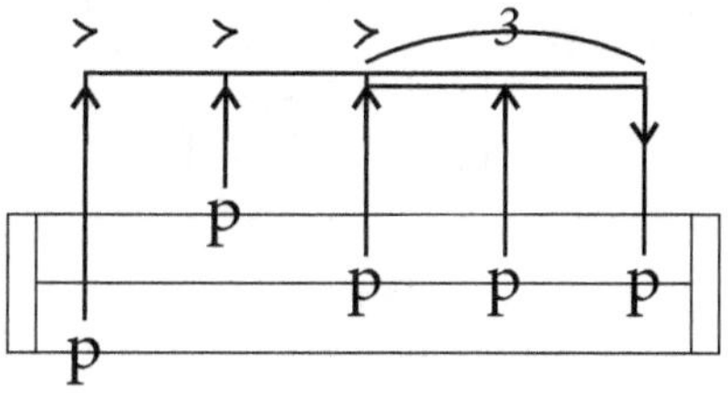

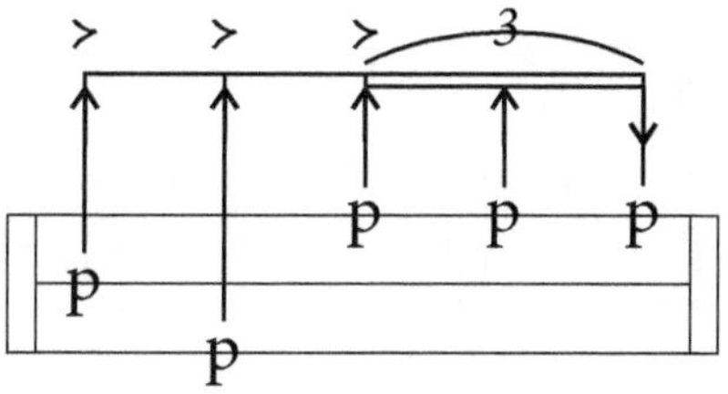

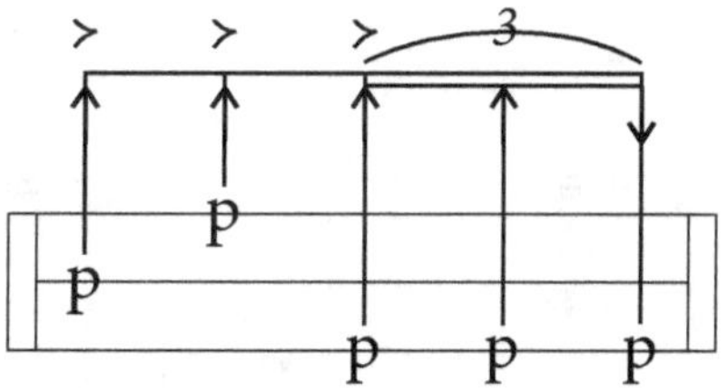

1st   2nd   3rd

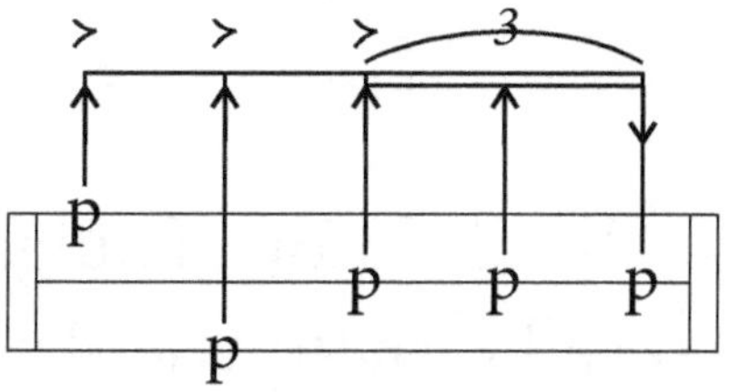

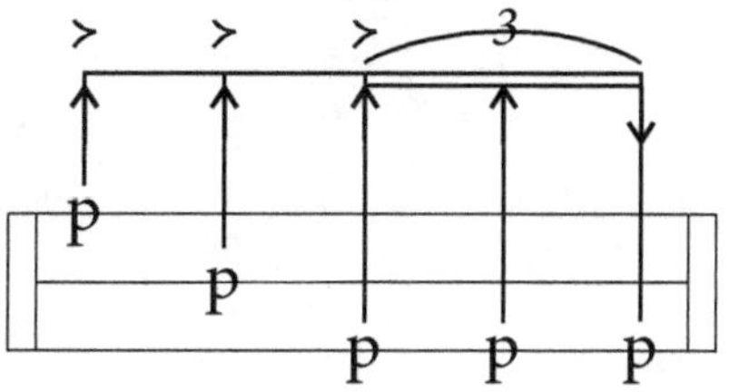

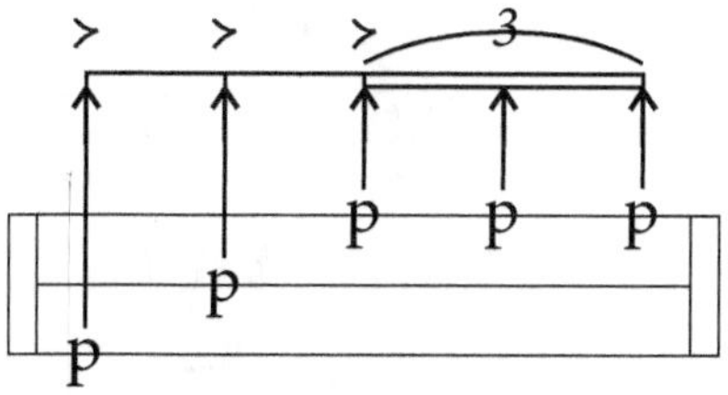

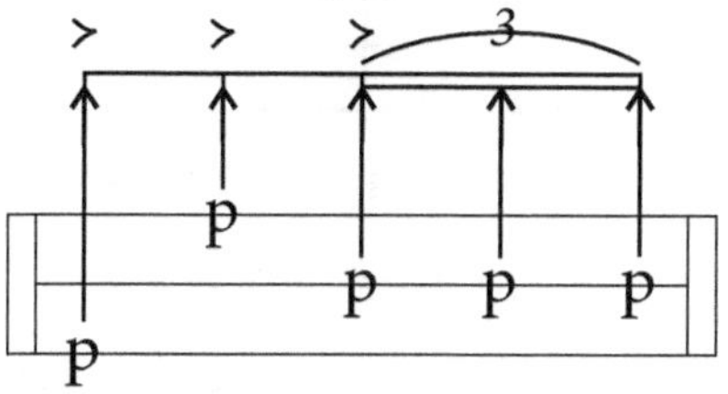

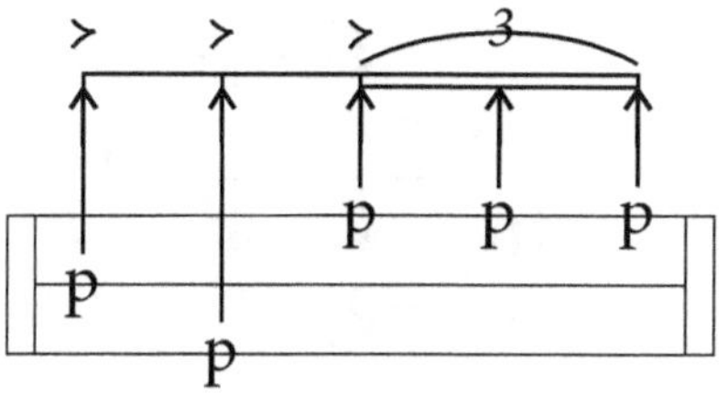

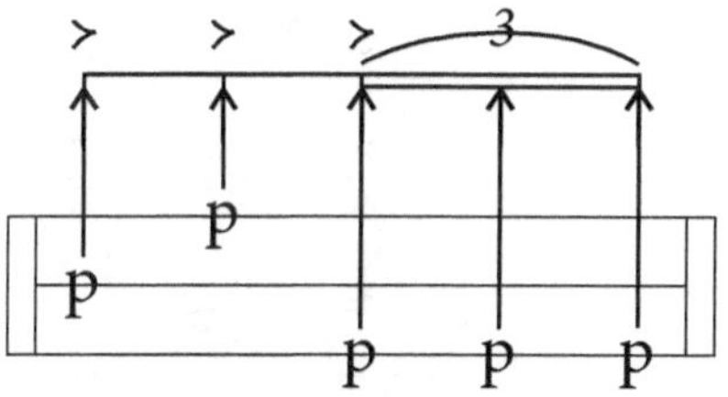

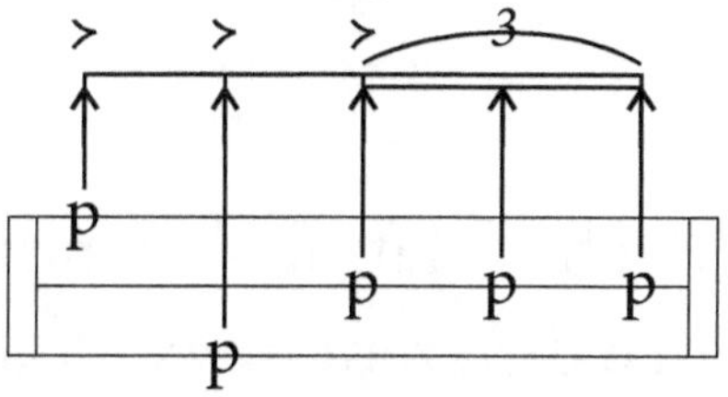

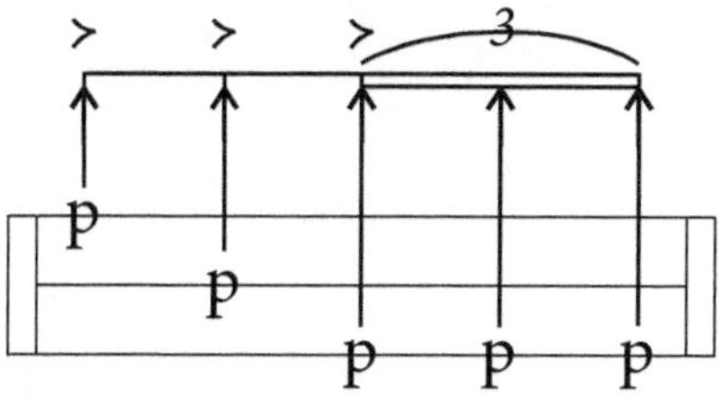

§ V

Exercise on pulgar on three adjacent strings with one single, one double and one triple (triplet) stroke. The single, double and triple stroke are isochronous. The exercise includes 6 variations depending on the position of the single, double and triple stroke within the Formula. The first Formula of each variation is cited below.

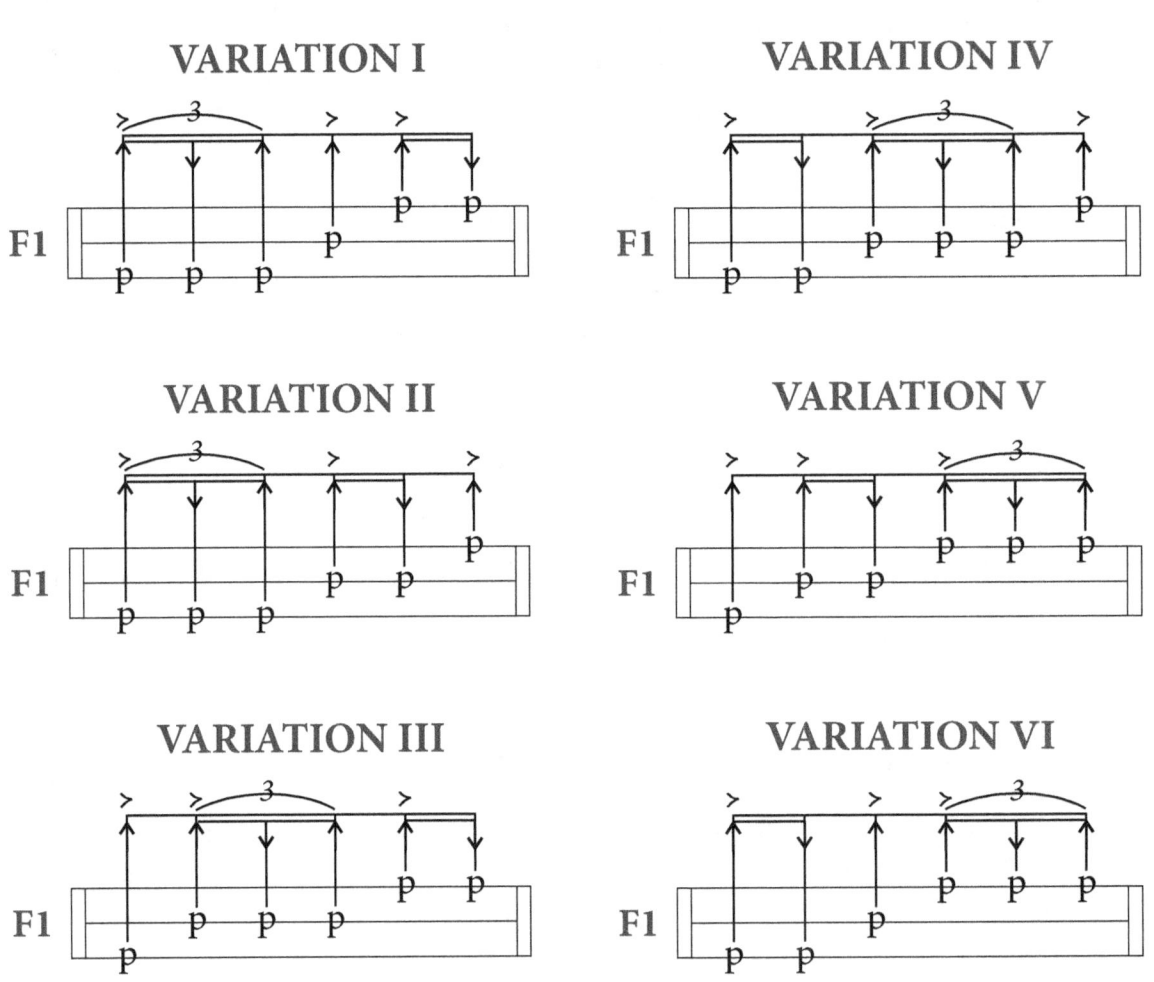

Each variation depending on the direction of pulgar stroke can be carried out in 6 different ways. Practice on all variations and in all different ways on three adjacent strings and also with inserted strings.

VARIATION I
WAYS OF PERFORMANCE

1st   **2nd**

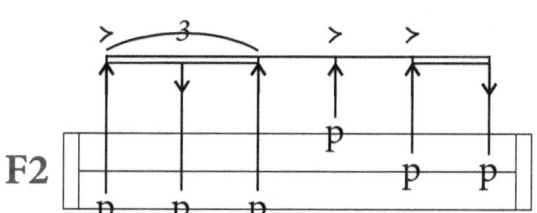 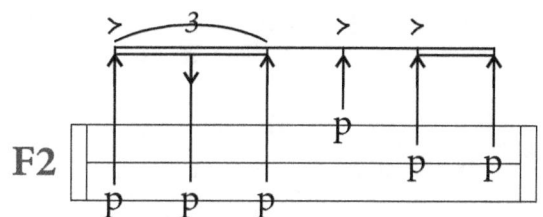

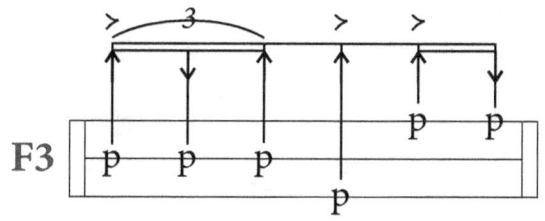 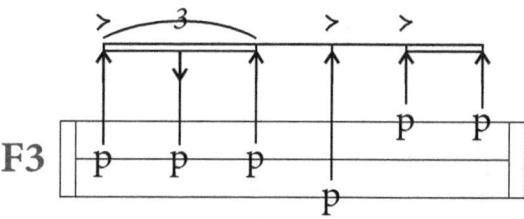

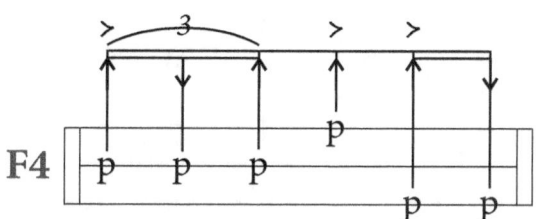 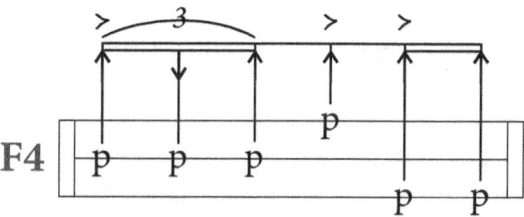

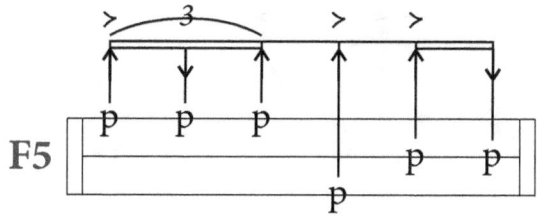 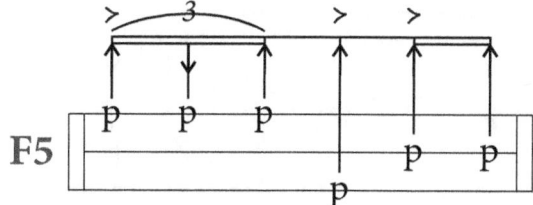

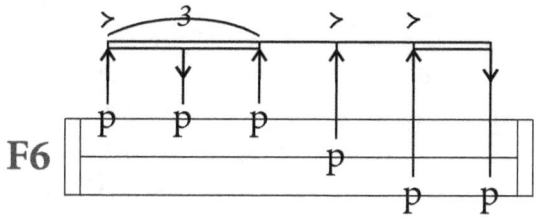 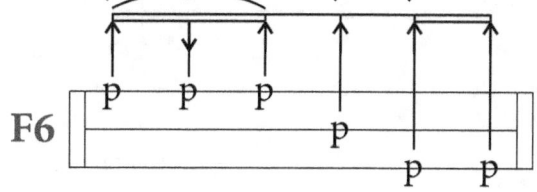

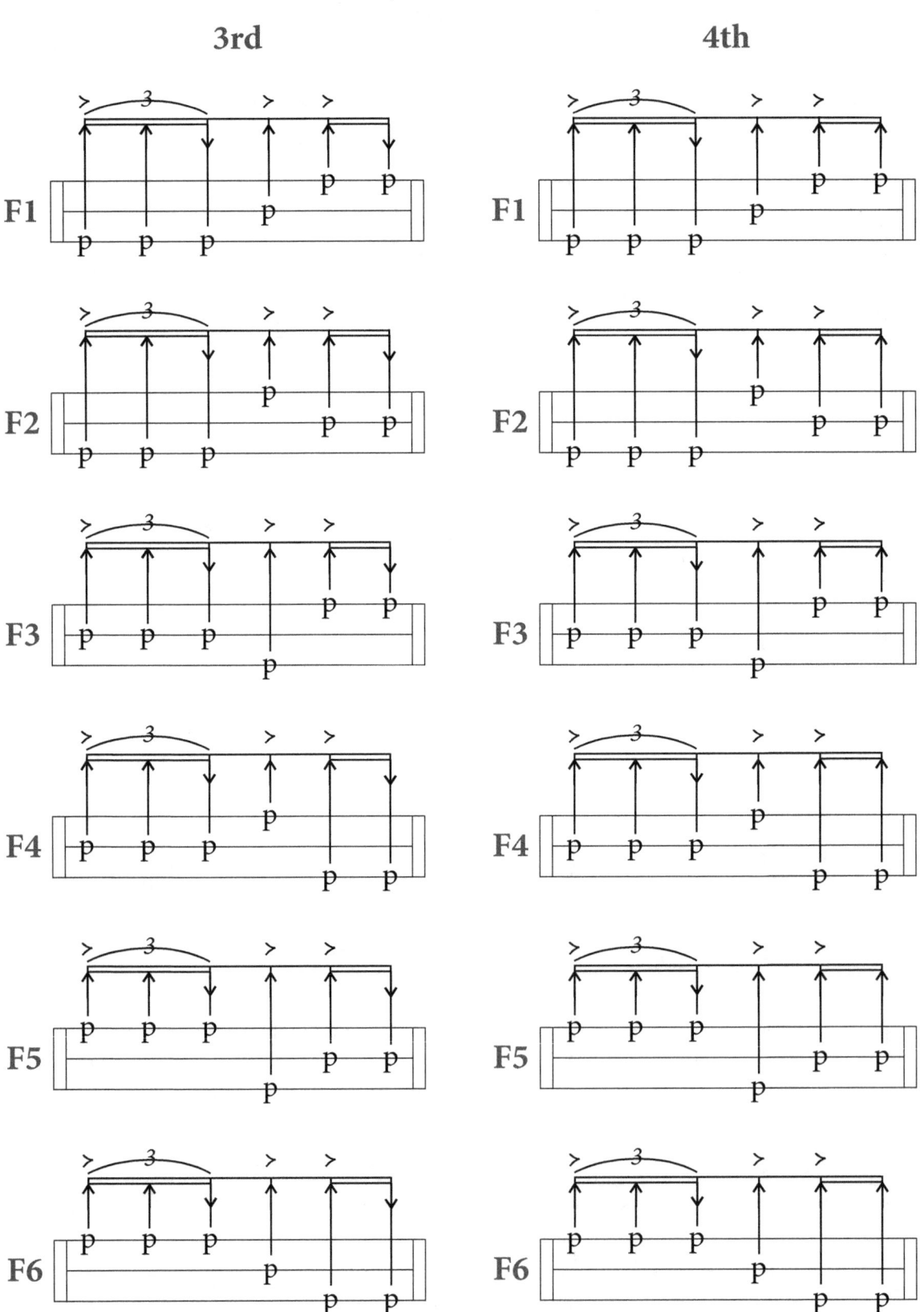

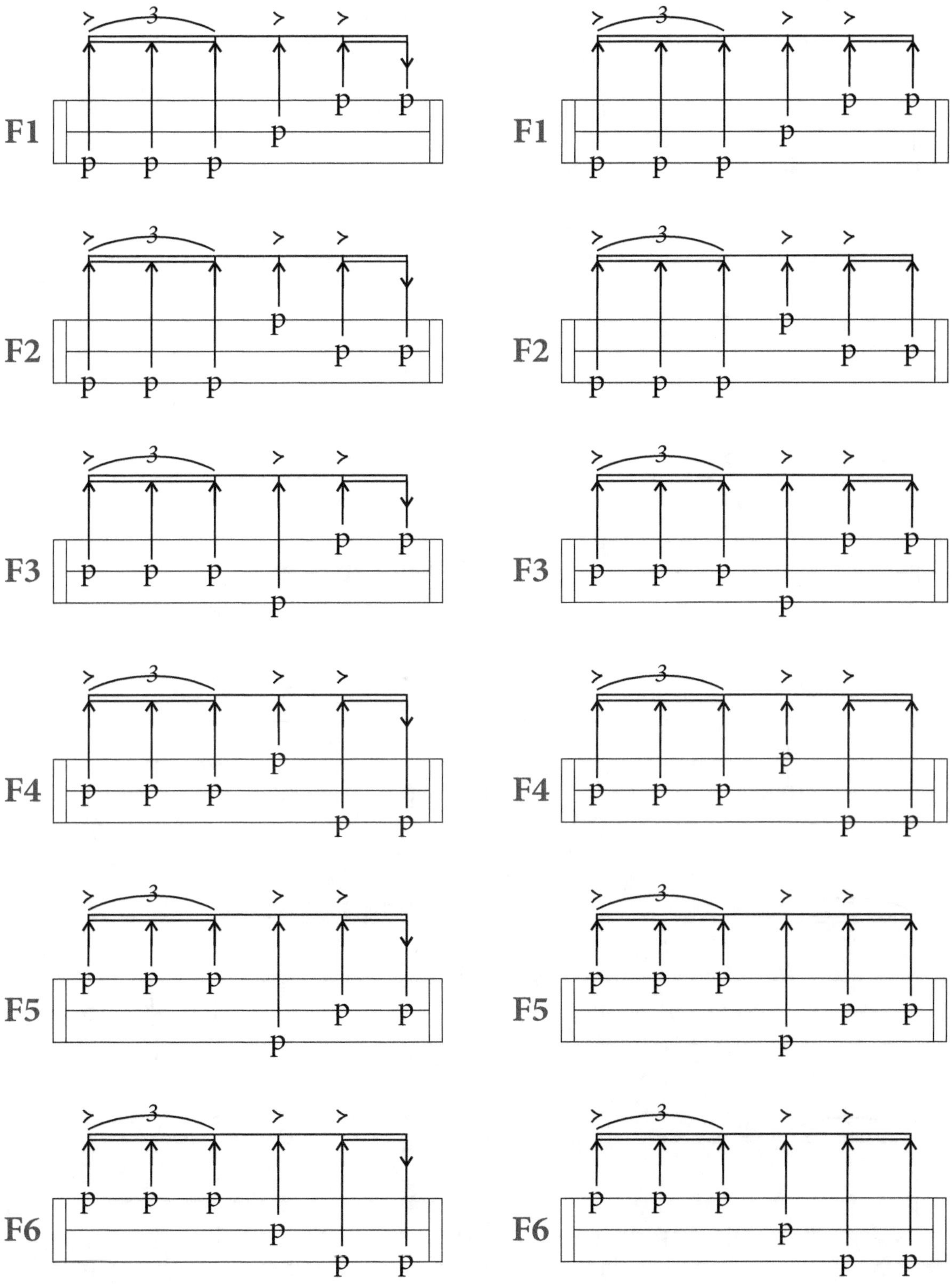

VARIATION II
WAYS OF PERFORMANCE

1st   **2nd**

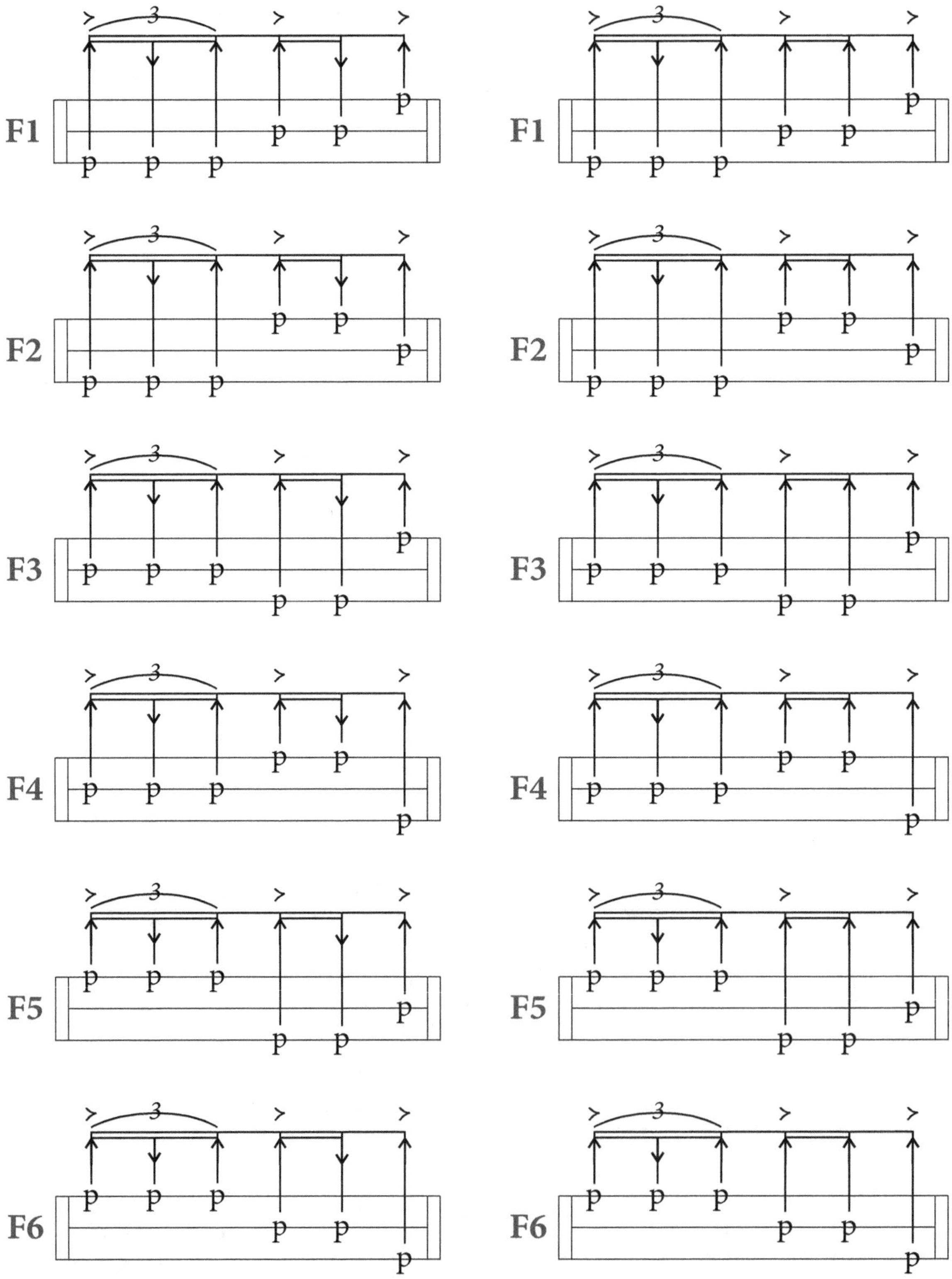

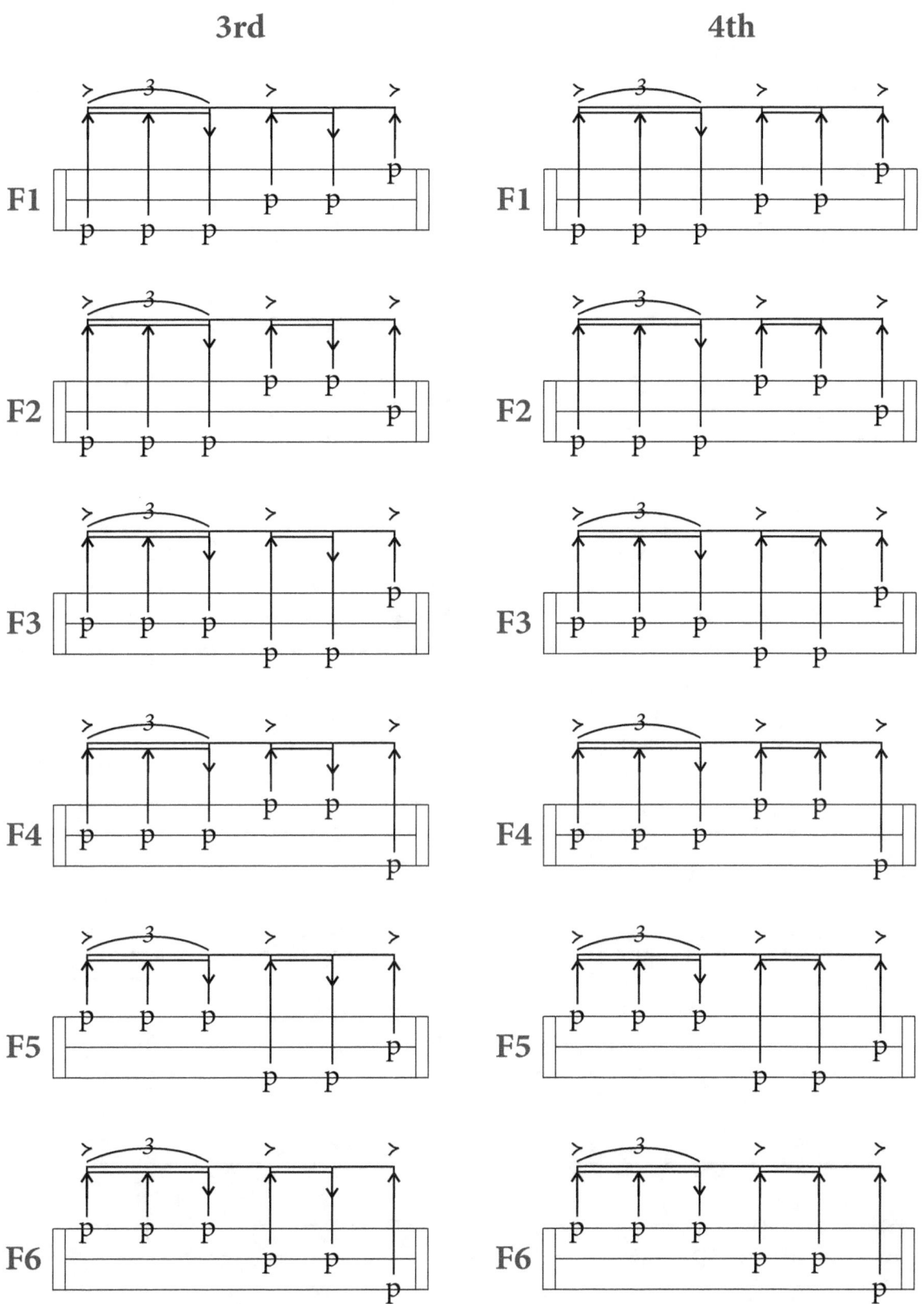

5th

F1
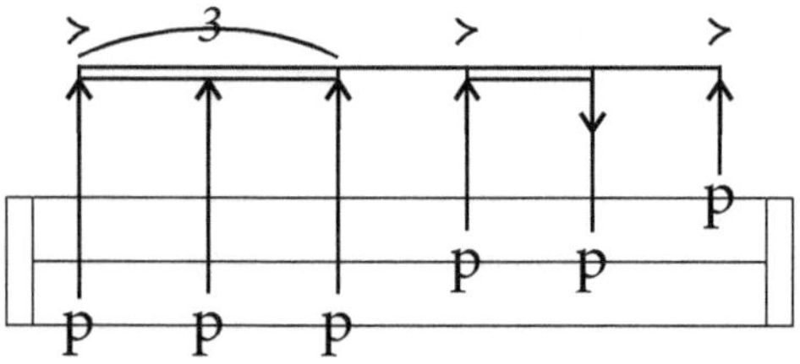

F2
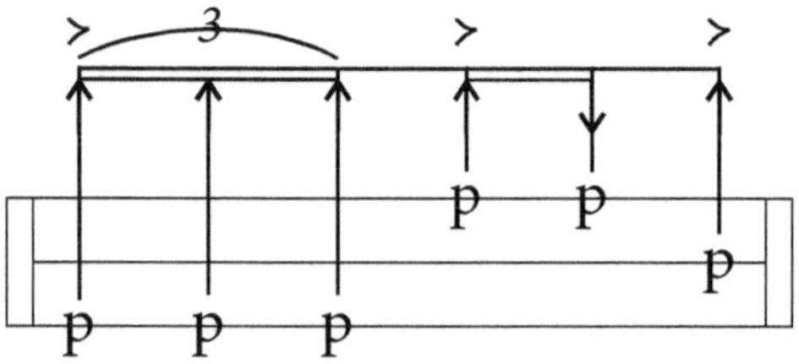

F3
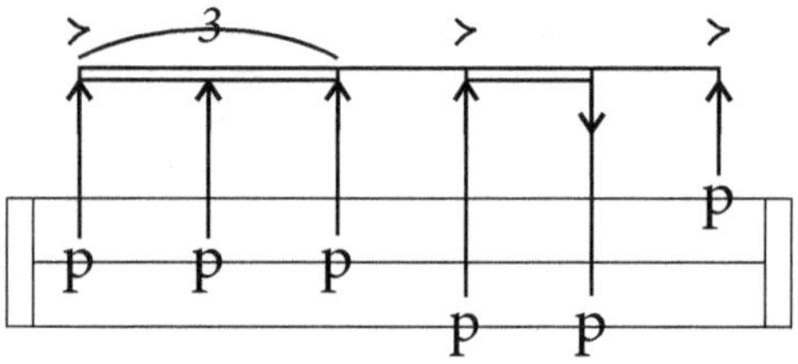

F4
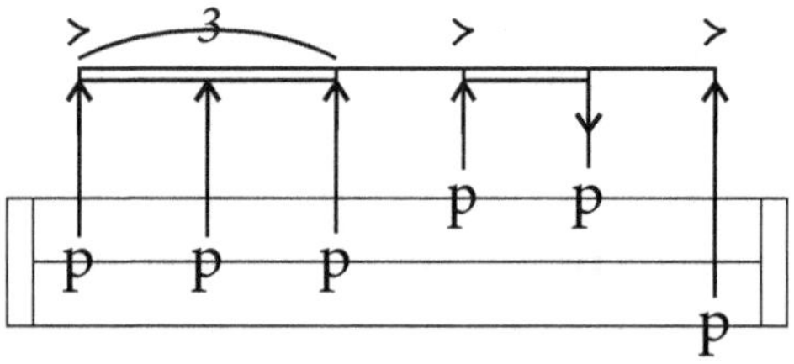

F5
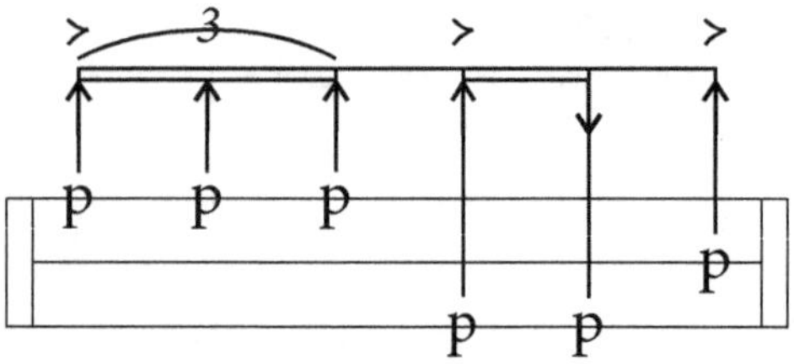

F6
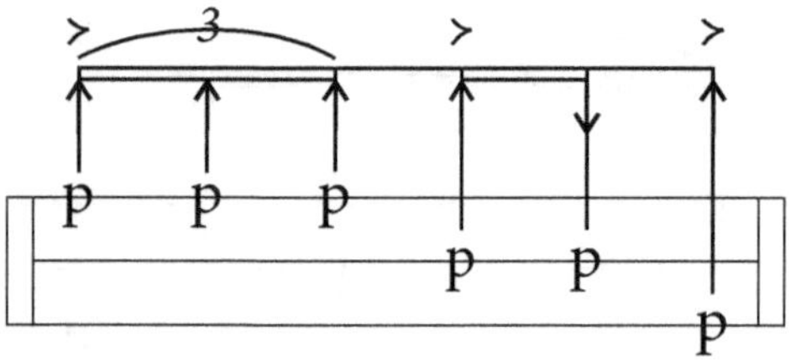

6th

F1
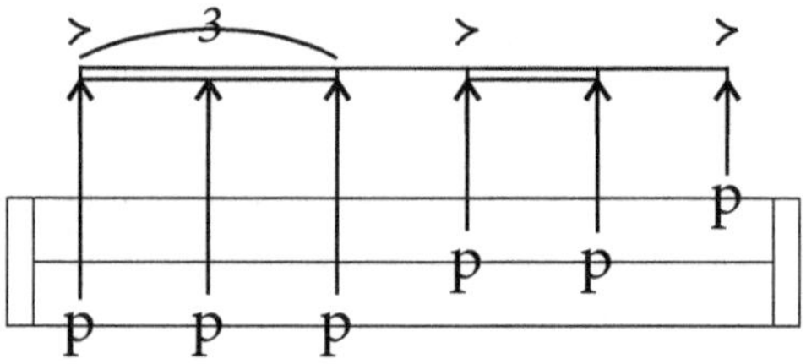

F2
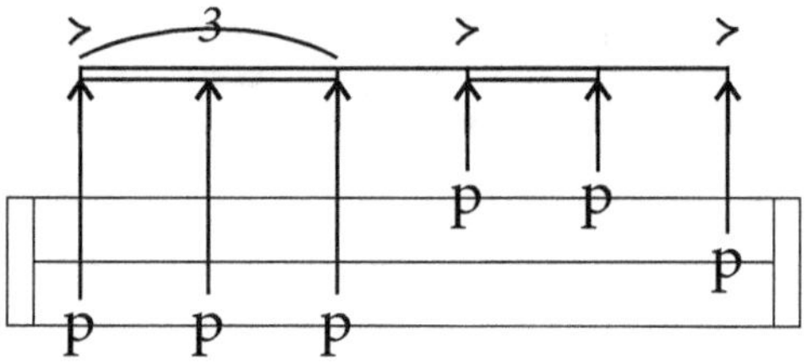

F3
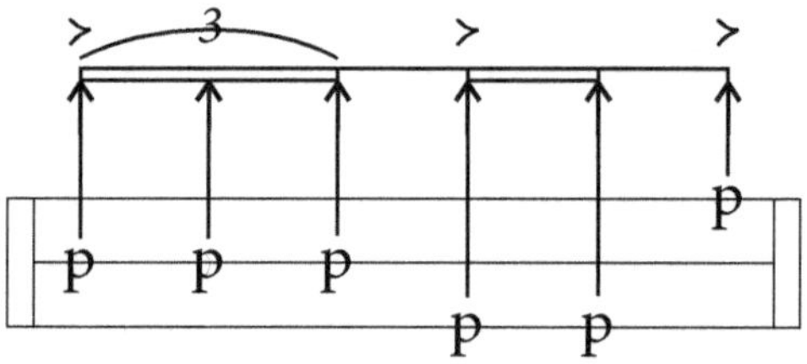

F4
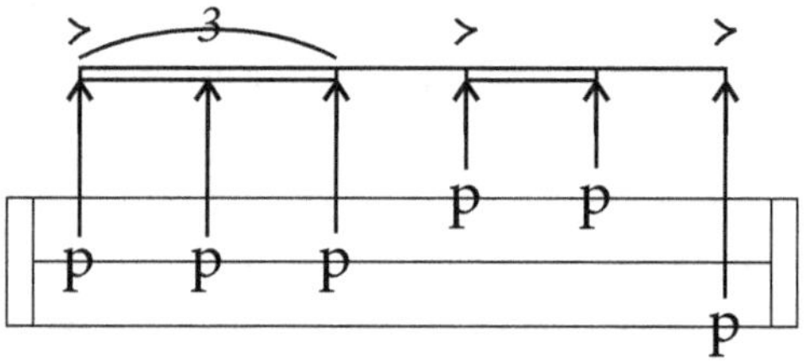

F5
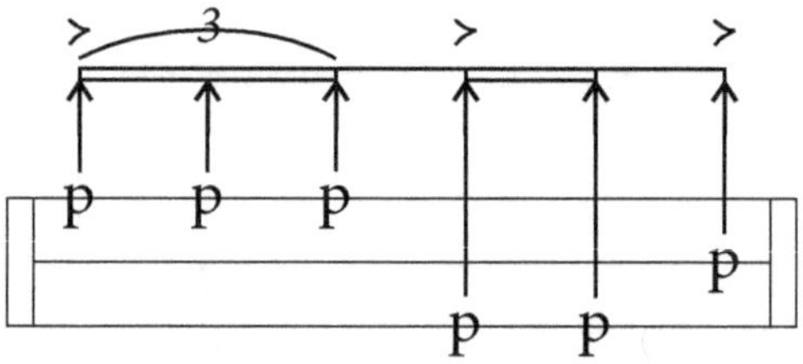

F6
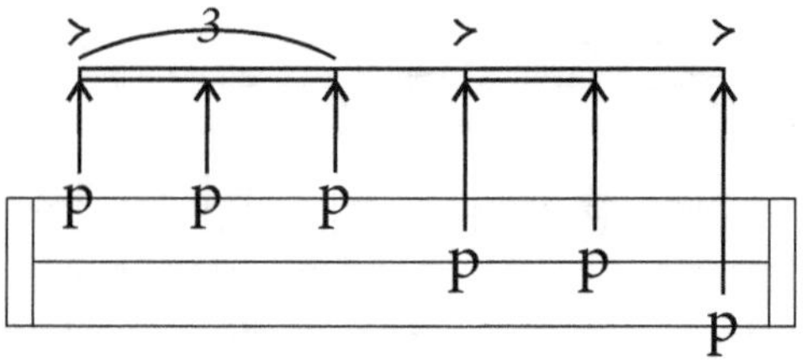

VARIATION III
WAYS OF PERFORMANCE

1st   **2nd**

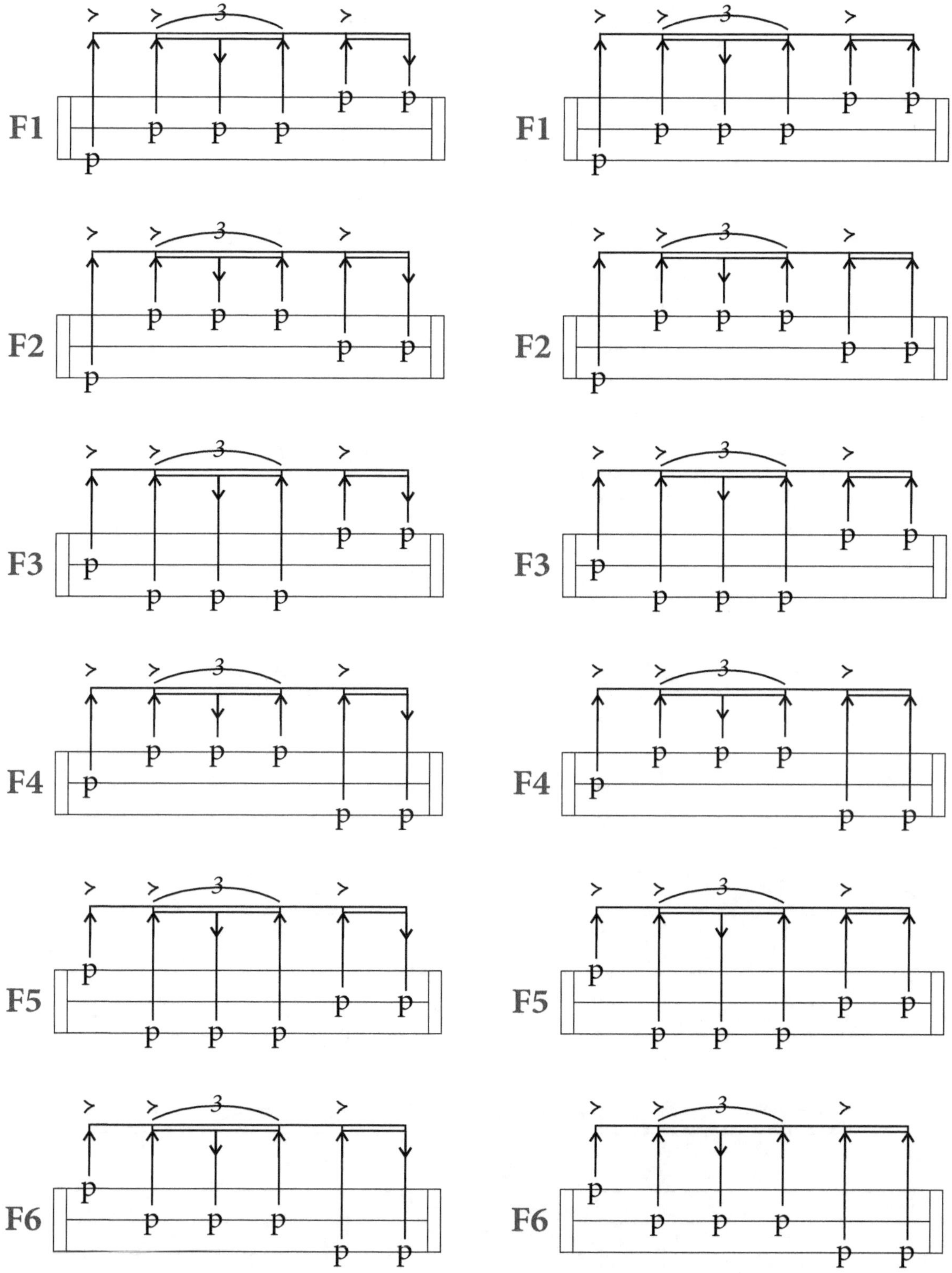

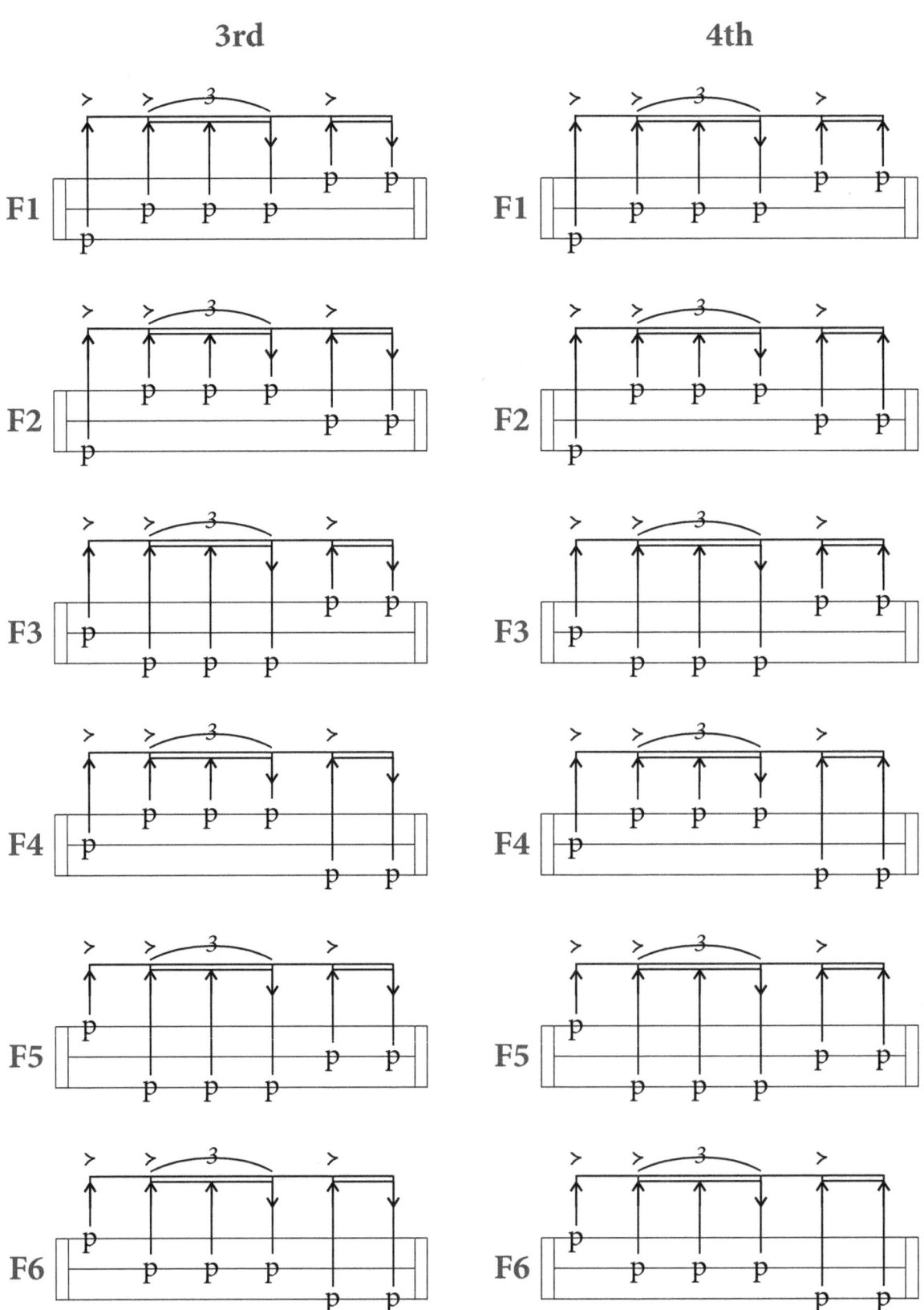

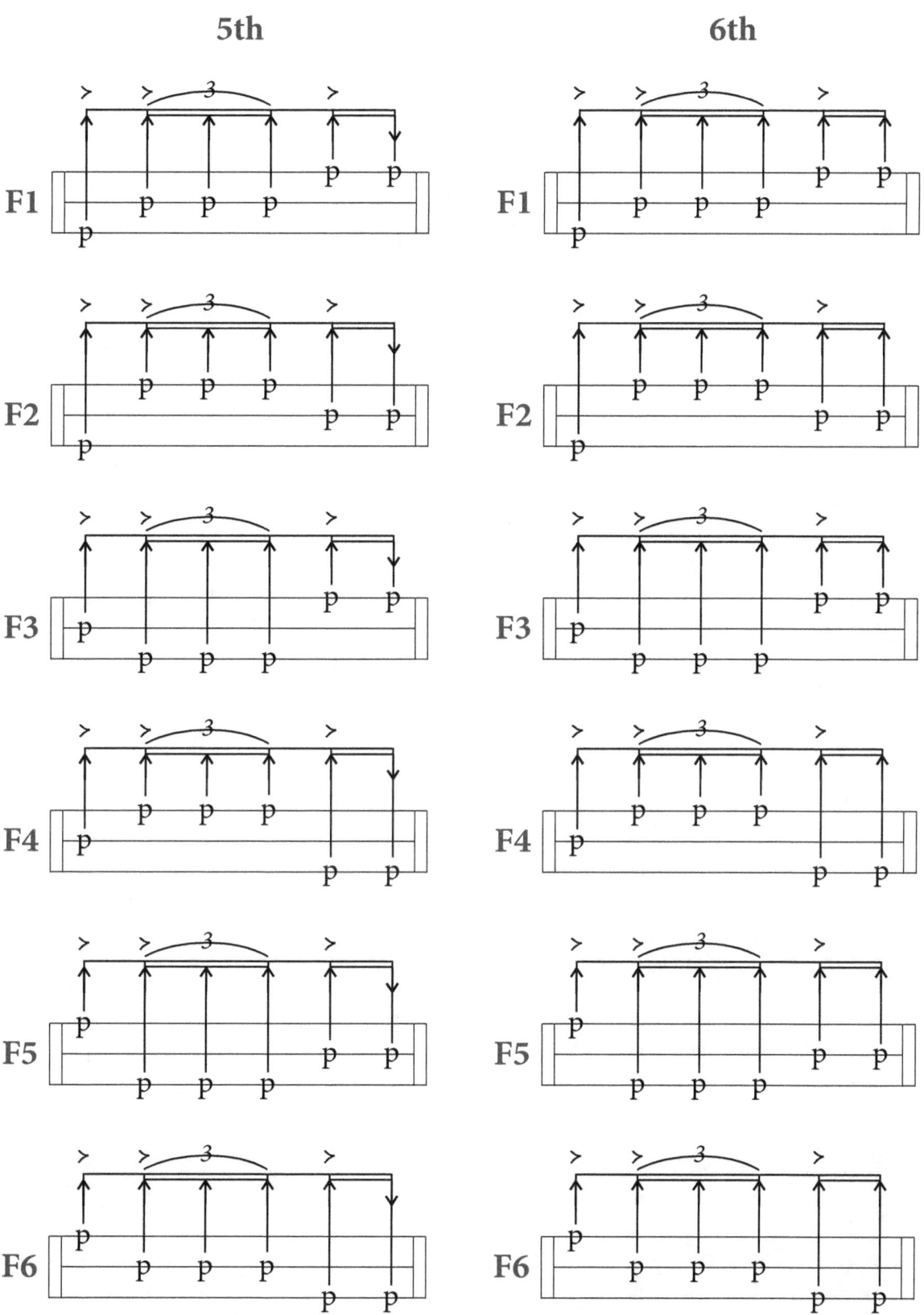

VARIATION IV
WAYS OF PERFORMANCE
1st   2nd

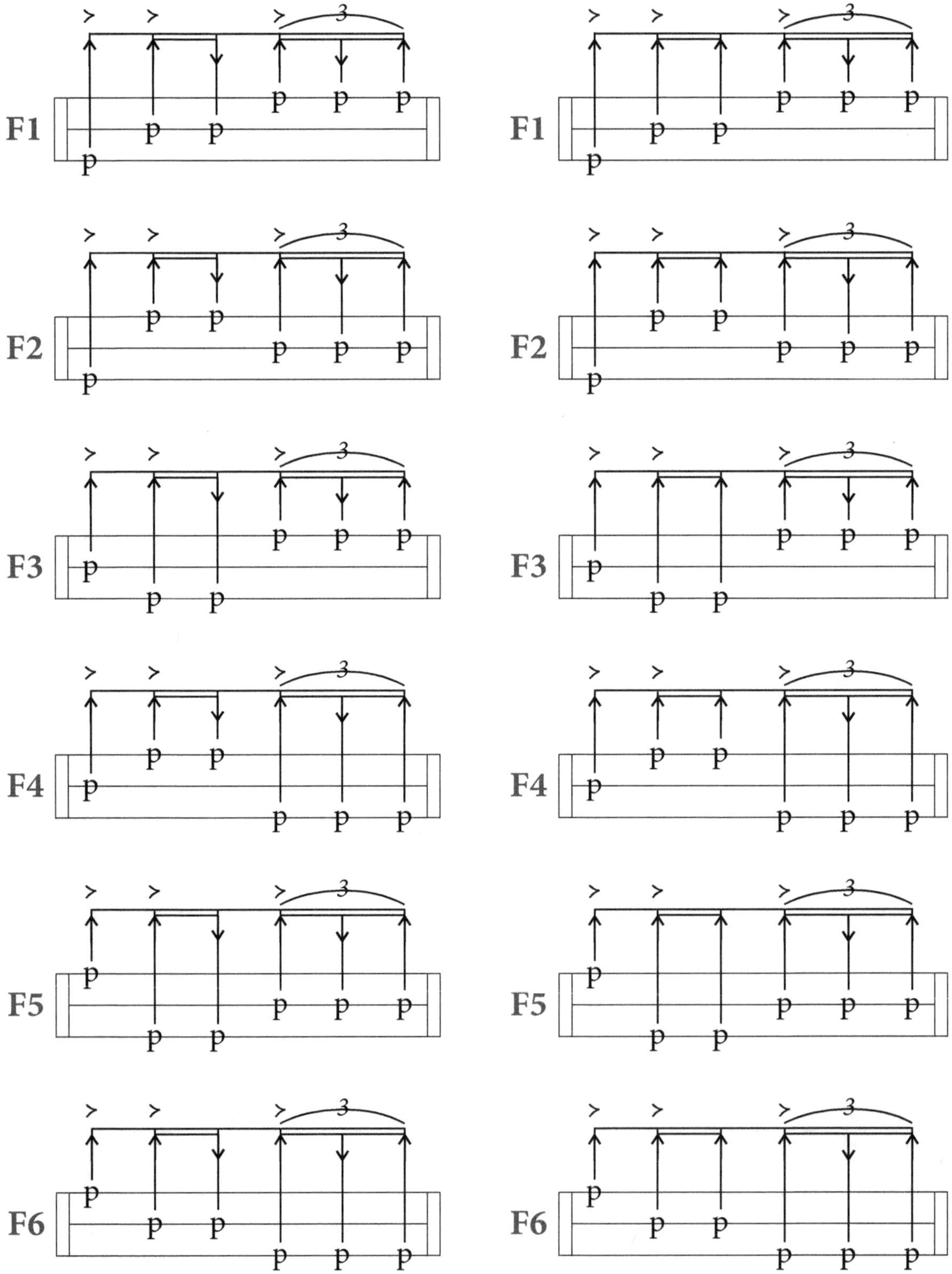

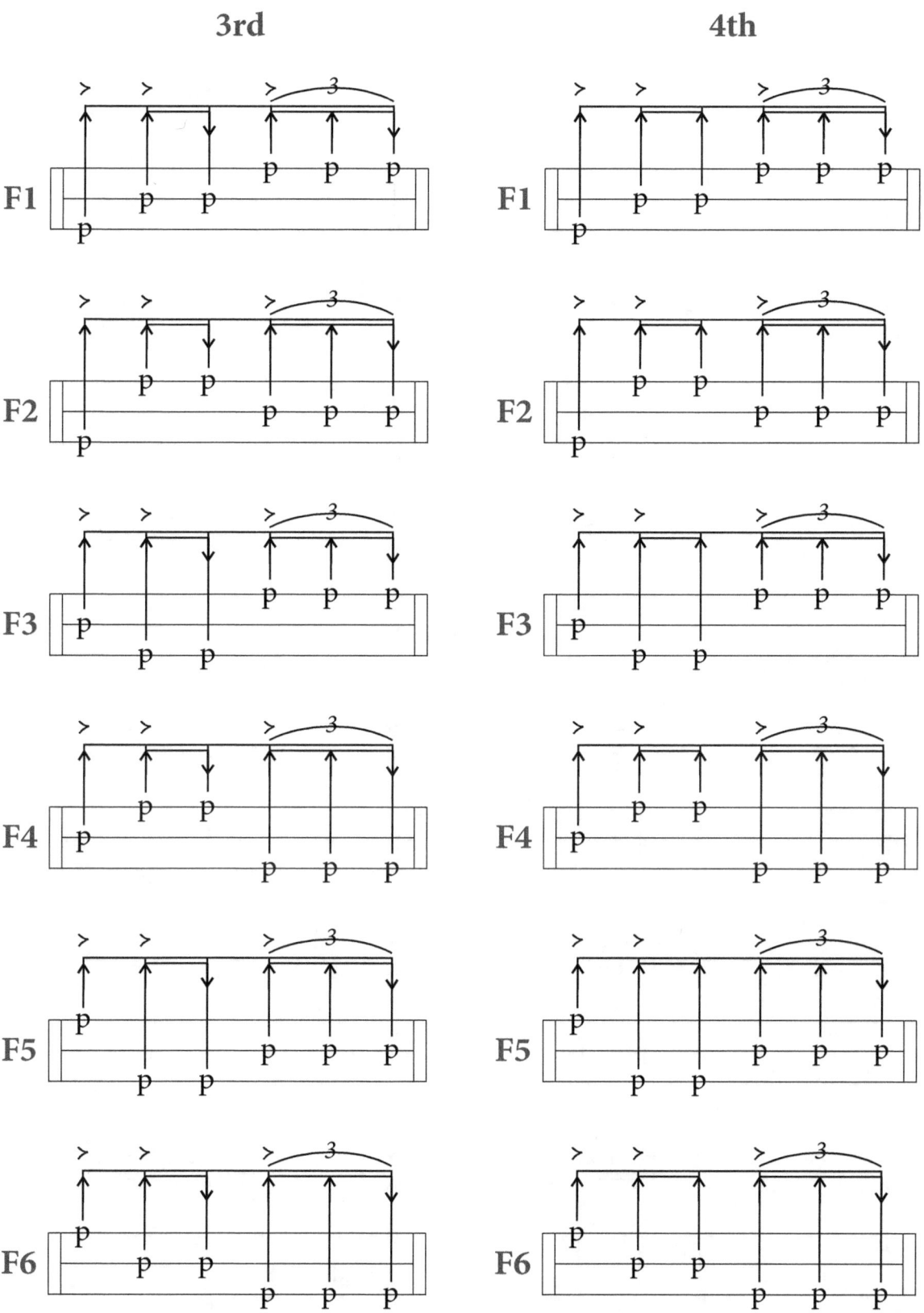

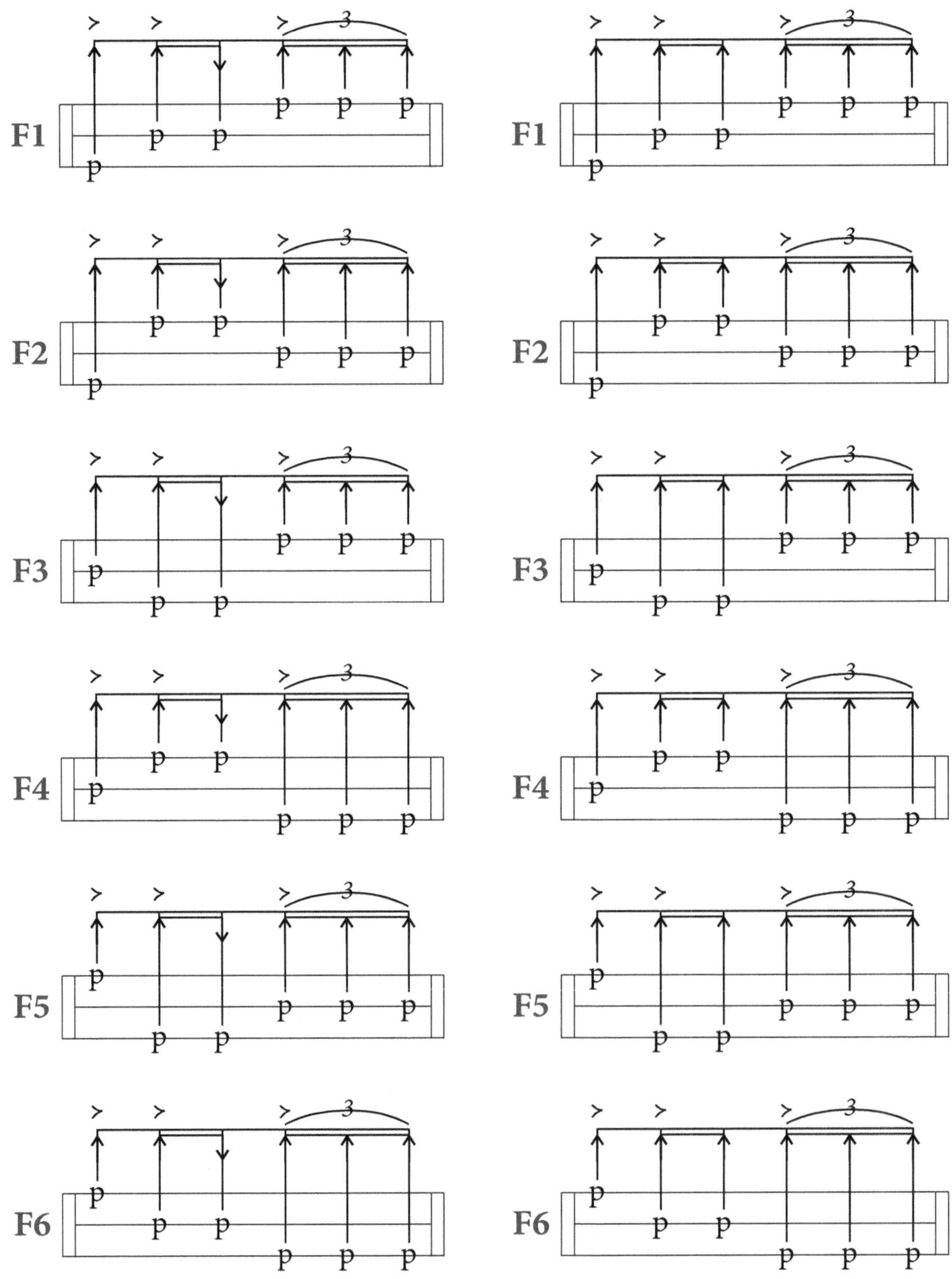

VARIATION V
WAYS OF PERFORMANCE

1st   **2nd**

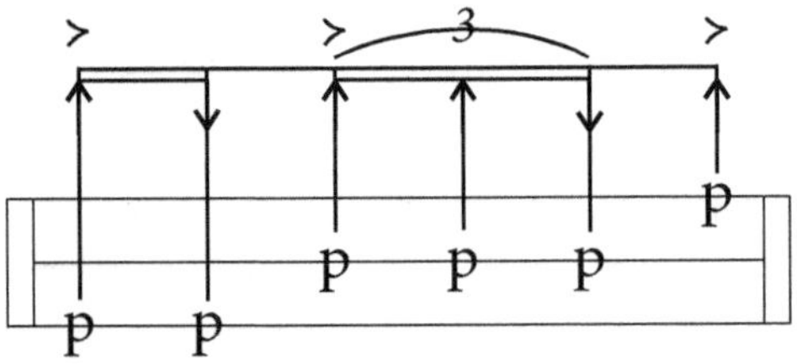

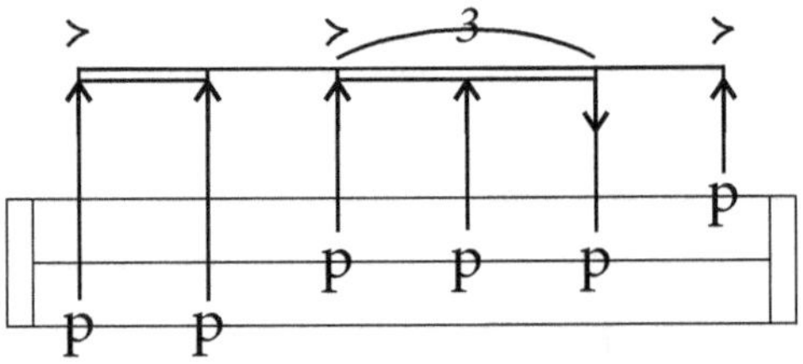

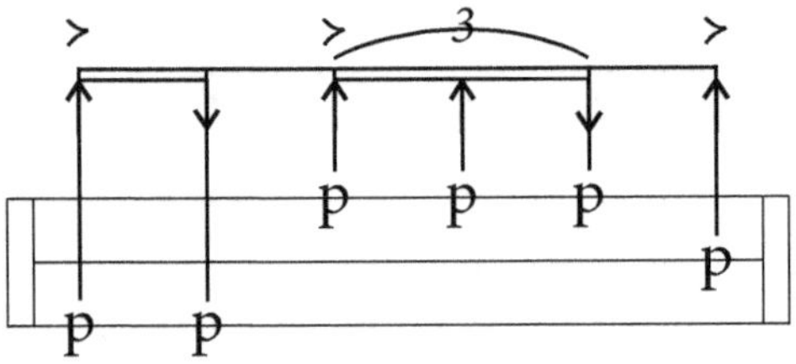

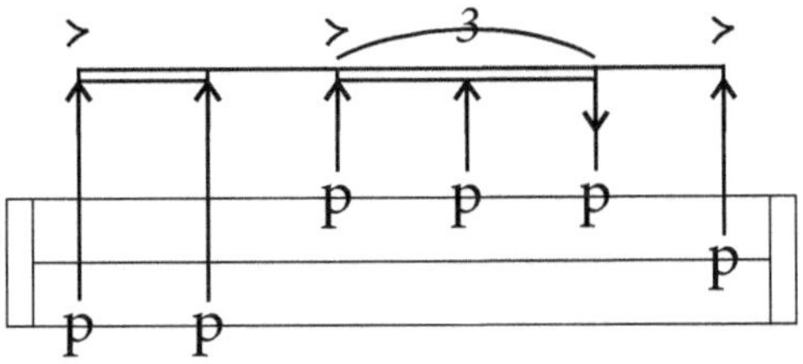

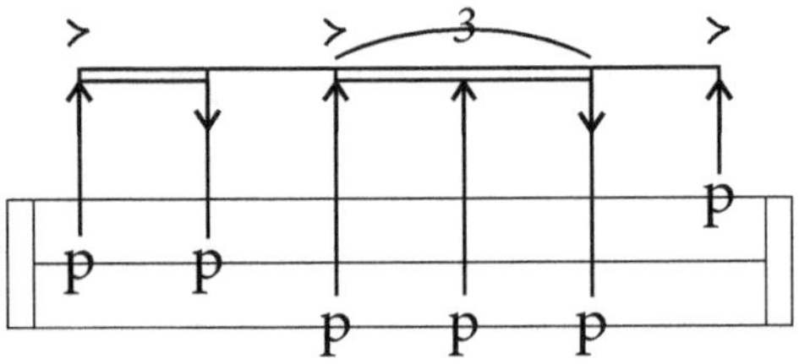

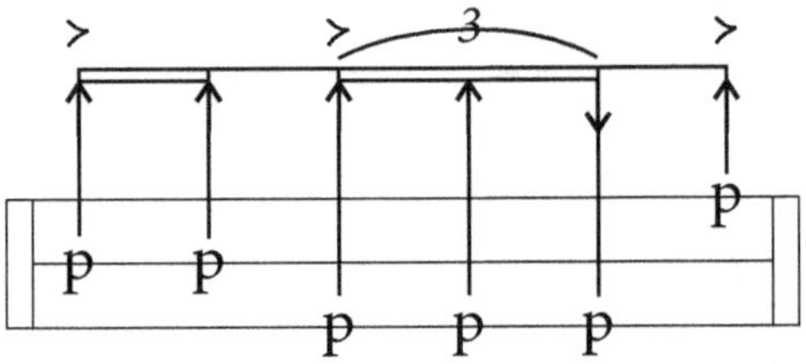

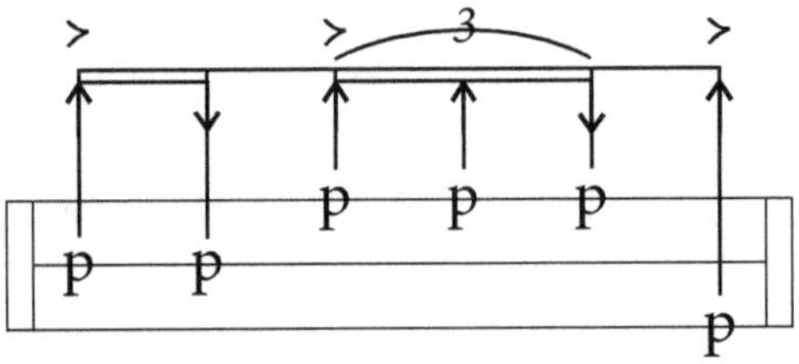

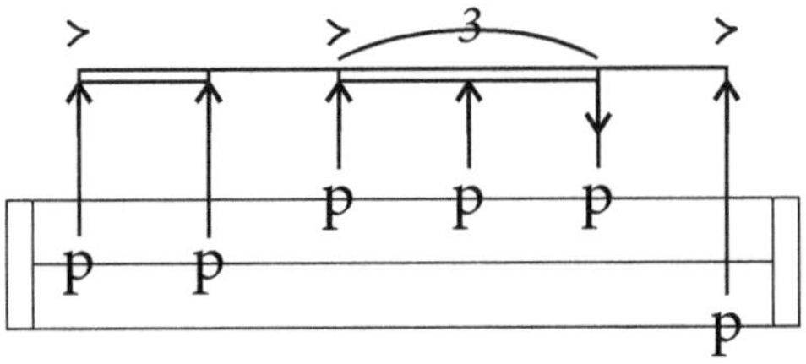

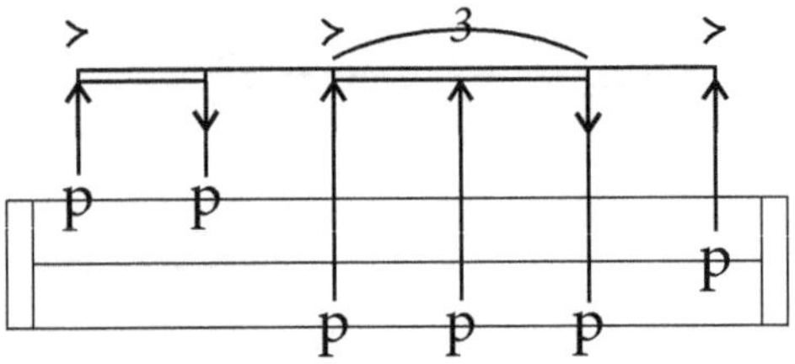

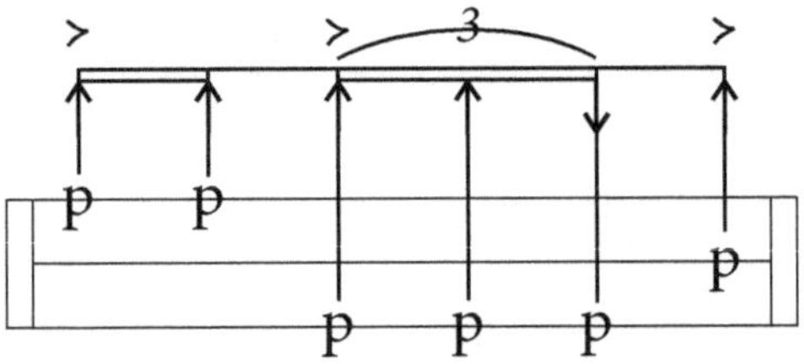

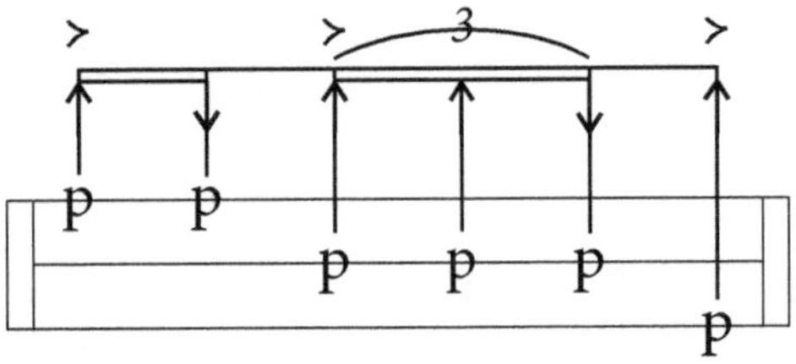

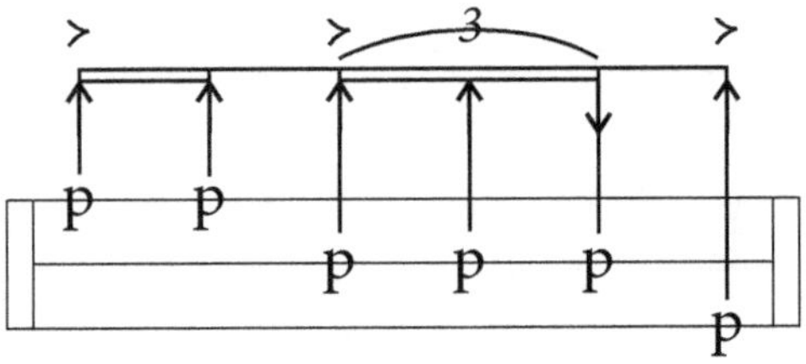

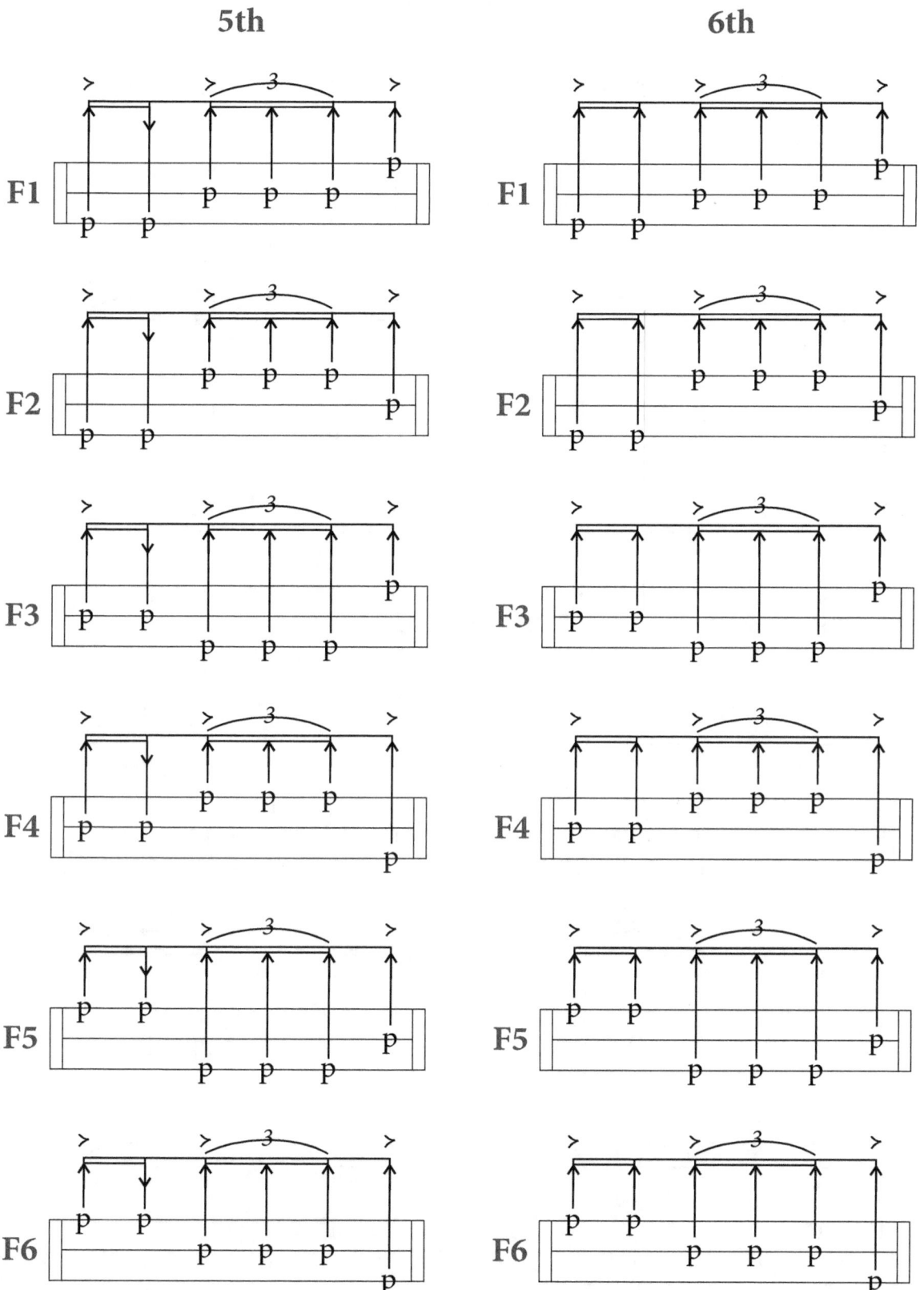

VARIATION VI
WAYS OF PERFORMANCE

1st | **2nd**

F1
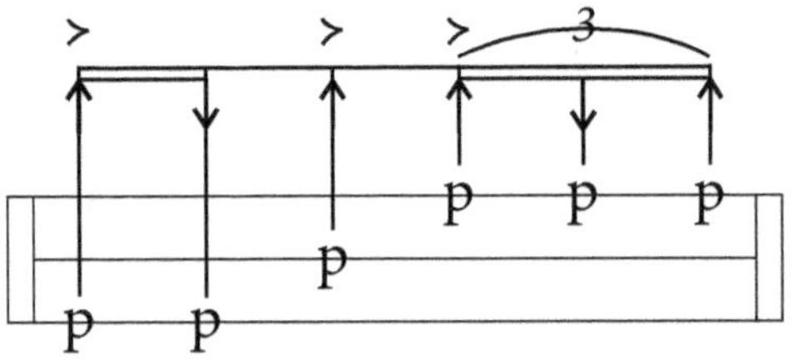
F1
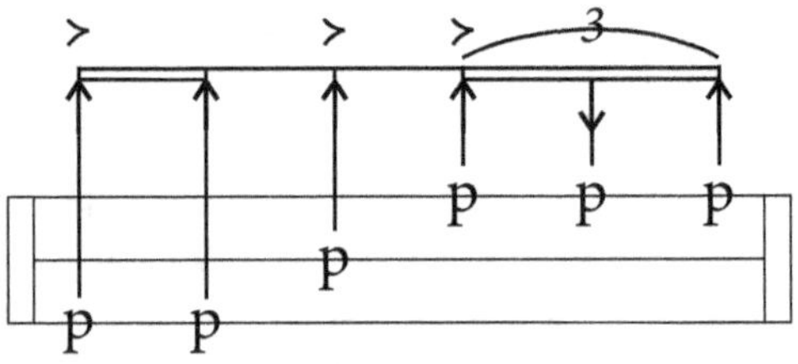

F2
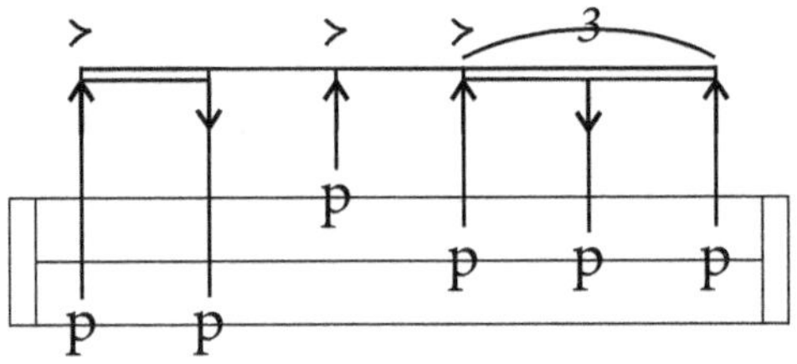
F2
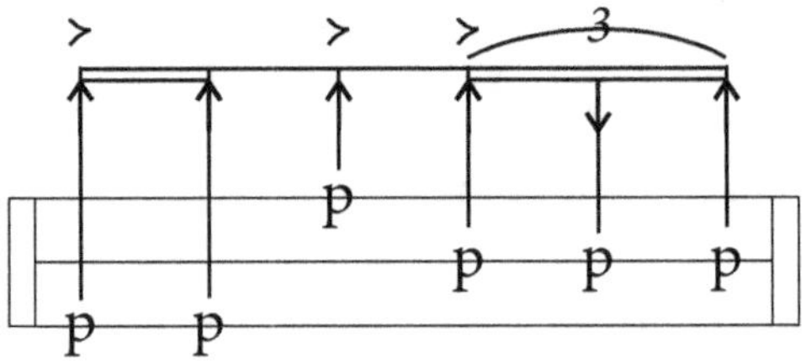

F3
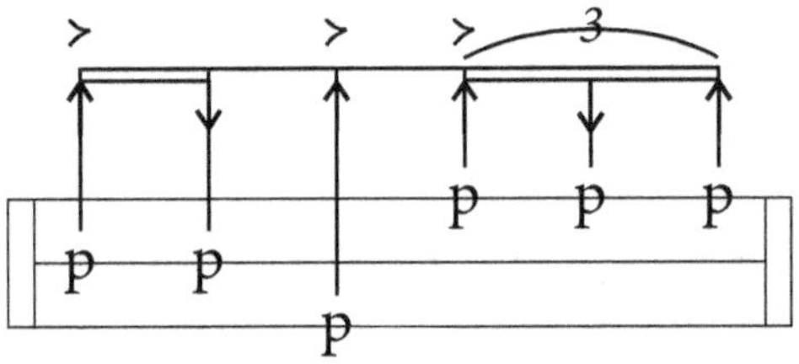
F3
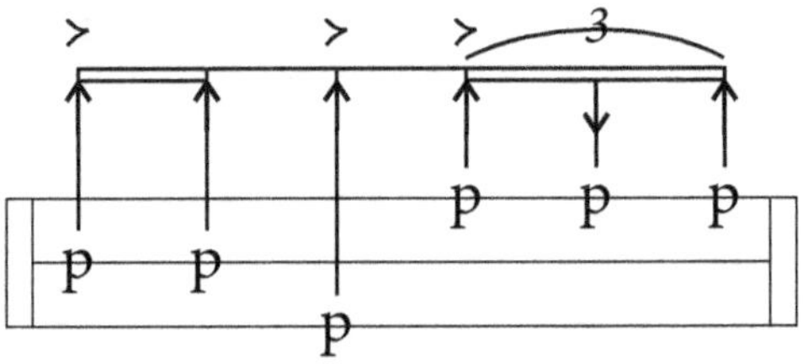

F4
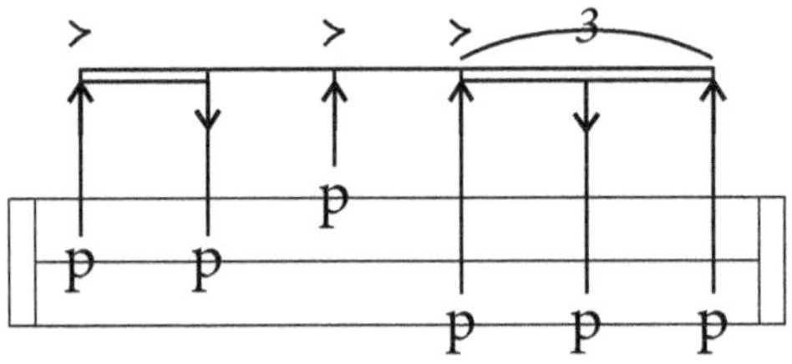
F4
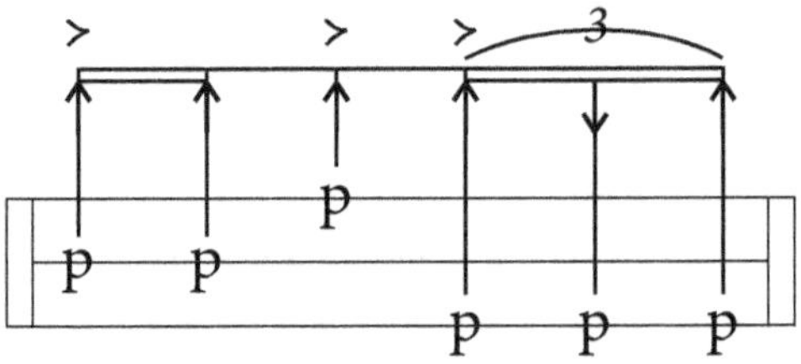

F5
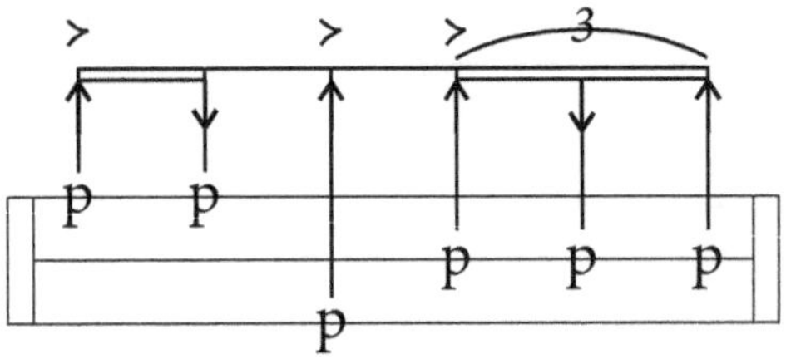
F5
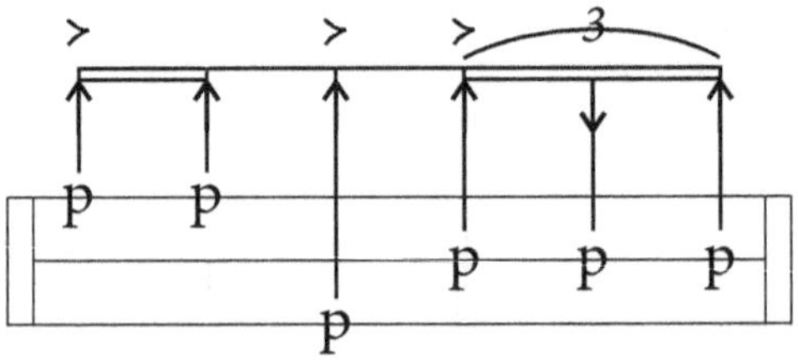

F6
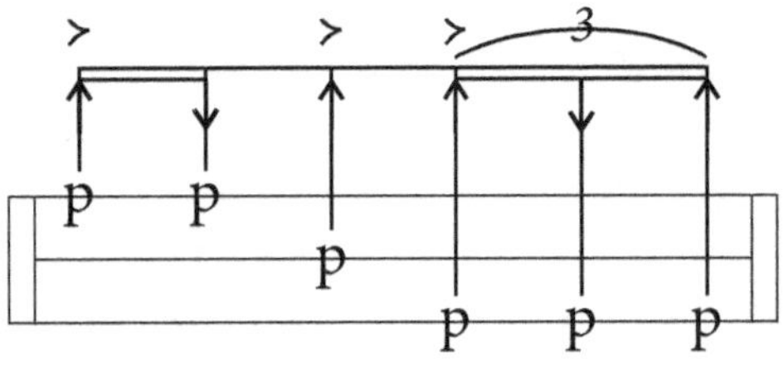
F6
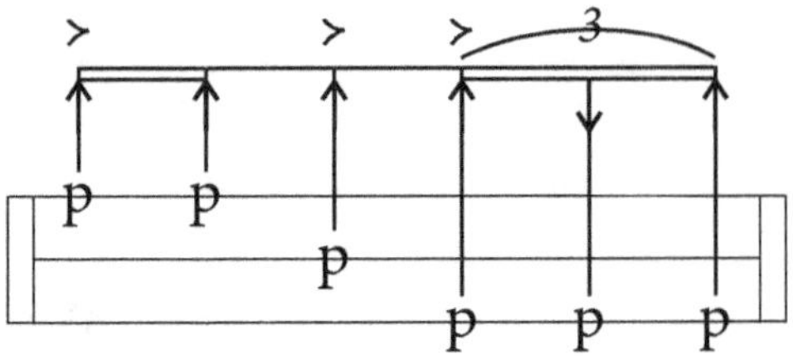

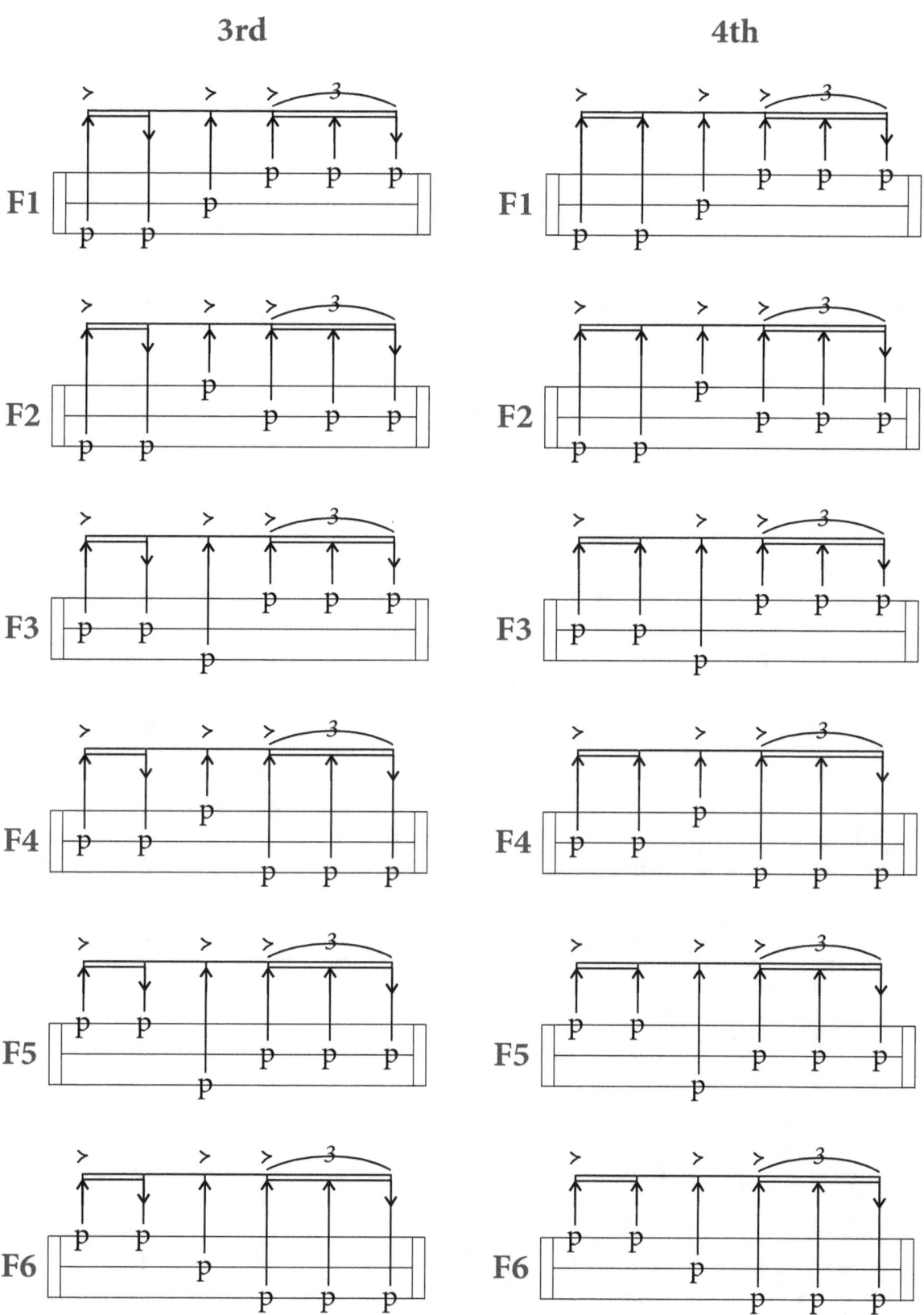

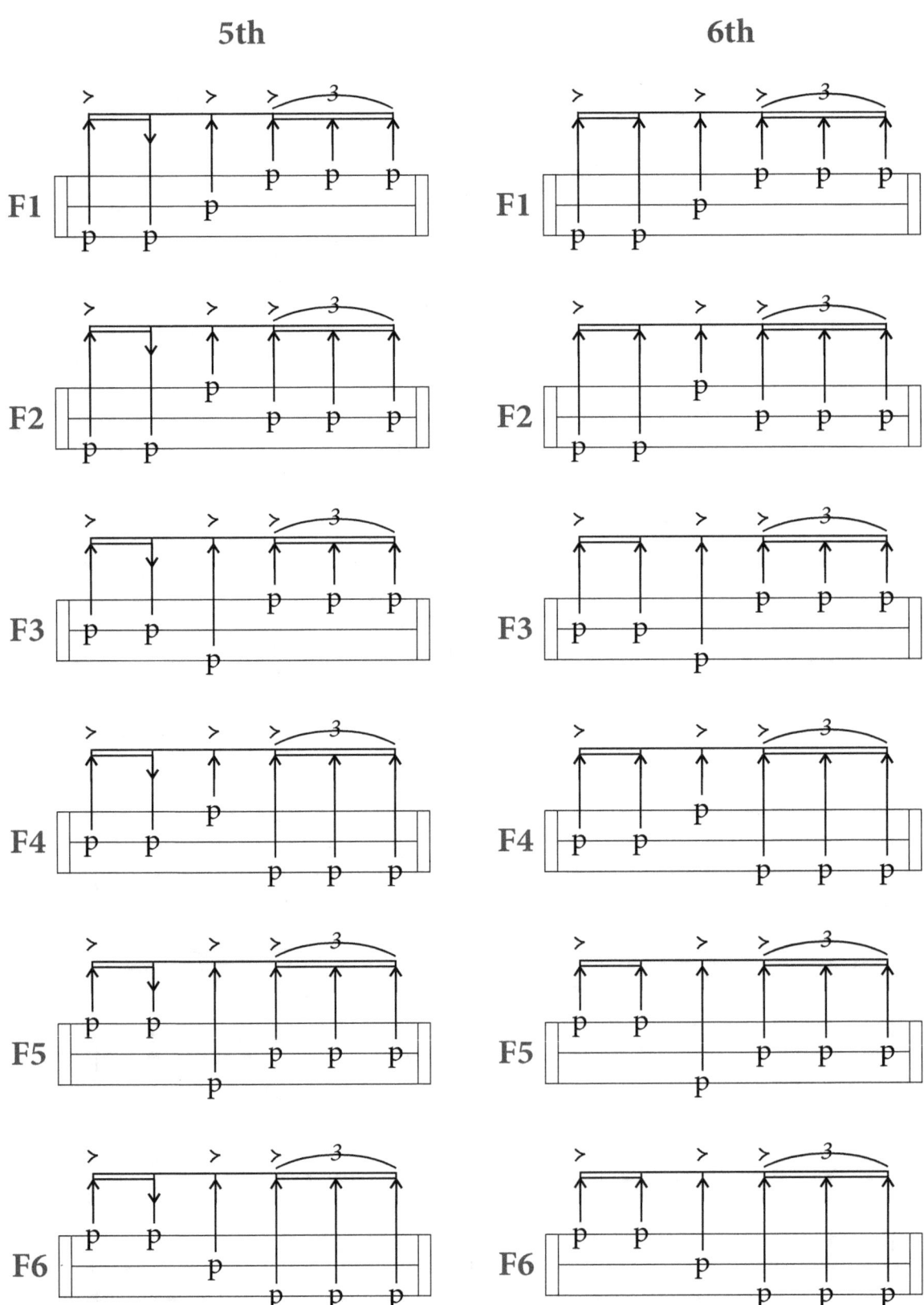

§ VI

Exercise on pulgar on three adjacent strings with one triple stroke (triplet) and two double strokes. The triple and double stroke are isochronous. The exercise includes three variations depending on the position of the triple and double strokes within the Formula. The first Formula of each variation is cited below.

VARIATION I

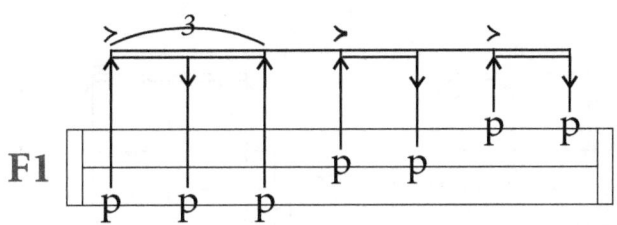

VARIATION II

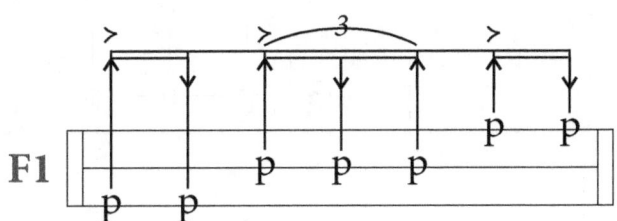

VARIATION III

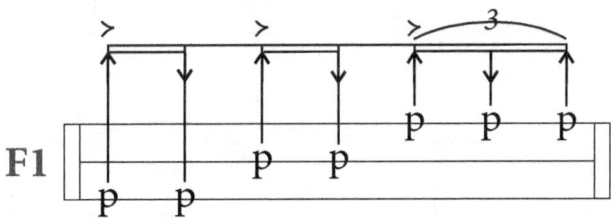

Each variation depending on the direction of pulgar stroke can be carried out in many different ways. 12 ways for each variation are cited below.

VARIATION I
WAYS OF PERFORMANCE
1st   2nd

3rd   4th

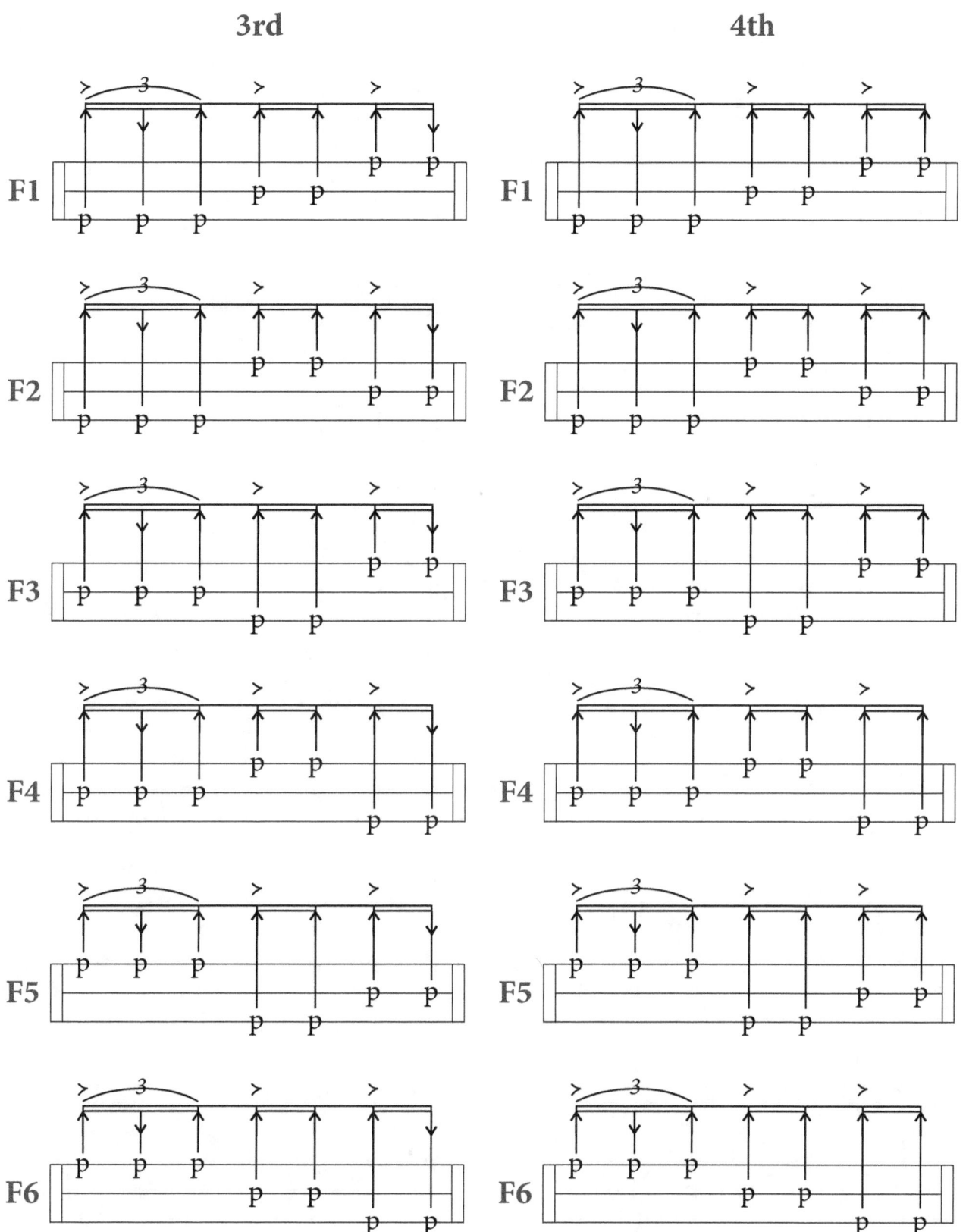

9

5th	6th

F1
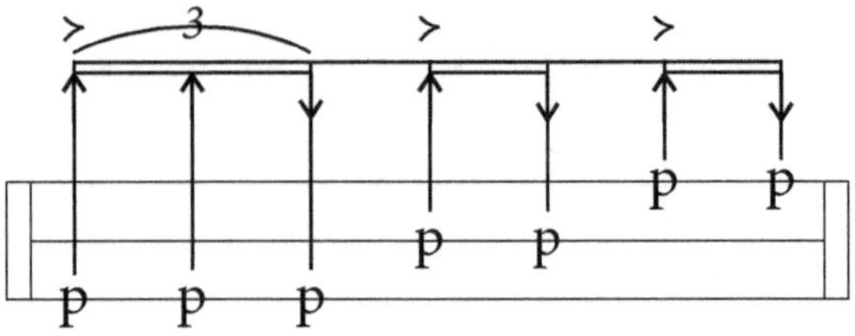

F1
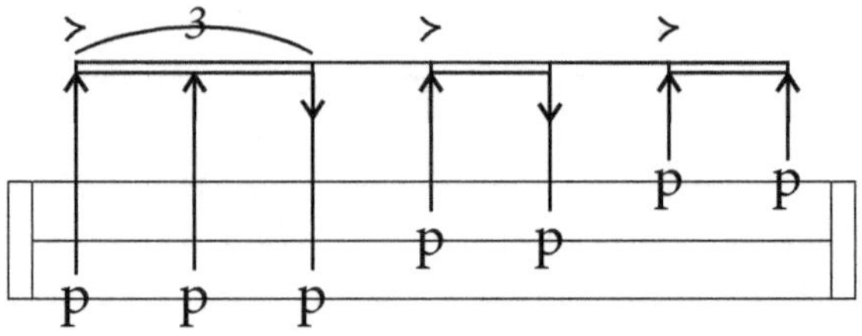

F2
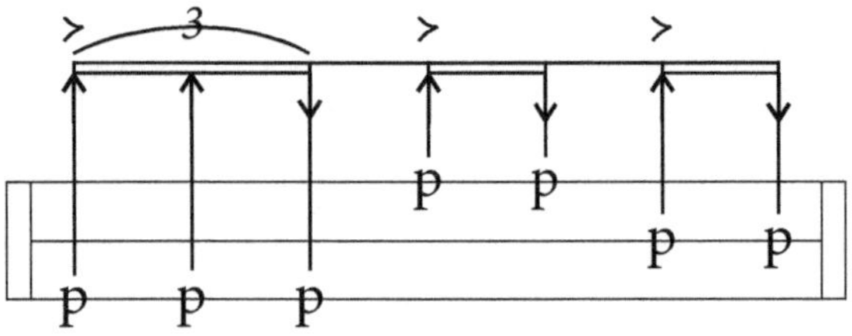

F2
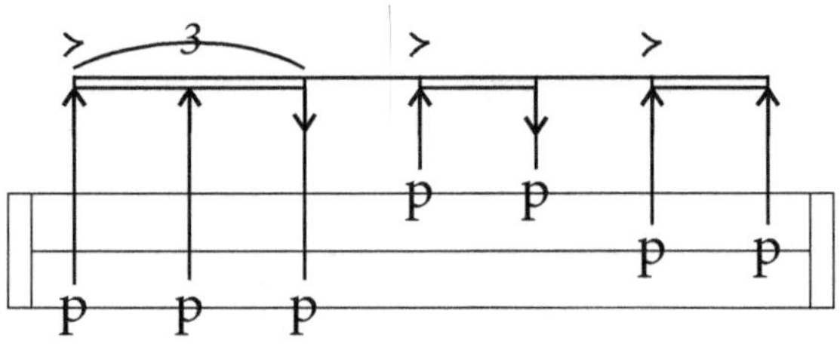

F3
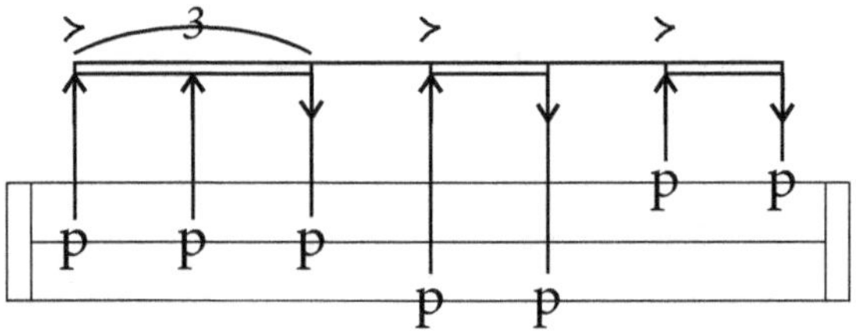

F3
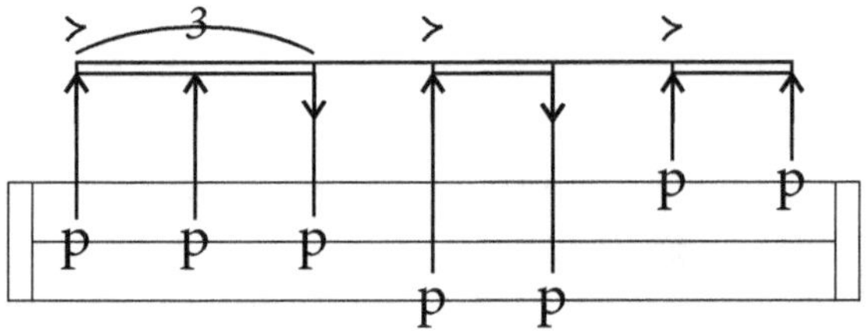

F4
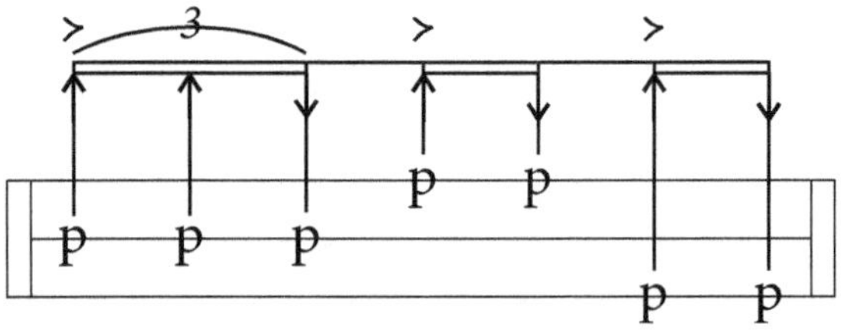

F4
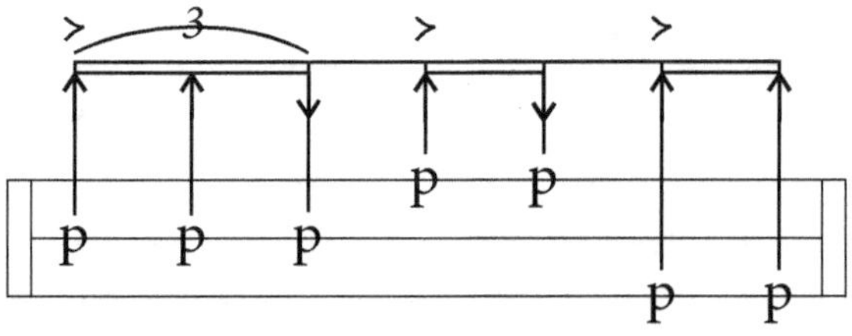

F5
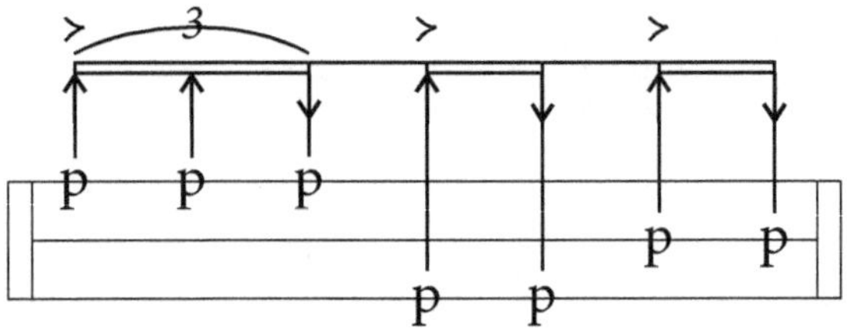

F5
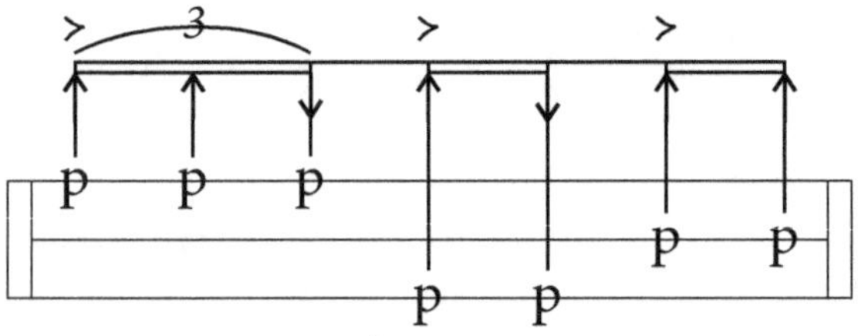

F6
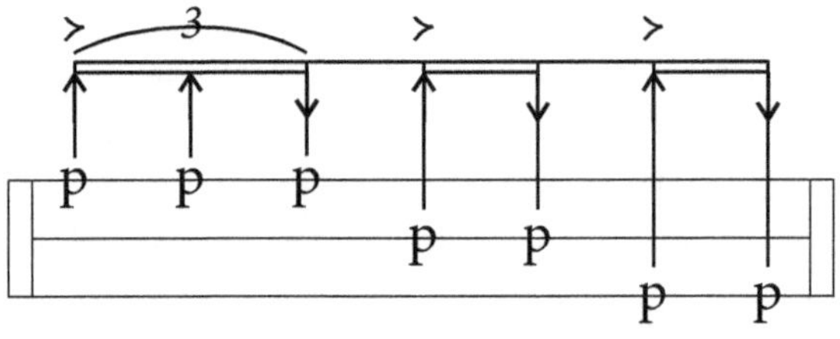

F6
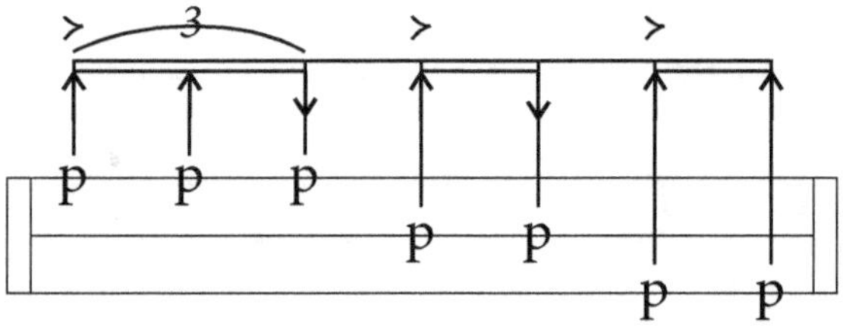

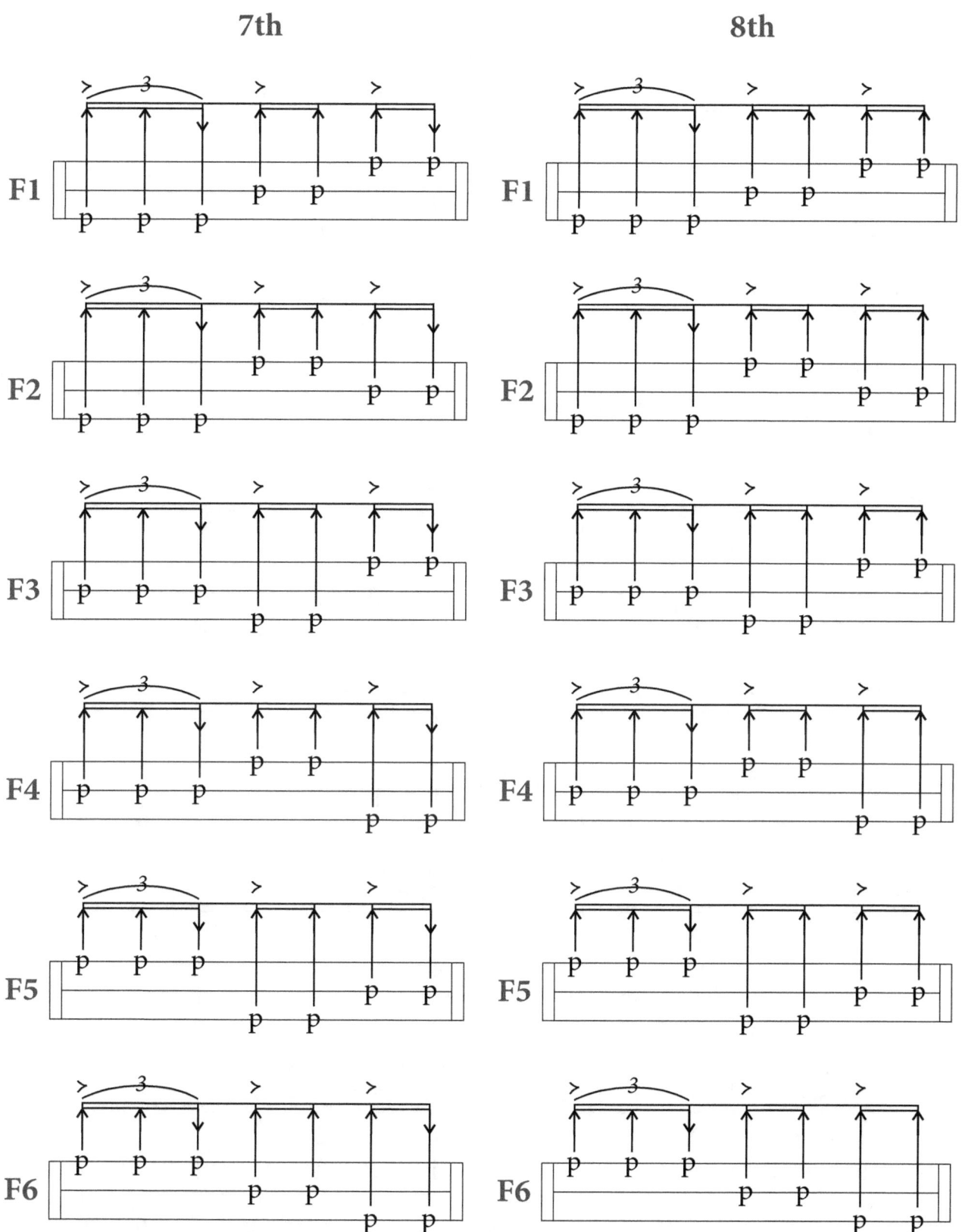

9th   10th

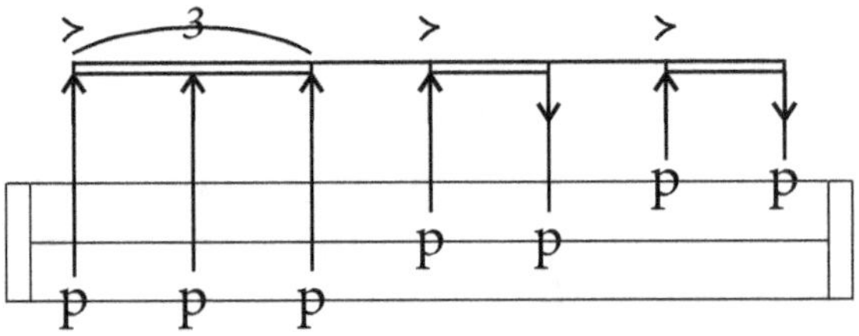

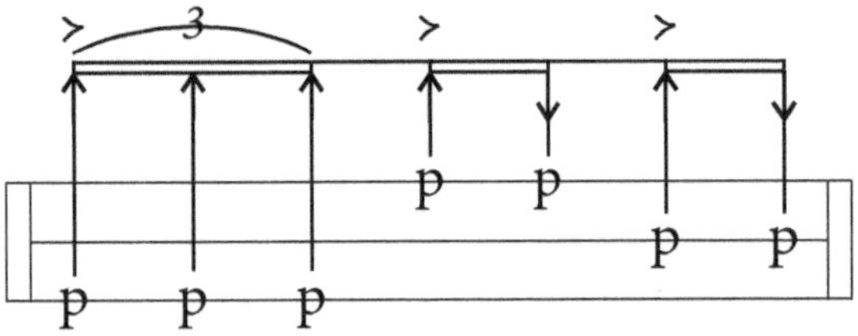

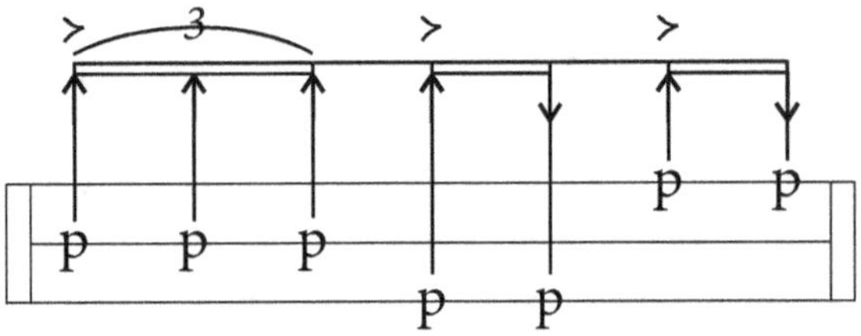

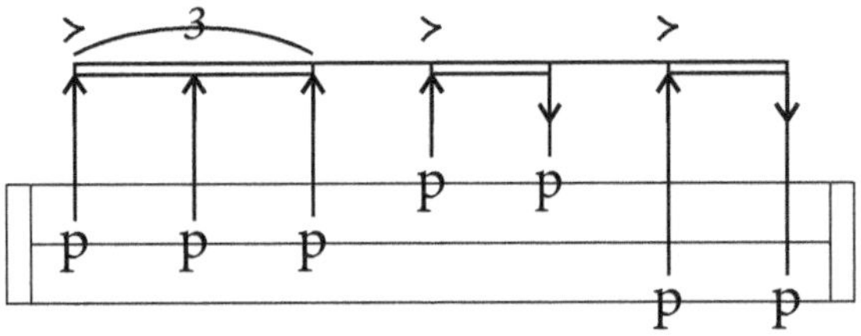

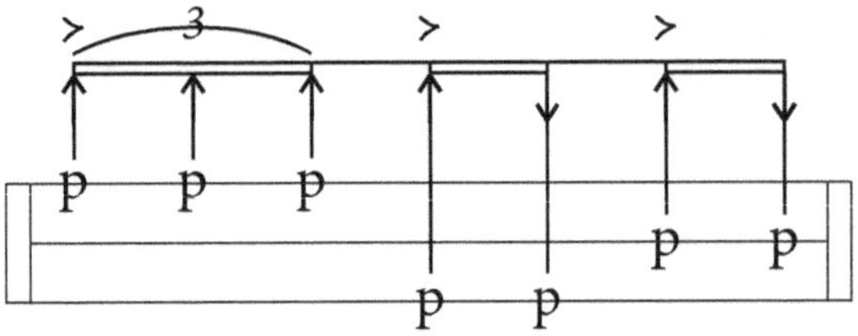

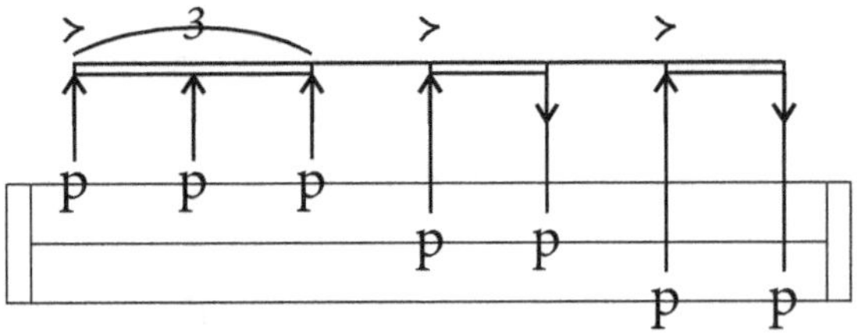

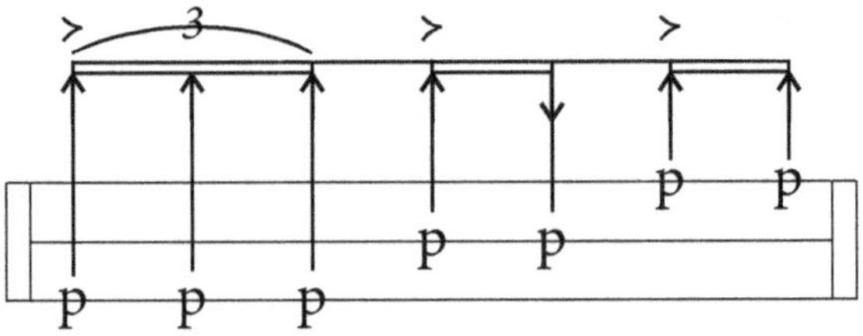

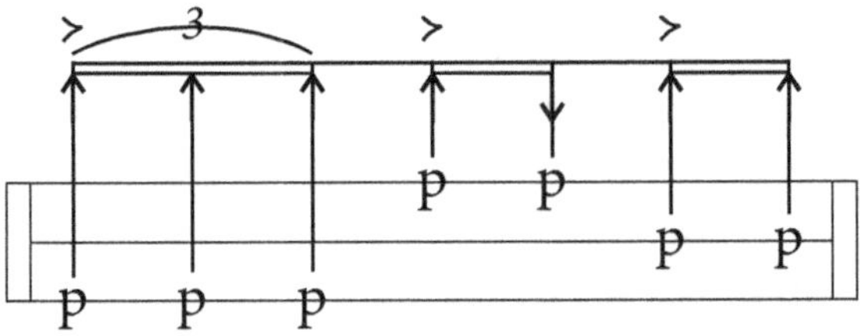

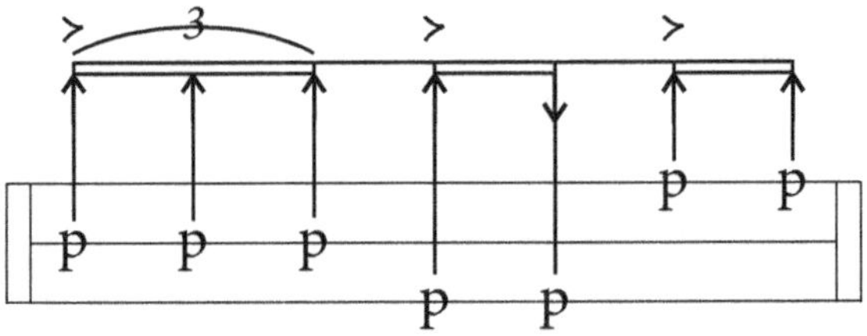

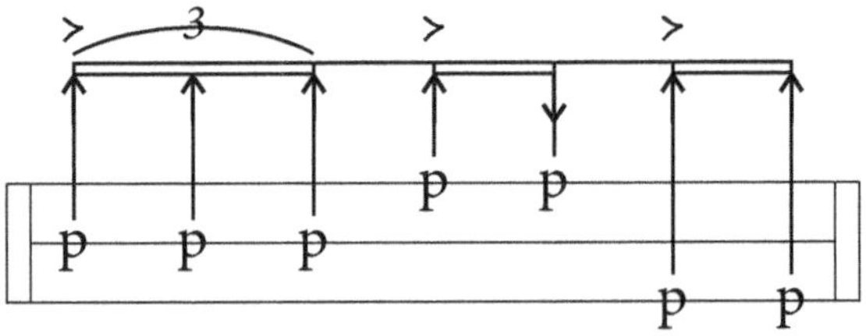

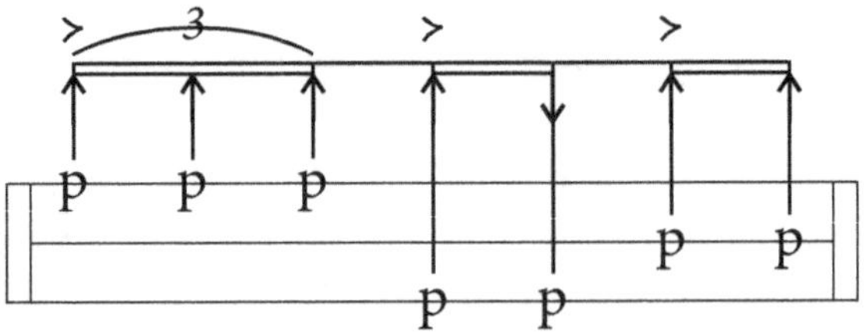

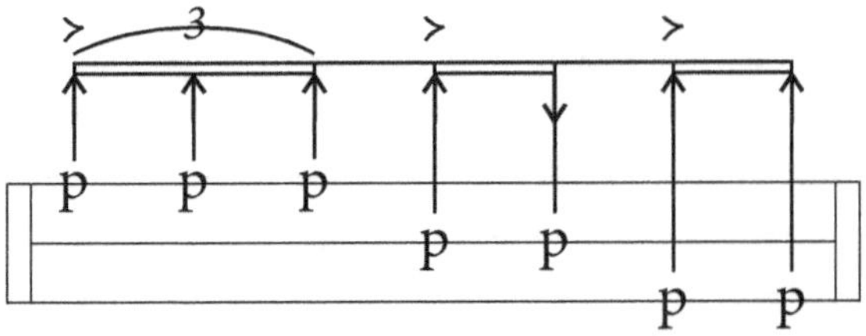

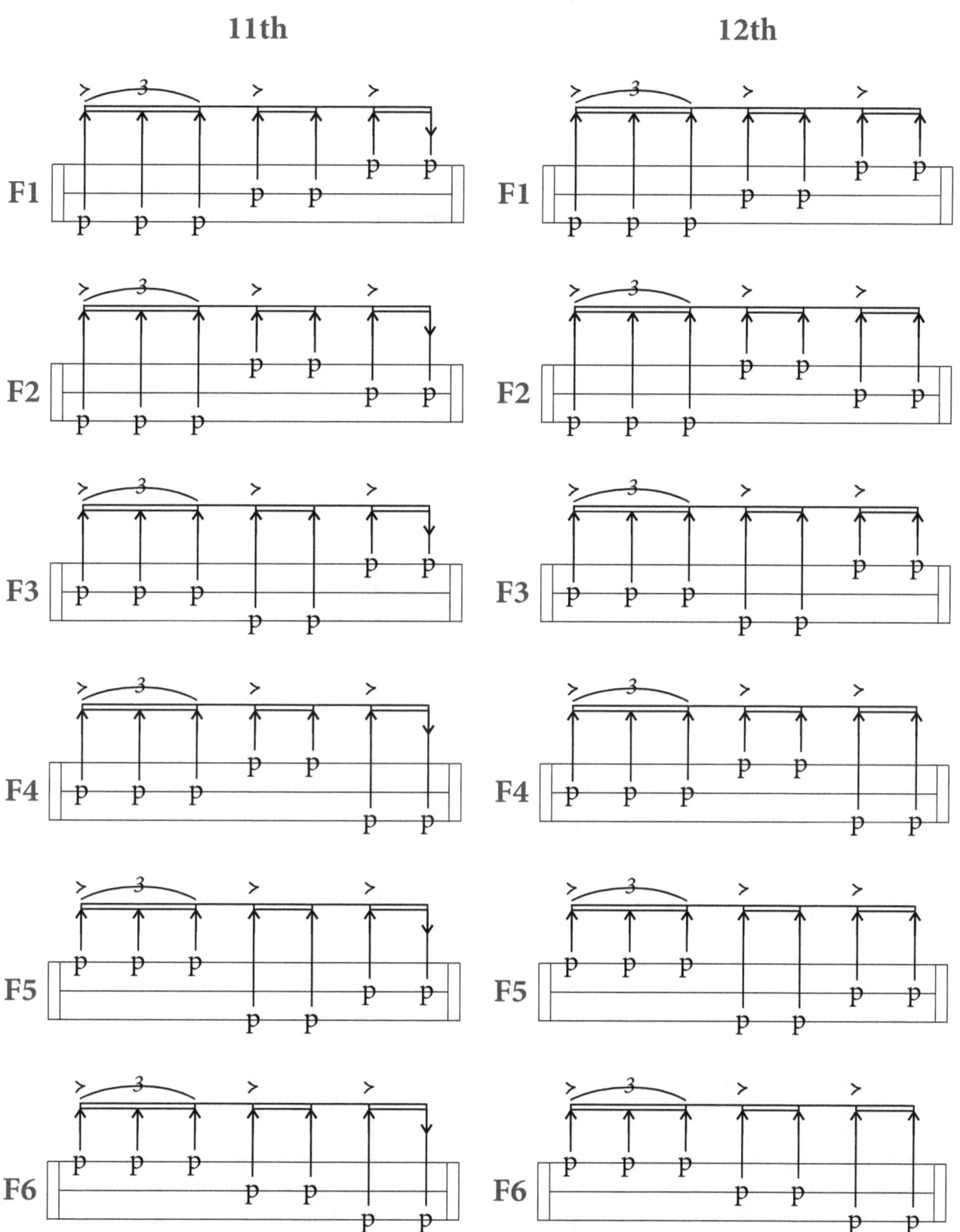

VARIATION II
WAYS OF PERFORMANCE

1st   **2nd**

F1

F2

F3

F4

F5

F6

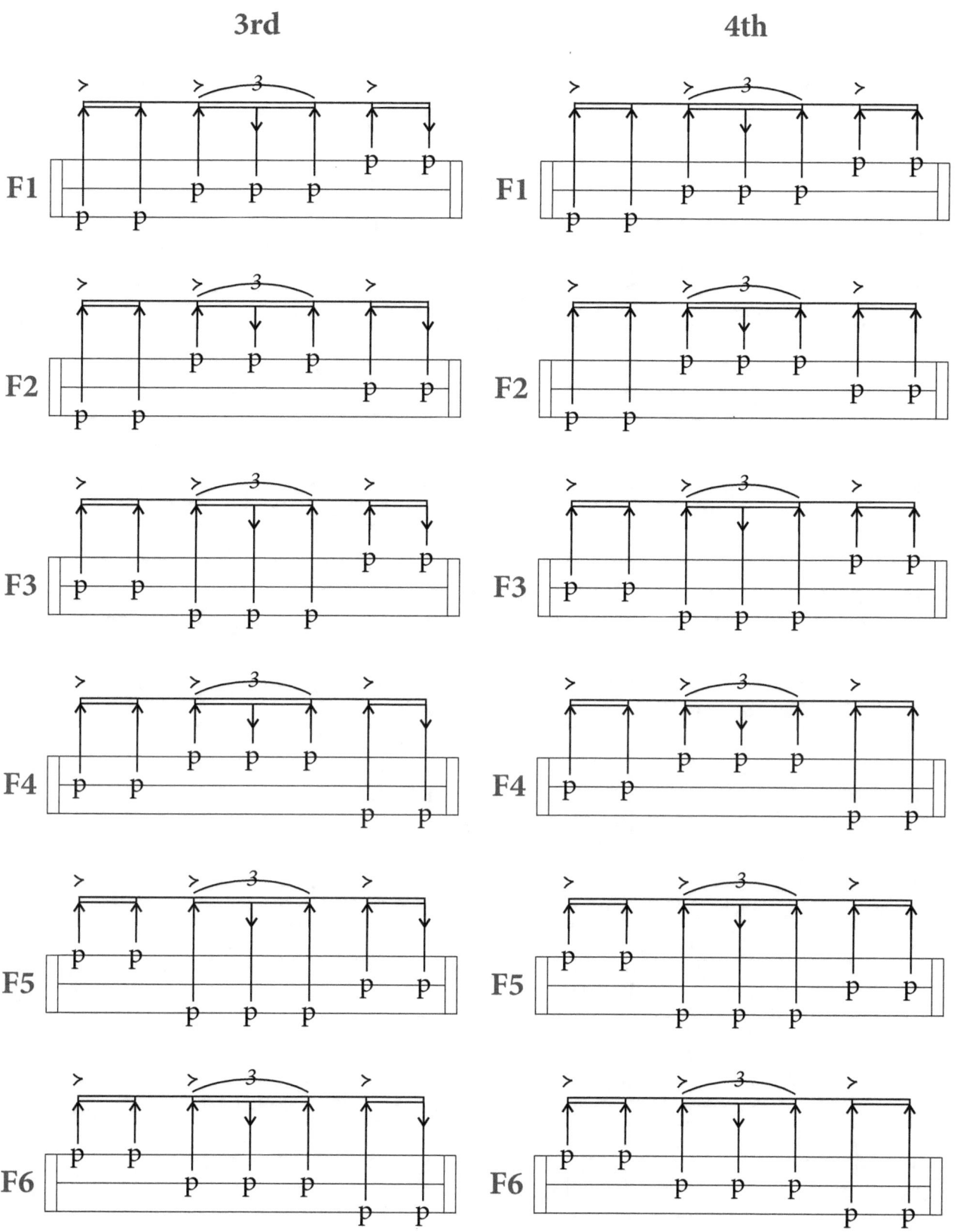

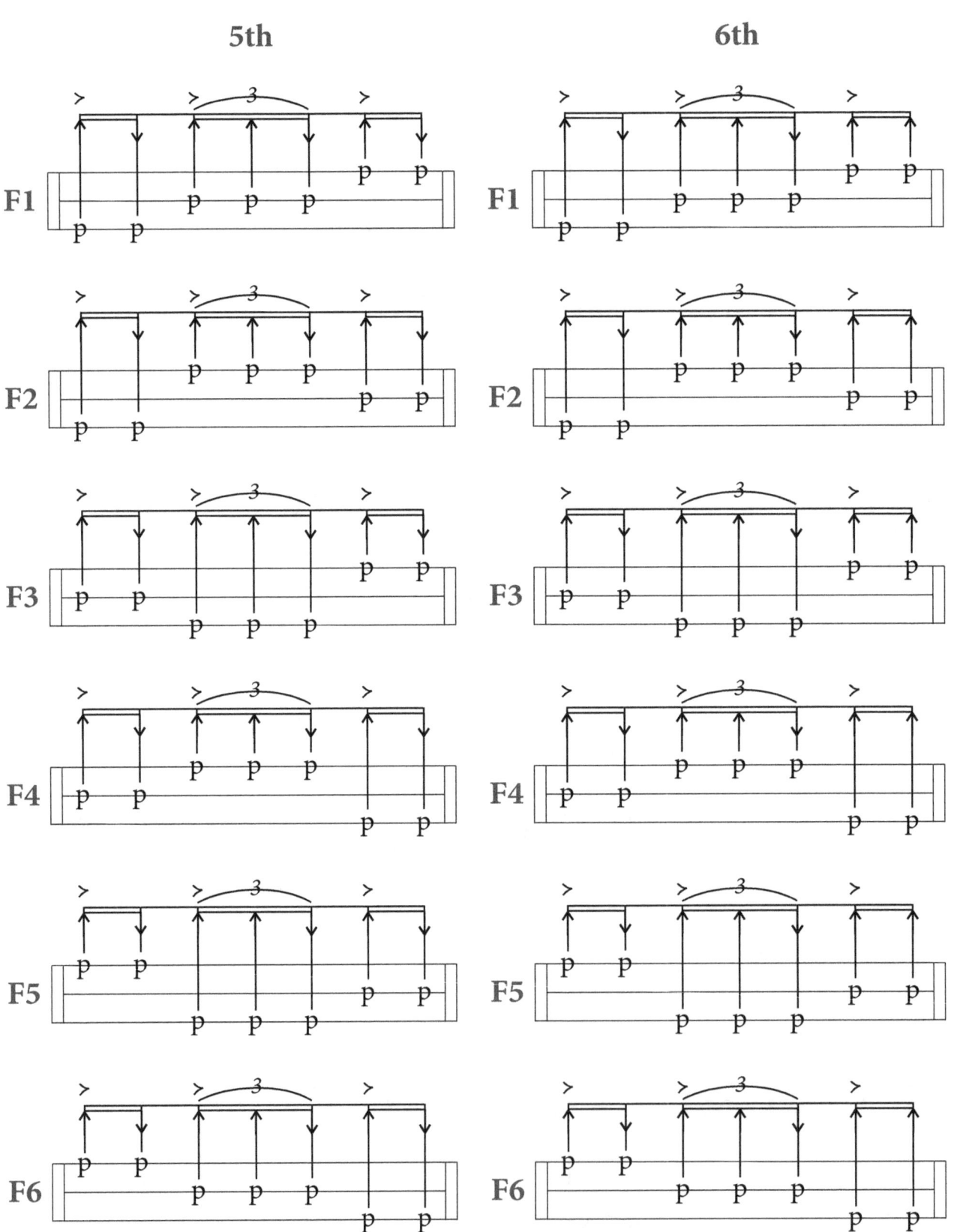

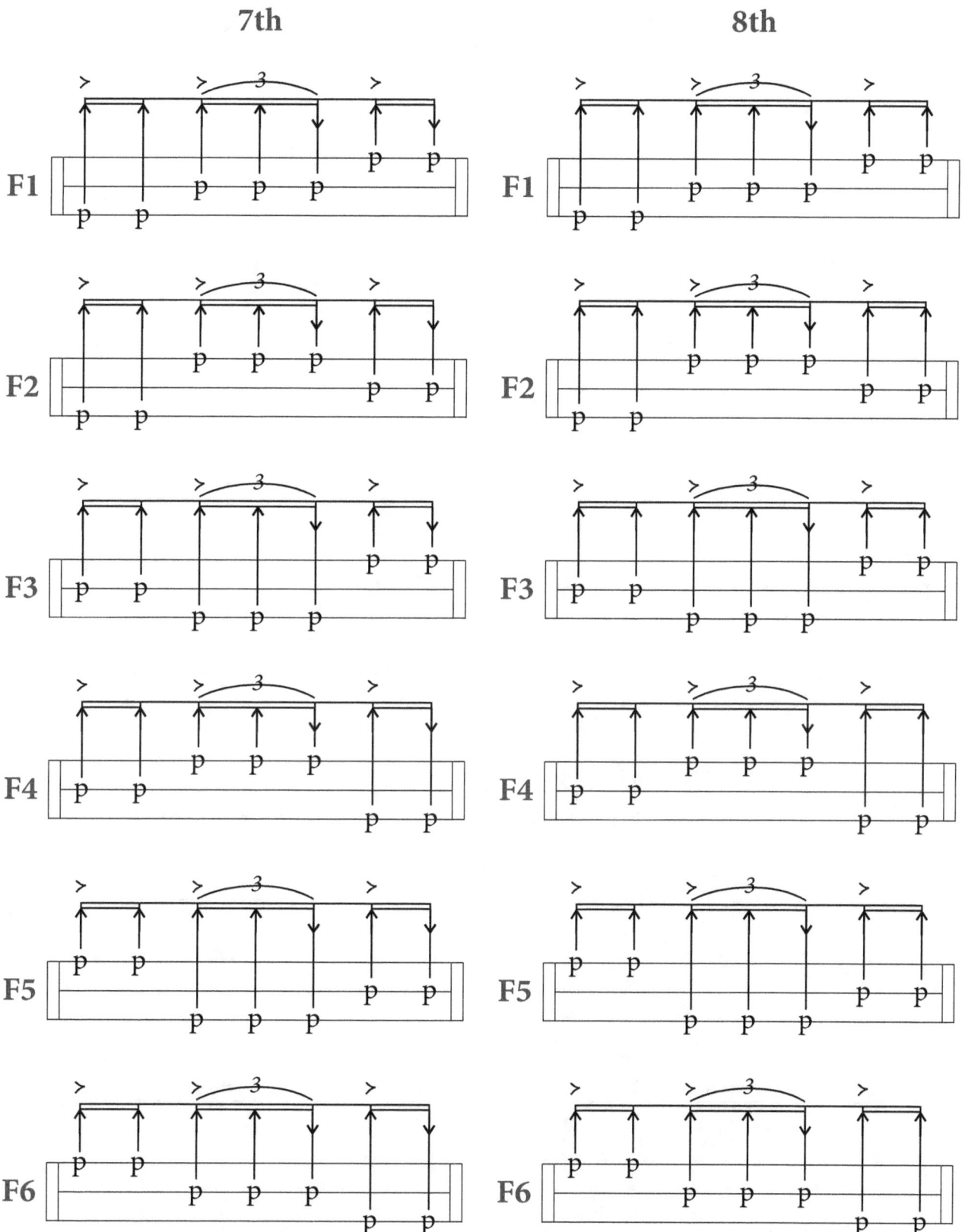

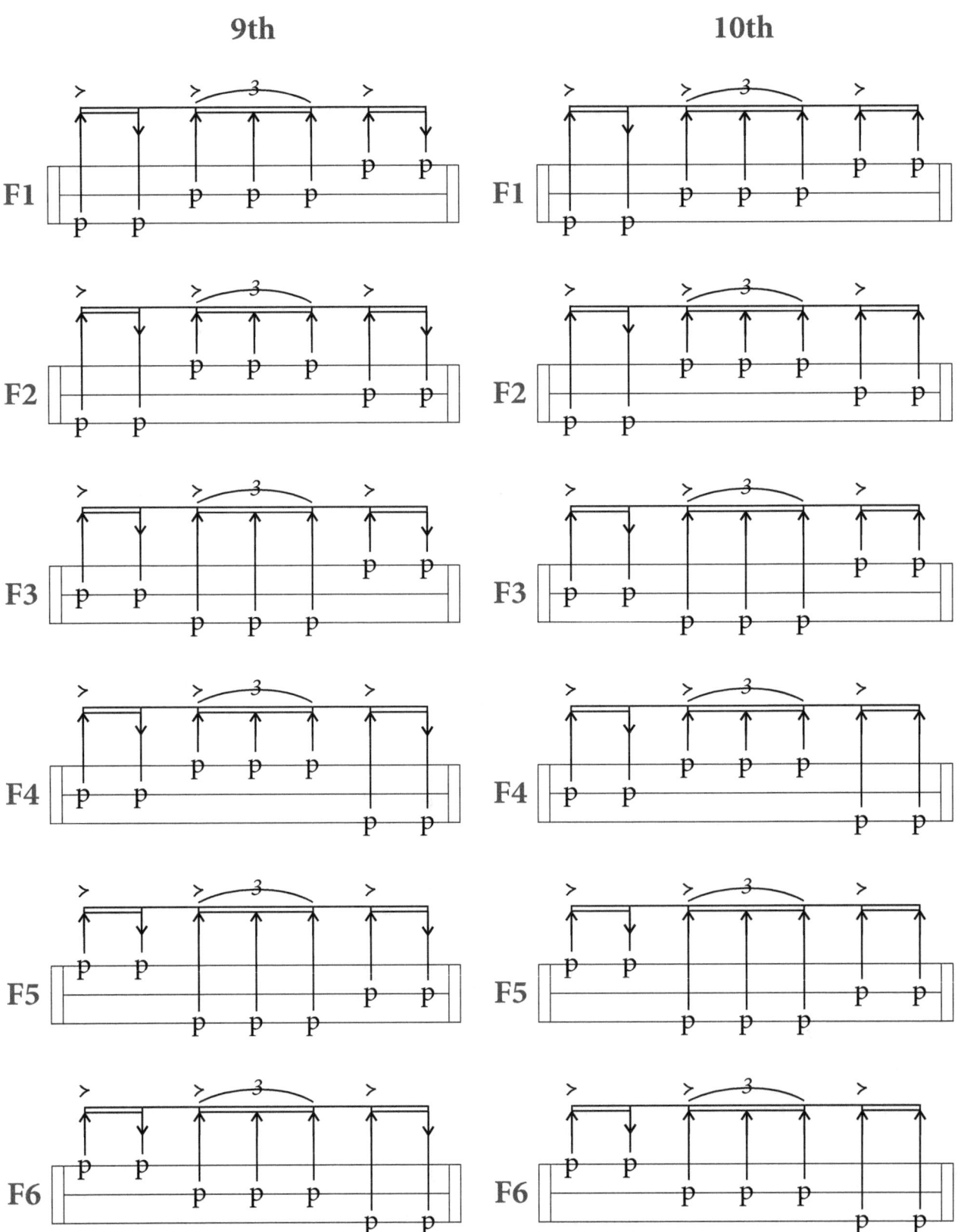

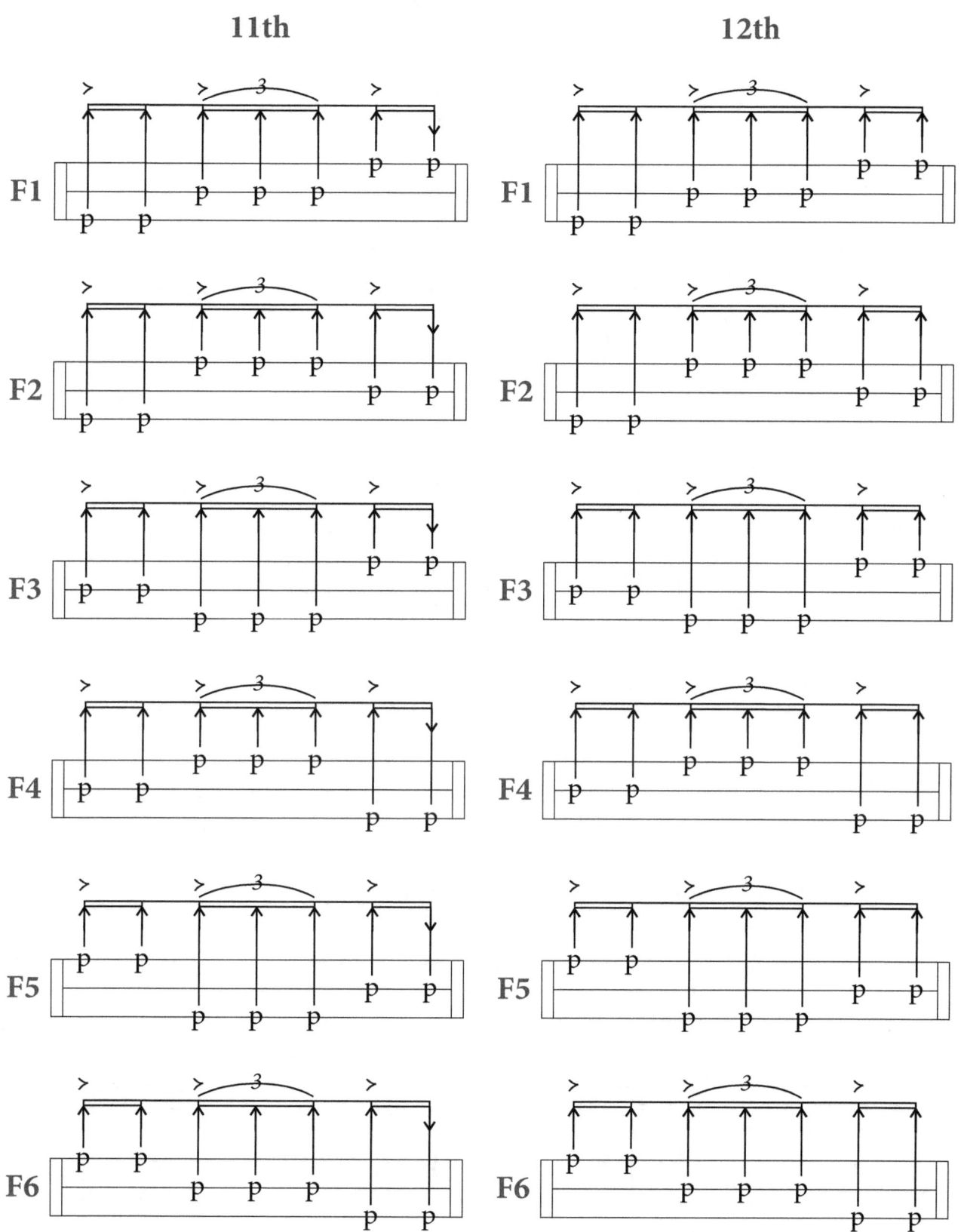

VARIATION III
WAYS OF PERFORMANCE

1st   **2nd**

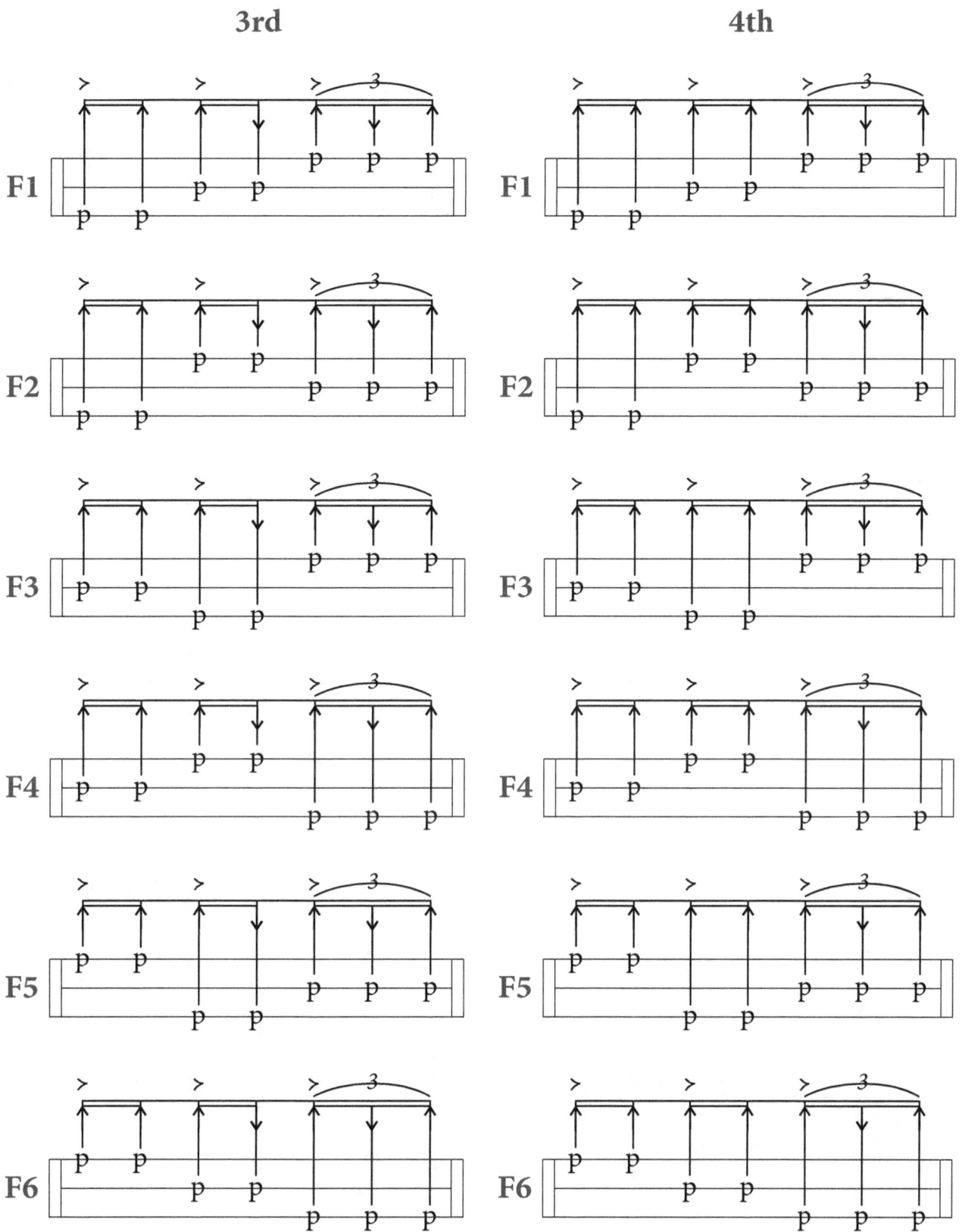

5th / 6th

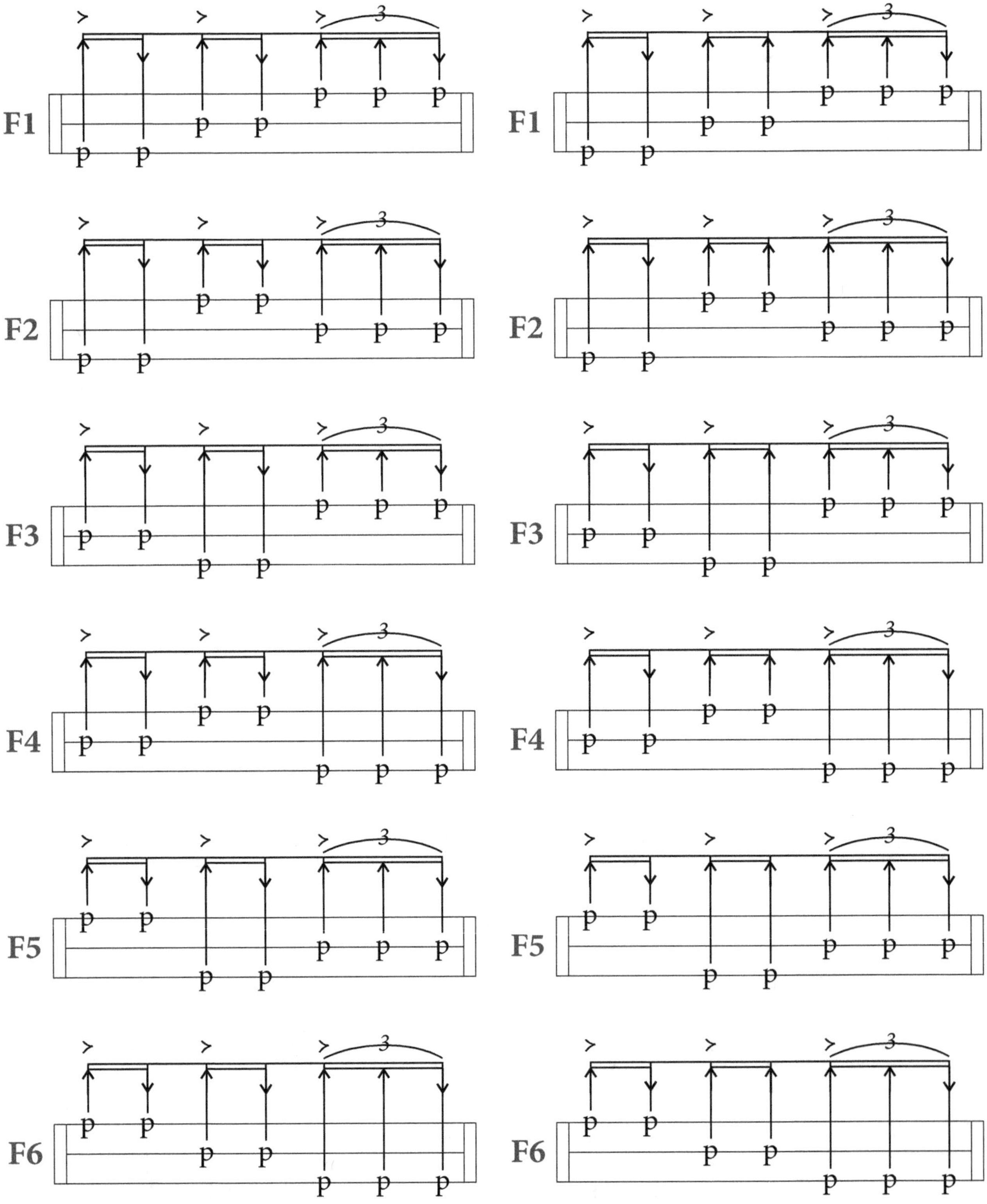

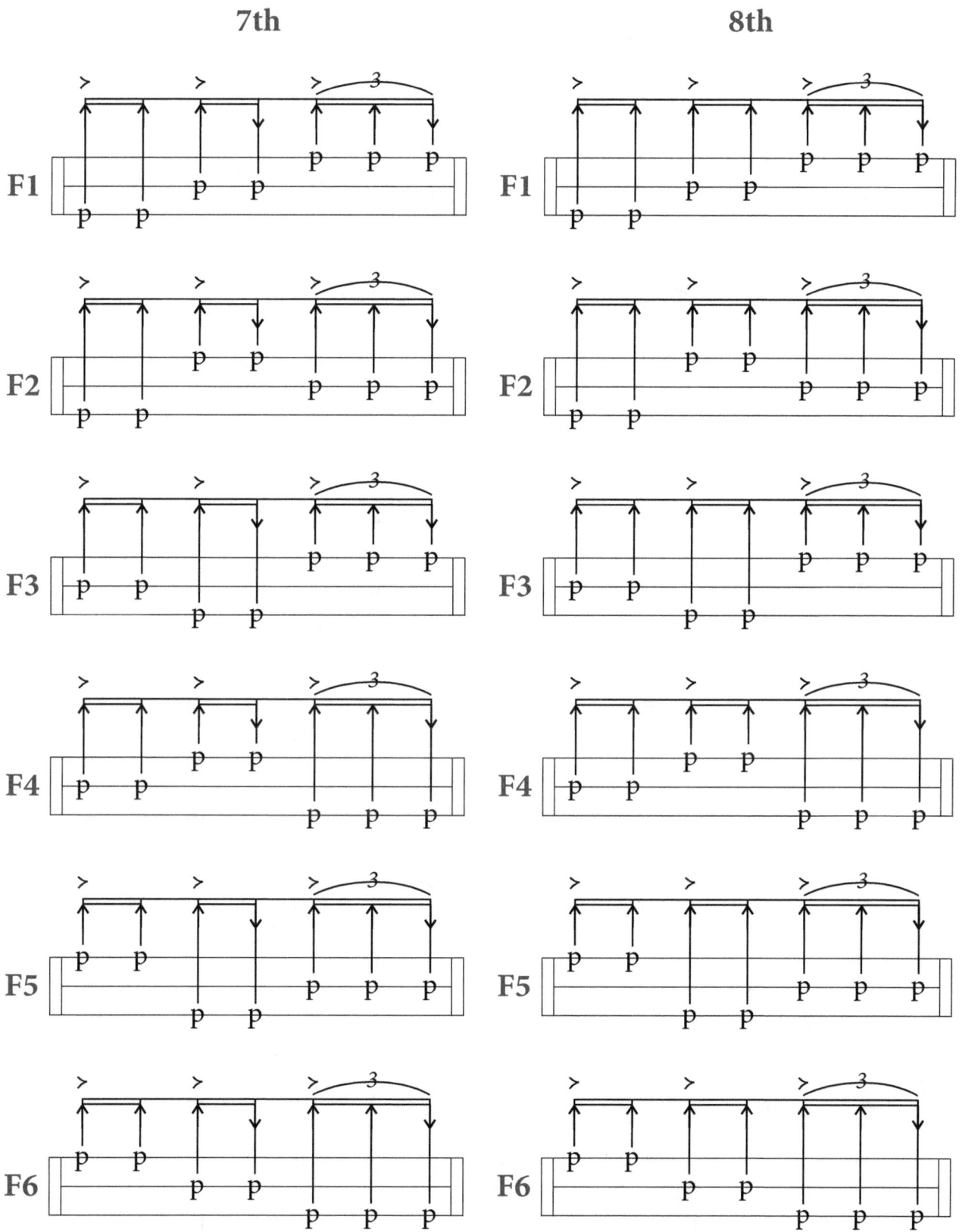

9th | **10th**

F1
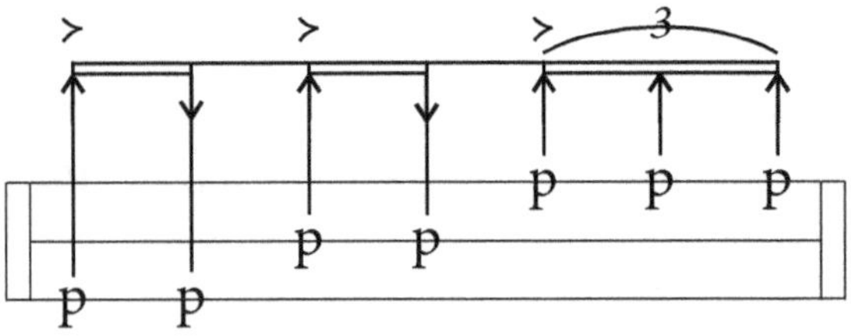

F1
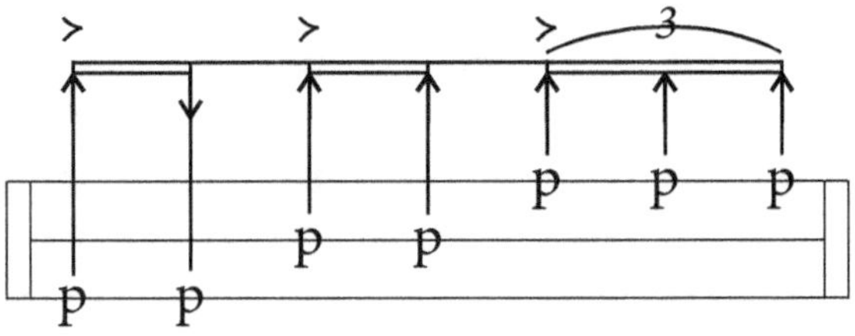

F2
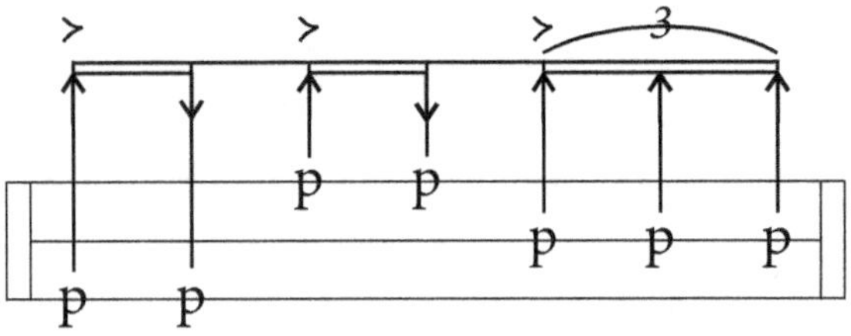

F2
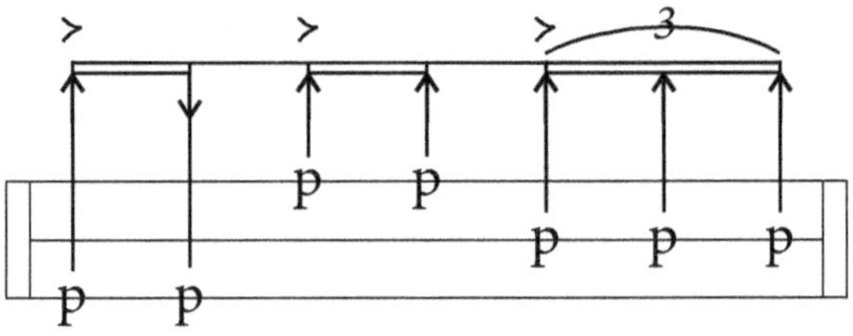

F3
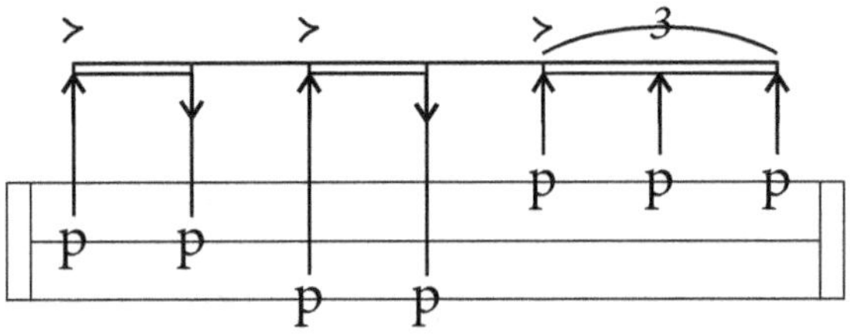

F3
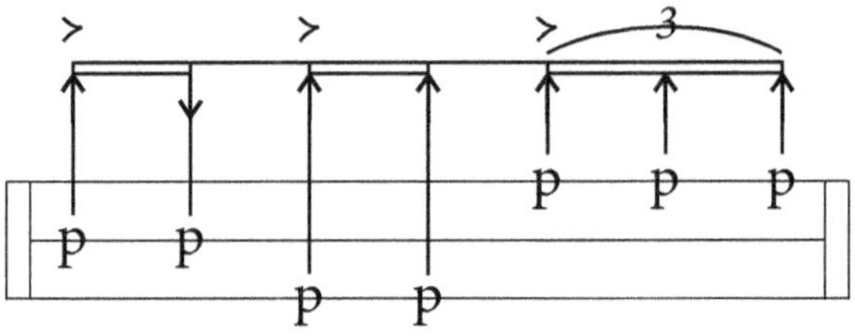

F4
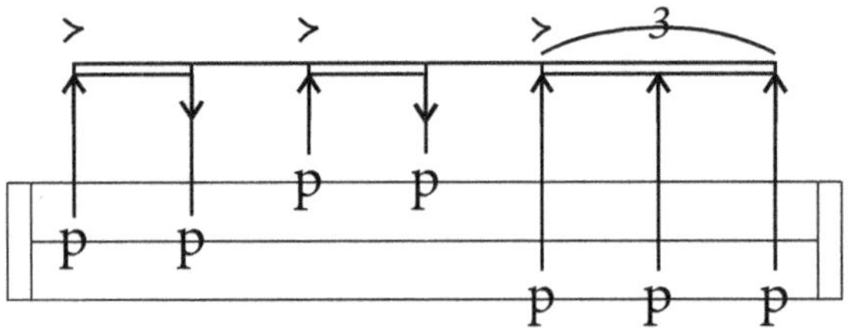

F4
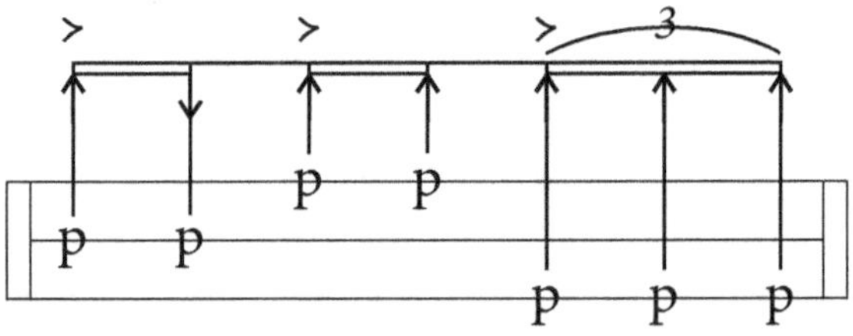

F5
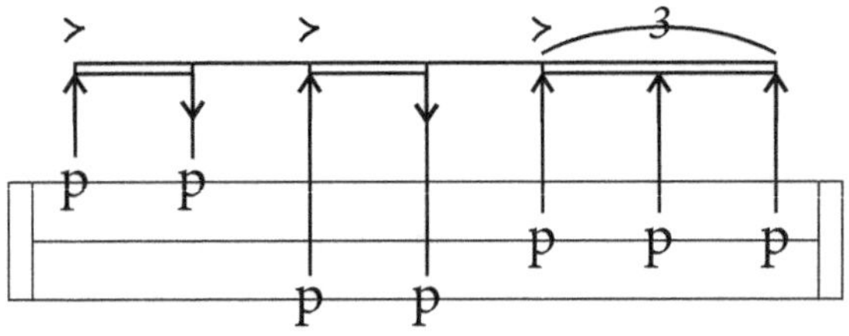

F5
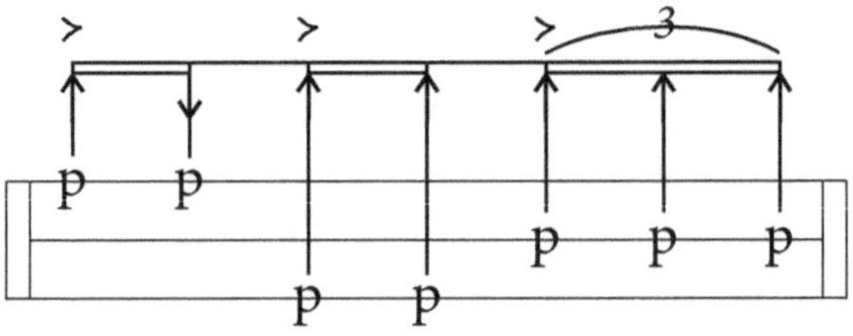

F6
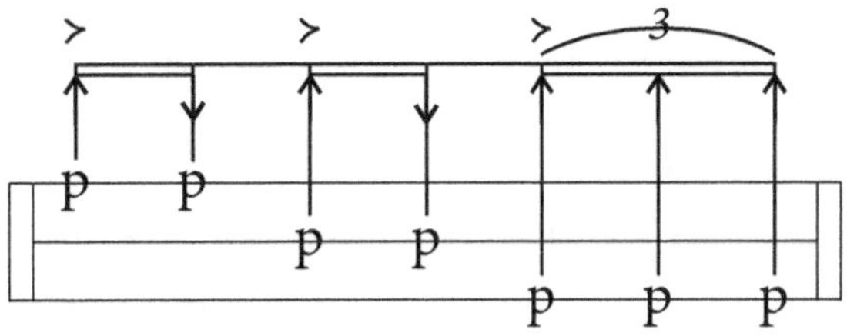

F6
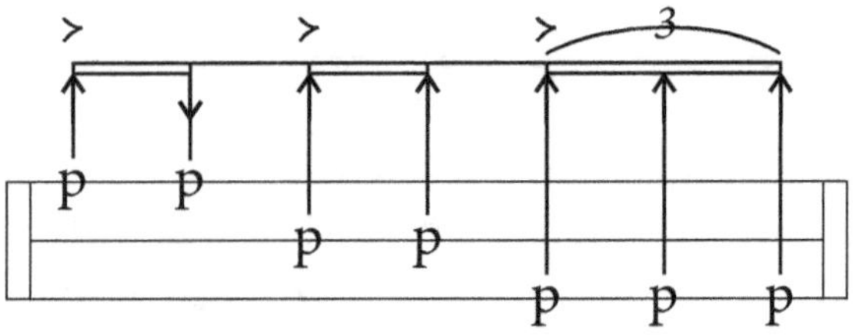

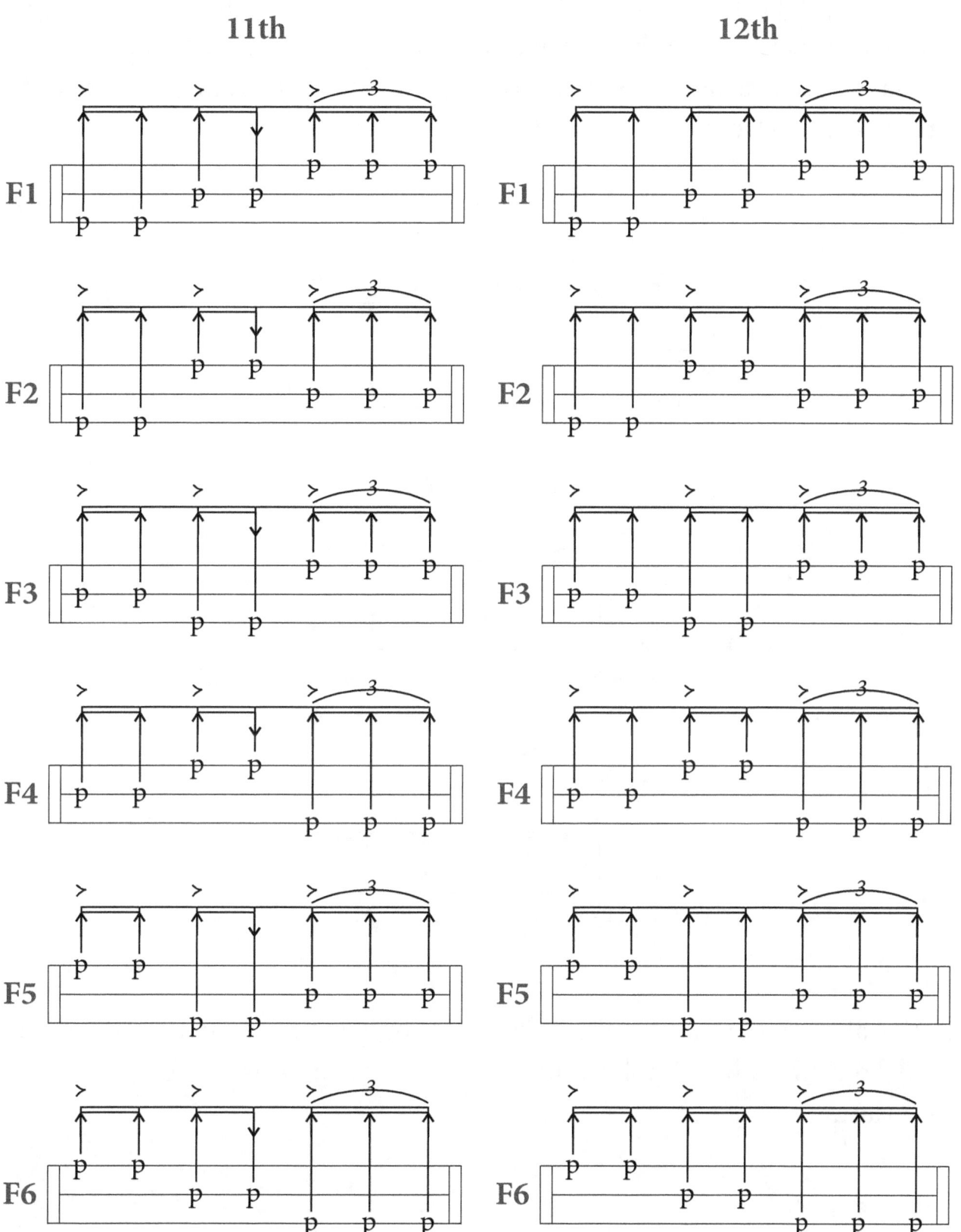

§ VII

Exercise on pulgar on three adjacent strings with two triple and one single stroke within each Formula. The exercise includes three variations with 6 Formulas in each variation. Isochronous playing of triplets and single stroke. The first Formula from each variation is cited below.

VARIATION I

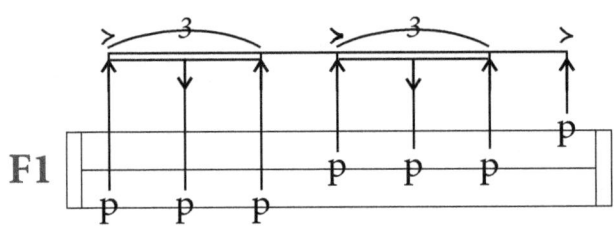

VARIATION II

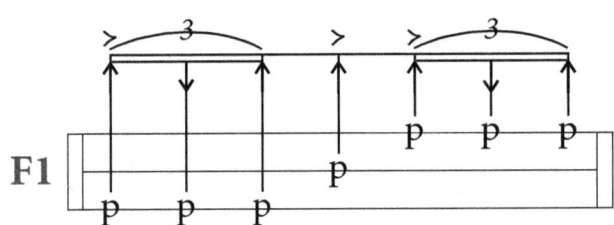

VARIATION III

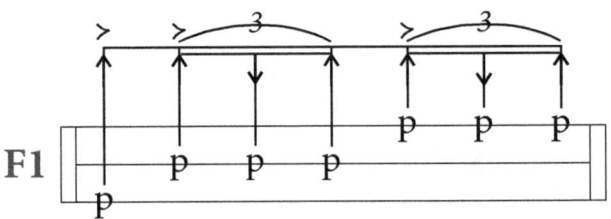

Each variation depending on the direction of pulgar stroke can be carried out in 9 different ways which follow. Practice on all variations and in all ways of each variation.

VARIATION I
WAYS OF PERFORMANCE

1st   **2nd**

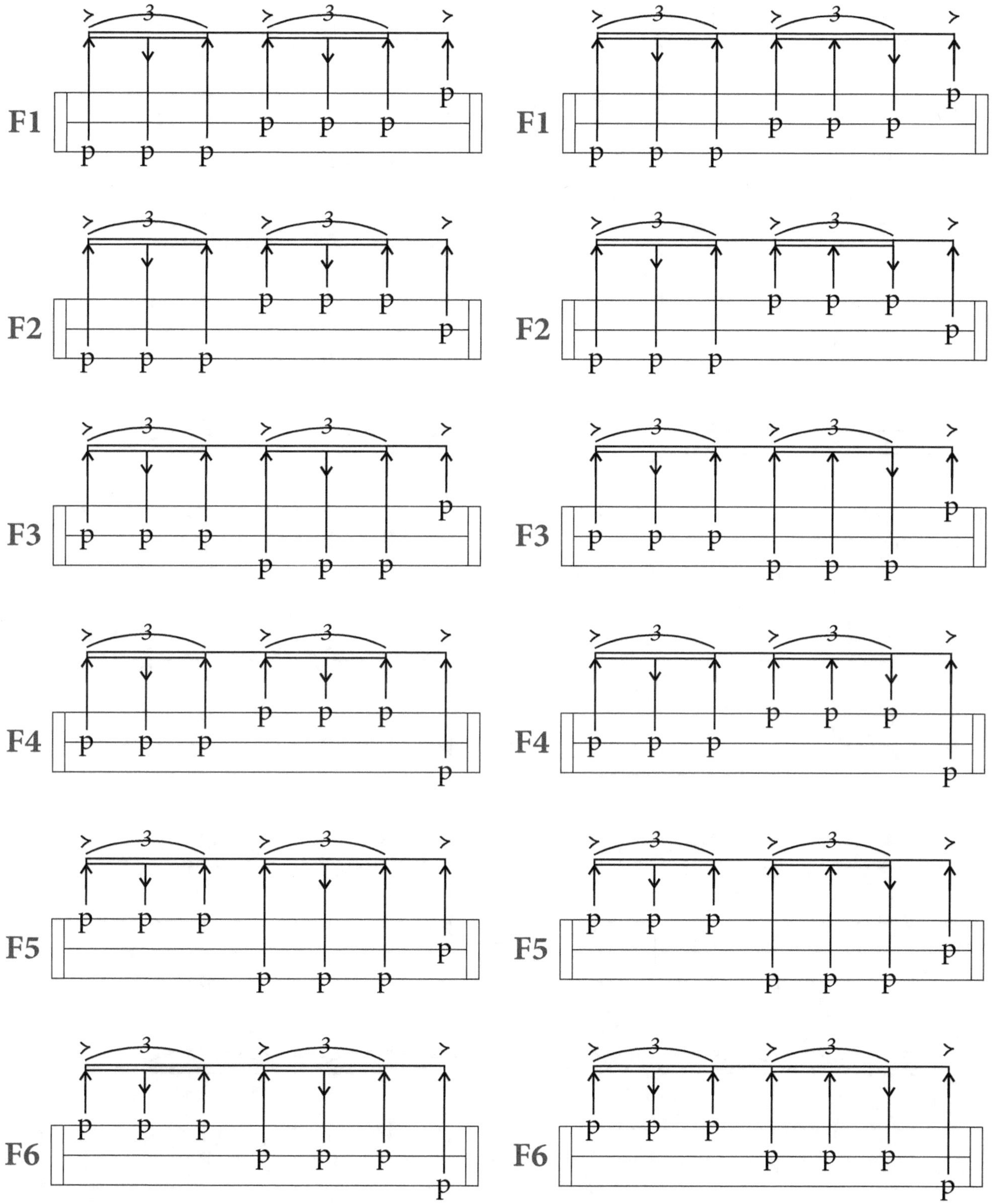

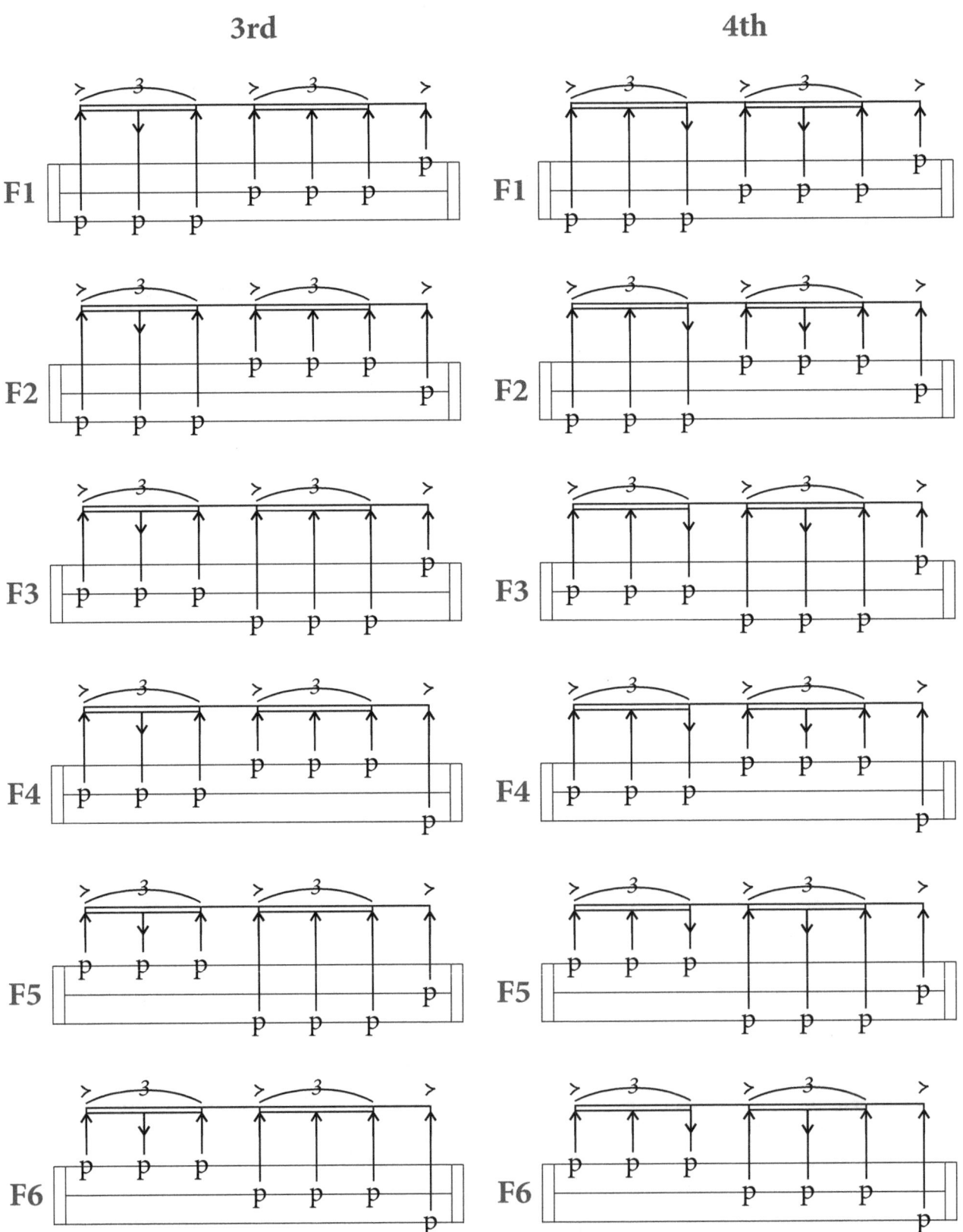

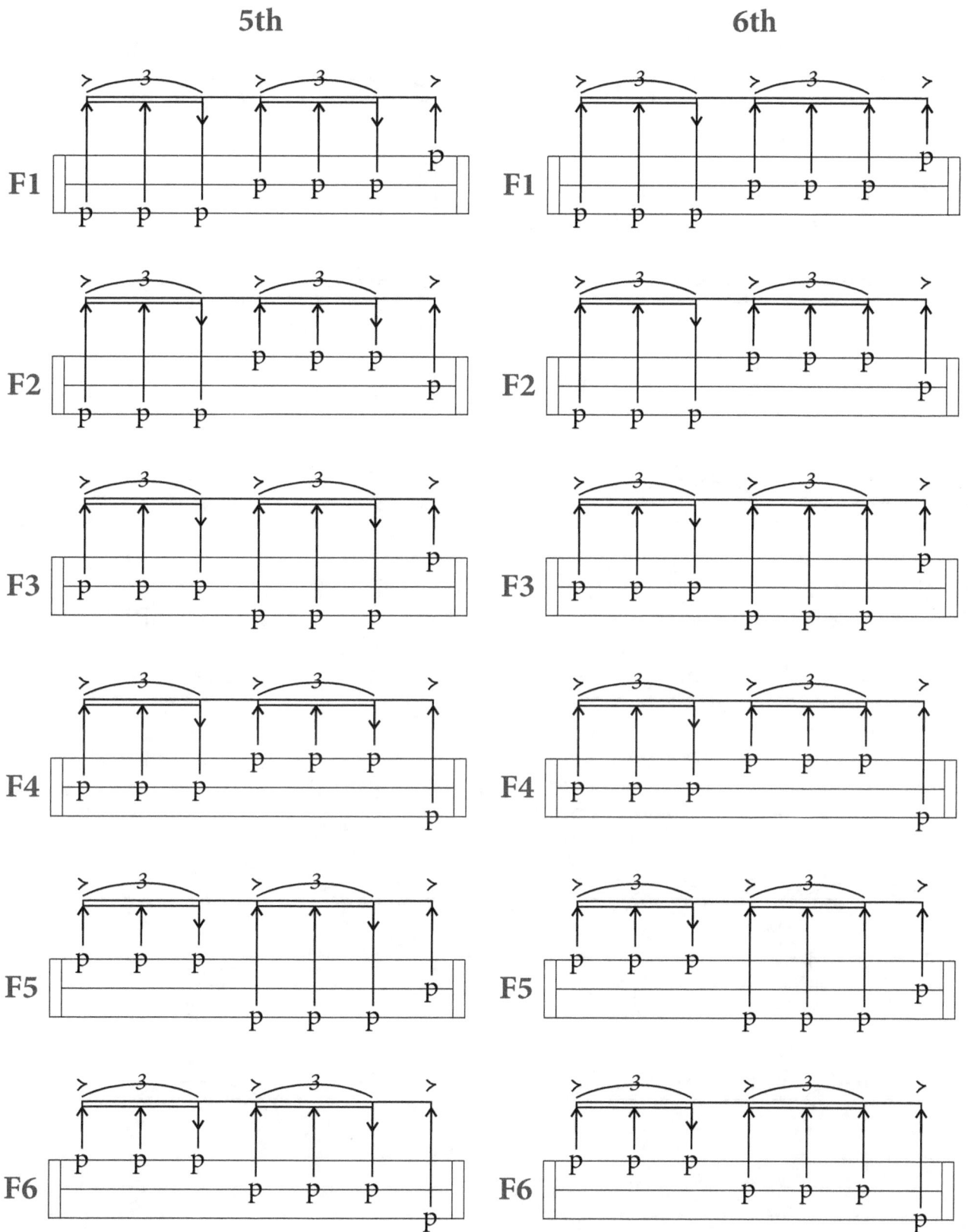

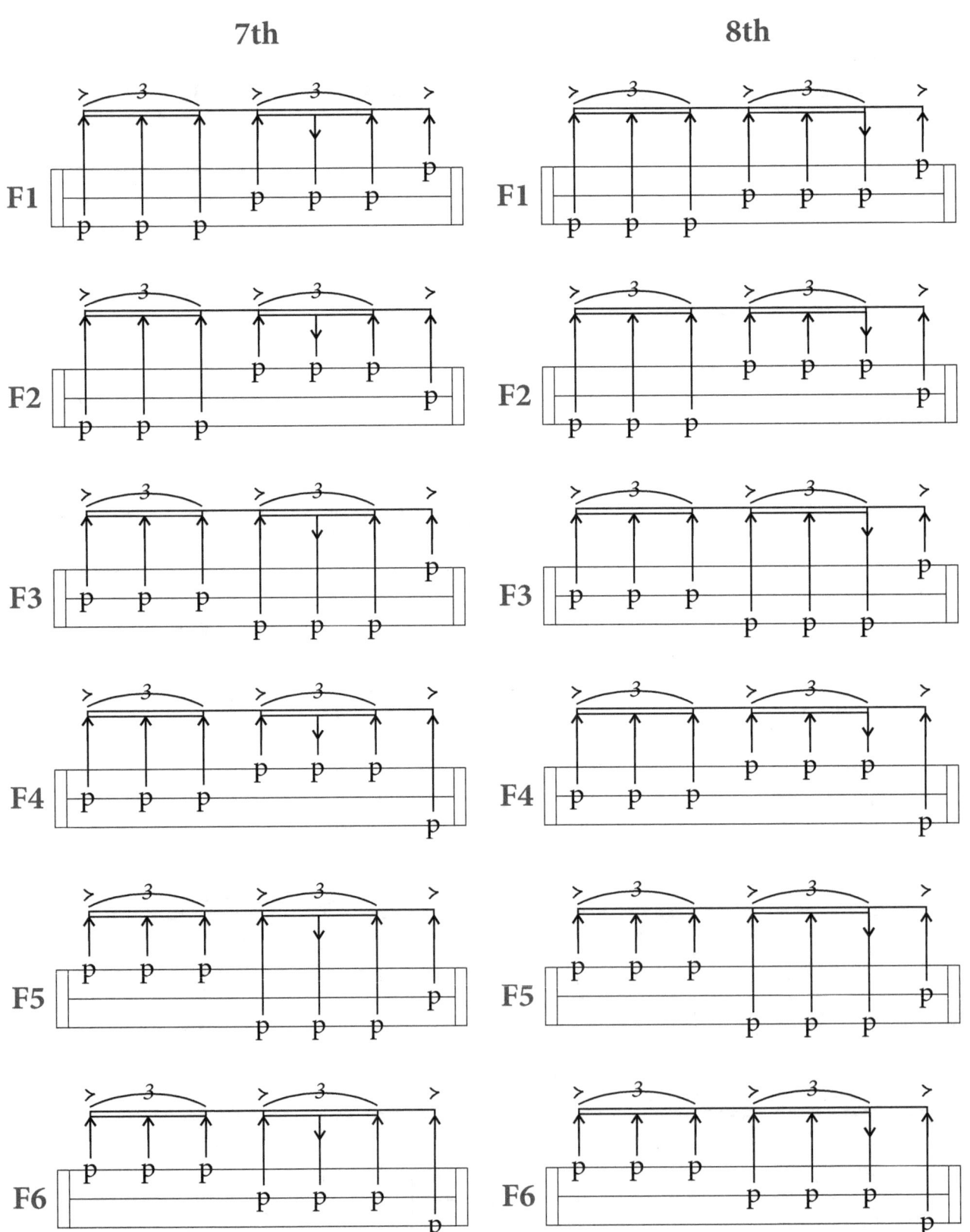

9th

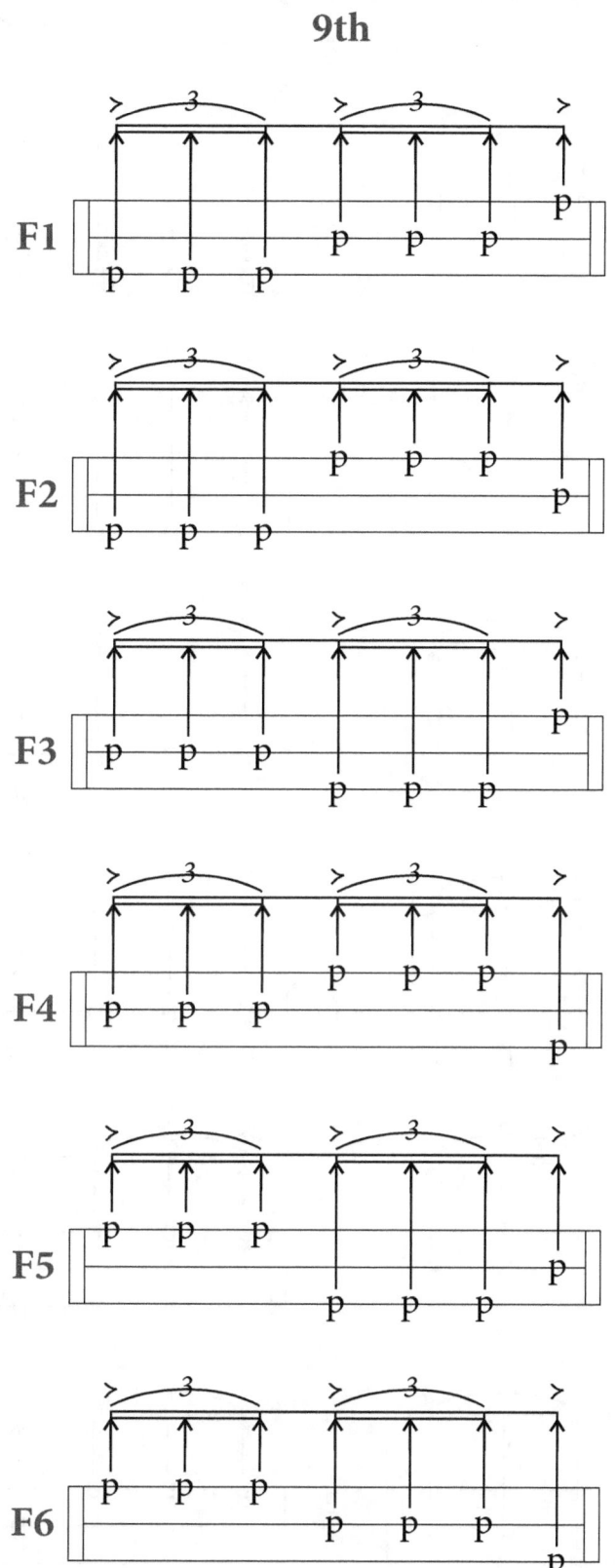

VARIATION II
WAYS OF PERFORMANCE

1st   **2nd**

3rd   4th

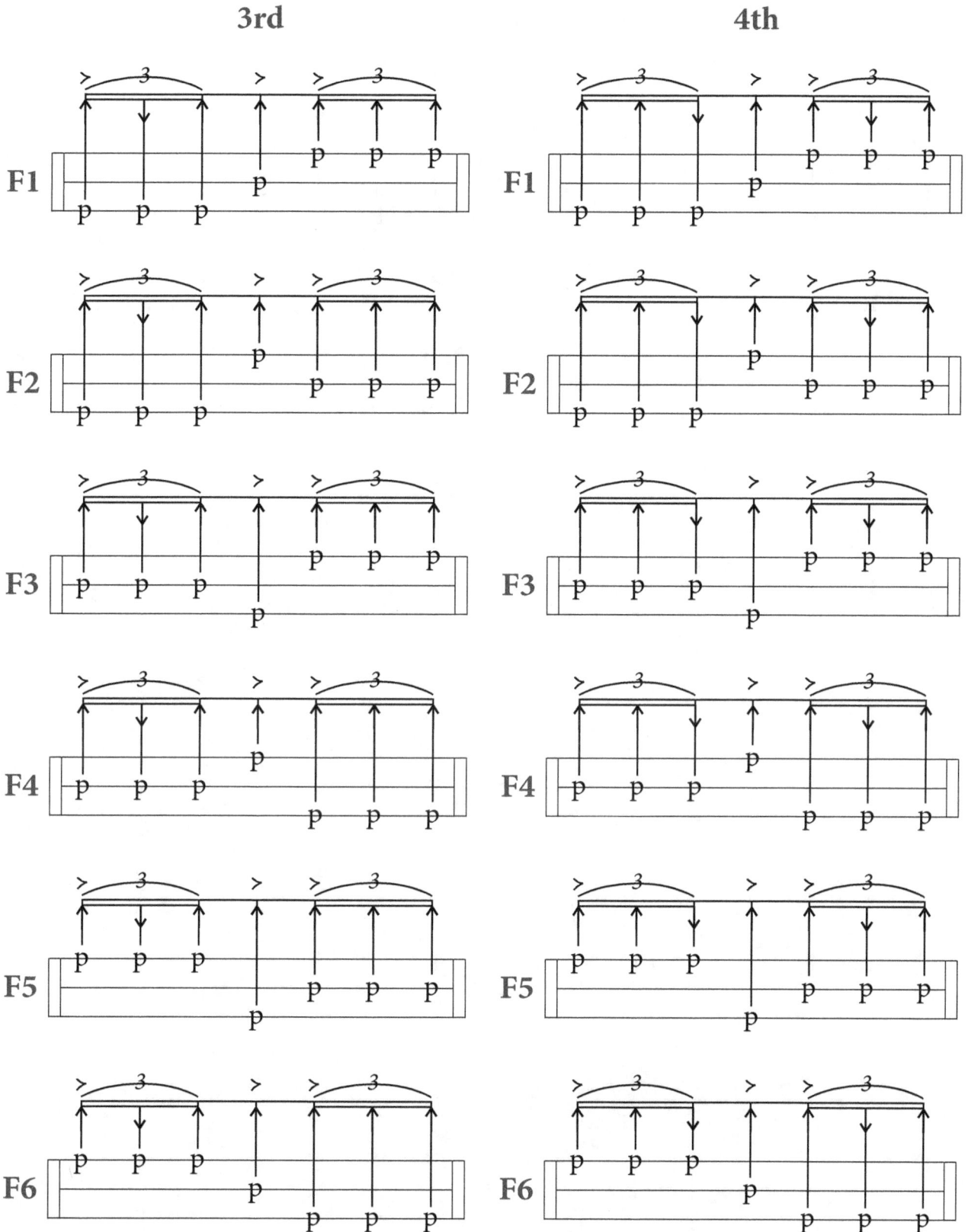

5th   6th

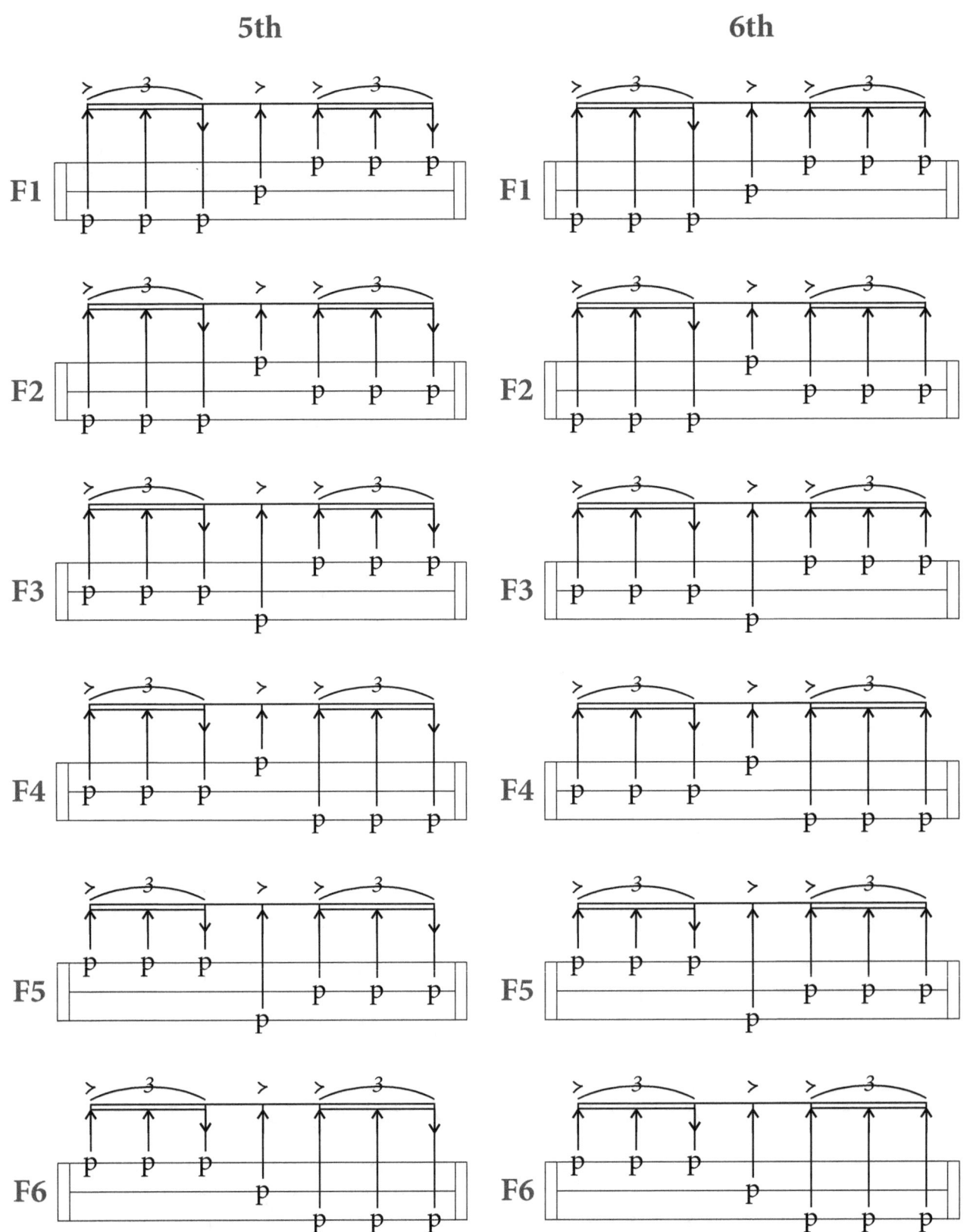

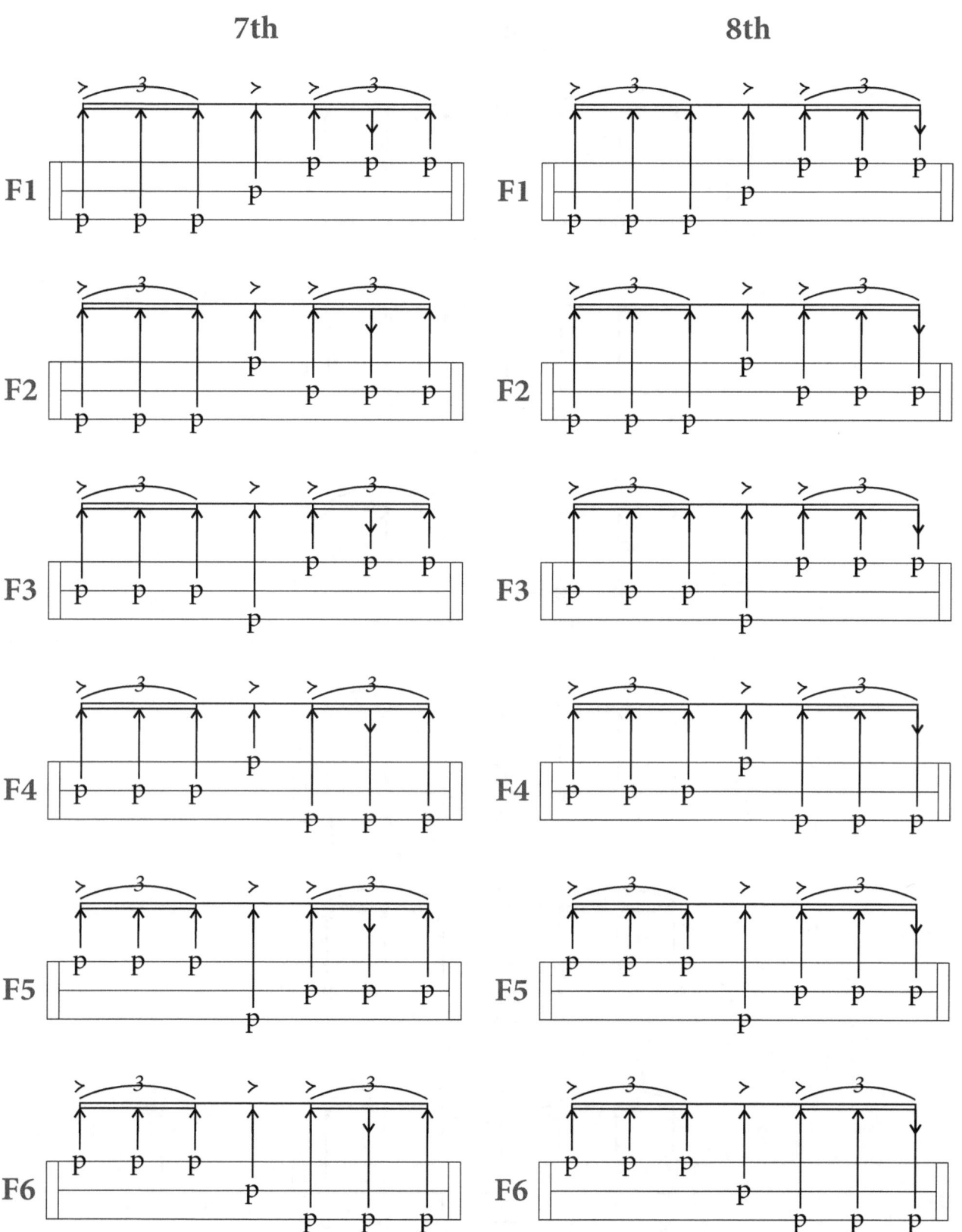

9th

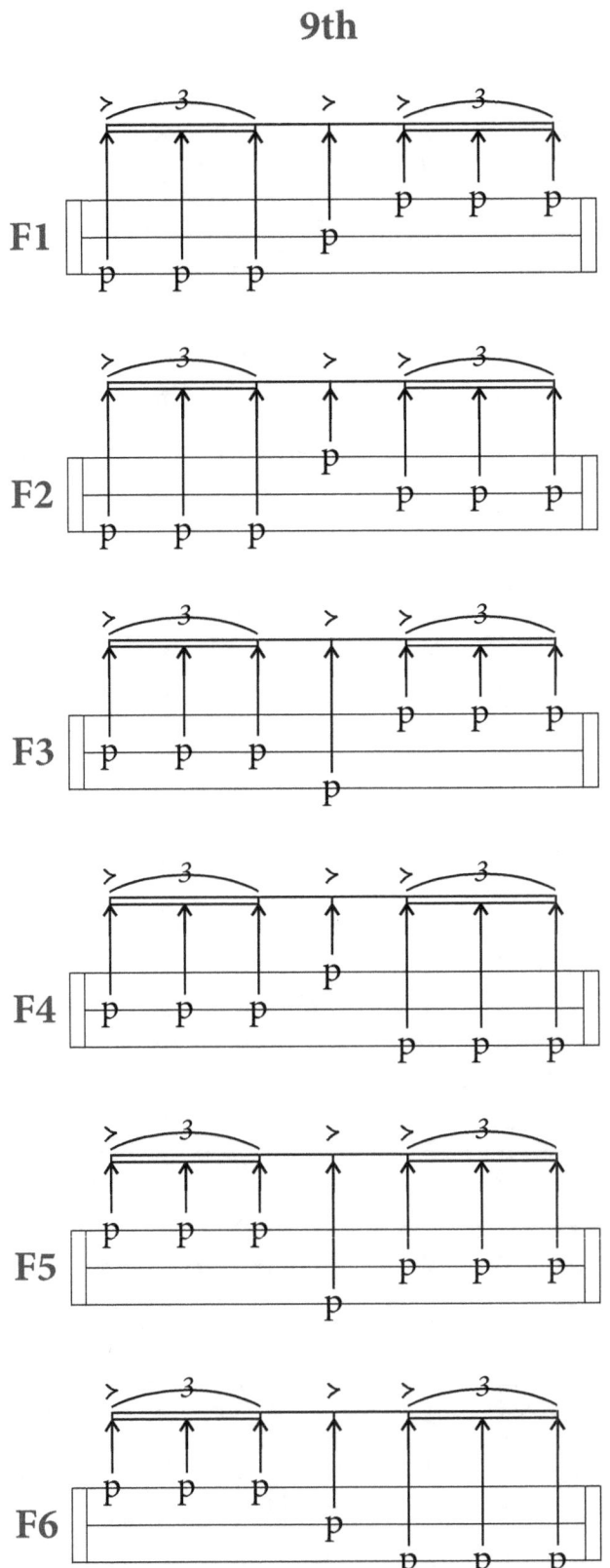

VARIATION III
WAYS OF PERFORMANCE

1st   **2nd**

9

3rd	4th

F1
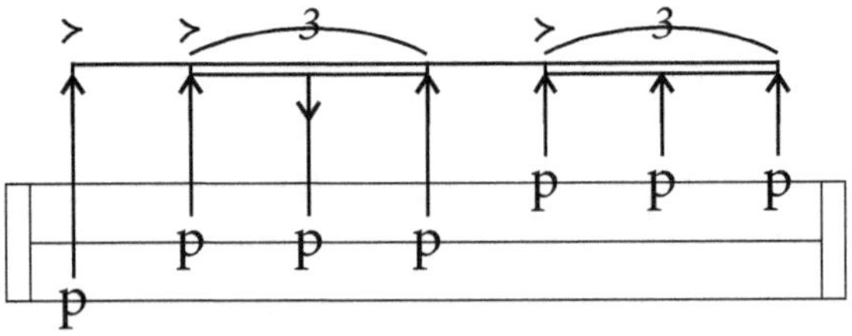
F1
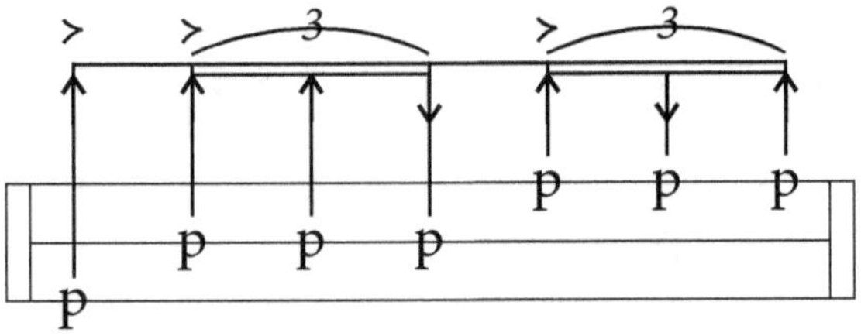

F2
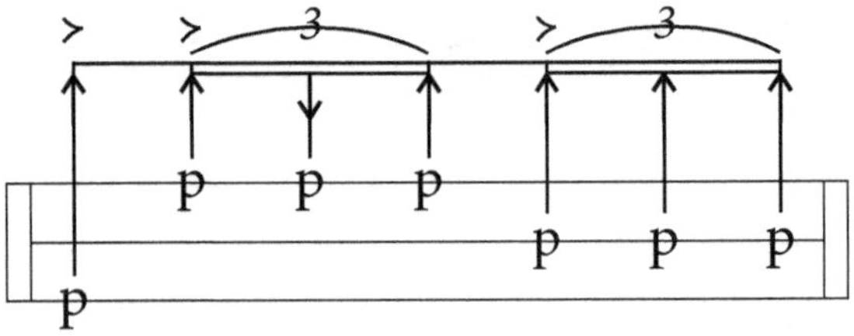
F2
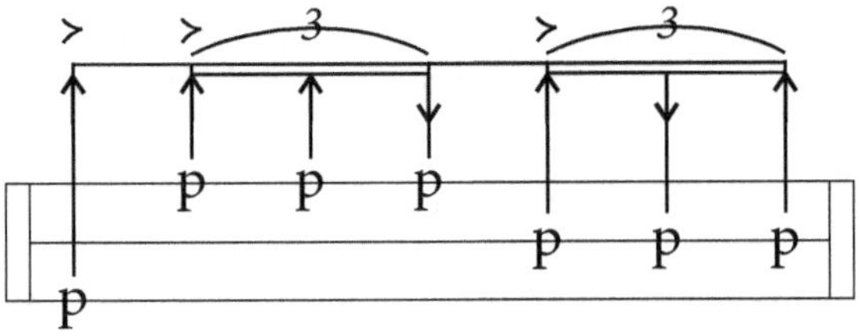

F3
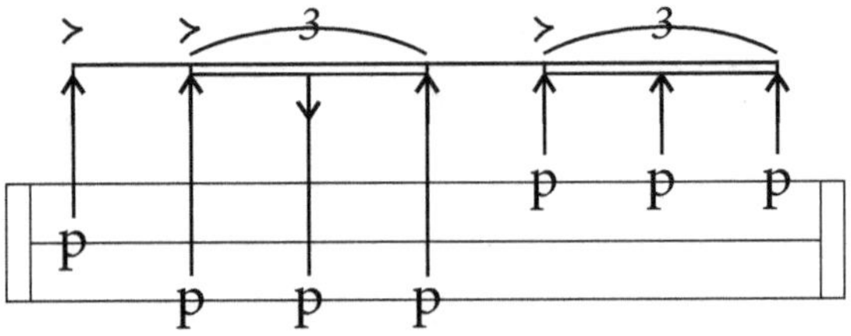
F3
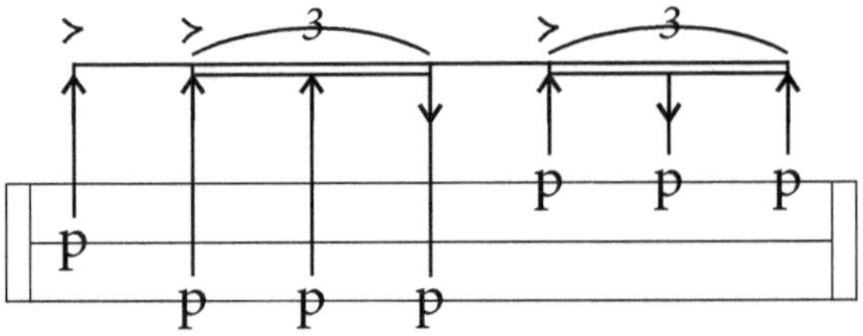

F4
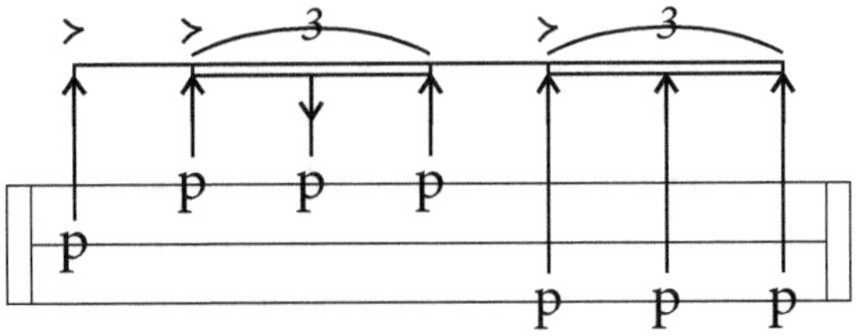
F4
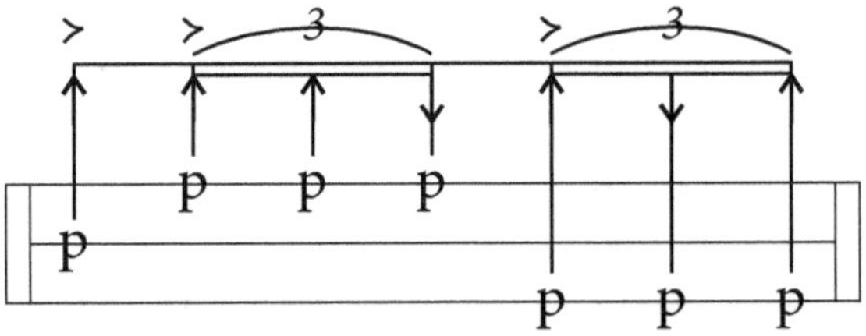

F5
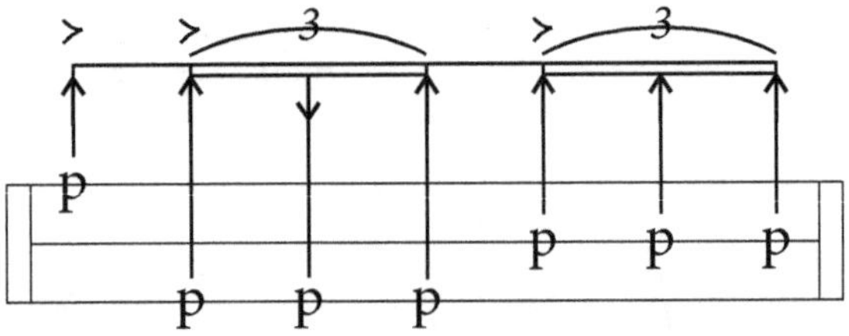
F5
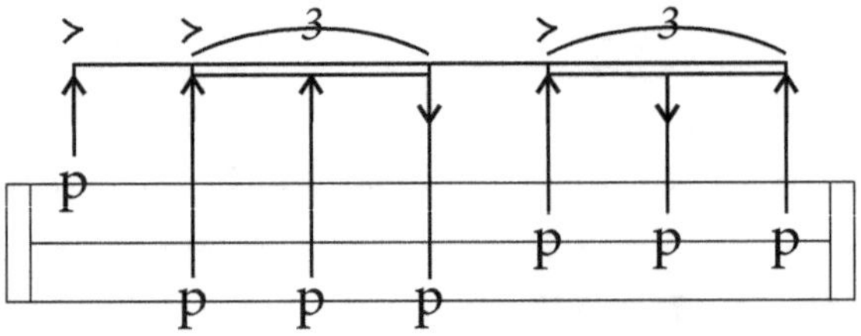

F6
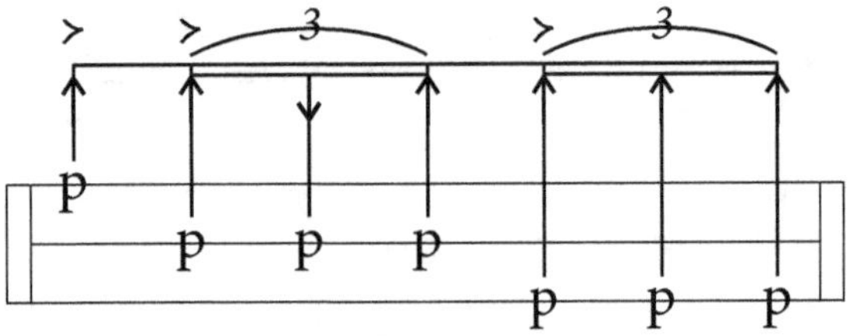
F6
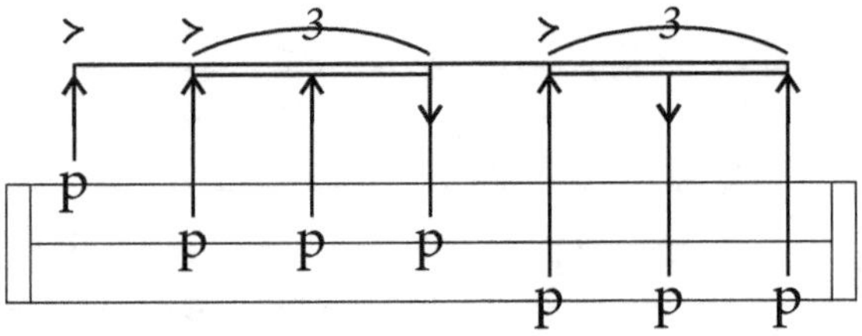

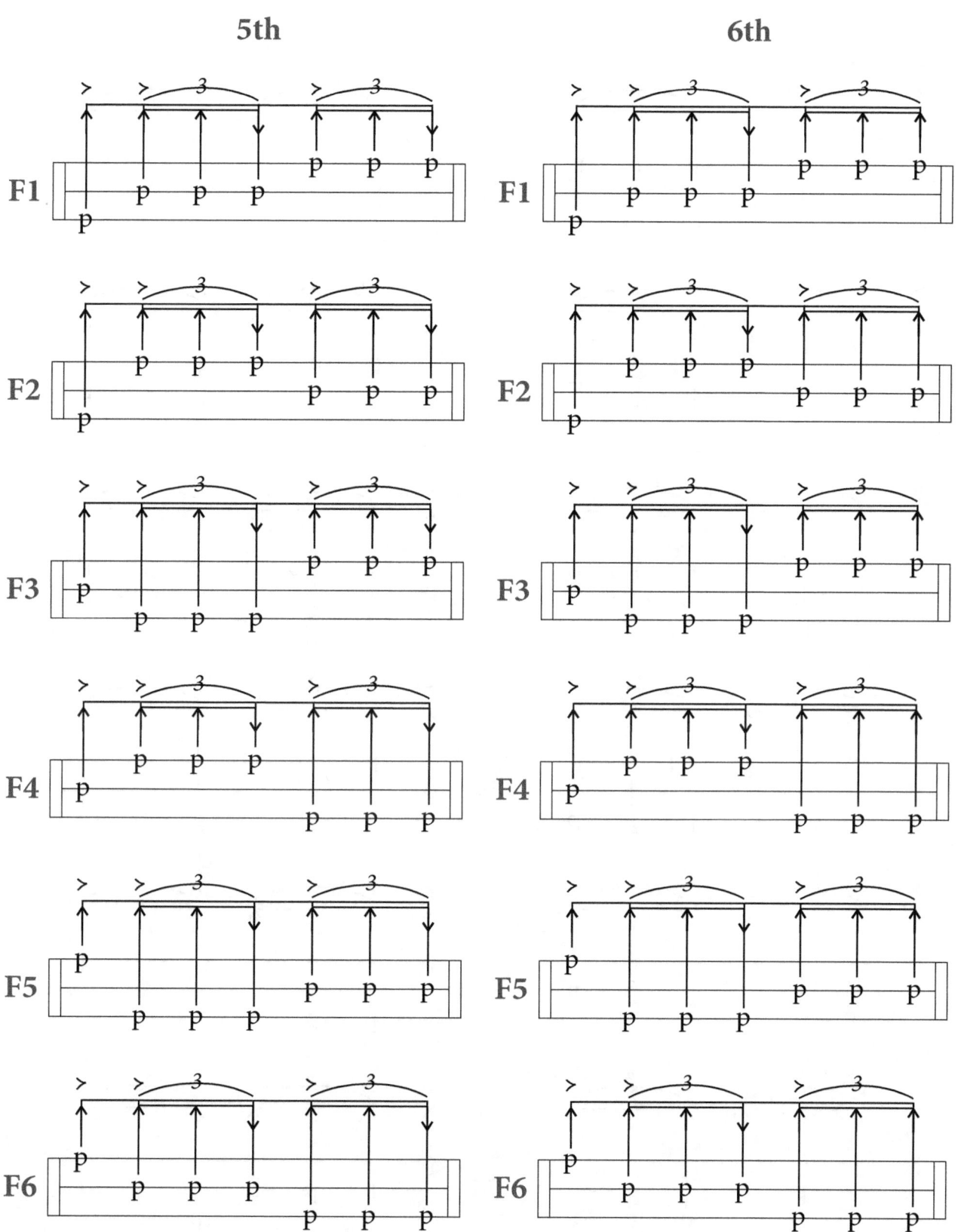

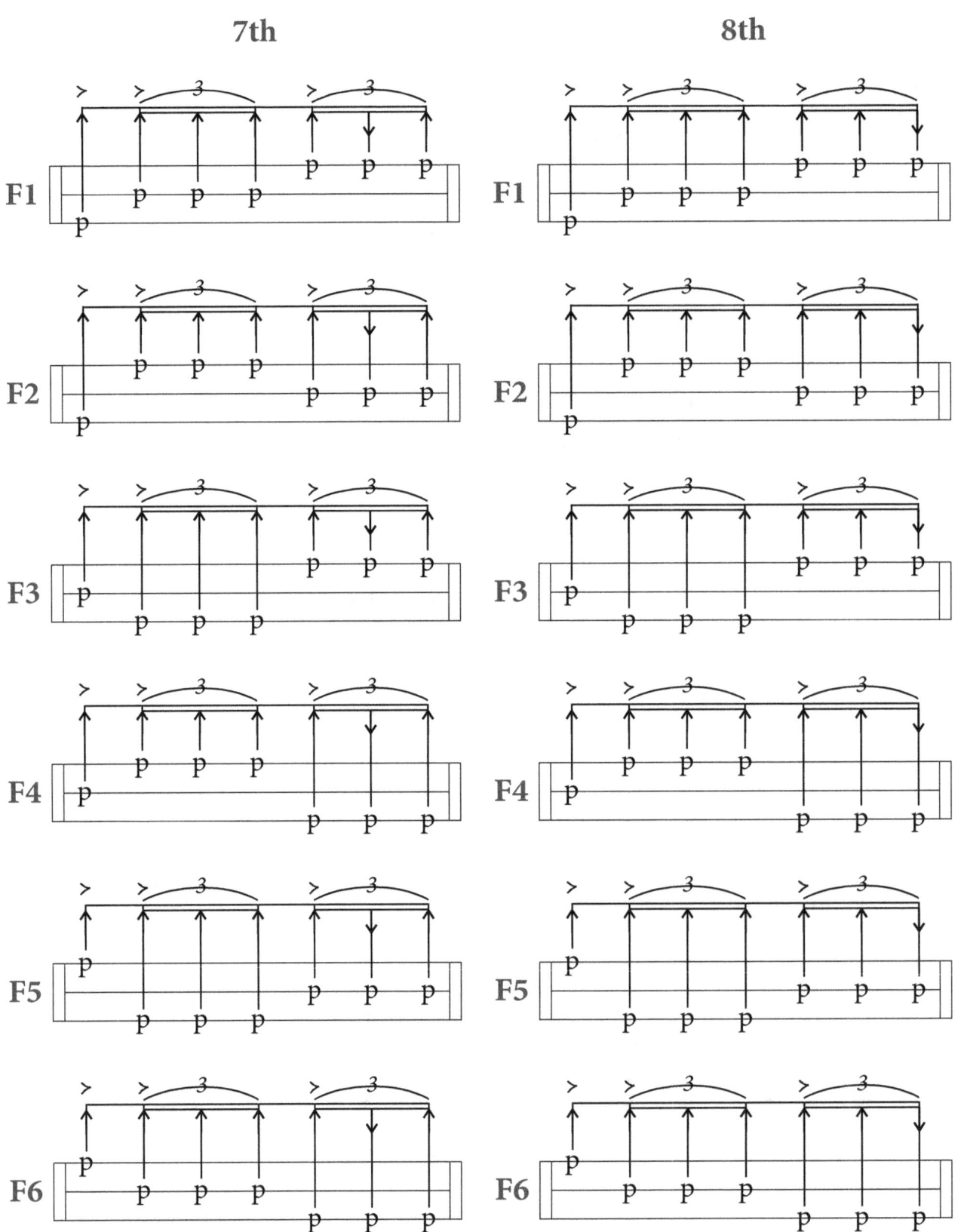

9th

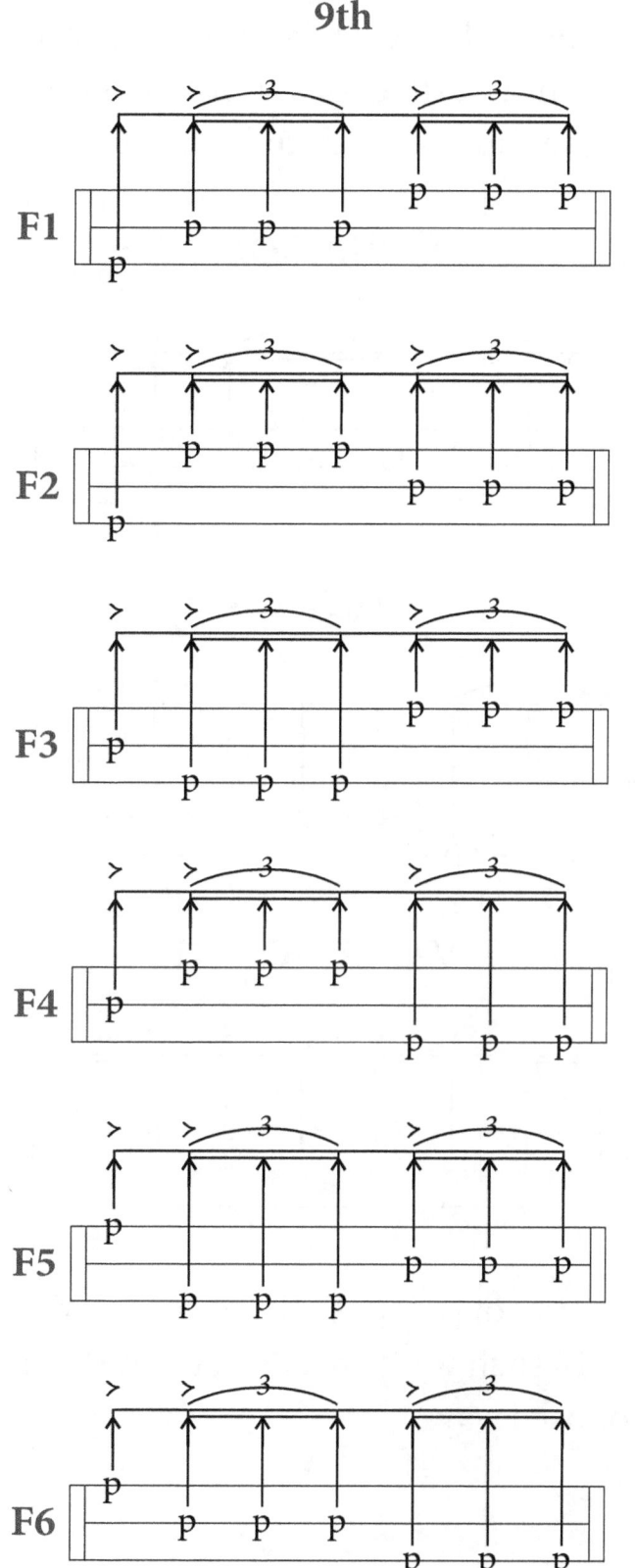

§ VIII

Exercise on pulgar on three adjacent strings with two triple and one double stroke within each Formula. The exercise contains three variations with 6 Formulas in each variation. The first Formula of each variation is cited below. Isochronous playing of the triplets and double stroke.

VARIATION I

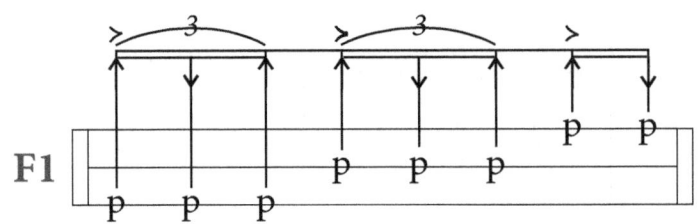

VARIATION II

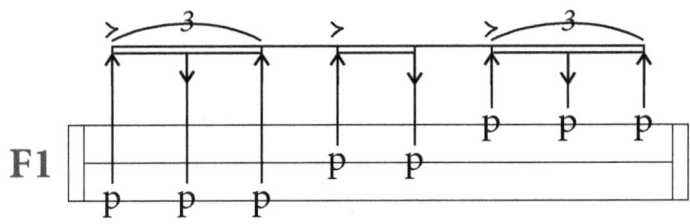

VARIATION III

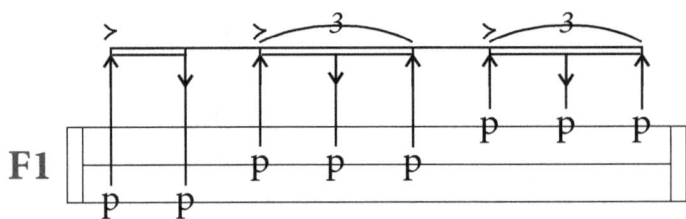

The change in the direction of pulgar stroke results in different performance ways of each variation. 18 such ways are cited below. Practice on all variations and in all different proposed ways.

VARIATION I
WAYS OF PERFORMANCE

1st   2nd

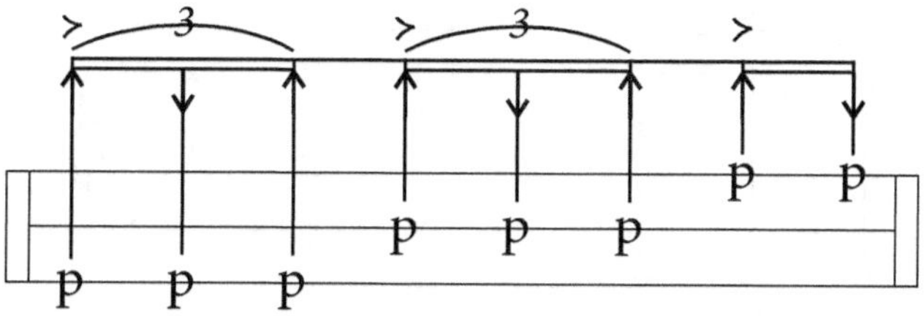

F1   F1

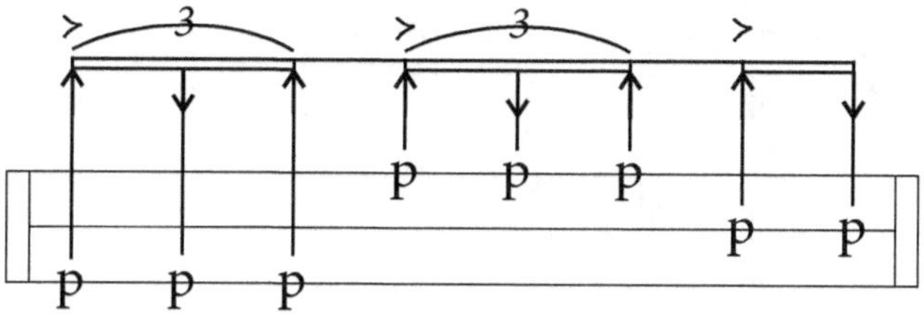

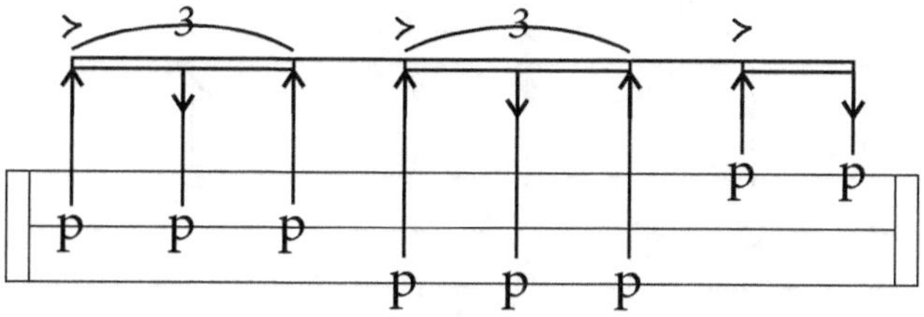

F2   F2

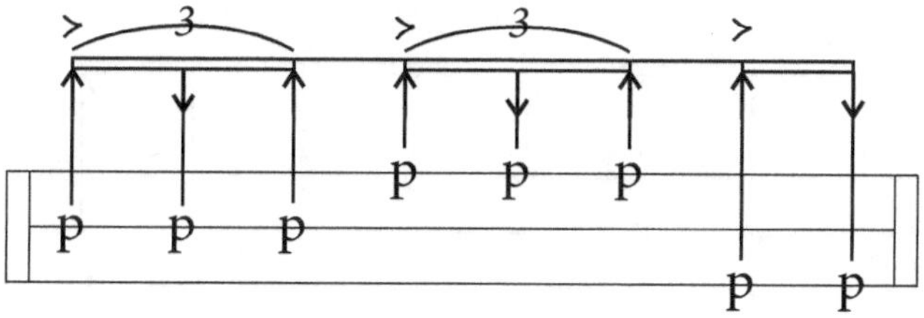

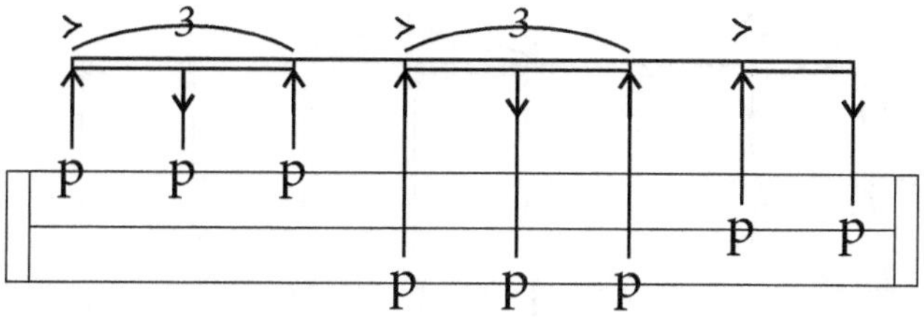

F3   F3

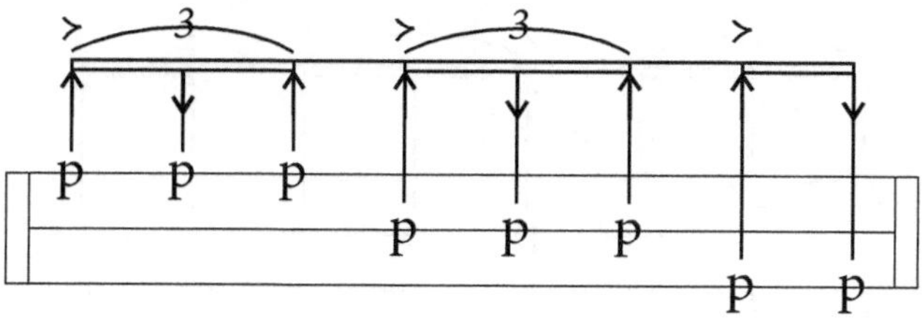

F4   F4

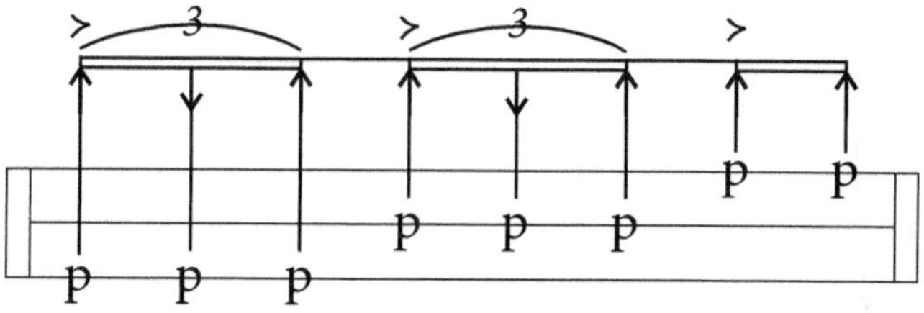

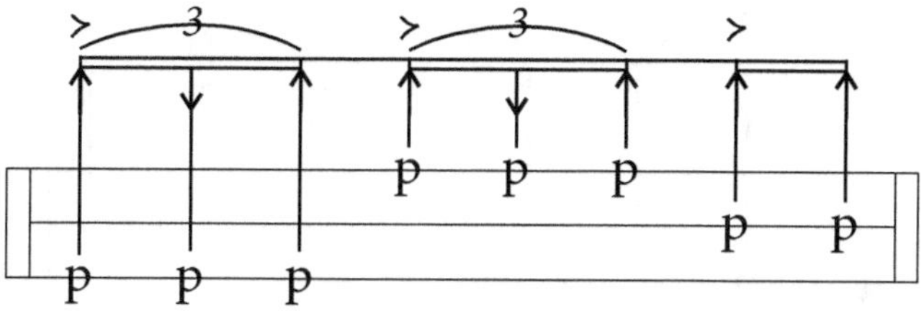

F5   F5

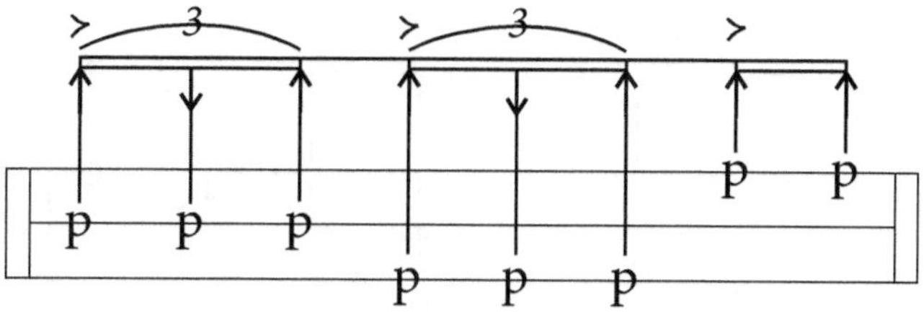

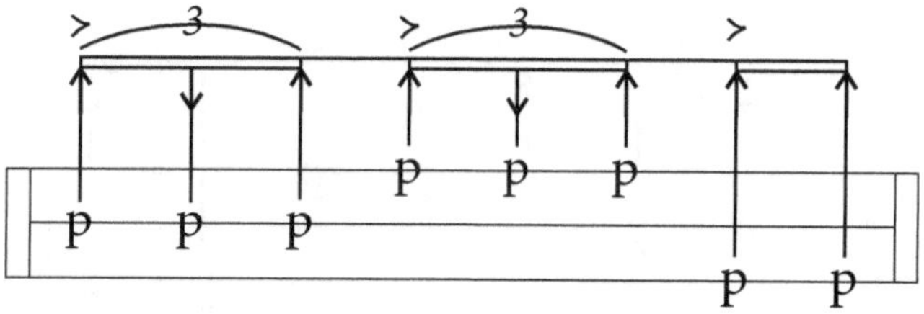

F6   F6

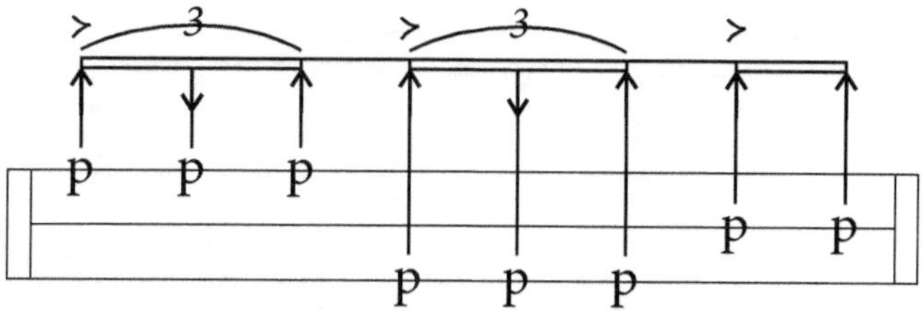

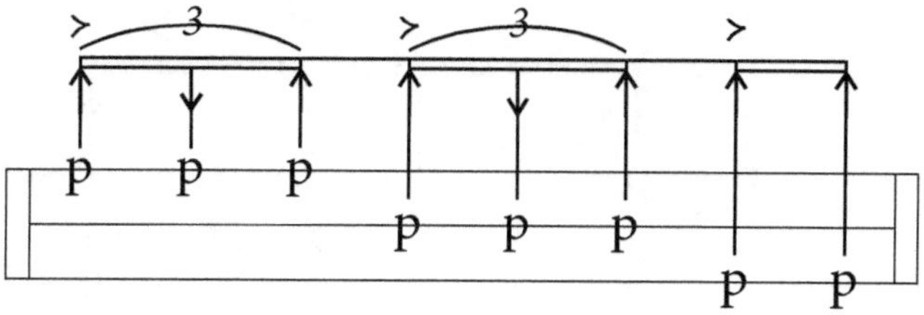

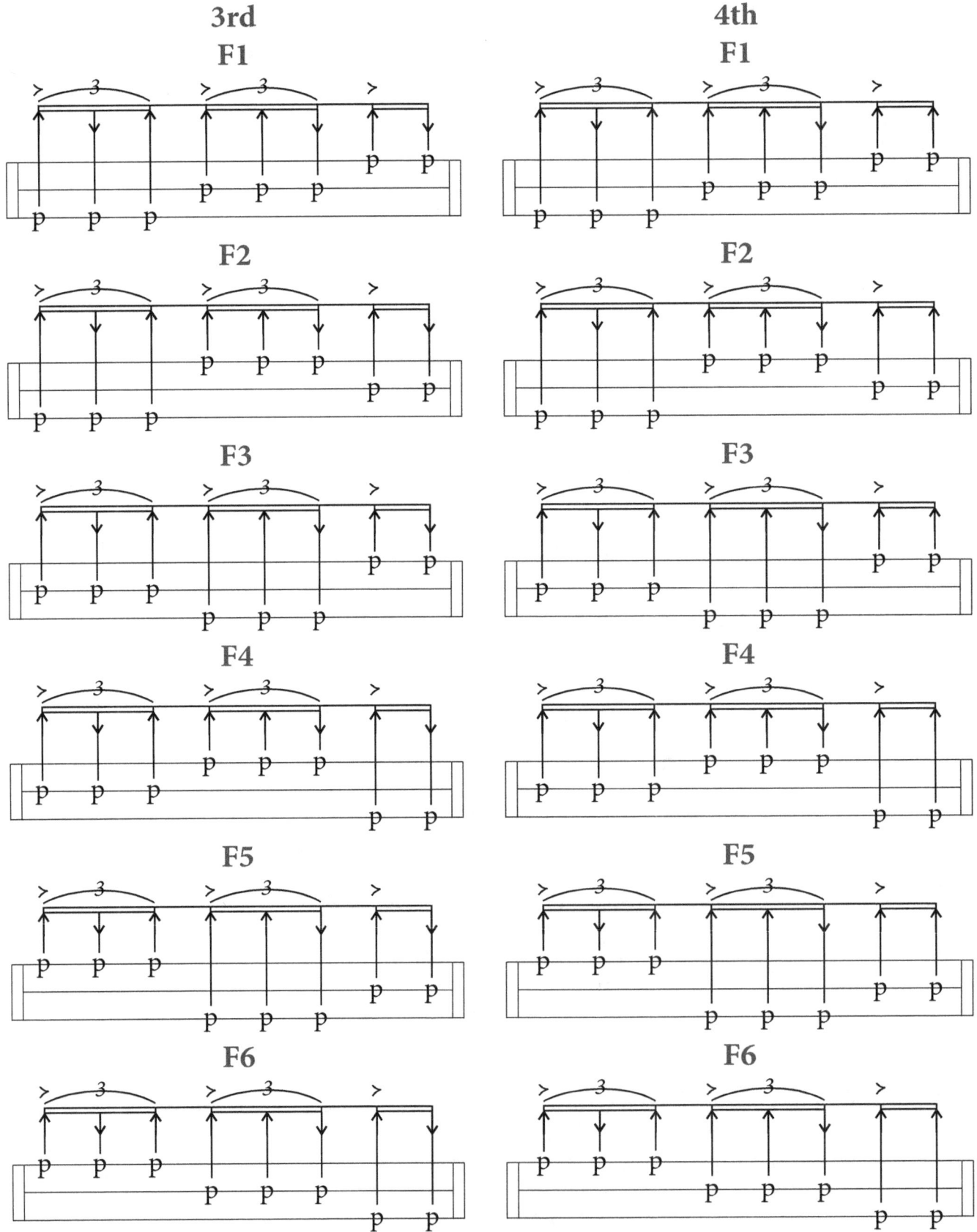

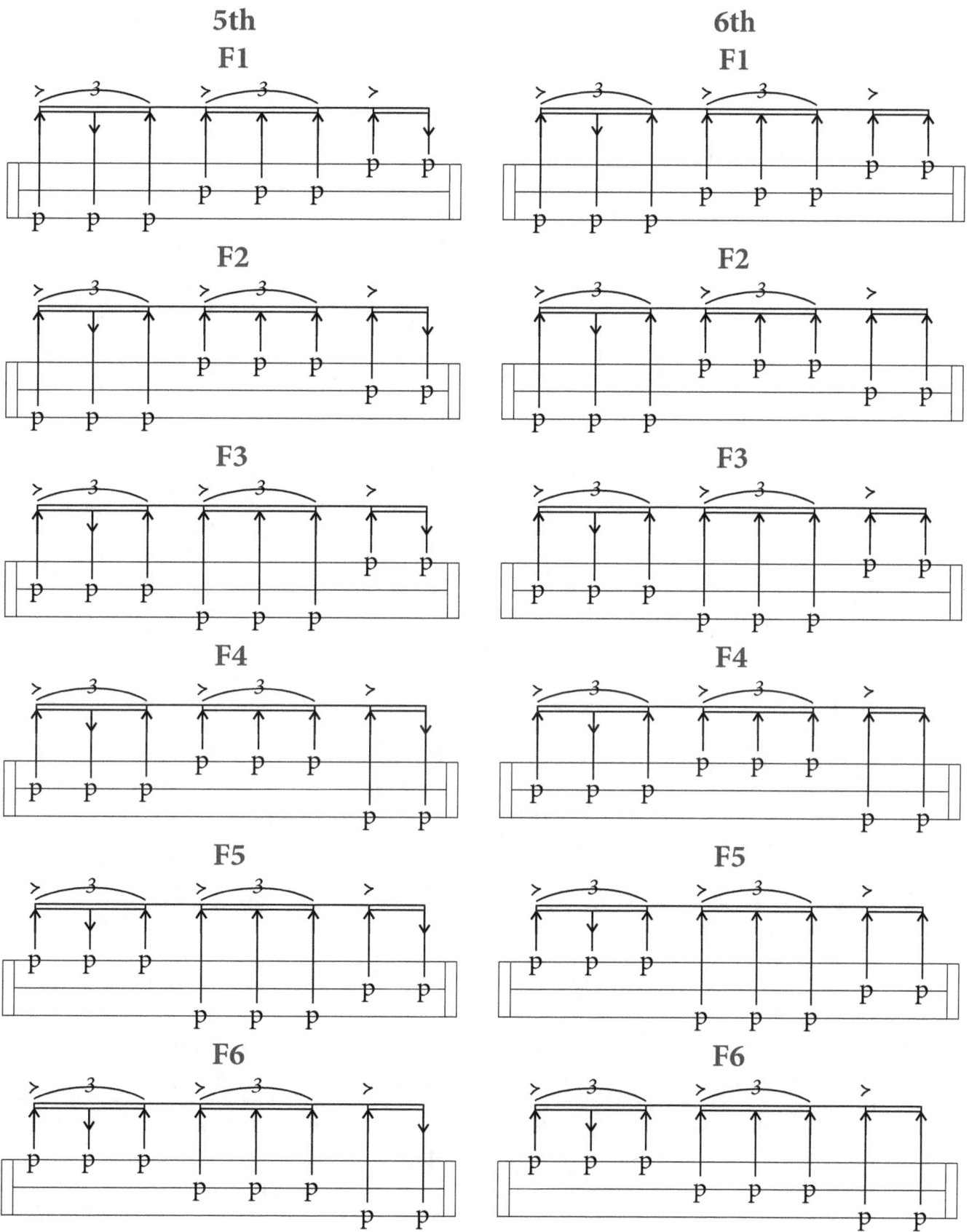

7th

F1

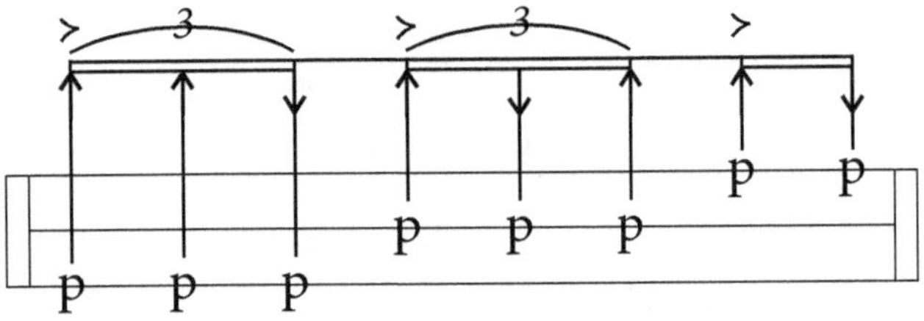

F2

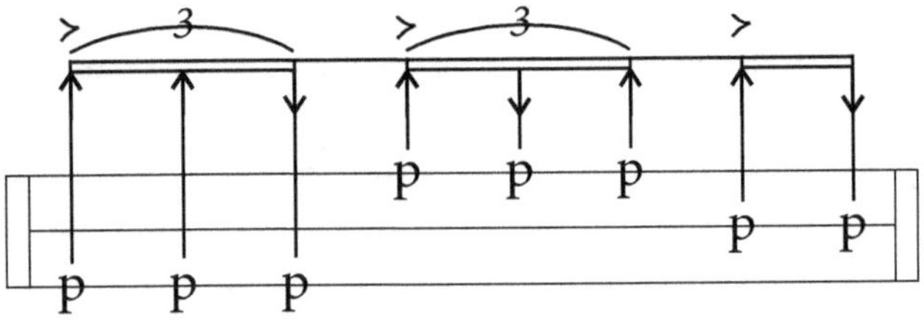

F3

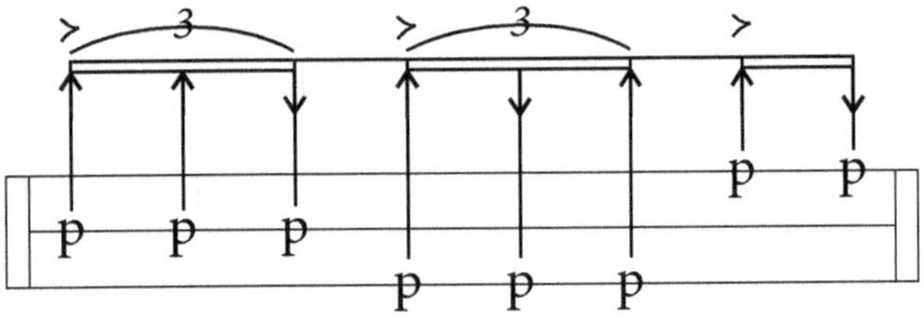

F4

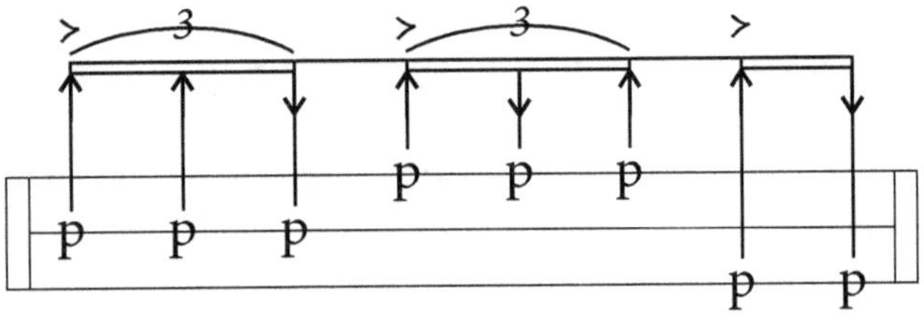

F5

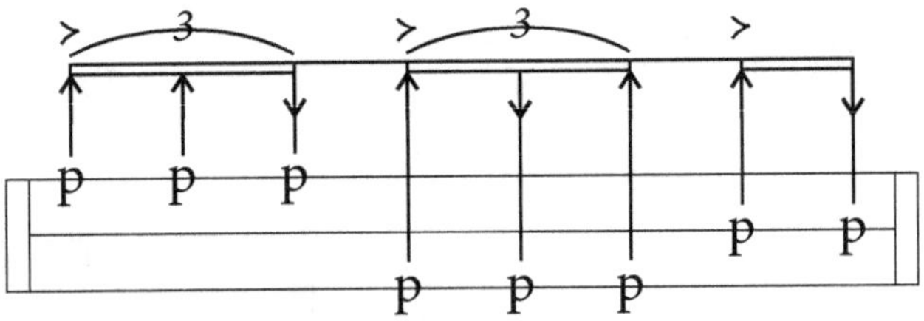

F6

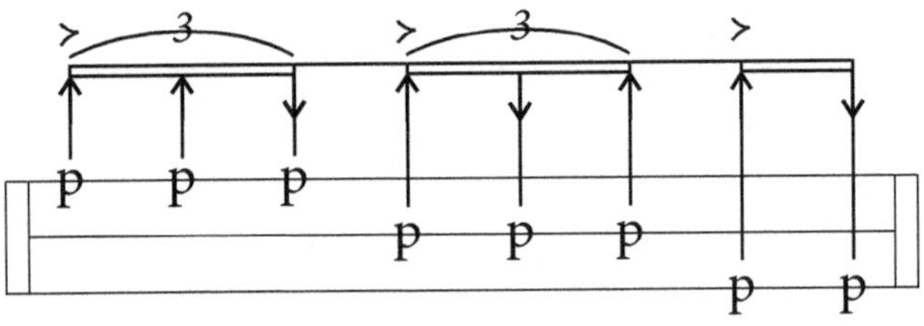

8th

F1

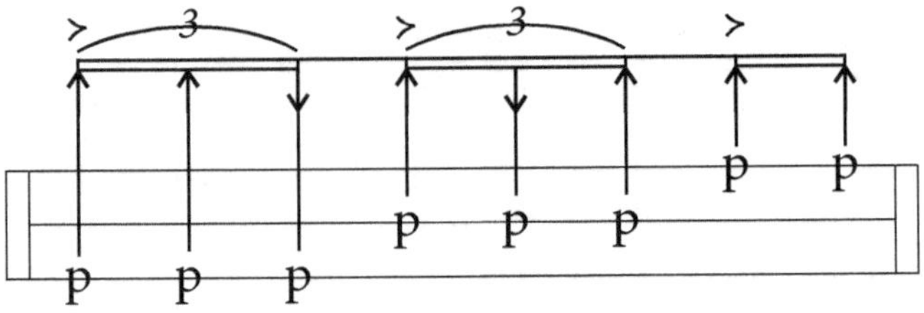

F2

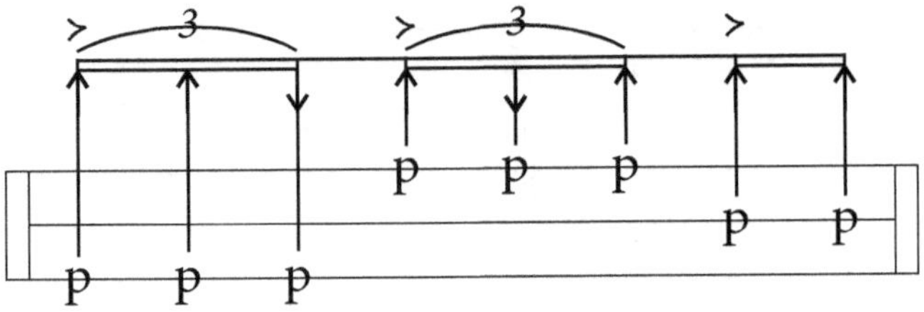

F3

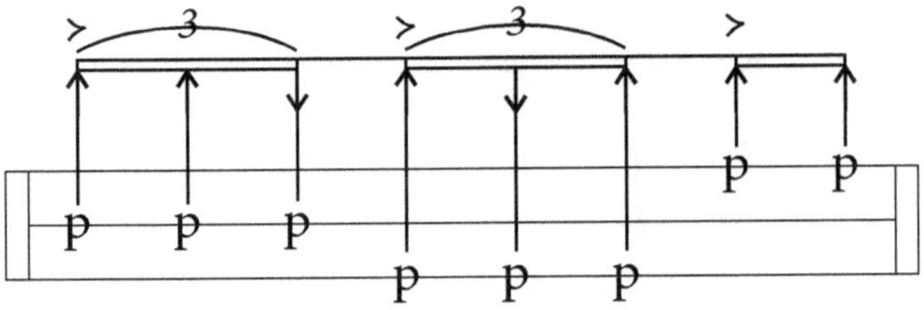

F4

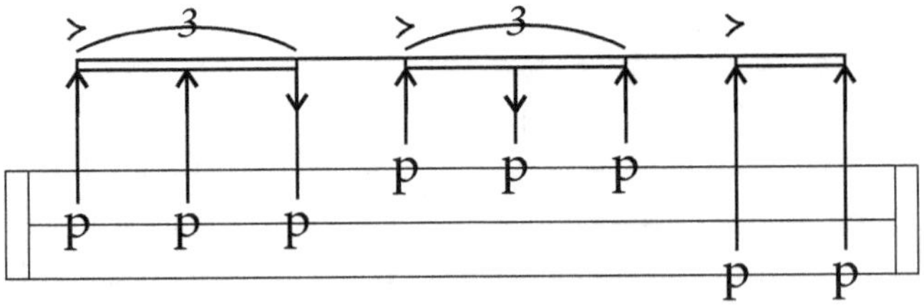

F5

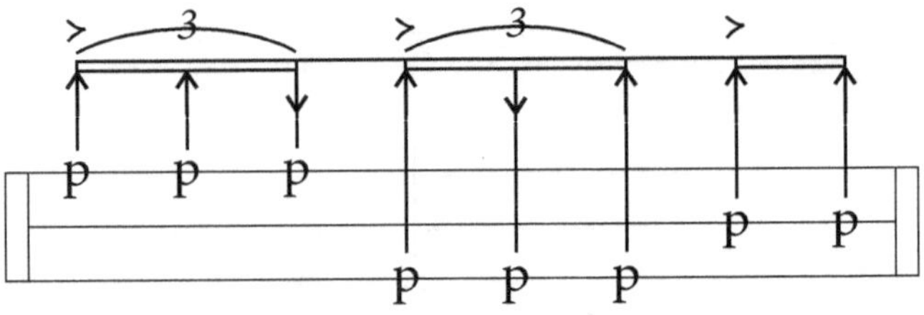

F6

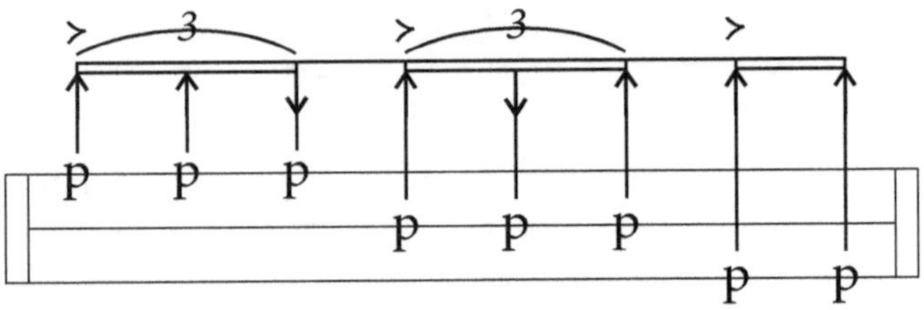

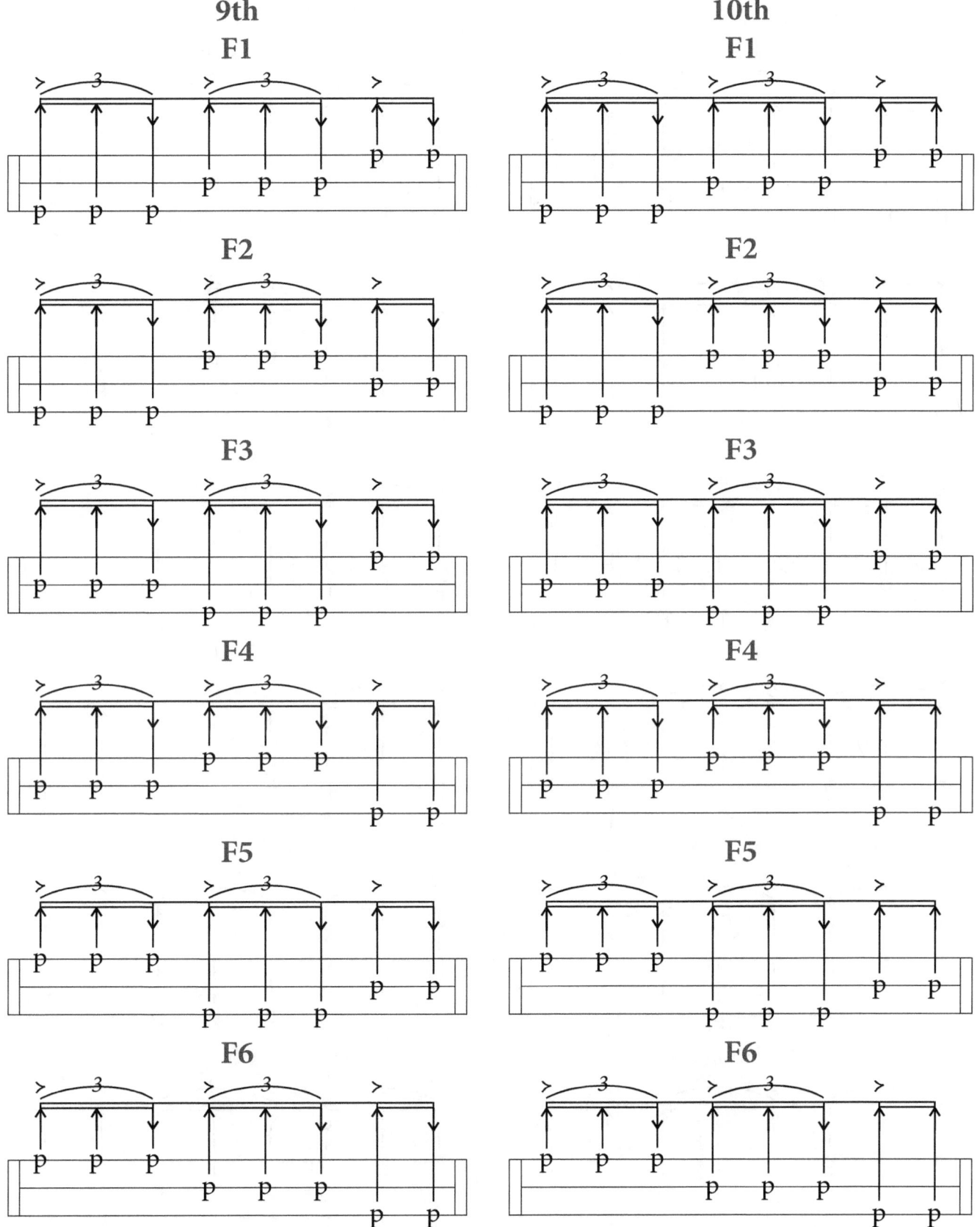

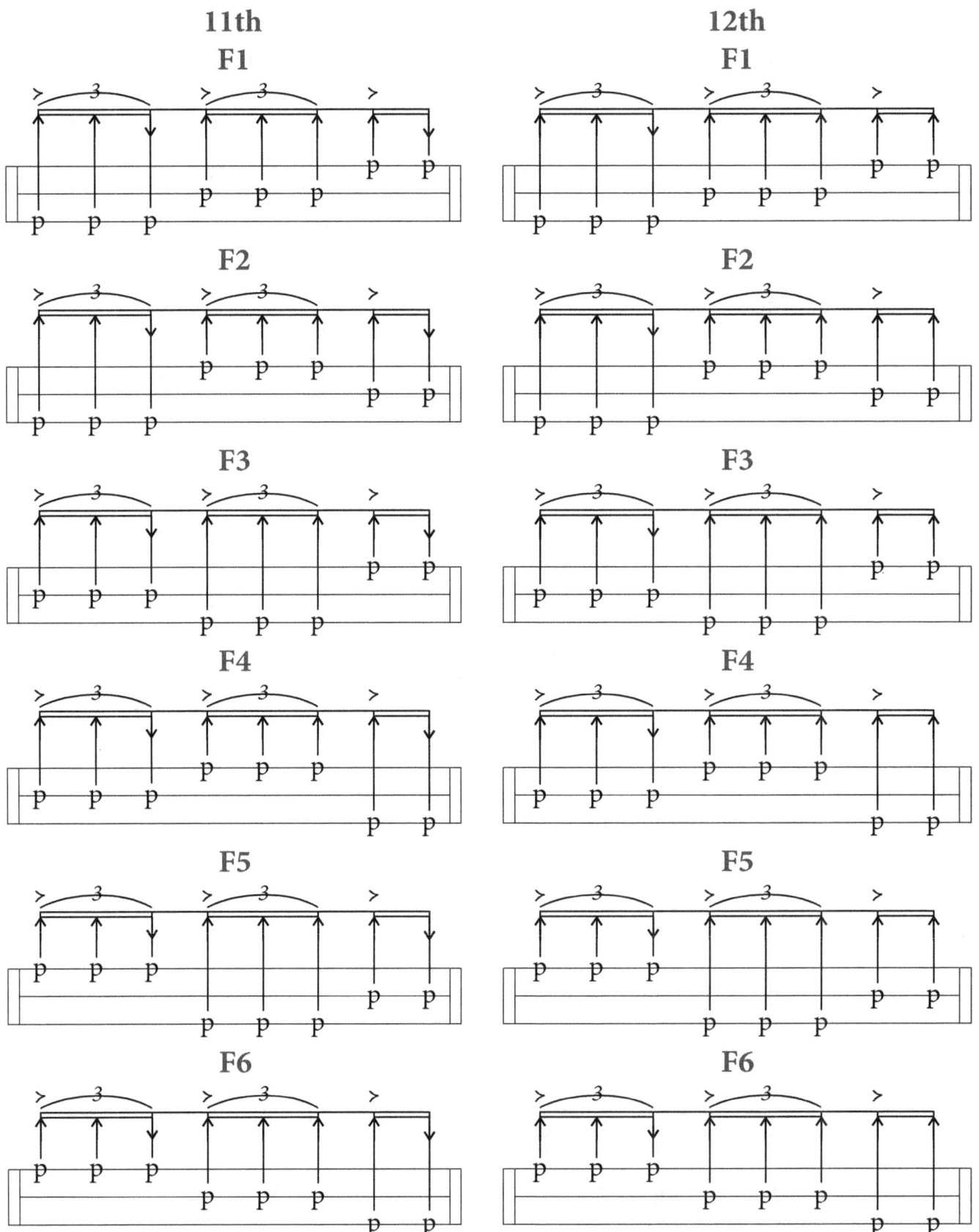

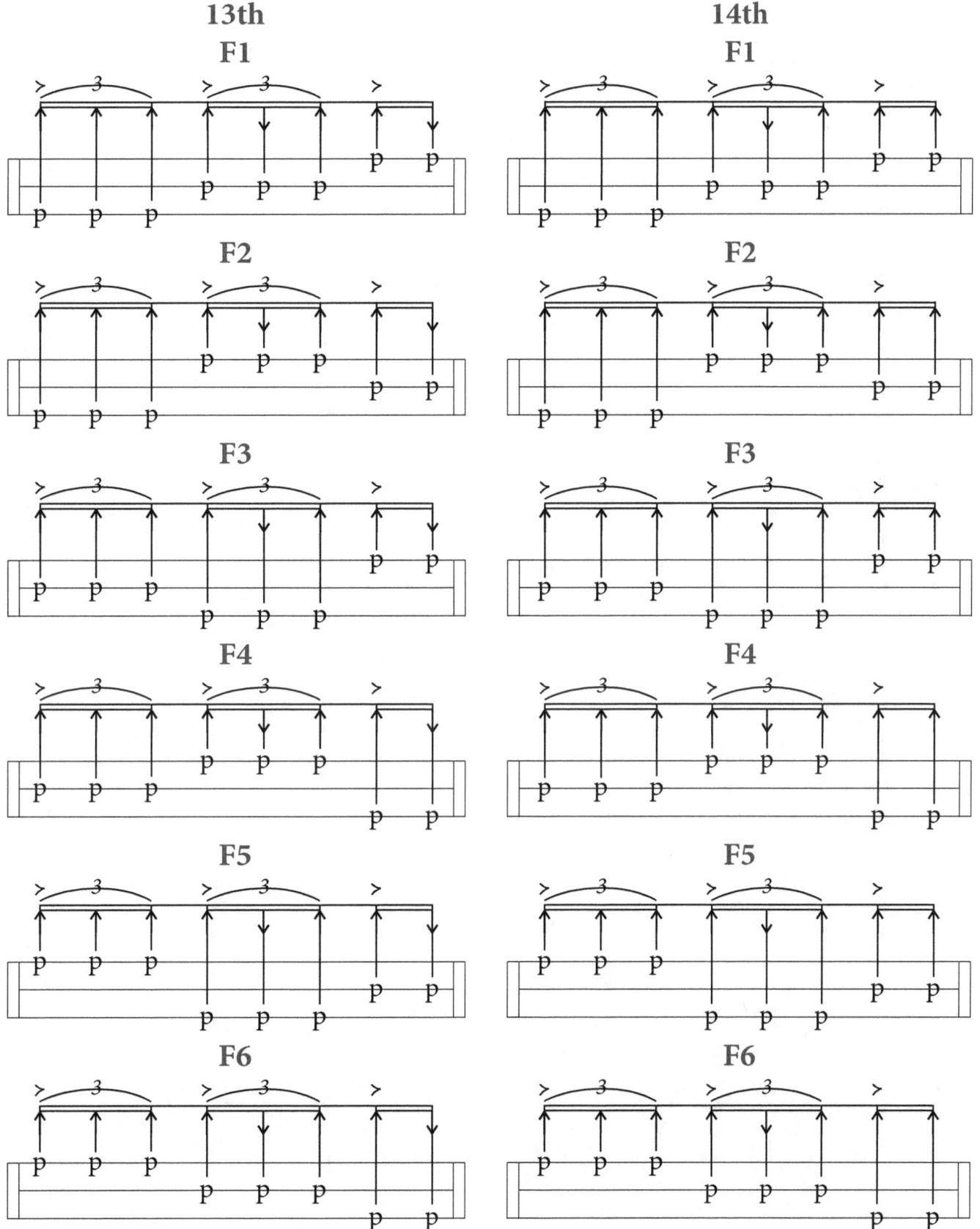

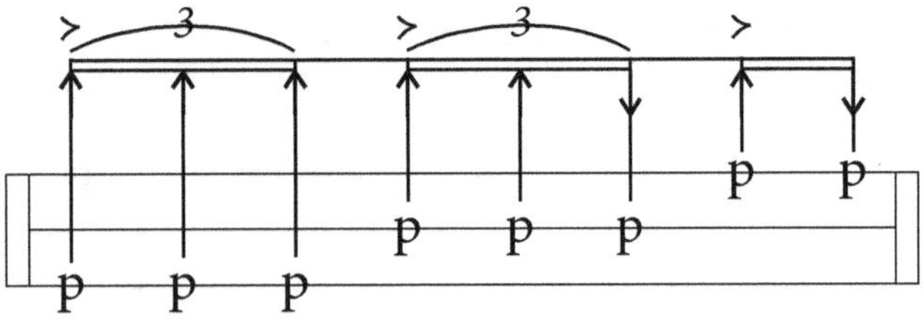

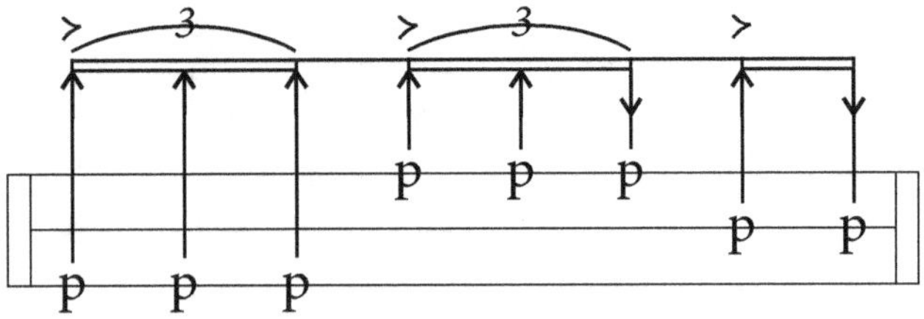

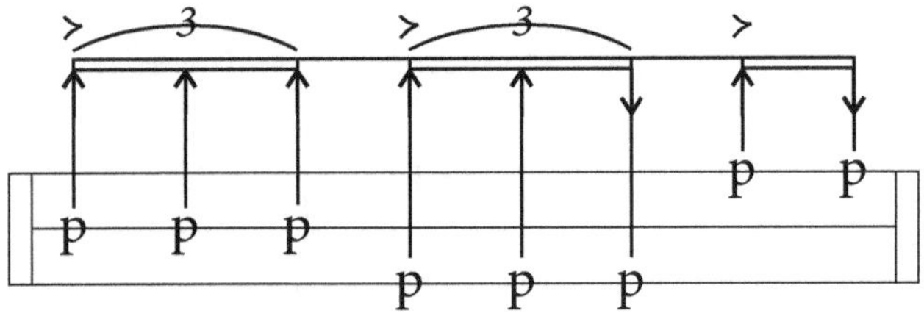

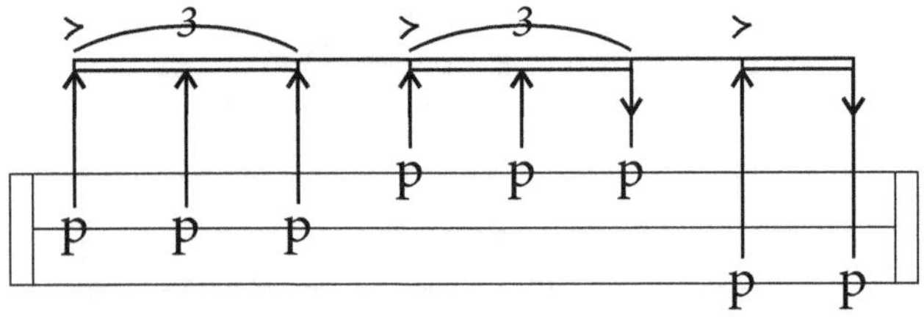

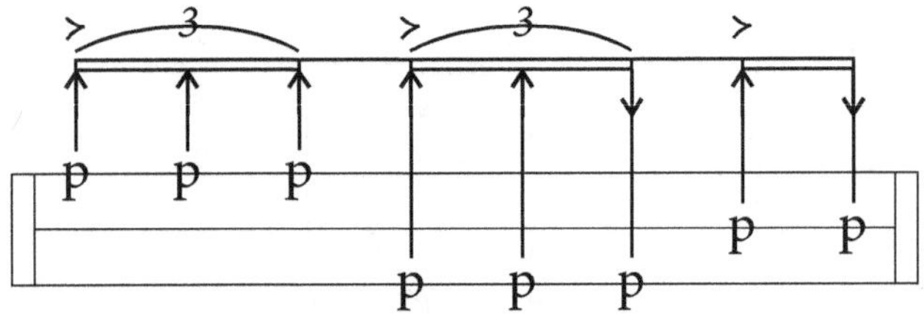

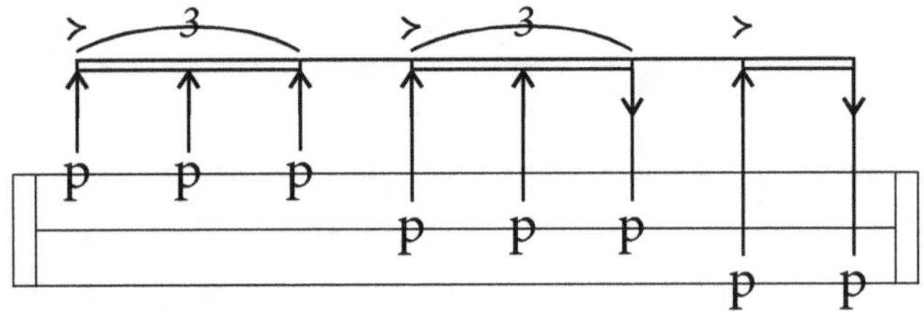

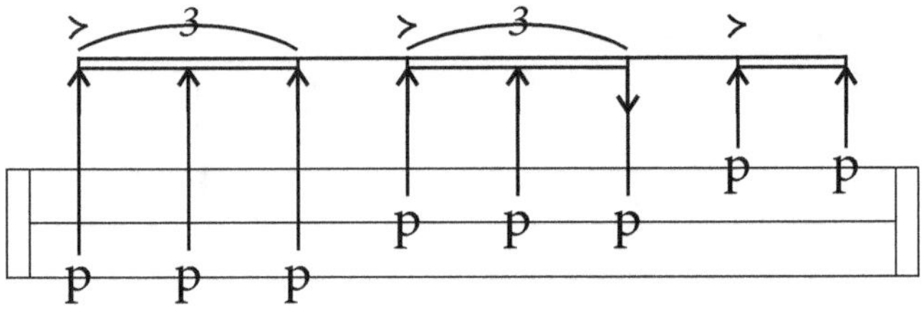

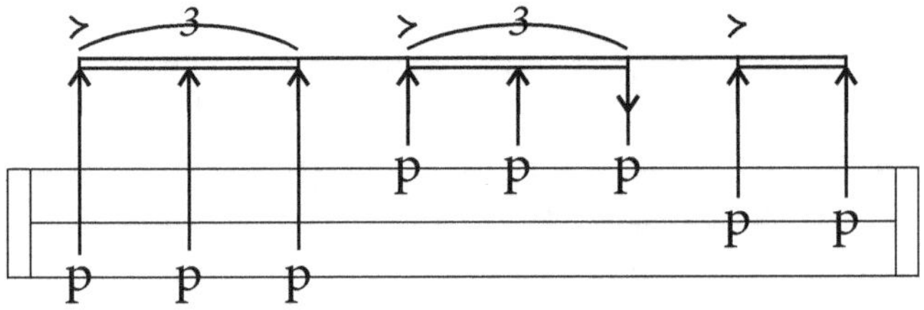

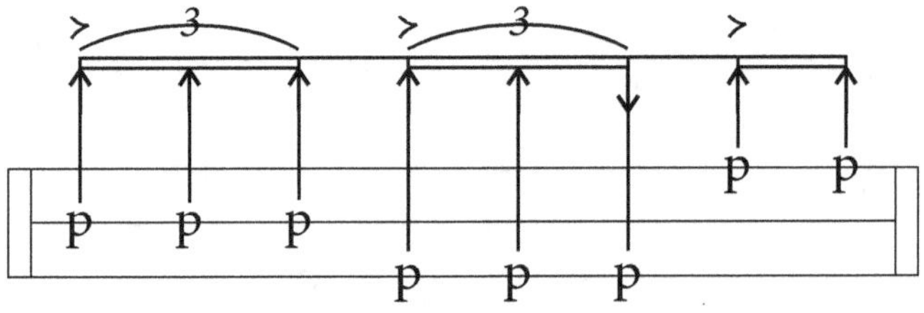

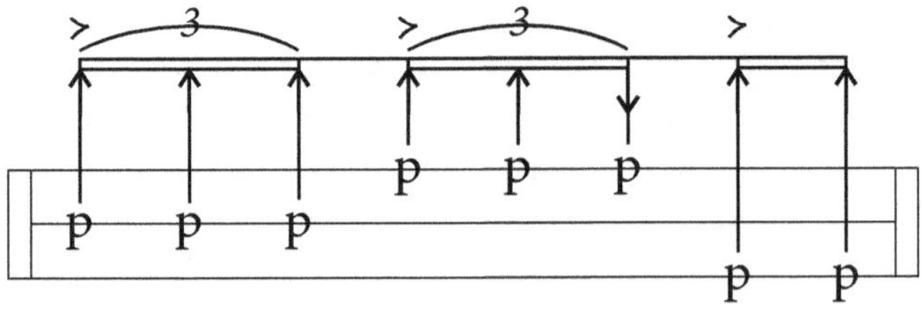

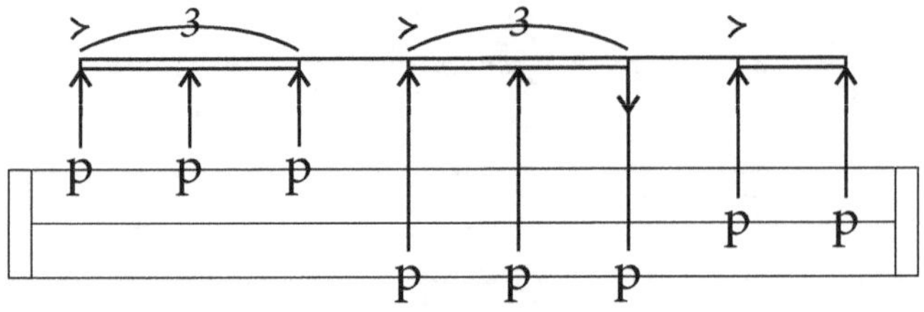

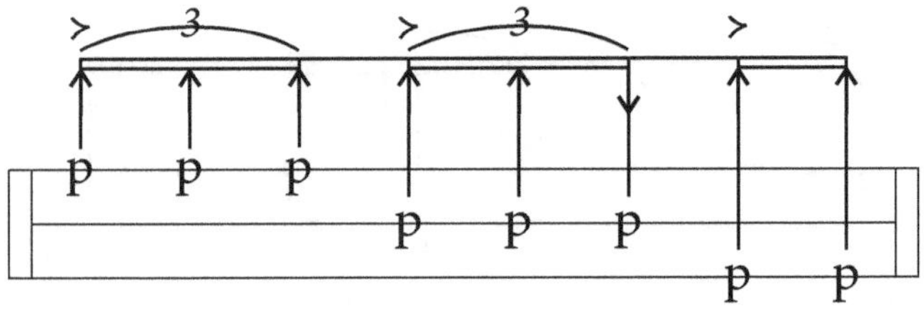

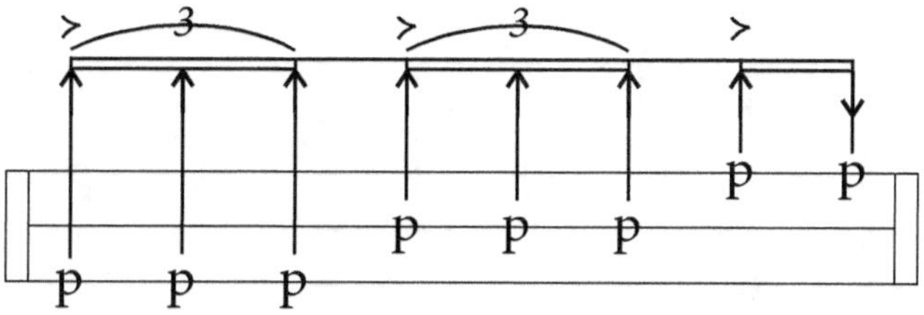

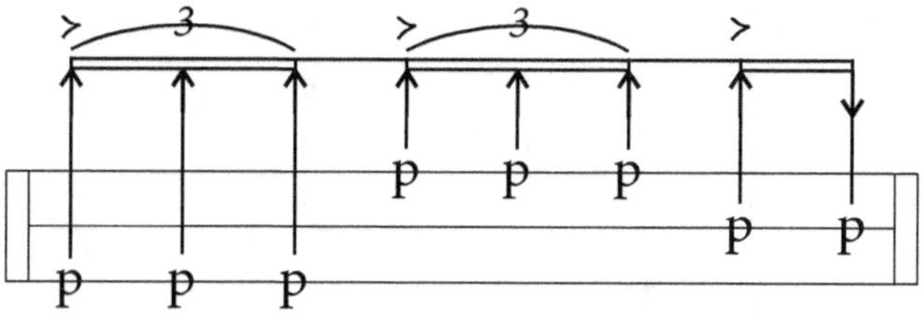

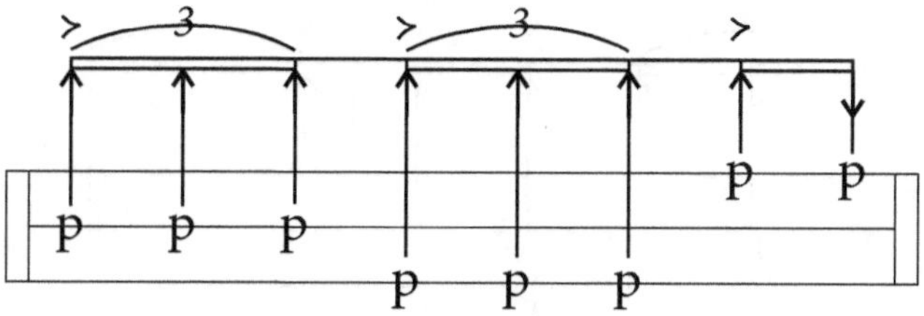

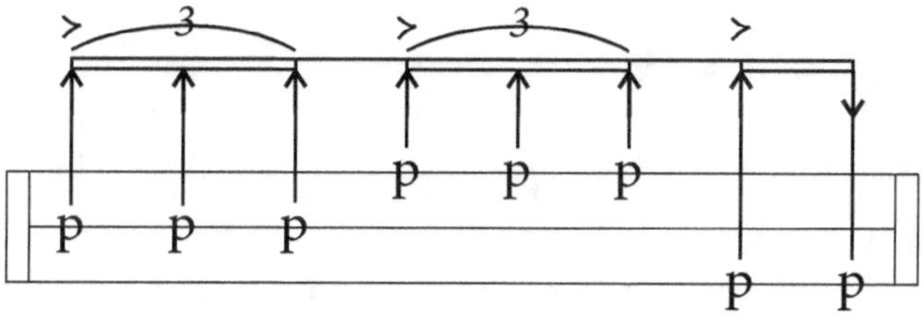

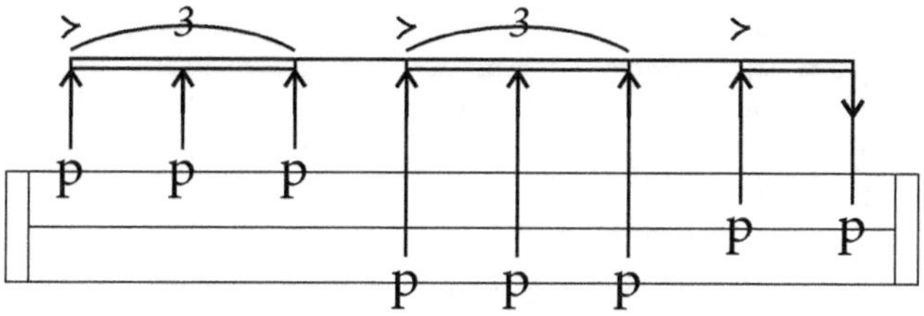

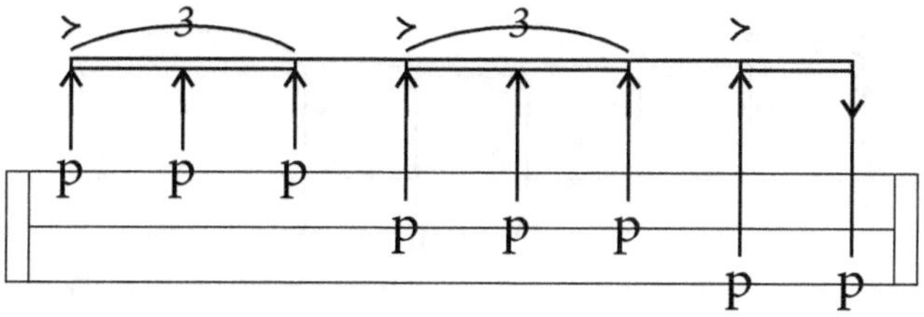

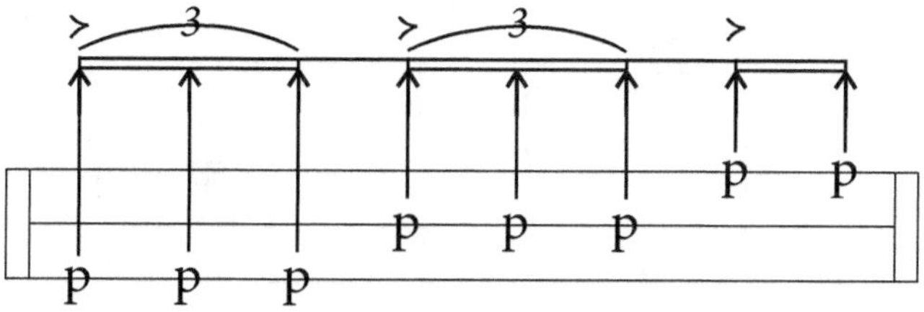

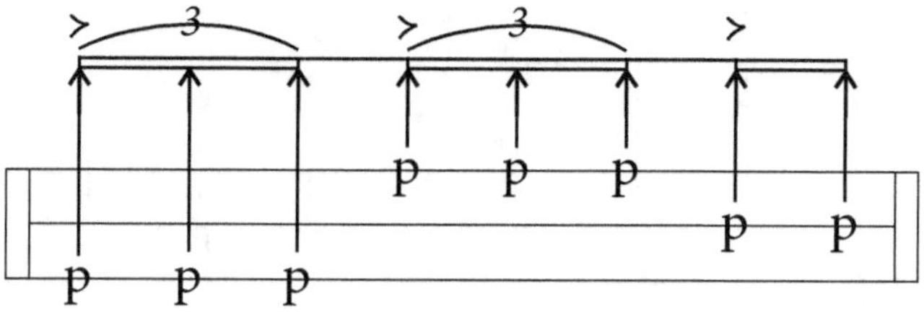

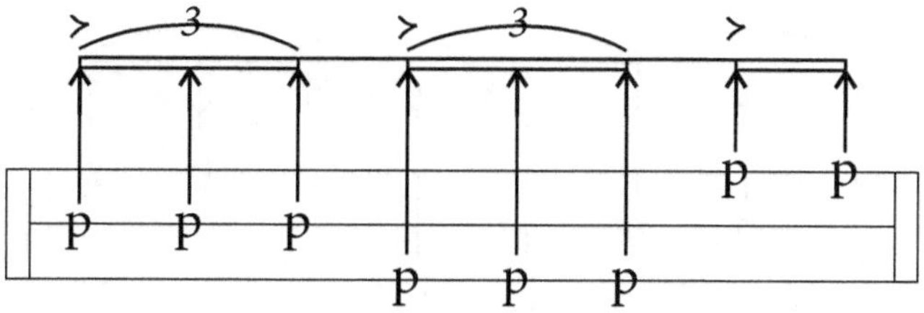

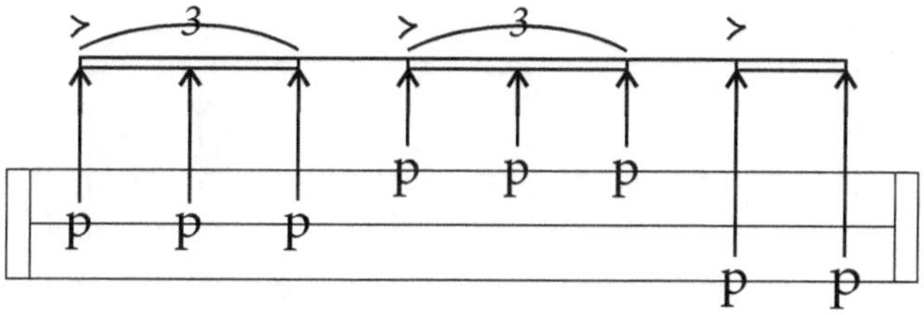

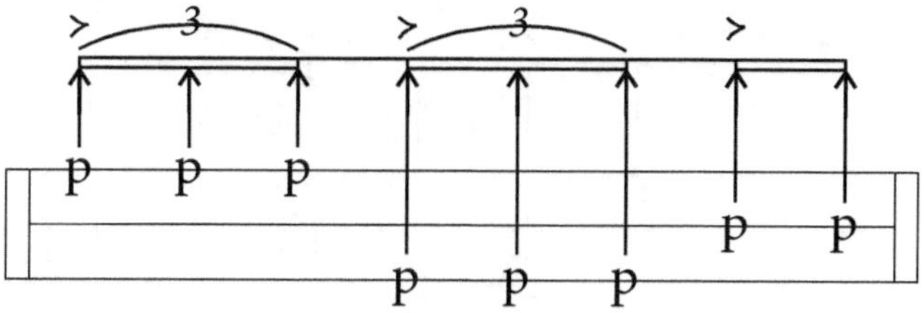

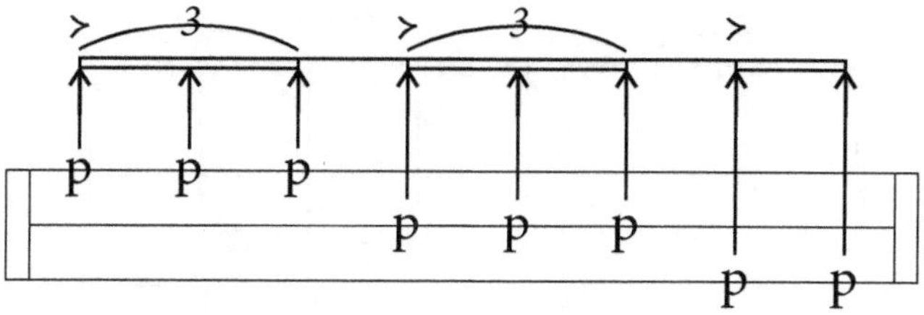

VARIATION II
WAYS OF PERFORMANCE

1st

F1

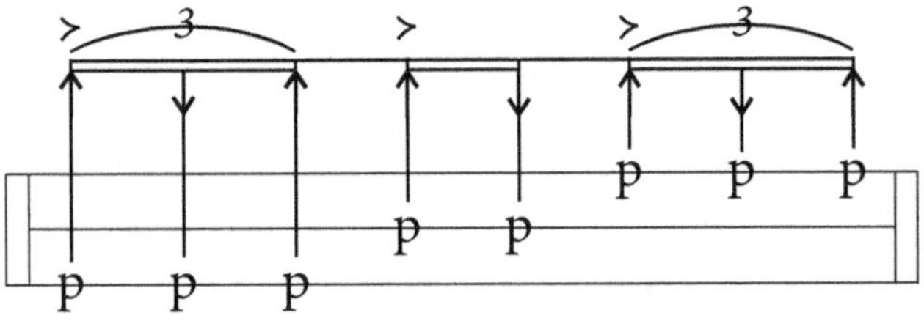

F2

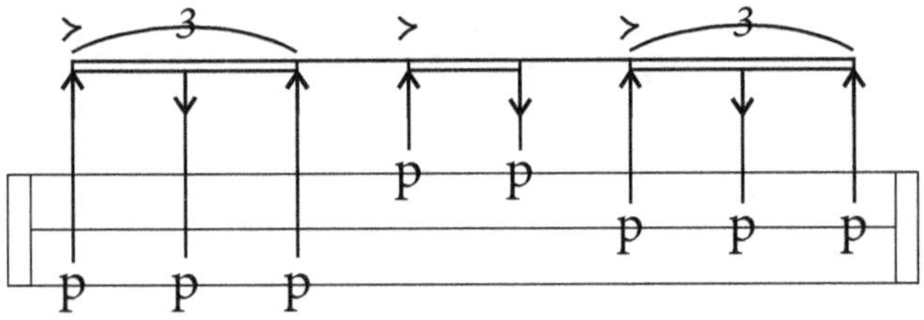

F3

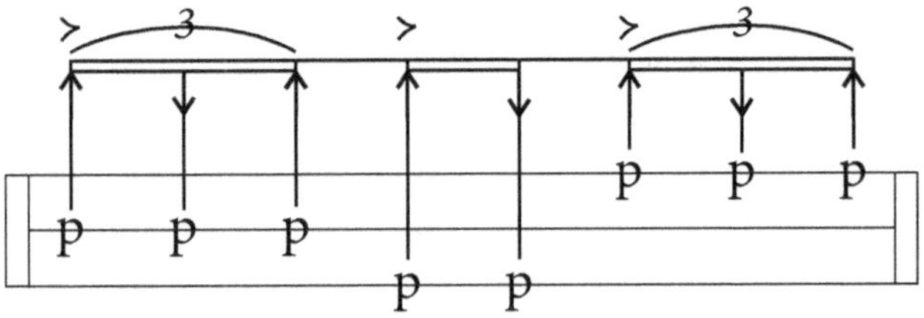

F4

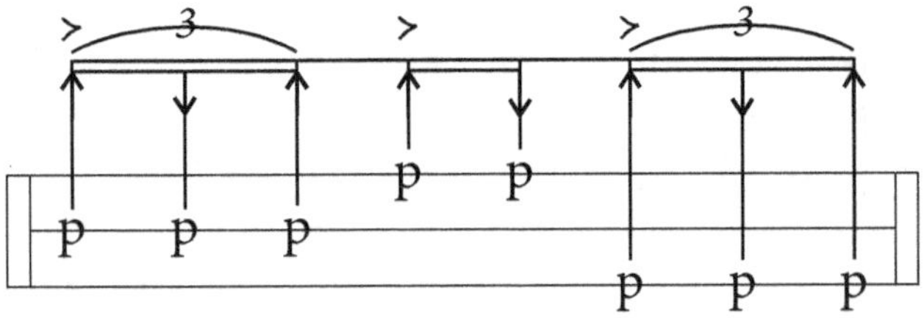

F5

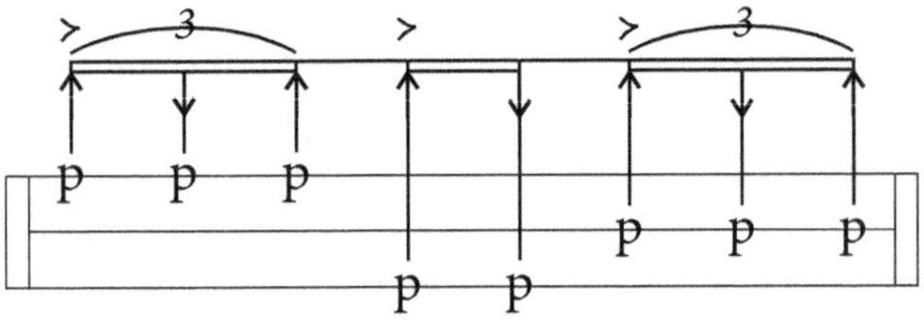

F6

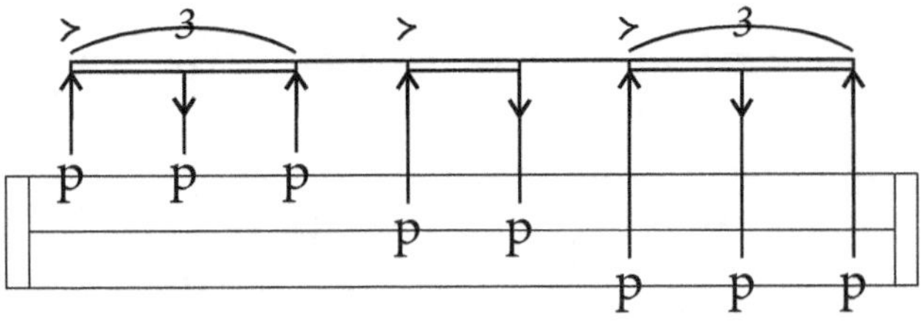

2nd

F1

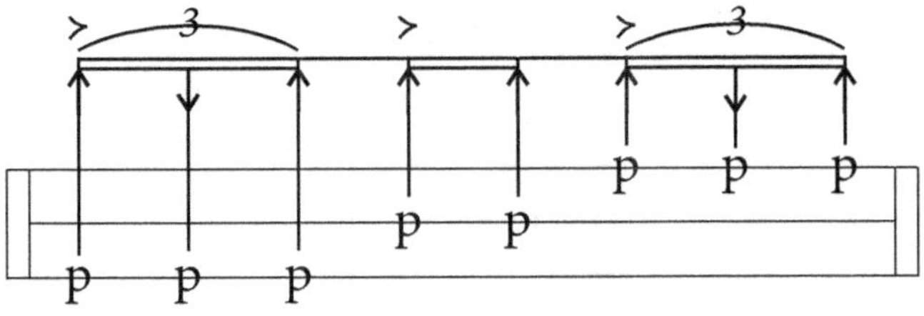

F2

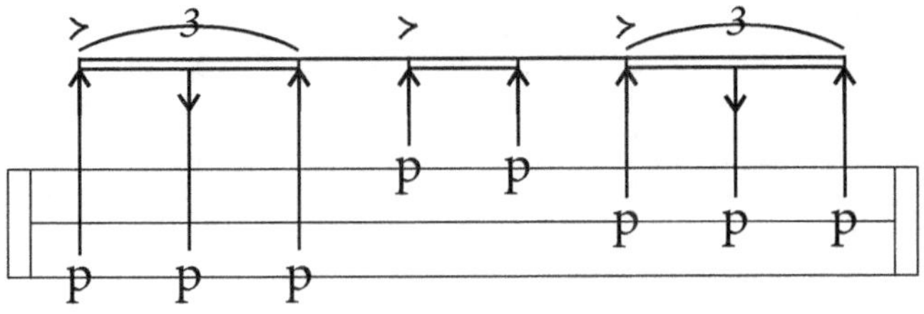

F3

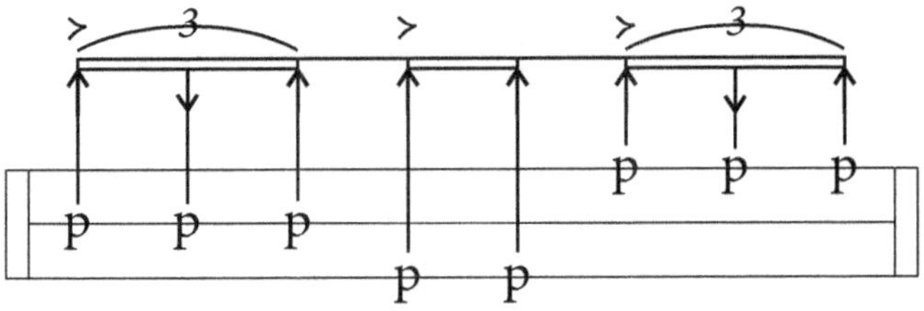

F4

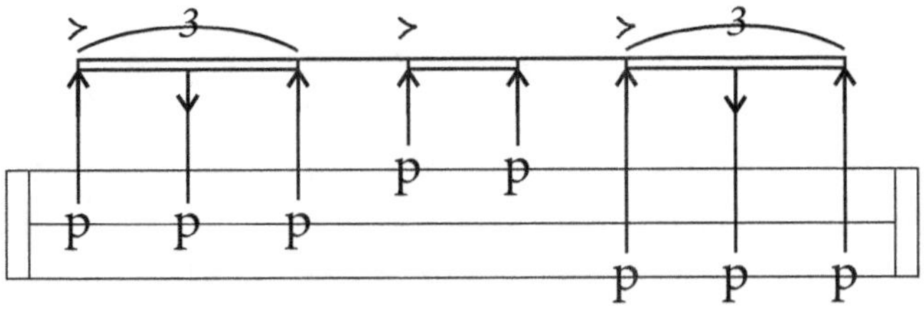

F5

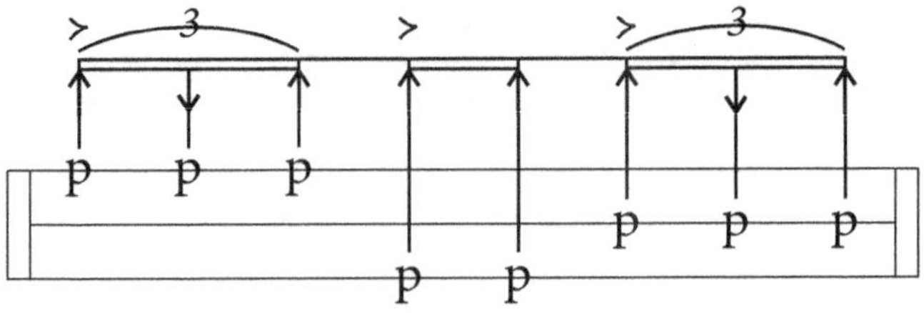

F6

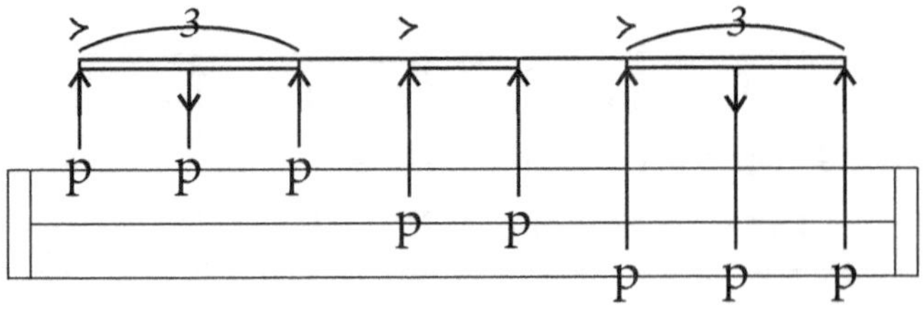

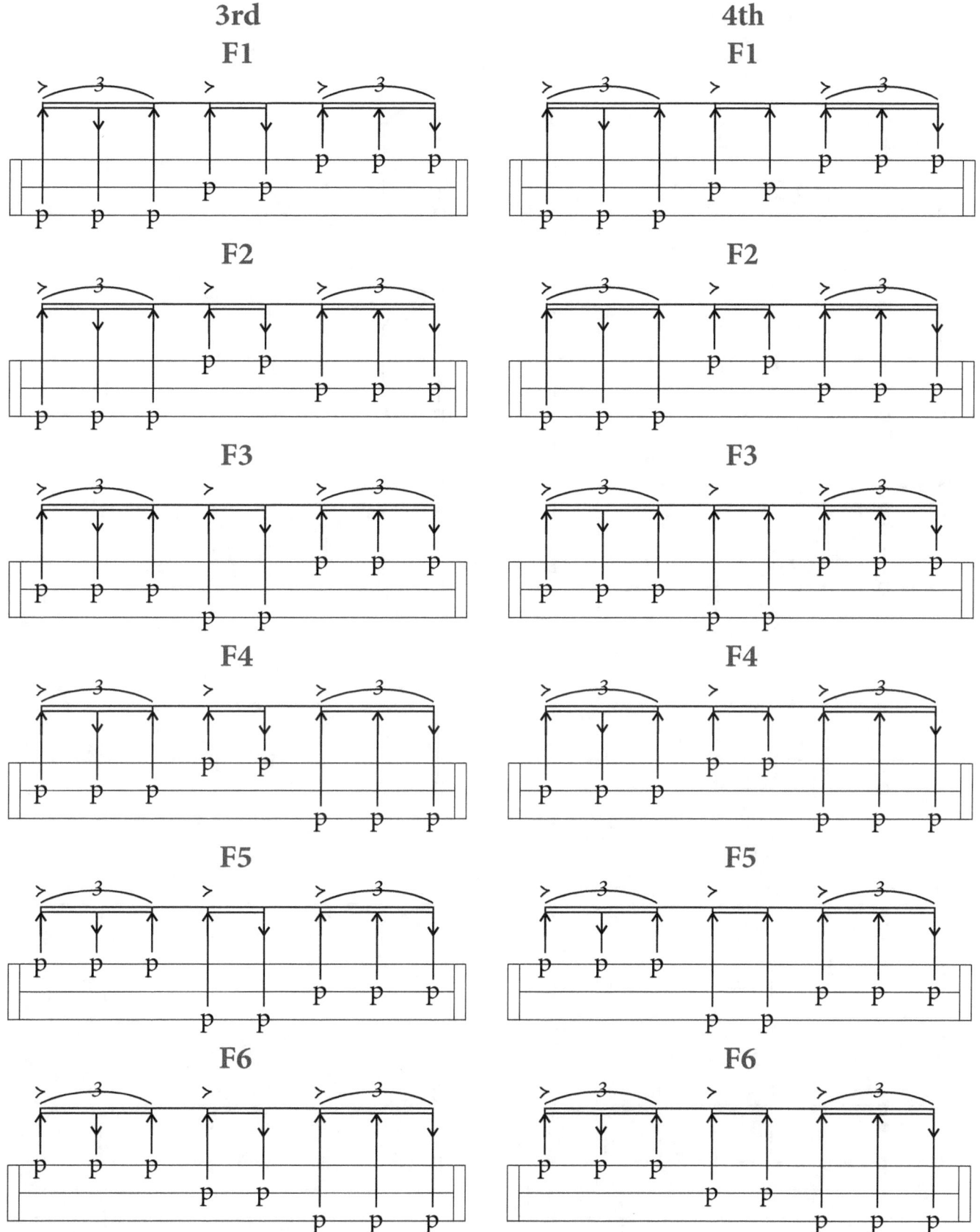

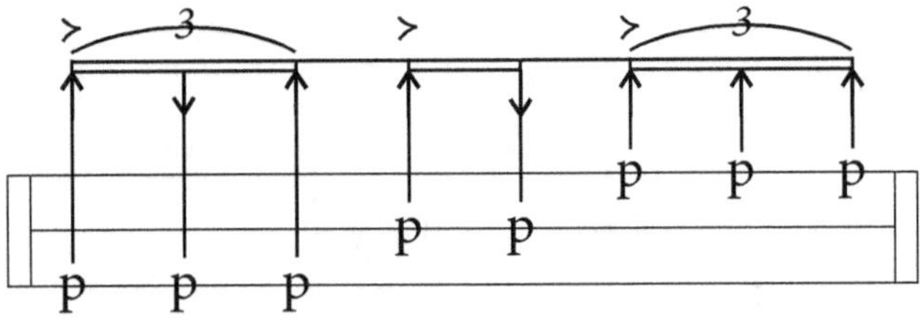

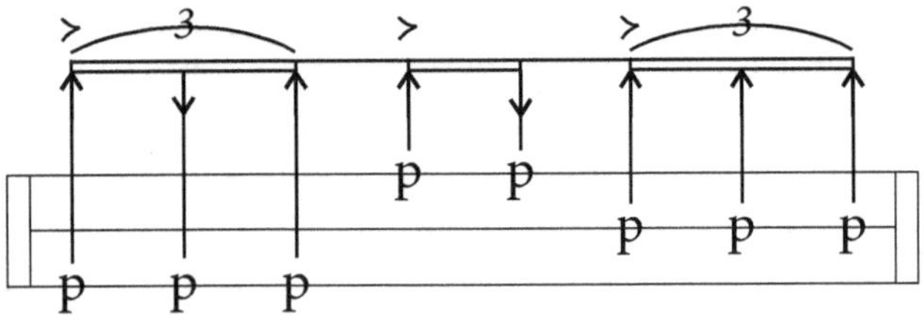

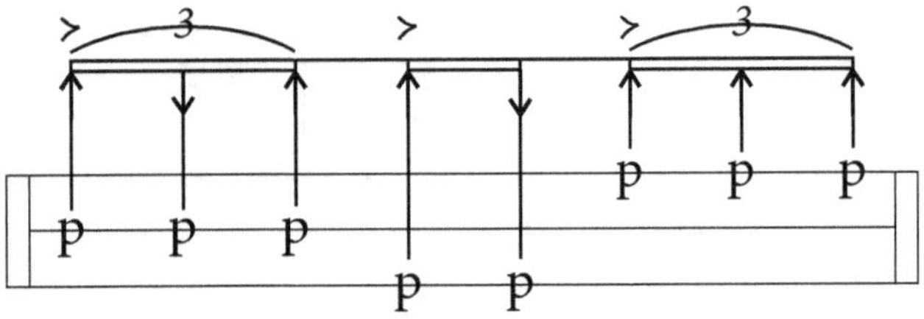

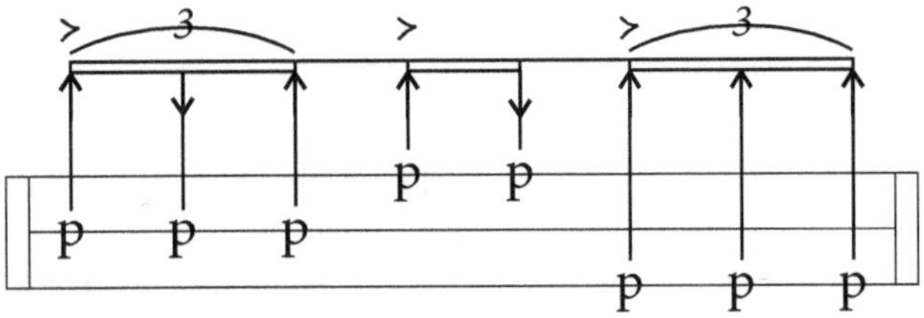

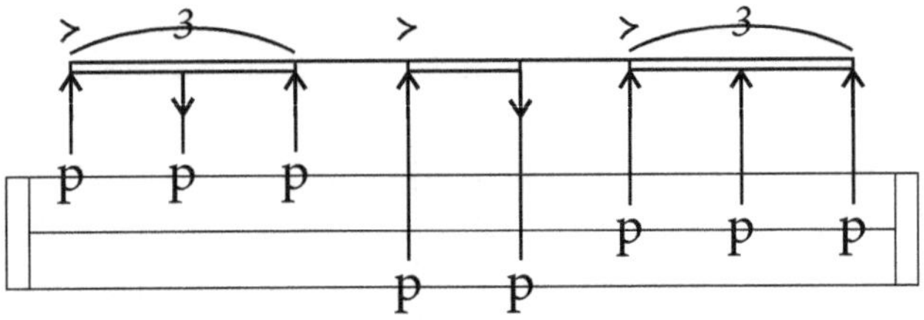

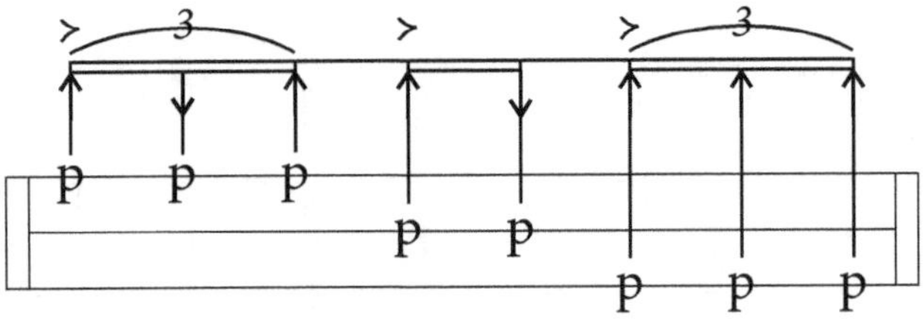

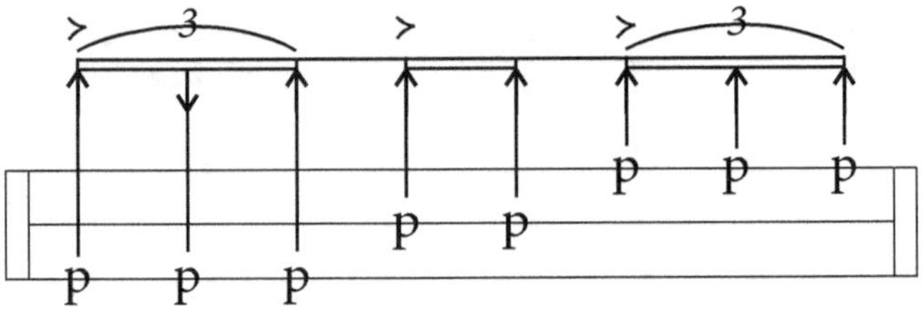

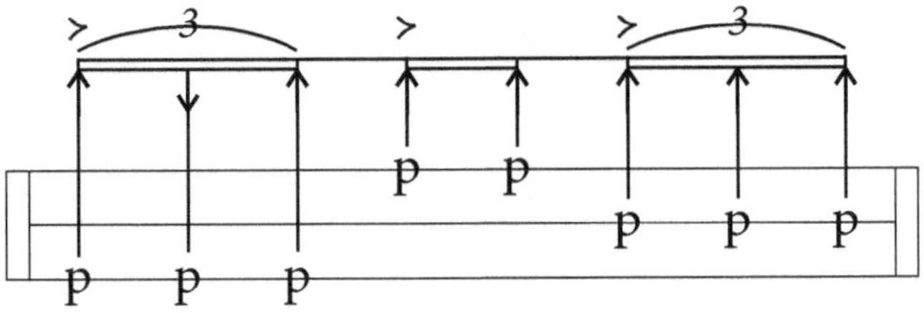

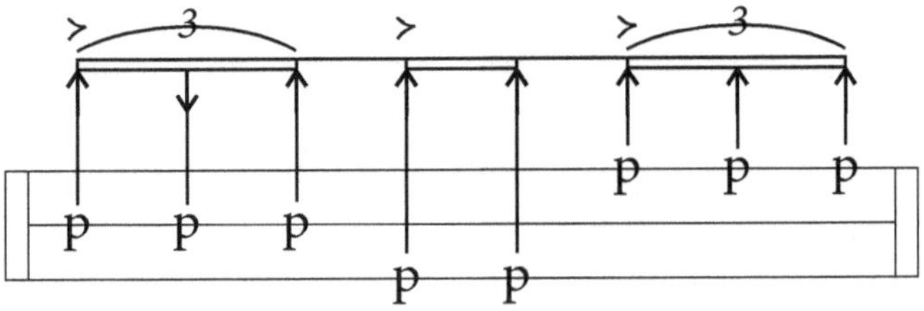

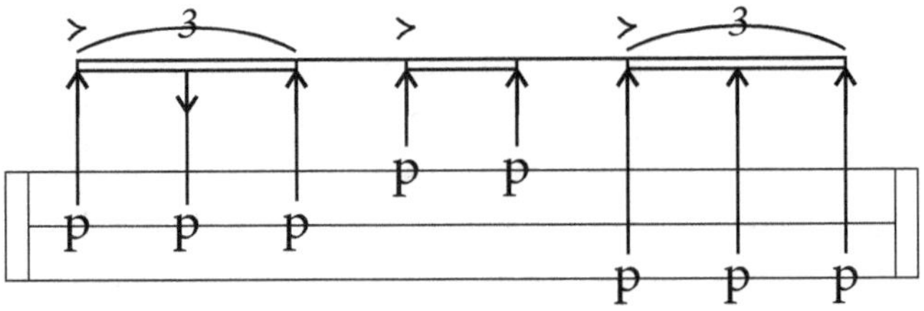

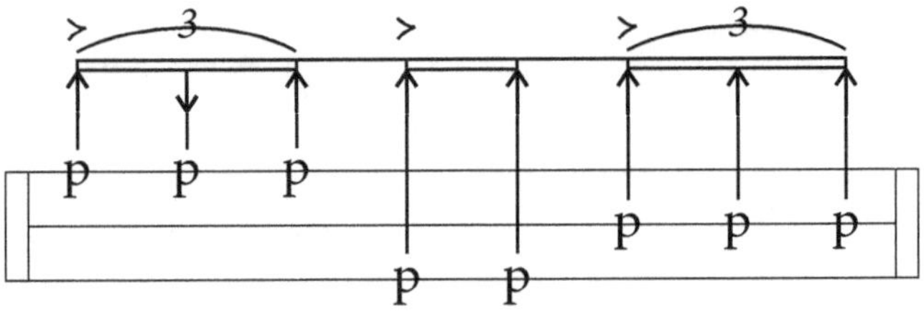

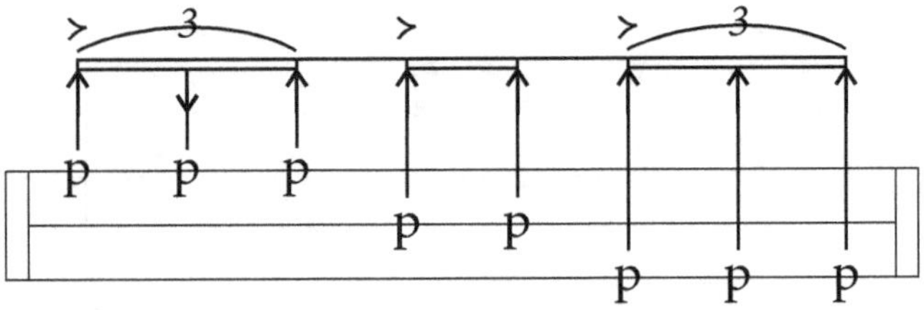

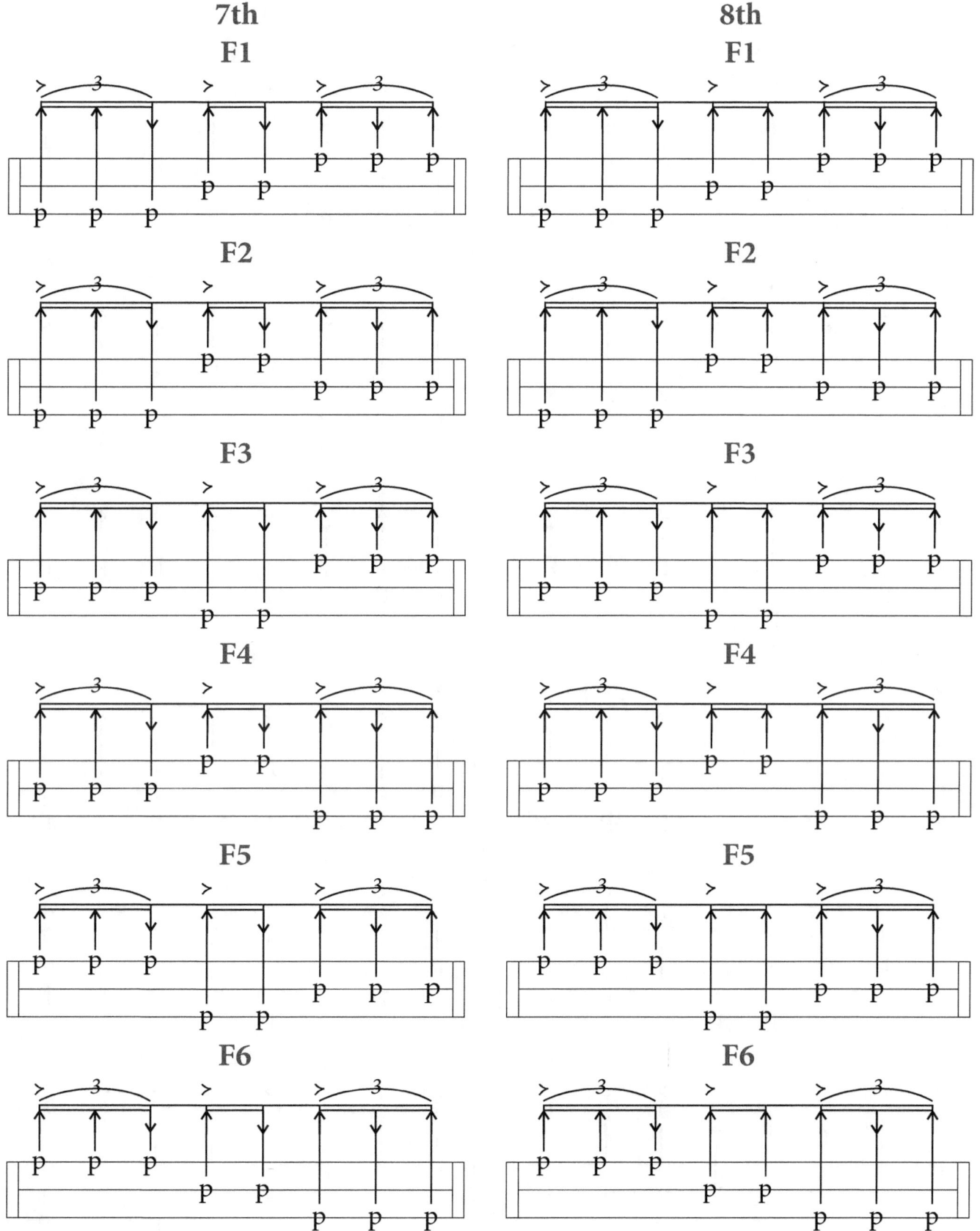

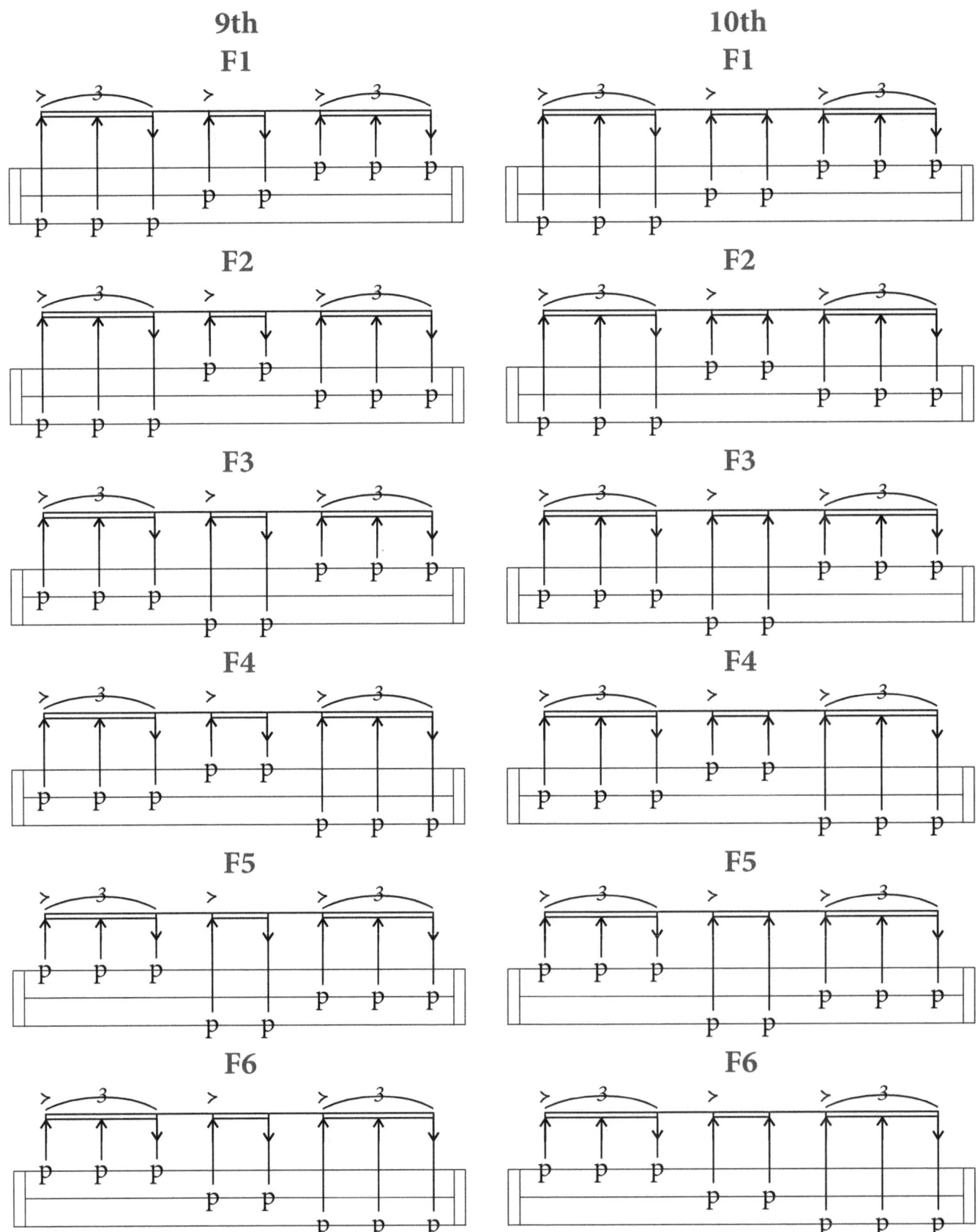

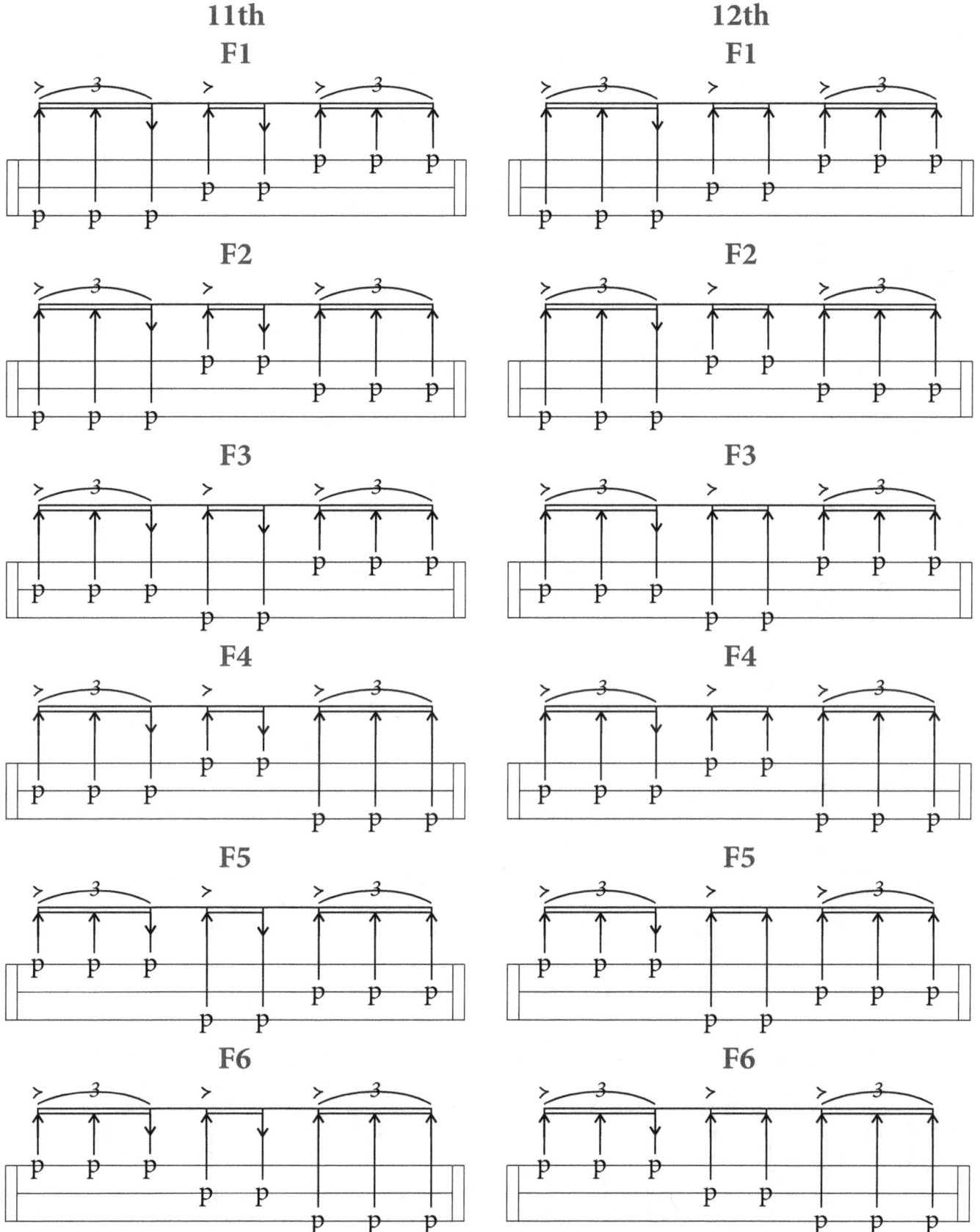

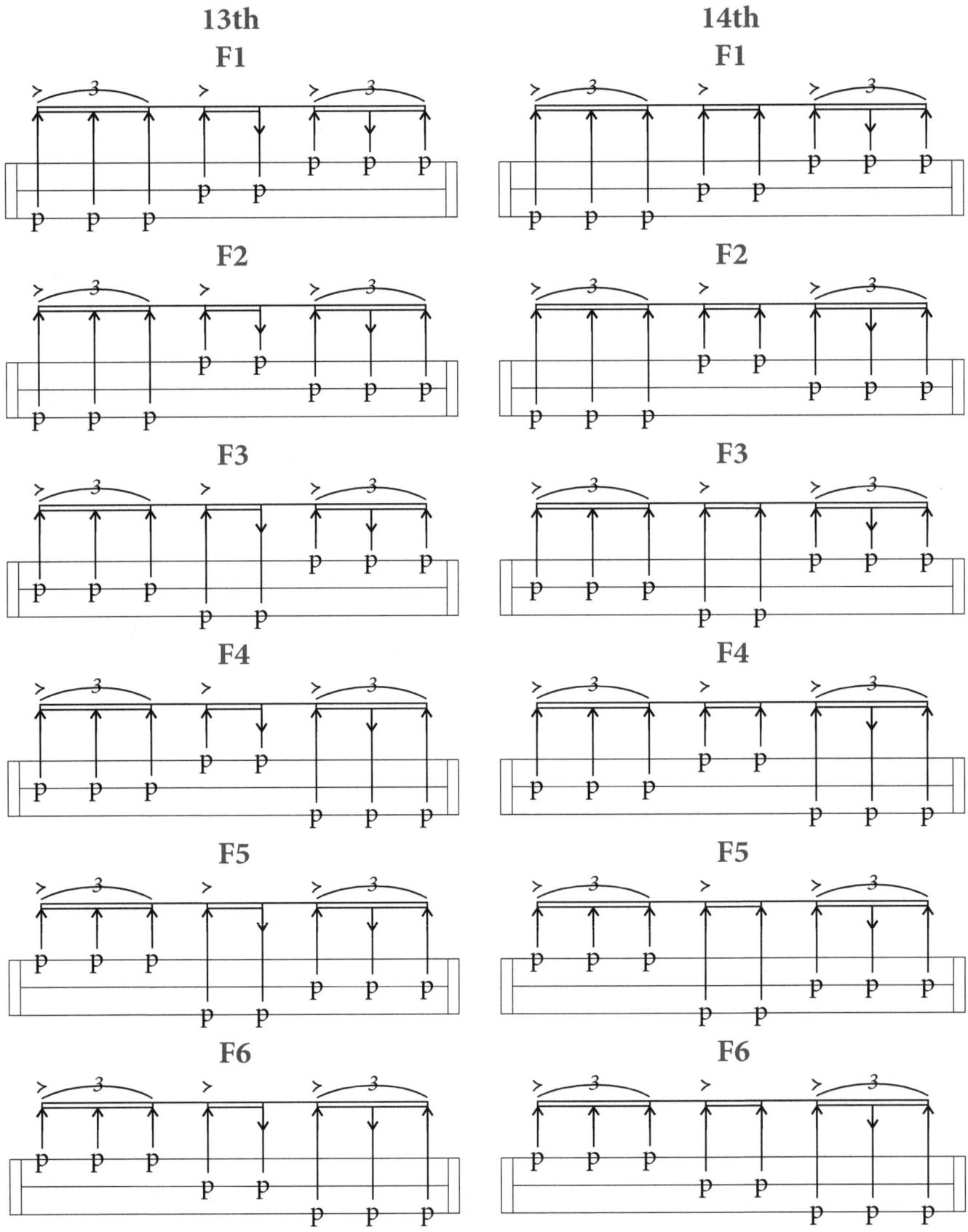

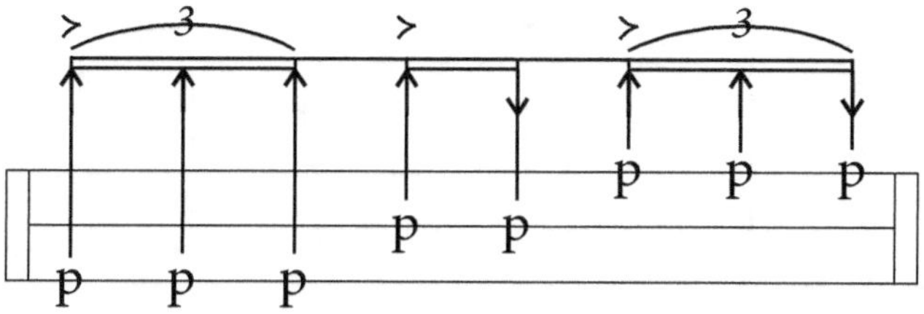

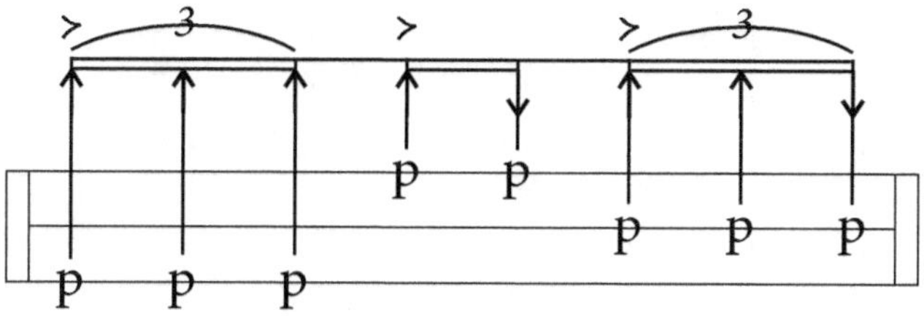

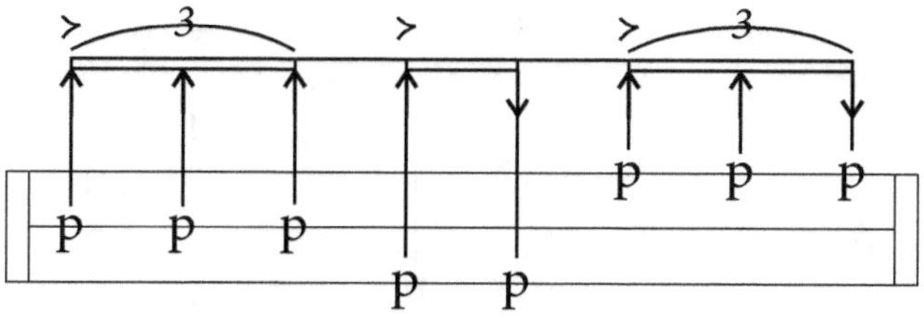

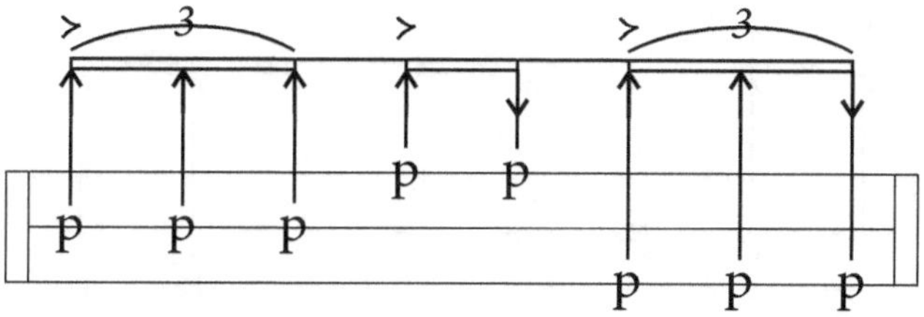

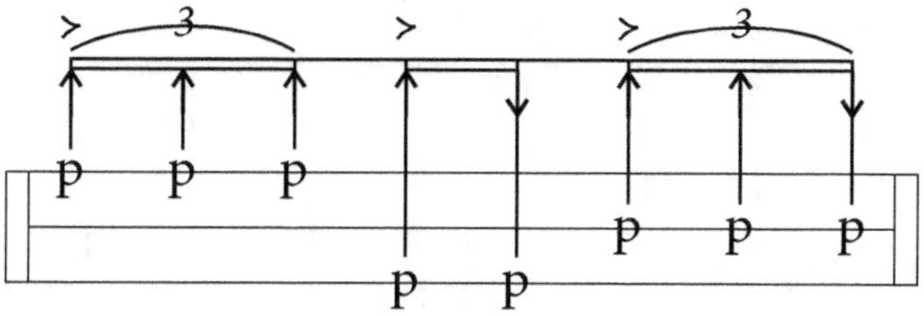

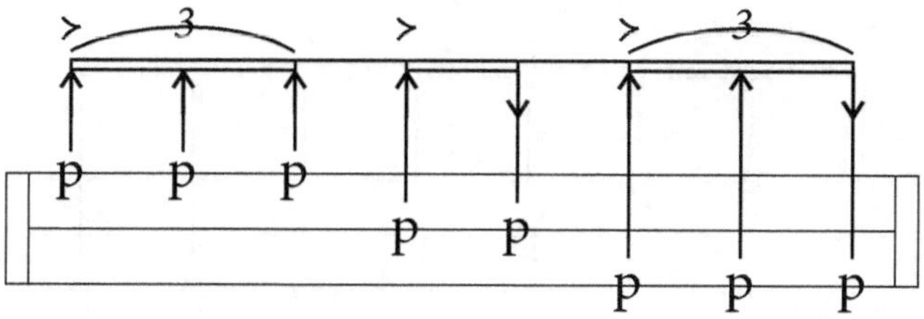

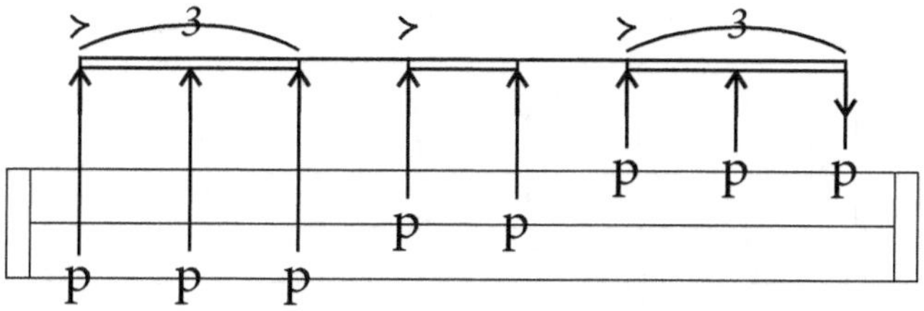

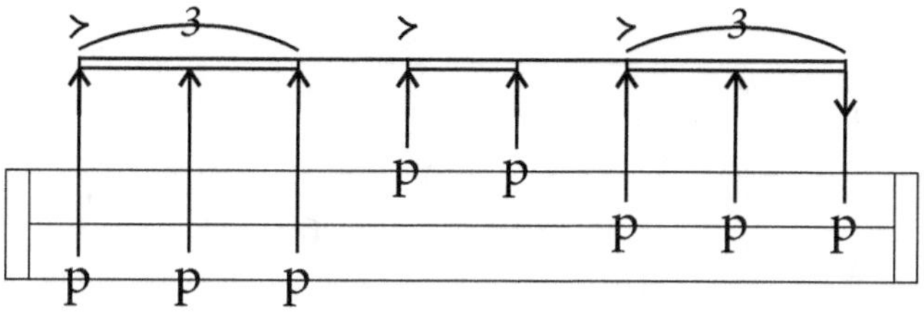

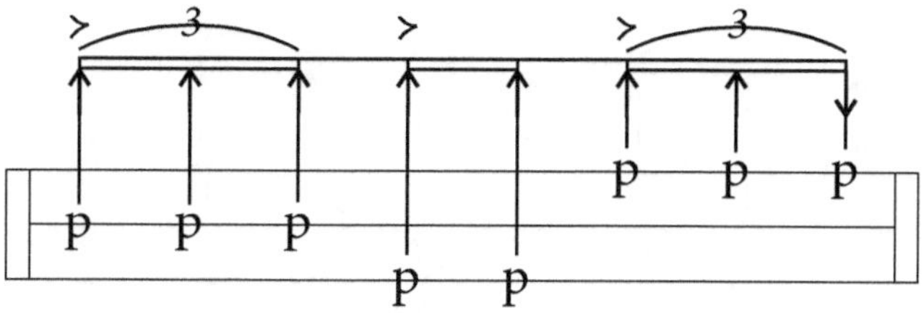

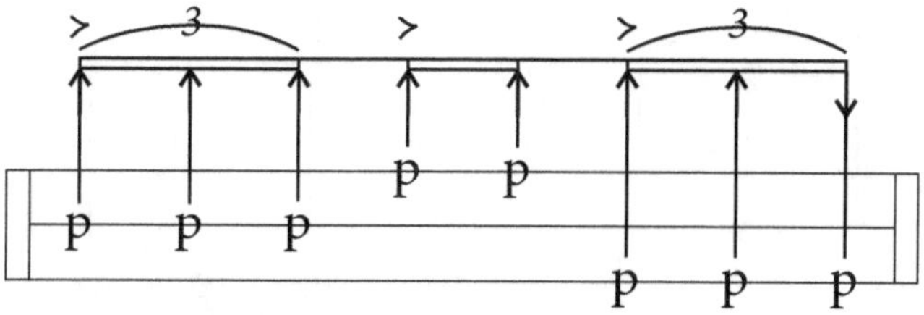

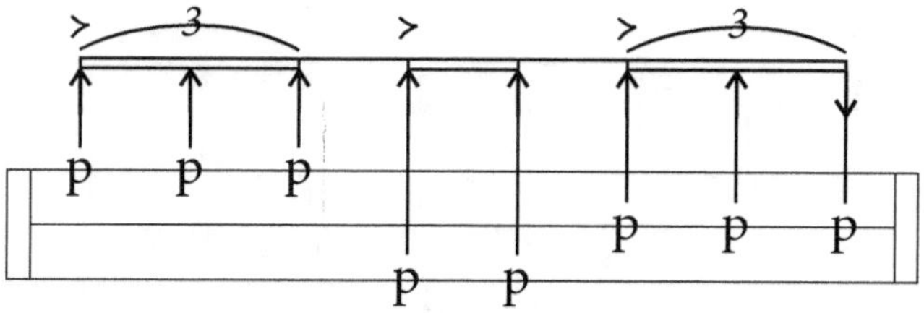

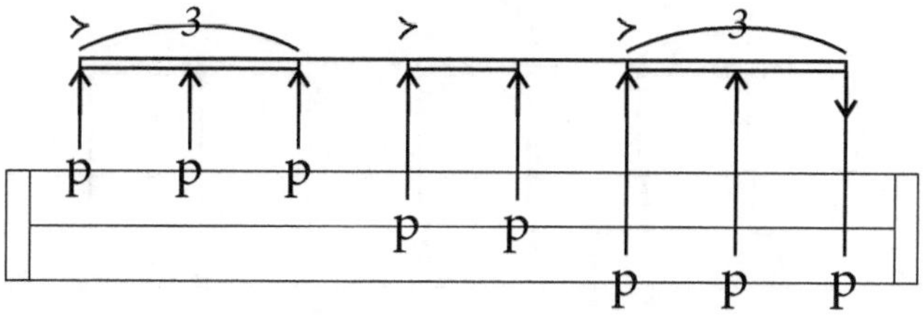

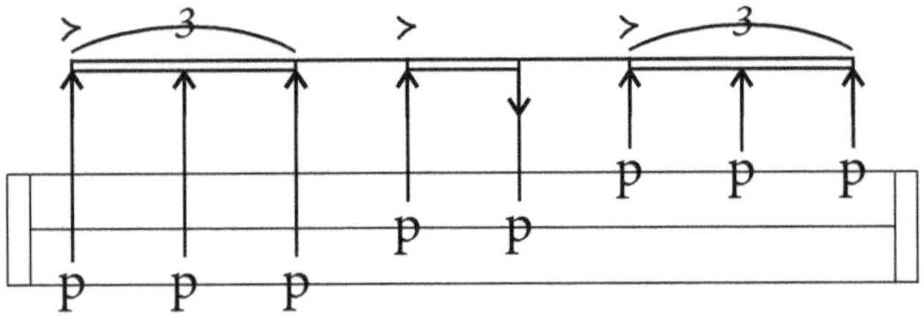

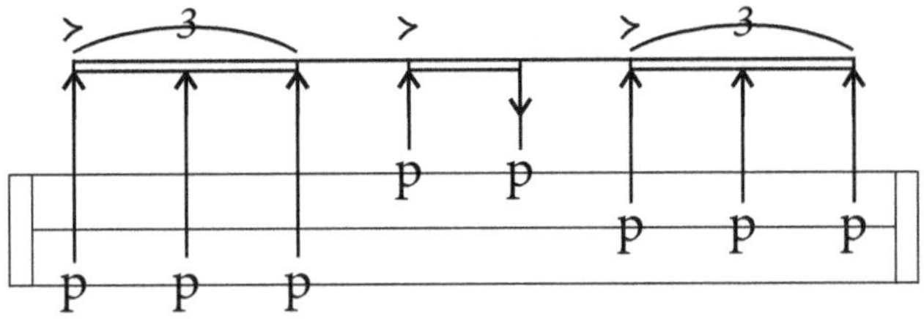

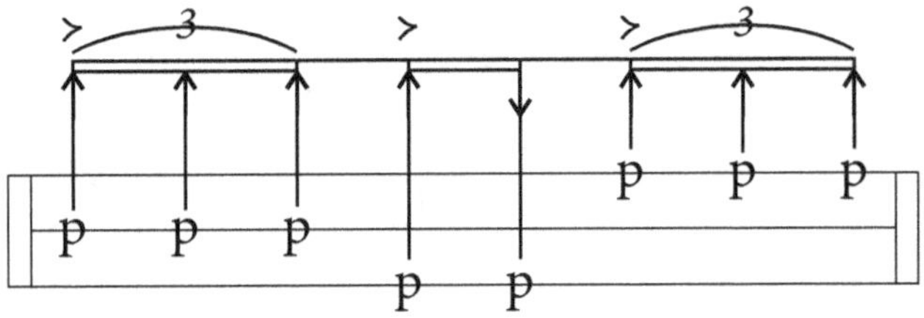

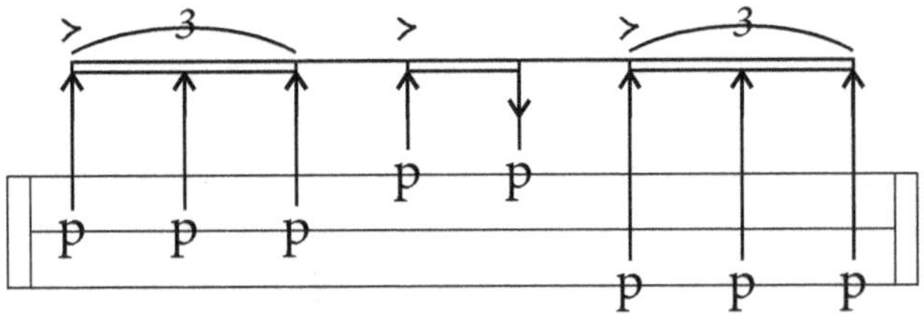

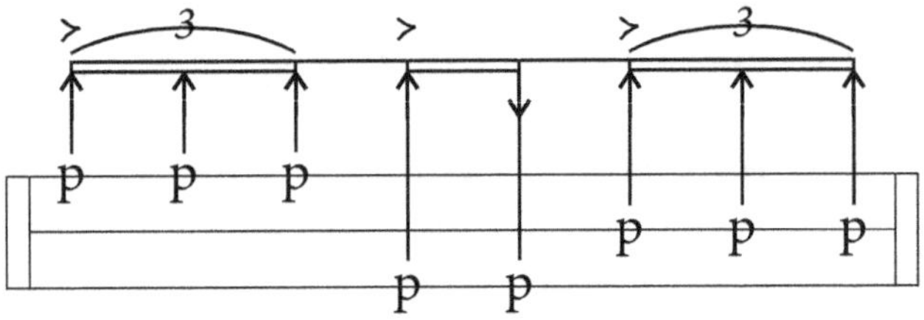

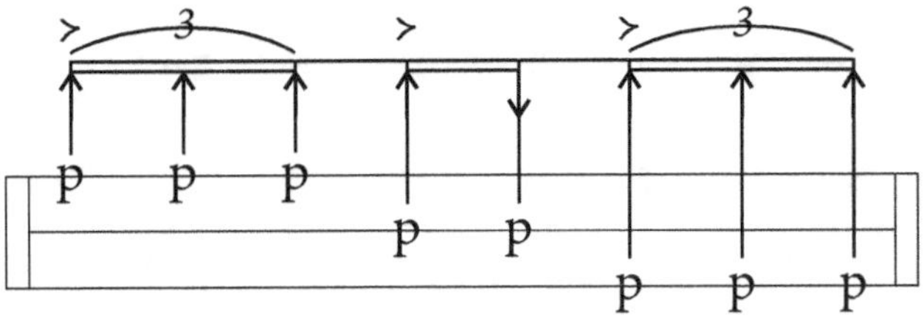

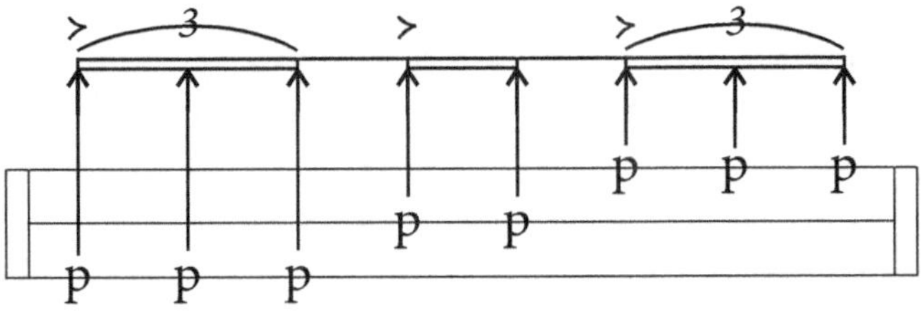

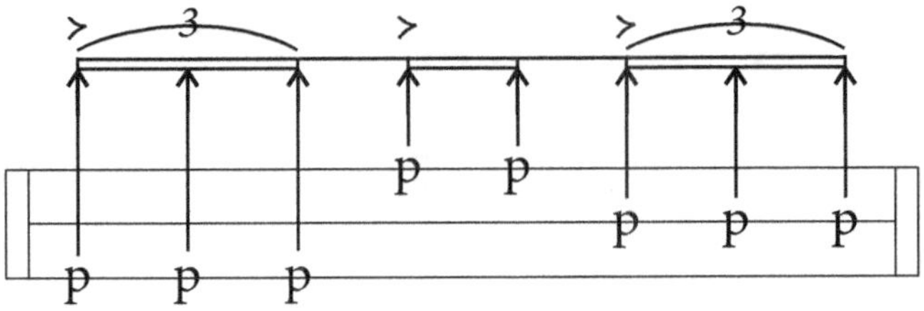

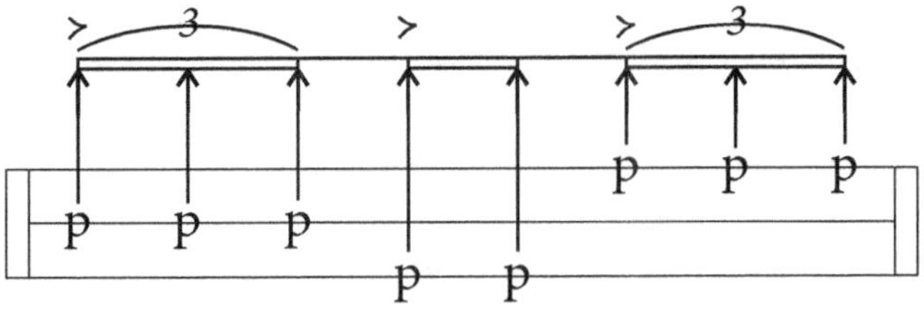

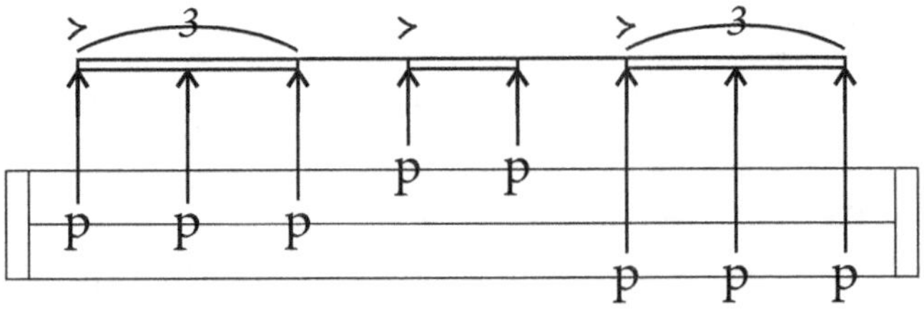

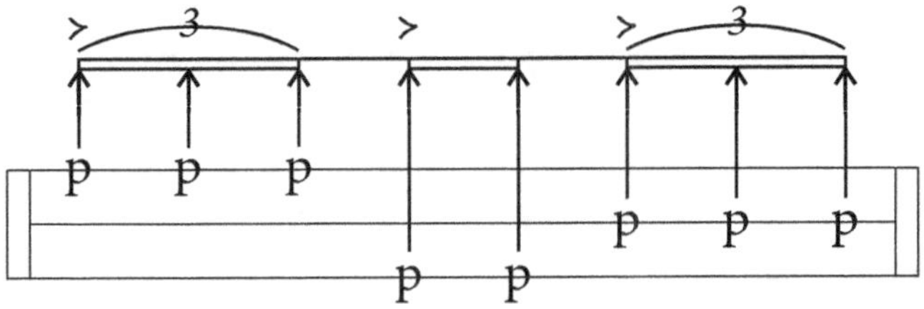

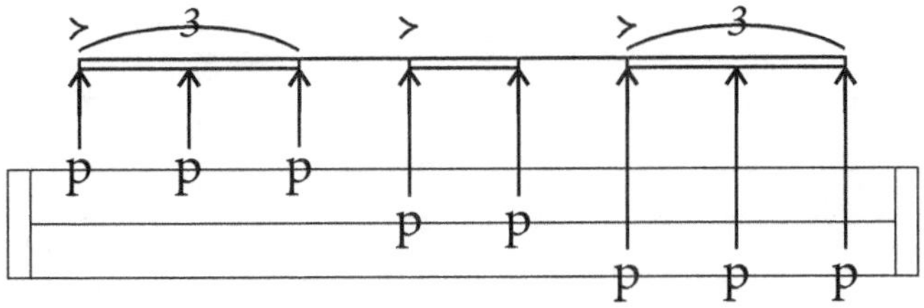

VARIATION III
WAYS OF PERFORMANCE

1st

F1
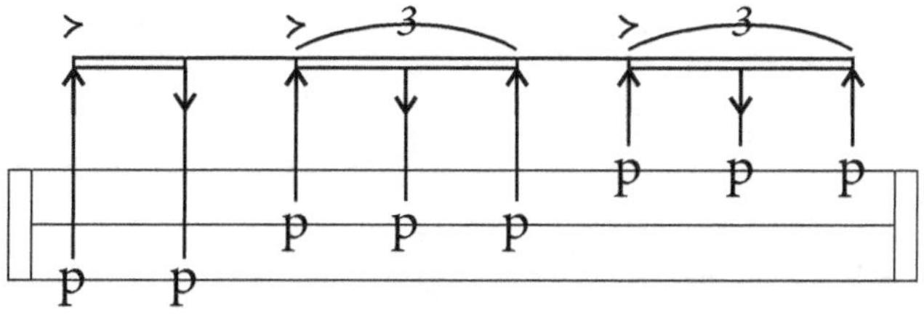

F2
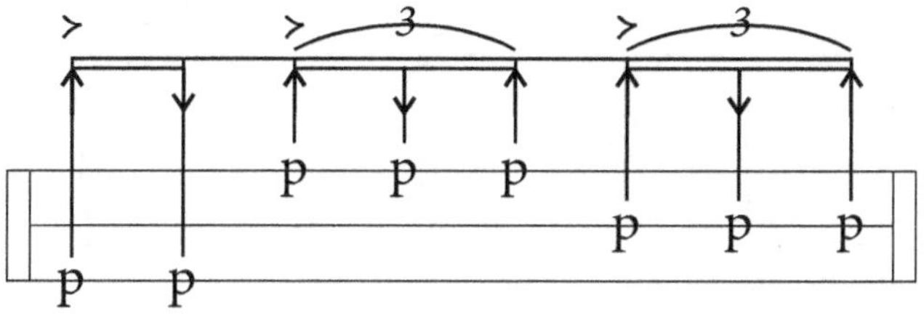

F3
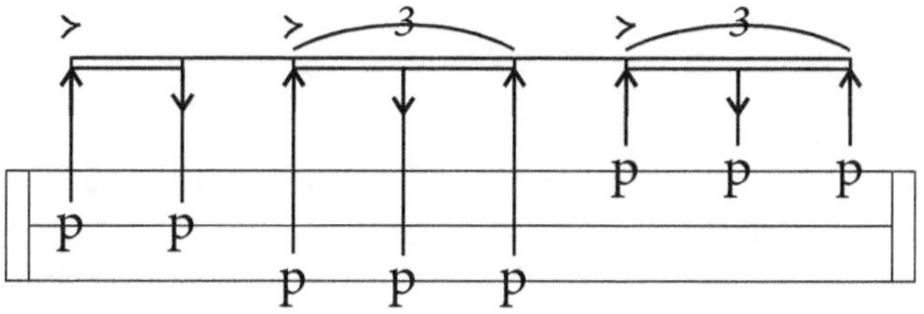

F4
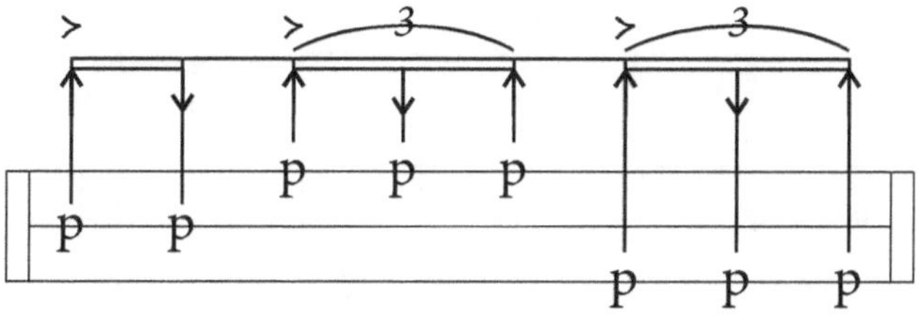

F5
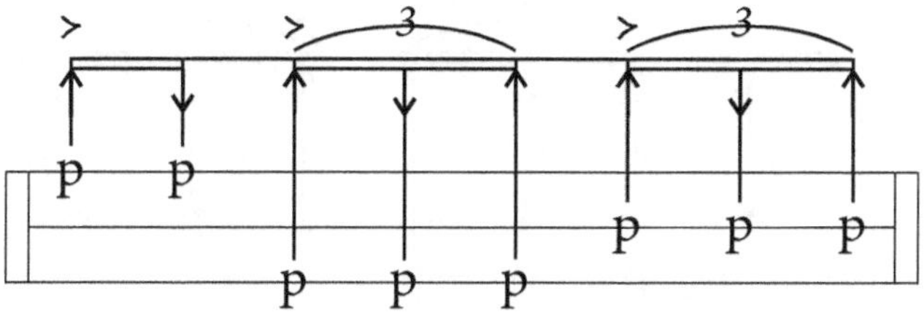

F6
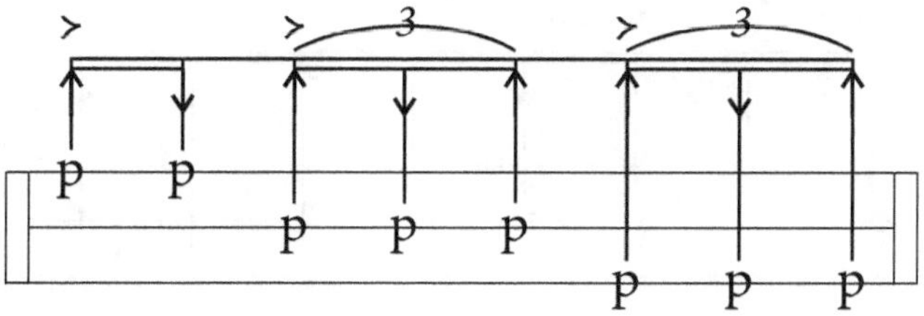

2nd

F1
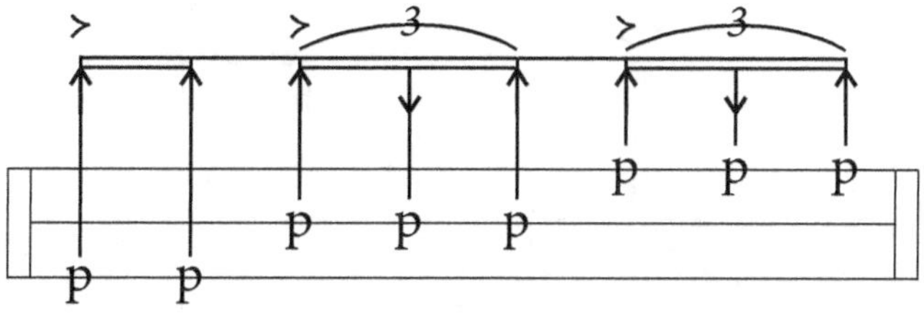

F2
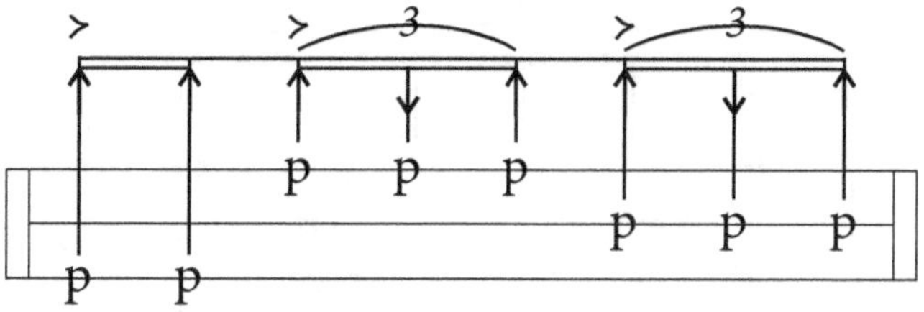

F3
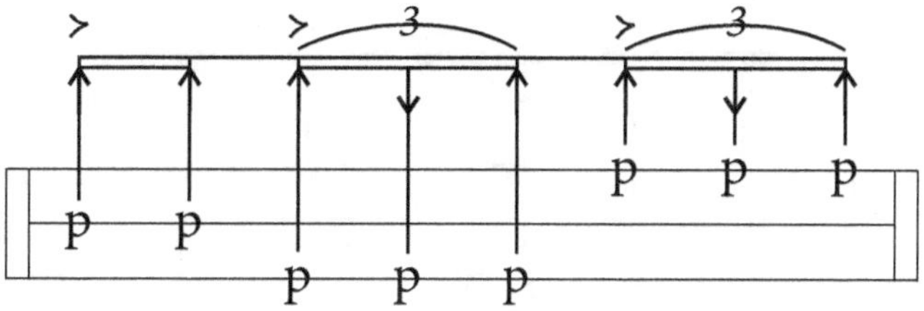

F4
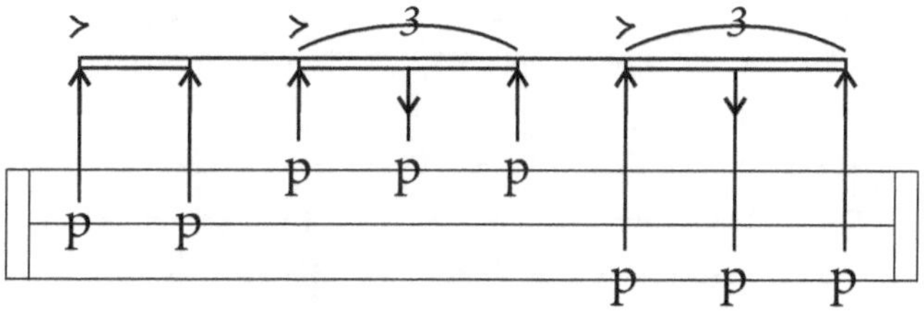

F5
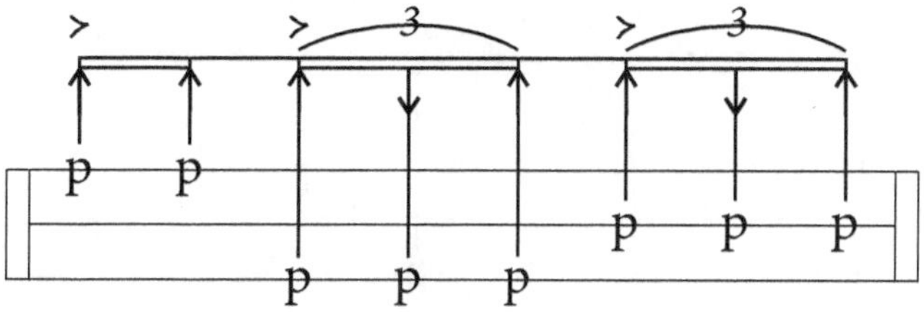

F6
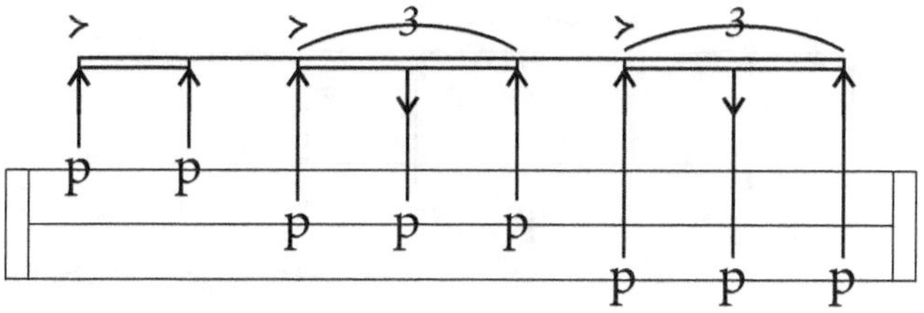

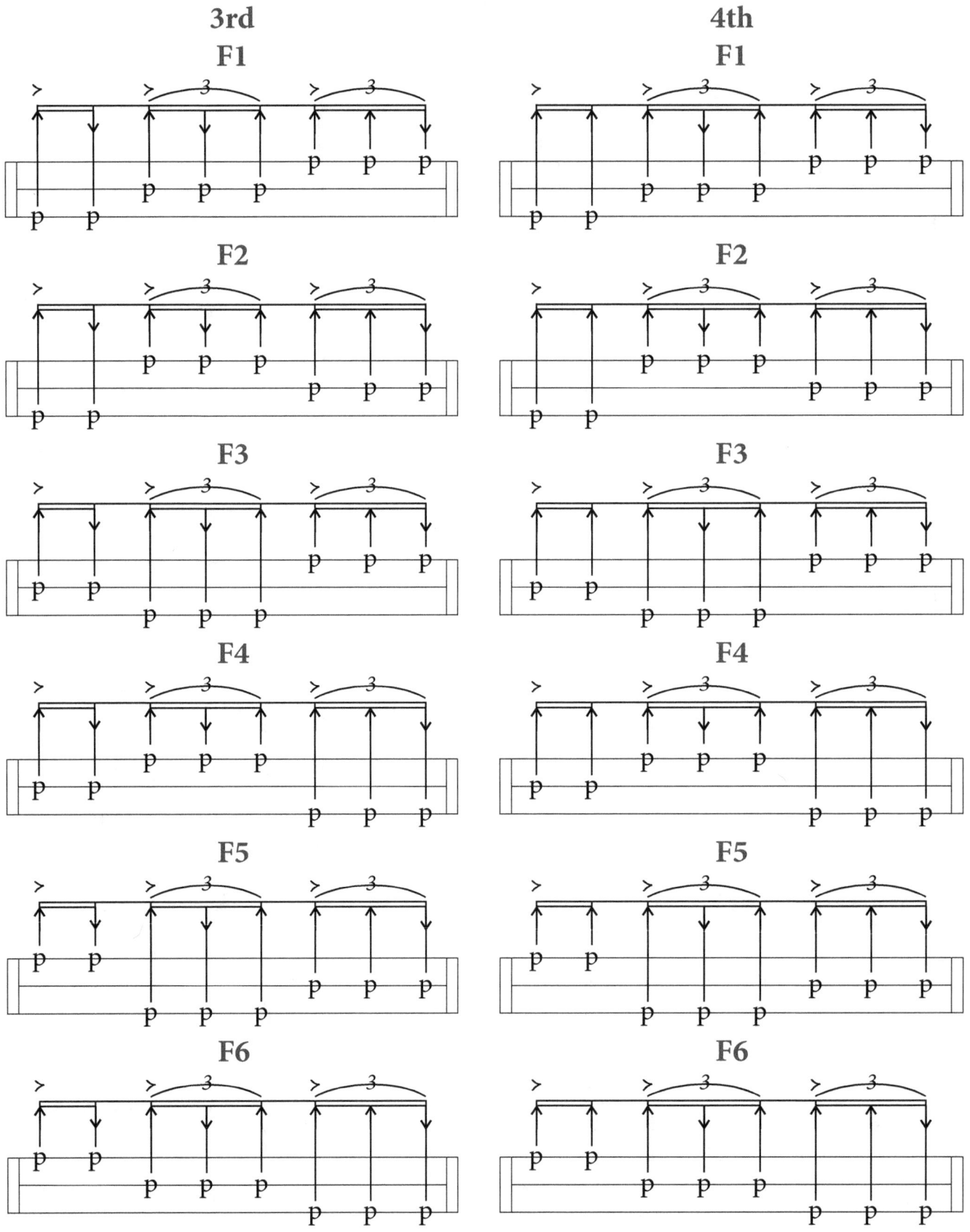

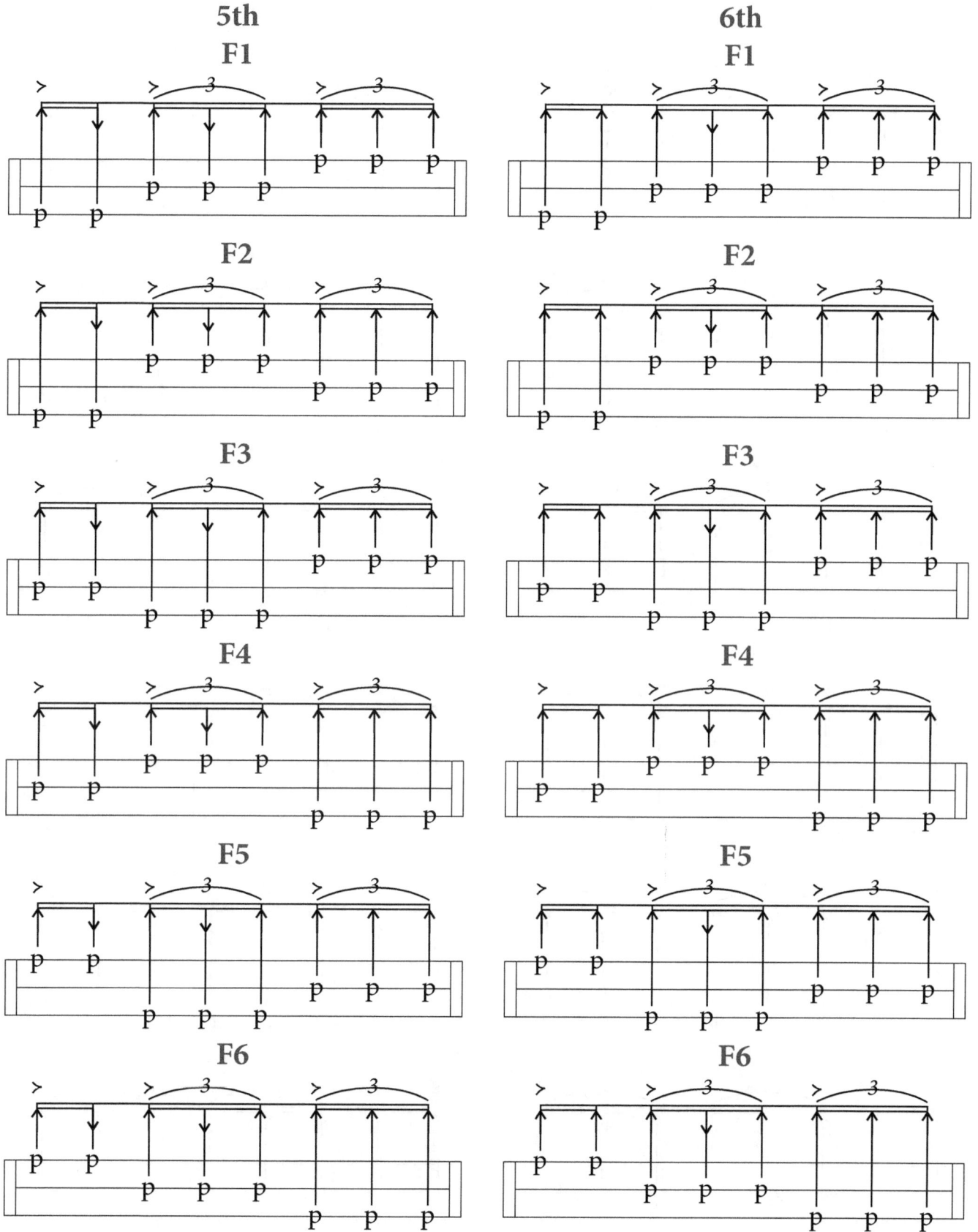

7th

F1

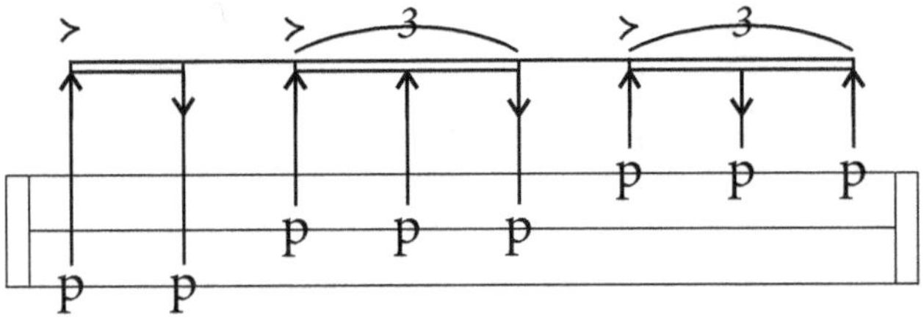

F2

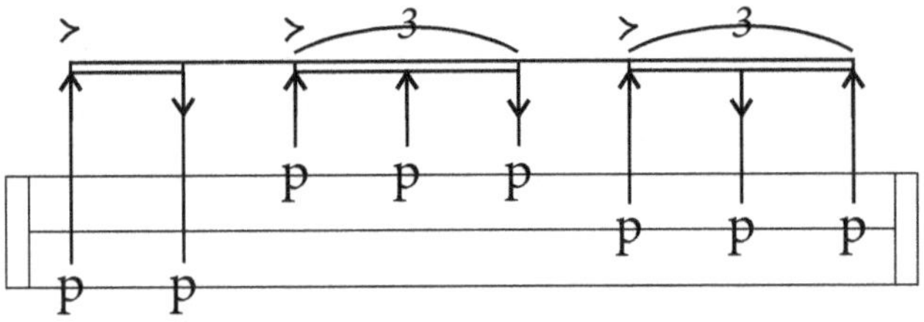

F3

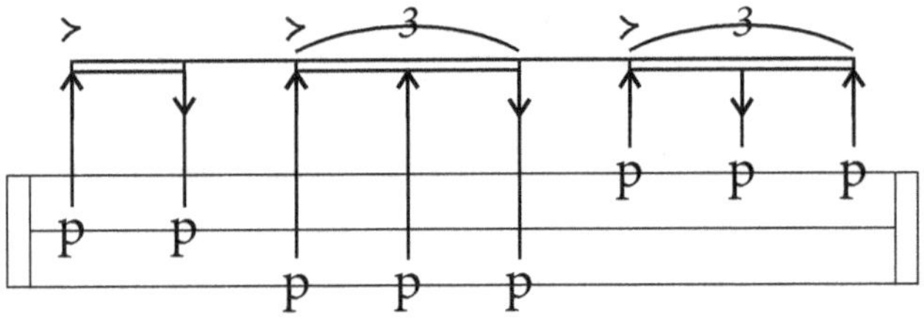

F4

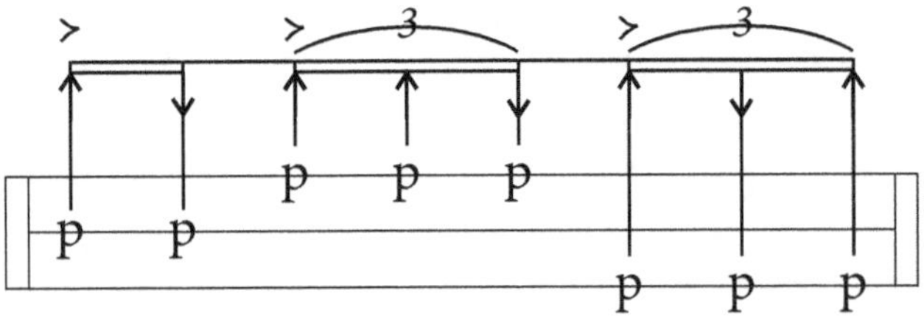

F5

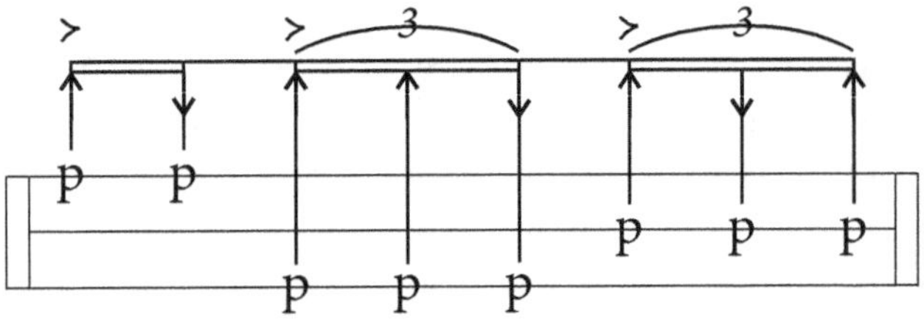

F6

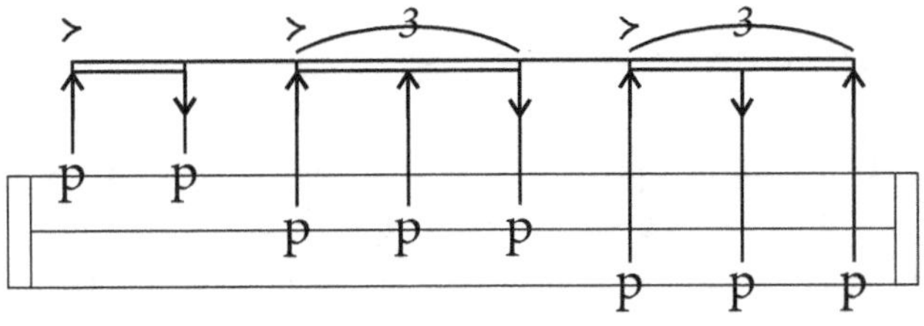

8th

F1

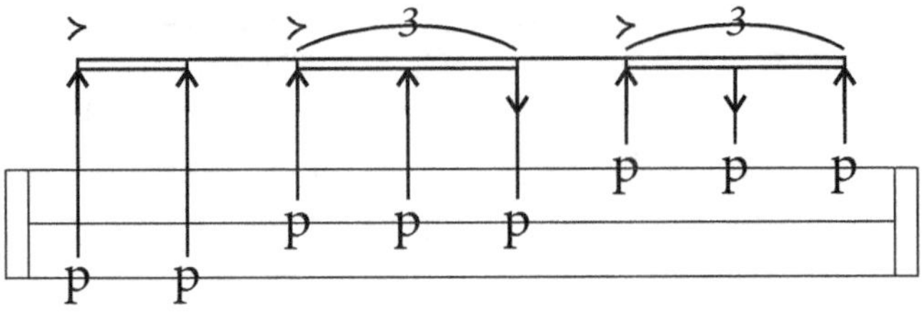

F2

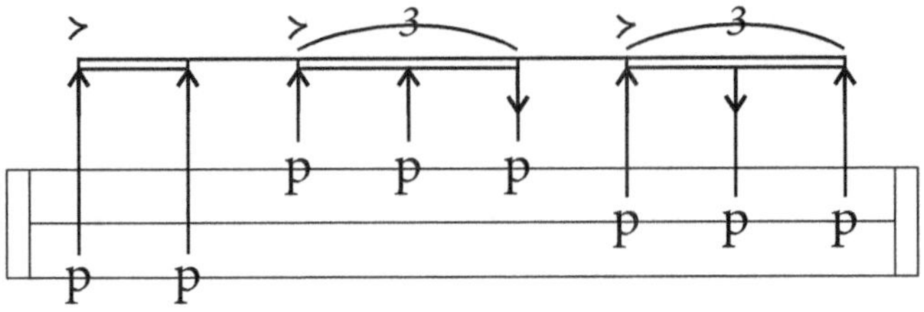

F3

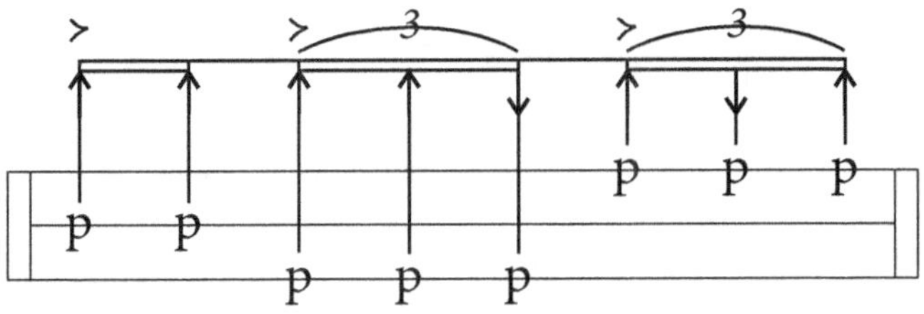

F4

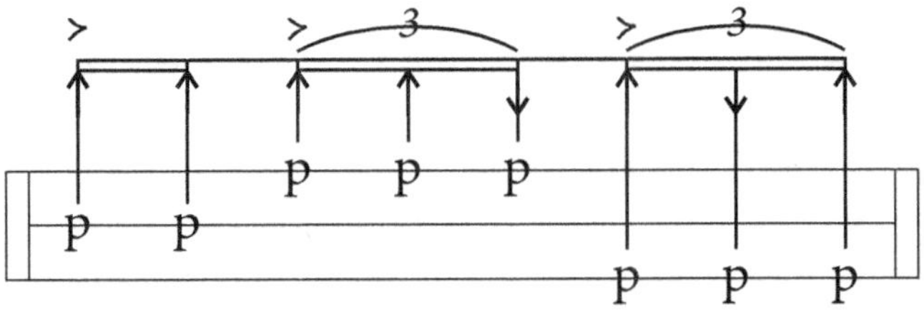

F5

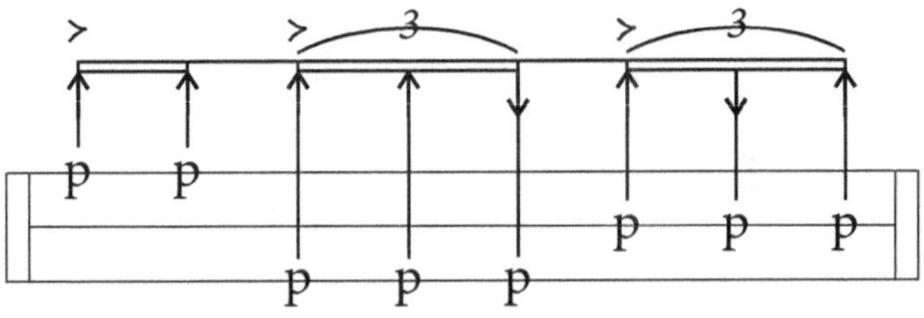

F6

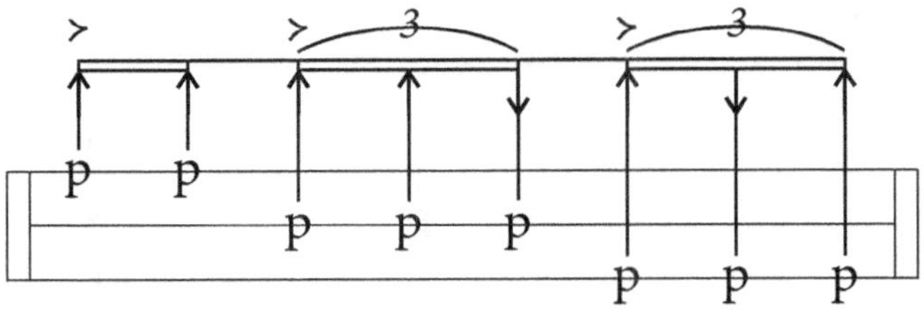

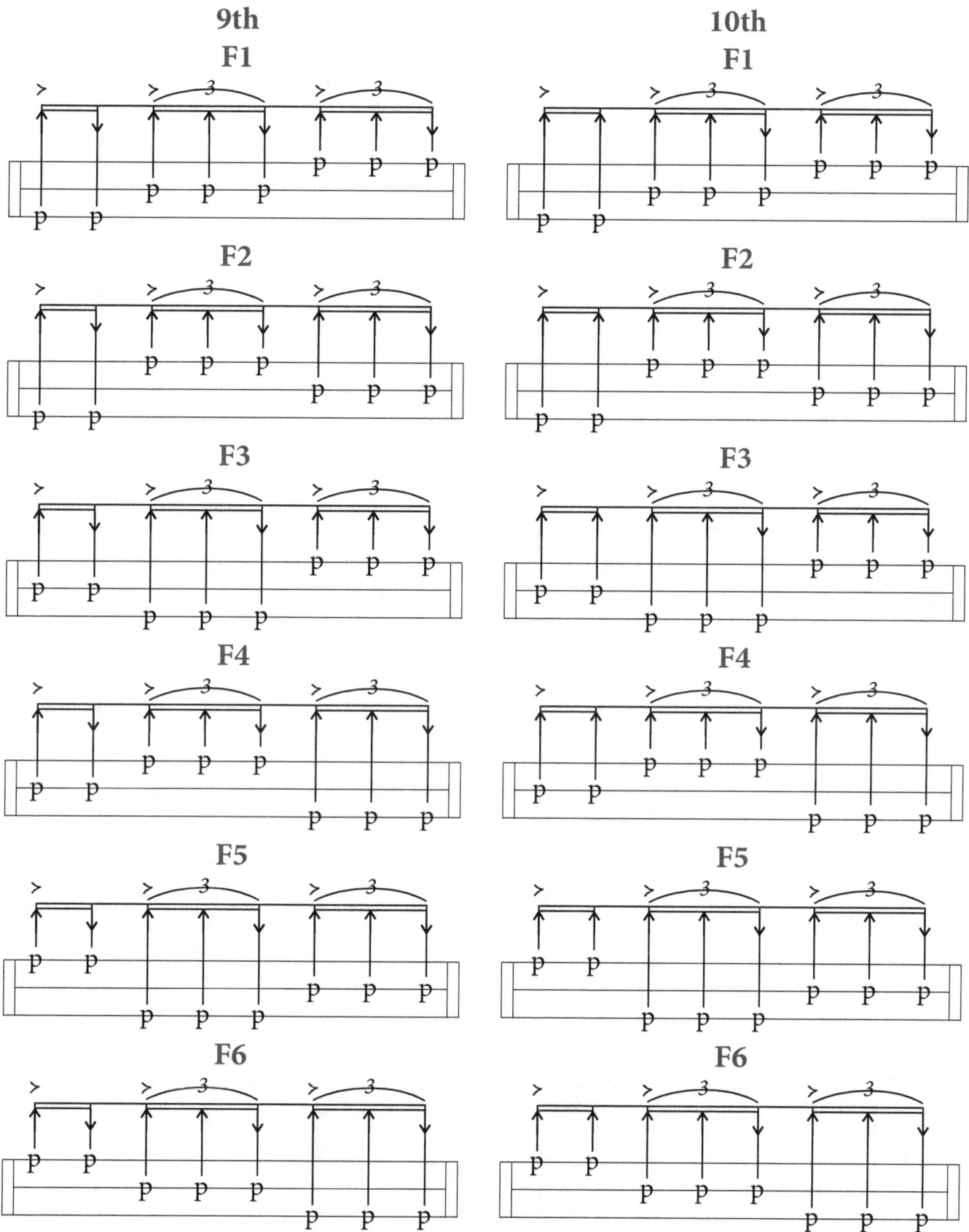

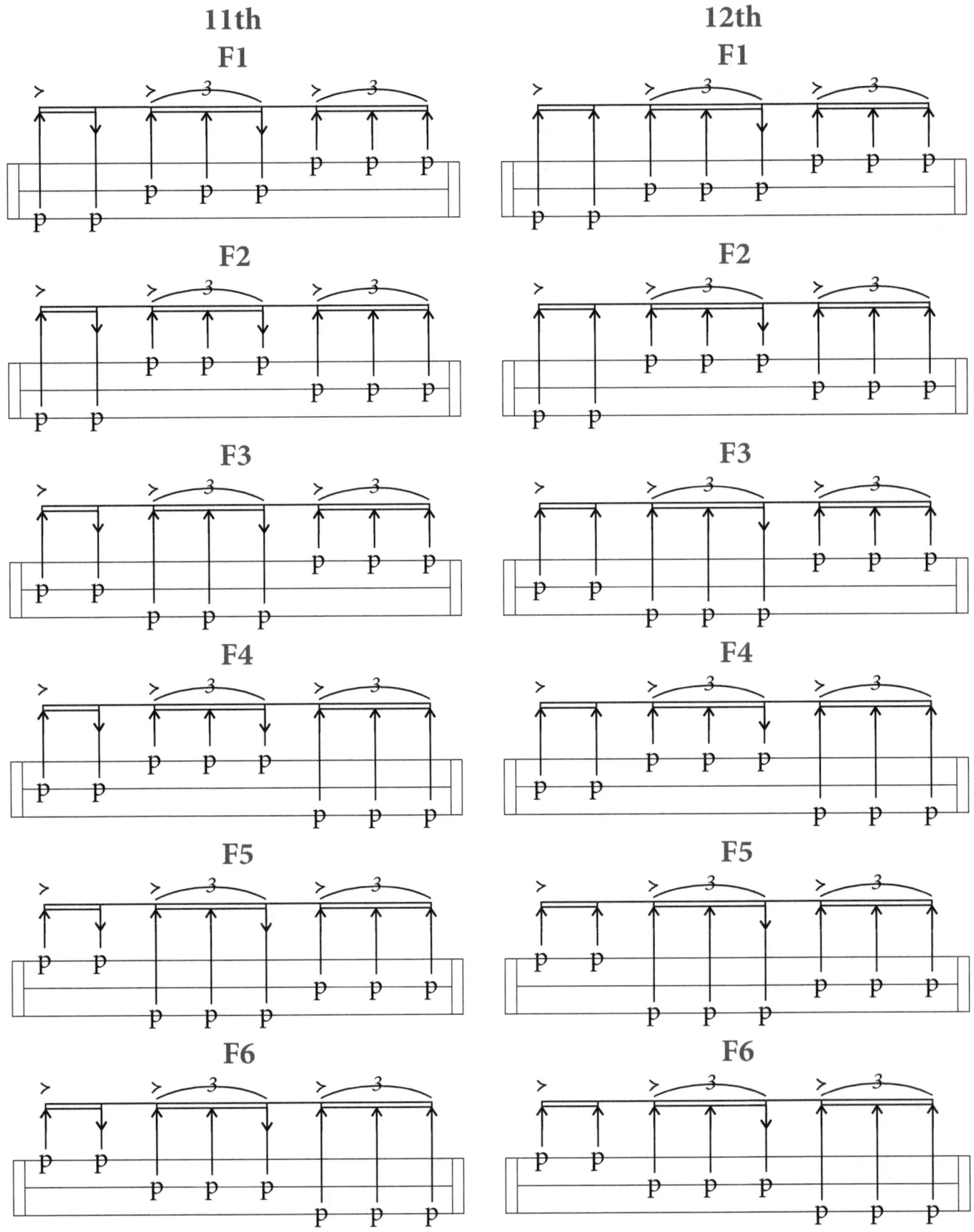

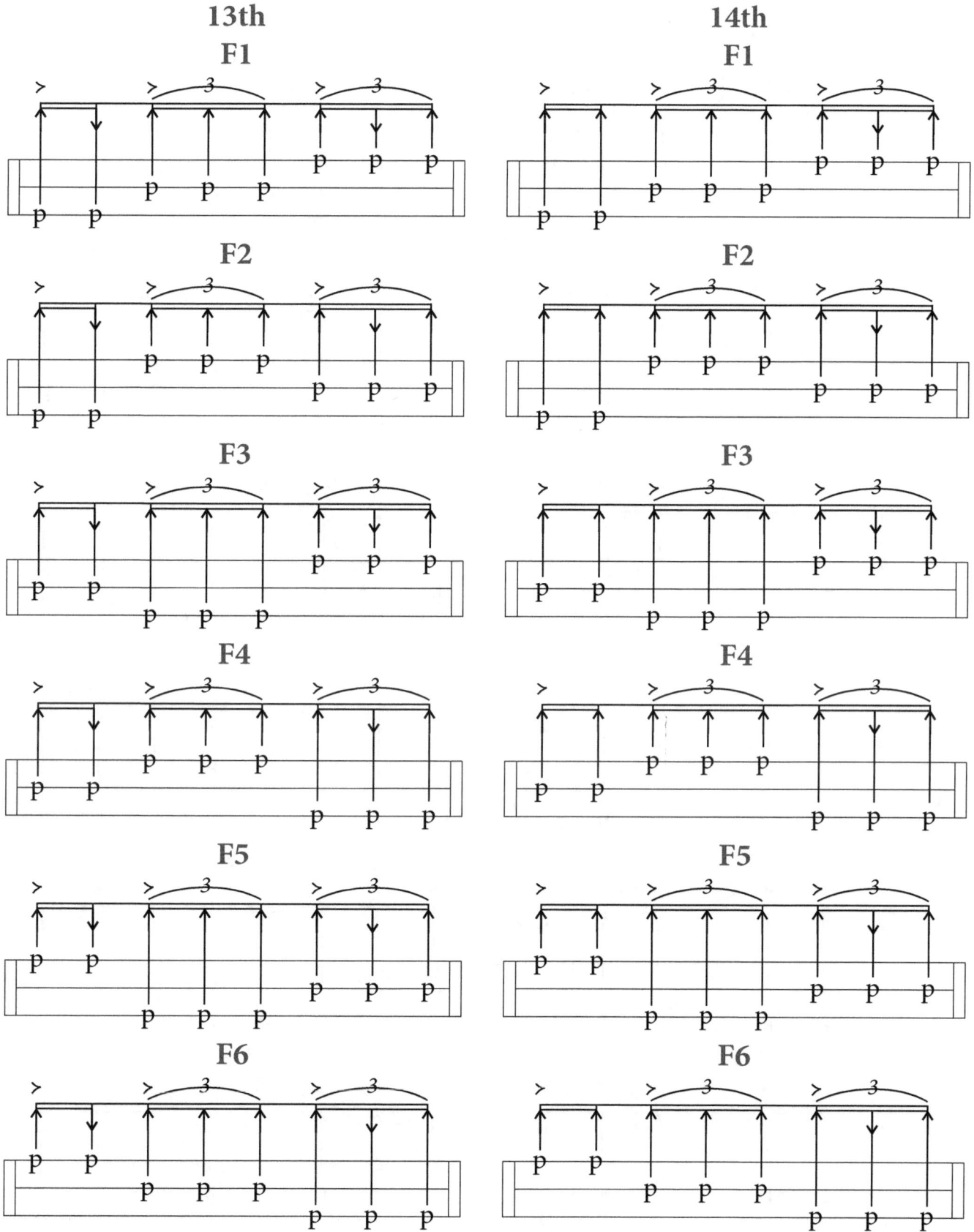

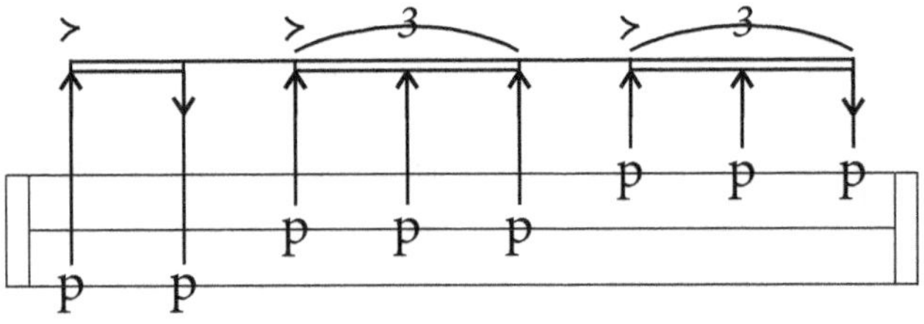

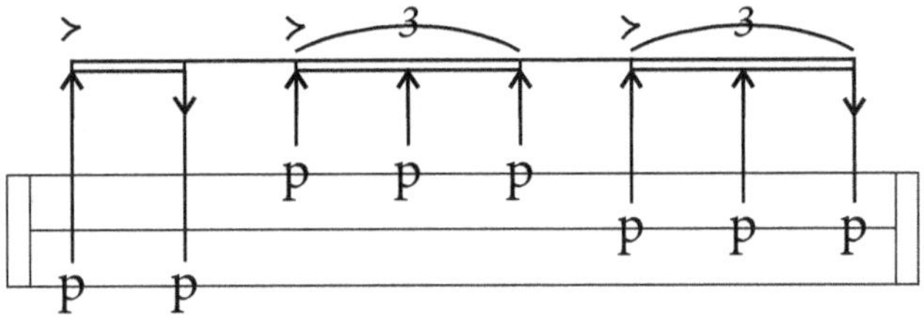

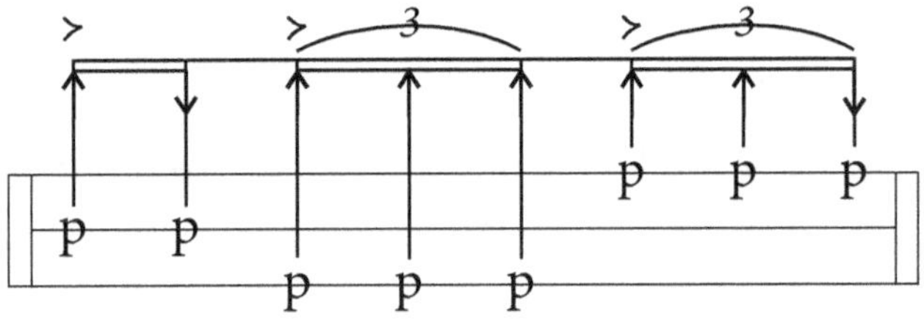

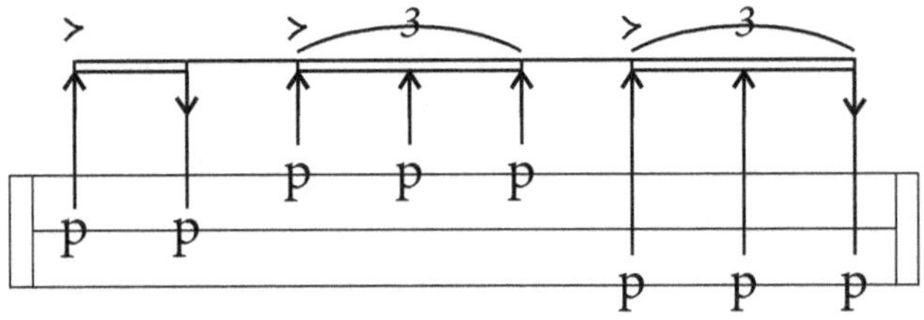

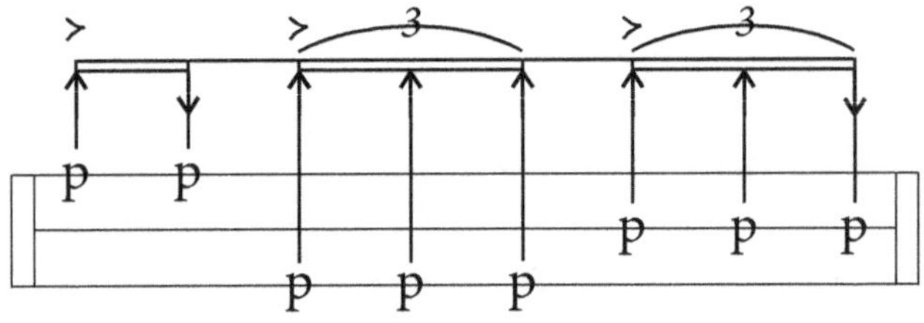

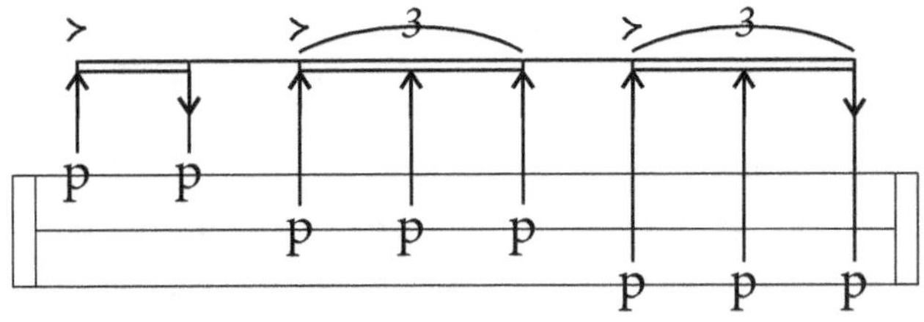

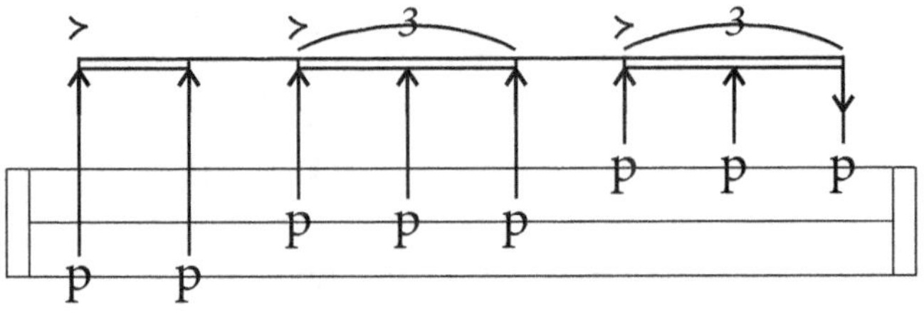

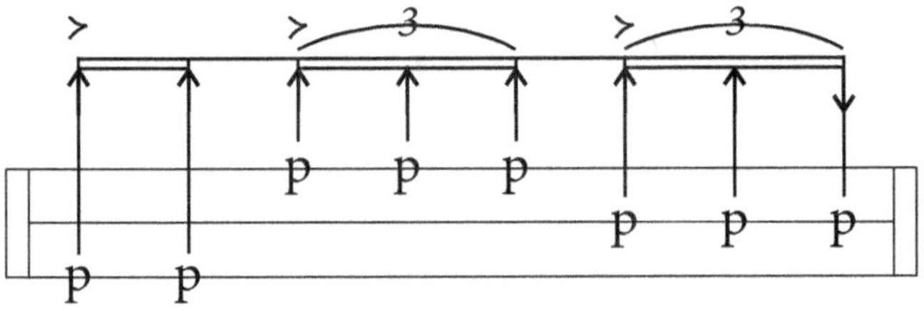

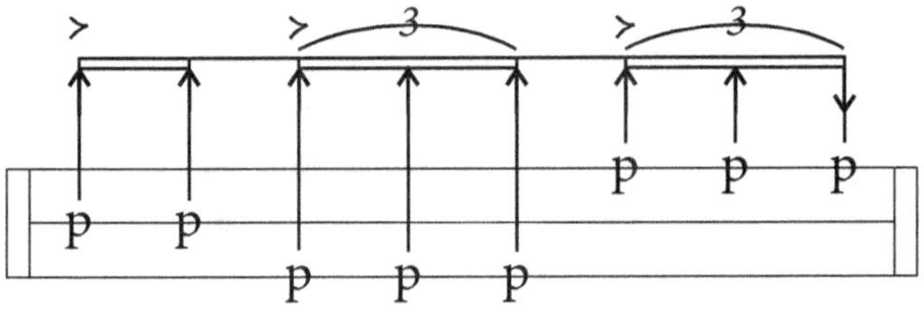

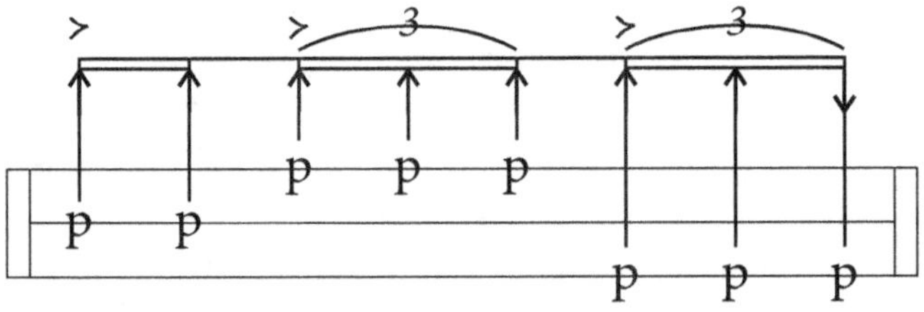

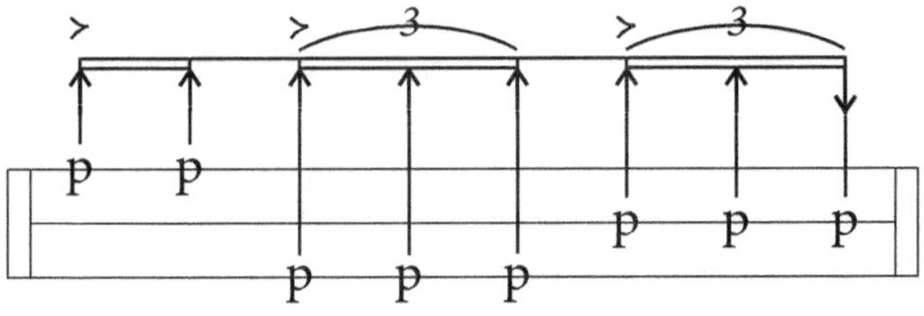

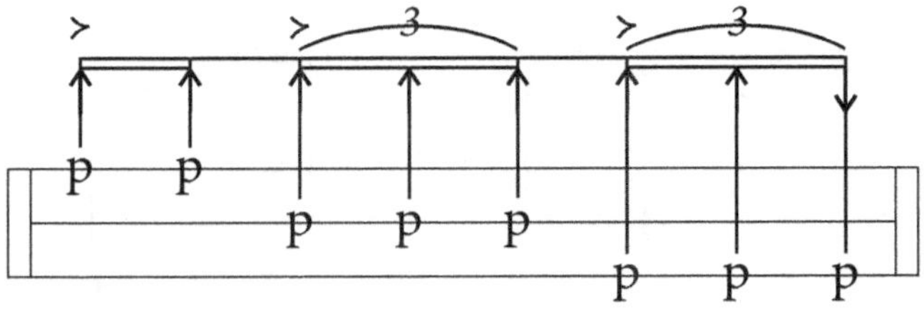

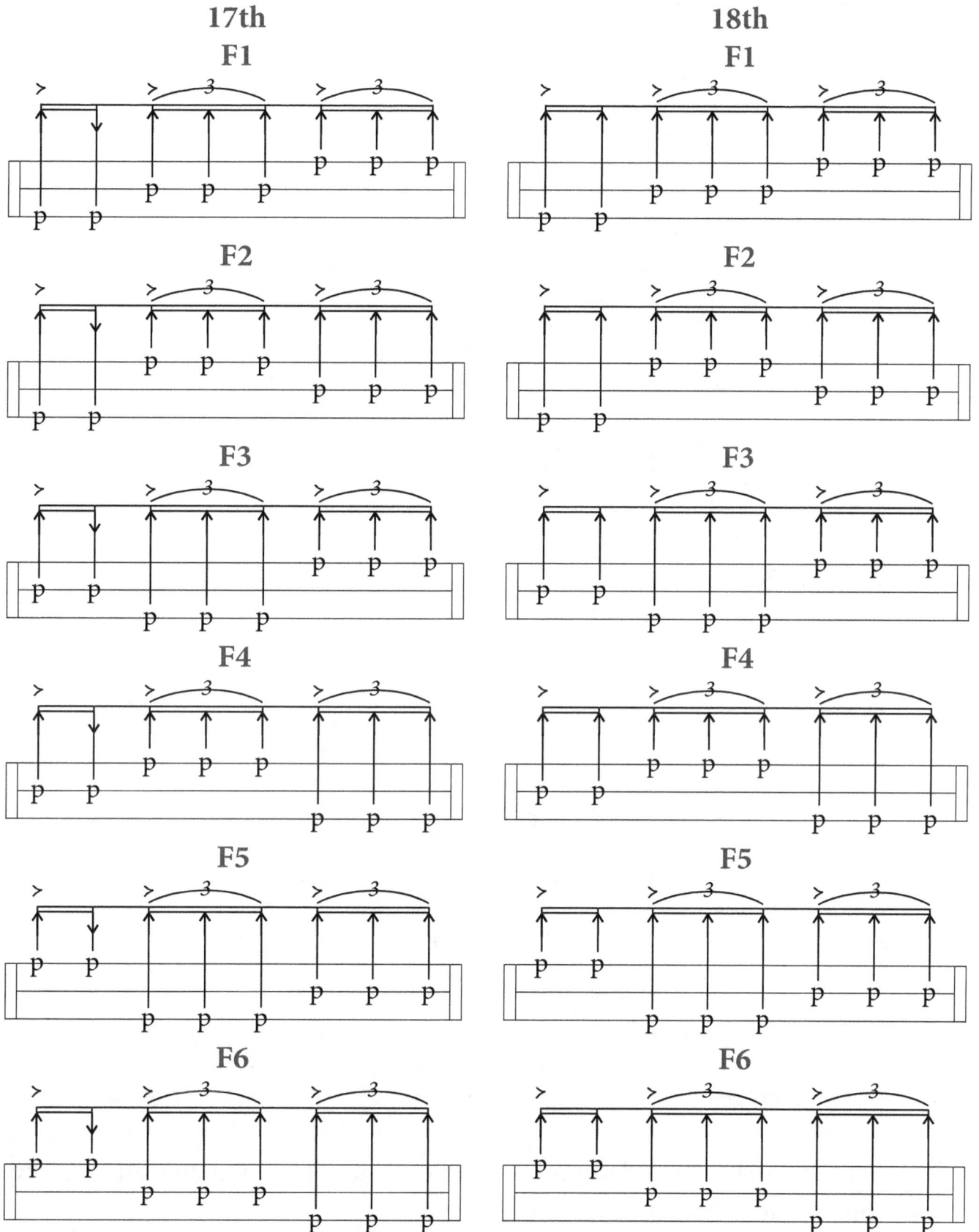

§ IX

Exercise on pulgar on three adjacent strings with three triple strokes within each Formula.

F1

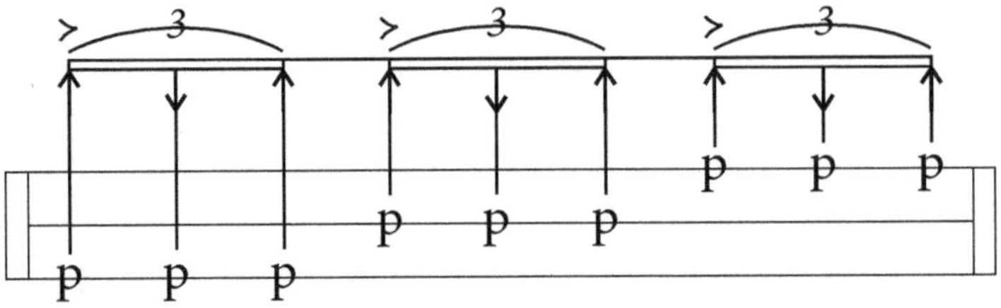

F2

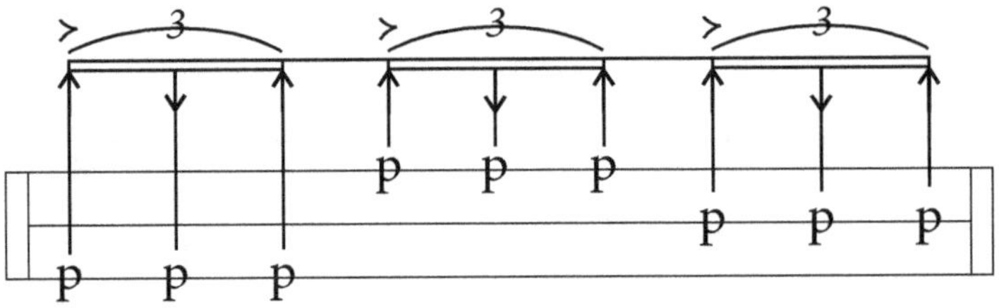

F3

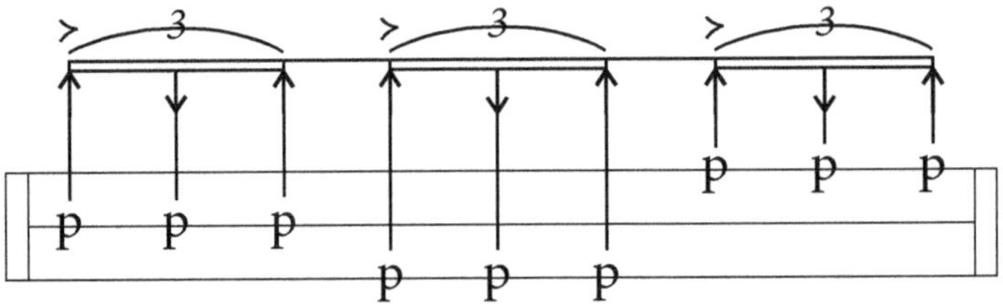

F4

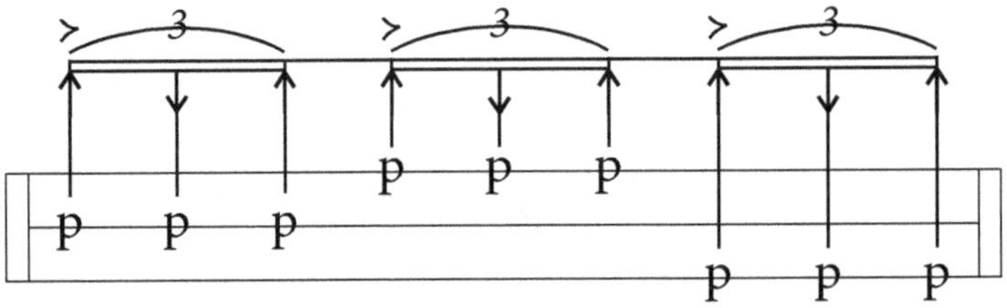

F5

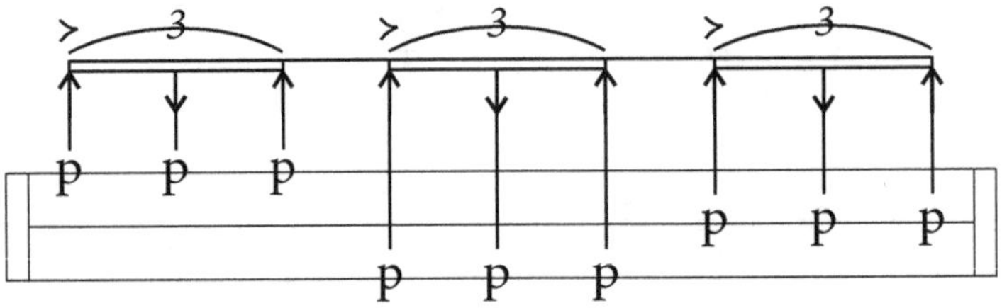

F6

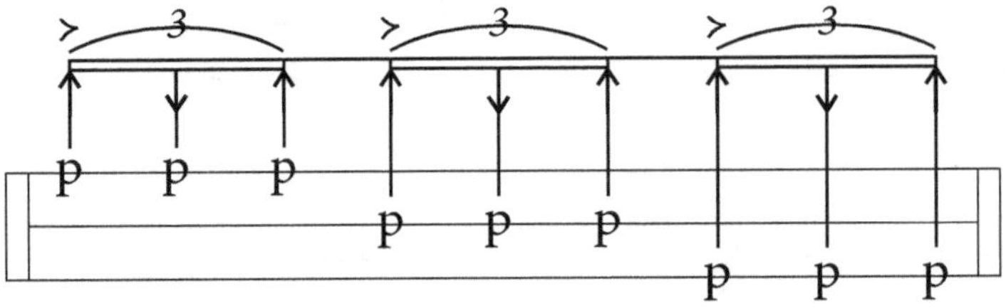

This exercise can be carried out in 24 different ways in total depending on the direction of pulgar stroke.

VARIATIONS

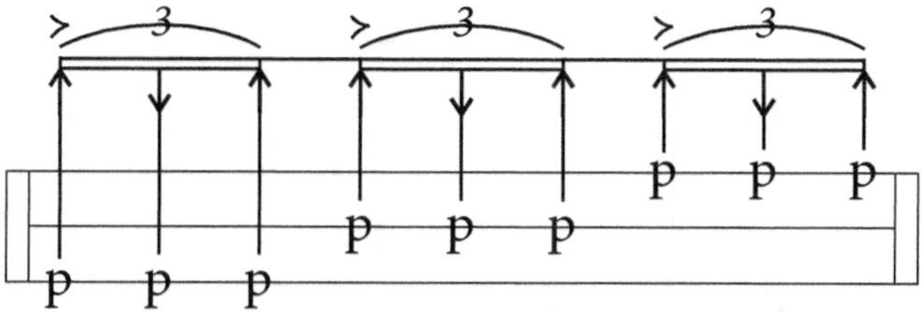

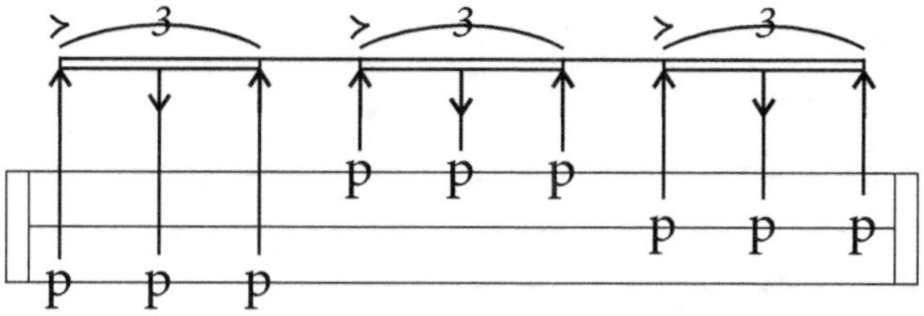

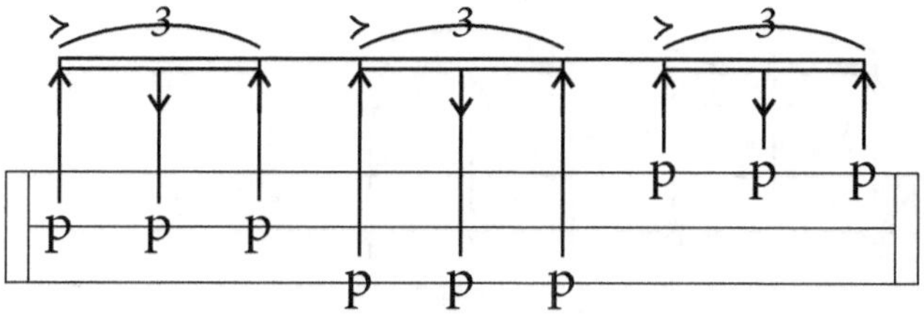

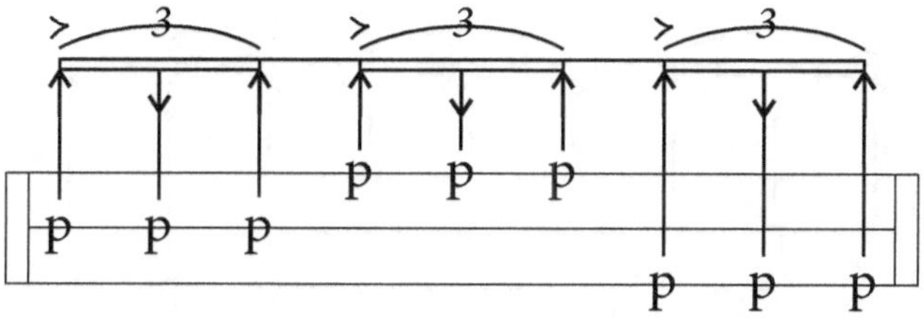

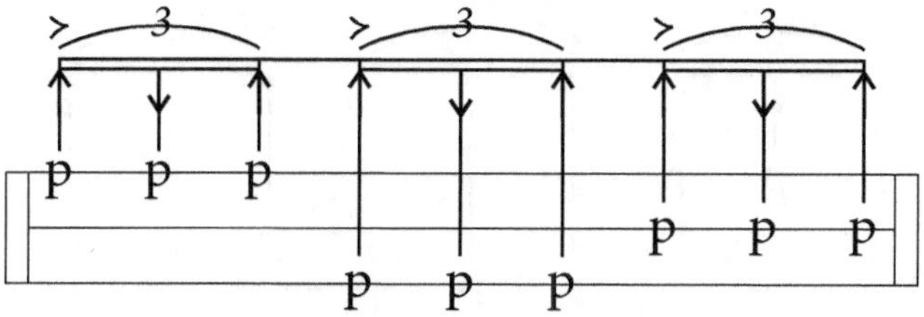

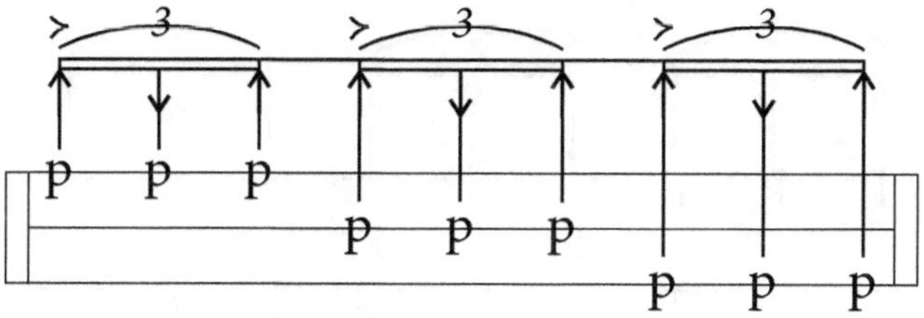

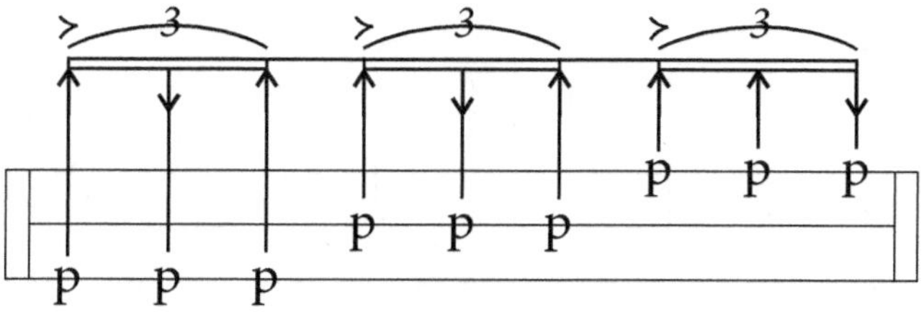

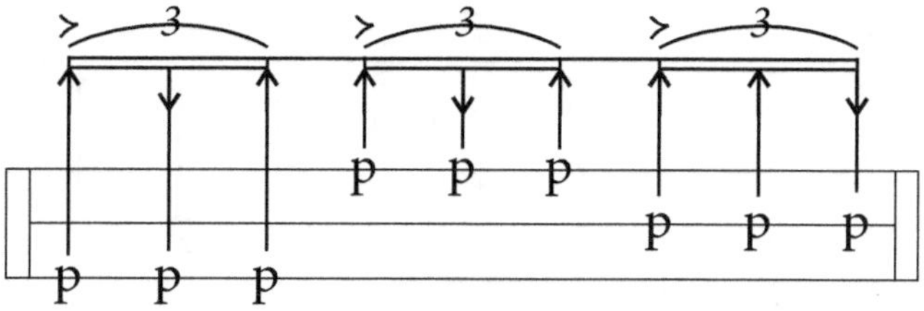

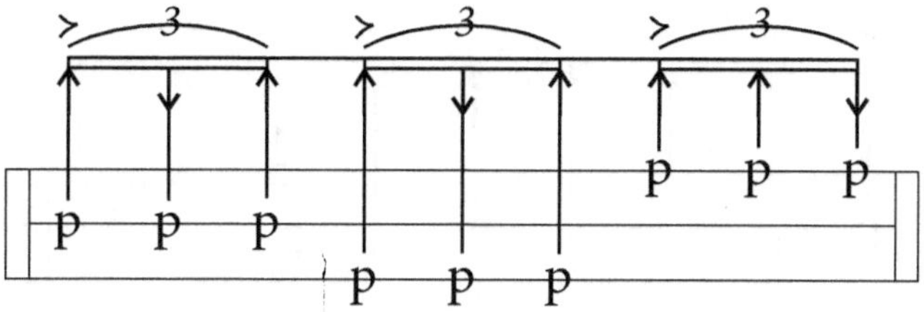

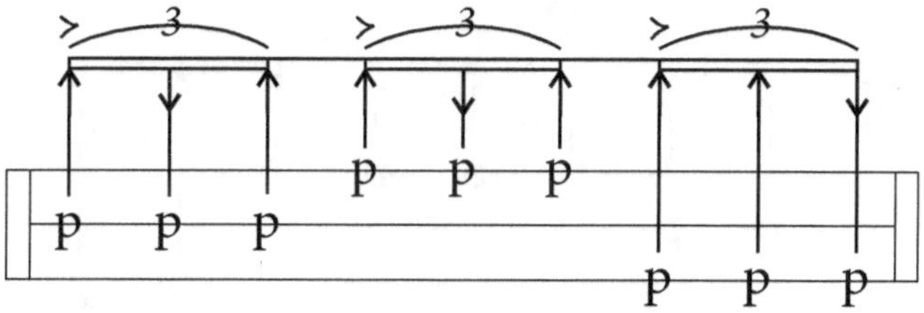

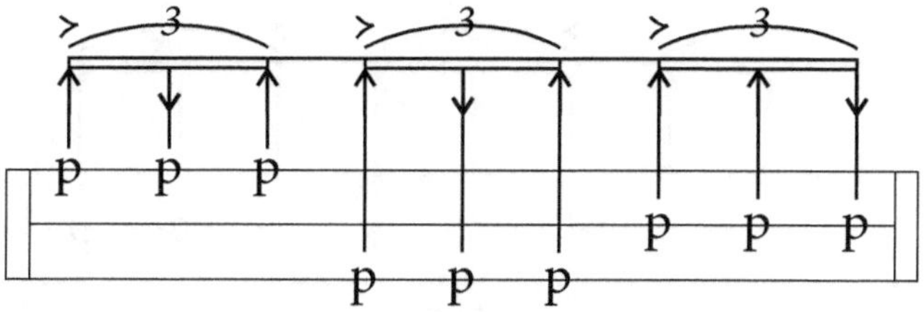

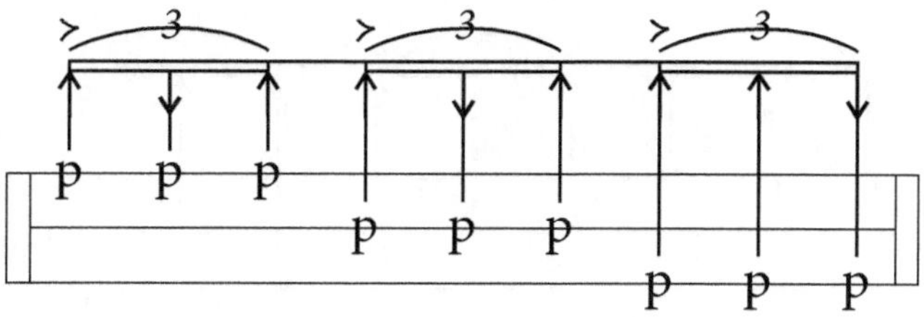

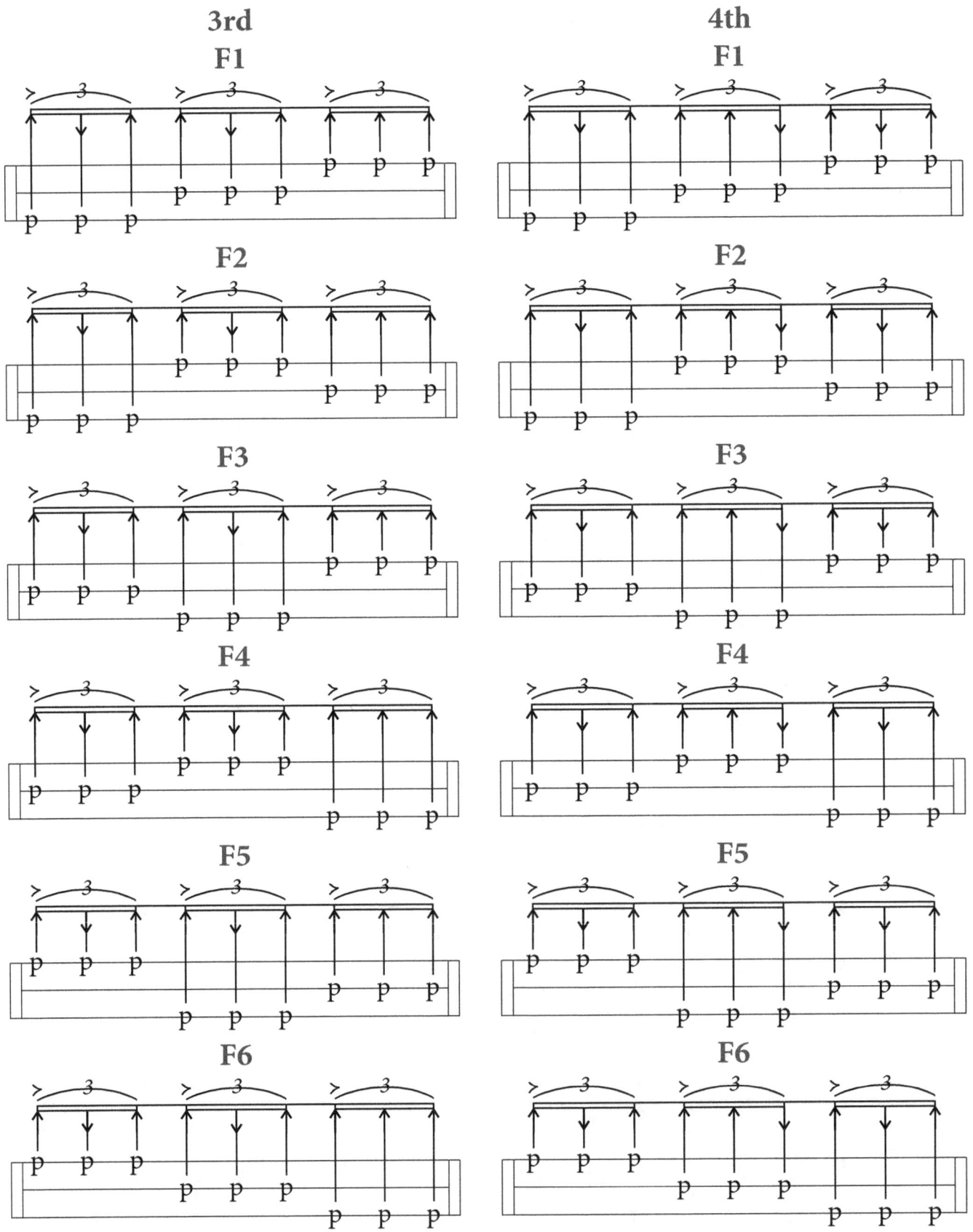

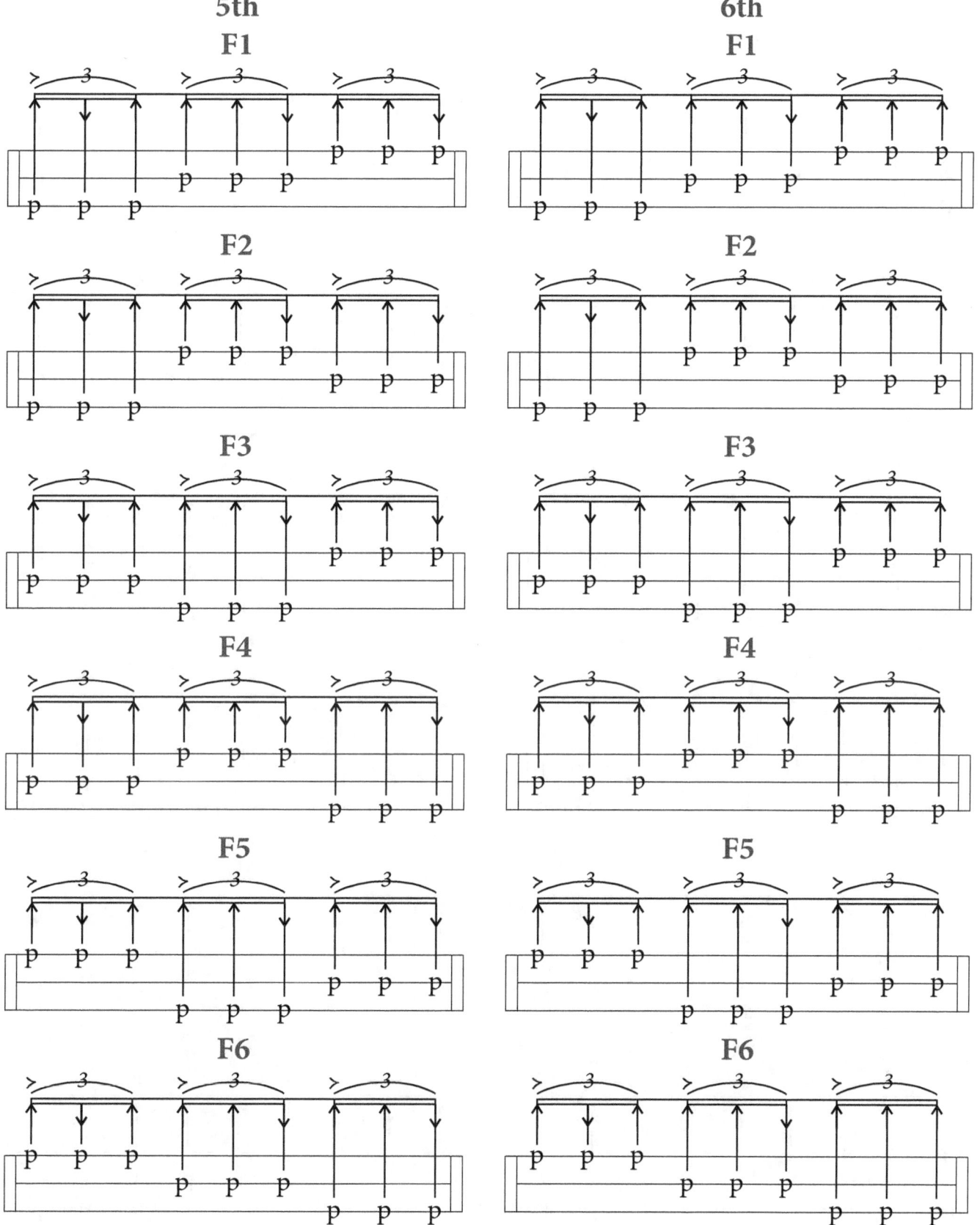

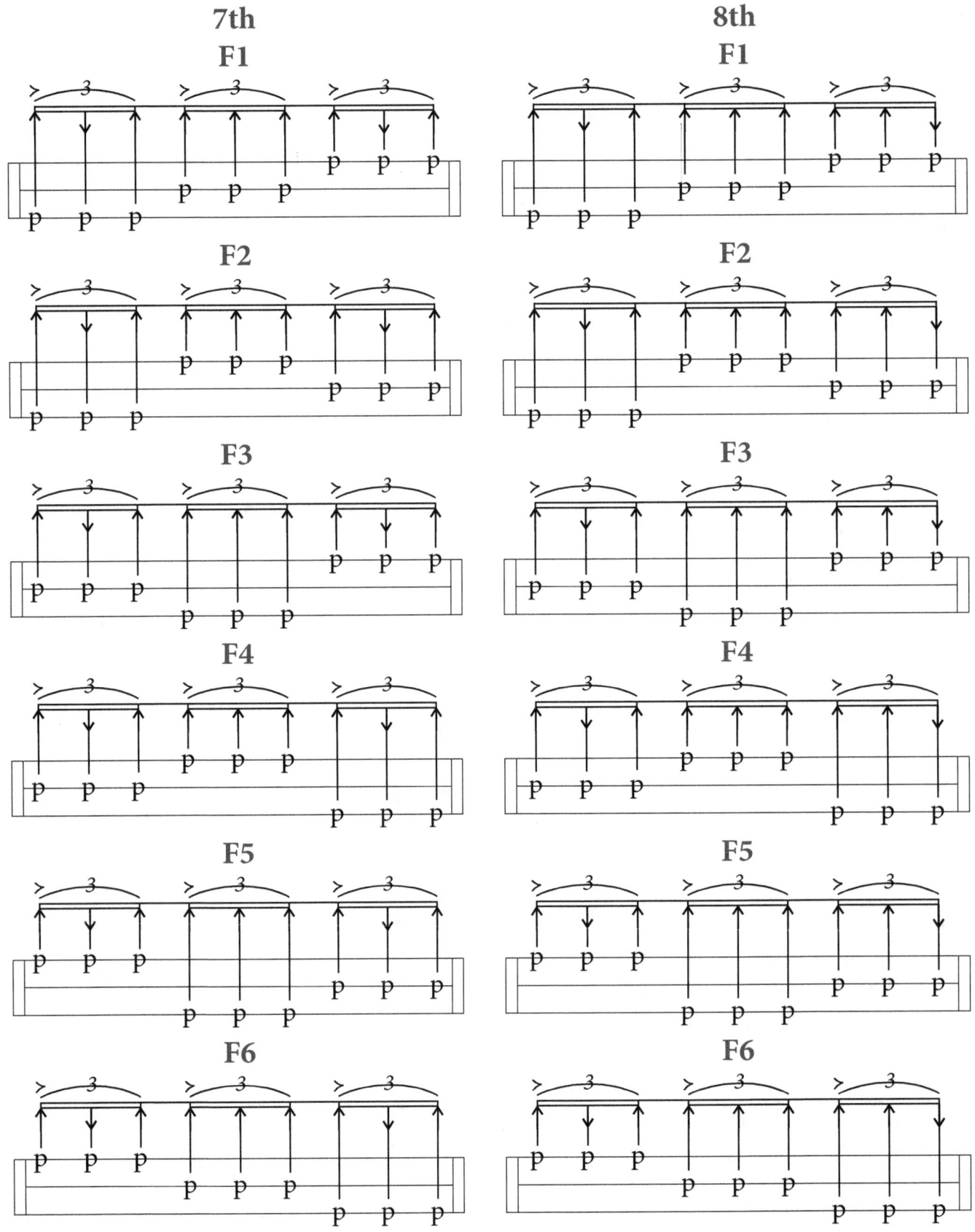

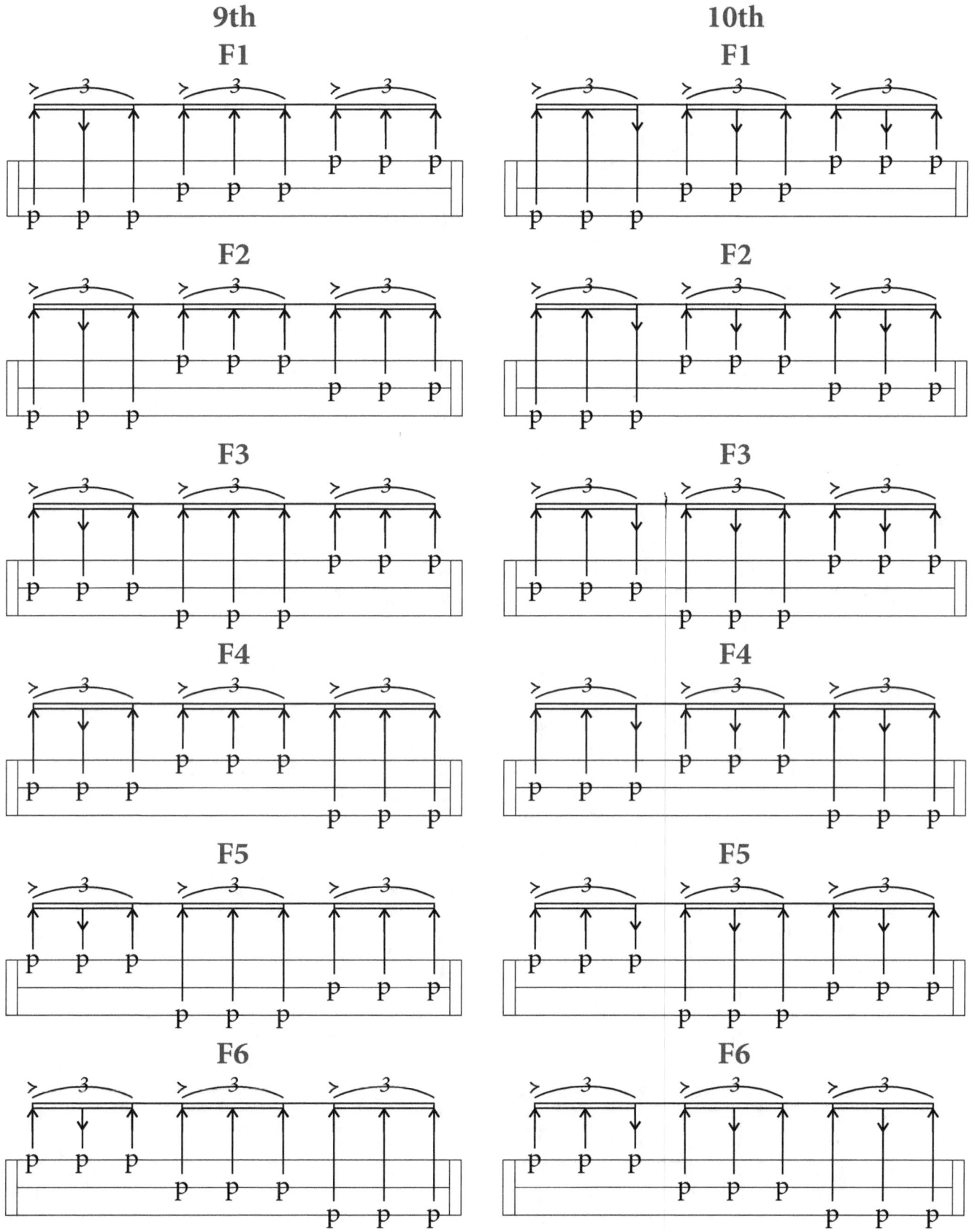

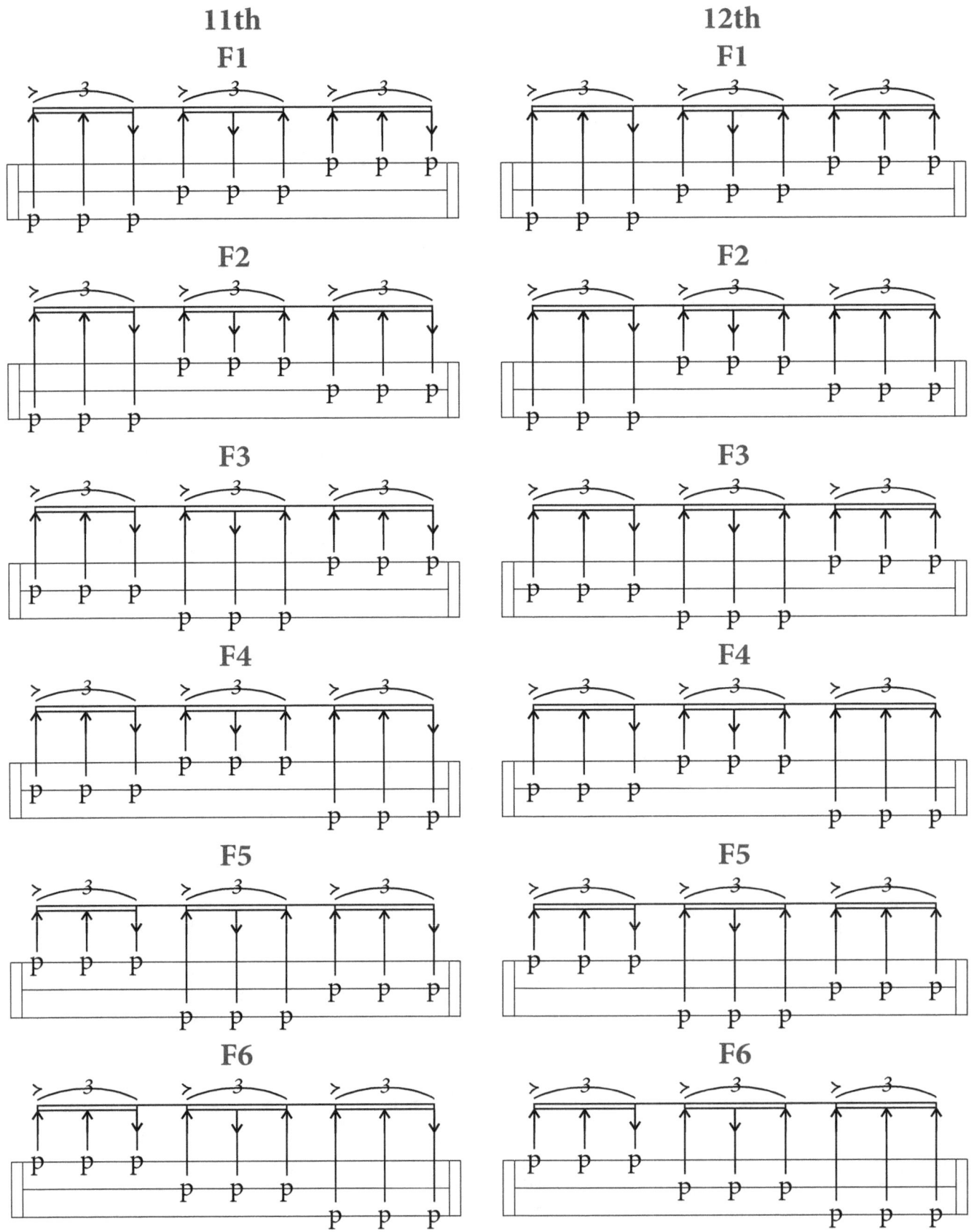

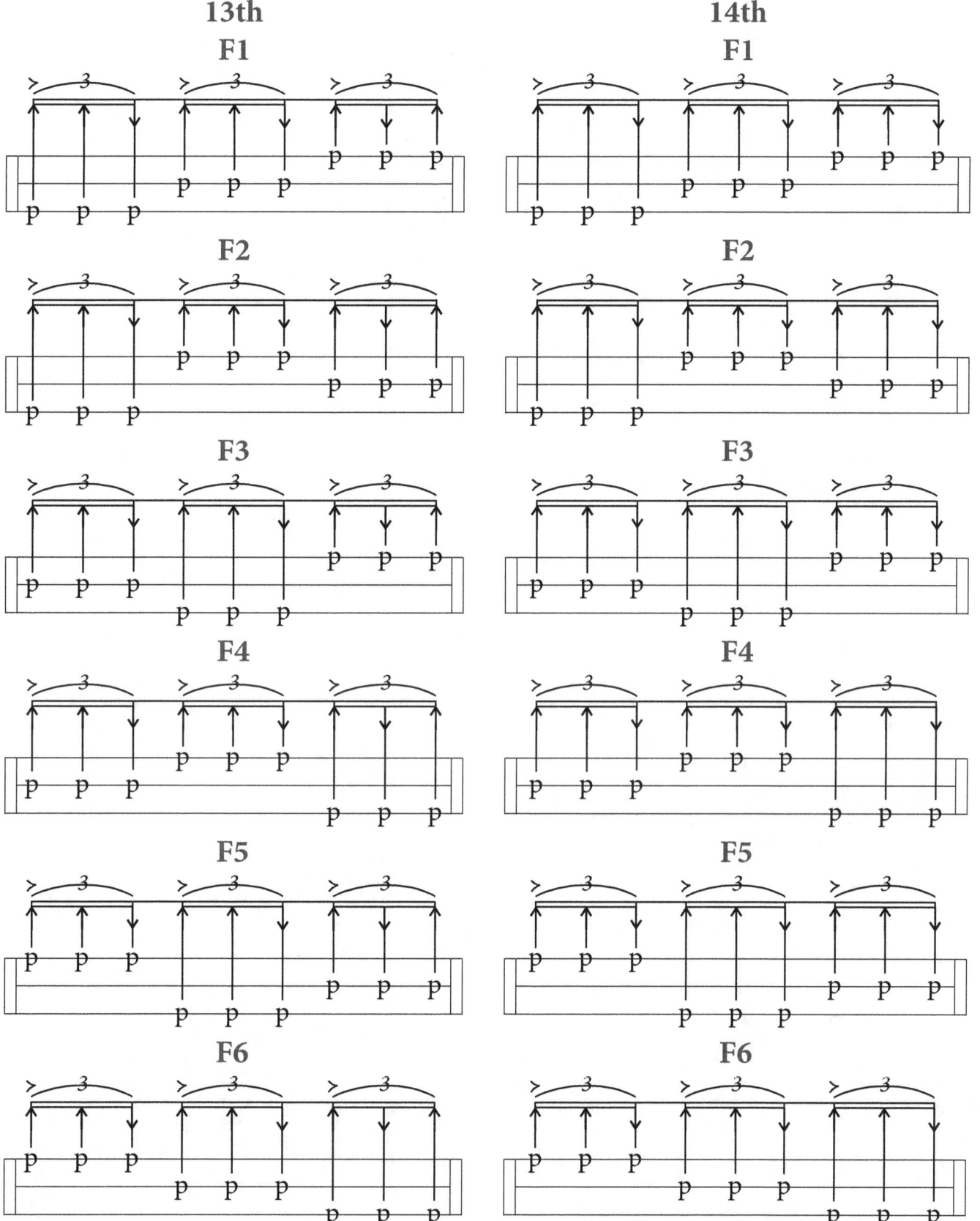

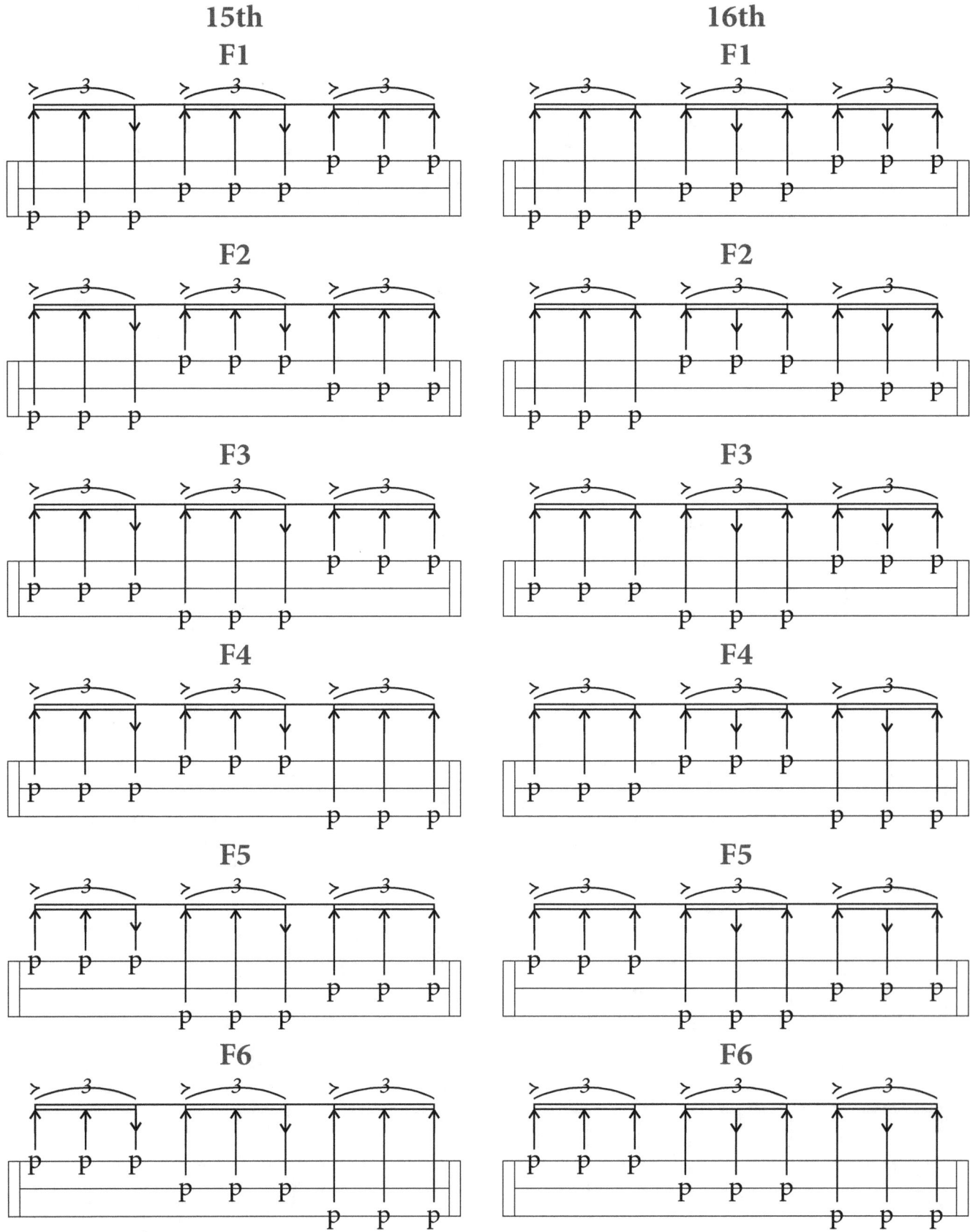

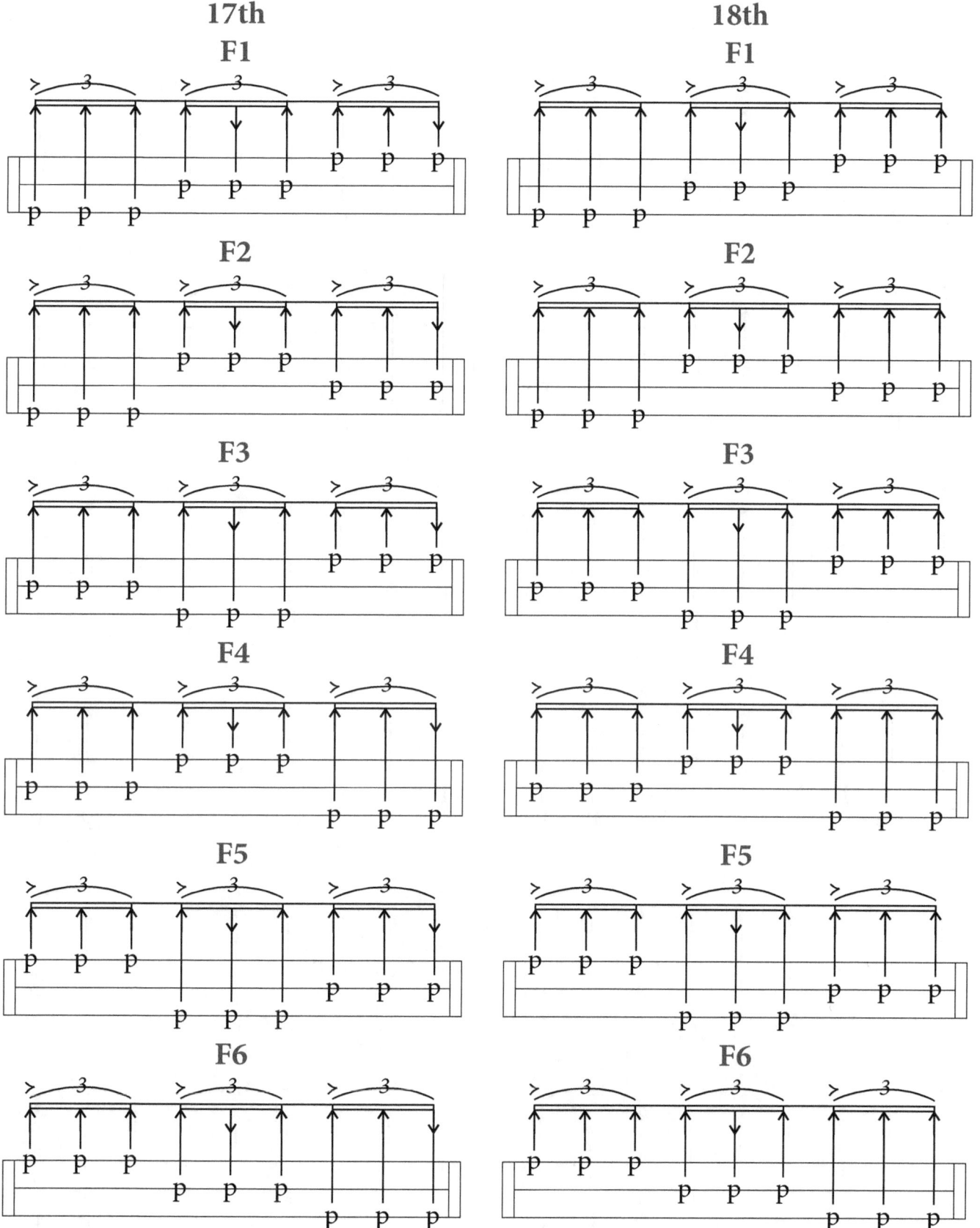

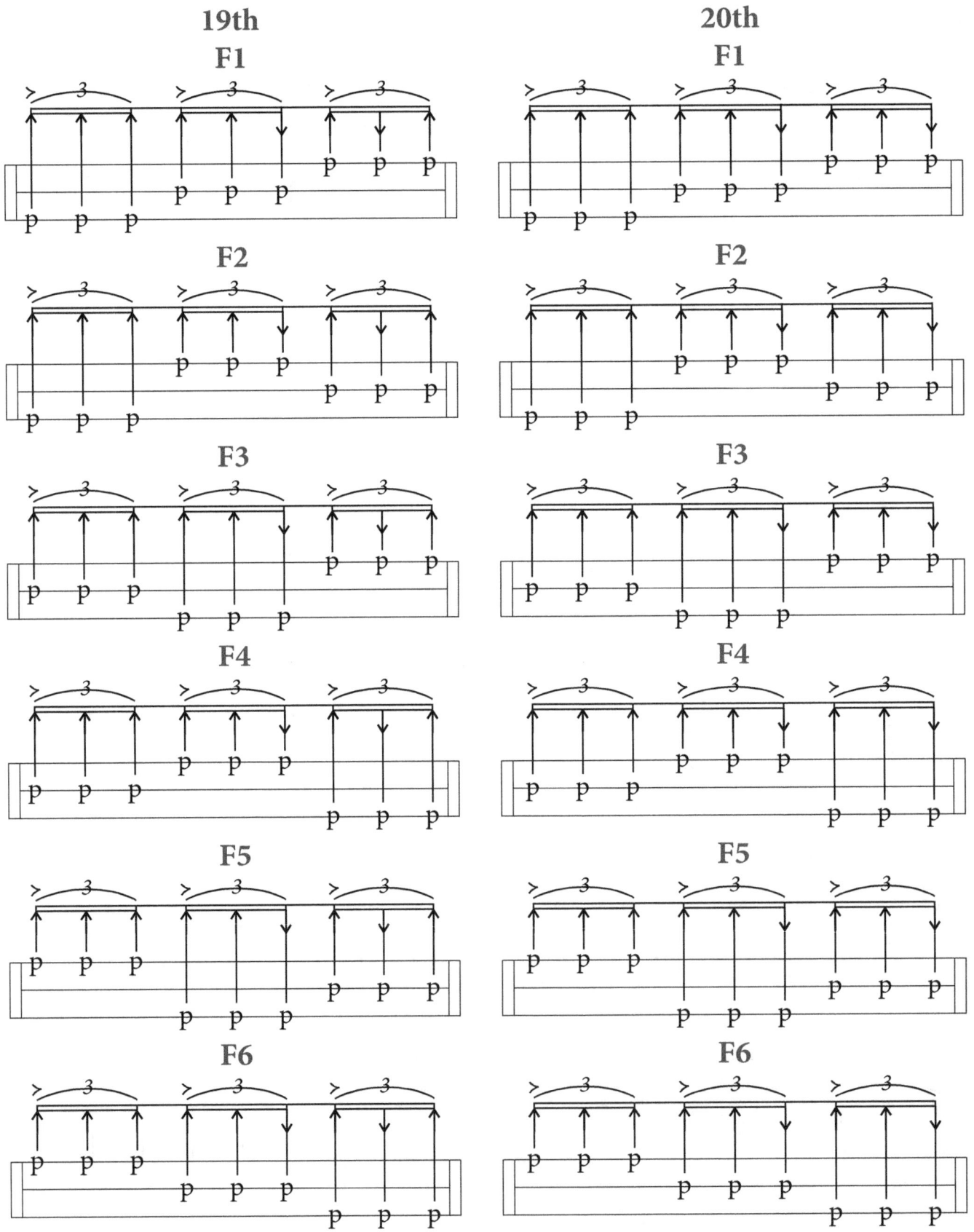

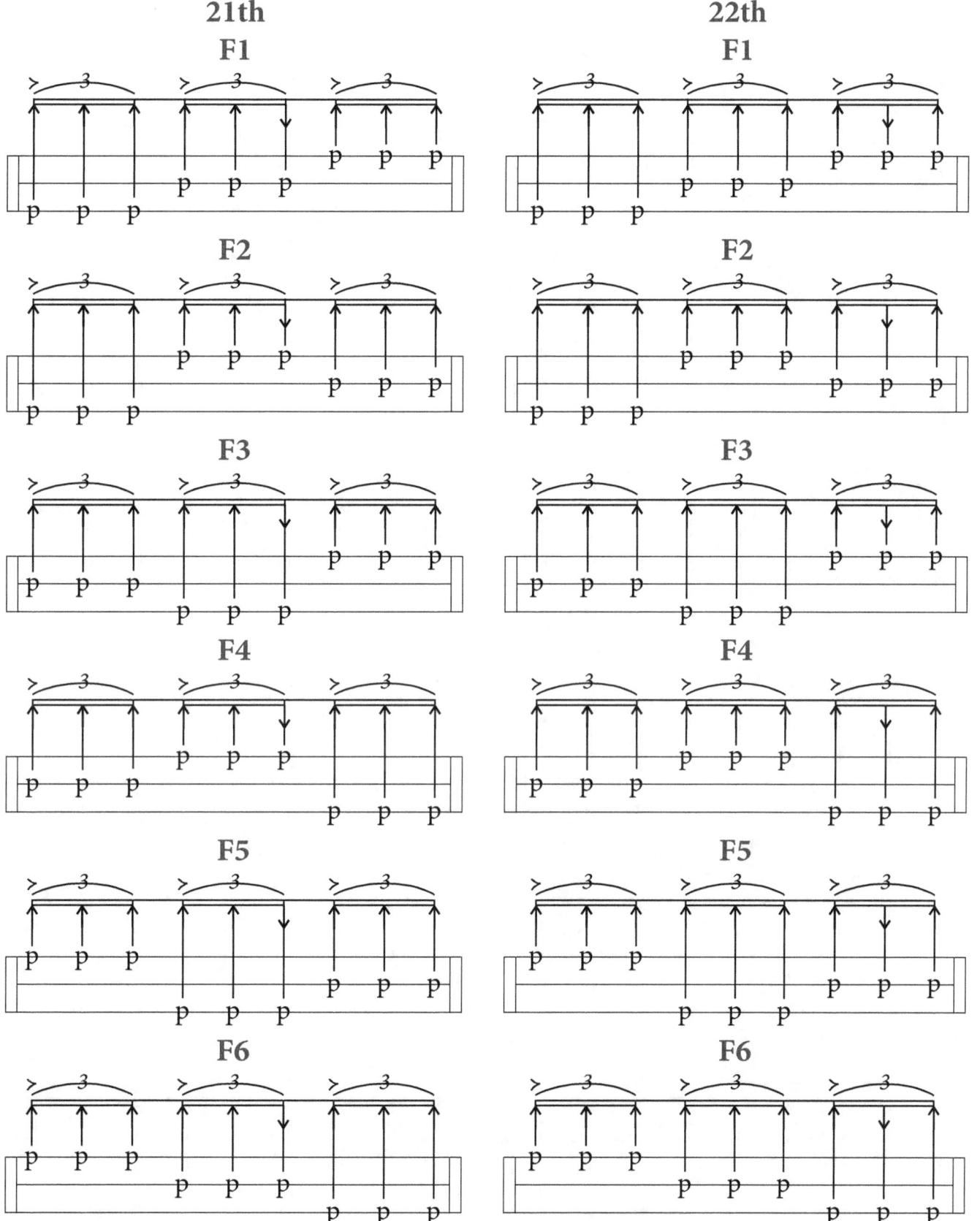

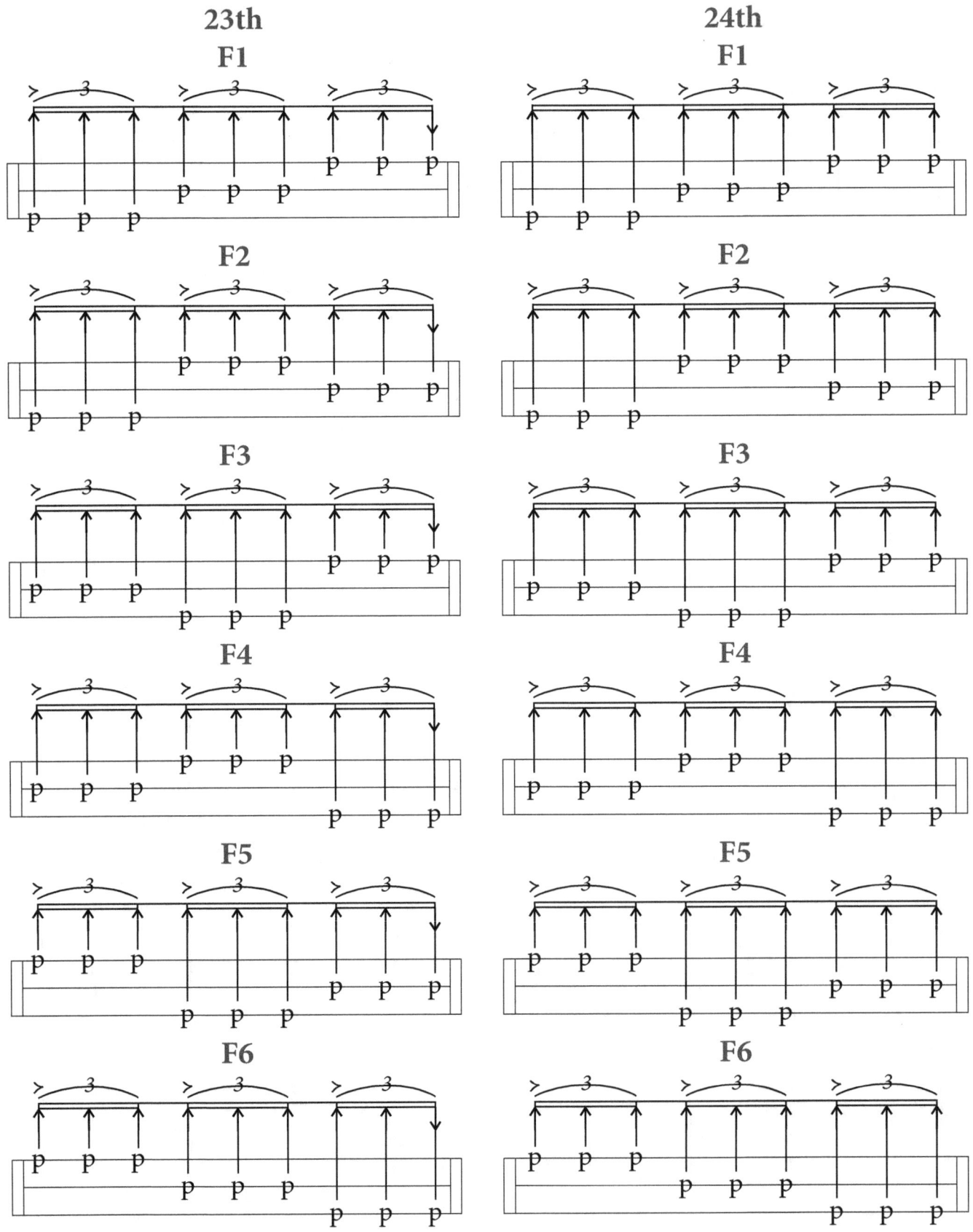

UNIT 2

Exercise on pulgar on three adjacent strings
which includes one, two or three quad strokes.
Different variations as far as the direction of pulgar stroke
and the combinations of strokes are concerned
(single + double + quad etc).

In unit 2 a fourth stroke is introduced in all previous Formulas. The fourth stroke is combined with single - double and triple strokes of the pulgar. Within each Formula all strokes are isochronous (single - double - triple and quad). All variations can be played either on adjacent strings (case A) or on remote strings (case B, C and D).

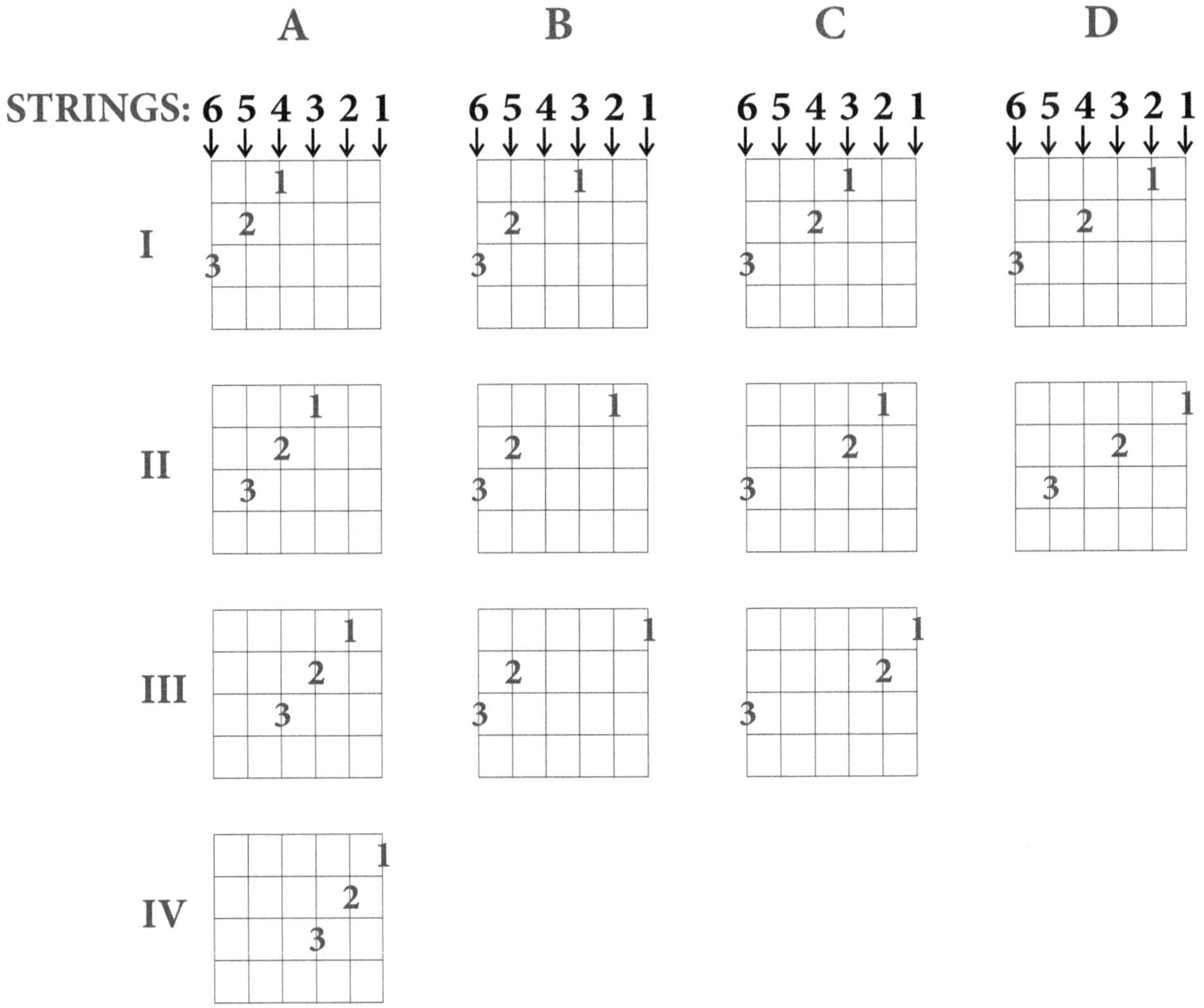

All the exercises of unit 2 that follow can be modified by changing the direction of pulgar stroke on the triple and quad stroke. The quad stroke apart from that mentioned in the exercises,

$$\begin{array}{cccc} p & p & p & p \\ \uparrow & \downarrow & \uparrow & \downarrow \end{array}$$

can be modified in 4 different ways:

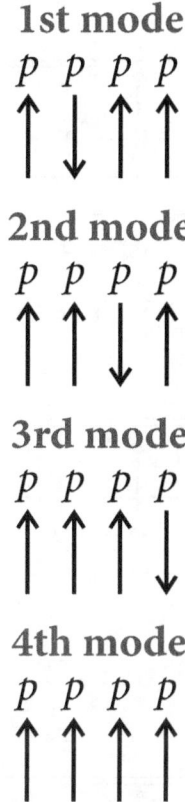

The triple stroke apart from that mentioned in the exercises,

$$\begin{array}{ccc} p & p & p \\ \uparrow & \downarrow & \uparrow \end{array}$$

can be modified in the following ways:

All the modifications (and their combinations) create additional material for the practice of the pulgar. These alternative ways of perfomance rely on the student to practice them.

§ I

Exercise on pulgar on three adjacent strings with one quad and two single strokes in each Formula. The exercise contains three variations with 6 Formulas in each variation. The first Formula of each variation is cited below. Isochronous playing of pulgar strokes (single and quad) within the Formula.

VARIATION I

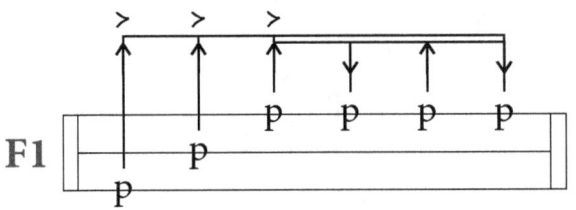

VARIATION II

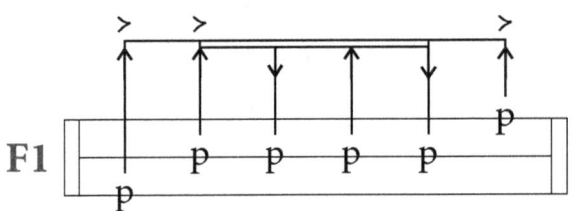

VARIATION III

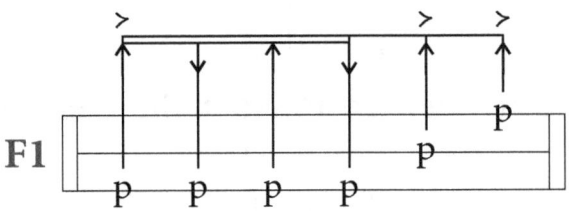

The change of direction of pulgar stroke results in 5 different performance ways for each variation. Practice on all variation and in all ways.

VARIATION I

WAYS OF PERFORMANCE

1st

F1
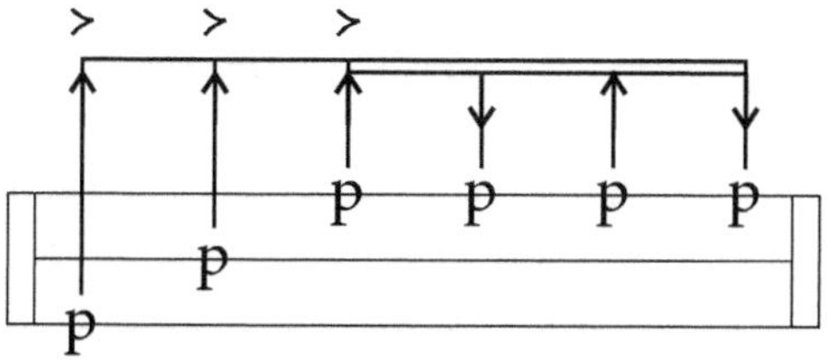

F2
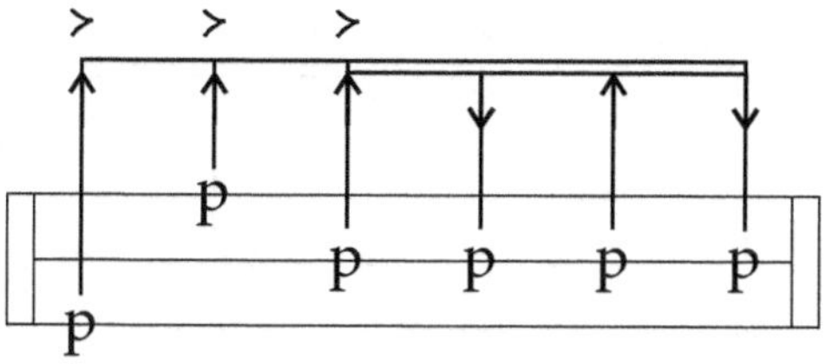

F3
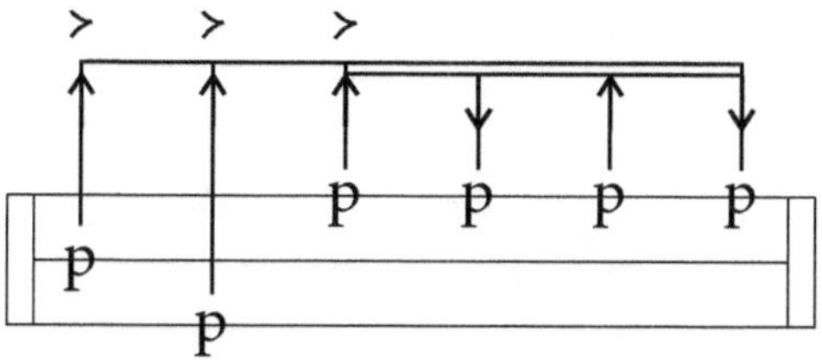

F4
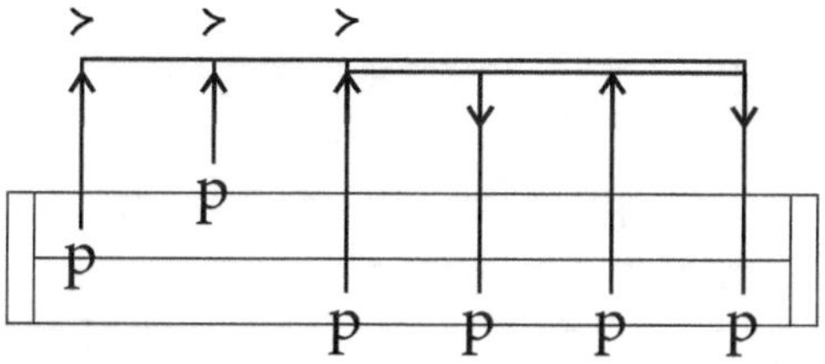

F5
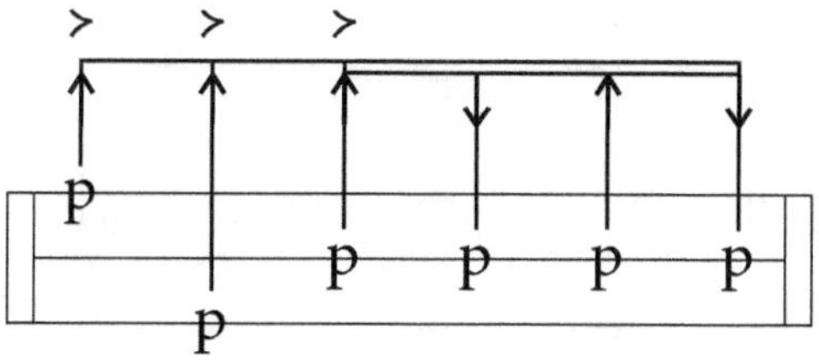

F6
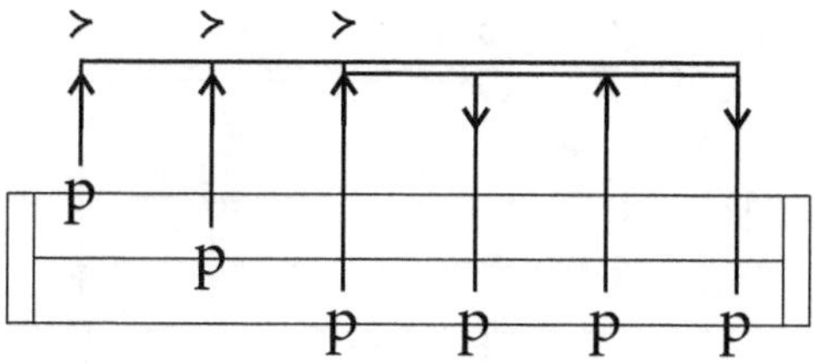

2nd

F1
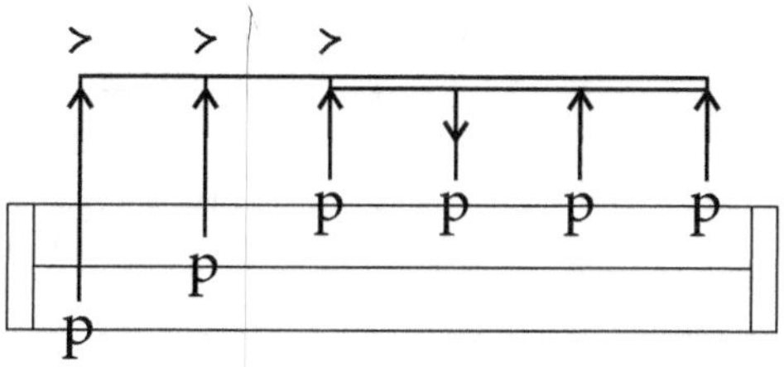

F2
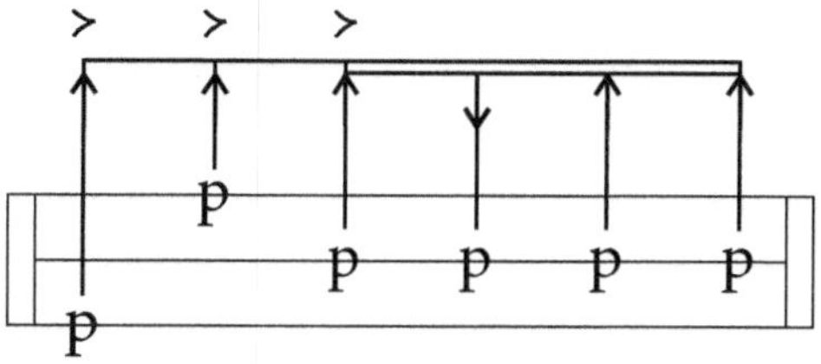

F3
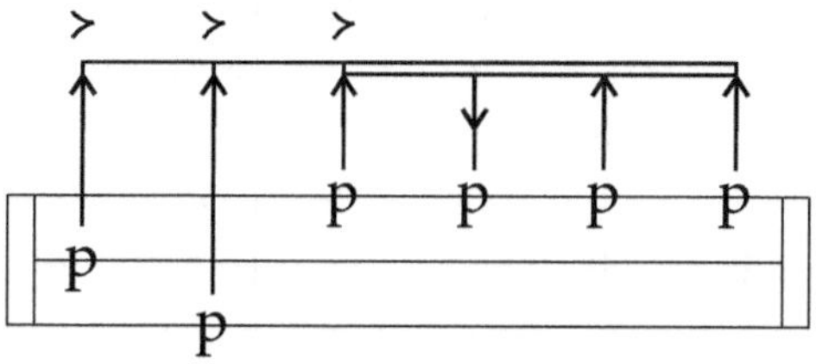

F4
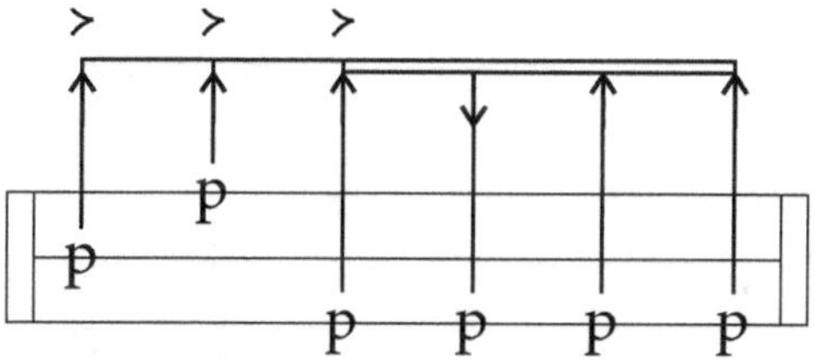

F5
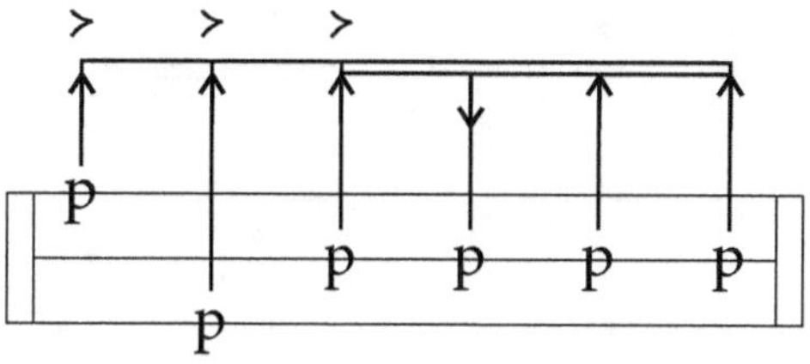

F6
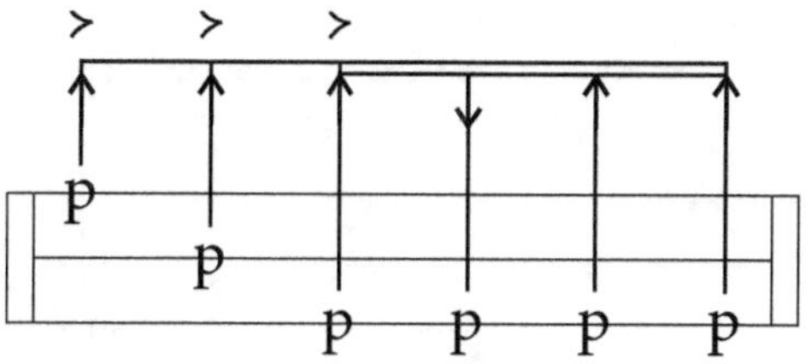

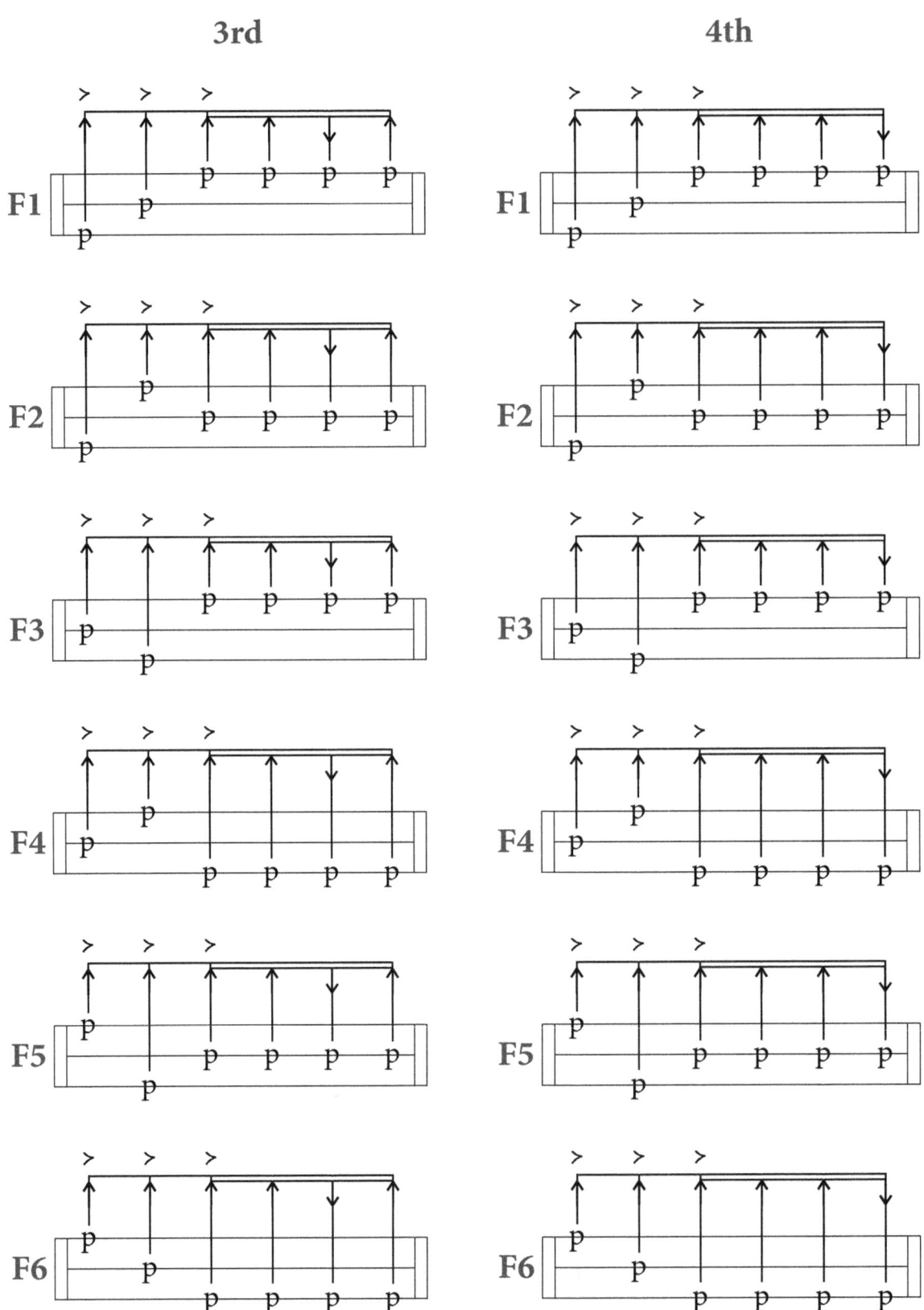

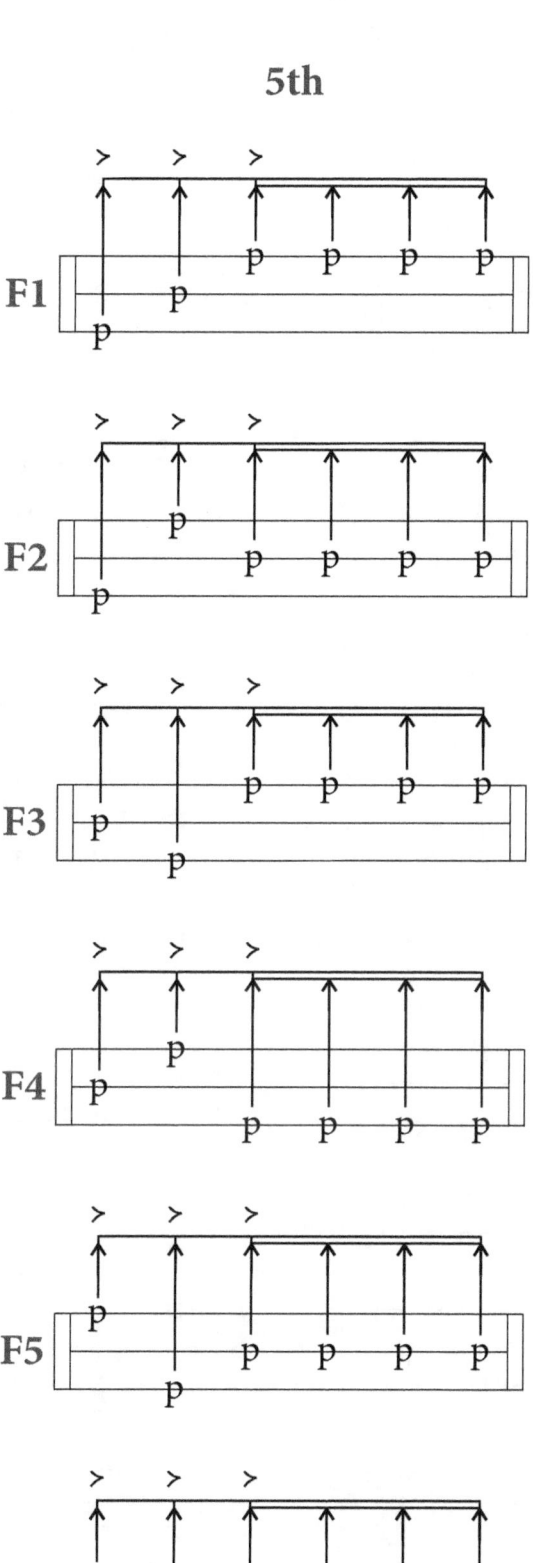

VARIATION II
WAYS OF PERFORMANCE

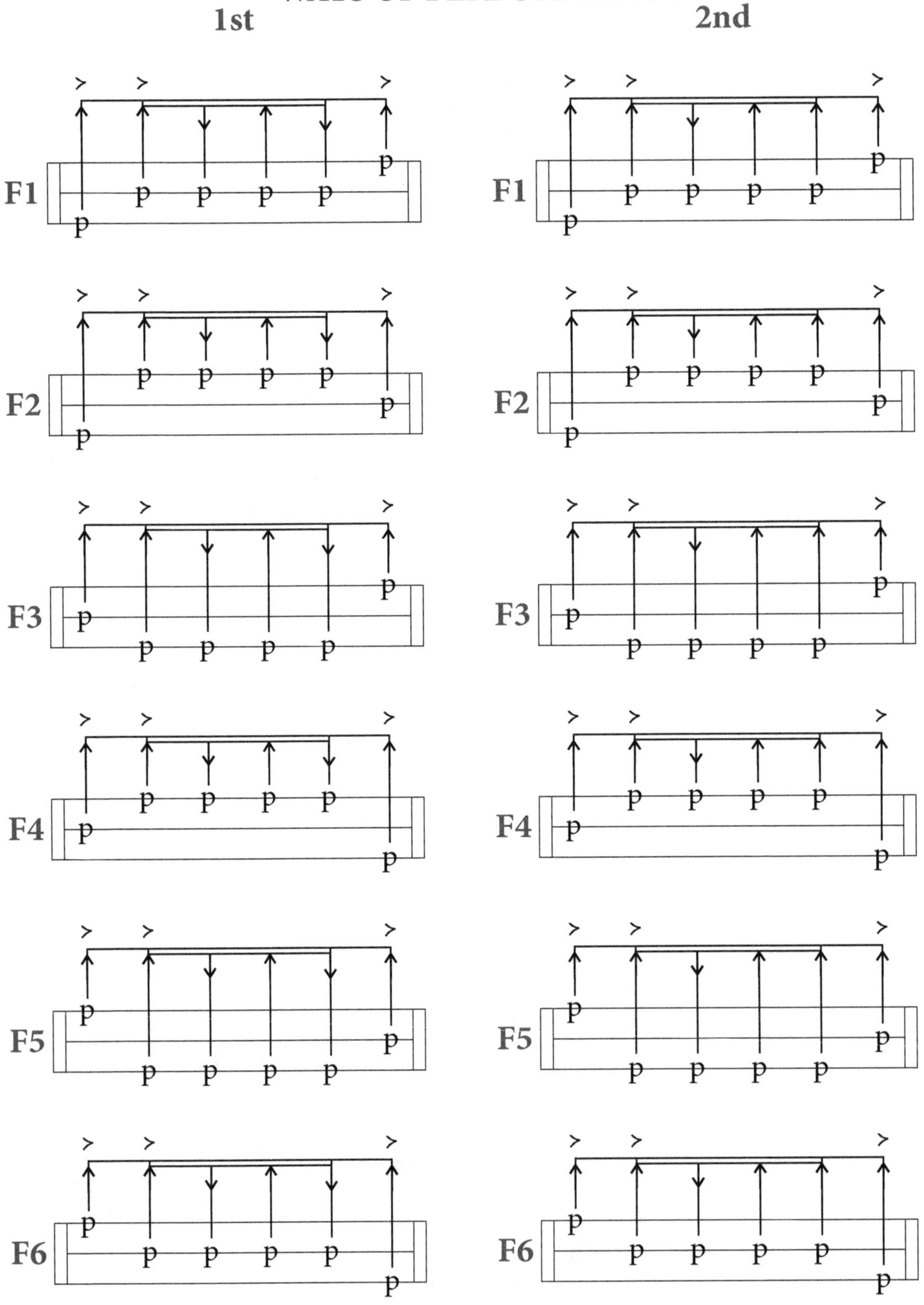

1st   **2nd**

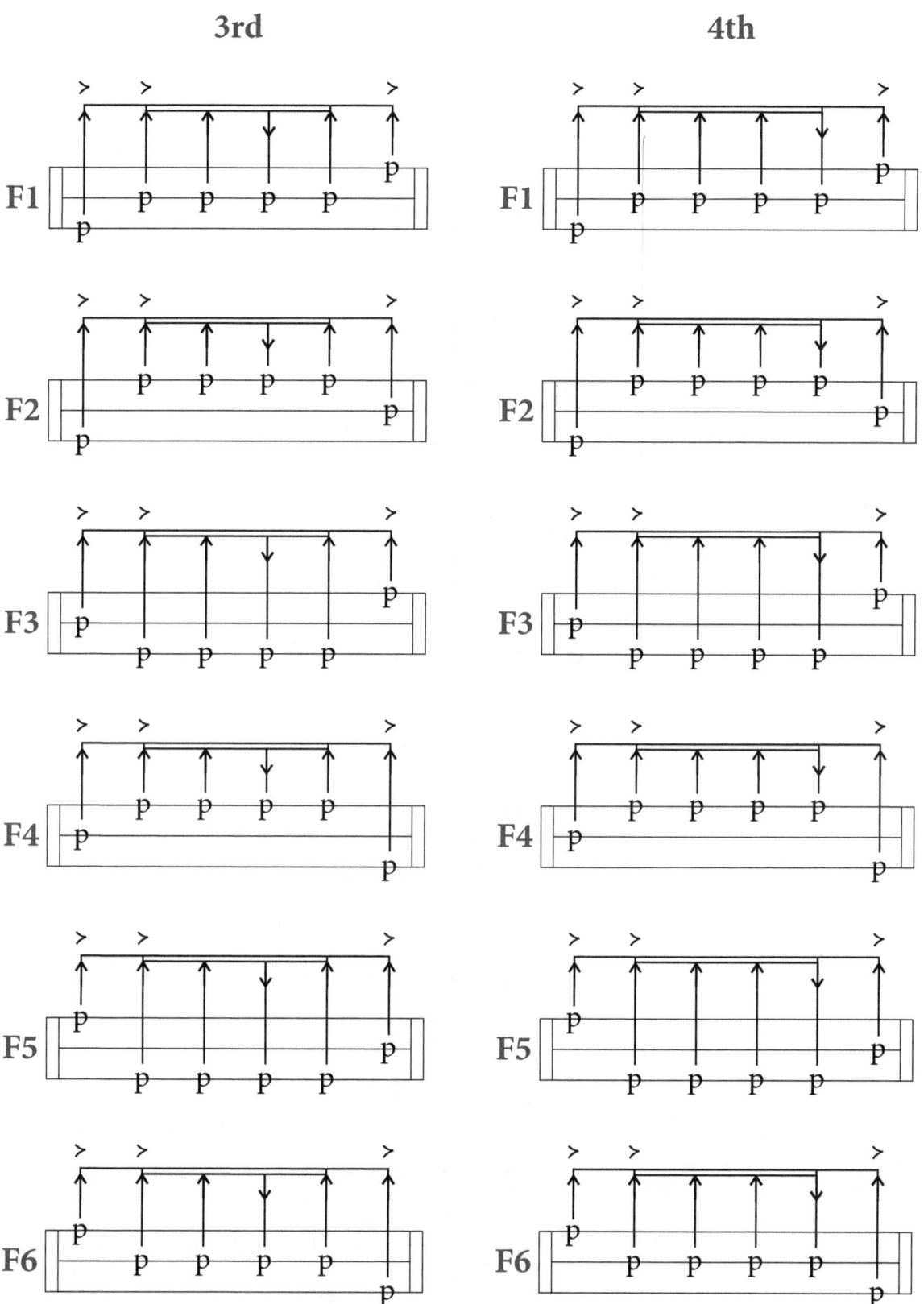

5th

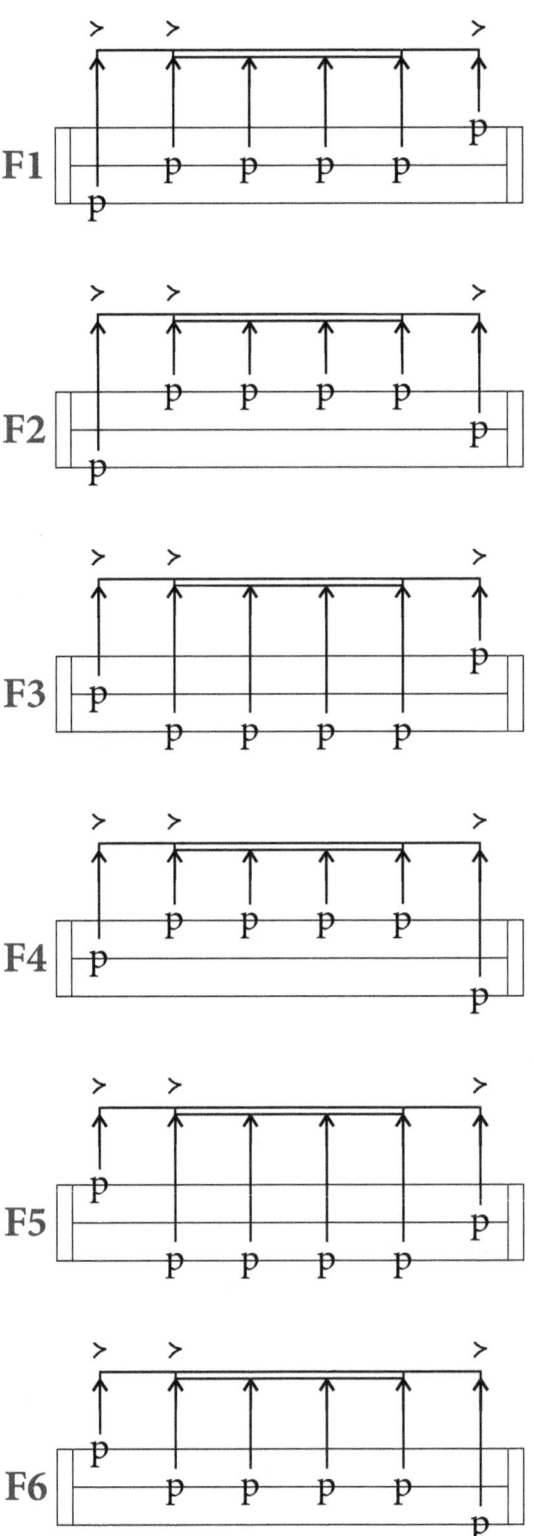

VARIATION III
WAYS OF PERFORMANCE

1st

F1
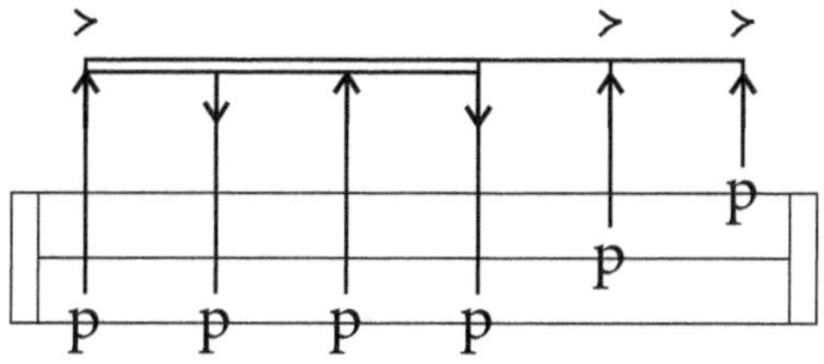

F2
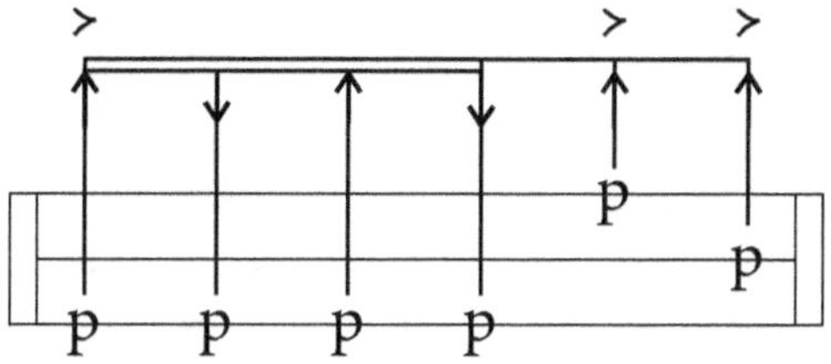

F3
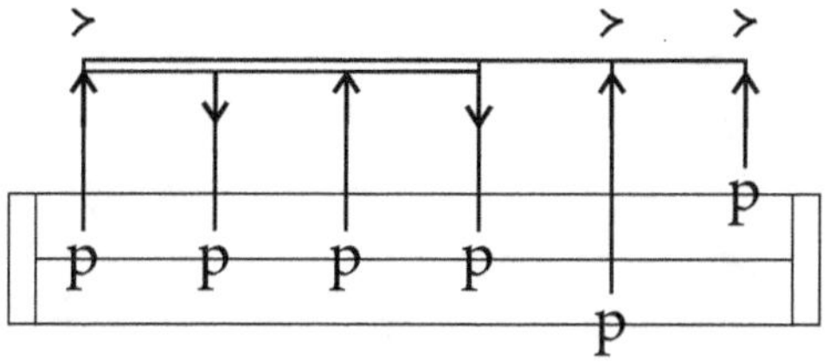

F4
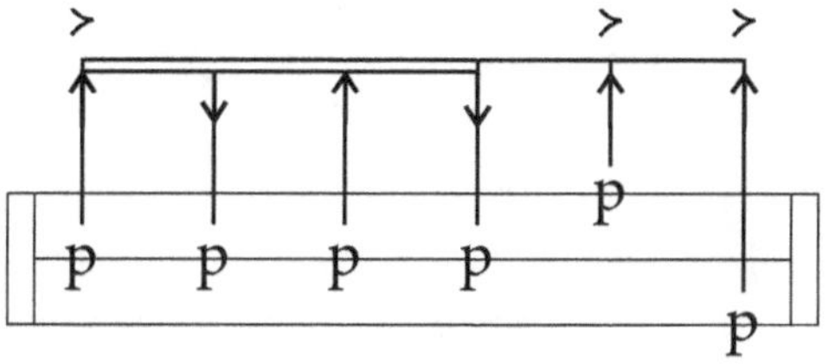

F5
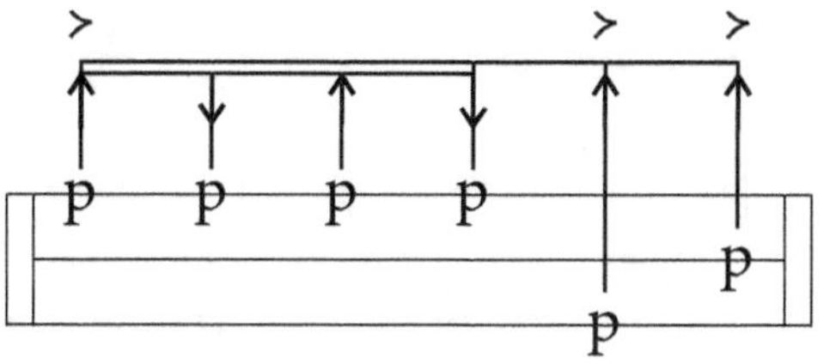

F6
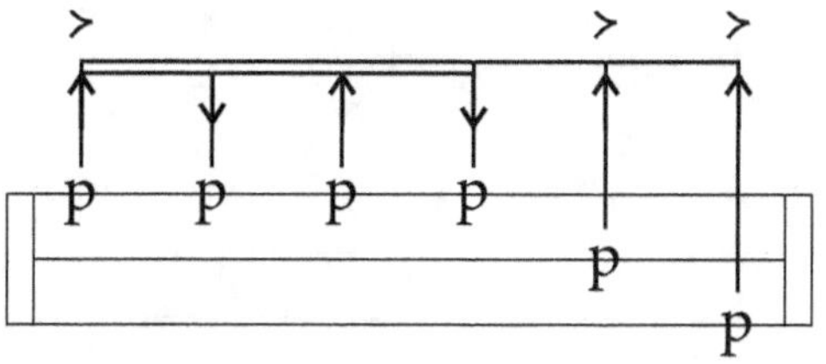

2nd

F1
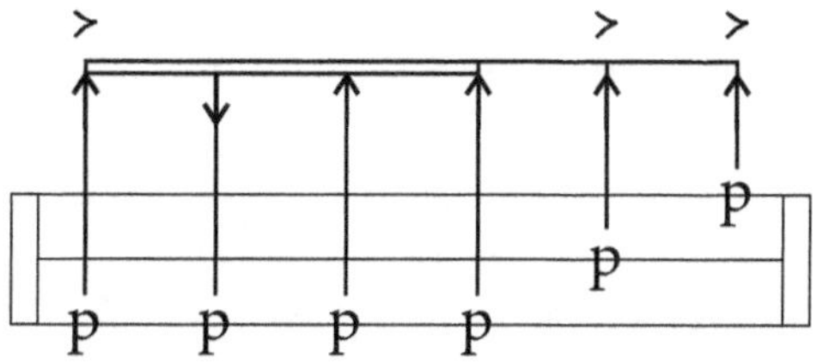

F2
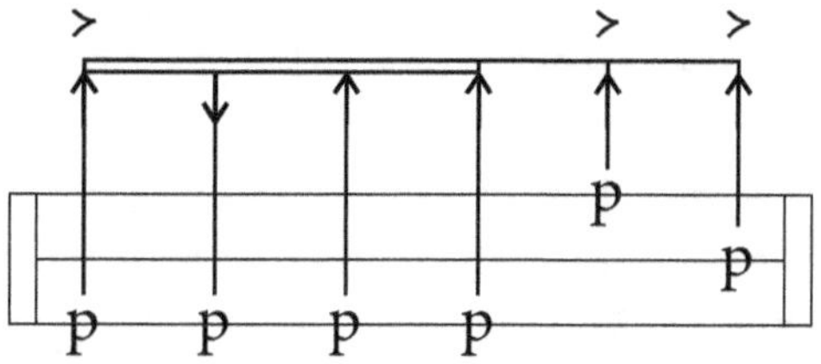

F3
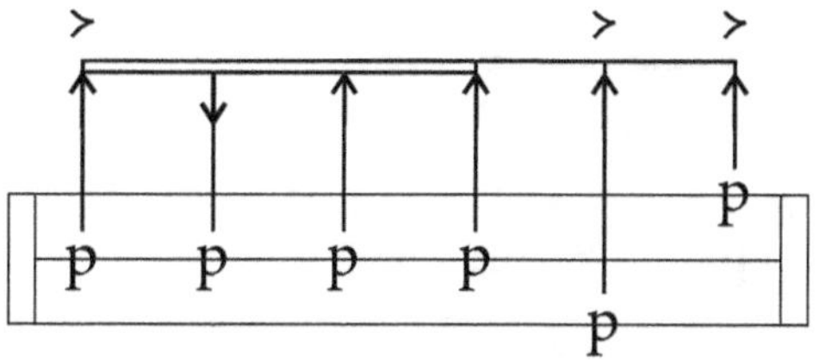

F4
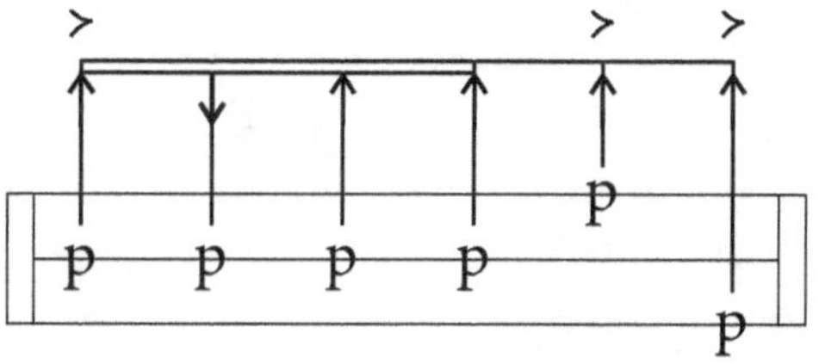

F5
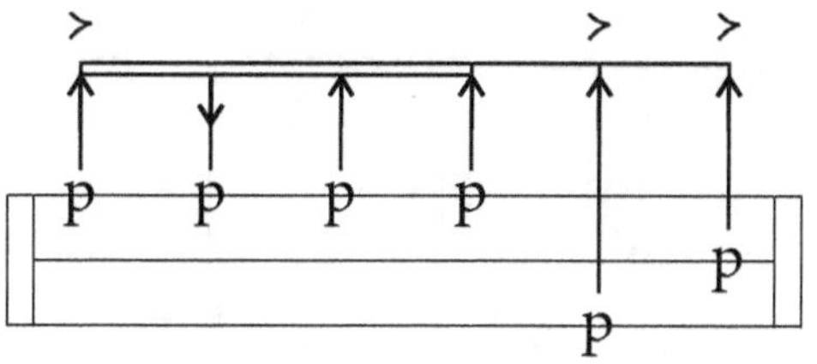

F6
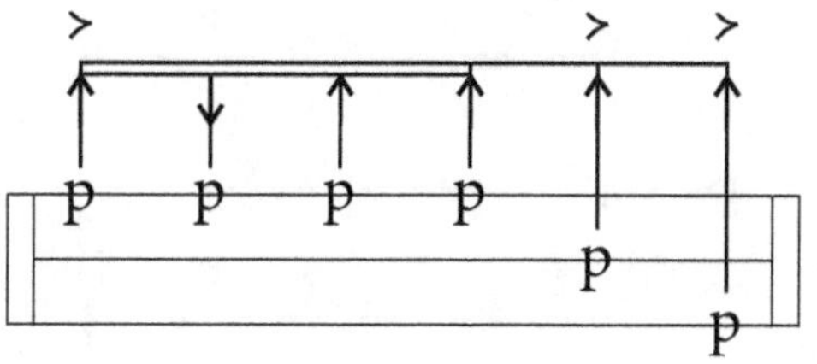

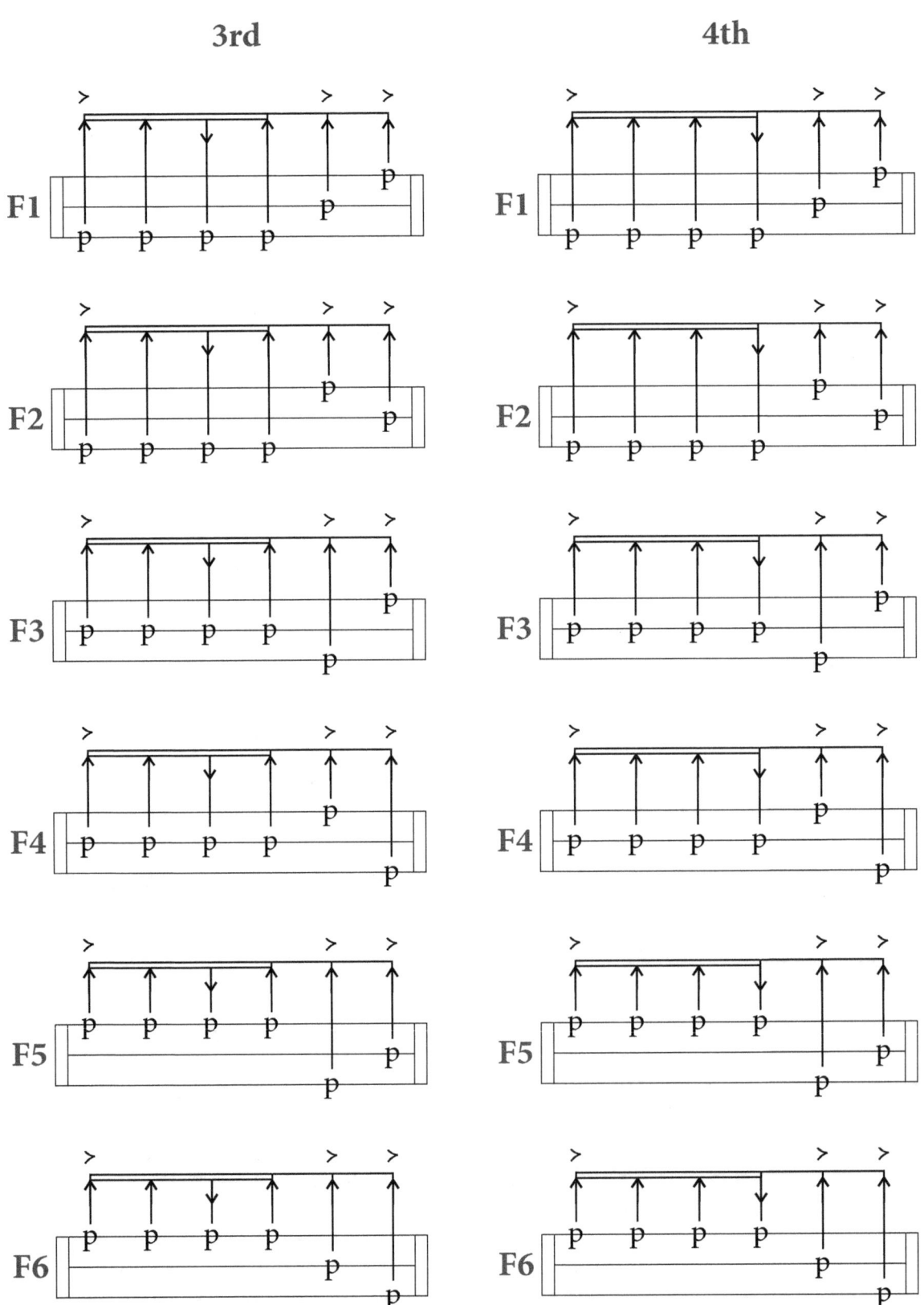

5th

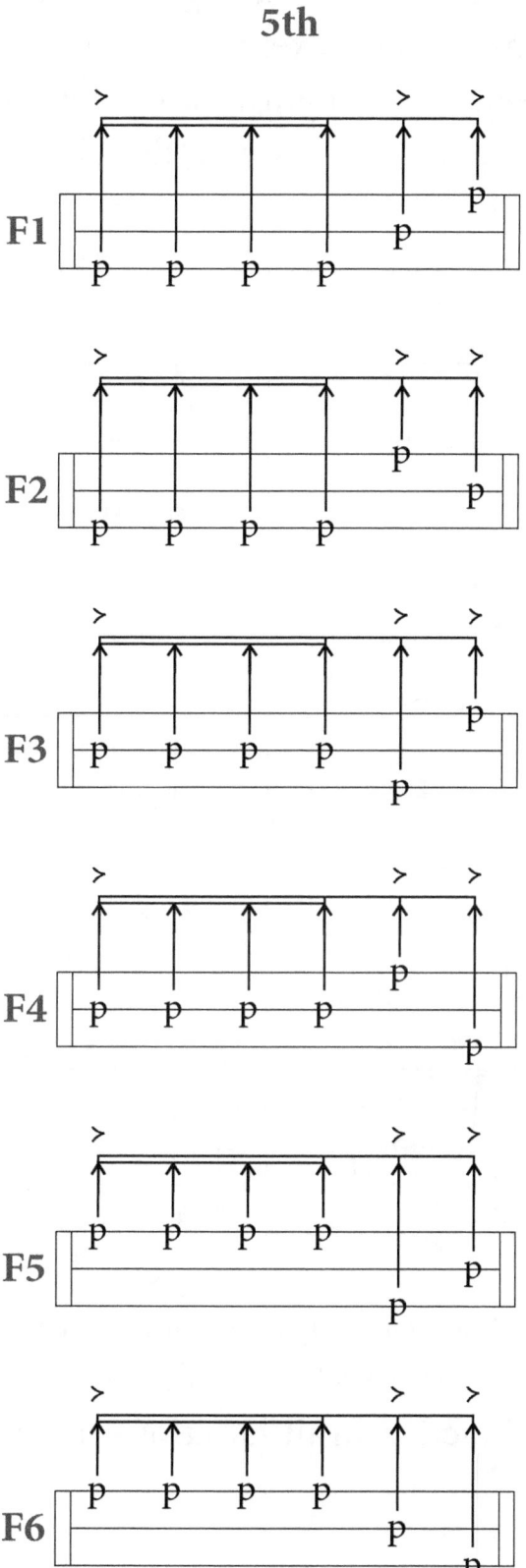

§ II

Exercise on pulgar on three adjacent strings with single, double and quad stroke within each Formula. The exercise contains six variations with 6 Formulas in each variation. The first Formula of each variation is cited below. Isochronous playing of pulgar strokes (single, double and quad).

VARIATION I

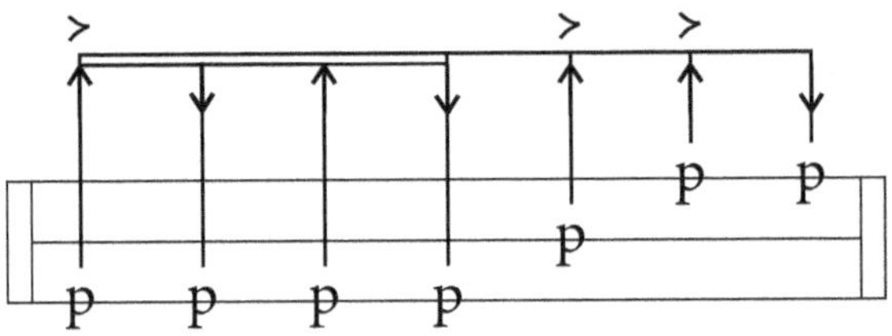

VARIATION II

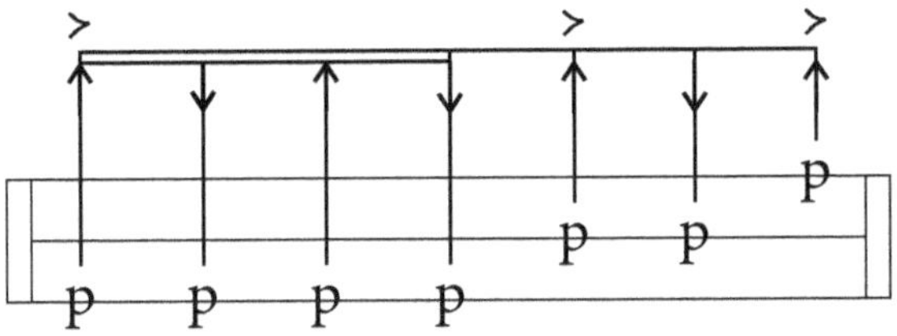

VARIATION III

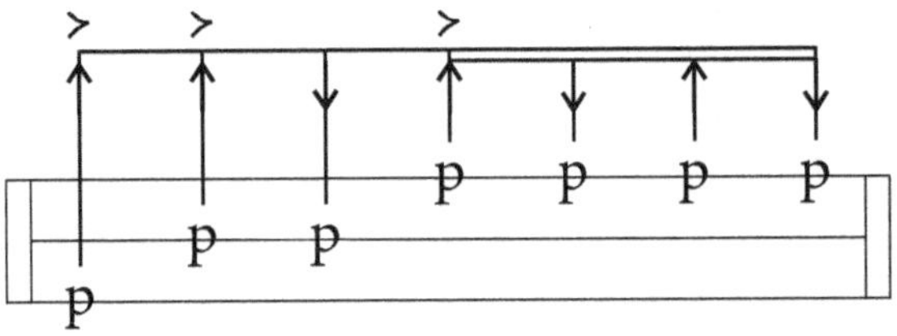

VARIATION IV

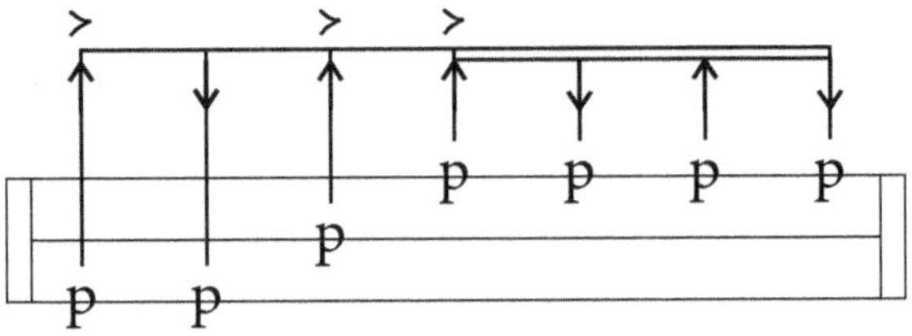

VARIATION V

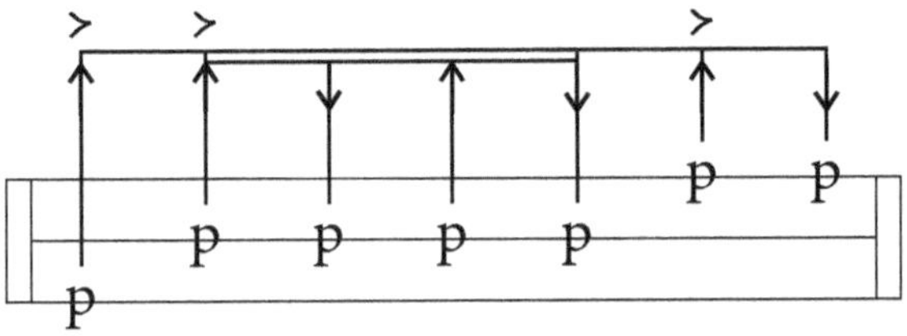

VARIATION VI

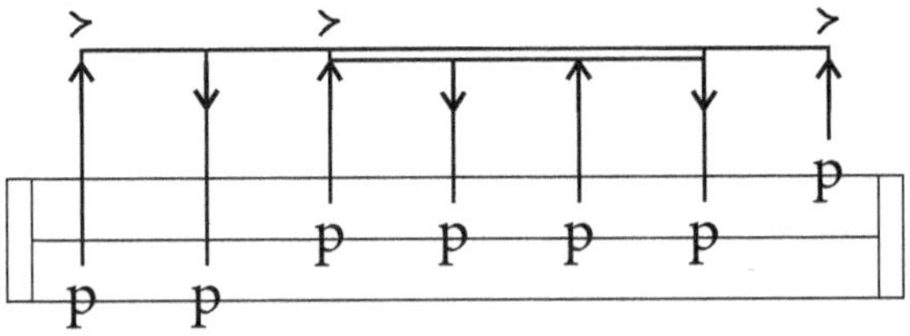

The change in the direction of pulgar stroke results in different ways of performance of each variation. In § II it results in 10 ways of performance all of which are cited below. Practice on all variations and in all ways.

VARIATION I
WAYS OF PERFORMANCE

1st   **2nd**

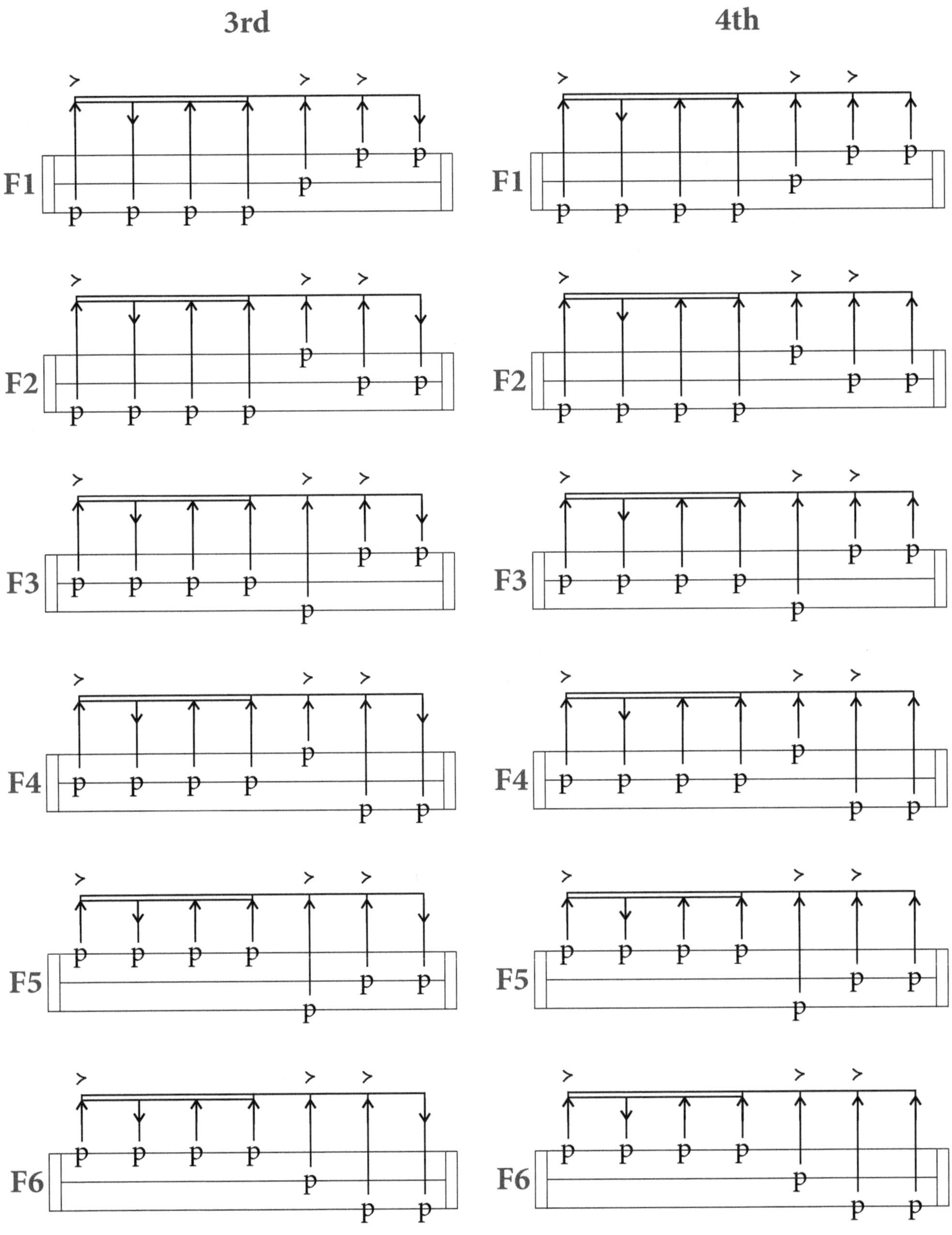

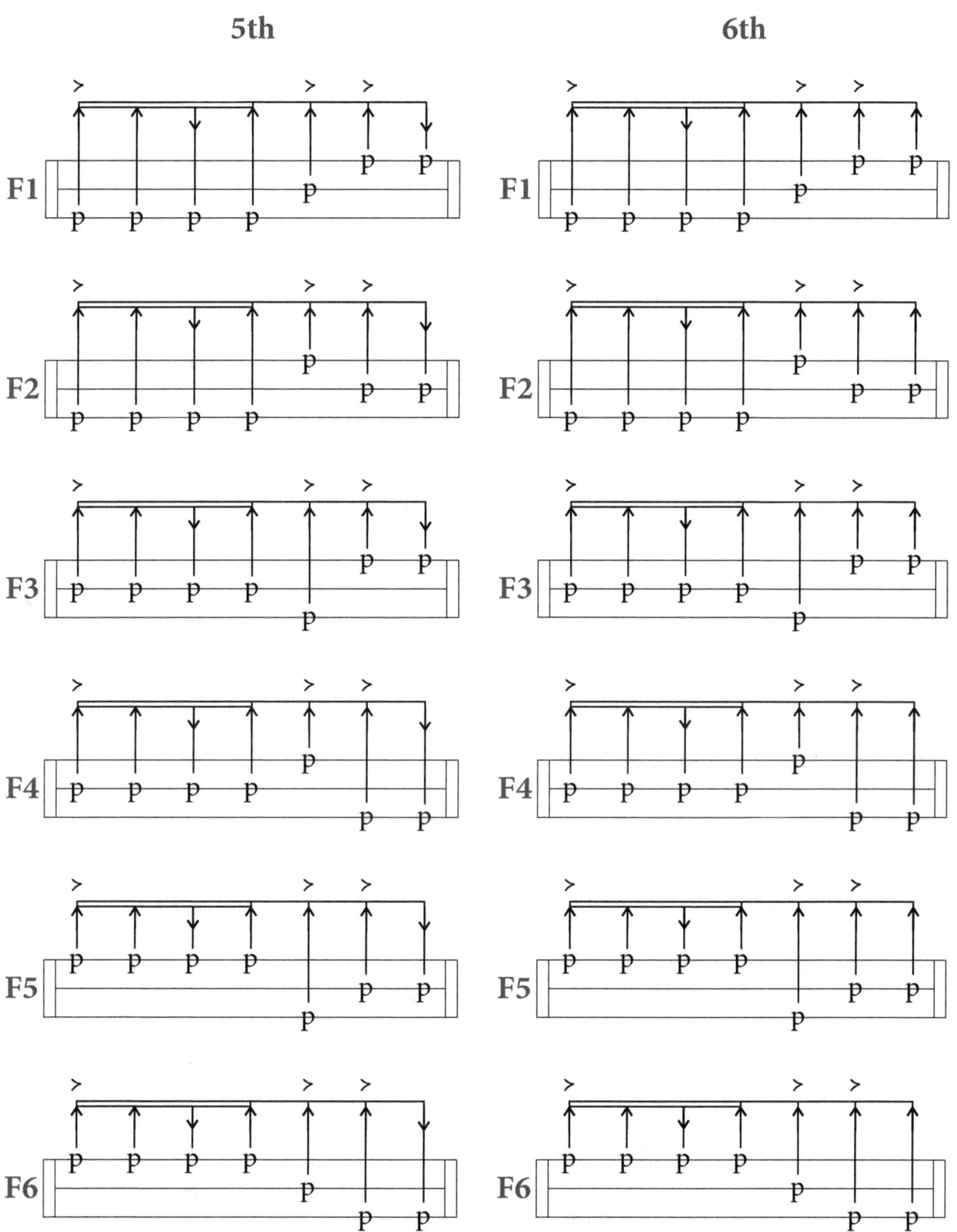

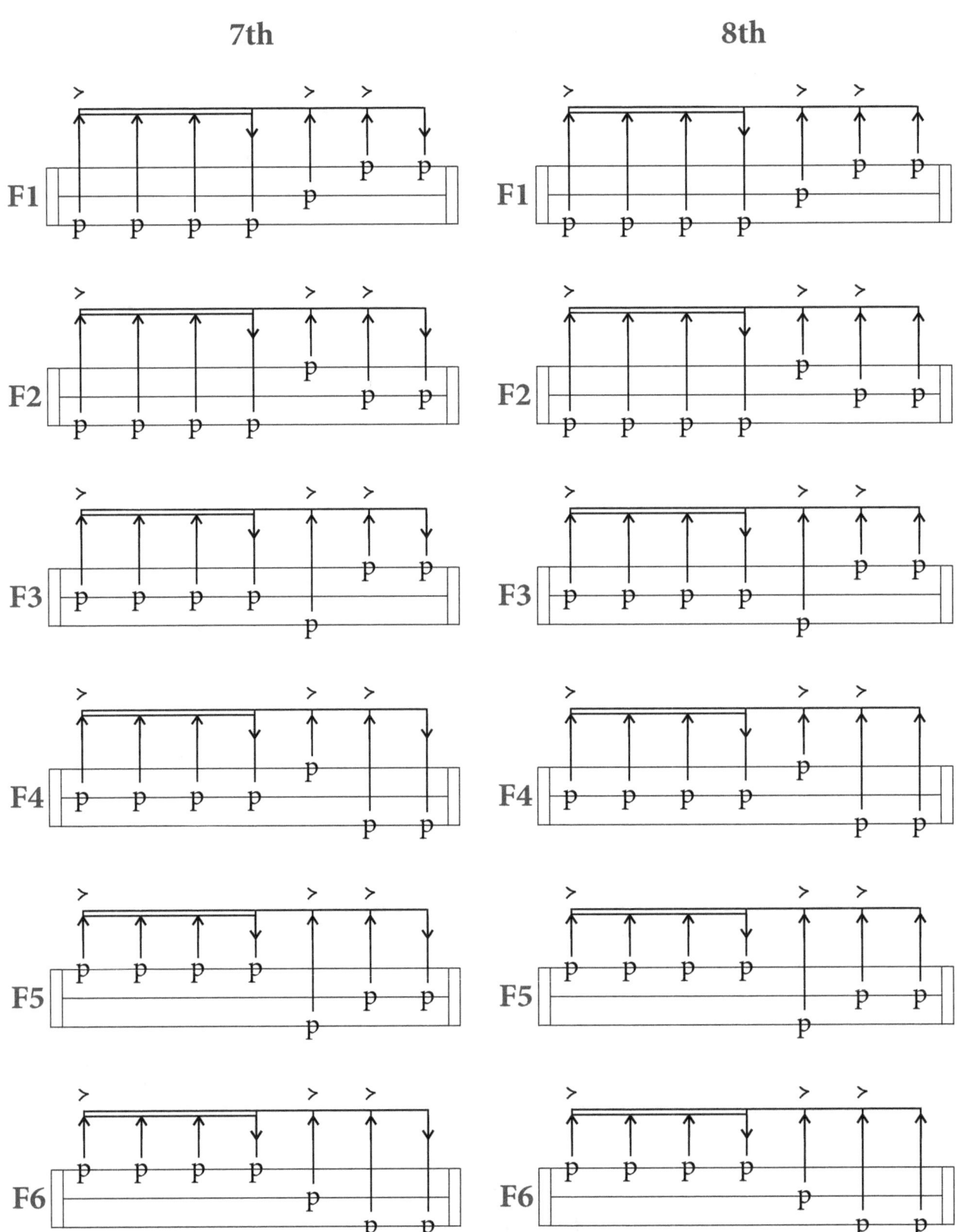

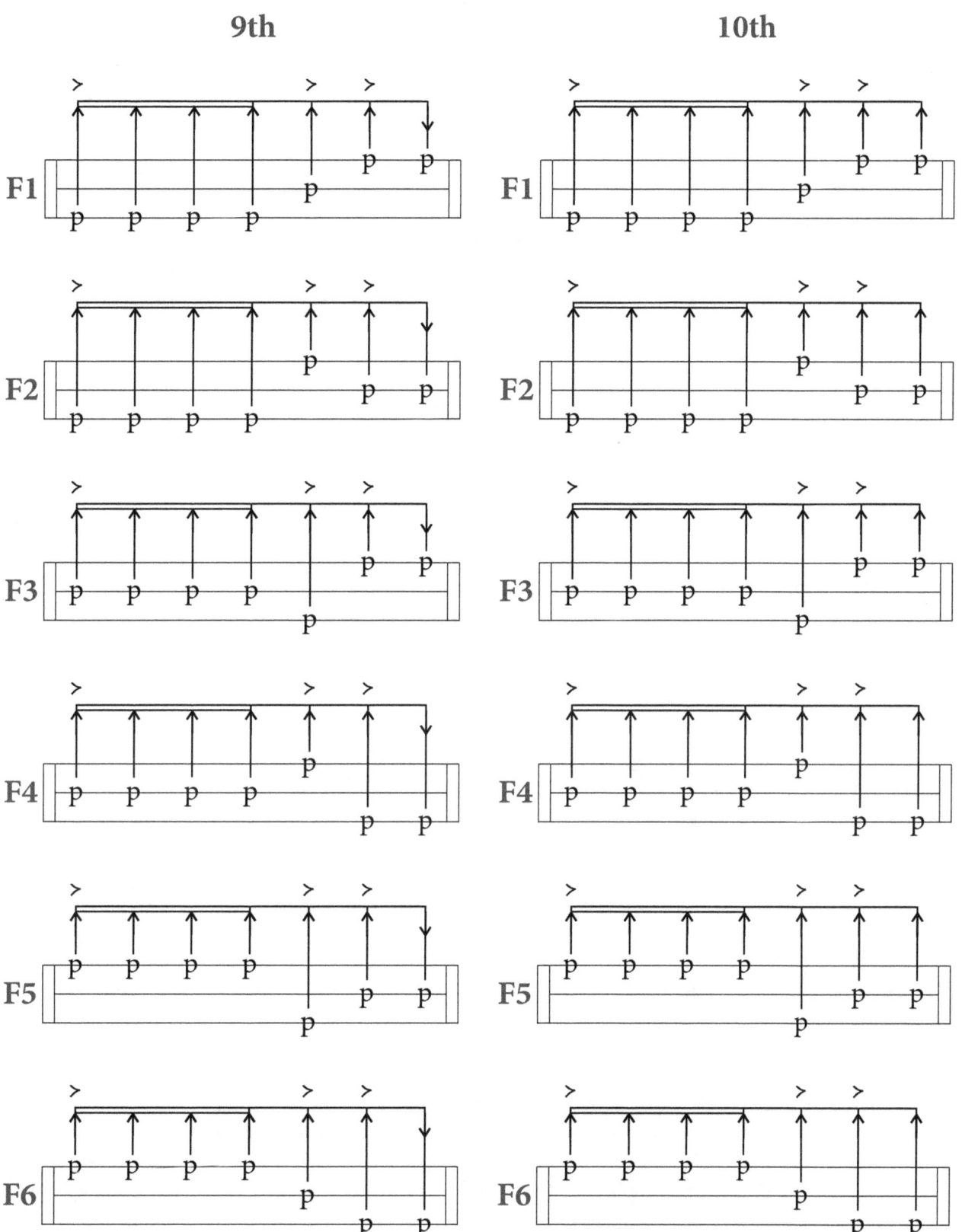

VARIATION II
WAYS OF PERFORMANCE

1st   **2nd**

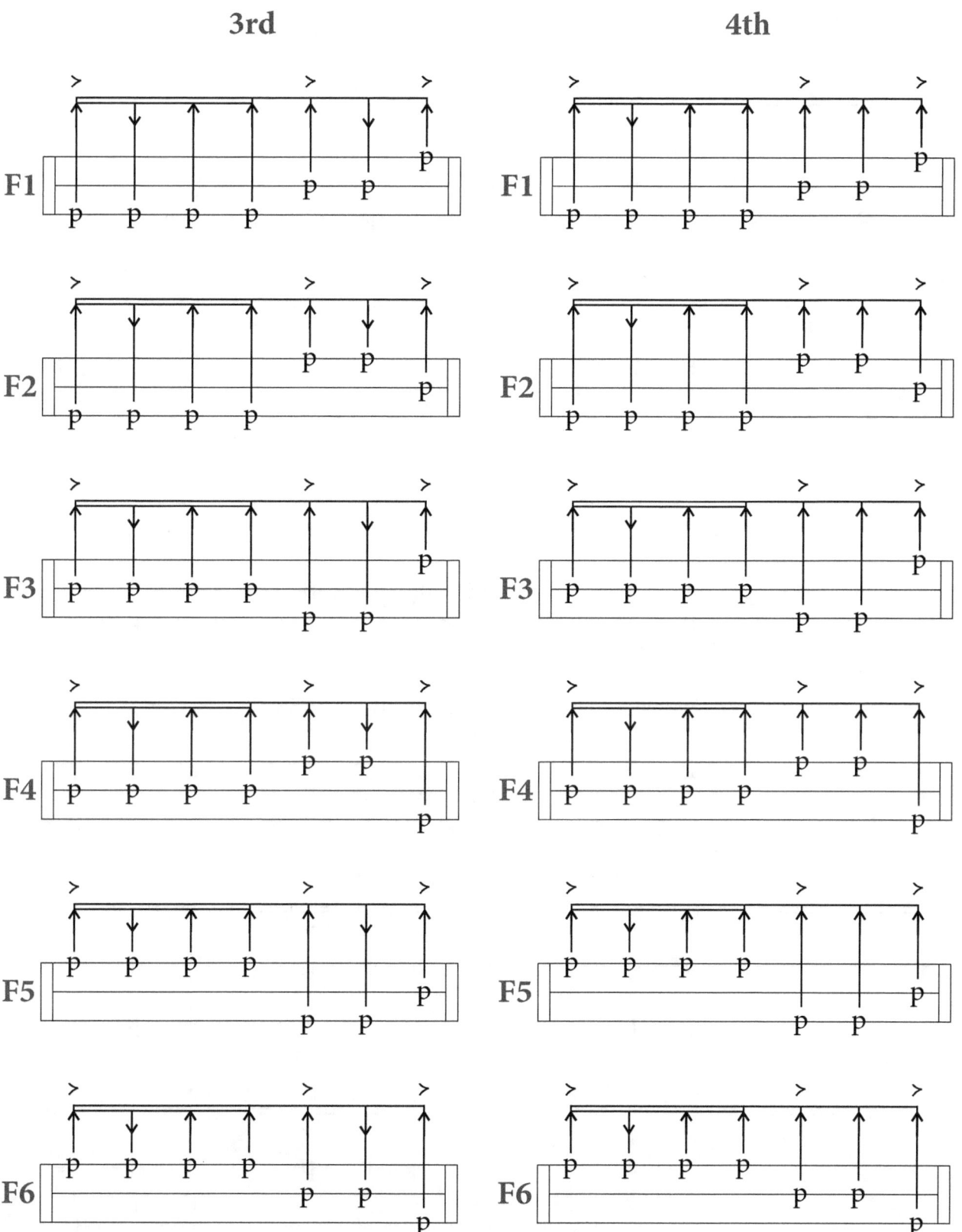

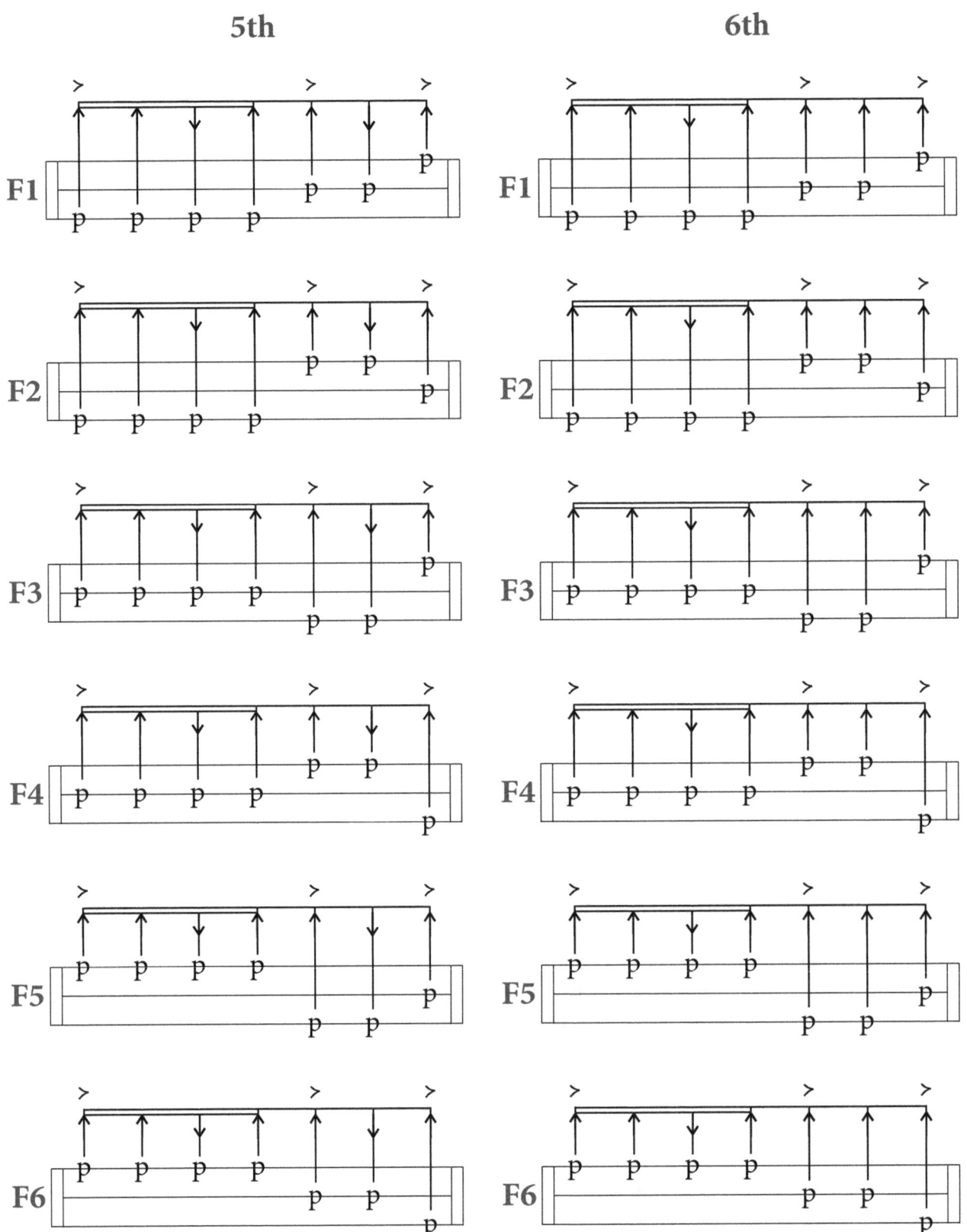

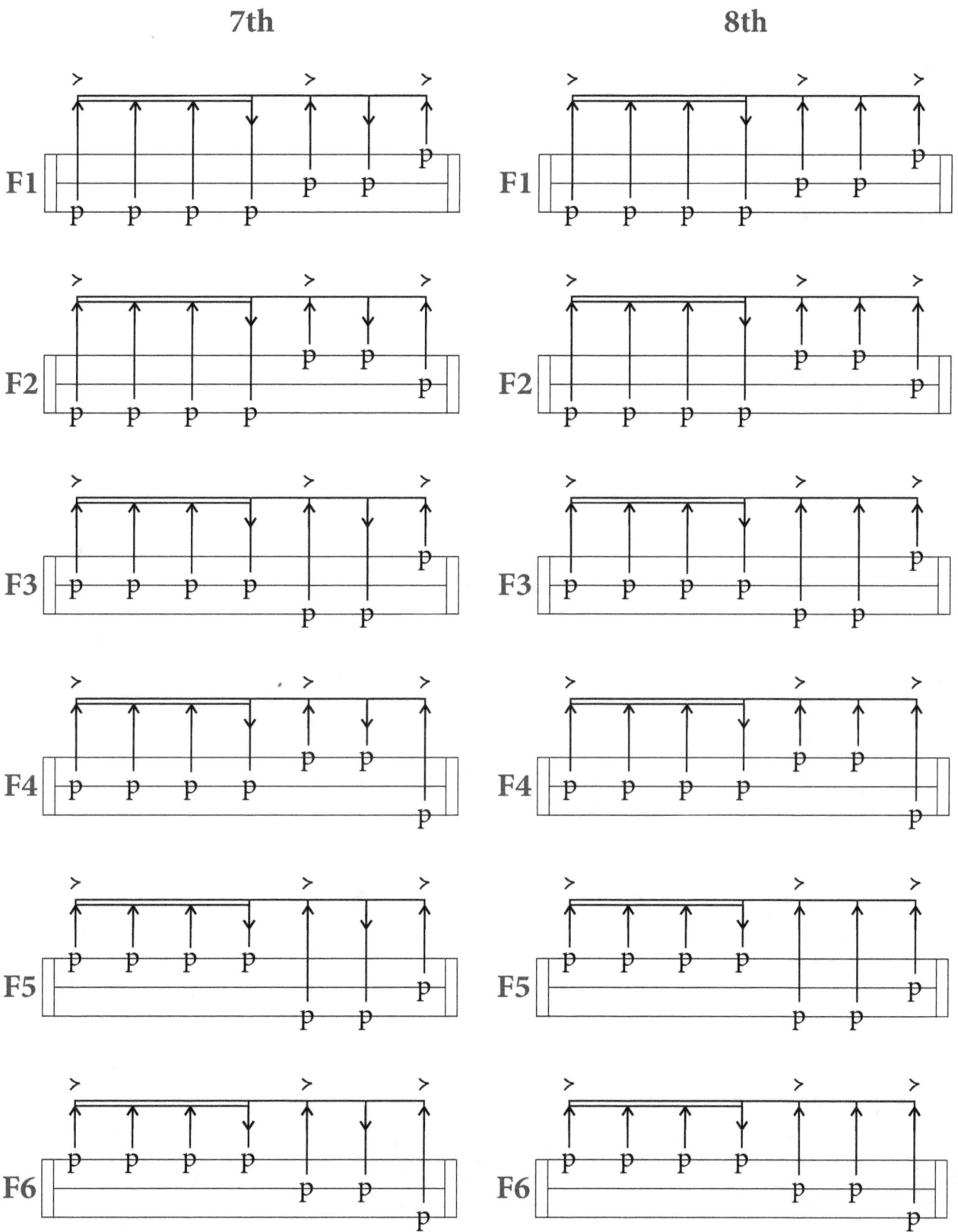

9th 10th

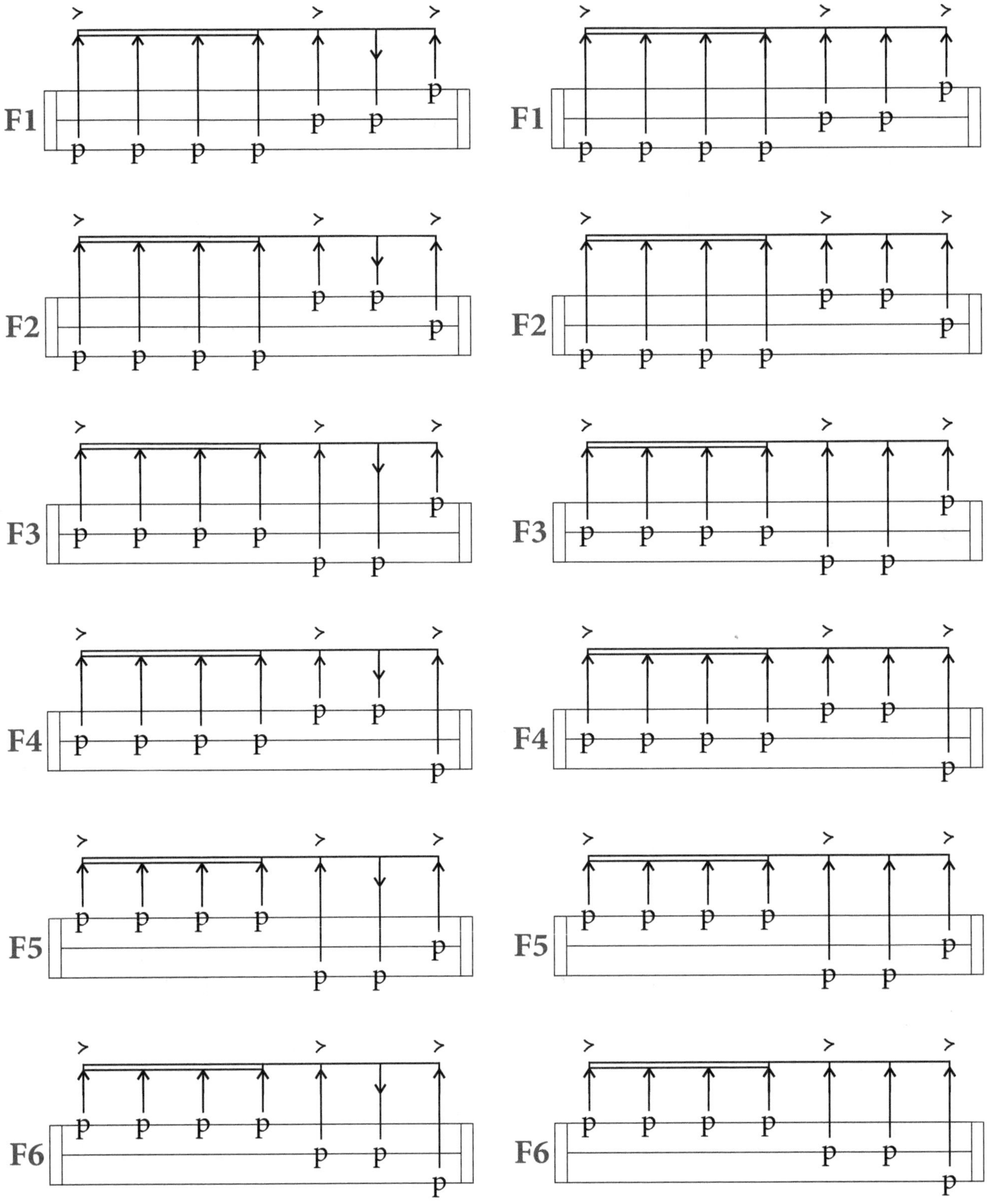

VARIATION III
WAYS OF PERFORMANCE

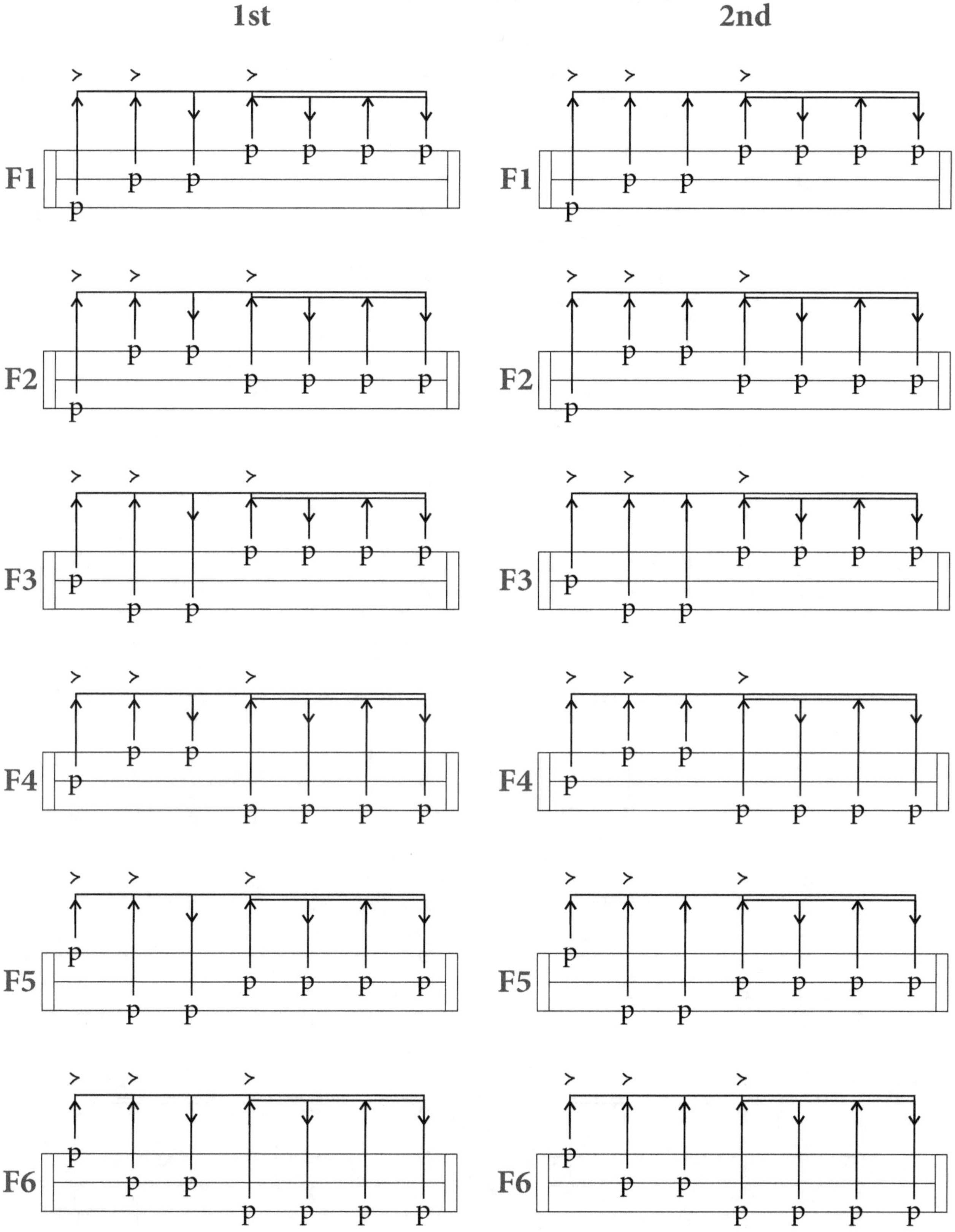

1st   2nd

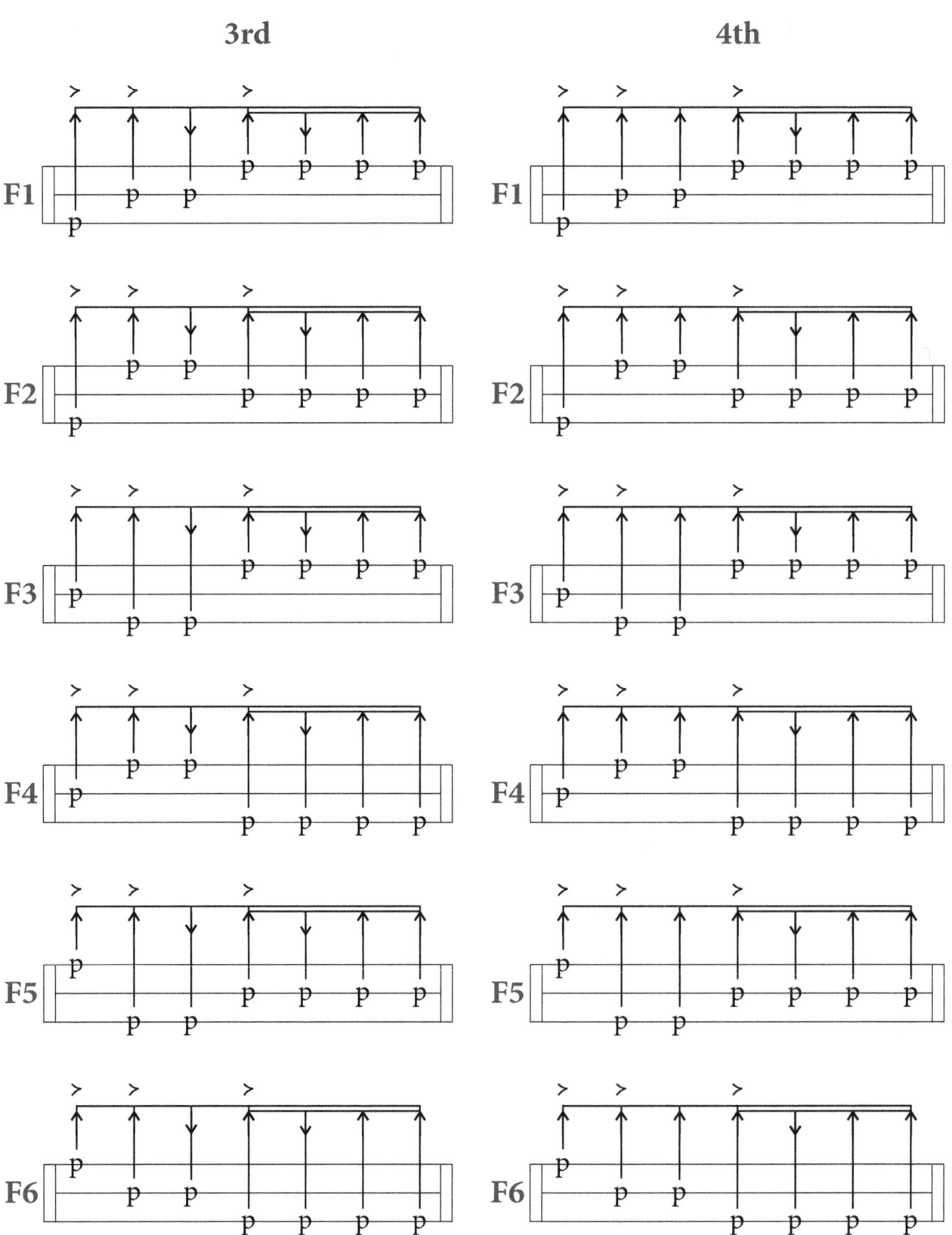

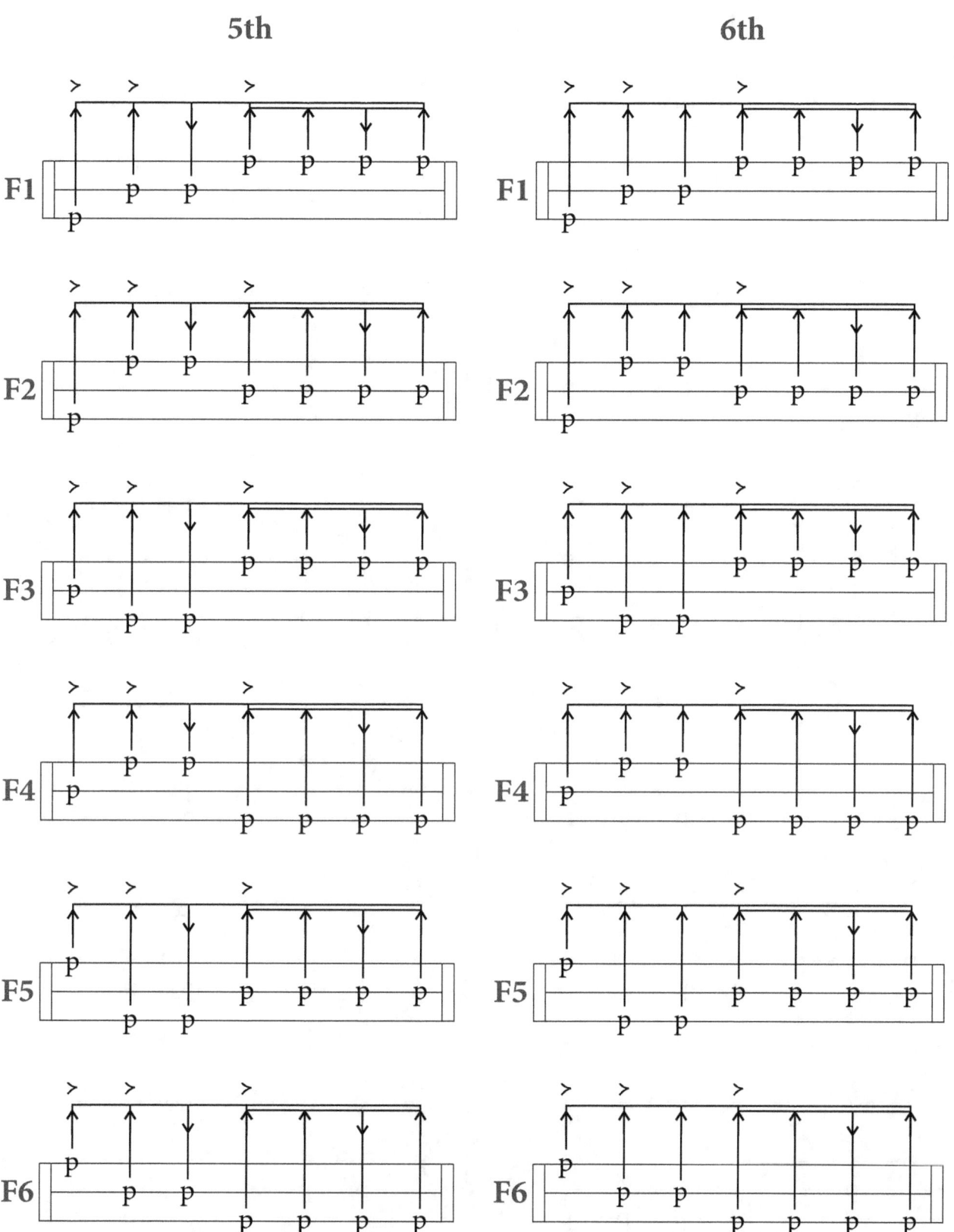

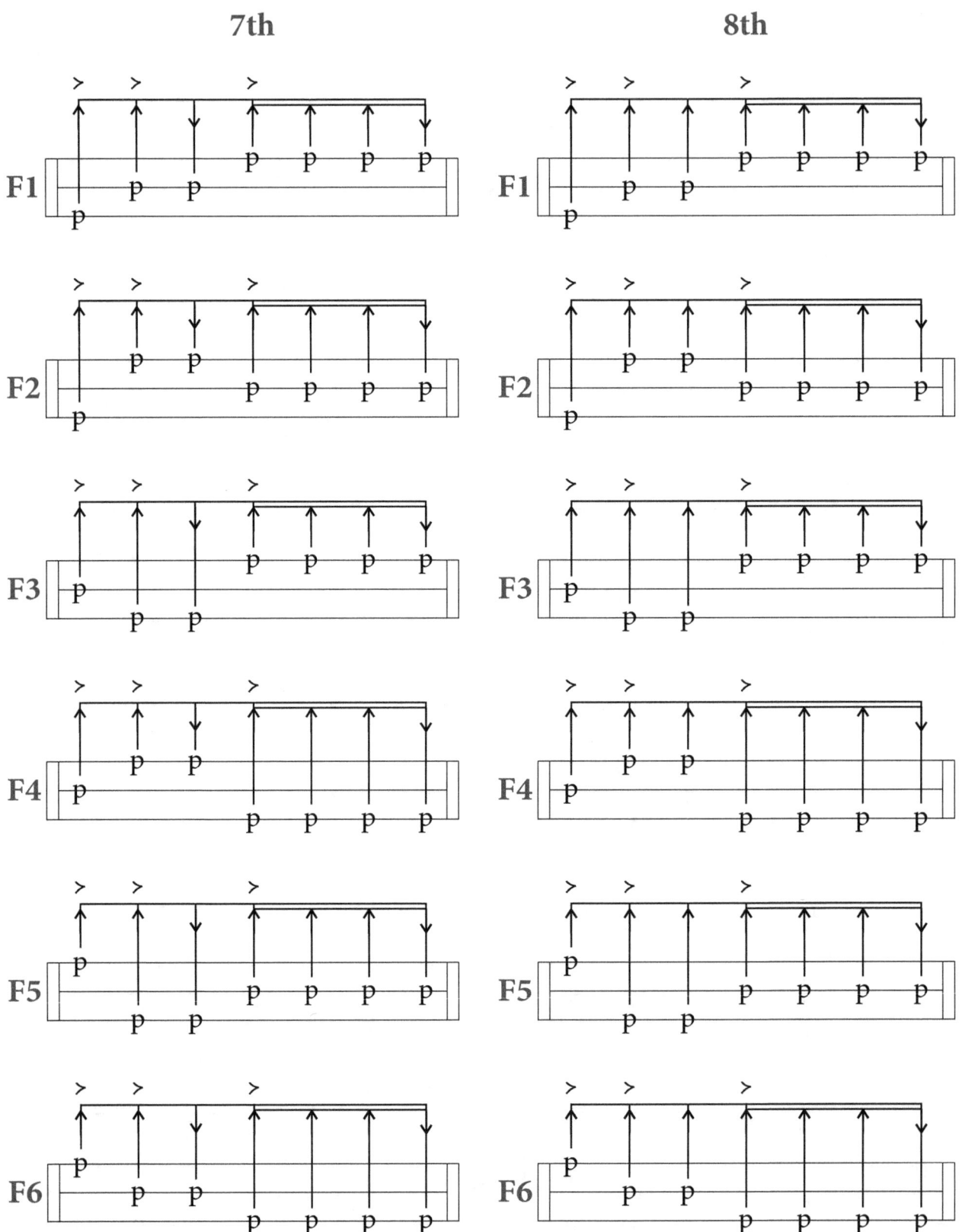

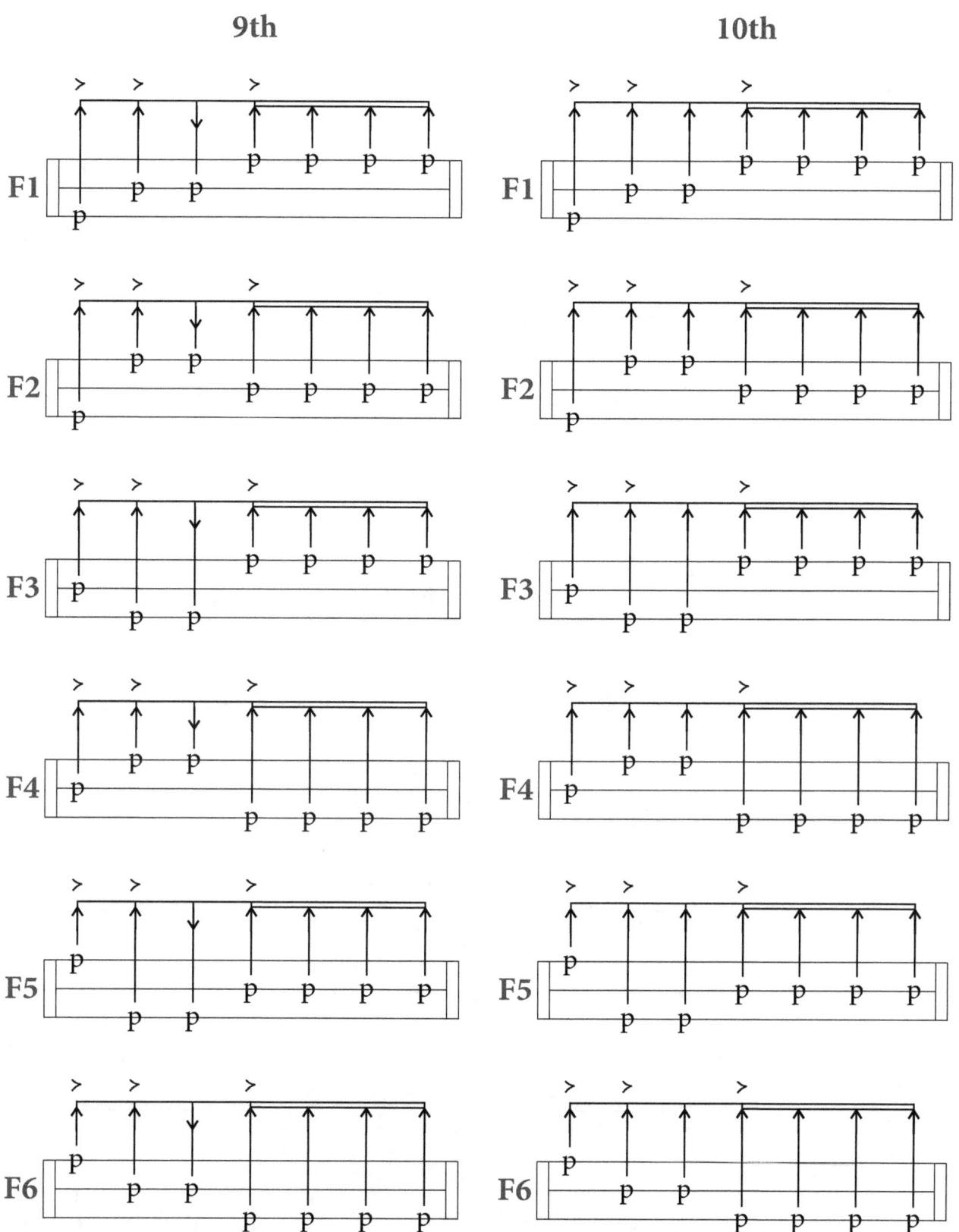

VARIATION IV
WAYS OF PERFORMANCE

1st   **2nd**

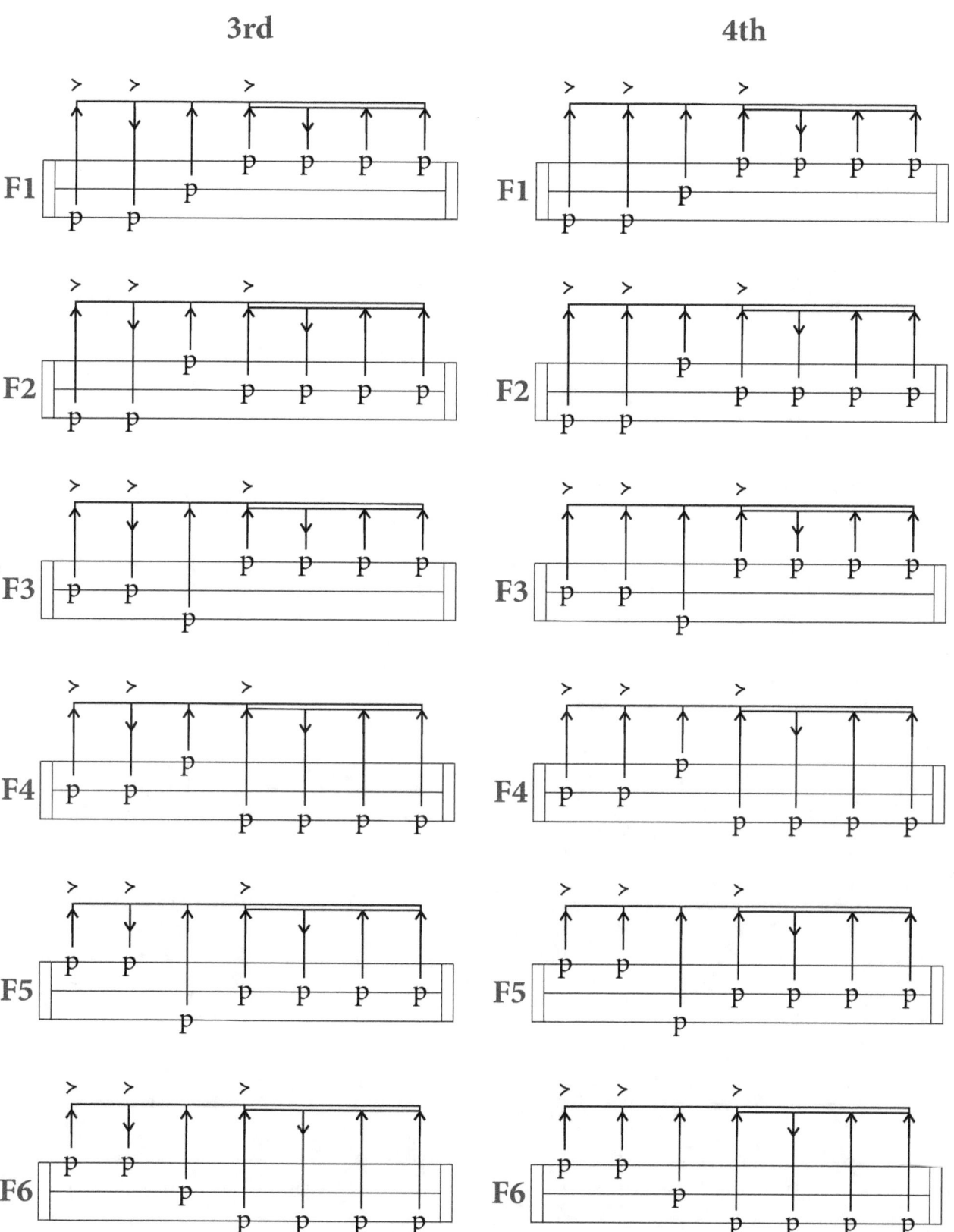

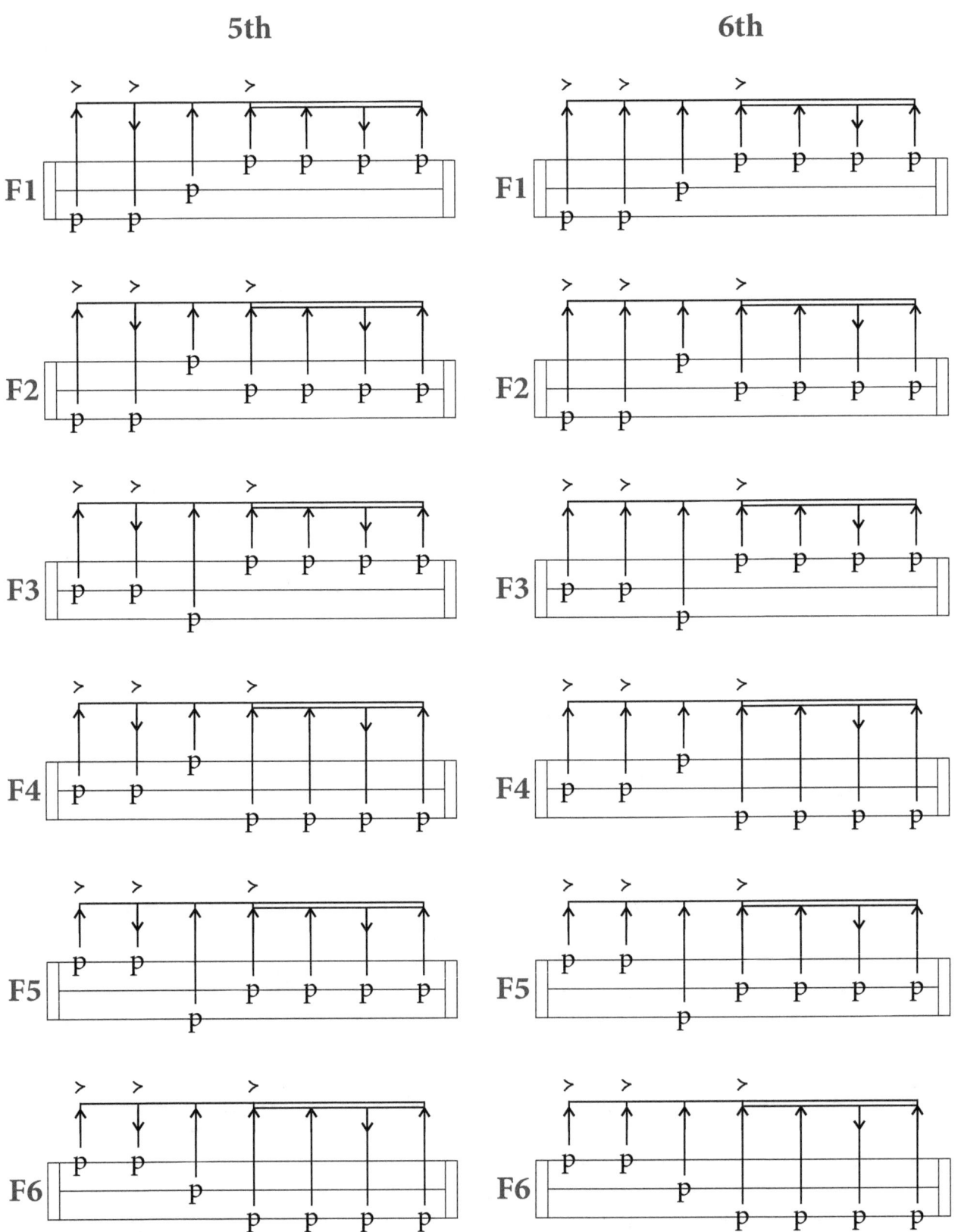

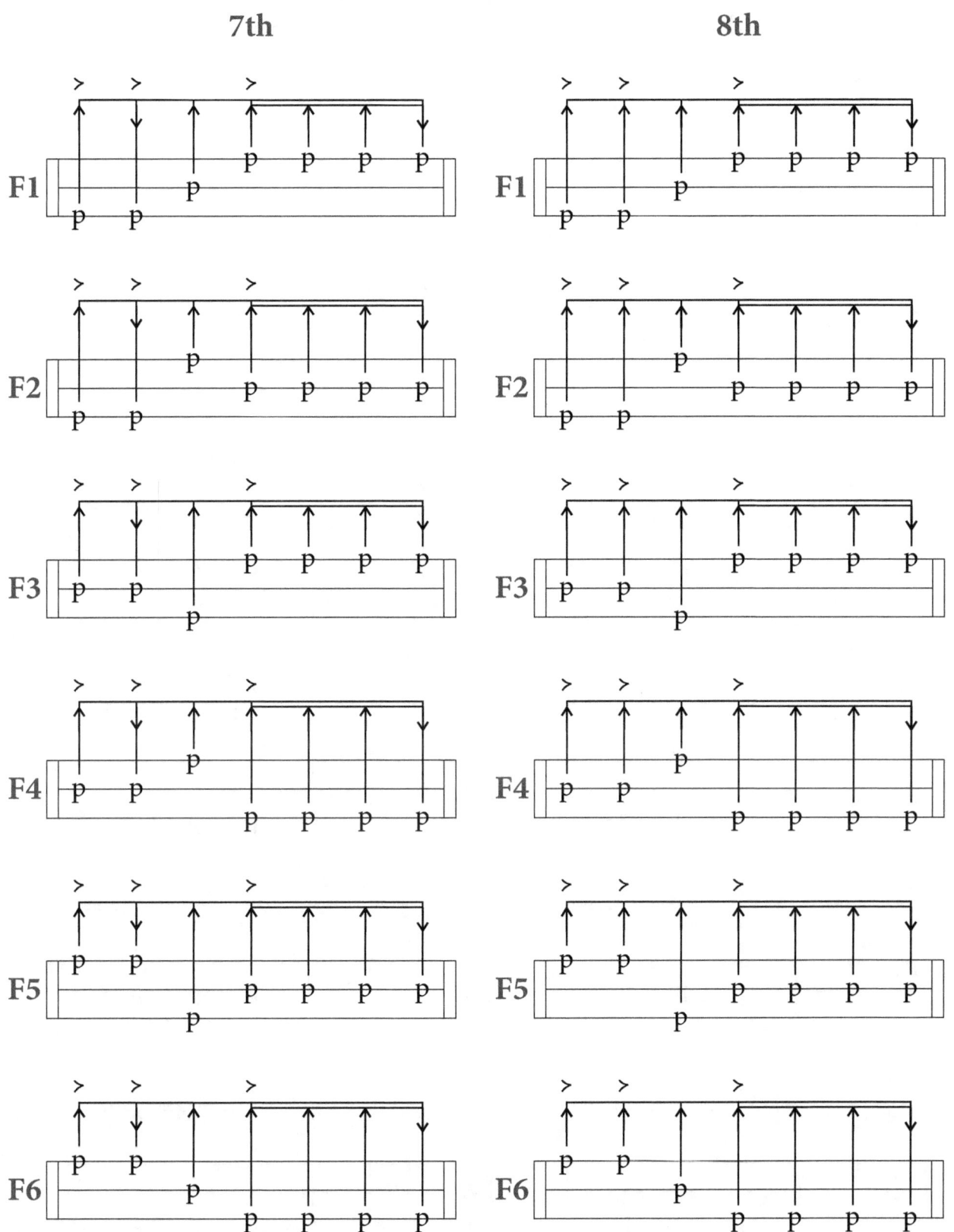

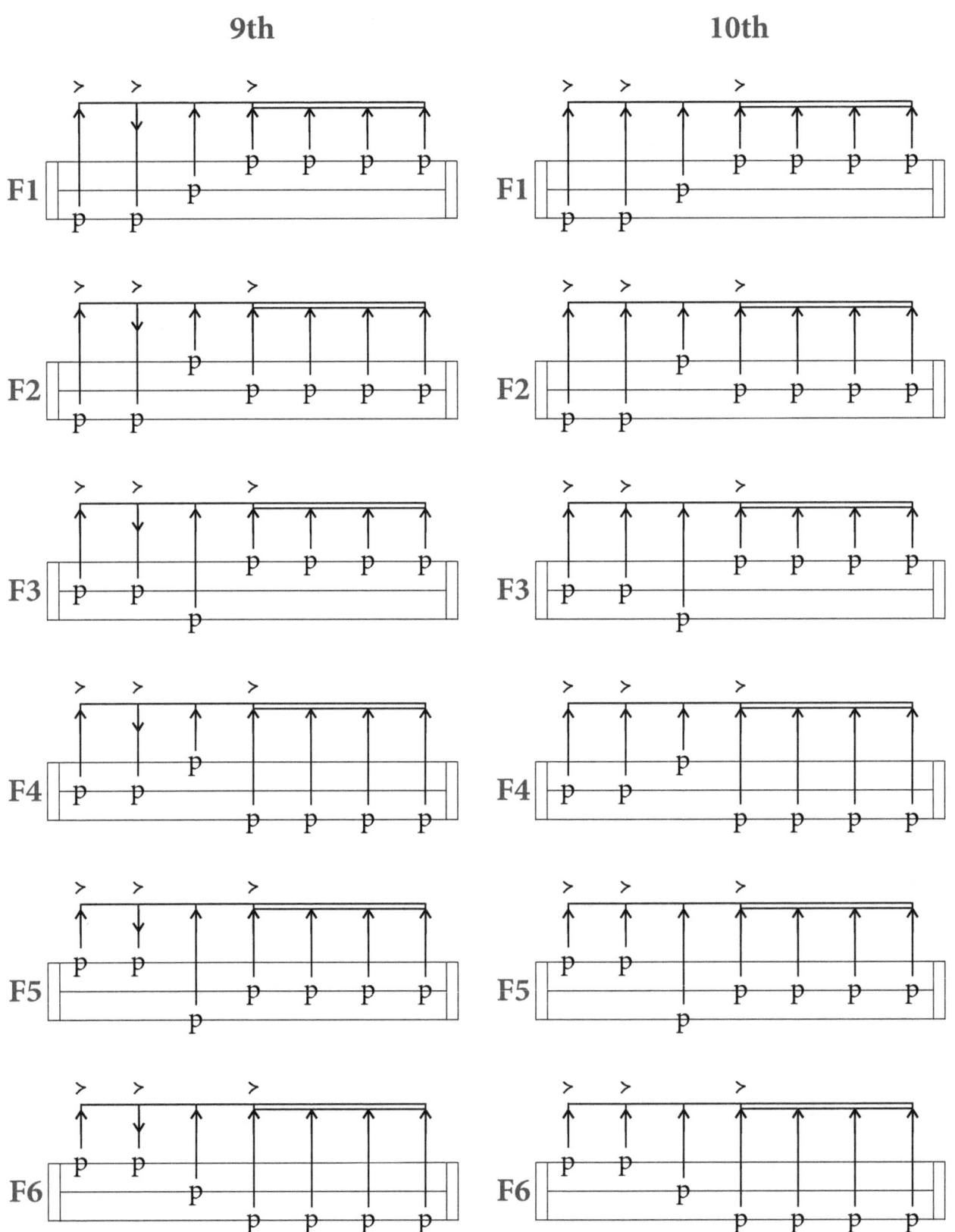

VARIATION V
WAYS OF PERFORMANCE

1st   2nd

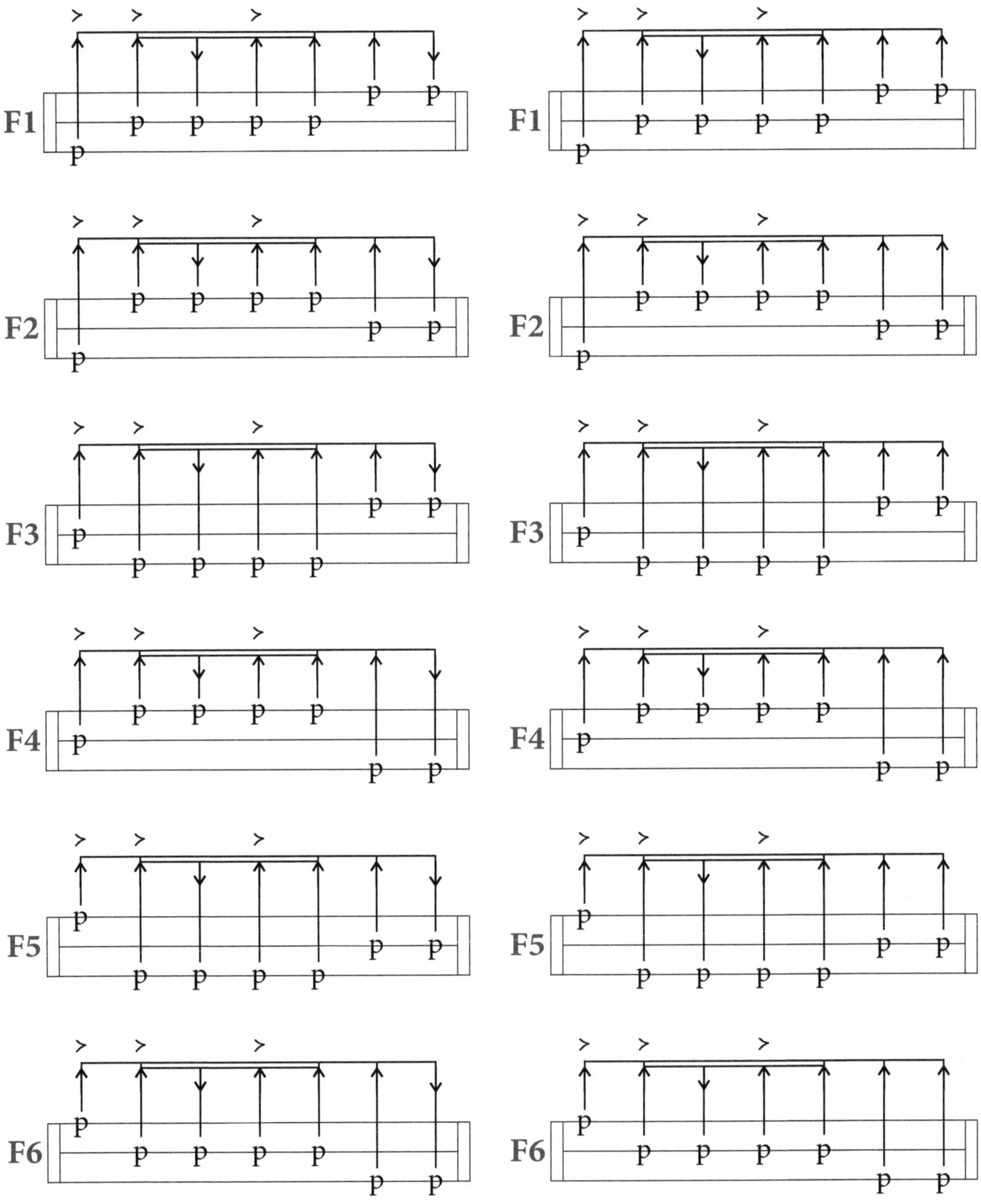

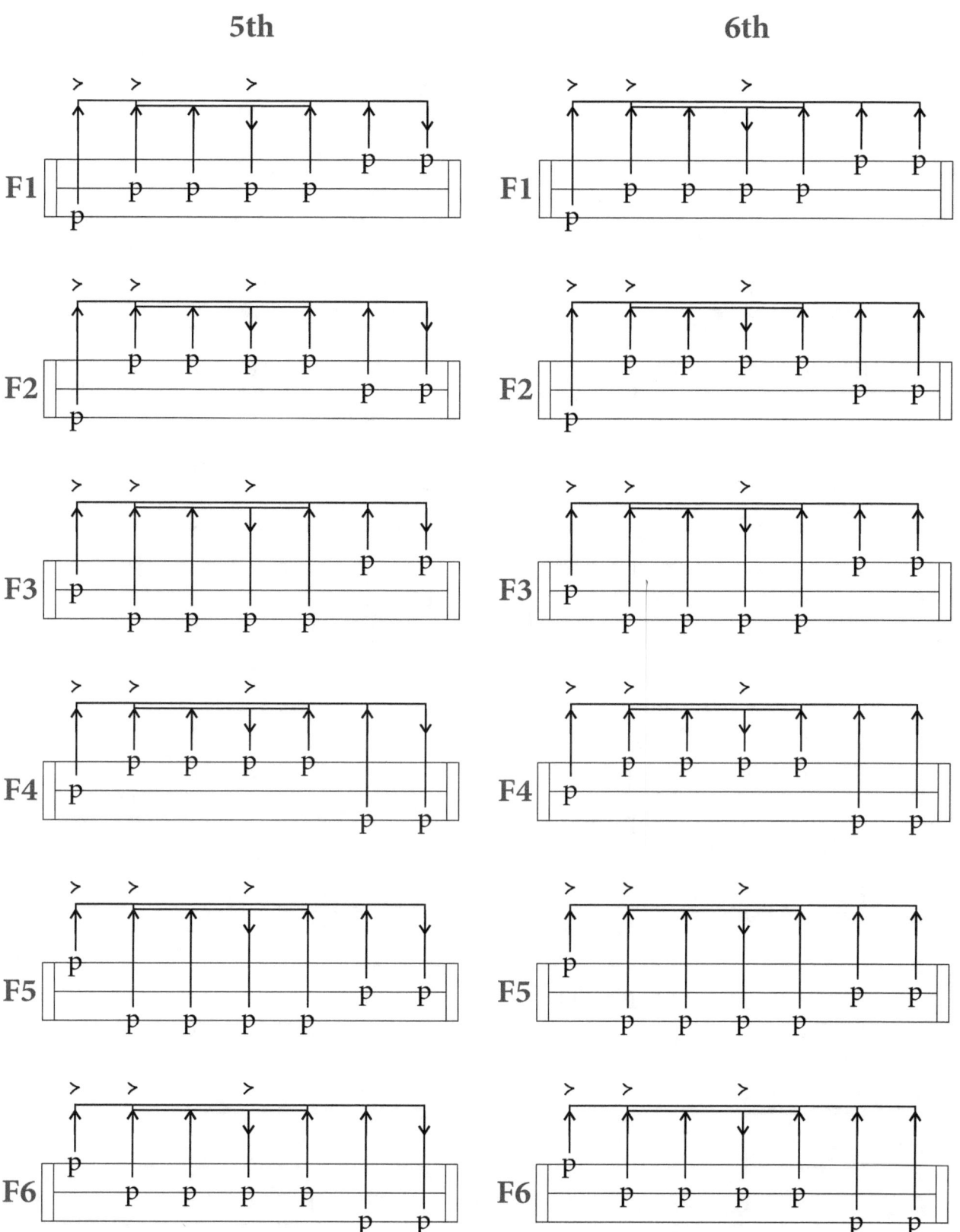

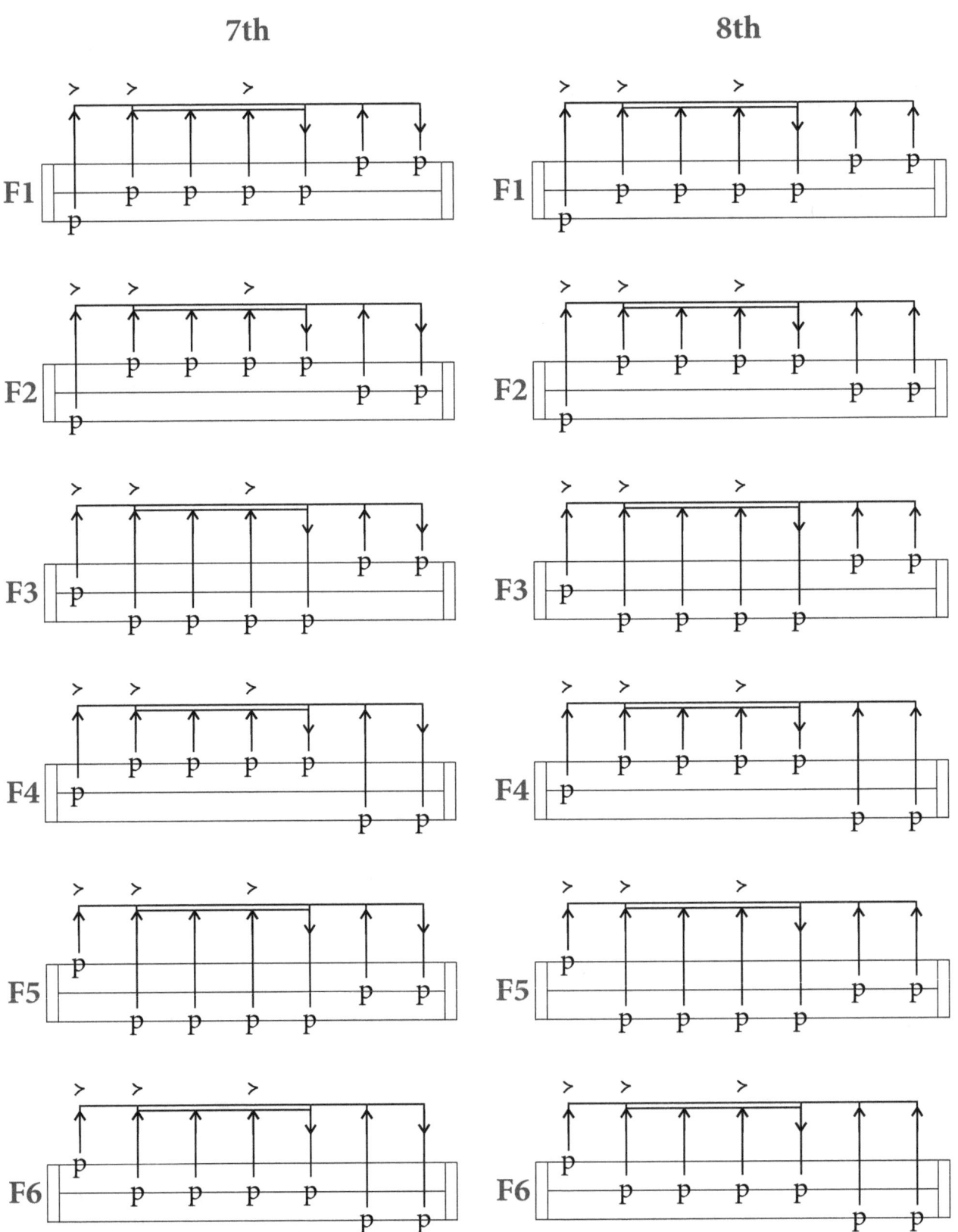

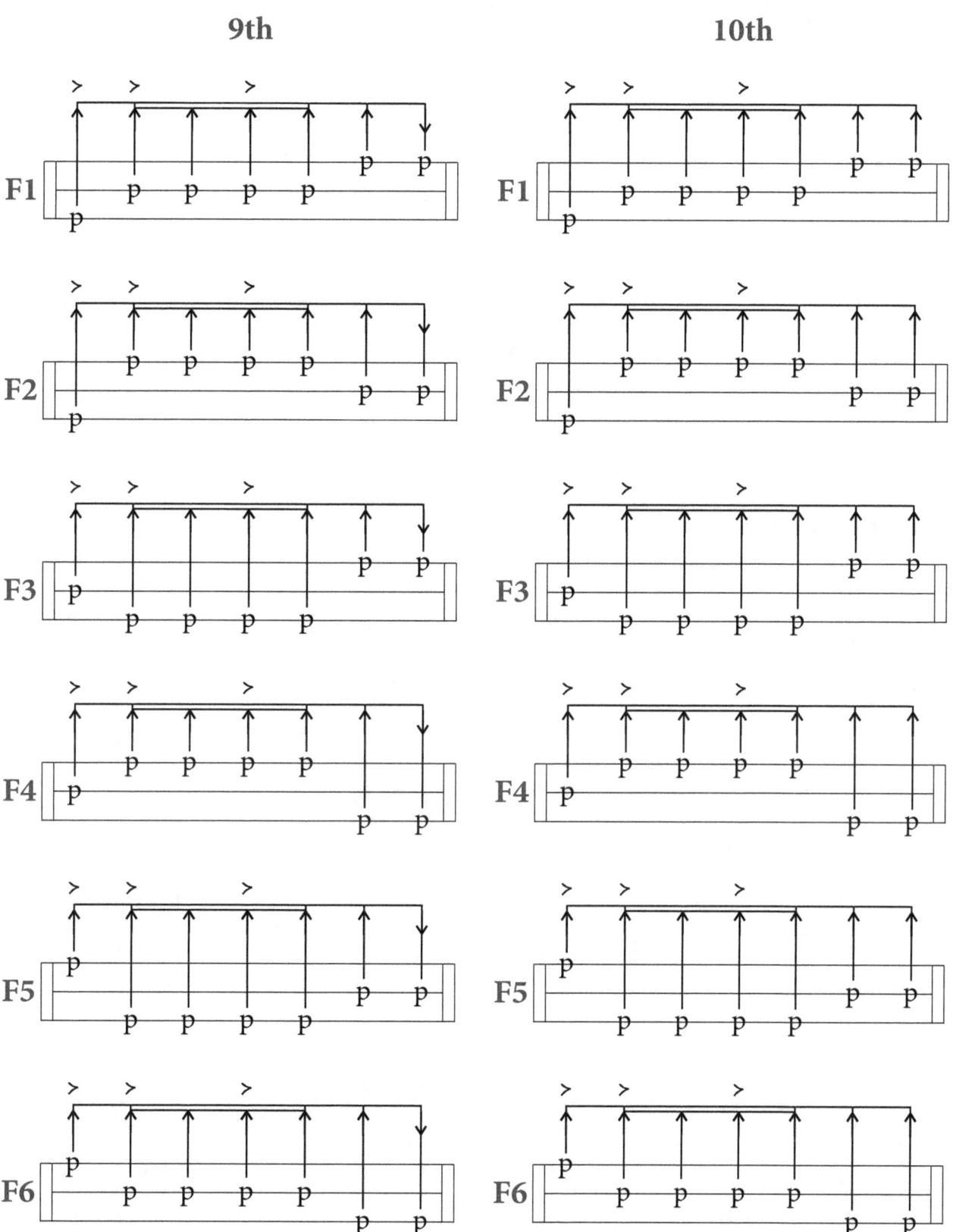

VARIATION VI
WAYS OF PERFORMANCE

1st　　　　　　　　　　　　　　　　　　**2nd**

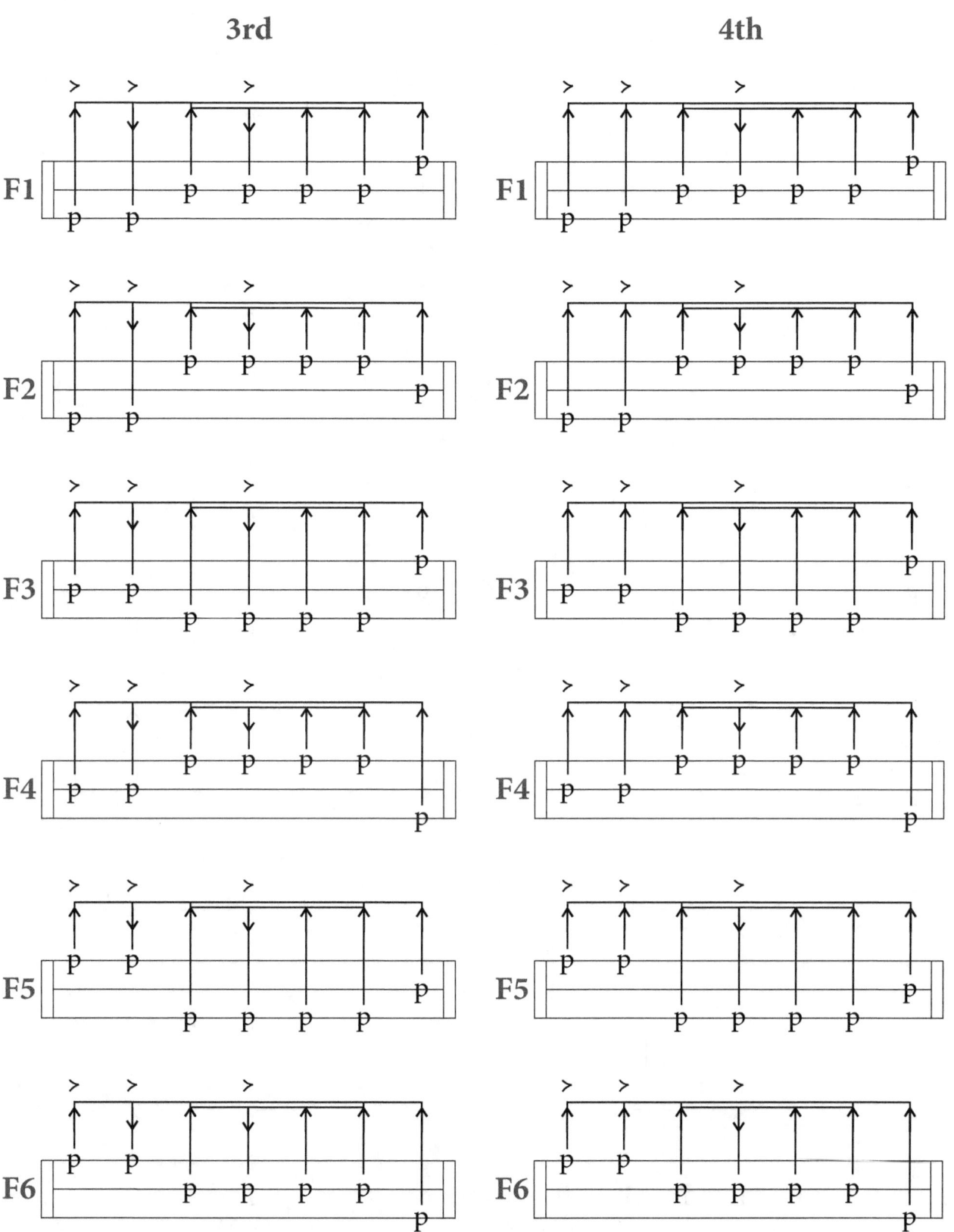

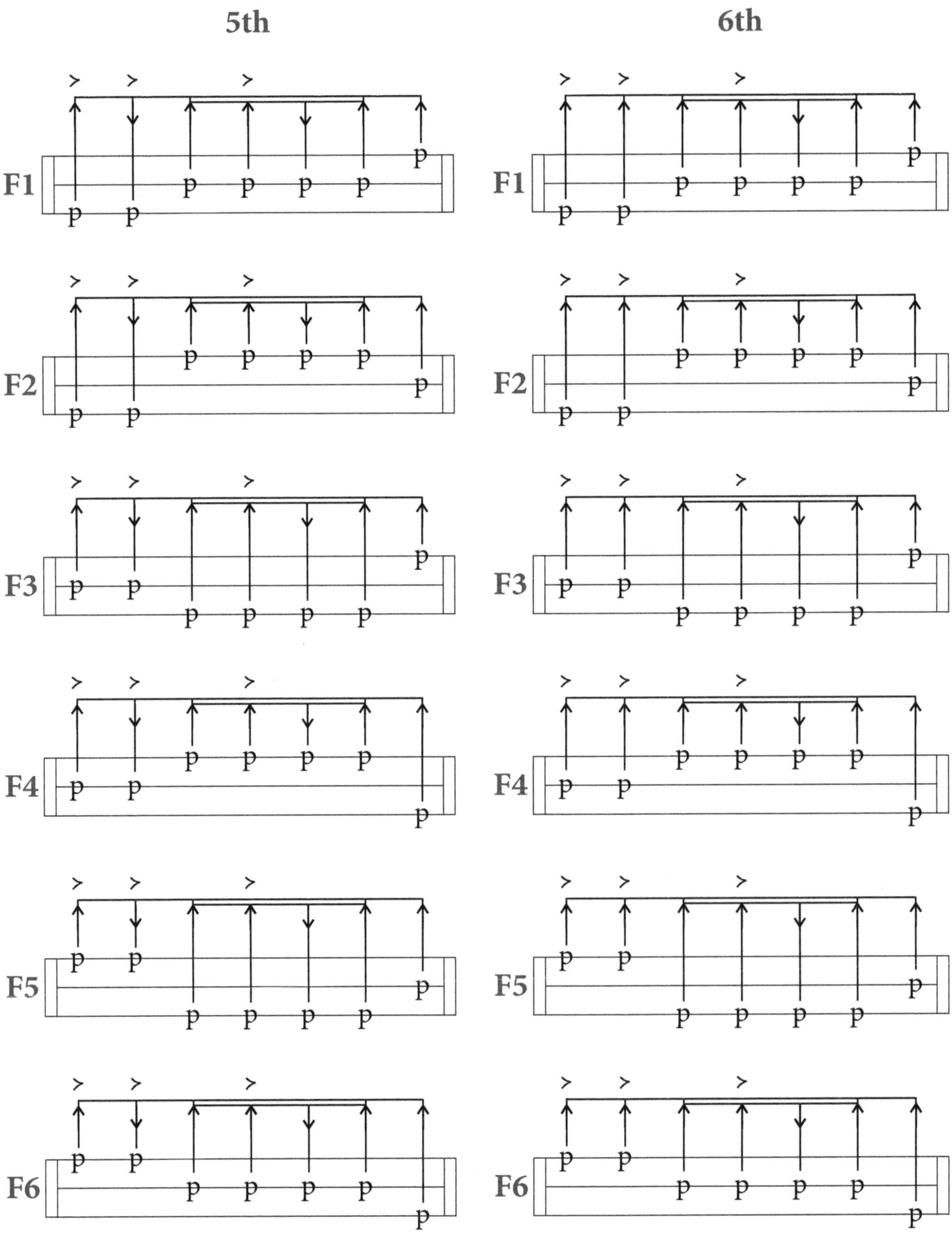

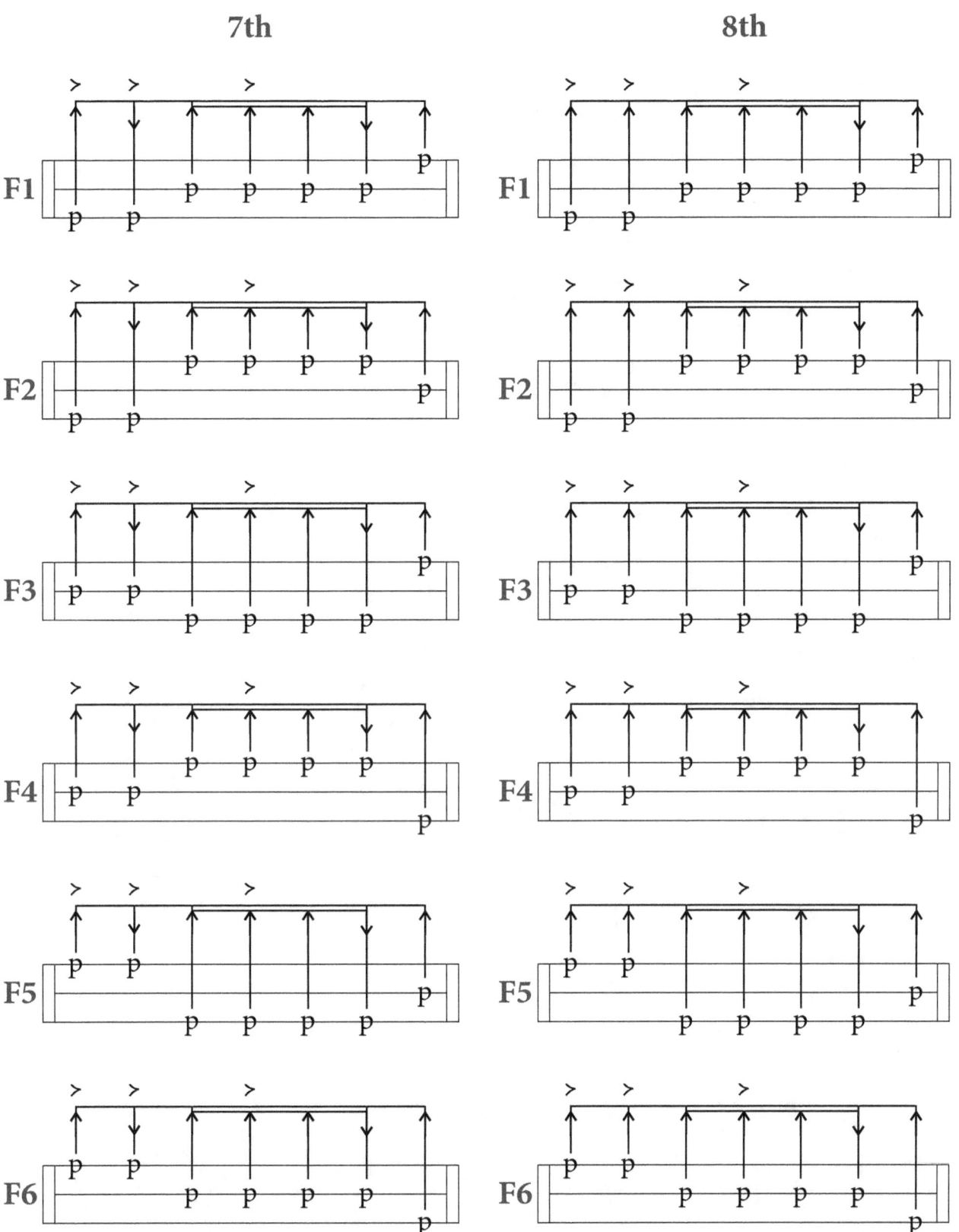

9

9th

F1
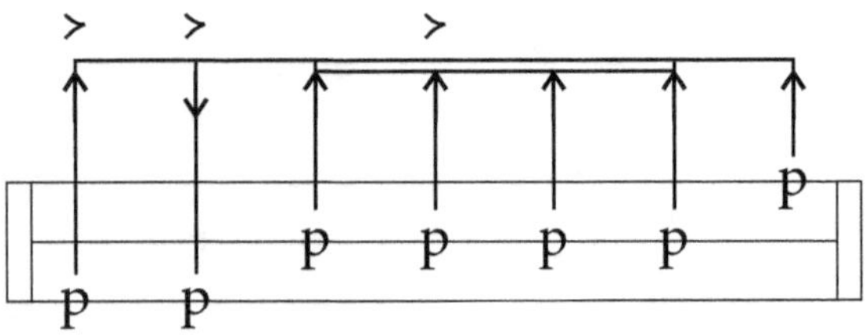

F2
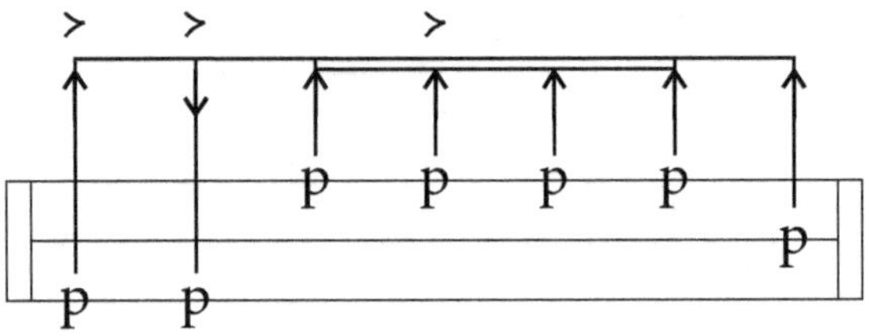

F3
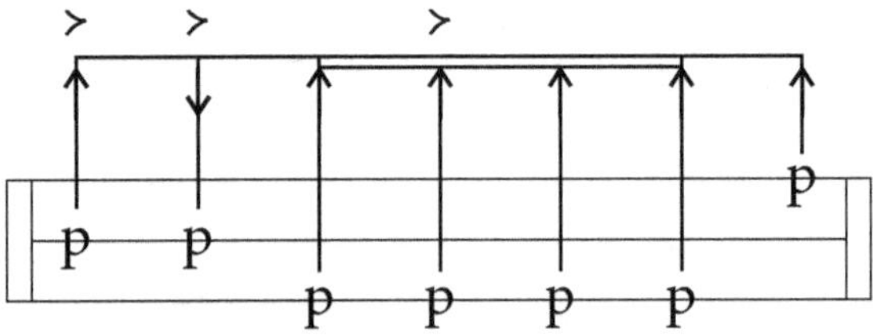

F4
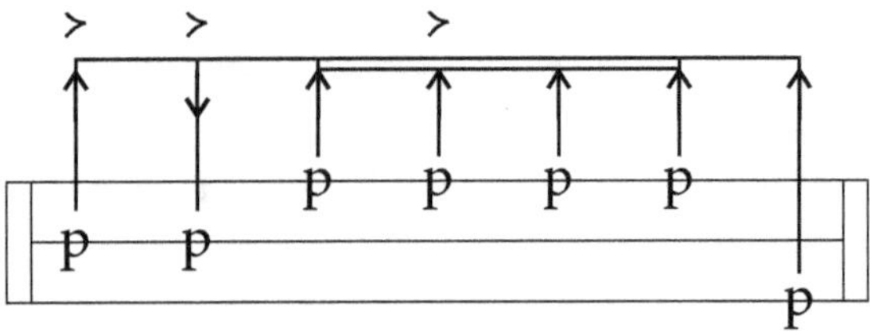

F5
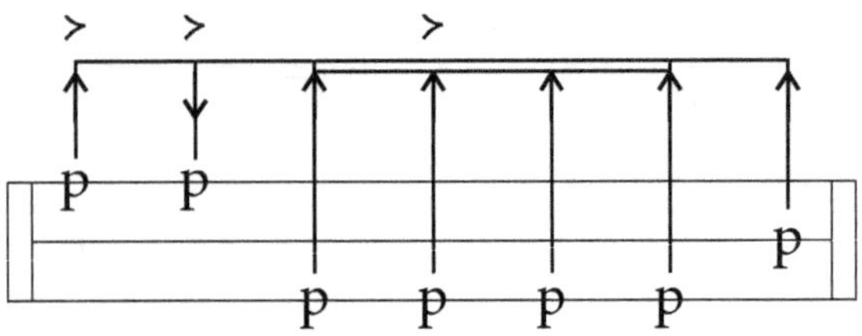

F6
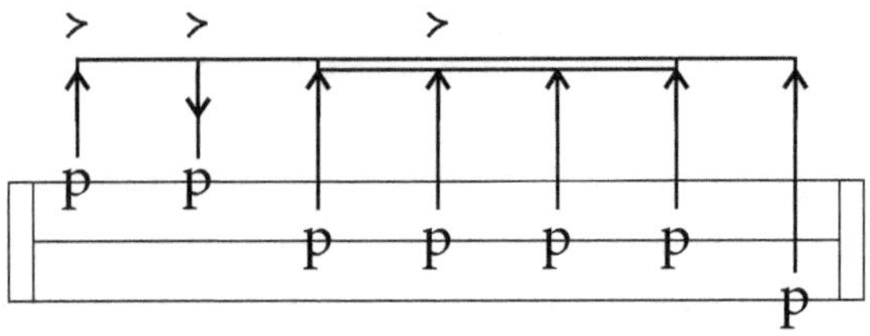

10th

F1
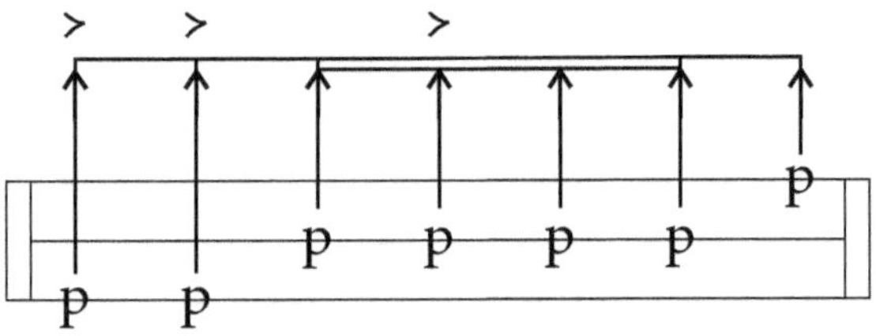

F2
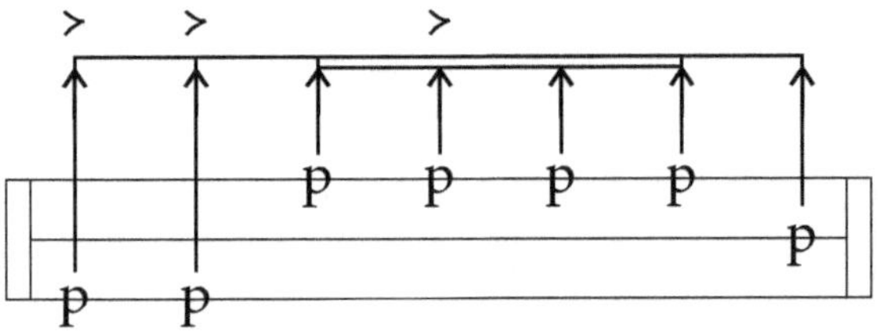

F3
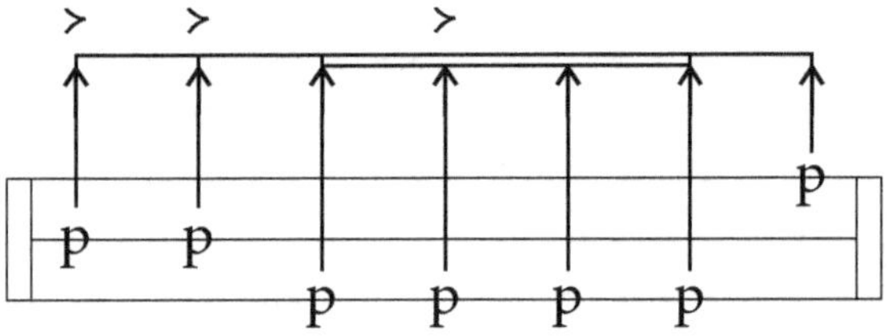

F4
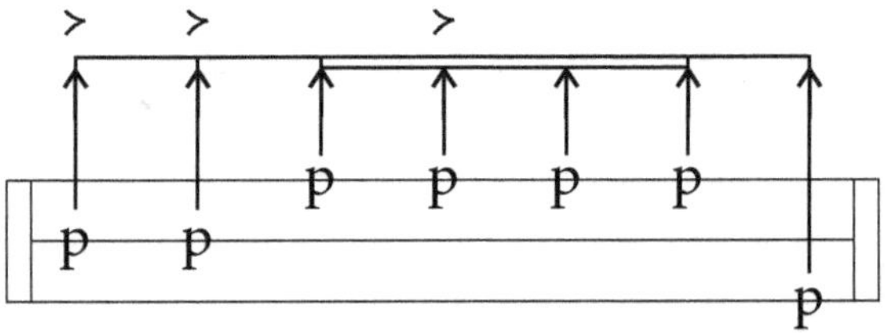

F5
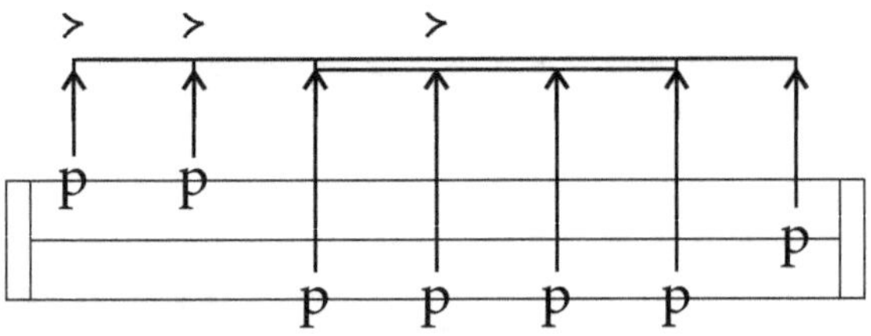

F6
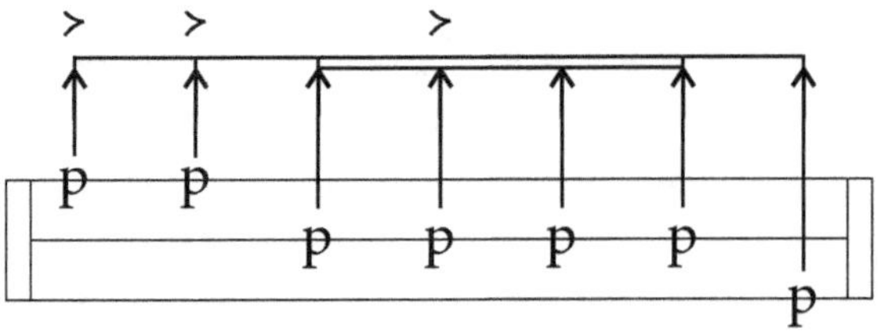

§ III

Exercise on pulgar on three adjacent strings with two double and one quad stroke within each Formula. The exercise contains three variations with 6 Formulas in each variation. The first Formula of each variation is cited below. Isochronous playing of pulgar strokes (double and quad).

VARIATION I

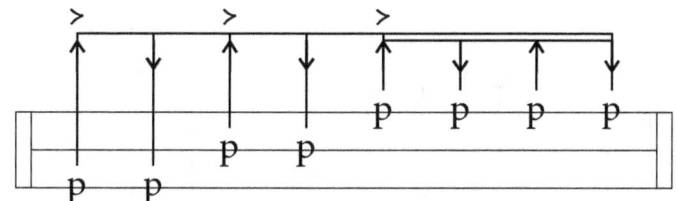

VARIATION II

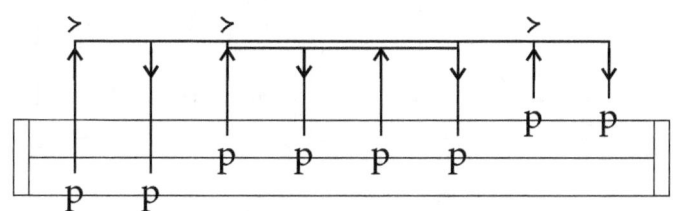

VARIATION III

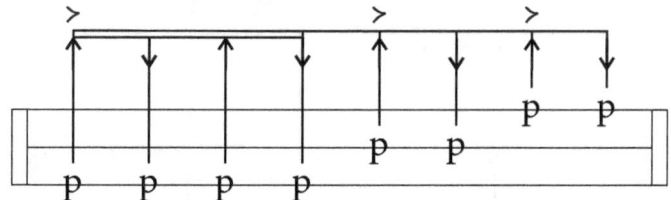

Each variation can be performed in 20 different ways depending on pulgar stroke. Practice on all variations and in all ways of performance either on three adjacent strings or with inserted strings.

VARIATION I
WAYS OF PERFORMANCE

1st   **2nd**

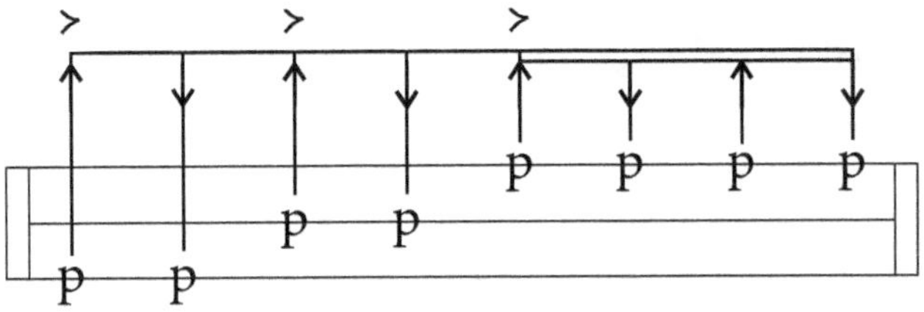

F1   F1

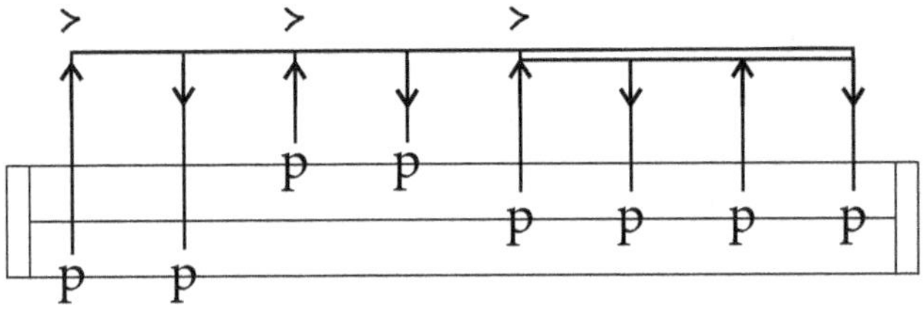

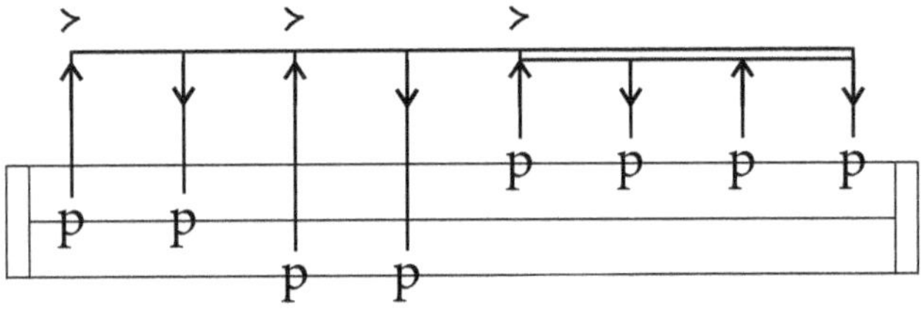

F2   F2

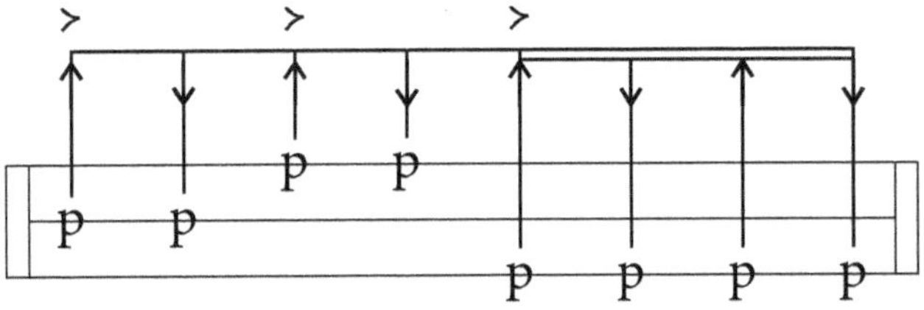

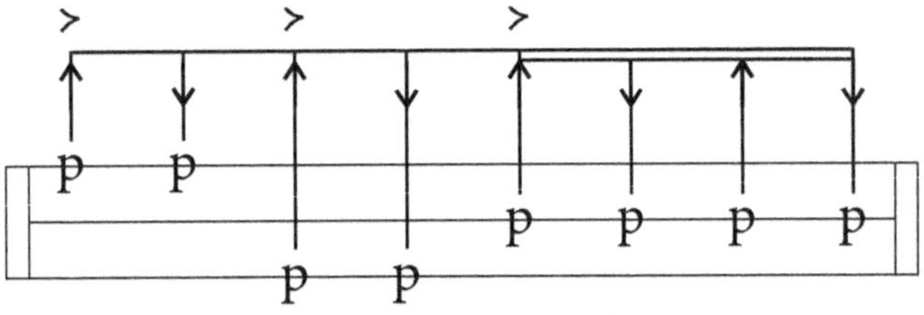

F3   F3

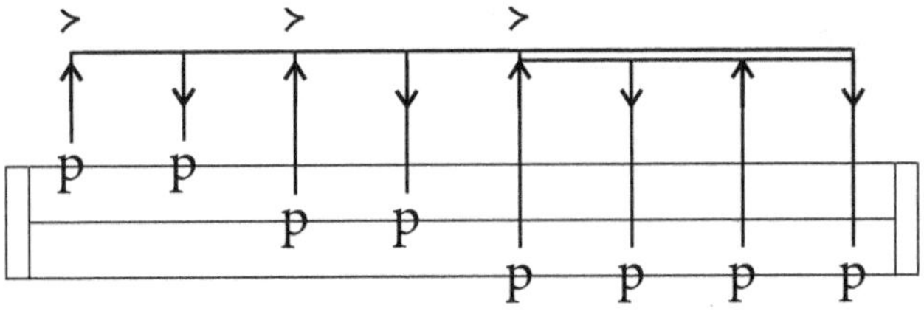

F4   F4

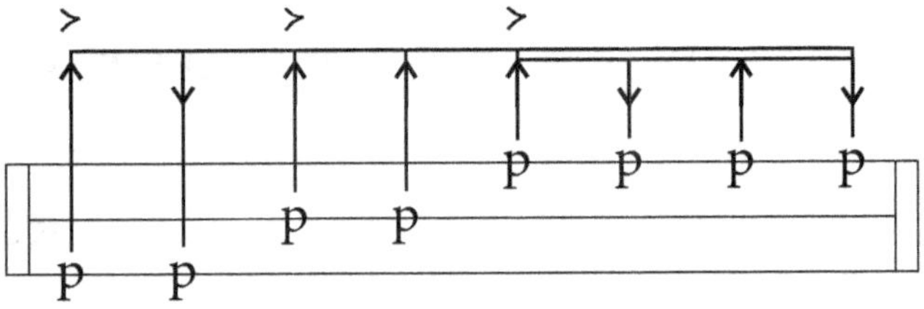

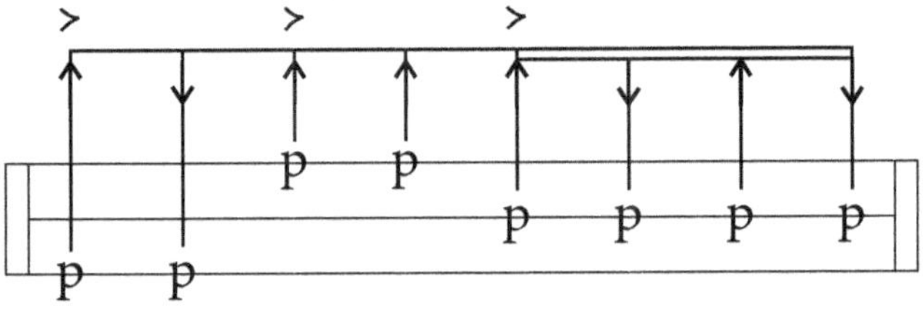

F5   F5

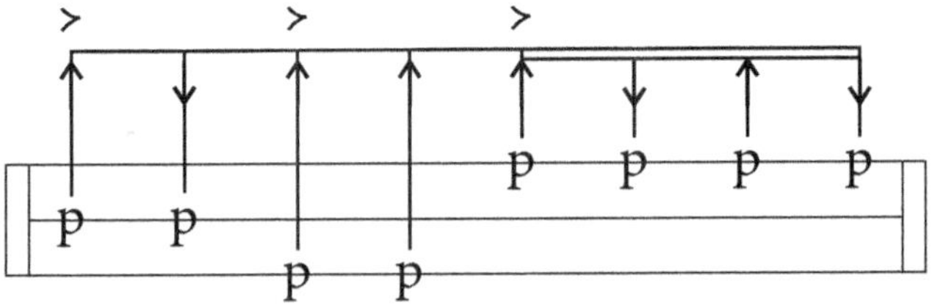

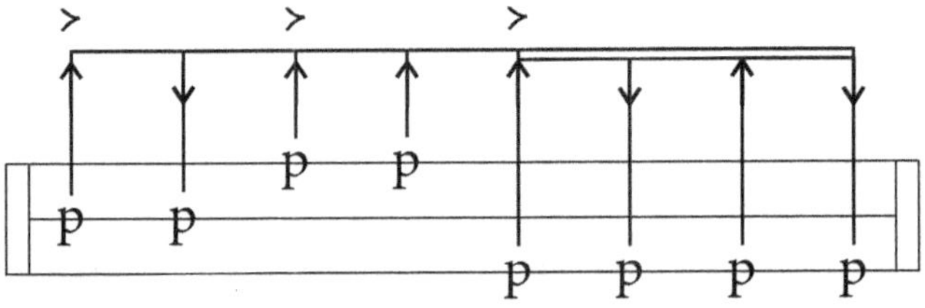

F6   F6

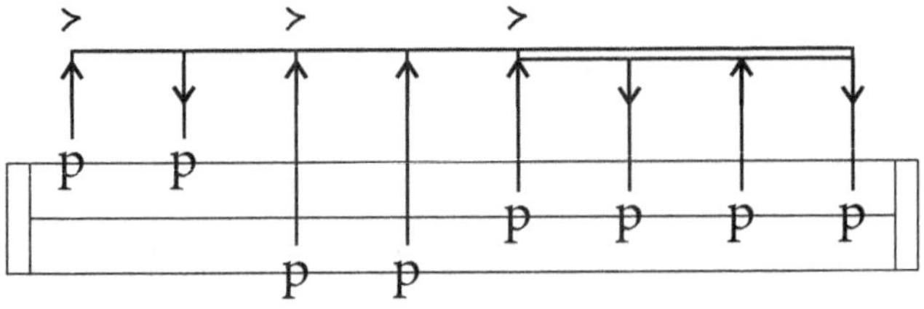

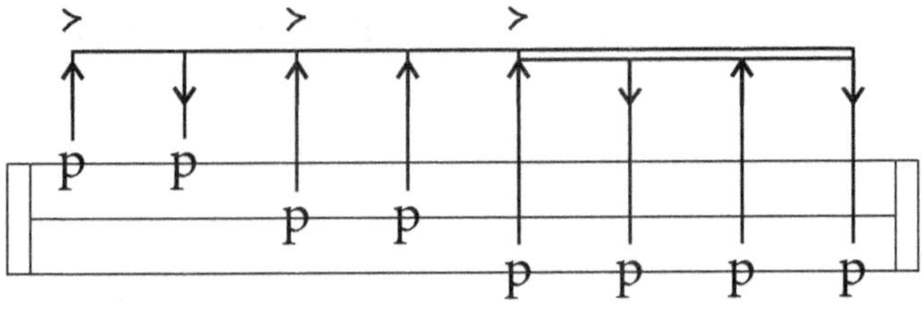

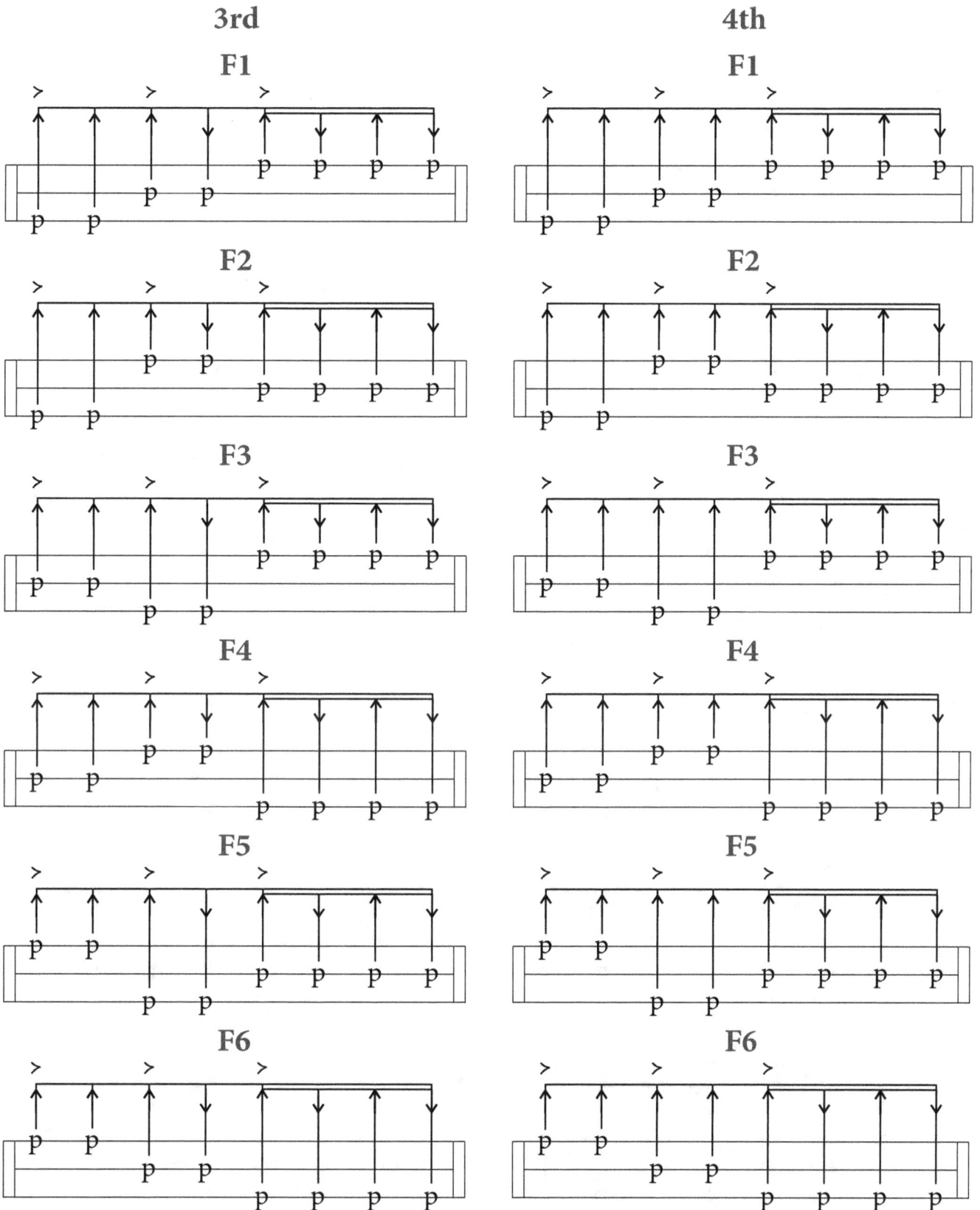

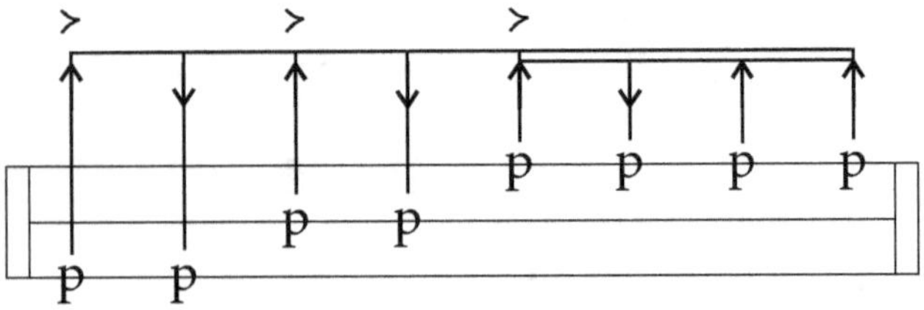

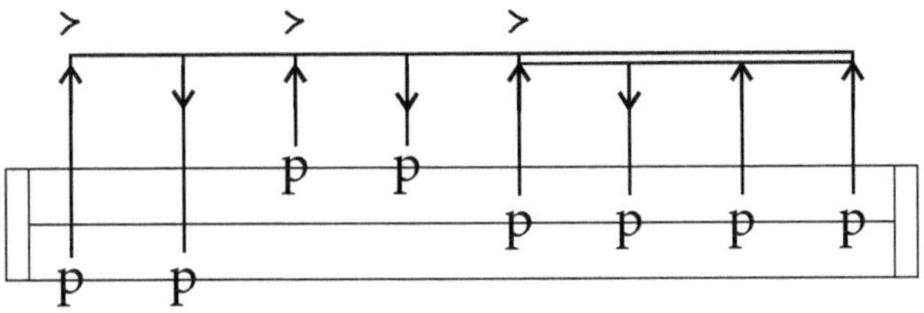

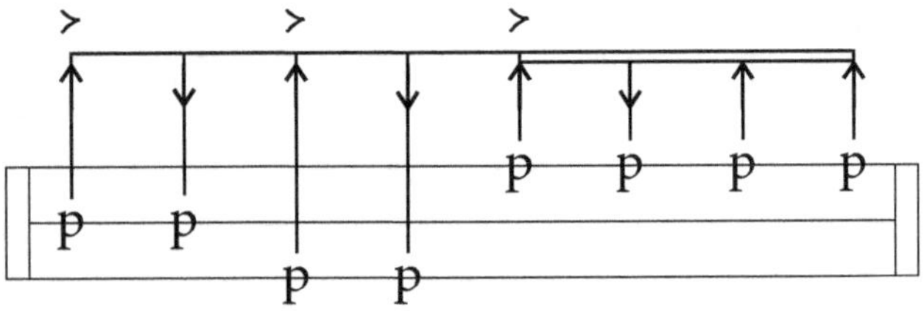

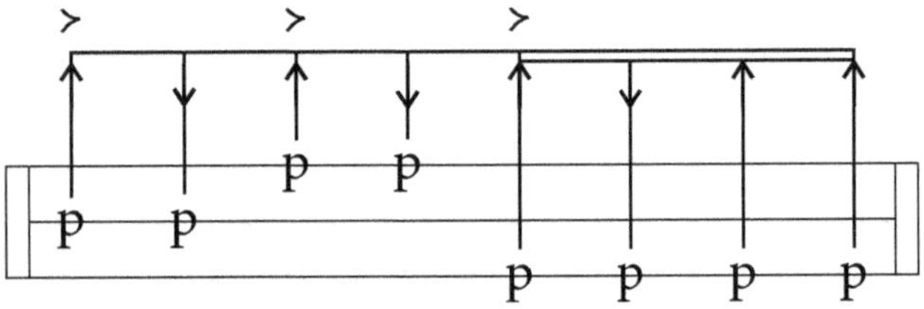

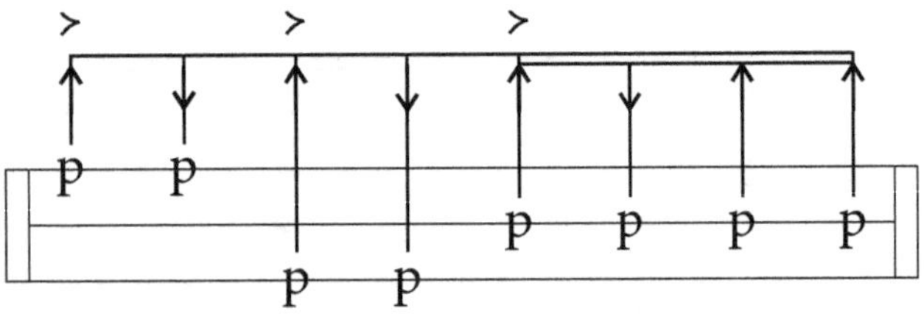

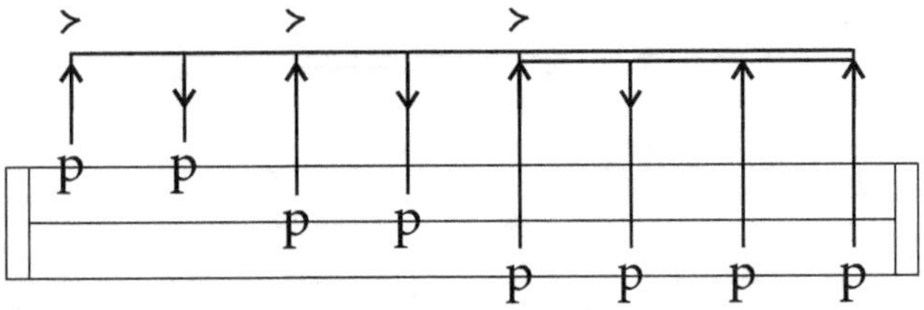

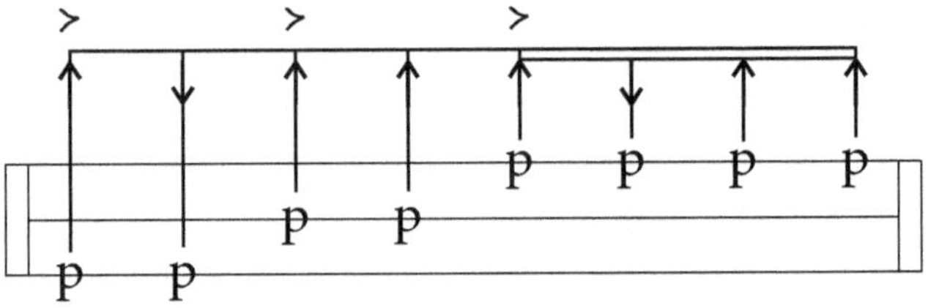

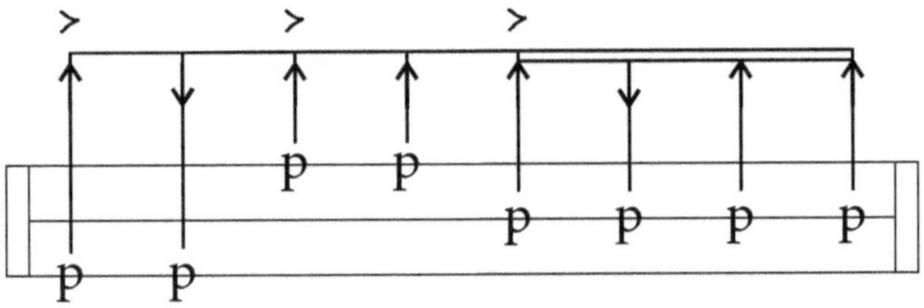

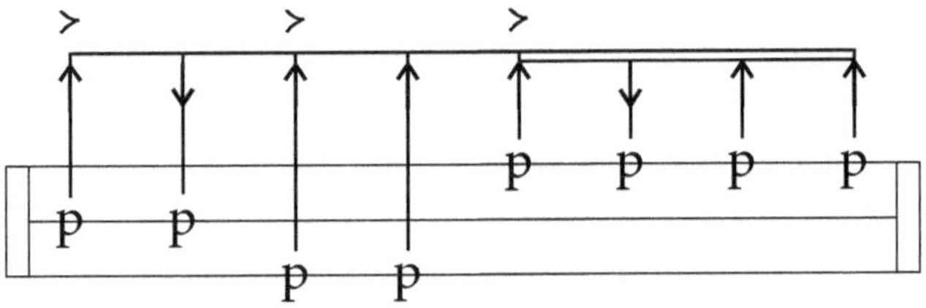

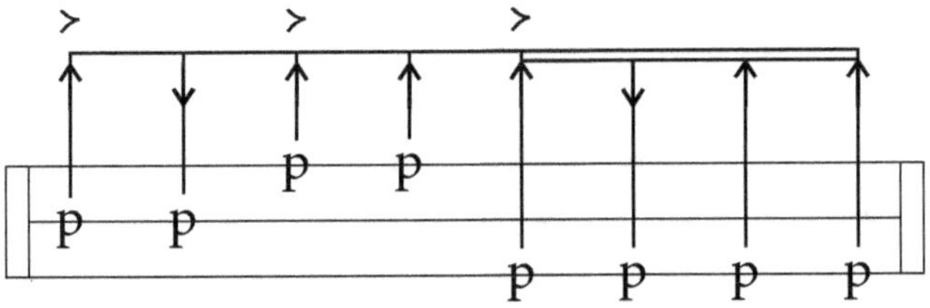

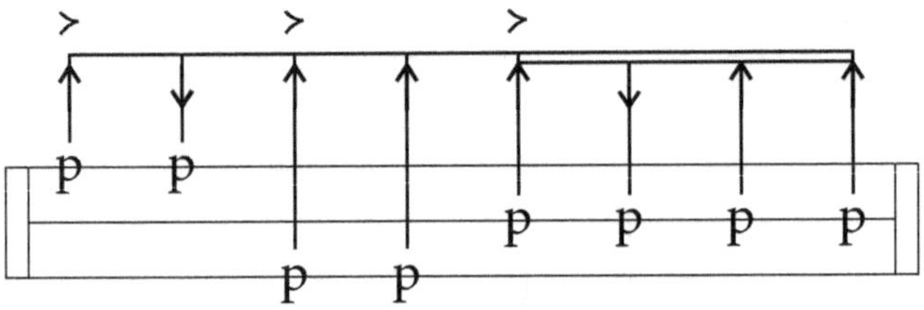

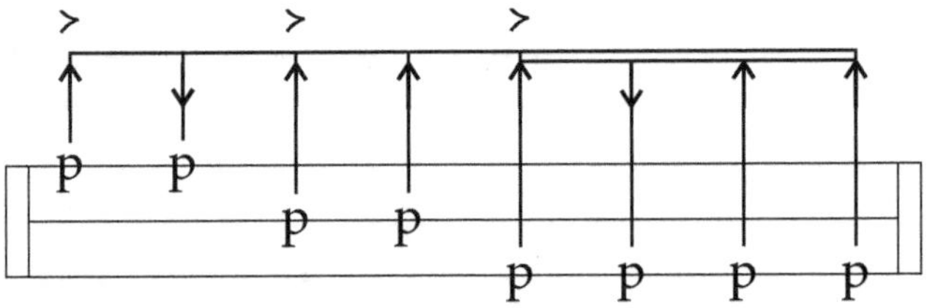

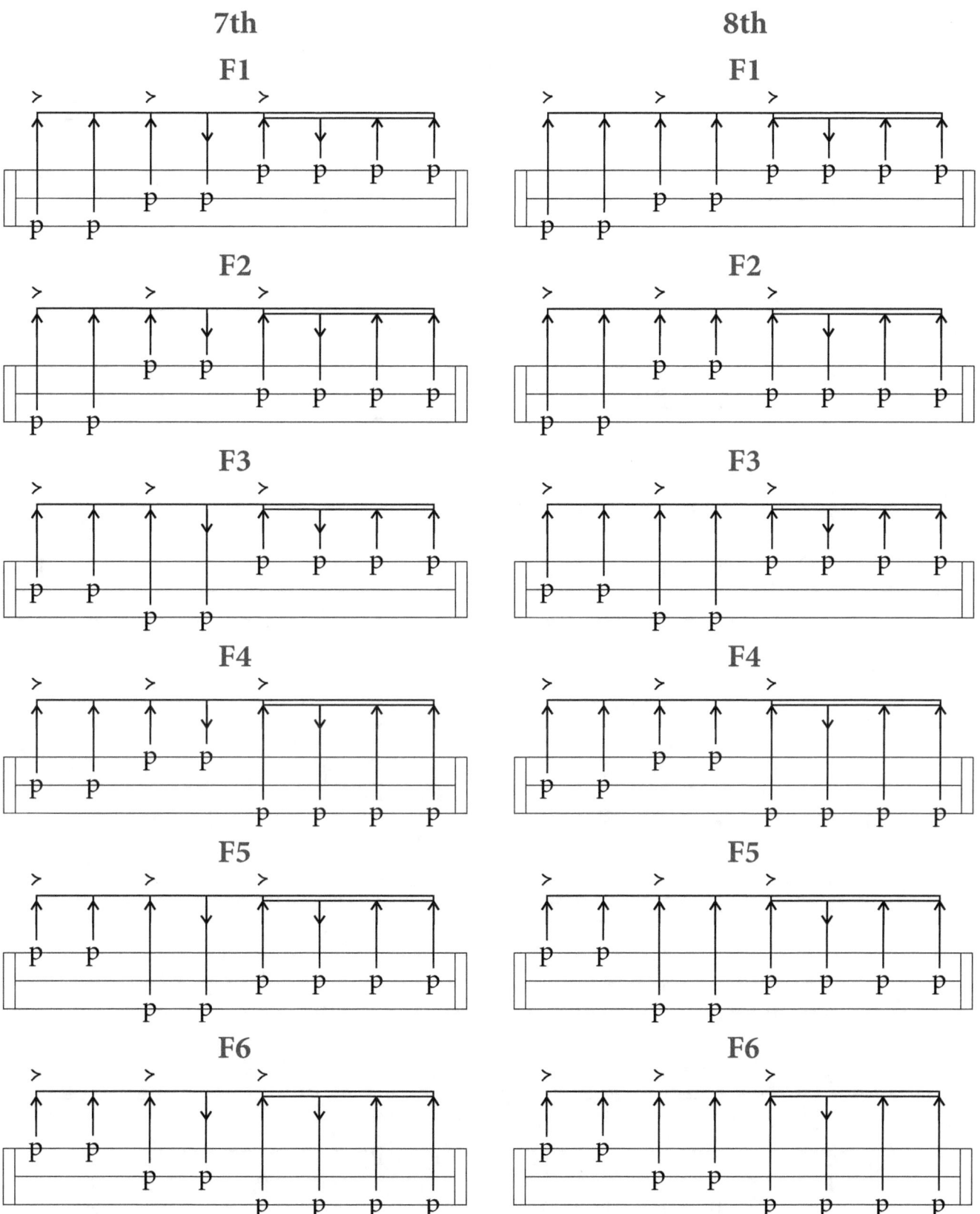

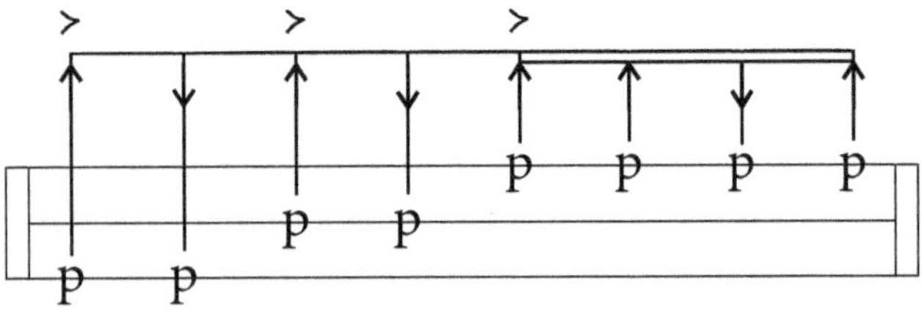

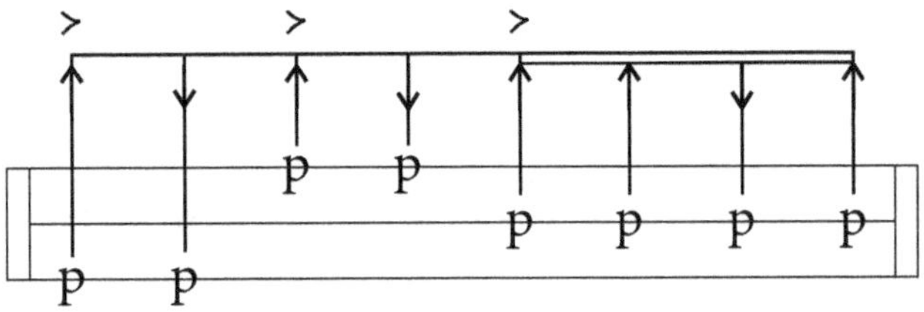

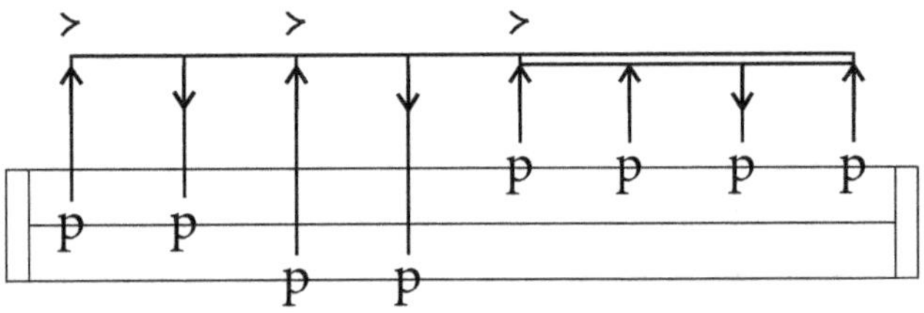

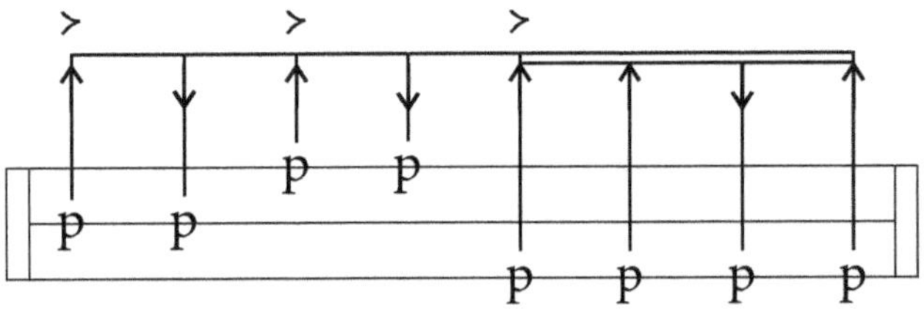

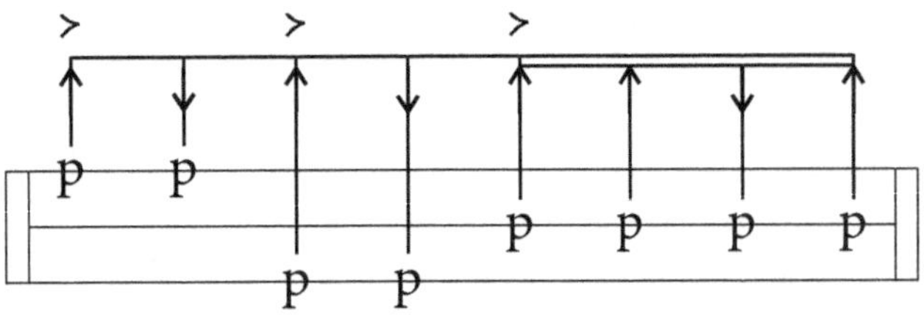

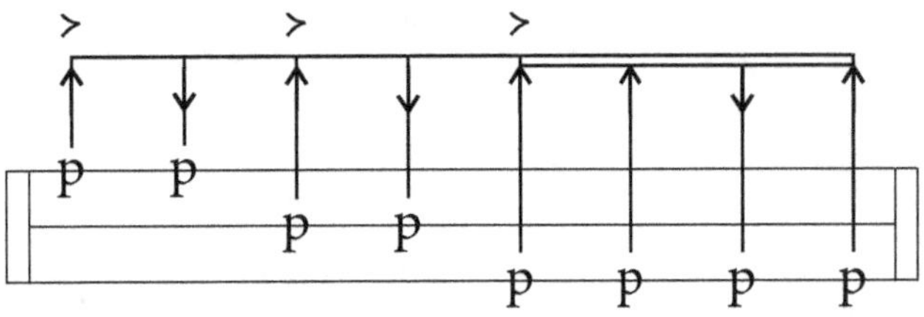

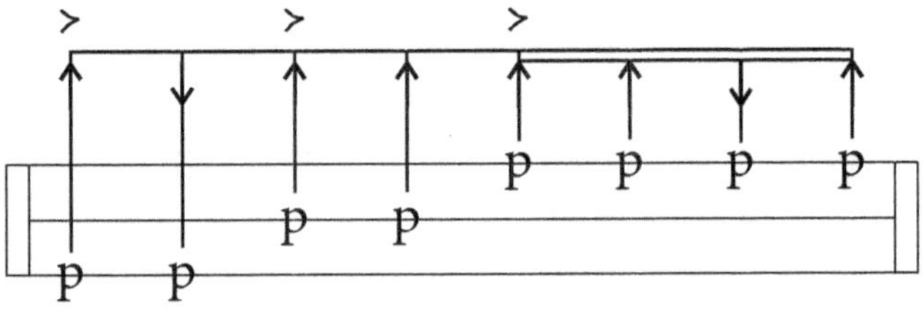

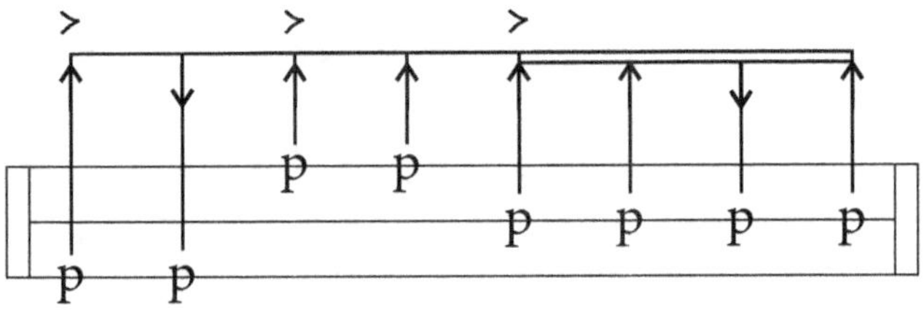

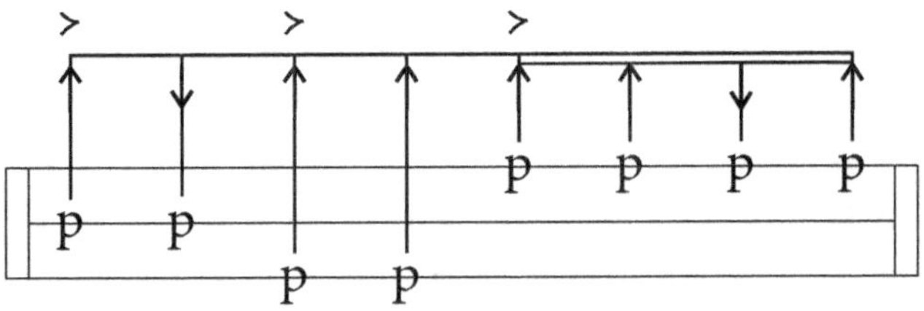

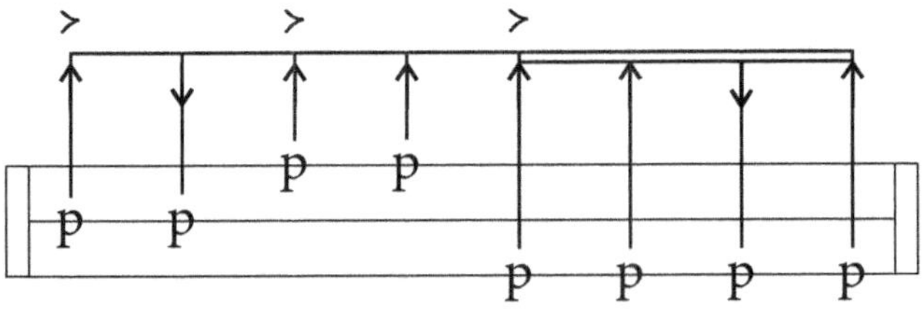

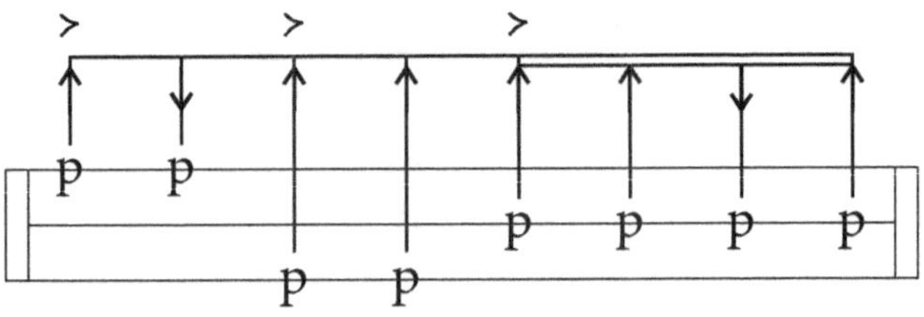

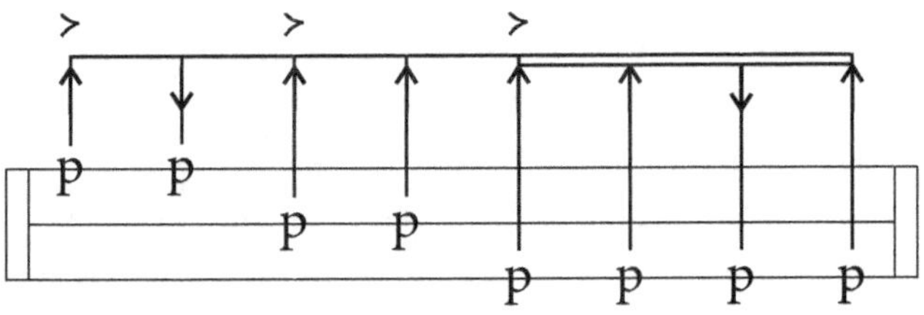

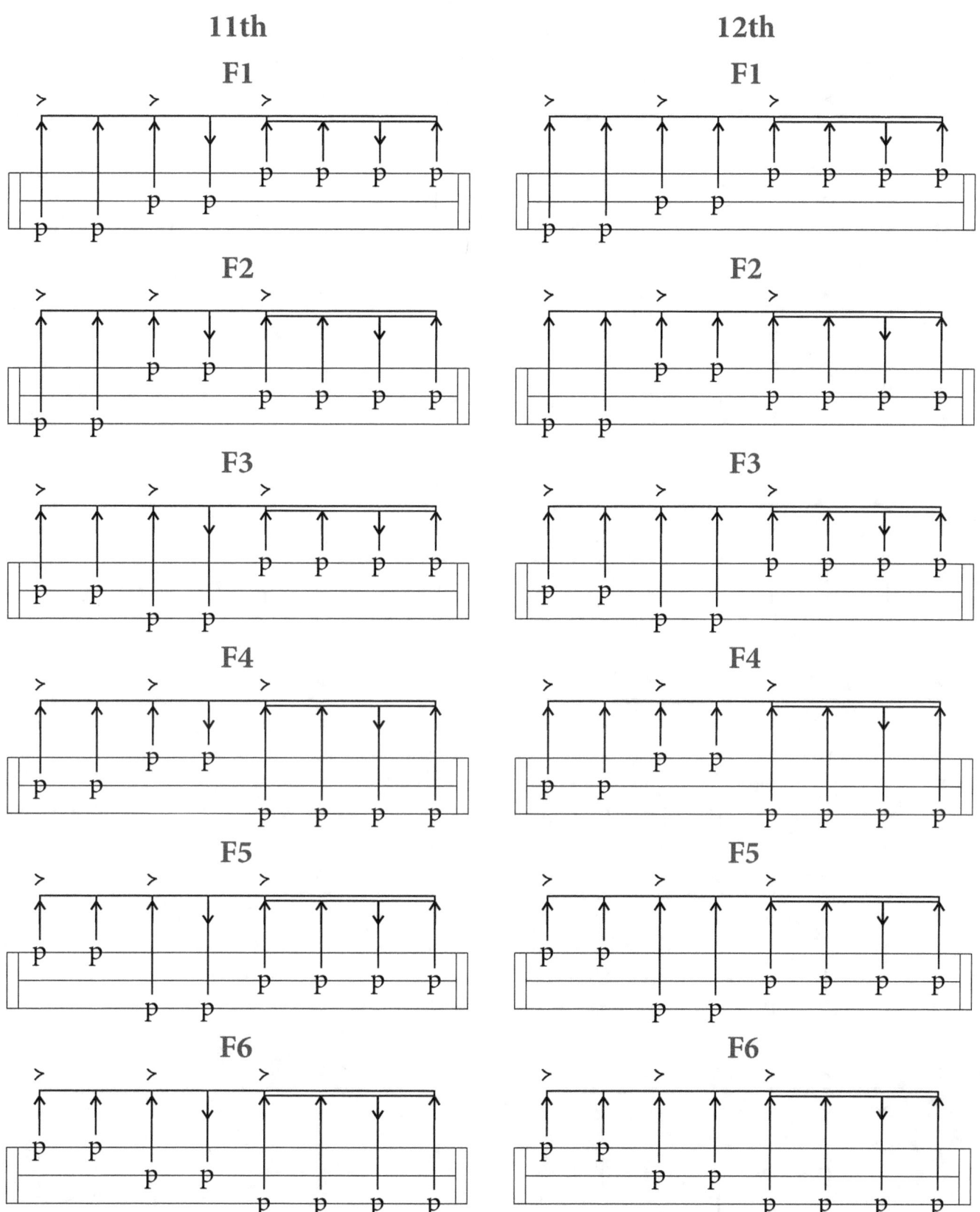

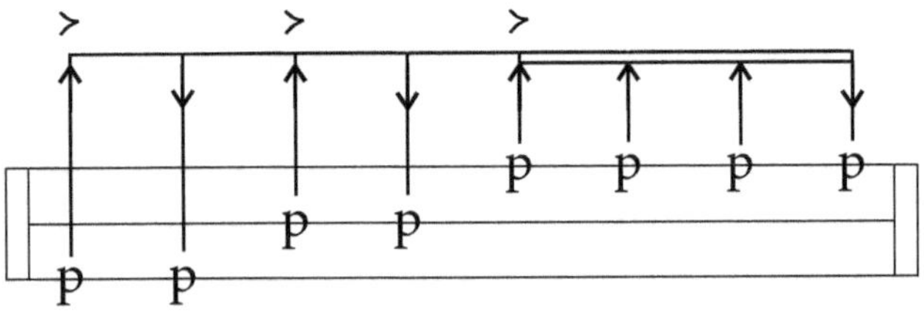

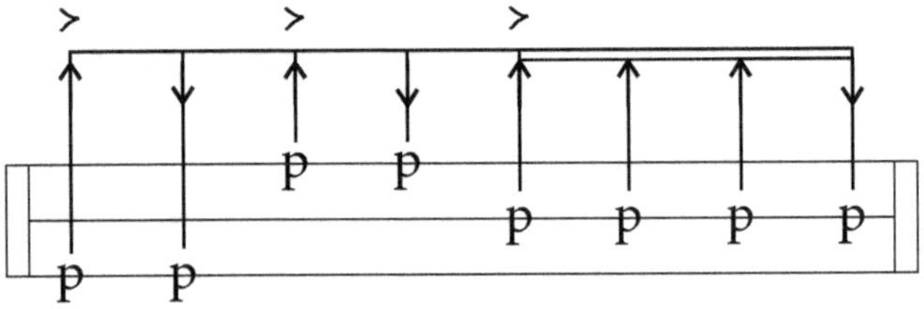

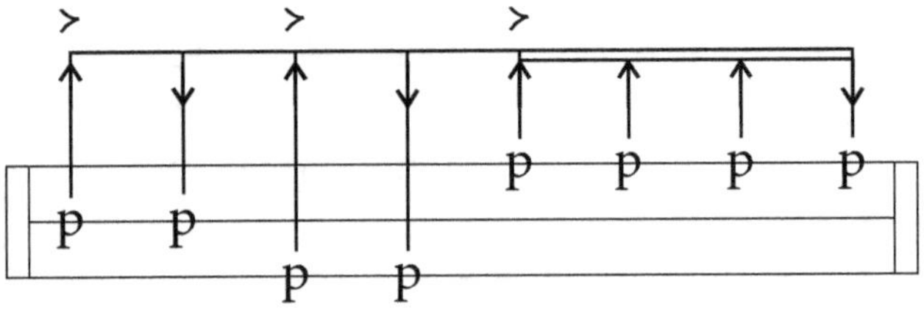

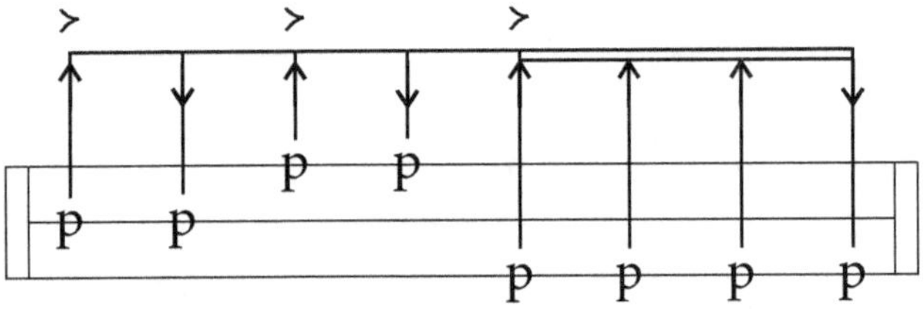

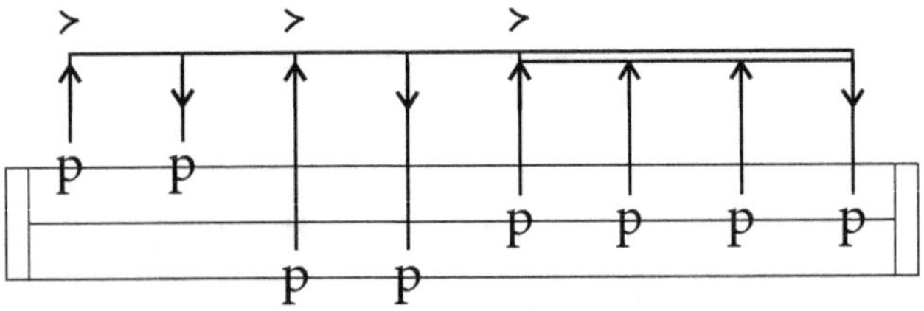

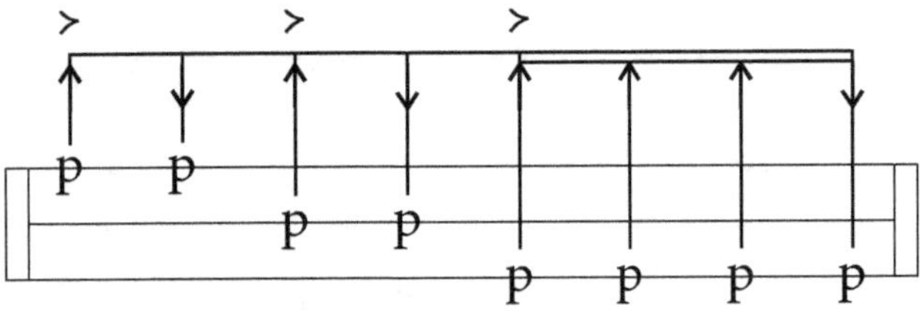

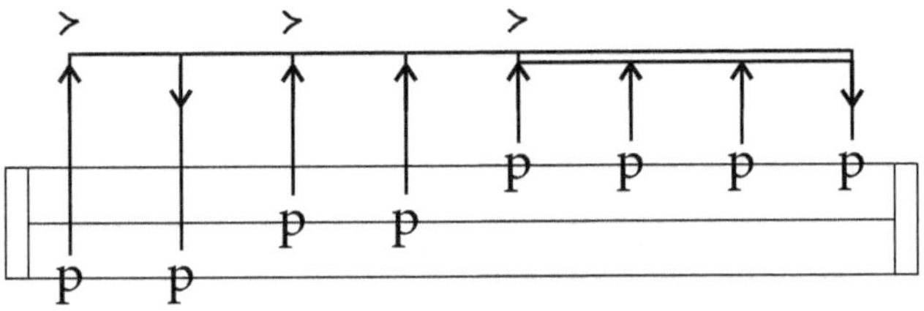

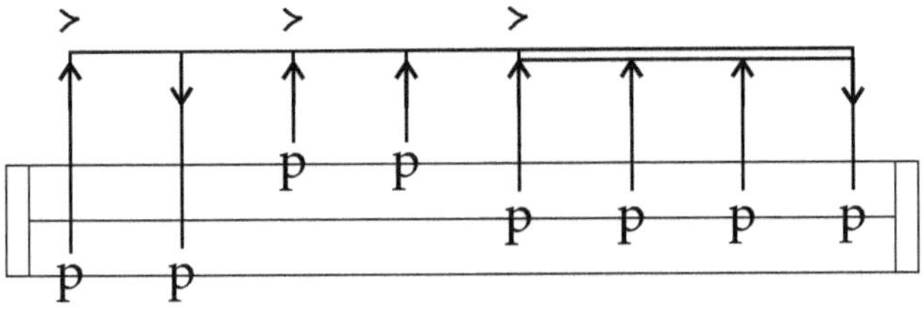

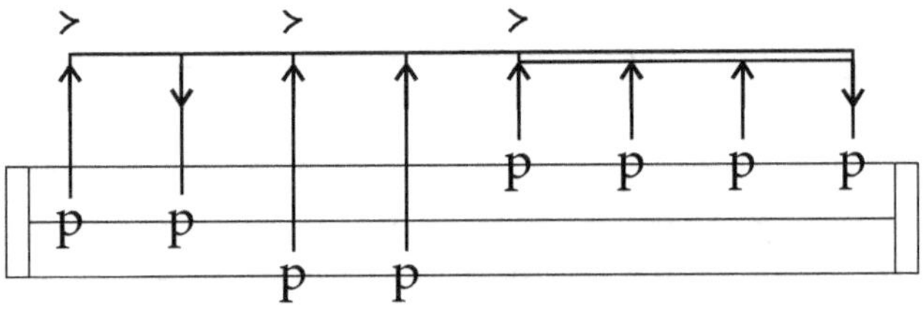

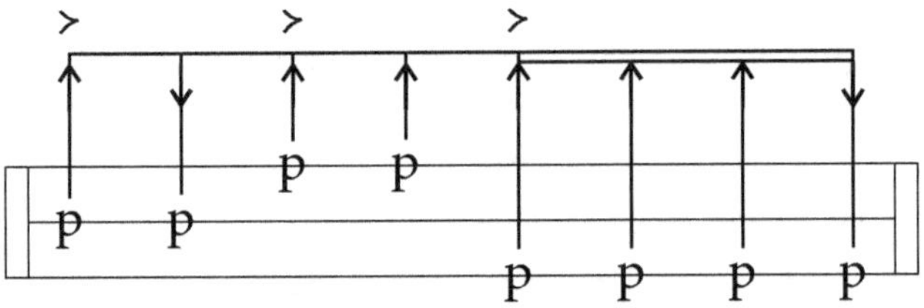

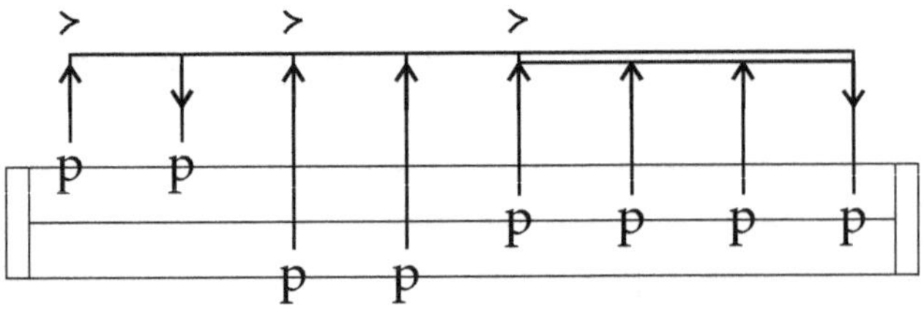

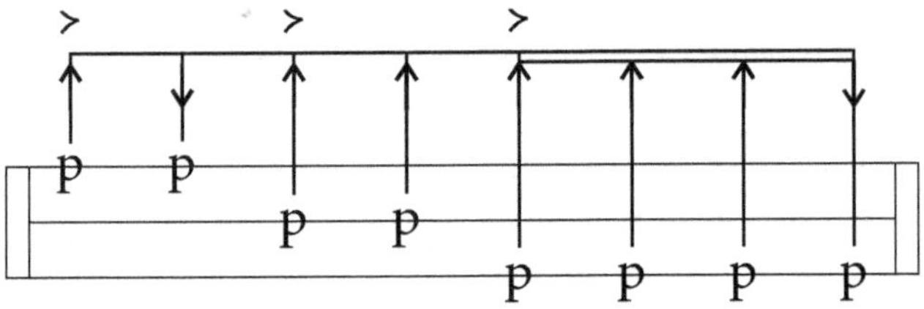

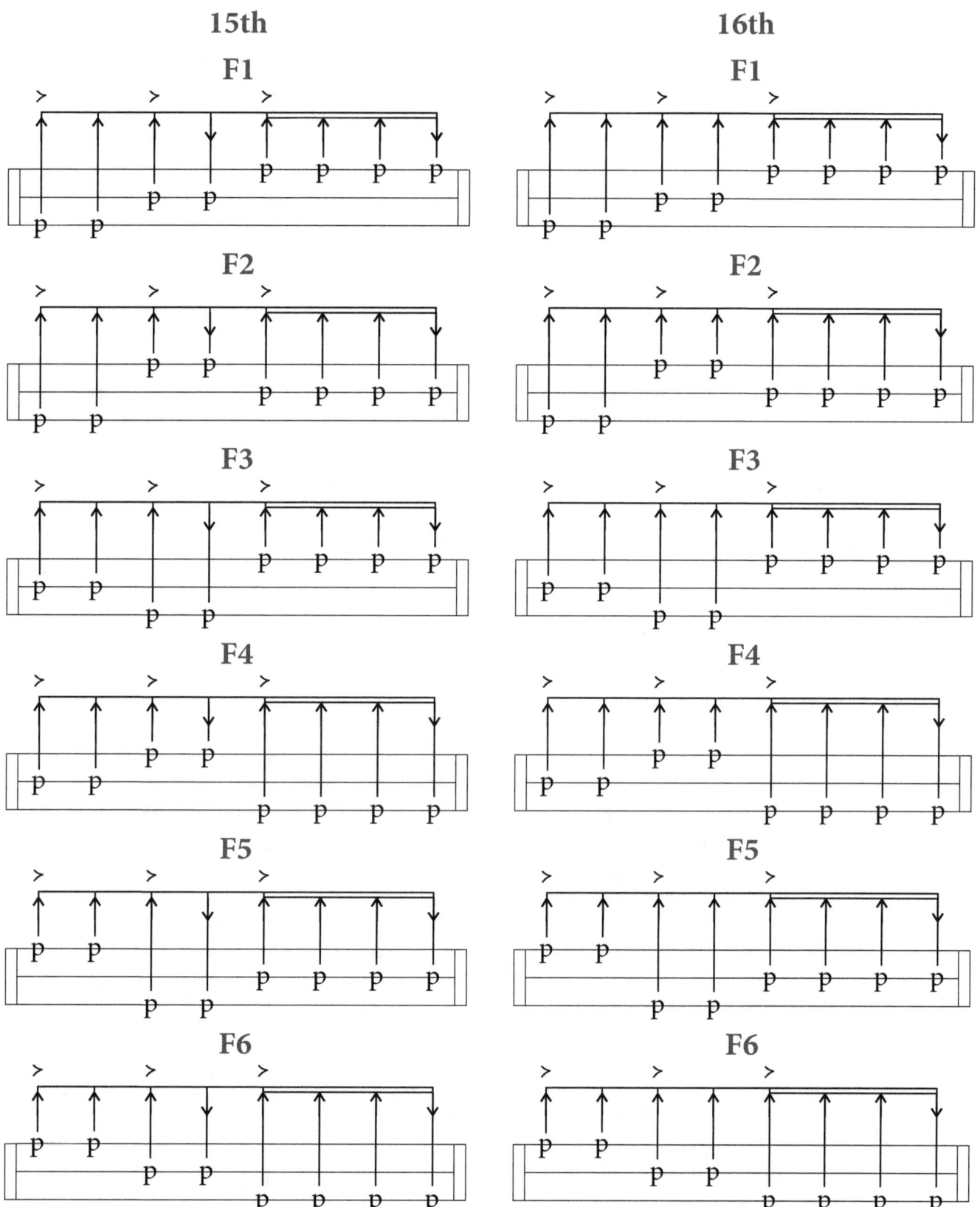

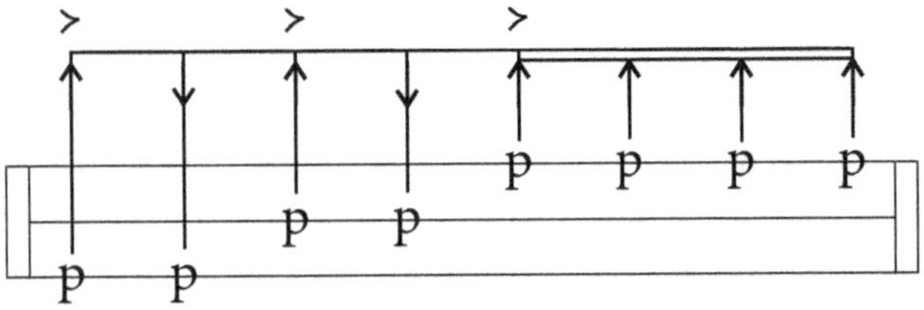

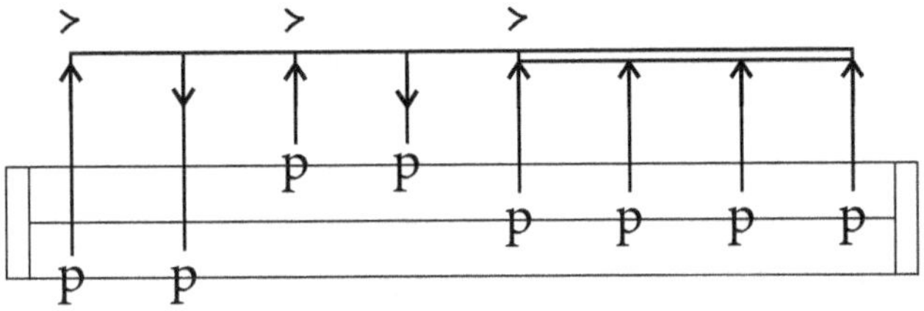

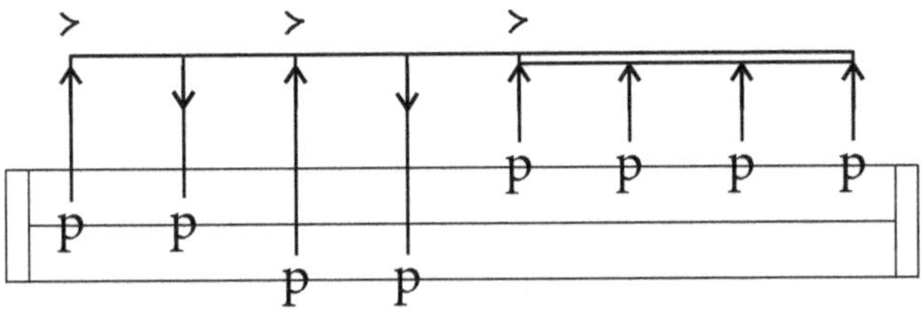

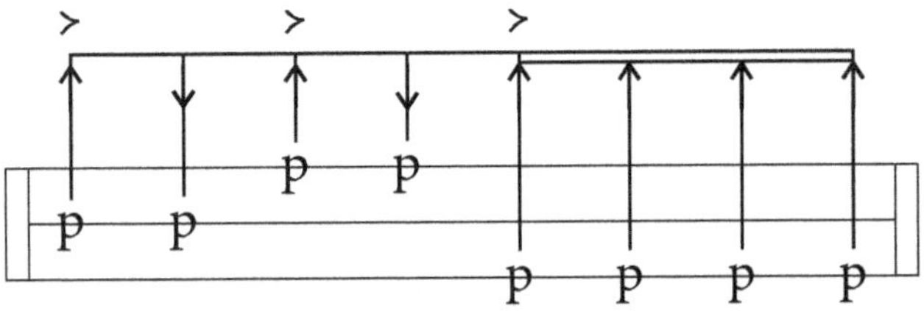

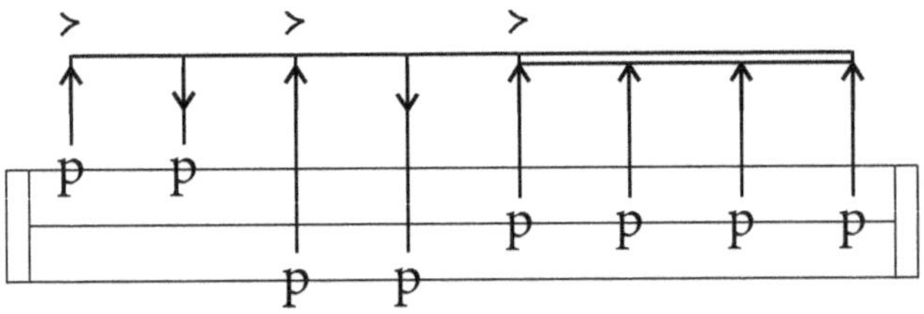

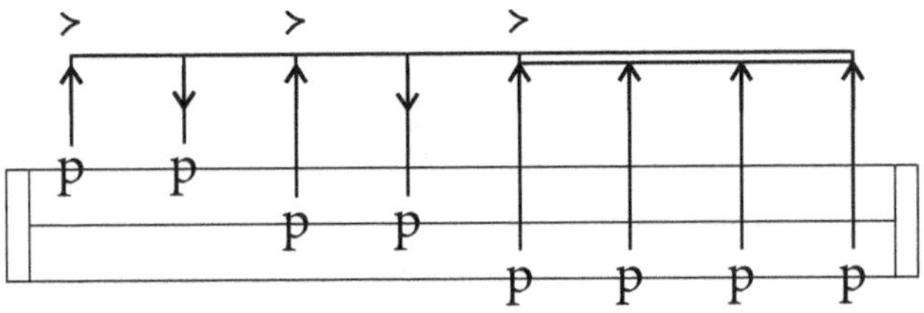

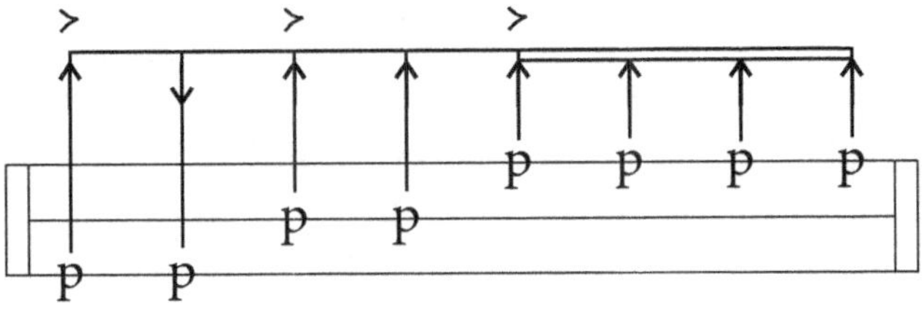

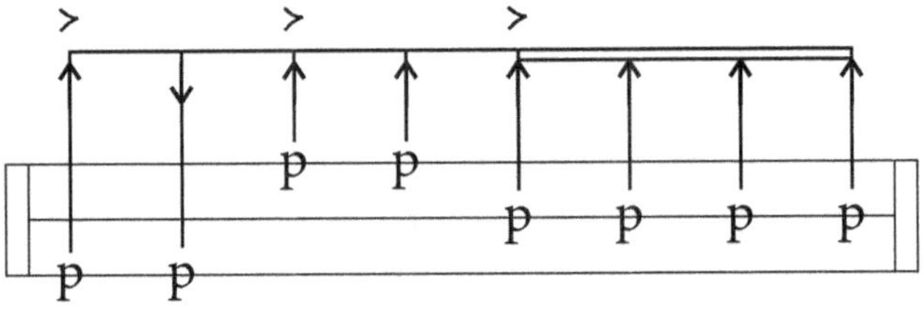

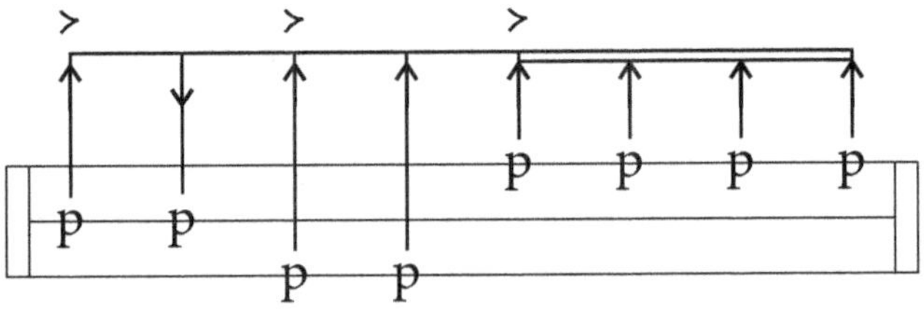

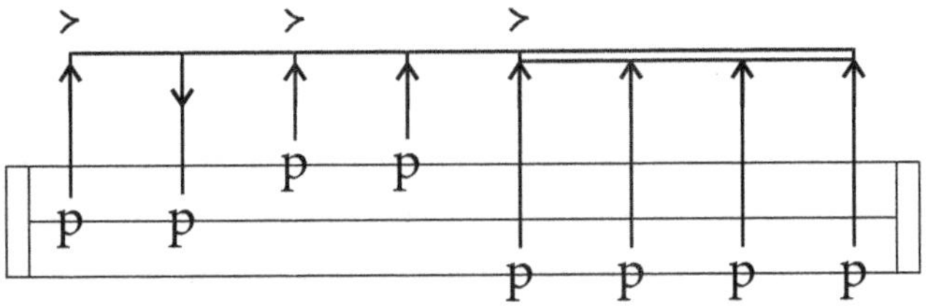

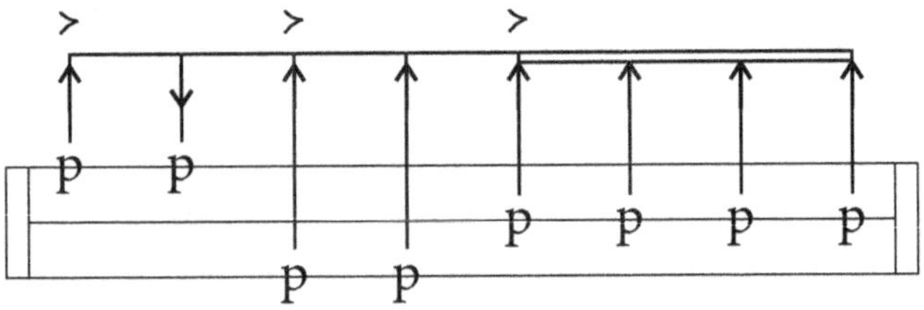

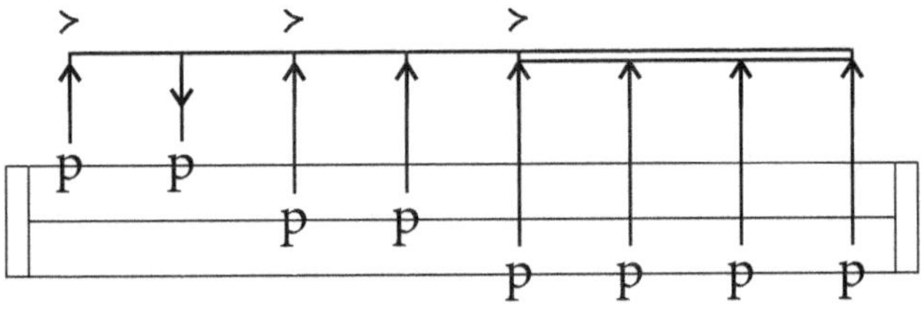

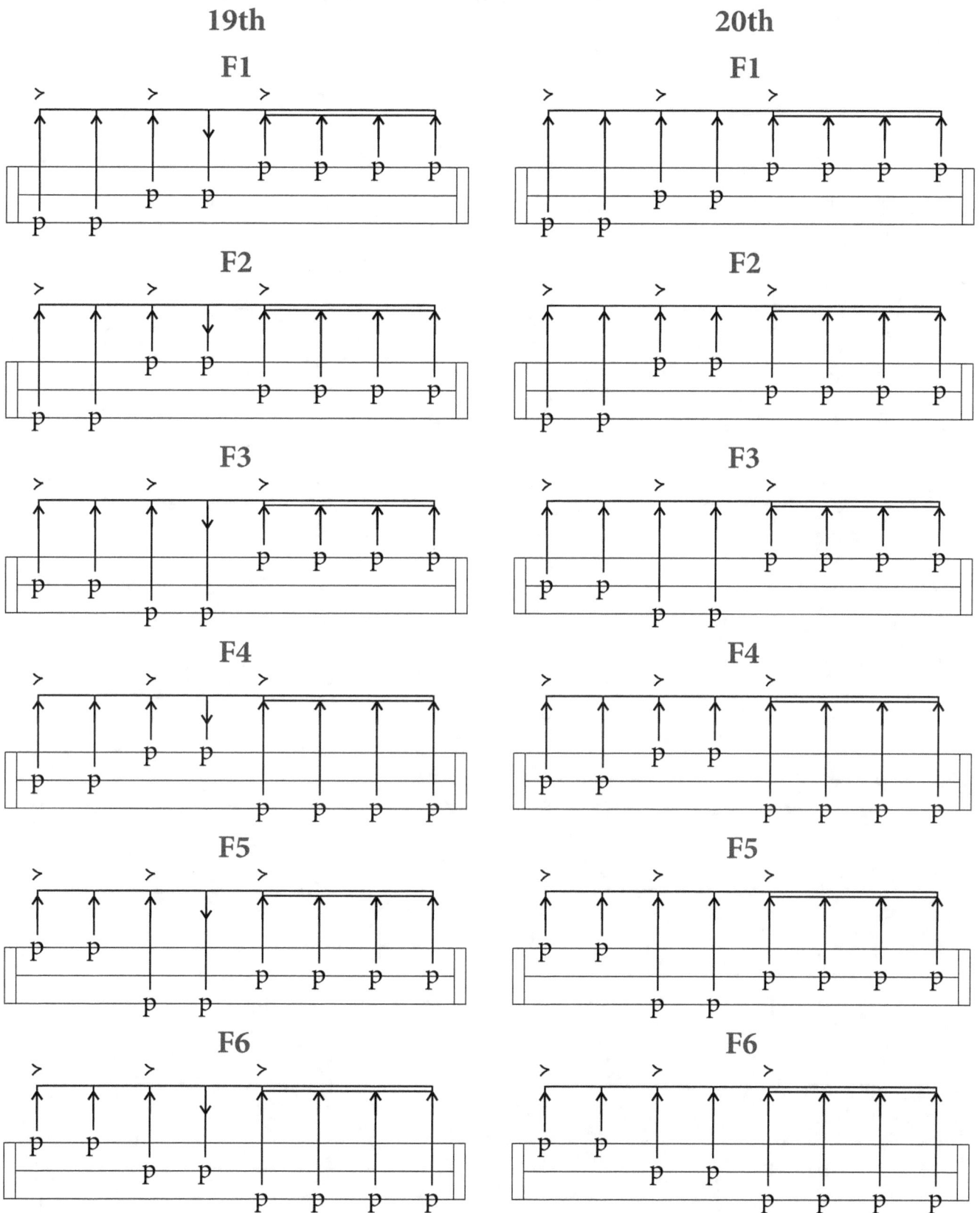

VARIATION II
WAYS OF PERFORMANCE

1st   **2nd**

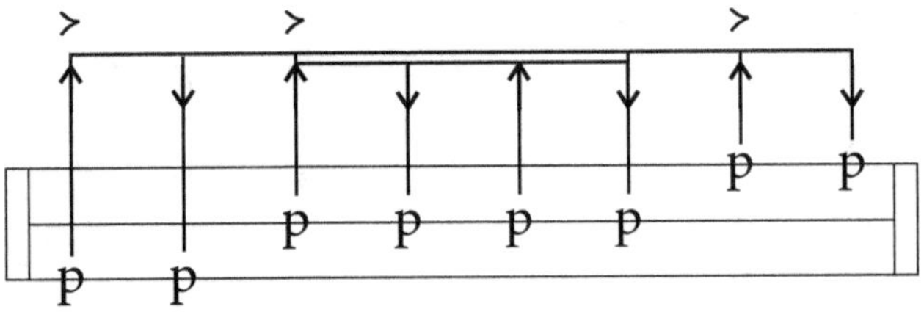

F1   F1

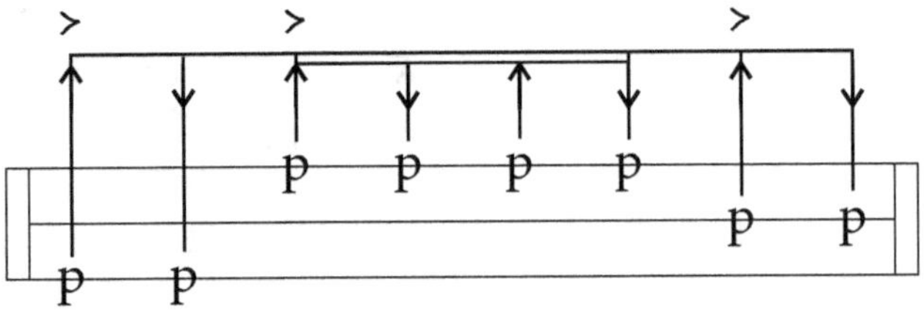

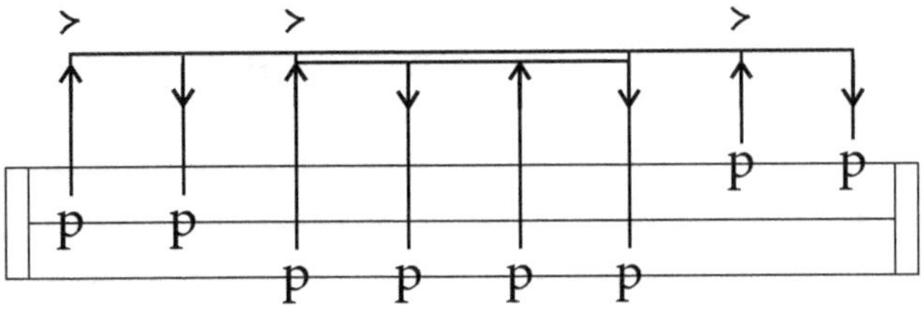

F2   F2

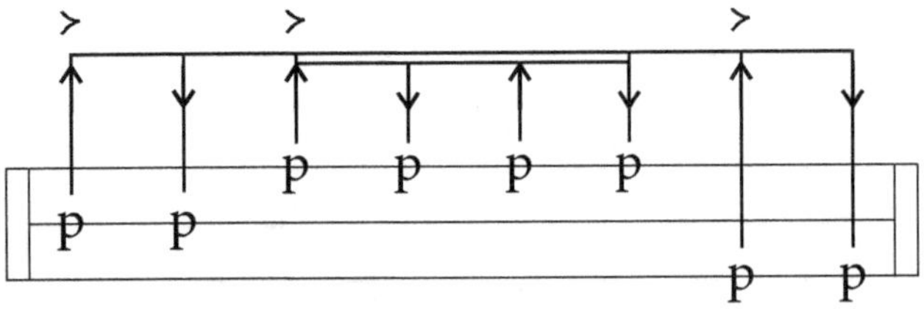

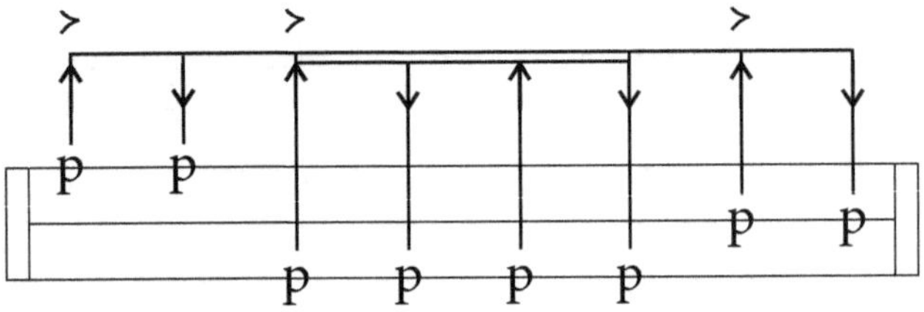

F3   F3

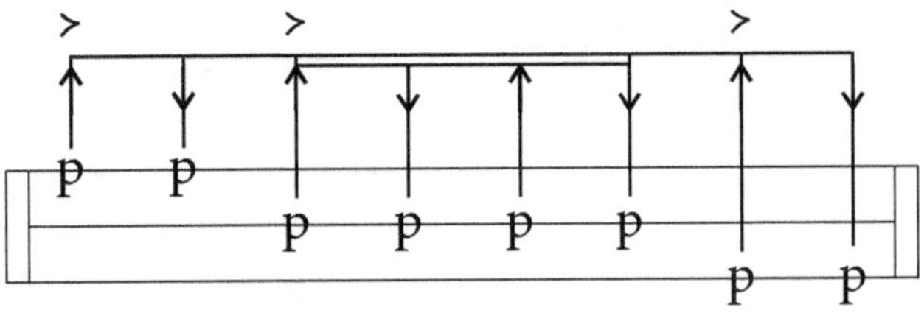

F4   F4

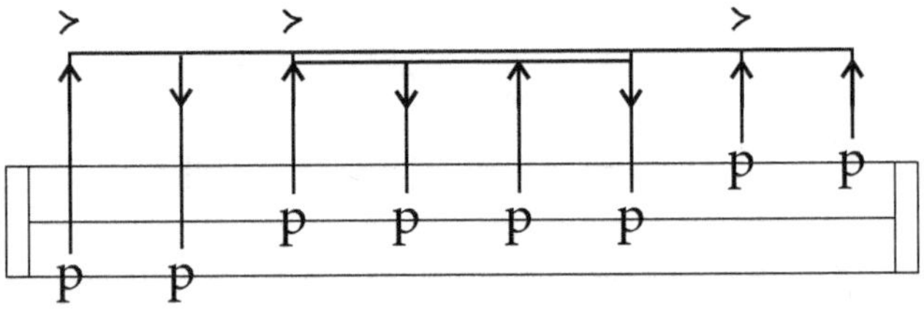

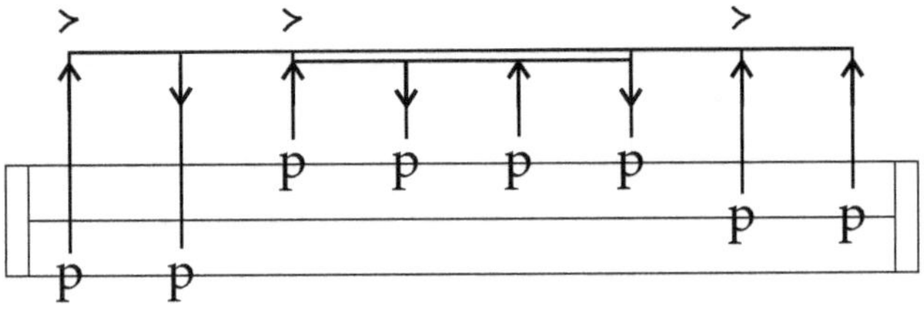

F5   F5

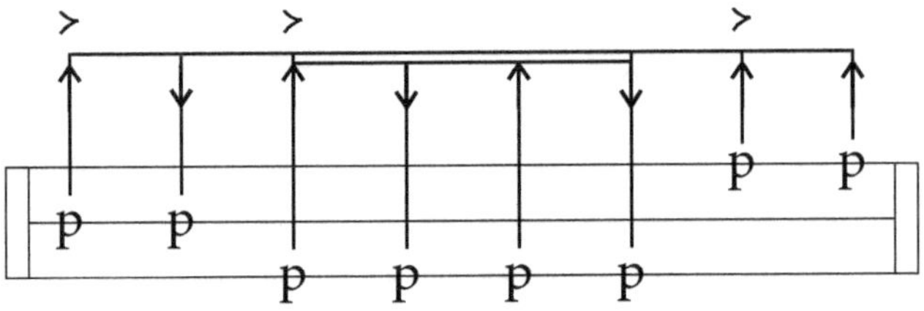

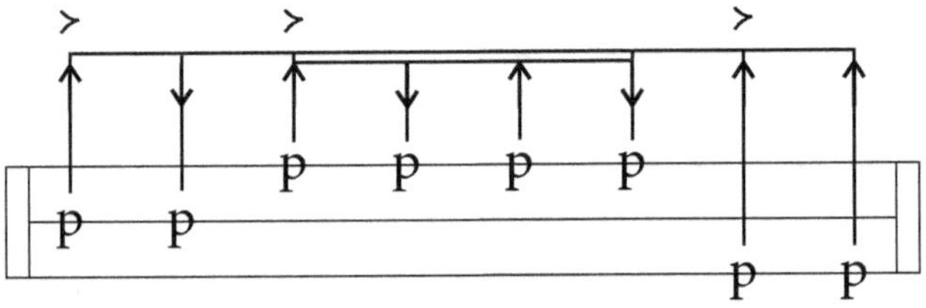

F6   F6

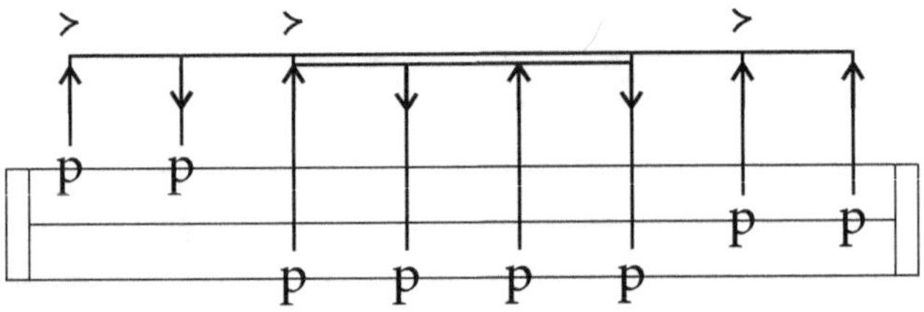

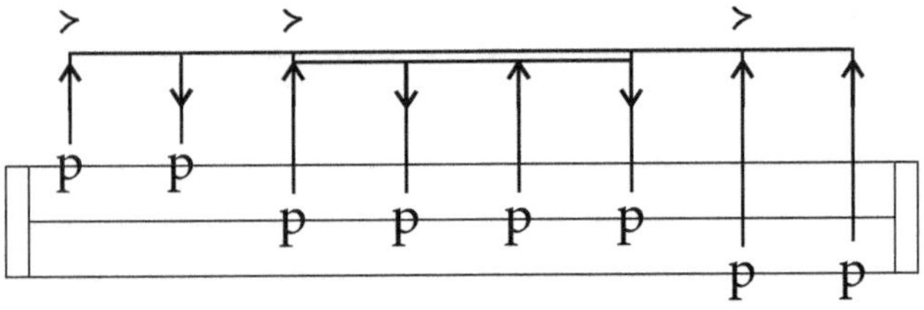

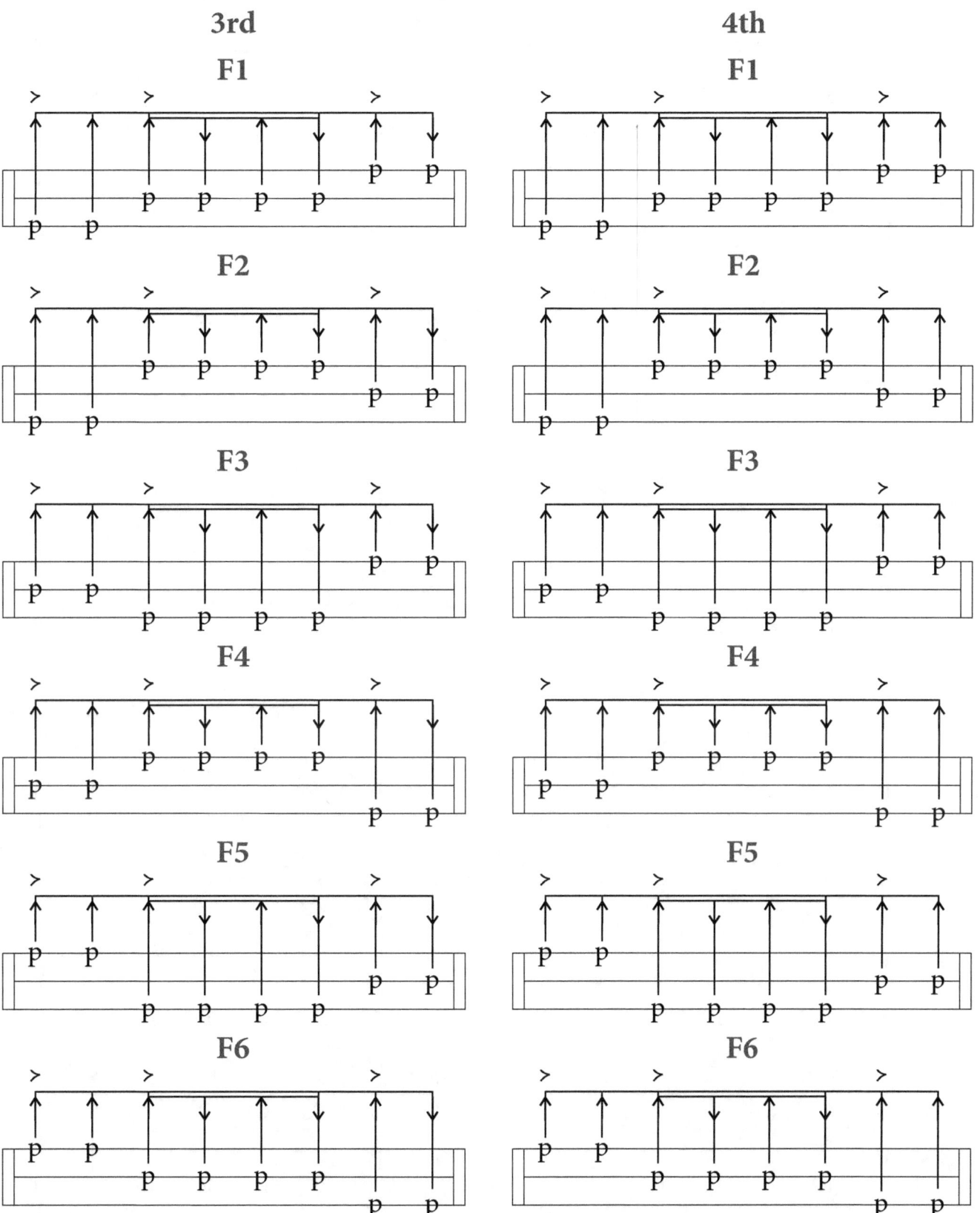

5th

F1

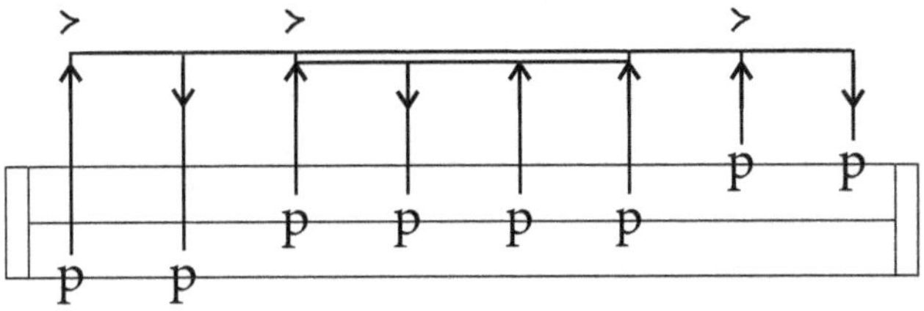

F2

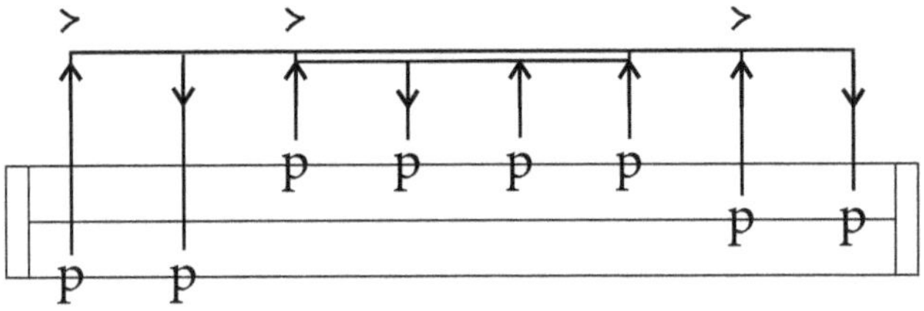

F3

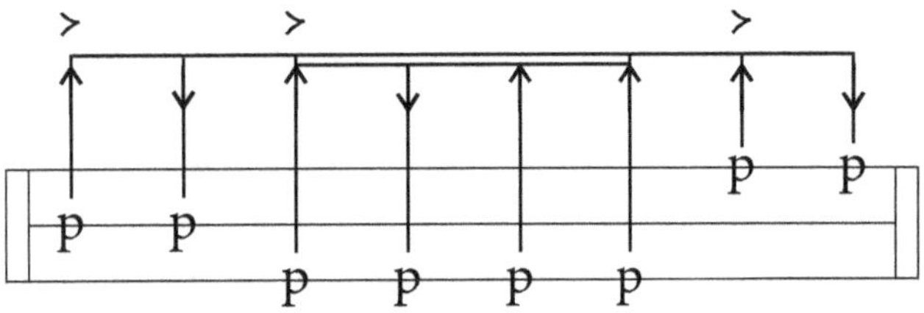

F4

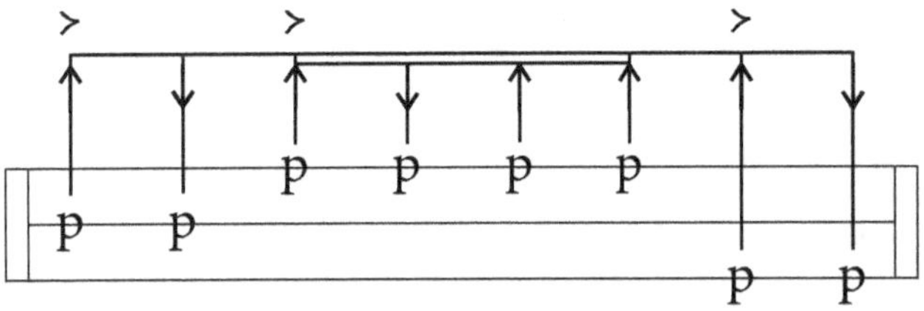

F5

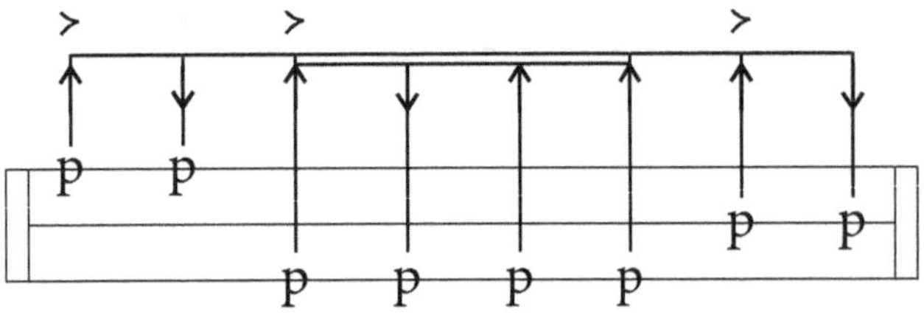

F6

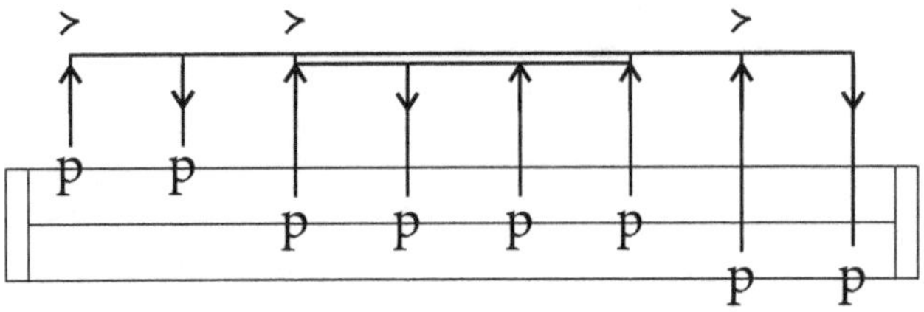

6th

F1

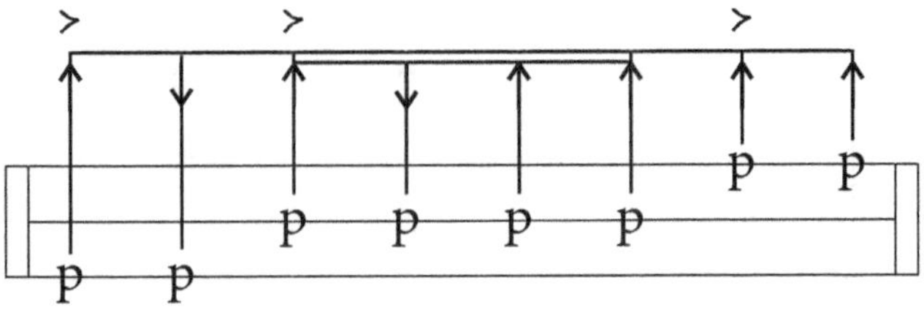

F2

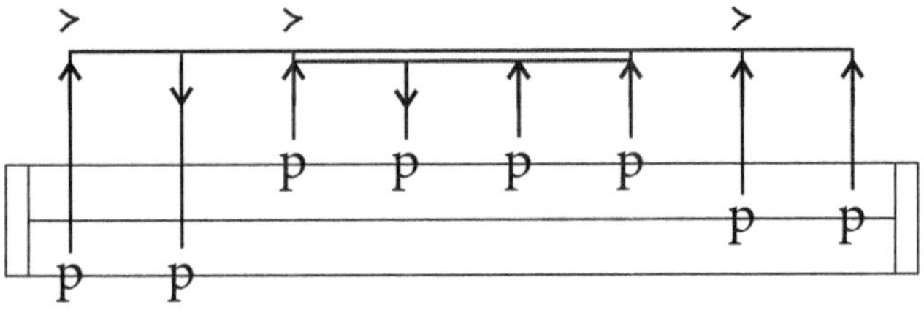

F3

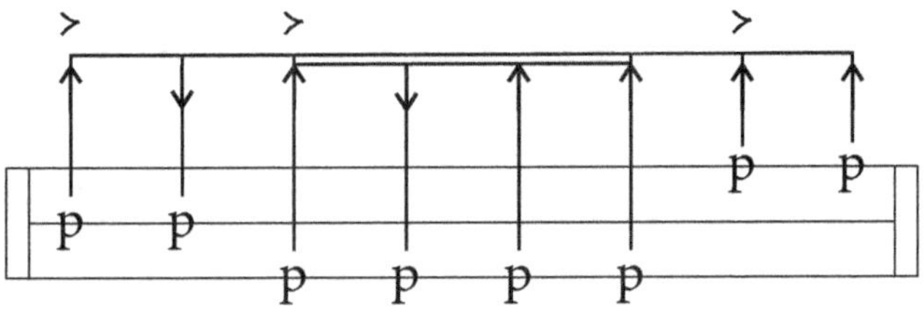

F4

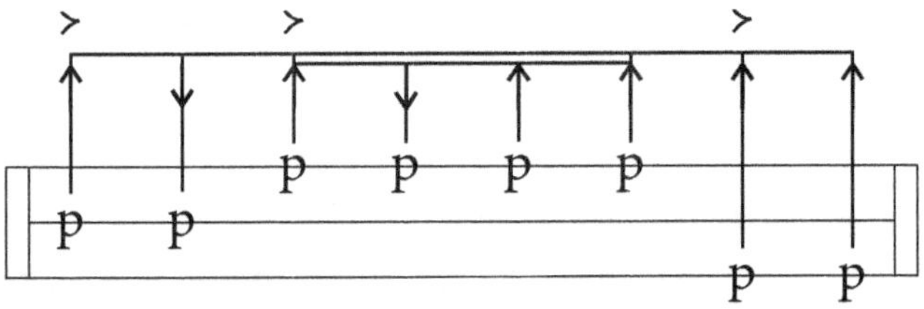

F5

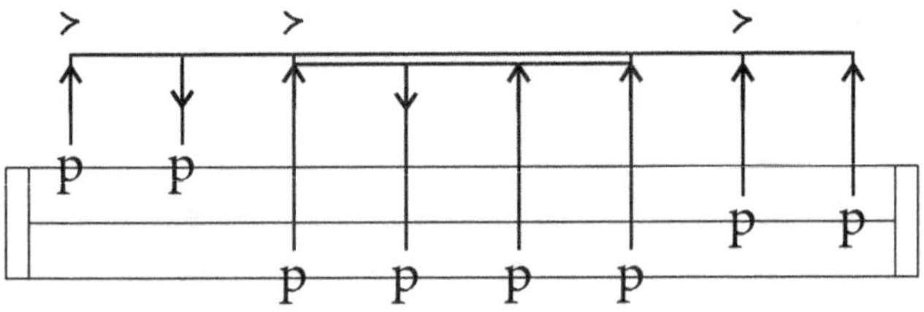

F6

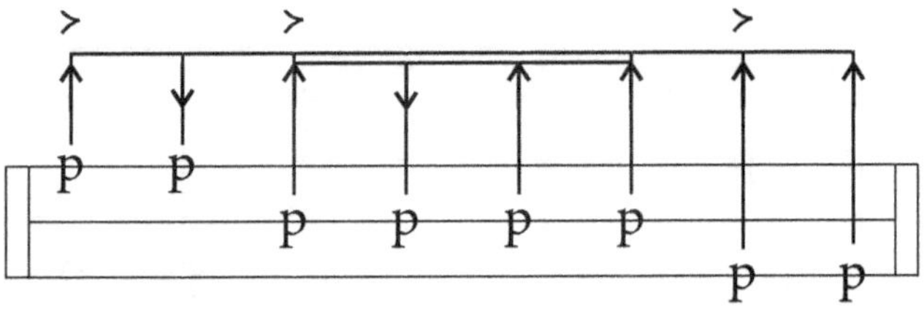

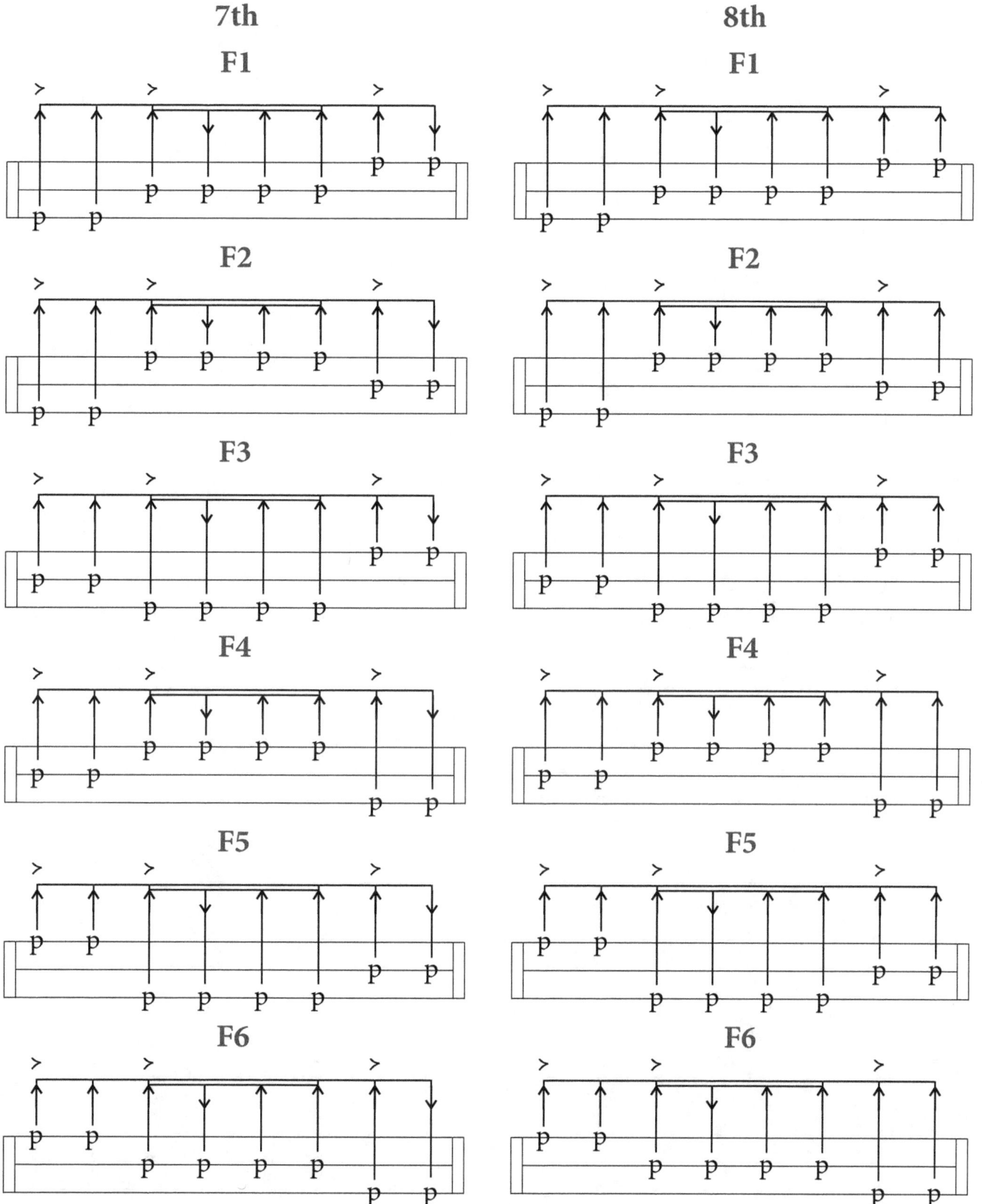

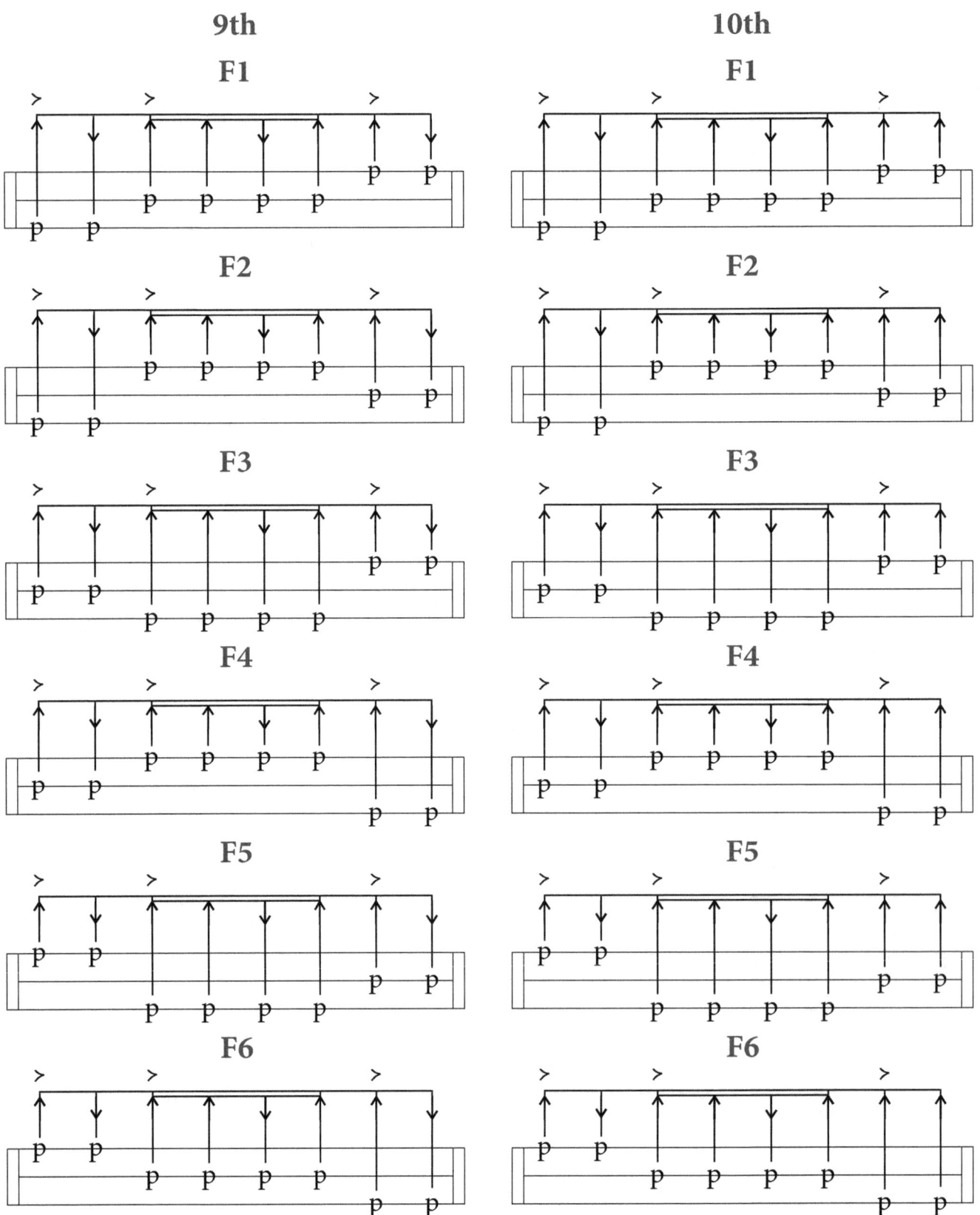

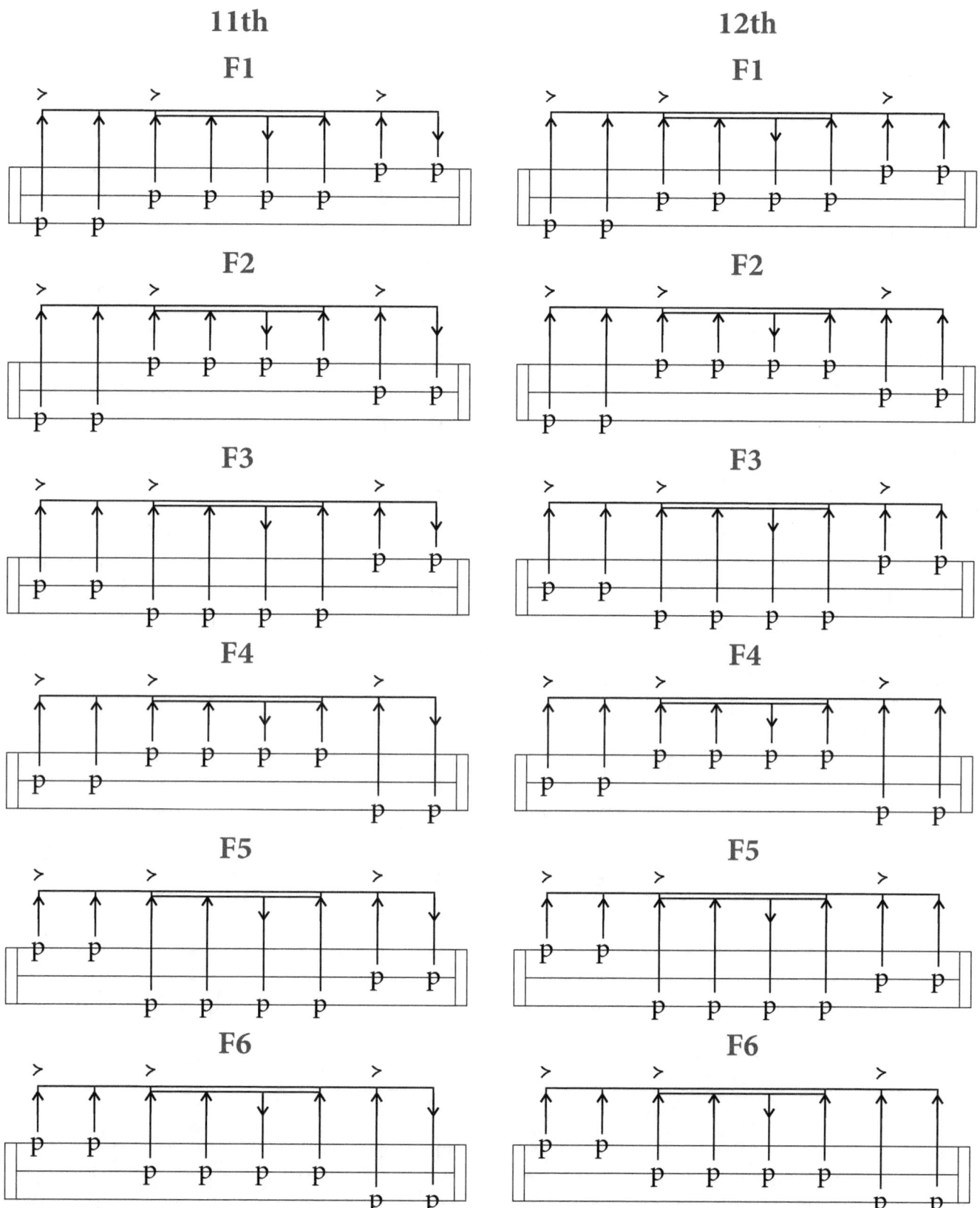

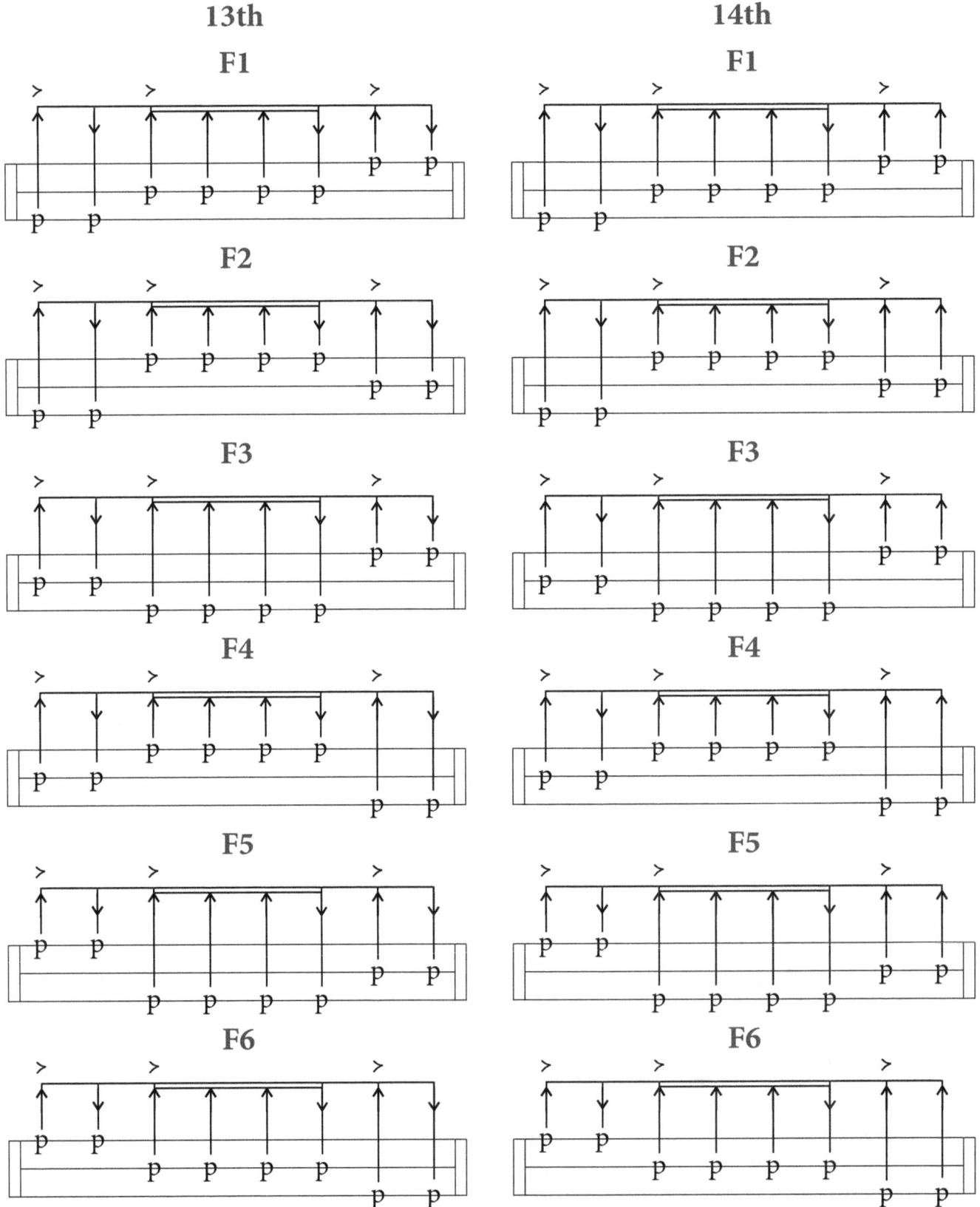

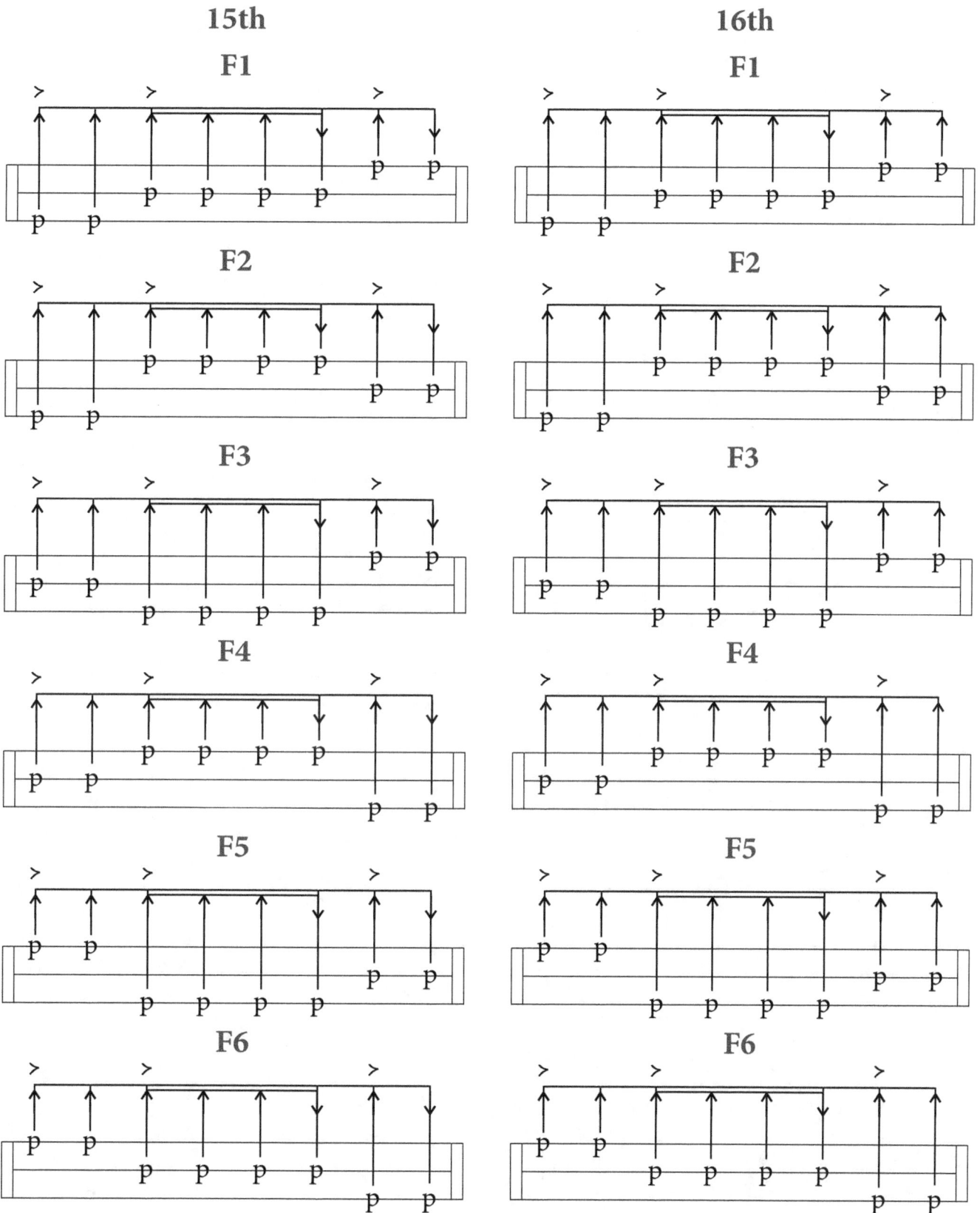

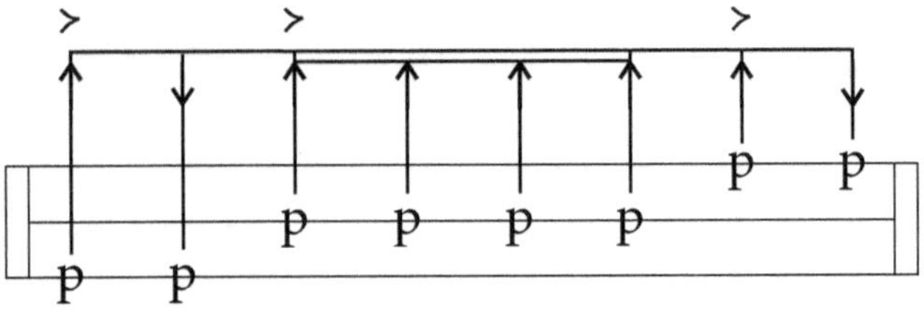

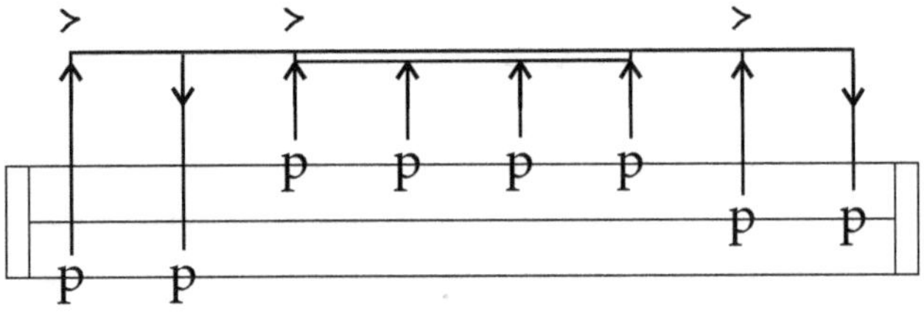

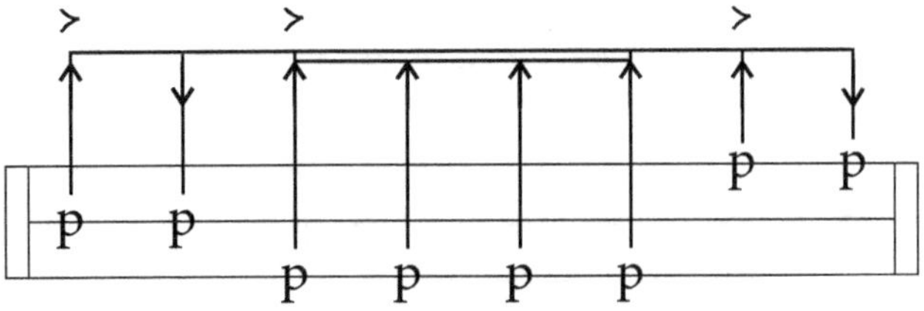

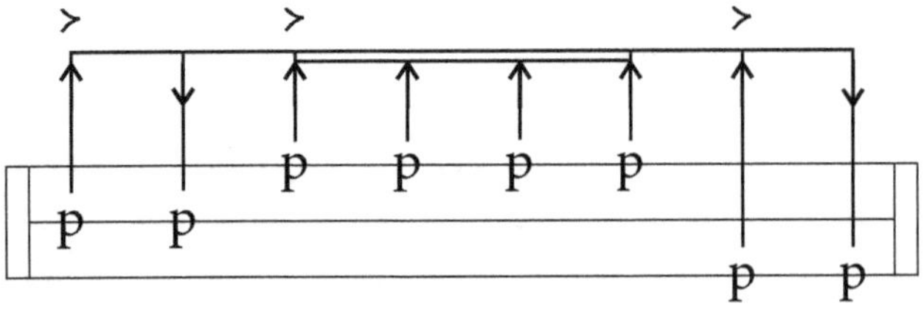

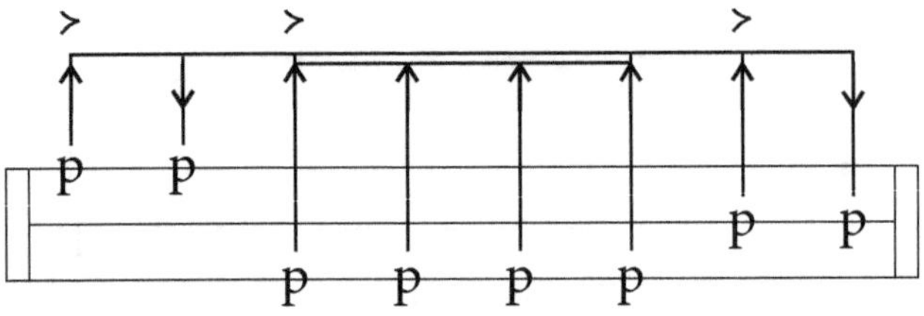

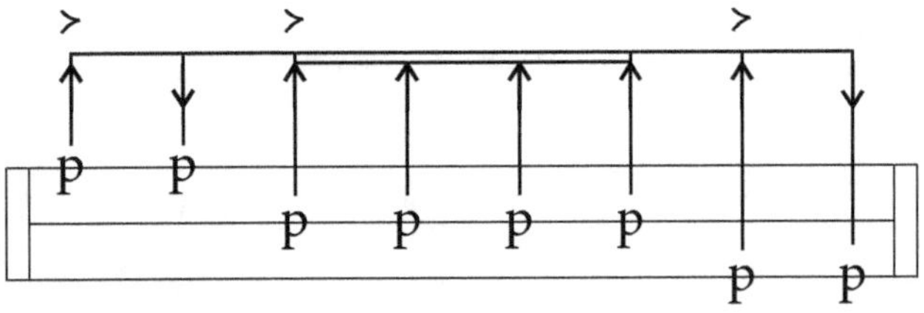

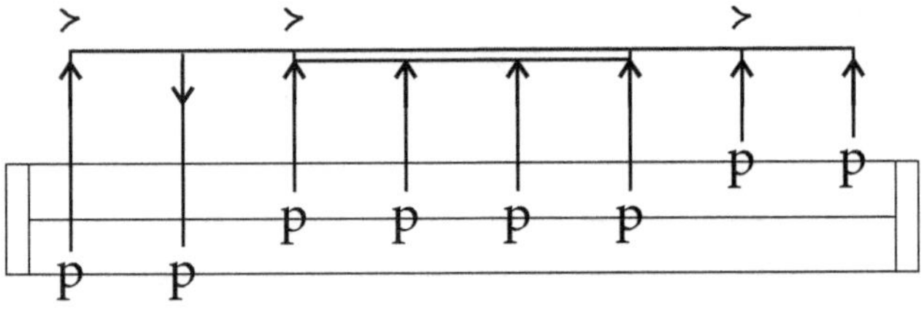

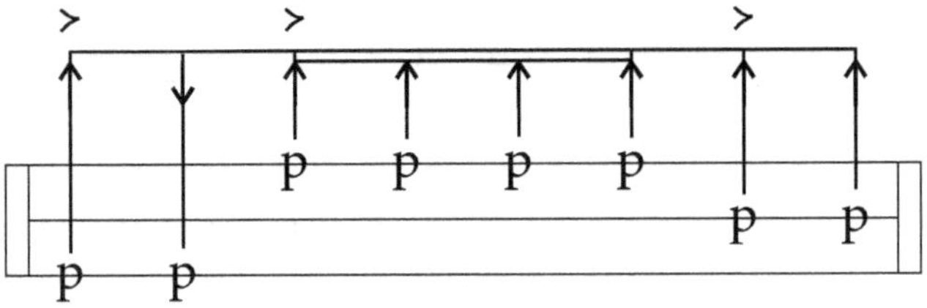

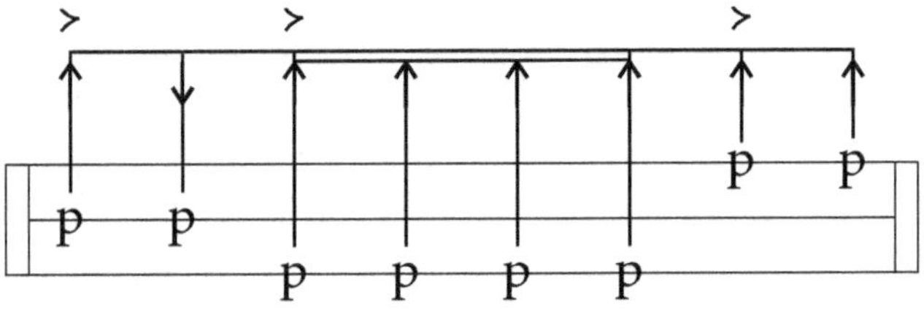

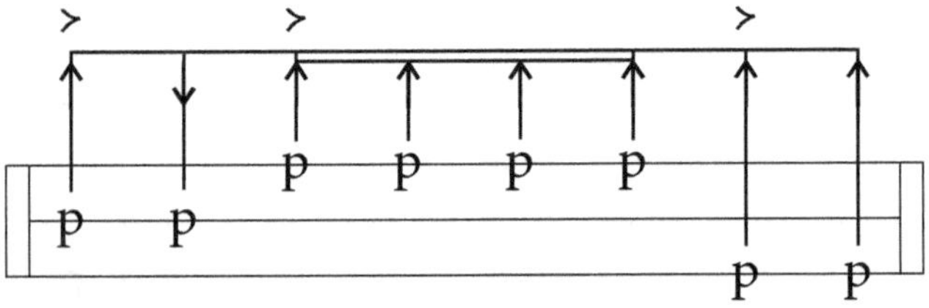

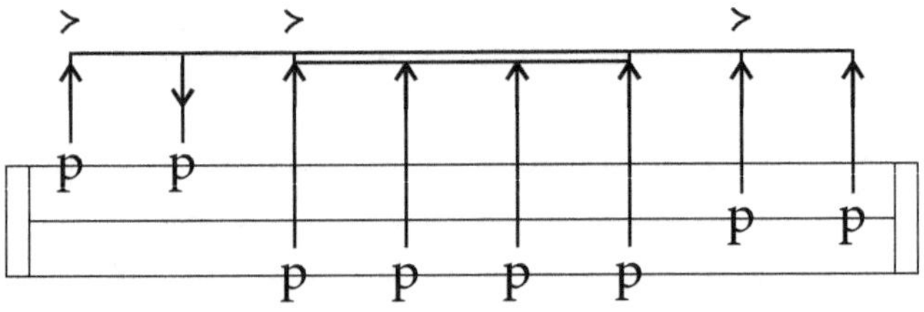

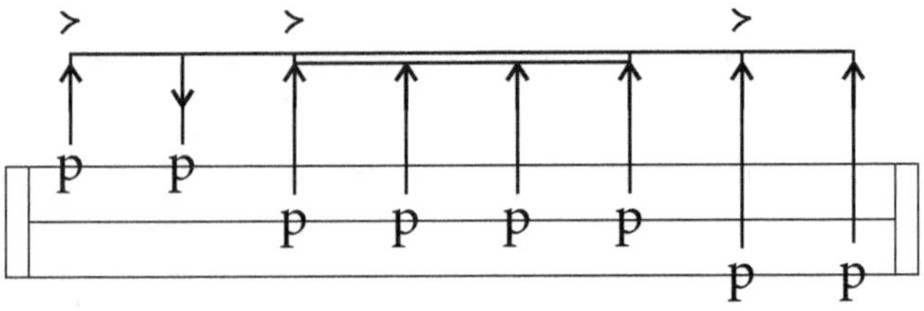

19th

F1
F2
F3
F4
F5
F6

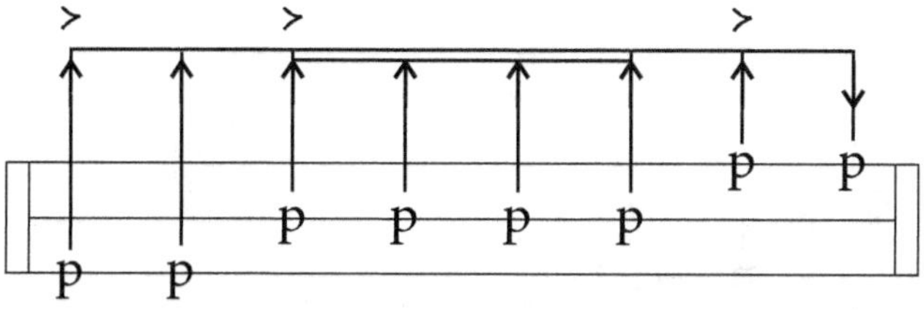

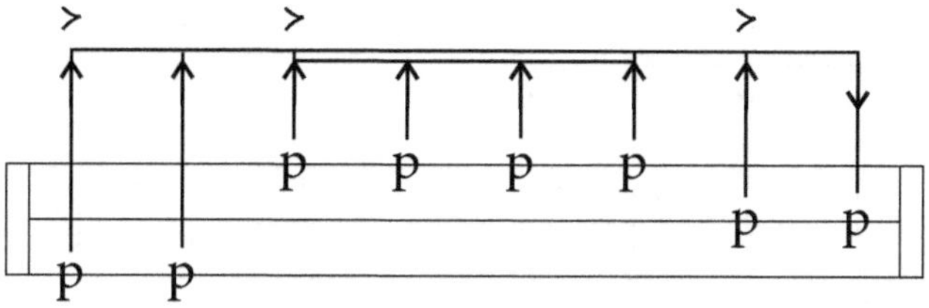

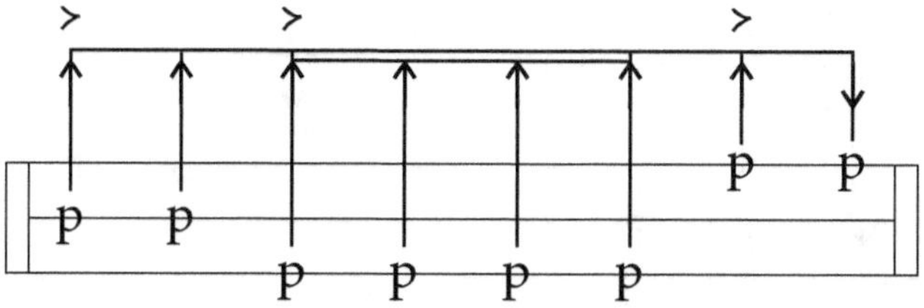

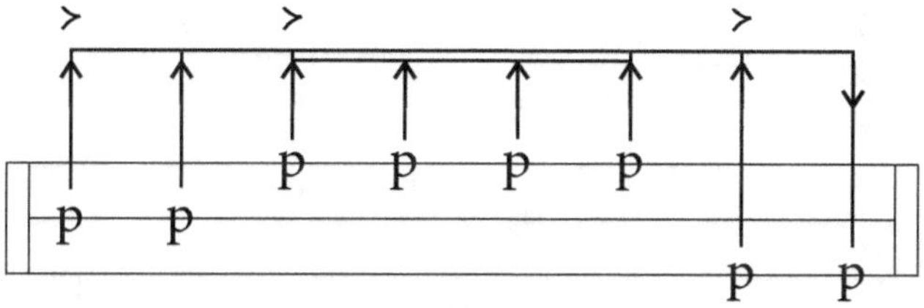

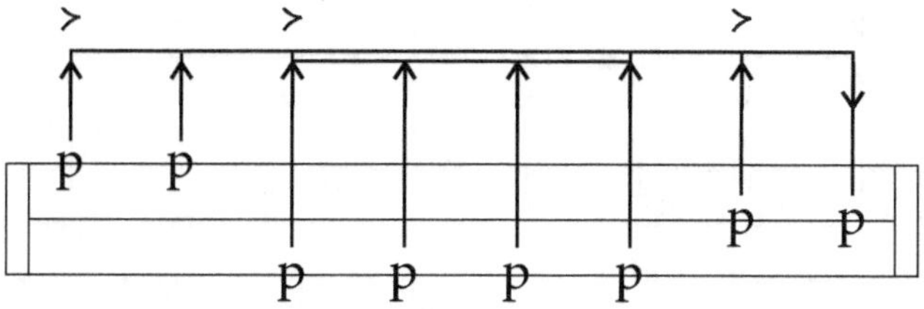

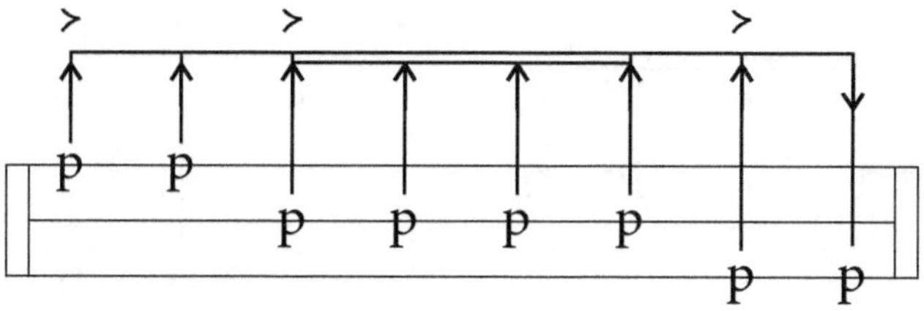

20th

F1
F2
F3
F4
F5
F6

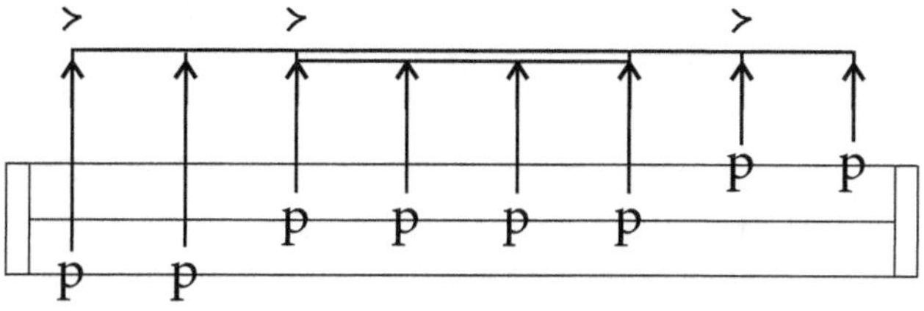

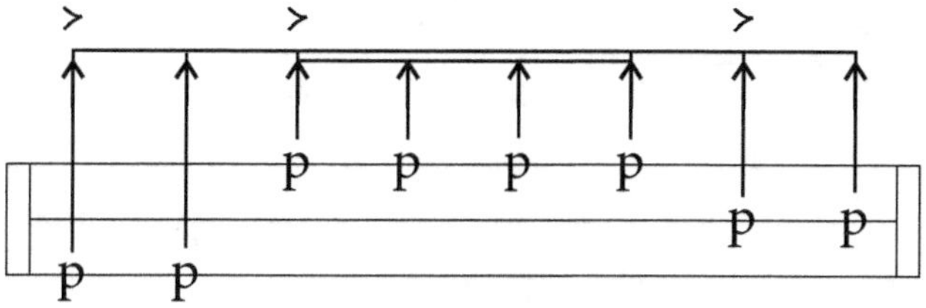

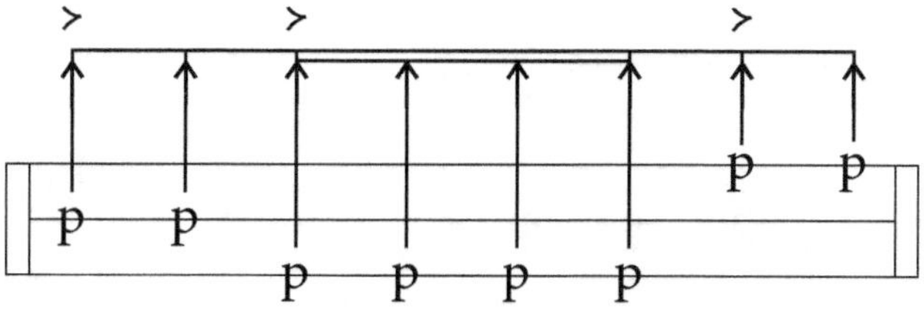

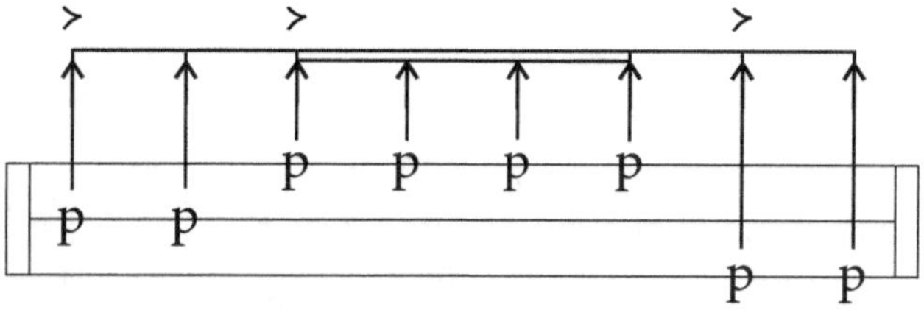

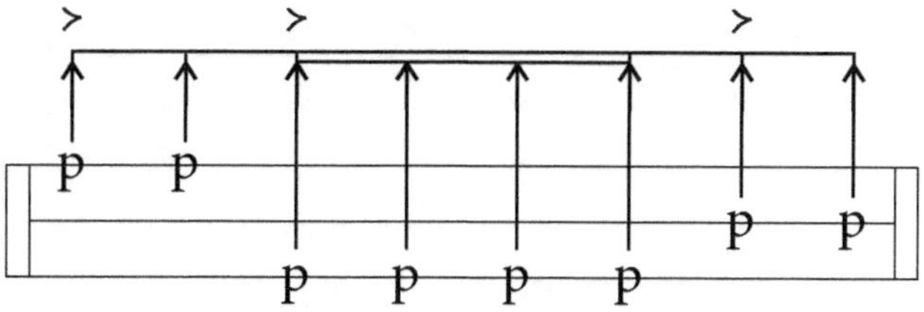

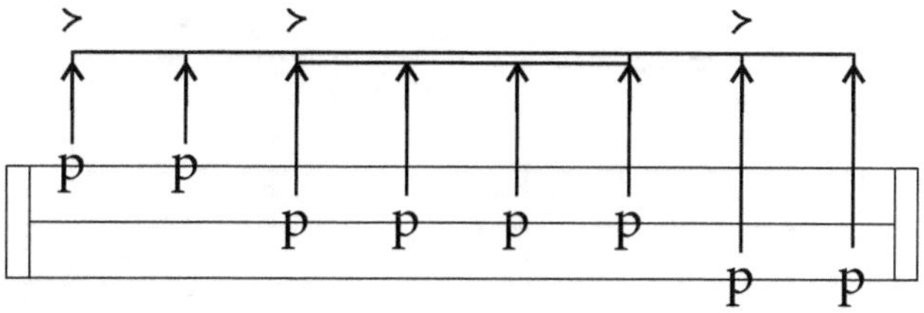

VARIATION III

WAYS OF PERFORMANCE

1st

F1

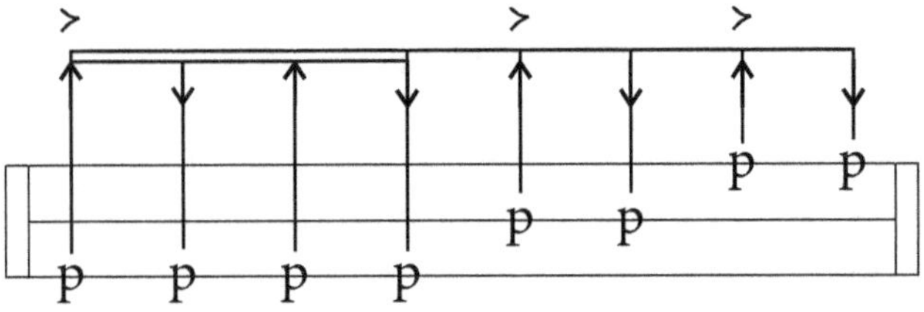

F2

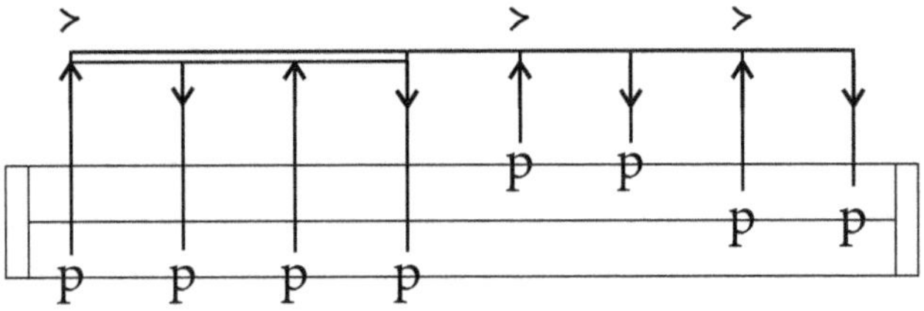

F3

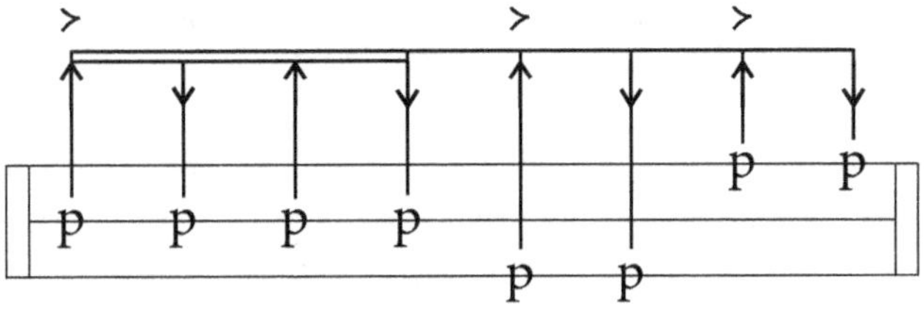

F4

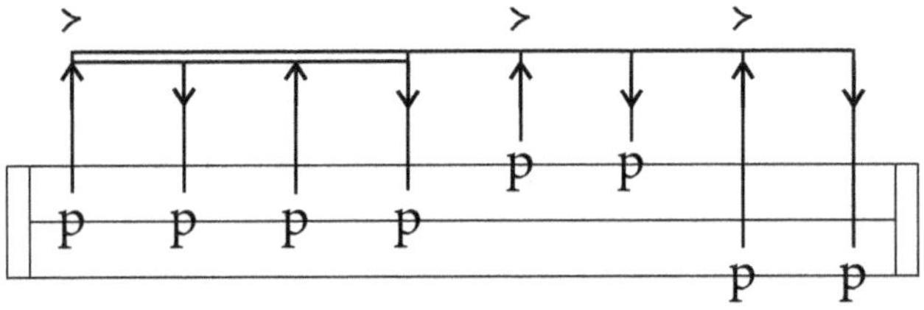

F5

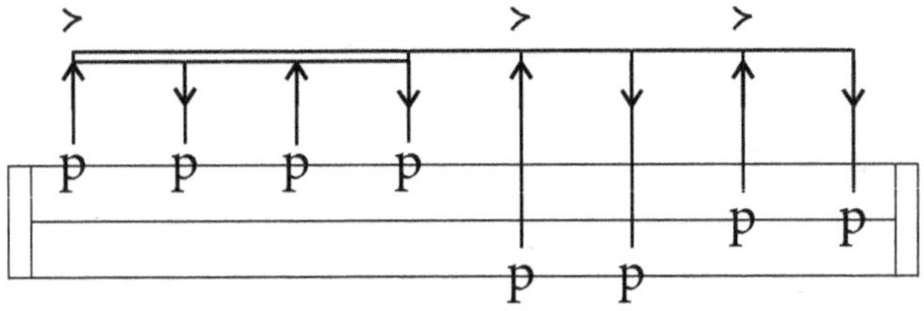

F6

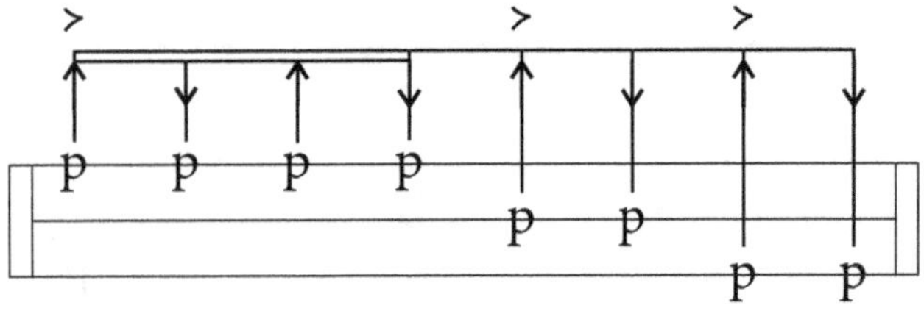

2nd

F1

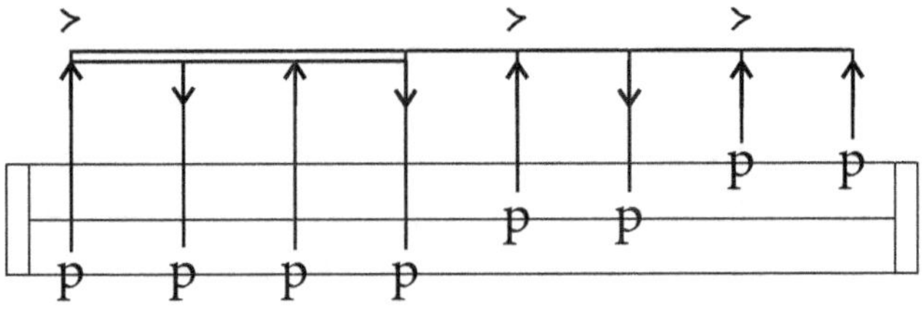

F2

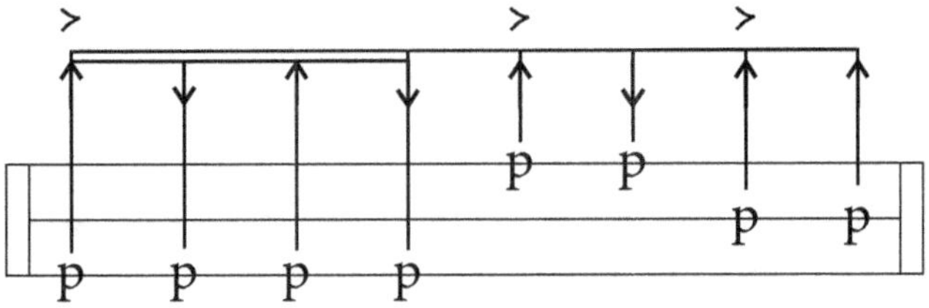

F3

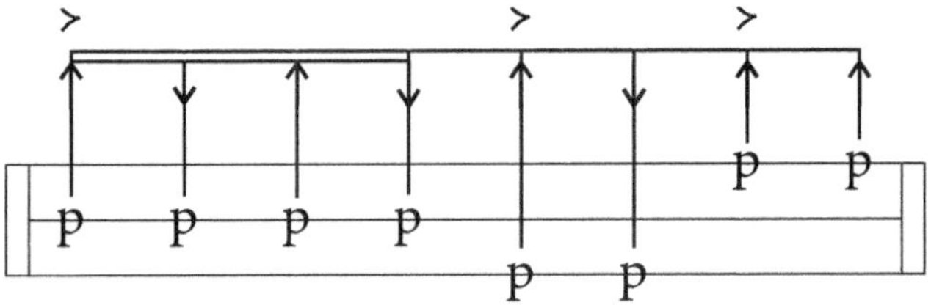

F4

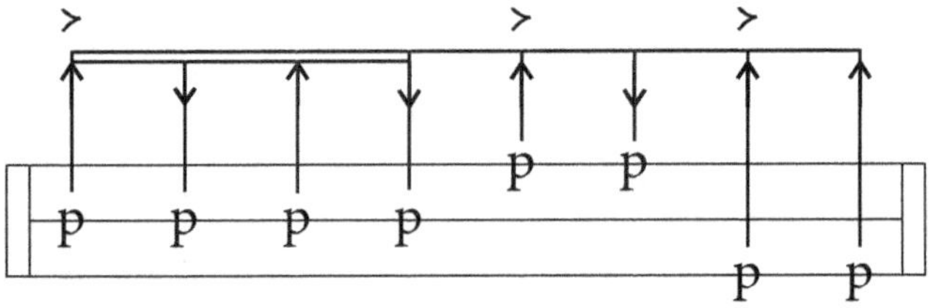

F5

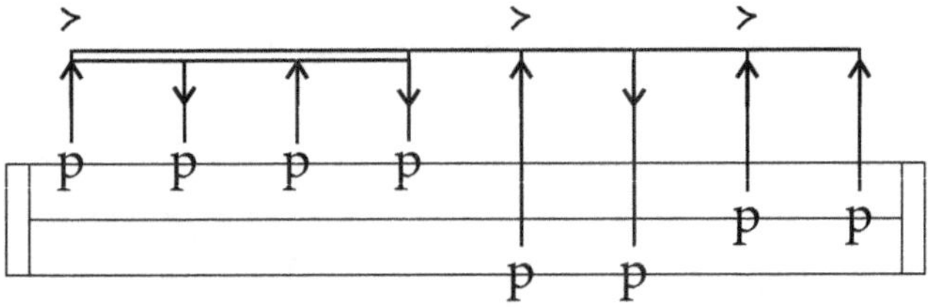

F6

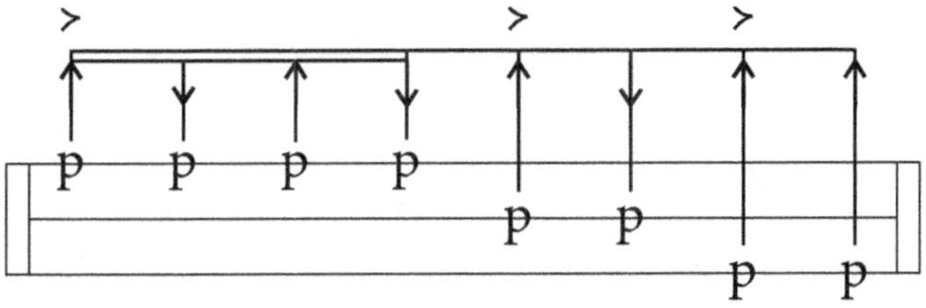

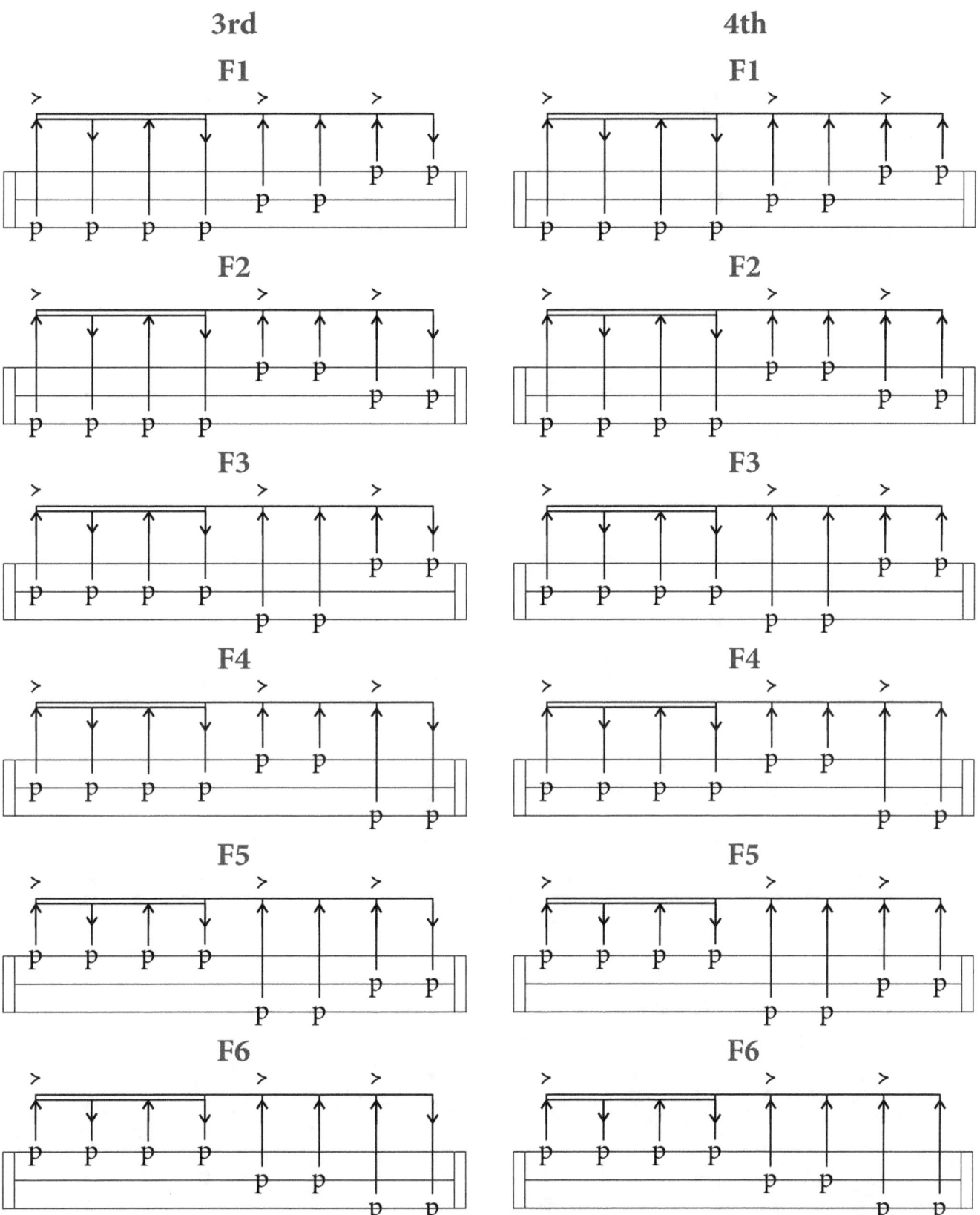

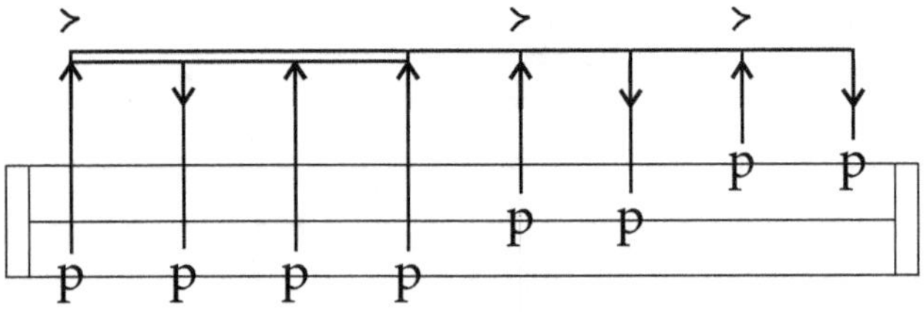

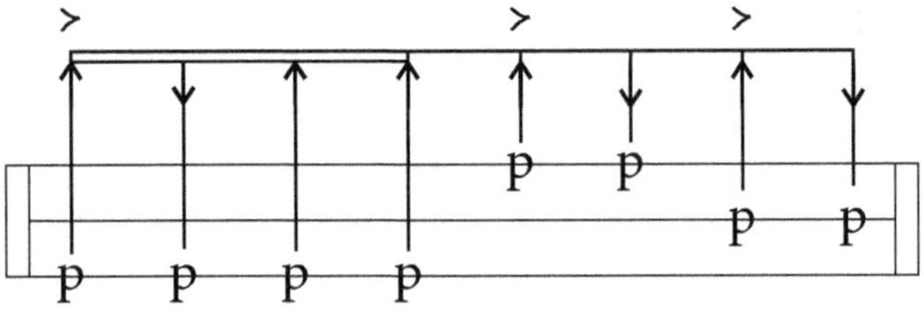

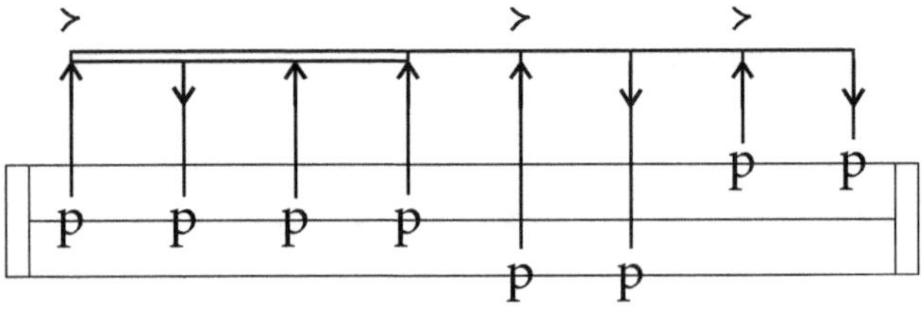

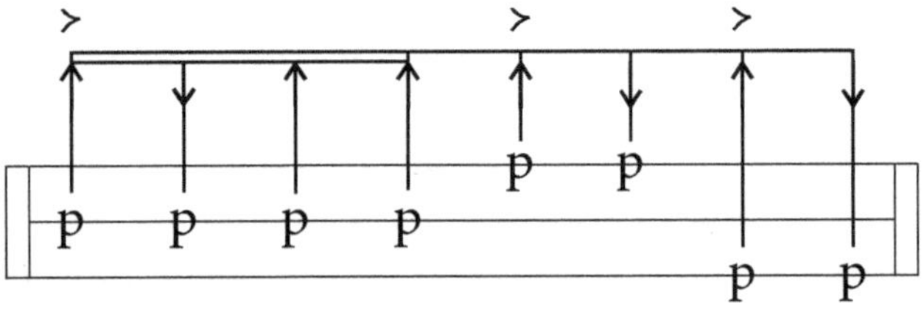

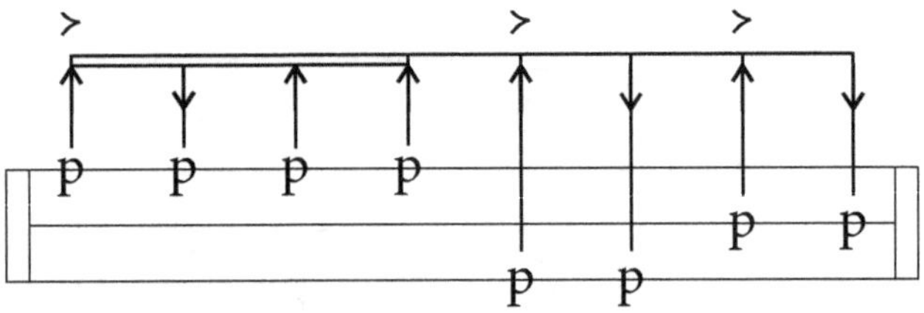

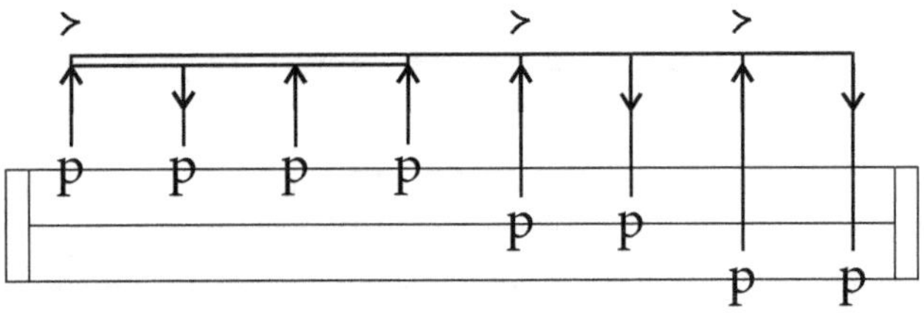

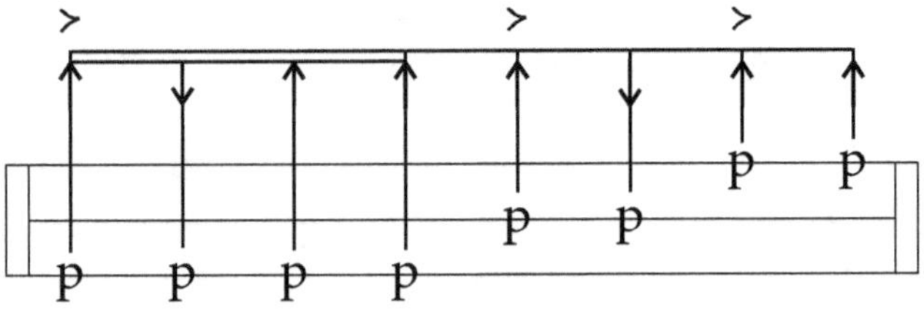

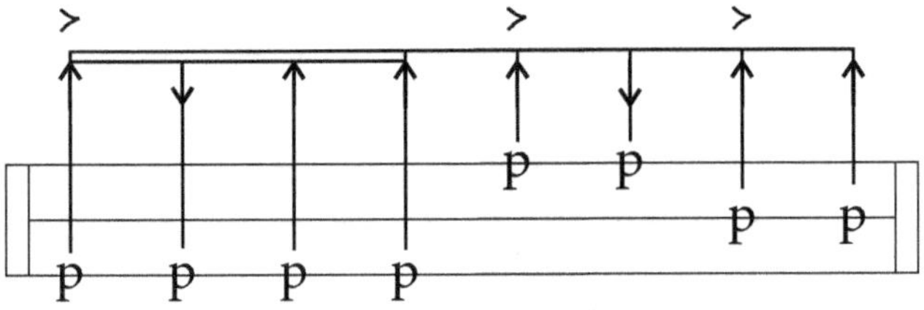

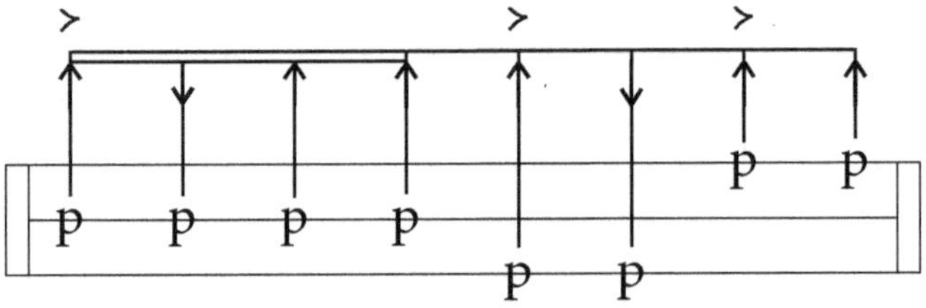

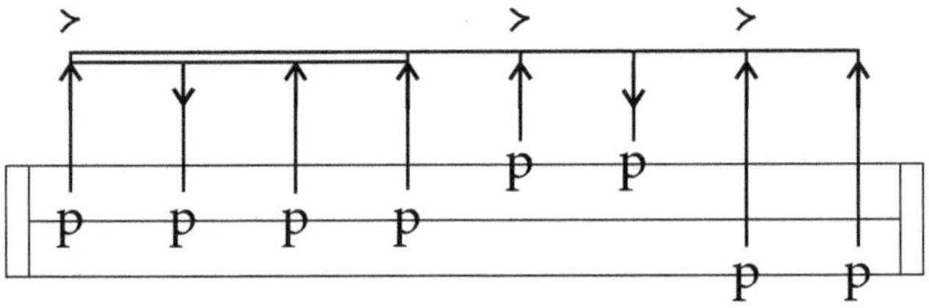

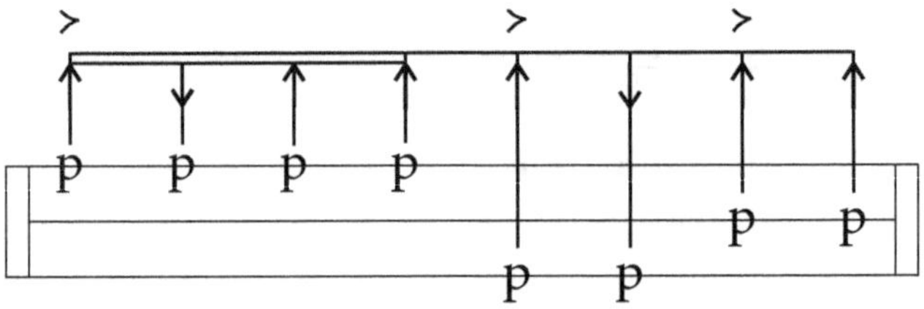

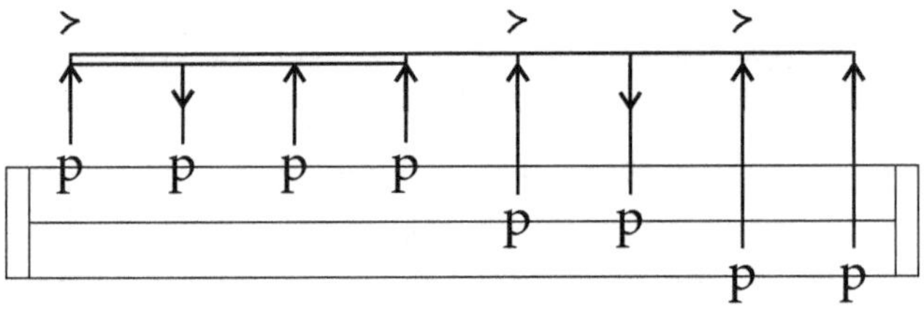

7th

F1
F2
F3
F4
F5
F6

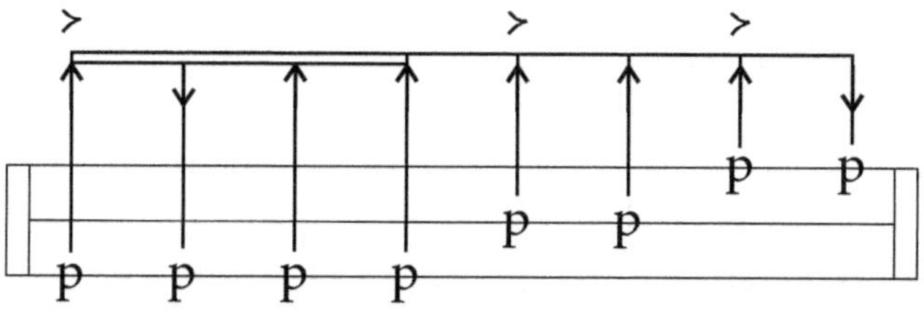

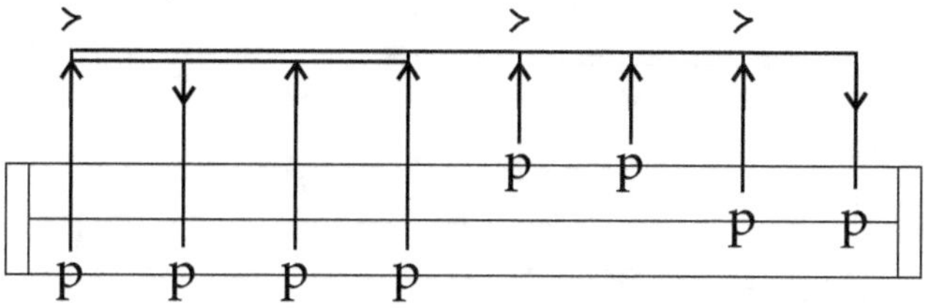

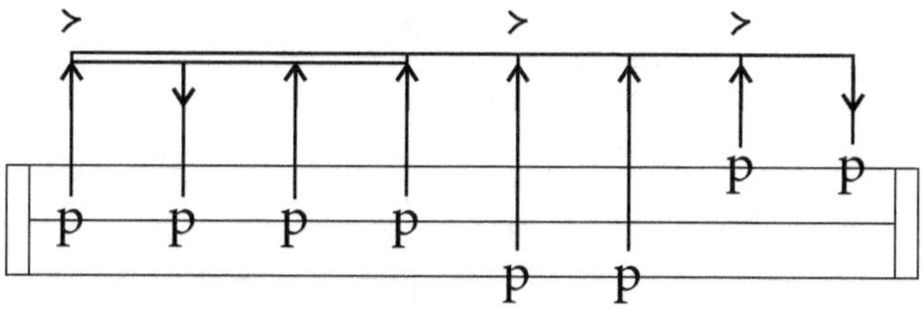

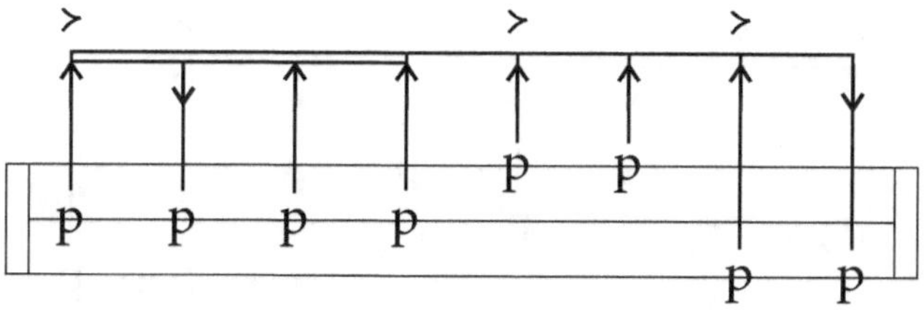

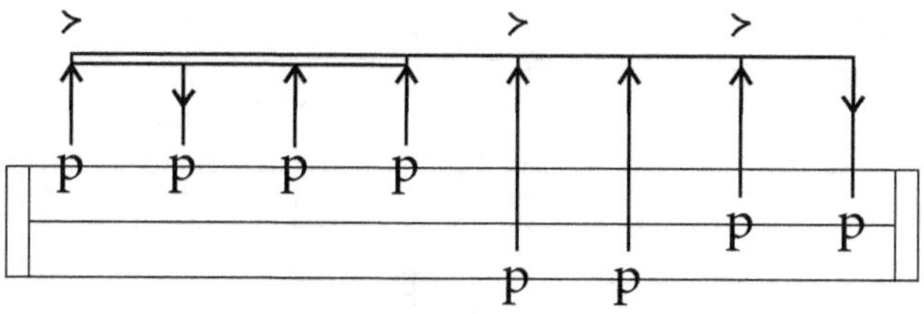

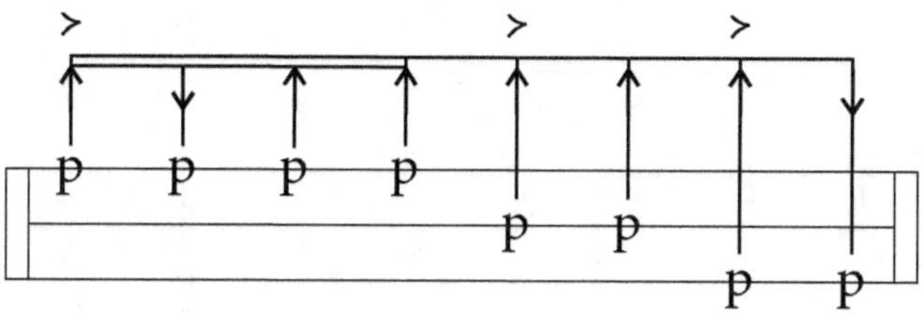

8th

F1
F2
F3
F4
F5
F6

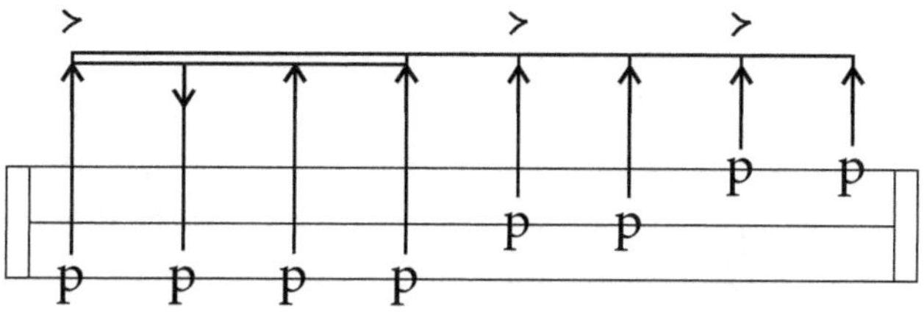

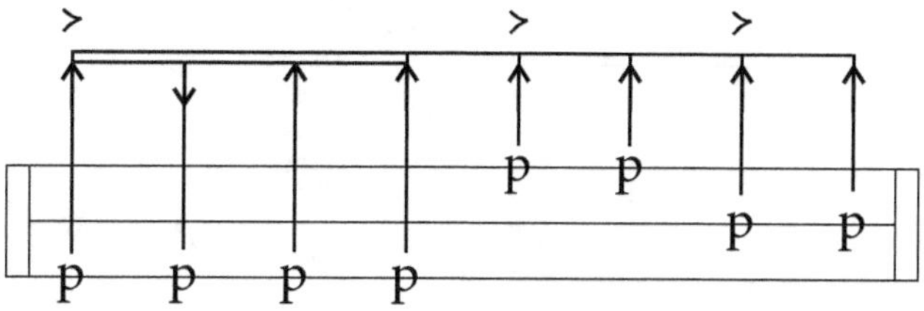

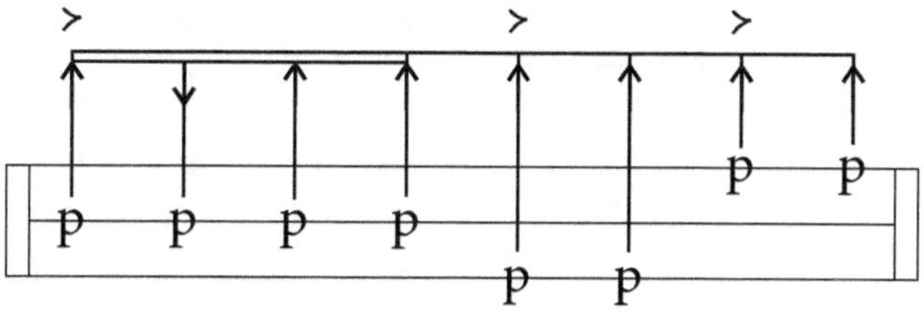

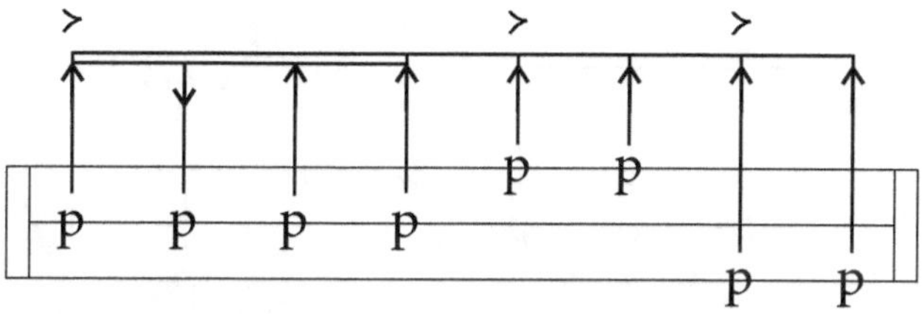

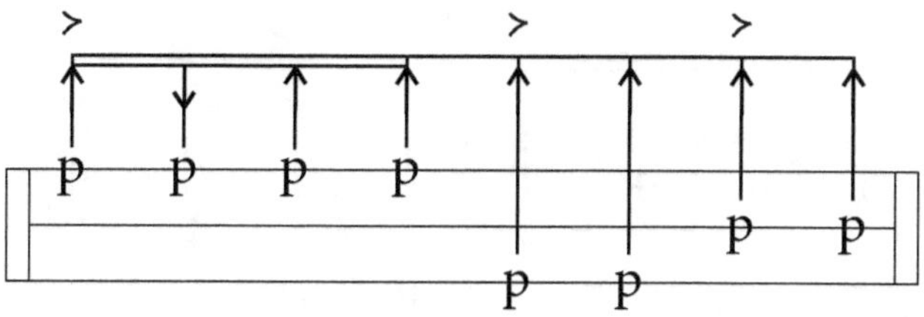

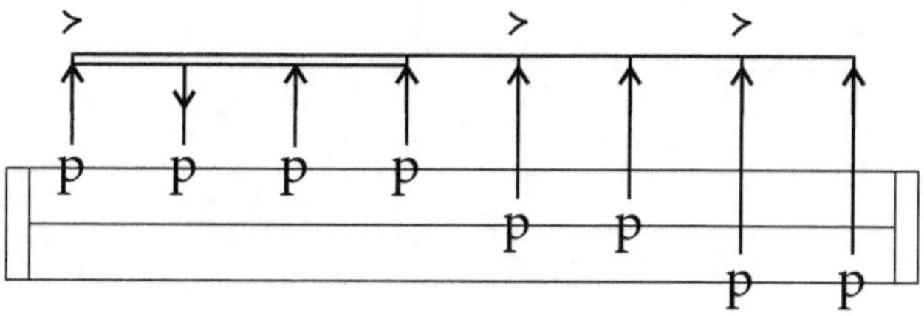

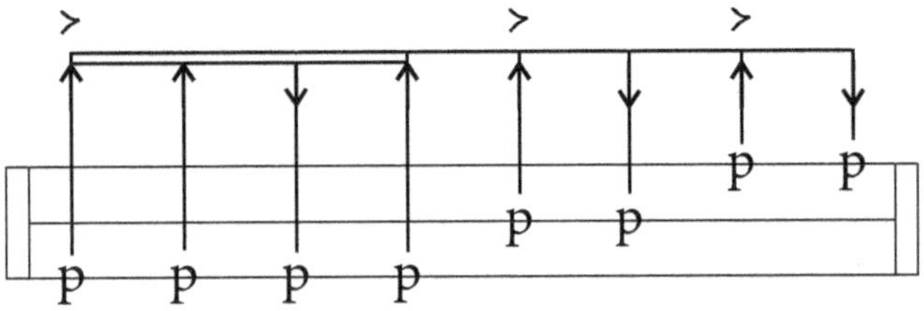

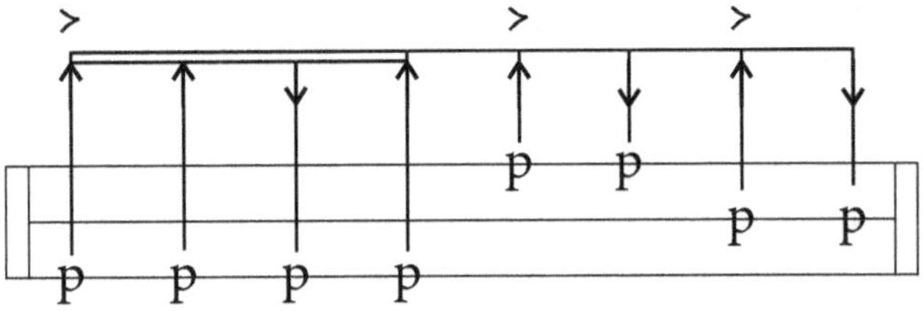

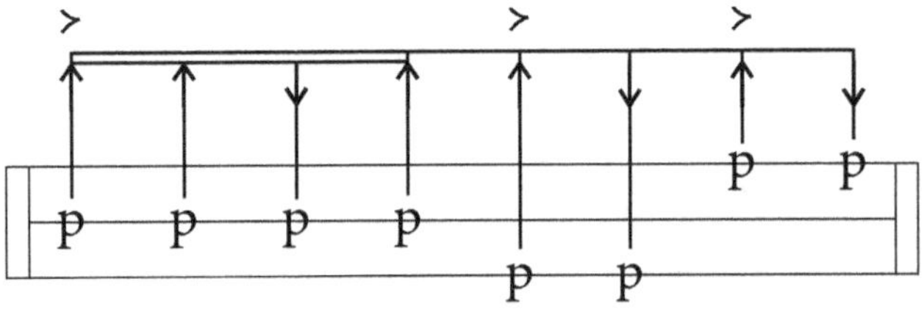

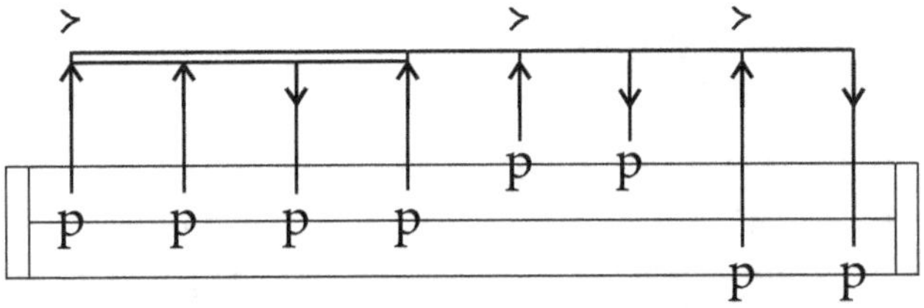

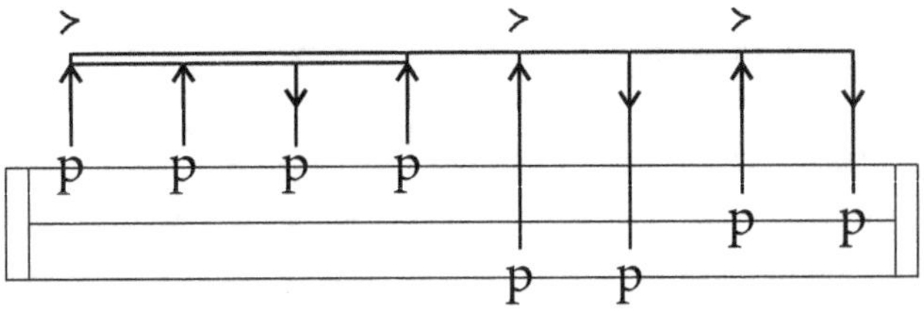

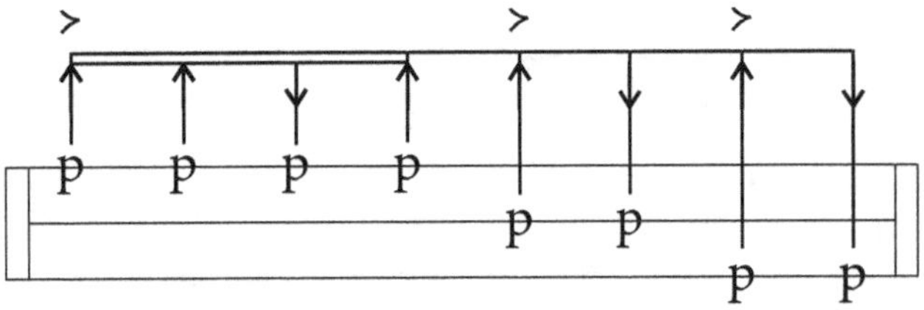

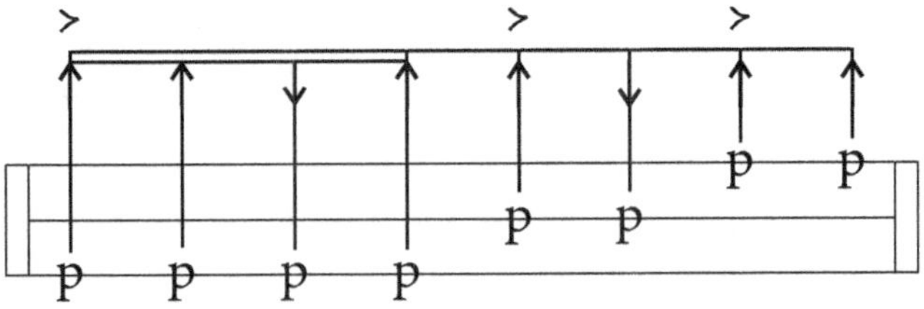

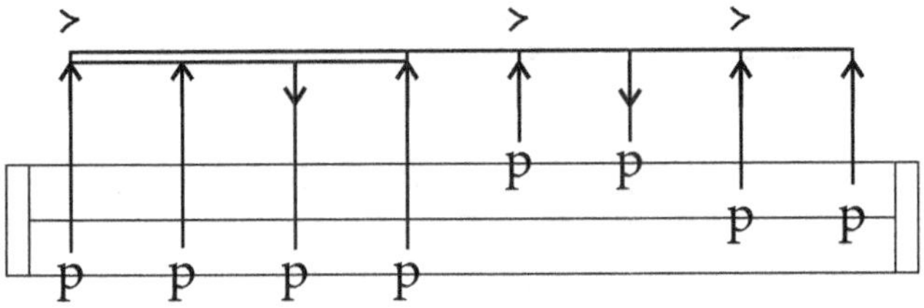

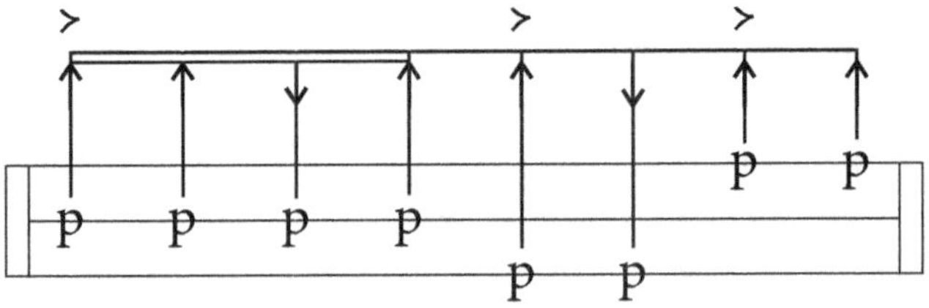

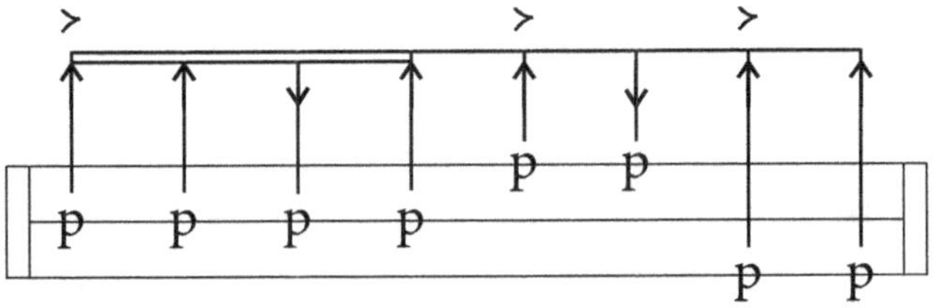

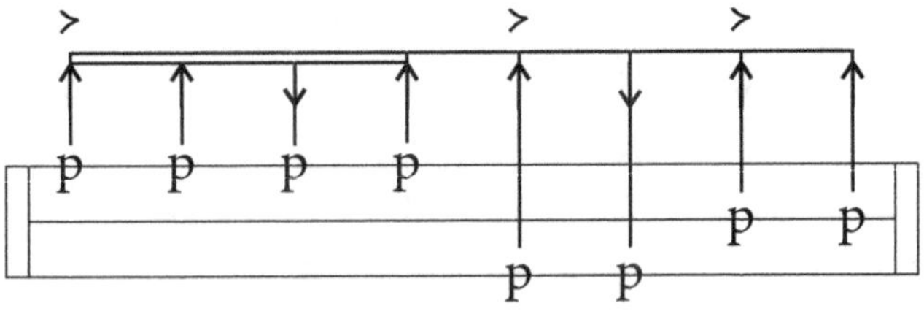

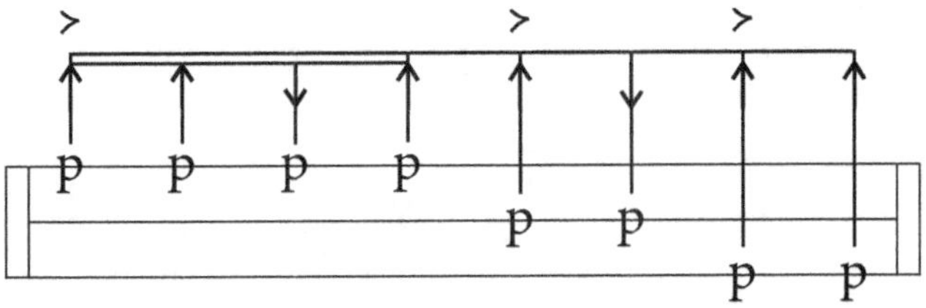

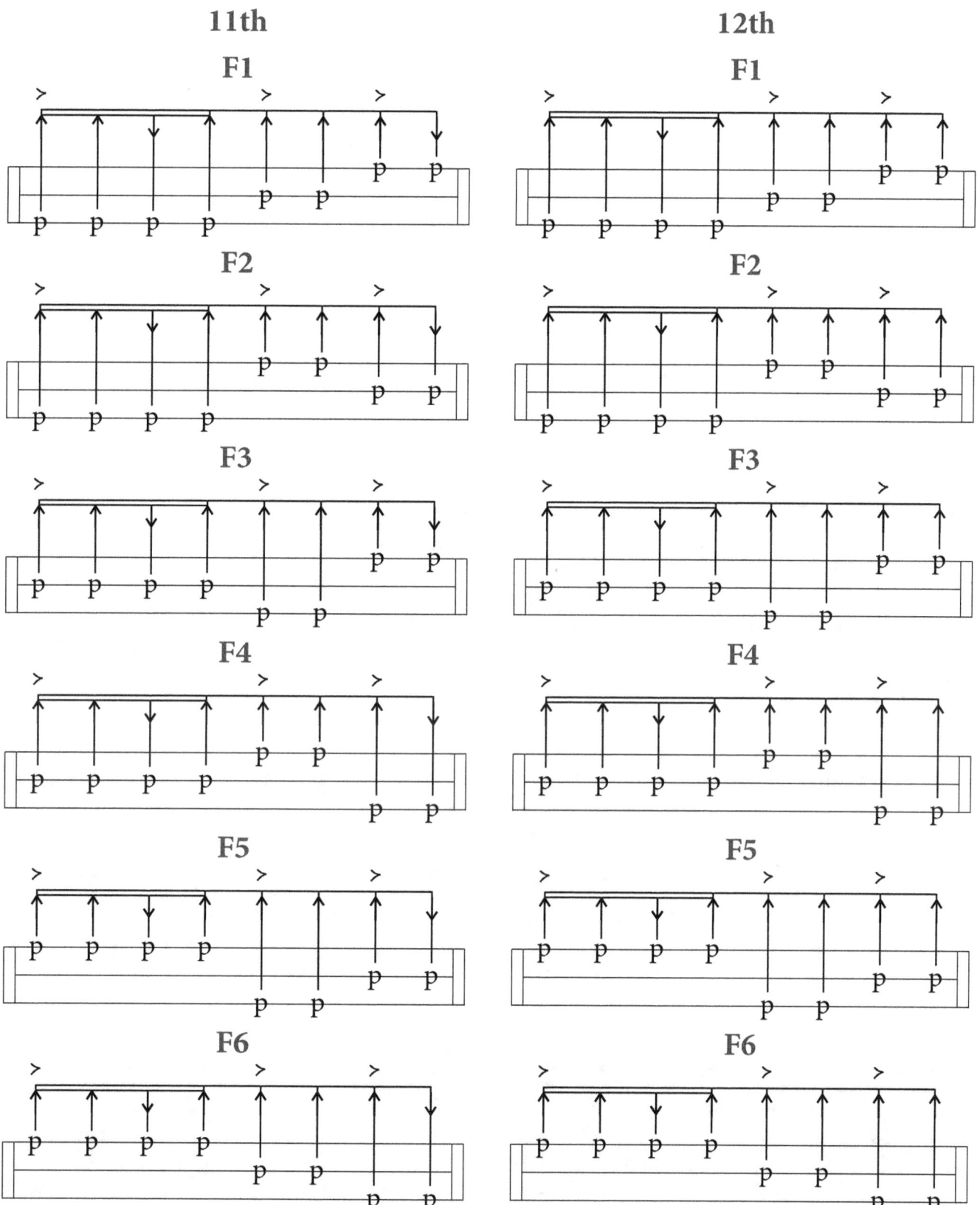

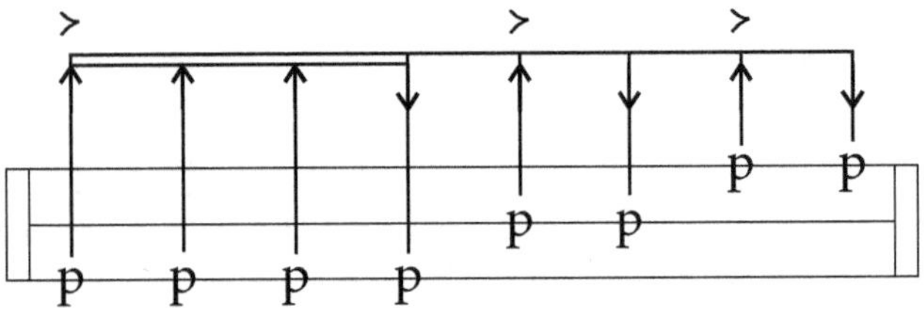

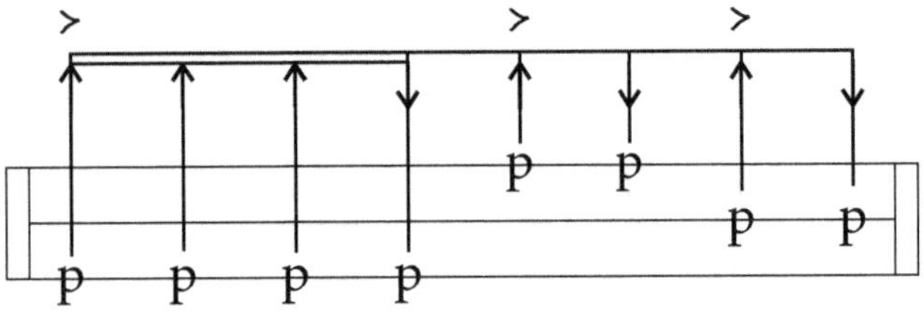

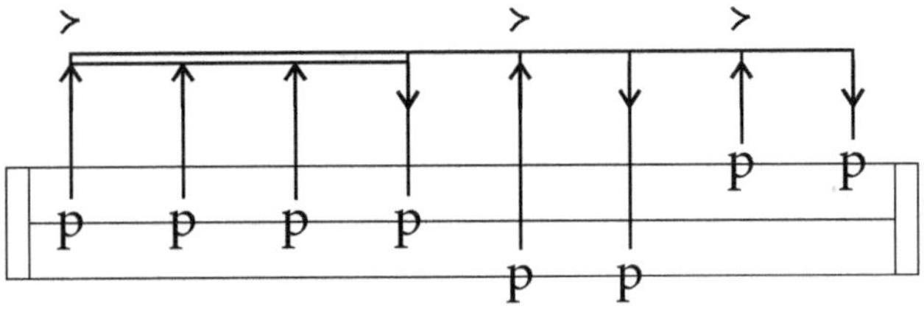

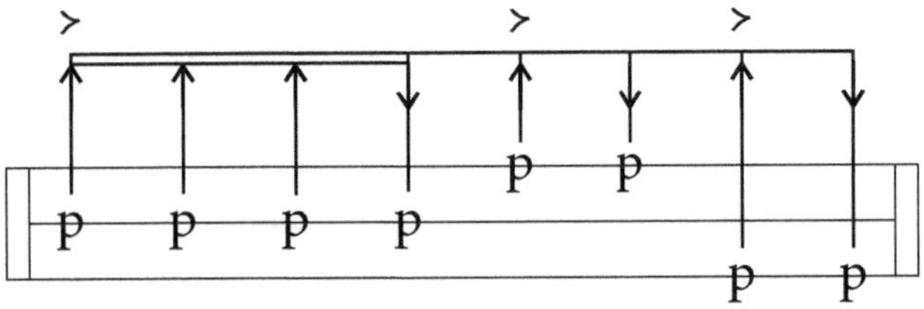

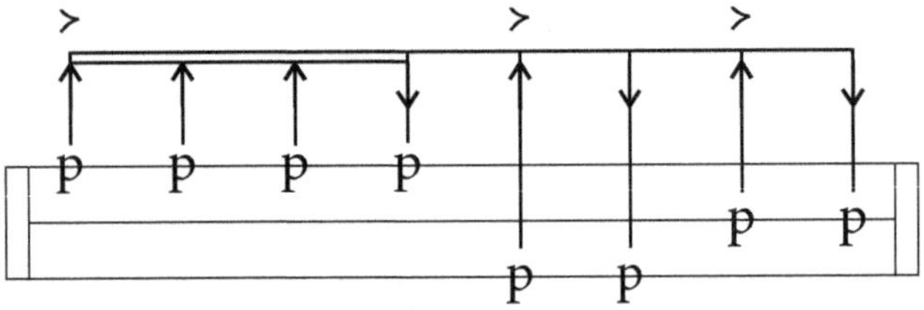

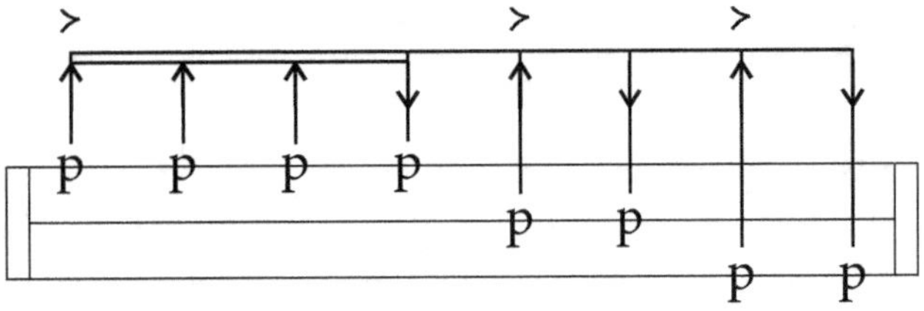

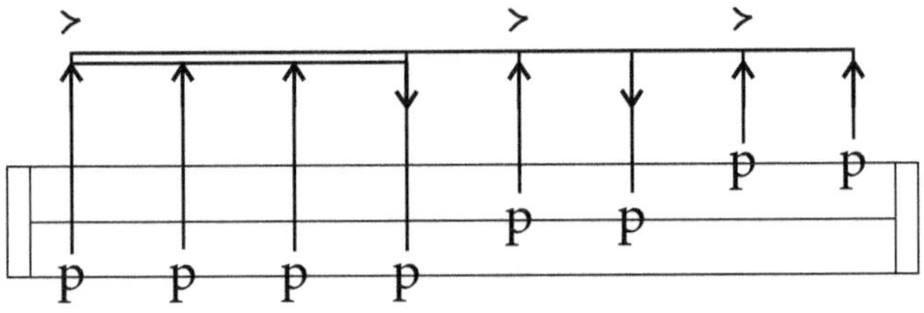

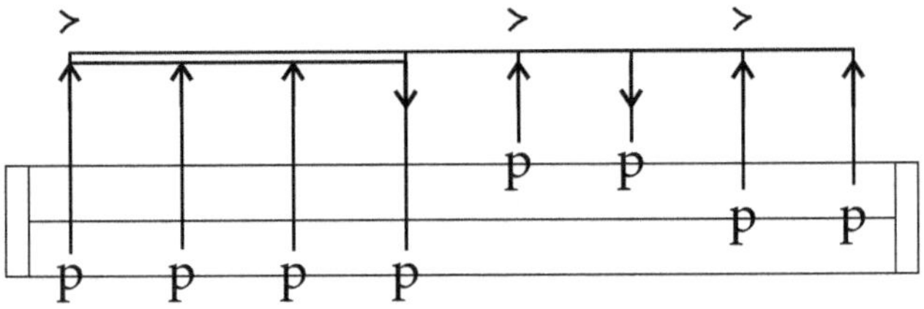

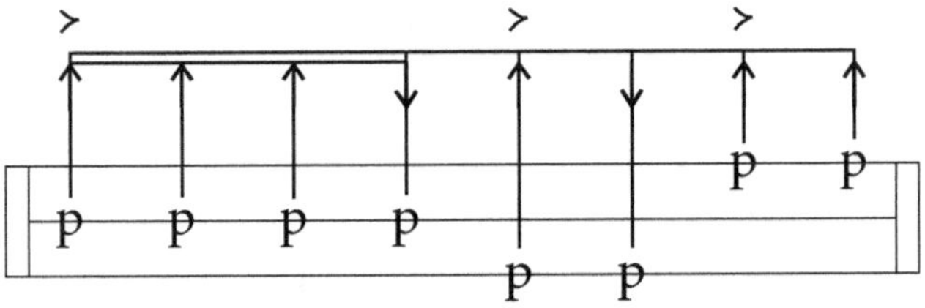

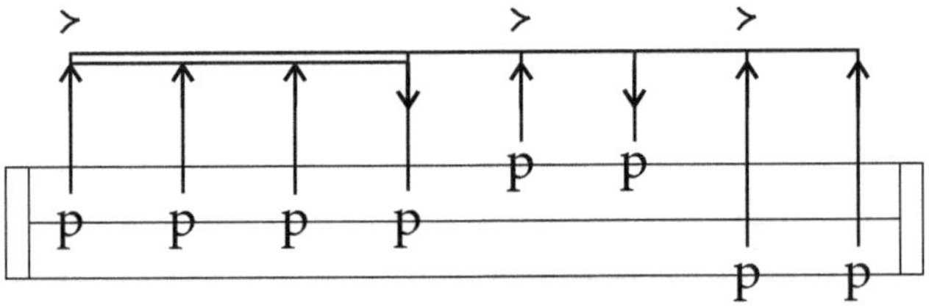

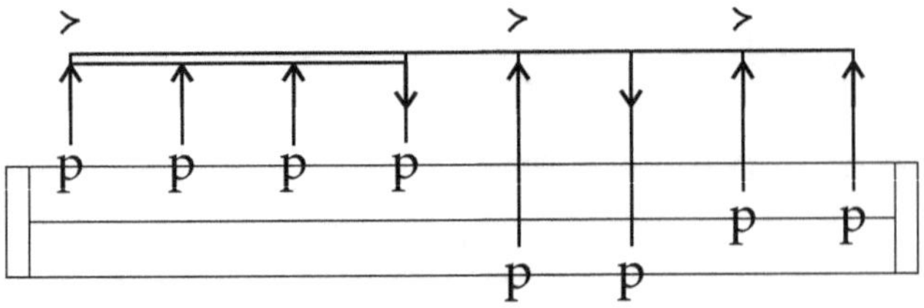

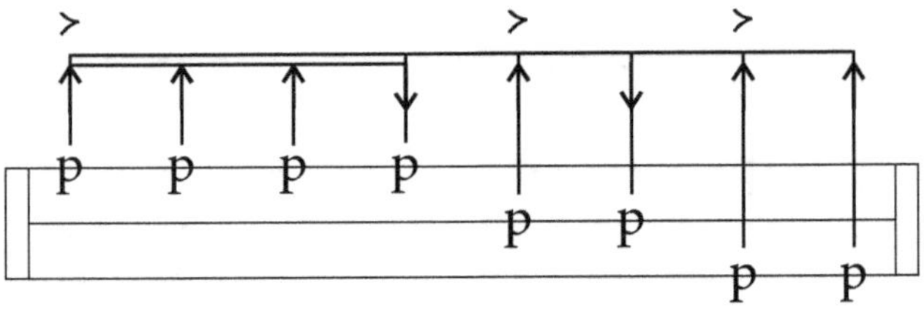

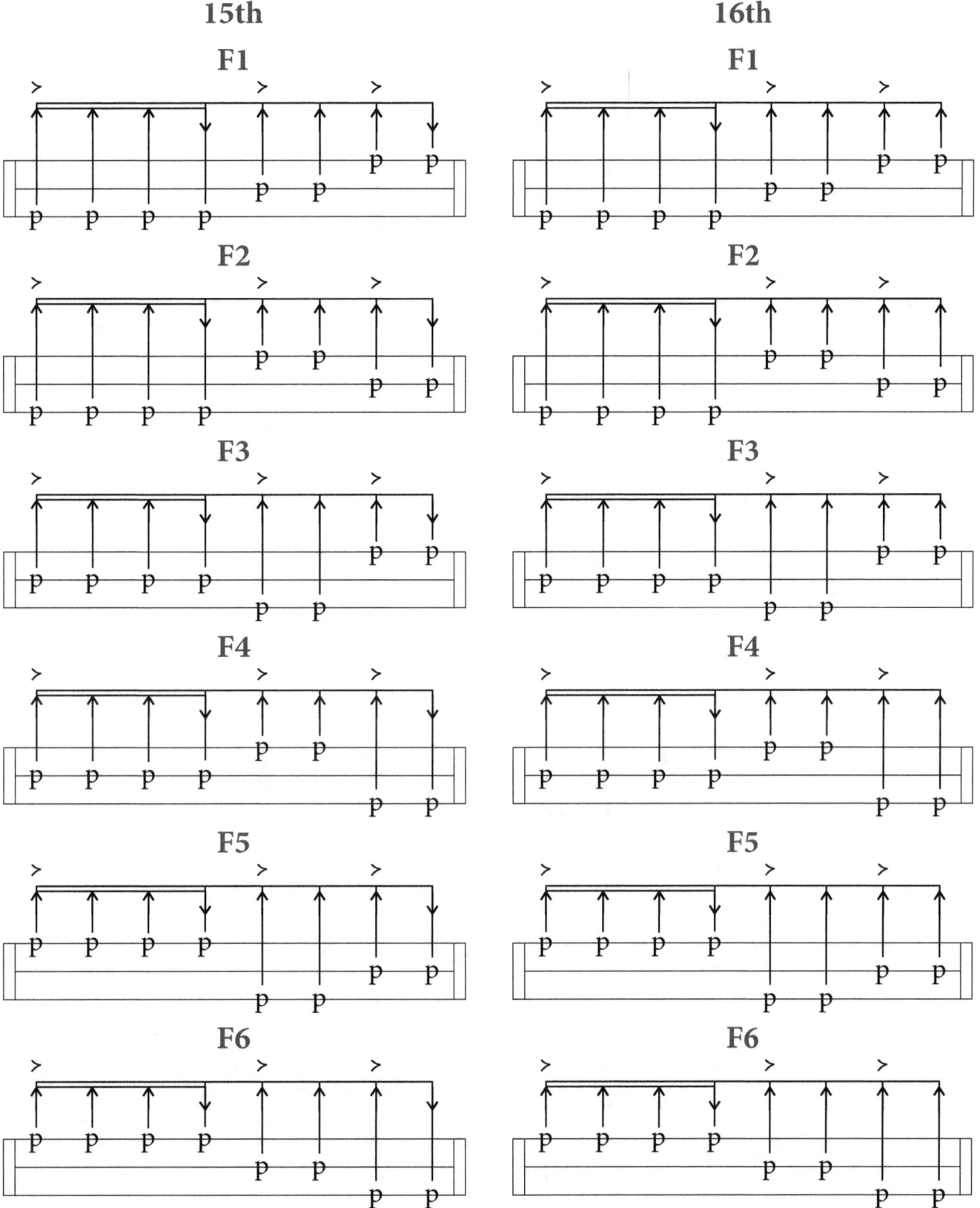

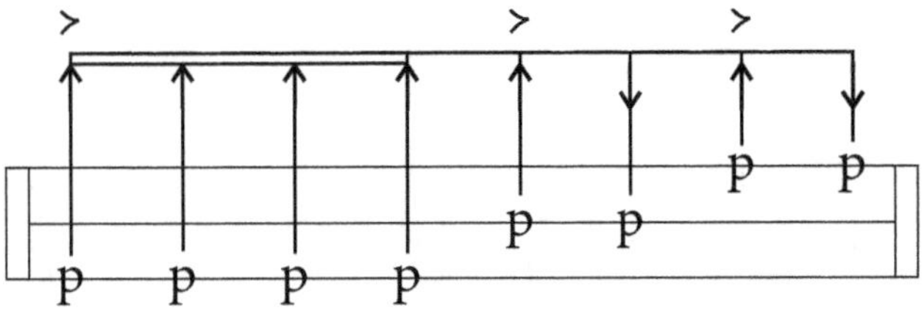

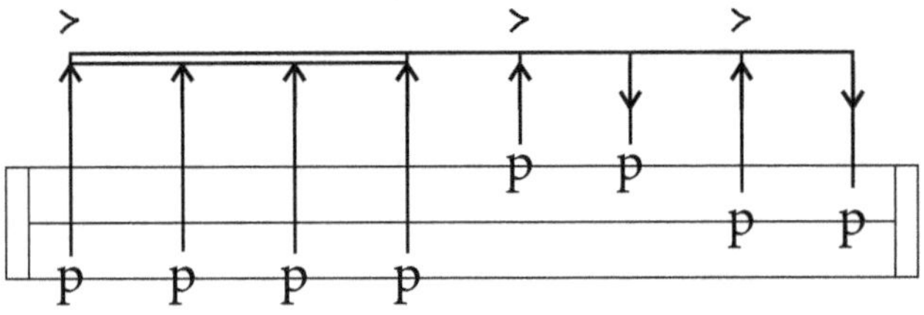

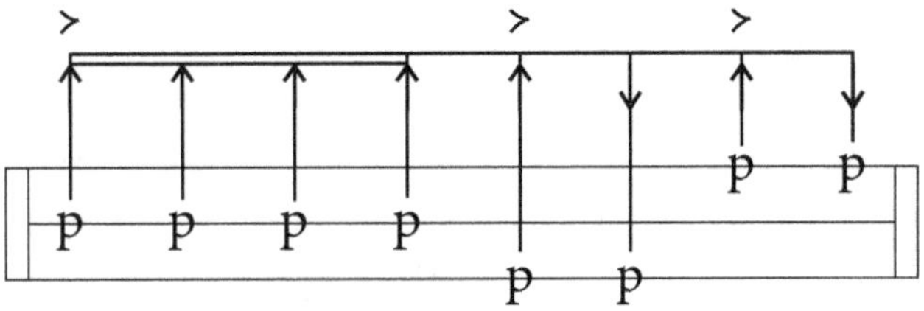

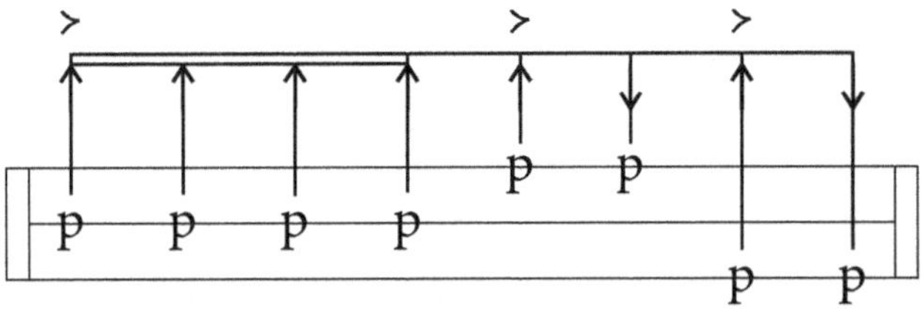

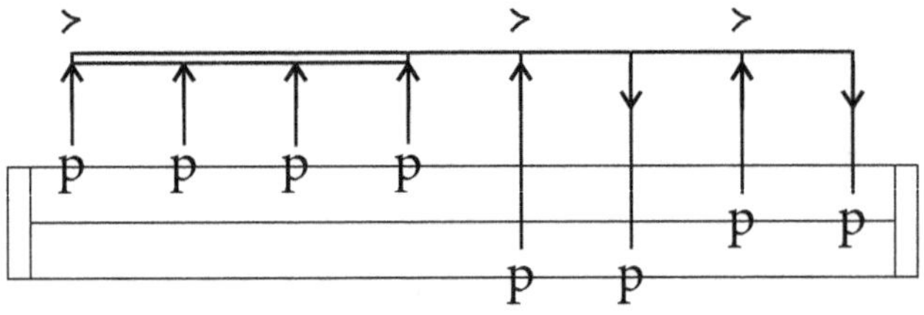

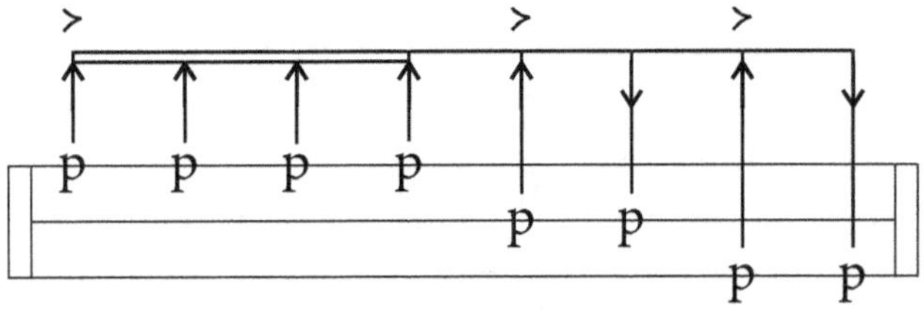

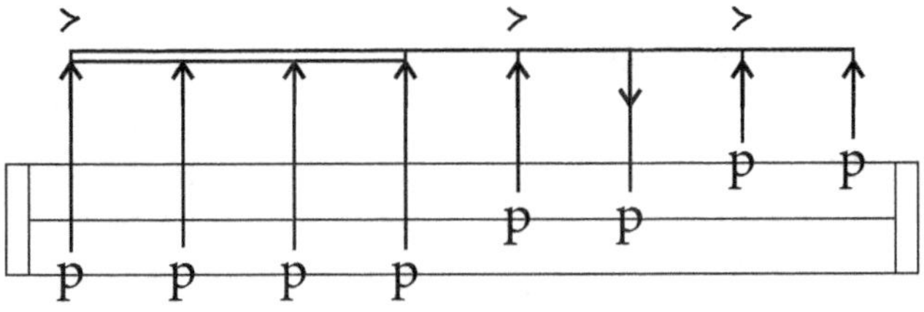

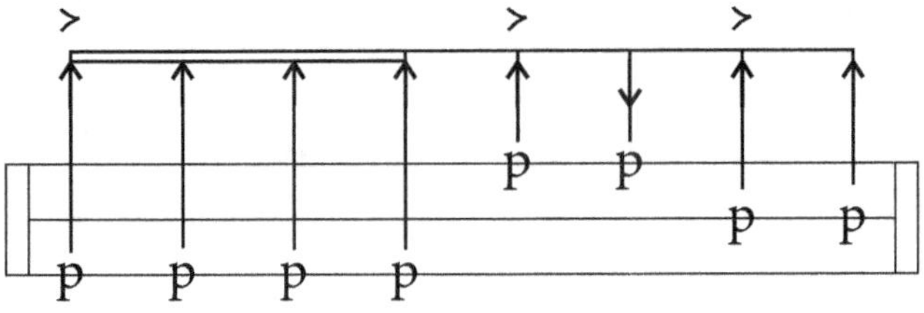

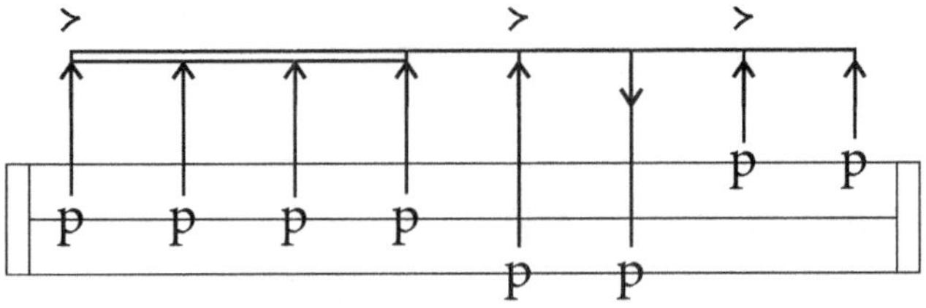

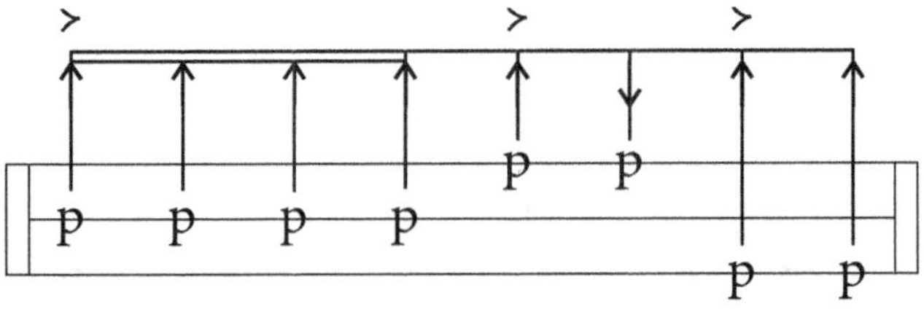

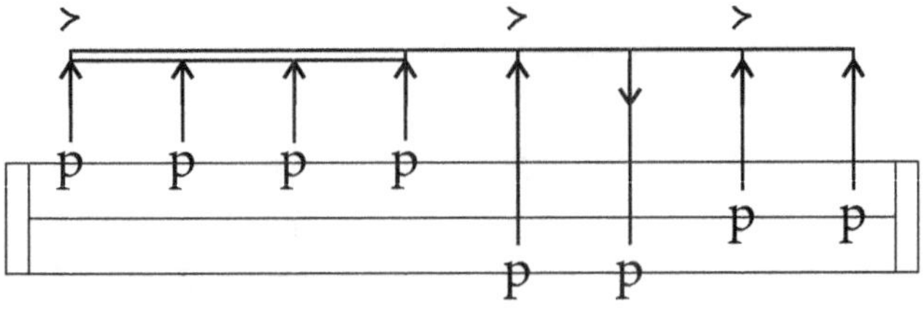

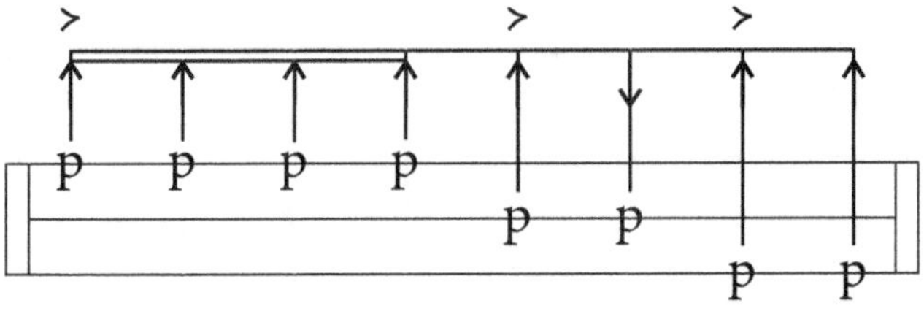

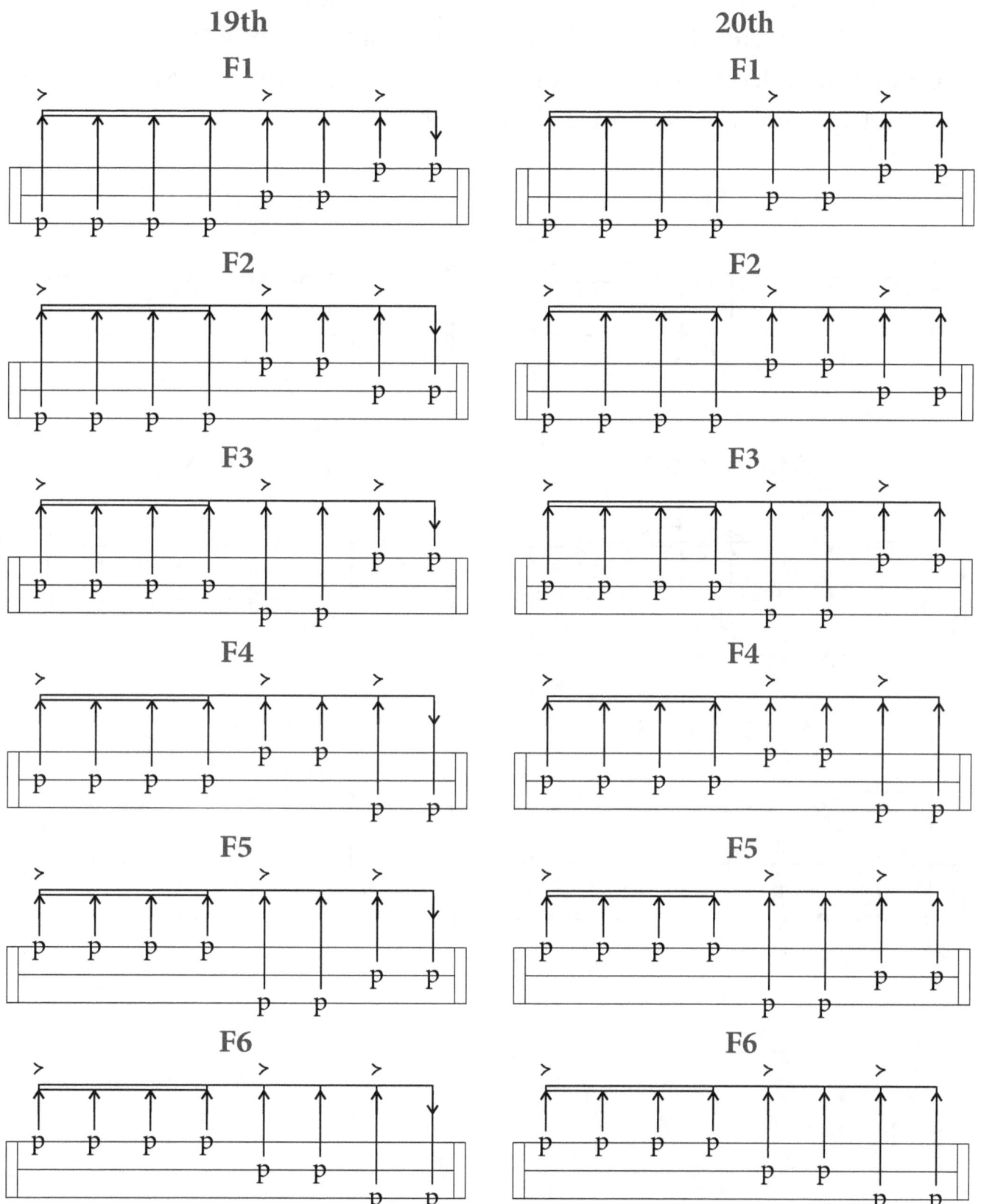

§ IV

Exercise on pulgar on three adjacent strings with double, triple (triplet) and quad stroke in each Formula. The exercise contains six variations with 6 Formulas in each one. The first Formula of each variation is cited below. The double, triple and quad strokes are isochronous.

VARIATION I

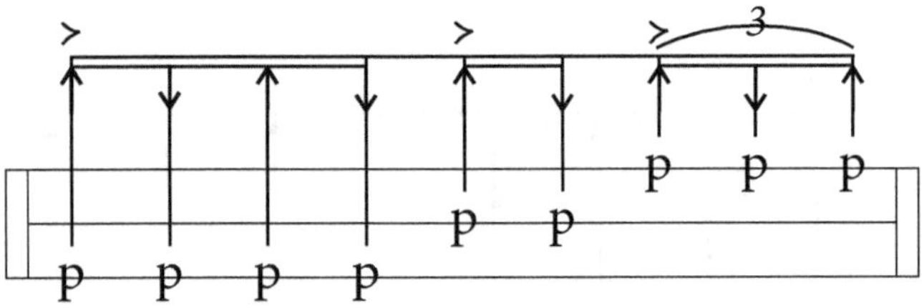

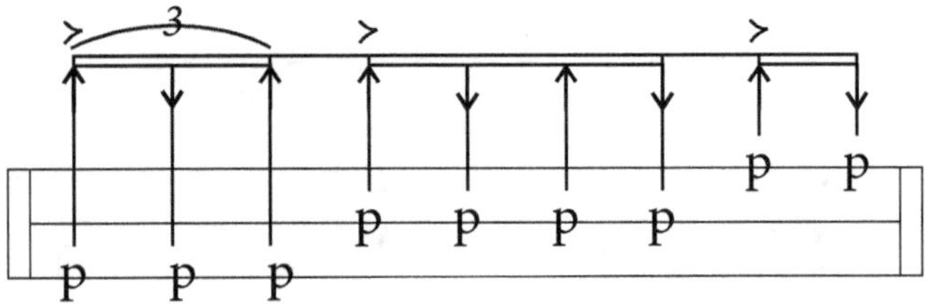

VARIATION IV

VARIATION II

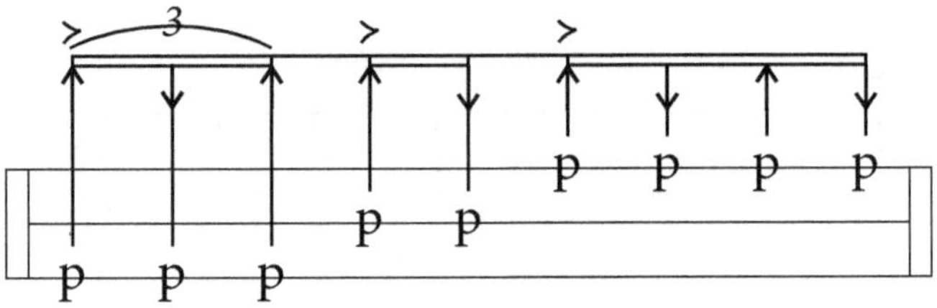

VARIATION V

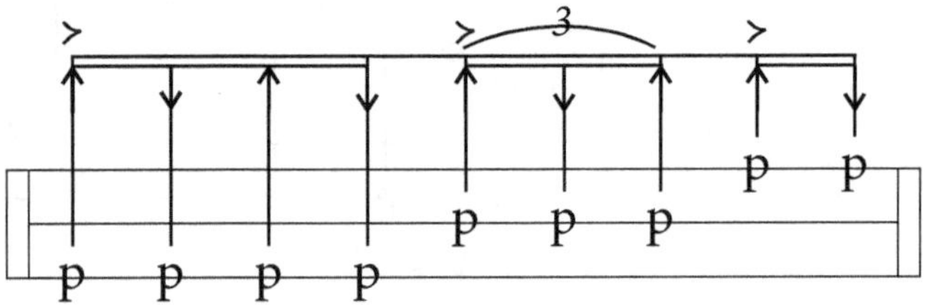

VARIATION III

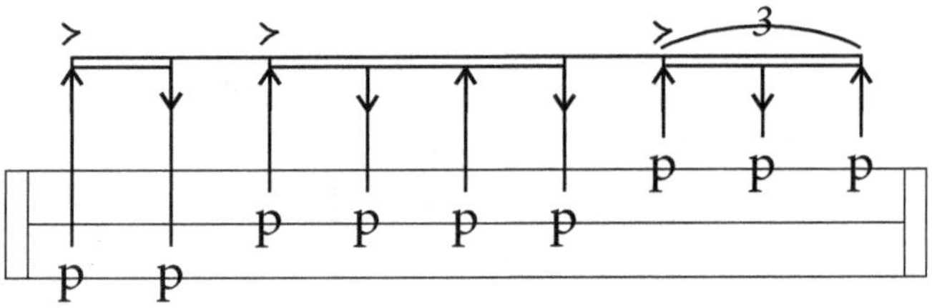

VARIATION VI

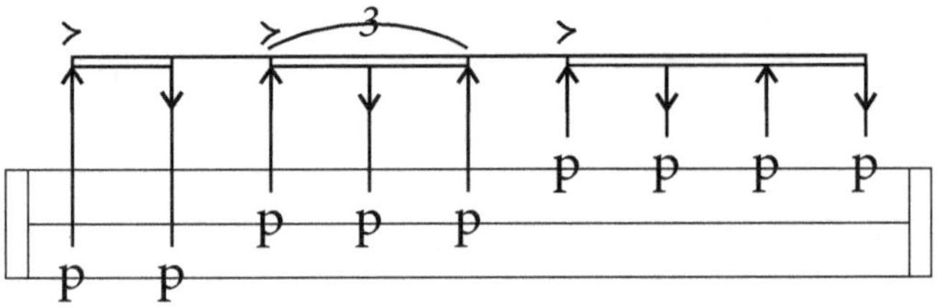

VARIATION I   VARIATION II

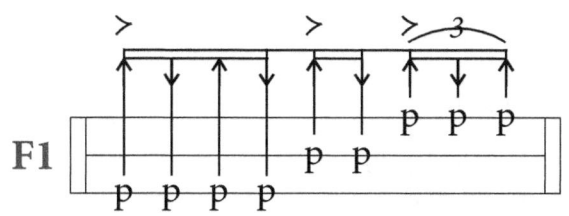 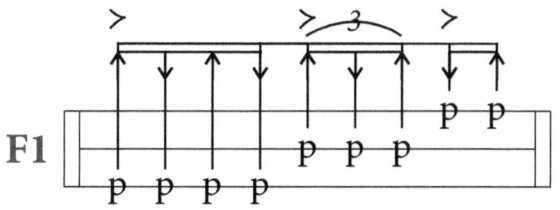

F1

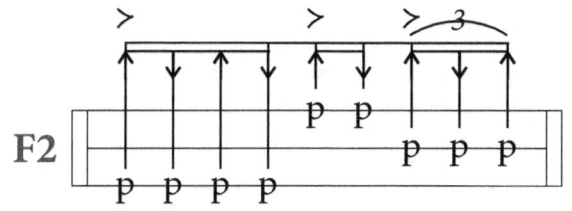 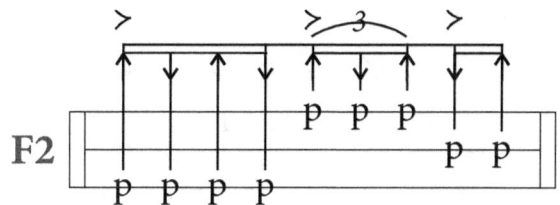

F2

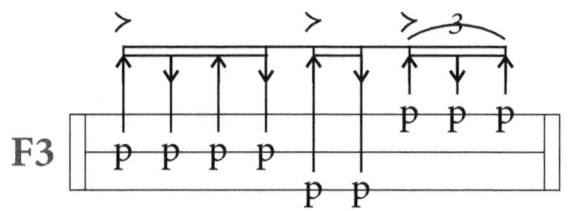 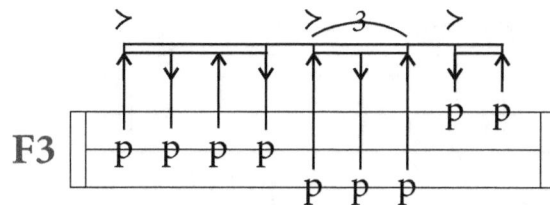

F3

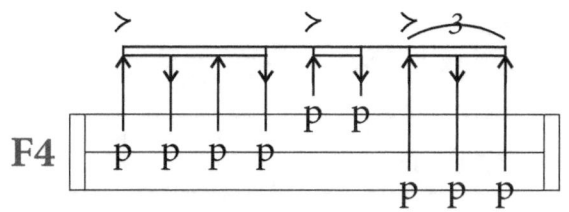 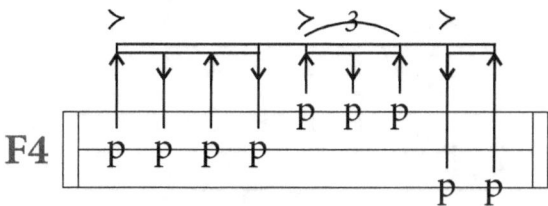

F4

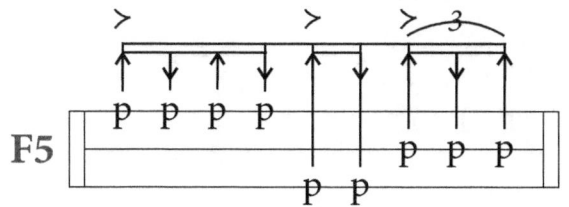 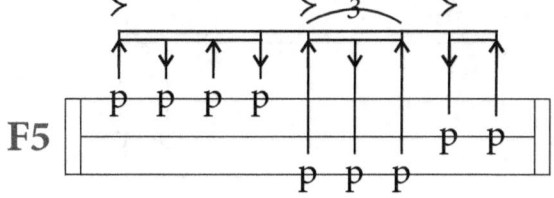

F5

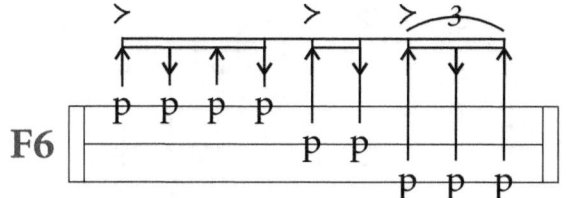 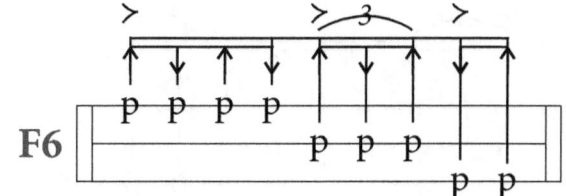

F6

VARIATION III   VARIATION IV

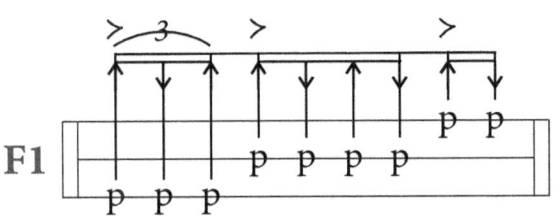 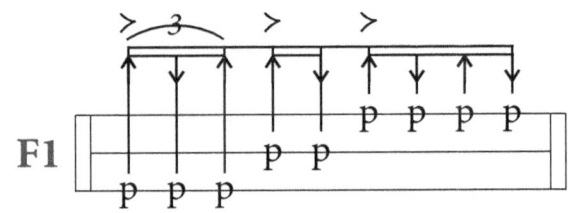

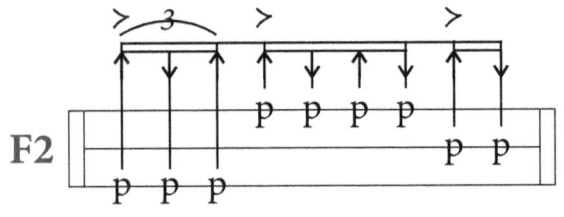 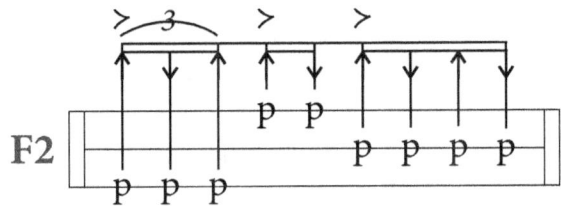

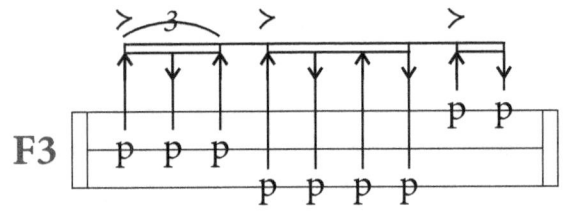 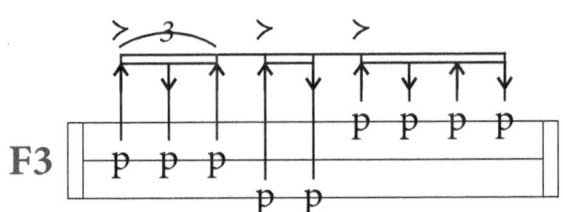

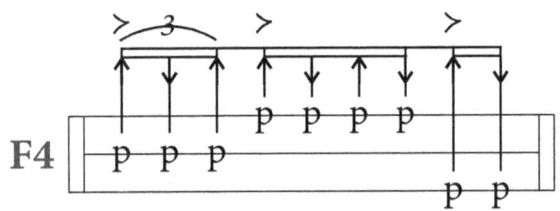 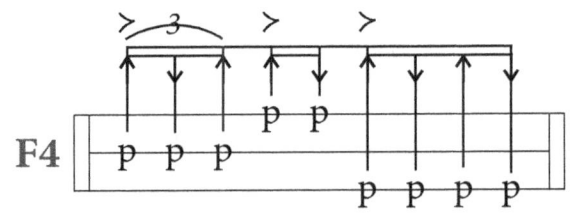

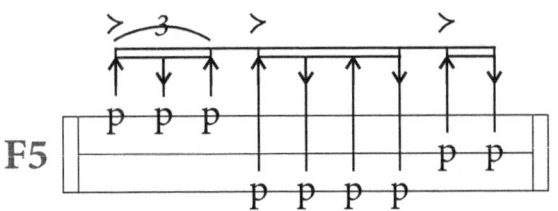 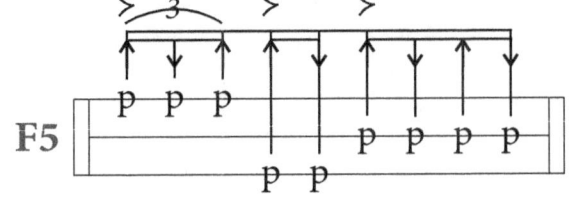

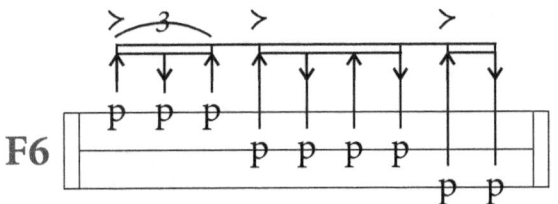 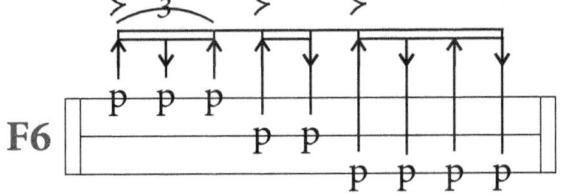

VARIATION V

VARIATION VI

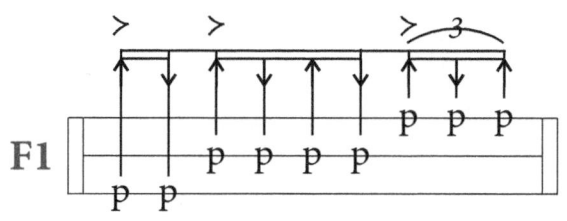

F1

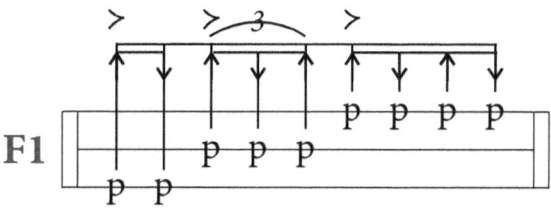

F1

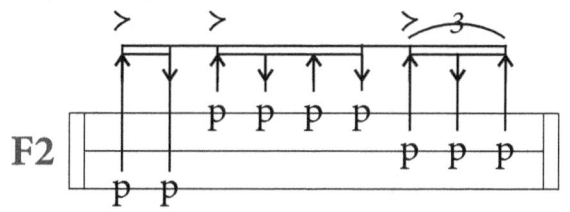

F2

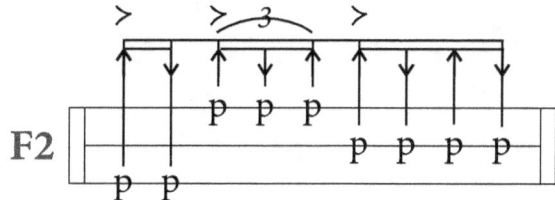

F2

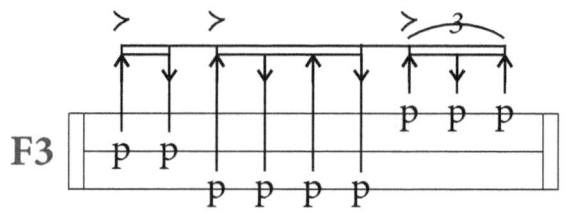

F3

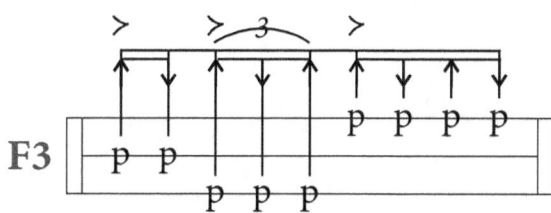

F3

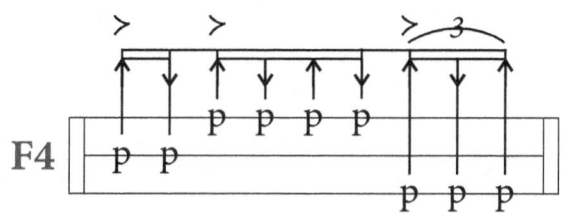

F4

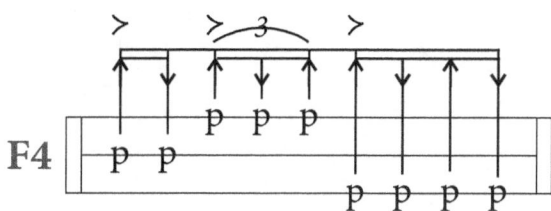

F4

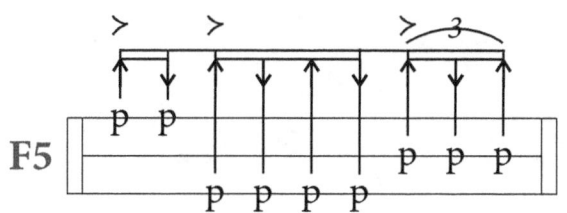

F5

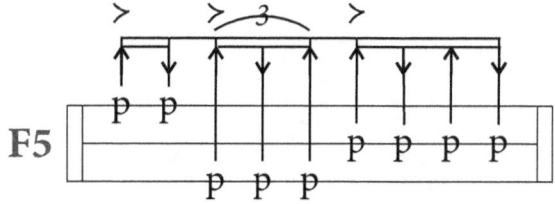

F5

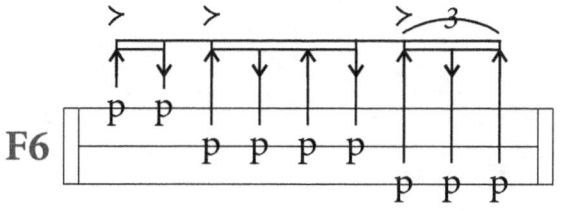

F6

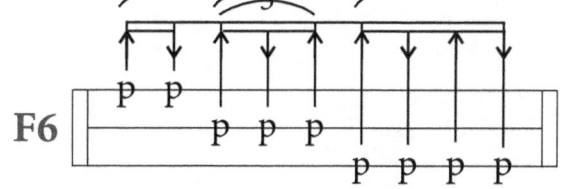

F6

30 ways of performance of variation I (in total) which result from the change in the direction of pulgar stroke are cited below.

VARIATION I
WAYS OF PERFORMANCE

1st — **A** — **2nd**

F1
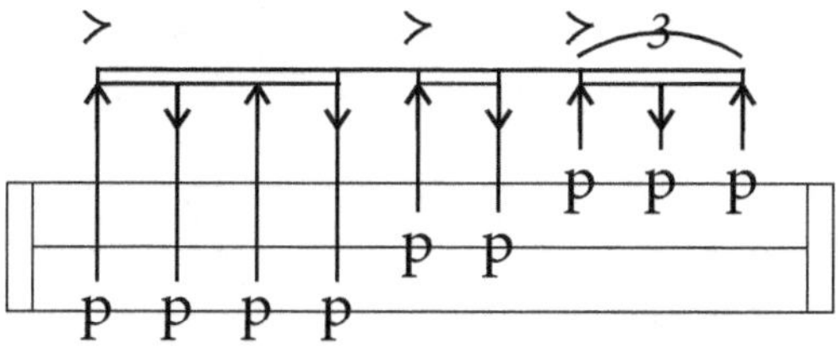

F1
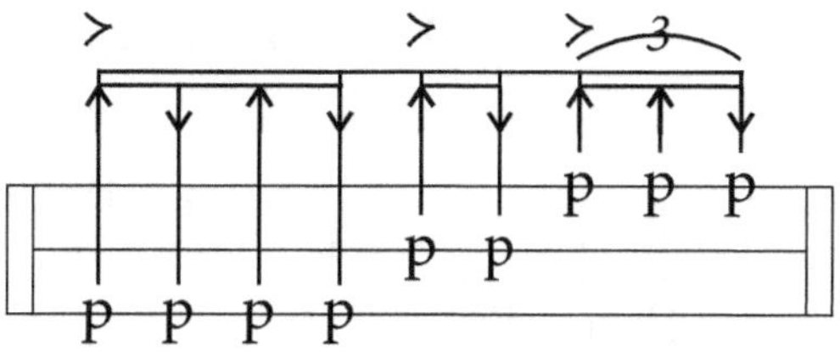

F2
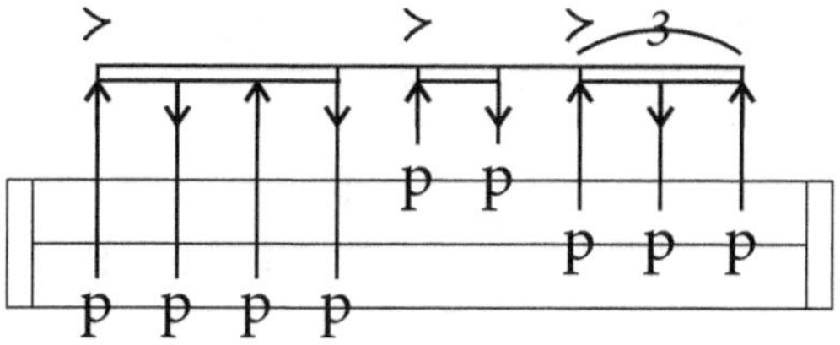

F2
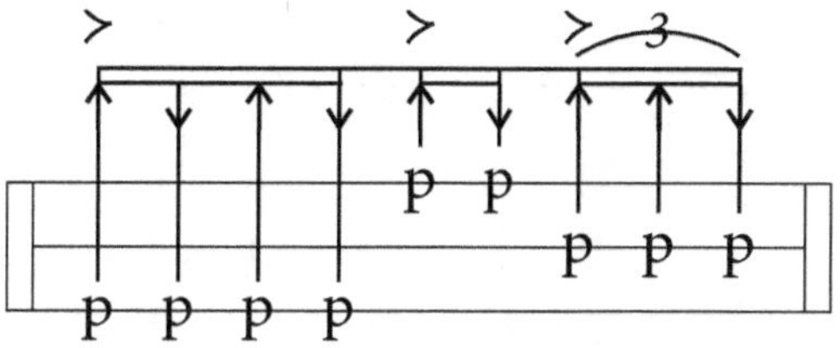

F3
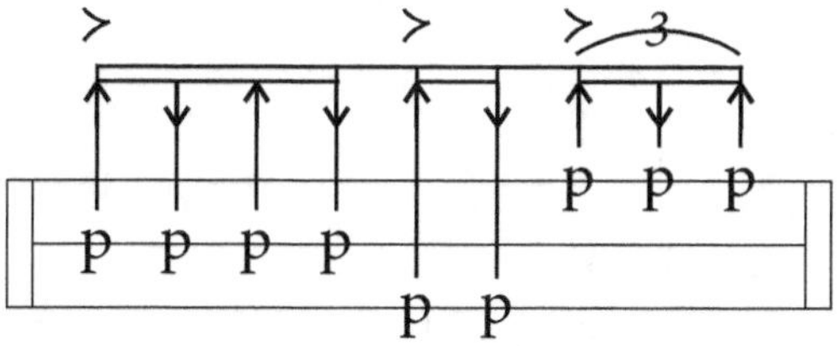

F3
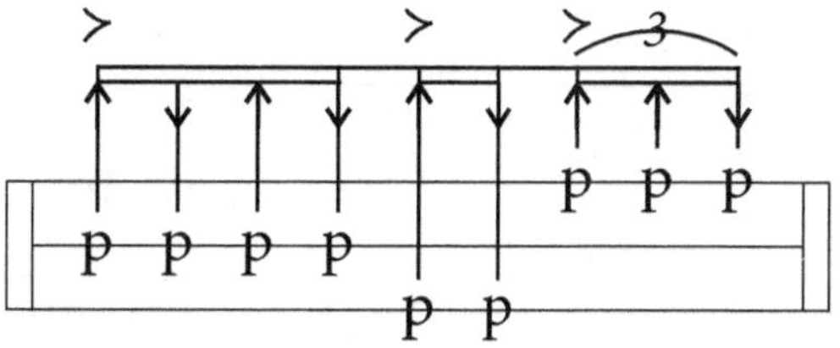

F4
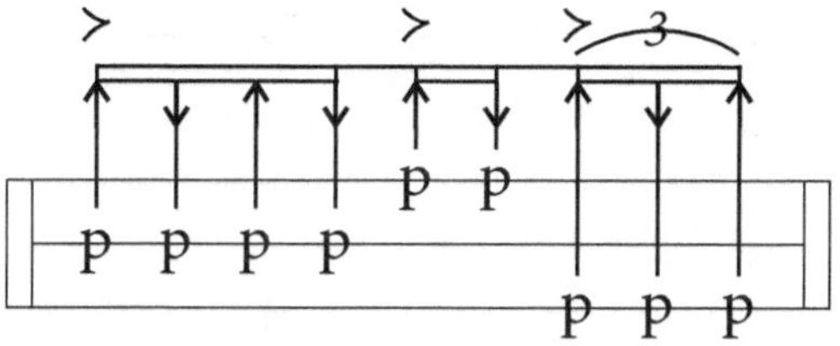

F4
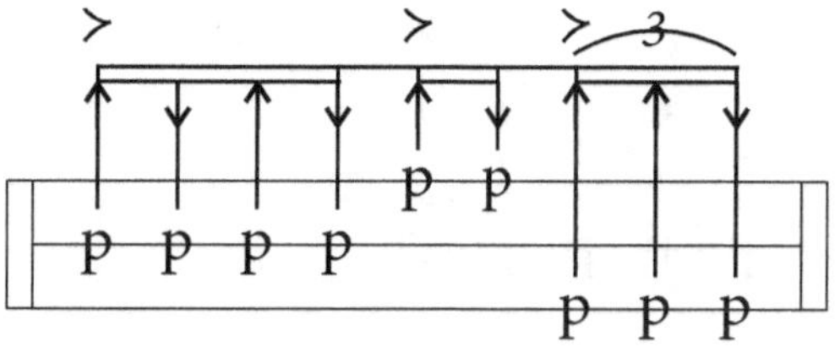

F5
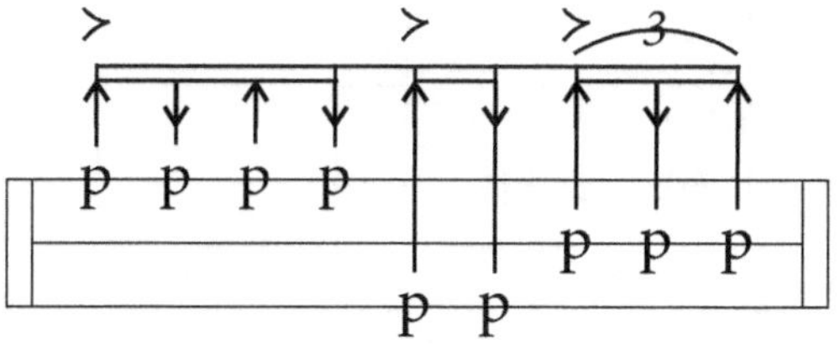

F5
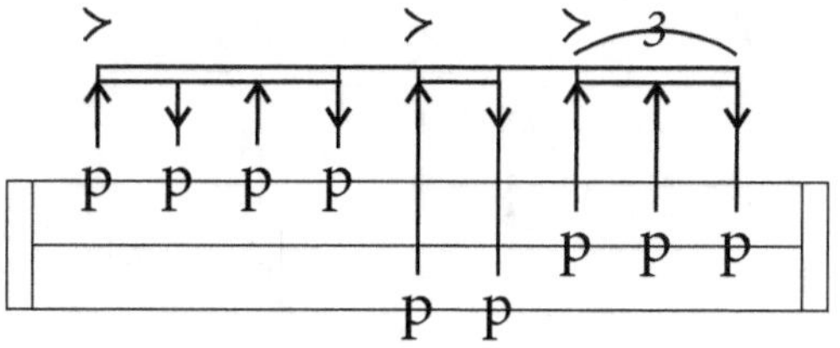

F6
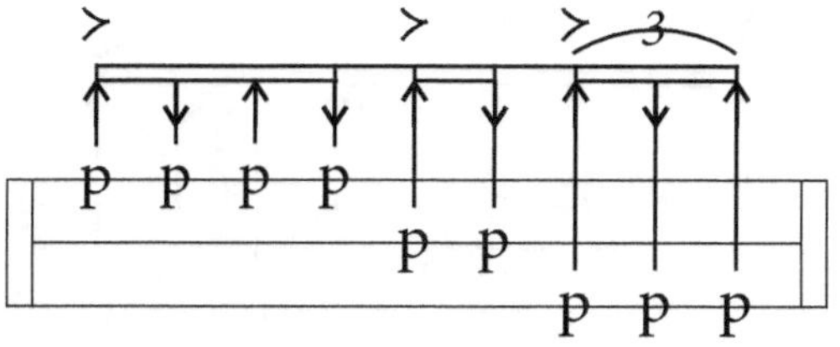

F6
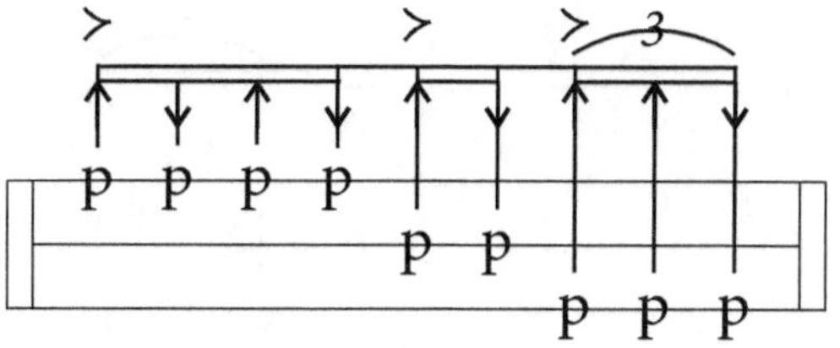

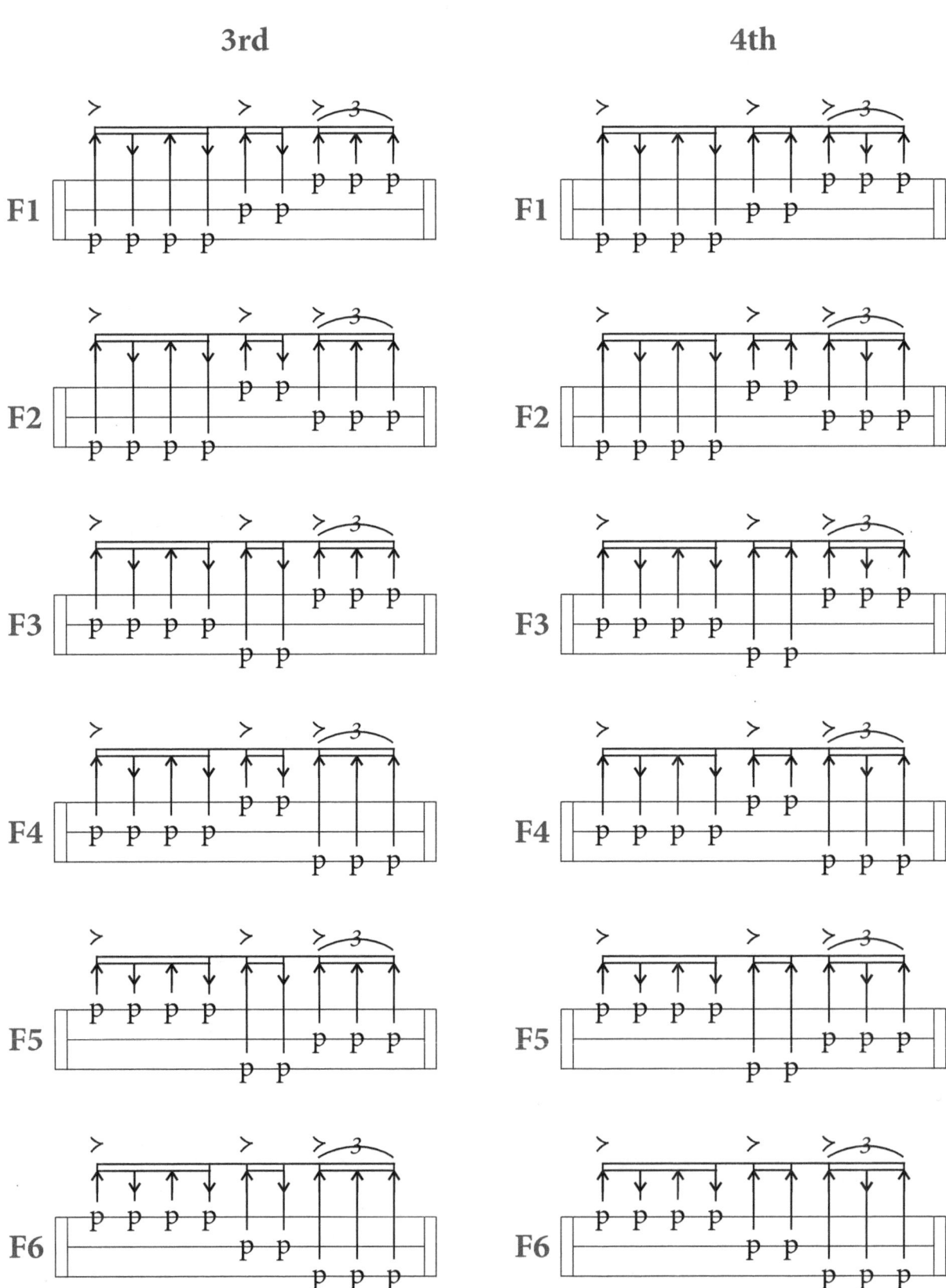

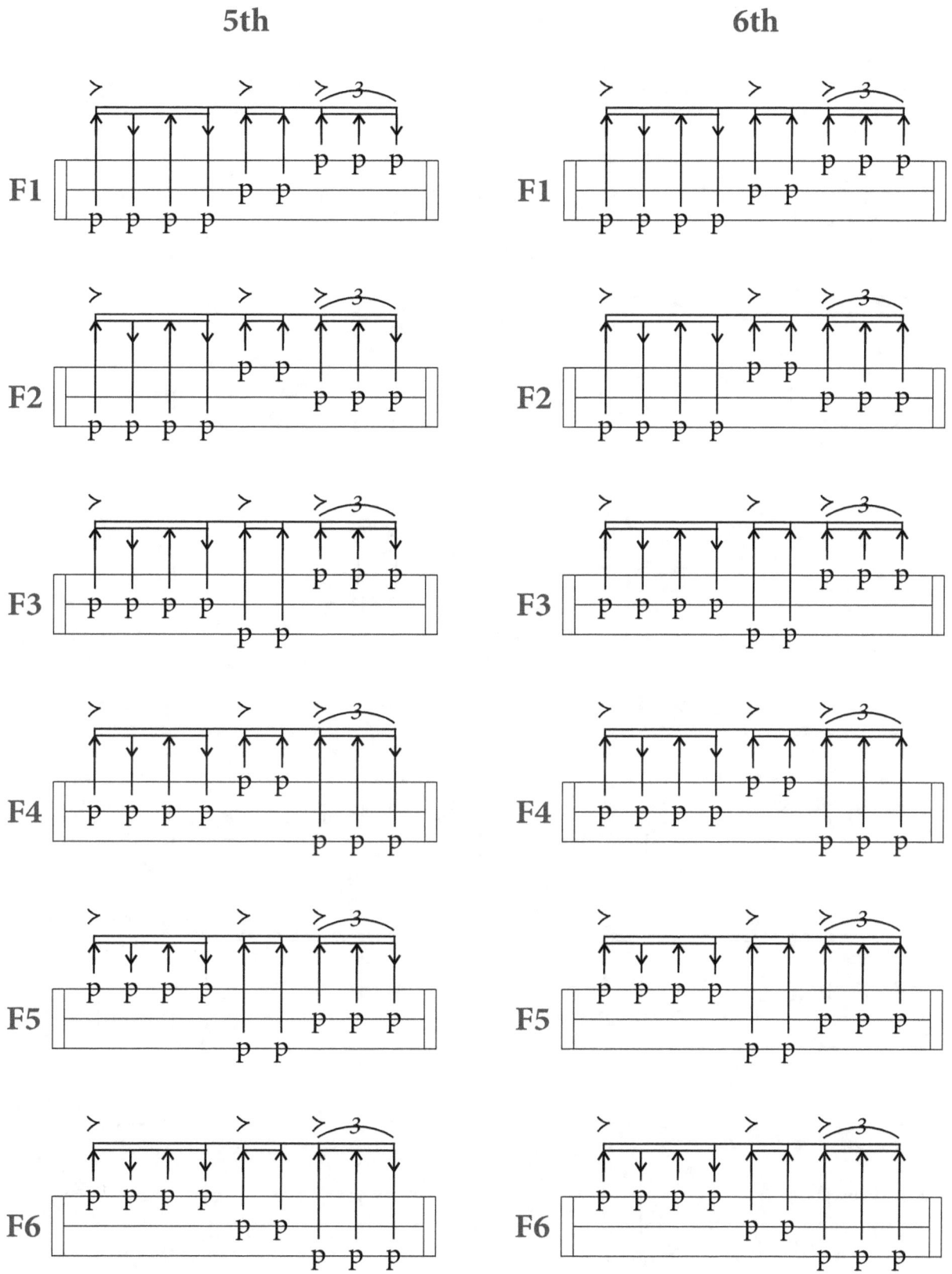

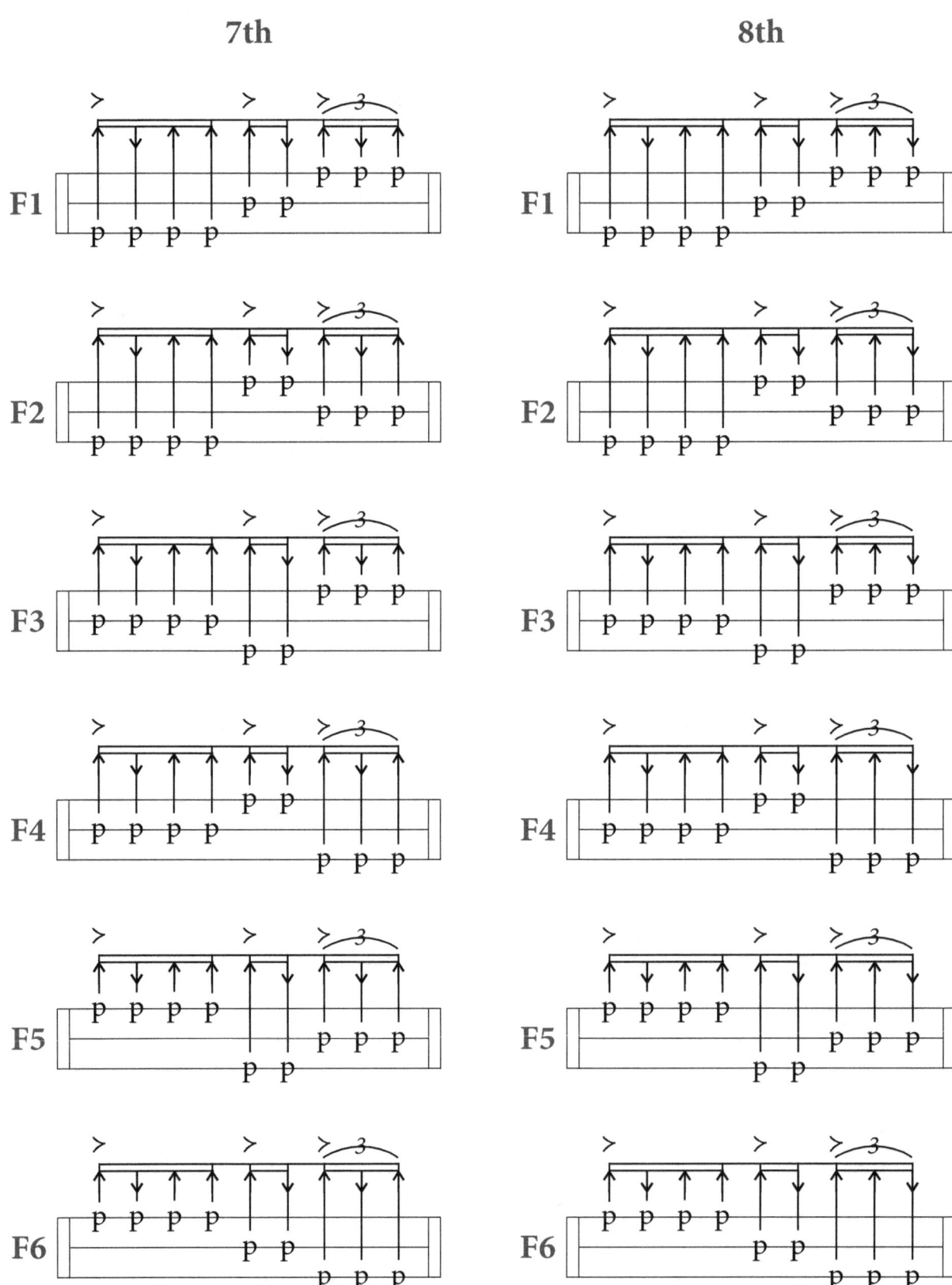

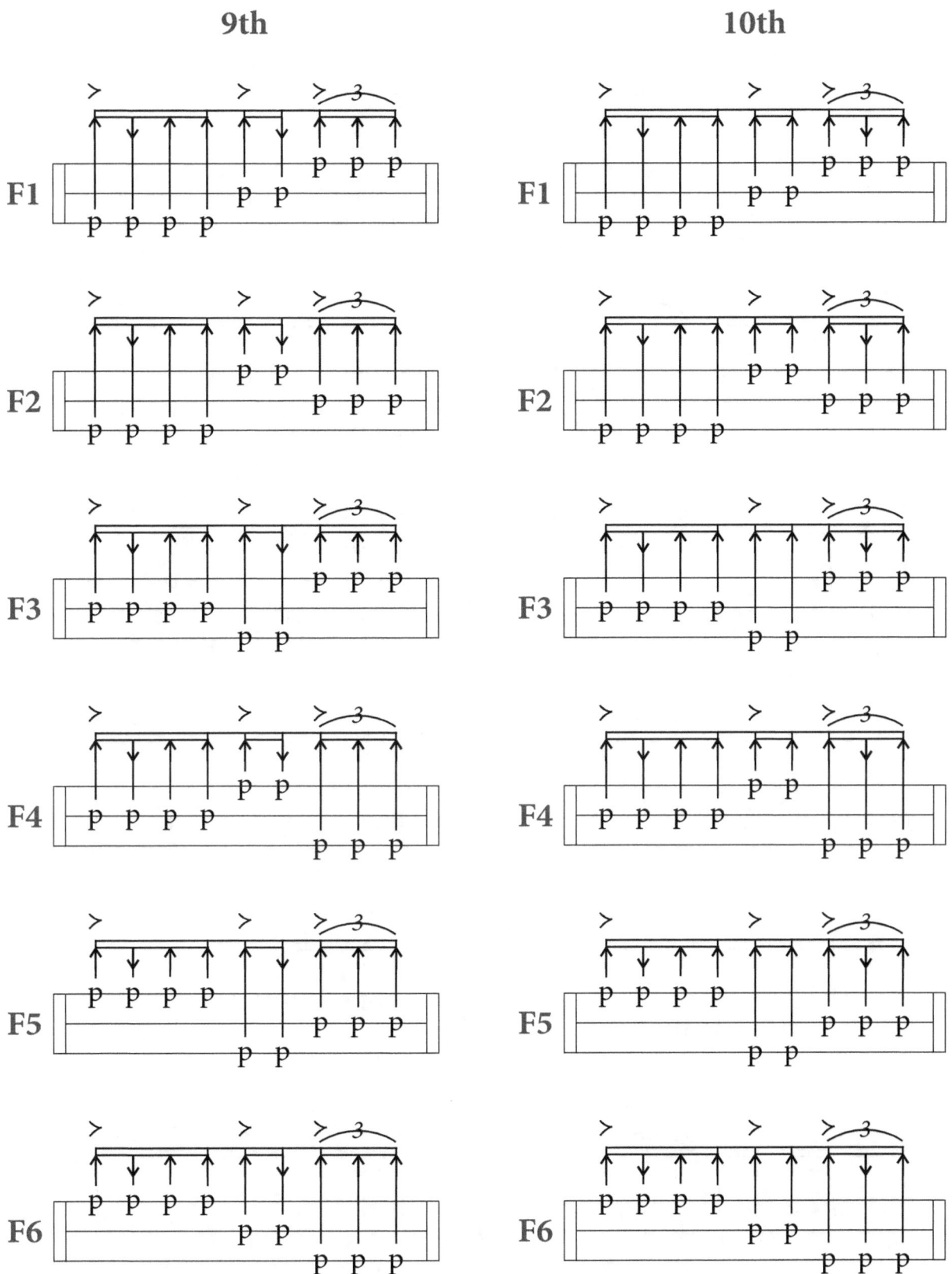

11th

F1 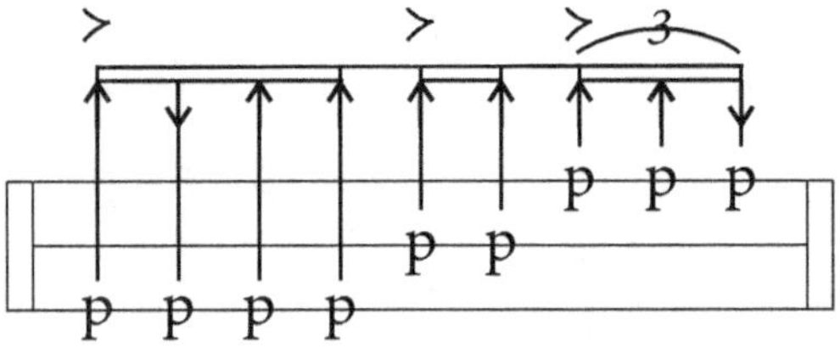

F2 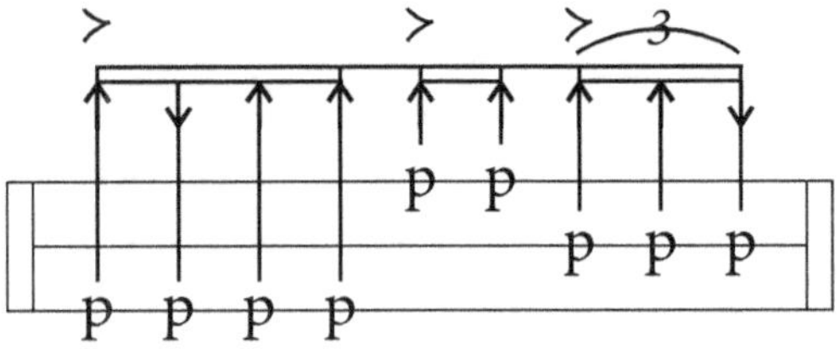

F3 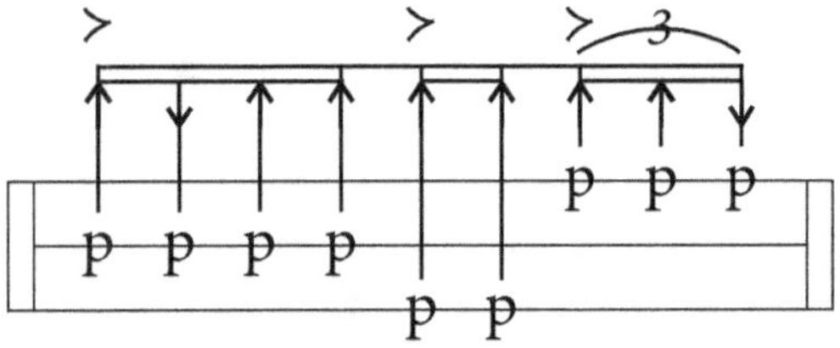

F4 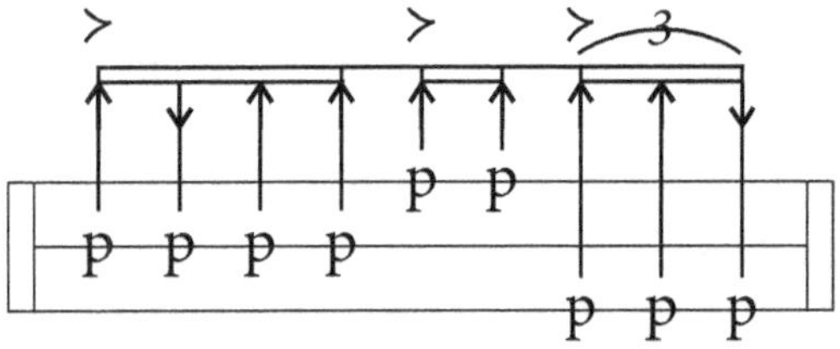

F5 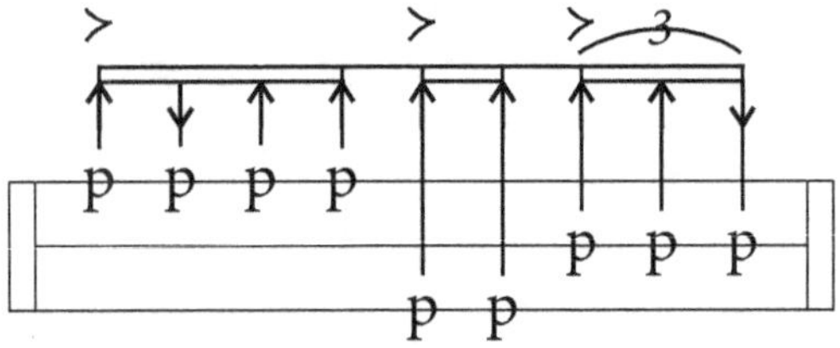

F6 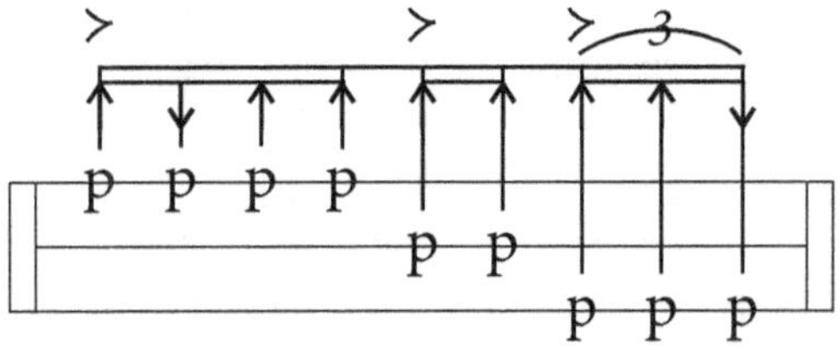

12th

F1 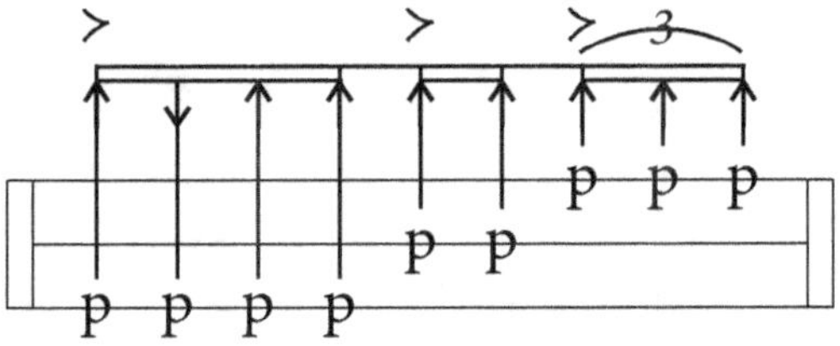

F2 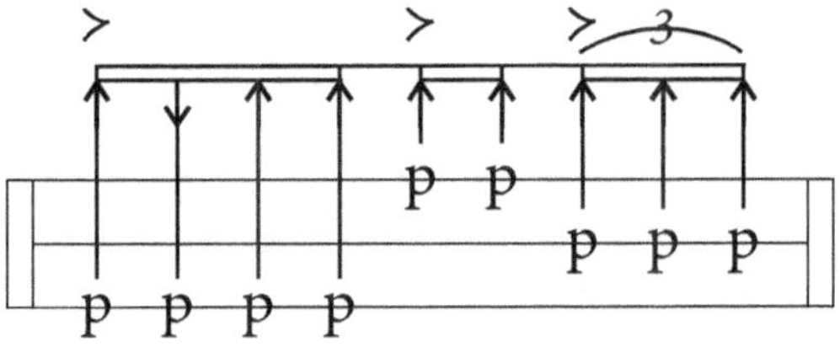

F3 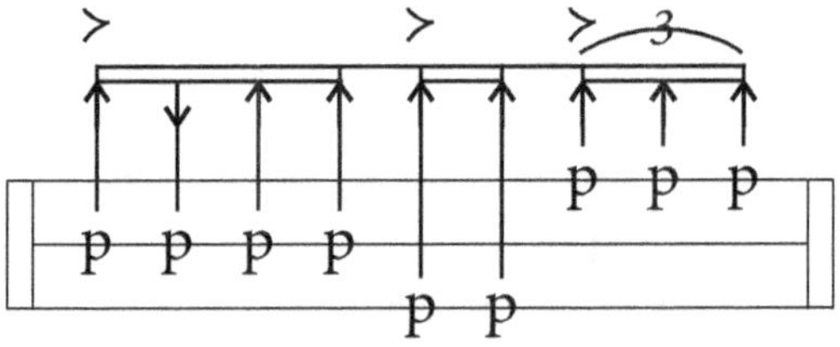

F4 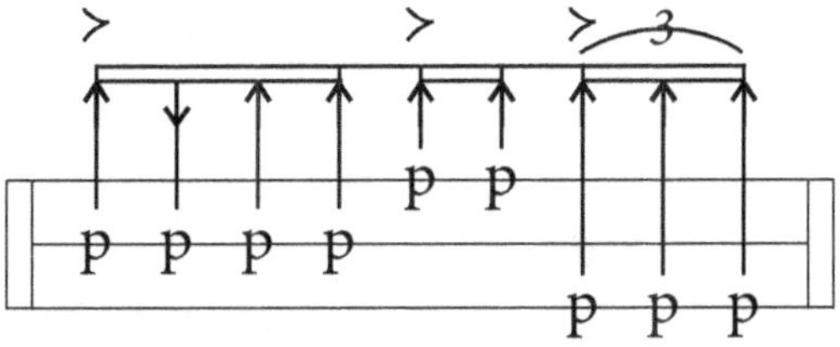

F5 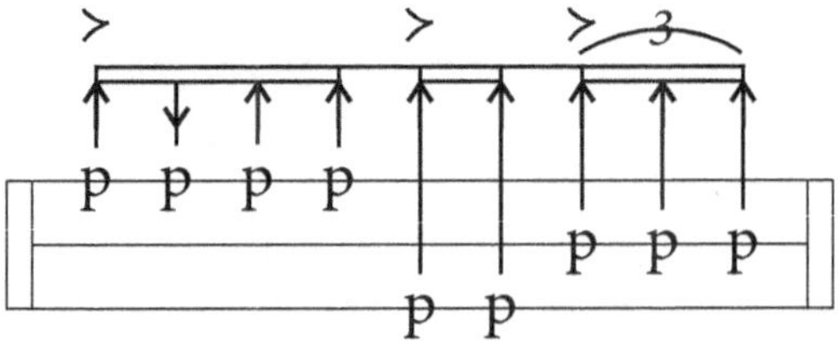

F6 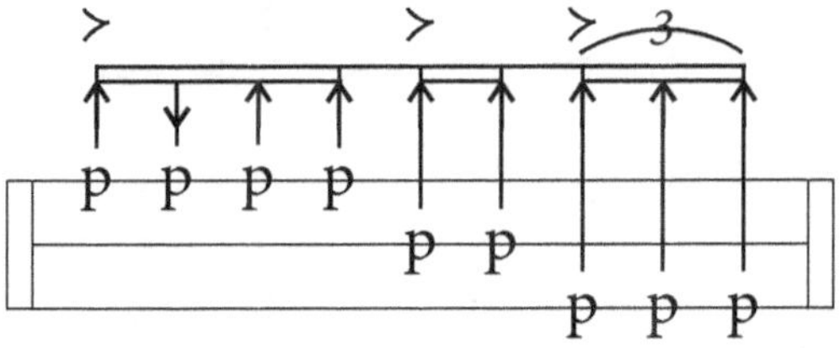

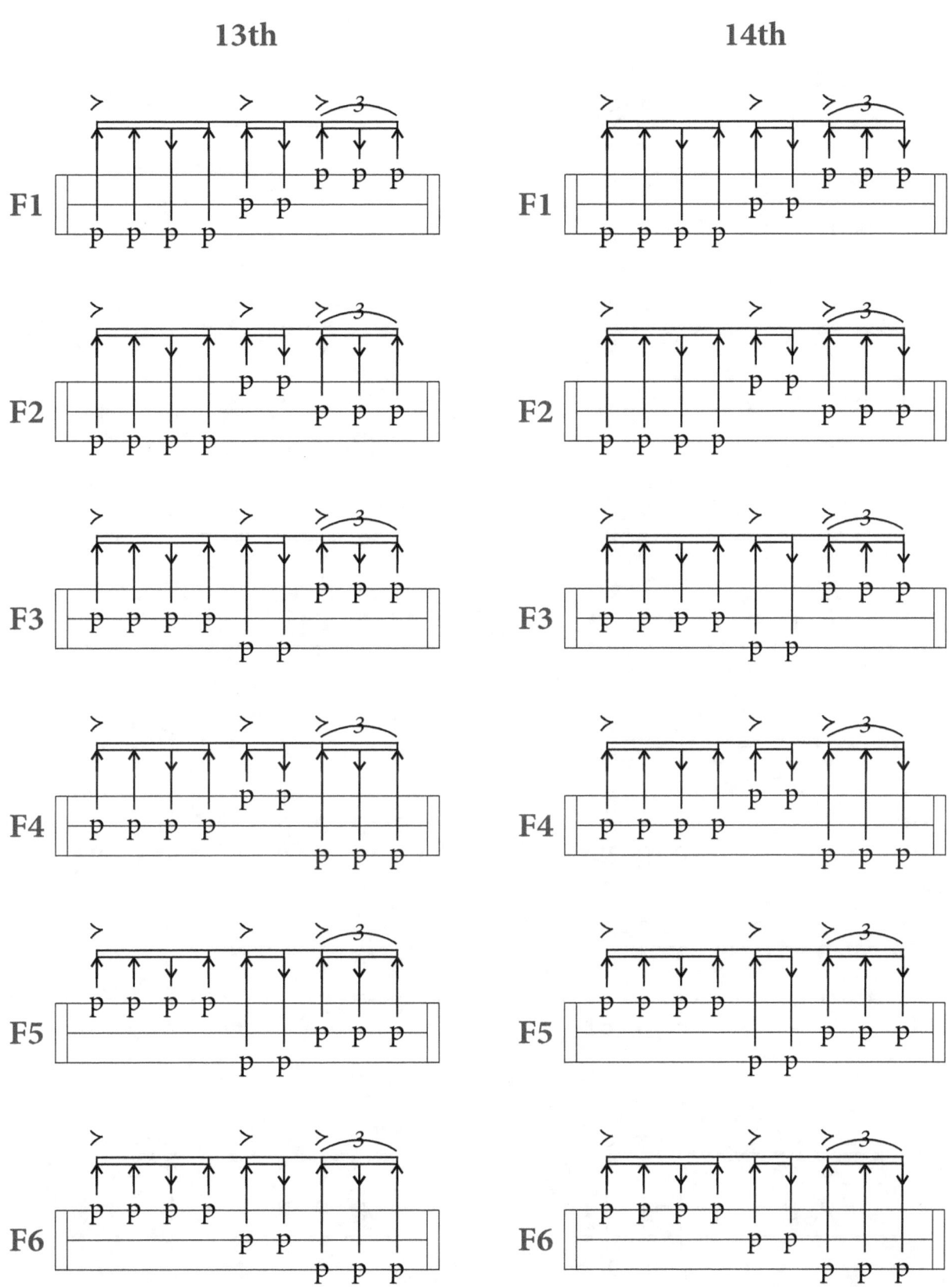

15th   **16th**

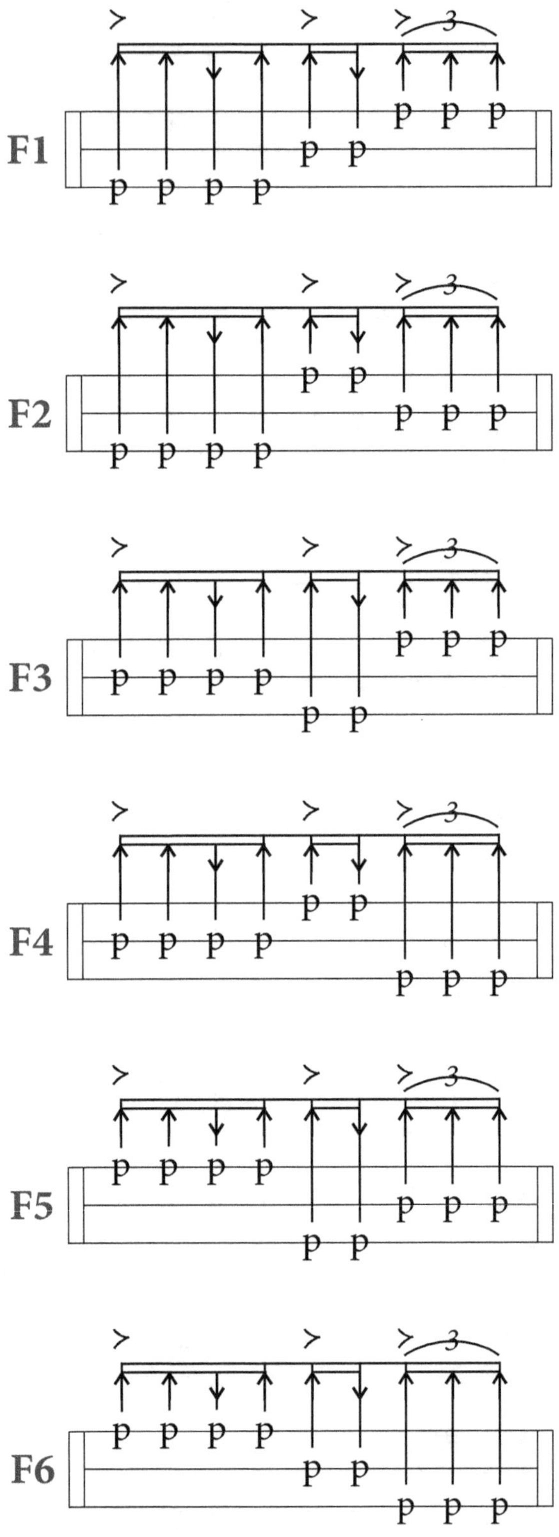

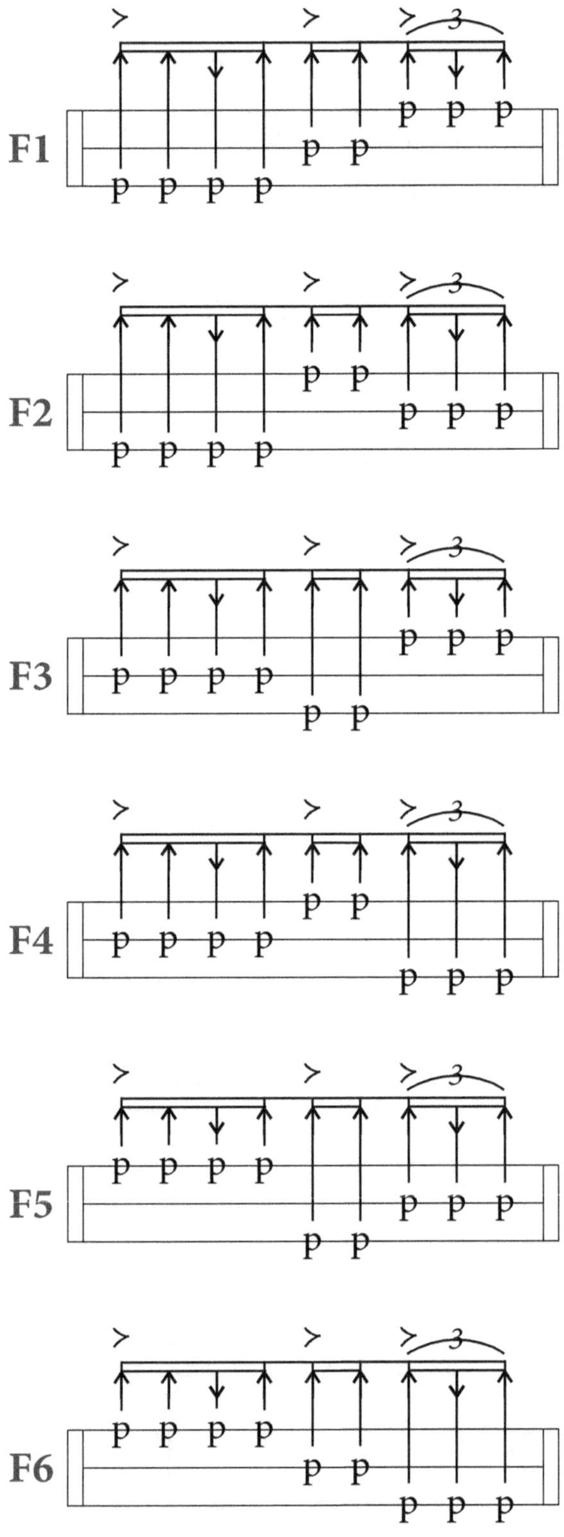

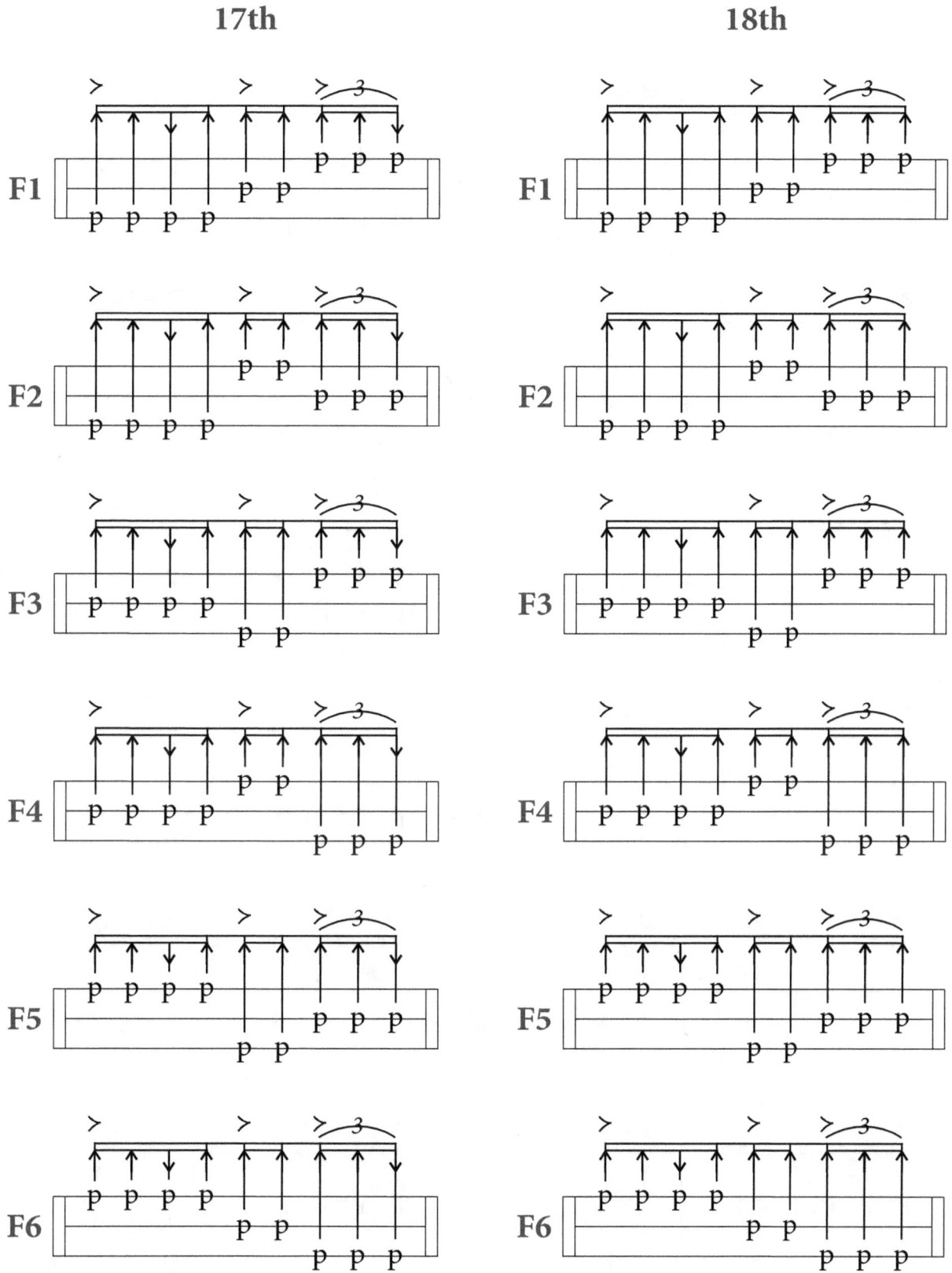

19th   20th

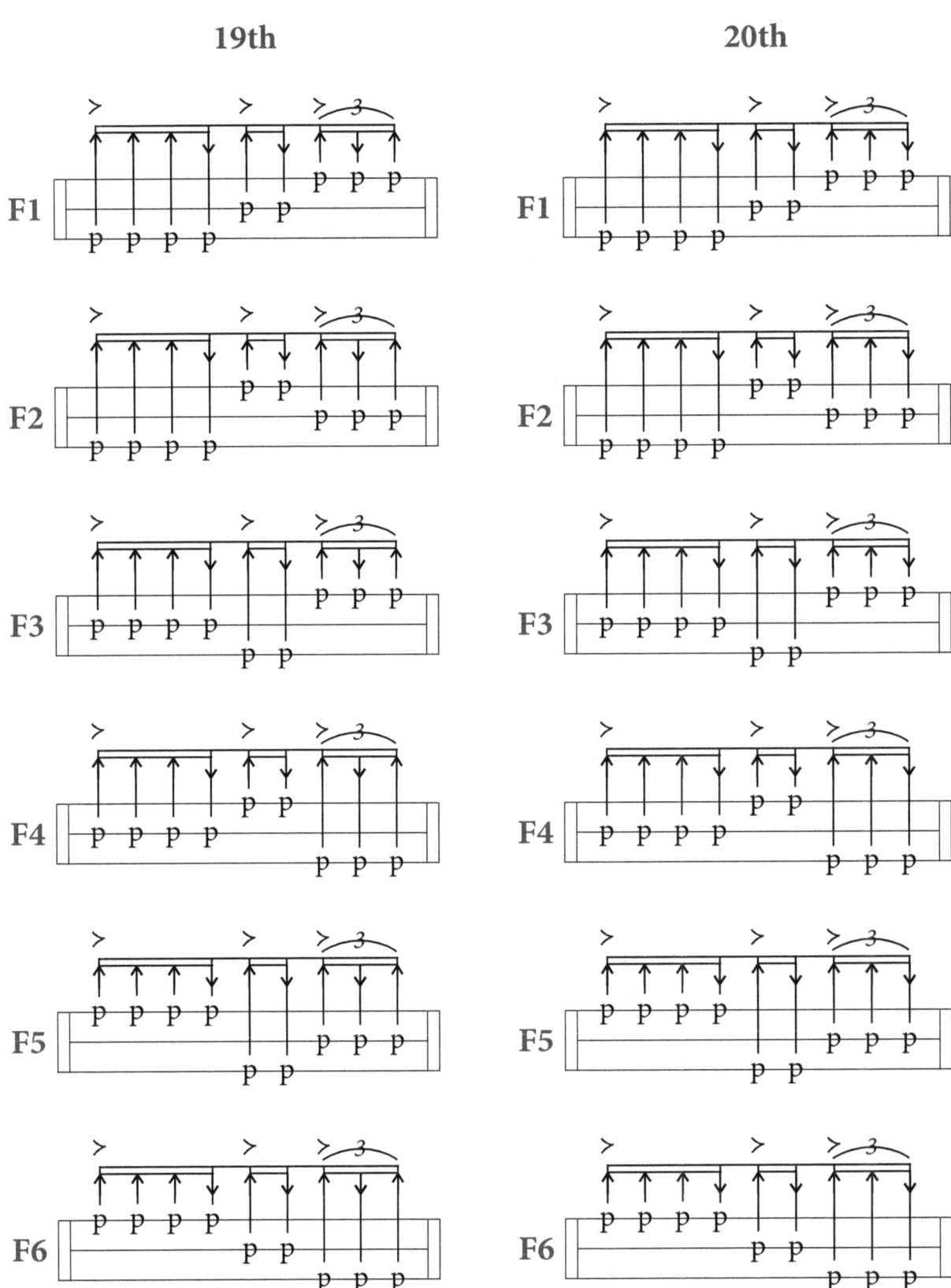

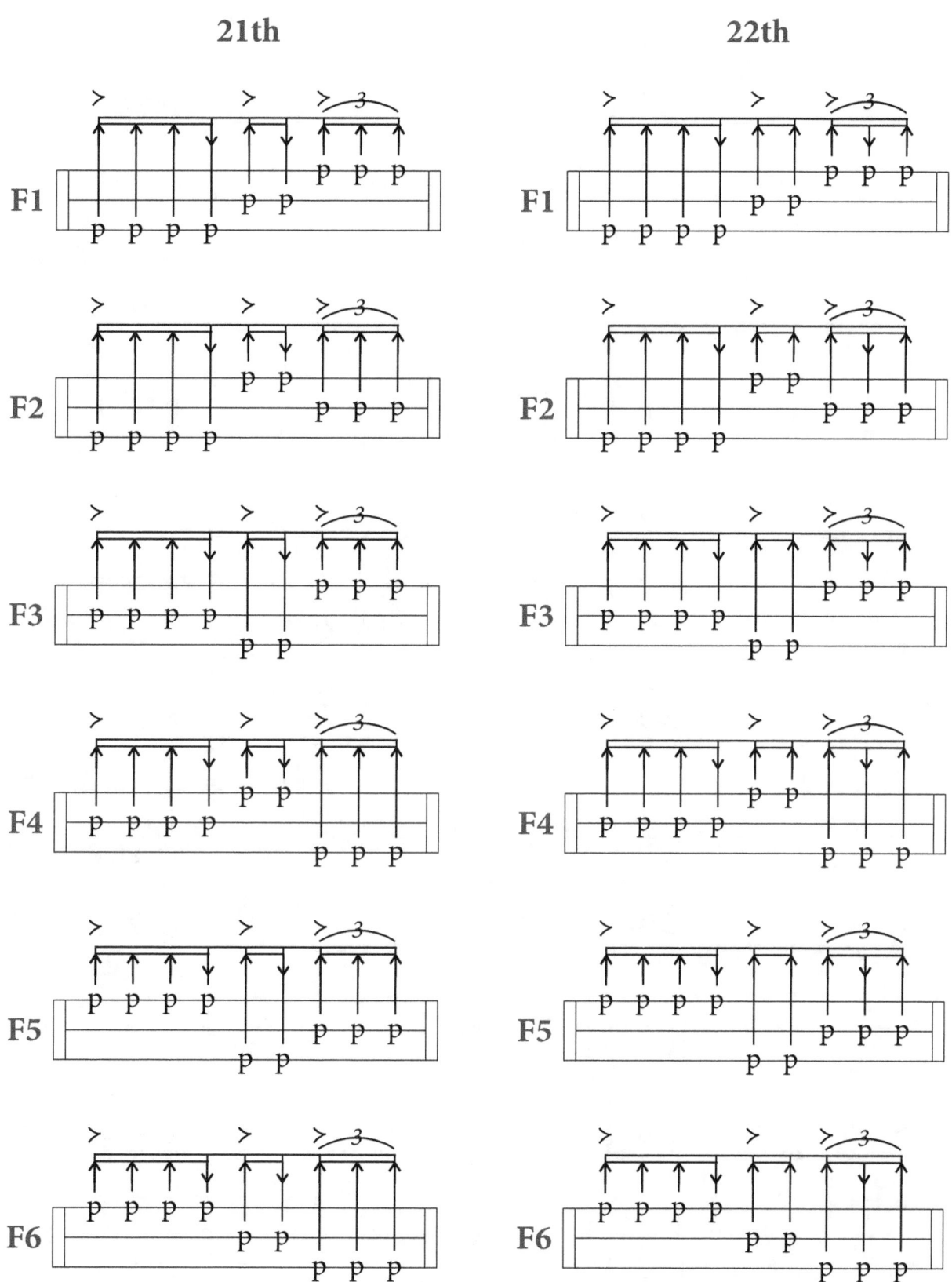

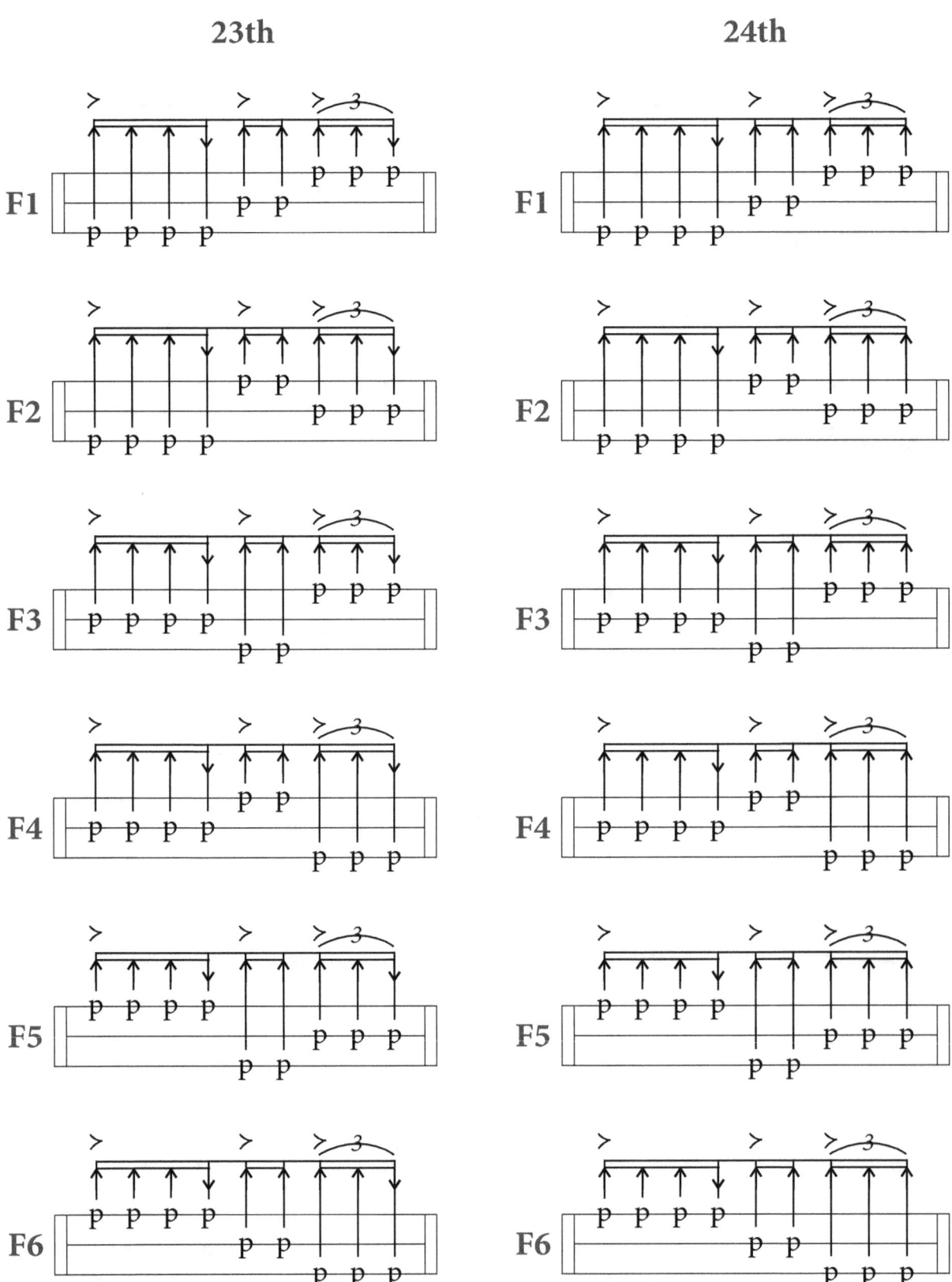

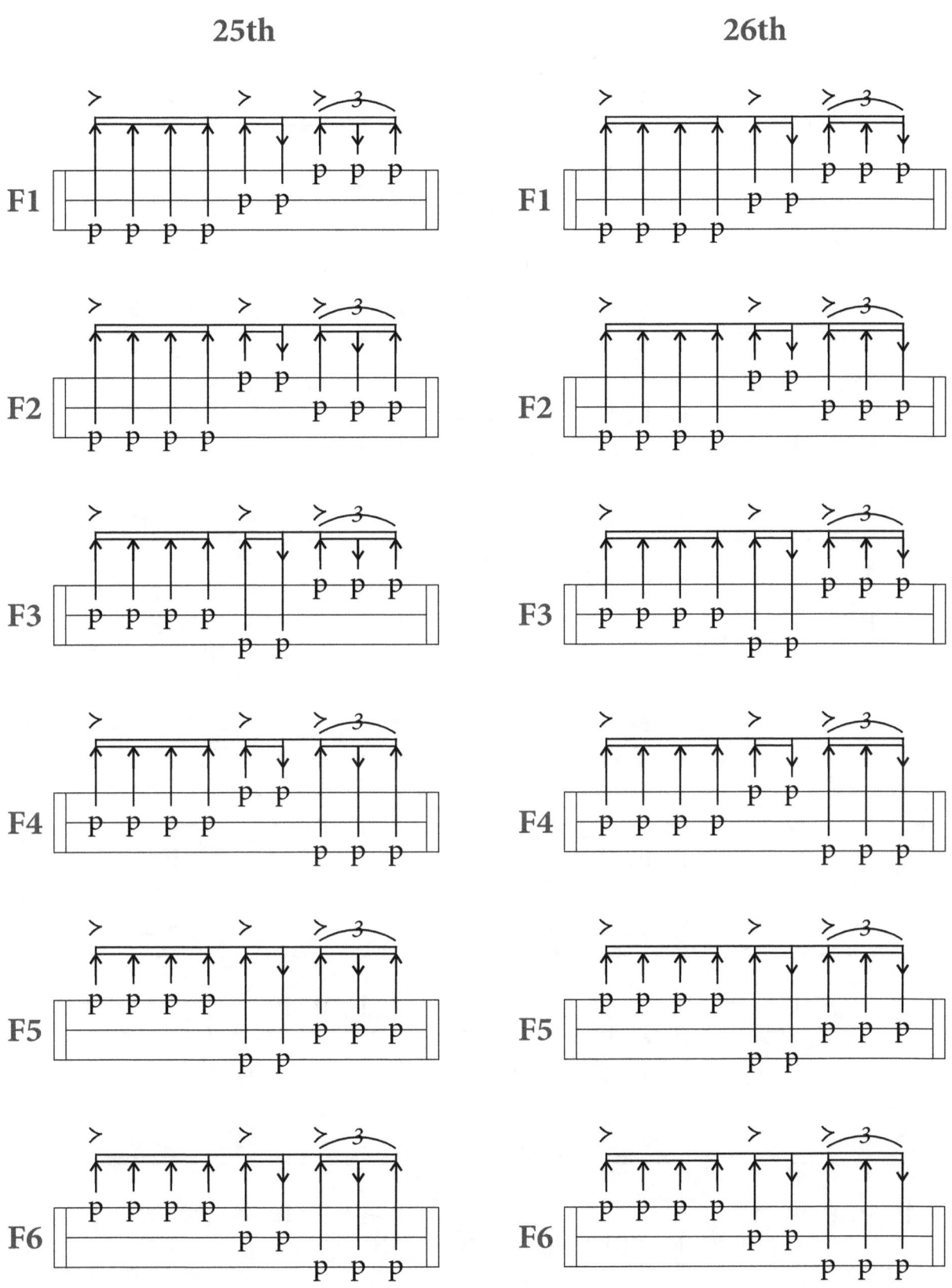

27th

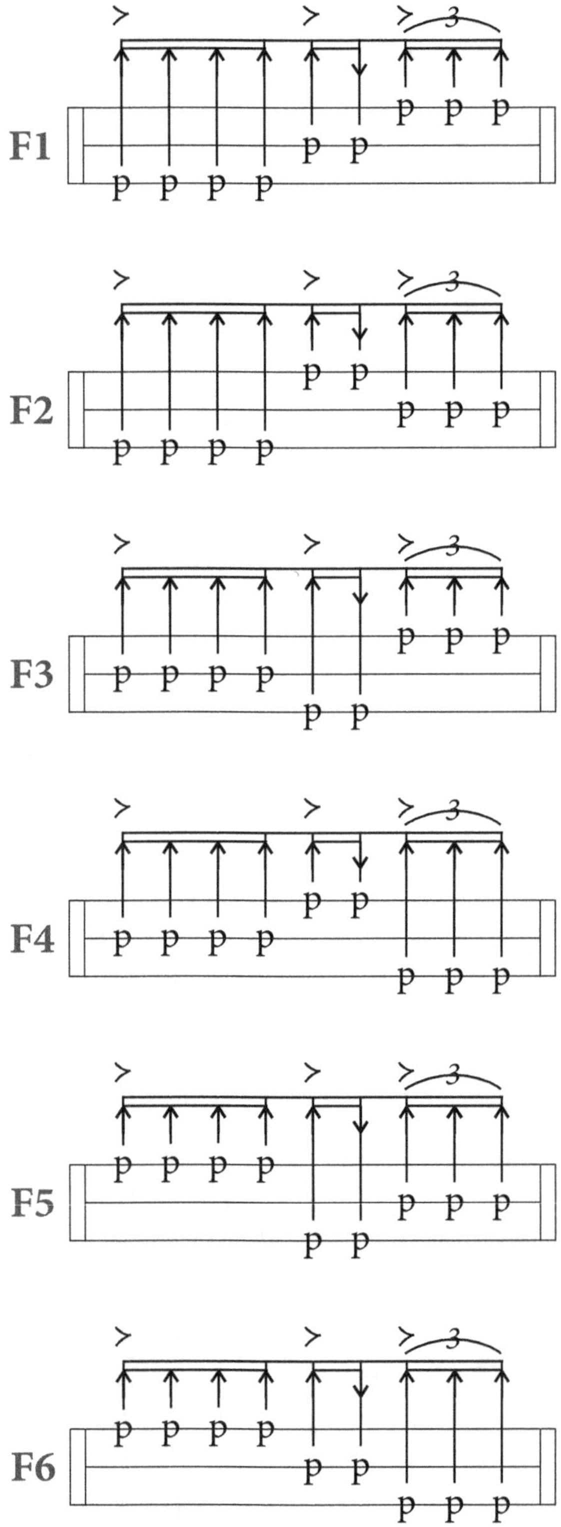
F1
p p p p p p p p p
F2
p p p p p p p p p
F3
p p p p p p p p p
F4
p p p p p p p p p
F5
p p p p p p p p p
F6
p p p p p p p p p

28th

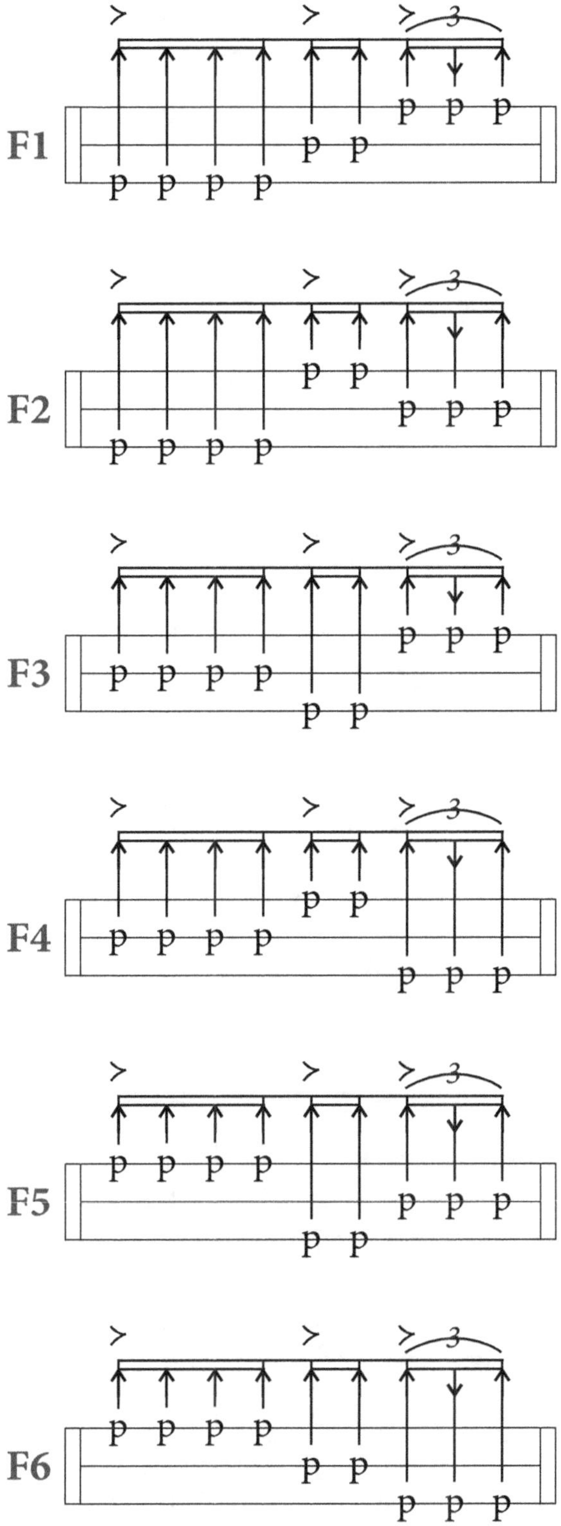
F1
p p p p p p p p p
F2
p p p p p p p p p
F3
p p p p p p p p p
F4
p p p p p p p p p
F5
p p p p p p p p p
F6
p p p p p p p p p

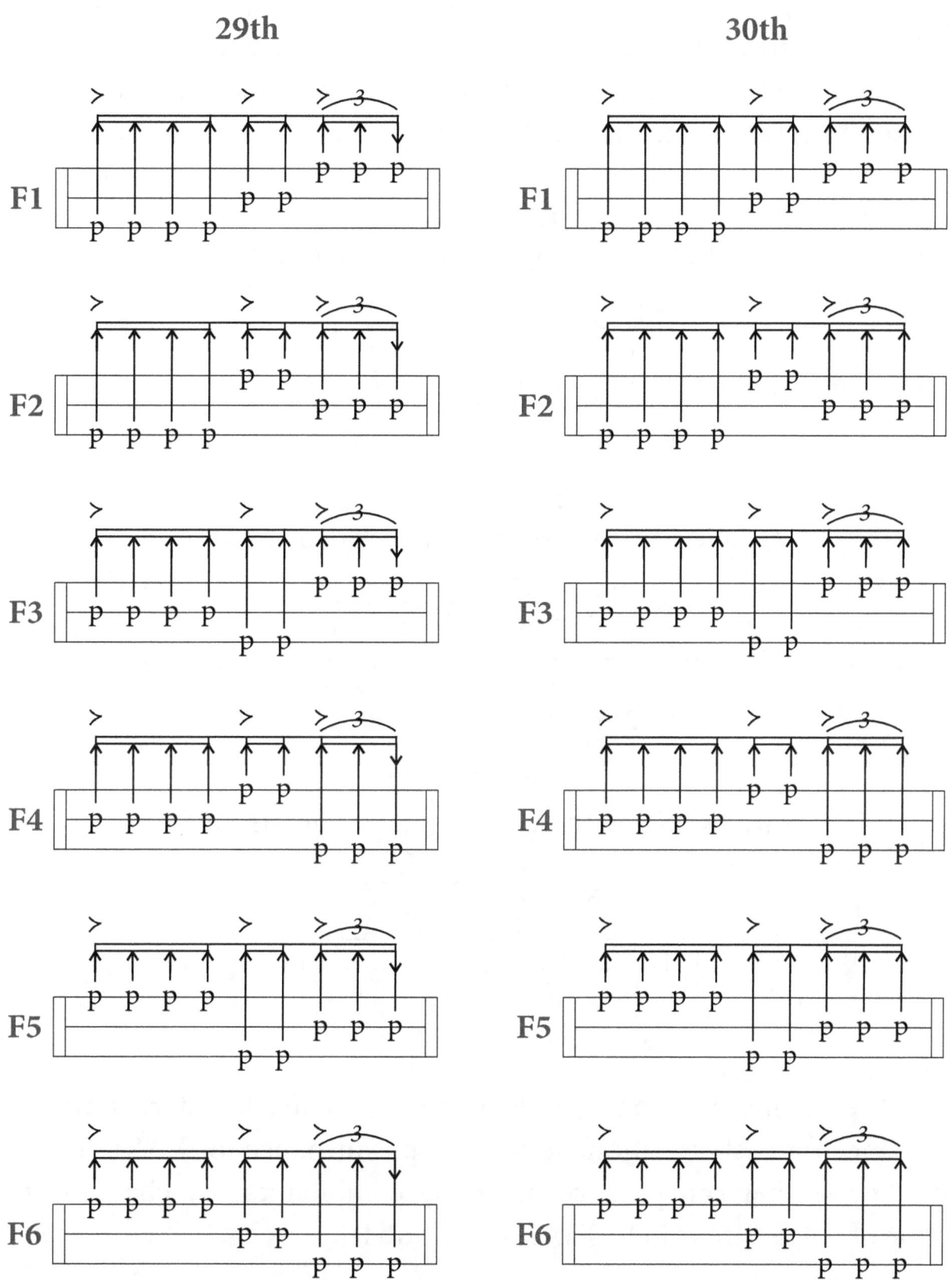

§ V

Exercise on pulgar on three adjacent strings with two triple strokes and one quad stroke within each Formula. The exercise includes three variations with 6 Formulas in each one. Isochronous playing of triple stroke (triplet) and quad stroke towards the mentioned direction.

VARIATION I
Variation I with triple - quad -triple stroke

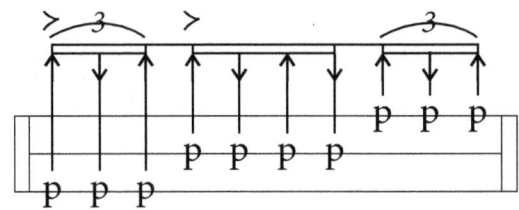

VARIATION II
Variation II with triple - triple - quad stroke

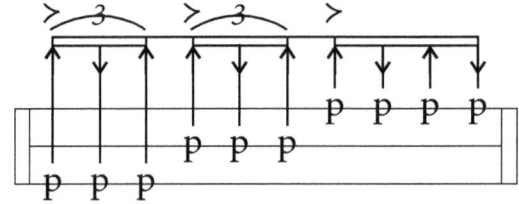

VARIATION III
Variation III with quad - triple - triple stroke

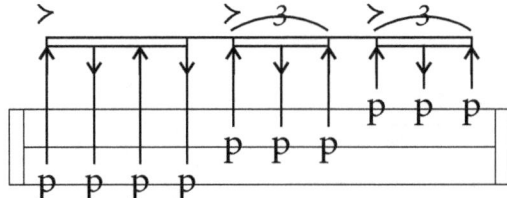

The change in the direction of pulgar stroke results in different ways of performance for each variation. 45 ways of performance for VARIATION I follow. The learner can practice on many combination by changing the direction of pulgar stroke in VARIATION II and III.

VARIATION I   VARIATION II

F1 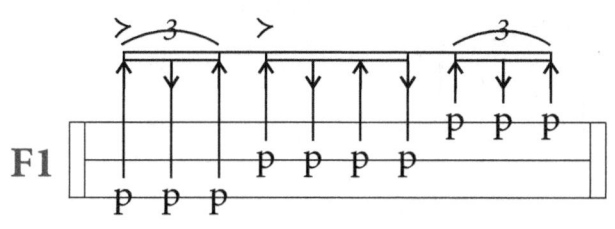   F1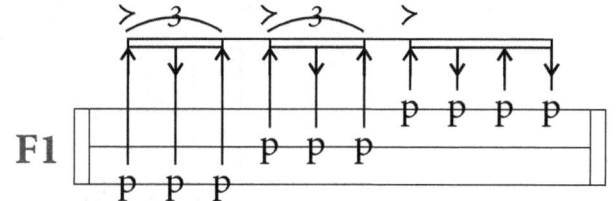

F2 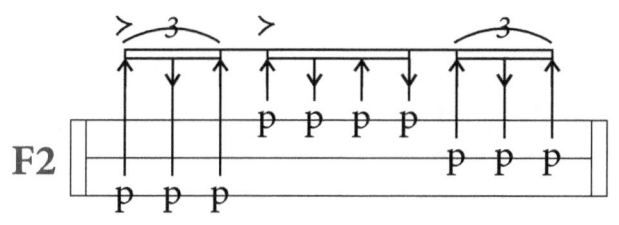   F2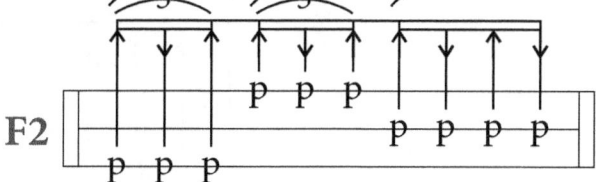

F3 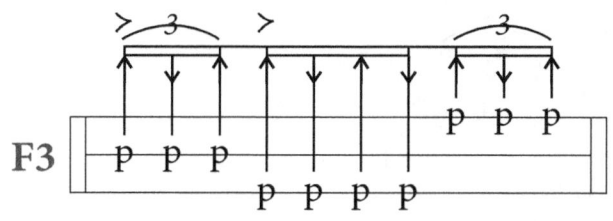   F3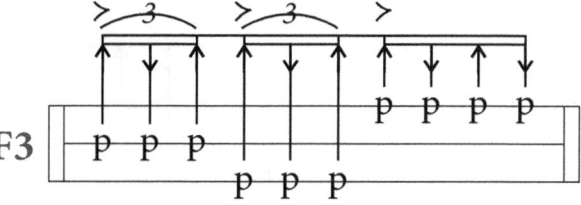

F4 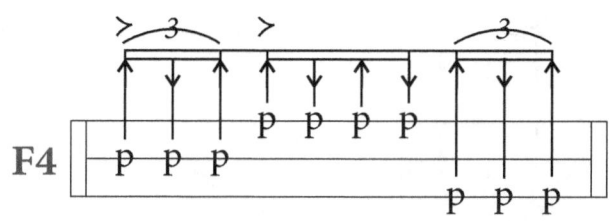   F4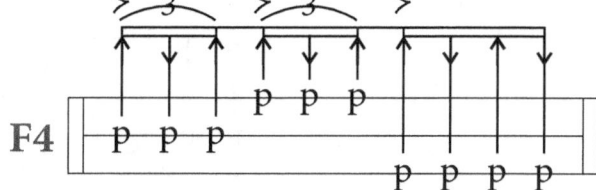

F5 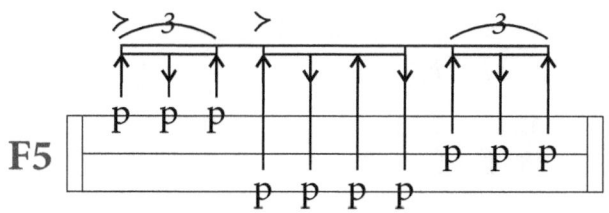   F5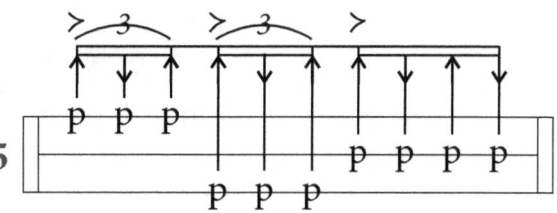

F6 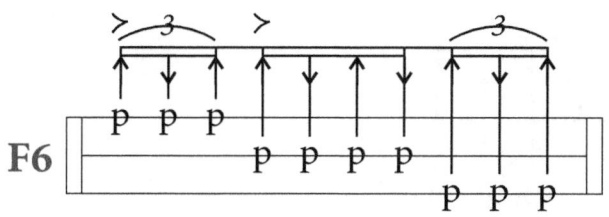   F6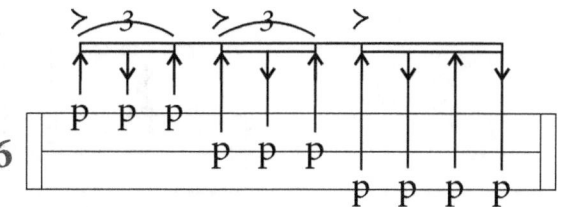

VARIATION
III

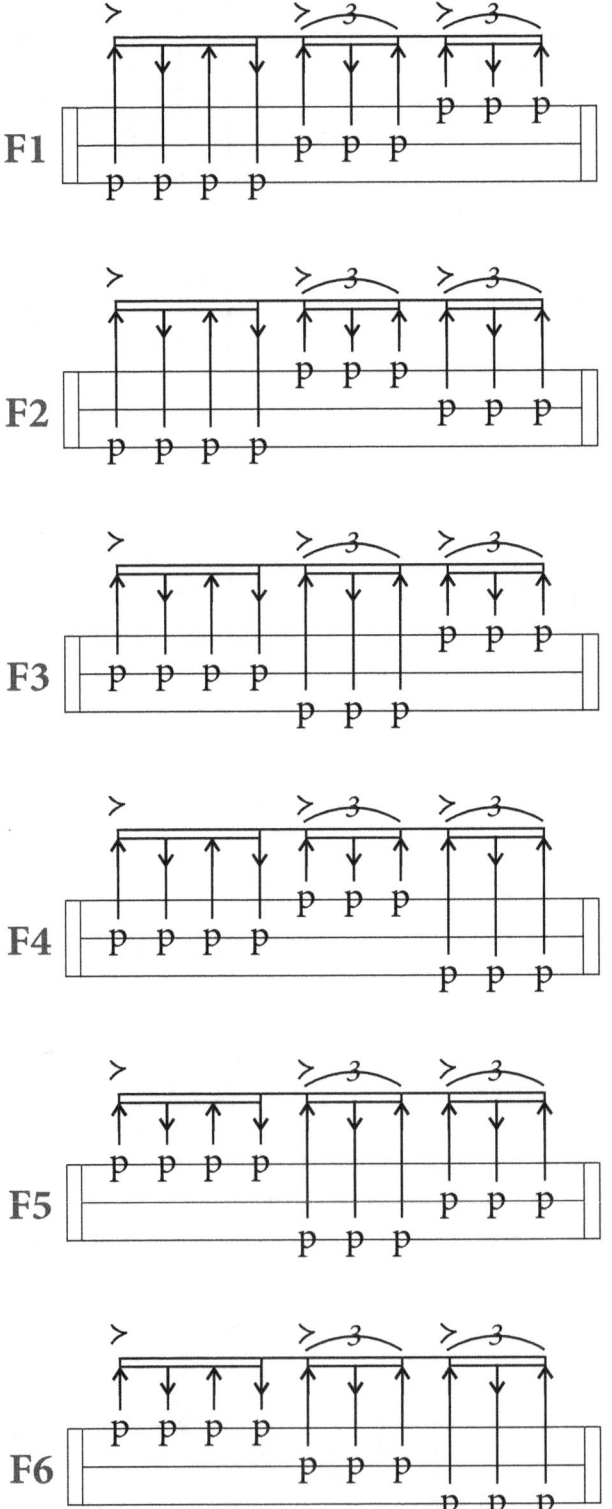

45 ways of performance of variation I which results from the change in the direction of pulgar stroke follow.

VARIATION I
WAYS OF PERFORMANCE

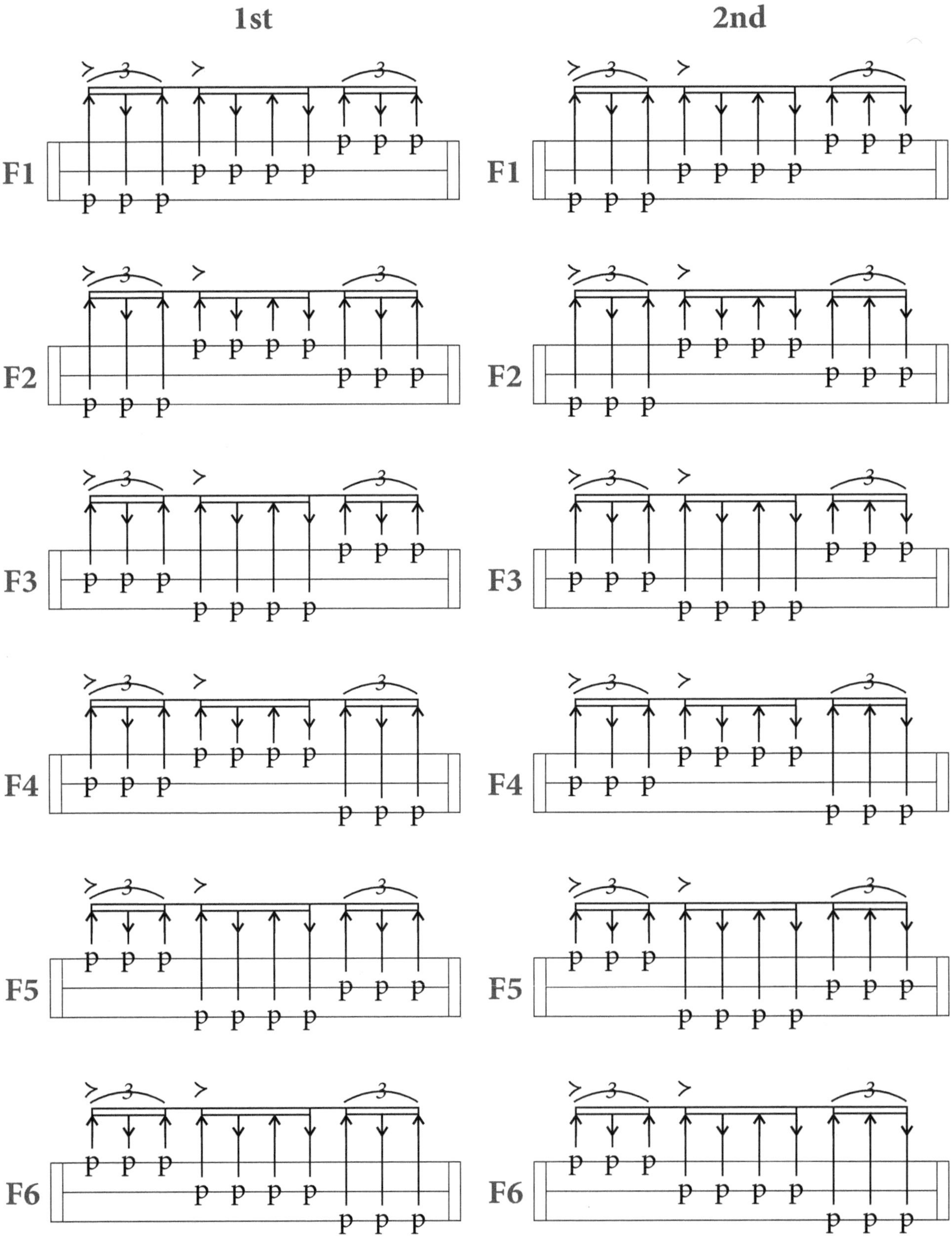

1st   **2nd**

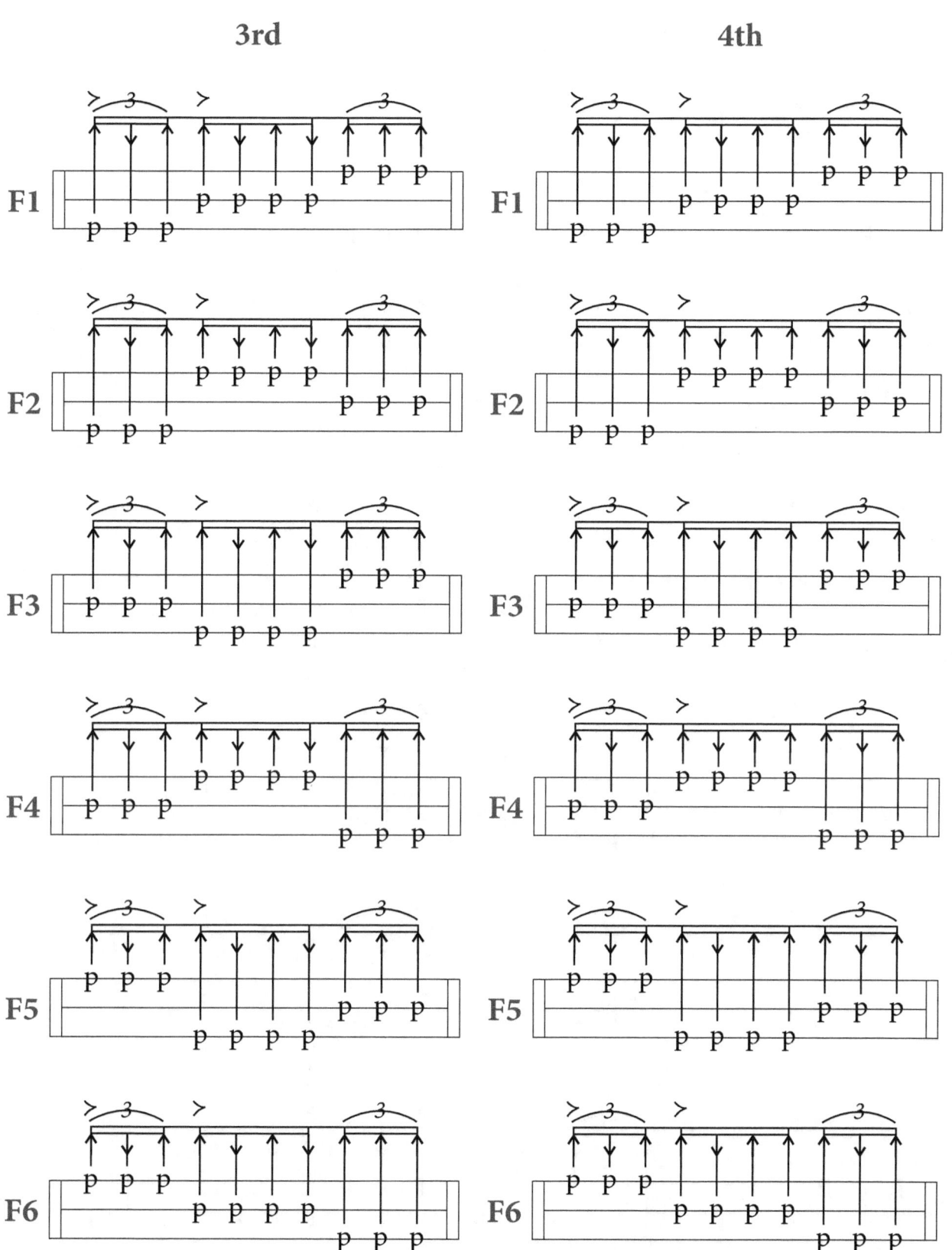

5th	6th

F1
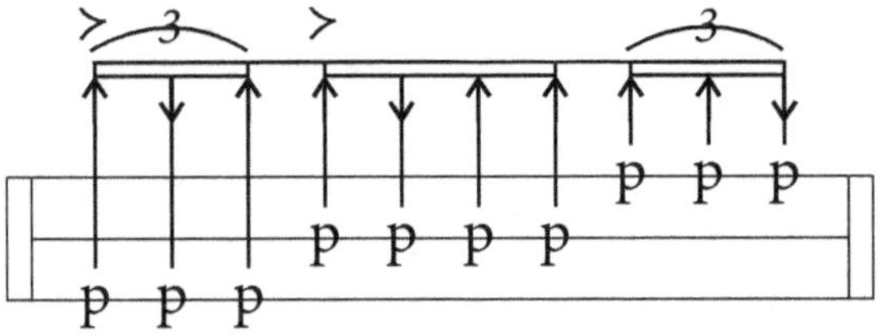
F1
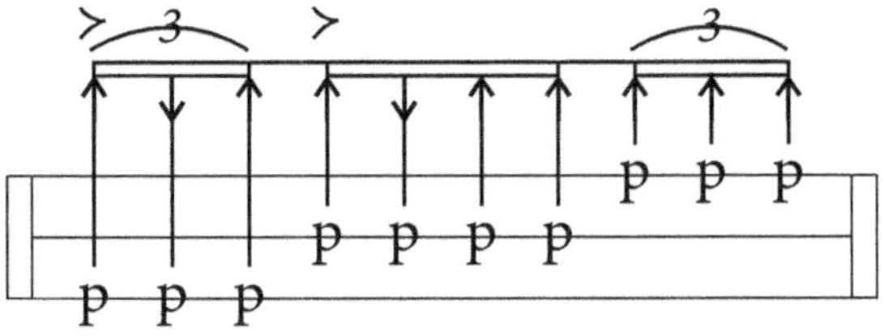

F2
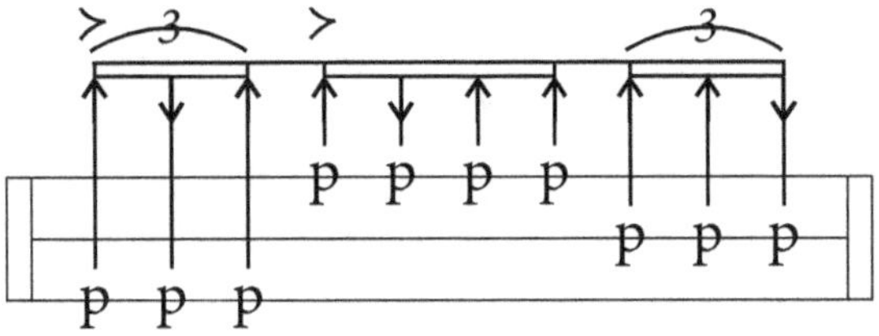
F2
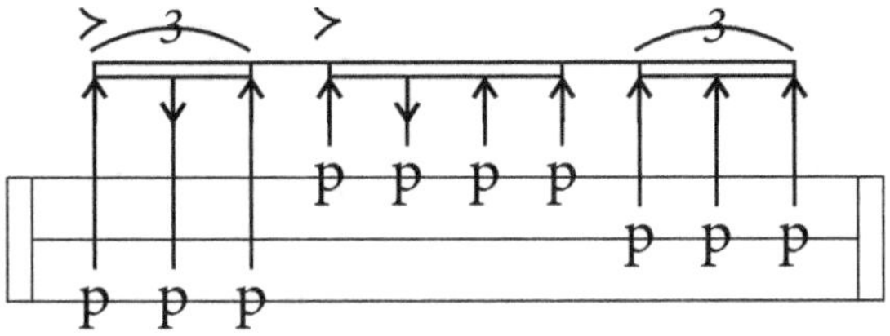

F3
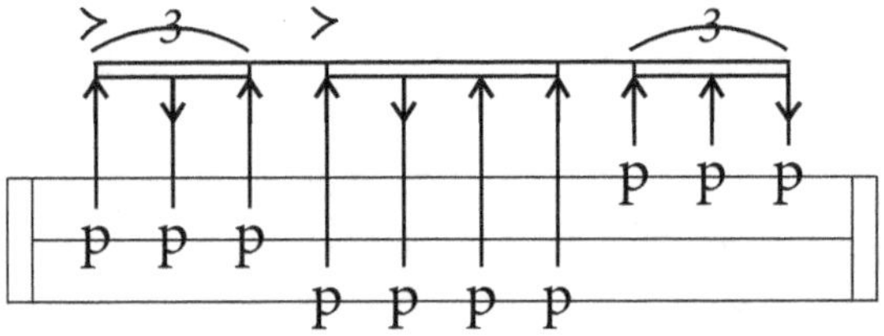
F3
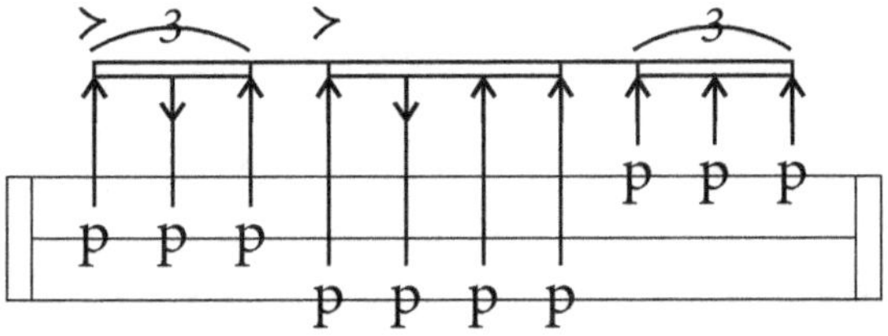

F4
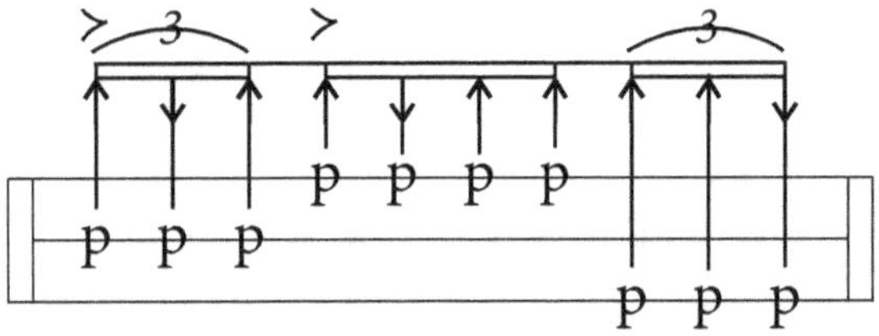
F4
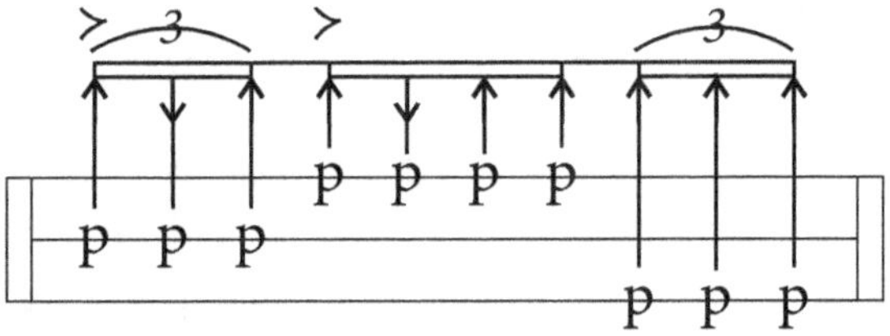

F5
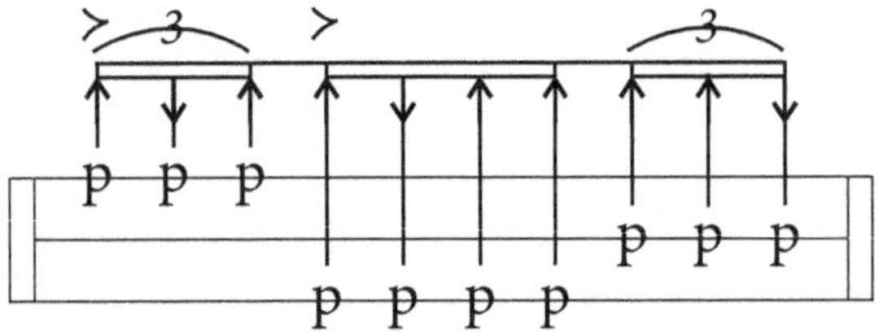
F5
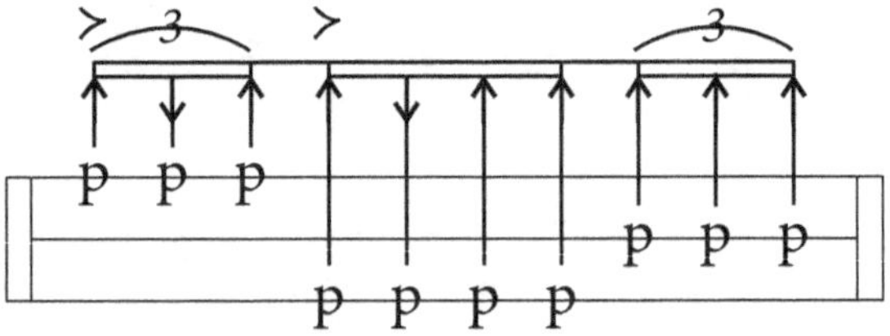

F6
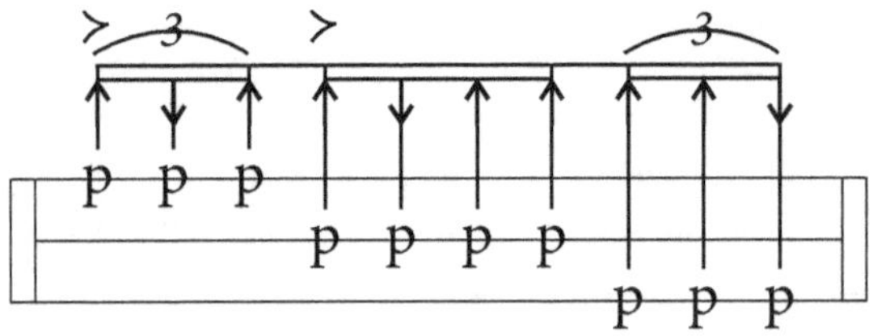
F6
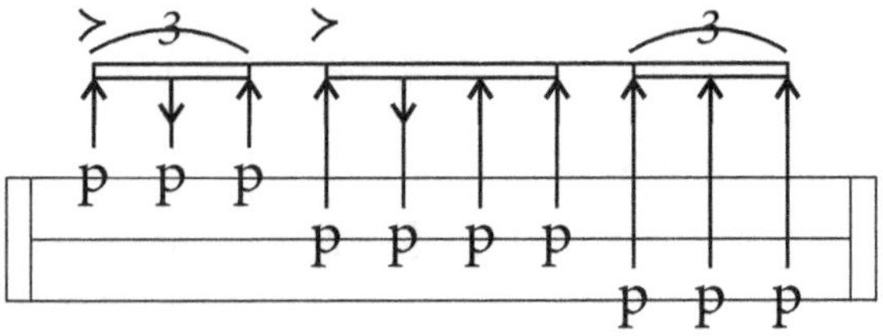

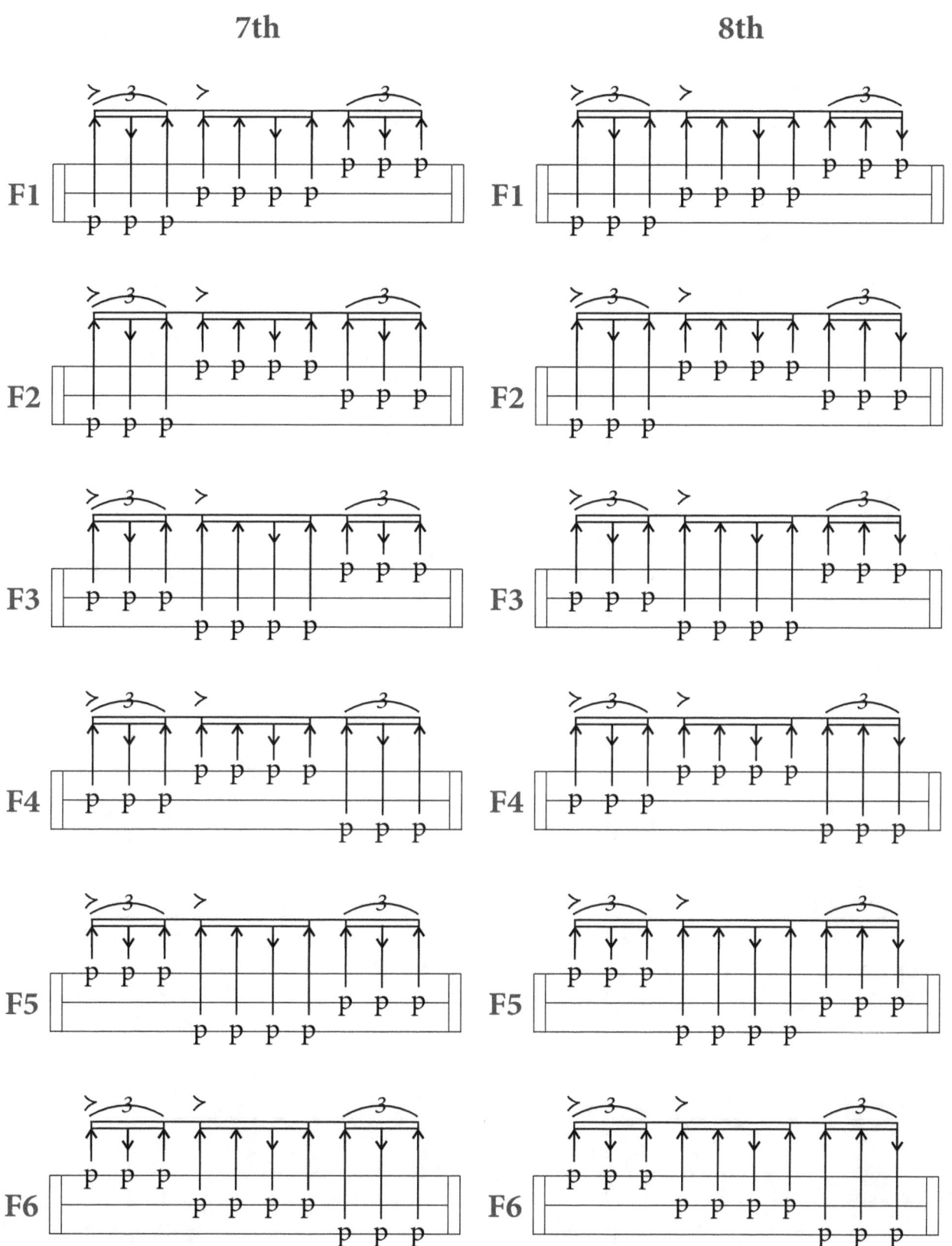

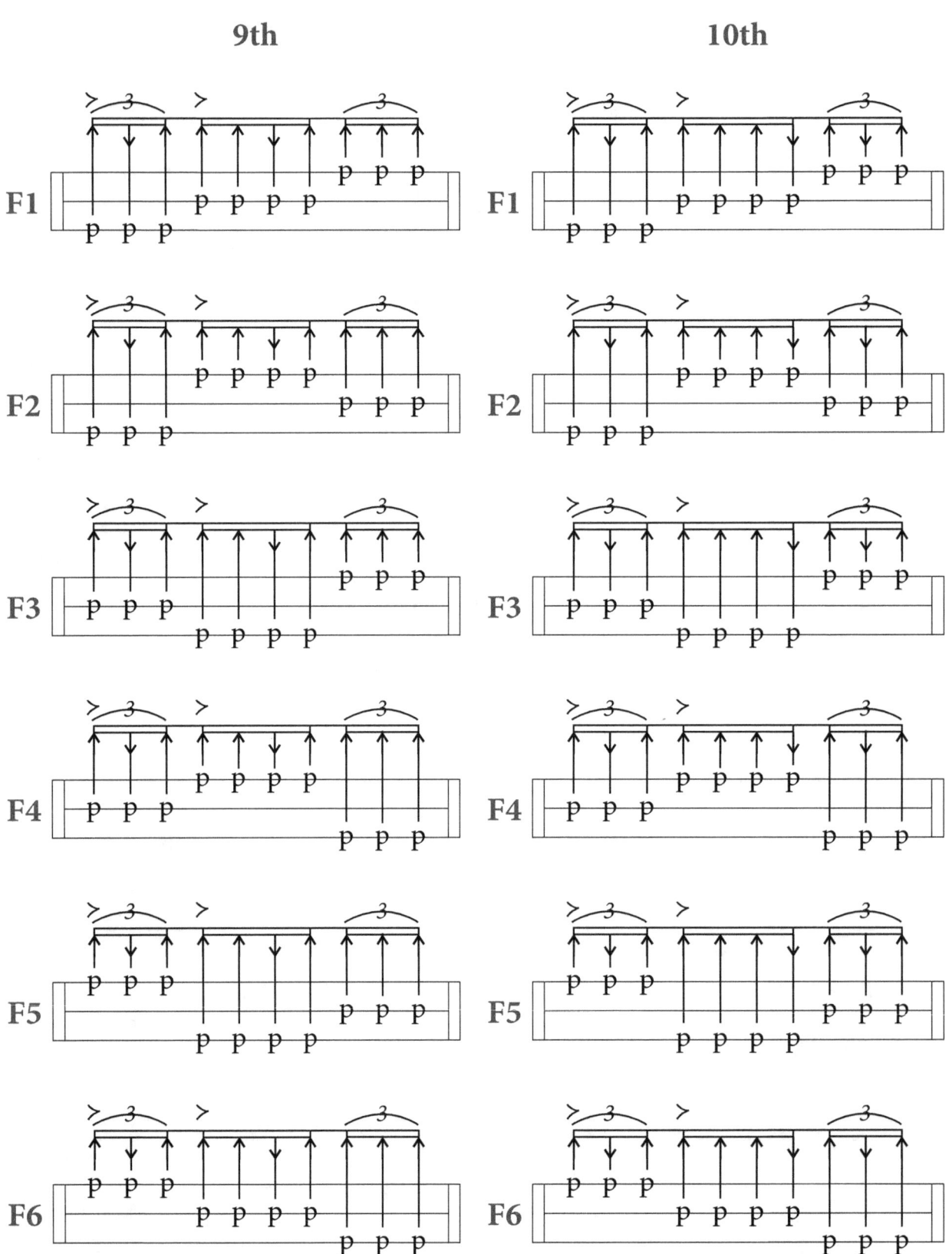

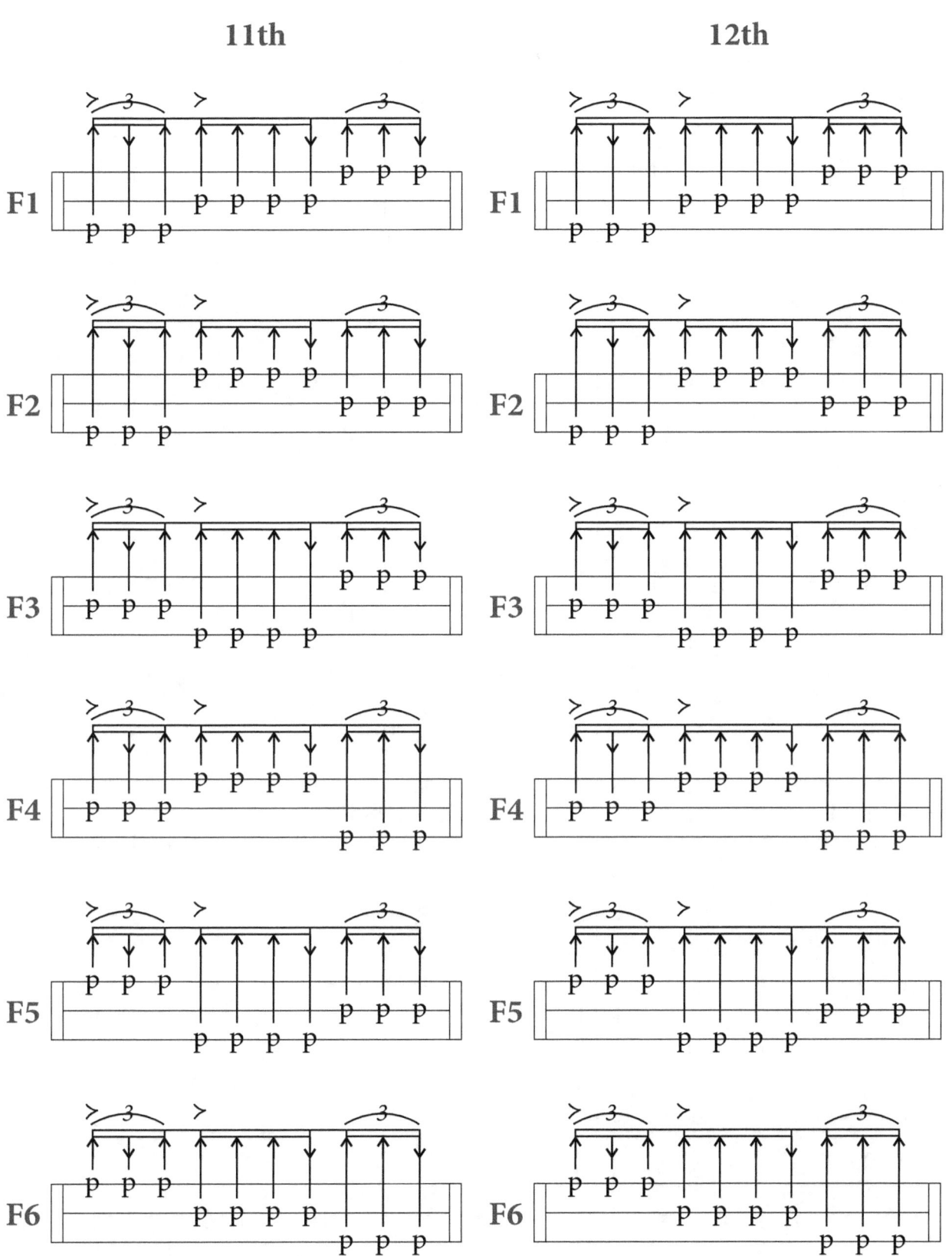

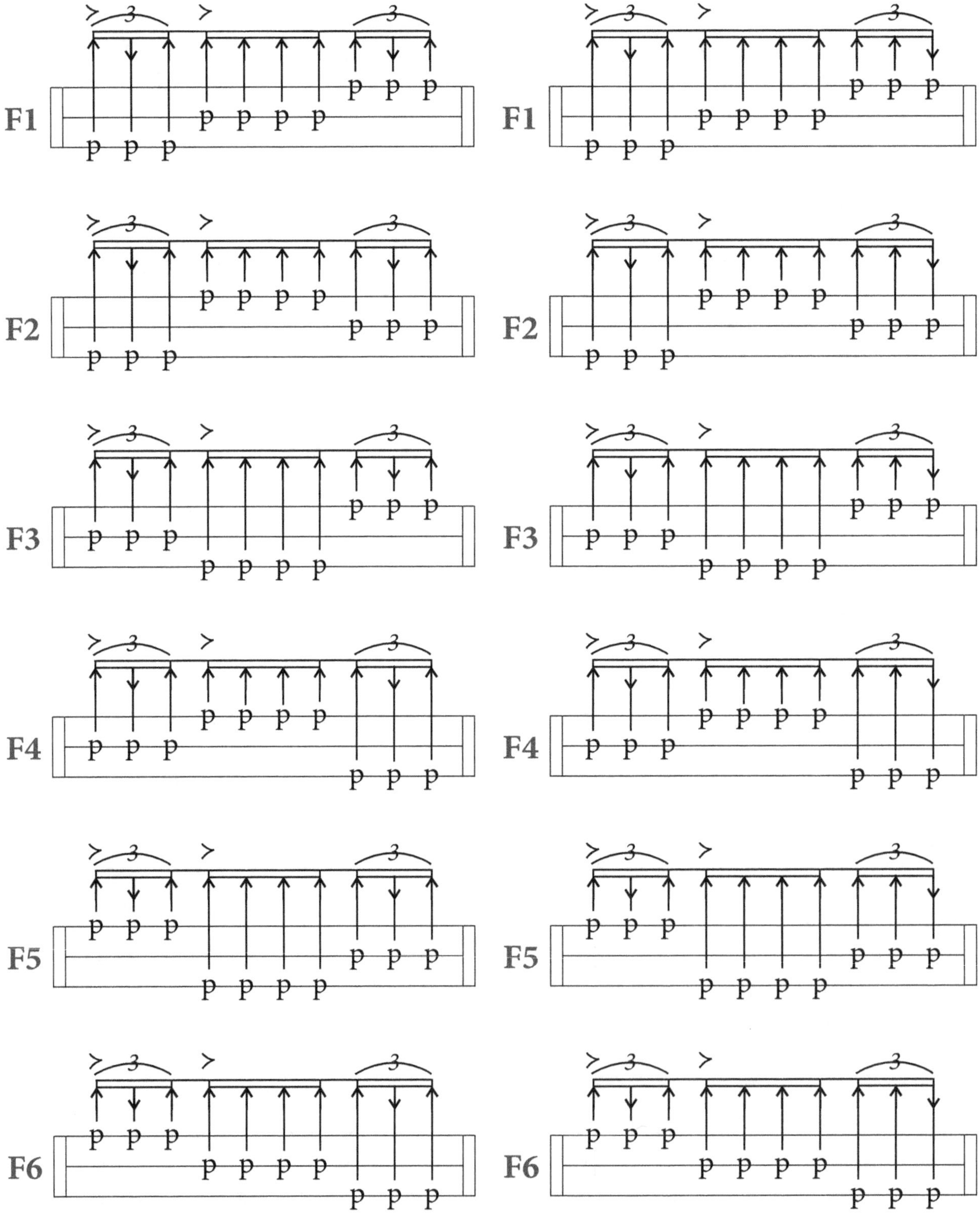

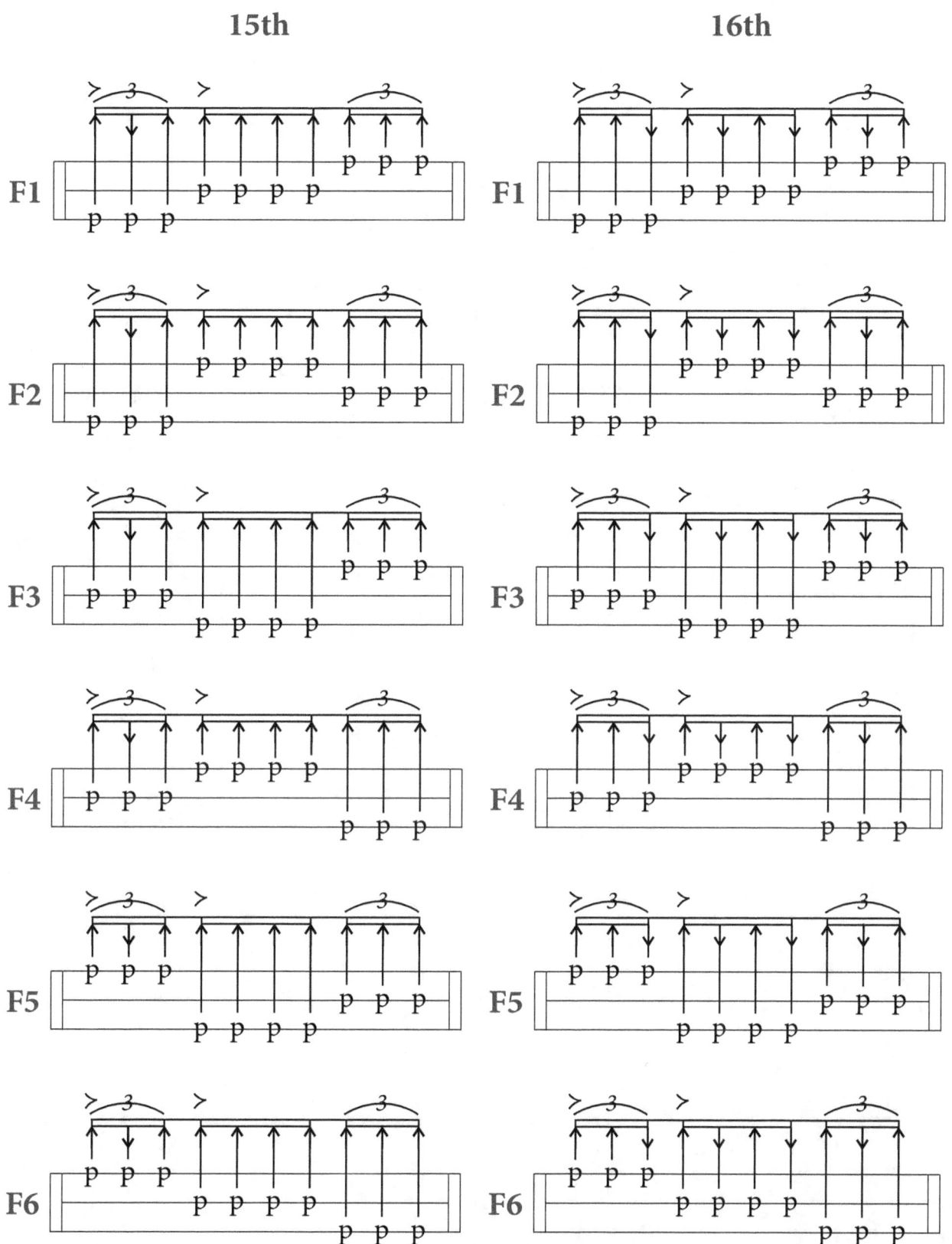

17th

F1
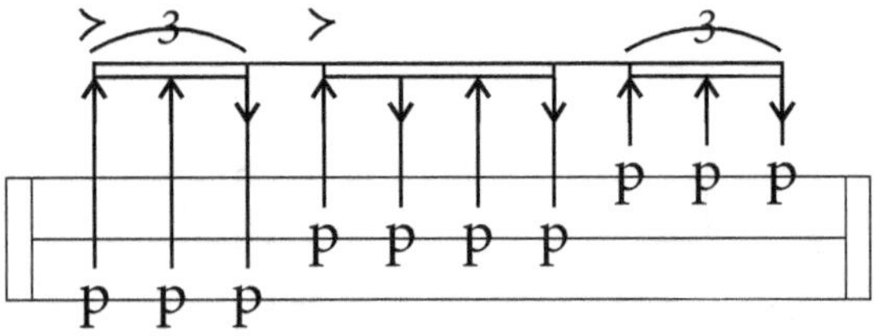

F2
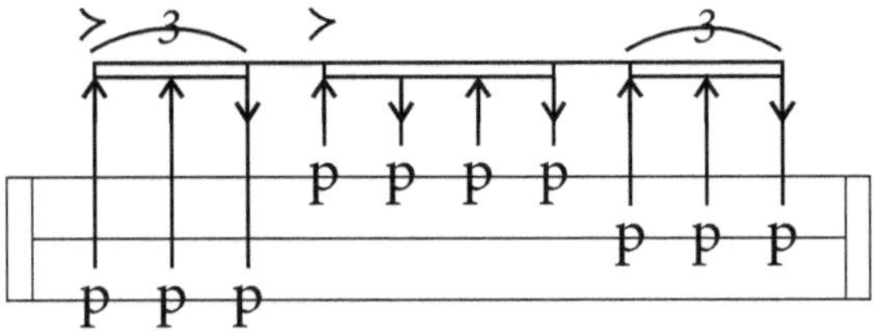

F3
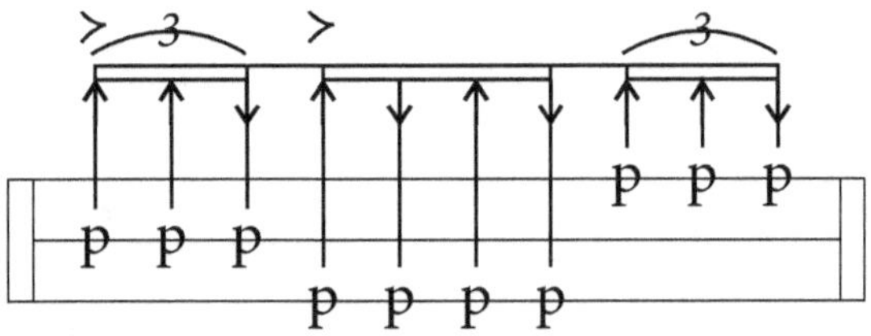

F4
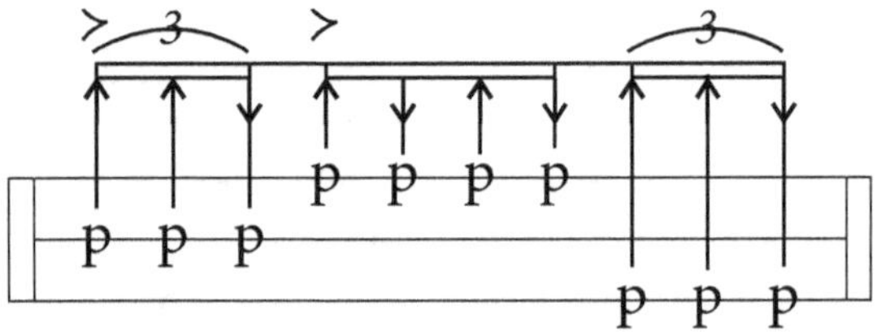

F5
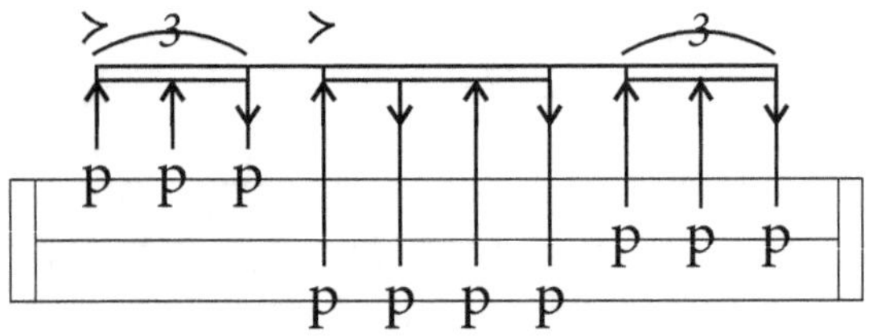

F6
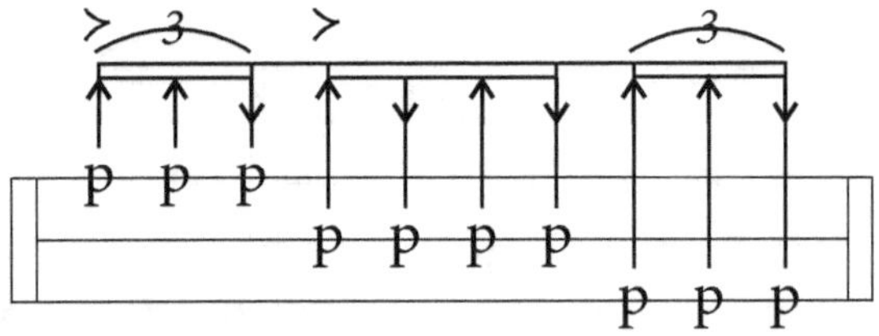

18th

F1
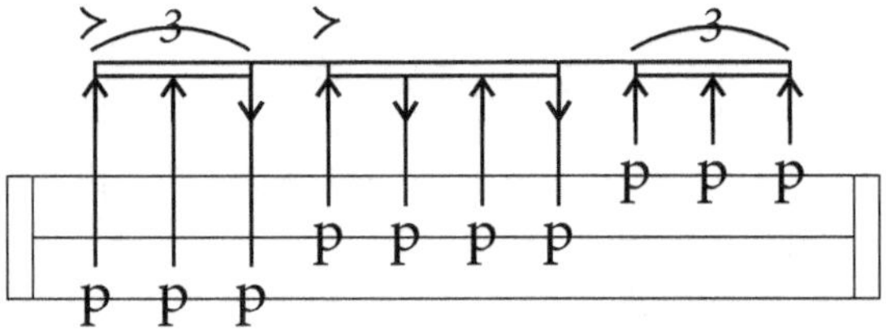

F2
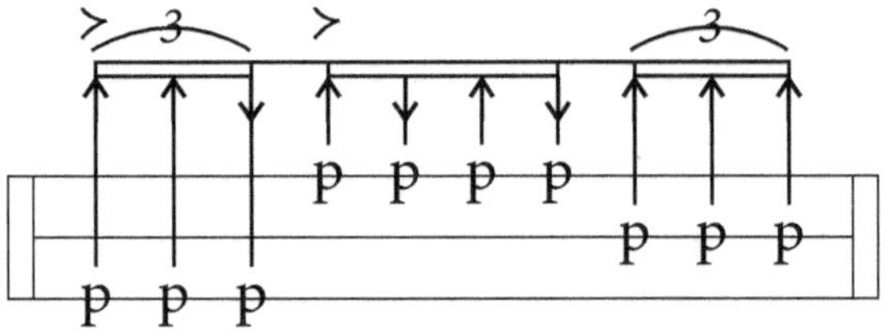

F3
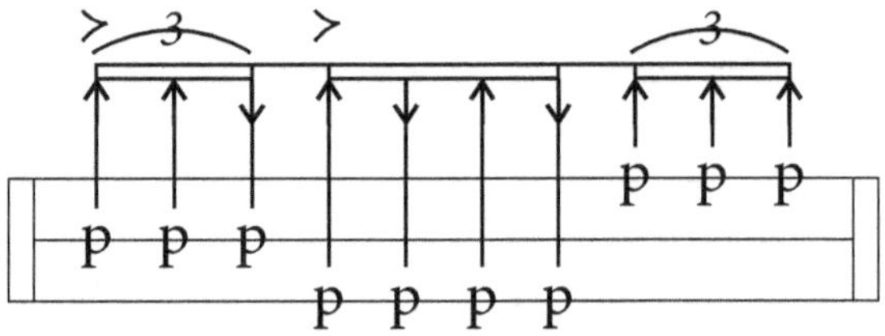

F4
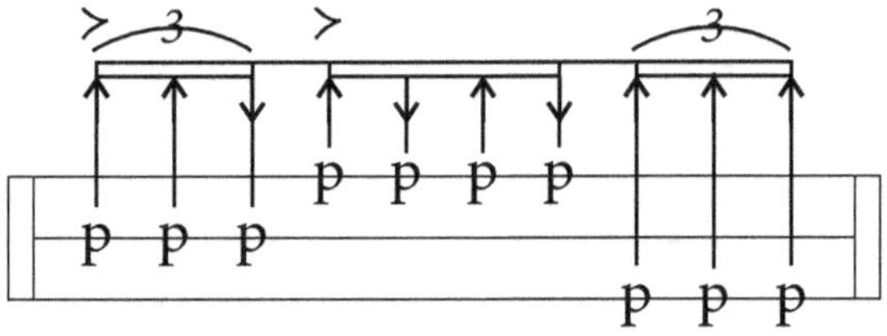

F5
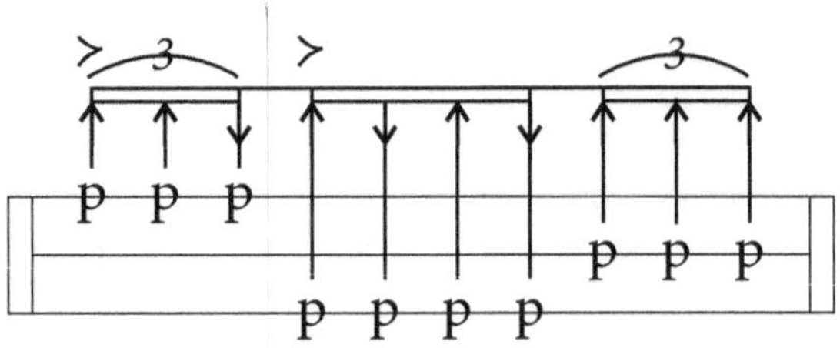

F6
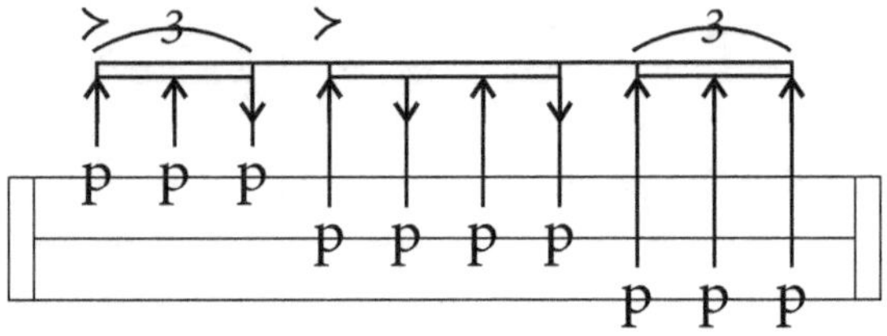

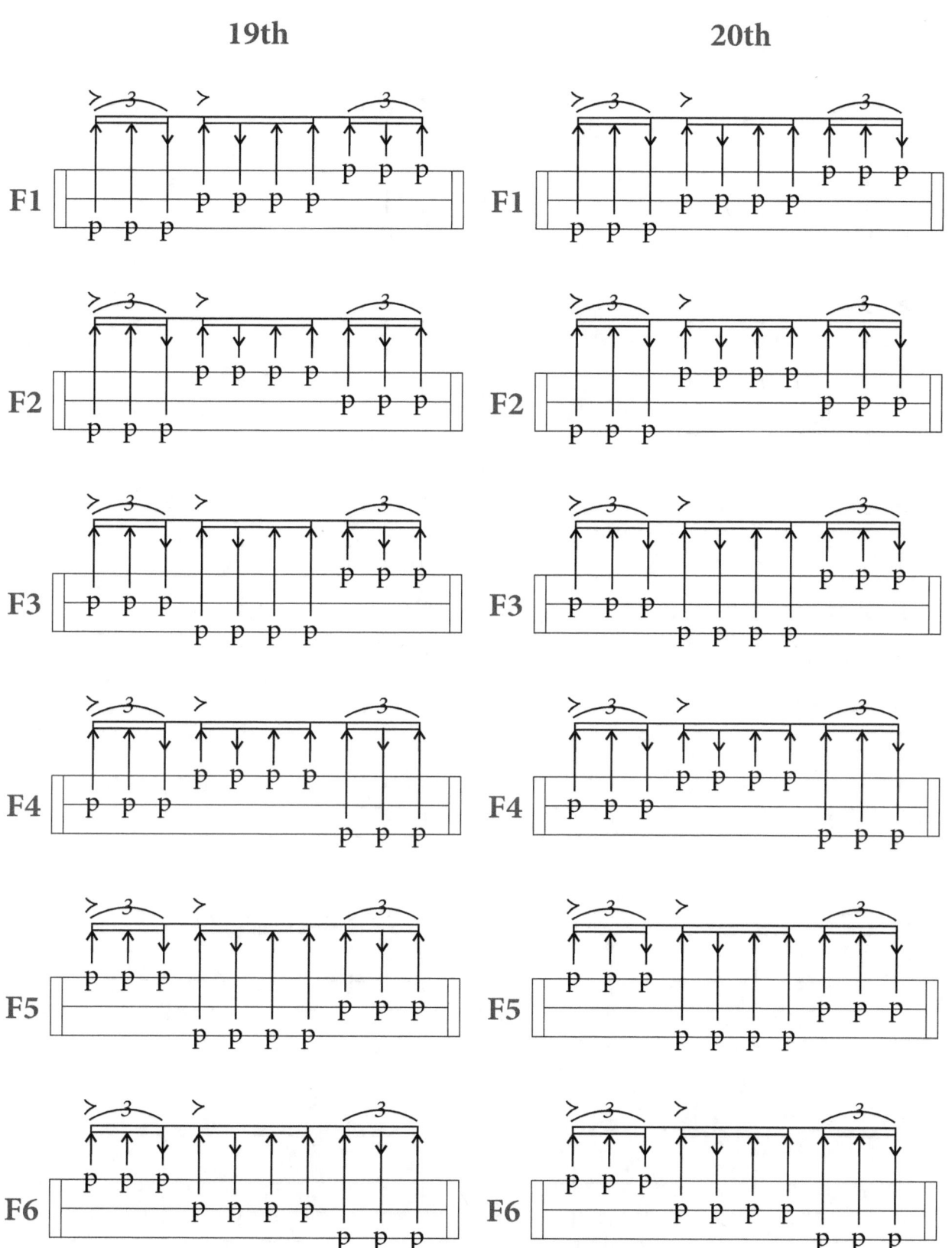

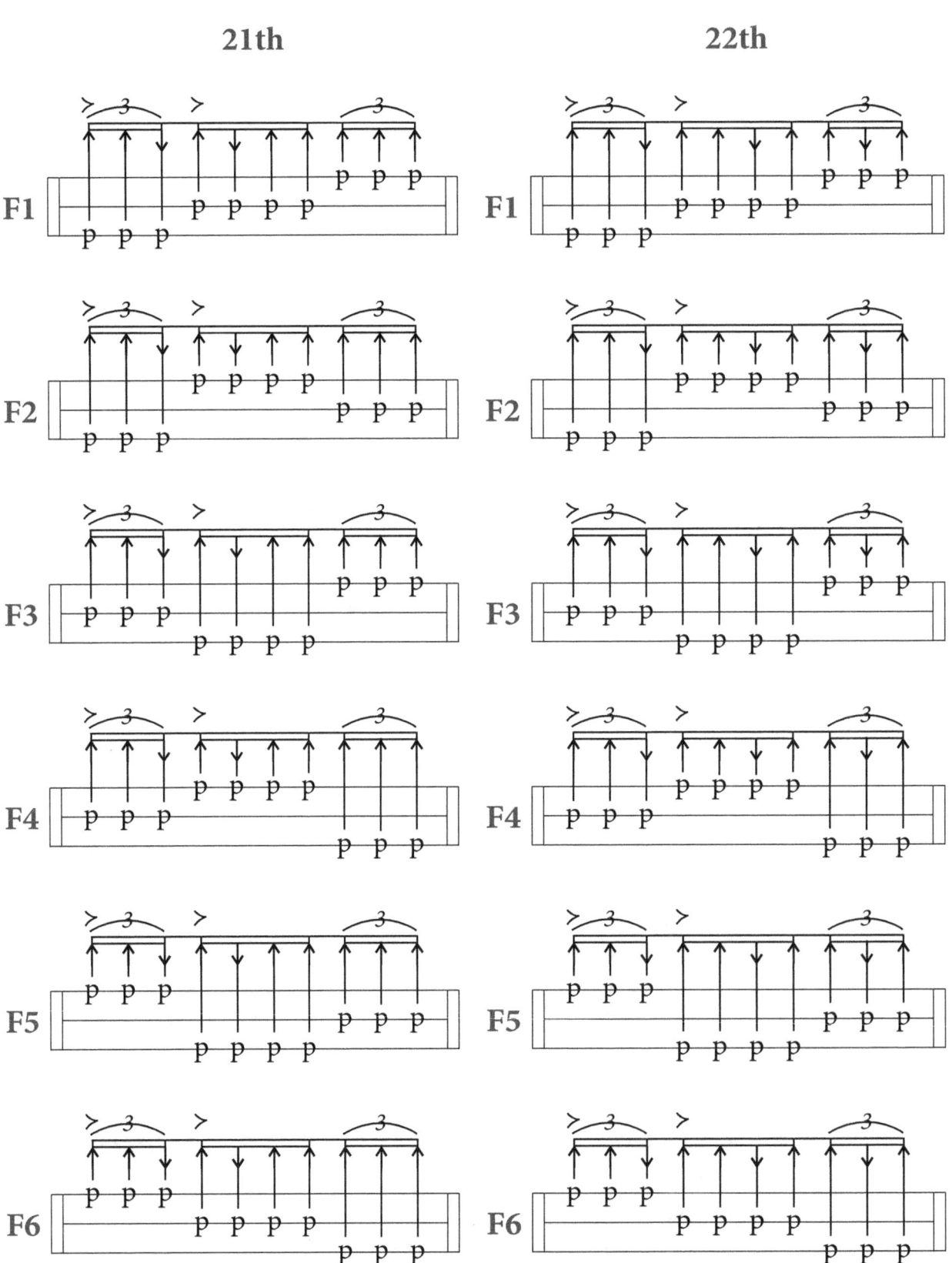

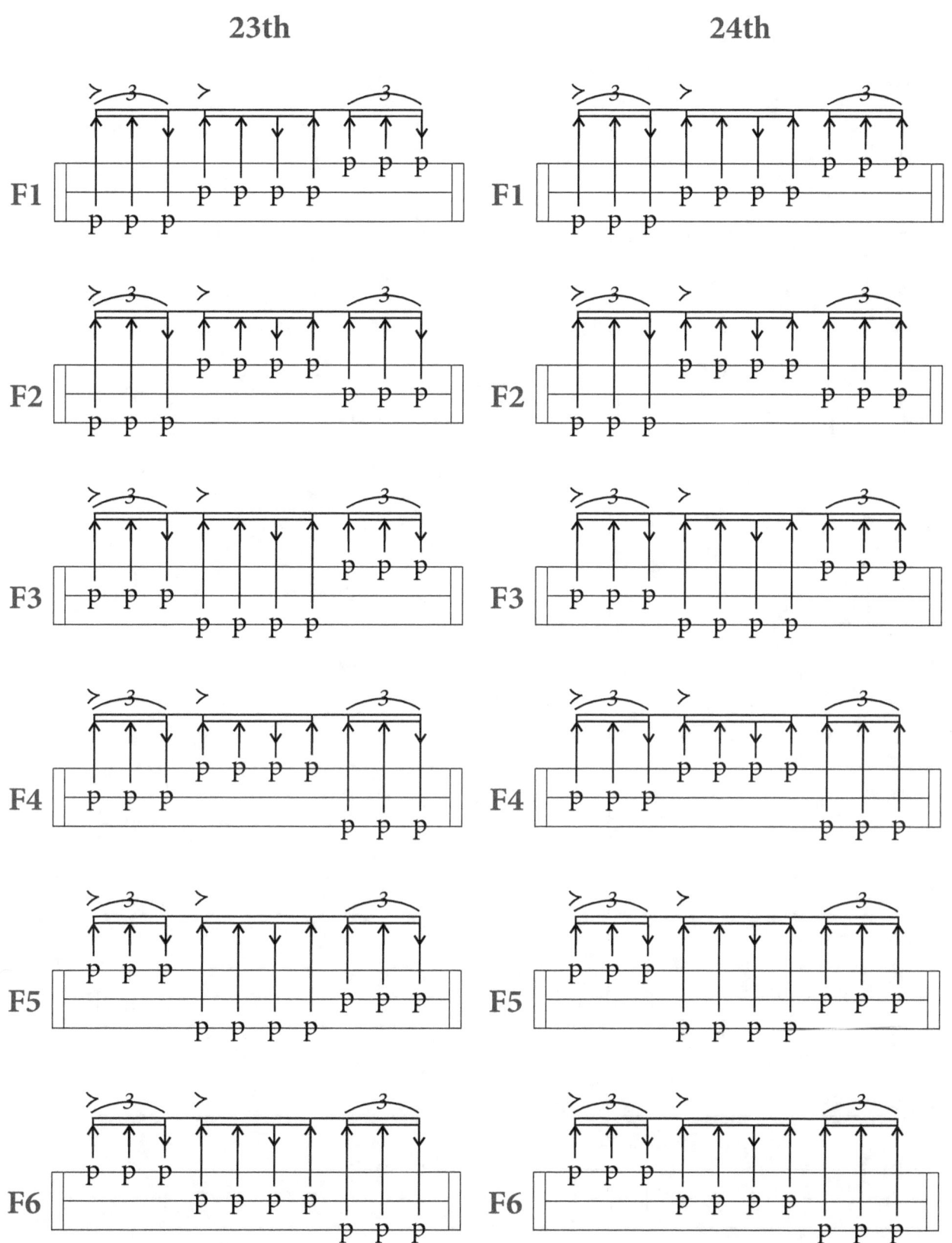

25th   26th

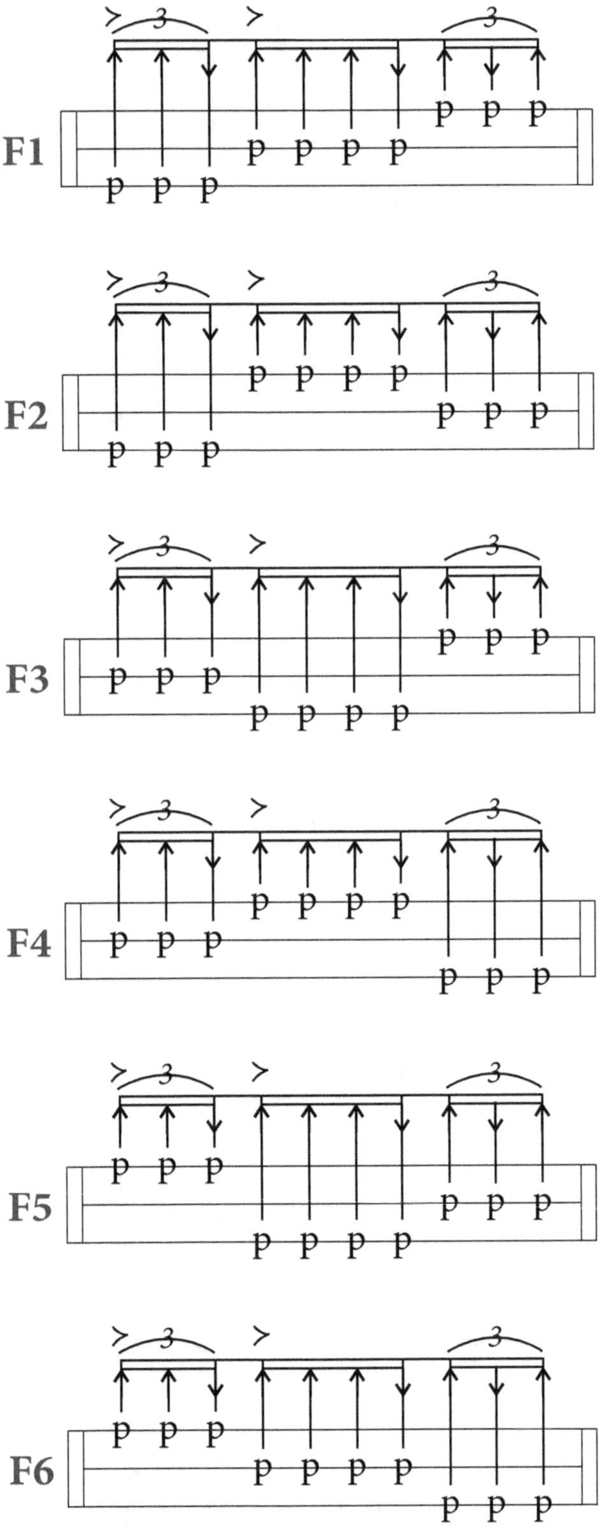

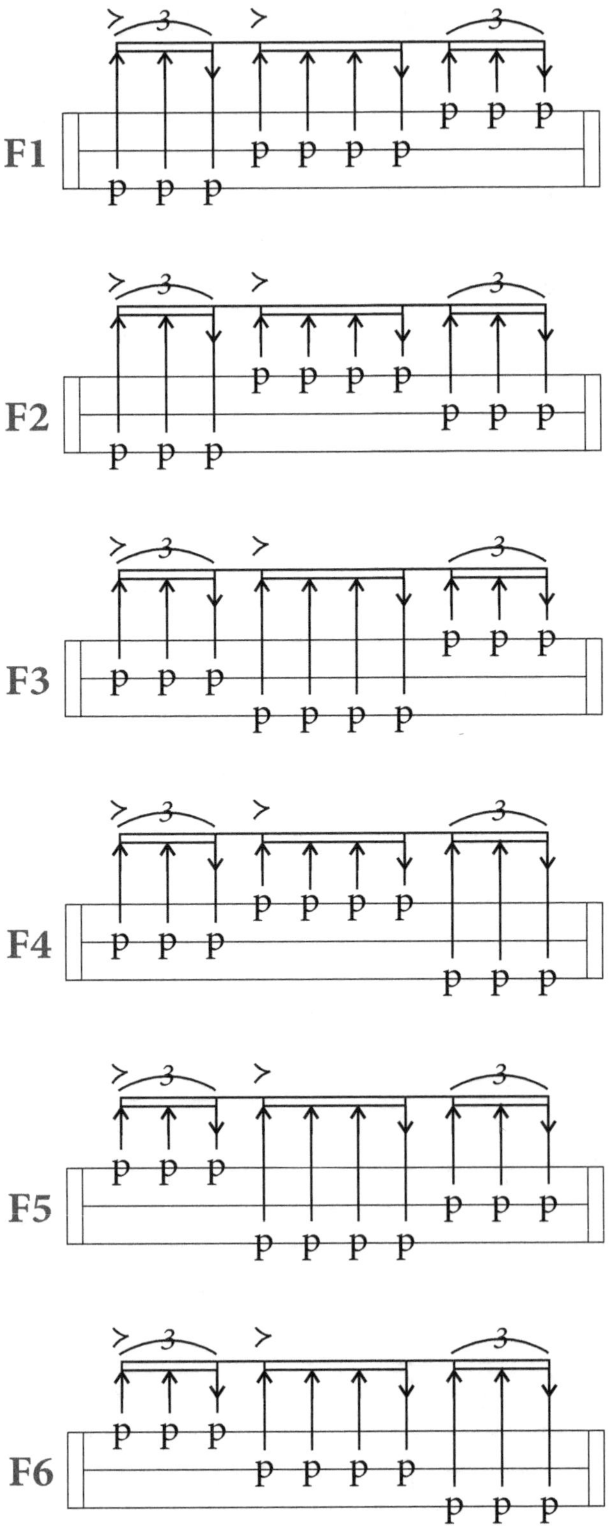

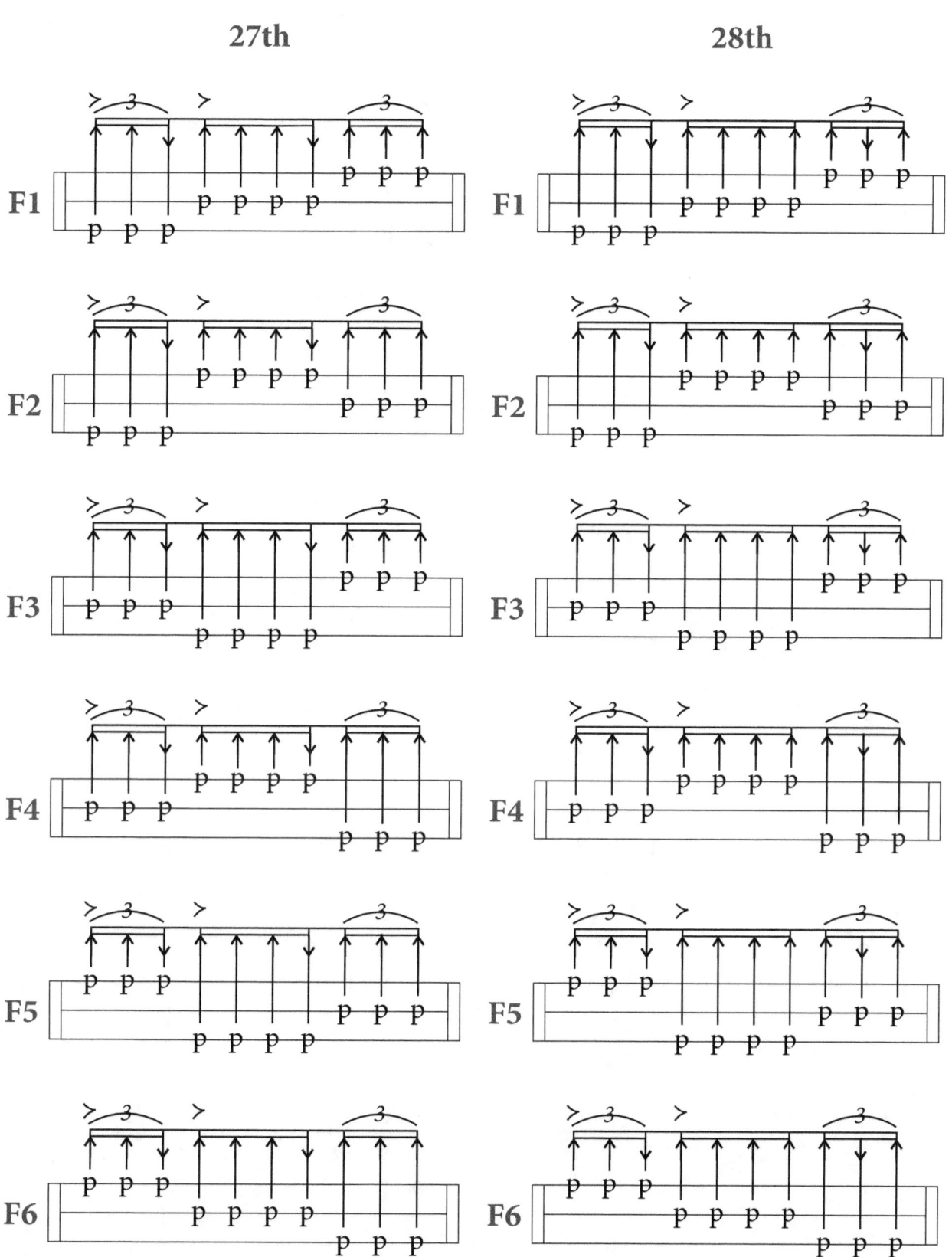

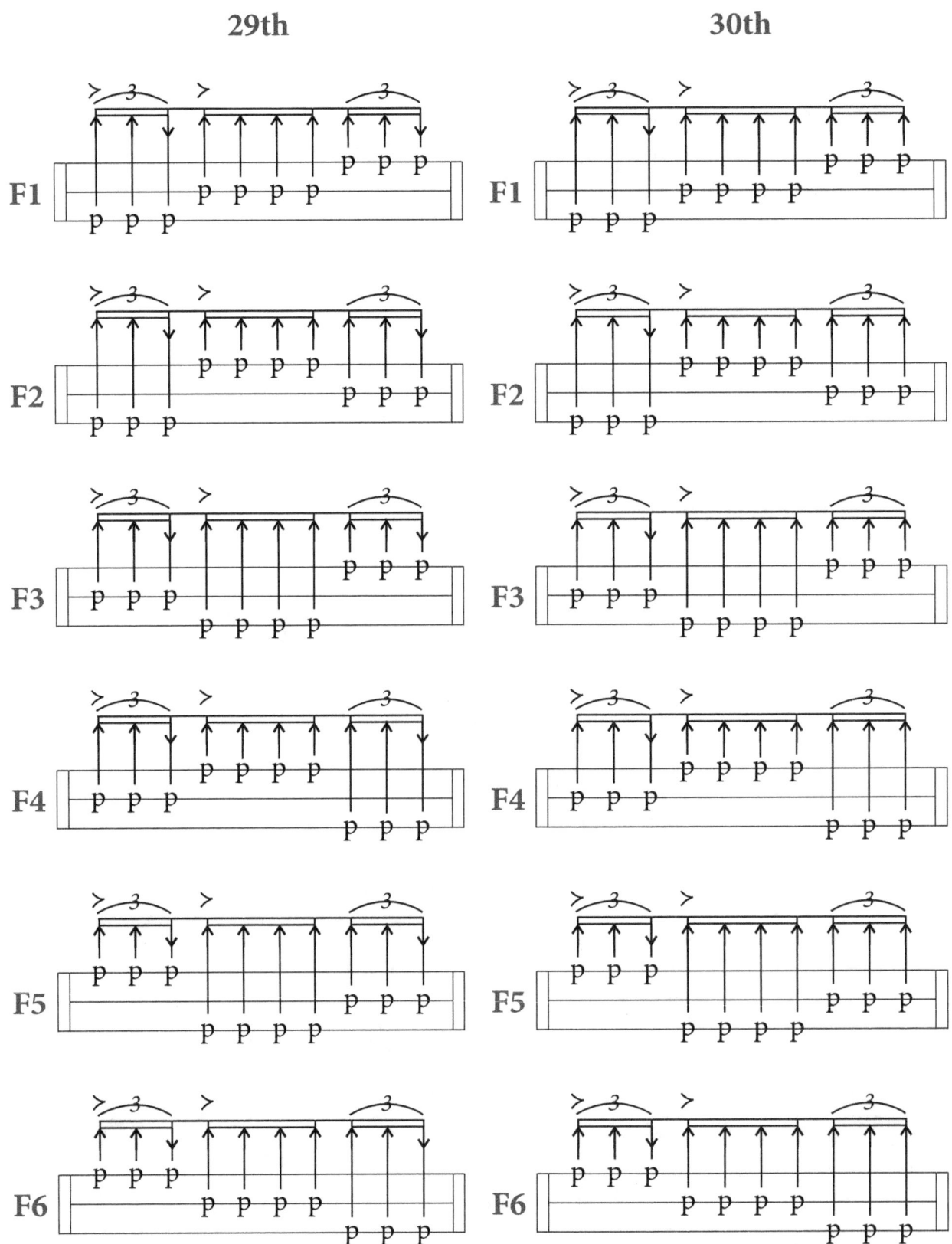

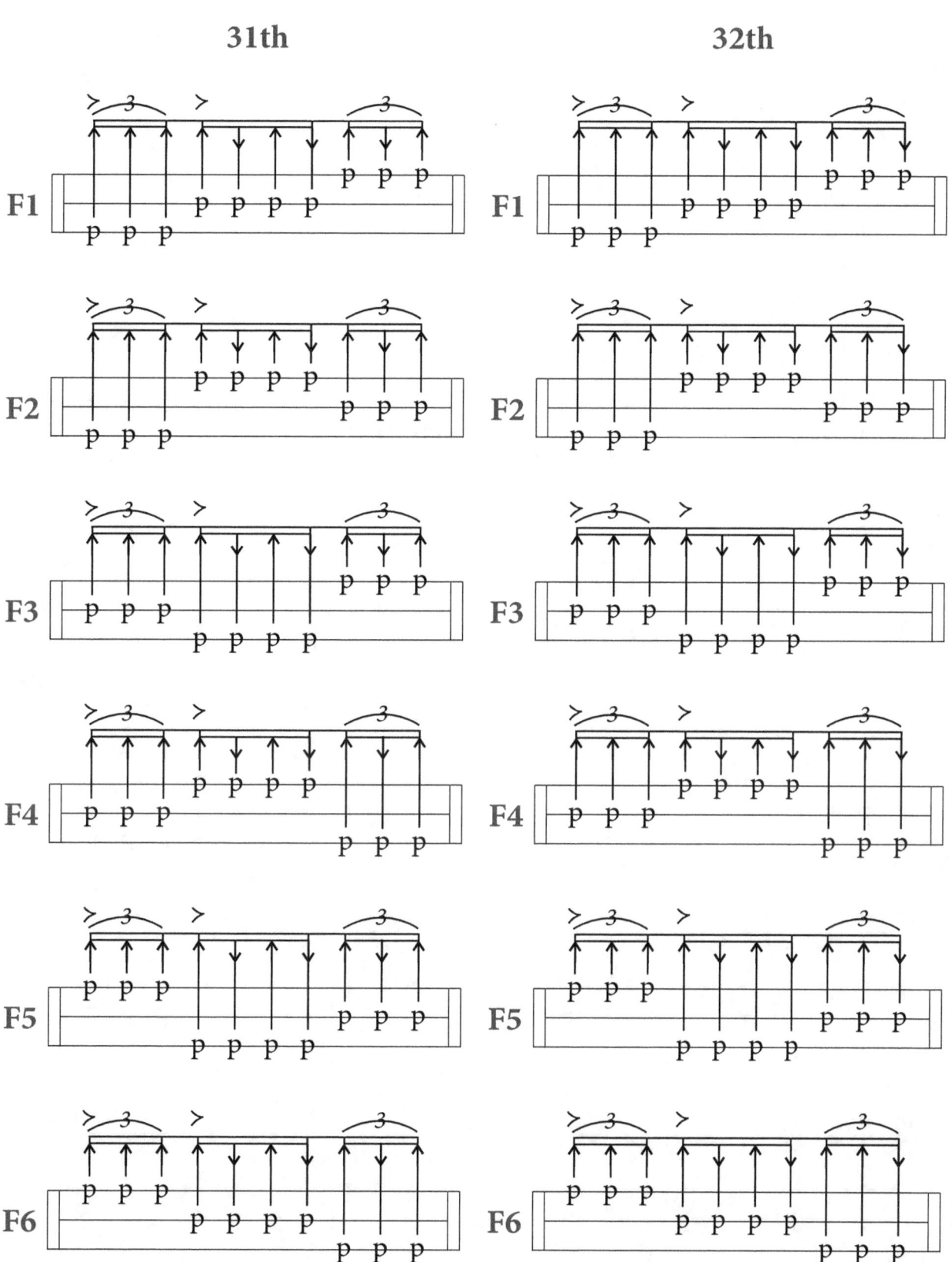

33th

F1
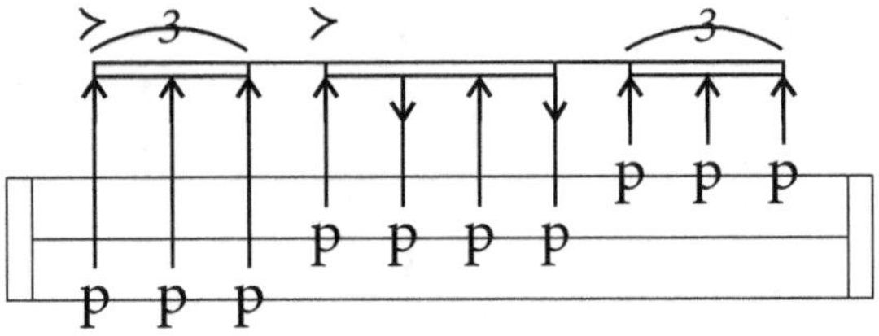

F2
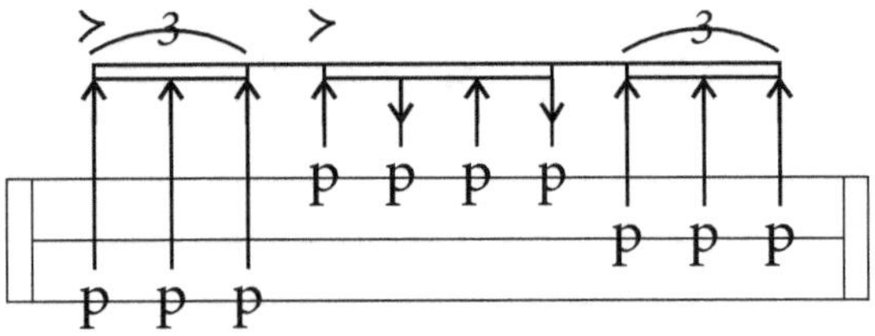

F3
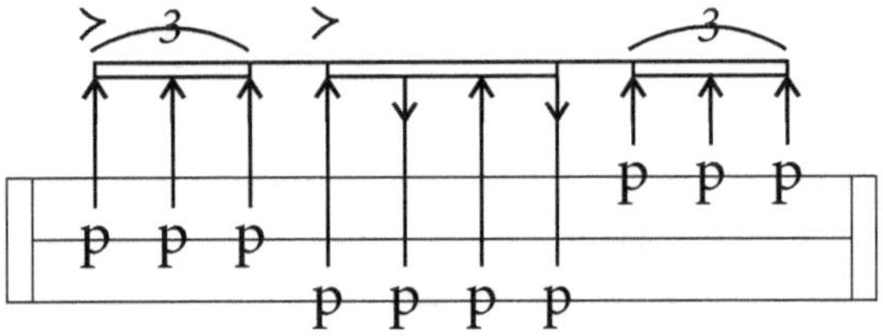

F4
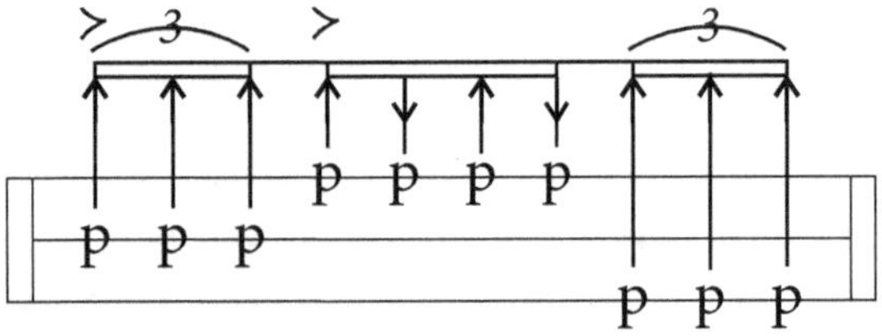

F5
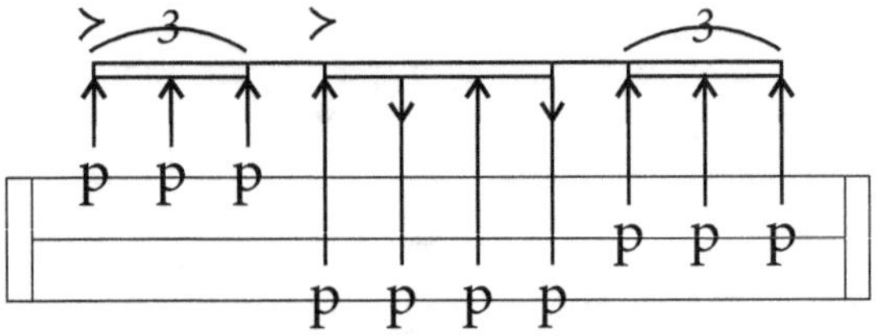

F6
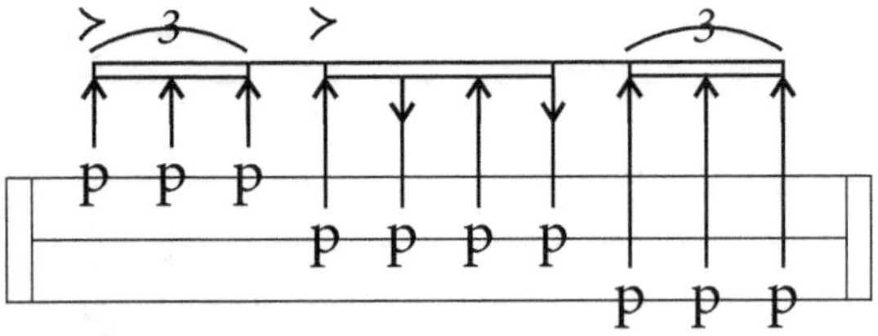

34th

F1
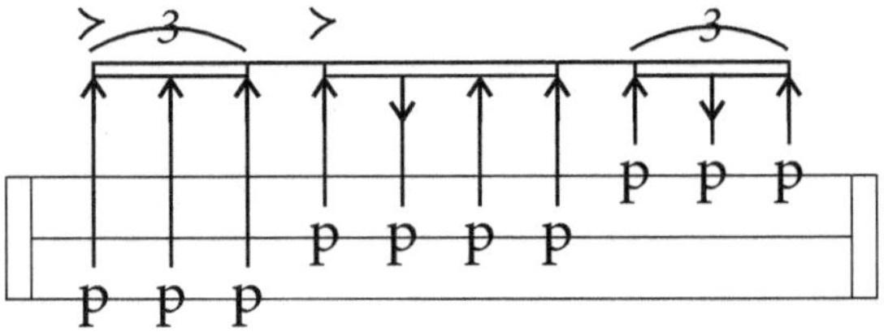

F2
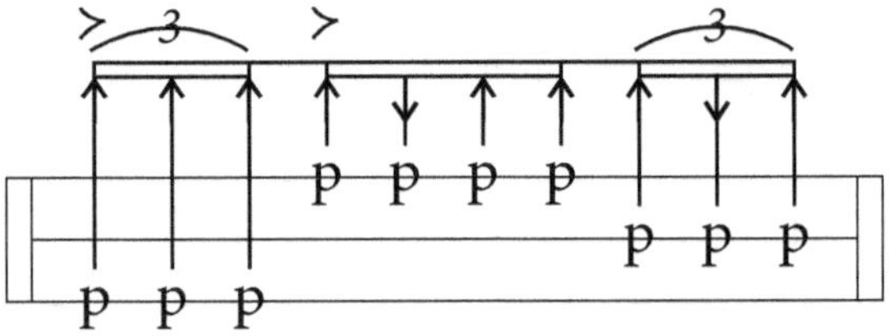

F3
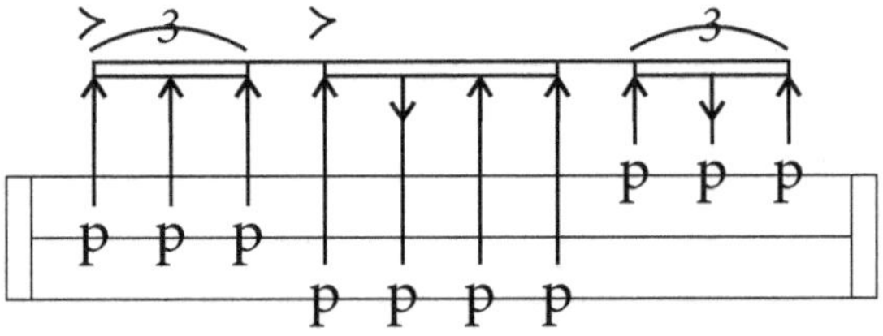

F4
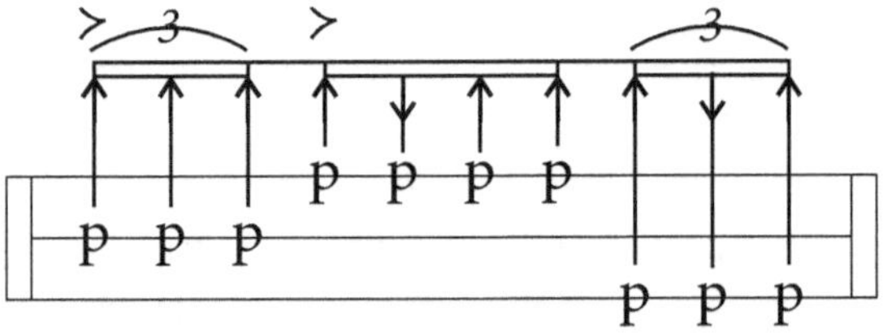

F5
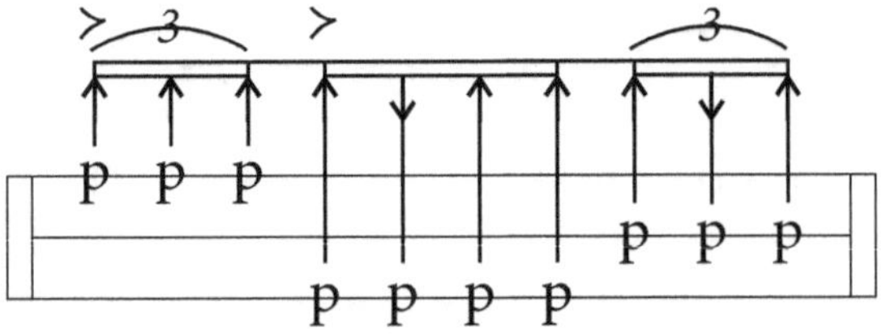

F6
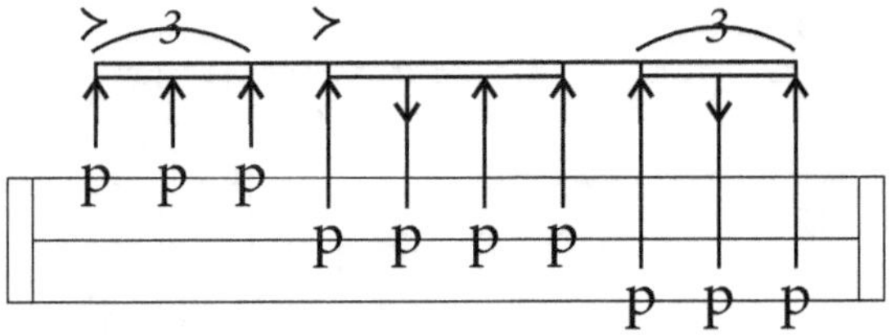

35th   36th

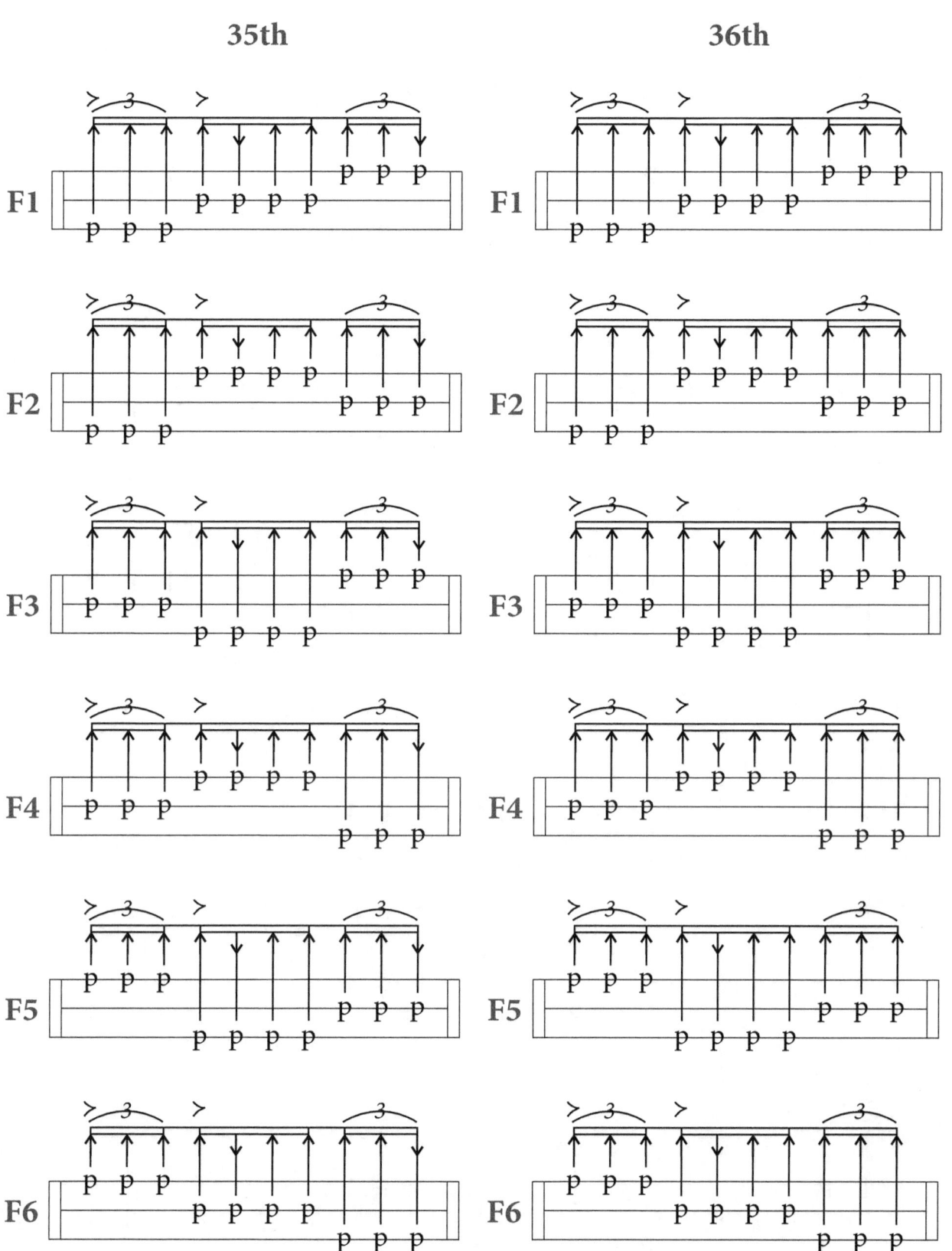

37th   38th

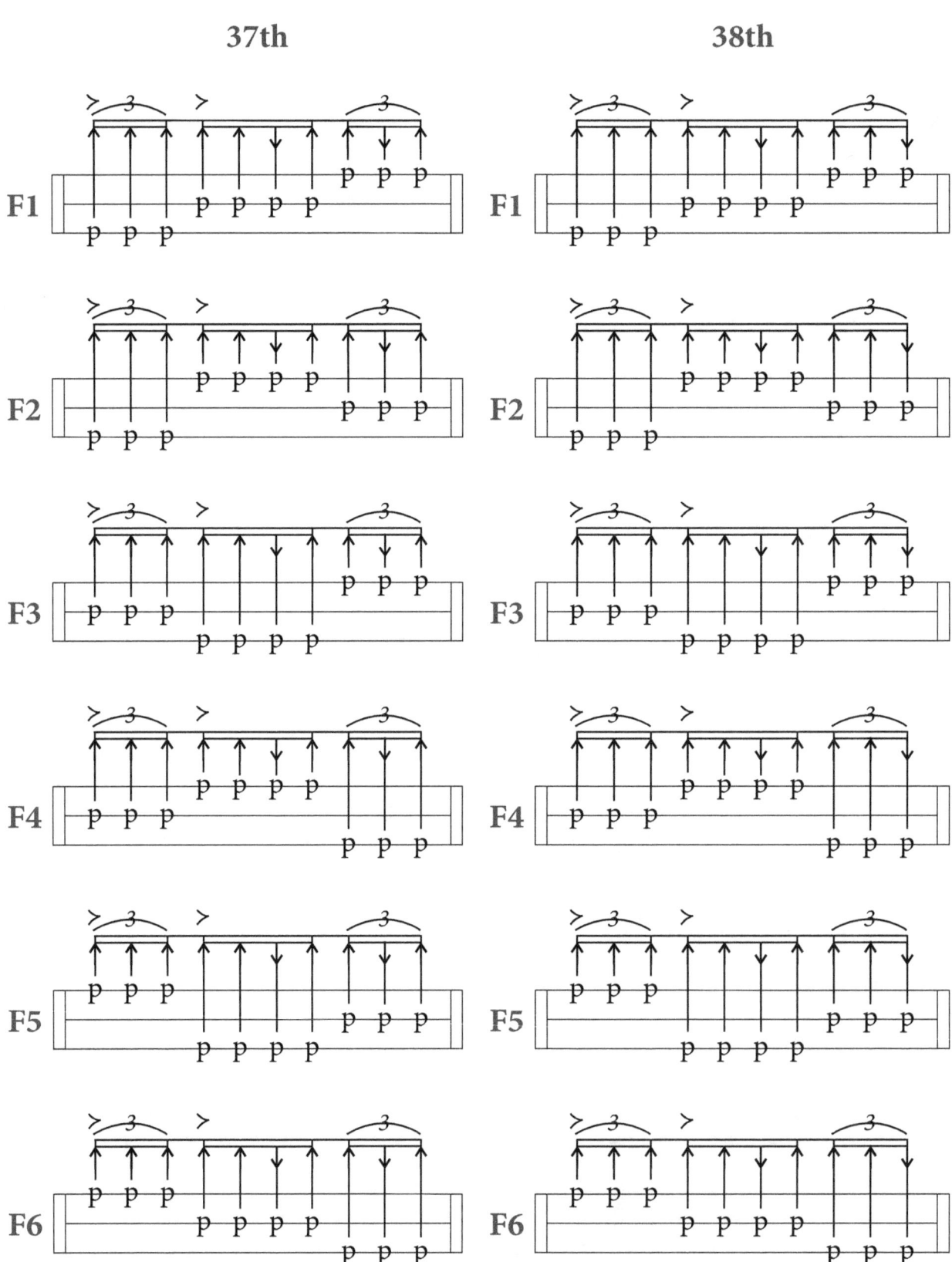

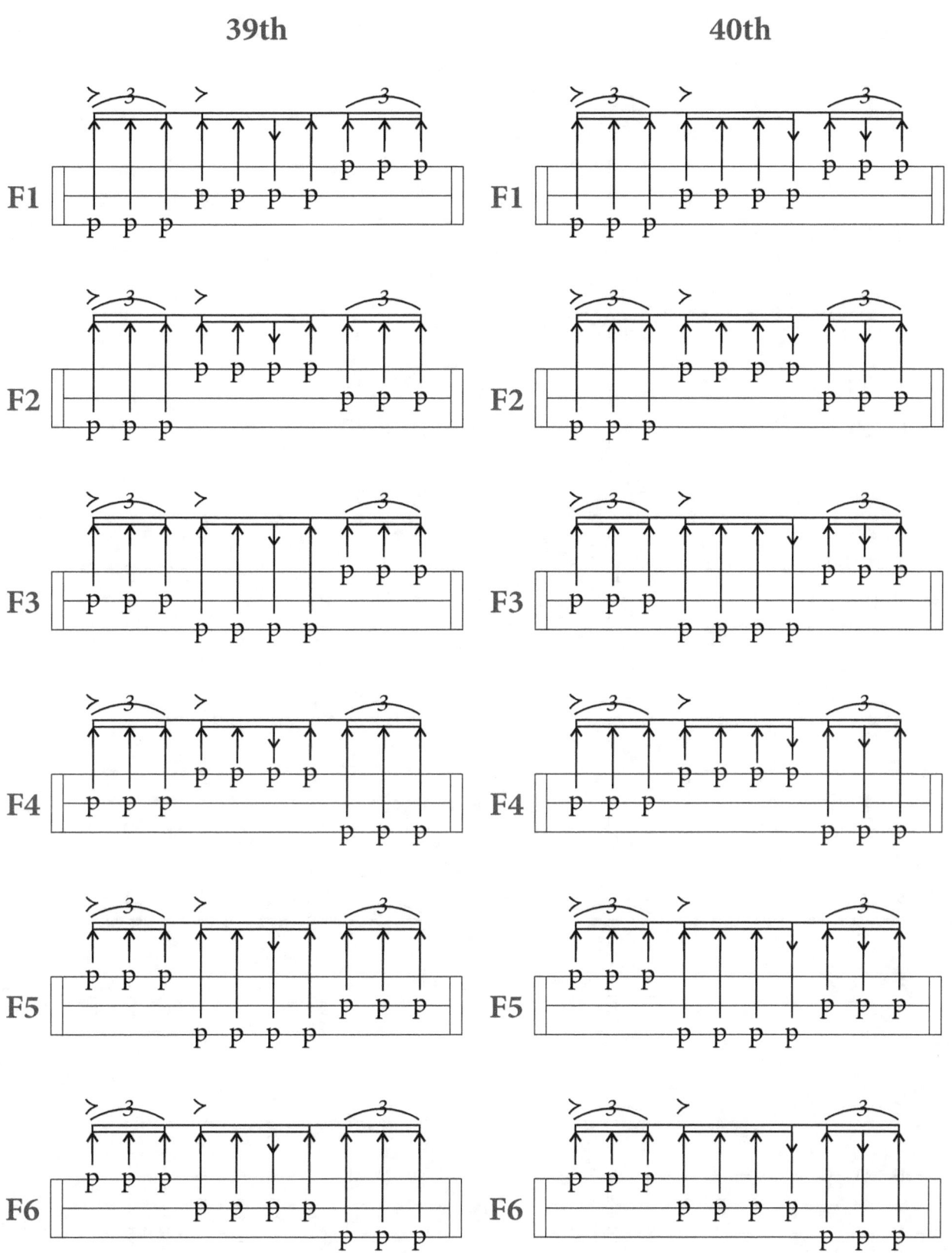

41th 42th

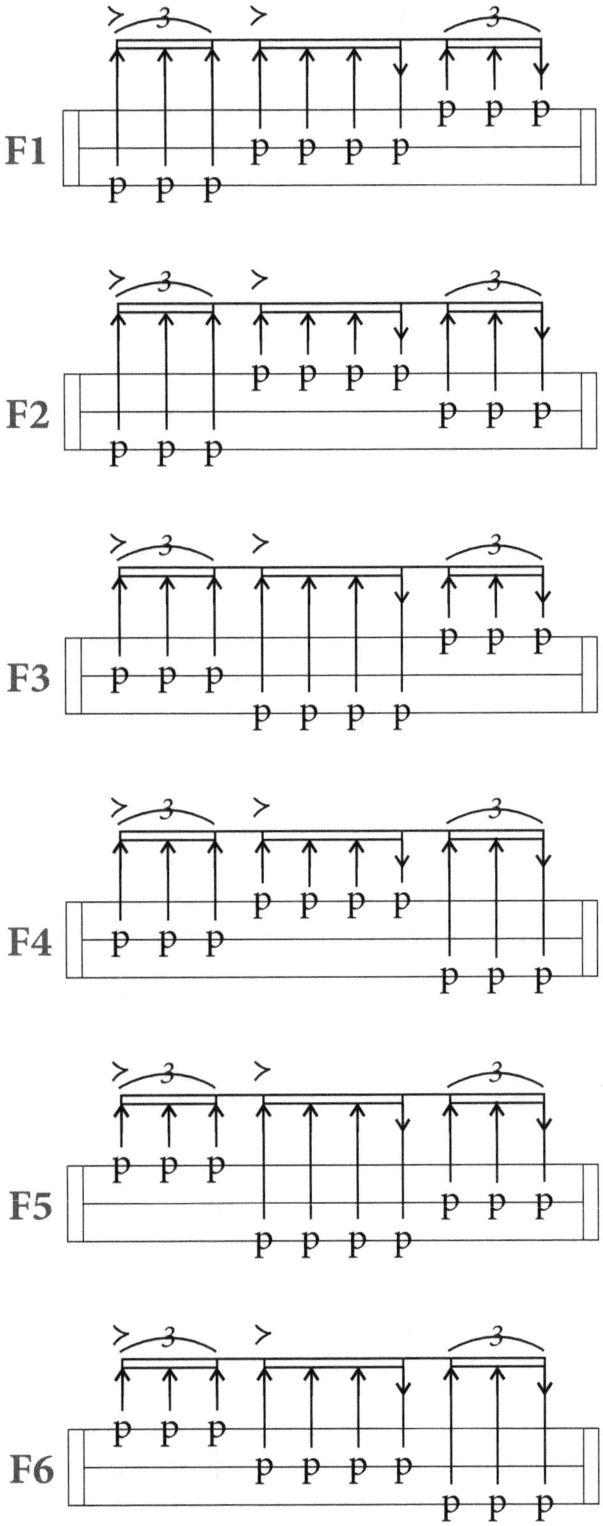

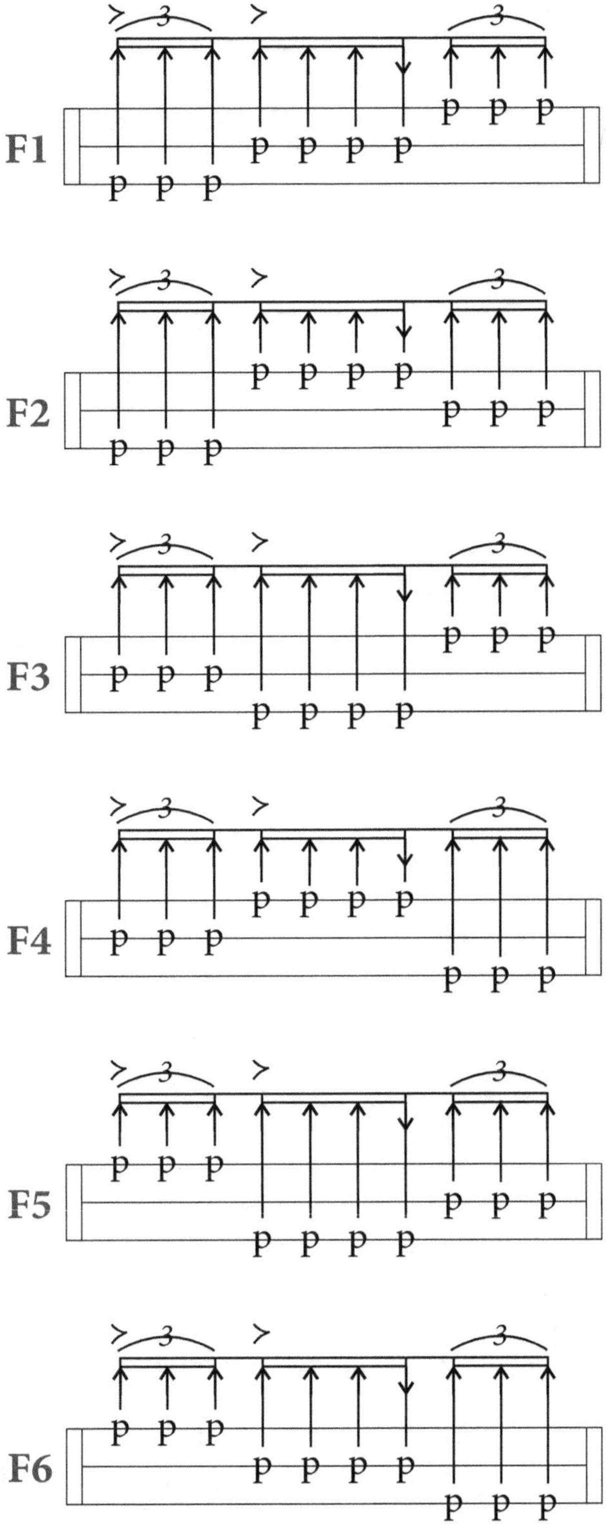

43th 44th

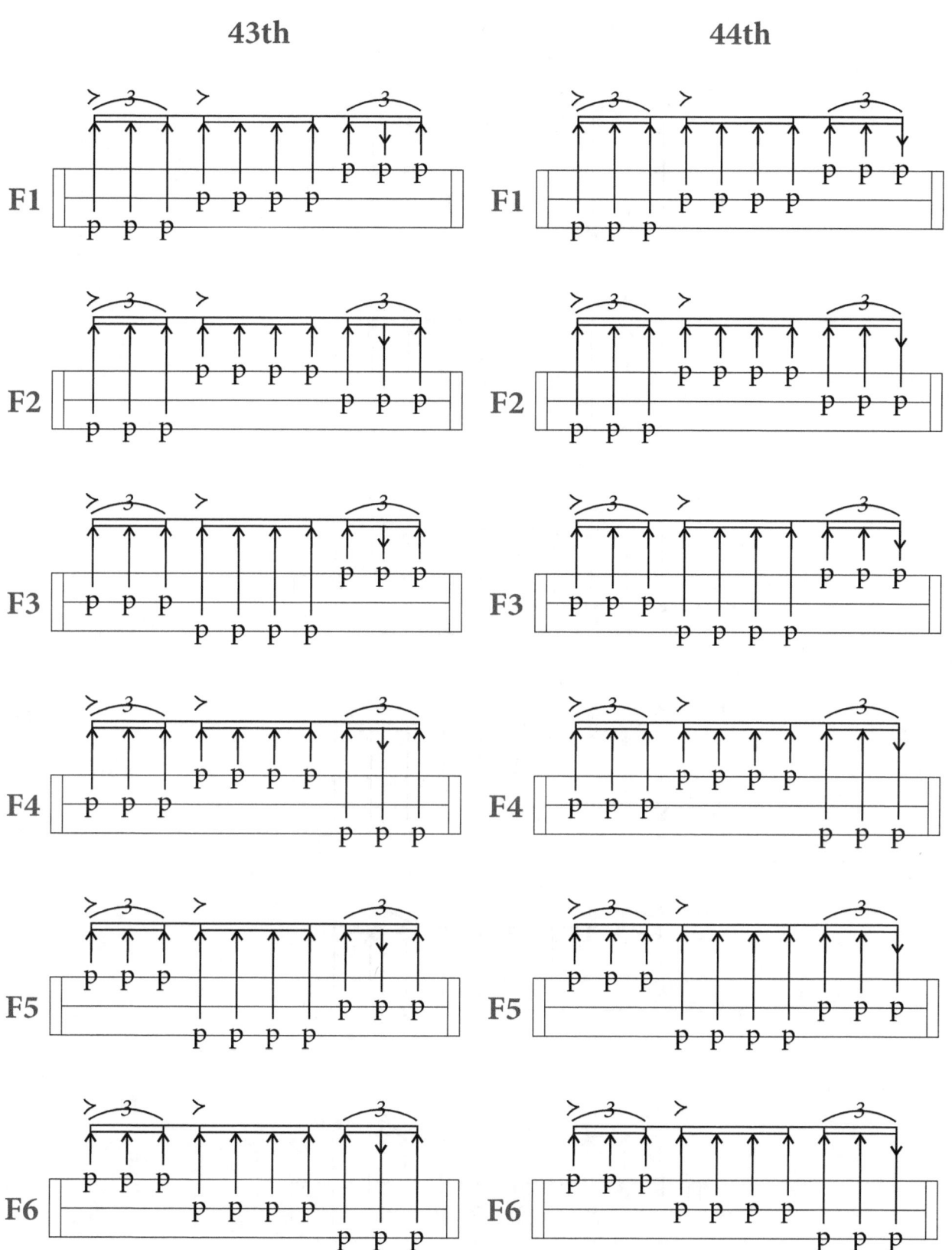

45th

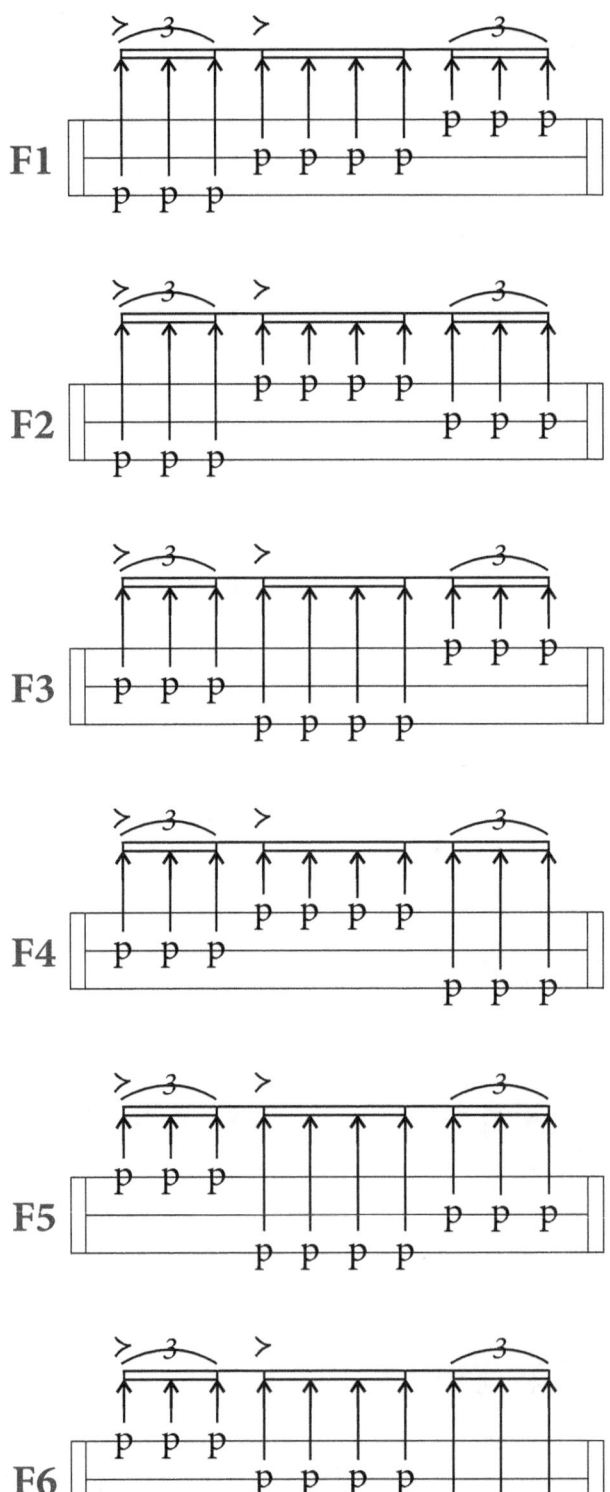

234

§ VI

Exercise on pulgar on three adjacent strings with two quad strokes and one triple stroke within each Formula. The exercise includes three variations with 6 Formulas in each one. The first Formula of each variation is cited below. Isochronous playing of triple and quad stroke.

VARIATION I
Variation I with quad - triple - quad stroke

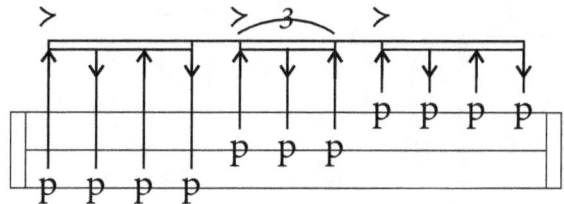

VARIATION II
Variation II with triple - quad - quad stroke

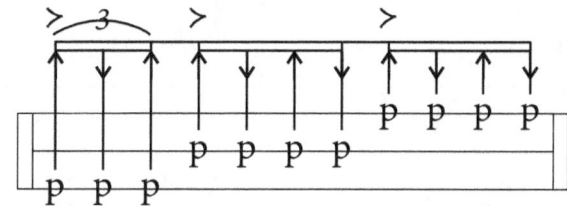

VARIATION III
Variation III with quad - quad - triple stroke

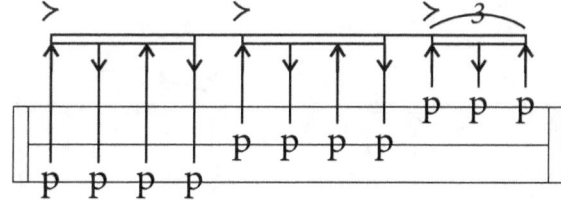

VARIATION I

F1
F2
F3
F4
F5
F6

VARIATION II

F1
F2
F3
F4
F5
F6

VARIATION
III

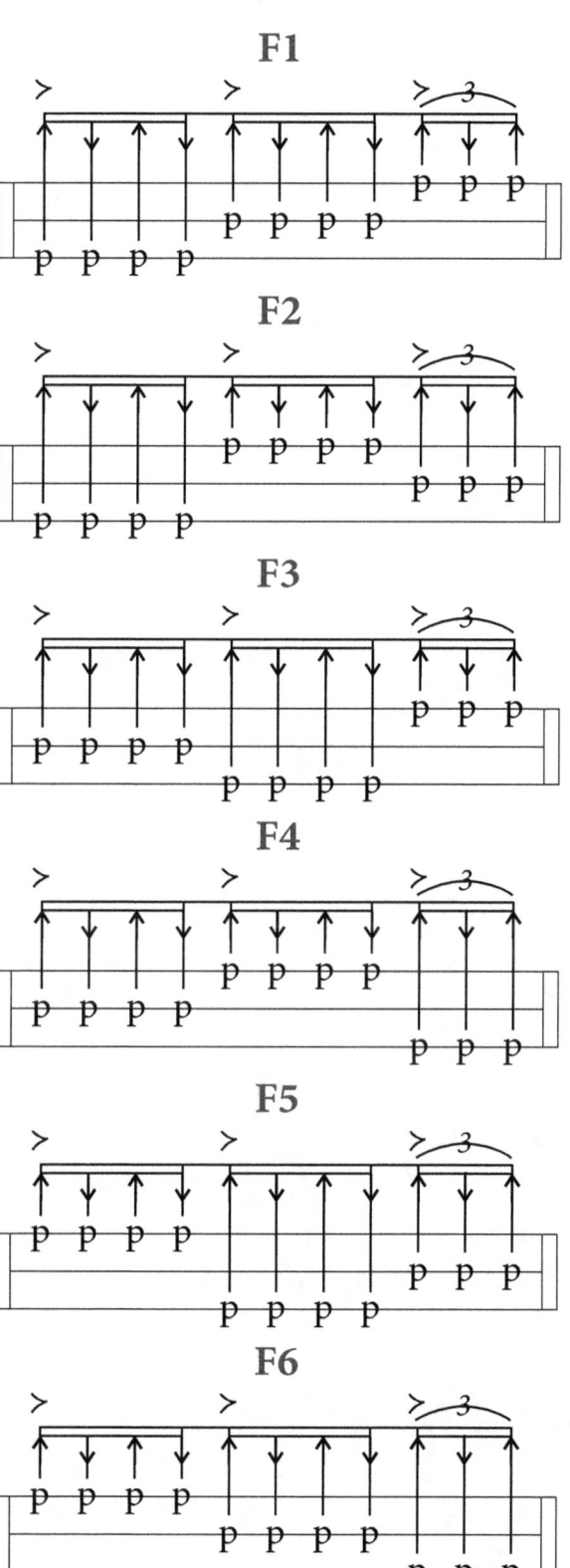

75 ways of performance of variation I which result from the change in the direction of pulgar stroke are cited below.

VARIATION I

WAYS OF PERFORMANCE

1st

F1

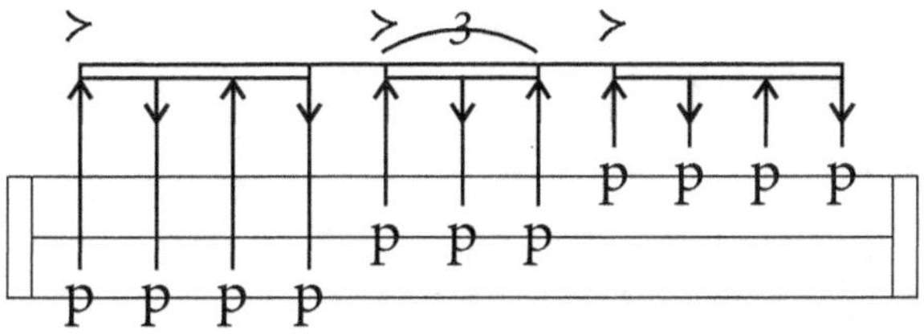

F2

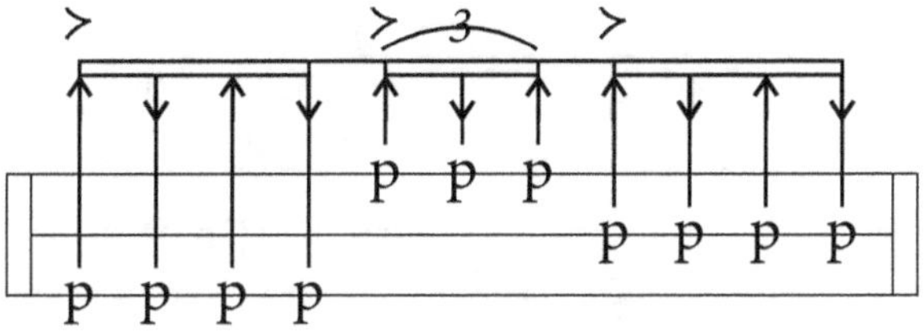

F3

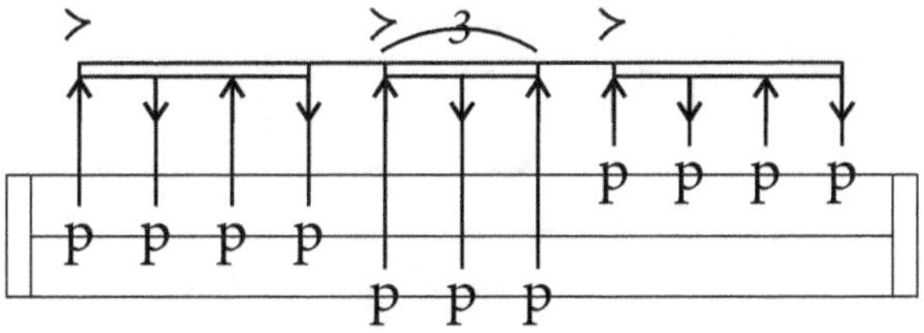

F4

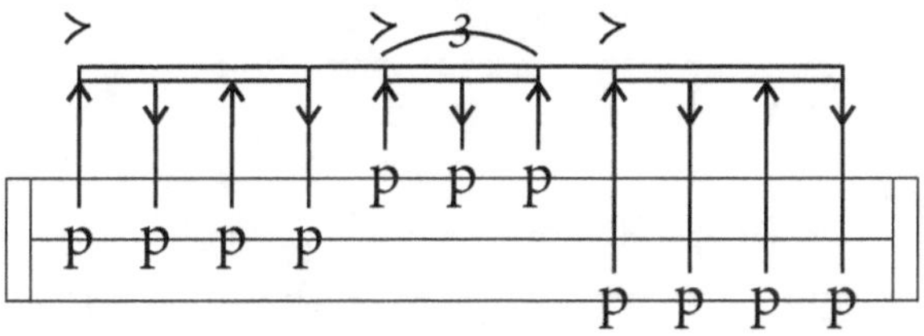

F5

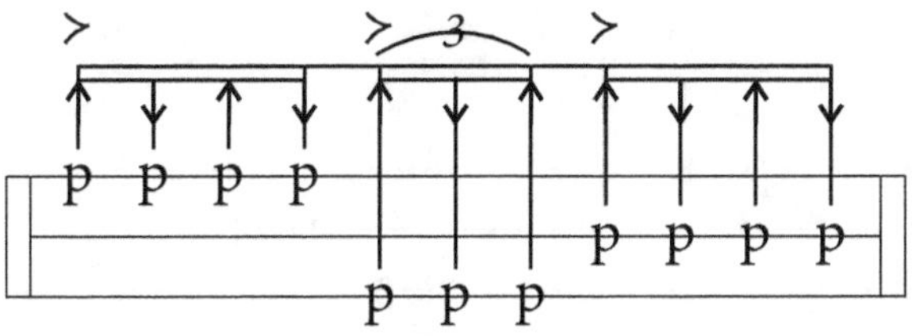

F6

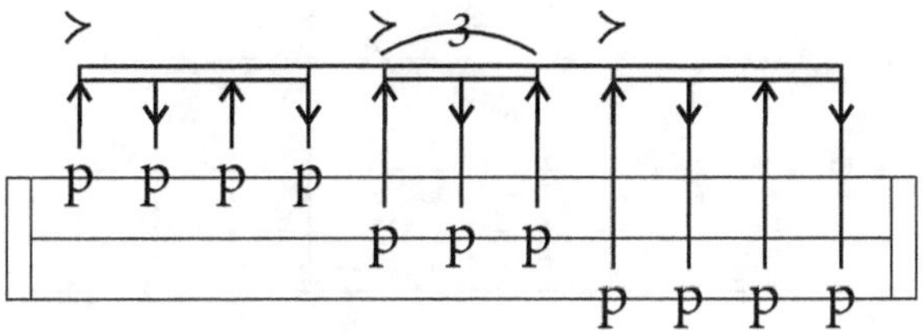

2nd

F1

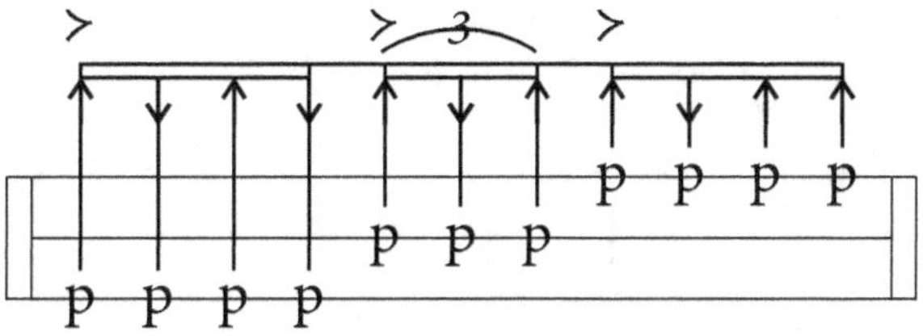

F2

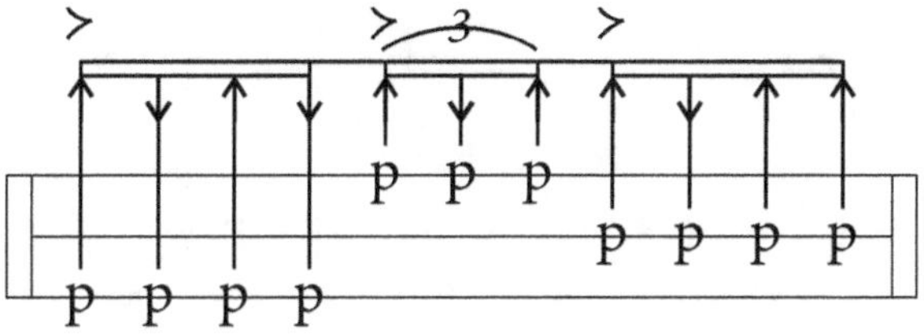

F3

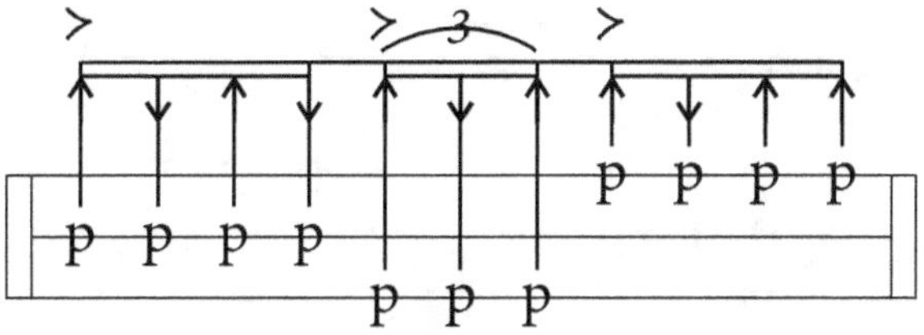

F4

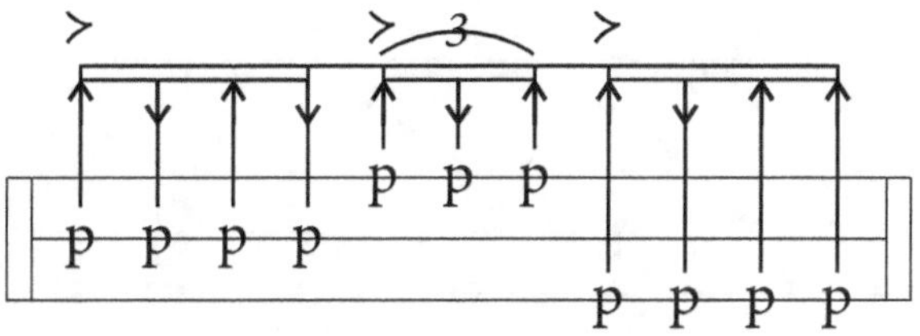

F5

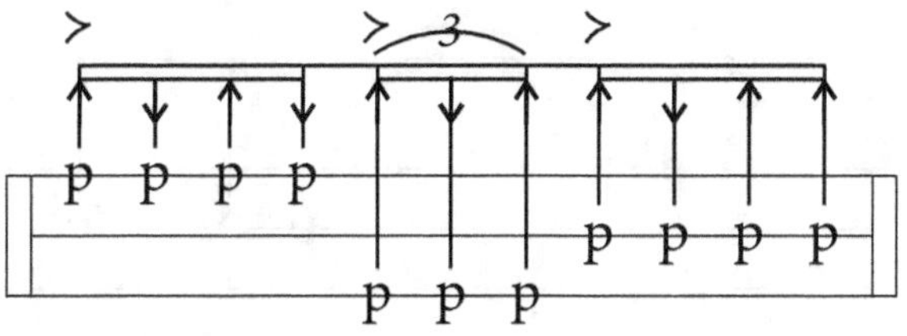

F6

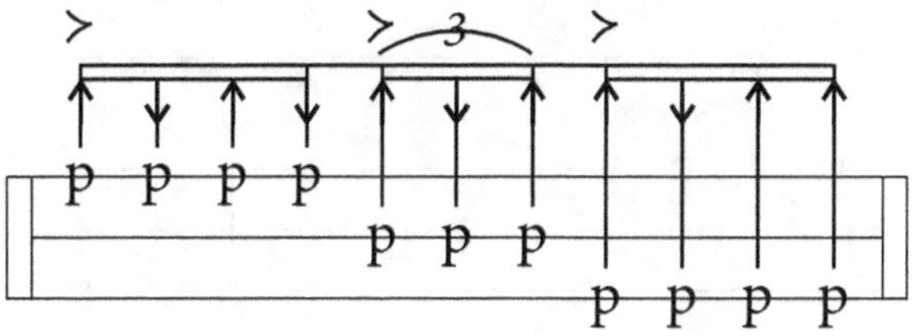

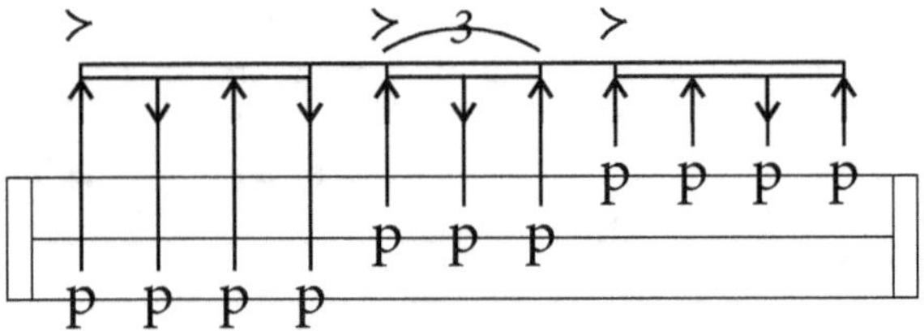

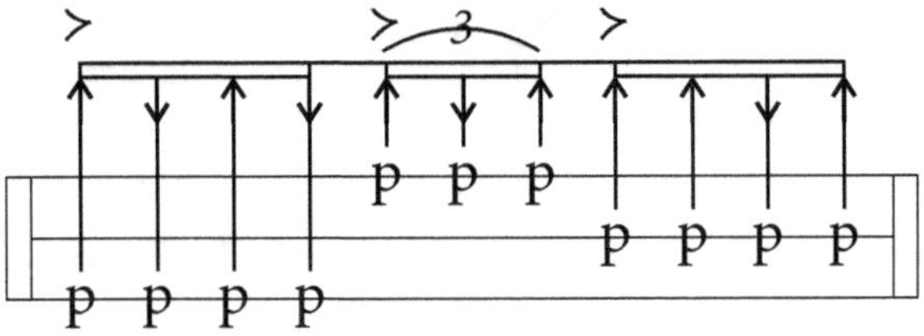

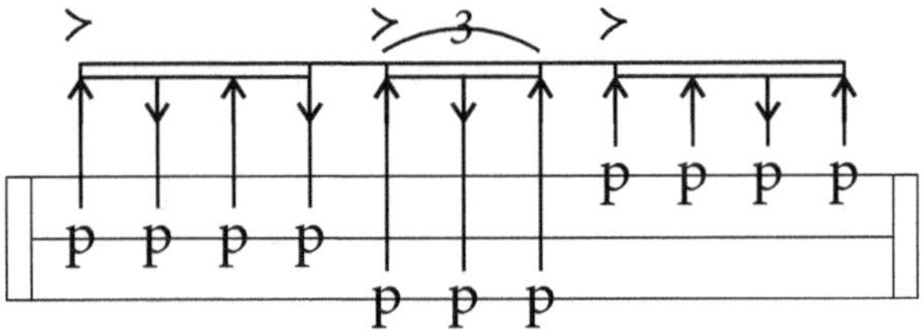

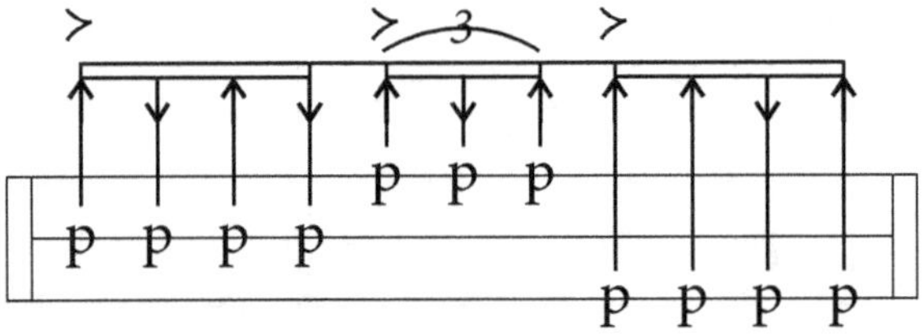

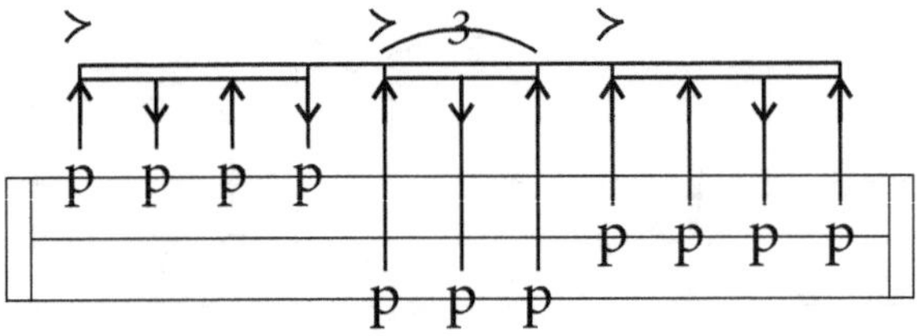

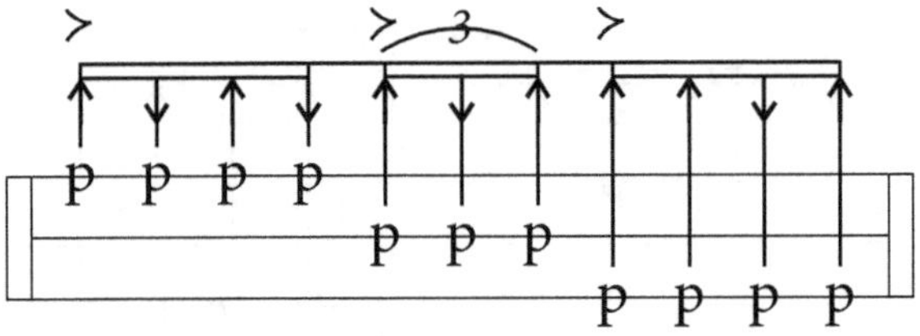

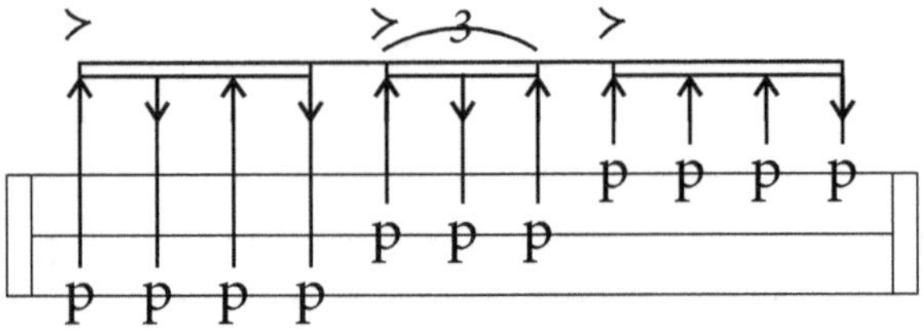

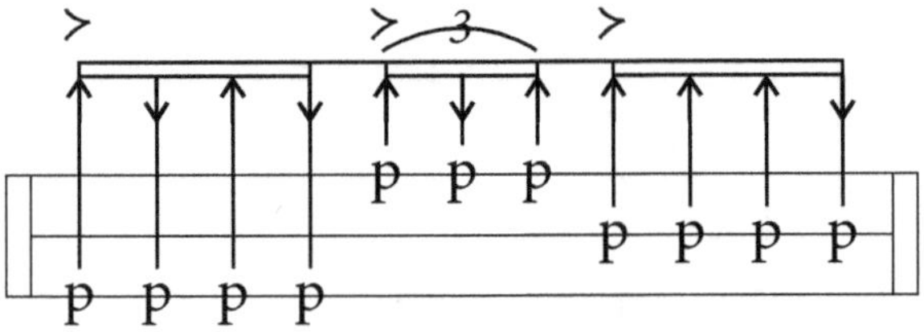

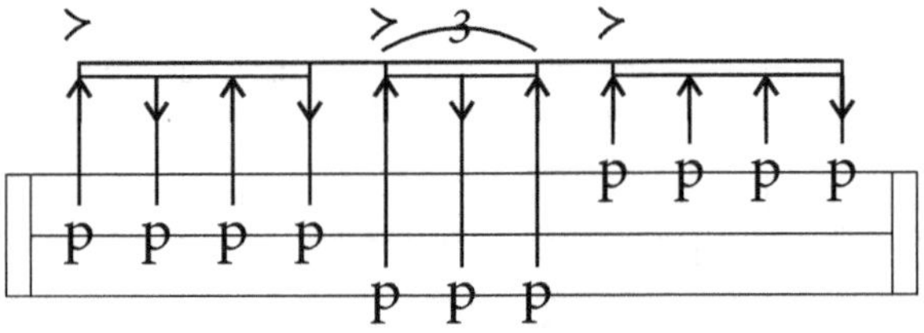

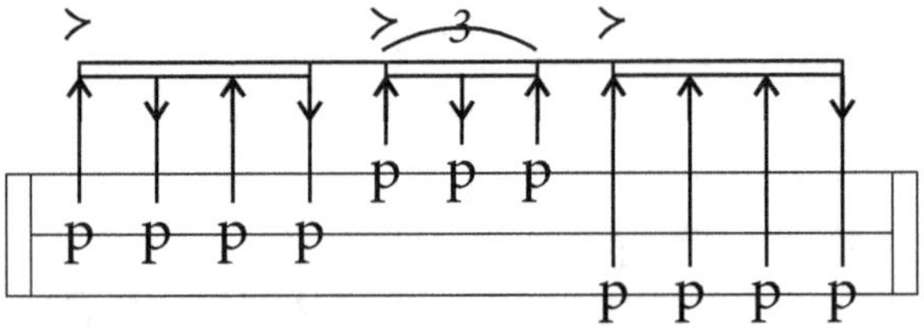

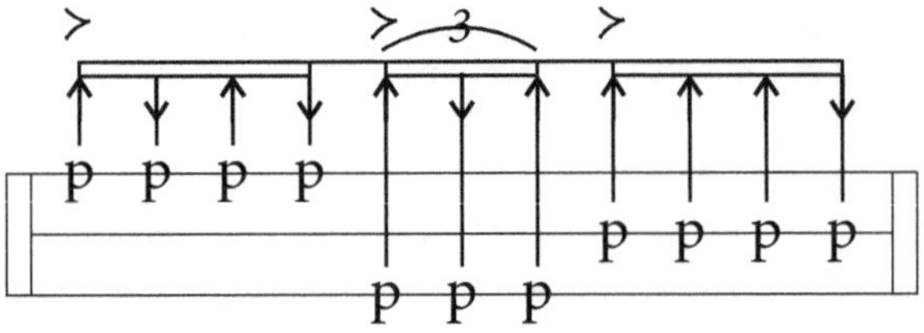

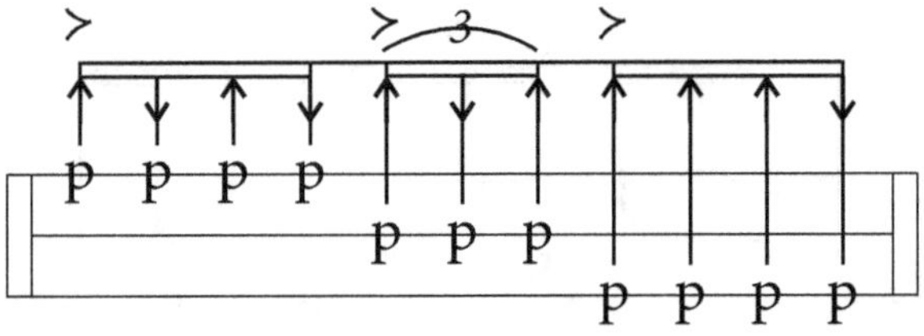

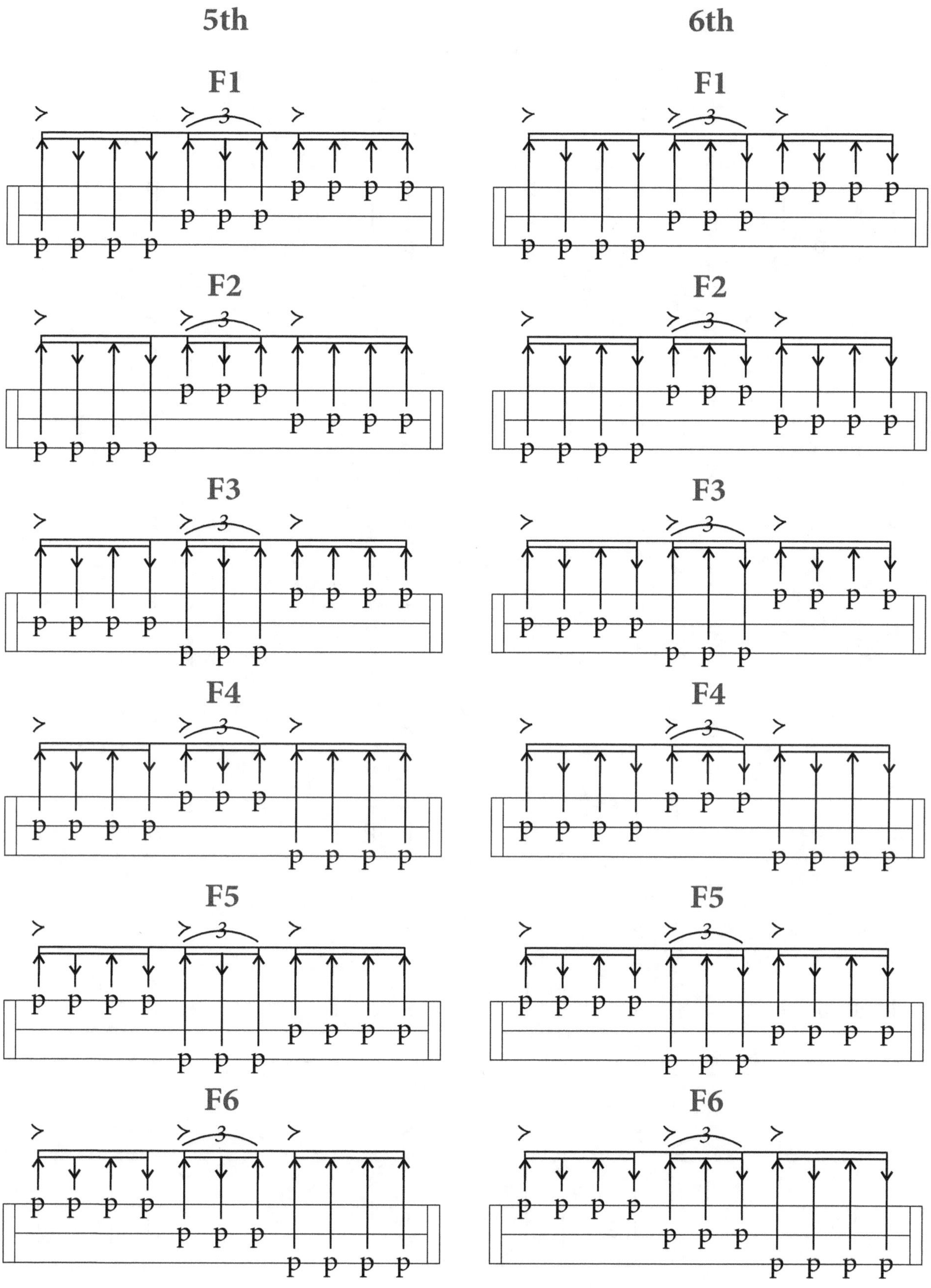

5th

F1
F2
F3
F4
F5
F6

6th

F1
F2
F3
F4
F5
F6

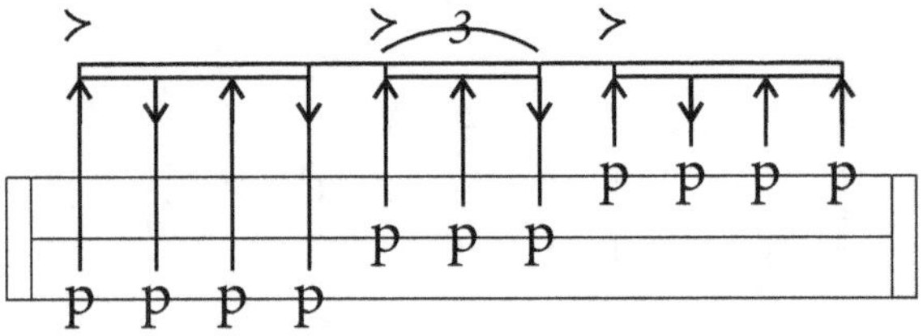

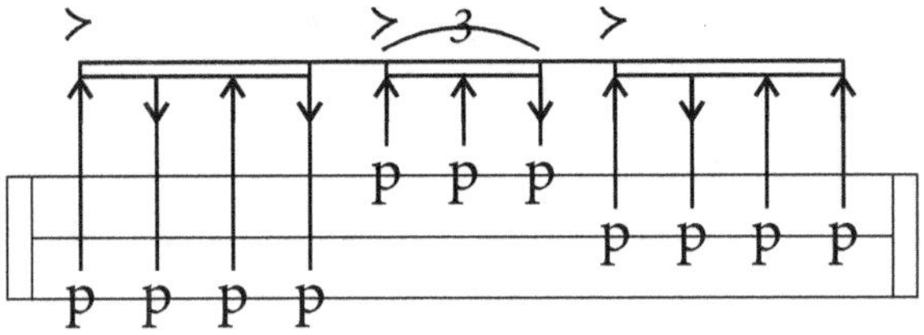

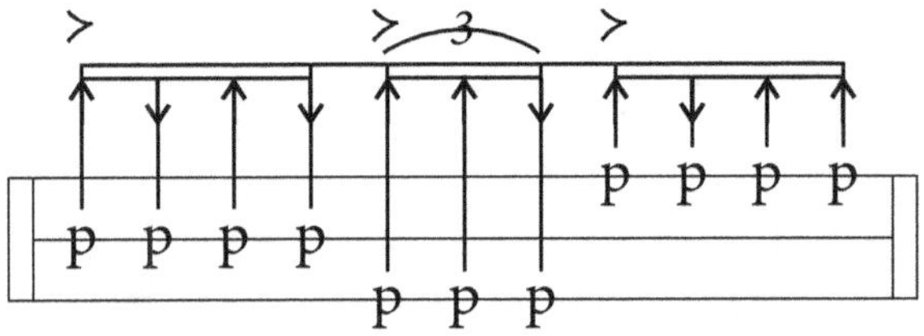

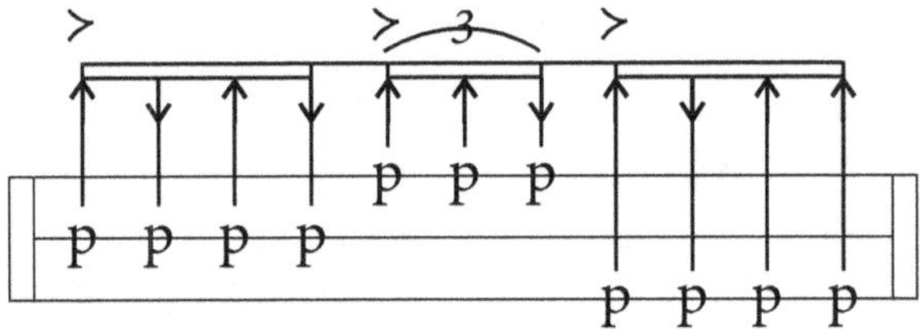

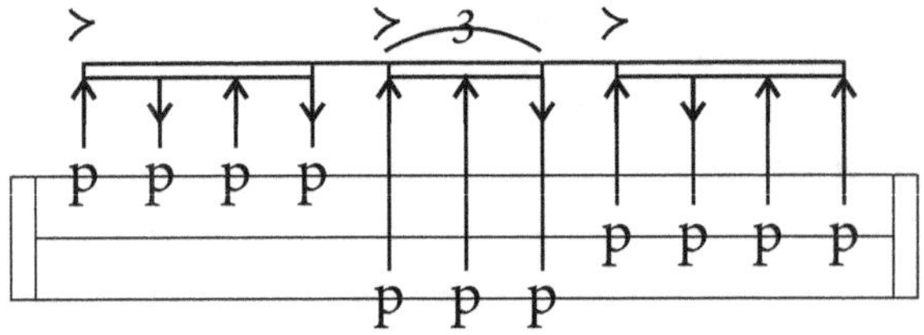

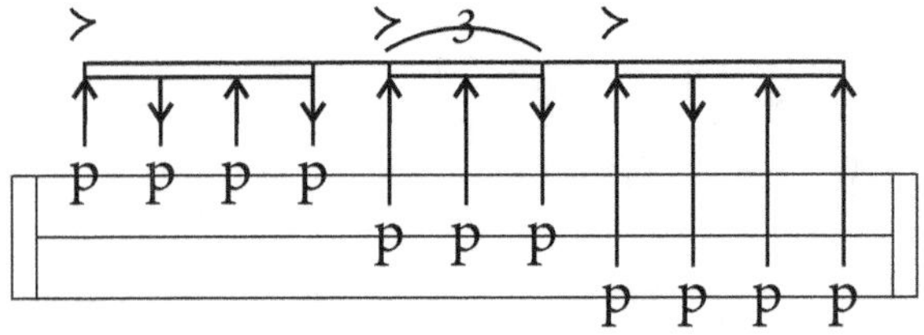

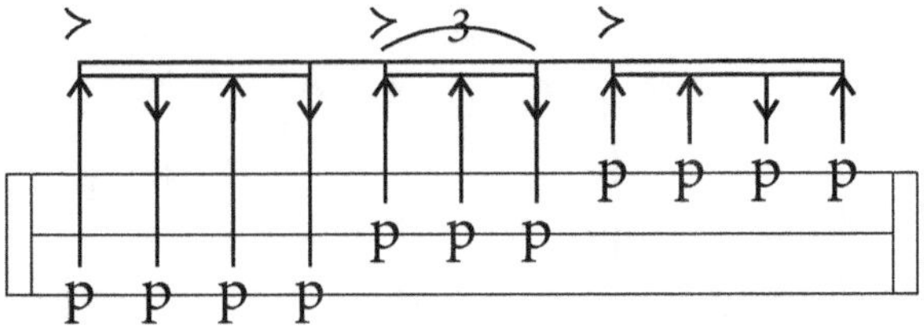

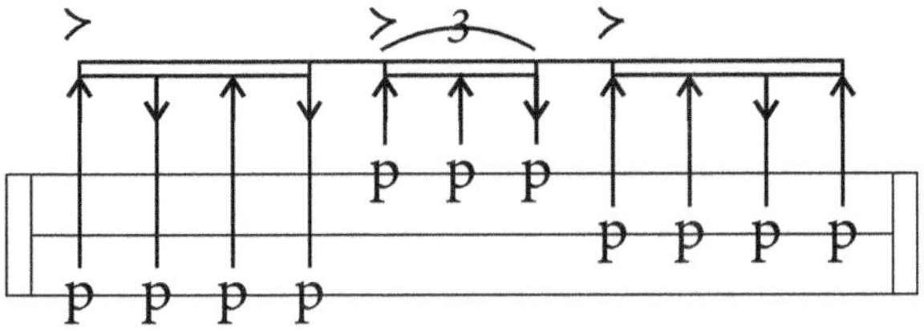

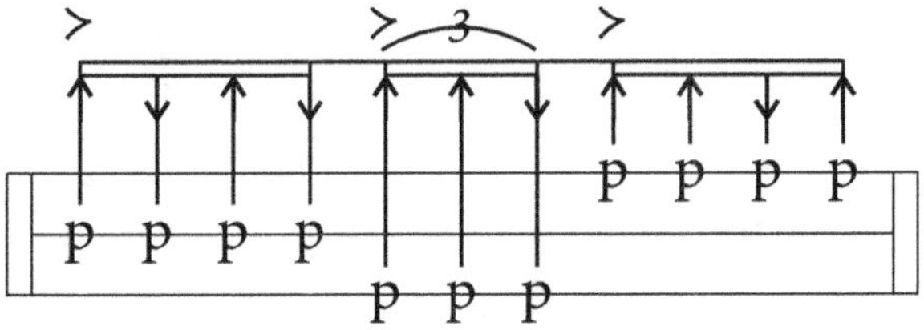

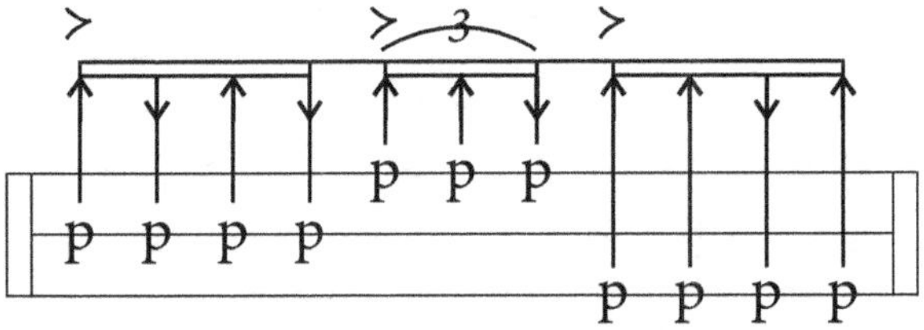

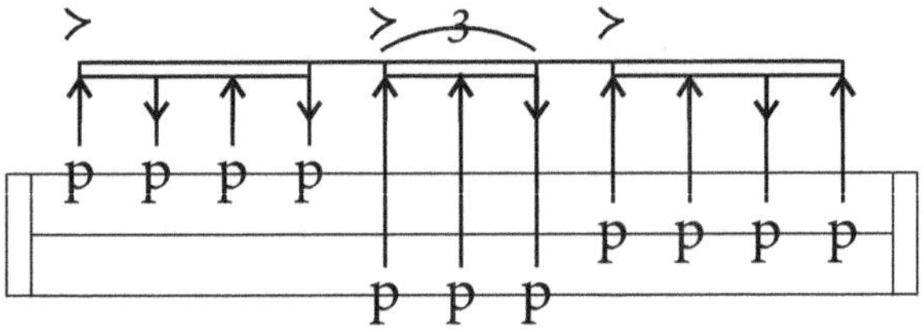

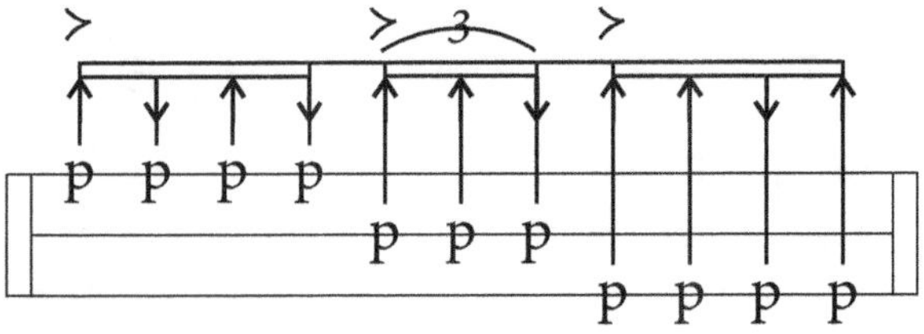

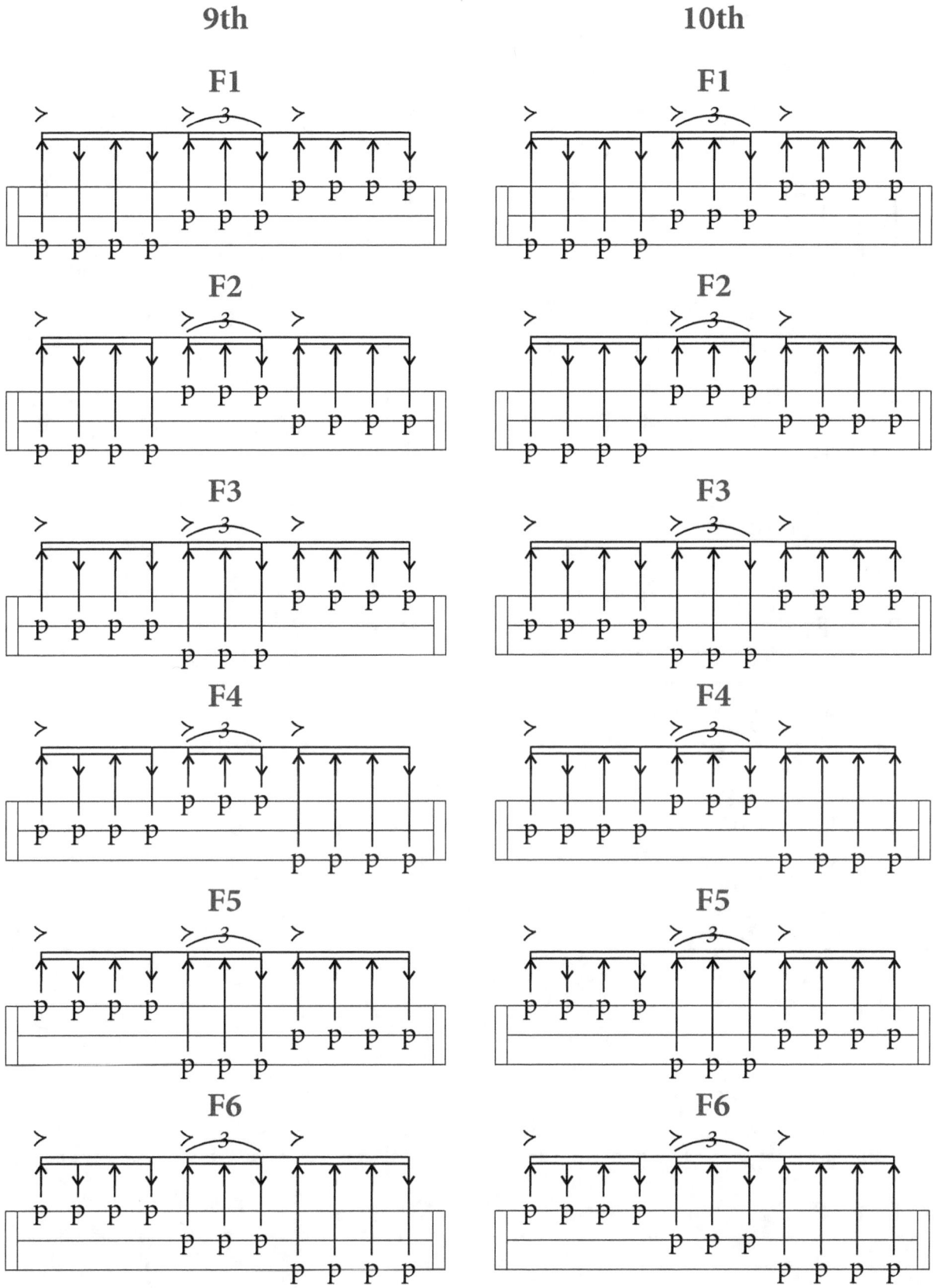

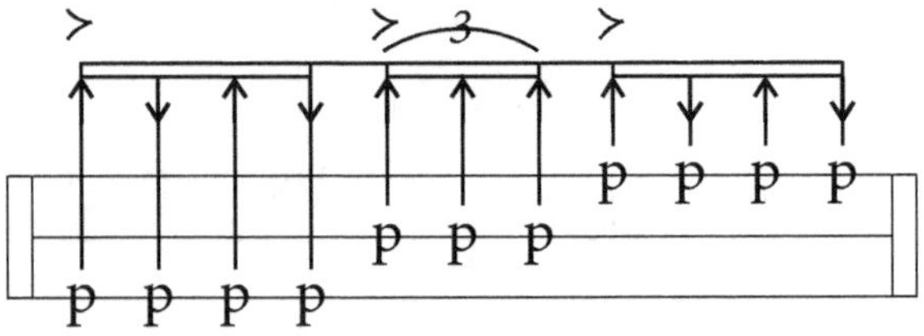

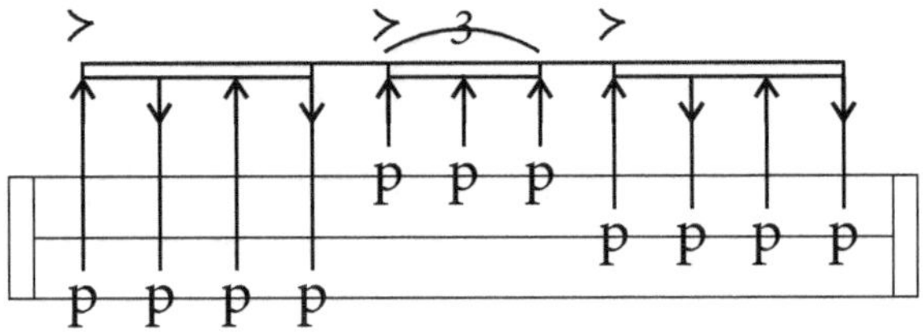

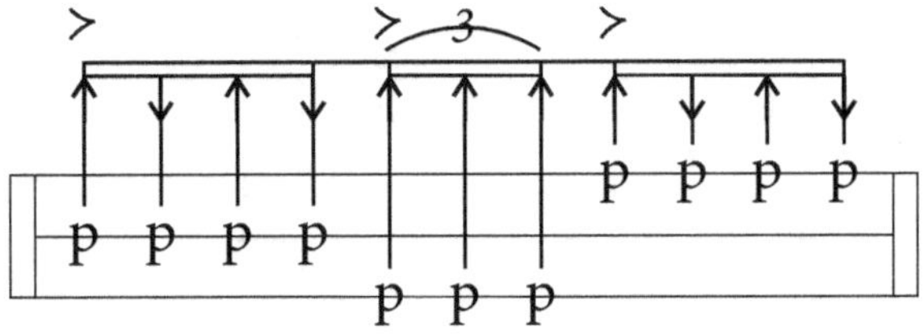

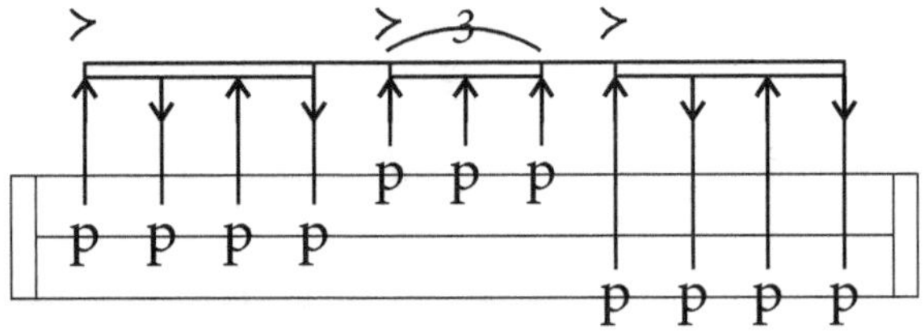

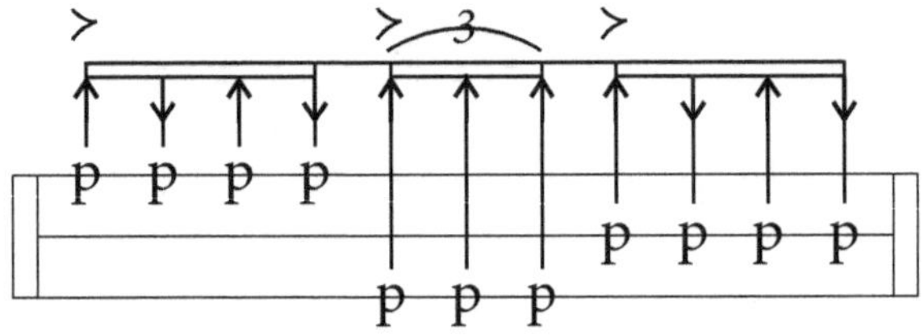

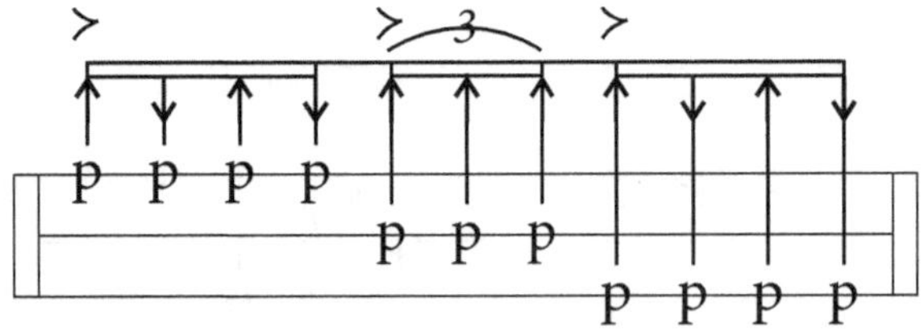

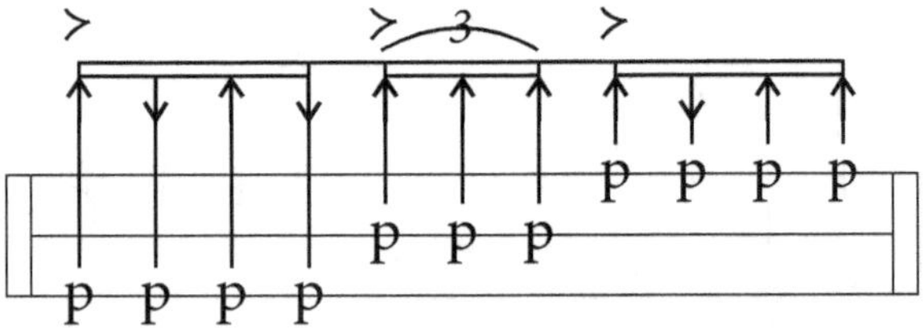

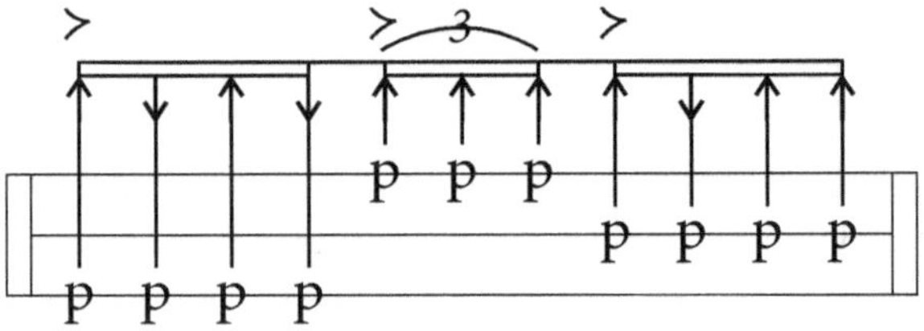

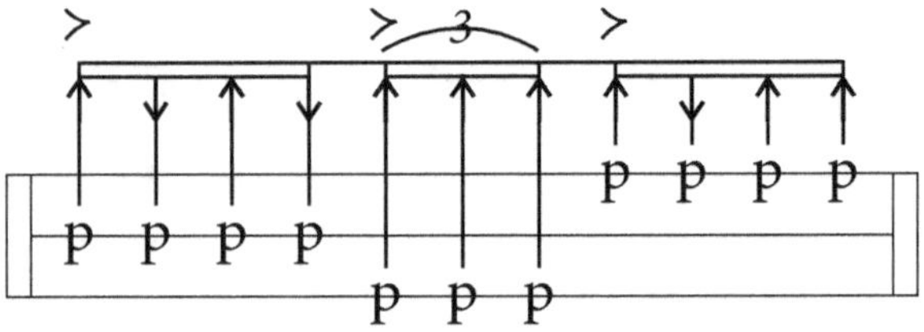

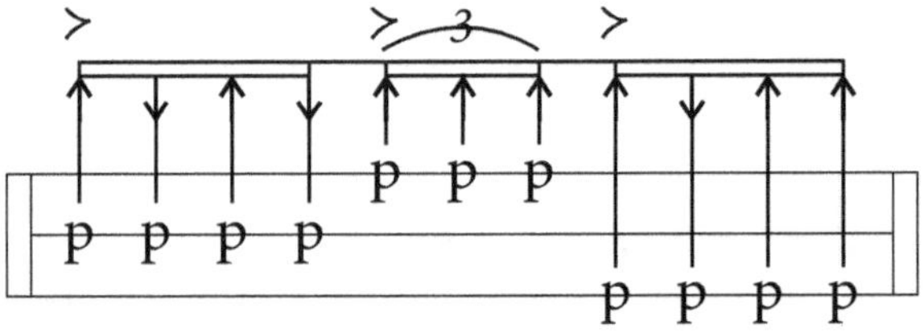

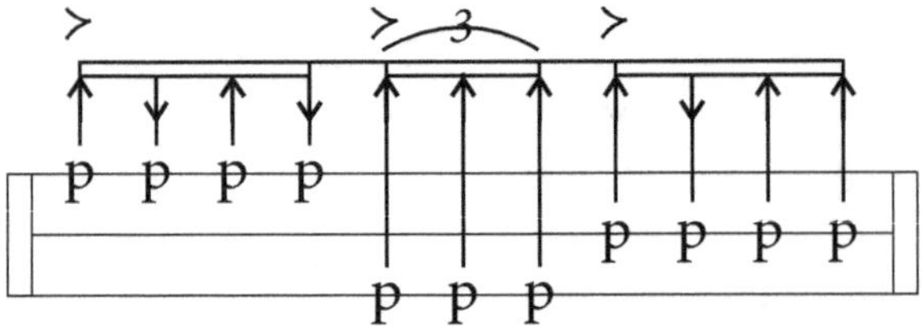

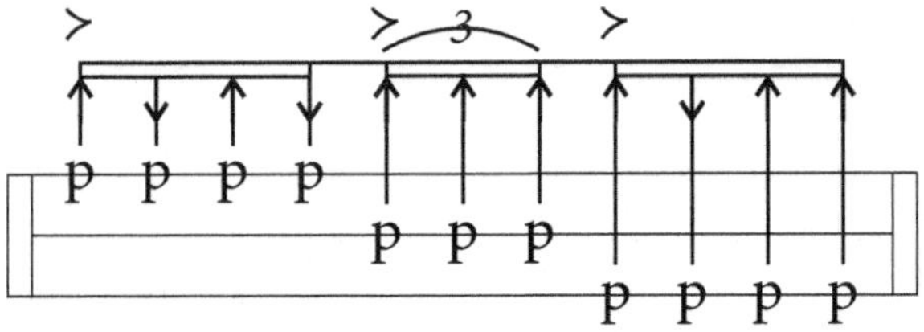

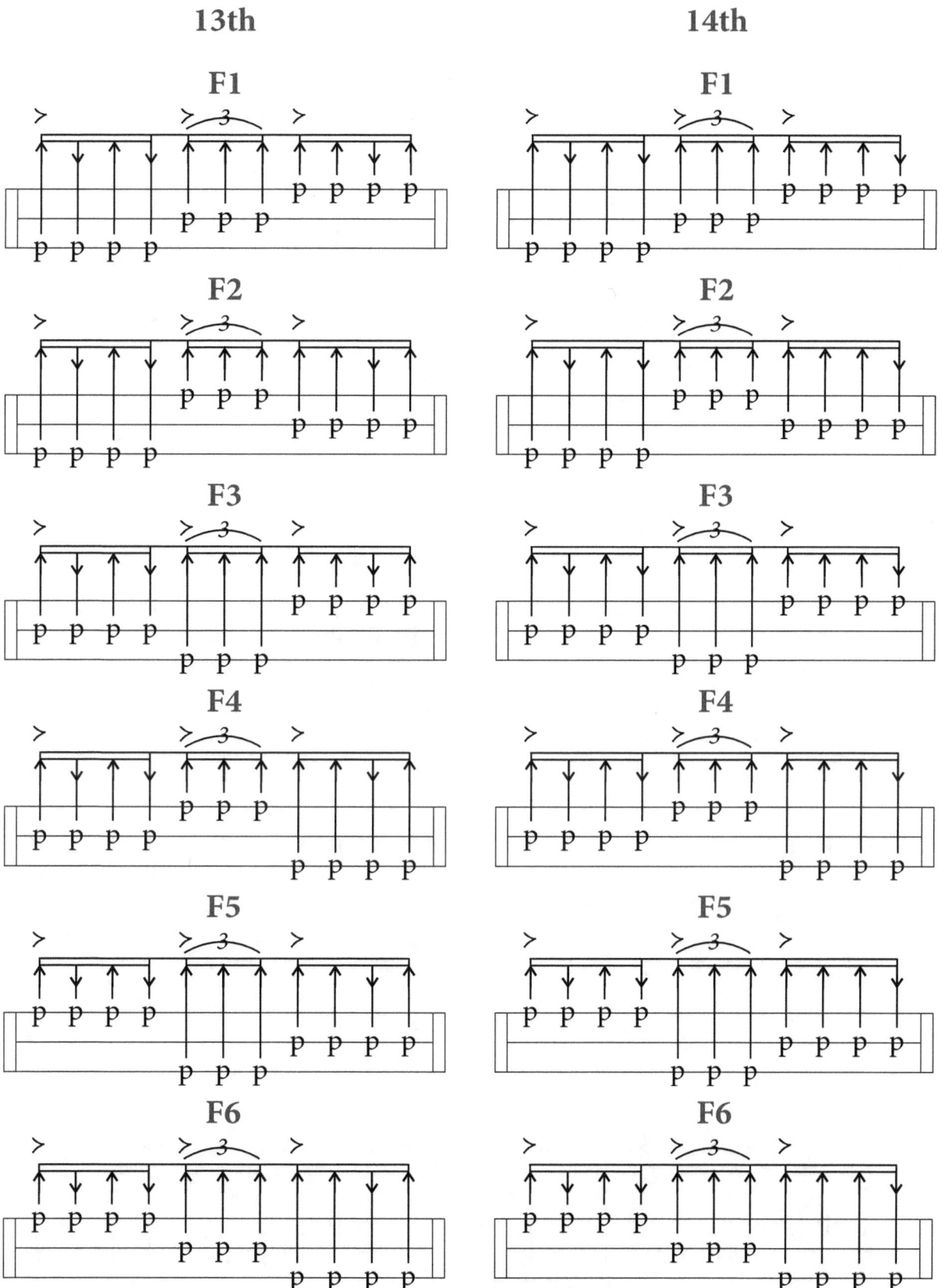

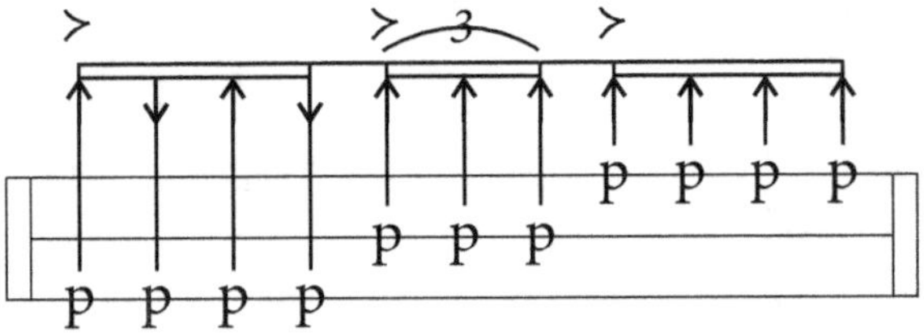

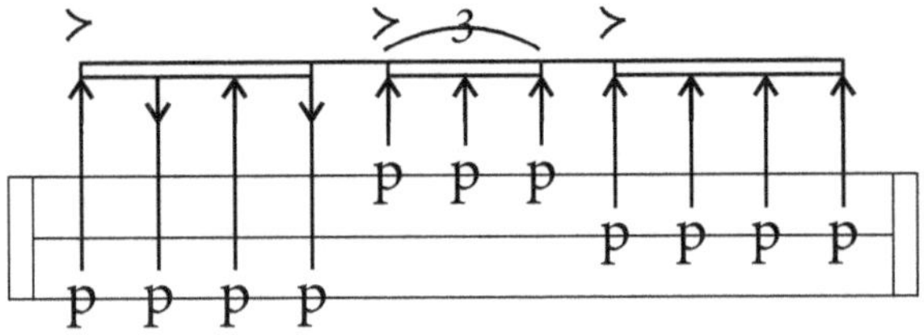

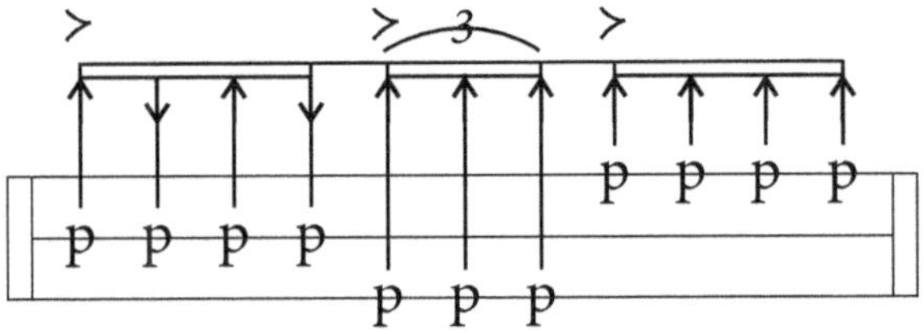

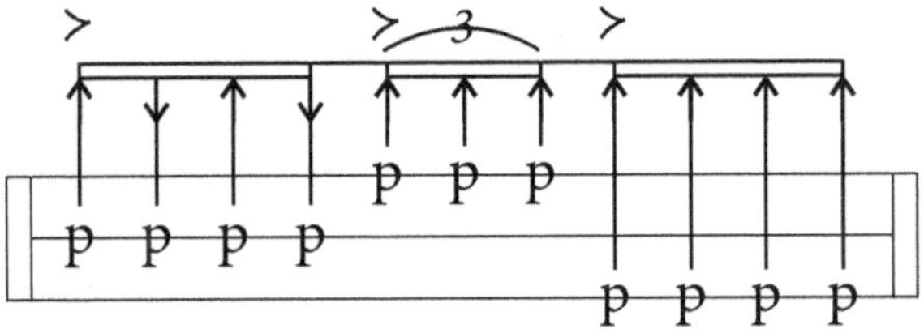

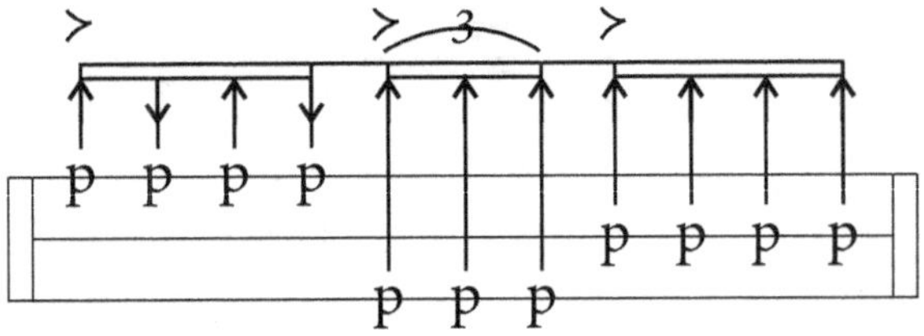

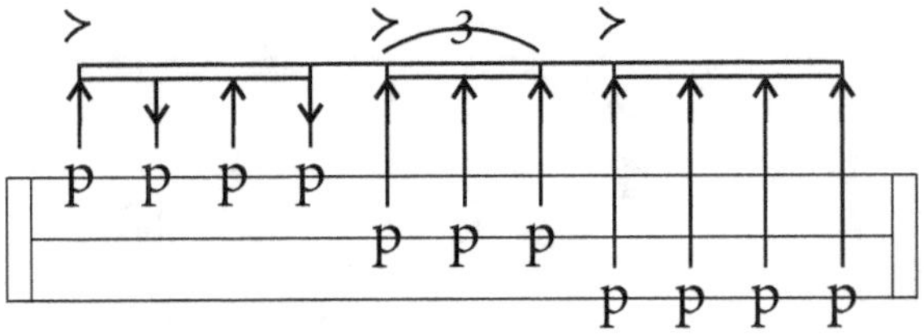

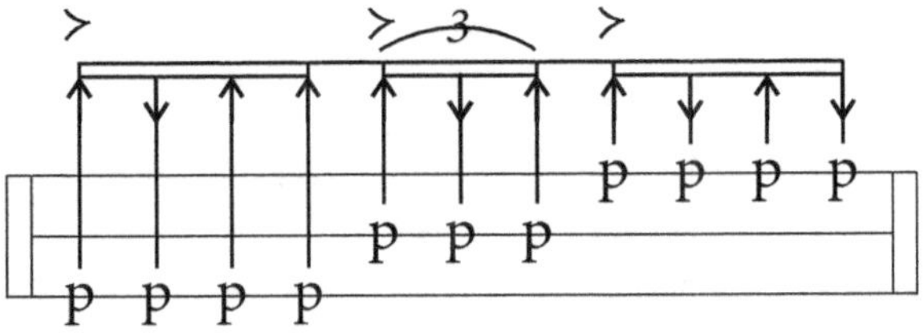

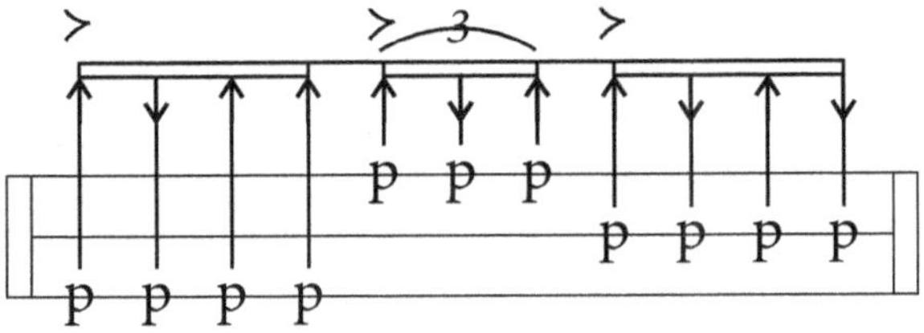

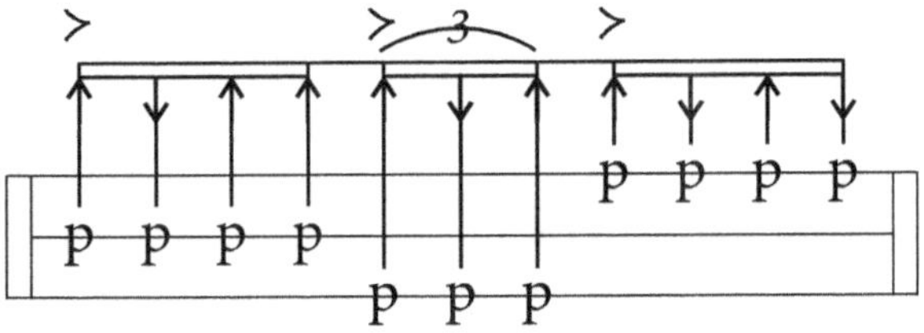

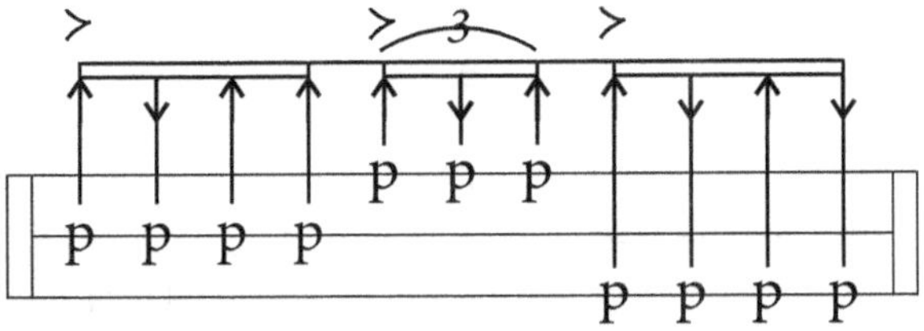

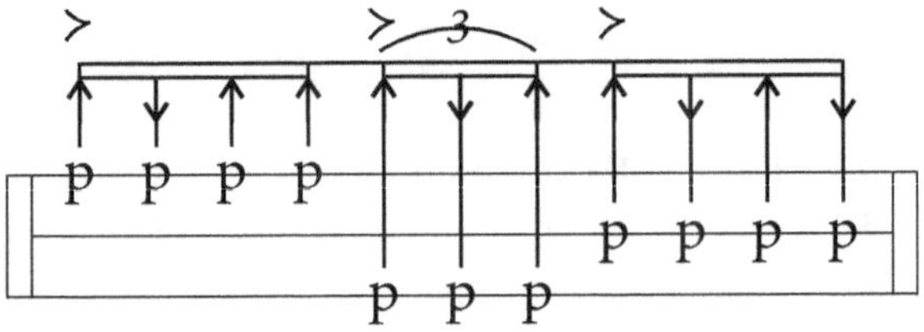

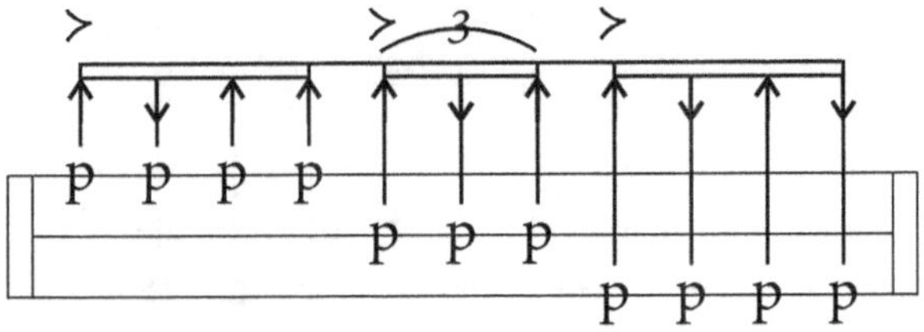

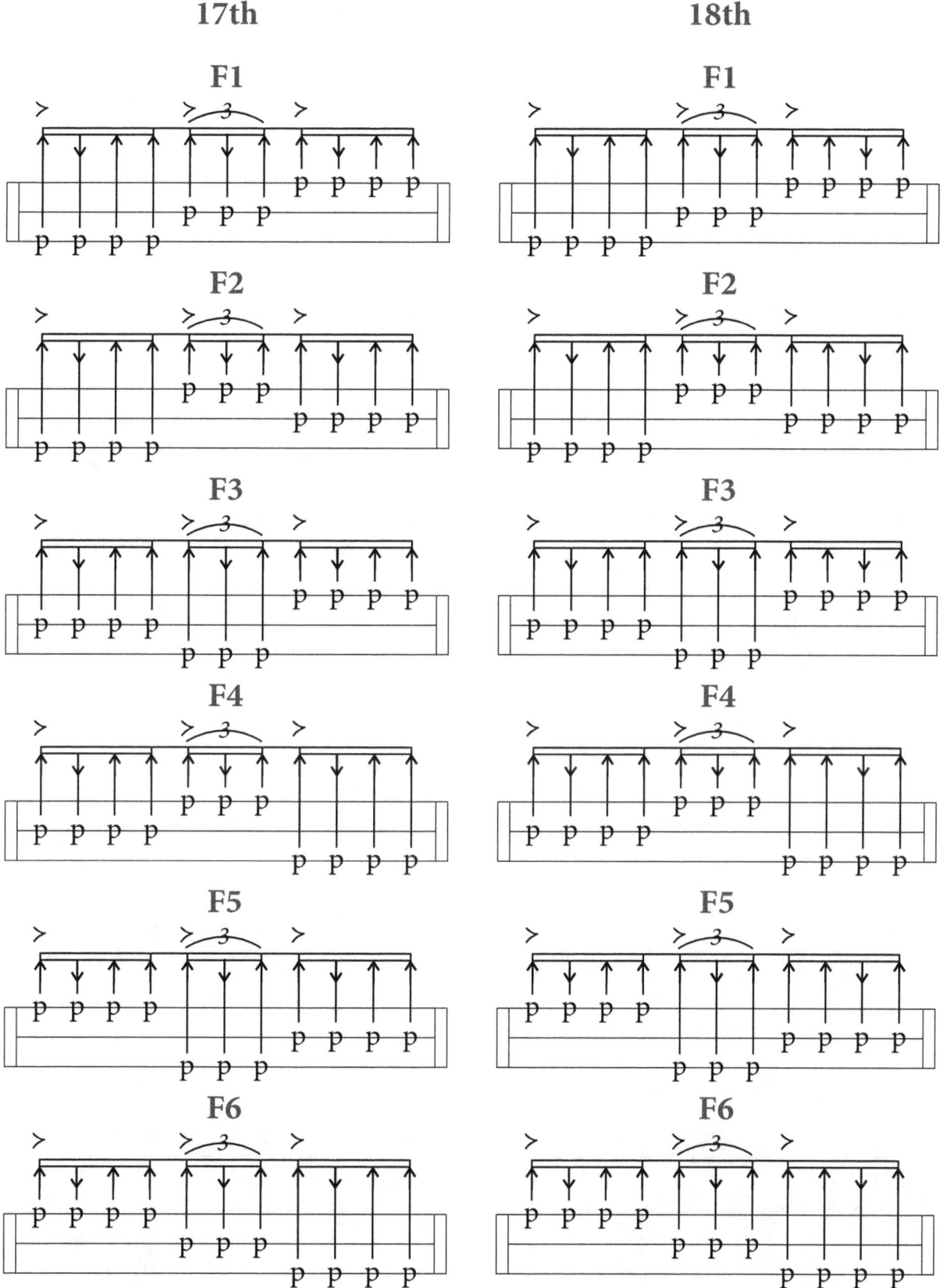

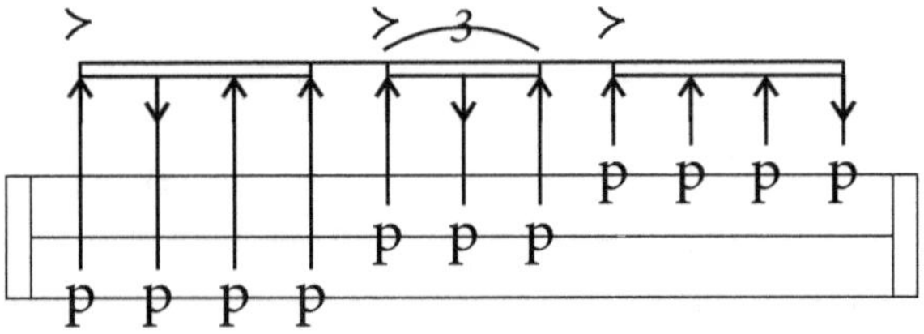

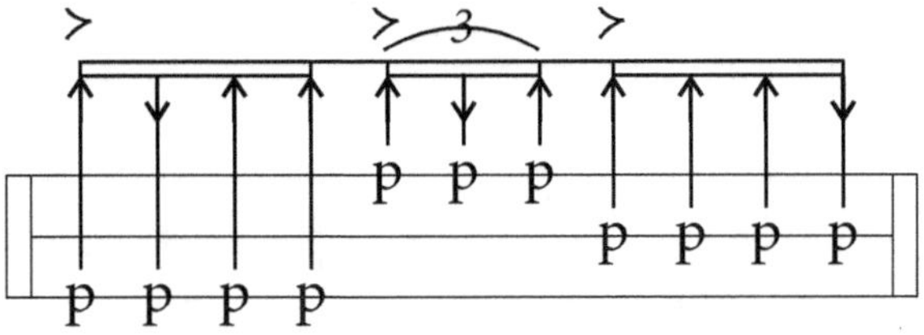

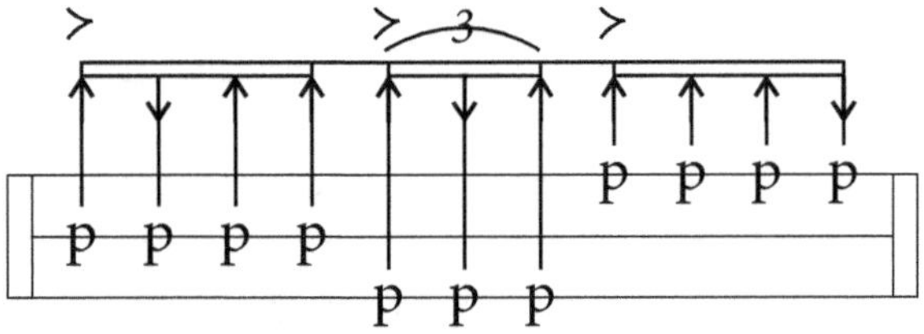

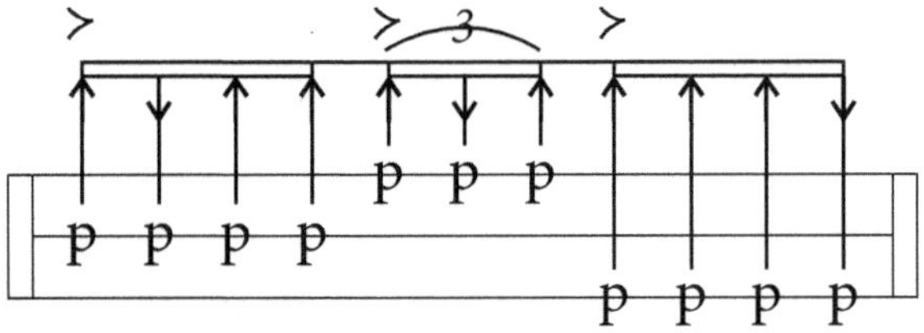

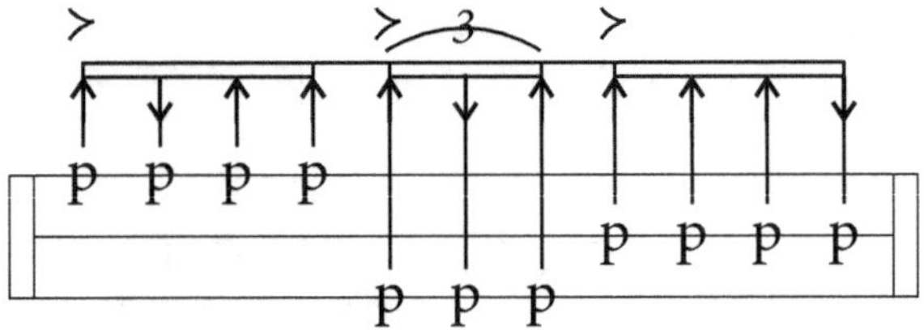

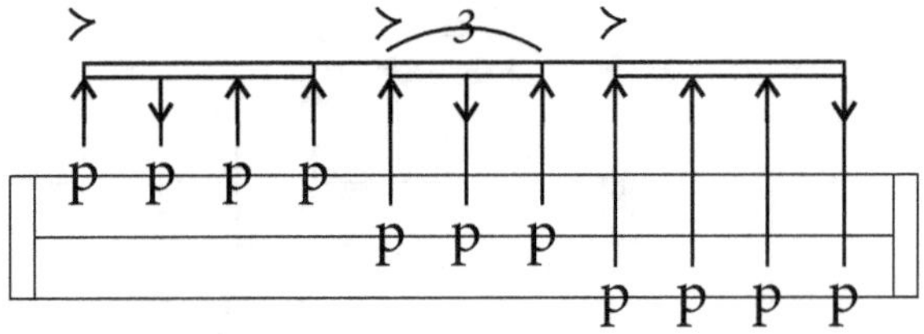

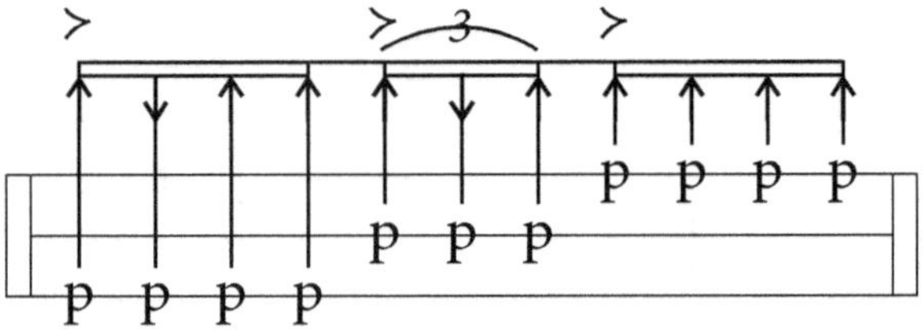

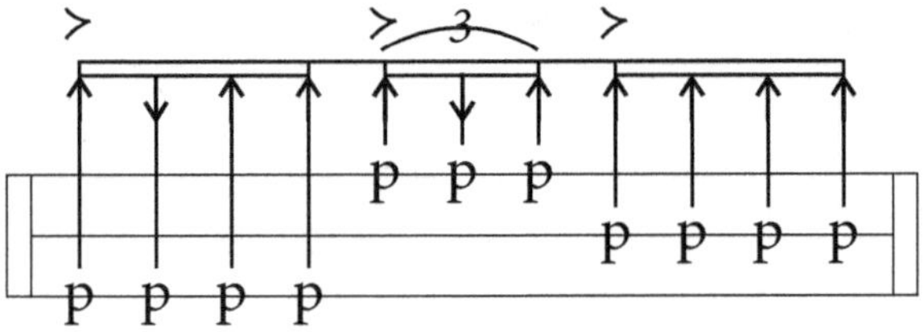

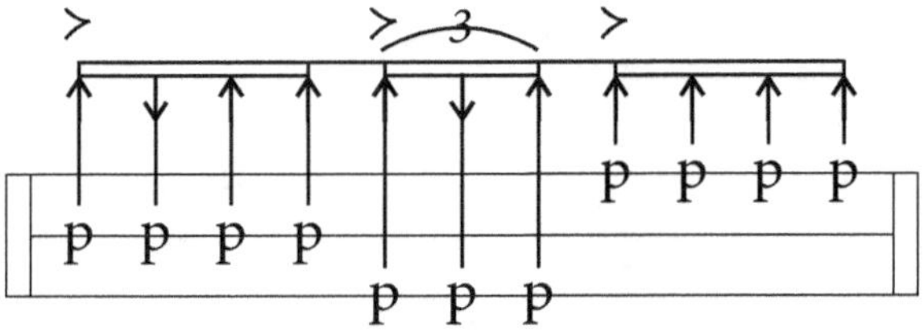

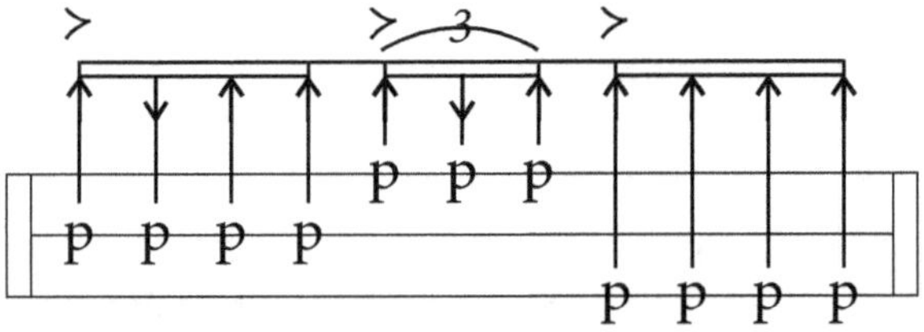

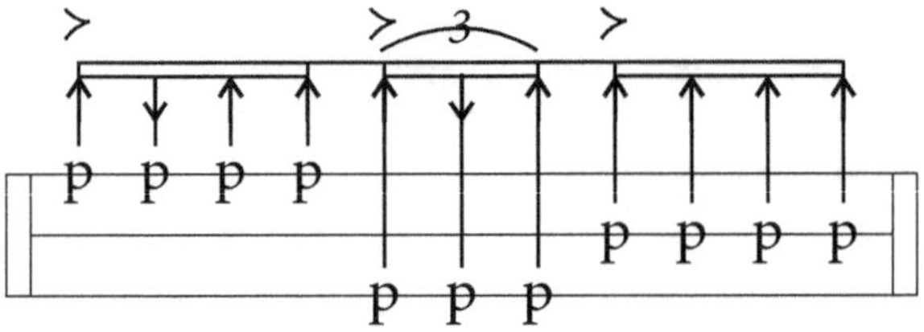

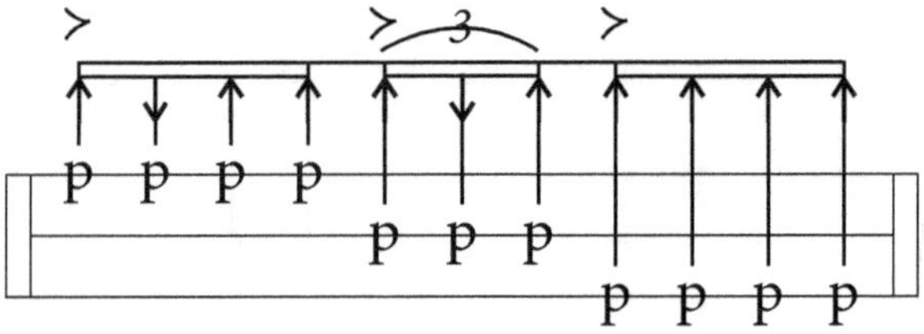

21th

F1

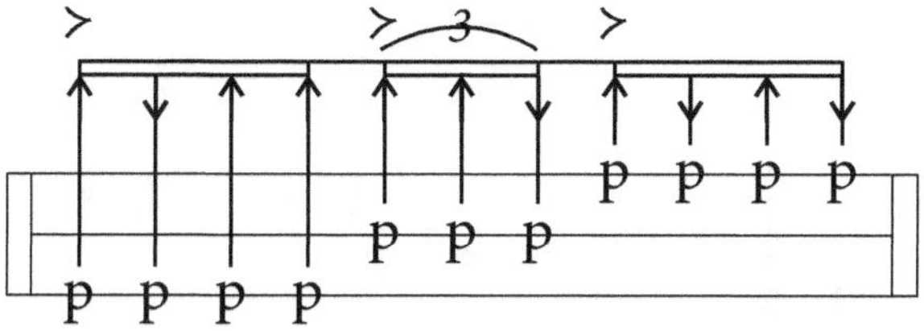

F2

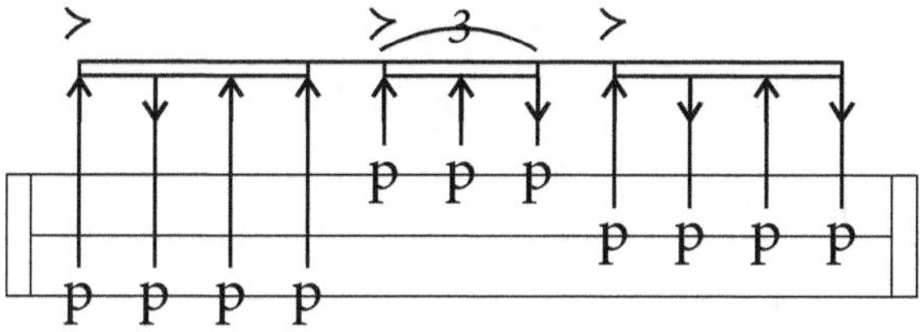

F3

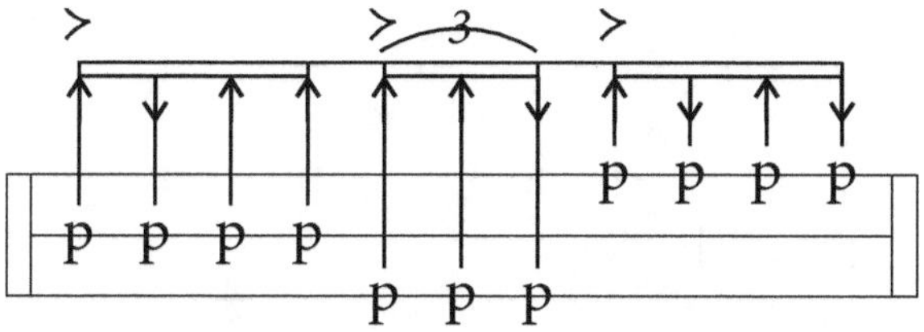

F4

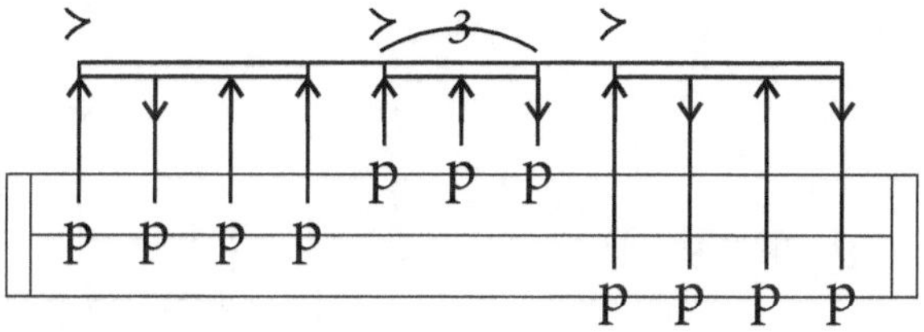

F5

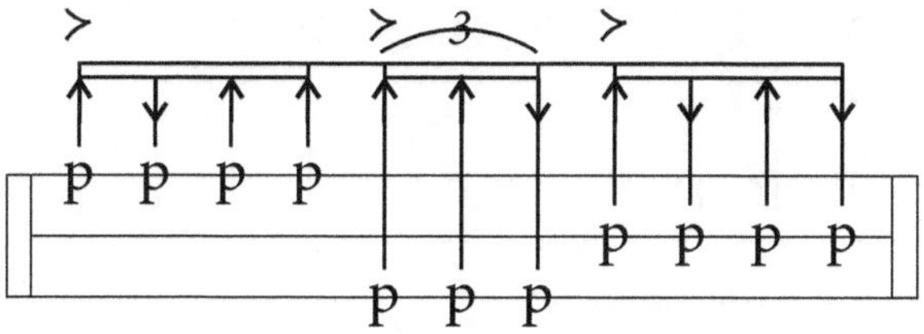

F6

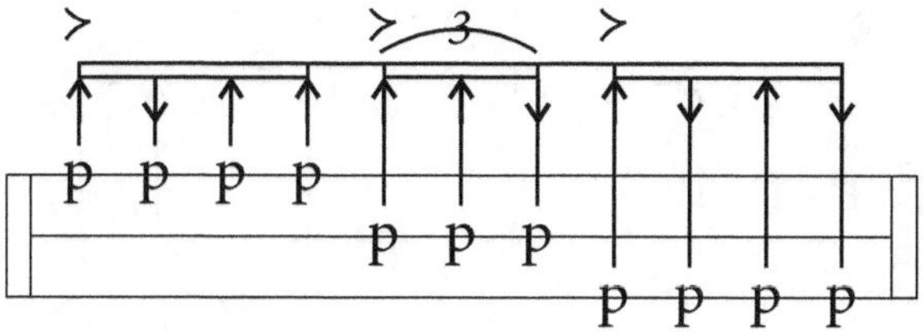

22th

F1

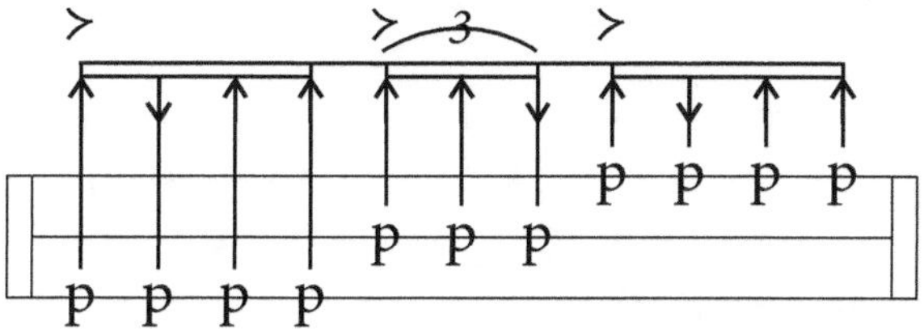

F2

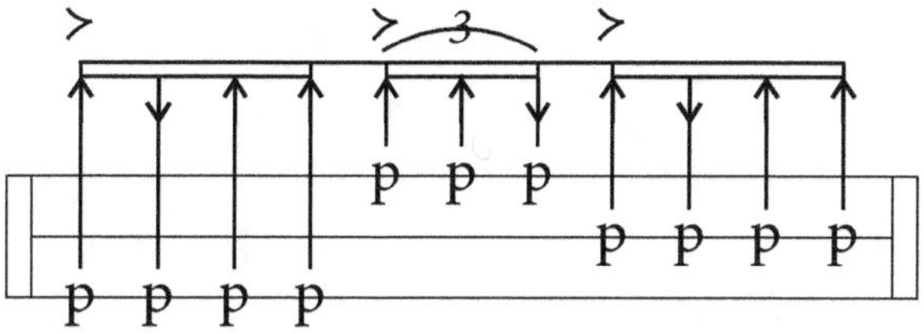

F3

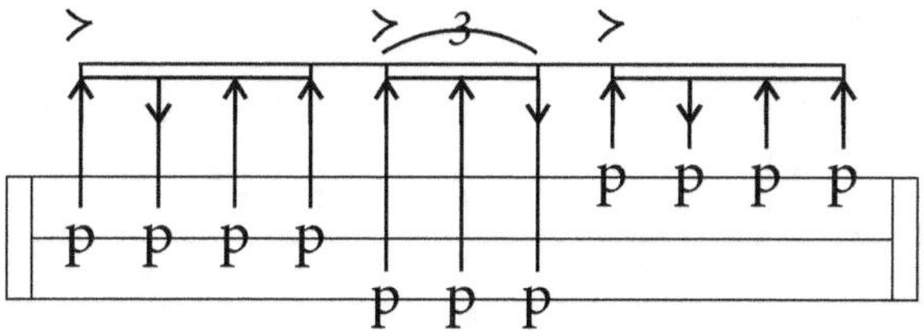

F4

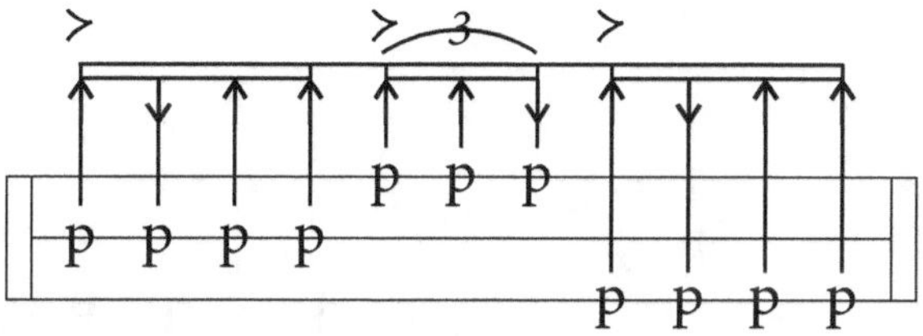

F5

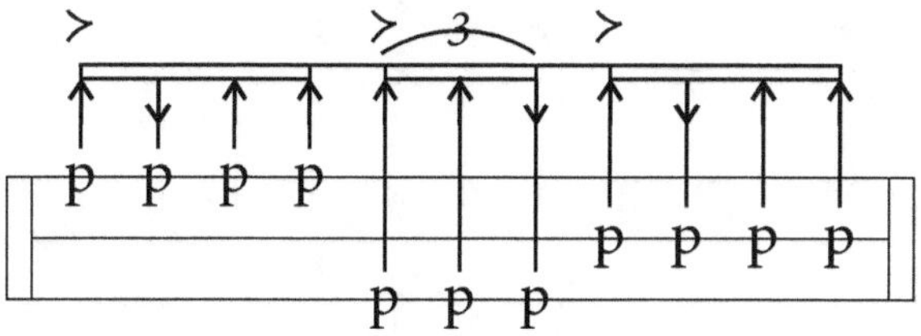

F6

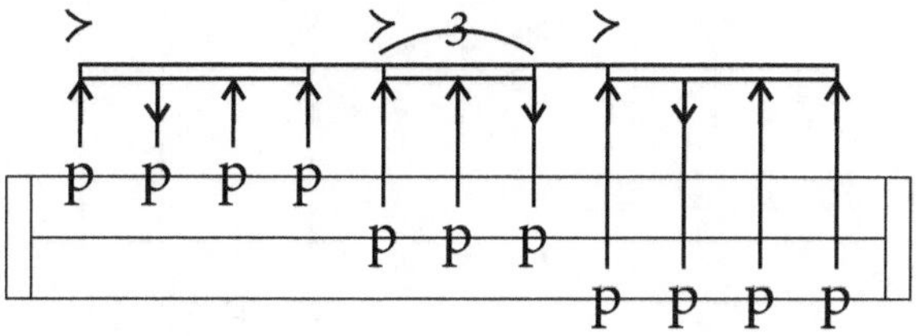

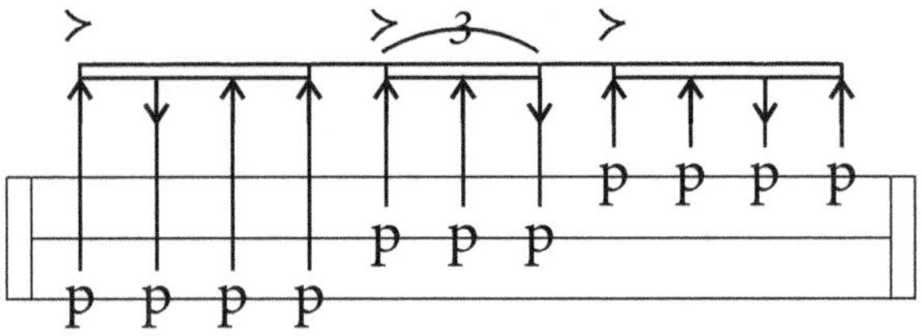

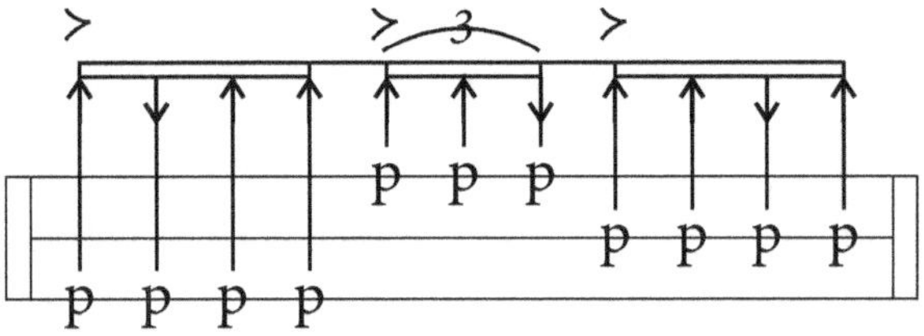

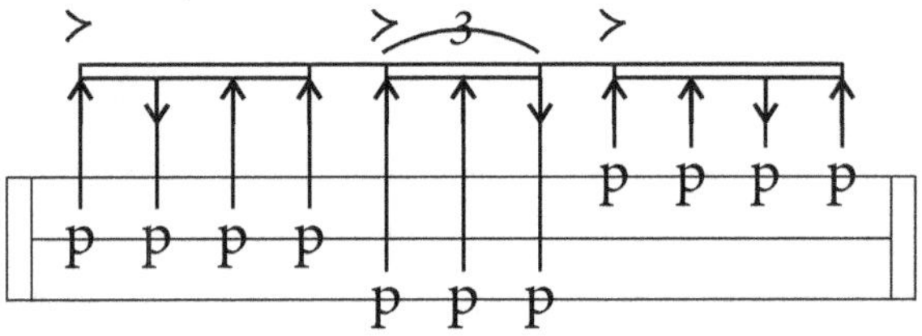

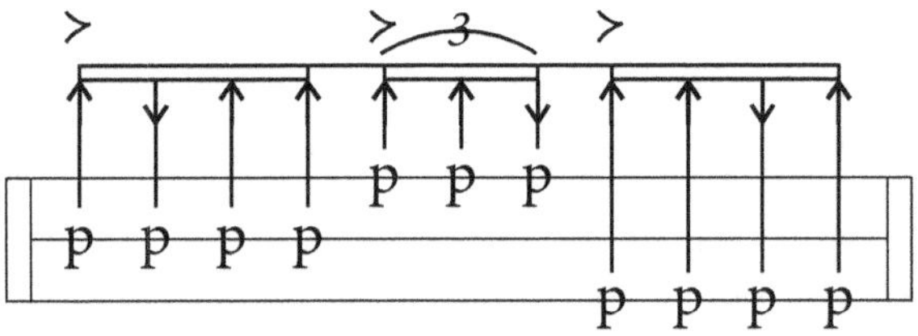

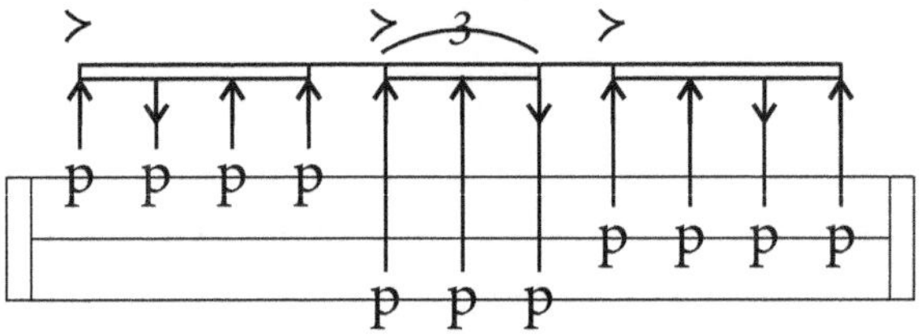

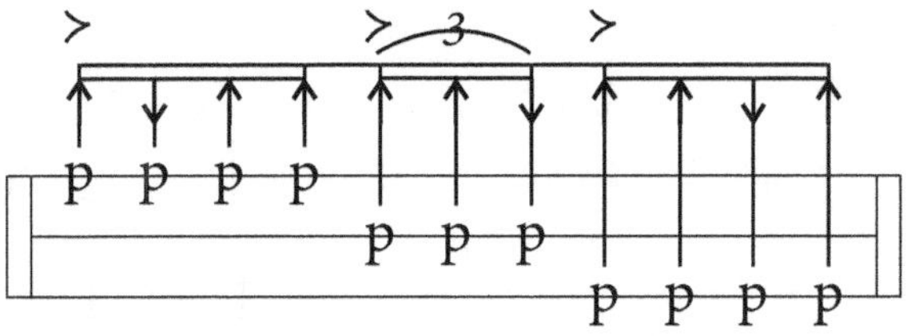

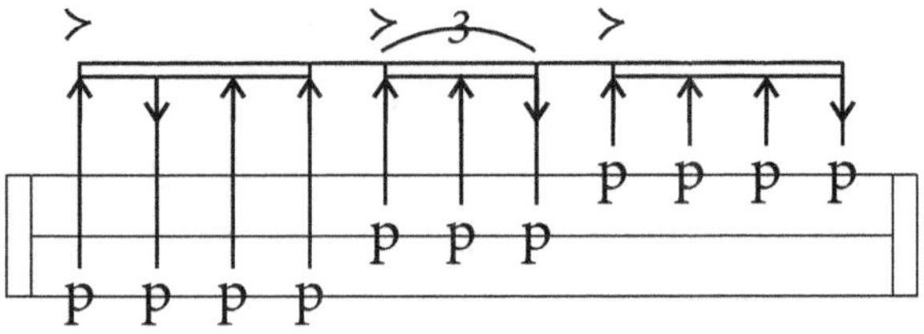

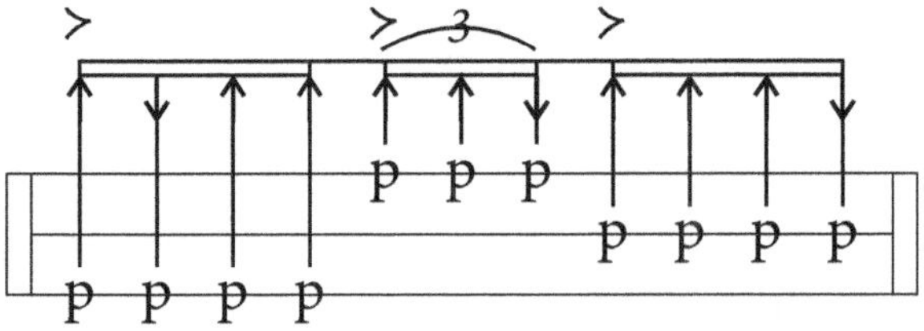

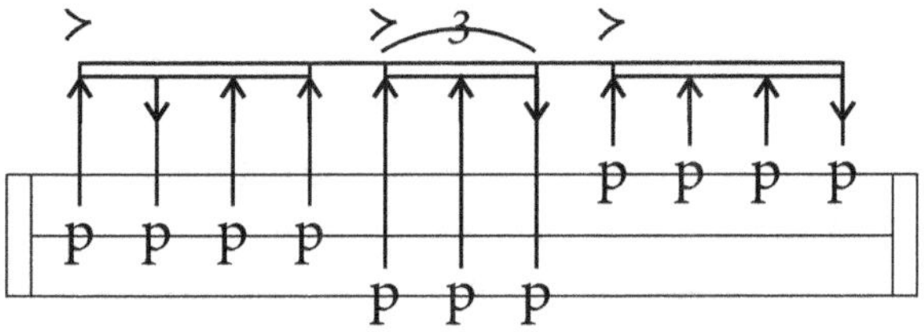

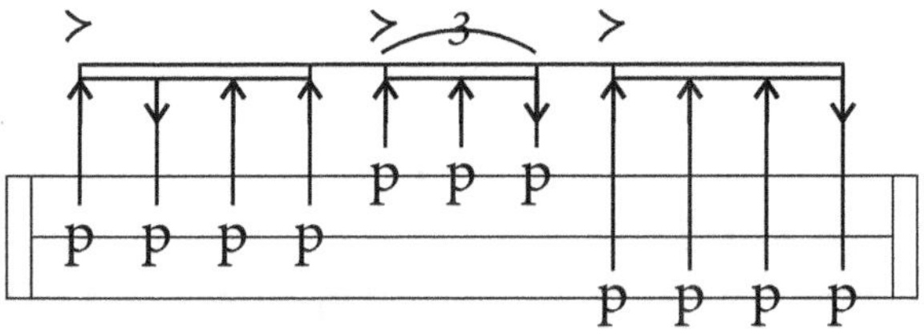

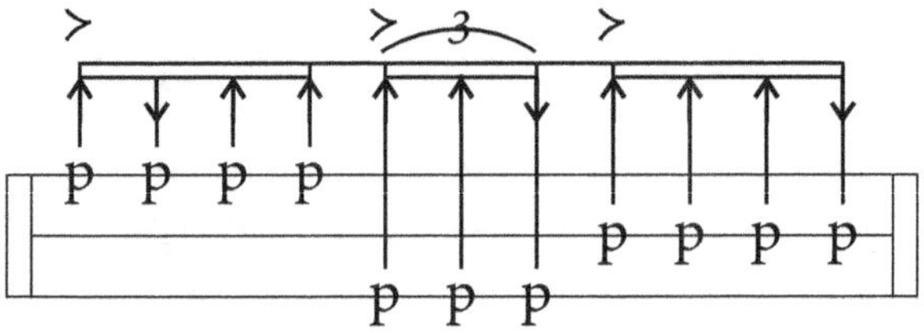

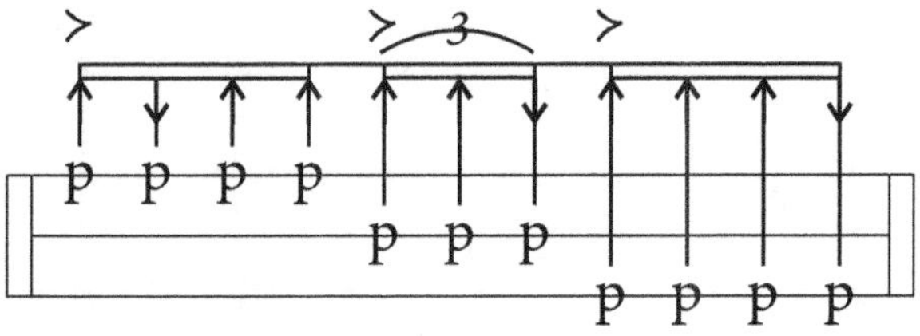

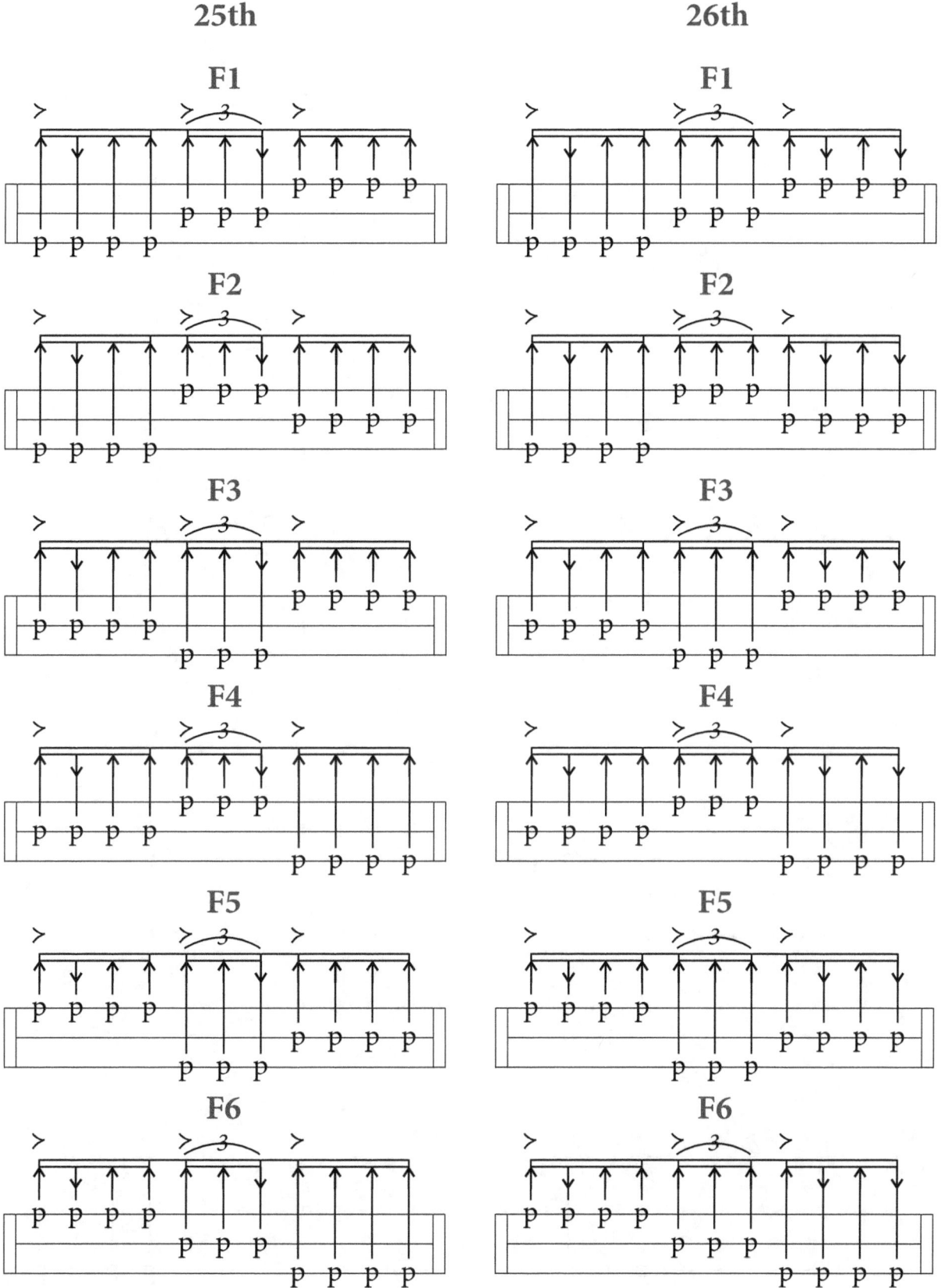

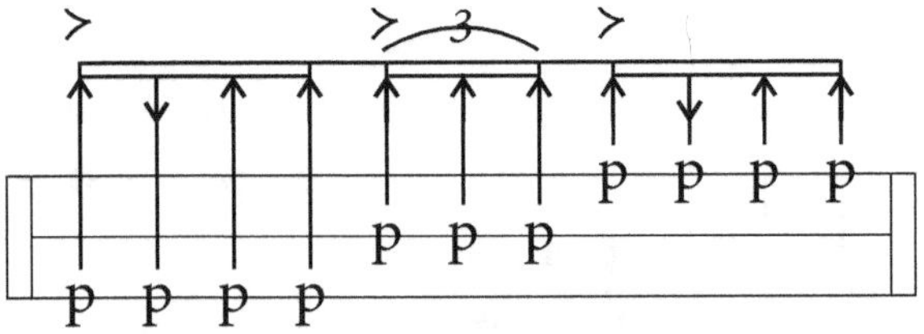

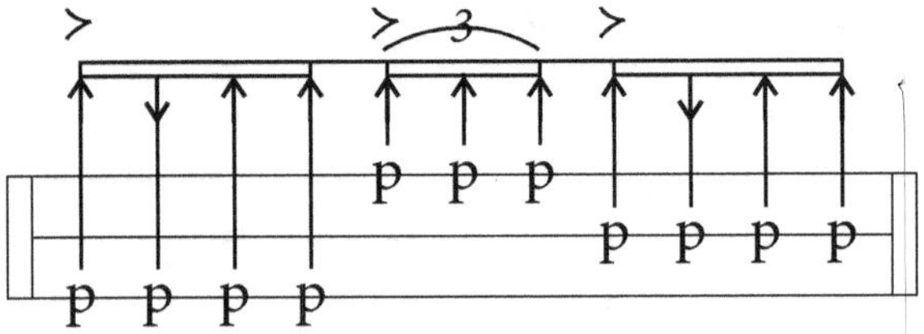

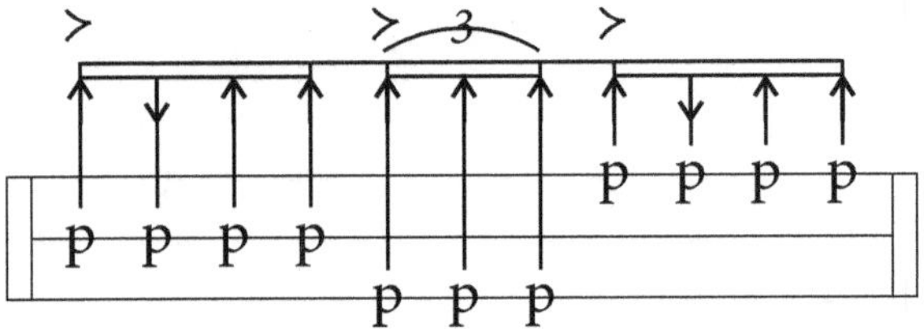

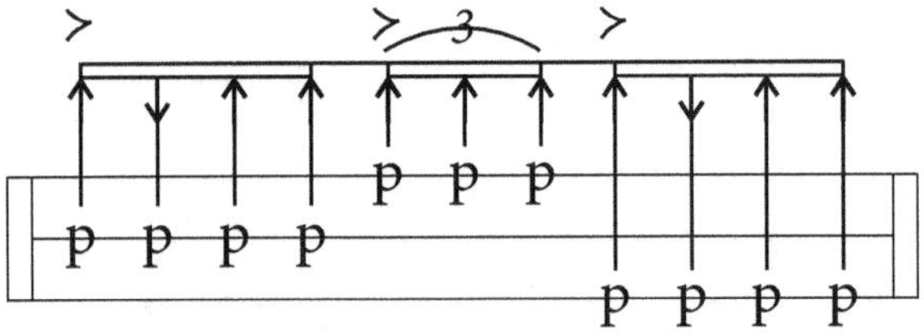

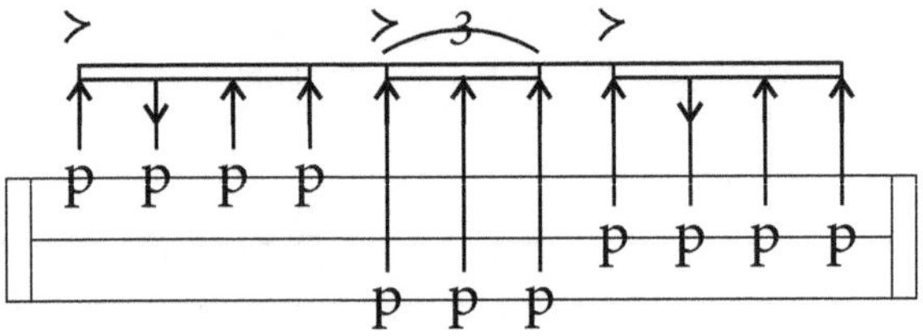

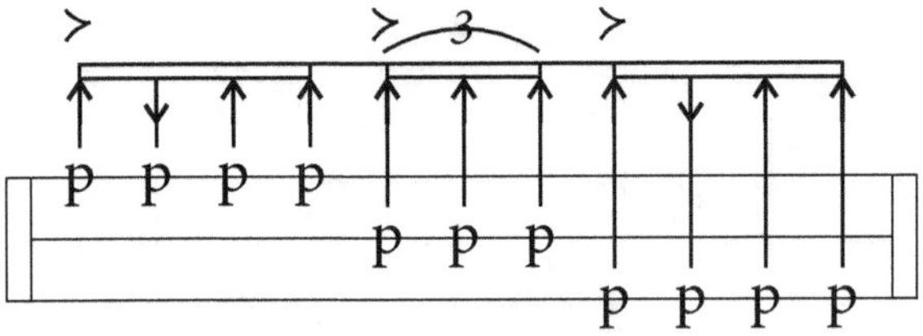

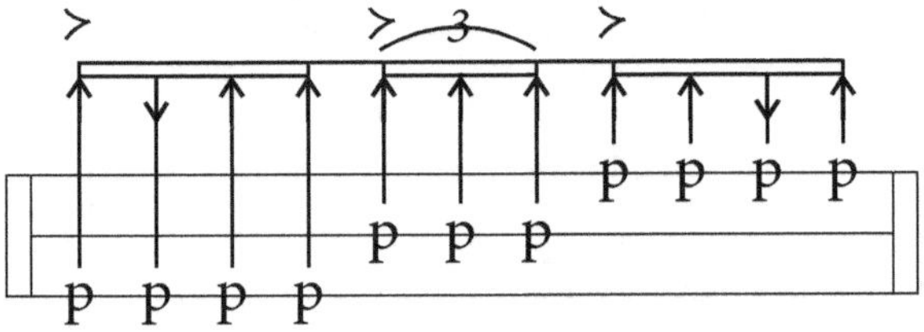

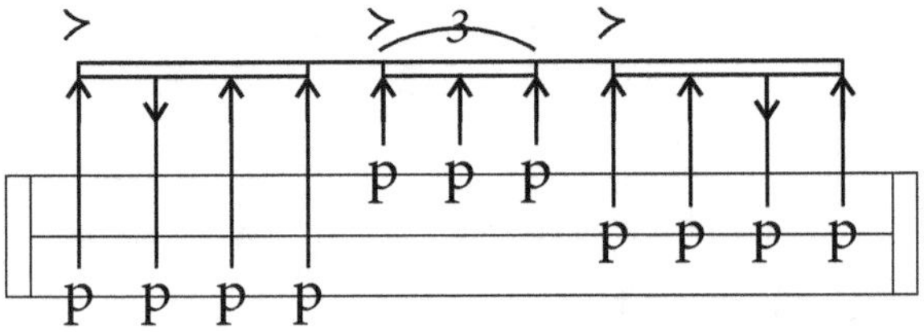

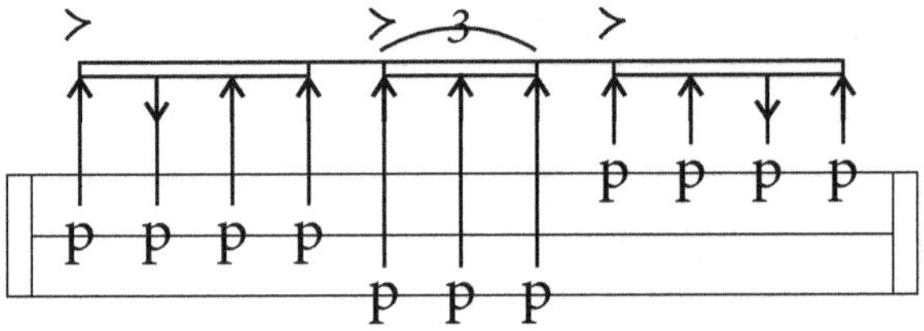

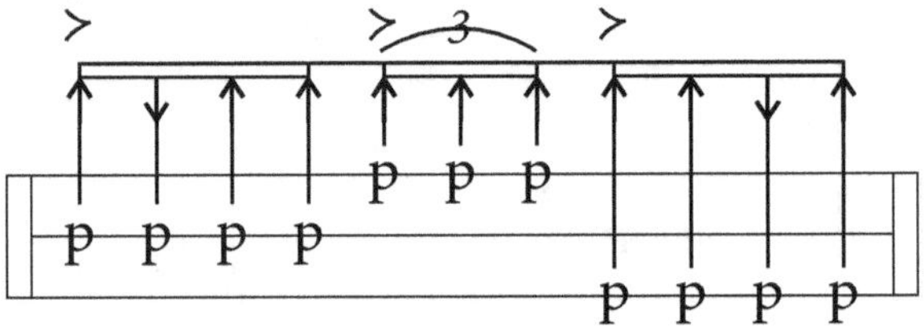

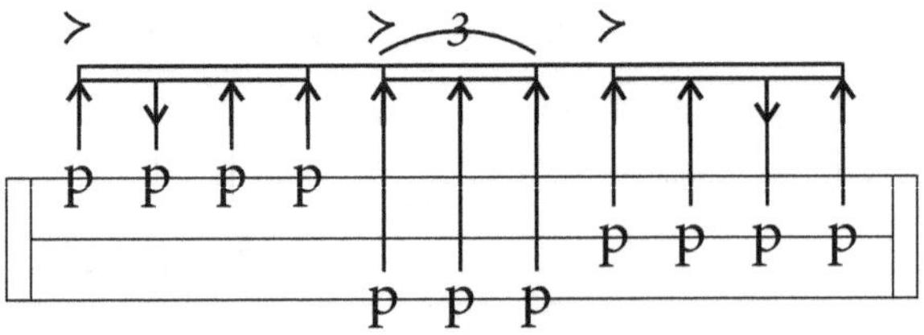

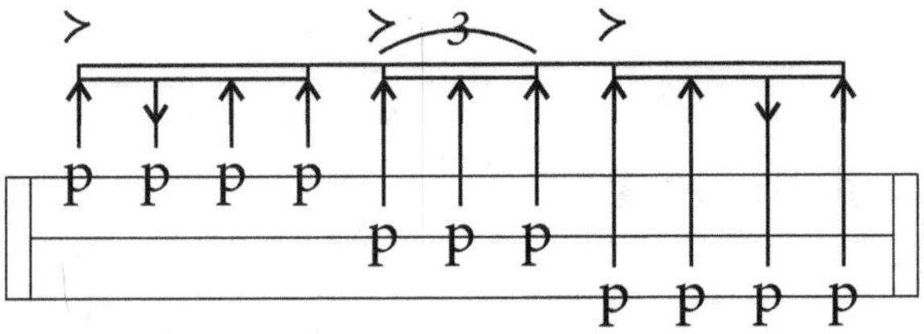

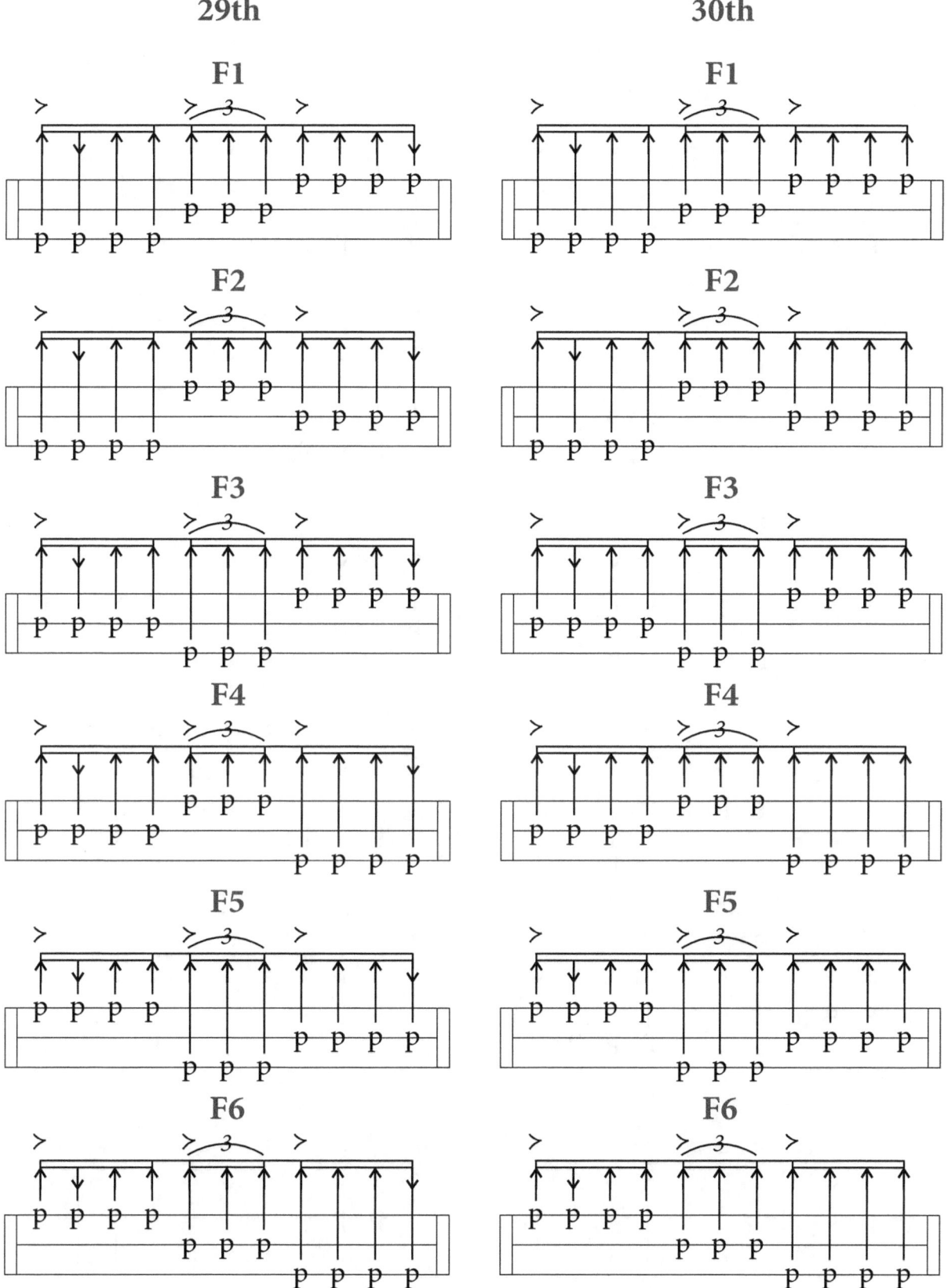

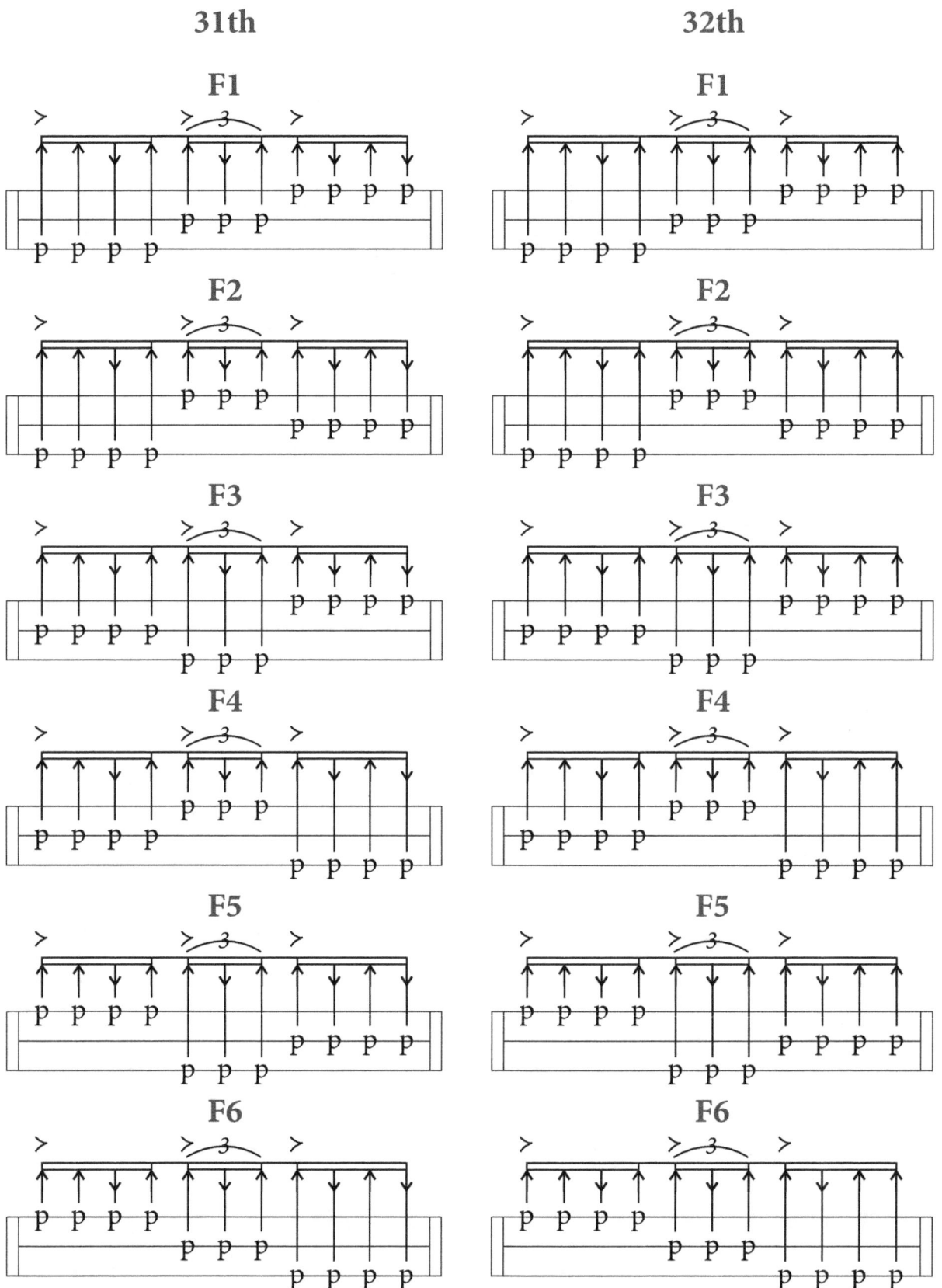

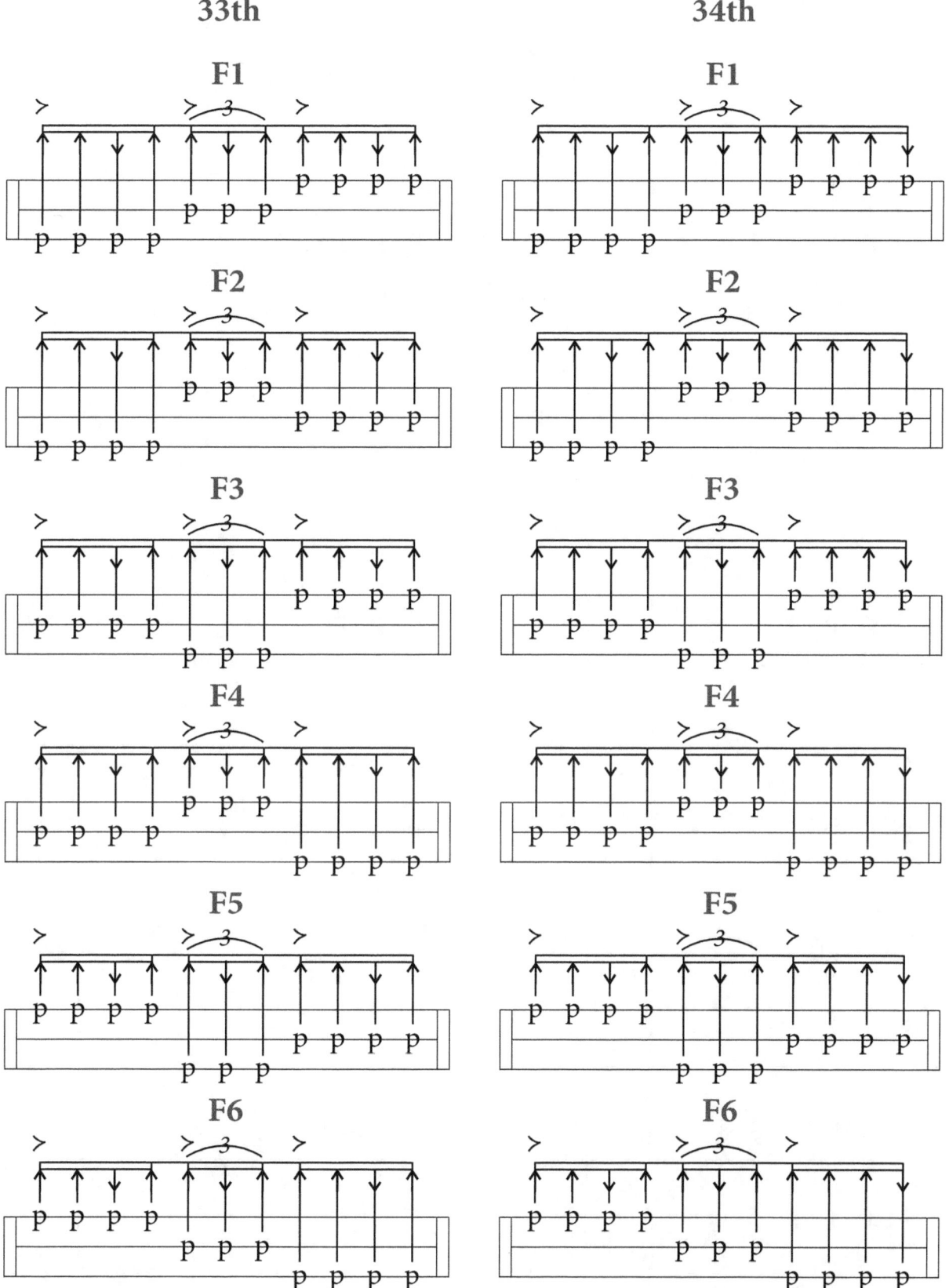

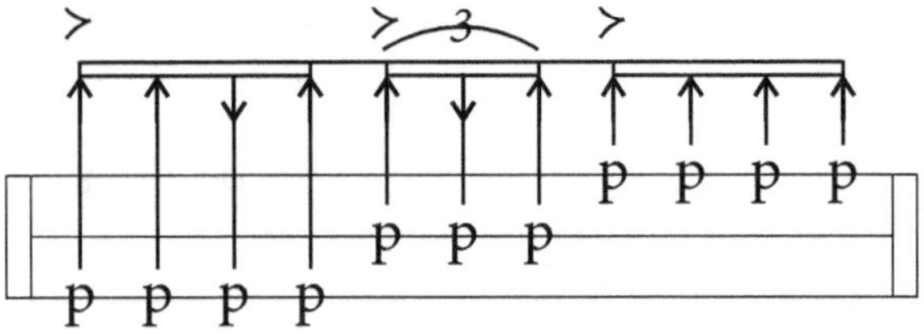

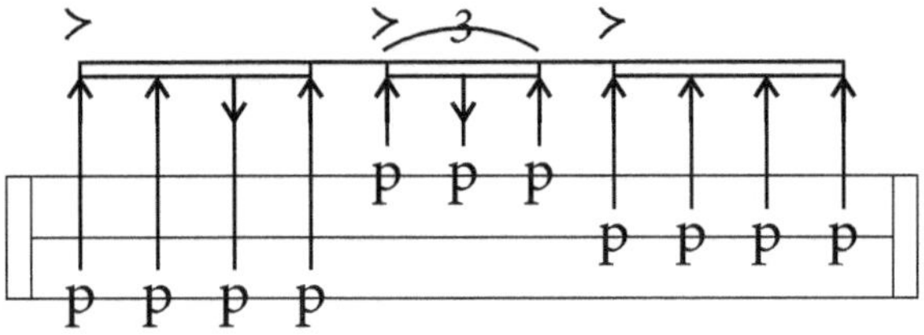

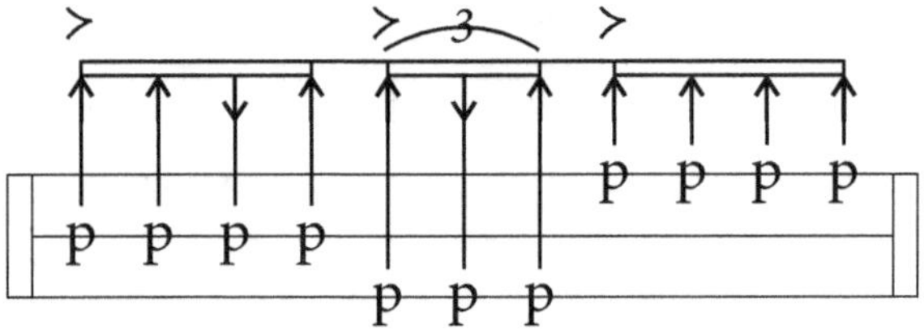

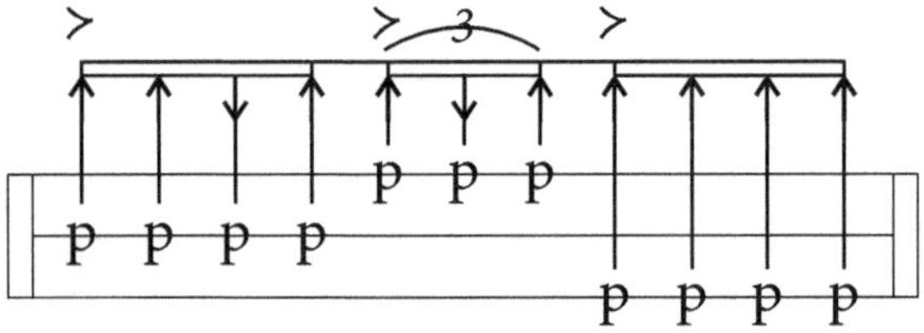

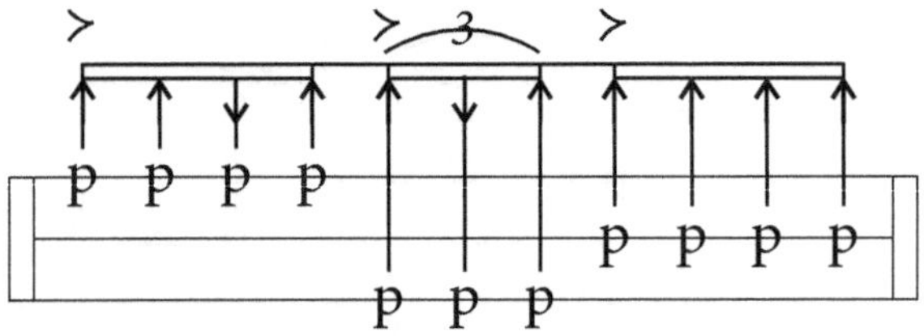

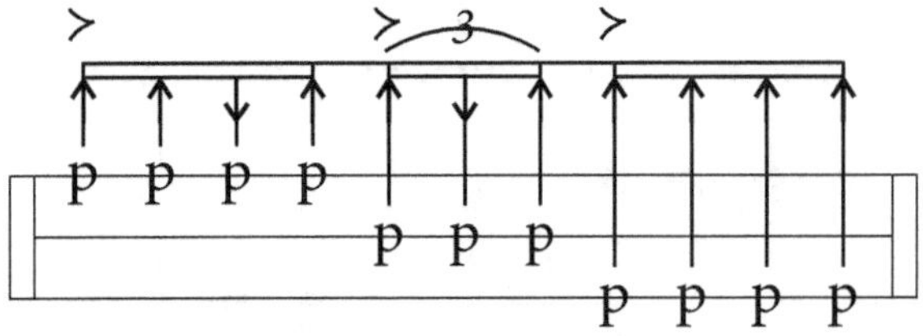

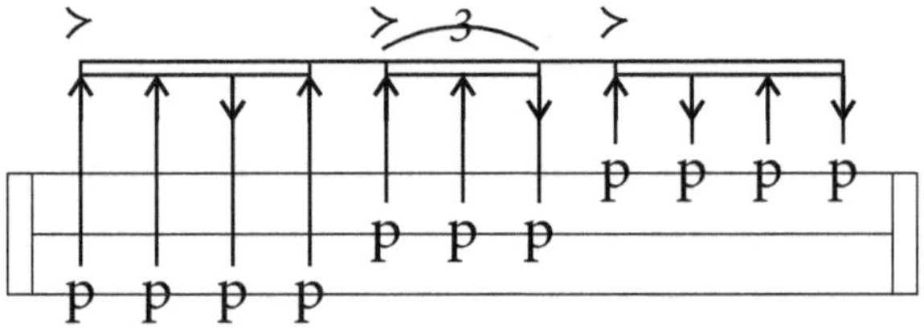

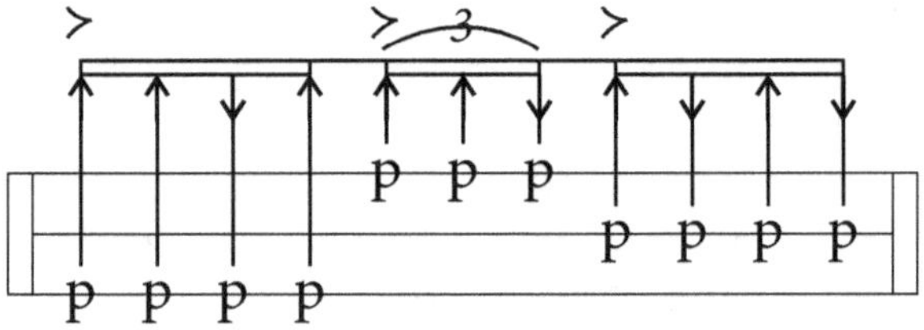

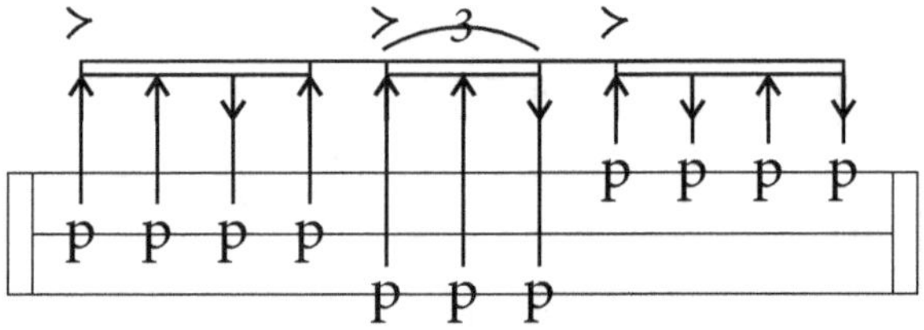

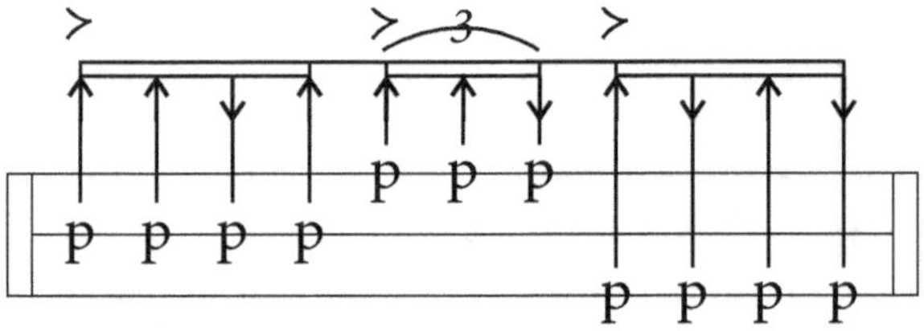

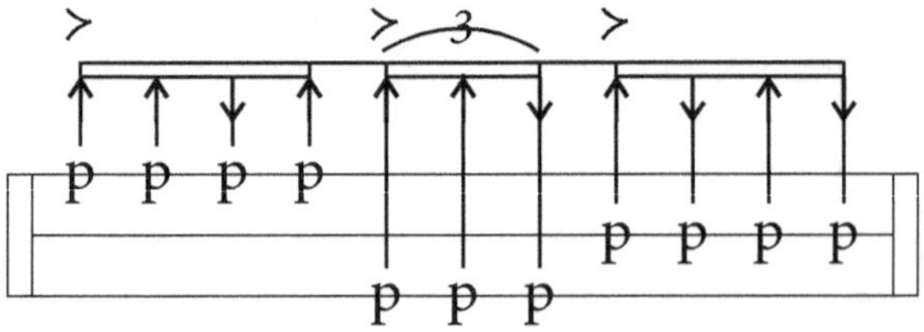

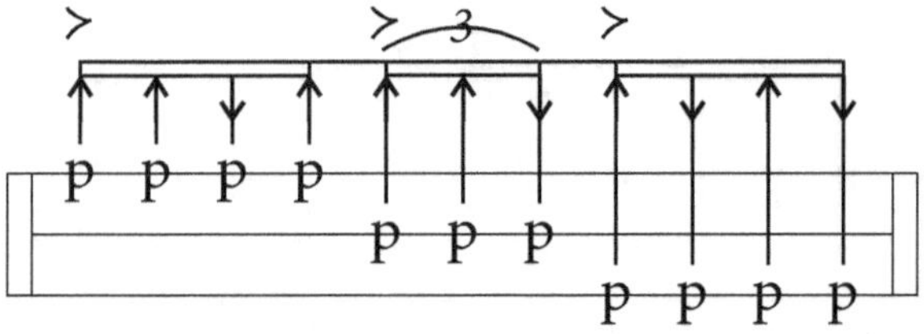

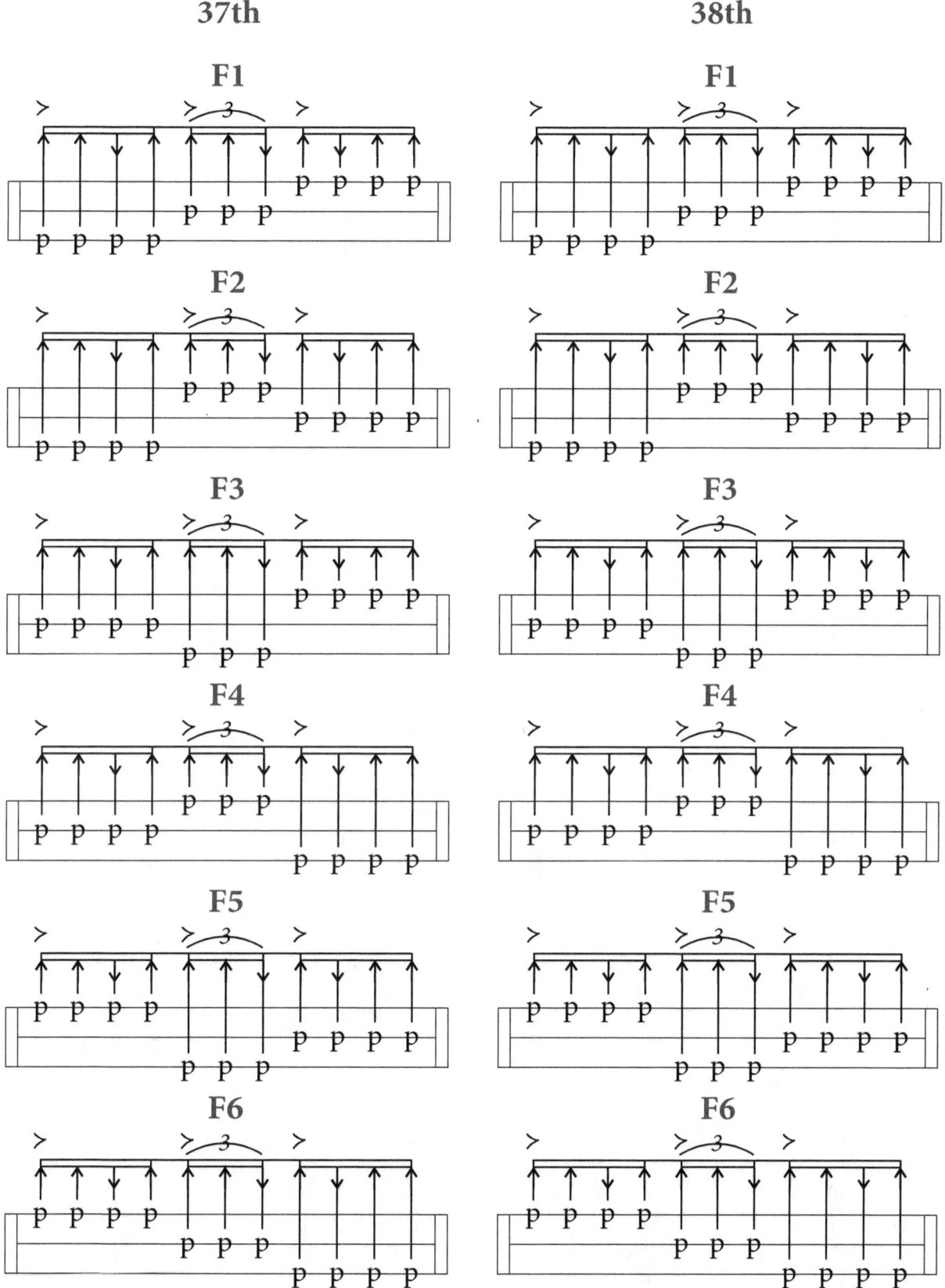

39th

F1
F2
F3
F4
F5
F6

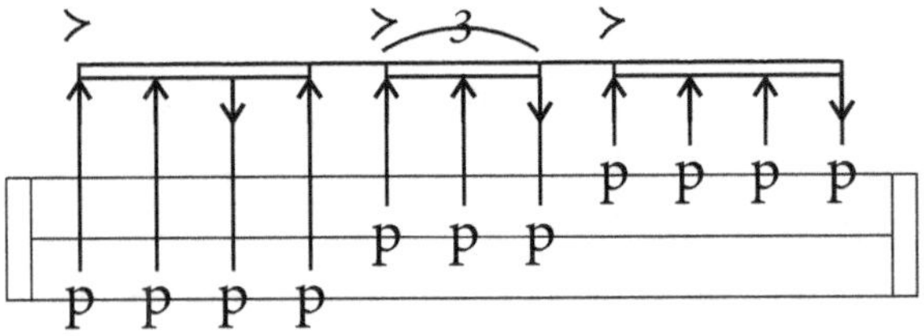

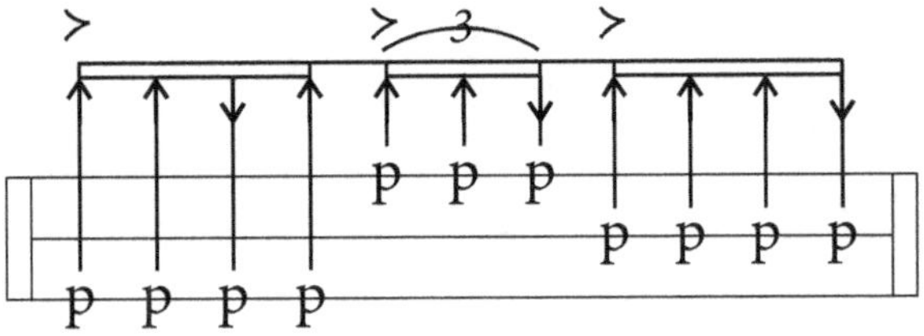

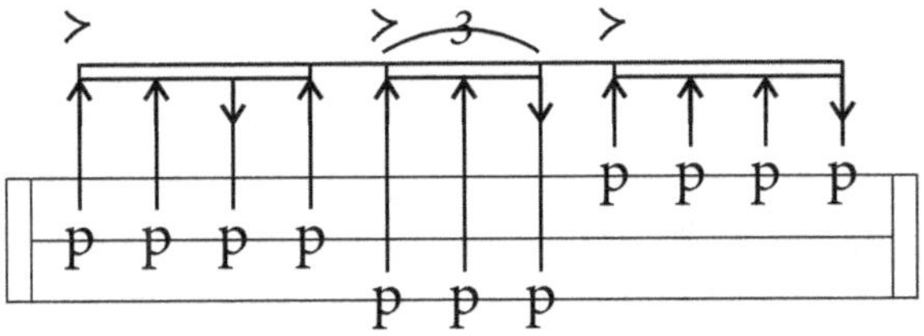

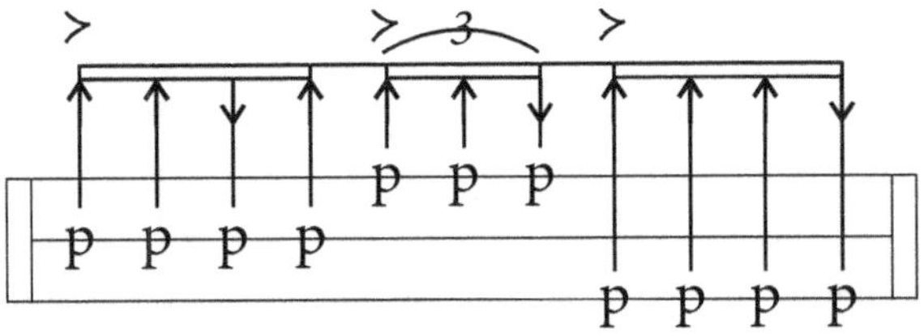

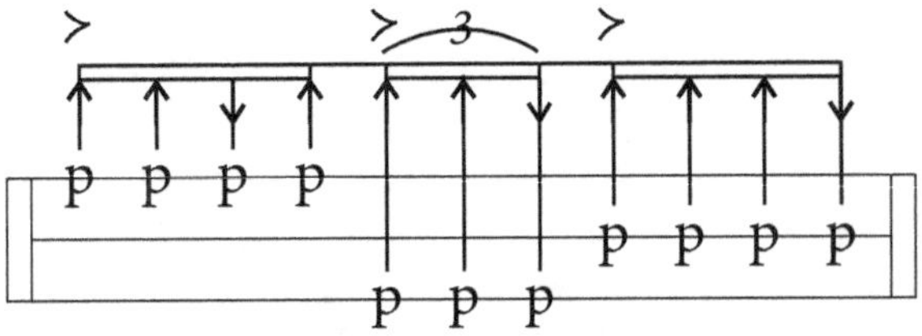

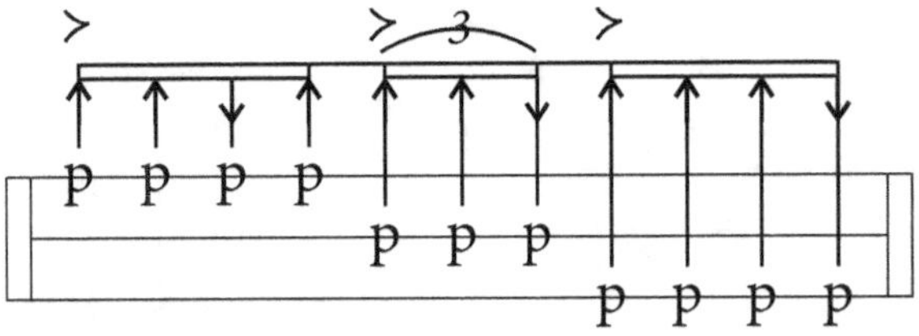

40th

F1
F2
F3
F4
F5
F6

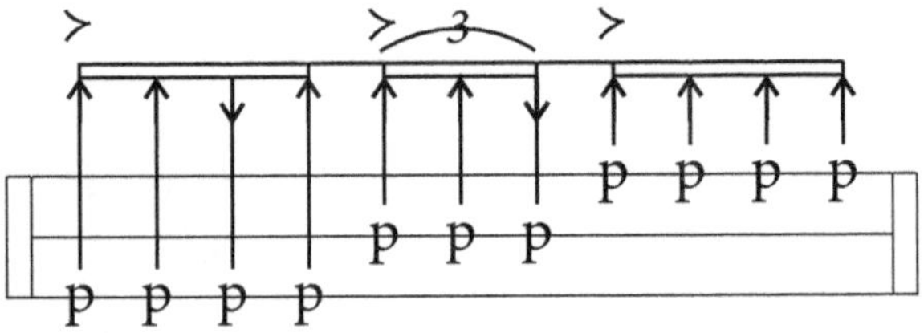

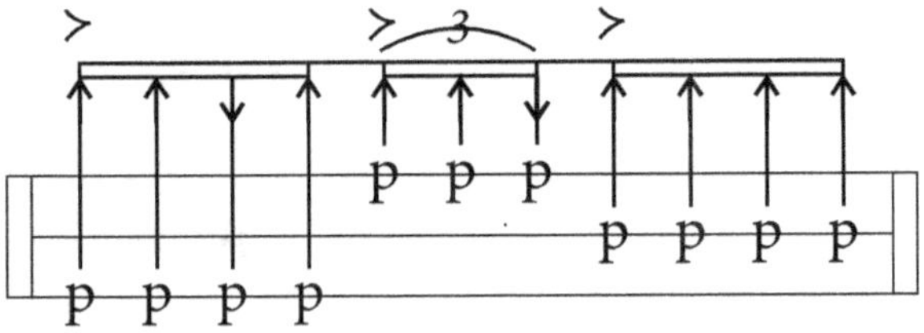

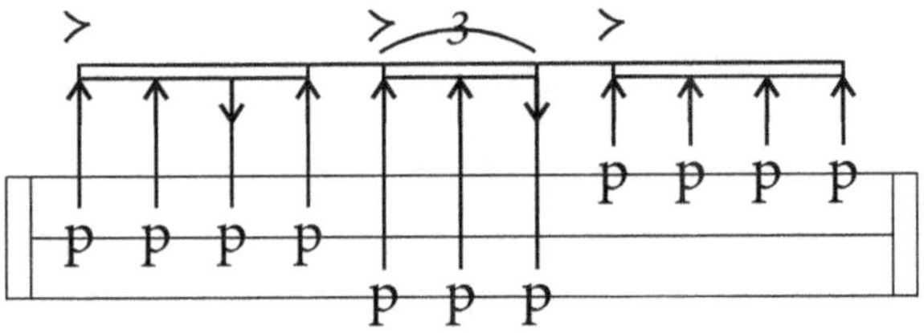

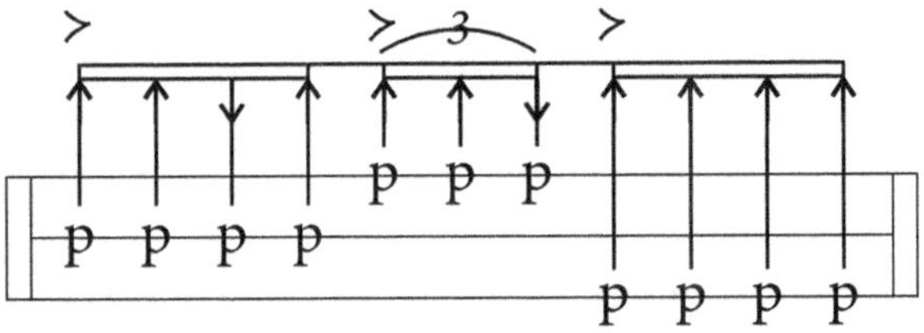

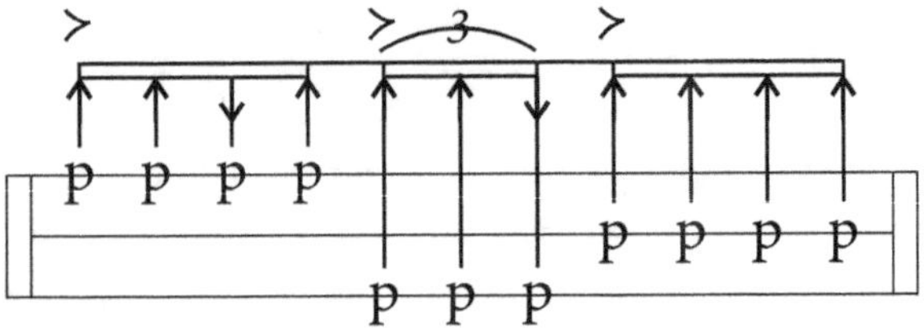

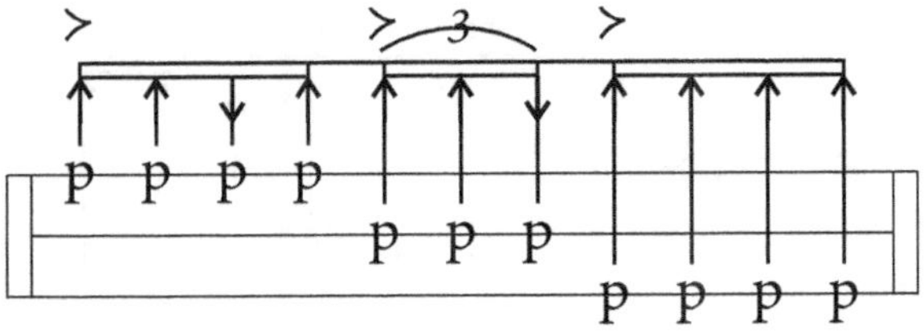

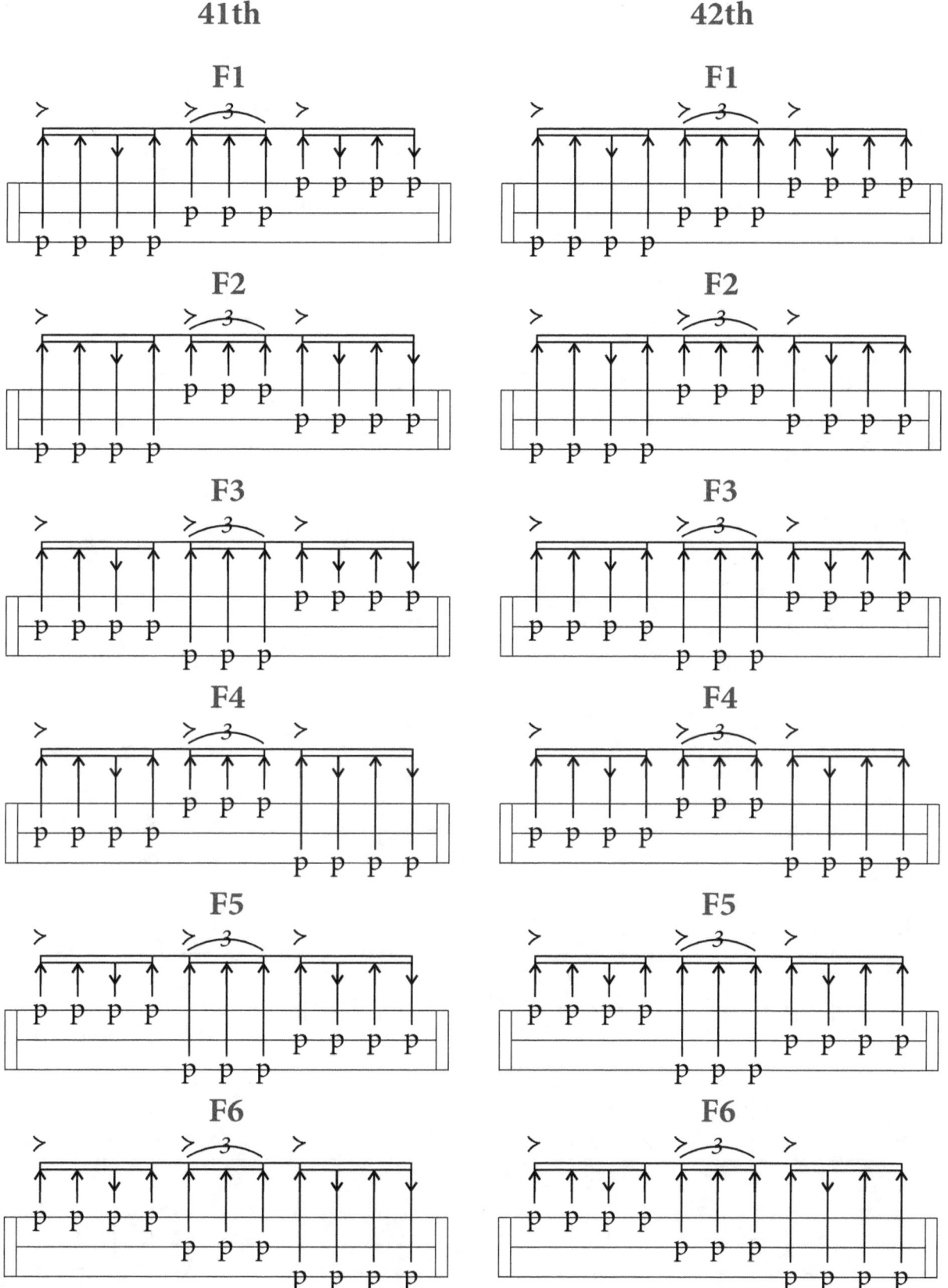

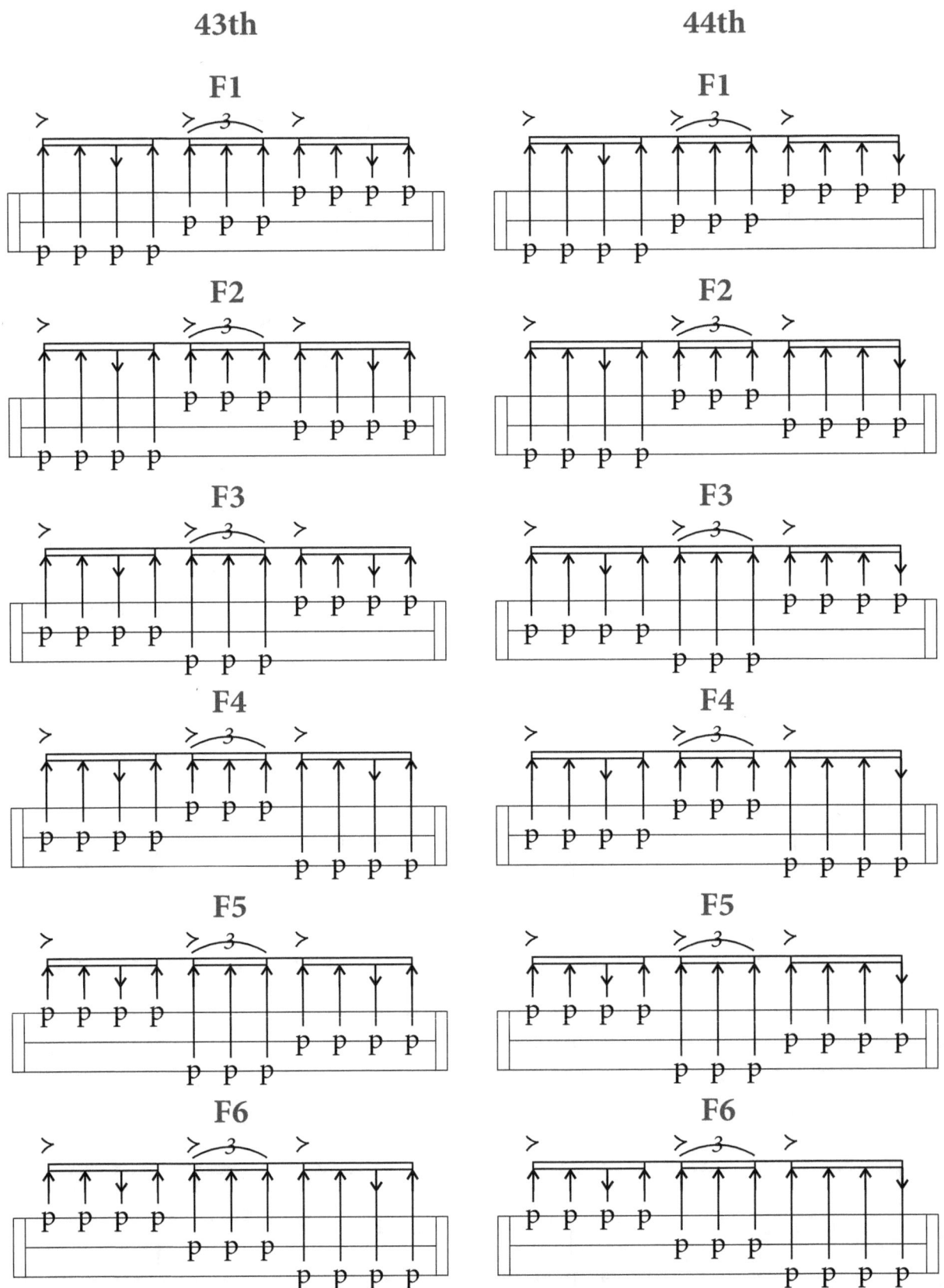

45th

F1

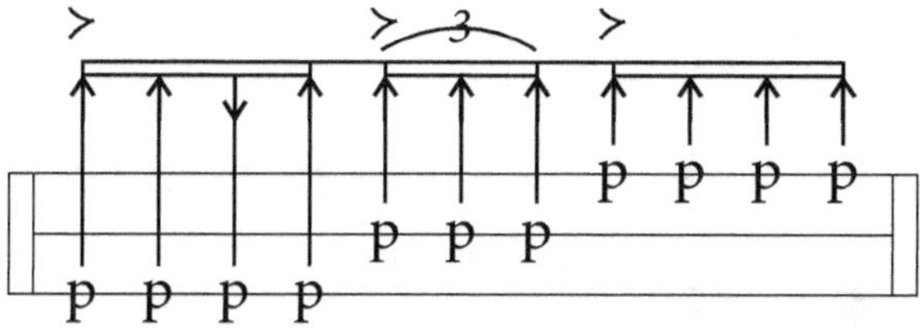

F2

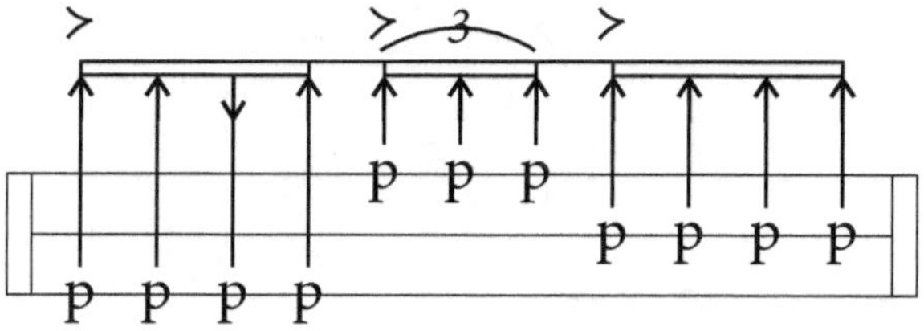

F3

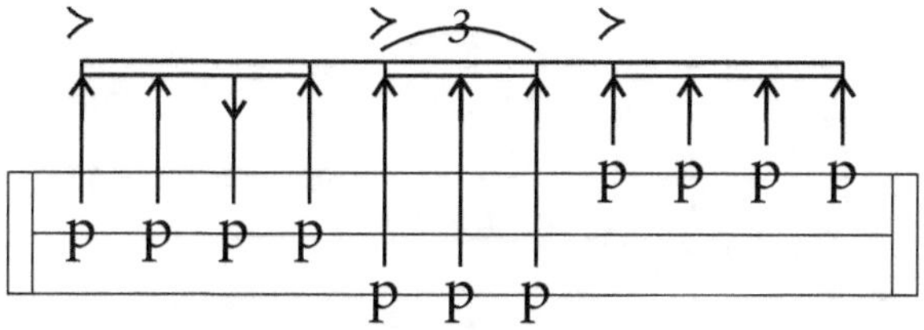

F4

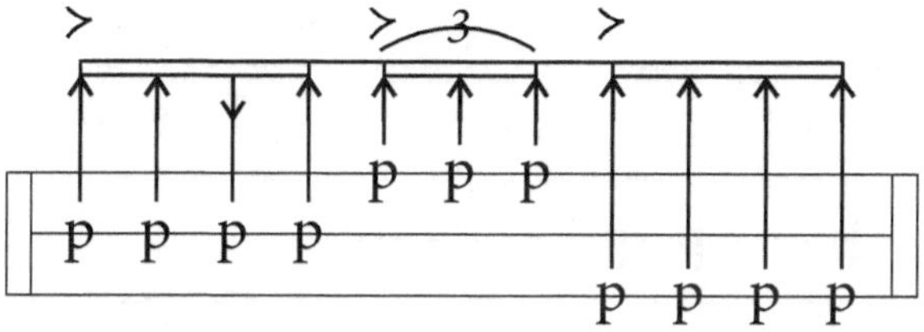

F5

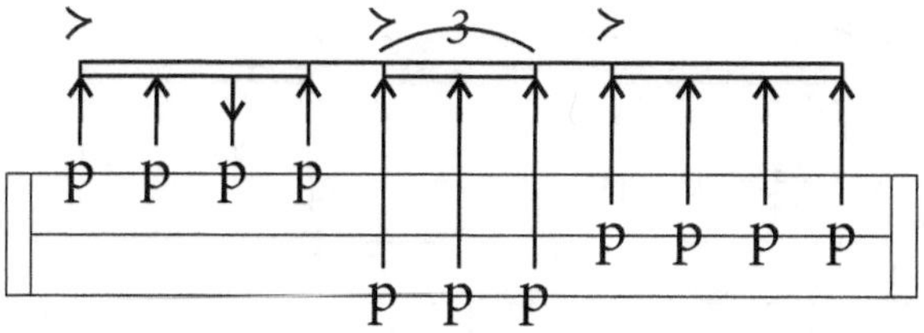

F6

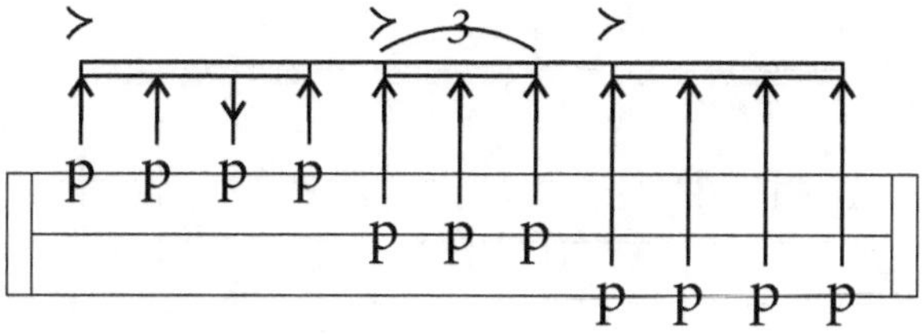

46th

F1

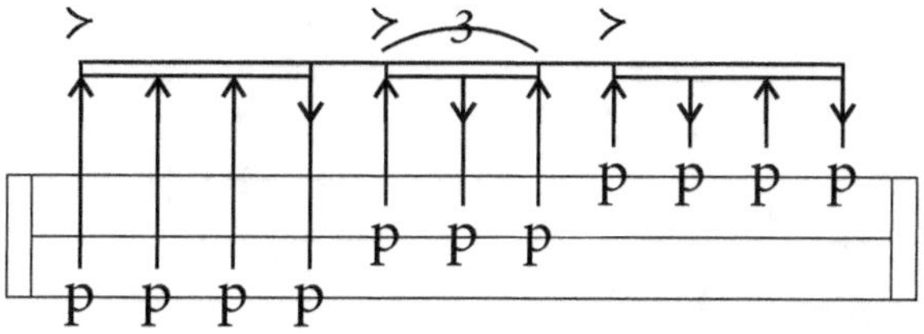

F2

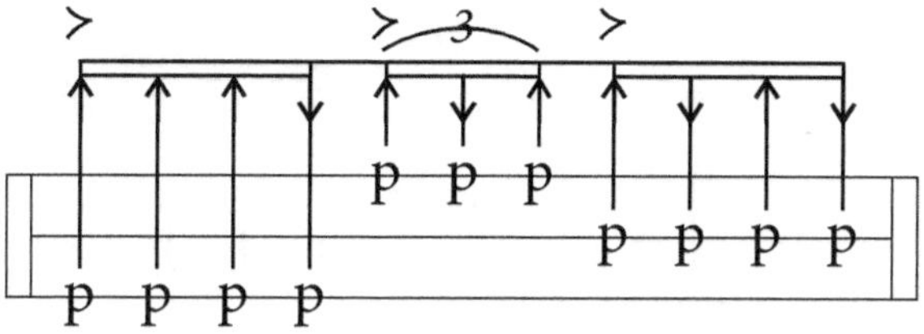

F3

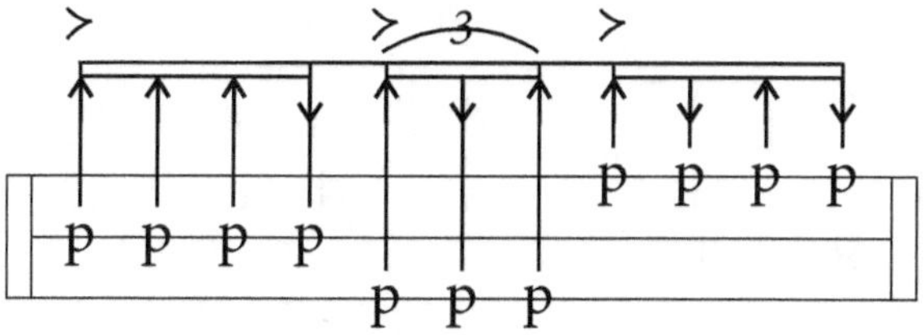

F4

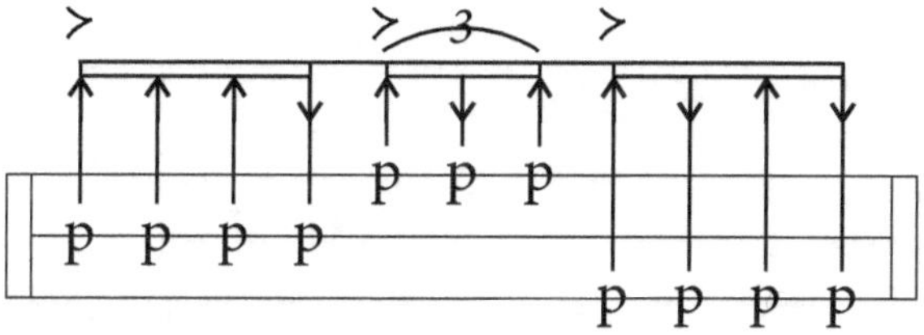

F5

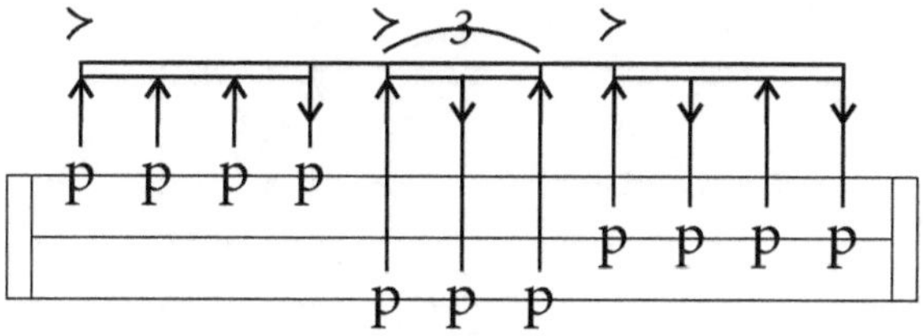

F6

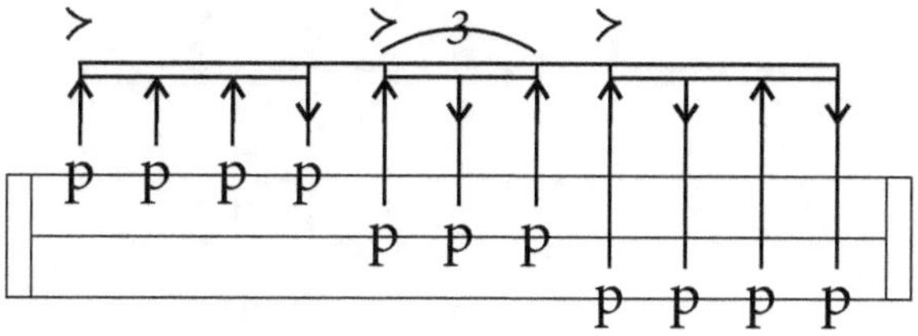

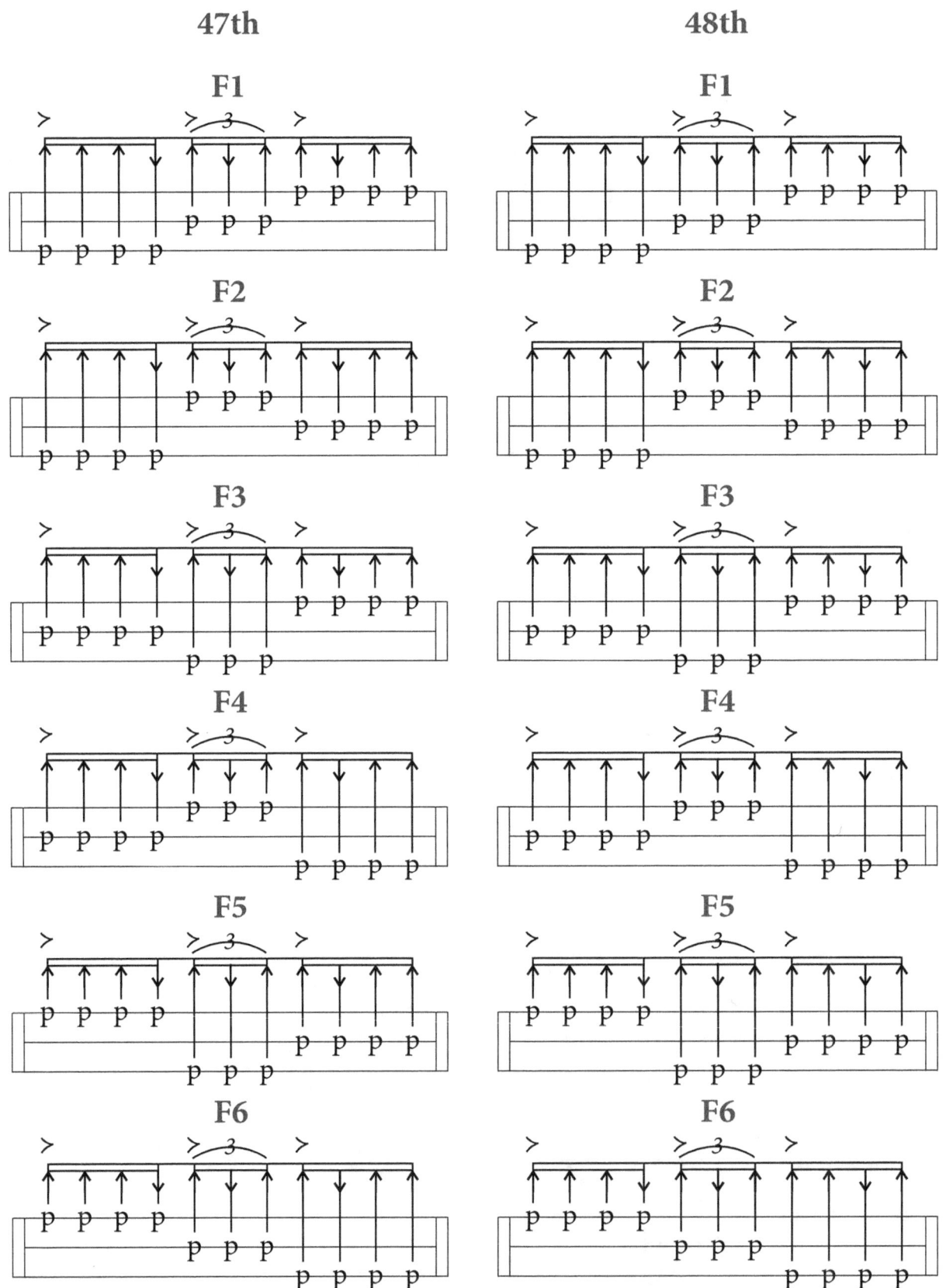

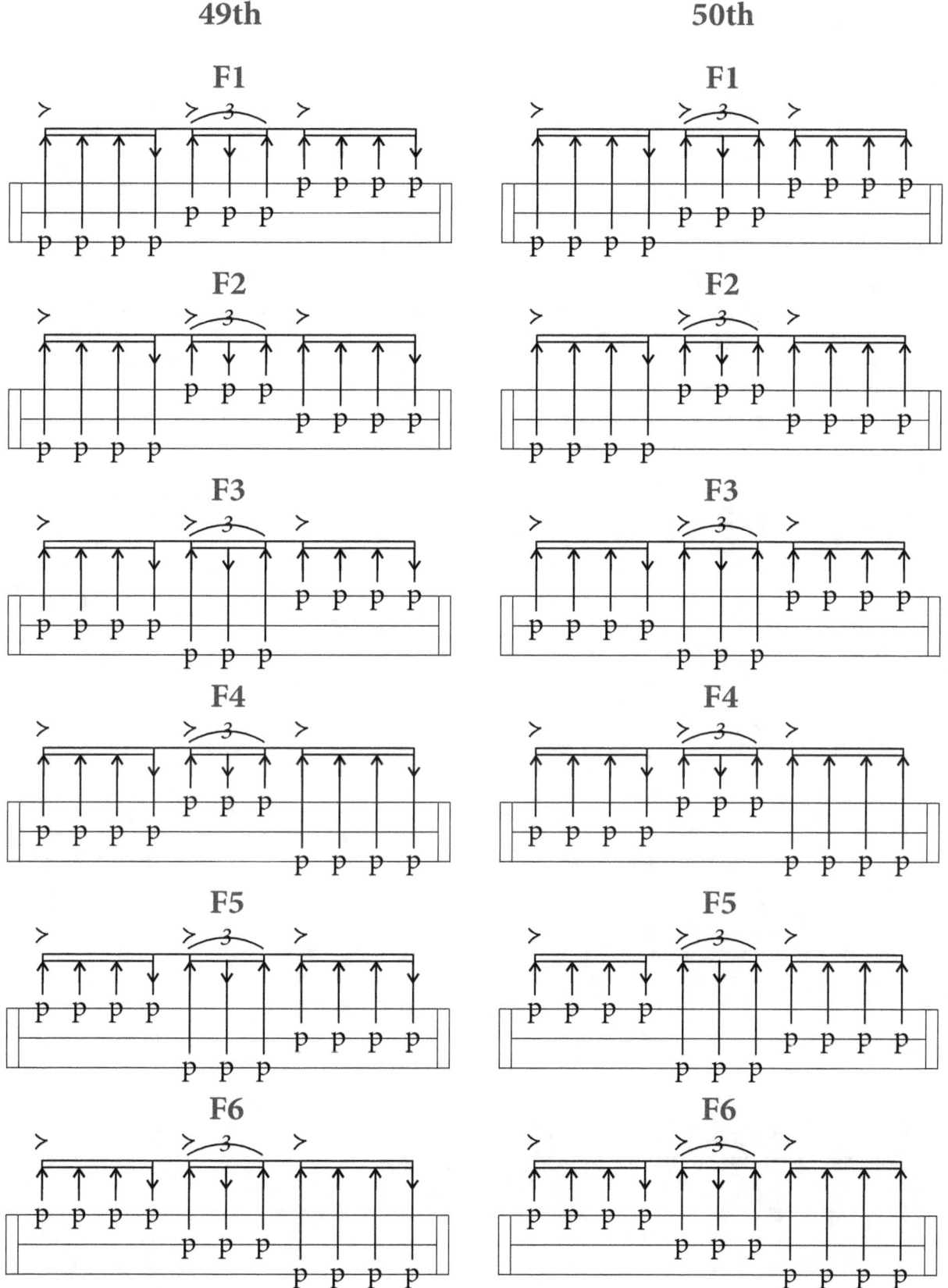

51th

F1
F2
F3
F4
F5
F6

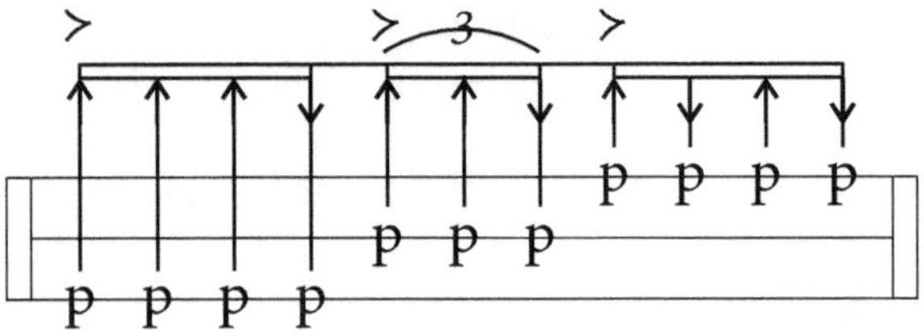

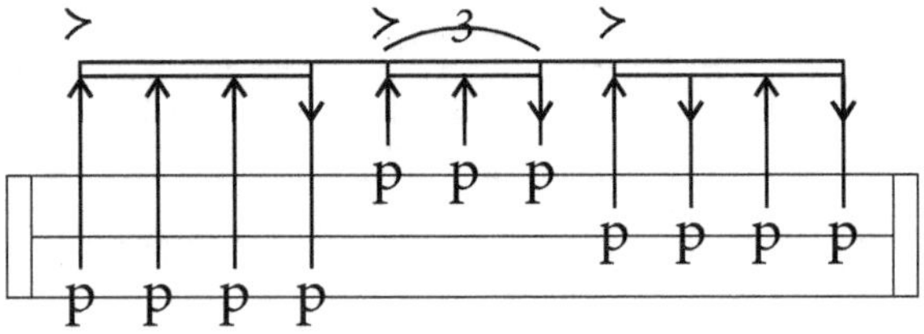

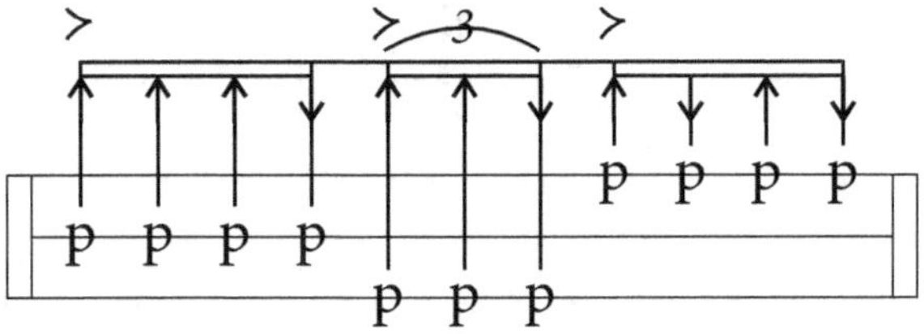

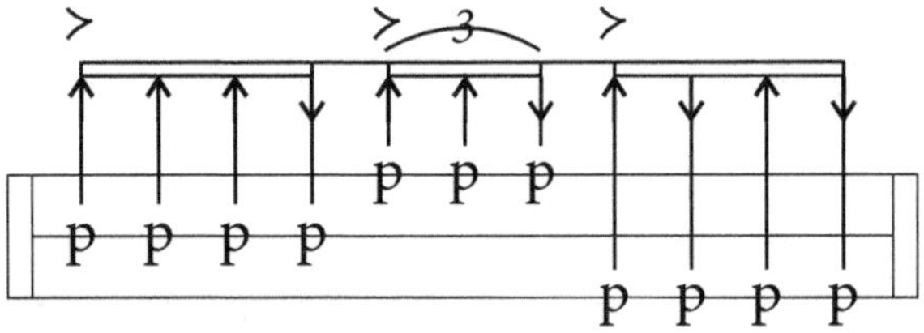

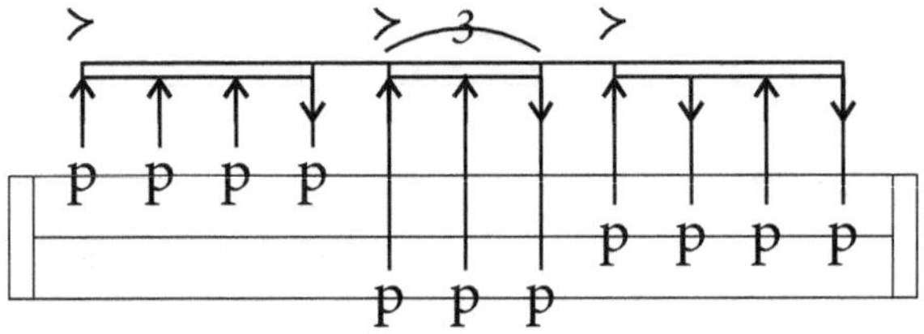

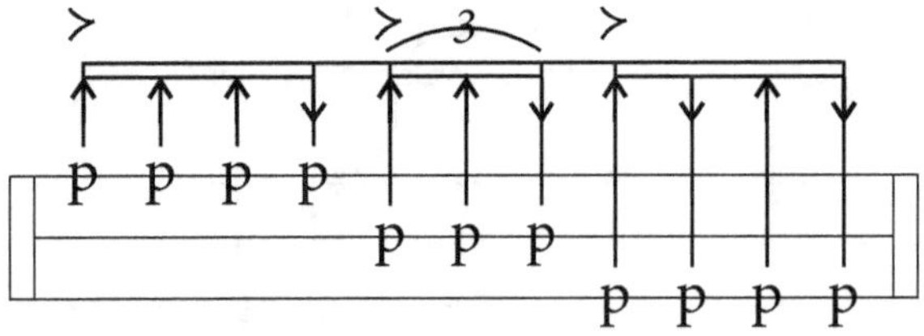

52th

F1
F2
F3
F4
F5
F6

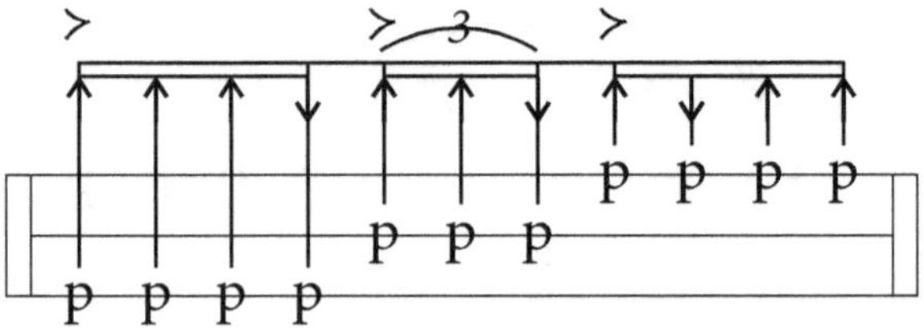

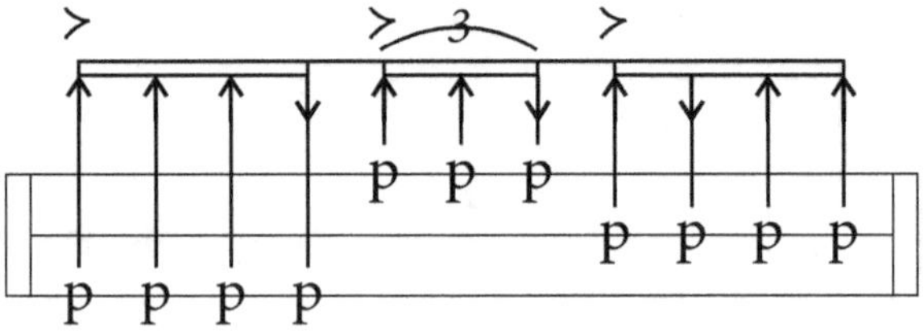

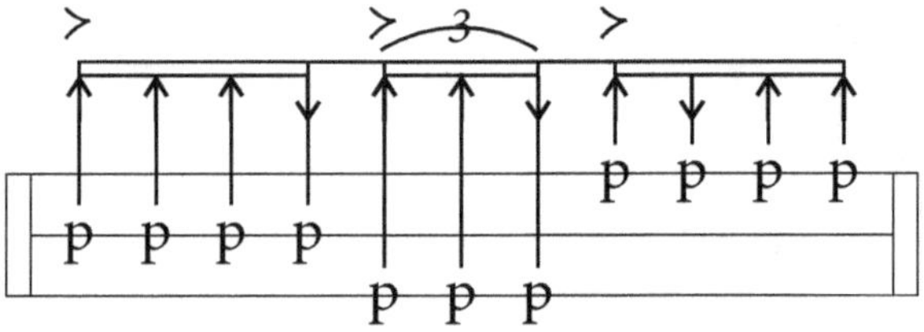

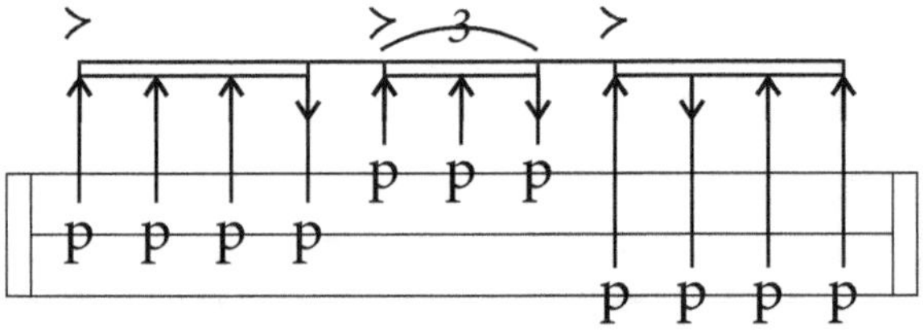

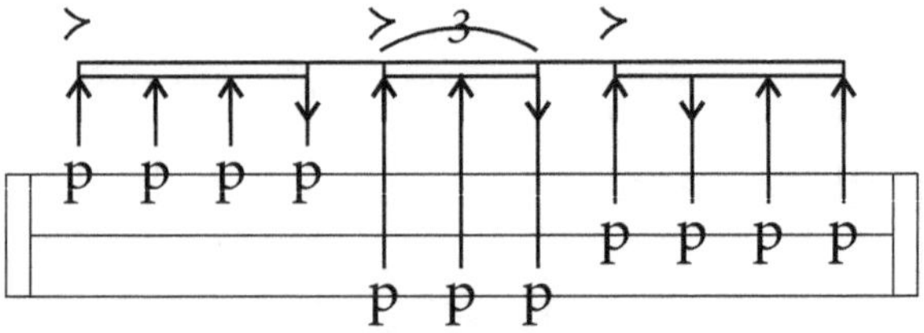

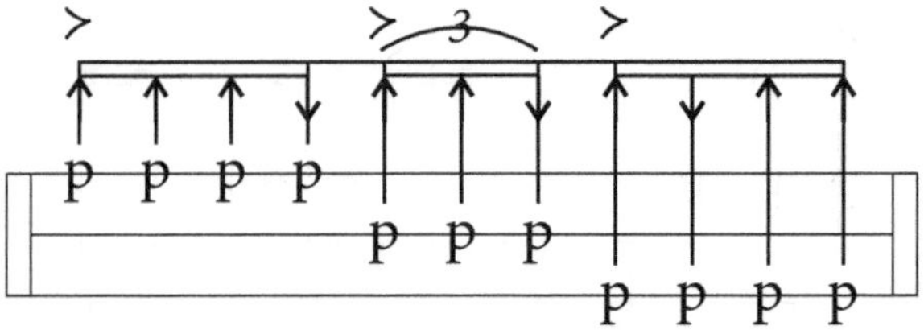

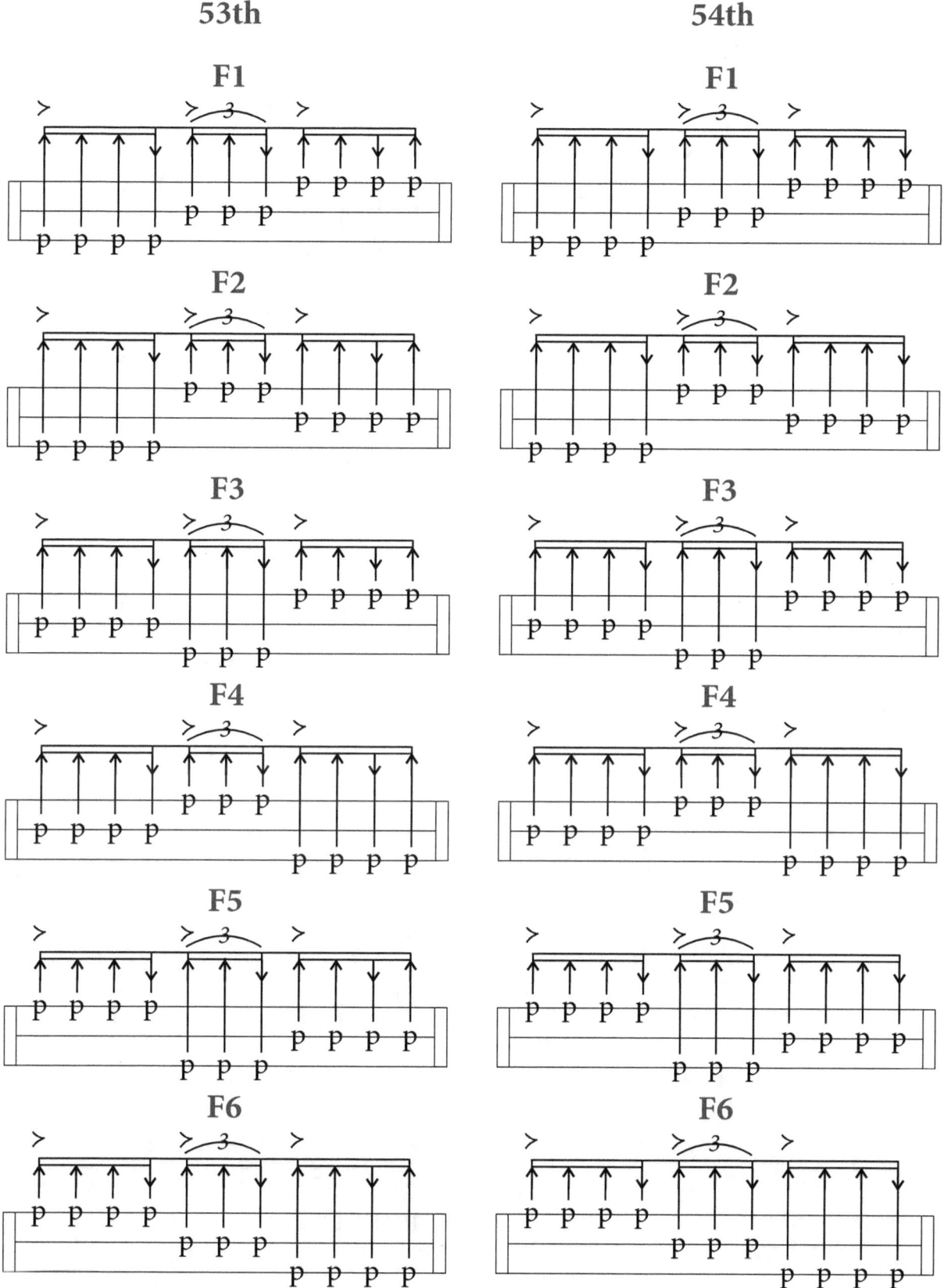

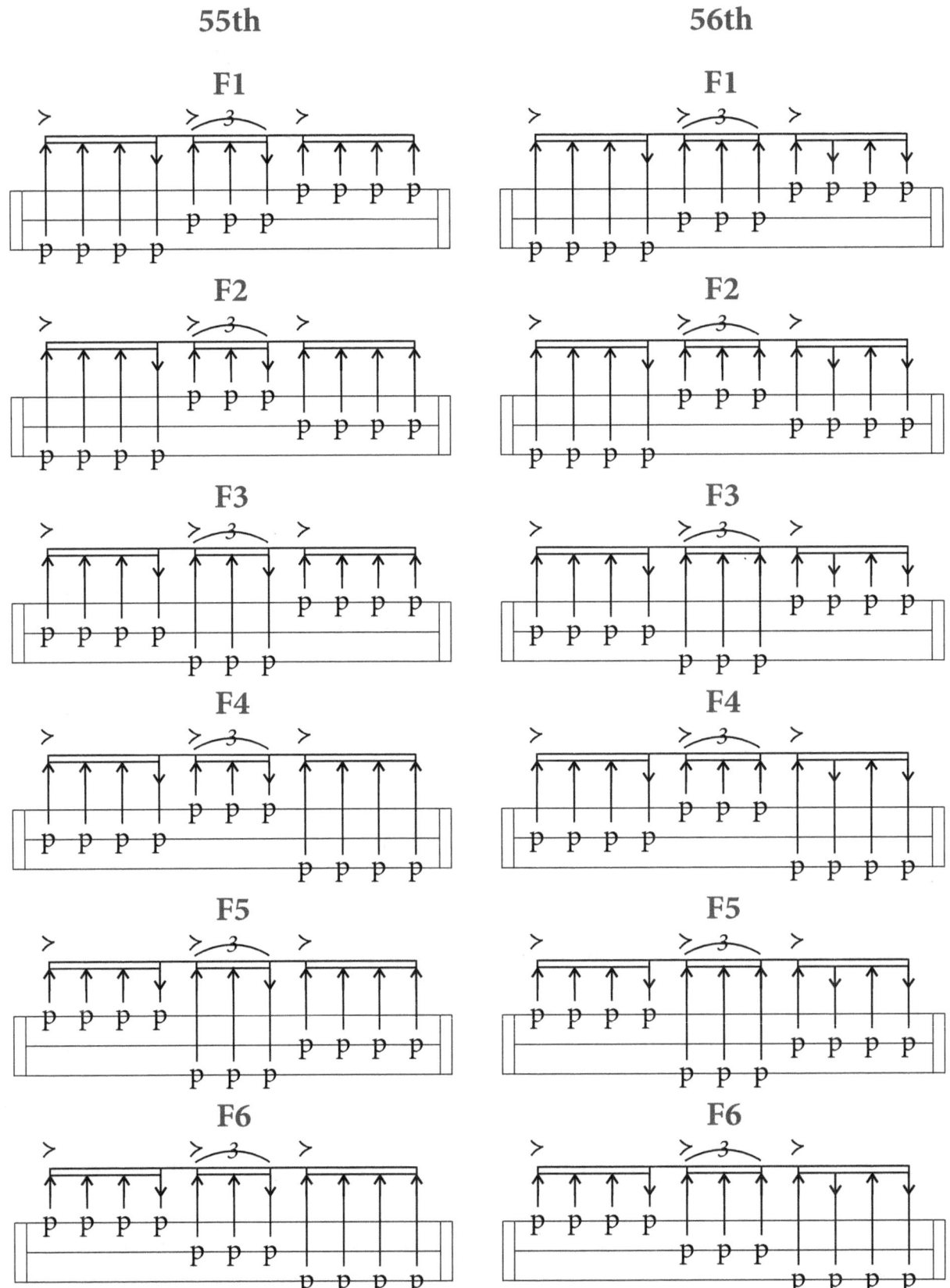

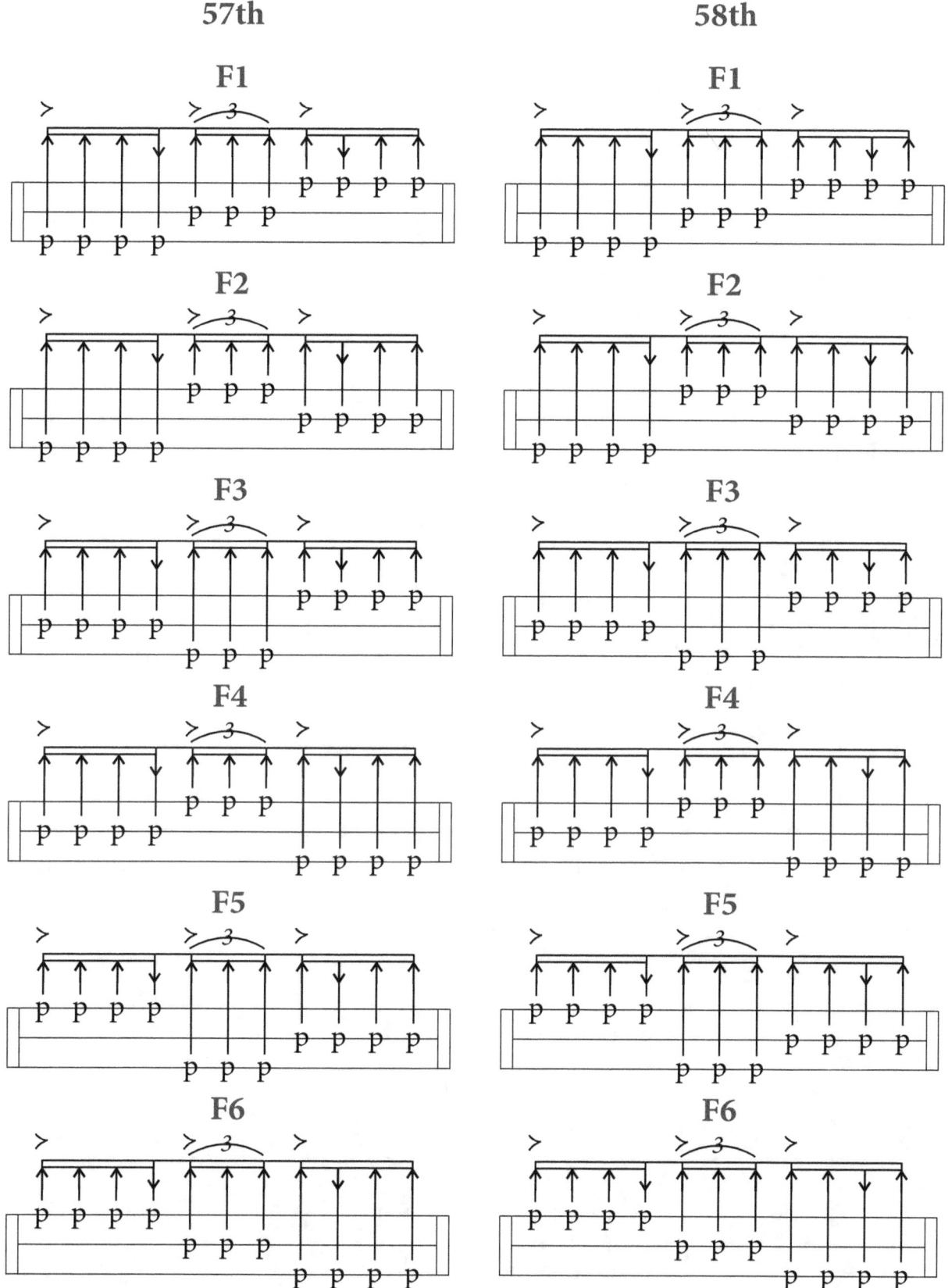

59th

F1

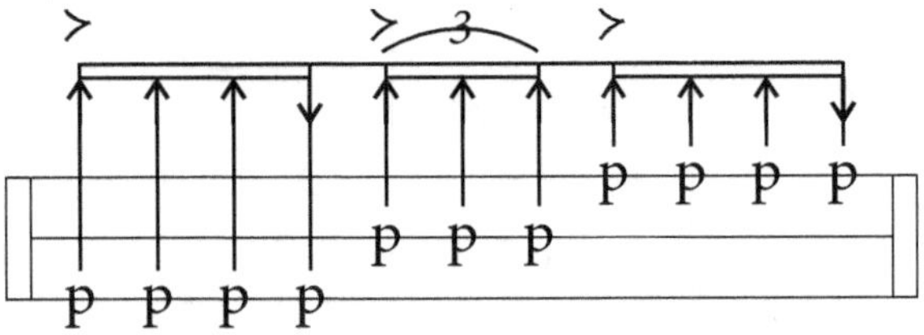

F2

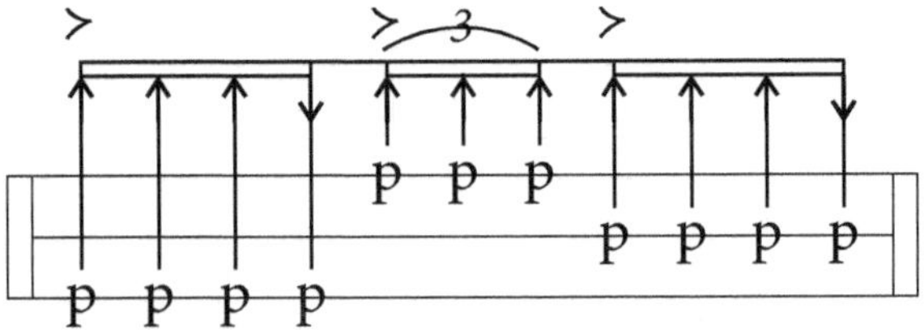

F3

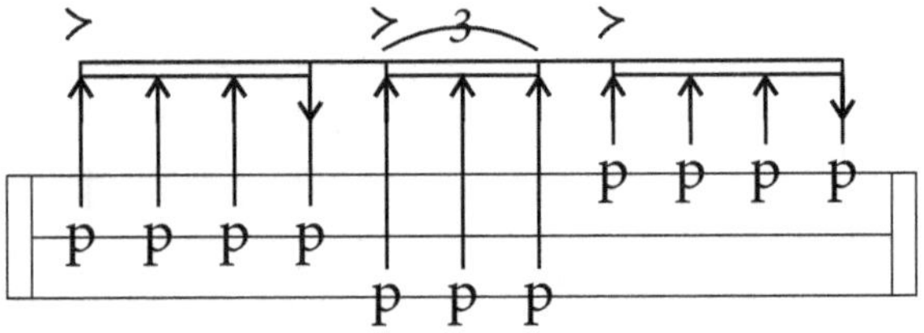

F4

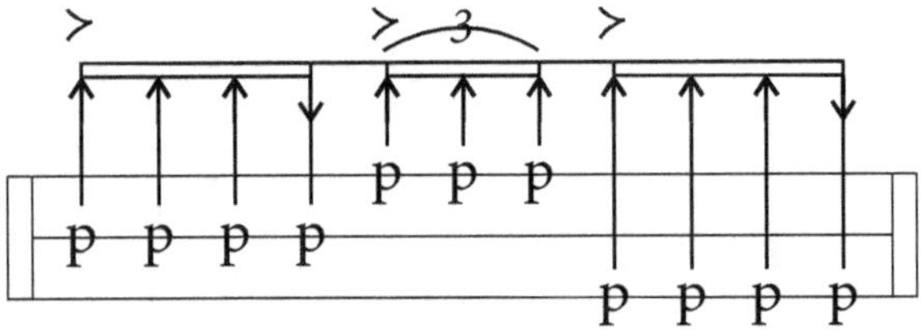

F5

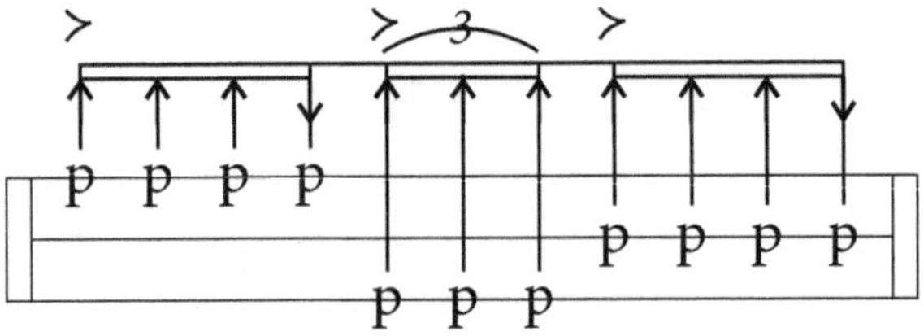

F6

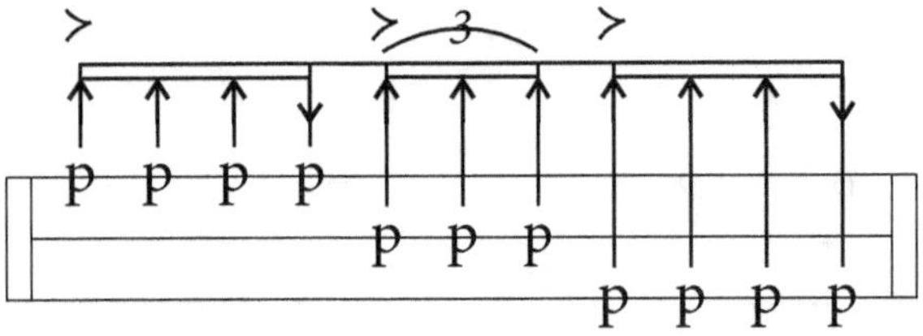

60th

F1

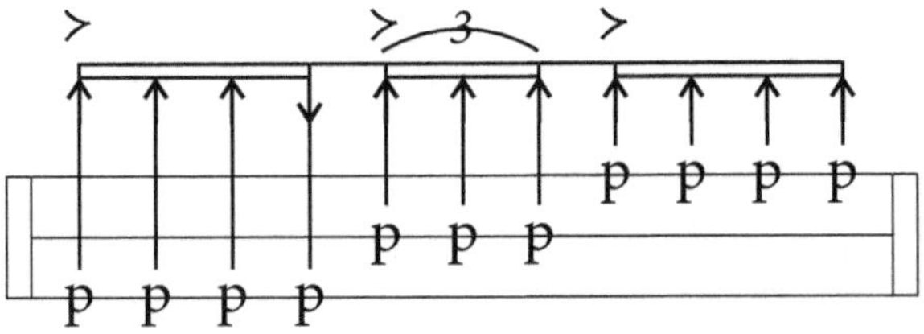

F2

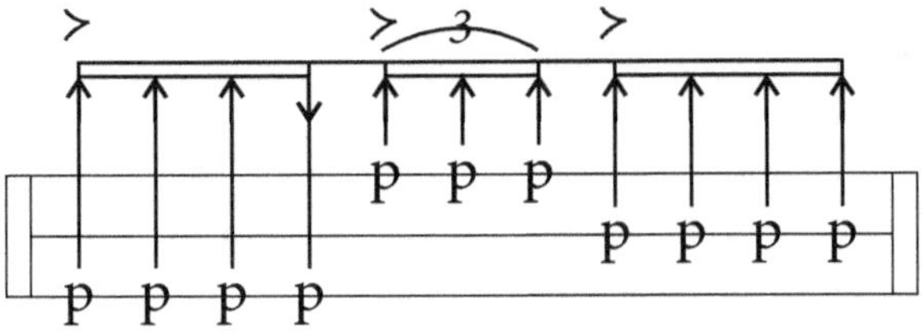

F3

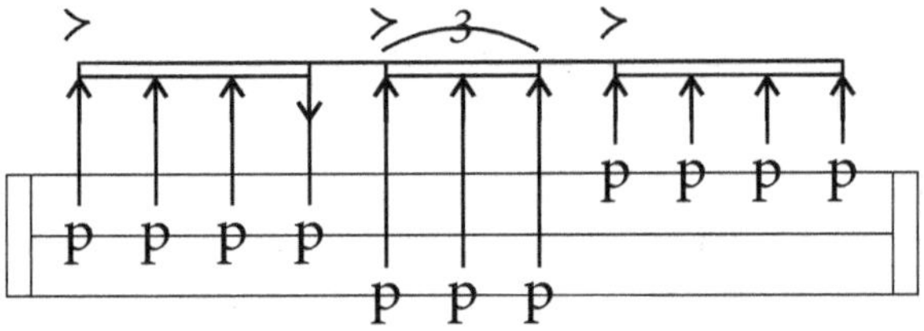

F4

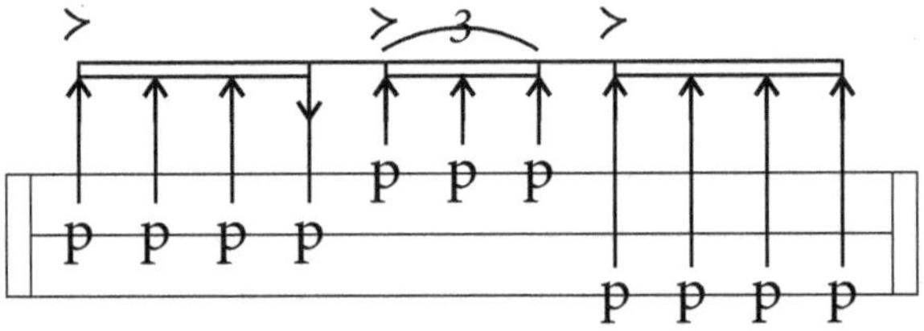

F5

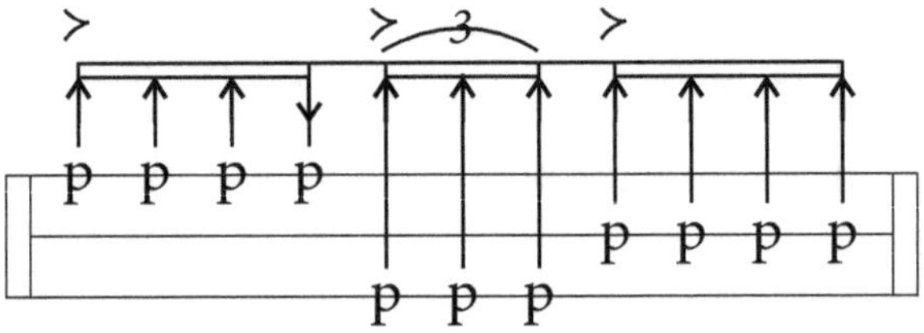

F6

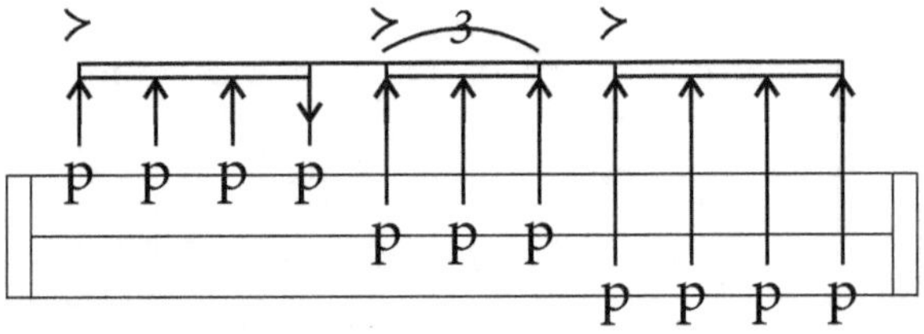

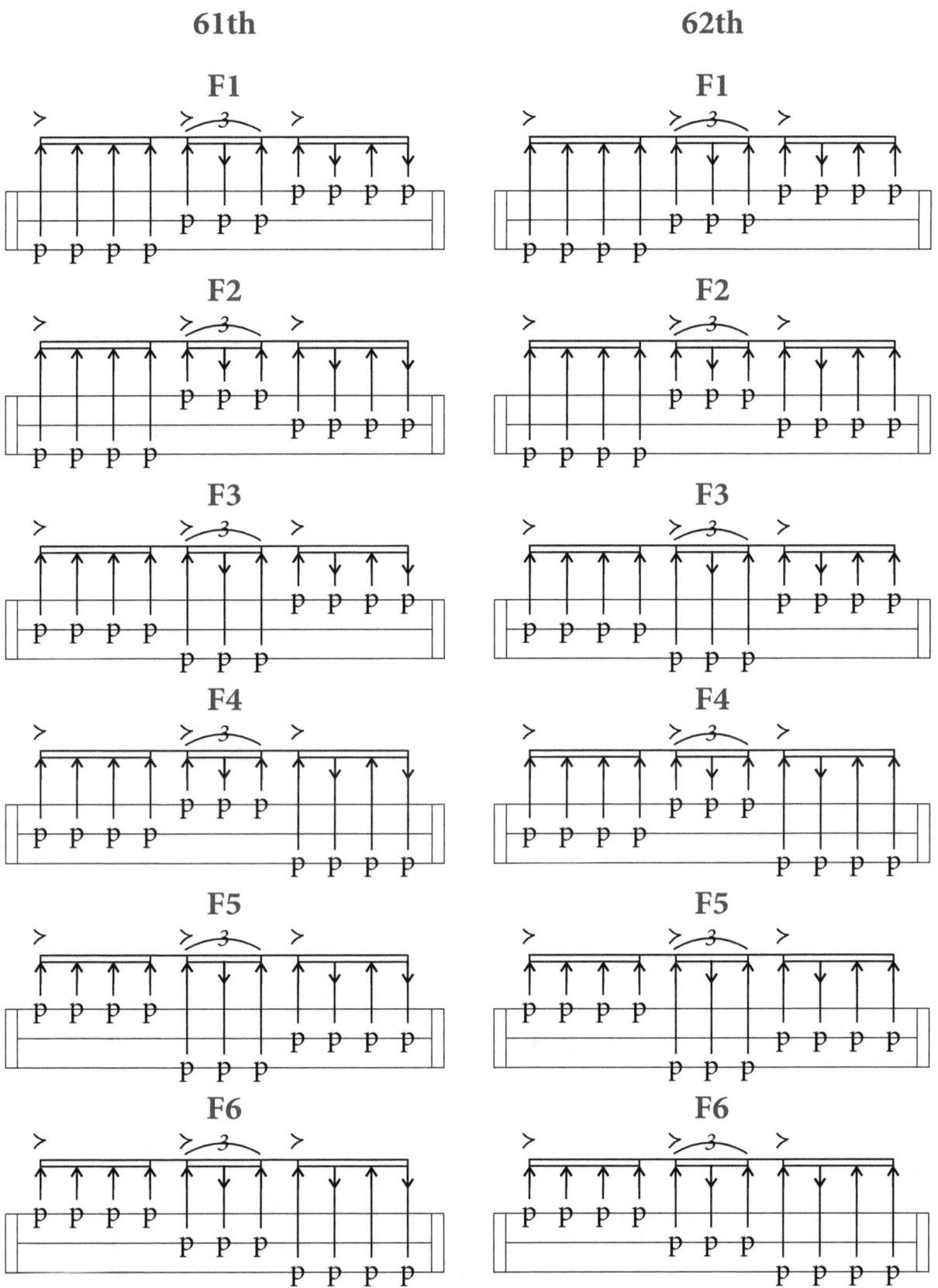

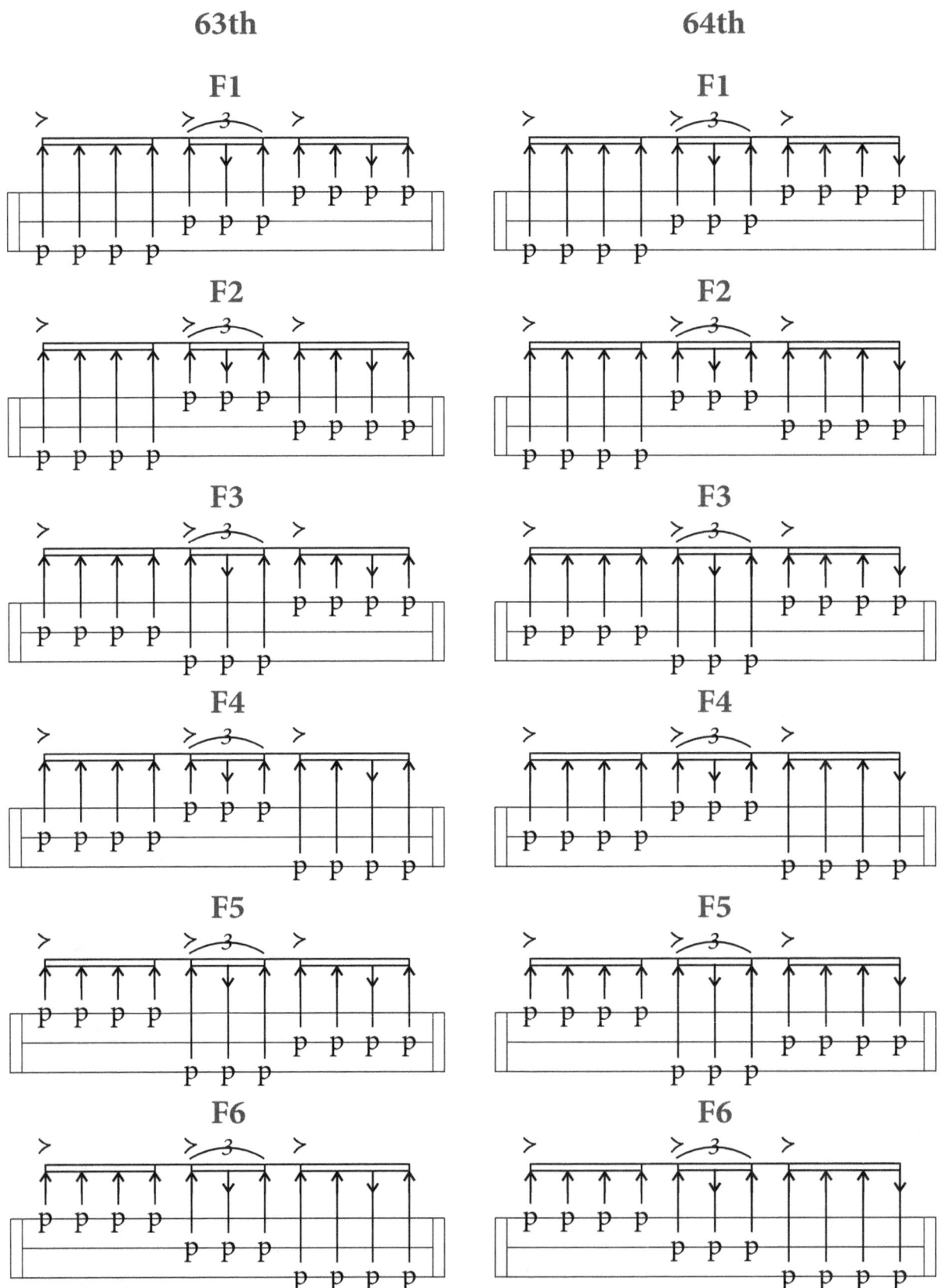

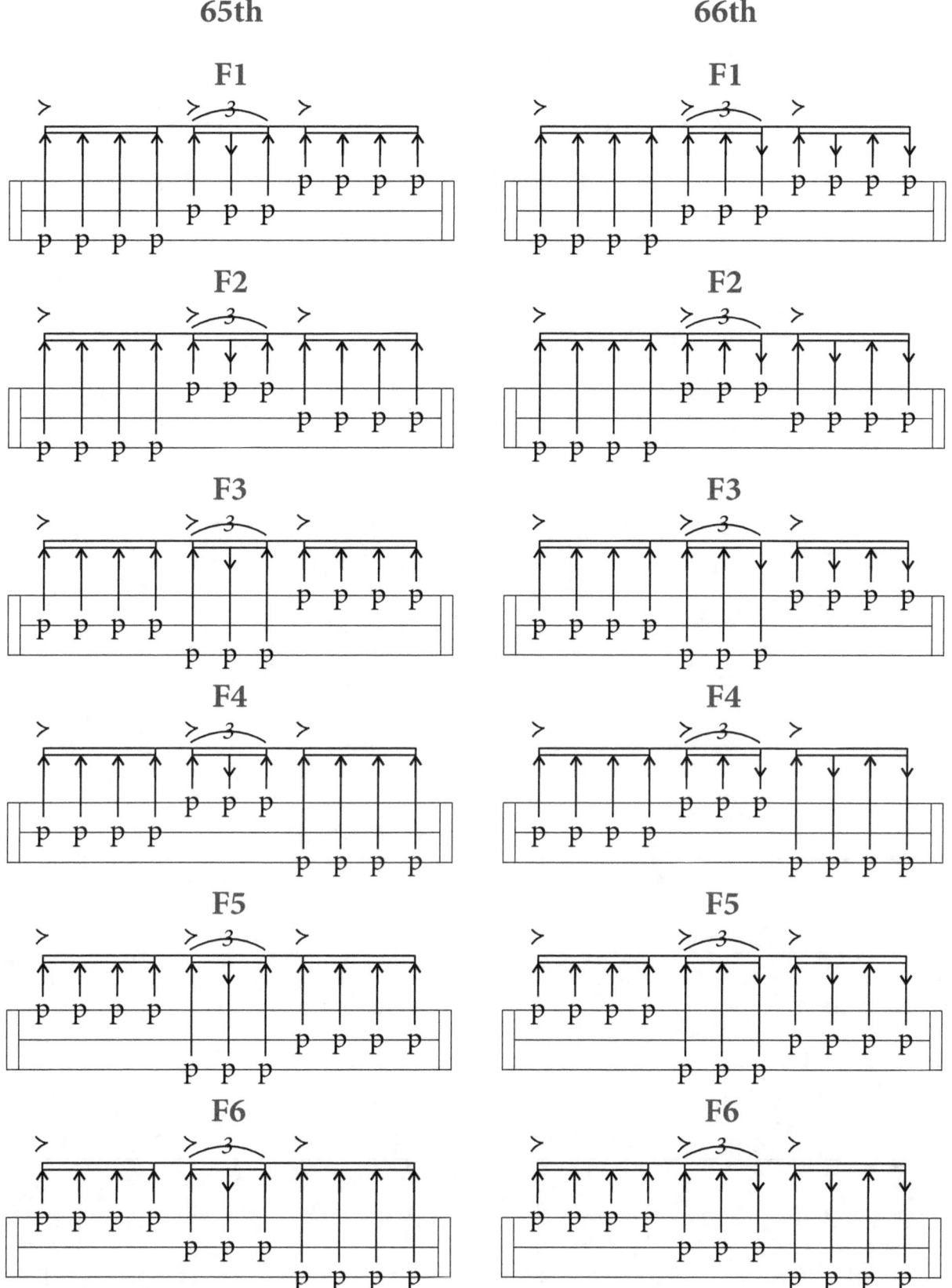

67th

F1
F2
F3
F4
F5
F6

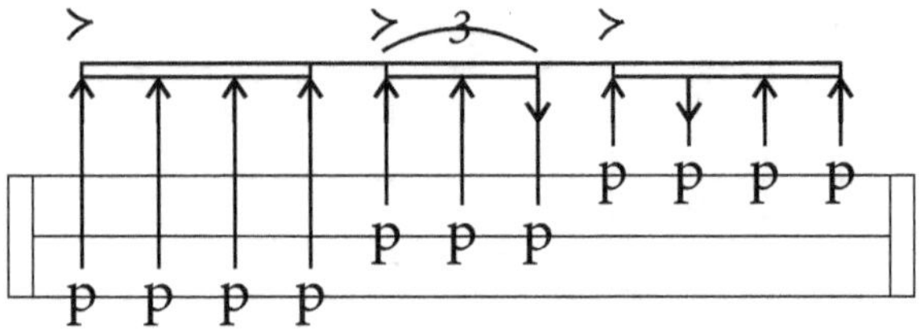

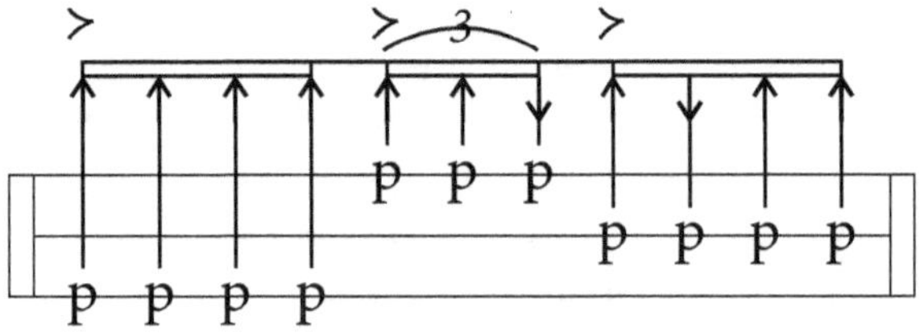

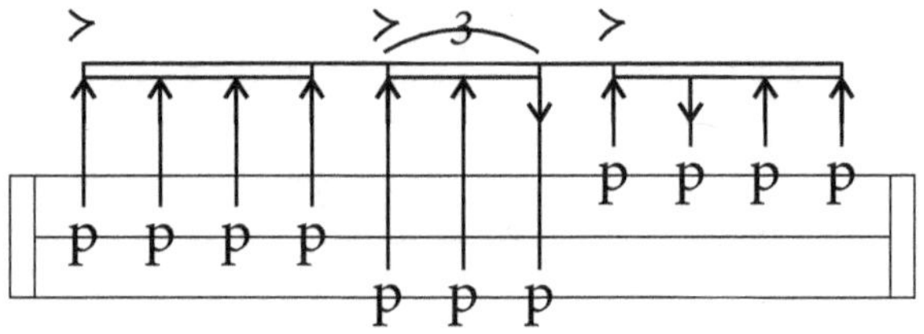

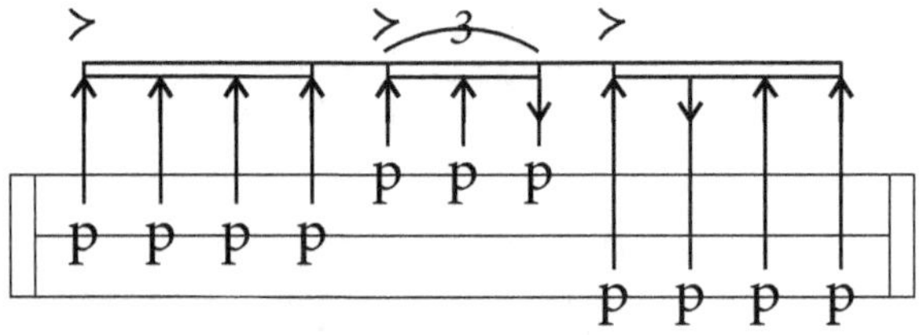

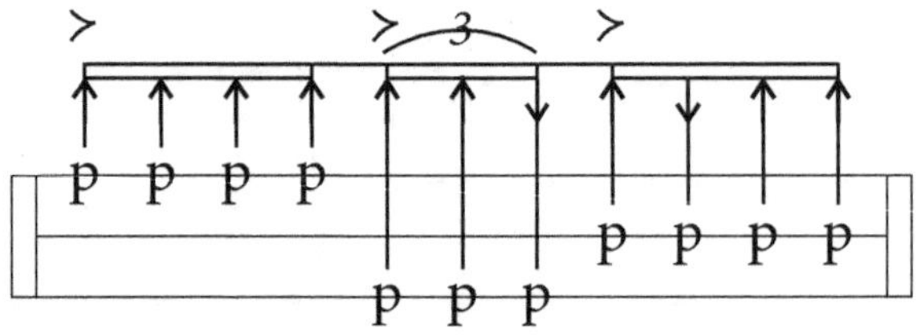

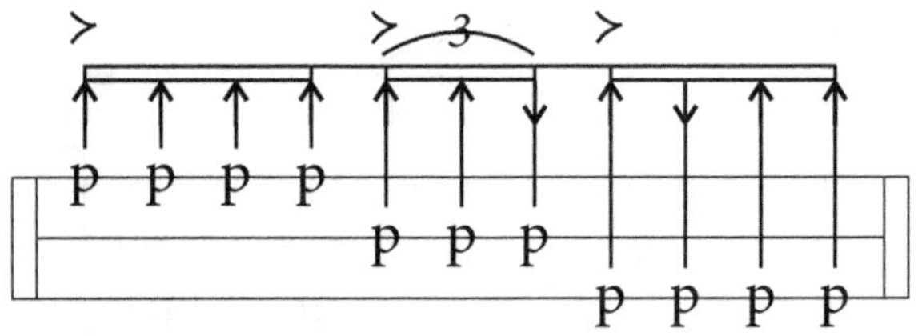

68th

F1
F2
F3
F4
F5
F6

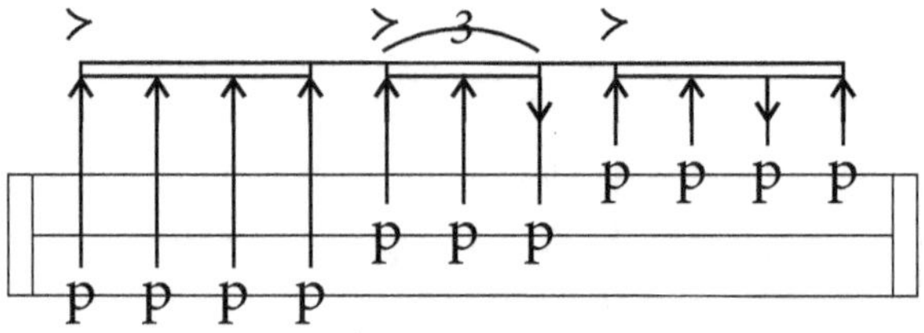

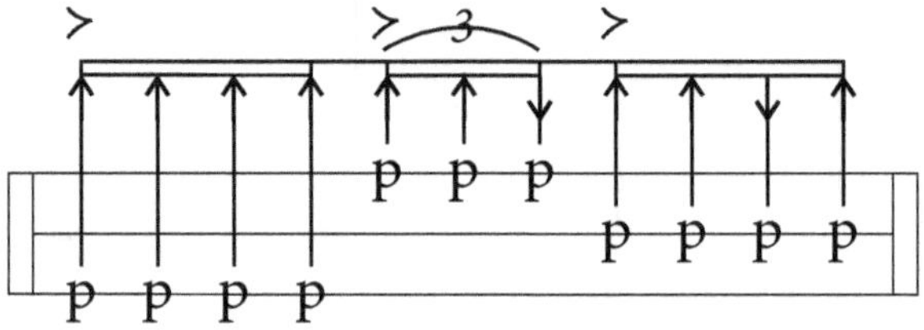

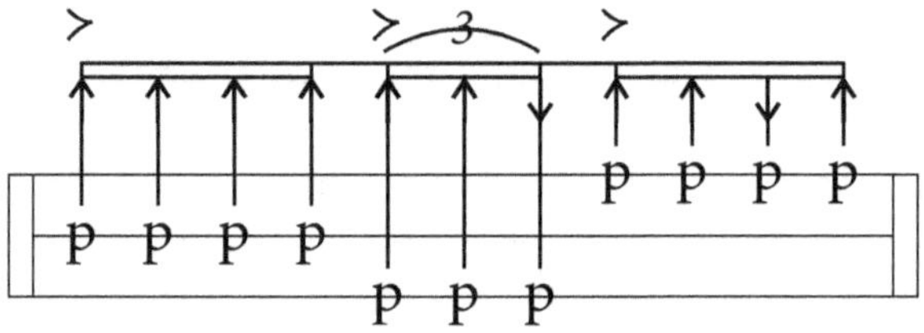

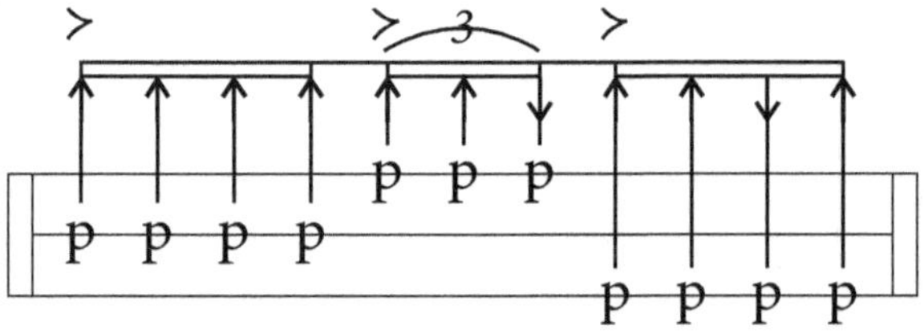

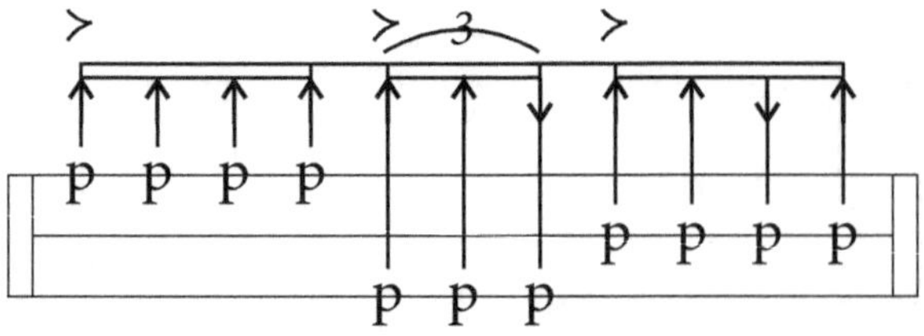

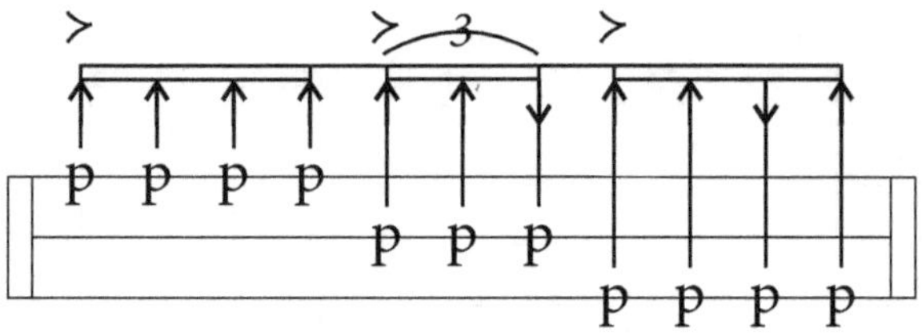

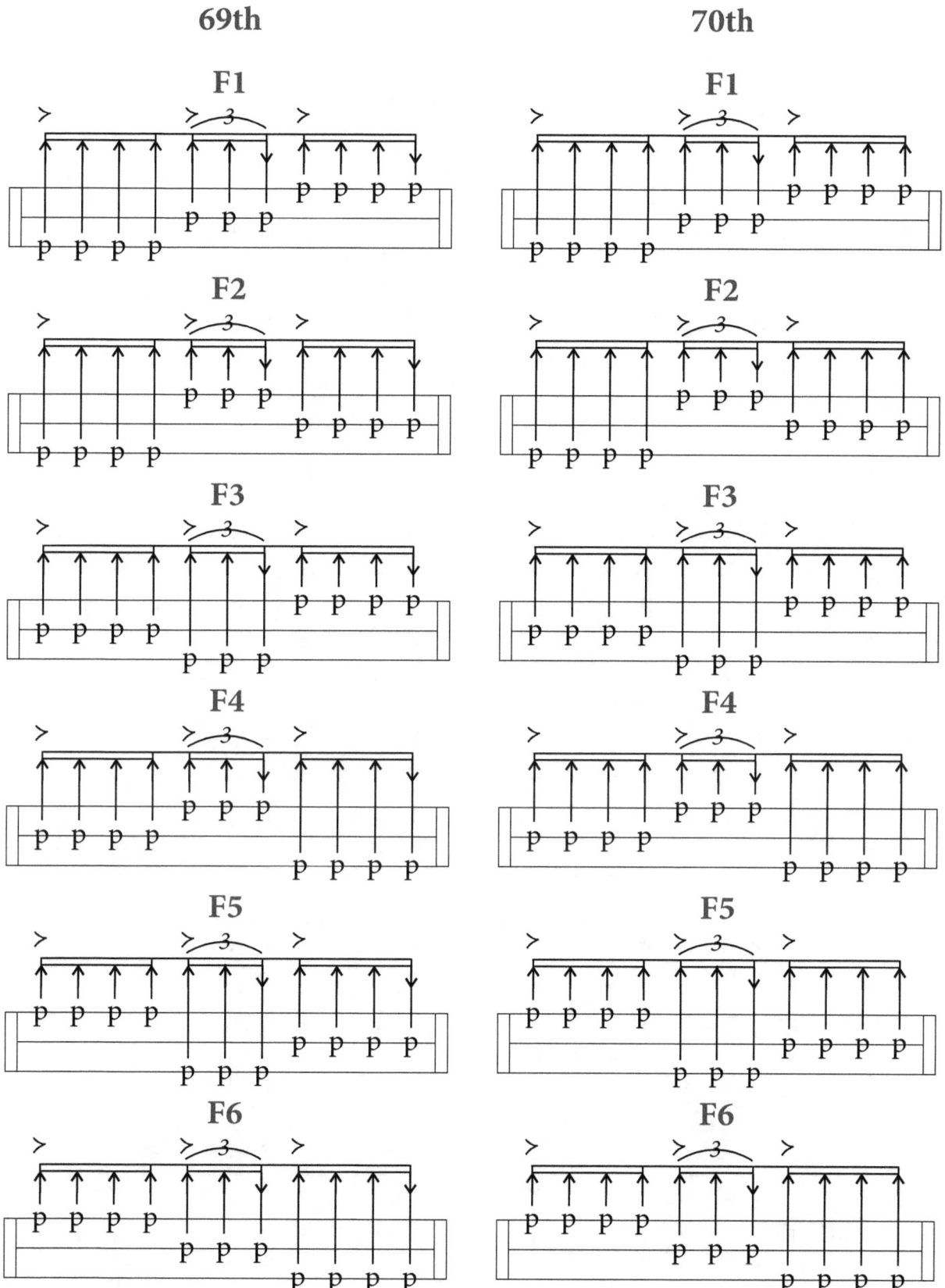

71th

F1
F2
F3
F4
F5
F6

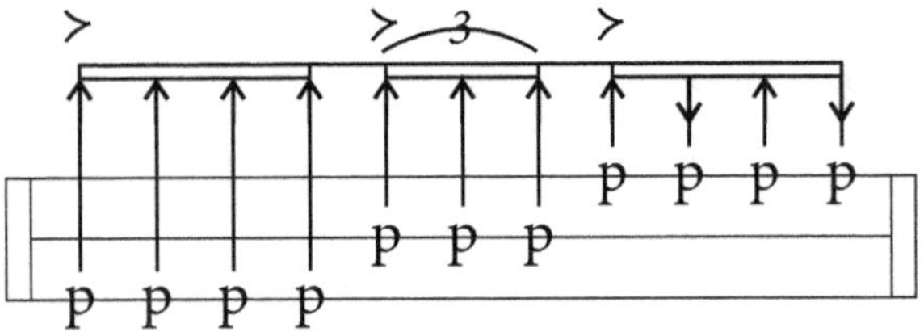

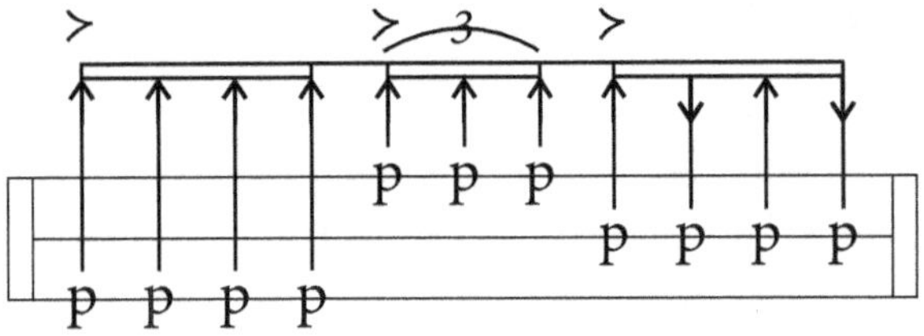

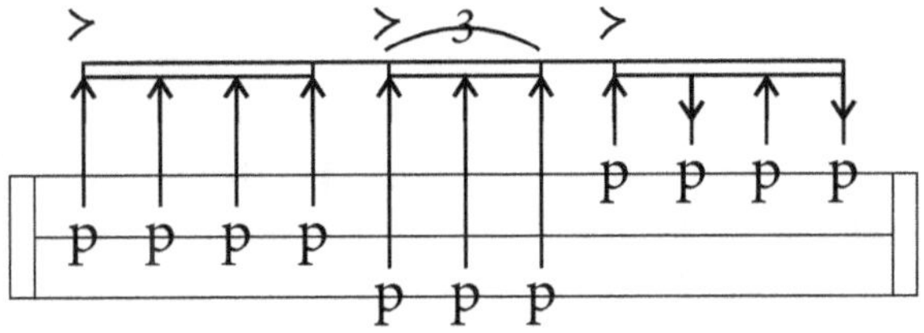

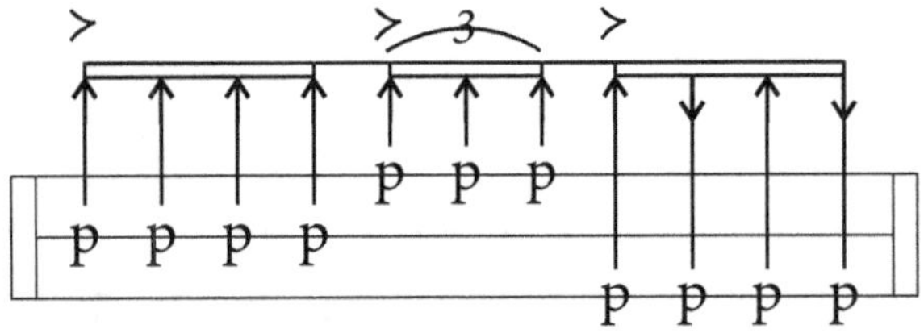

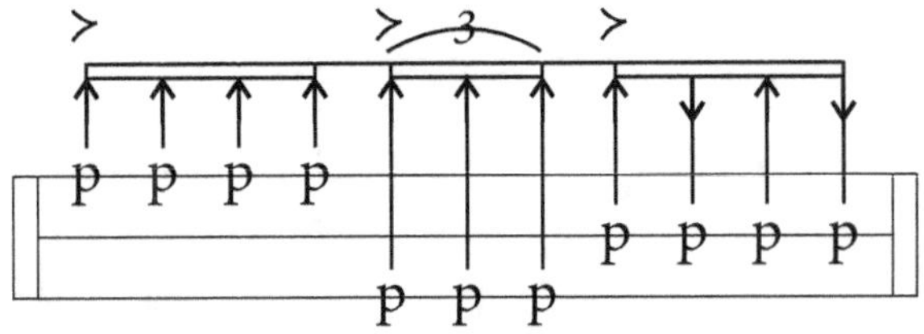

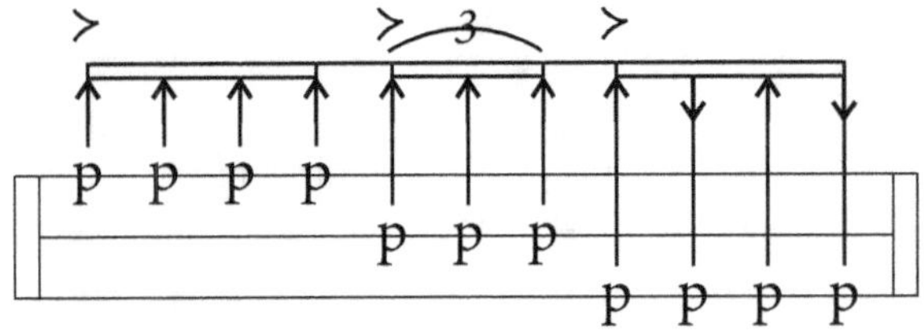

72th

F1
F2
F3
F4
F5
F6

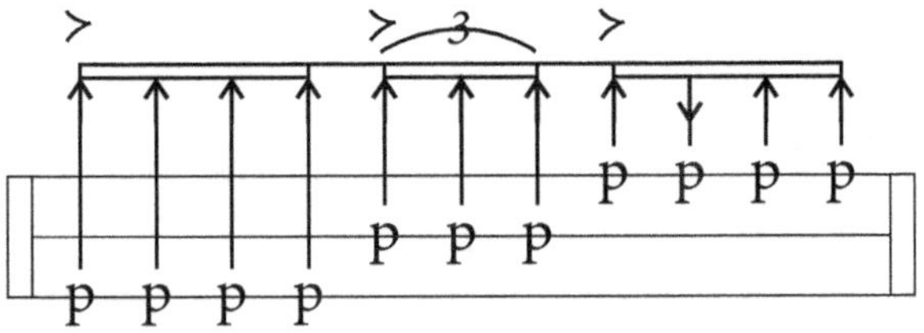

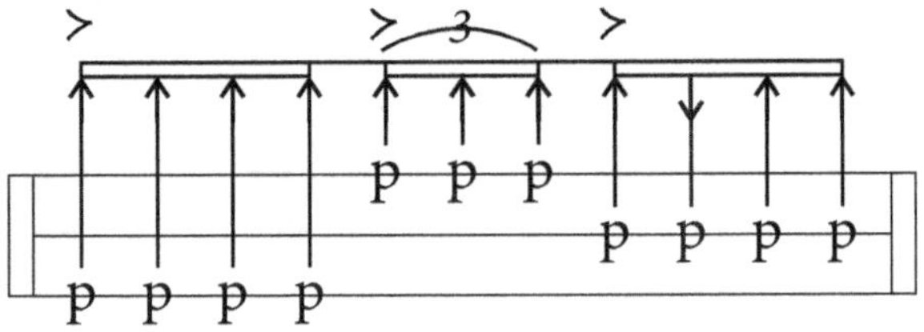

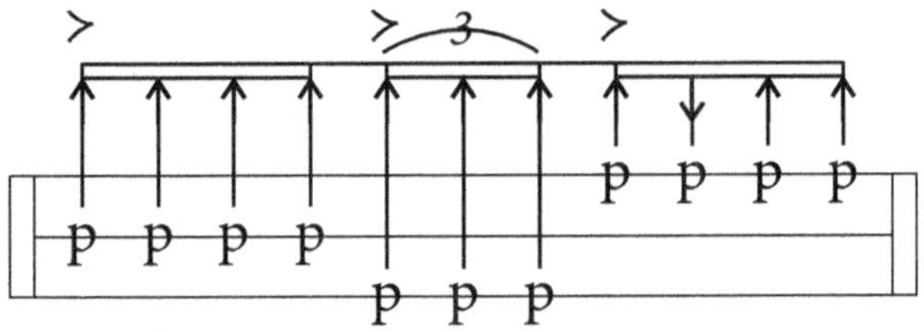

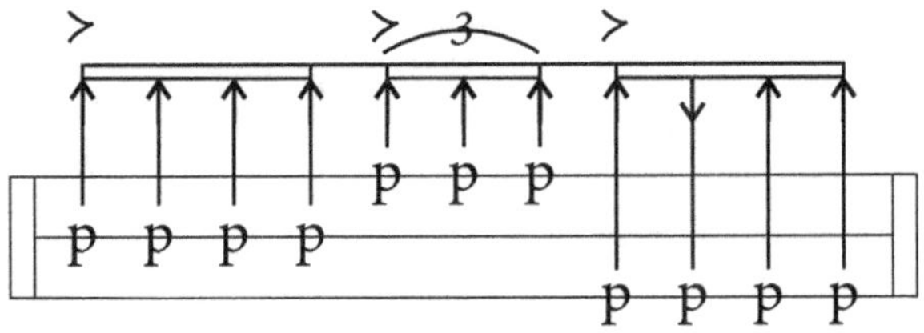

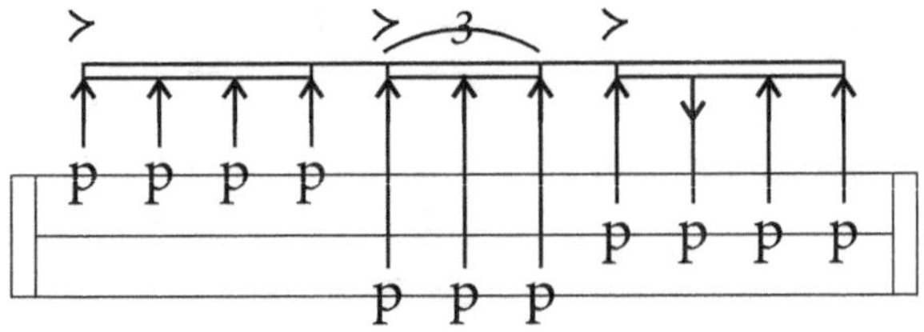

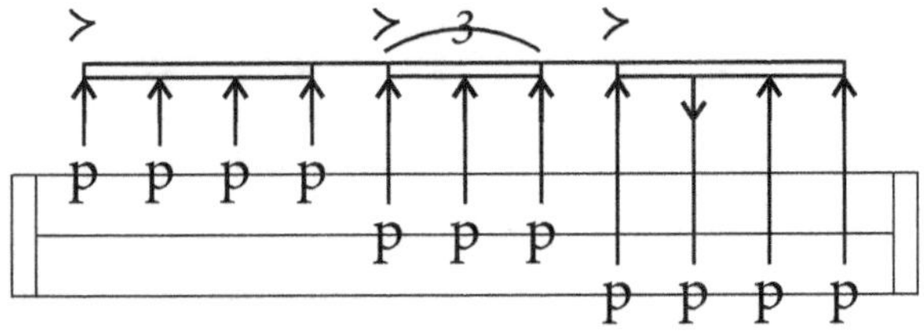

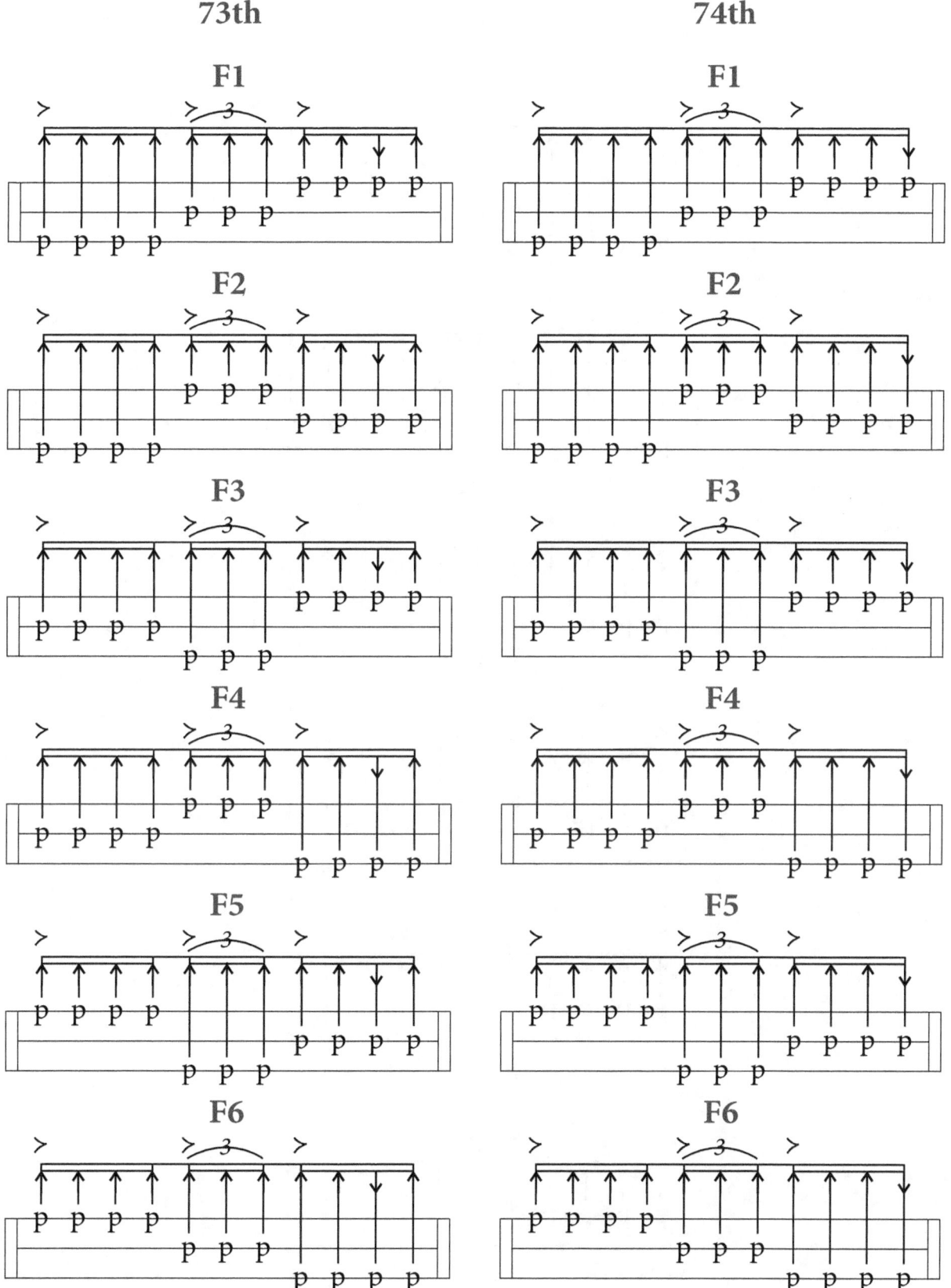

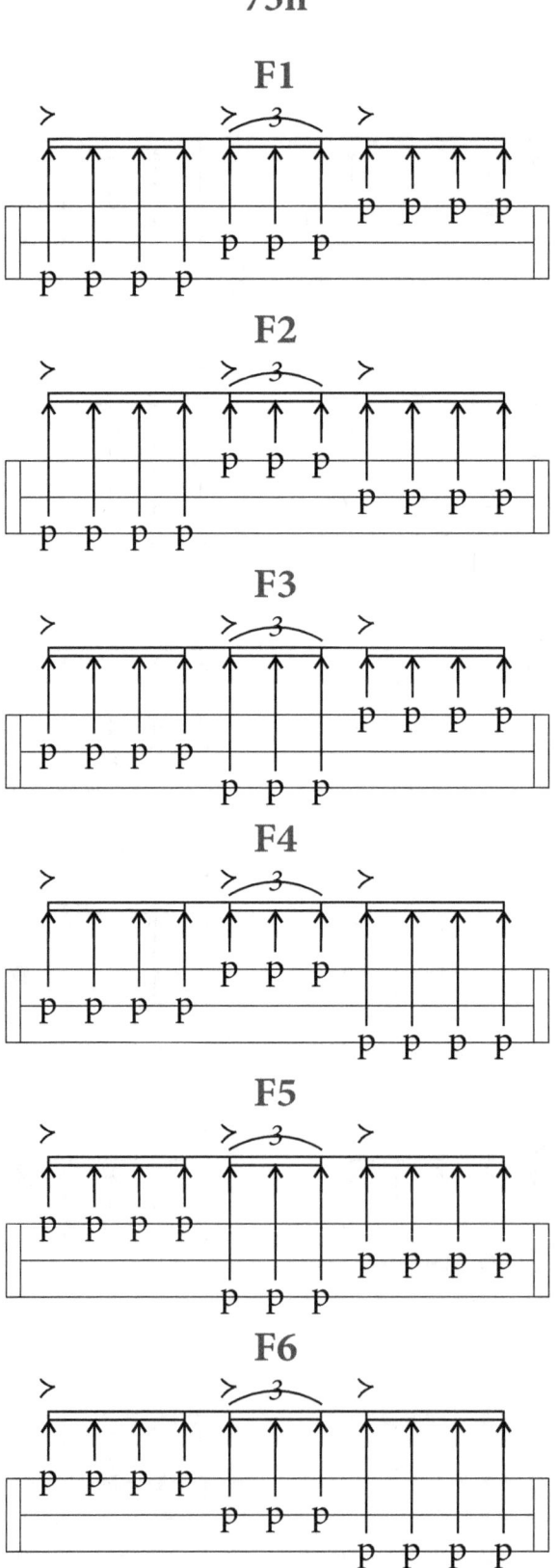

§ VII

Exercise on pulgar on three adjacent strings with three quad strokes in each Formula. Here are the 5 basic ways of pulgar stroke in regard to the direction of stroke. The first Formula of each basic way is cited below:

WAYS OF PERFORMANCE

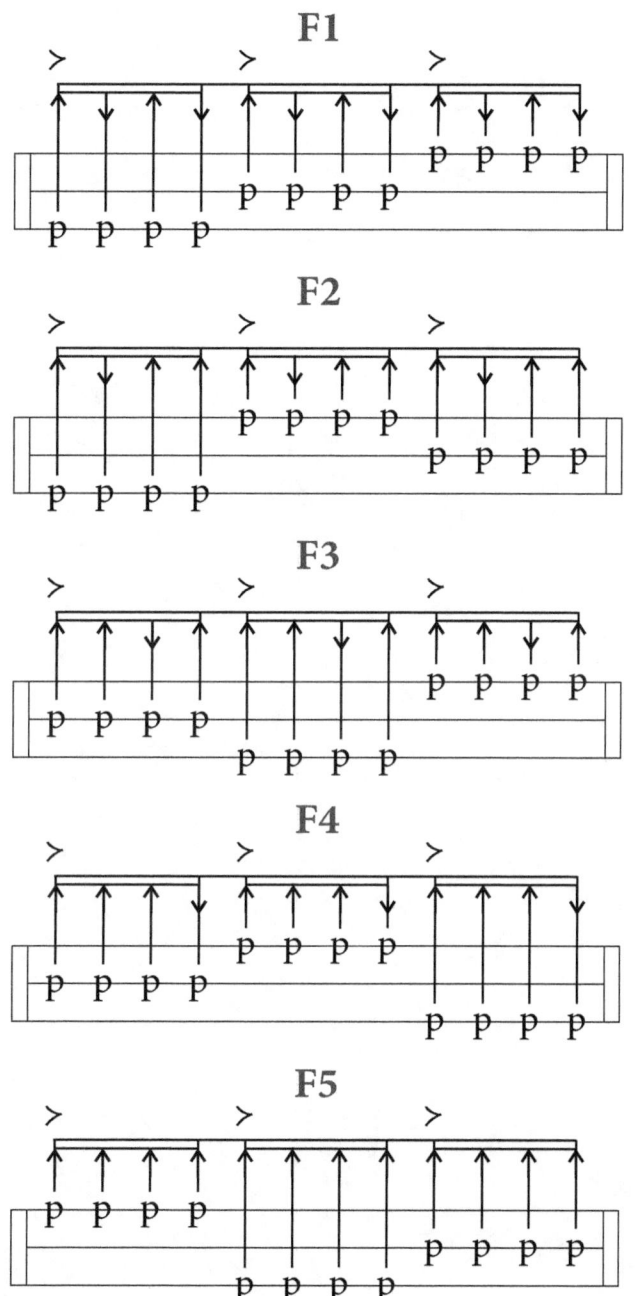

The change in the direction of pulgar stroke results in many different ways of performance. Here are some of them (24) for practice.

VARIATION 1

F1
F2
F3
F4
F5
F6

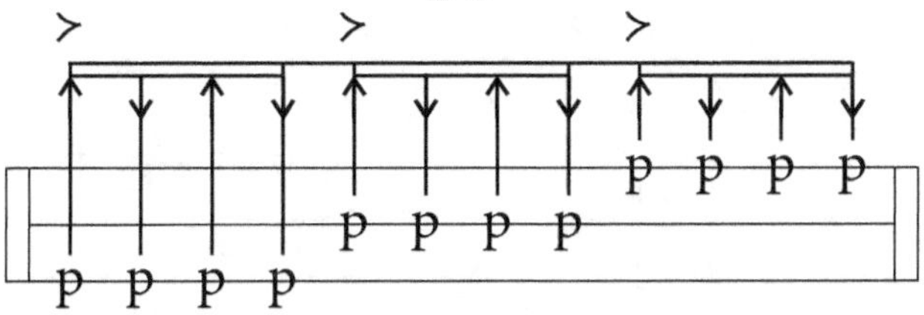

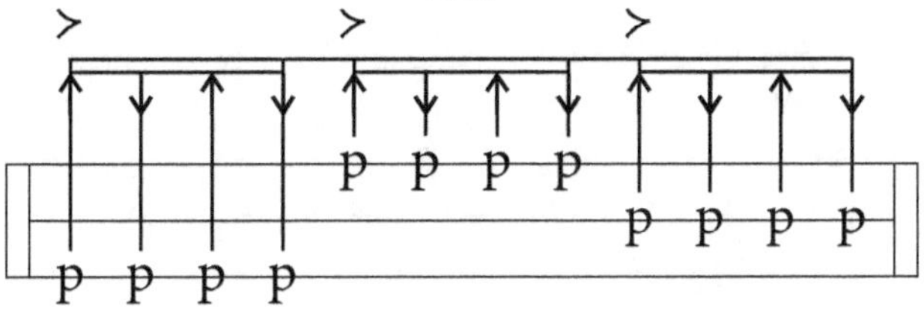

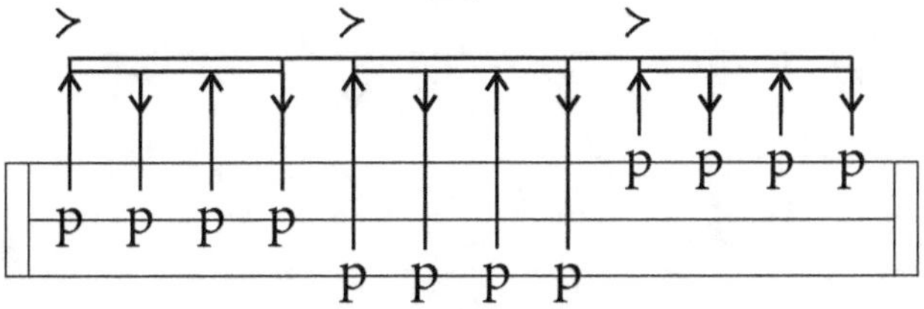

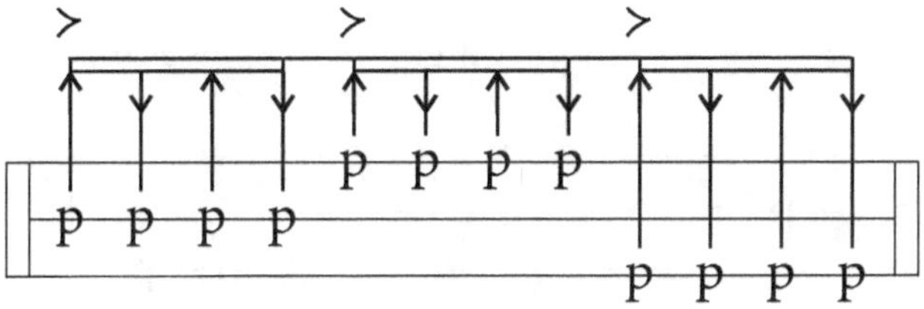

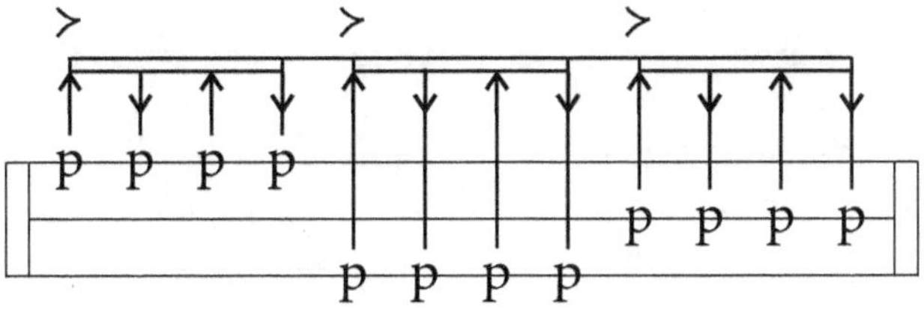

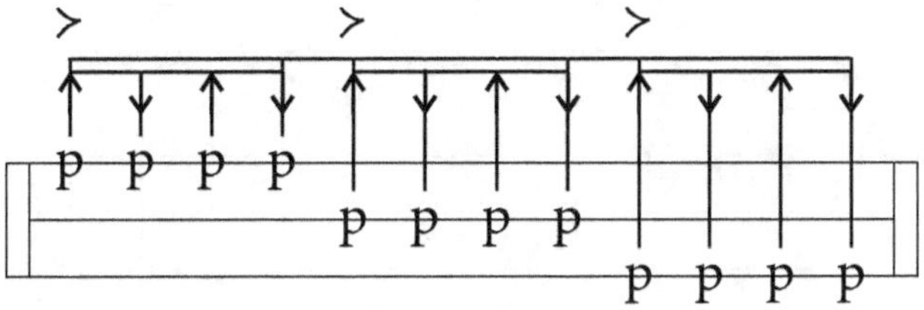

VARIATION 2

F1
F2
F3
F4
F5
F6

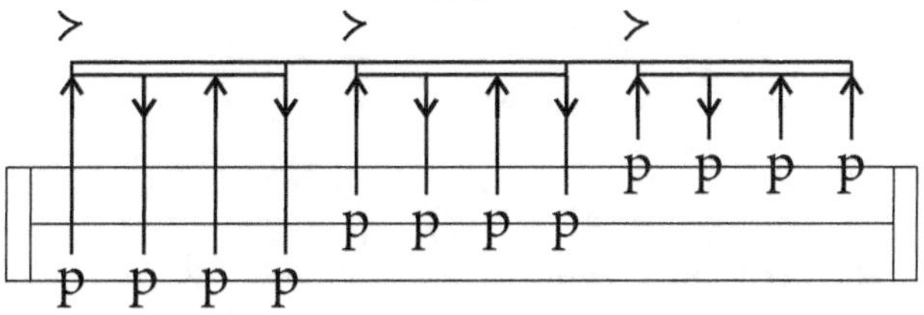

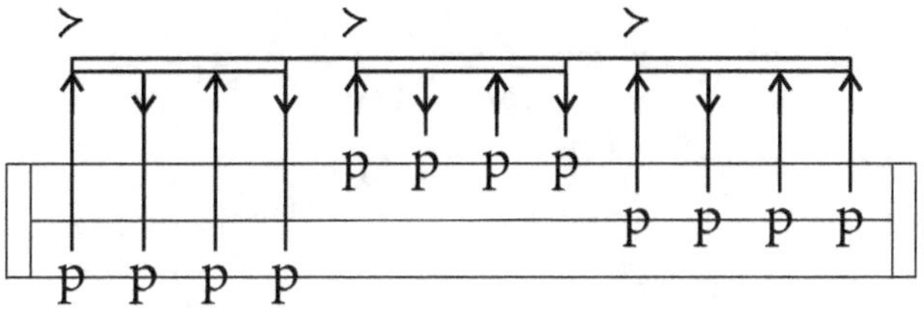

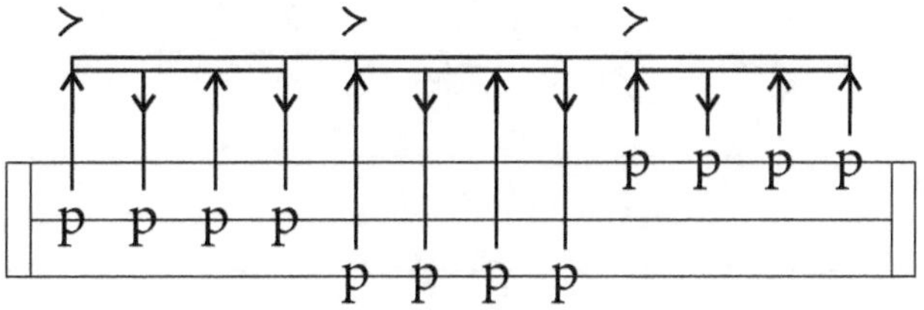

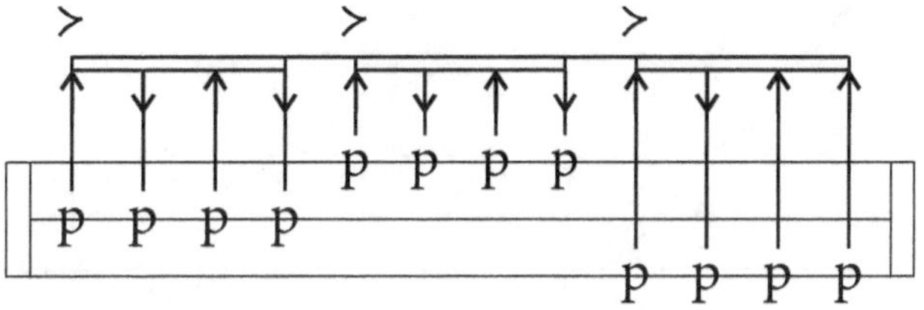

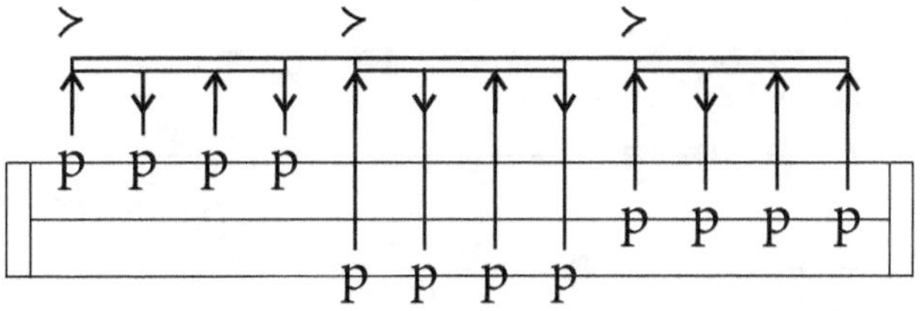

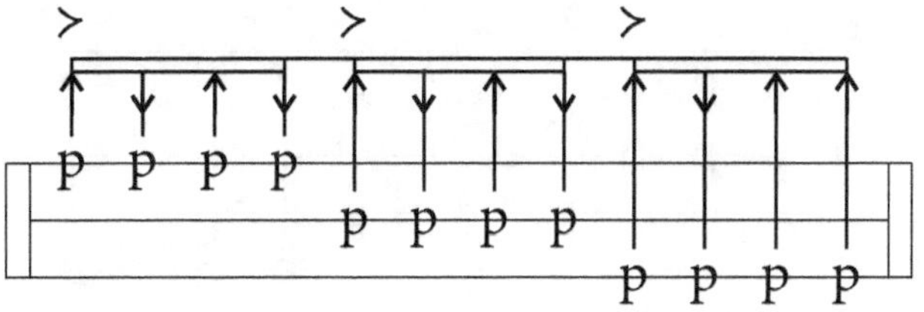

VARIATION 3

F1
F2
F3
F4
F5
F6

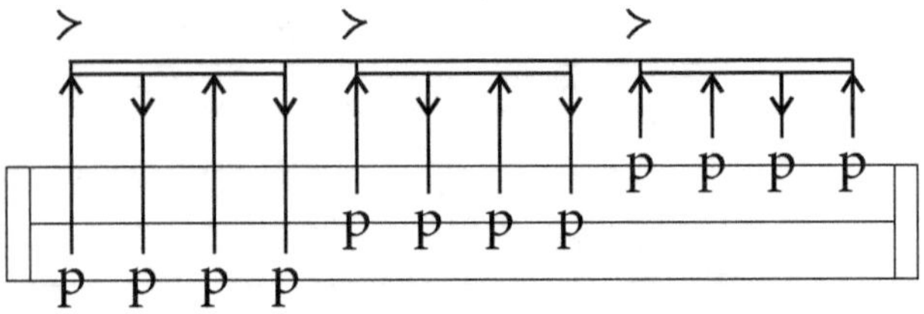

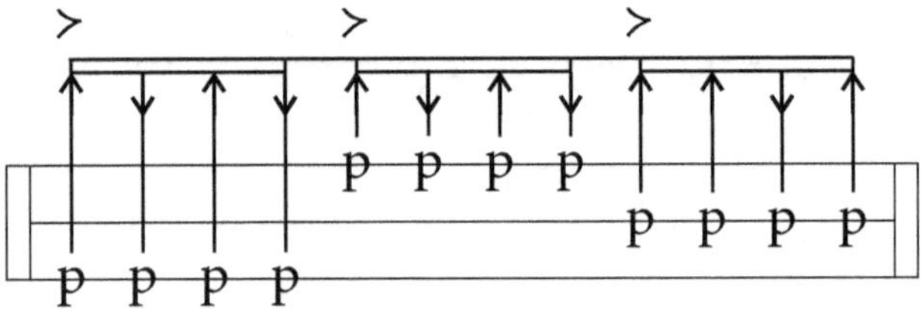

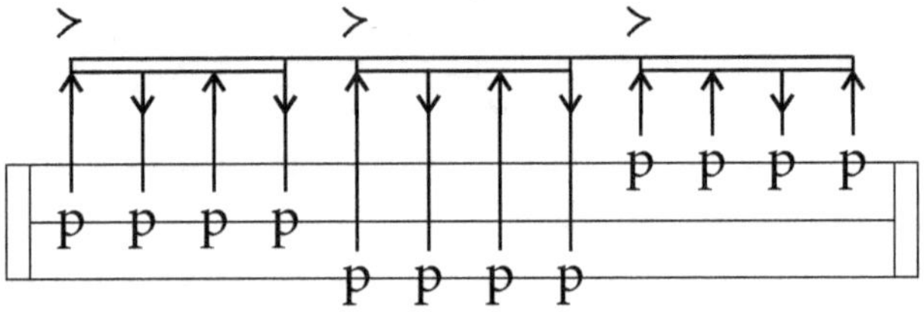

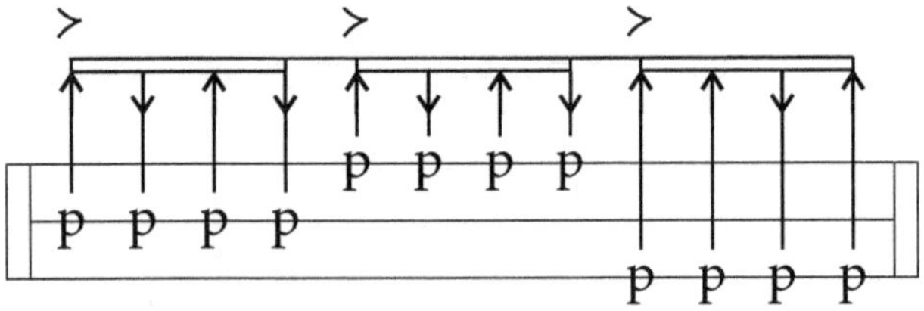

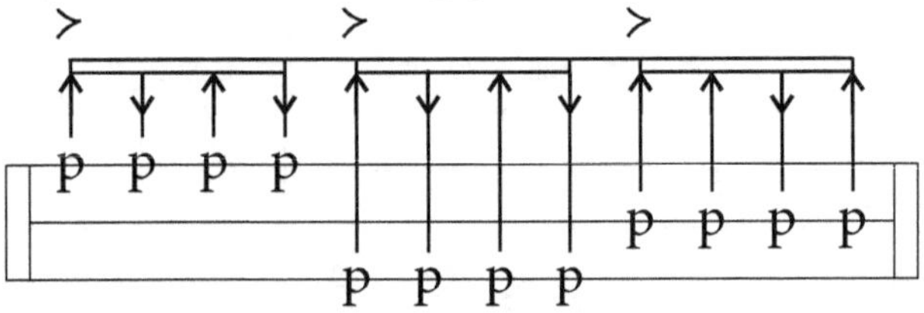

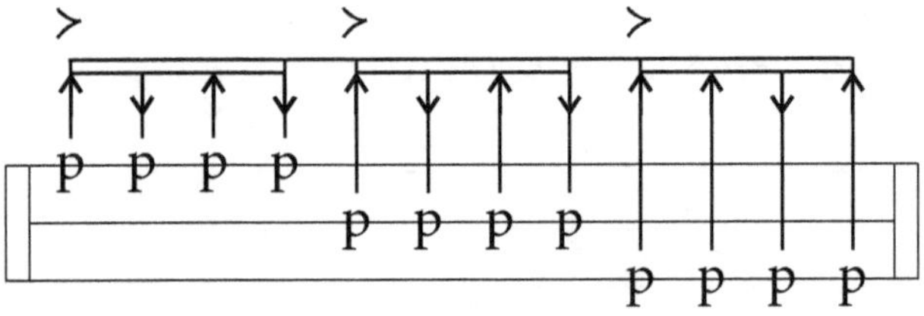

VARIATION 4

F1
F2
F3
F4
F5
F6

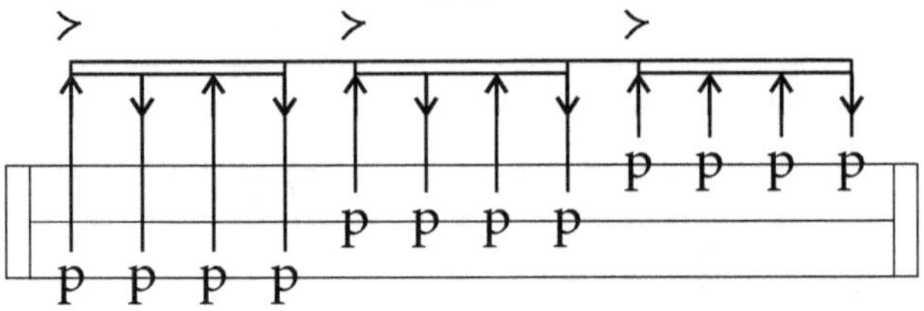

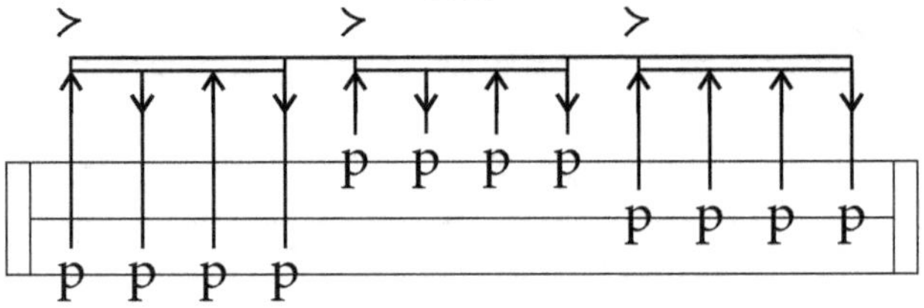

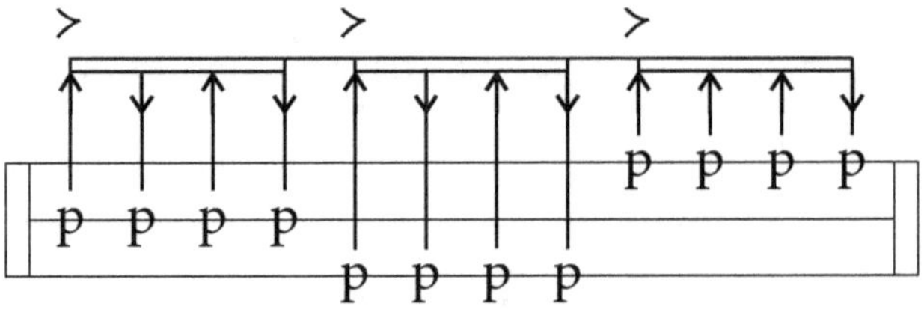

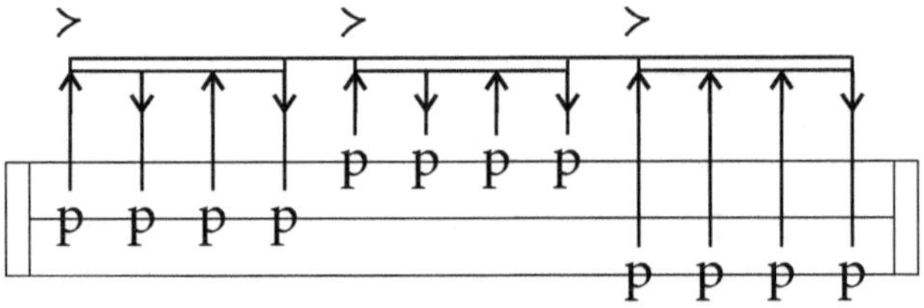

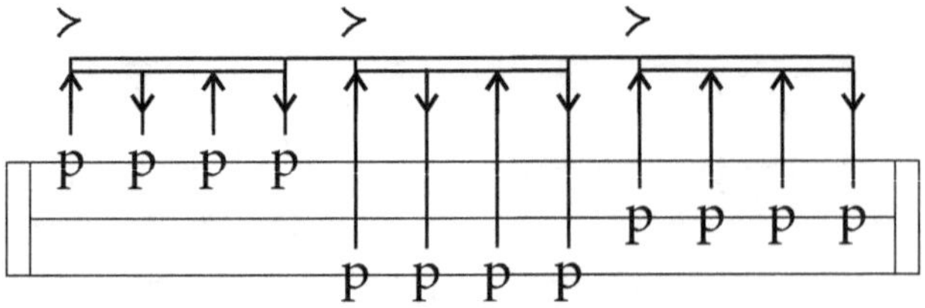

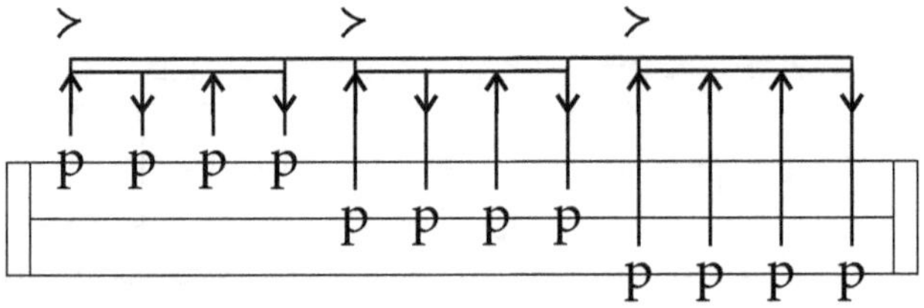

VARIATION 5

F1
F2
F3
F4
F5
F6

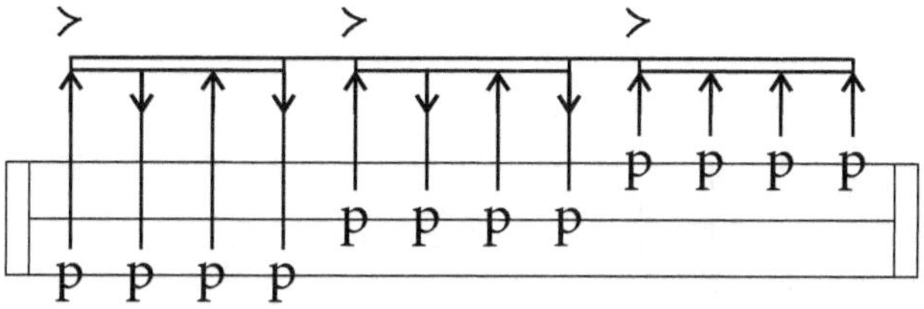

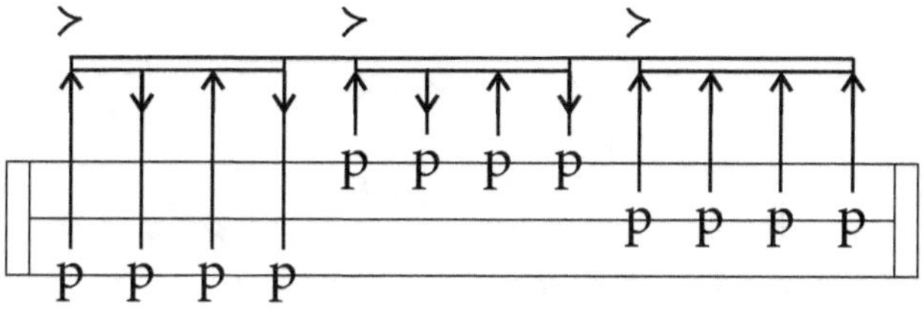

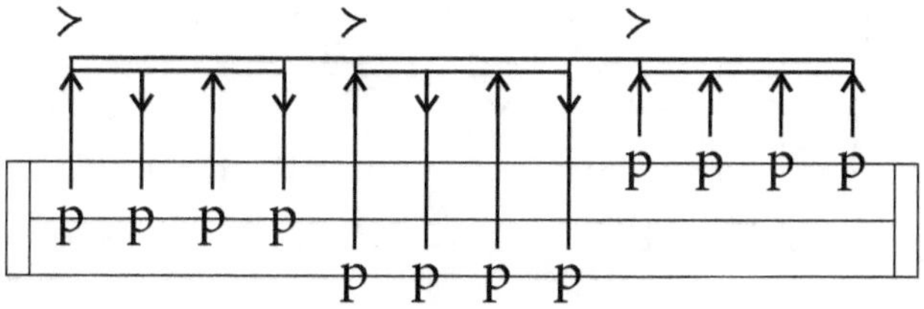

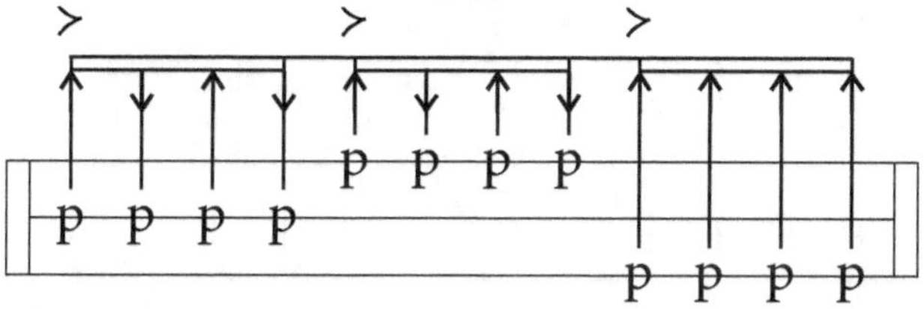

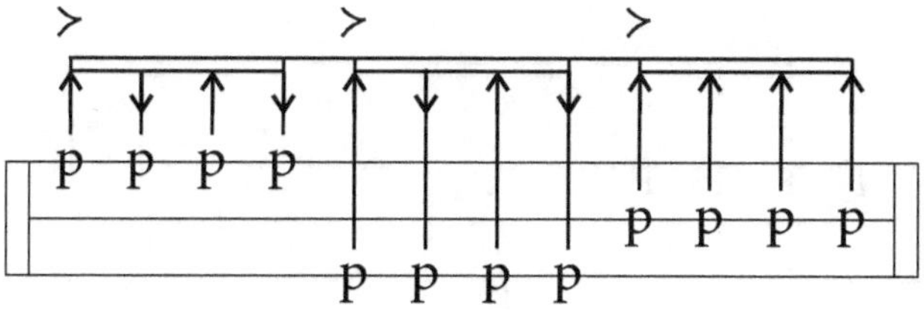

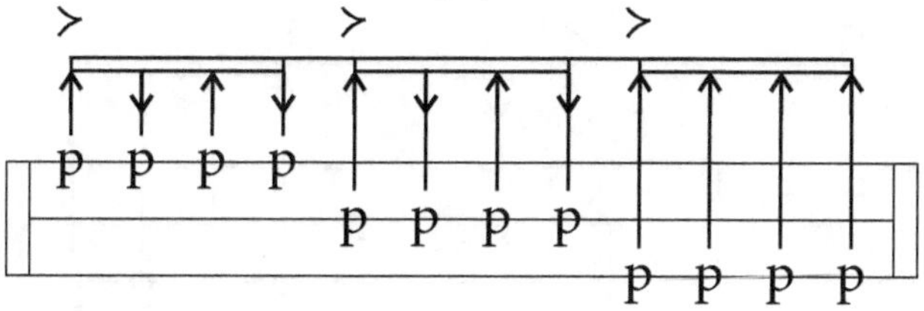

VARIATION 6

F1
F2
F3
F4
F5
F6

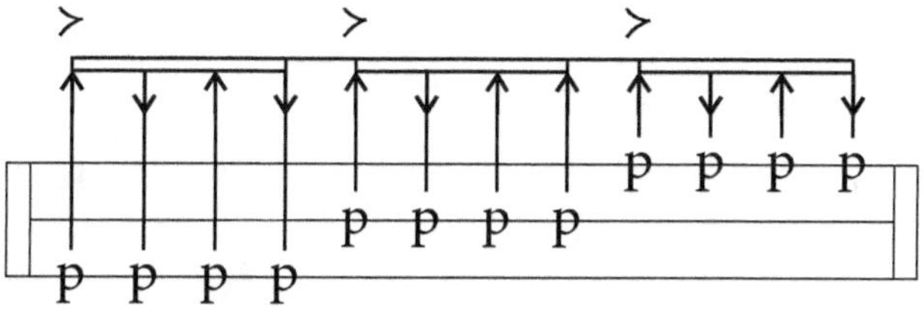

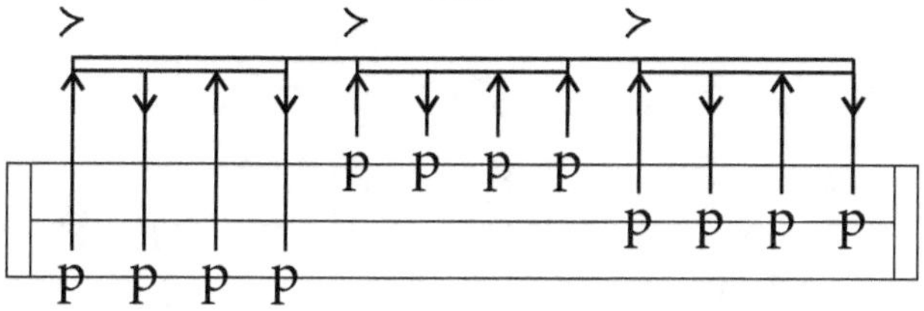

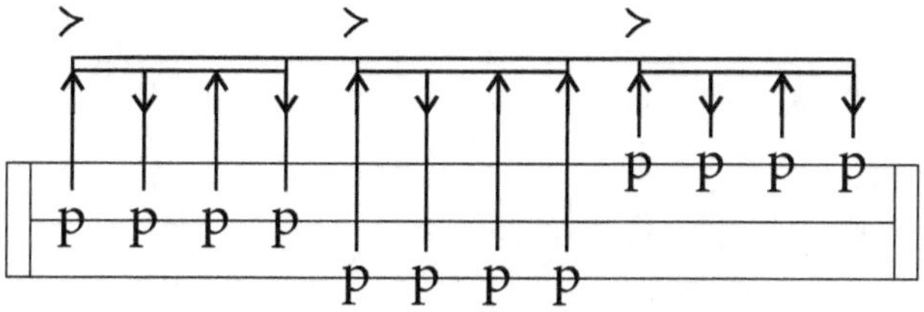

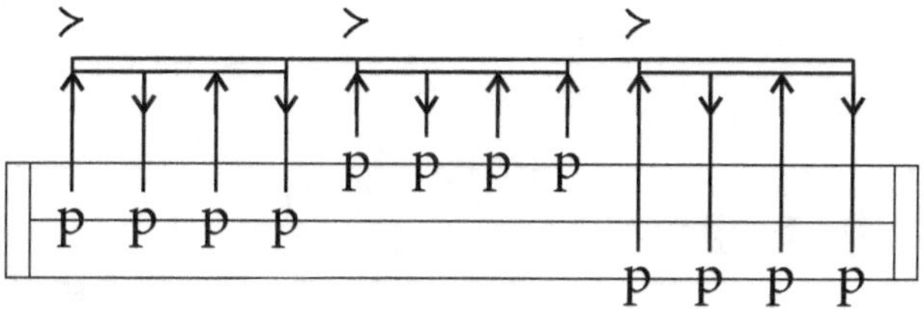

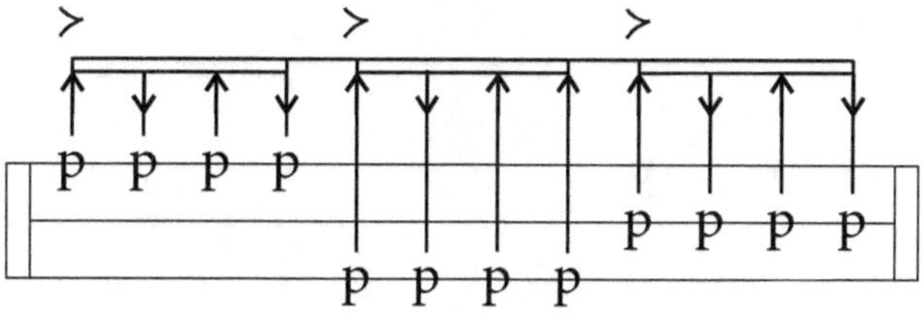

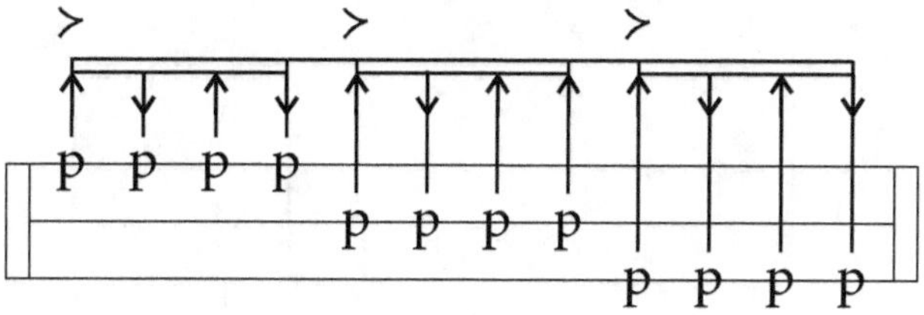

VARIATION 7

F1

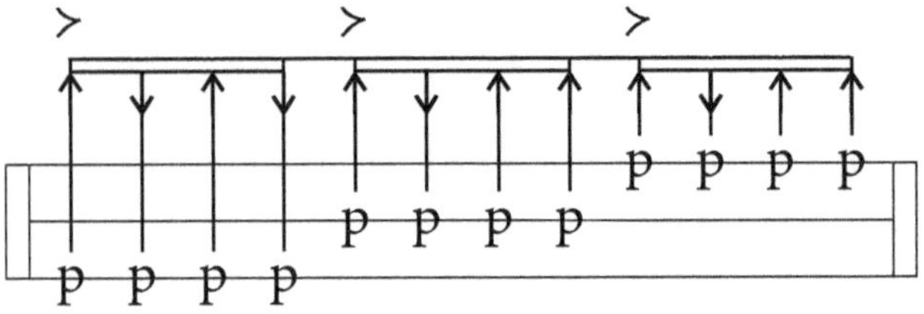

F2

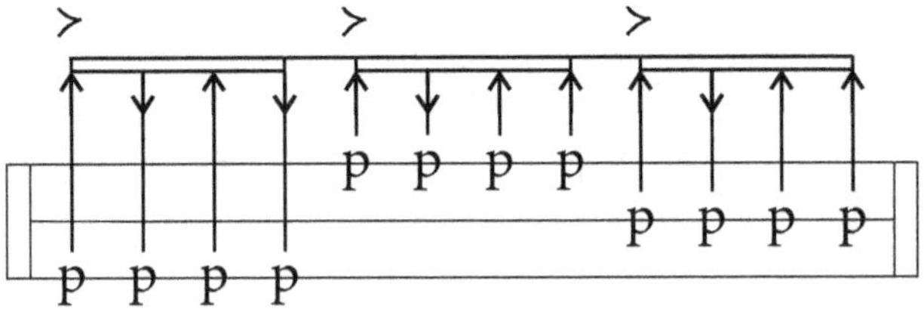

F3

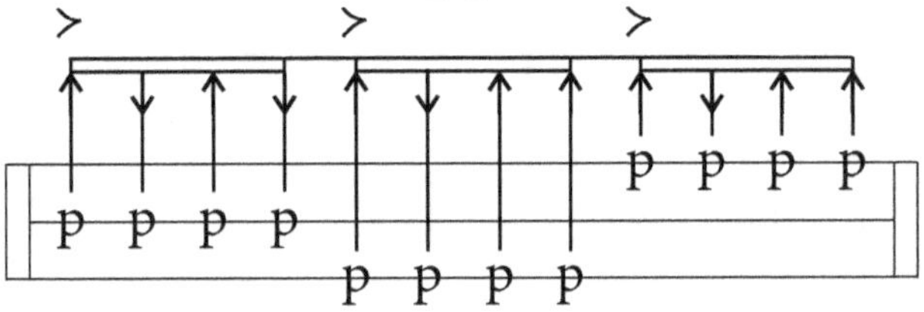

F4

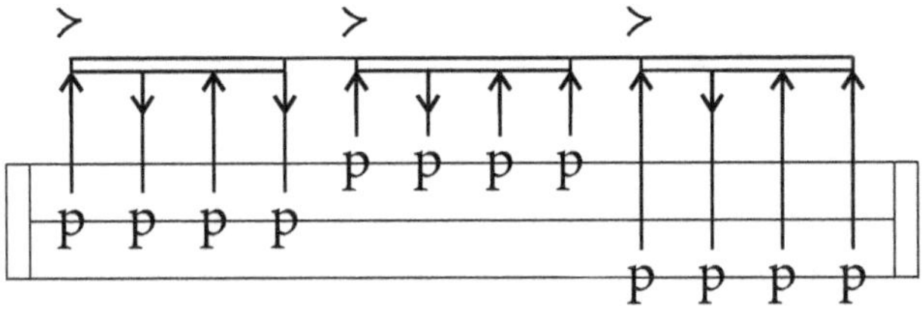

F5

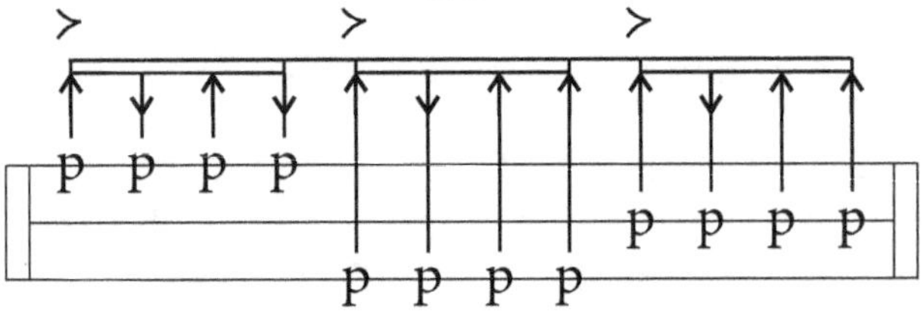

F6

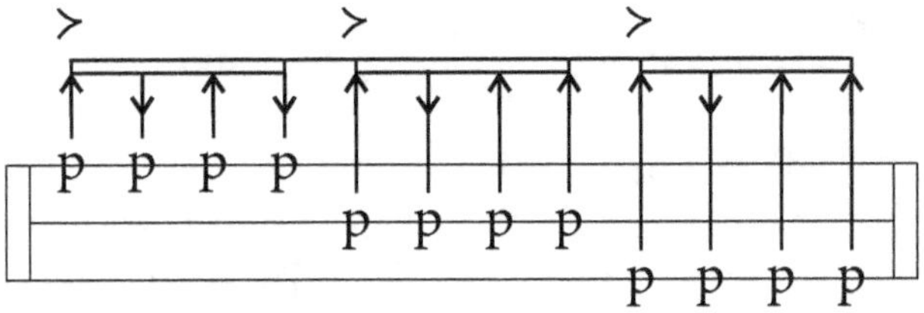

VARIATION 8

F1

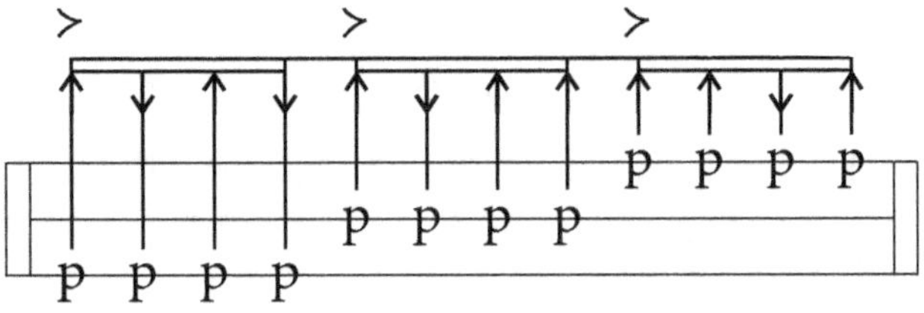

F2

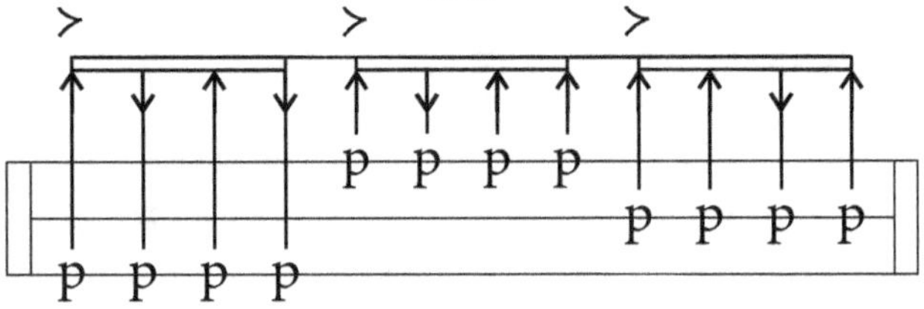

F3

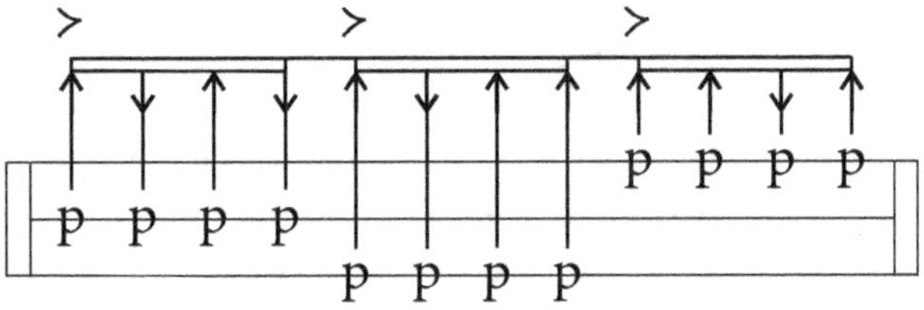

F4

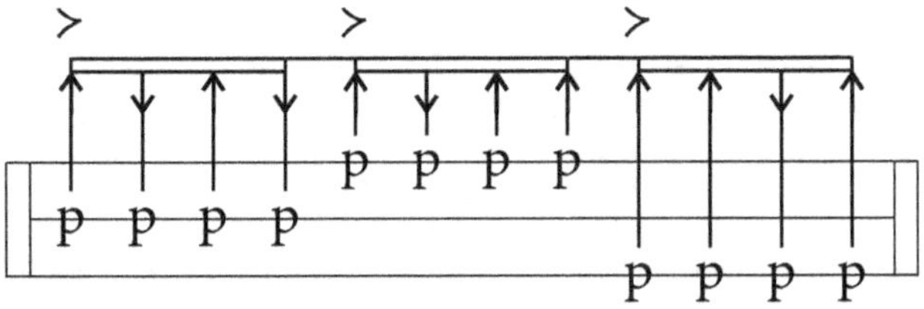

F5

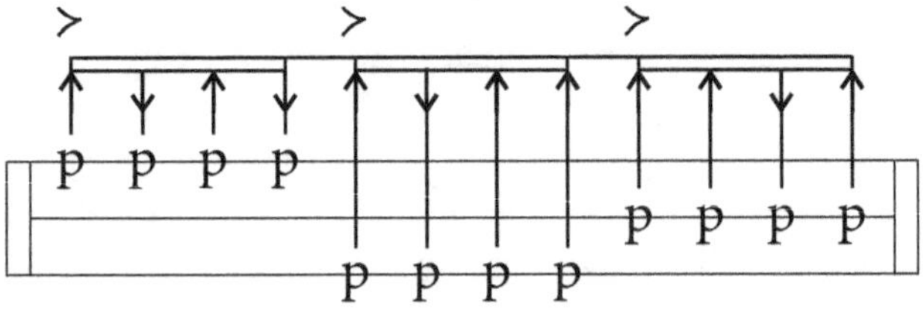

F6

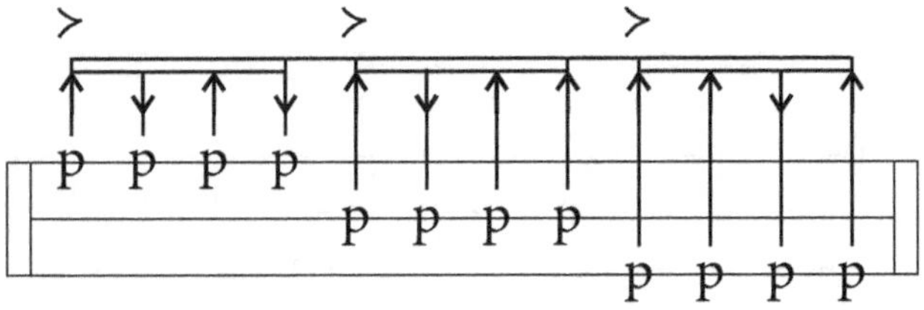

VARIATION 9

F1
F2
F3
F4
F5
F6

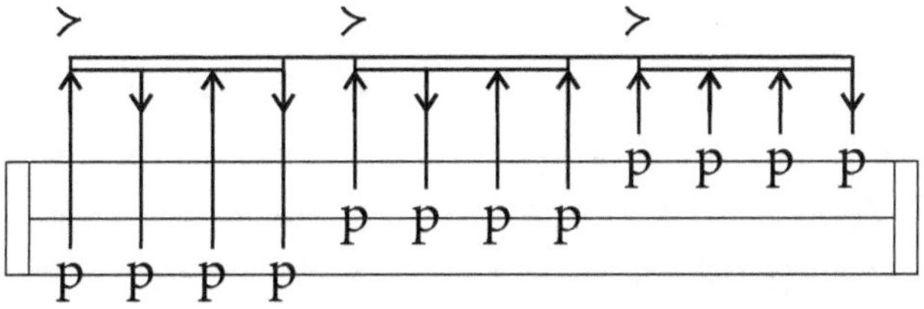

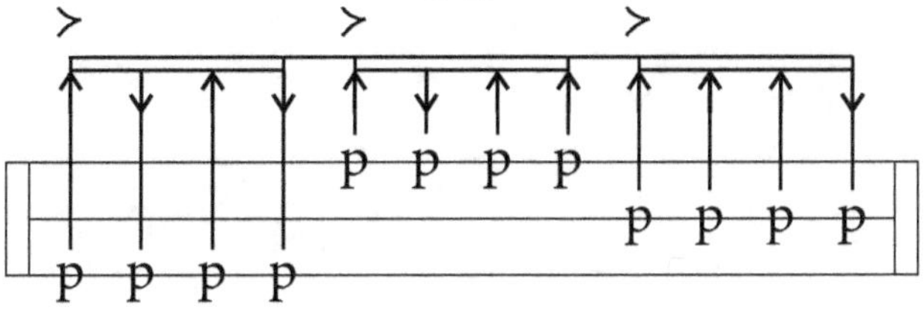

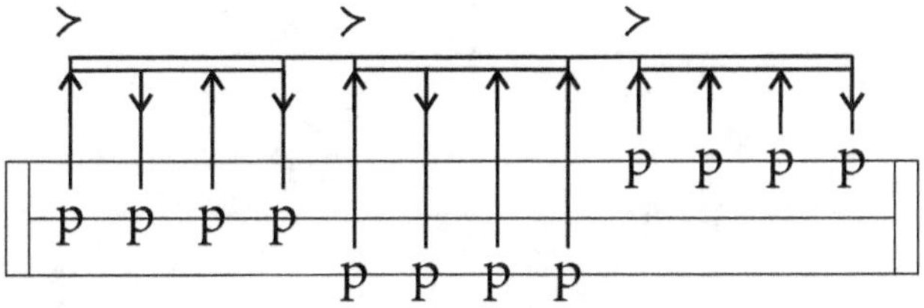

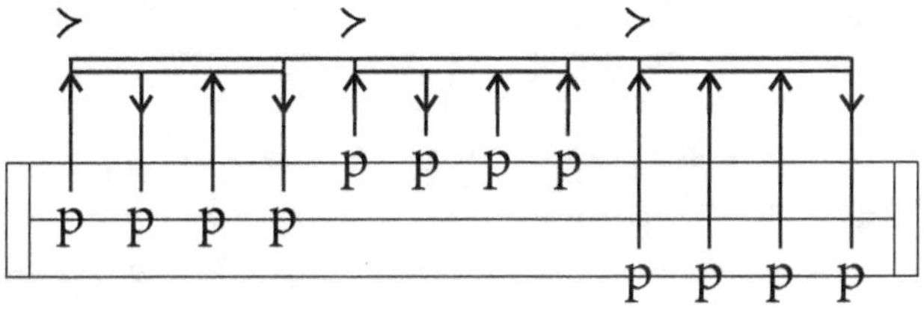

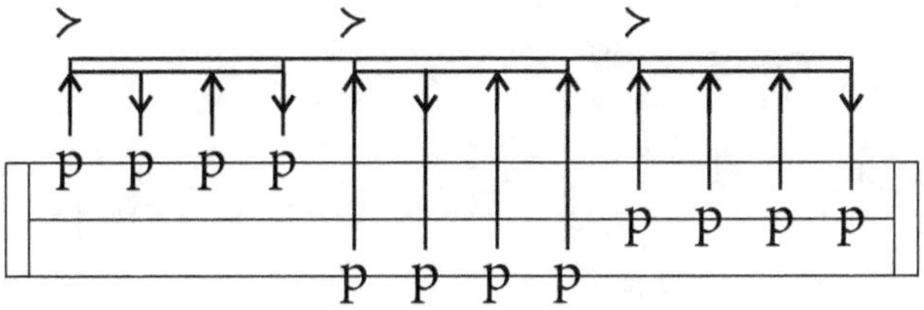

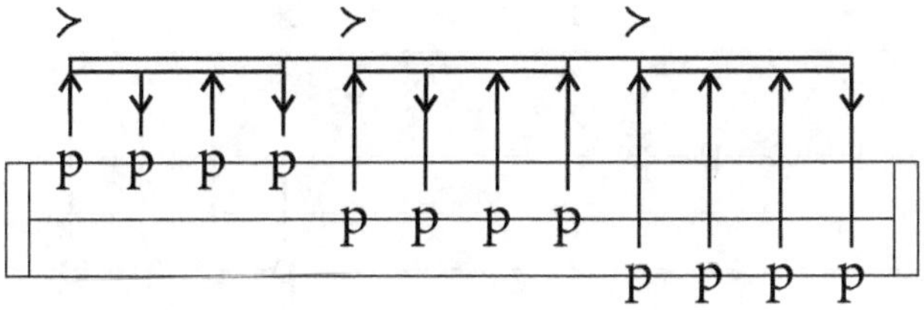

VARIATION 10

F1
F2
F3
F4
F5
F6

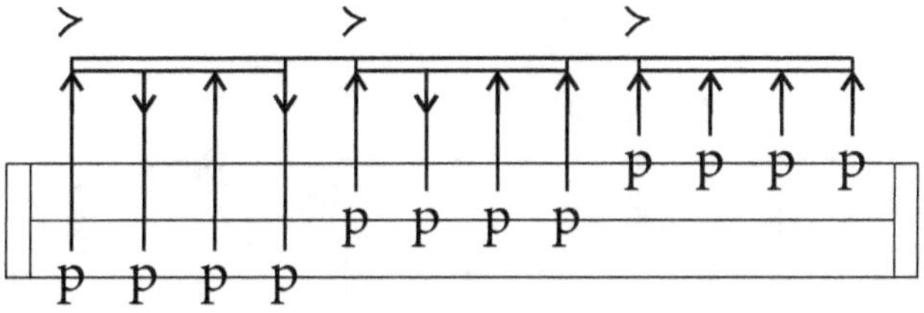

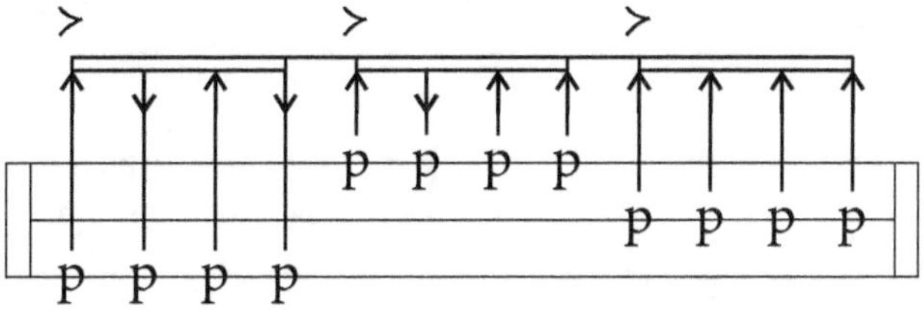

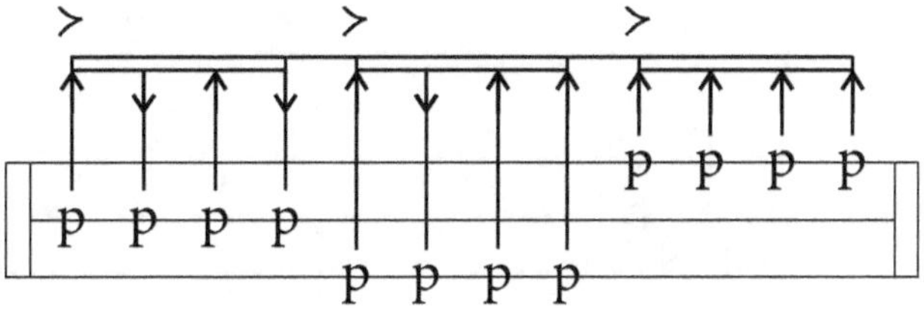

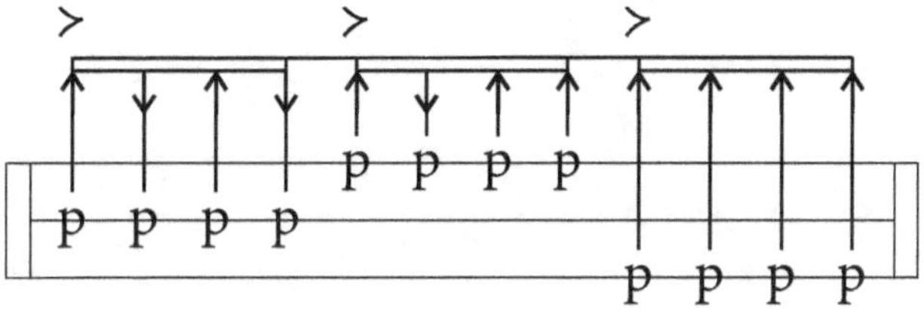

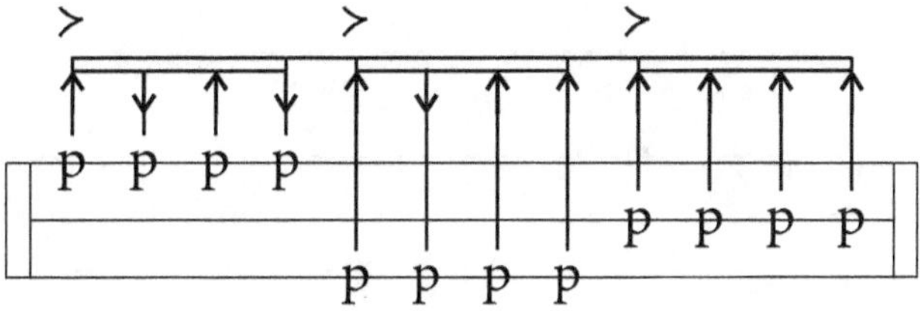

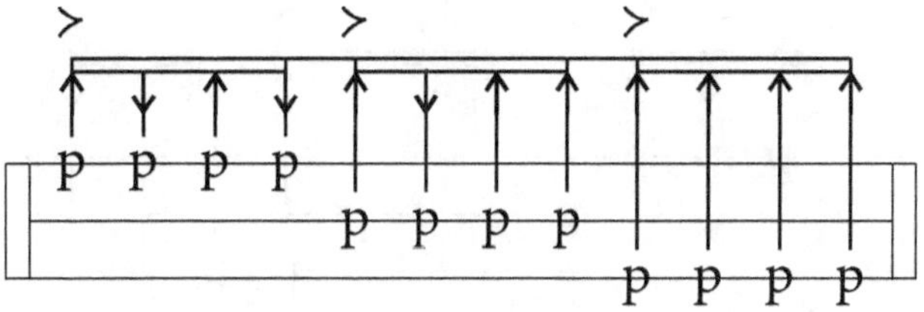

VARIATION 11

F1
F2
F3
F4
F5
F6

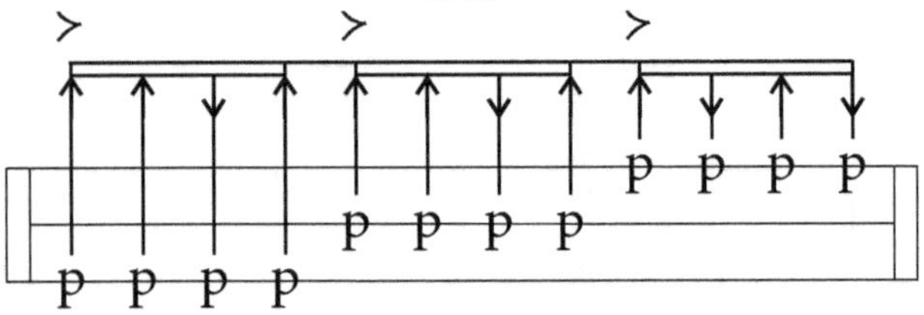

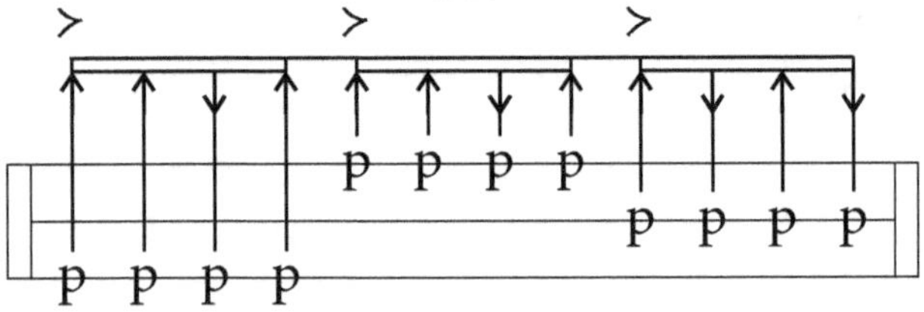

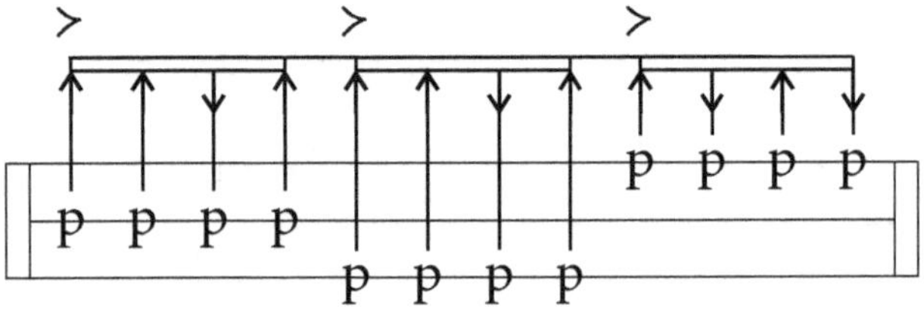

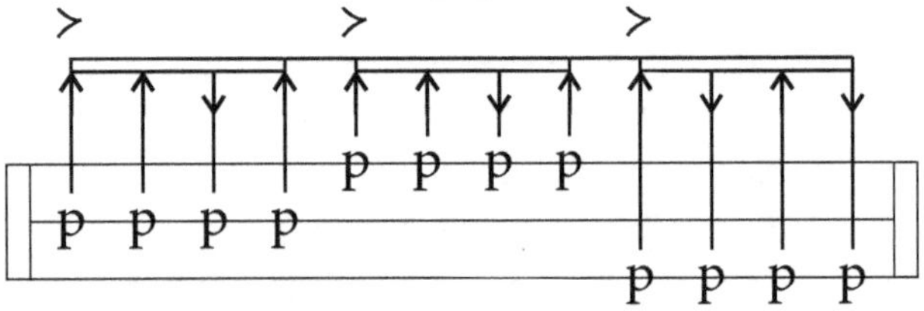

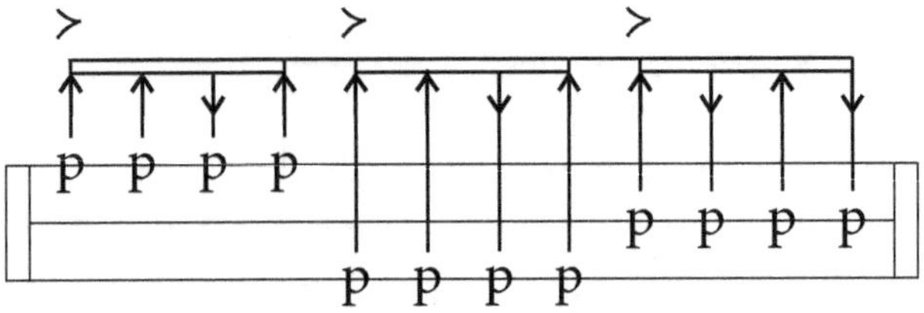

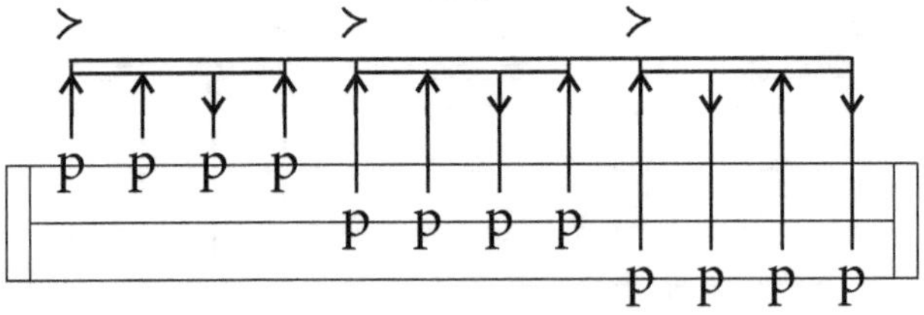

VARIATION 12

F1
F2
F3
F4
F5
F6

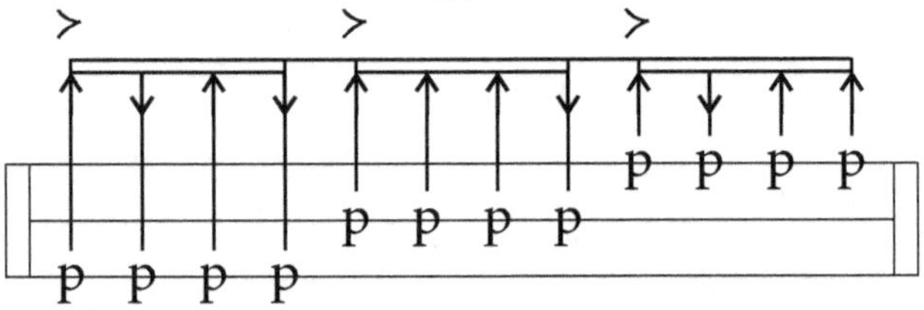

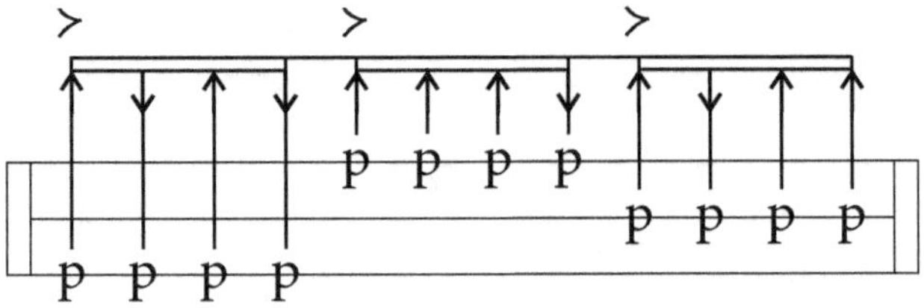

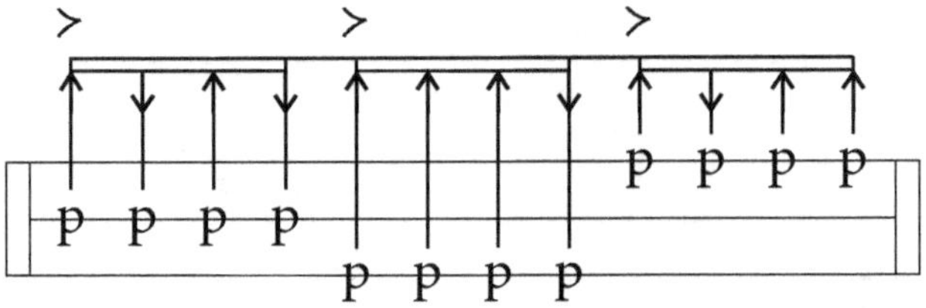

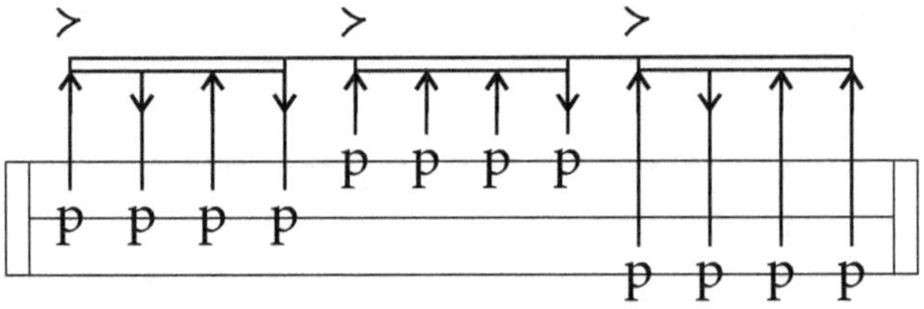

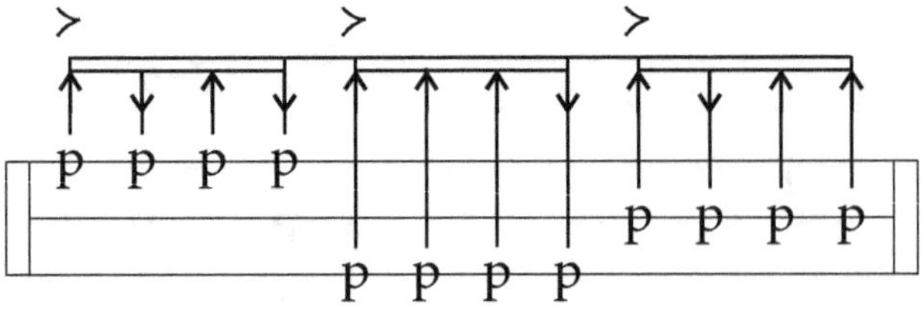

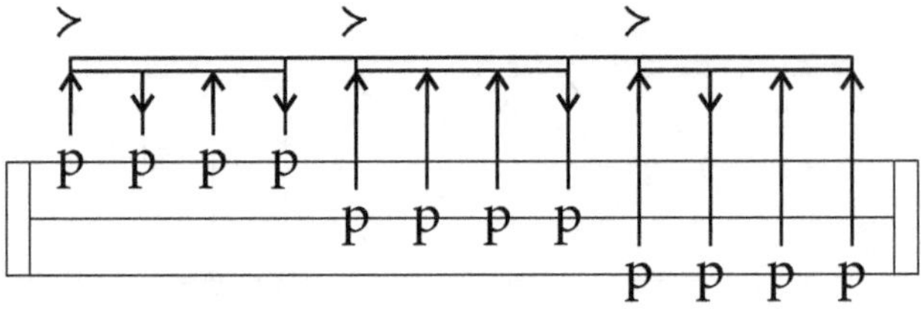

VARIATION 13

F1

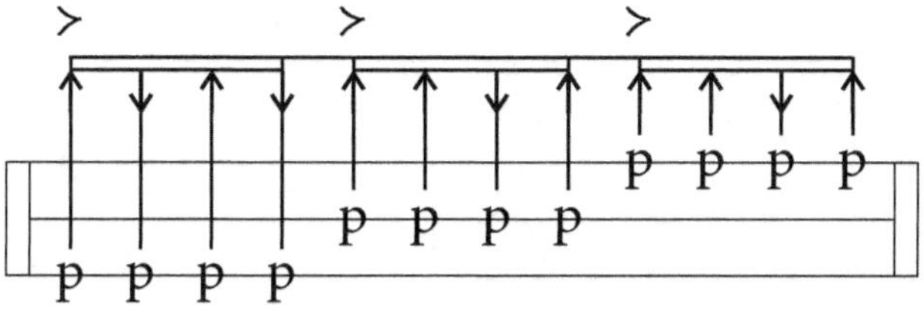

F2

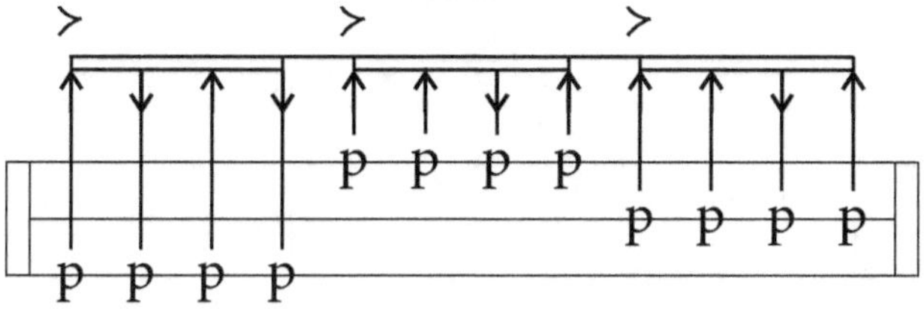

F3

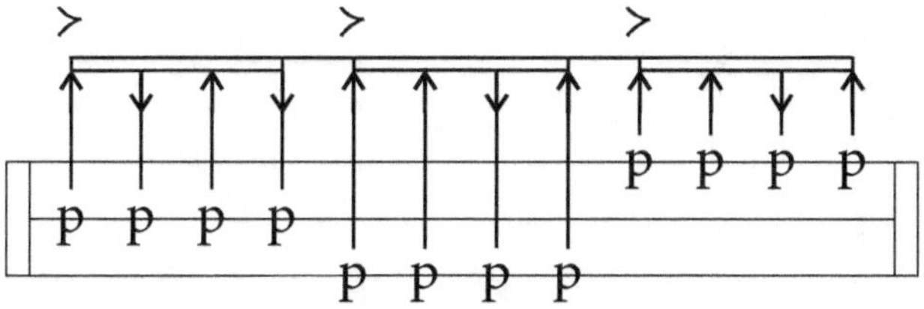

F4

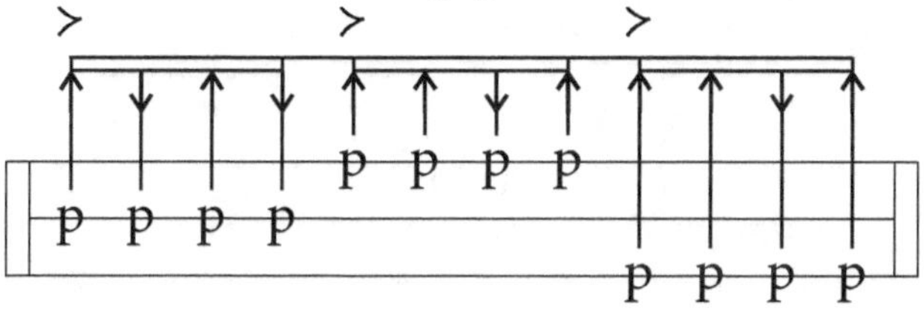

F5

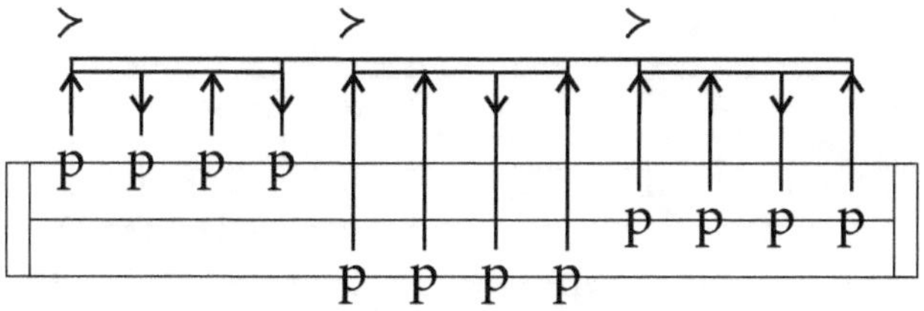

F6

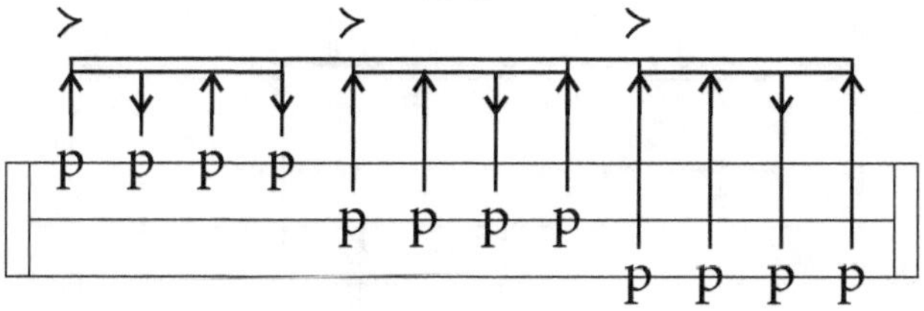

VARIATION 14

F1

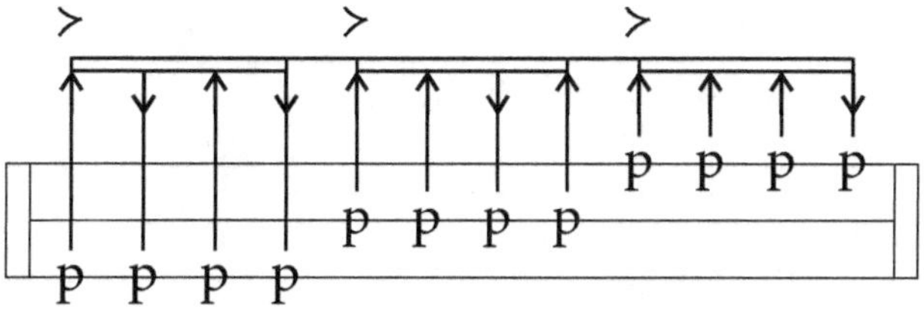

F2

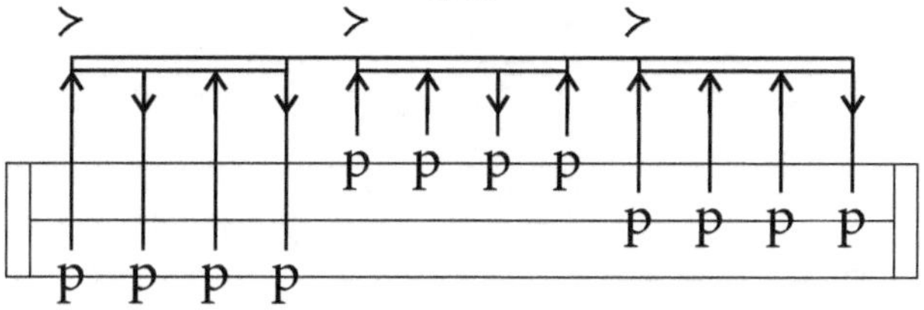

F3

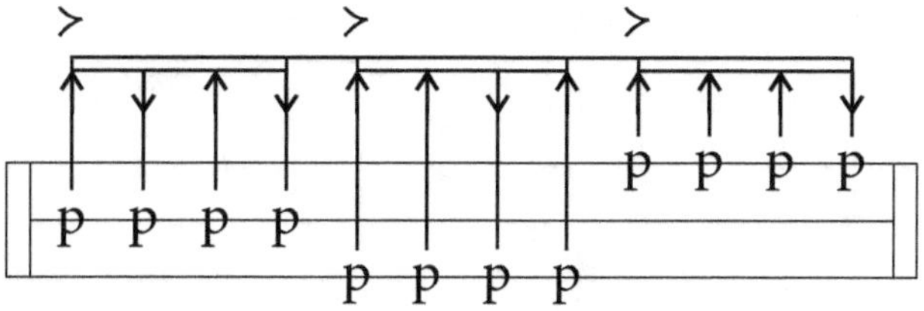

F4

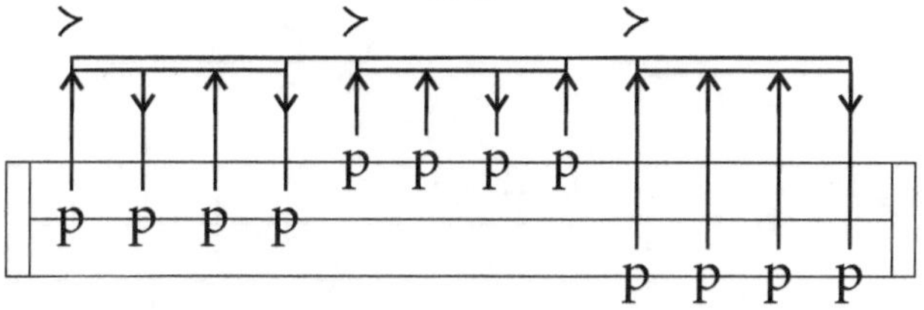

F5

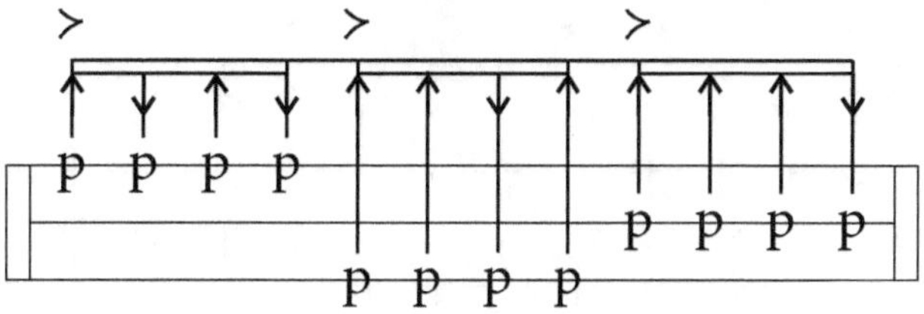

F6

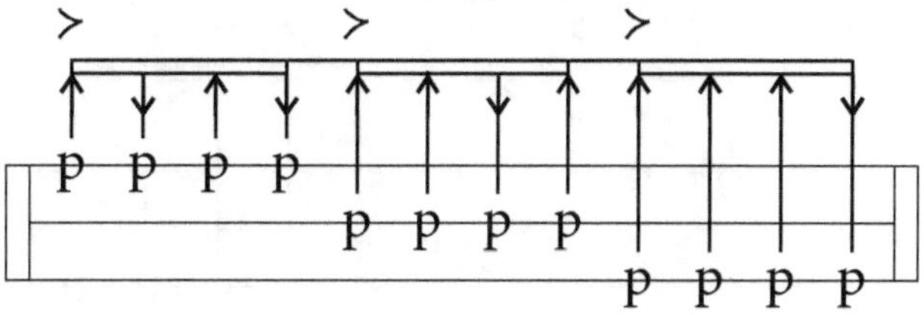

VARIATION 15

F1

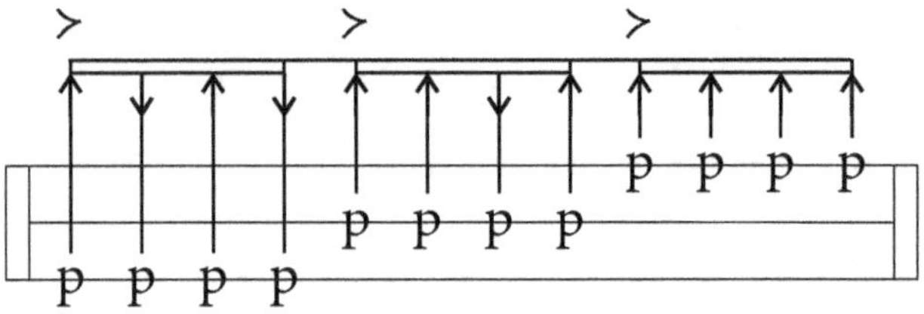

F2

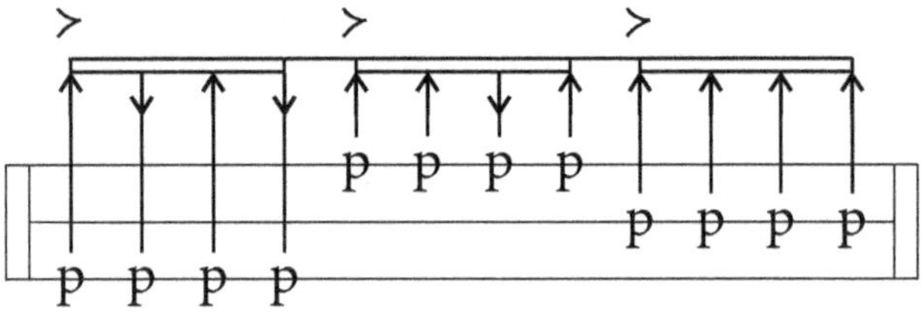

F3

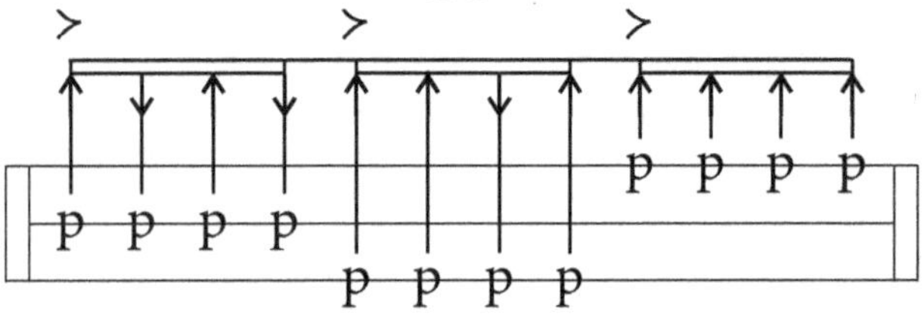

F4

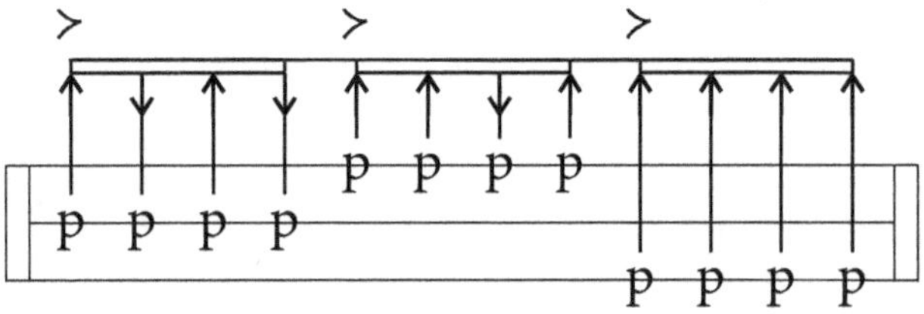

F5

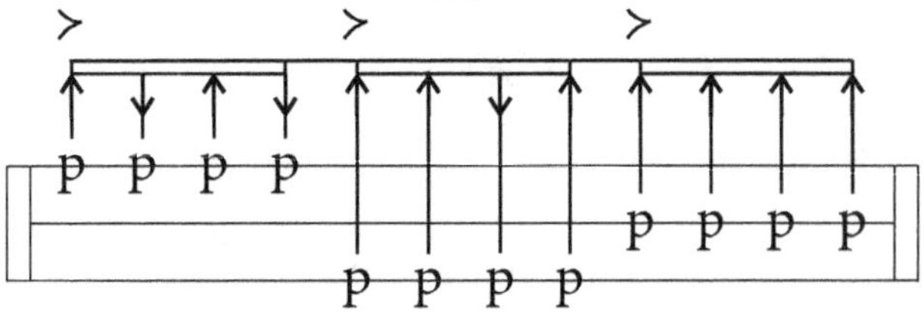

F6

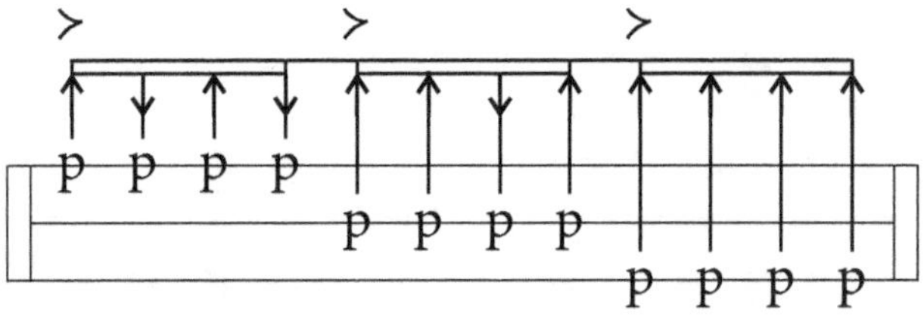

VARIATION 16

F1

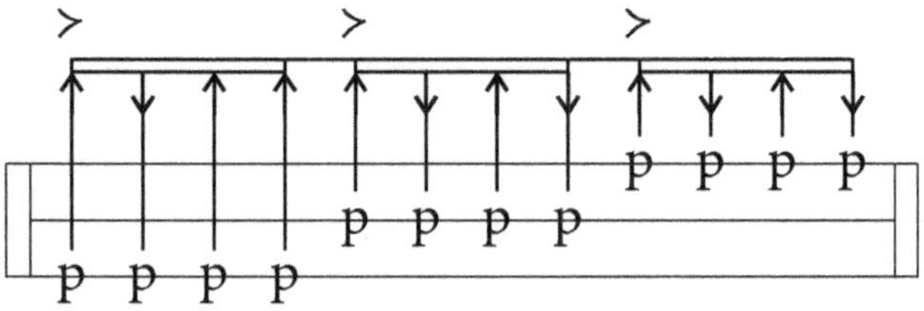

F2

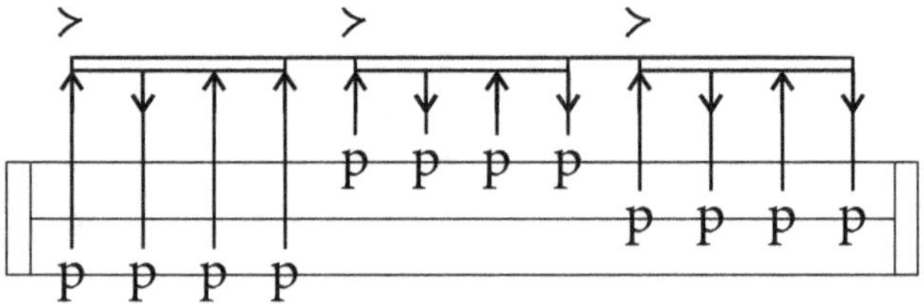

F3

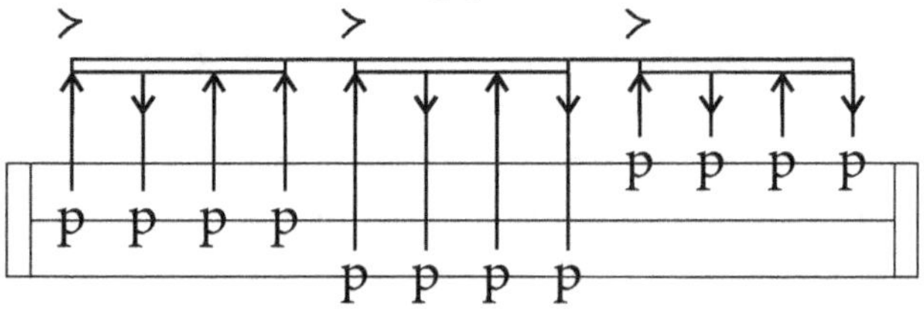

F4

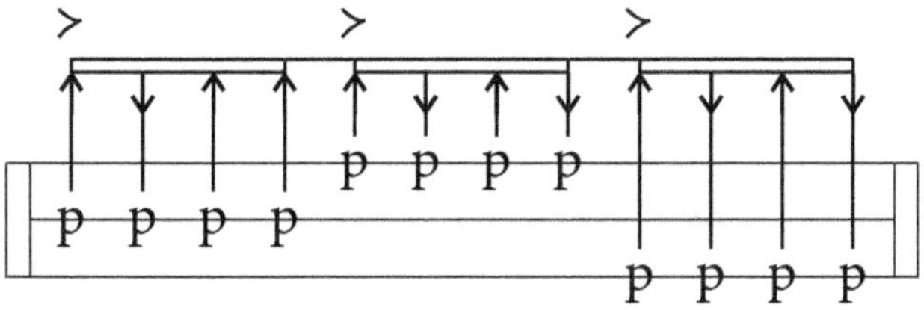

F5

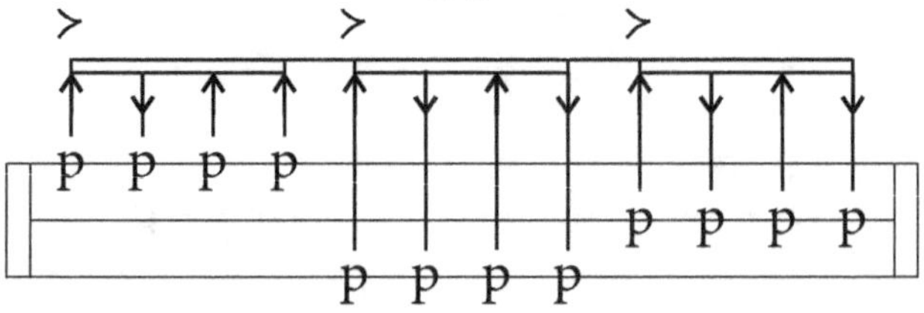

F6

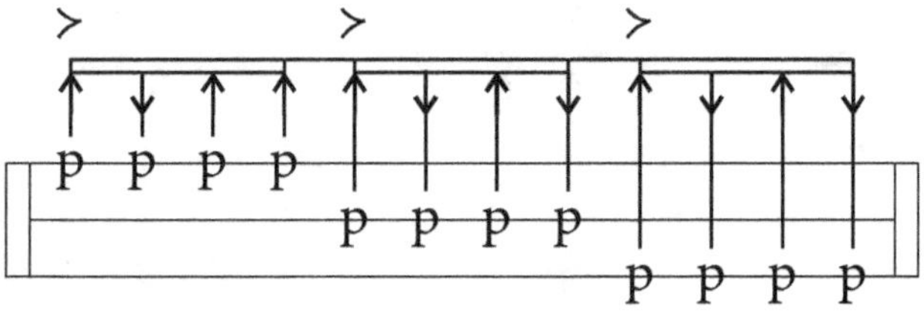

VARIATION 17

F1

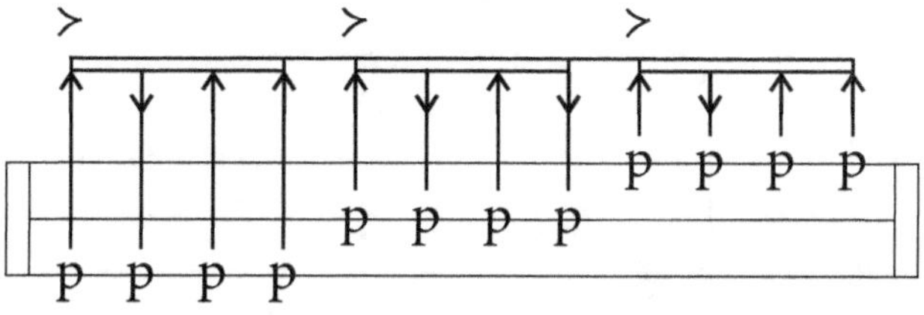

F2

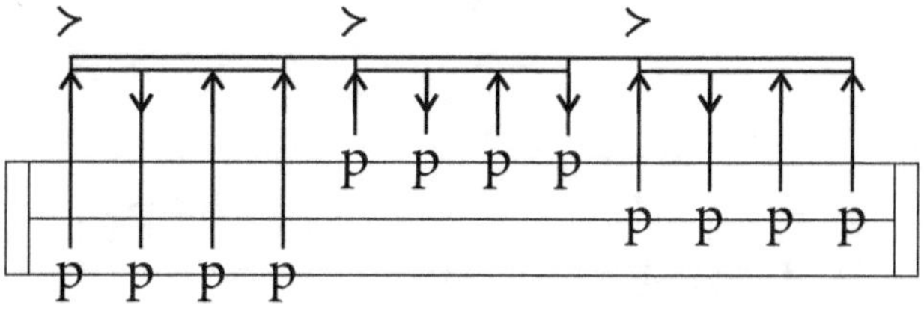

F3

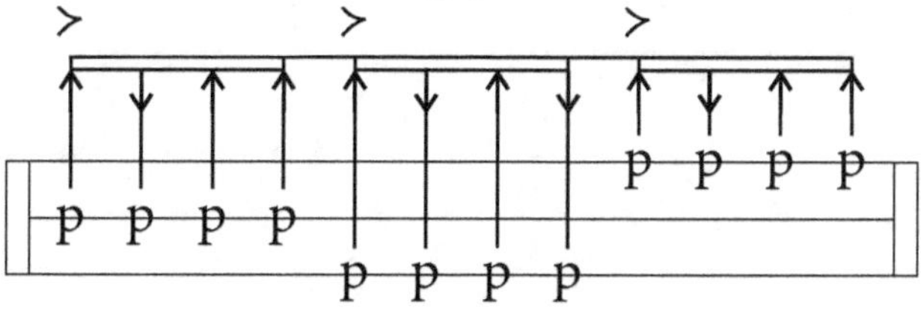

F4

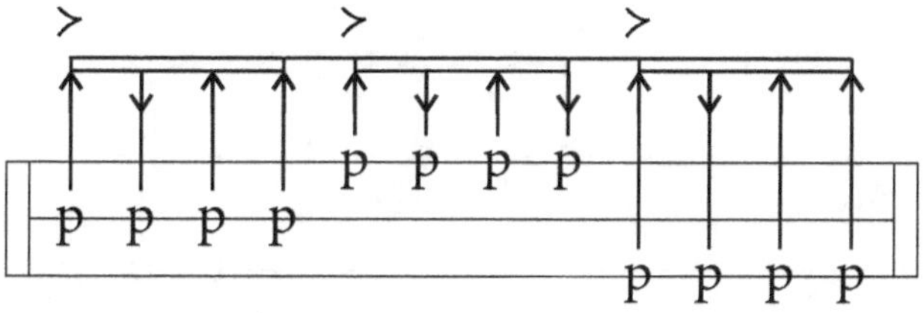

F5

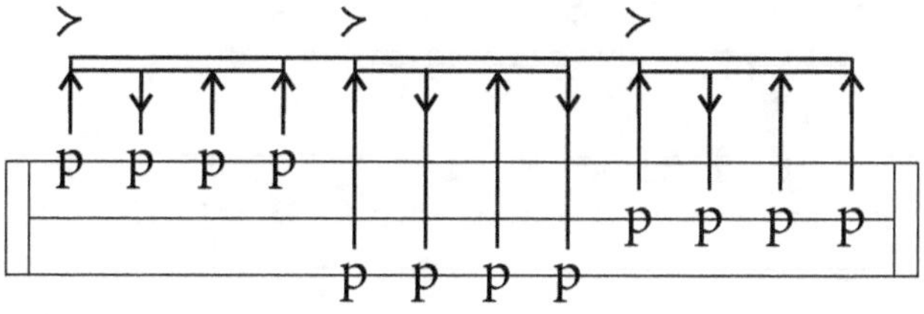

F6

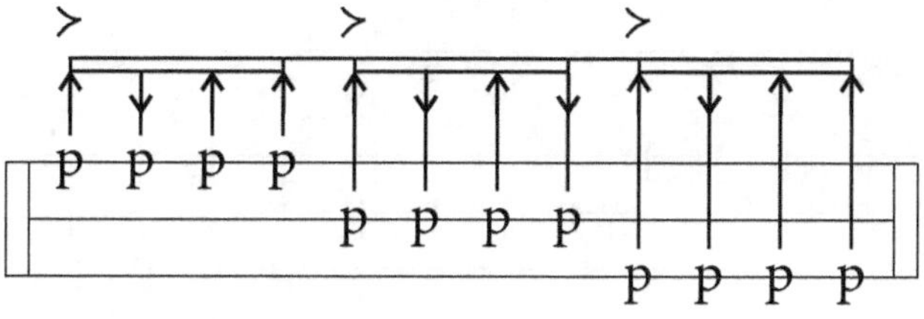

VARIATION 18

F1

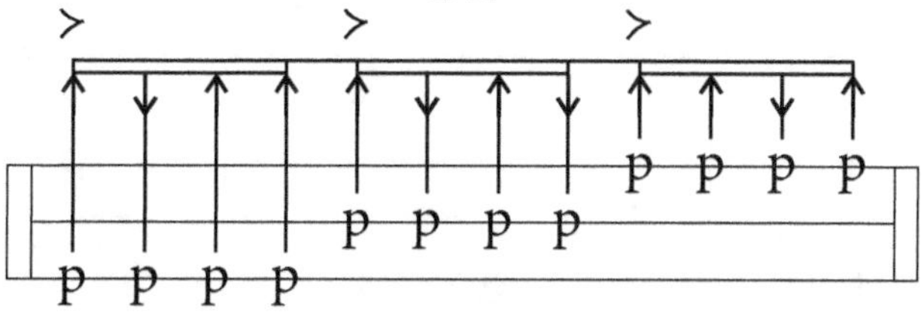

F2

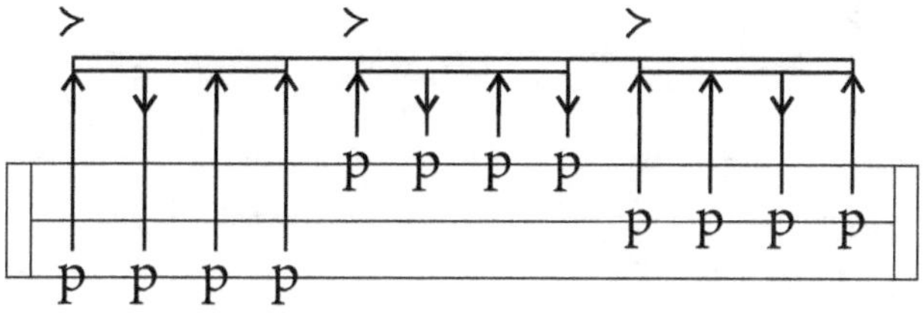

F3

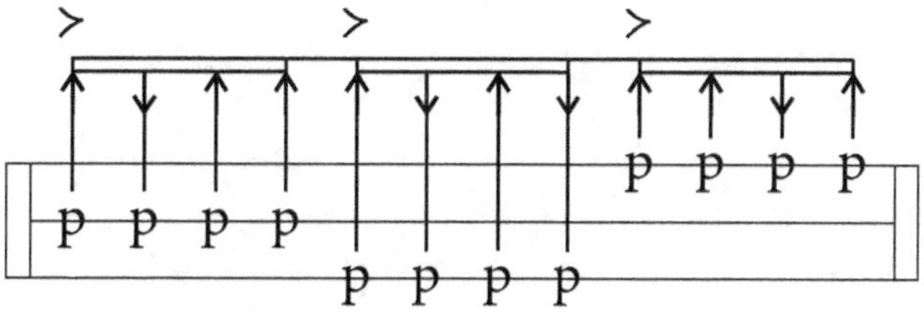

F4

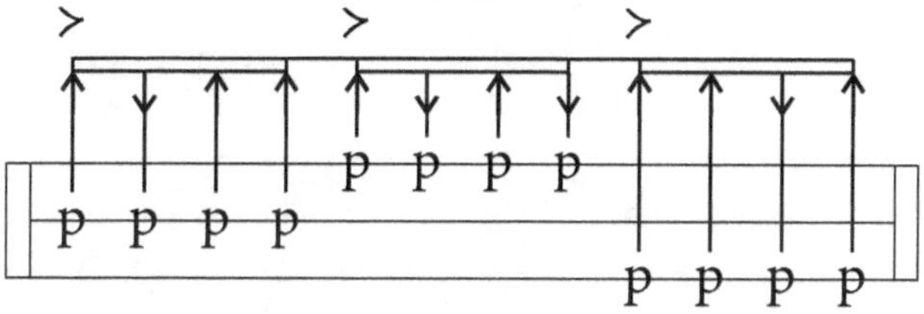

F5

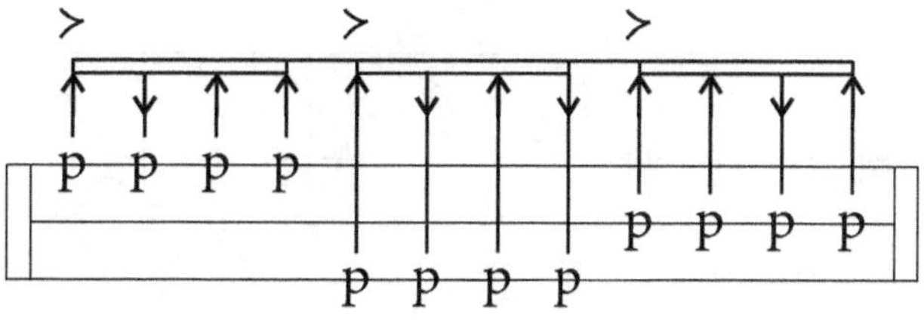

F6

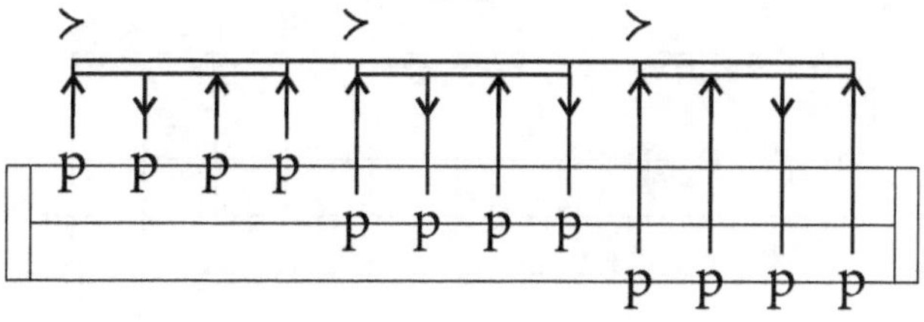

VARIATION 19

F1
F2
F3
F4
F5
F6

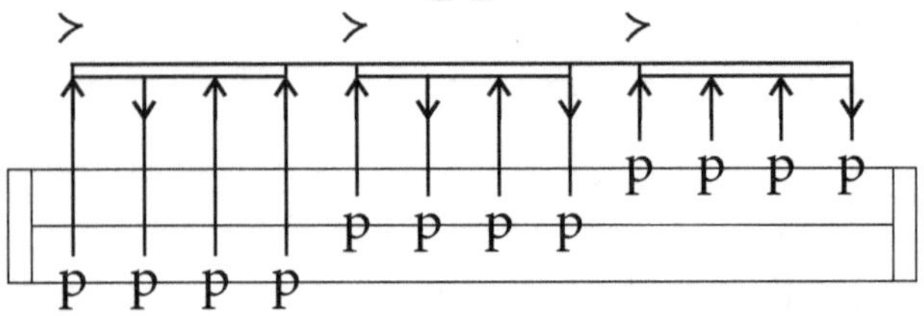

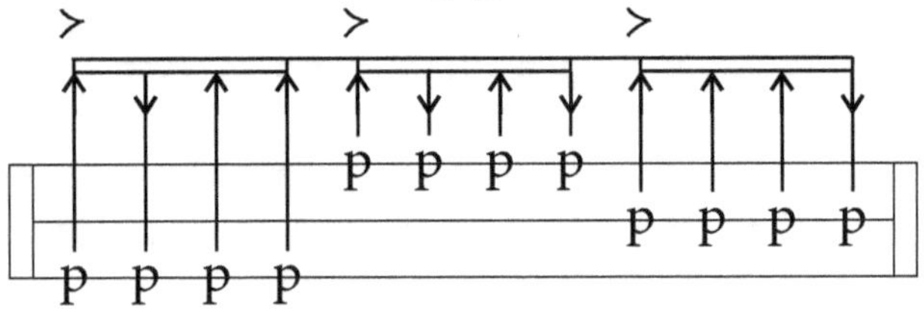

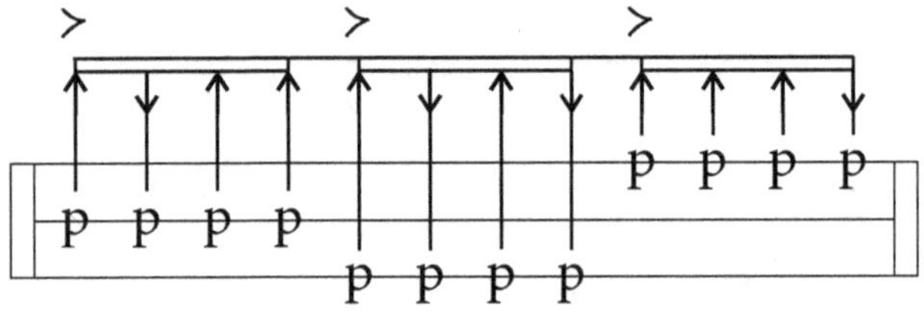

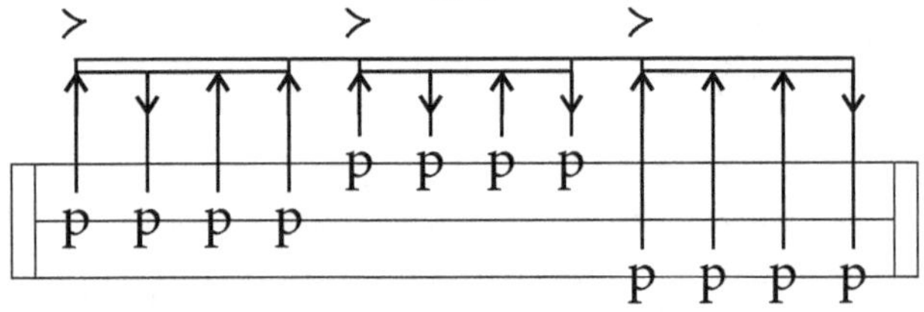

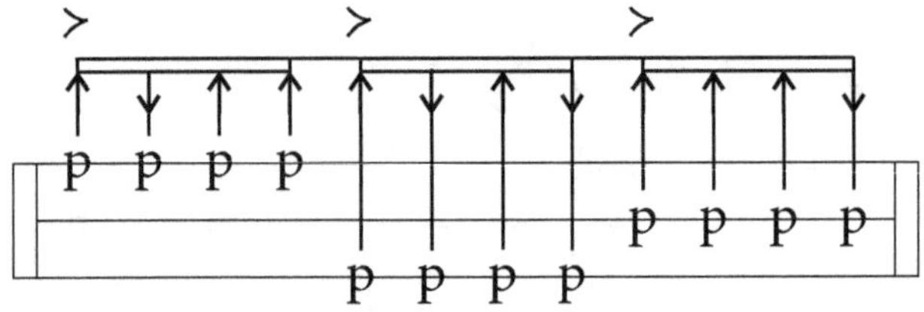

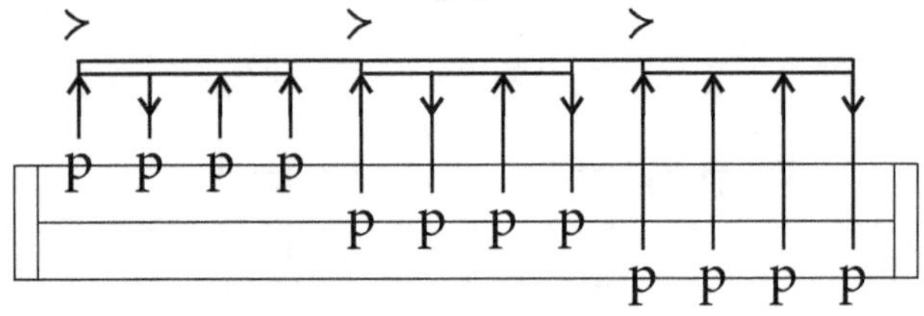

VARIATION 20

F1
F2
F3
F4
F5
F6

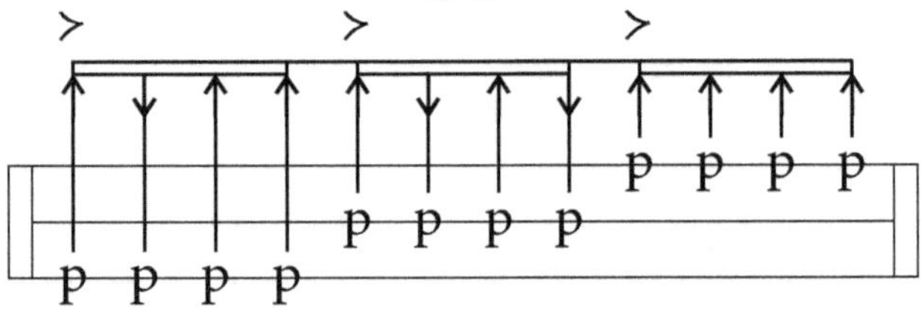

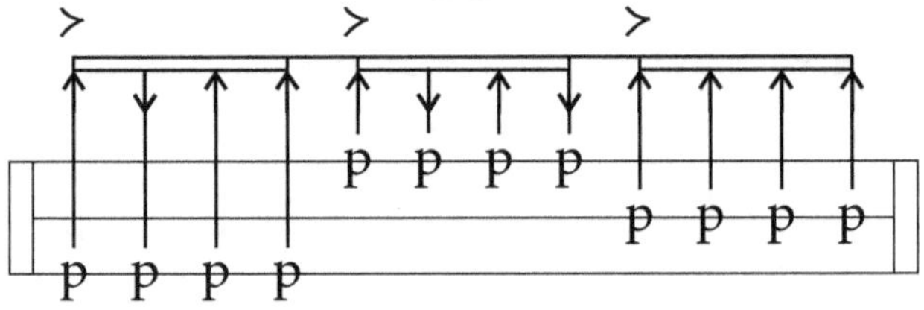

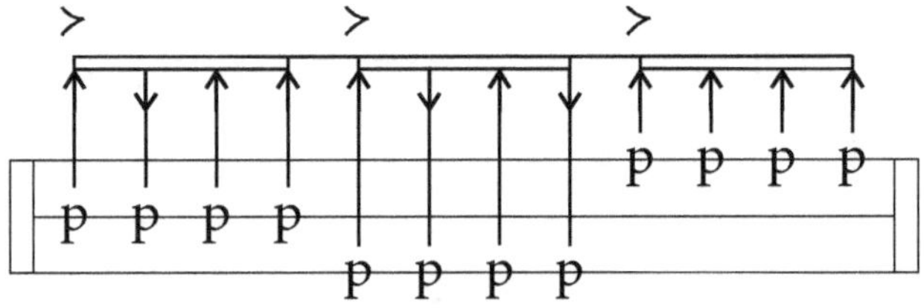

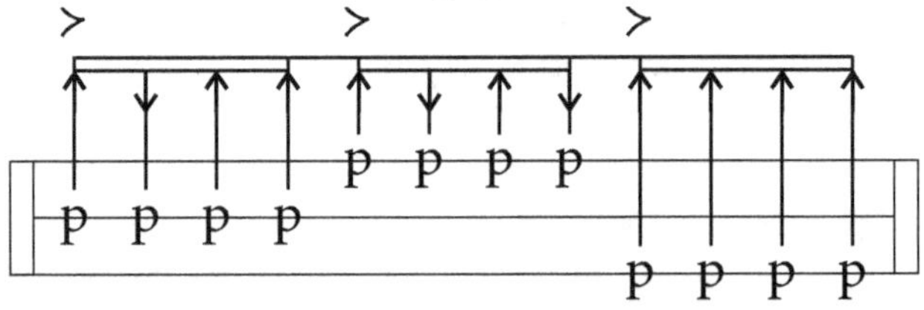

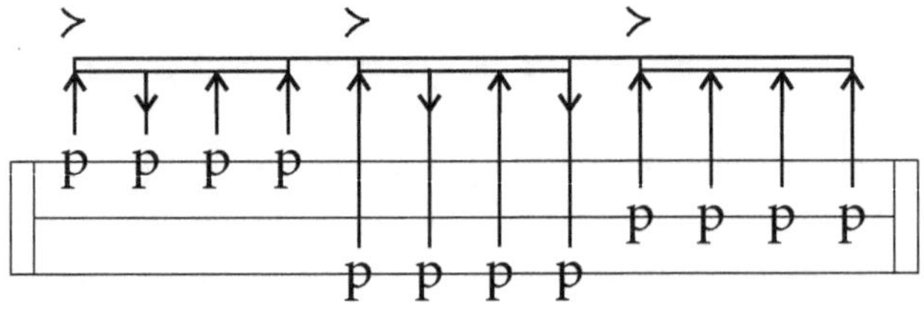

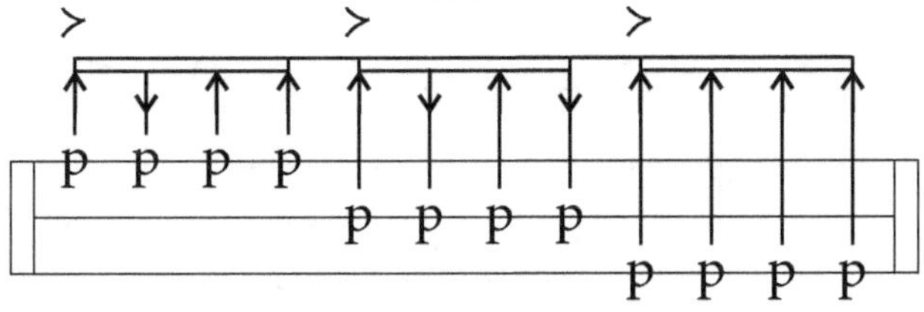

VARIATION 21

F1

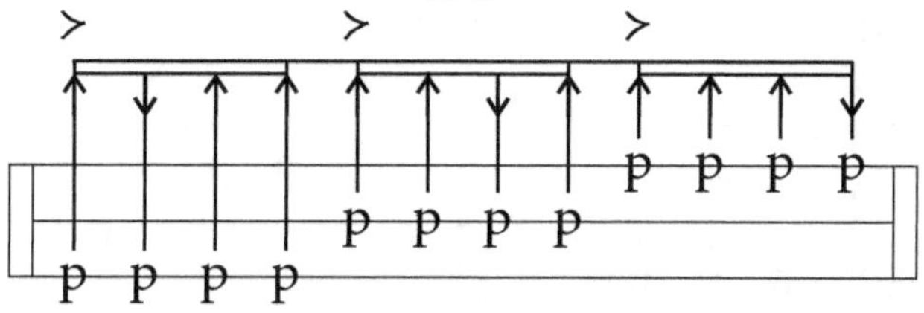

F2

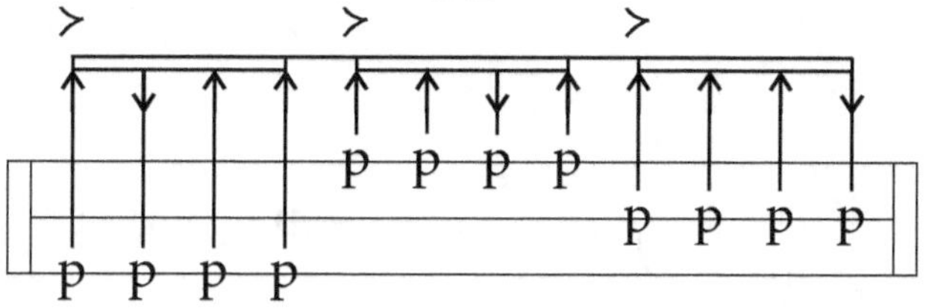

F3

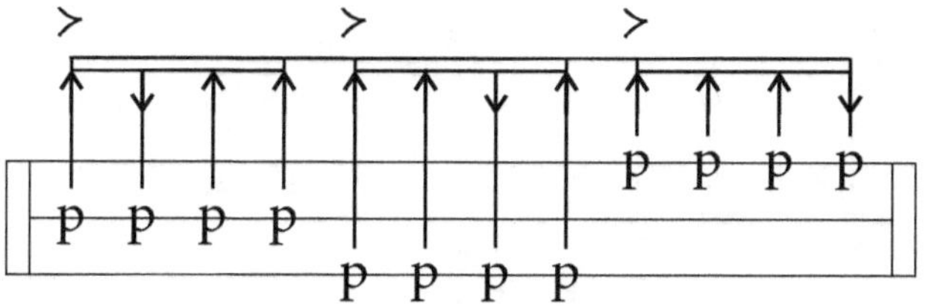

F4

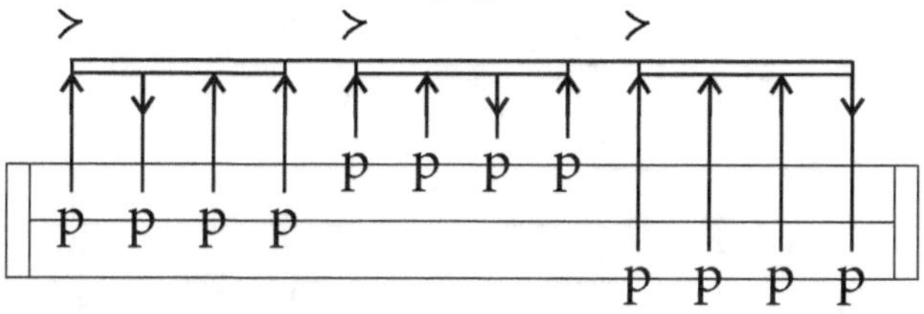

F5

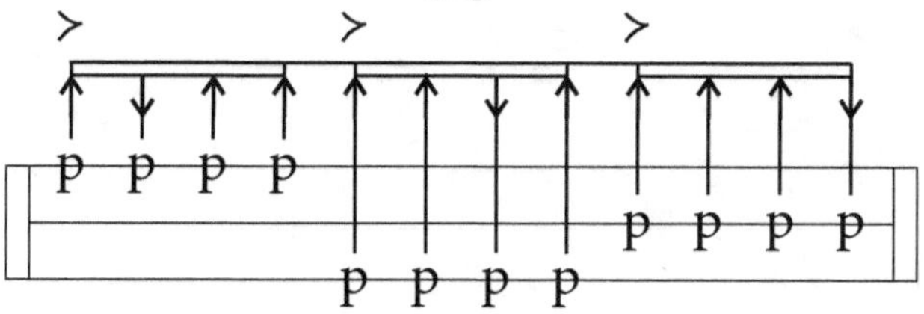

F6

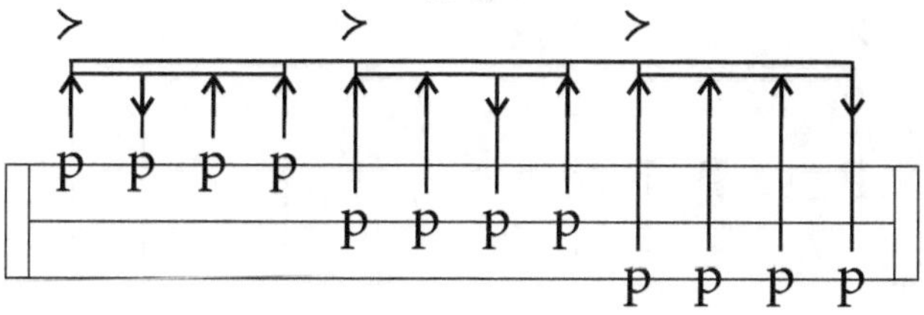

VARIATION 22

F1

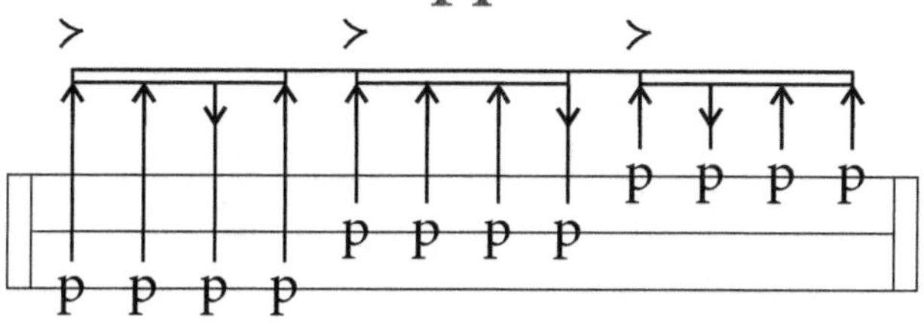

F2

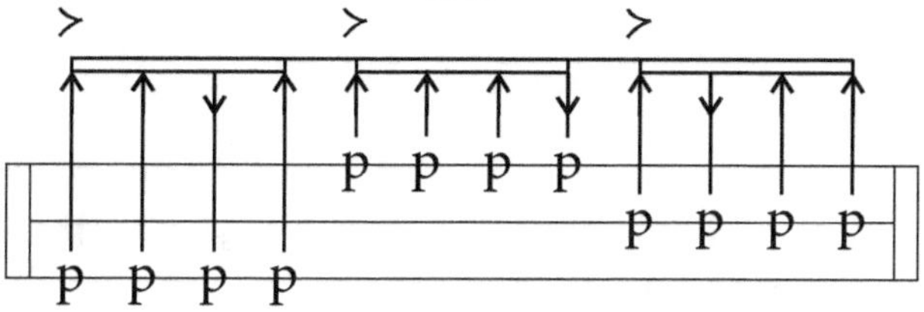

F3

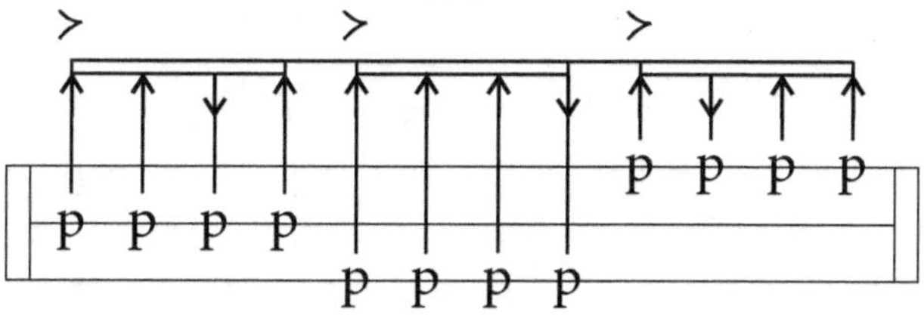

F4

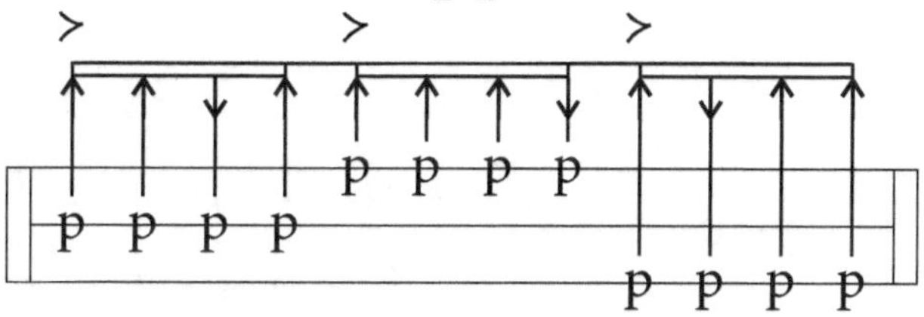

F5

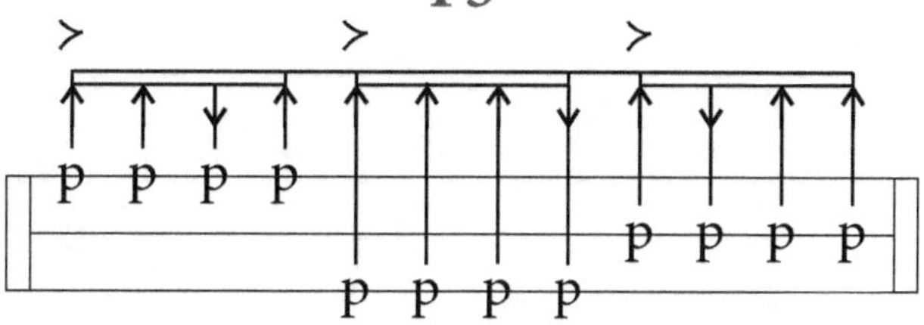

F6

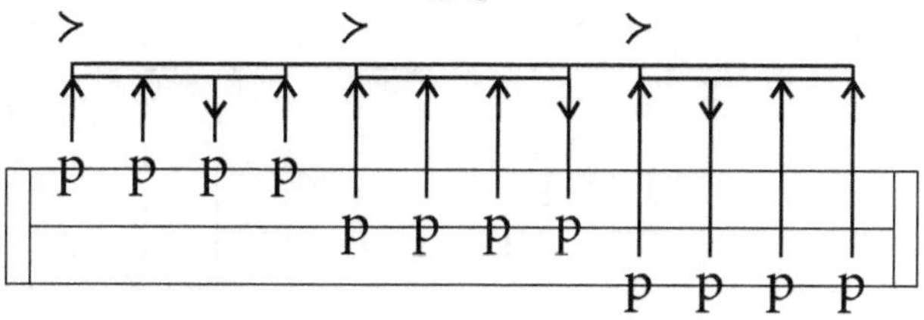

VARIATION 23

F1
F2
F3
F4
F5
F6

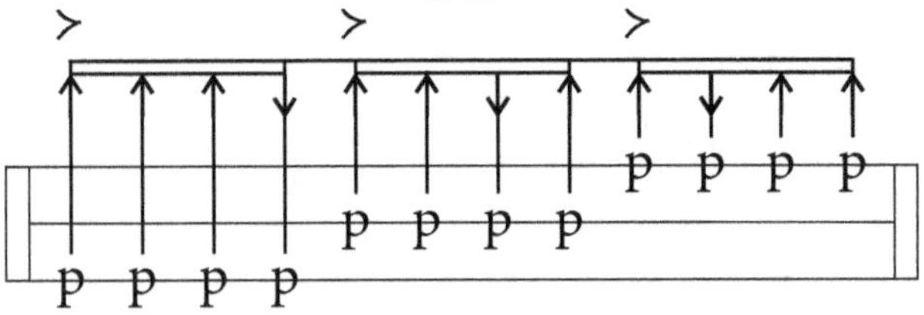

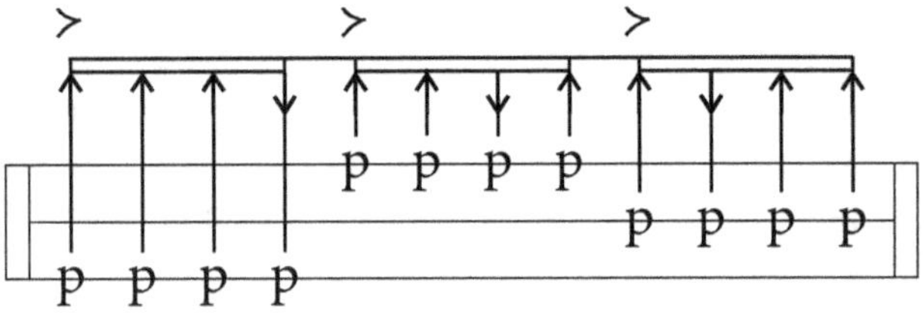

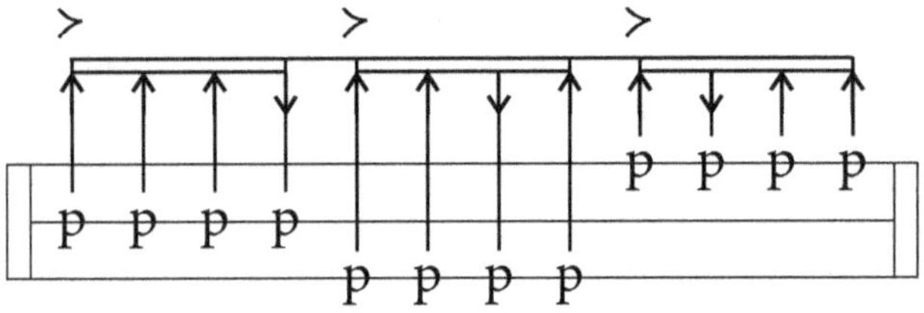

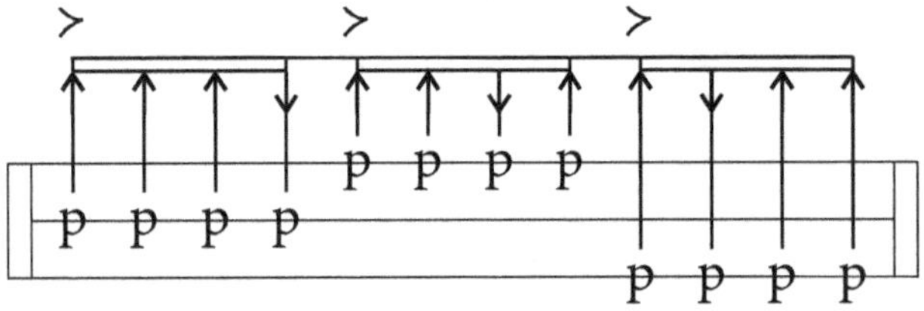

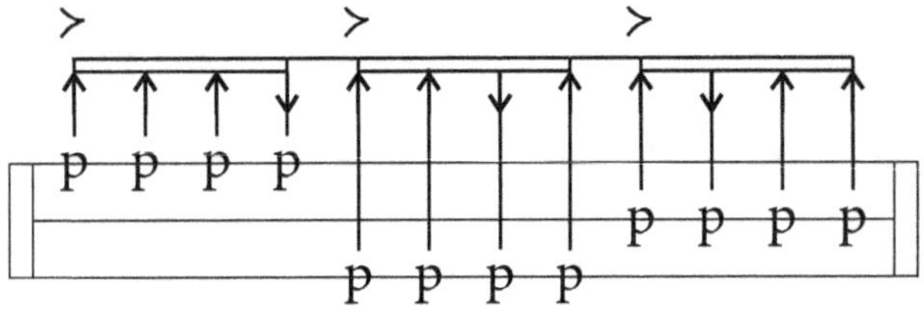

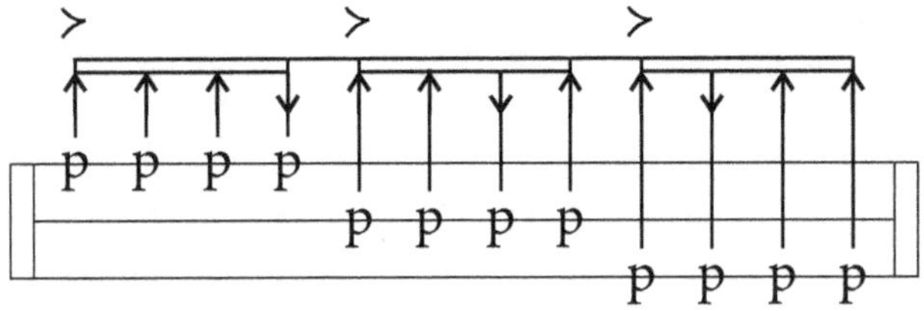

VARIATION 24

F1
F2
F3
F4
F5
F6

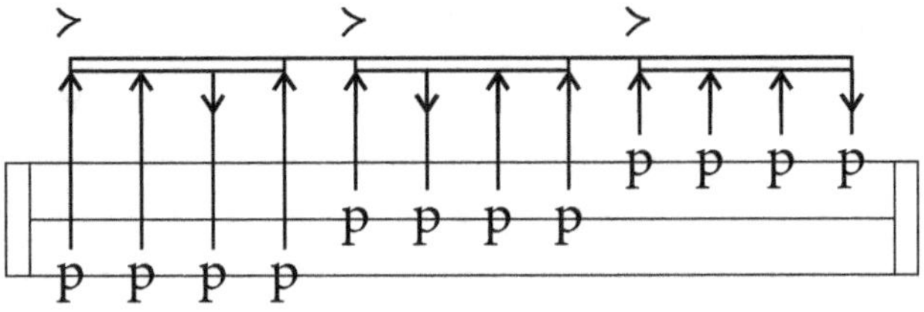

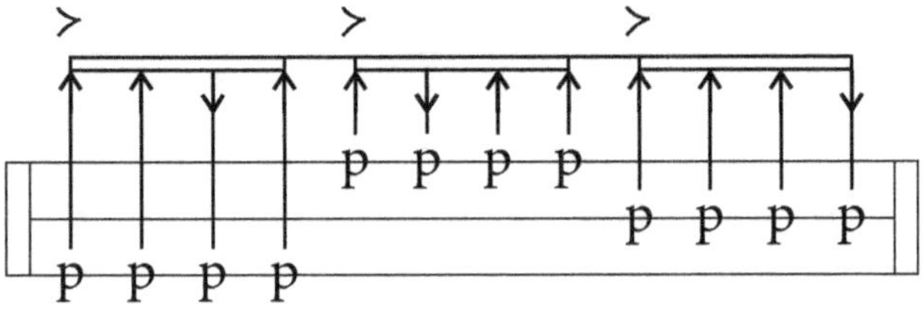

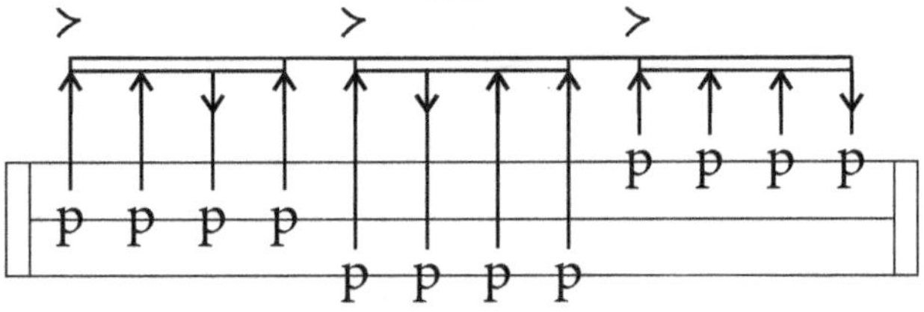

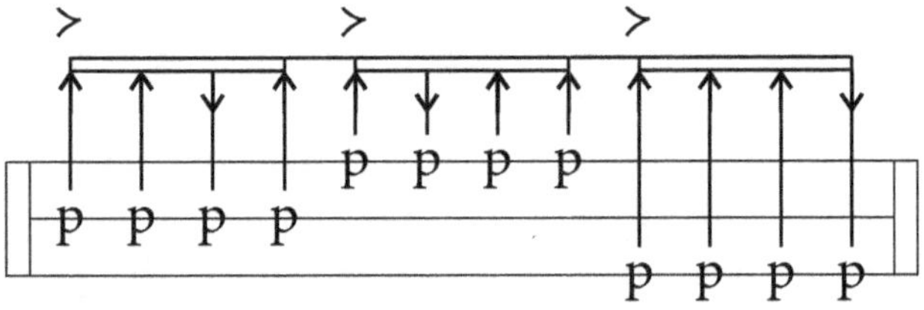

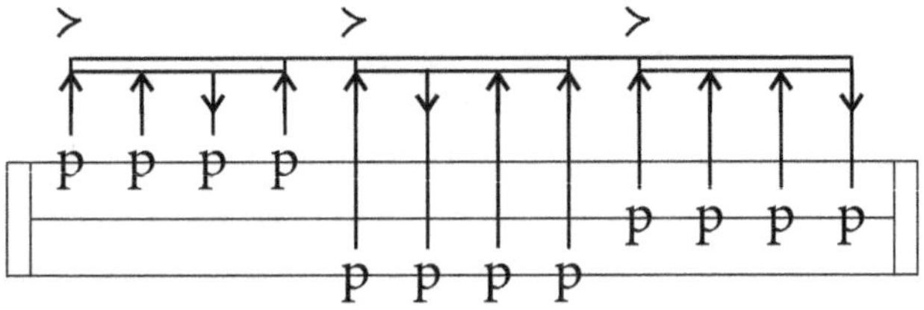

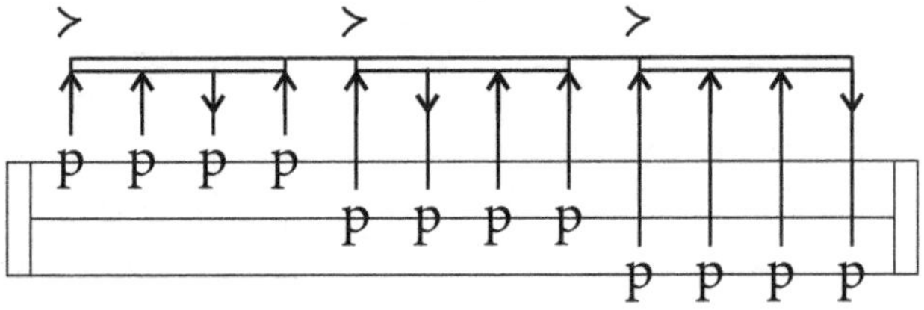

CHAPTER 2

SINGLE - DOUBLE - TRIPLE AND QUAD PULGAR STROKE
ON THREE ADJACENT STRINGS
IN VARIOUS STROKE COMBINATIONS AND WITH CHANGES
IN THE DIRECTION OF THE PULGAR STROKE

§ I

Exercise on pulgar on three adjacent strings with single strokes within each Formula. The exercise includes 18 Formulas in total. Isochronous playing on pulgar strokes.

§ II

Exercise on pulgar on three adjacent strings with four double strokes within each Formula. The exercise includes 18 Formulas in total. Isochronous playing on pulgar strokes.

§ I

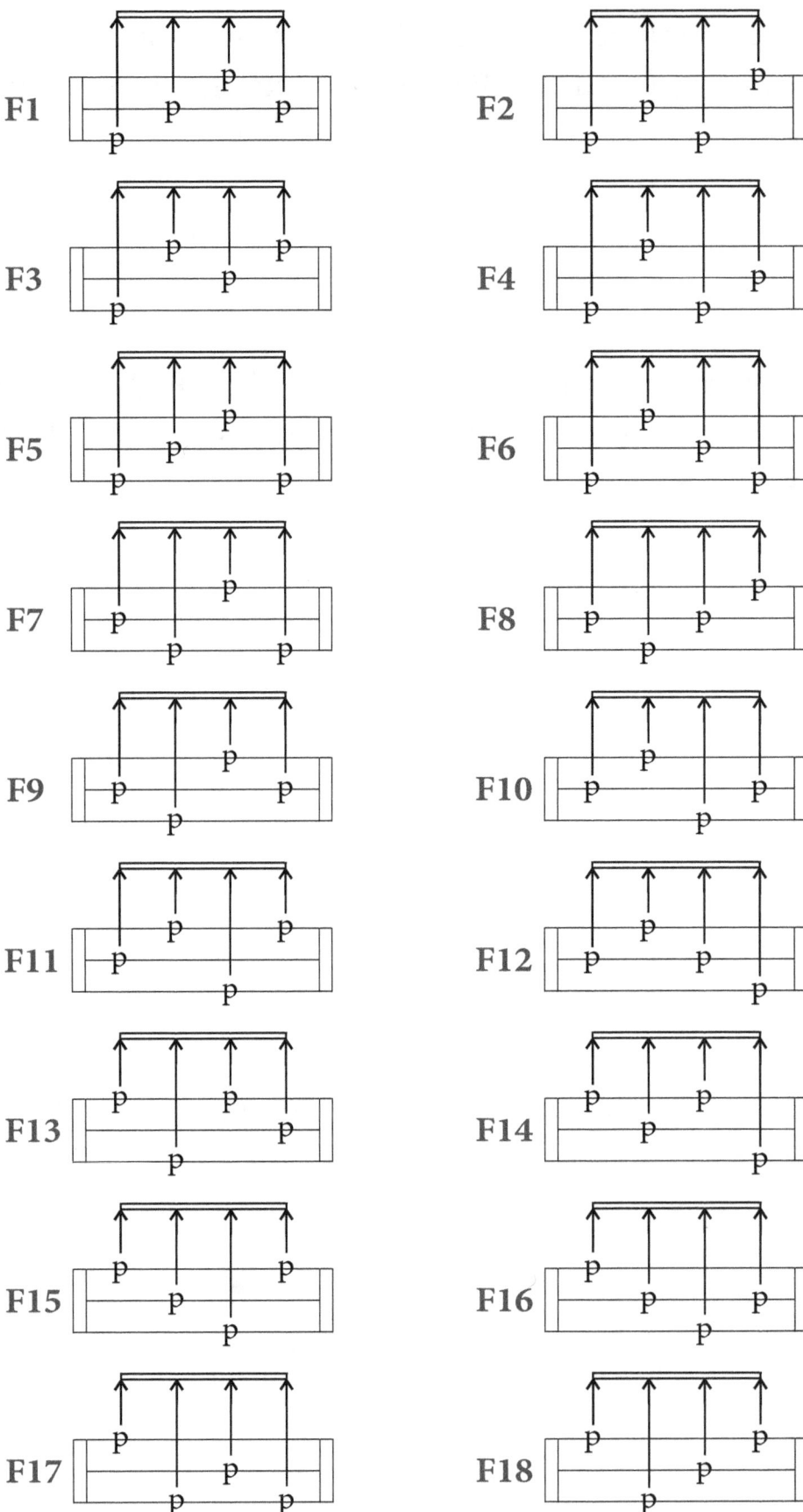

§ II

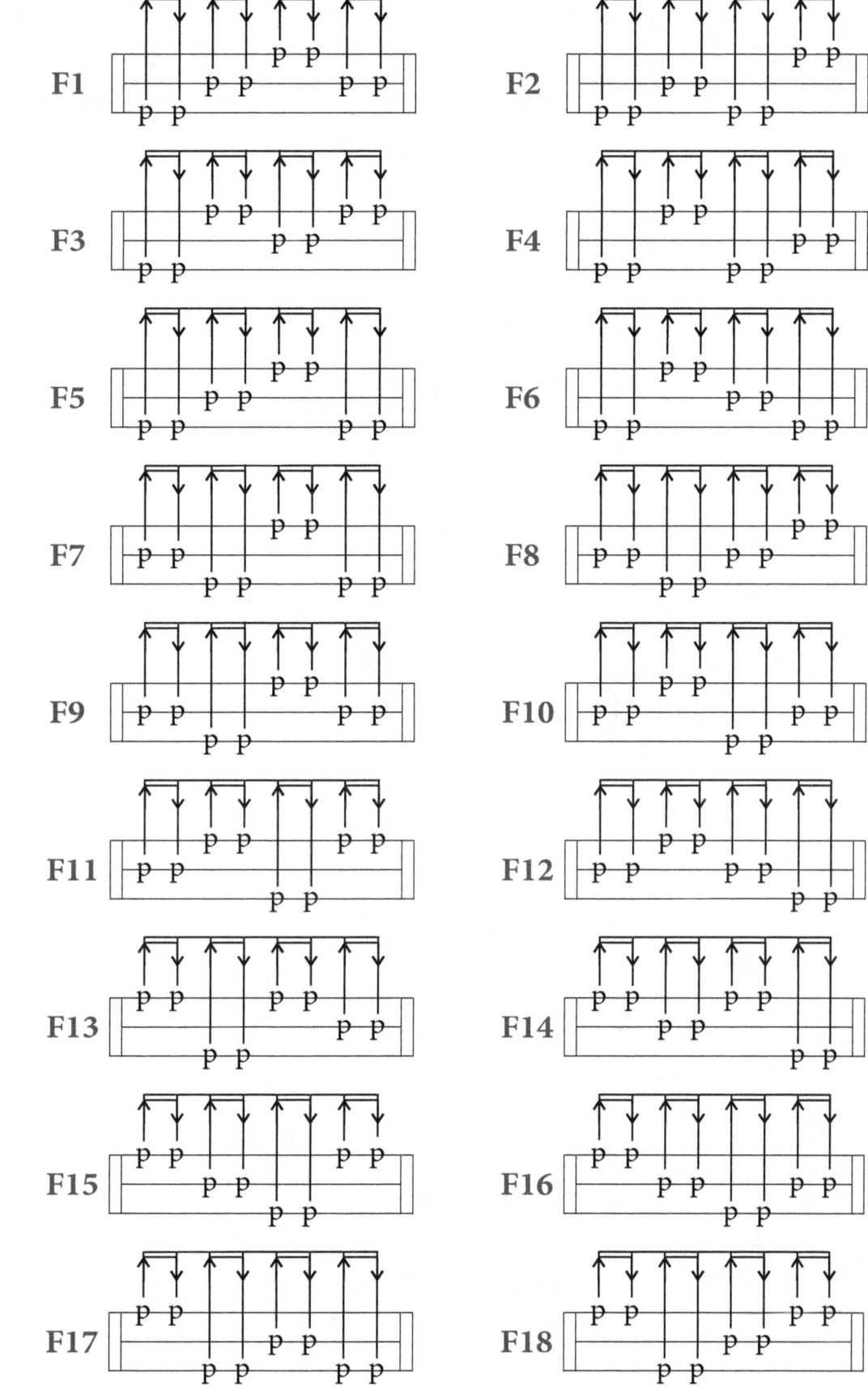

§ III

Exercise on pulgar on three adjacent strings with one double and three single strokes within each Formula. The exercise includes four variations with 18 Formulas in each. The first Formula of each variation is cited below. Isochronous playing of single and double pulgar strokes.

VARIATION I

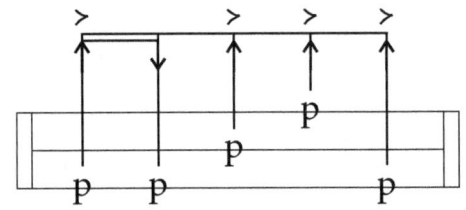

VARIATION II

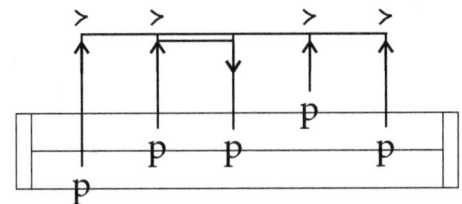

VARIATION III

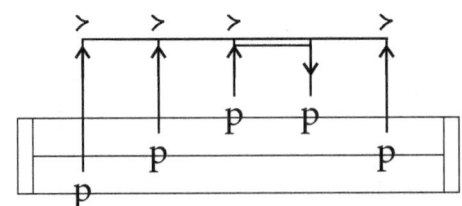

VARIATION IV

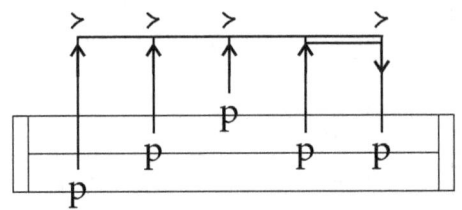

VARIATION I

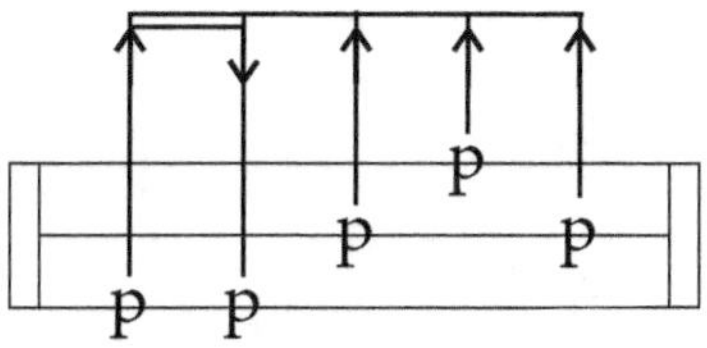

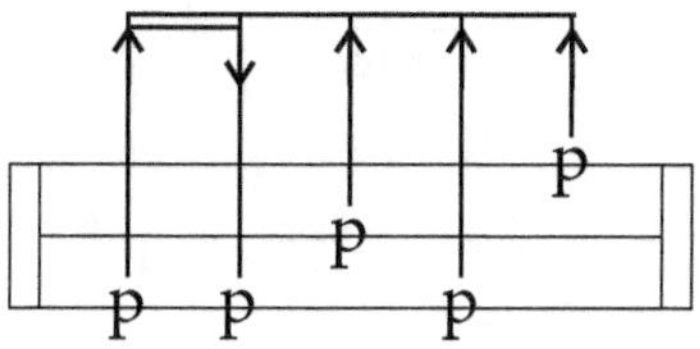

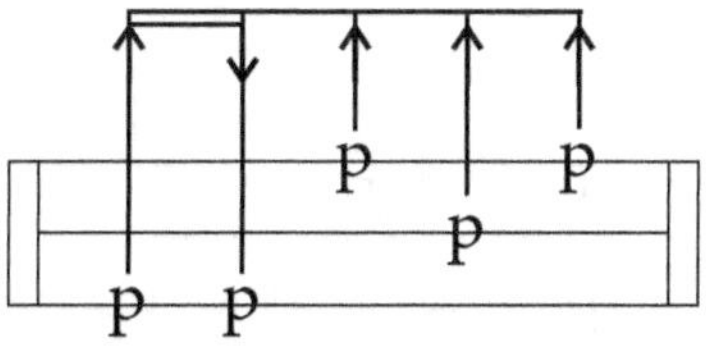

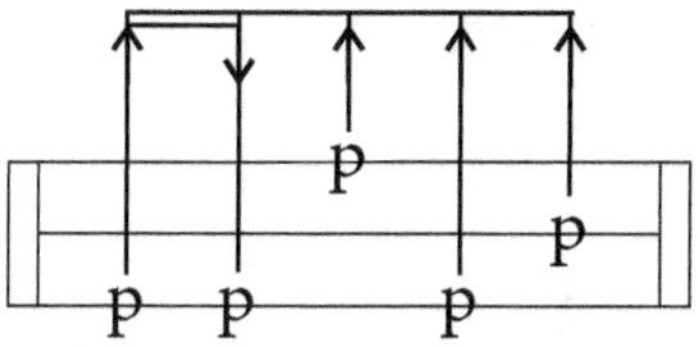

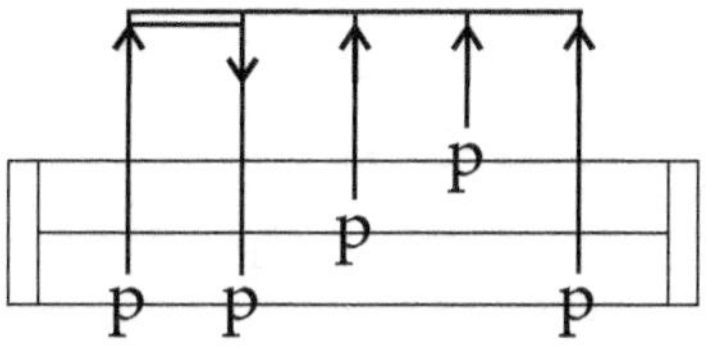

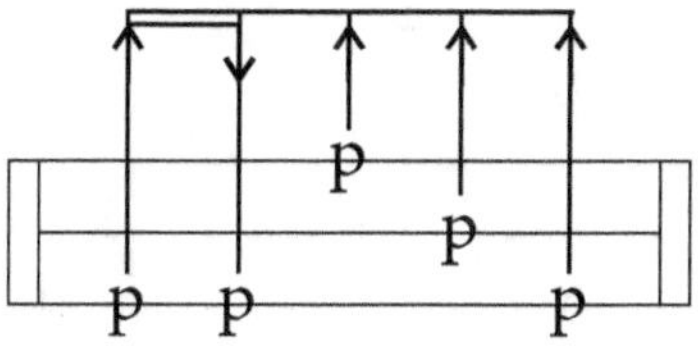

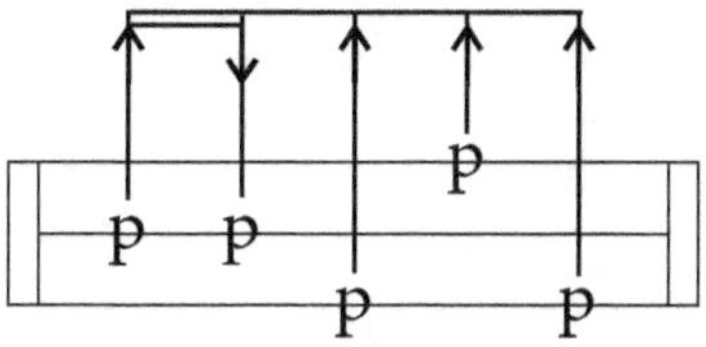

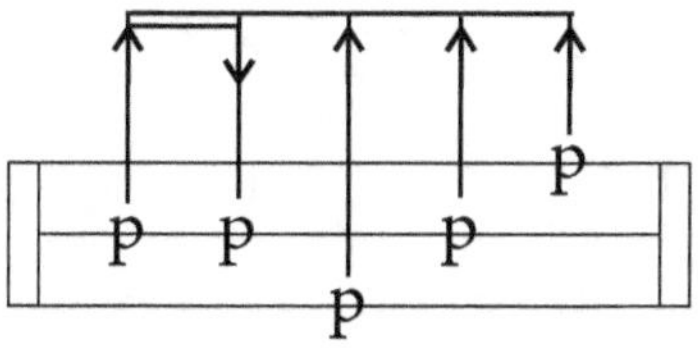

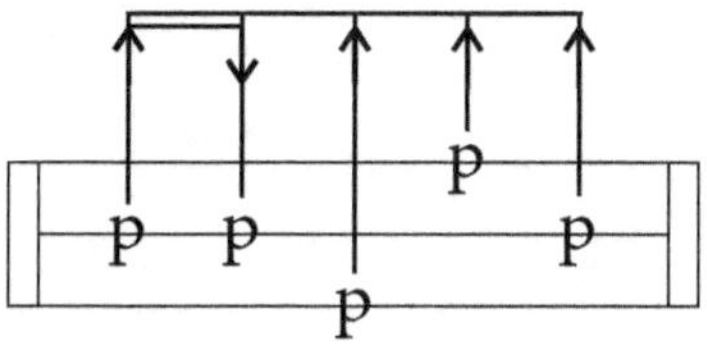

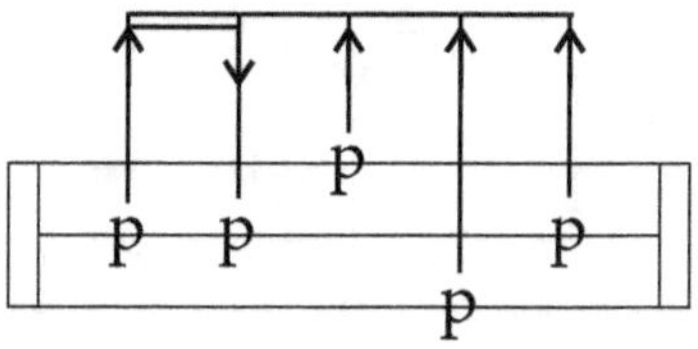

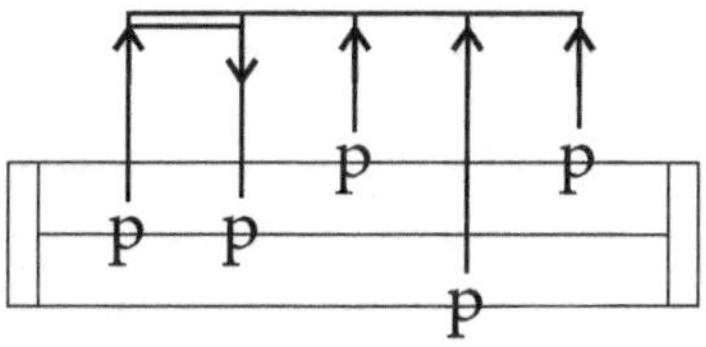

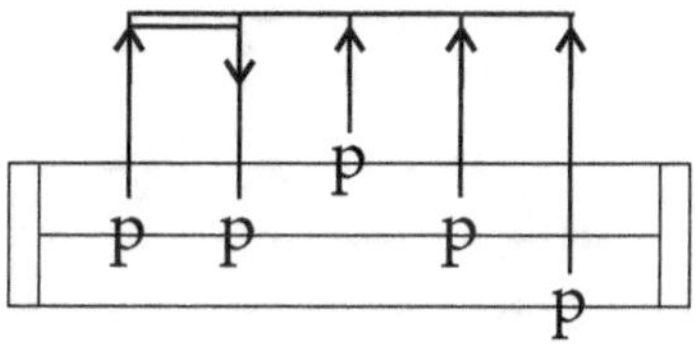

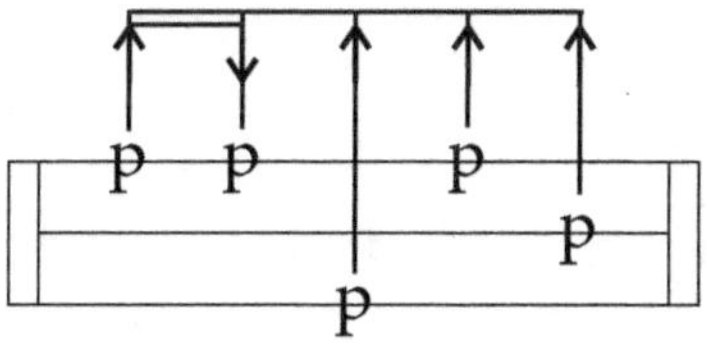

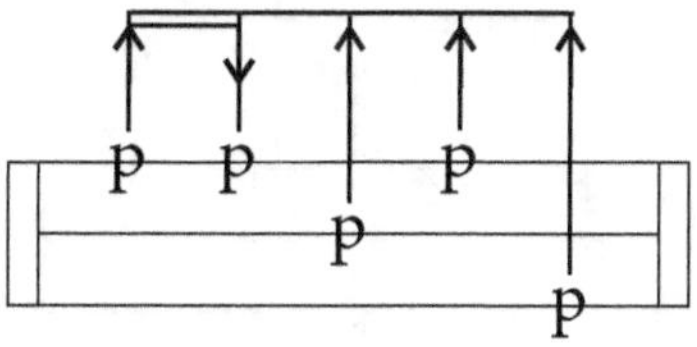

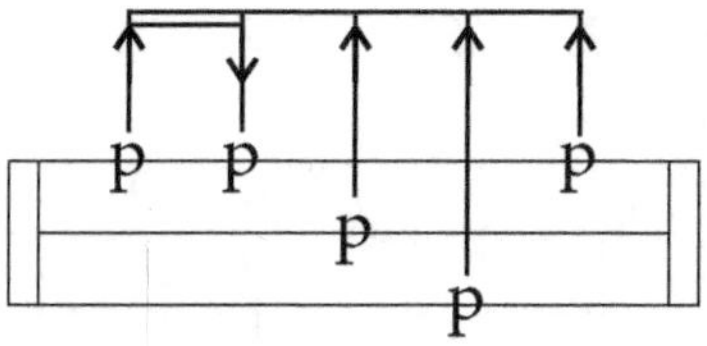

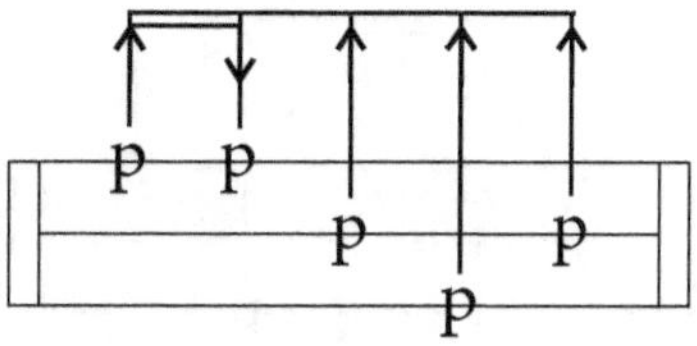

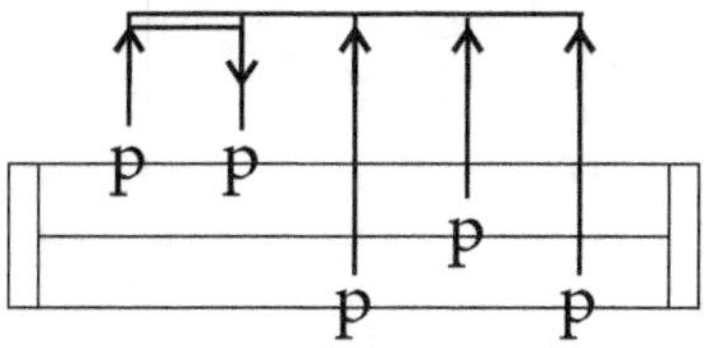

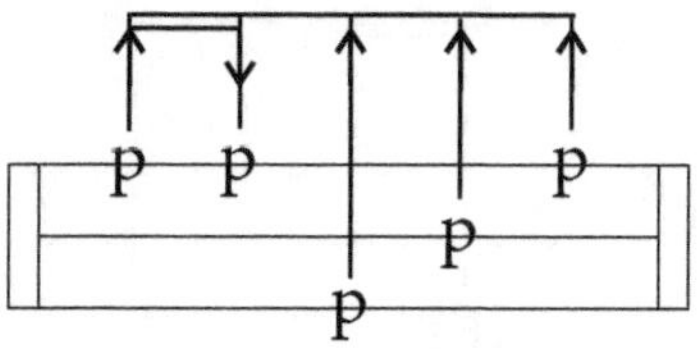

VARIATION II

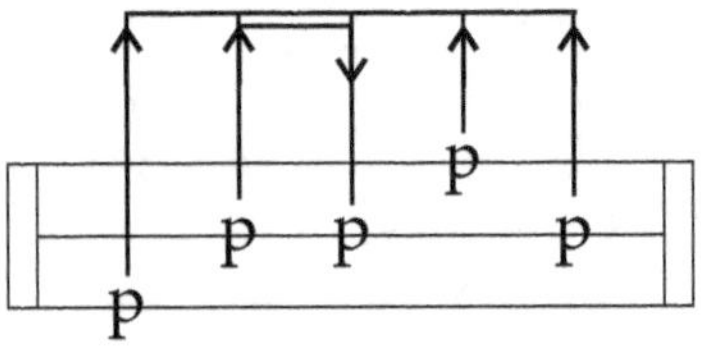

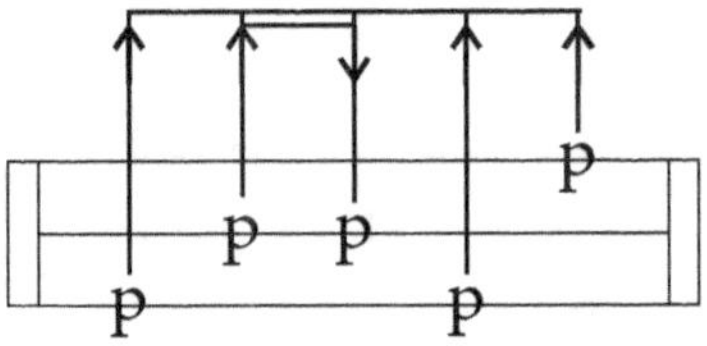

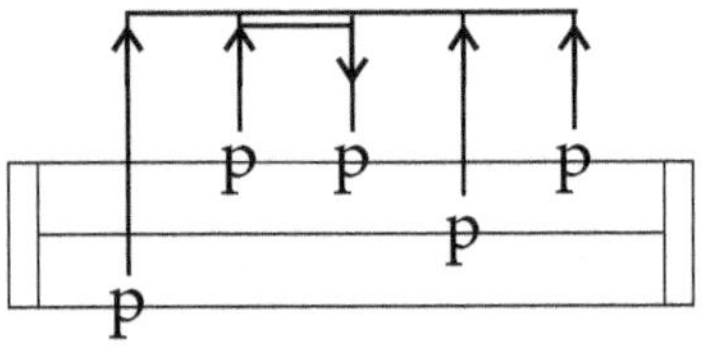

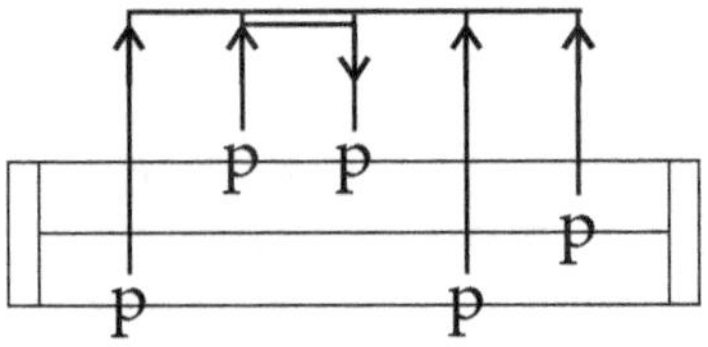

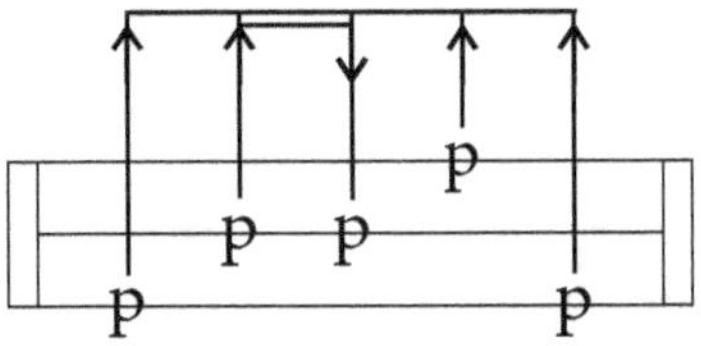

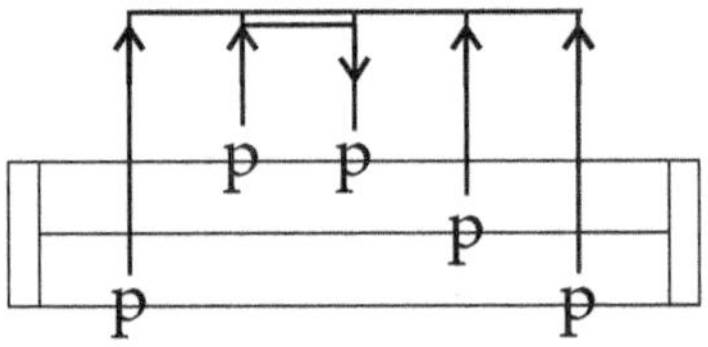

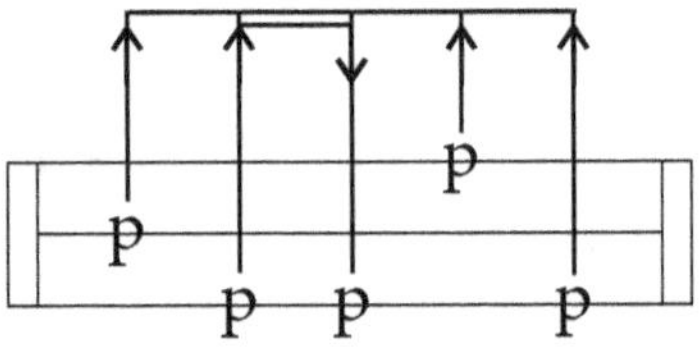

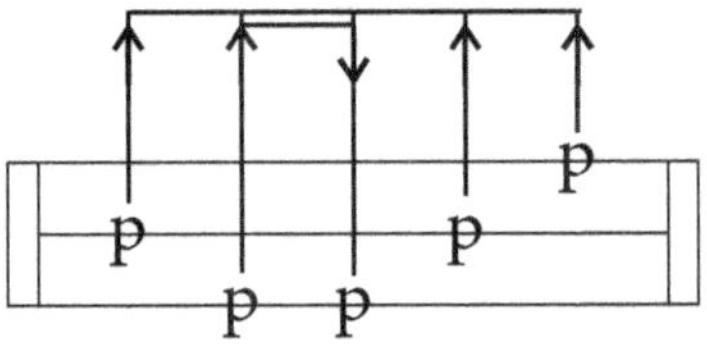

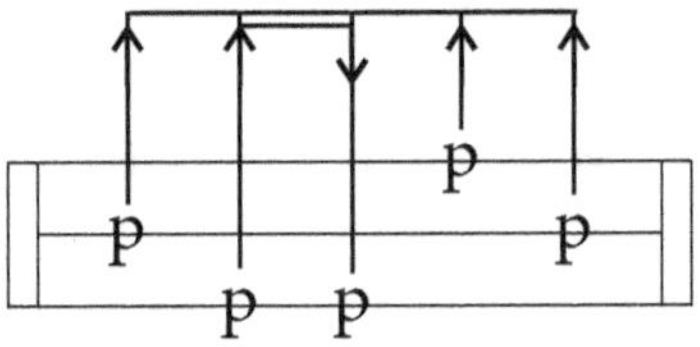

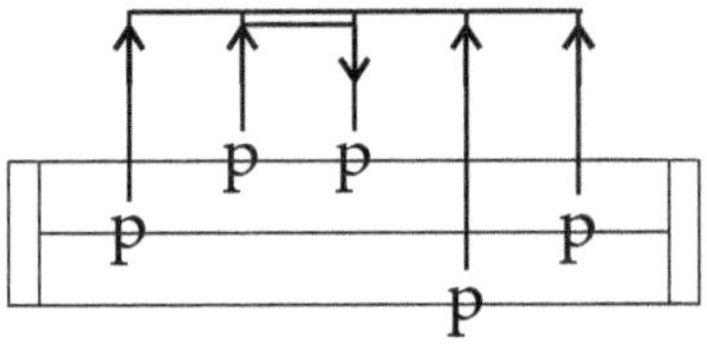

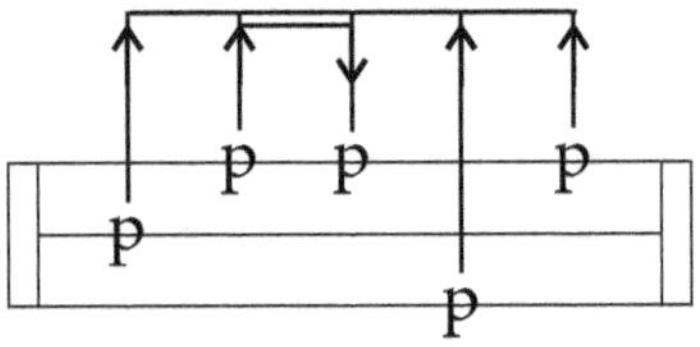

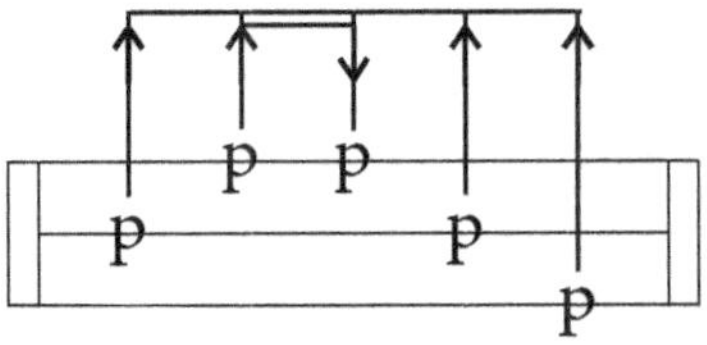

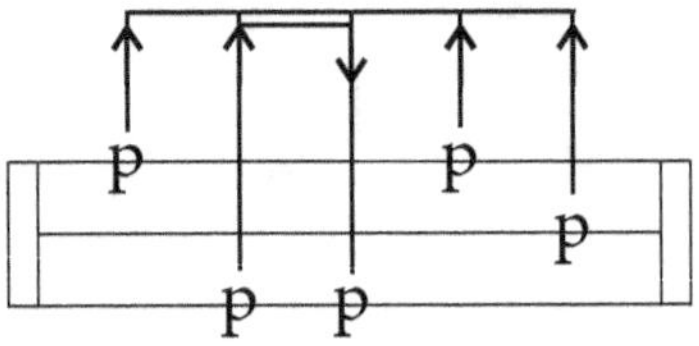

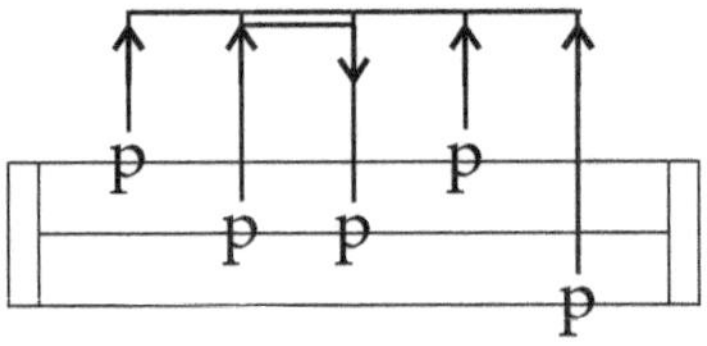

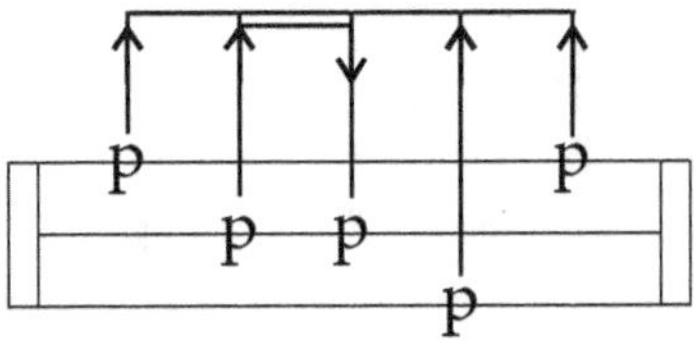

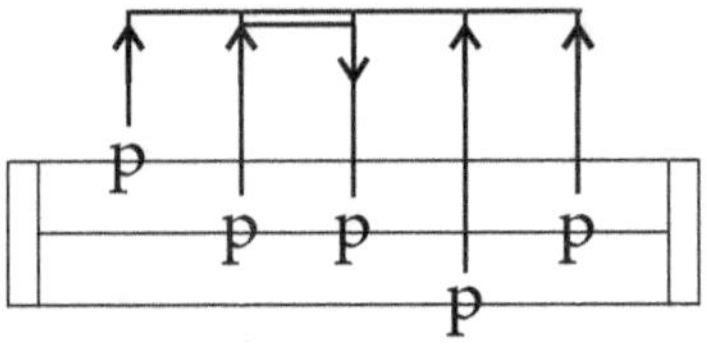

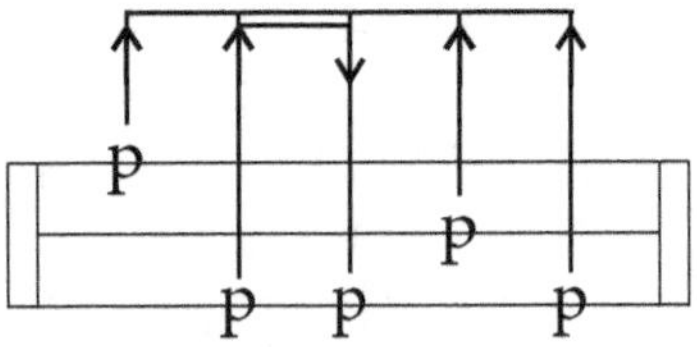

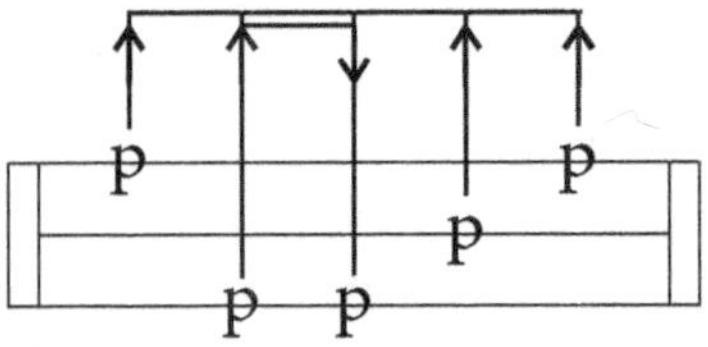

VARIATION III

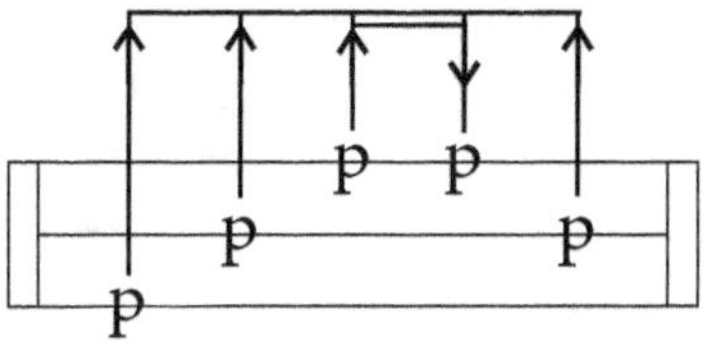

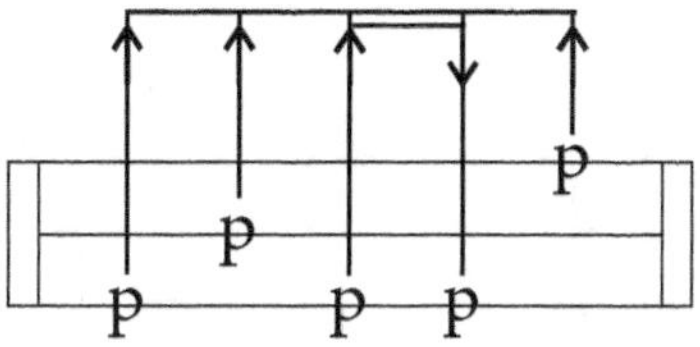

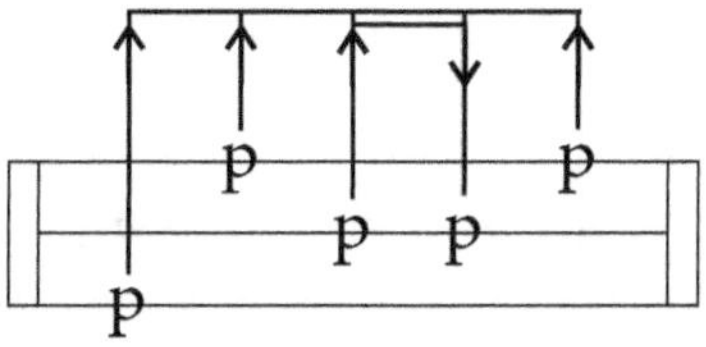

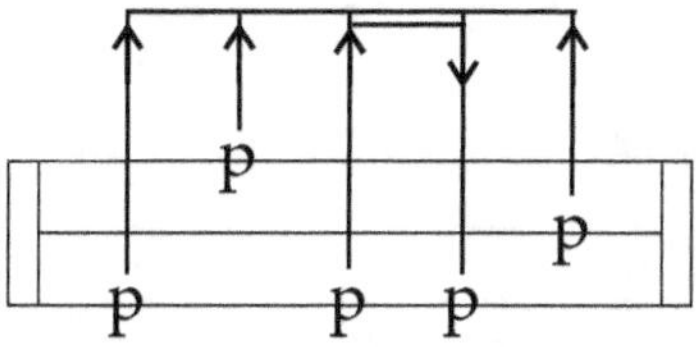

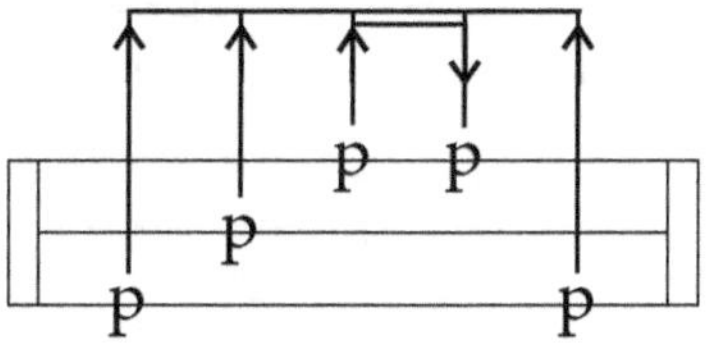

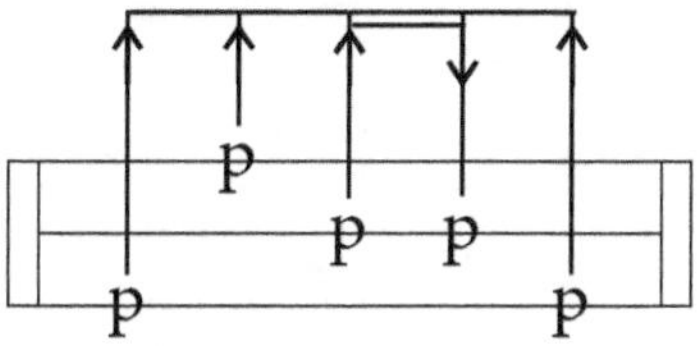

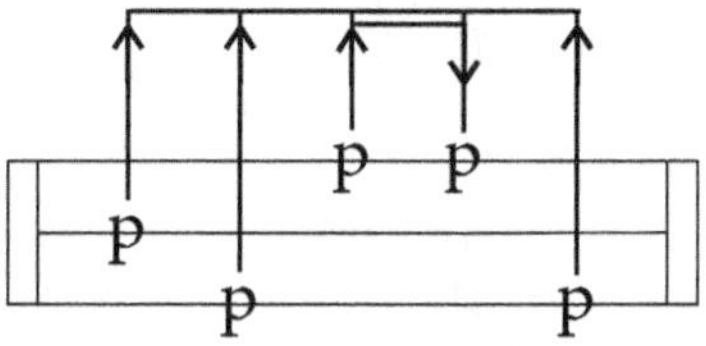

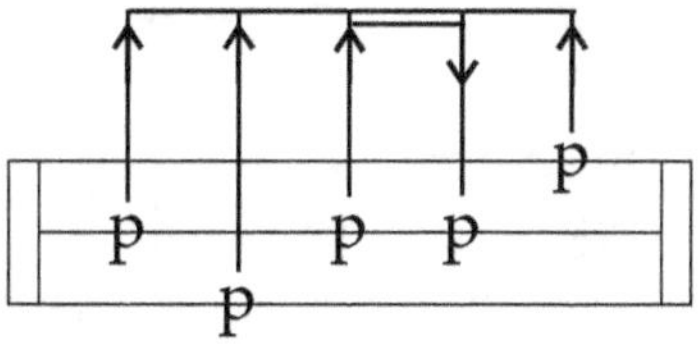

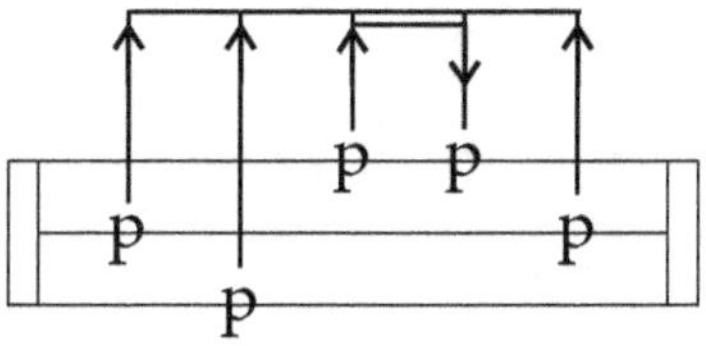

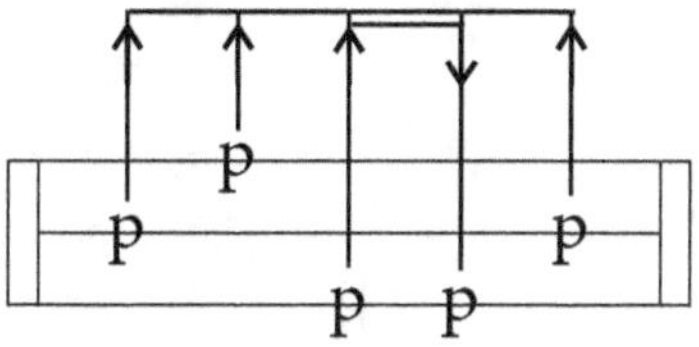

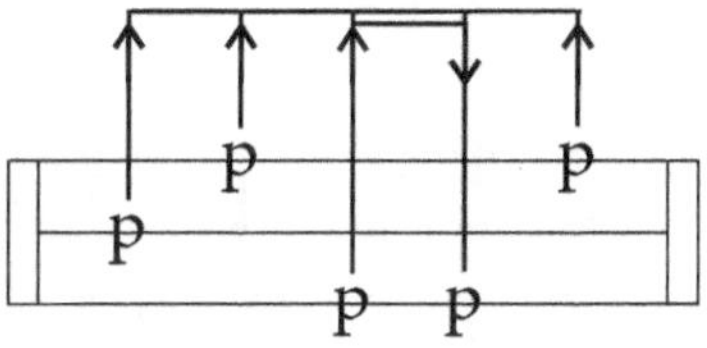

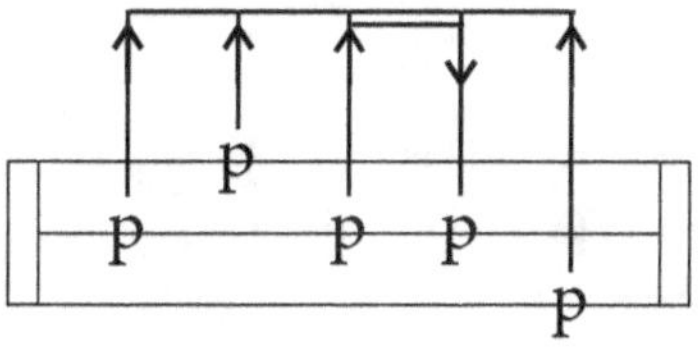

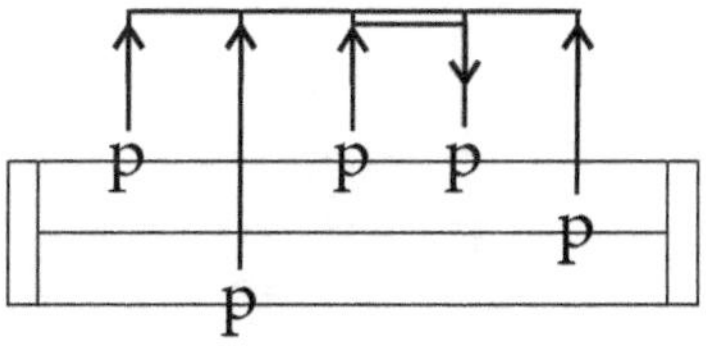

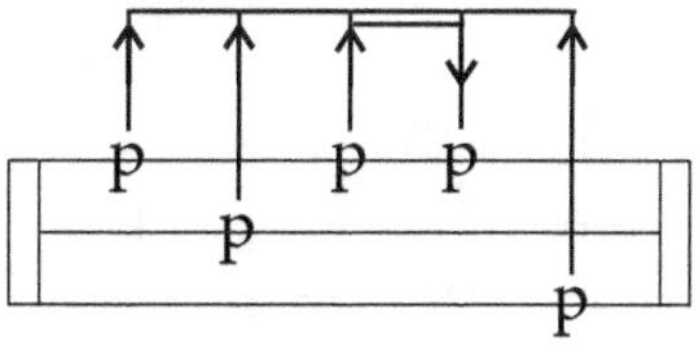

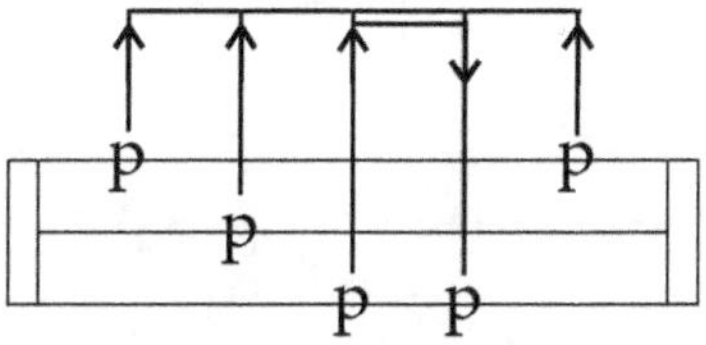

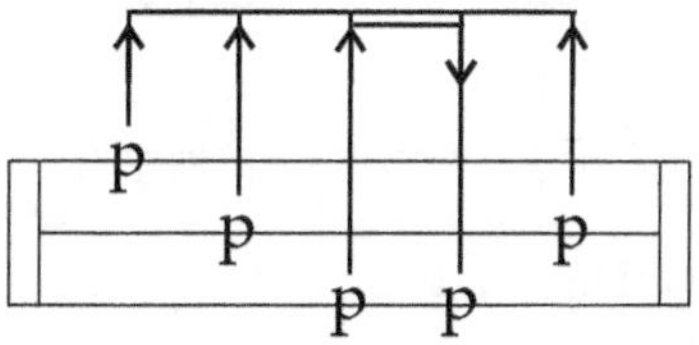

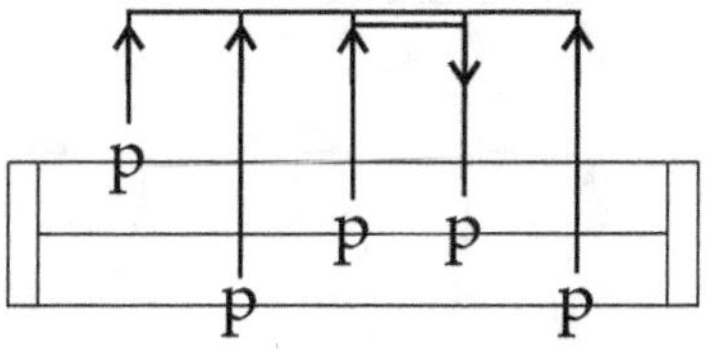

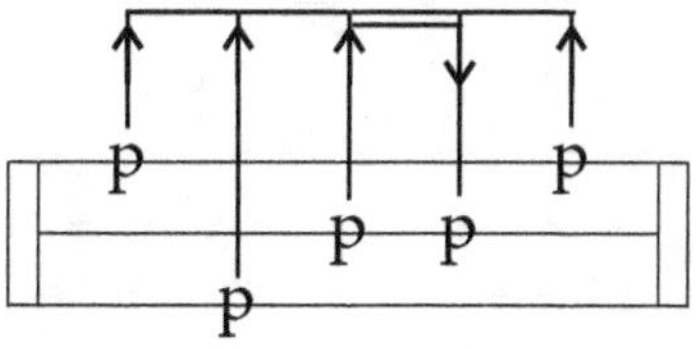

VARIATION IV

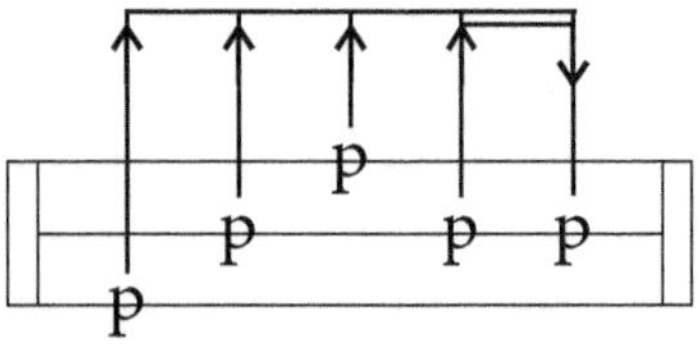

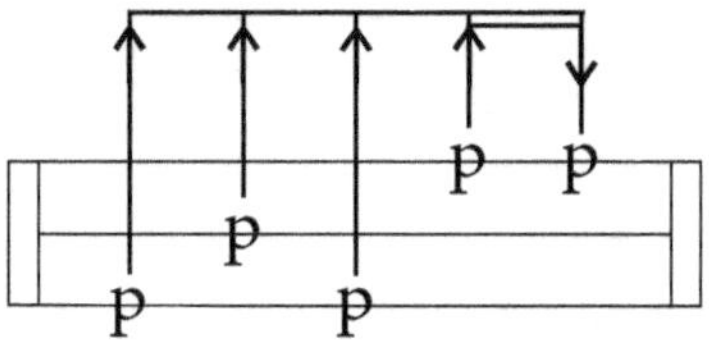

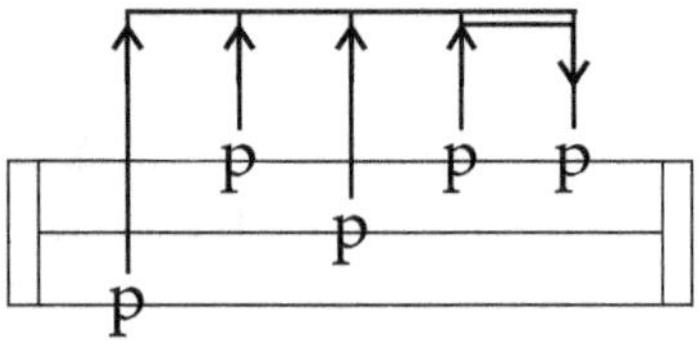

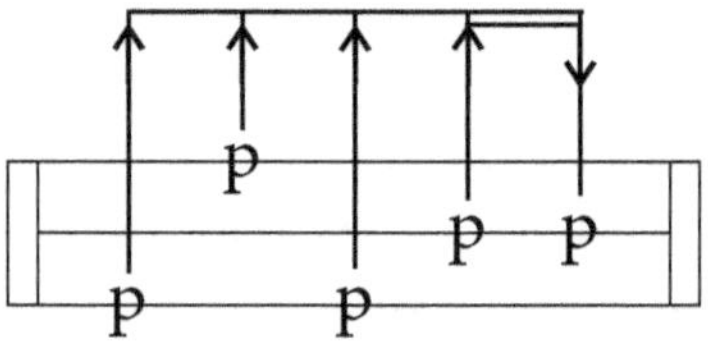

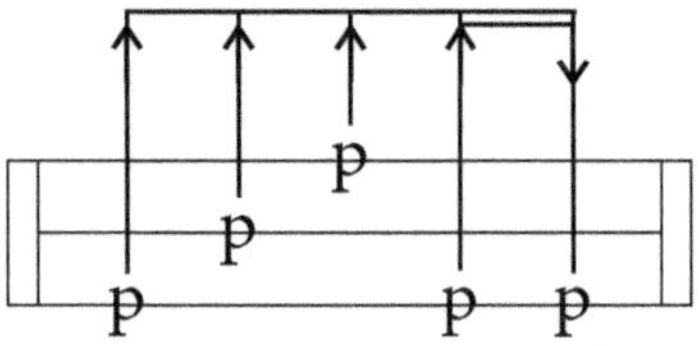

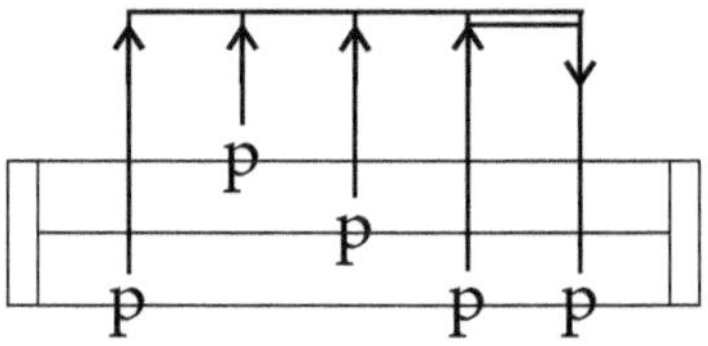

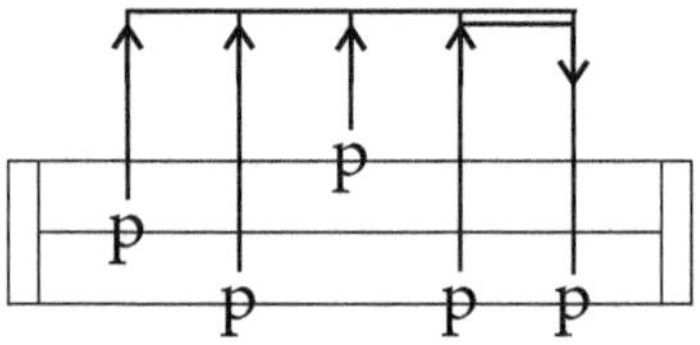

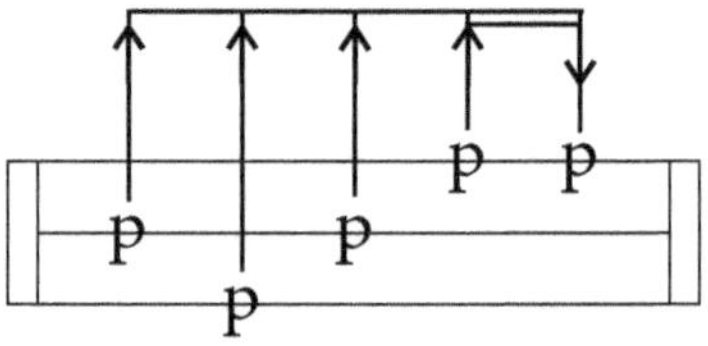

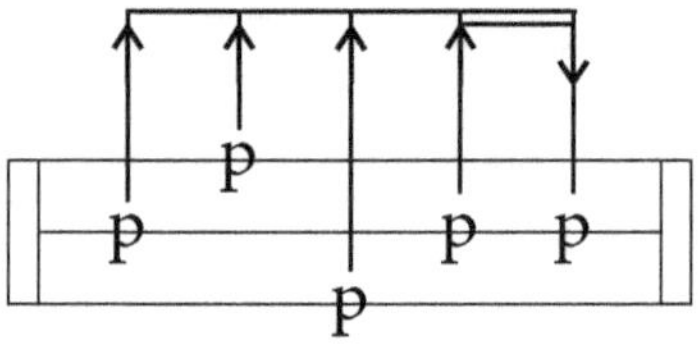

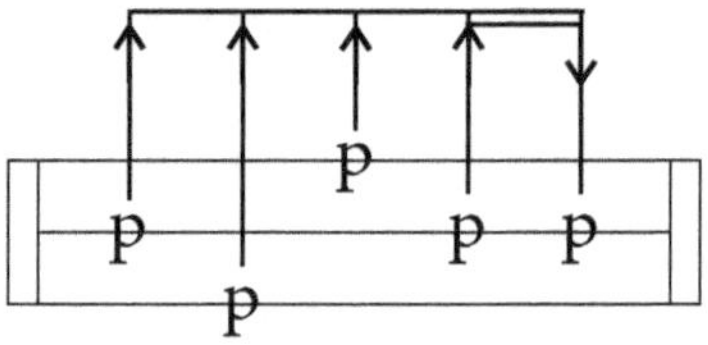

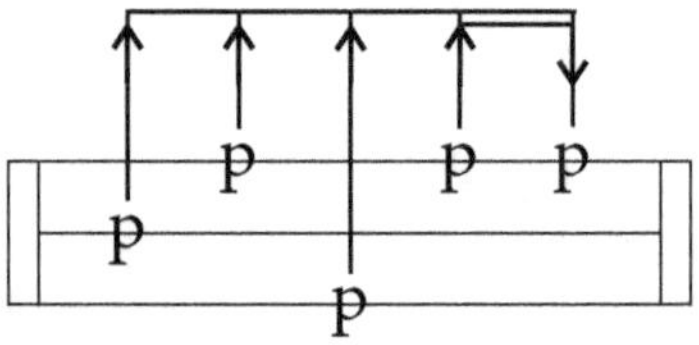

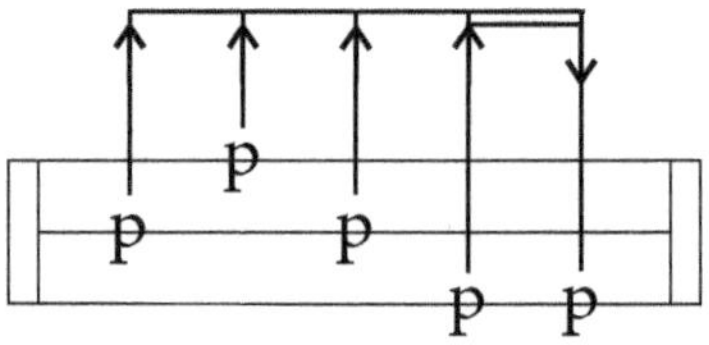

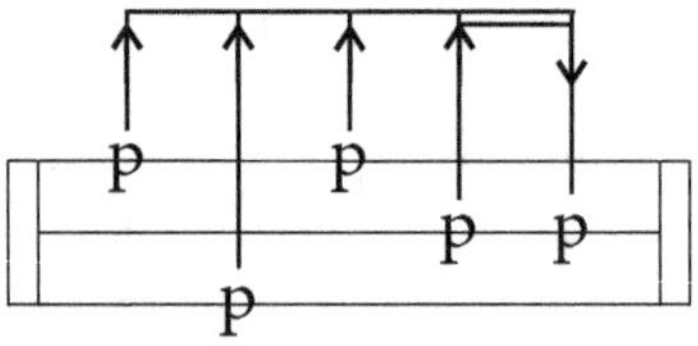

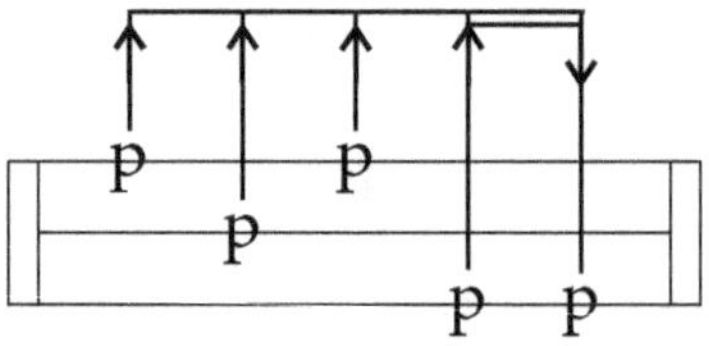

300

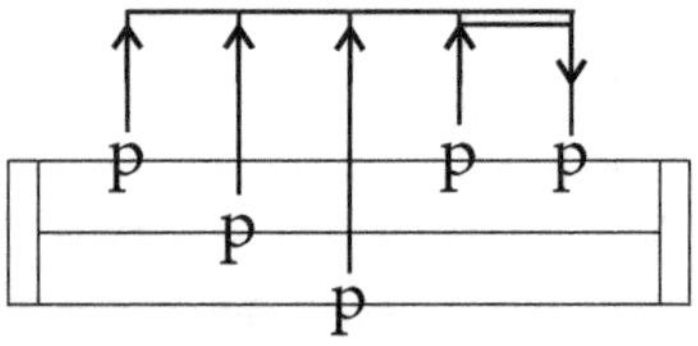

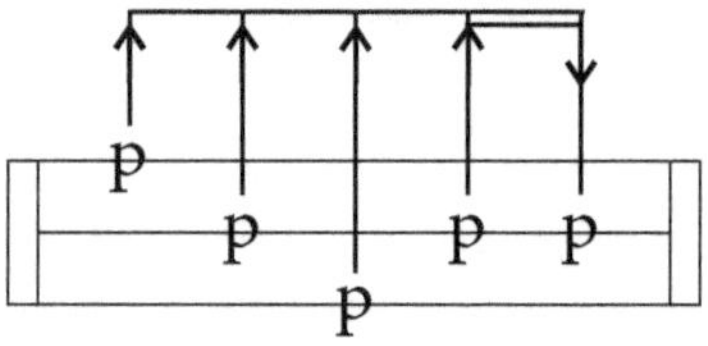

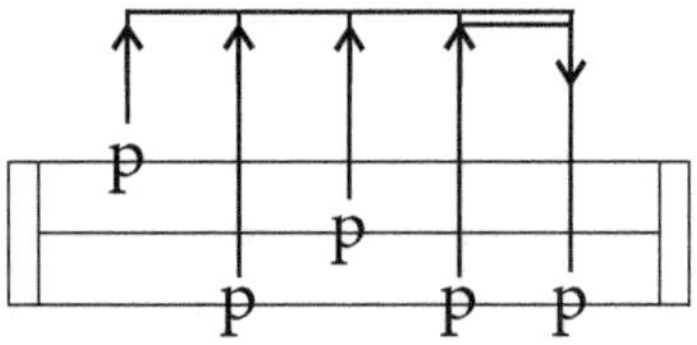

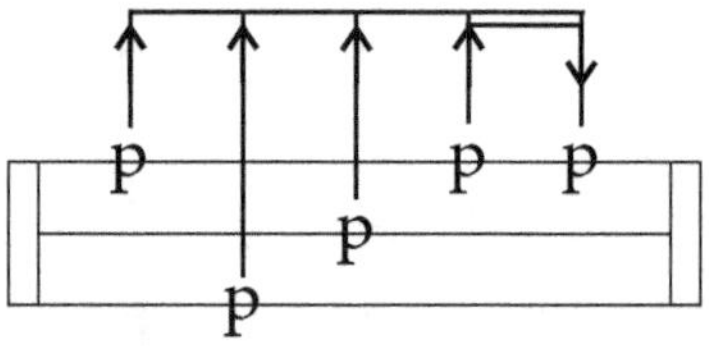

§ IV

Exercise on pulgar on three adjacent strings with two double and two single strokes within each Formula. The single strokes only (↑) and the double strokes (↑↓). The exercise contains six variations with 18 Formulas in each one. The first Formula of each variation is cited below. Isochronous playing of pulgar strokes.

VARIATION I

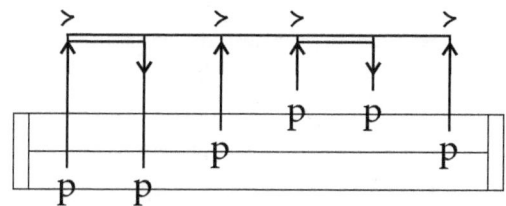

VARIATION IV

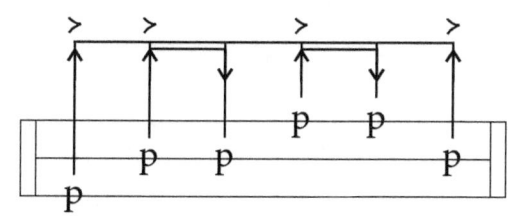

VARIATION II

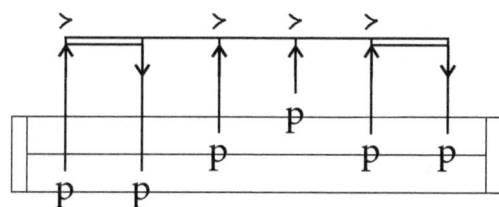

VARIATION V

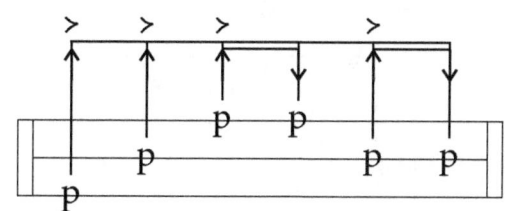

VARIATION III

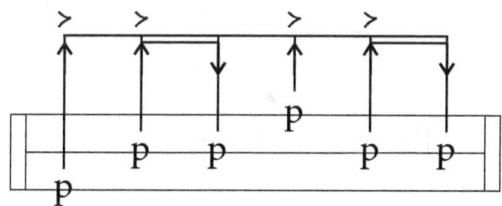

VARIATION VI

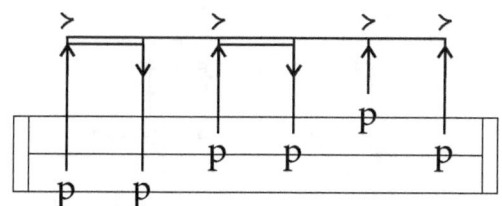

VARIATION I

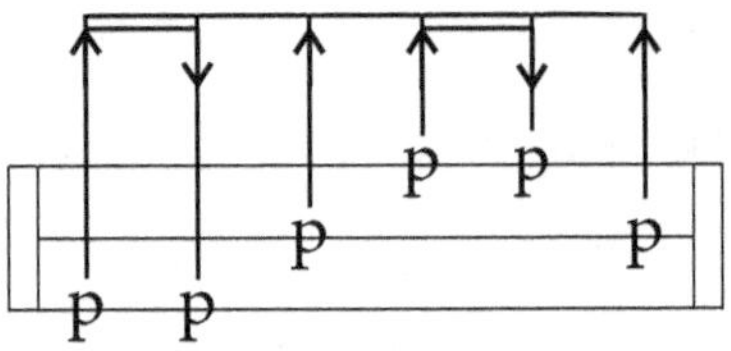

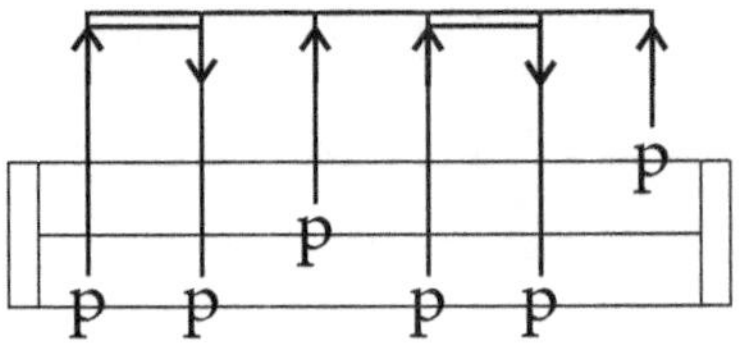

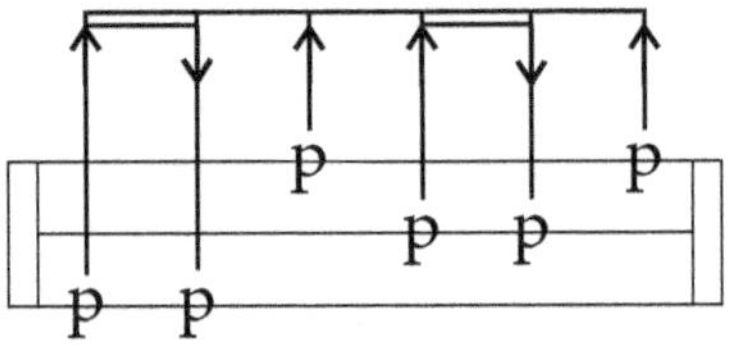

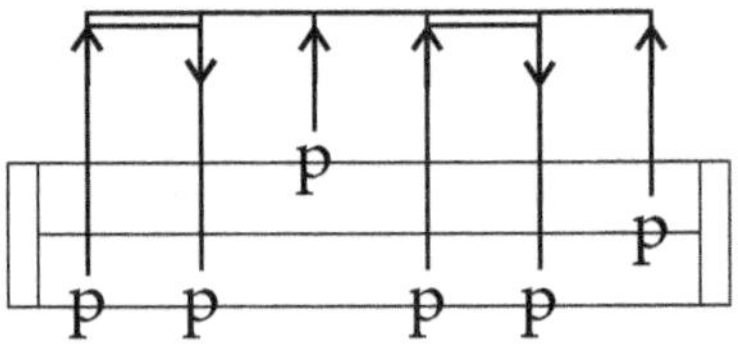

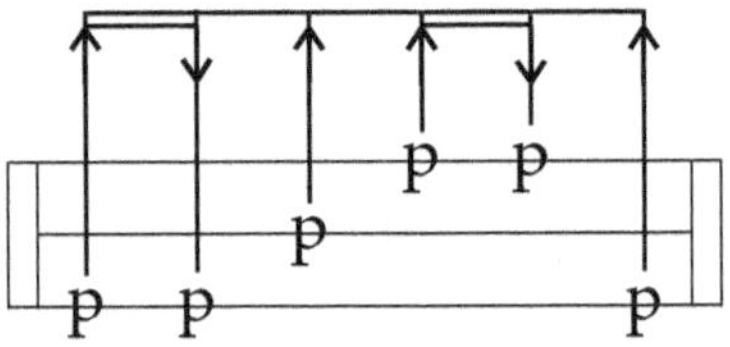

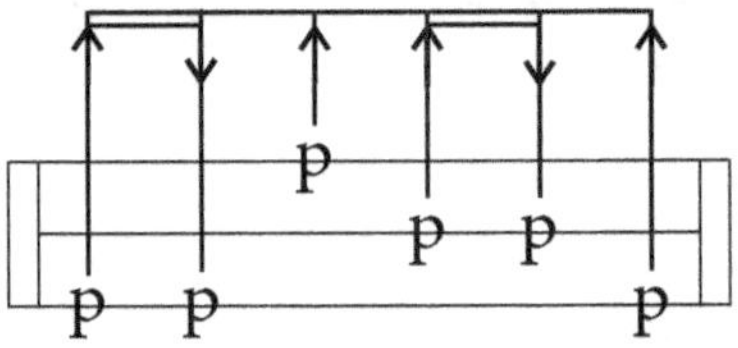

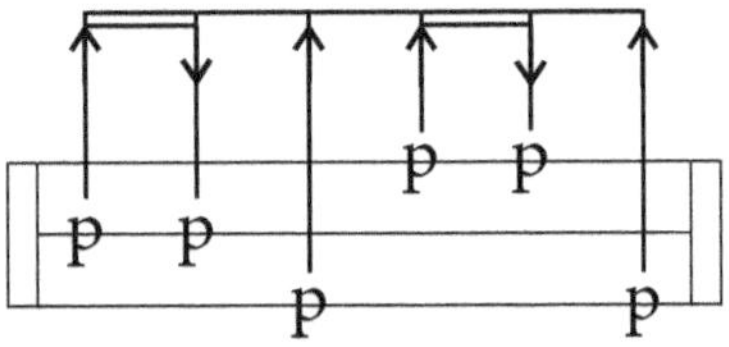

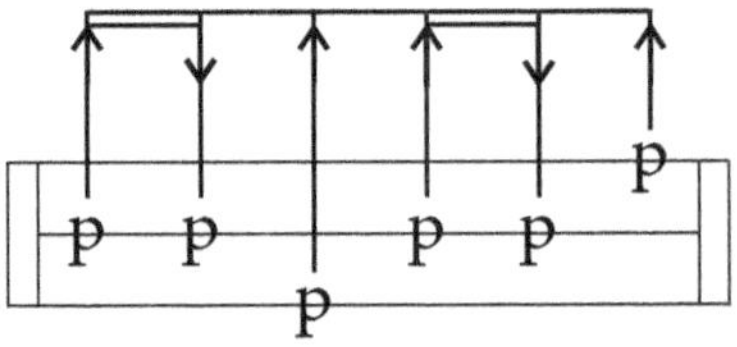

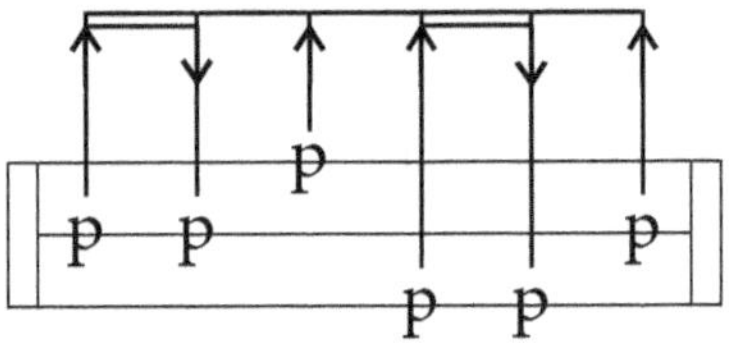

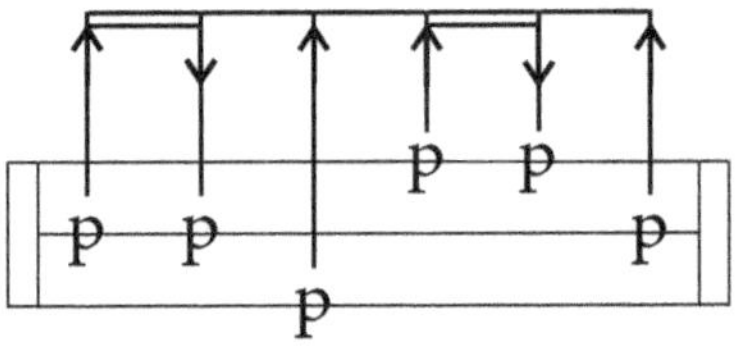

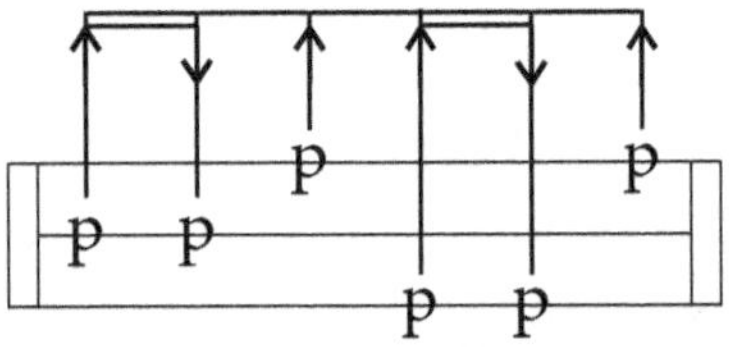

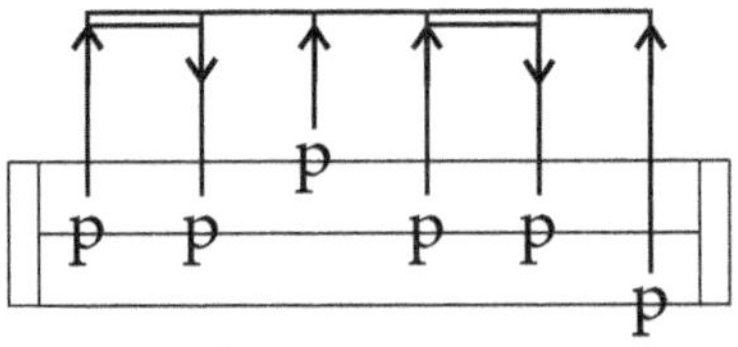

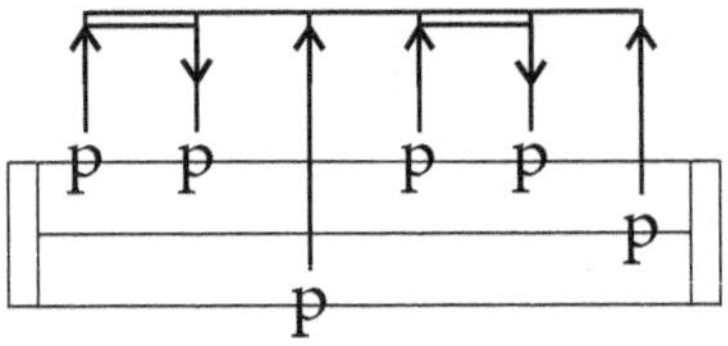

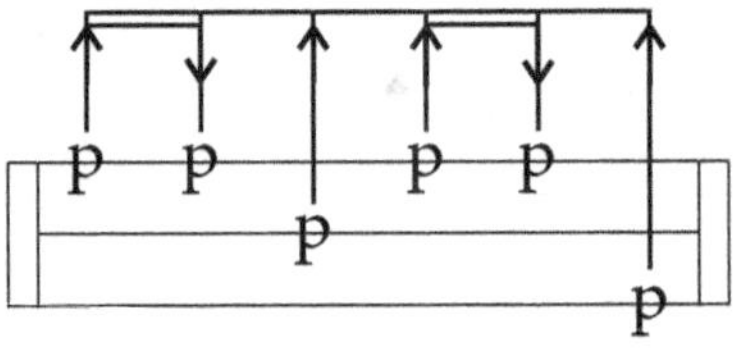

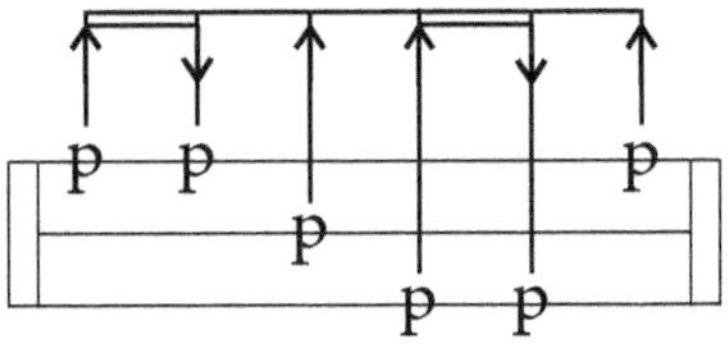

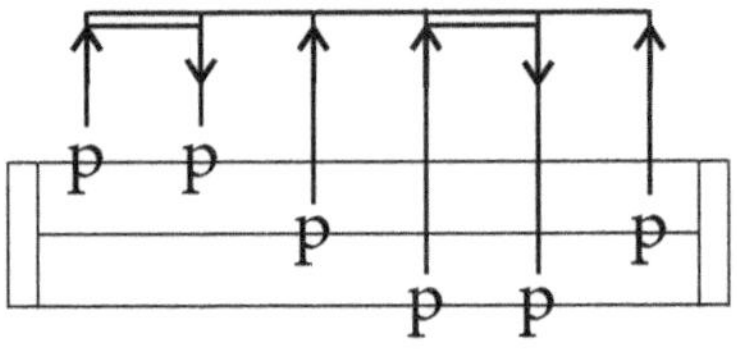

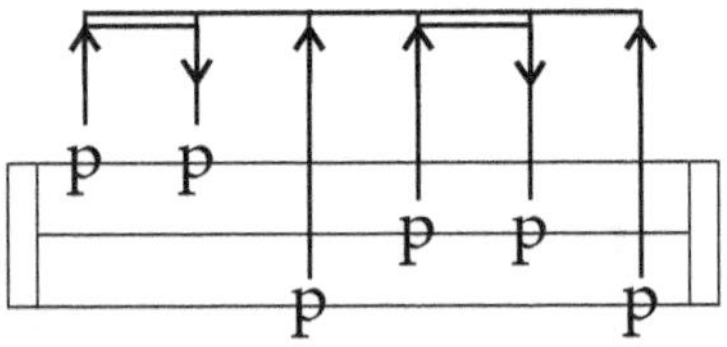

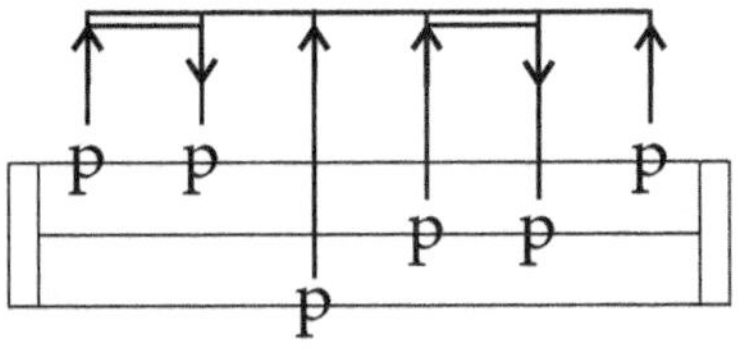

VARIATION II

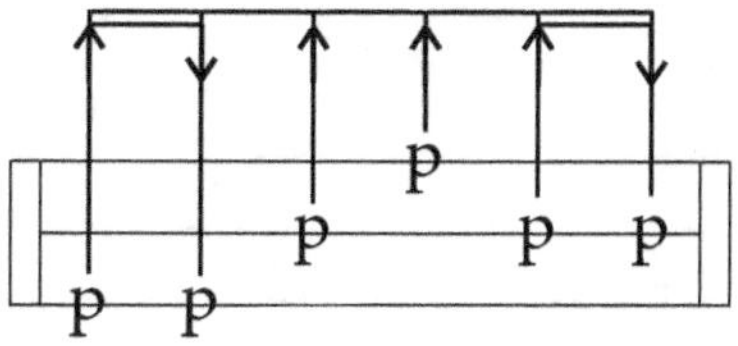

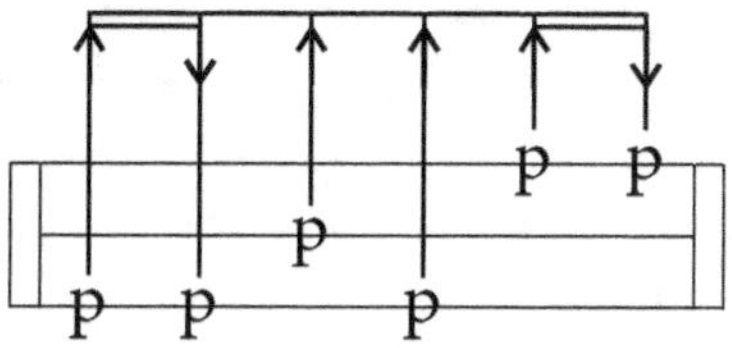

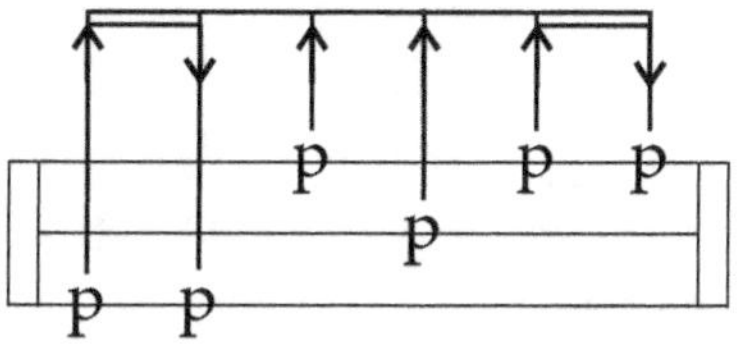

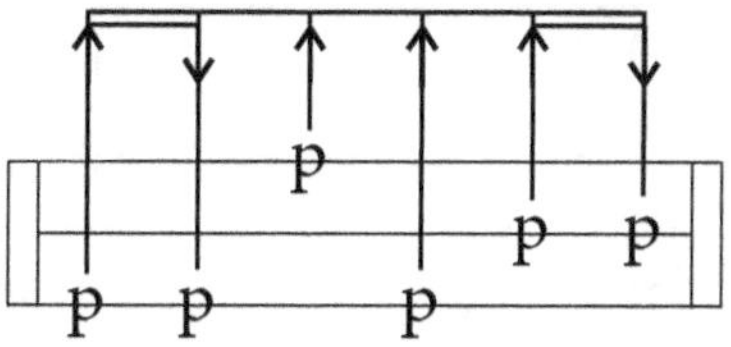

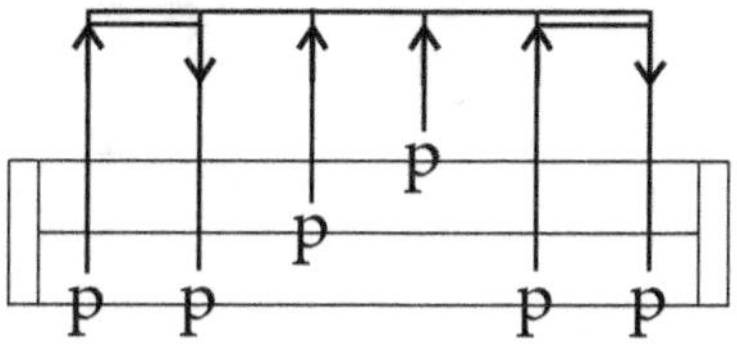

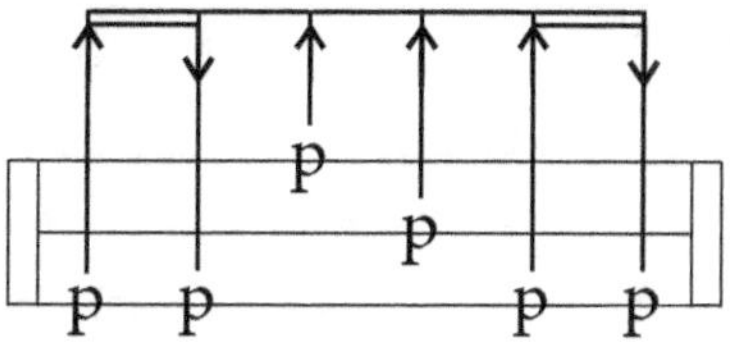

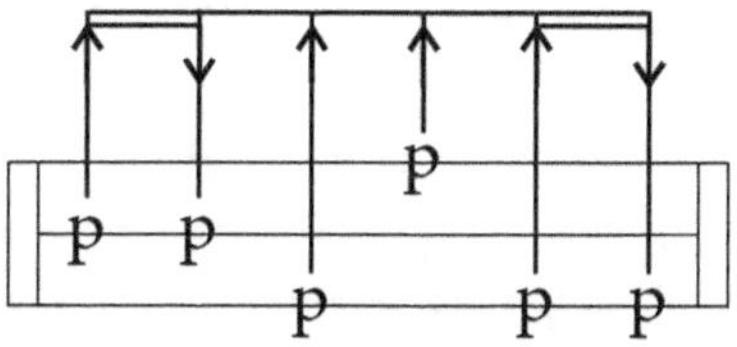

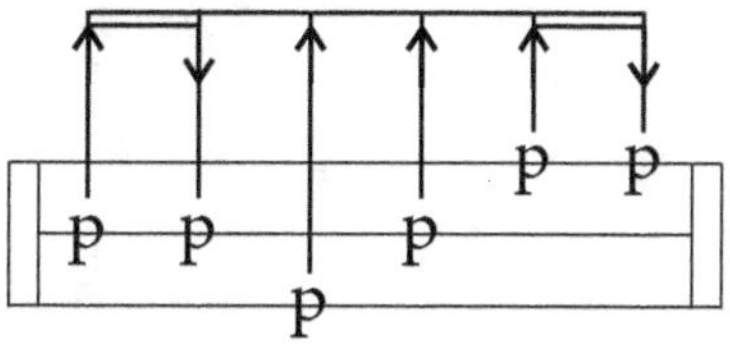

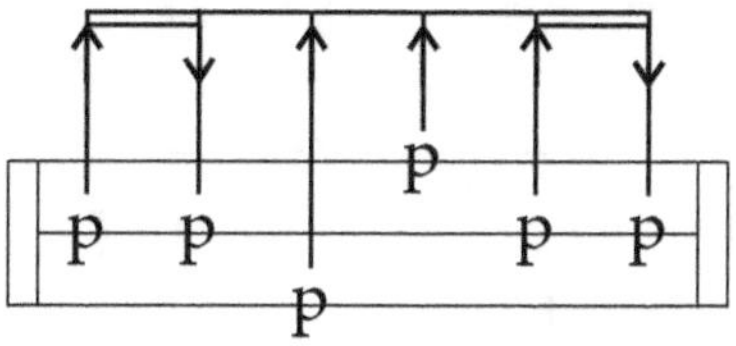

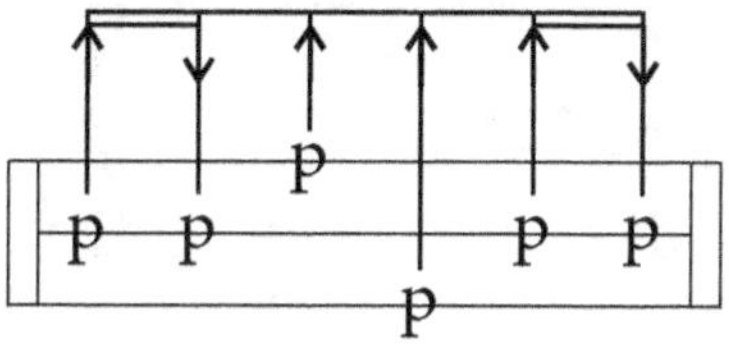

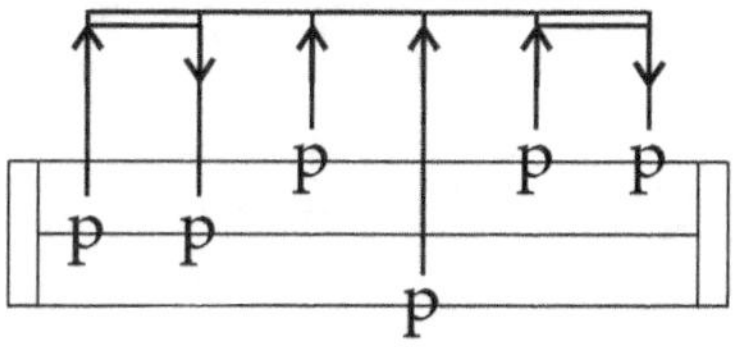

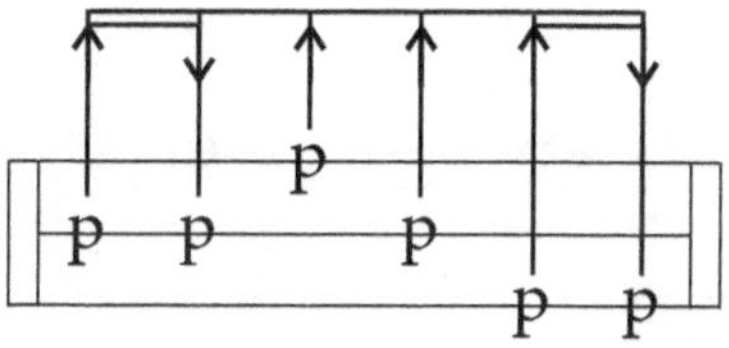

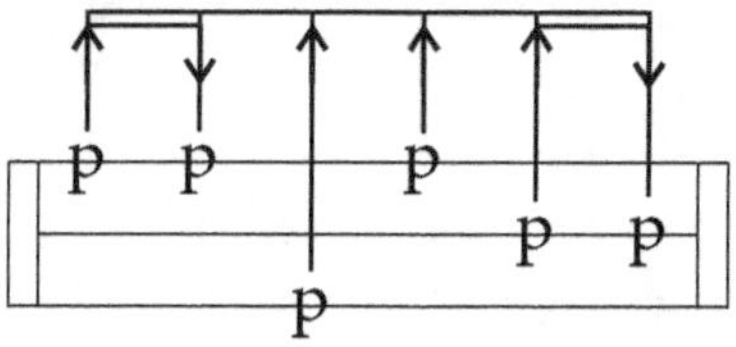

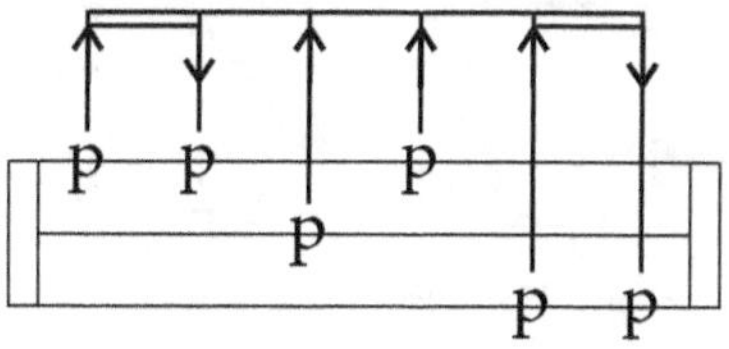

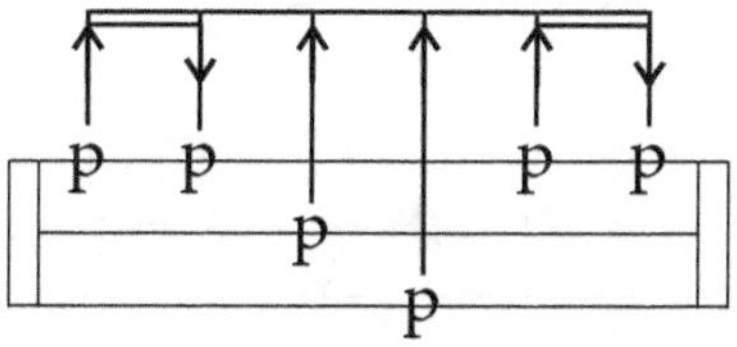

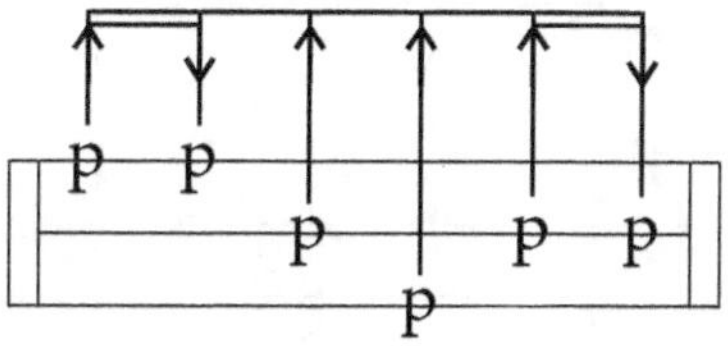

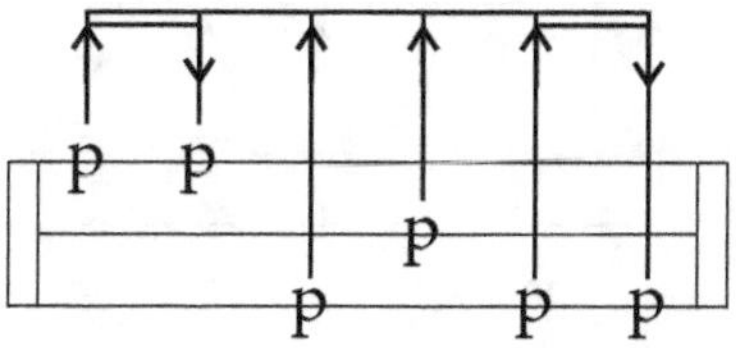

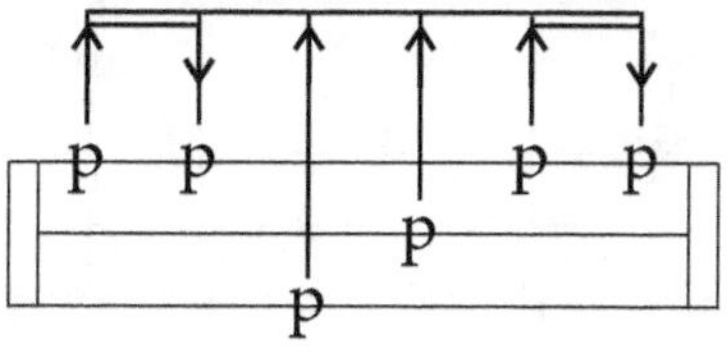

VARIATION III

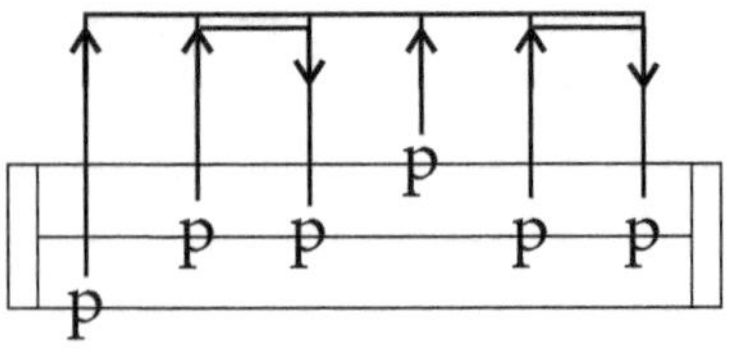

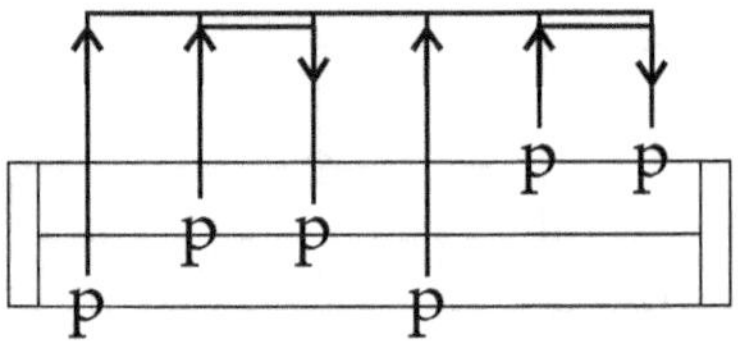

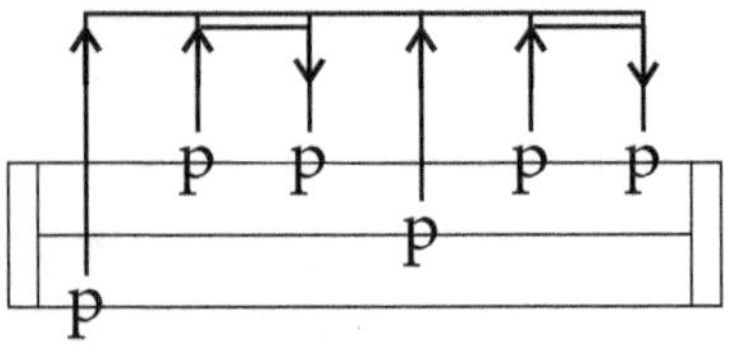

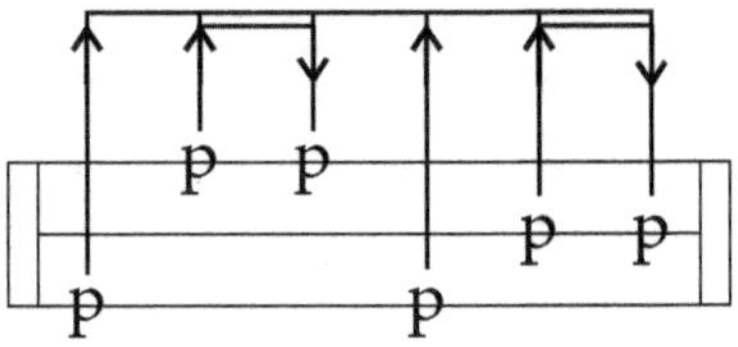

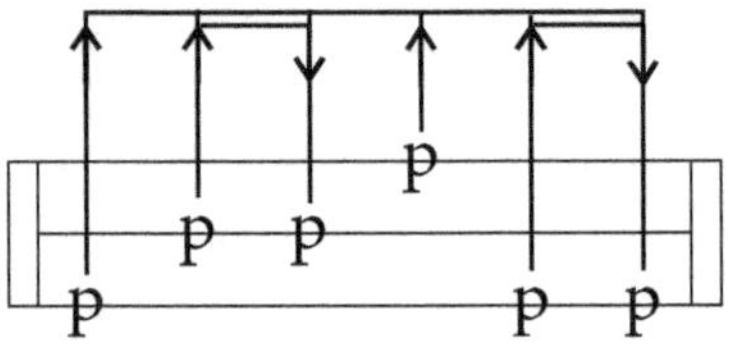

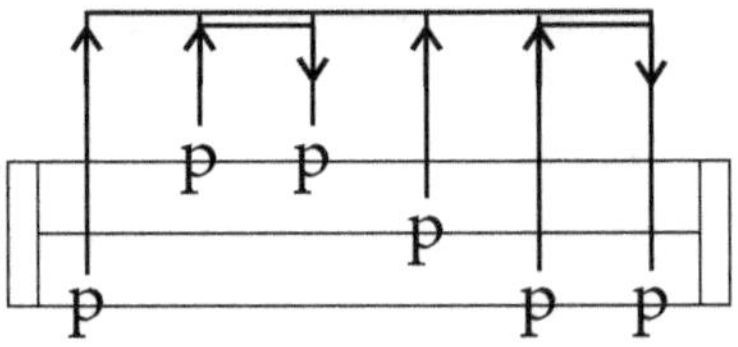

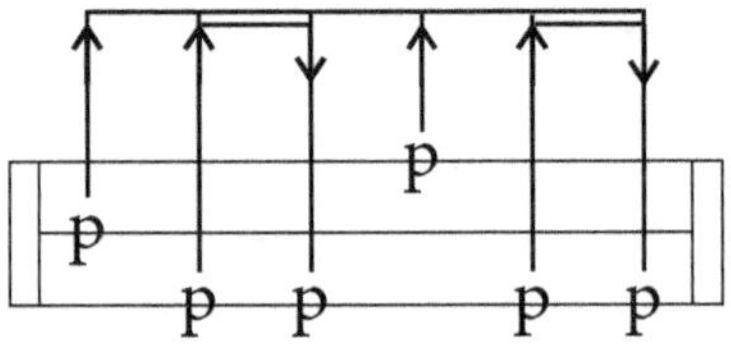

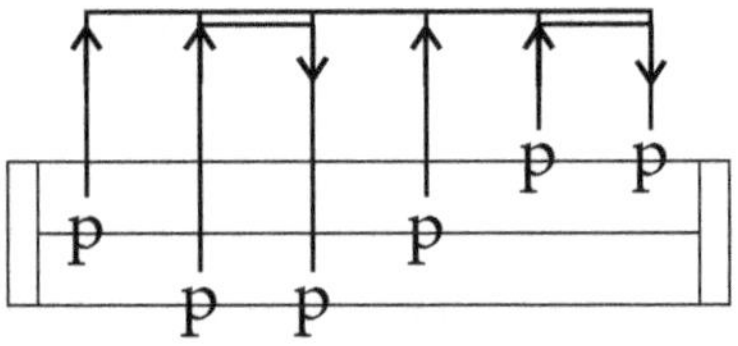

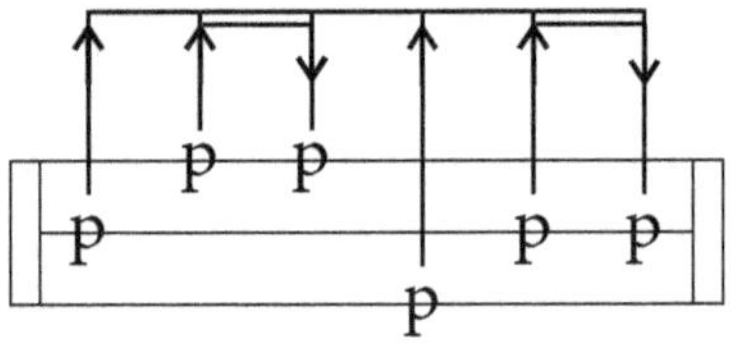

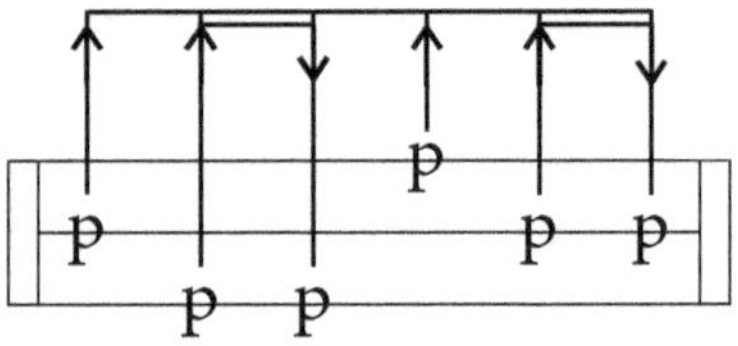

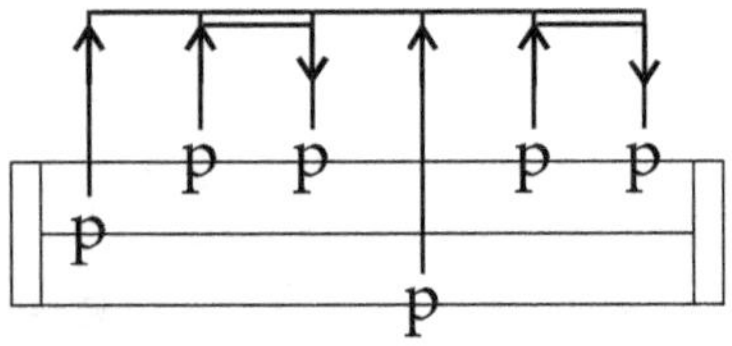

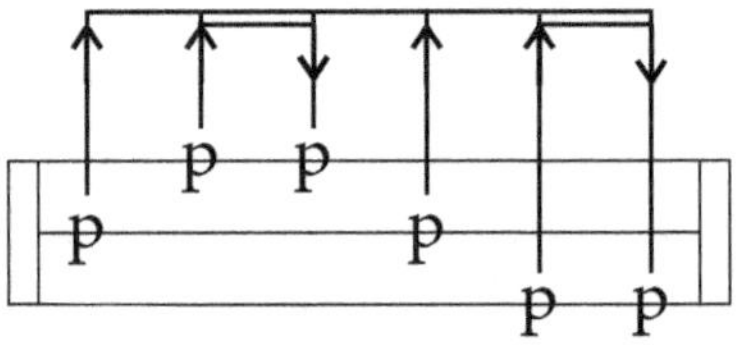

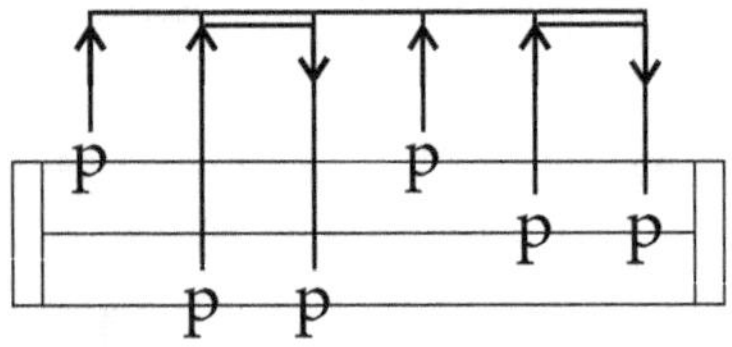

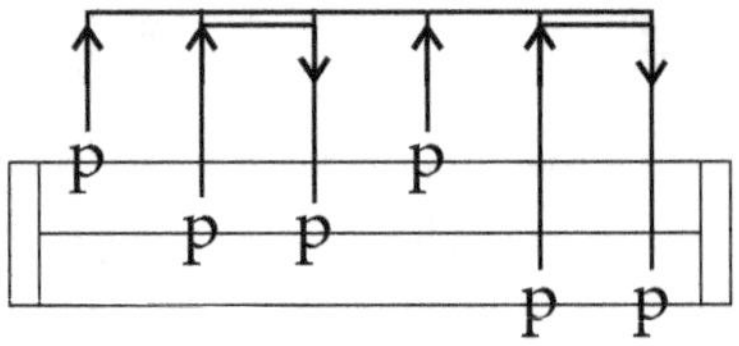

304

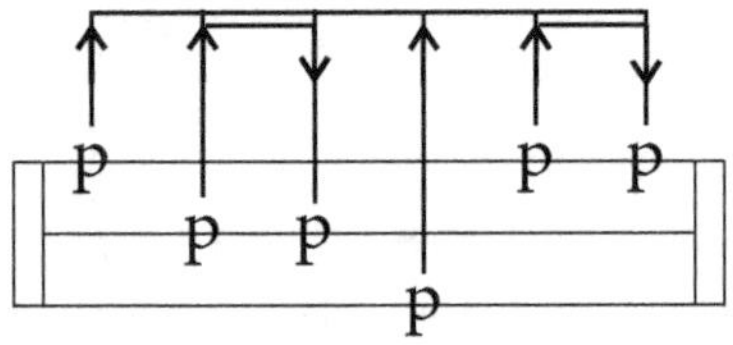

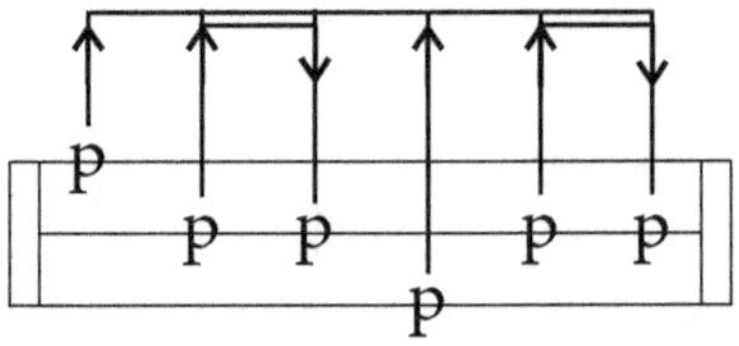

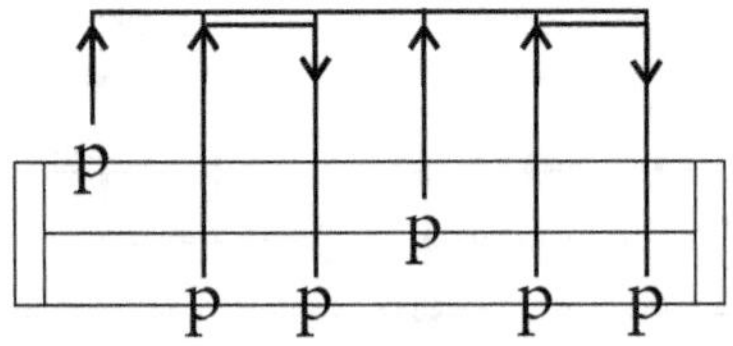

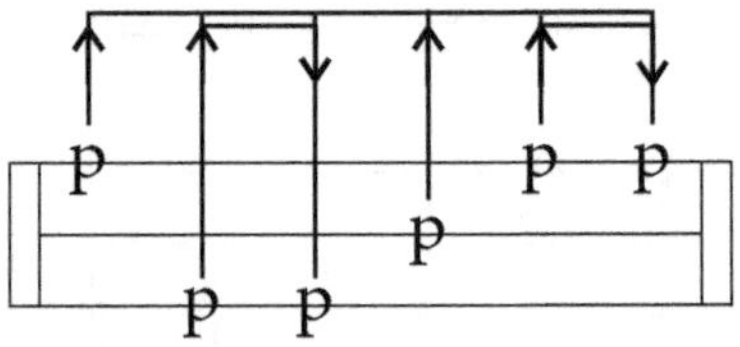

VARIATION IV

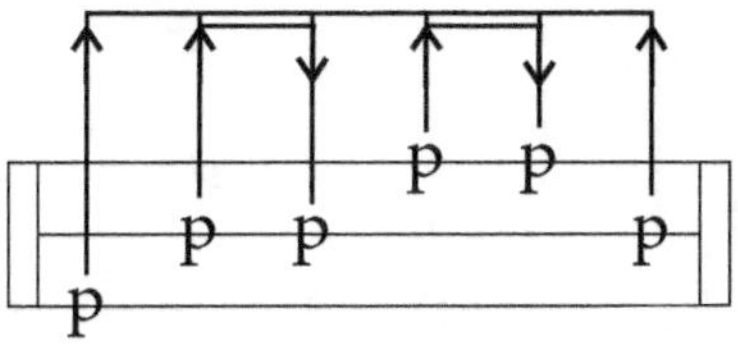

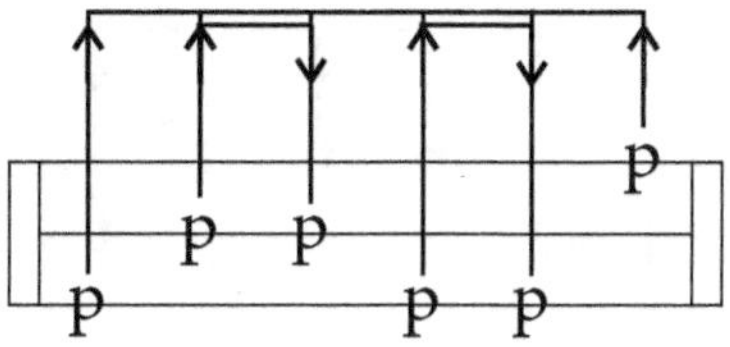

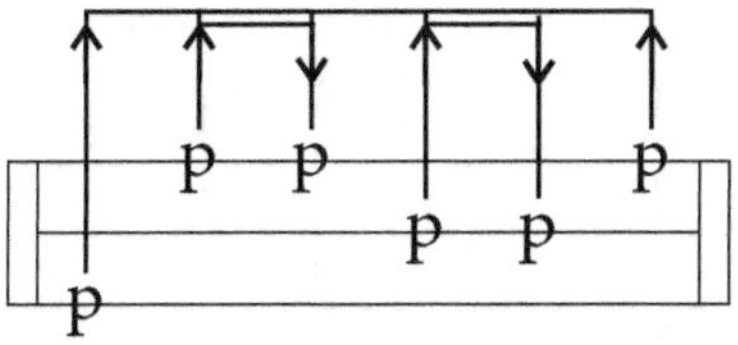

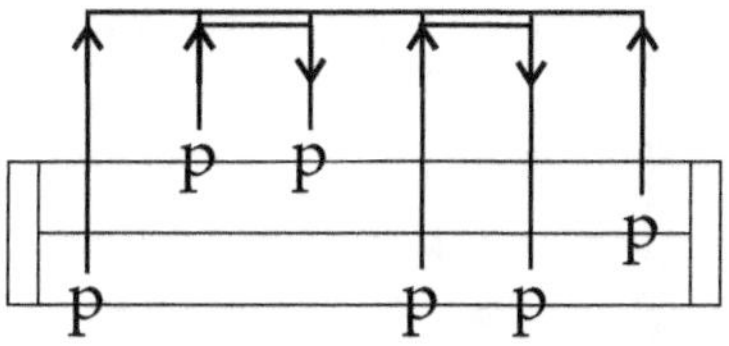

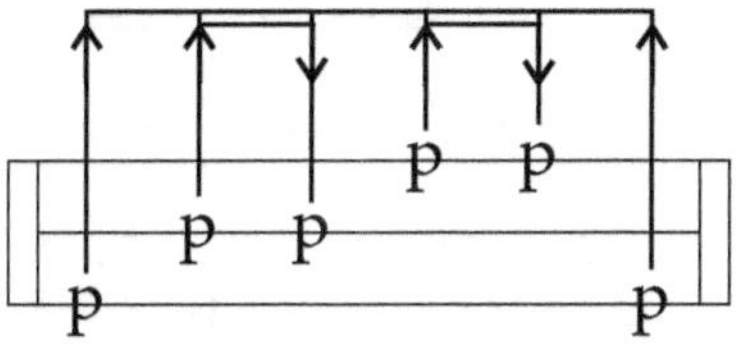

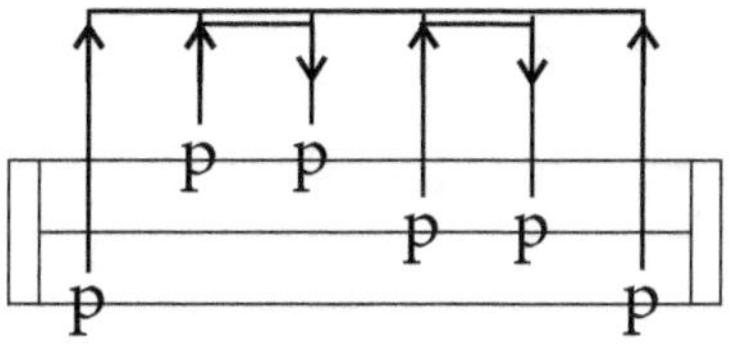

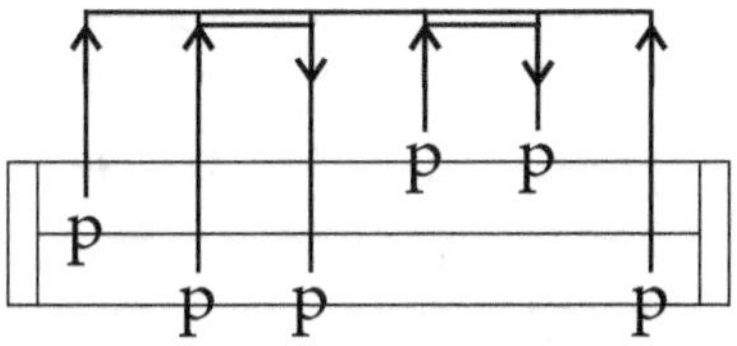

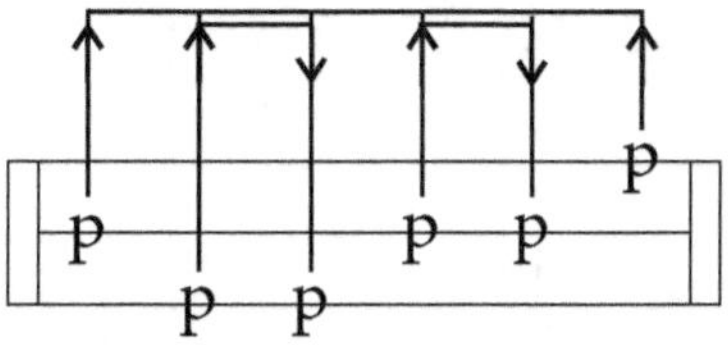

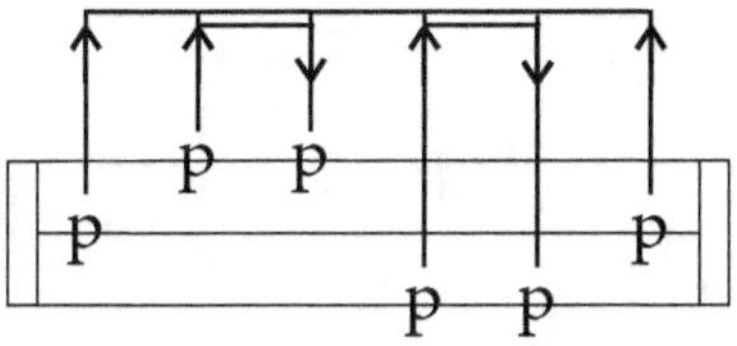

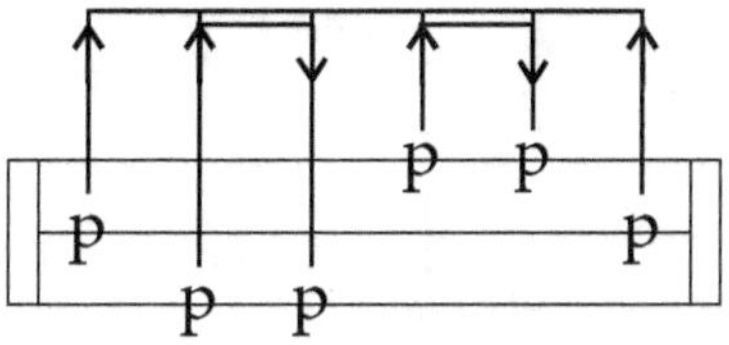

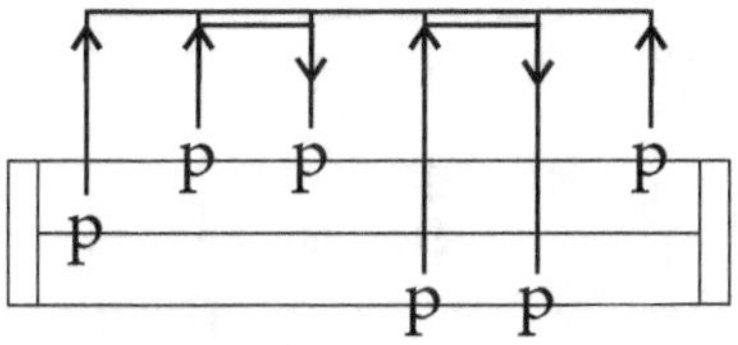

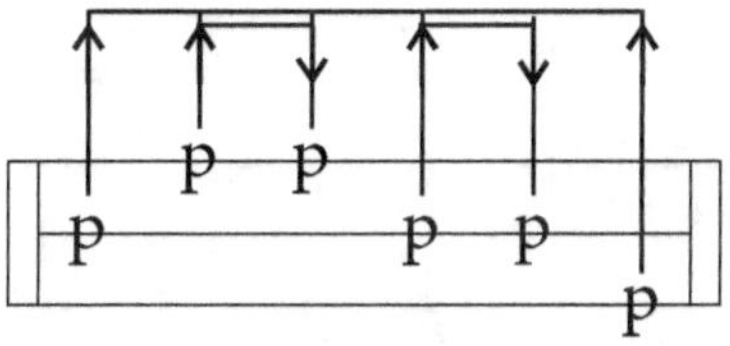

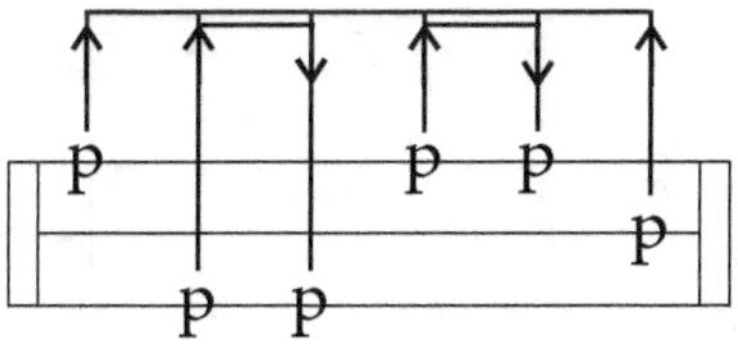

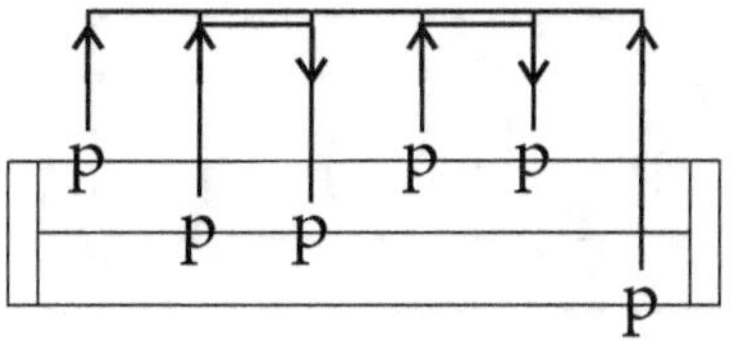

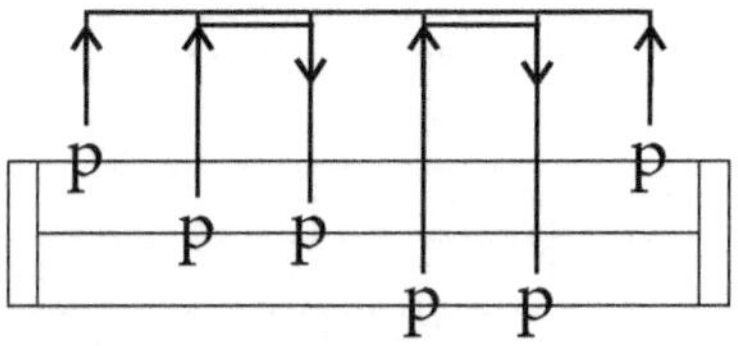

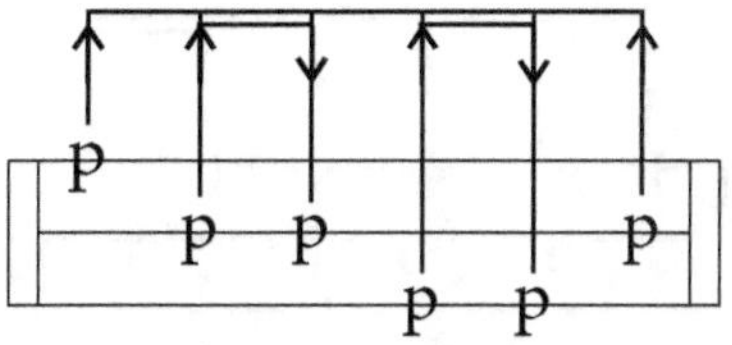

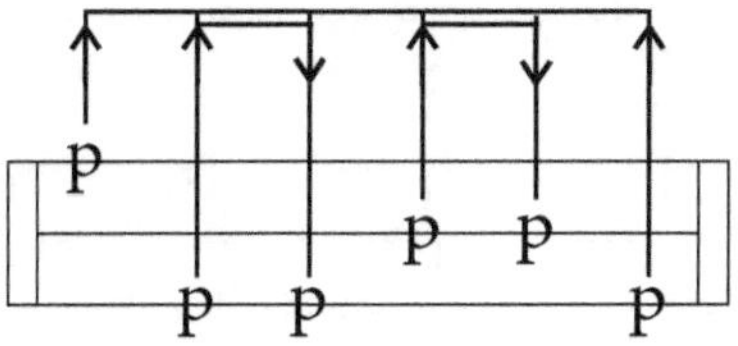

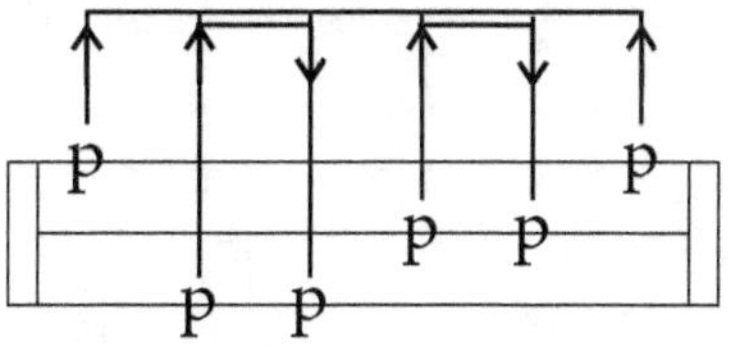

VARIATION V

F1 F2 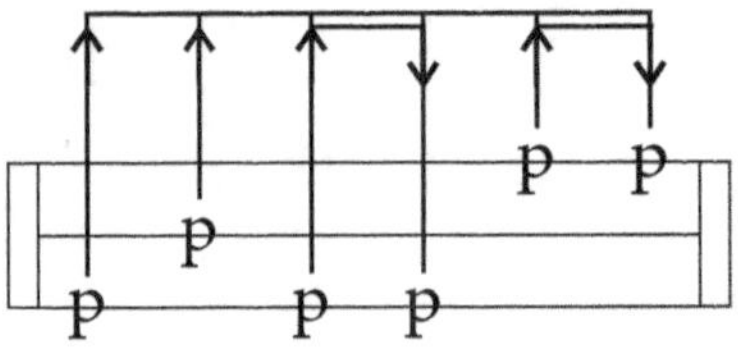
F3 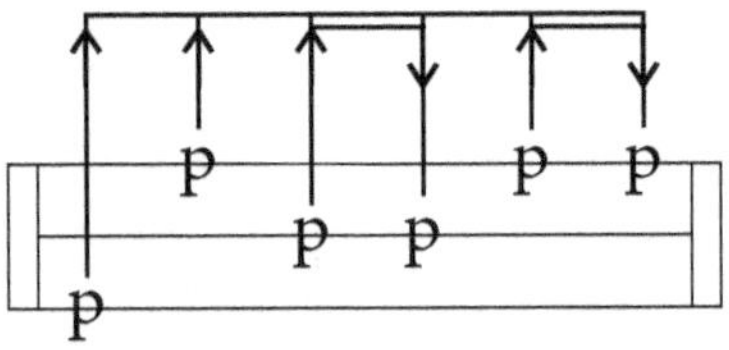 F4 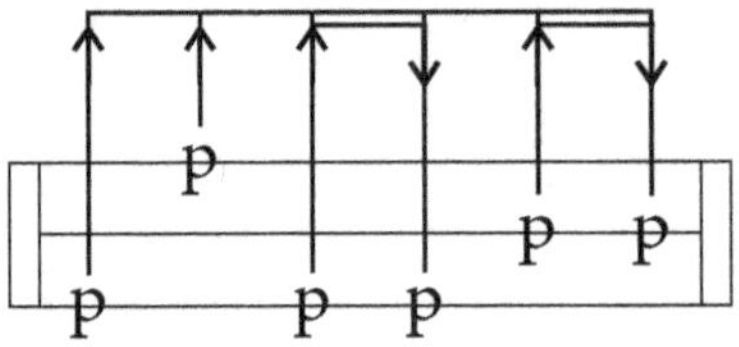
F5 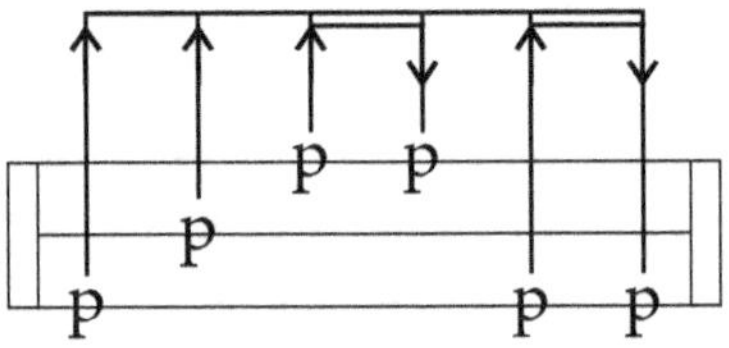 F6 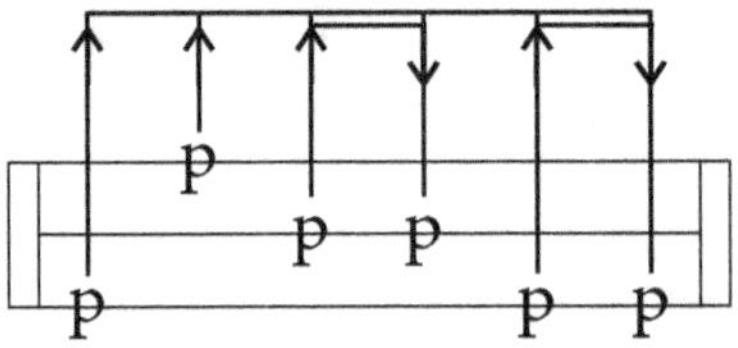
F7 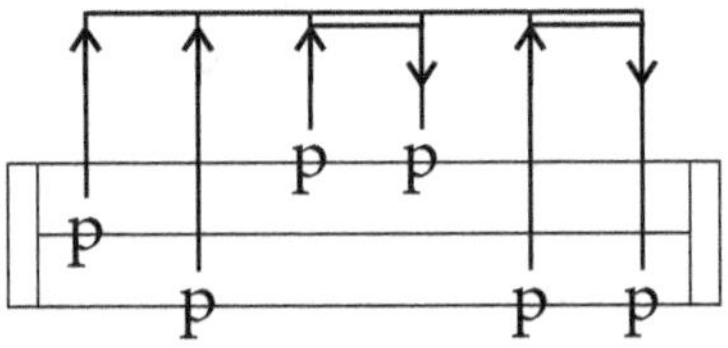 F8 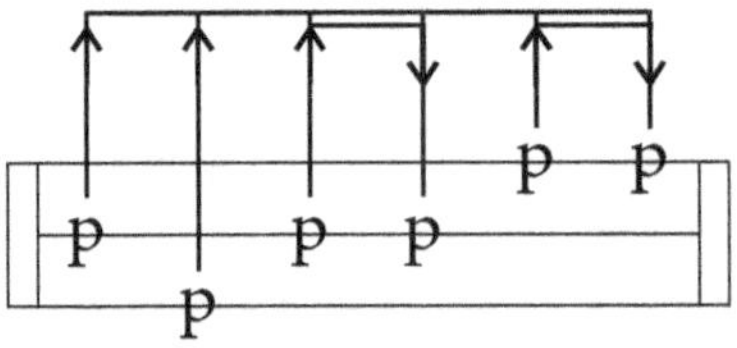
F9 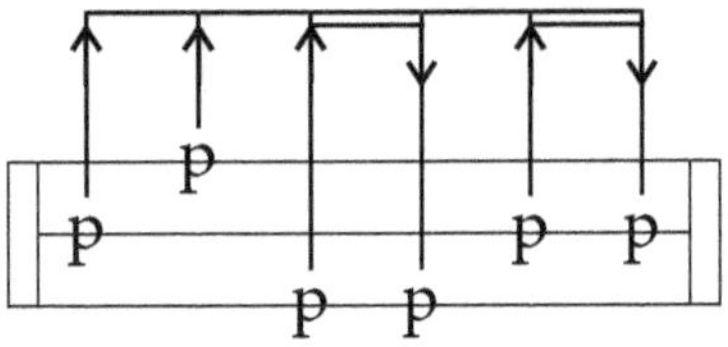 F10 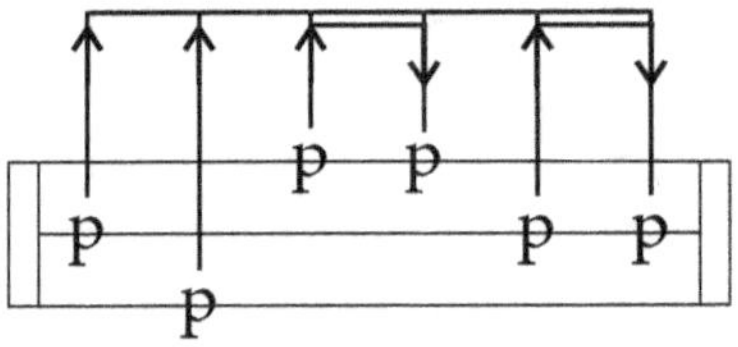
F11 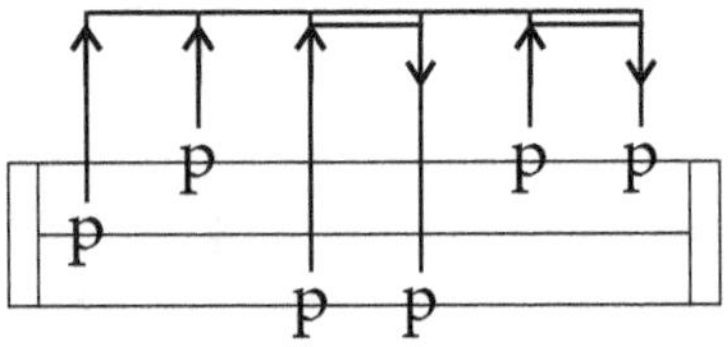 F12 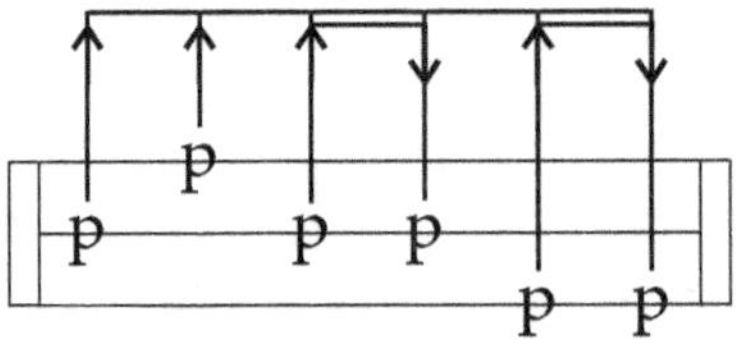
F13 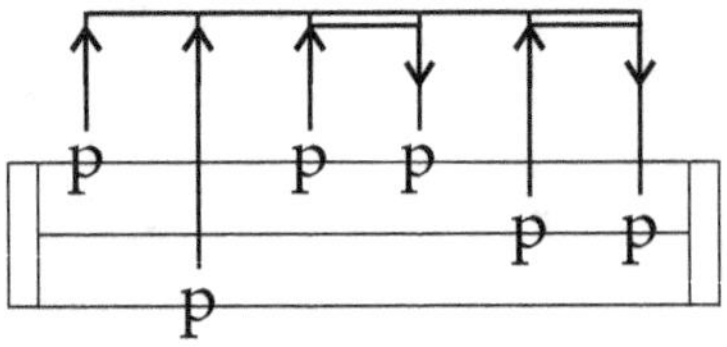 F14 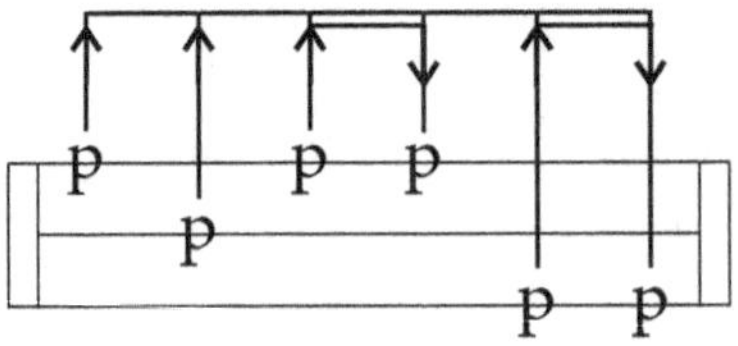
F15 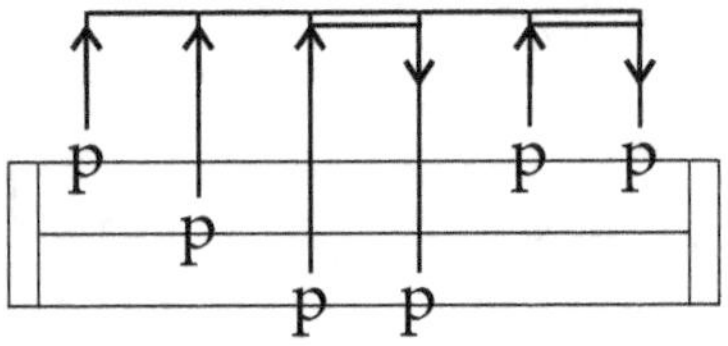 F16 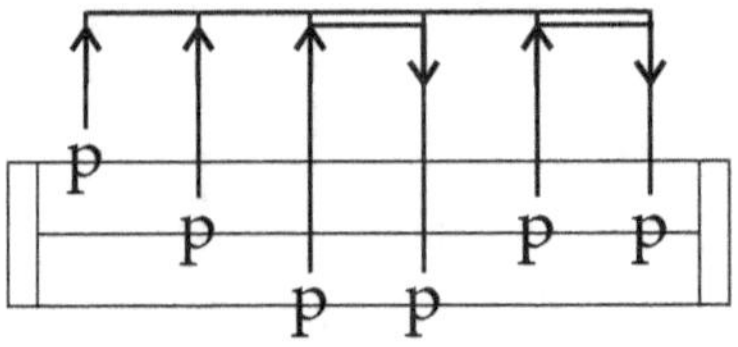
F17 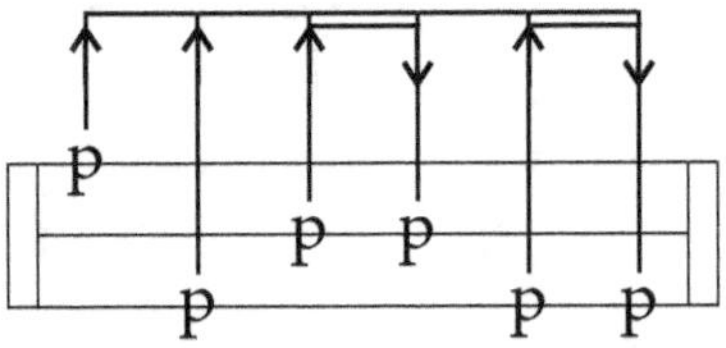 F18

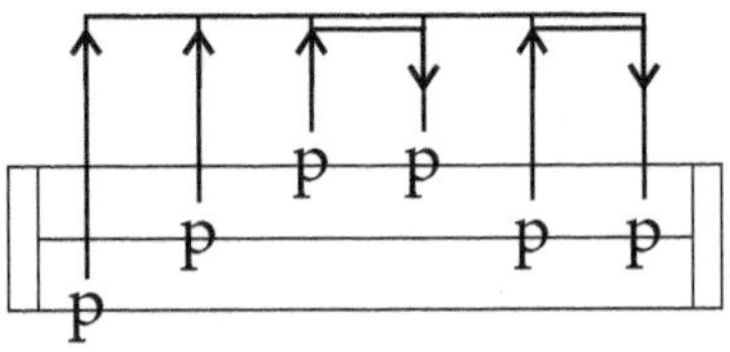

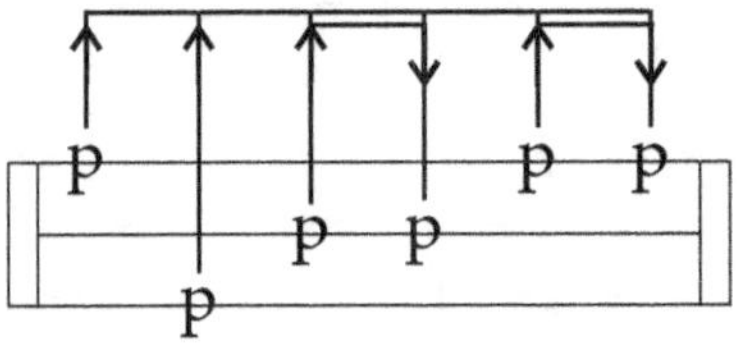

VARIATION VI

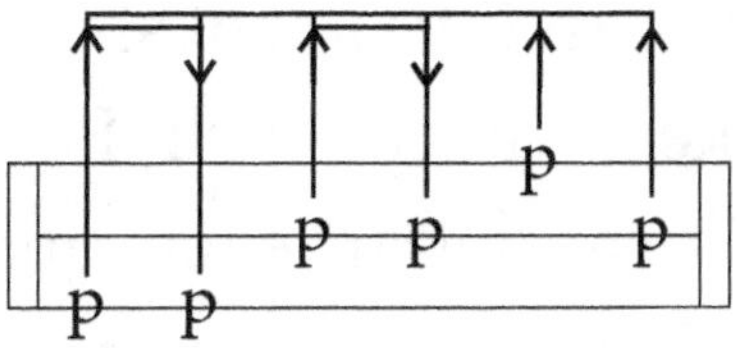

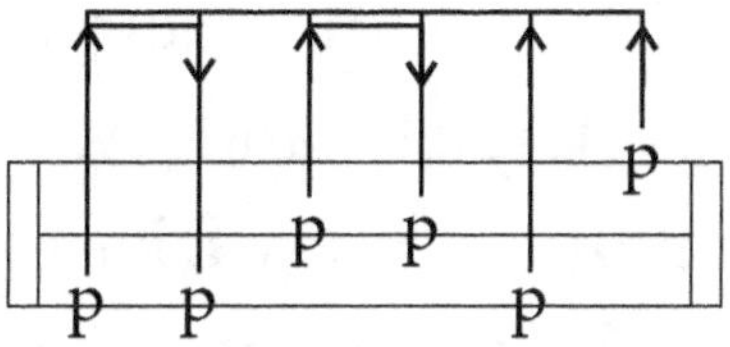

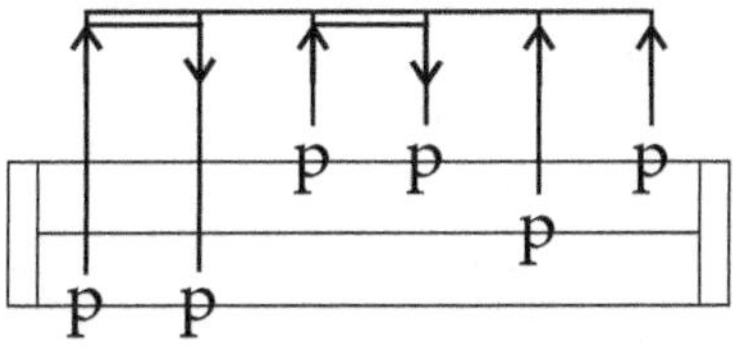

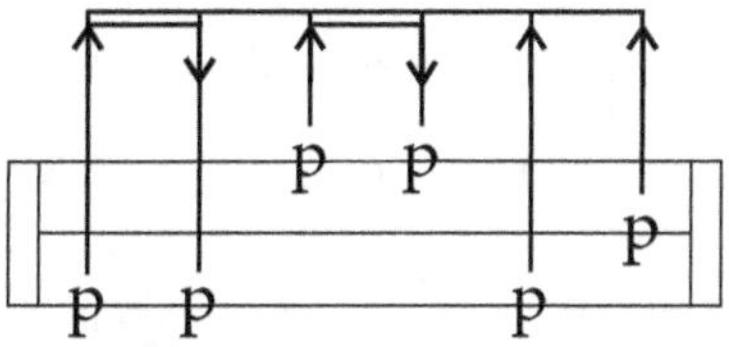

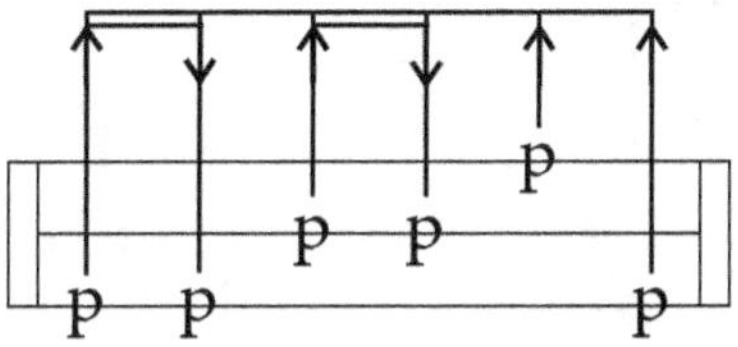

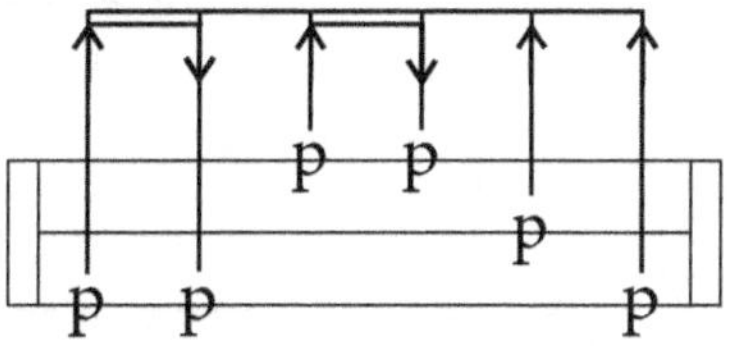

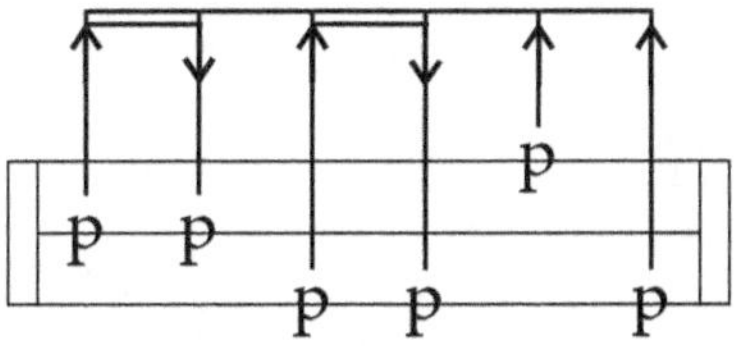

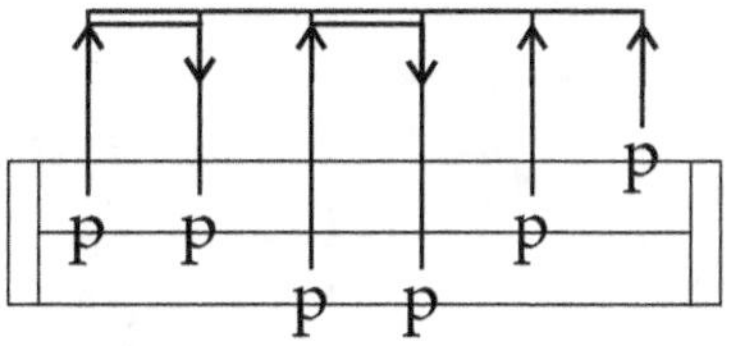

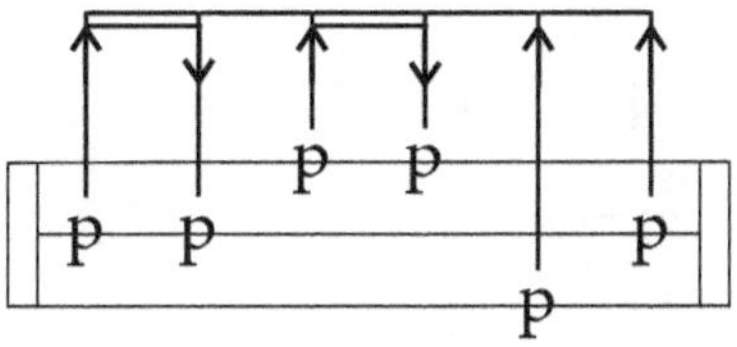

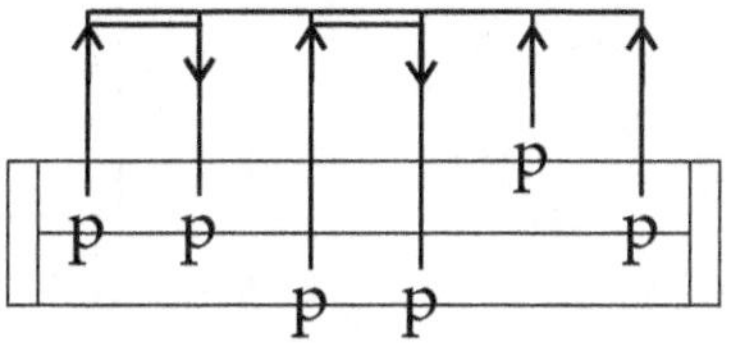

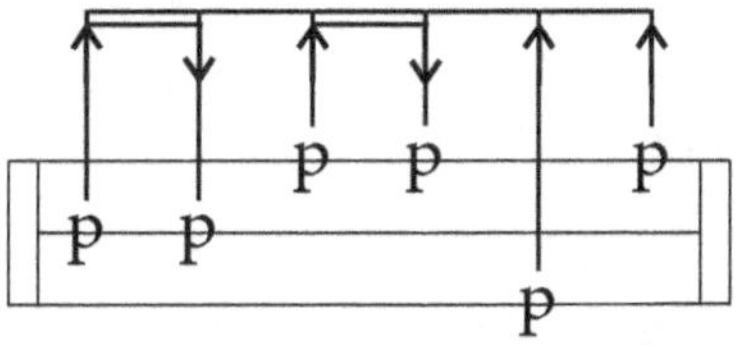

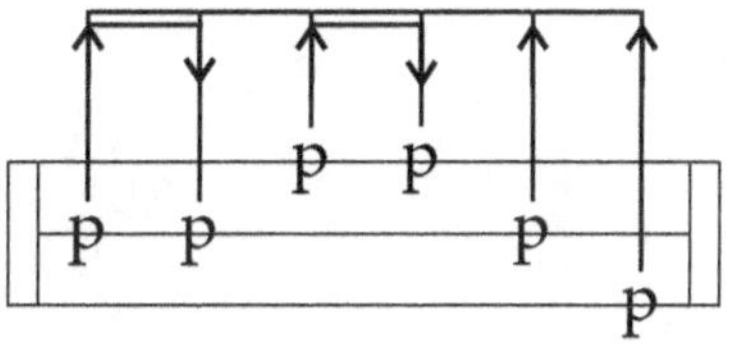

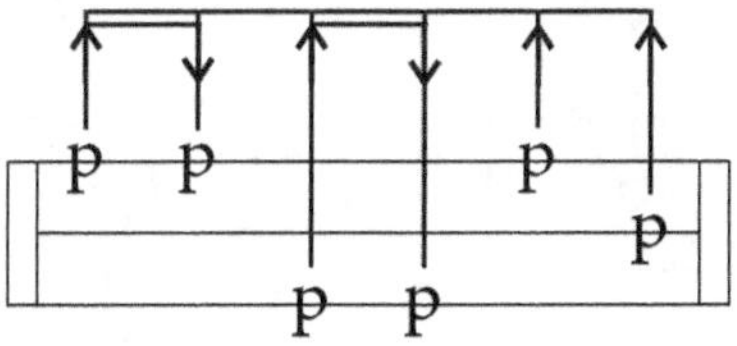

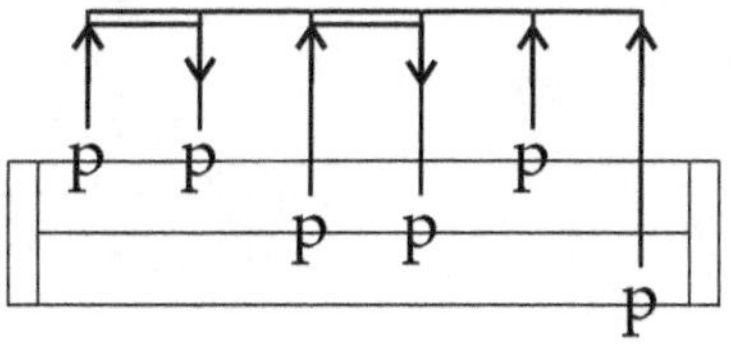

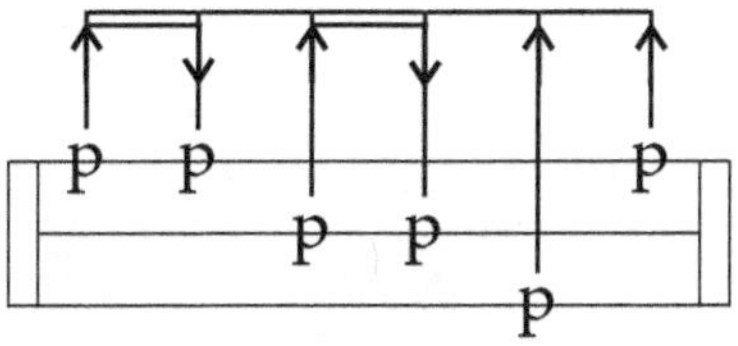

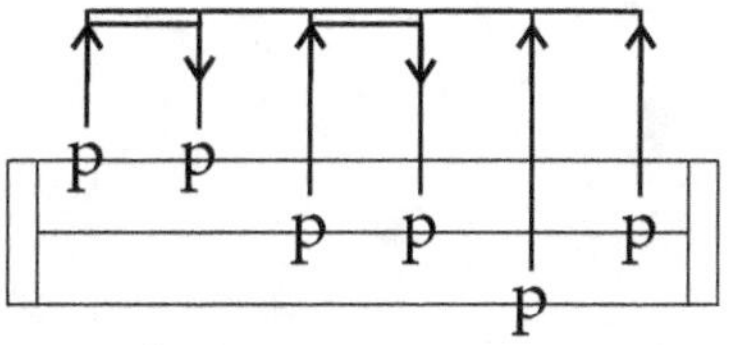

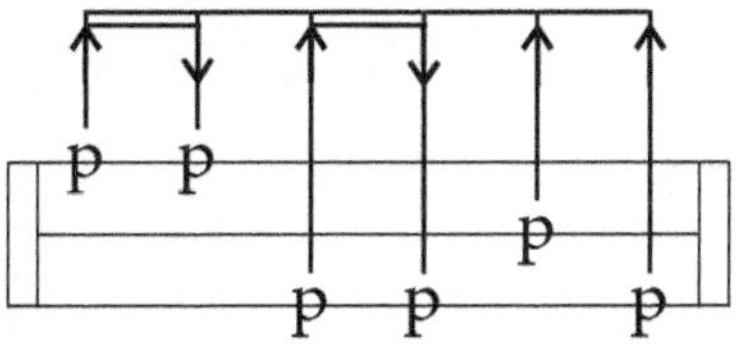

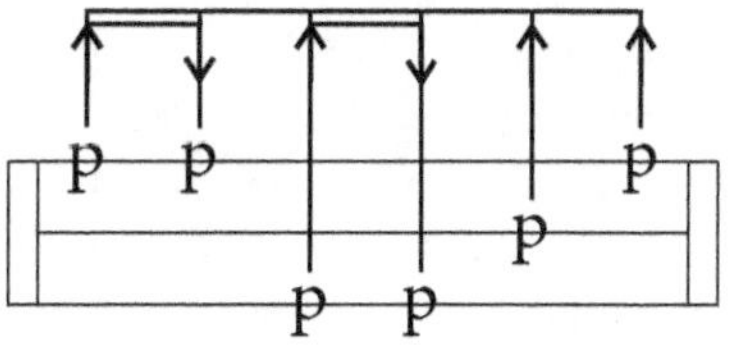

§ V

Modification of previous exercise on pulgar on three adjacent strings with one triple stroke (triplet) and two single strokes within each Formula. The exercise contains three variations with 18 Formulas in each one. The first Formula of each variation is cited below. Isochronous playing of single and triple (triplet) pulgar strokes.

VARIATION I

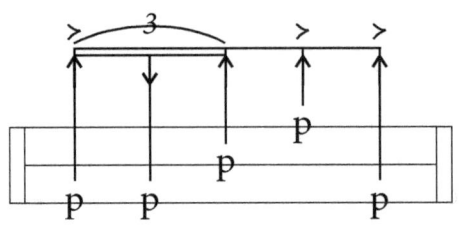

VARIATION II

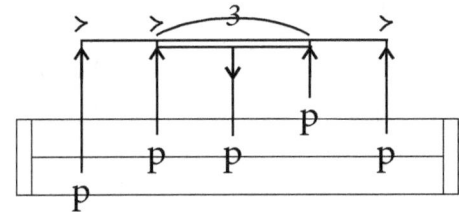

VARIATION III

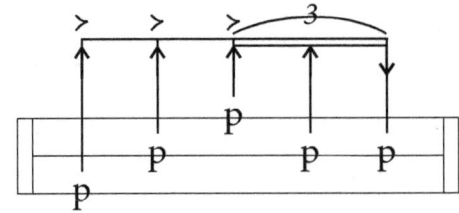

VARIATION I

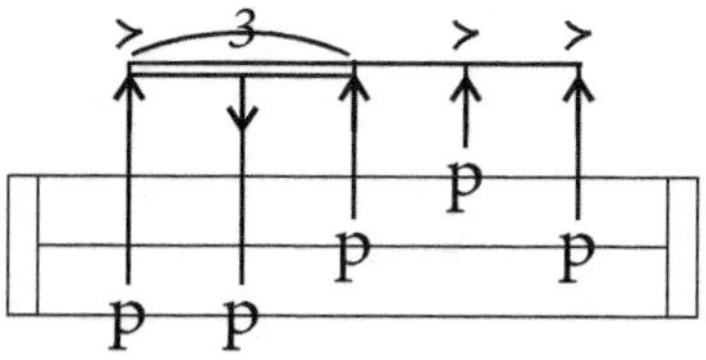

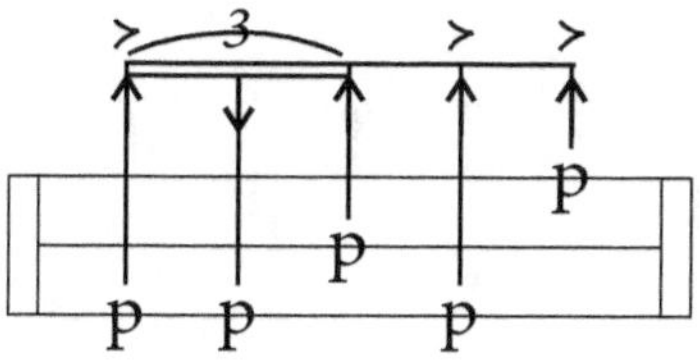

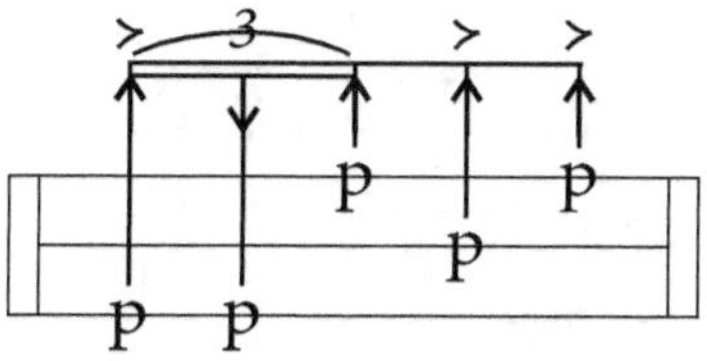

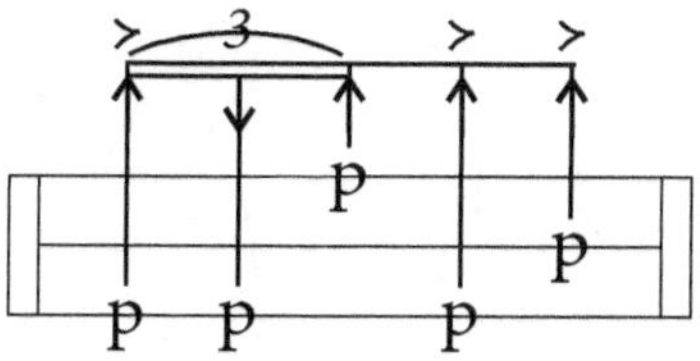

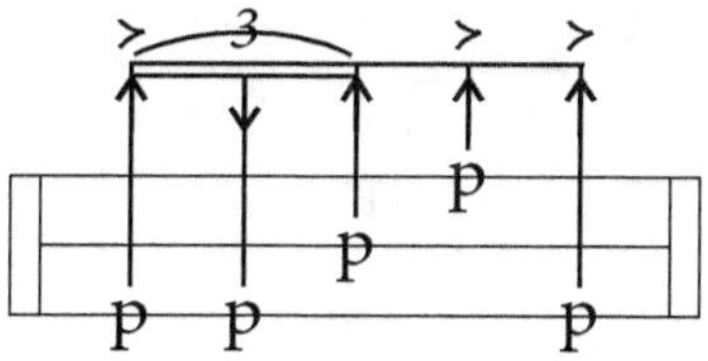

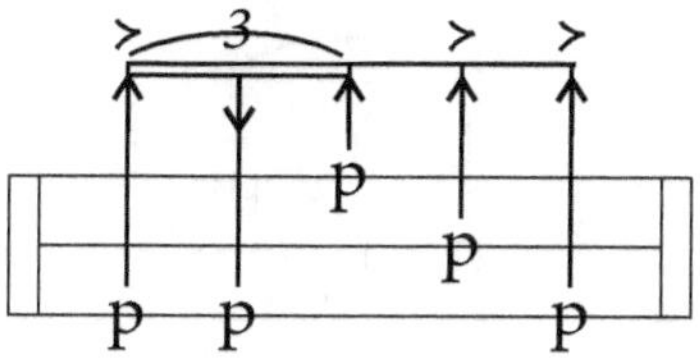

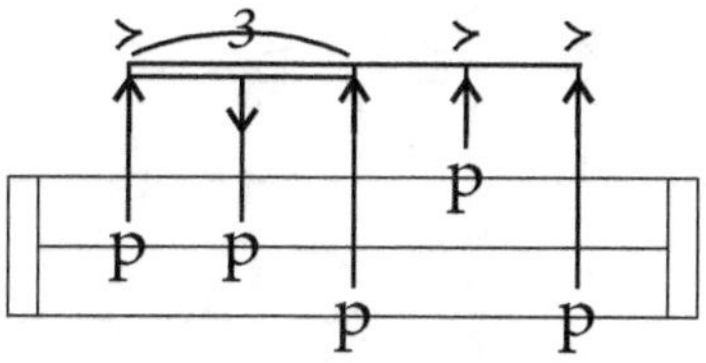

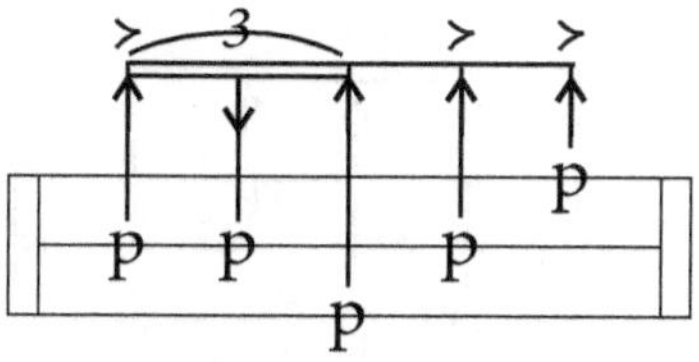

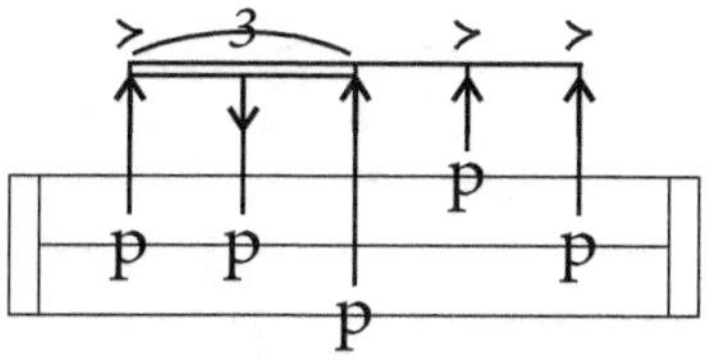

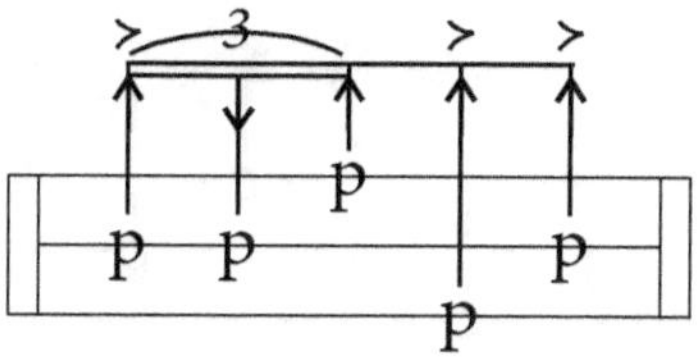

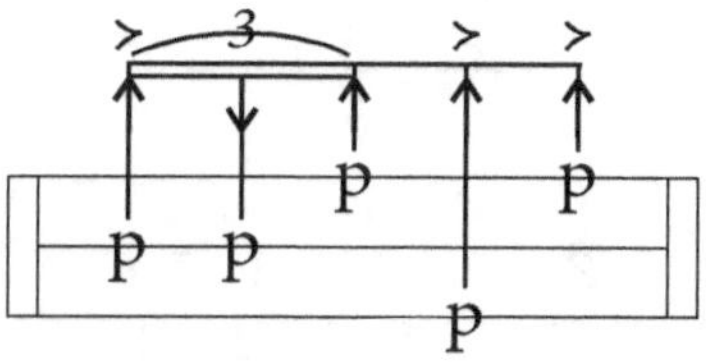

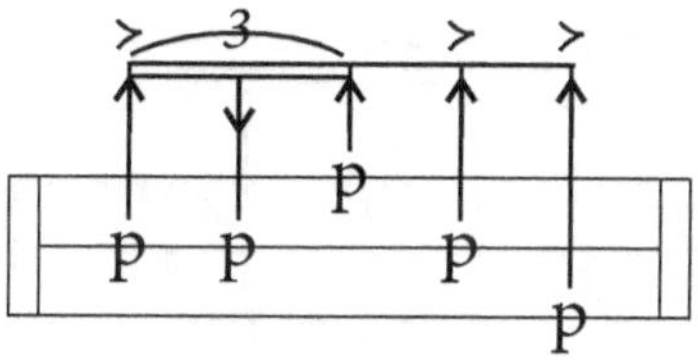

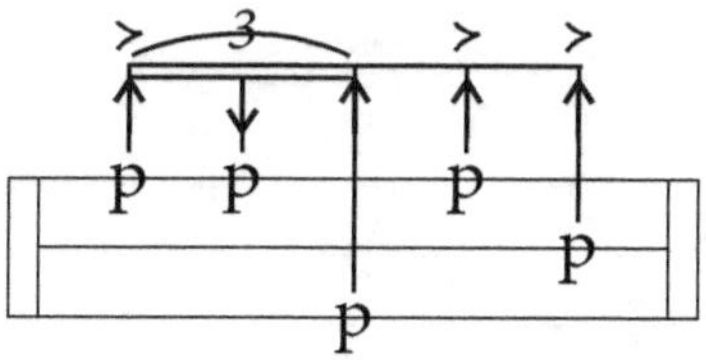

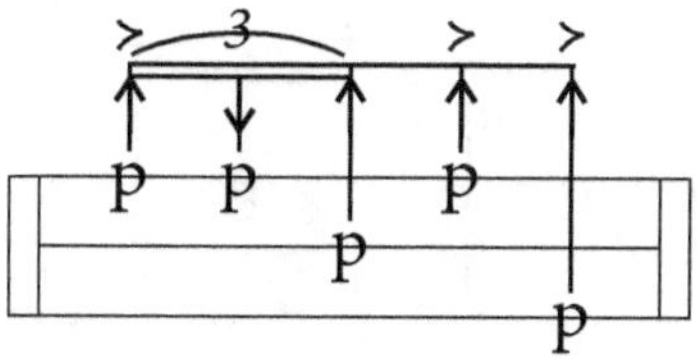

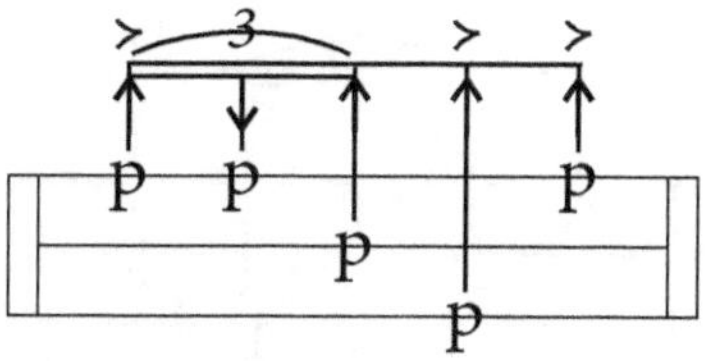

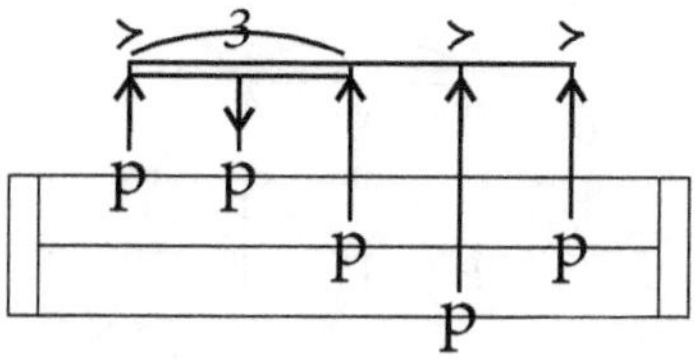

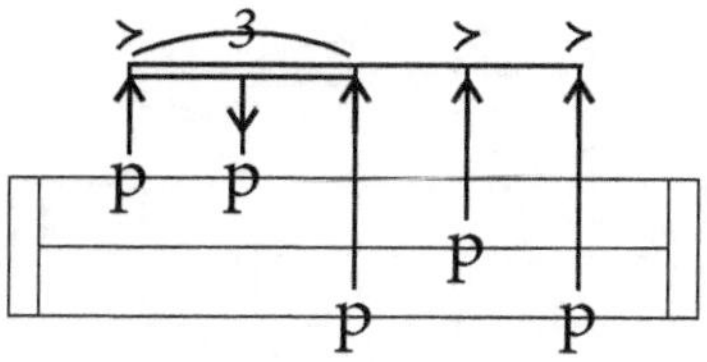

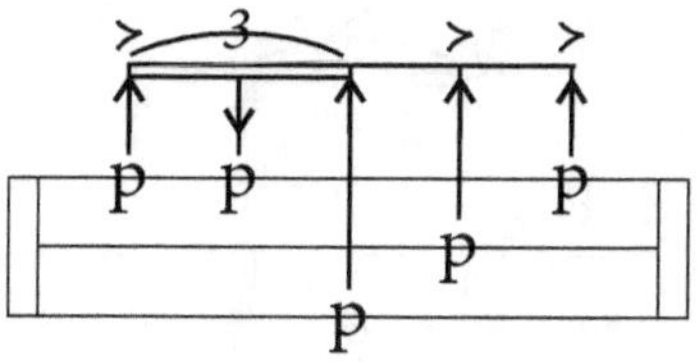

VARIATION II

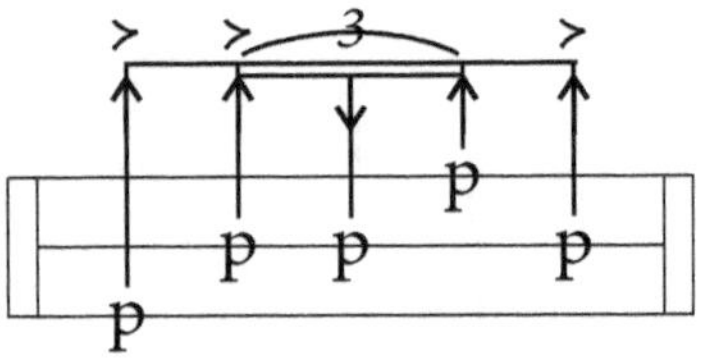

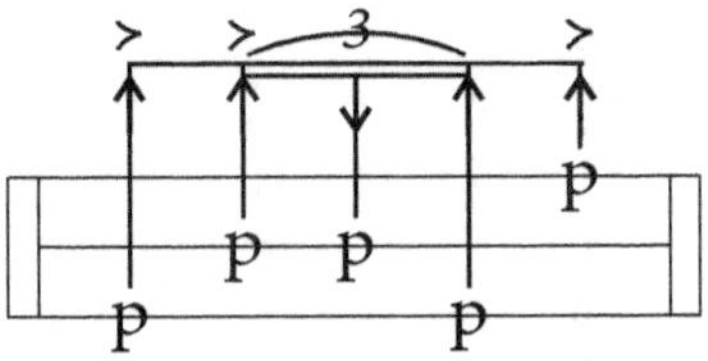

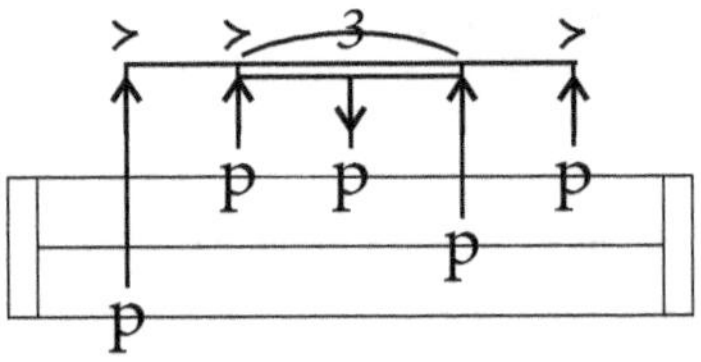

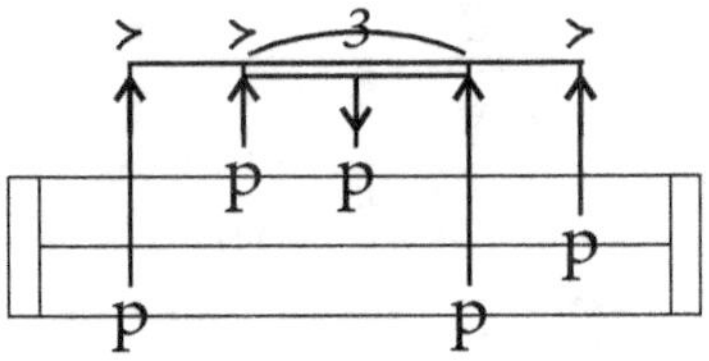

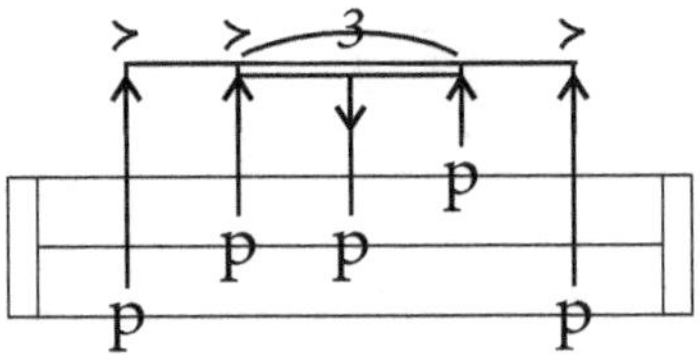

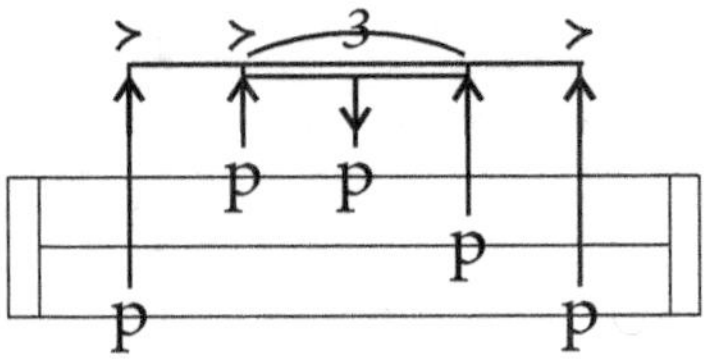

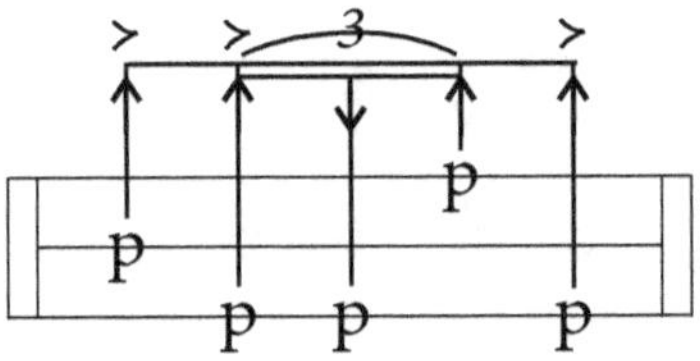

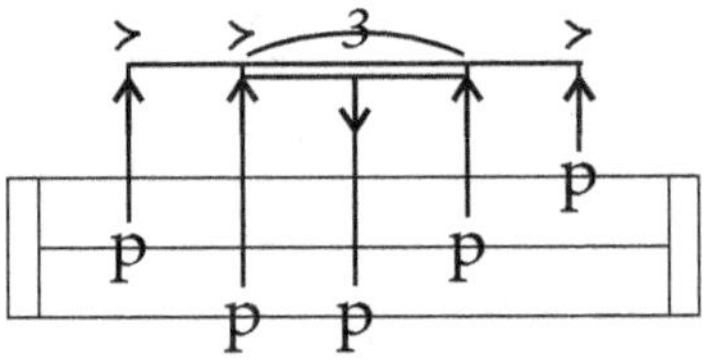

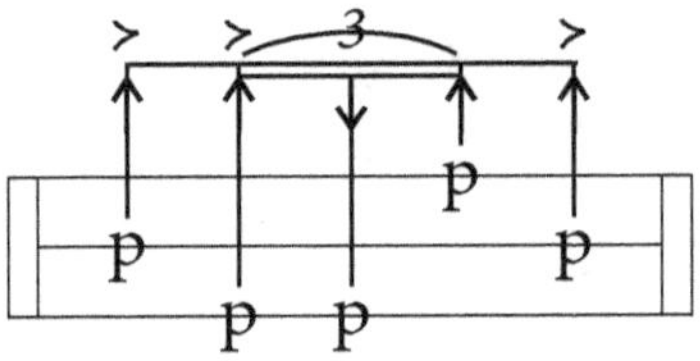

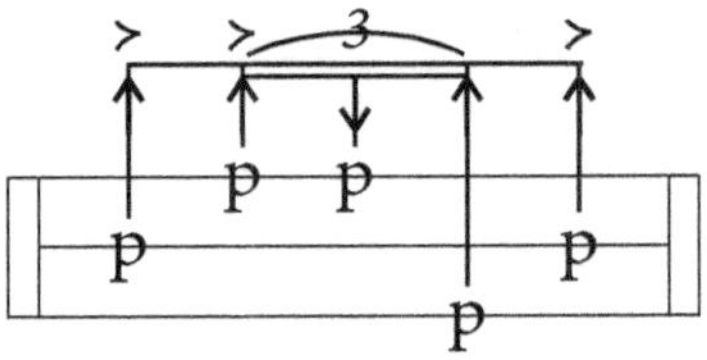

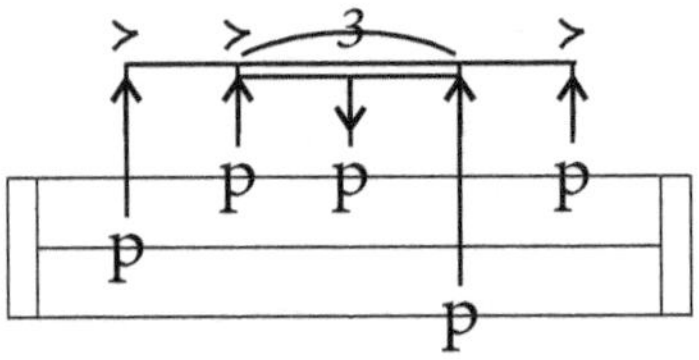

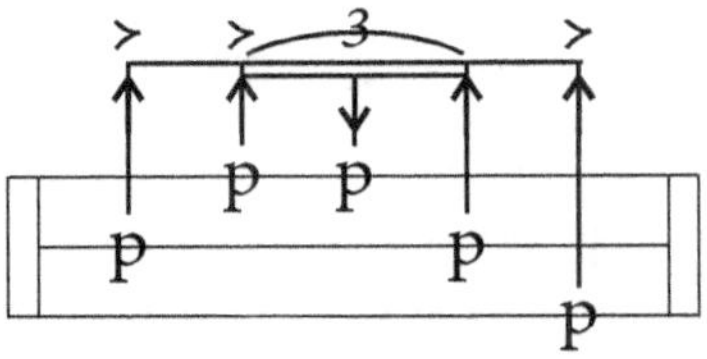

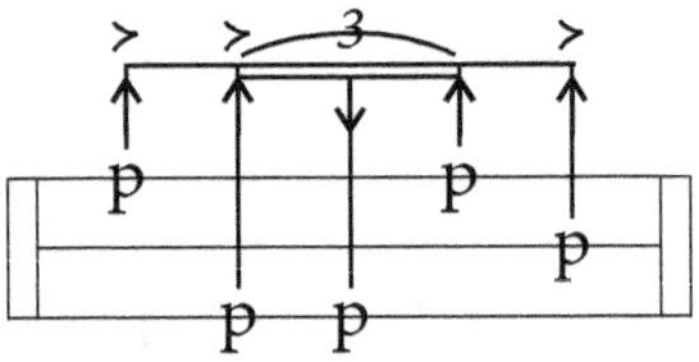

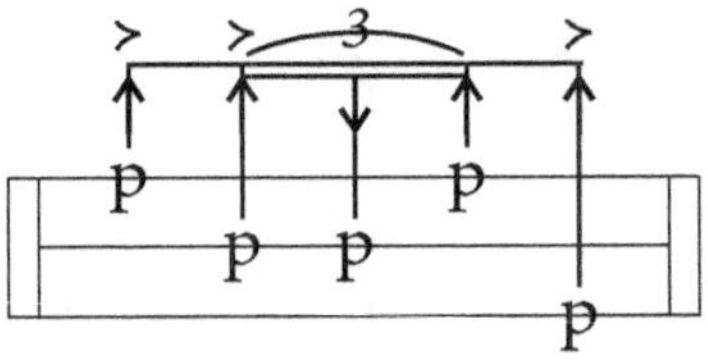

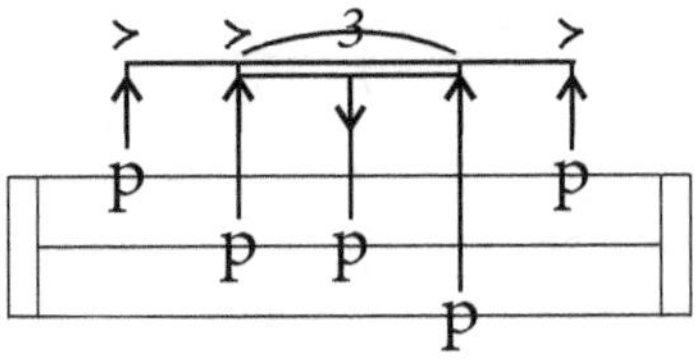

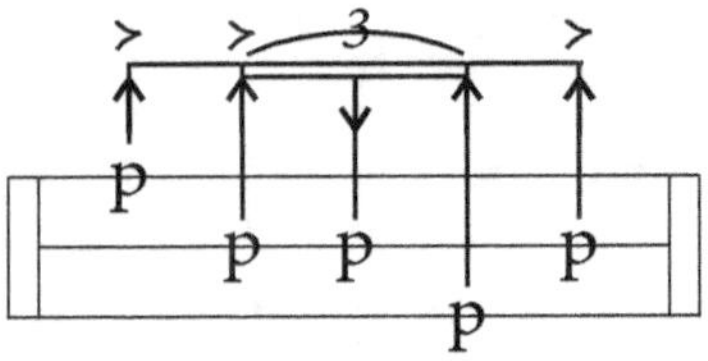

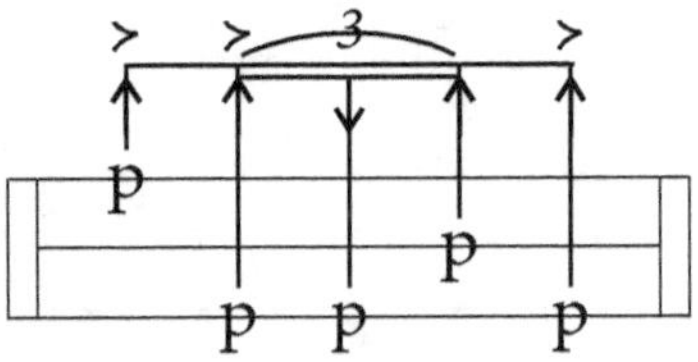

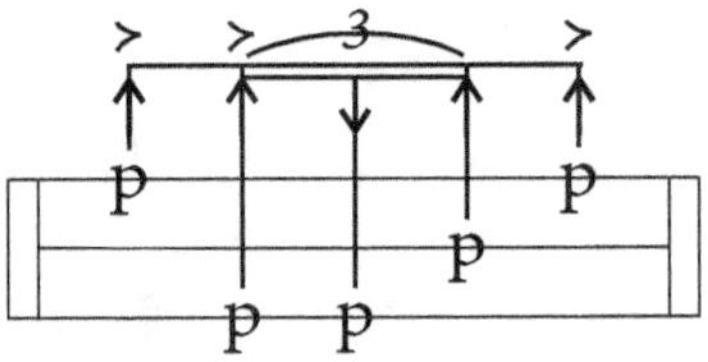

VARIATION III

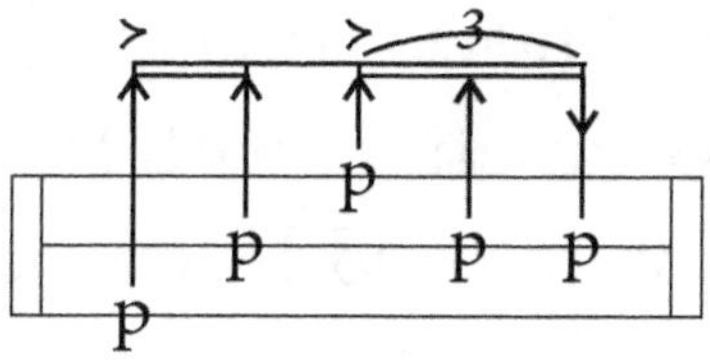

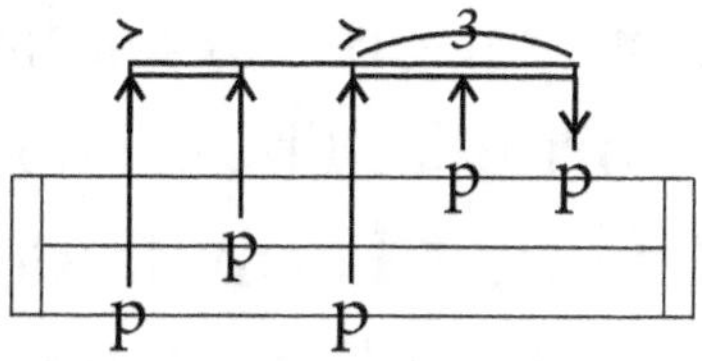

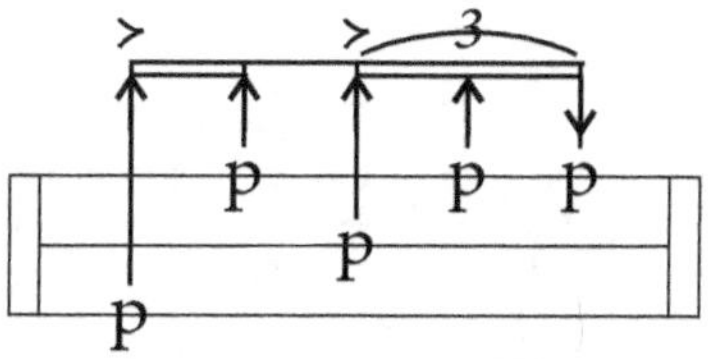

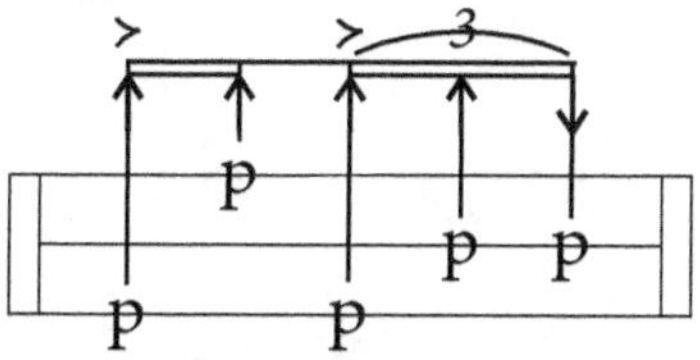

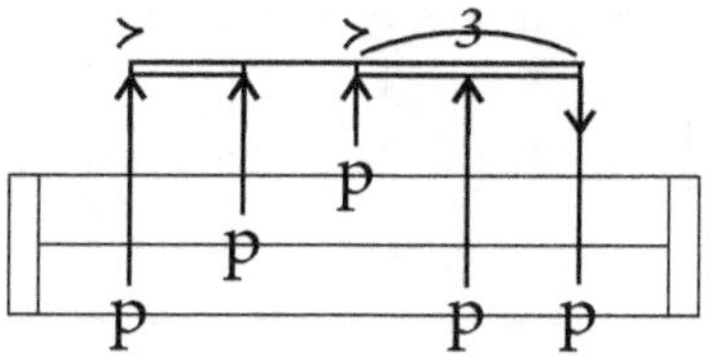

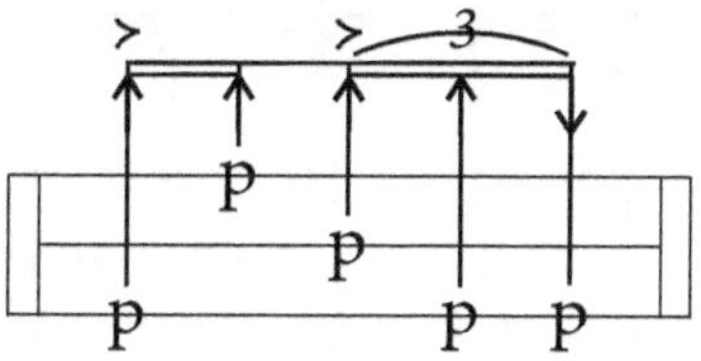

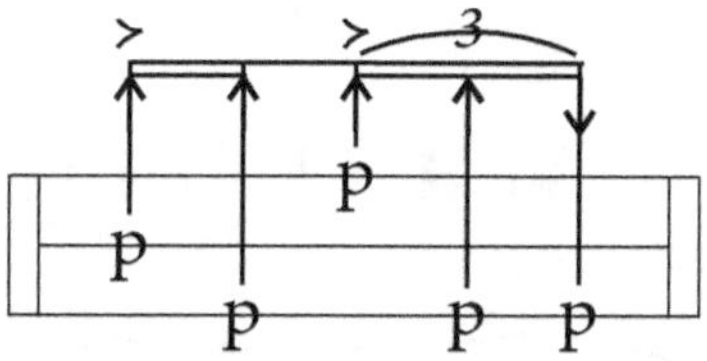

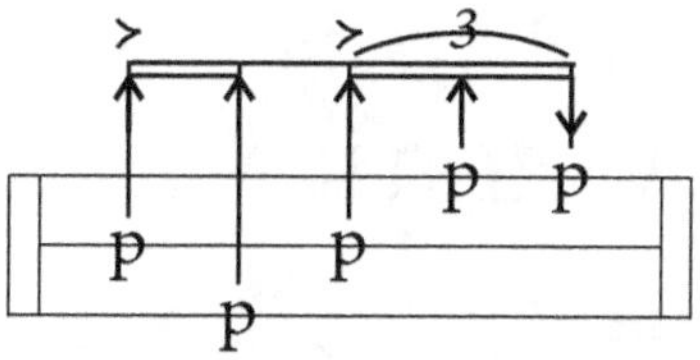

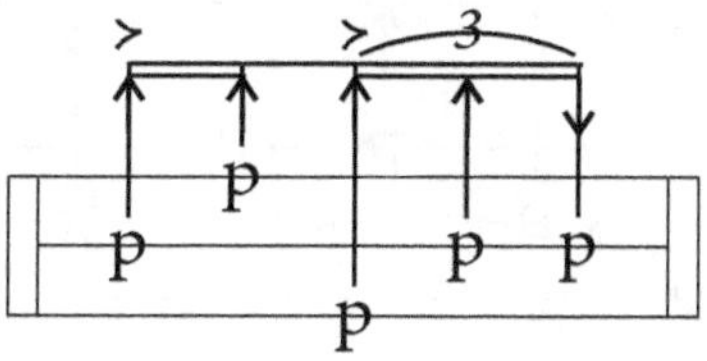

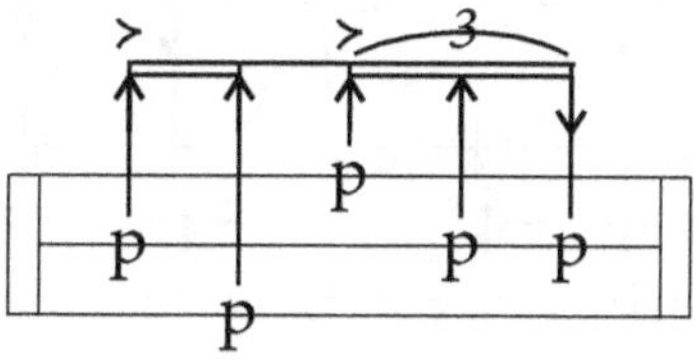

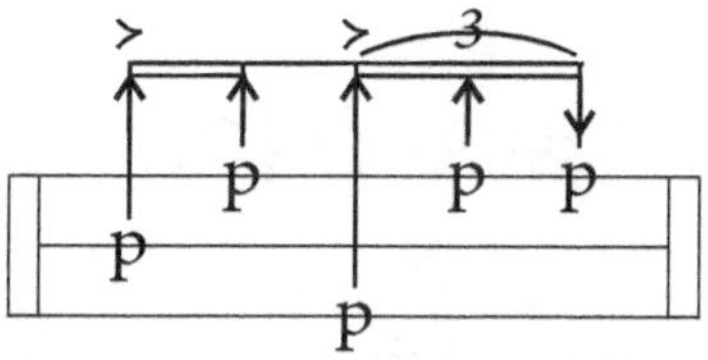

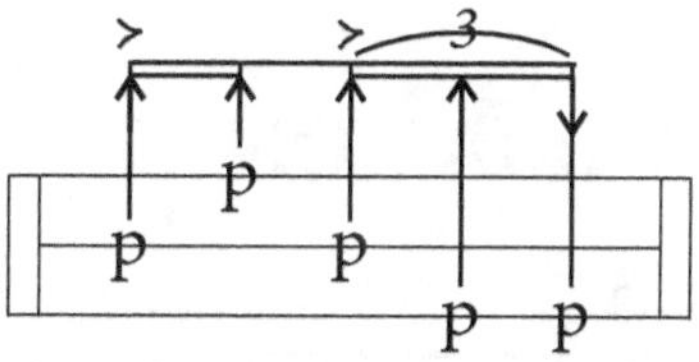

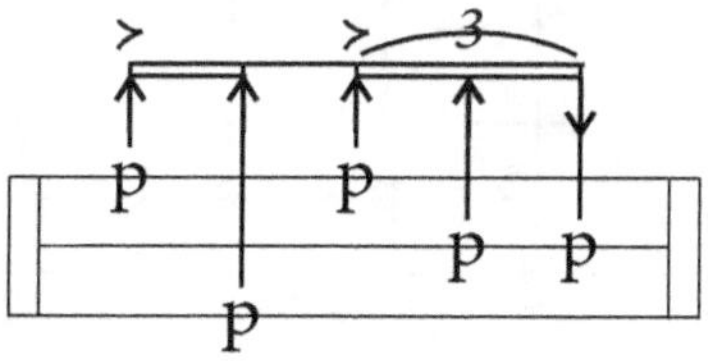

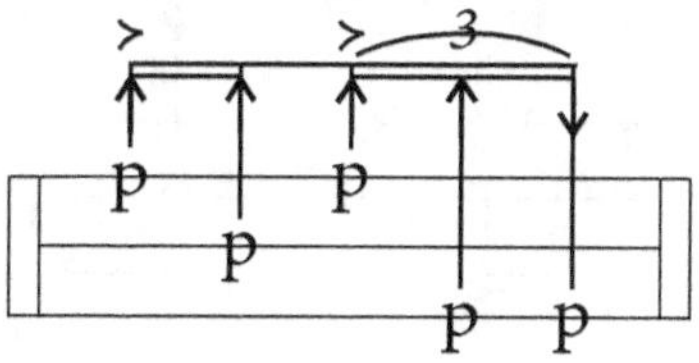

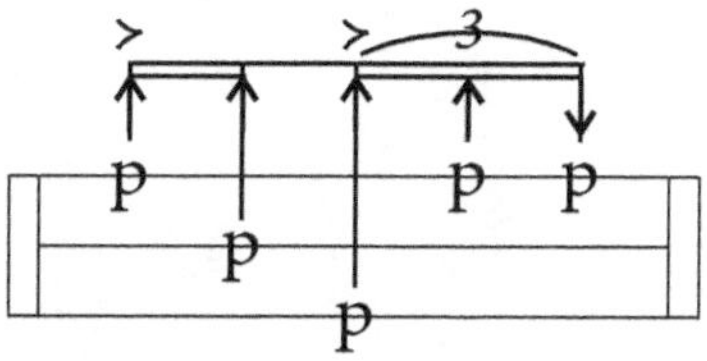

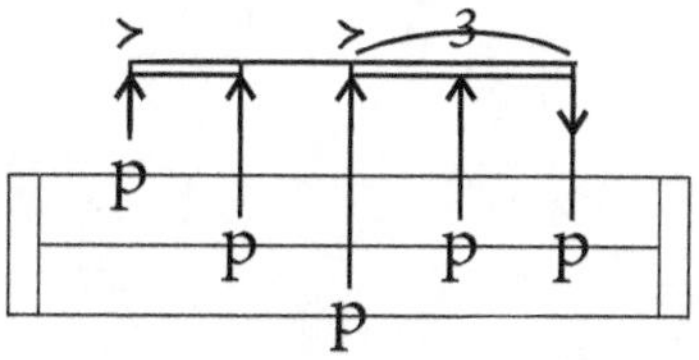

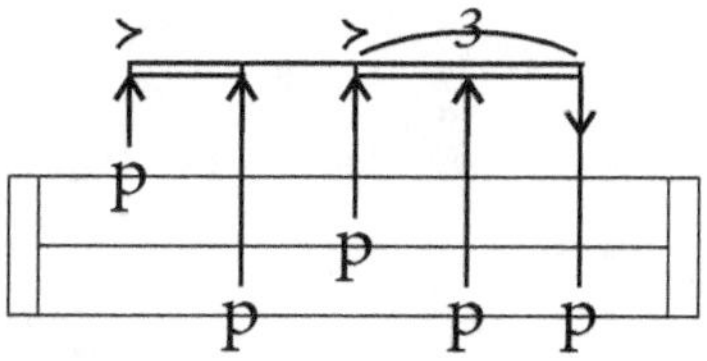

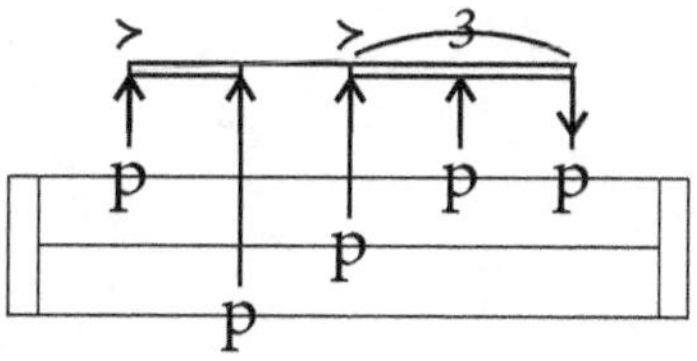

§ VI

Exercise on pulgar on three adjacent strings with two triple (triplet) strokes within each Formula. The exercise contains six variations with 18 Formulas in each one. The first Formula of each variation is cited below. Isochronous playing of pulgar strokes (of the triplets).

VARIATION I

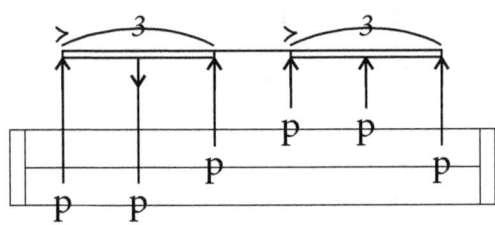

VARIATION IV

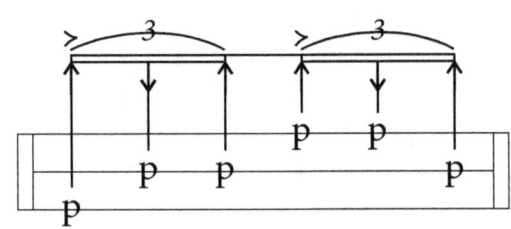

VARIATION II

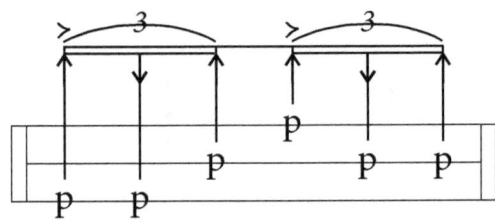

VARIATION V

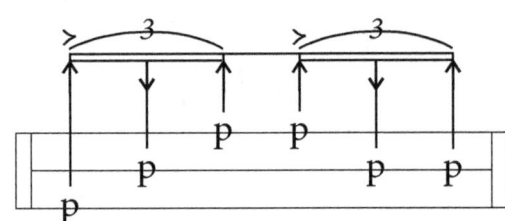

VARIATION III

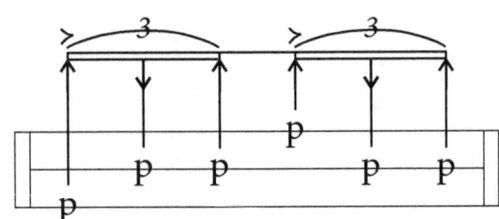

VARIATION VI

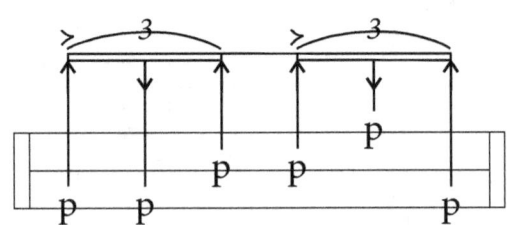

VARIATION I

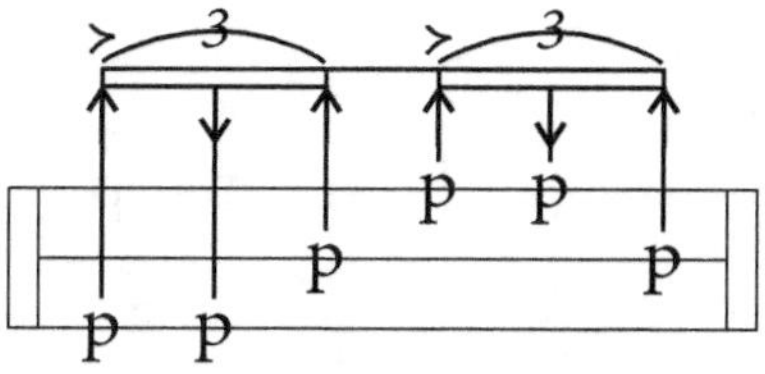

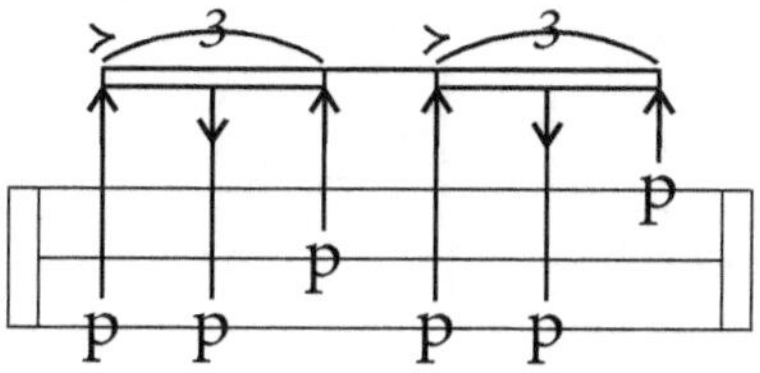

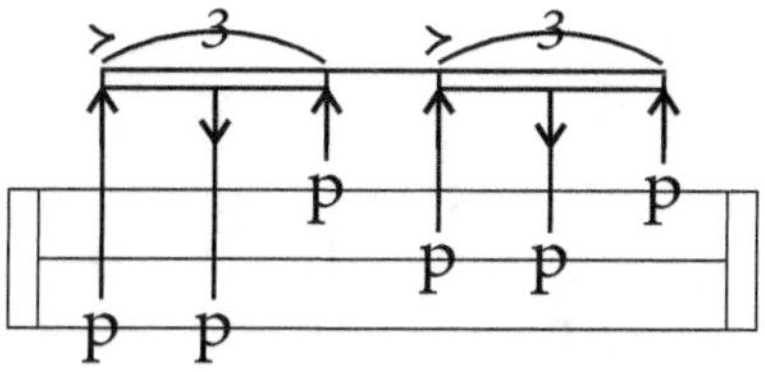

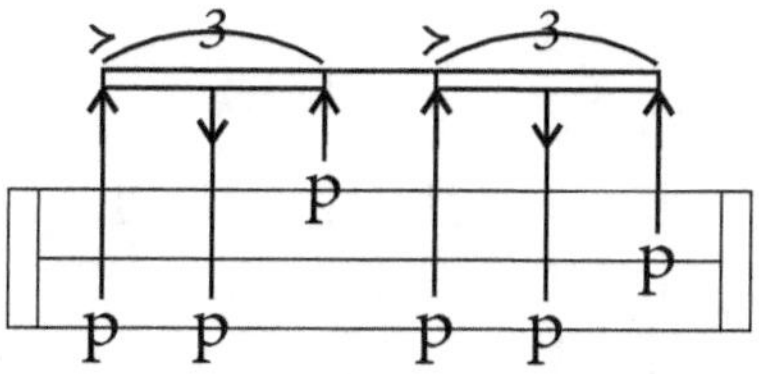

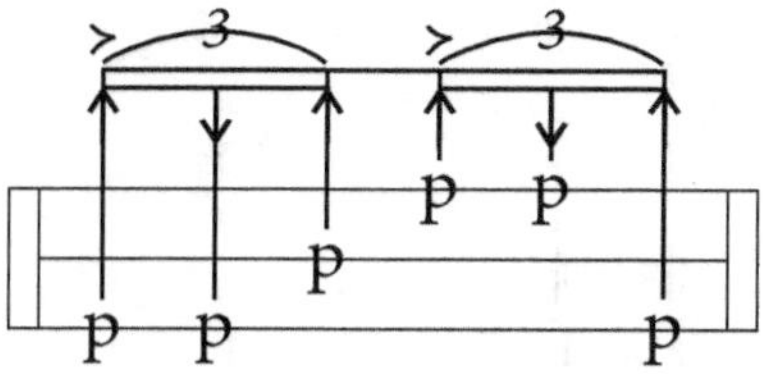

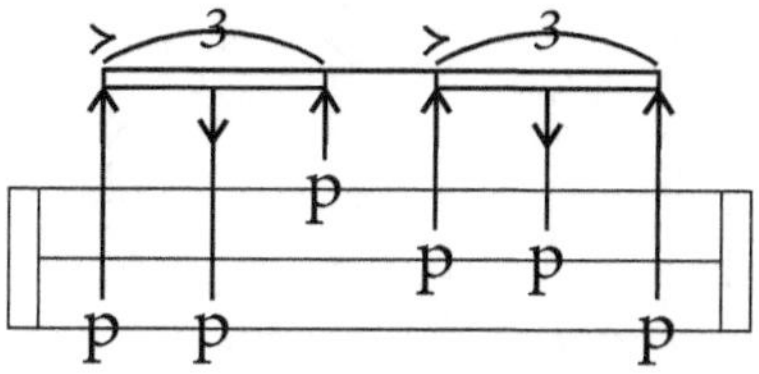

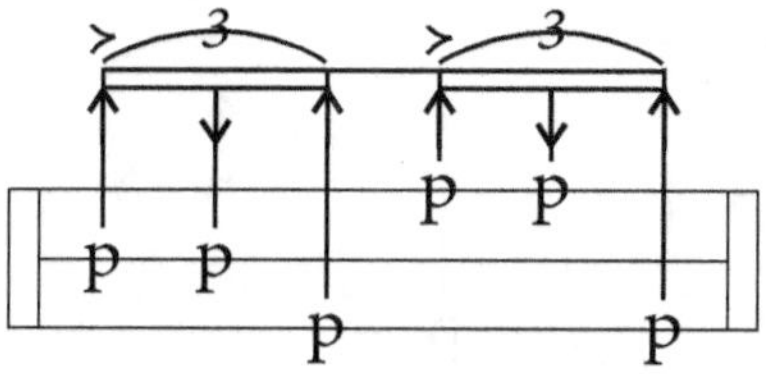

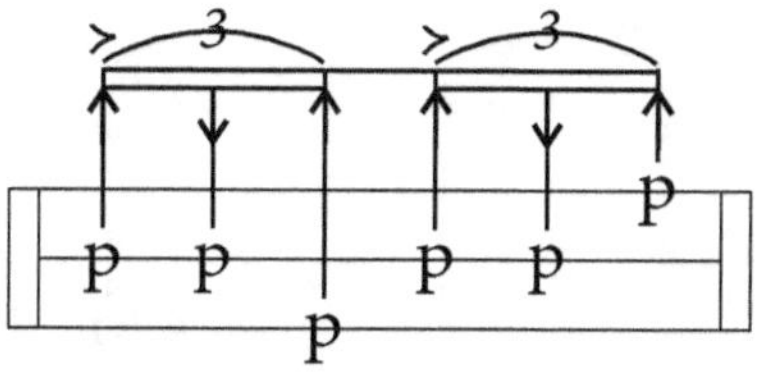

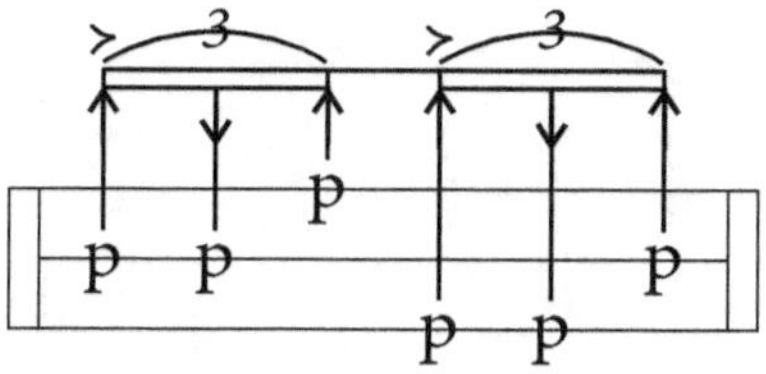

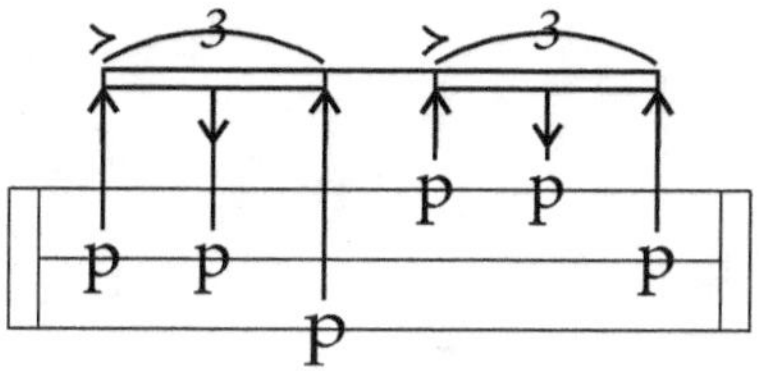

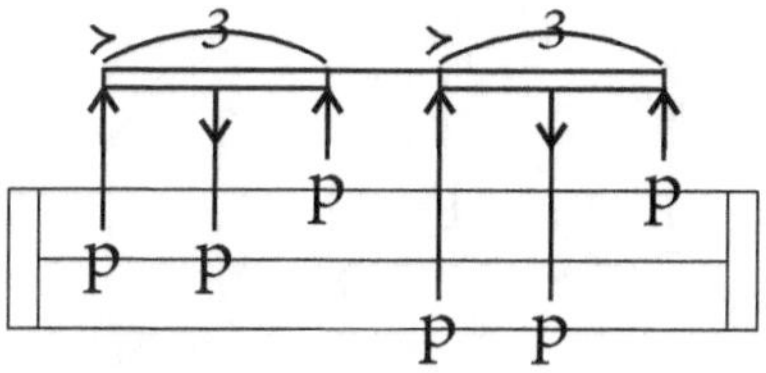

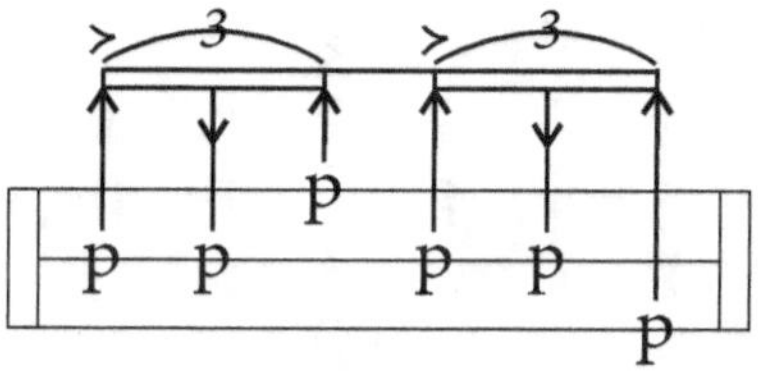

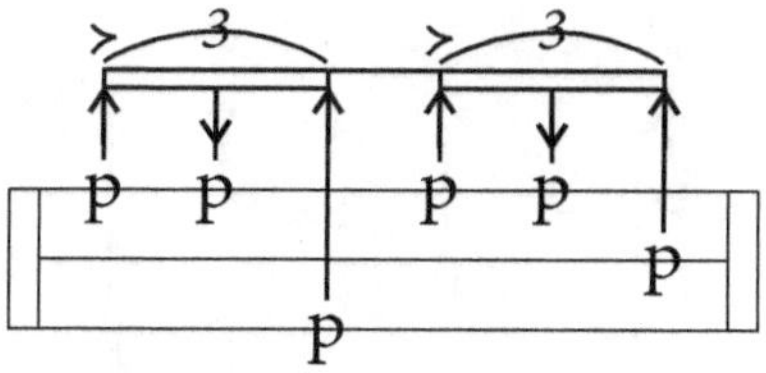

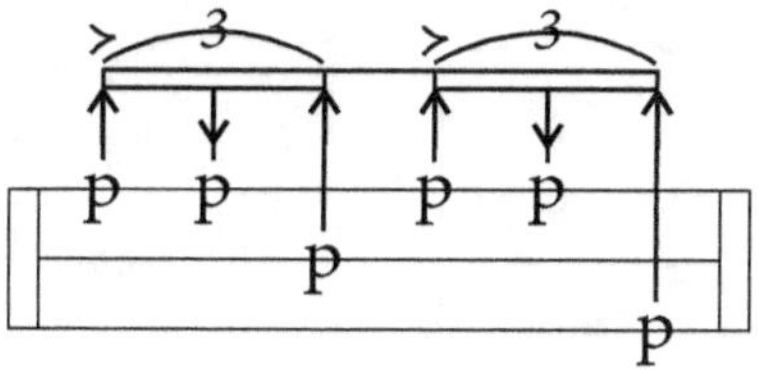

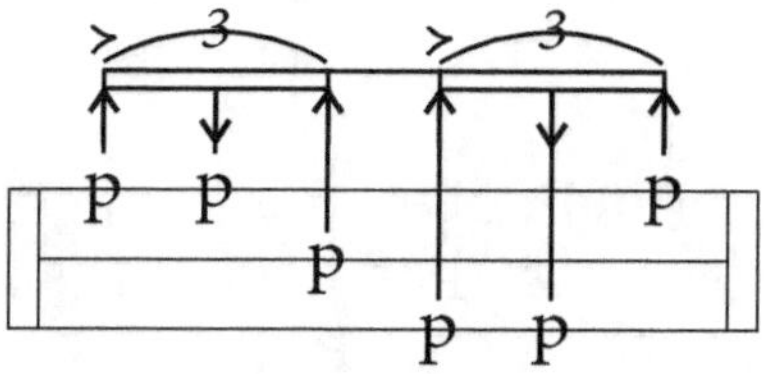

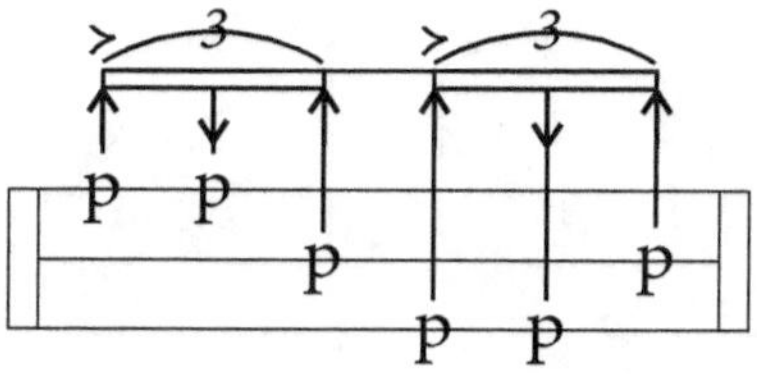

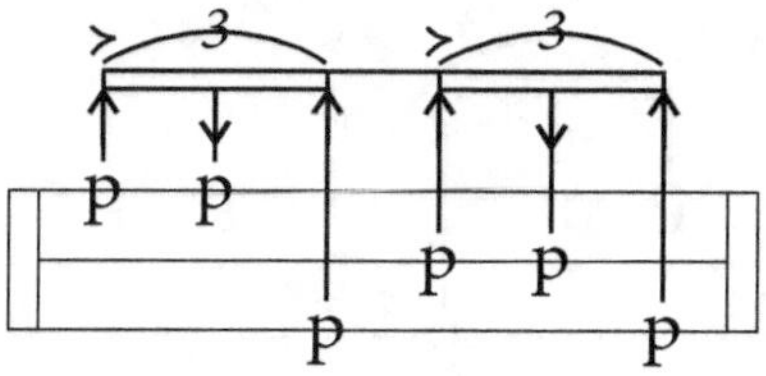

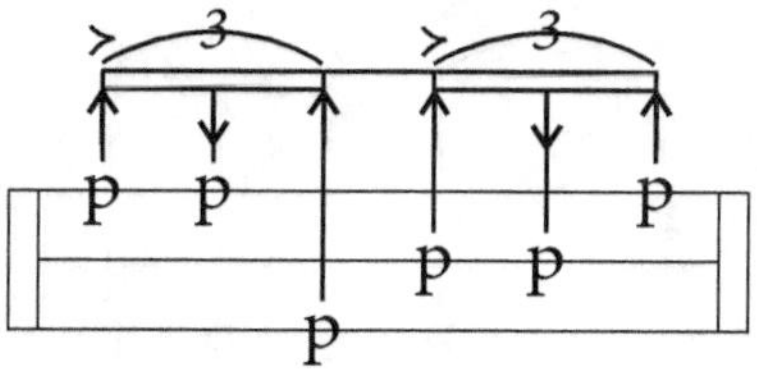

VARIATION II

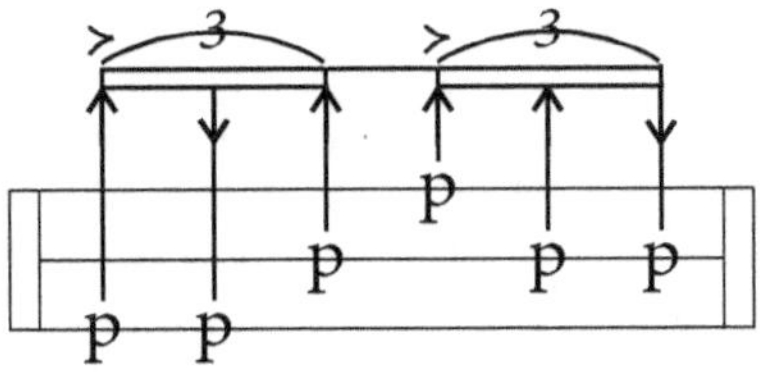

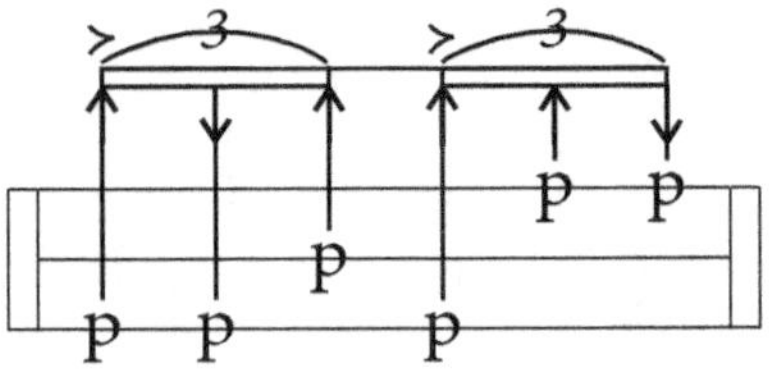

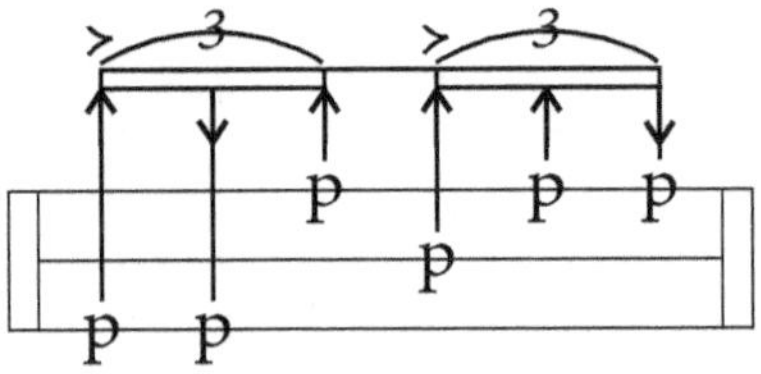

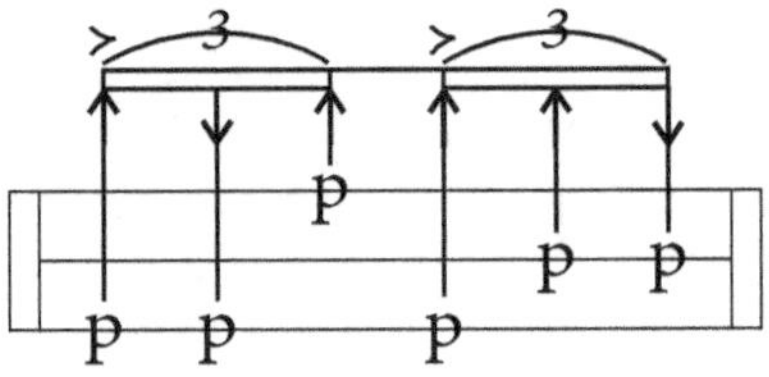

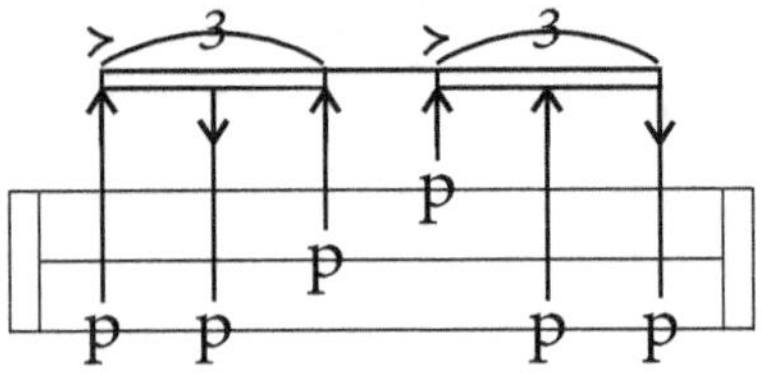

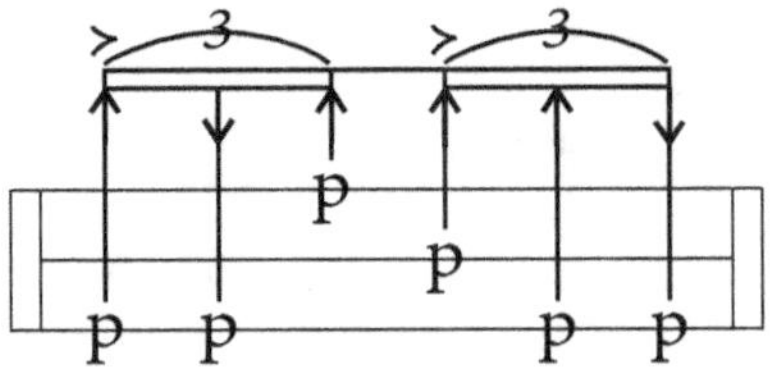

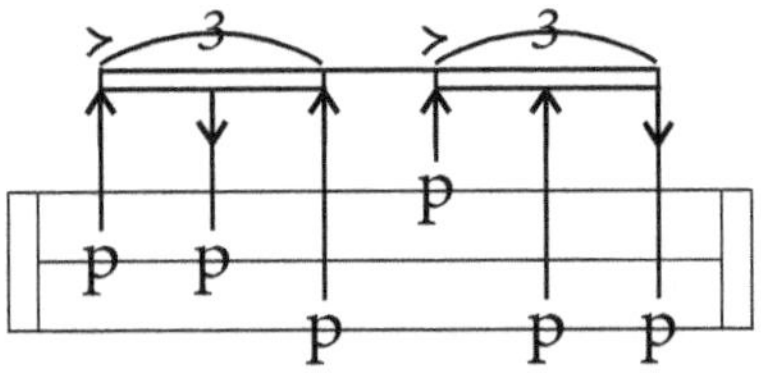

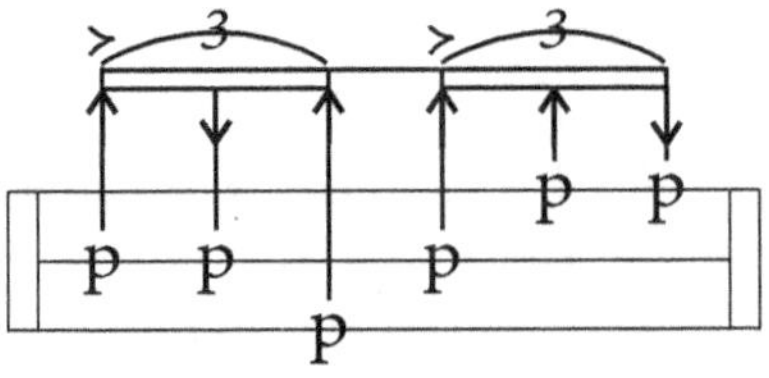

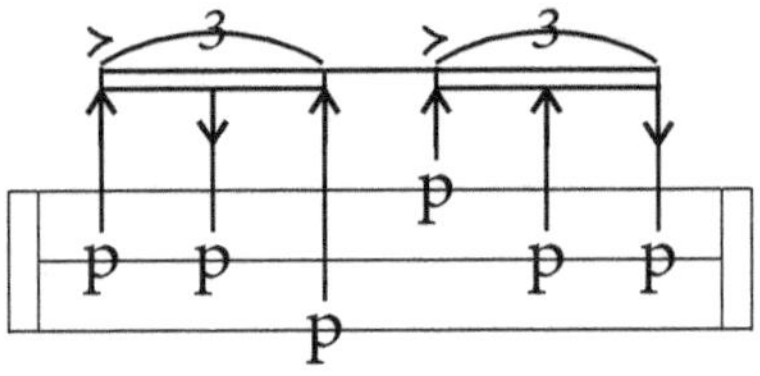

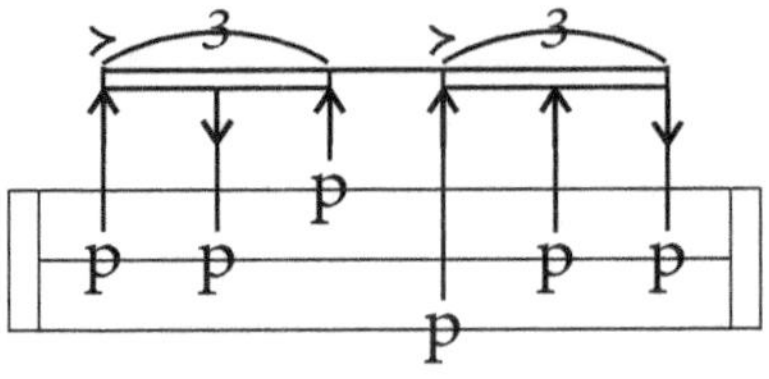

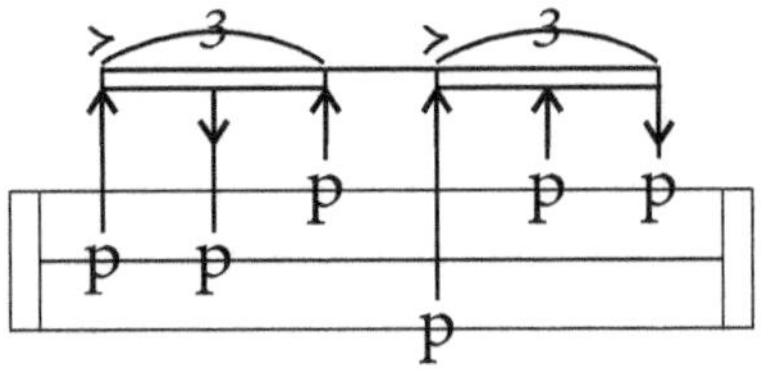

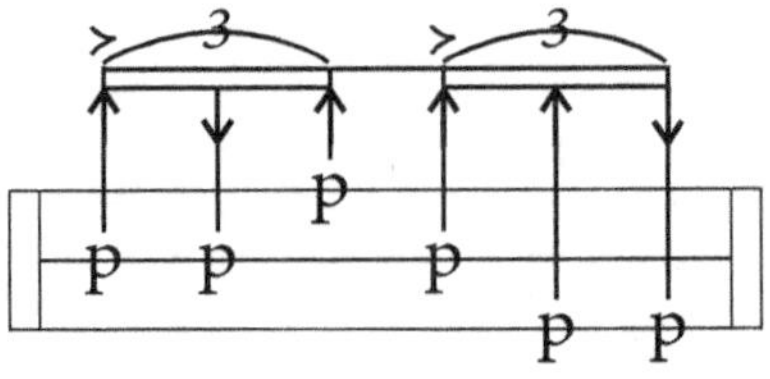

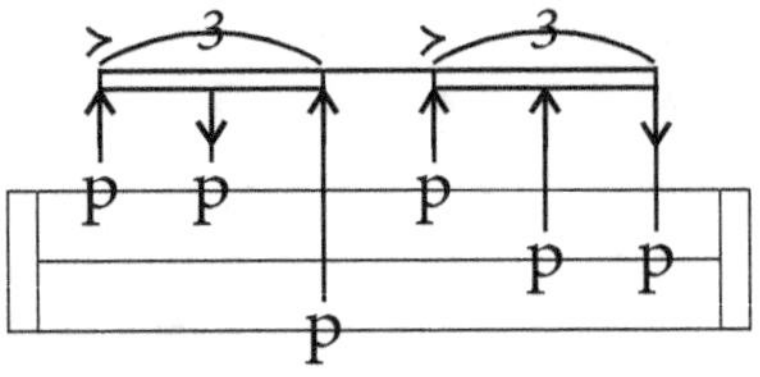

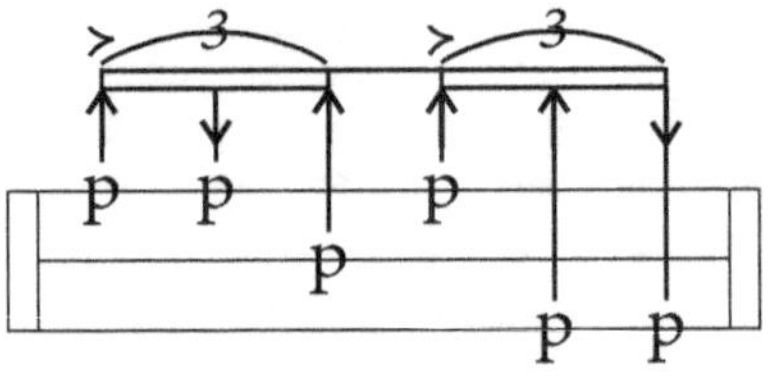

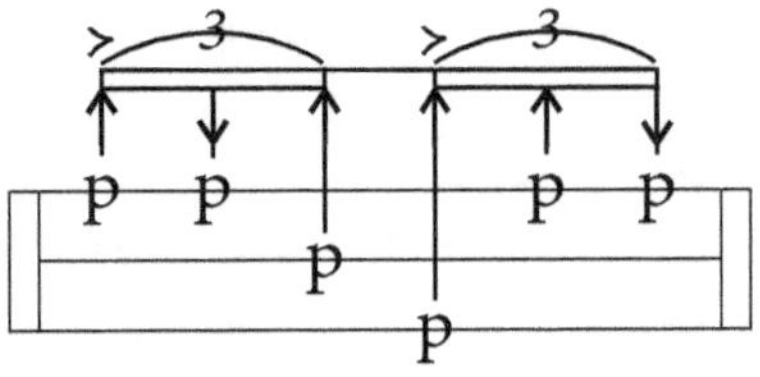

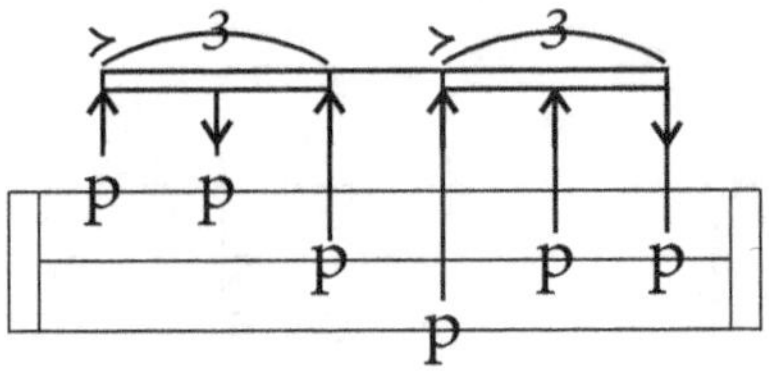

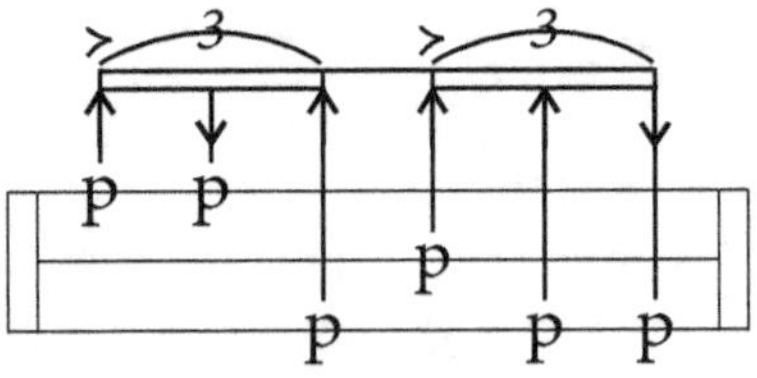

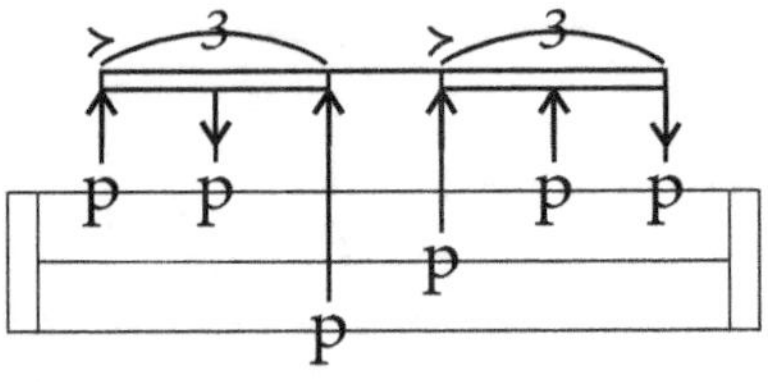

VARIATION III

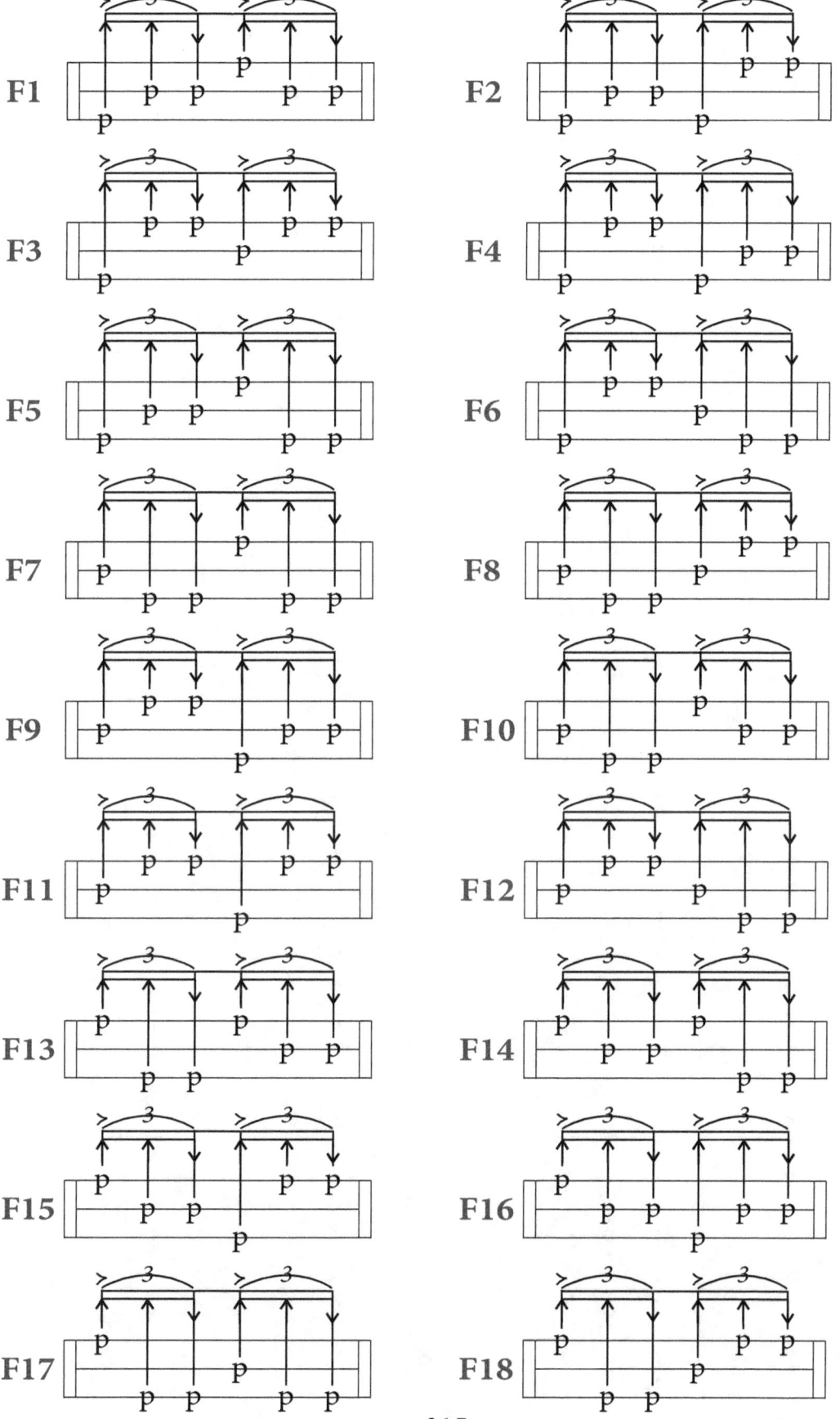

VARIATION IV

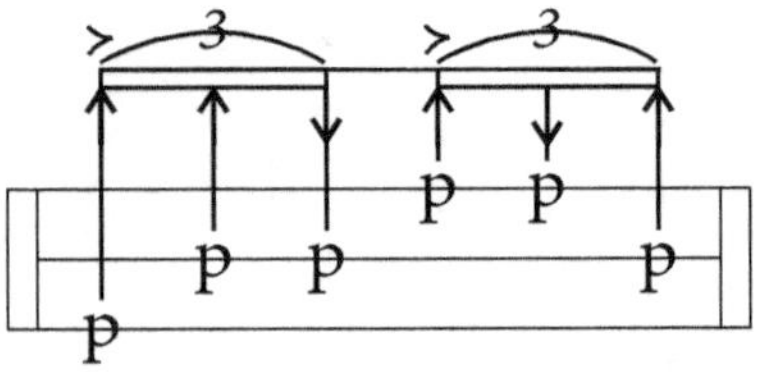

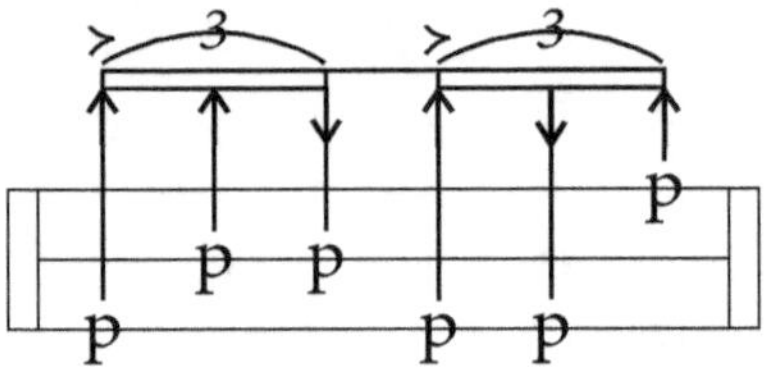

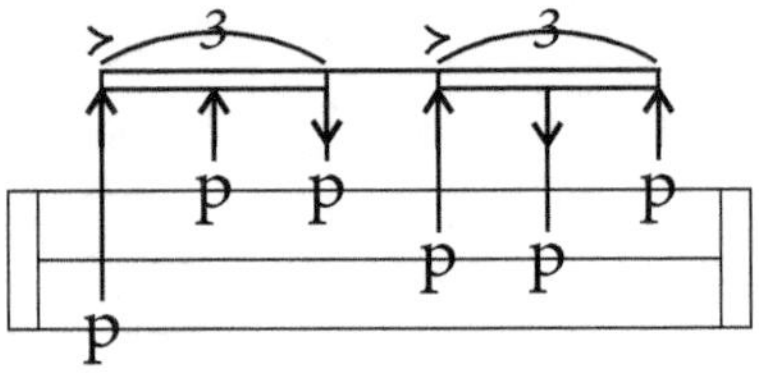

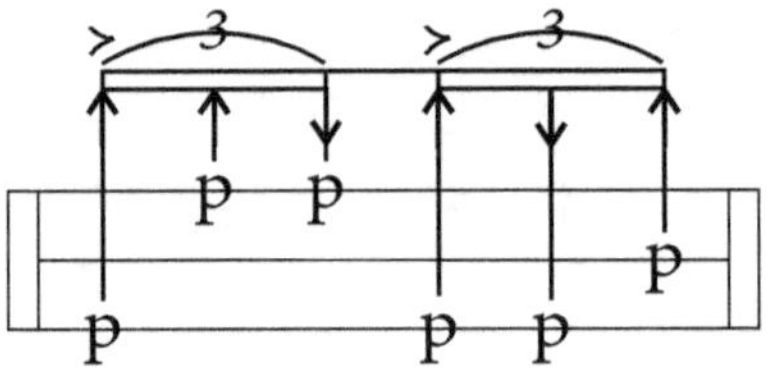

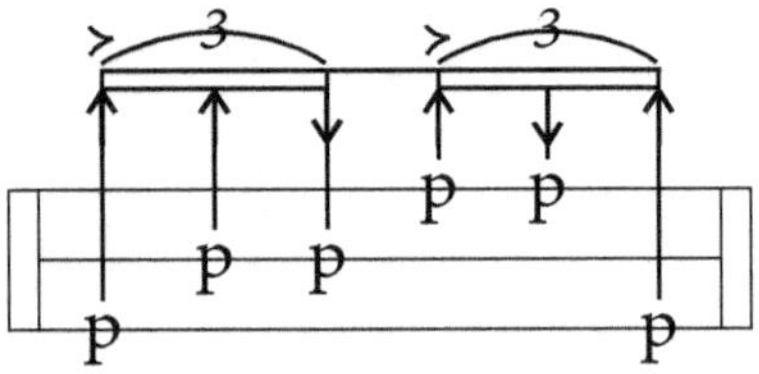

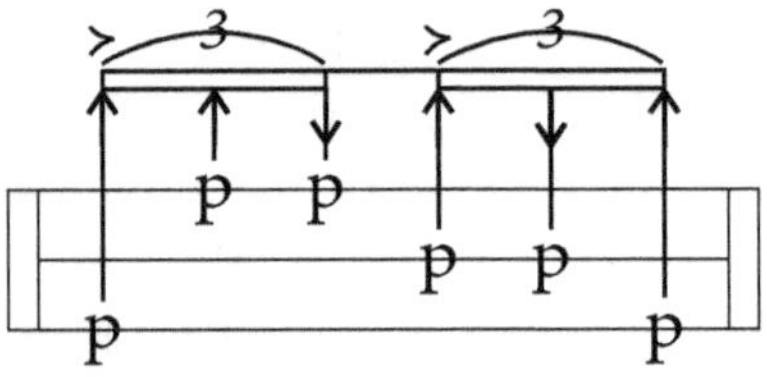

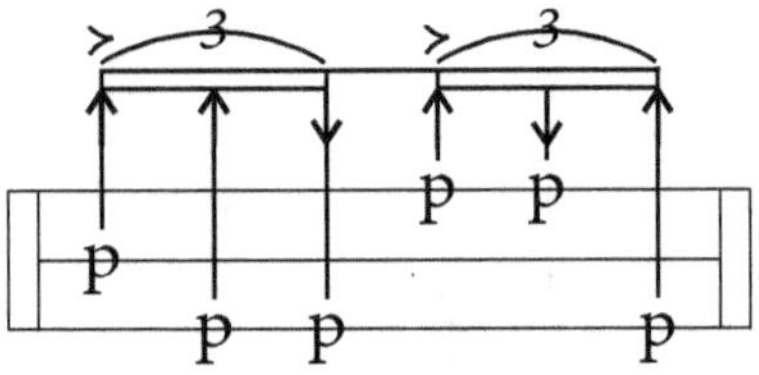

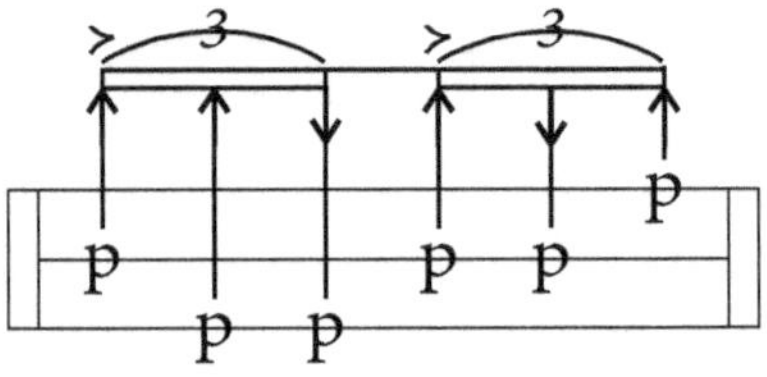

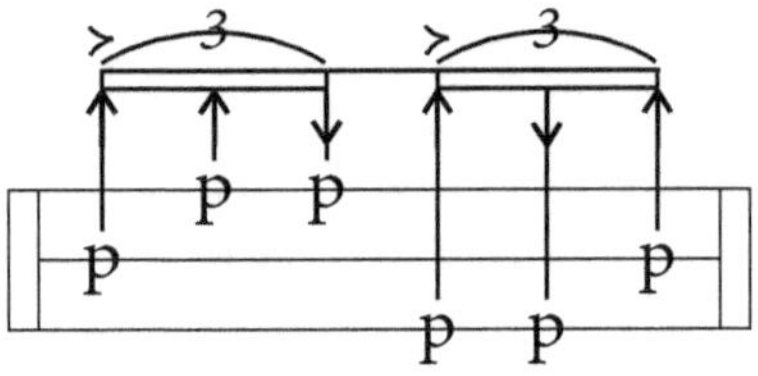

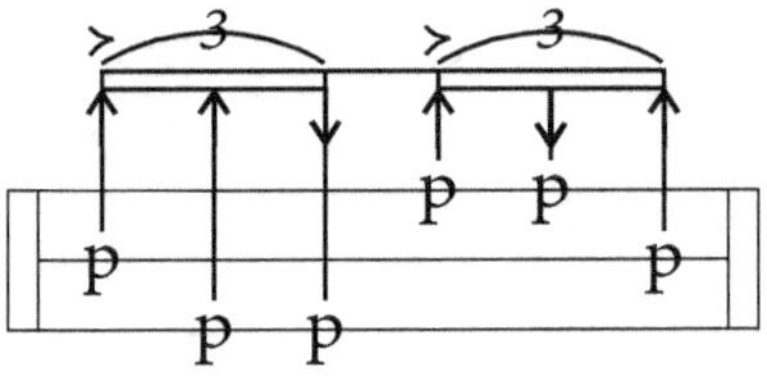

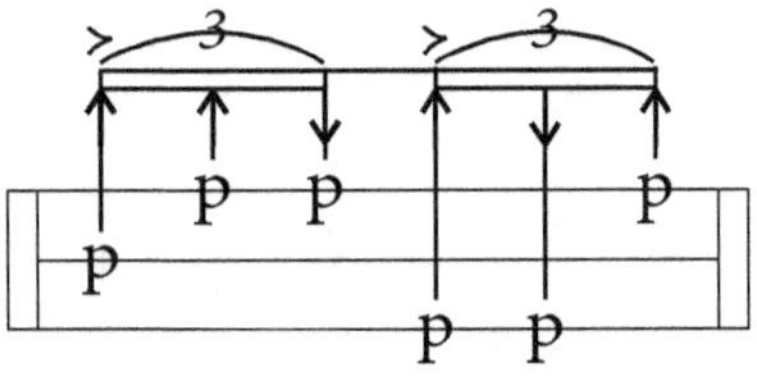

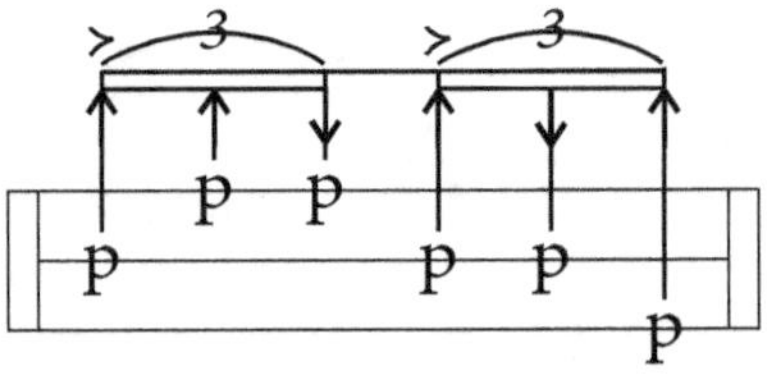

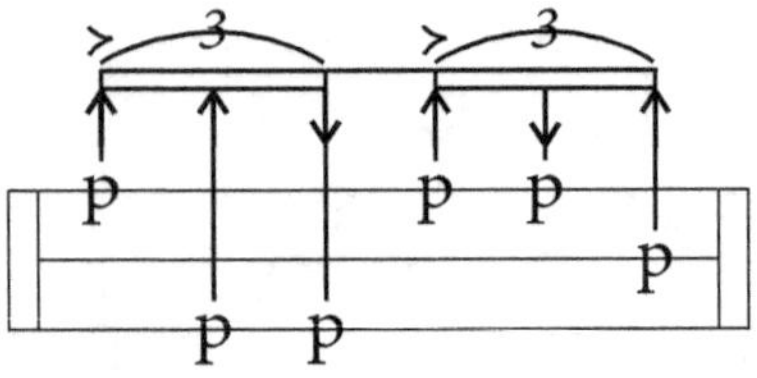

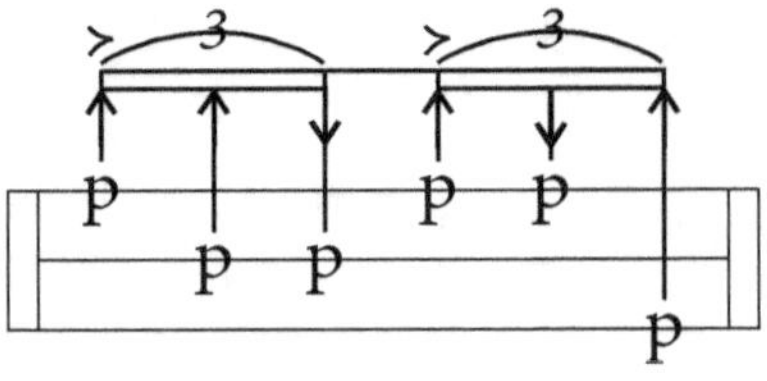

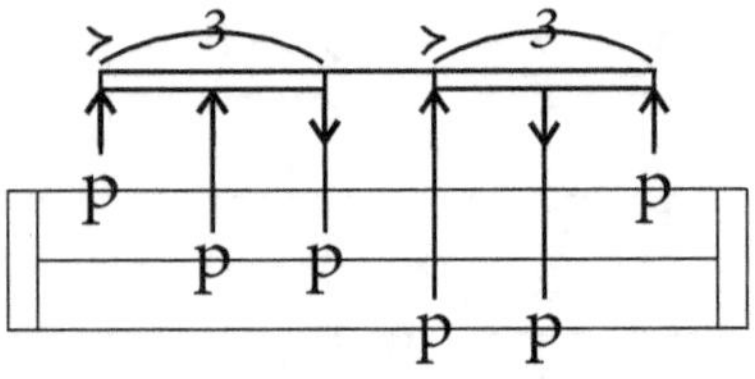

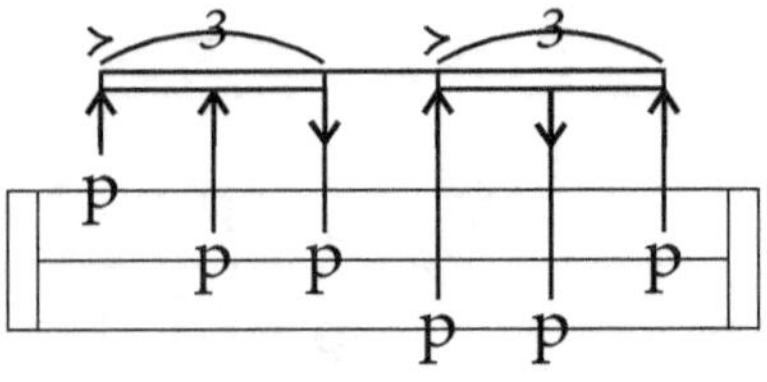

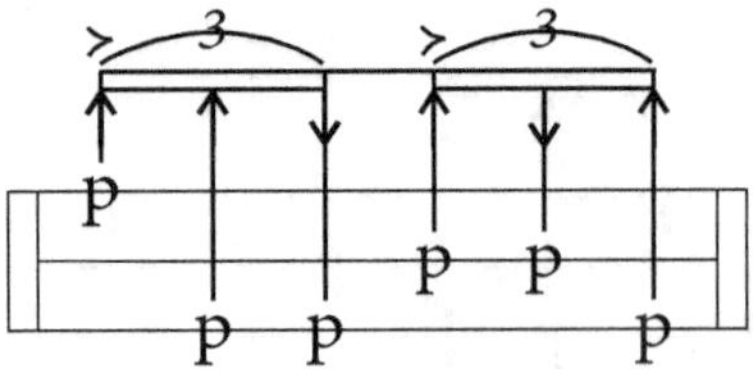

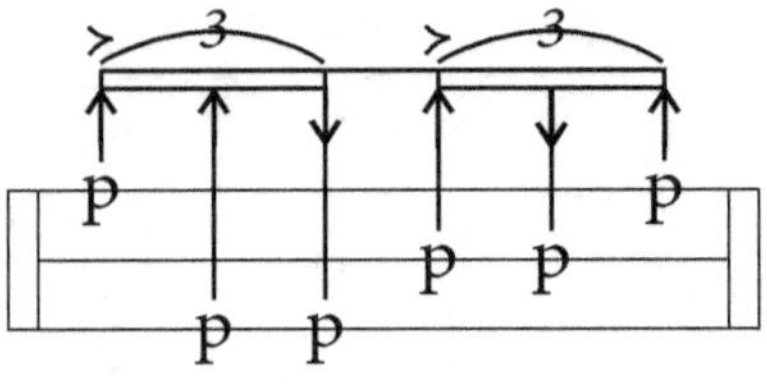

VARIATION V

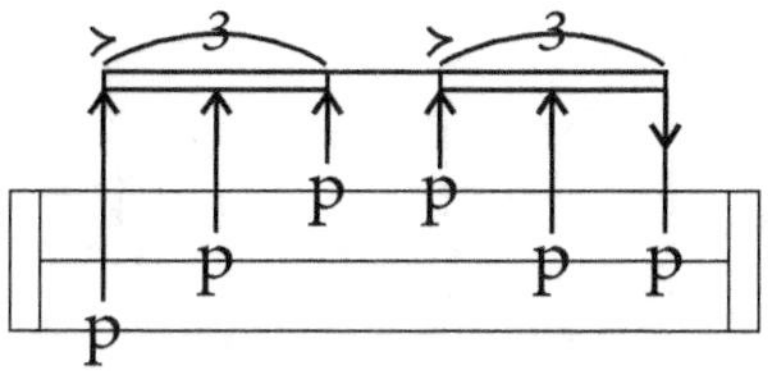

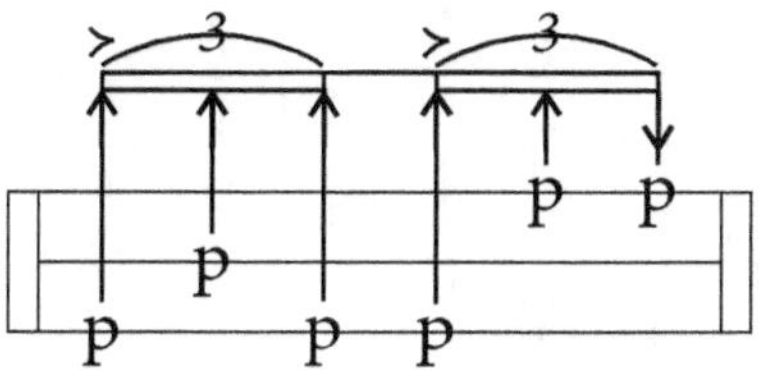

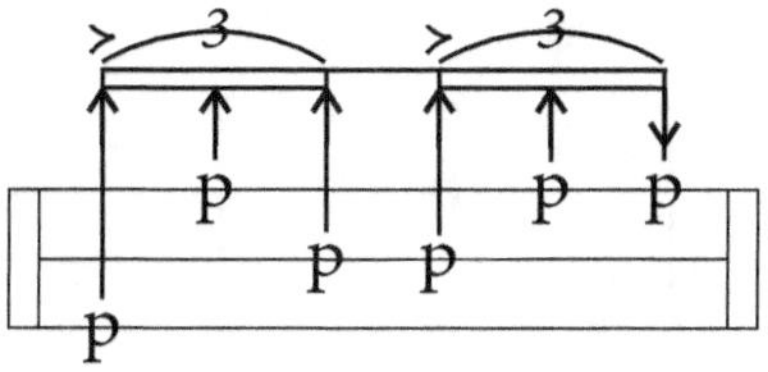

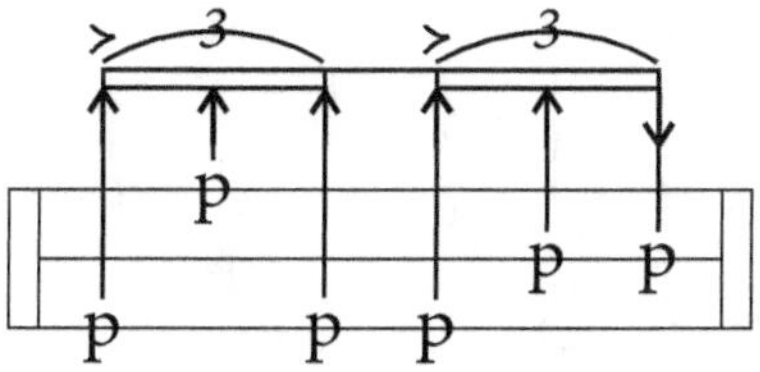

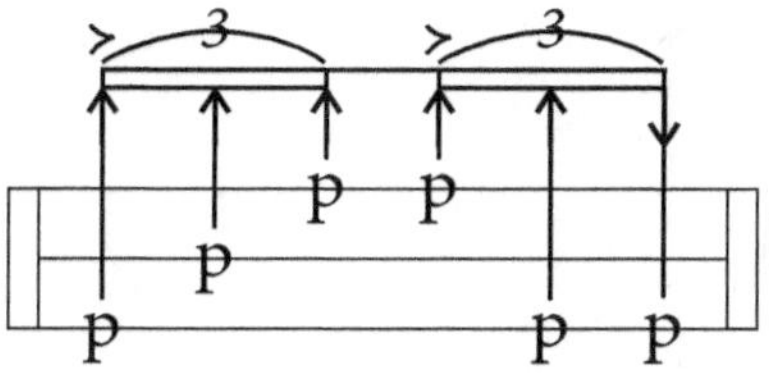

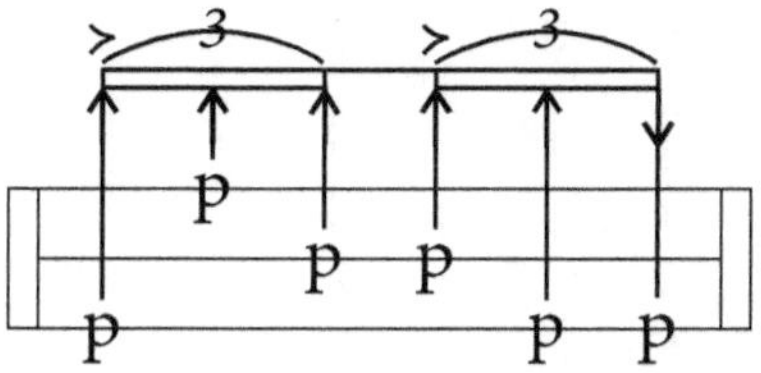

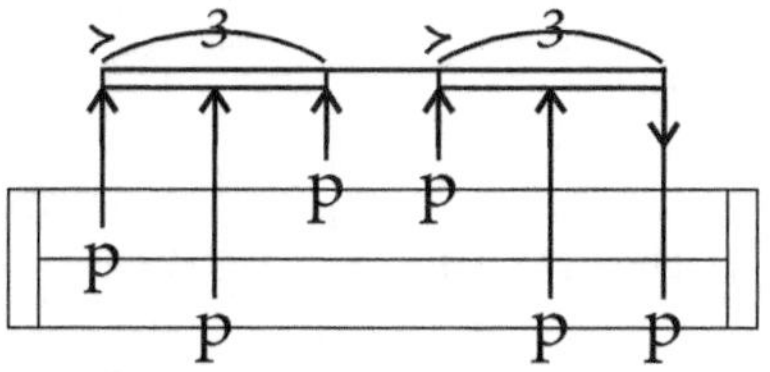

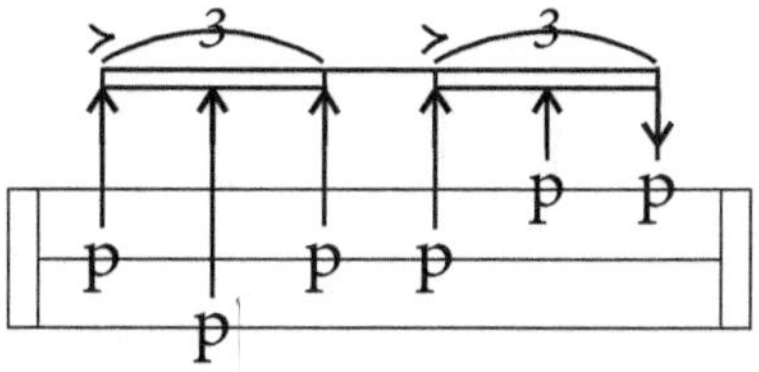

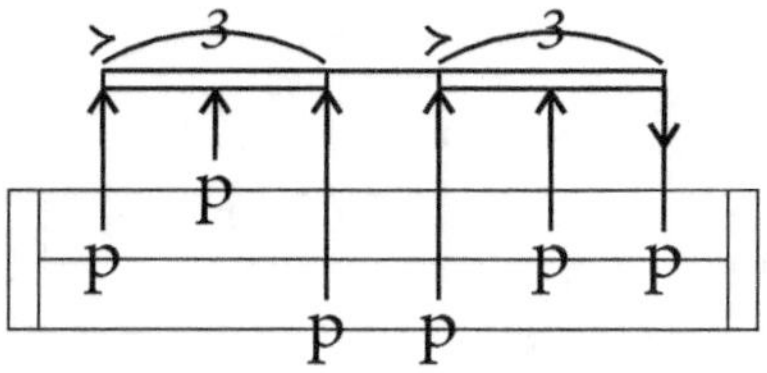

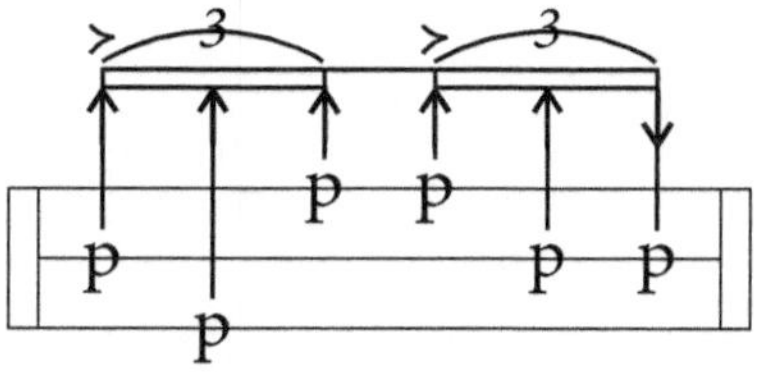

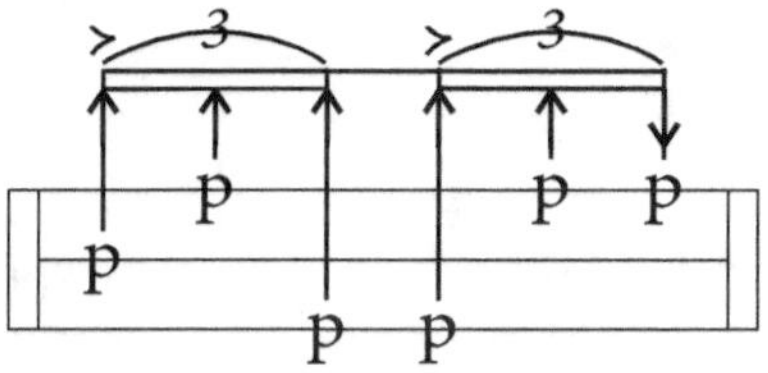

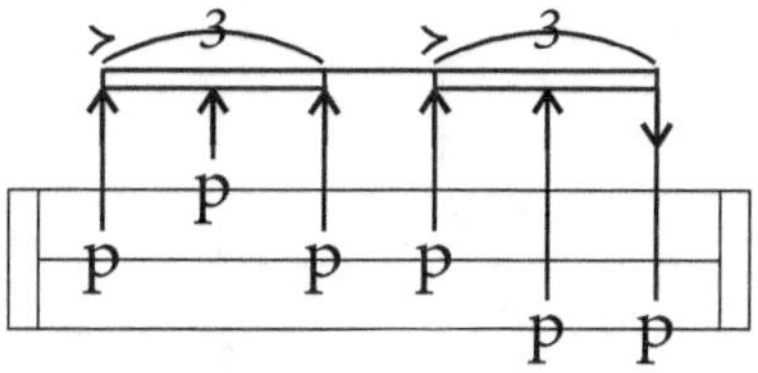

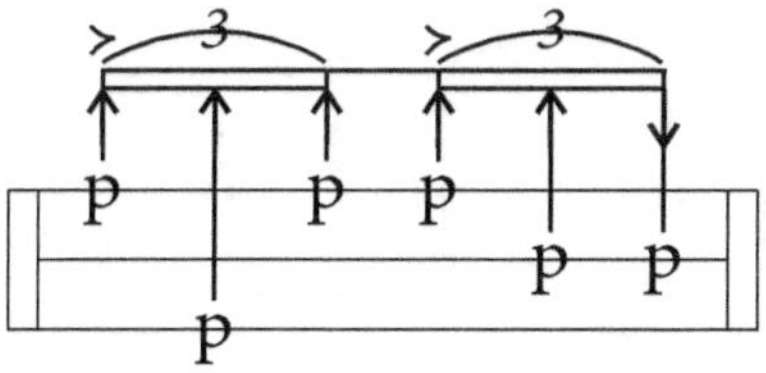

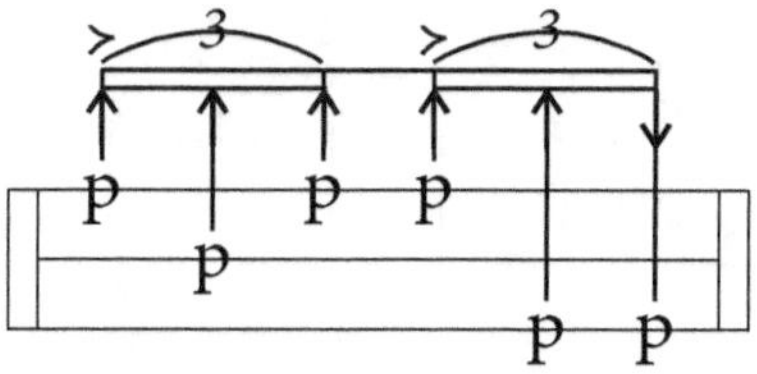

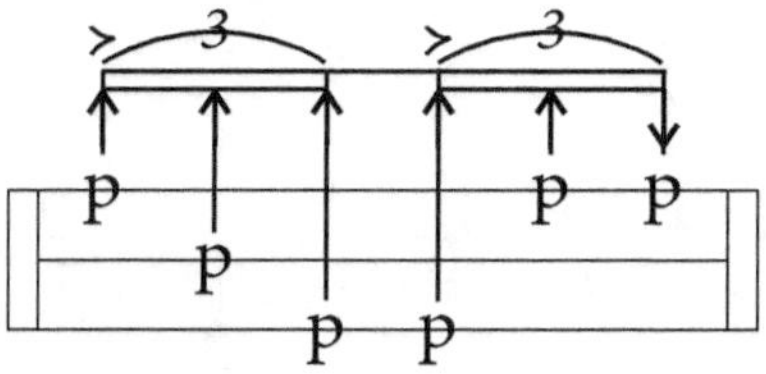

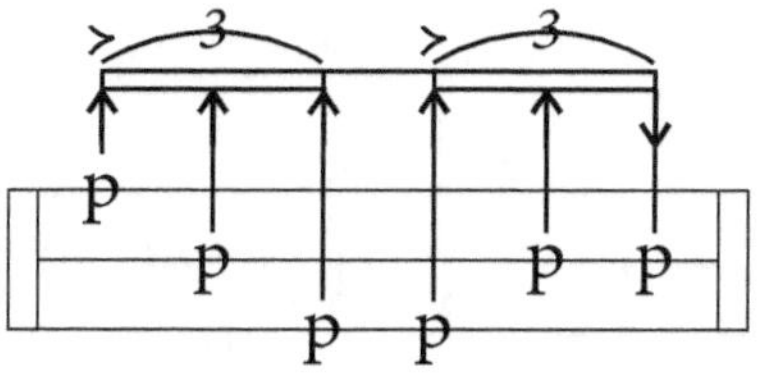

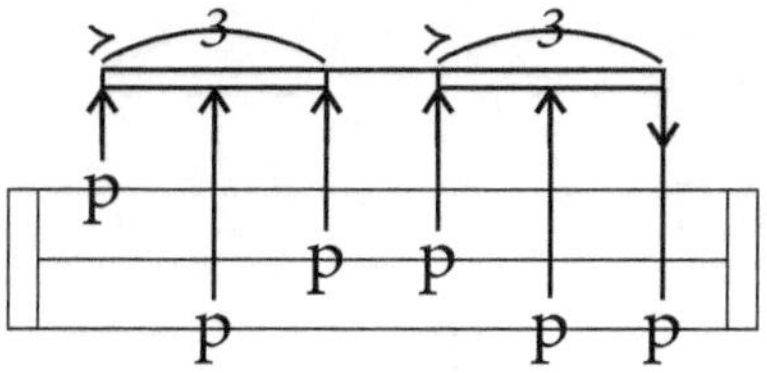

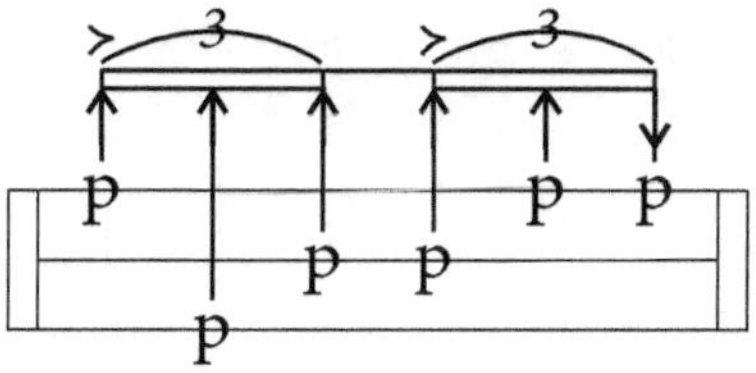

VARIATION VI

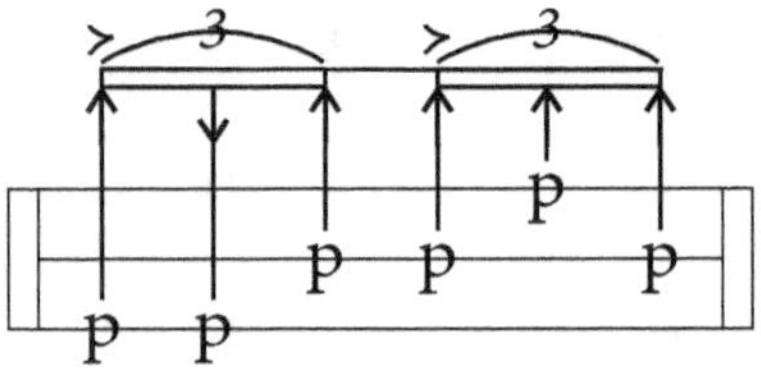

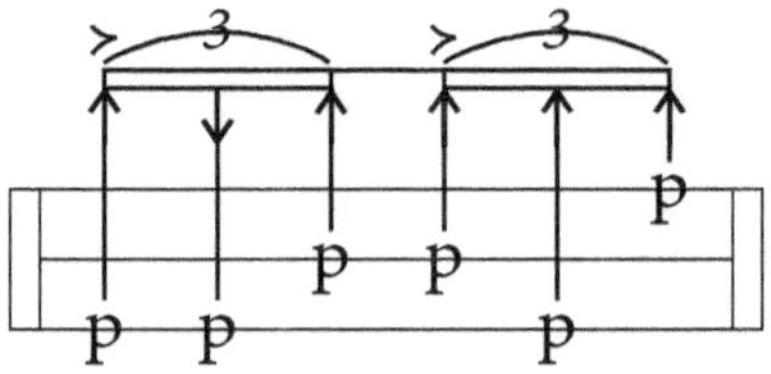

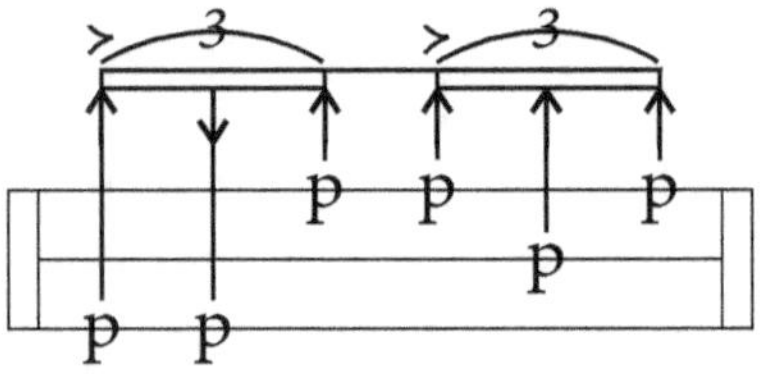

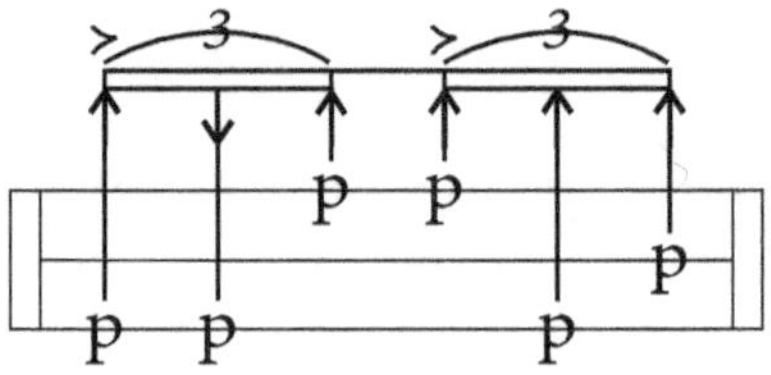

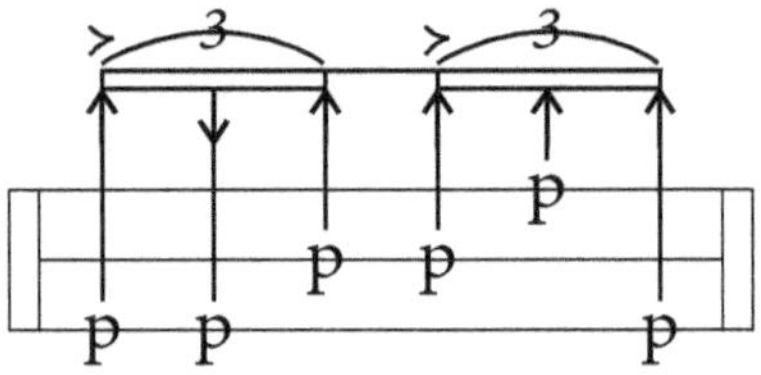

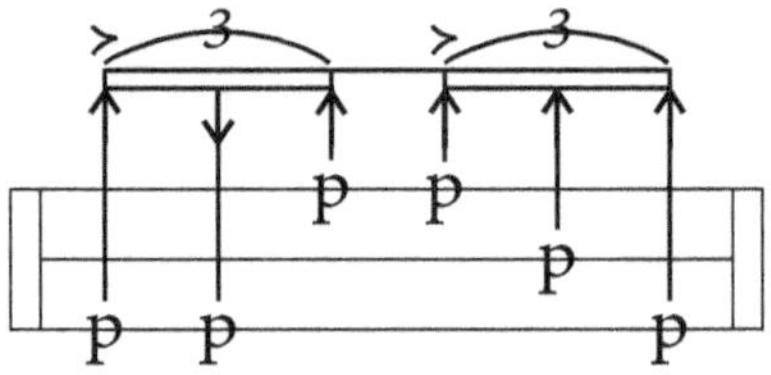

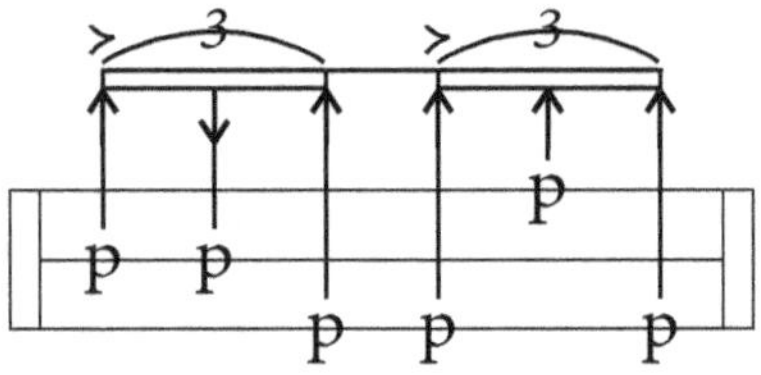

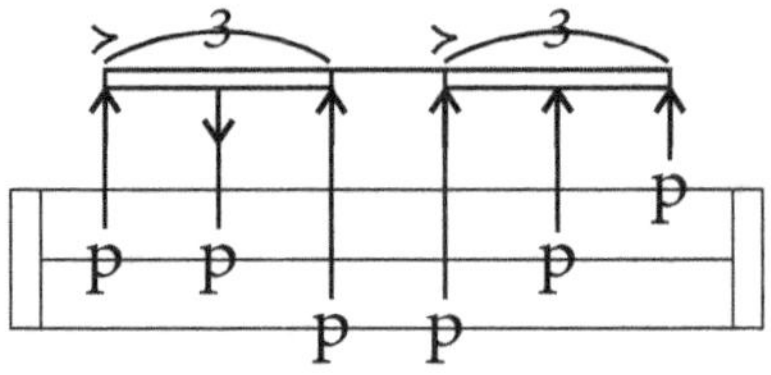

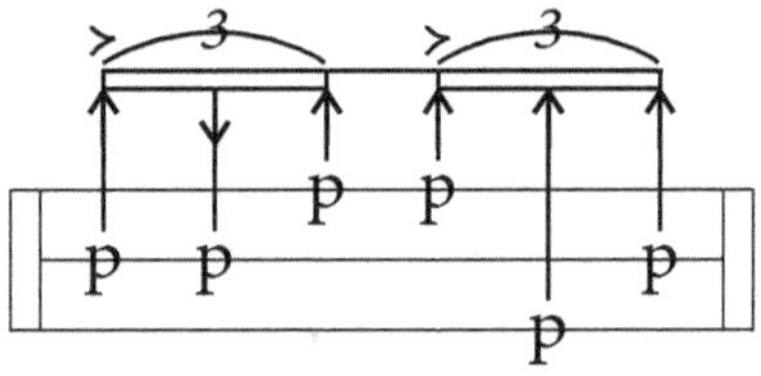

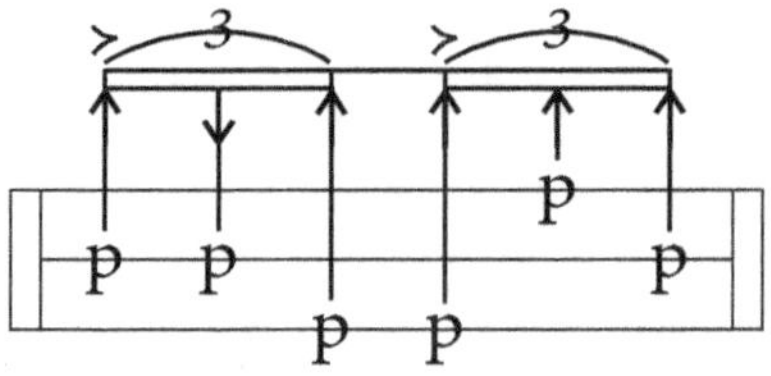

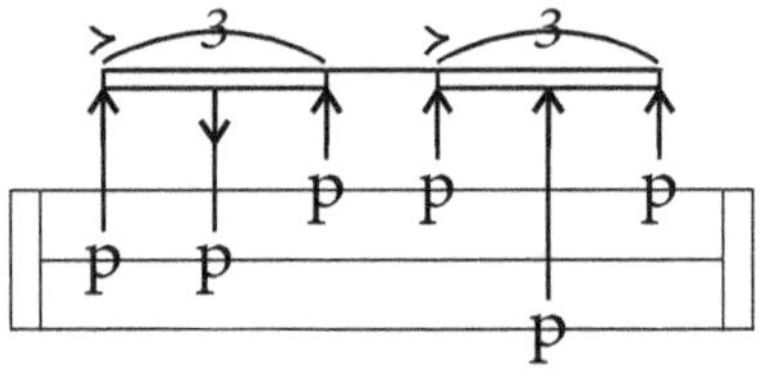

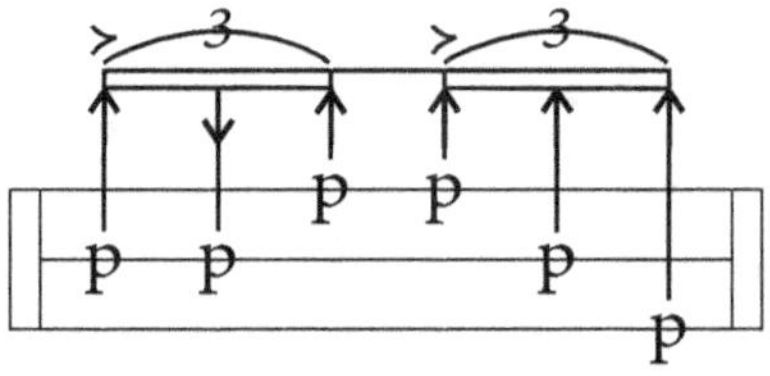

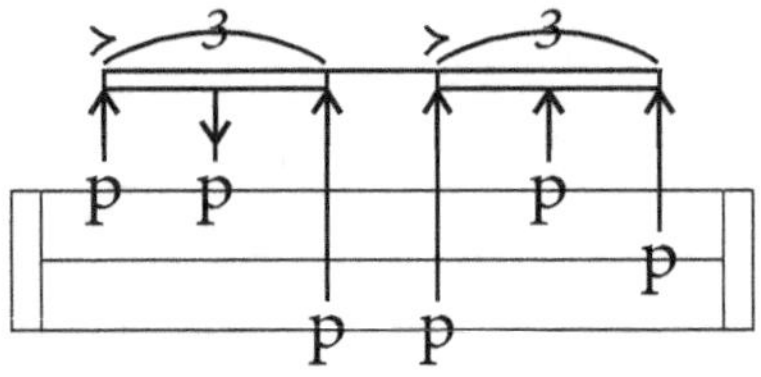

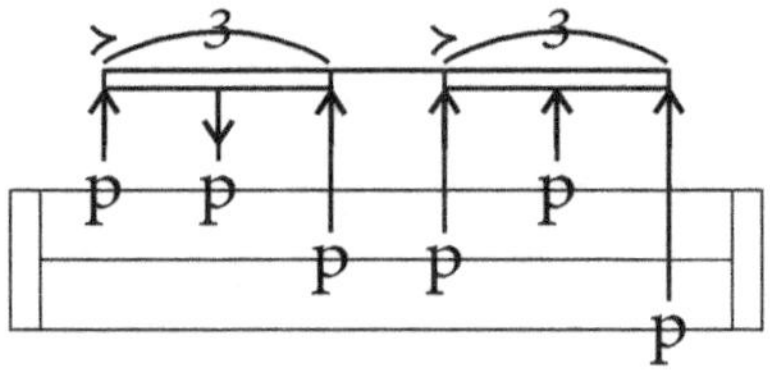

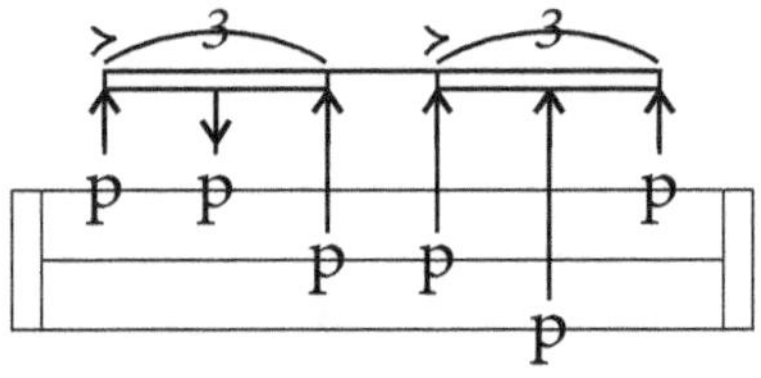

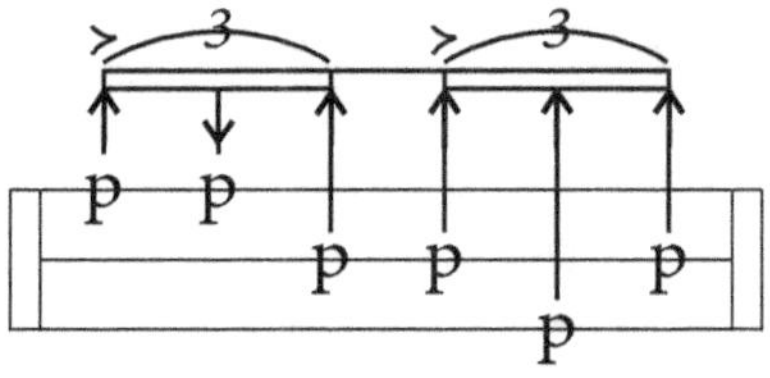

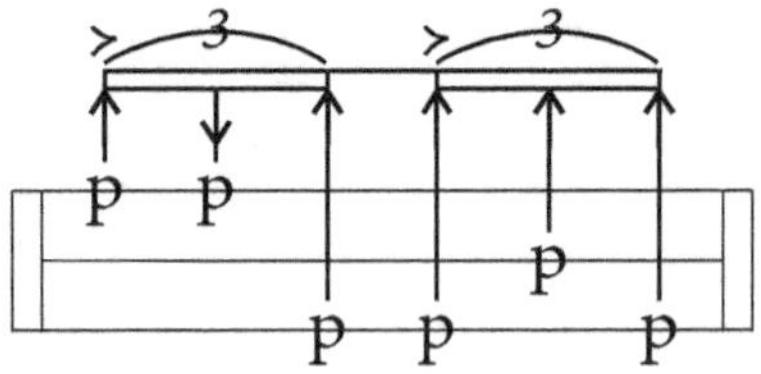

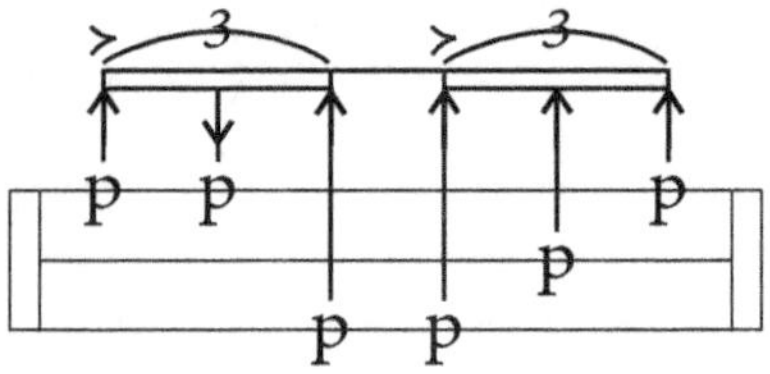

§ VII

Exercise on pulgar on three adjacent strings with two triple (triplets) strokes and one double stroke within each Formula. The exercise contains three variations with 18 Formulas in each one. The first Formula of each variation is cited below. The triple (triplet) and double strokes are isochronous.

VARIATION I

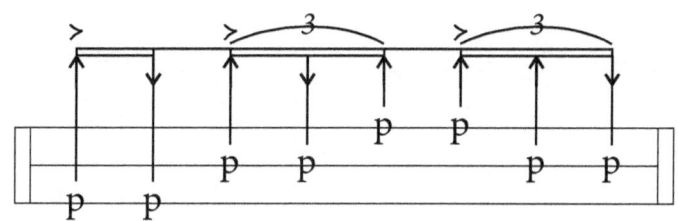

VARIATION II

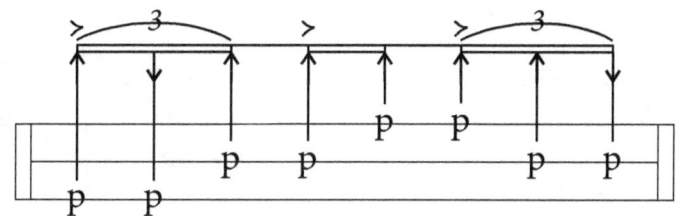

VARIATION III

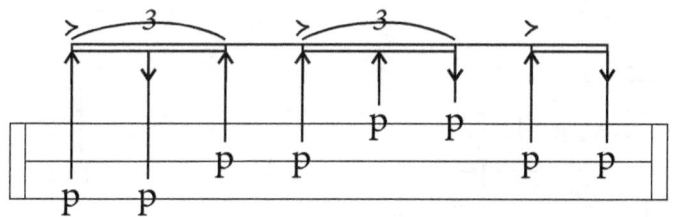

VARIATION I

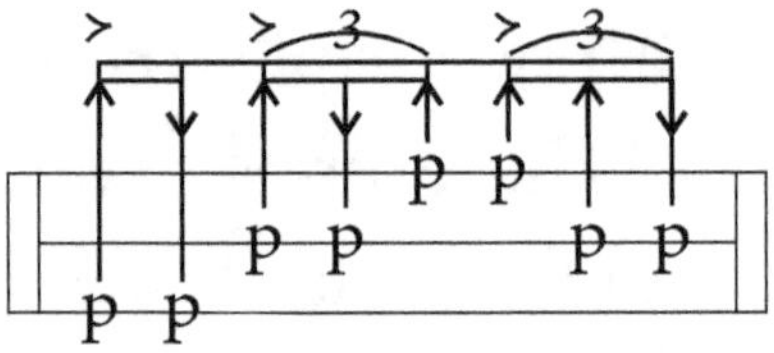

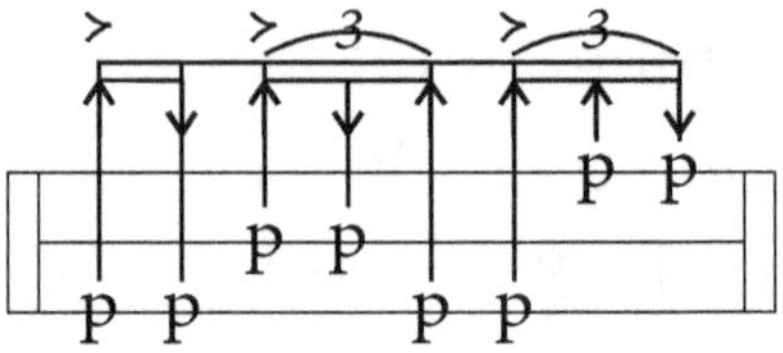

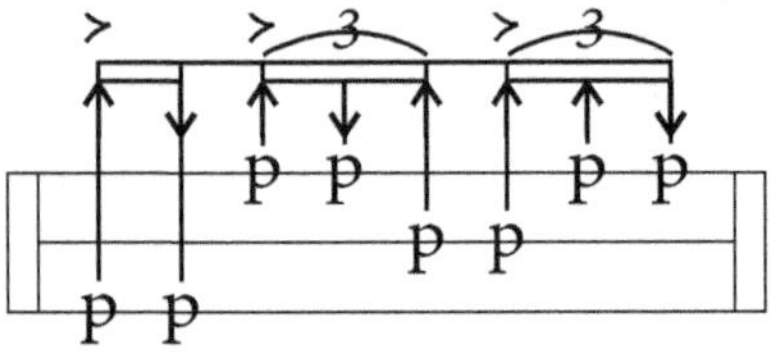

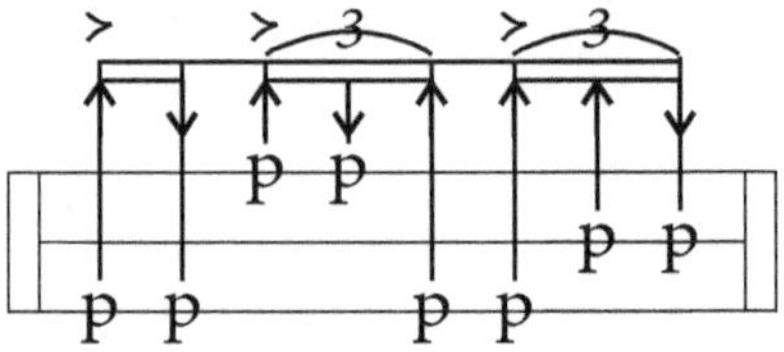

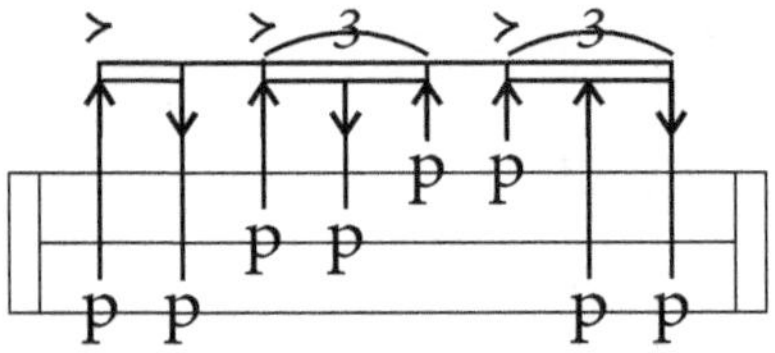

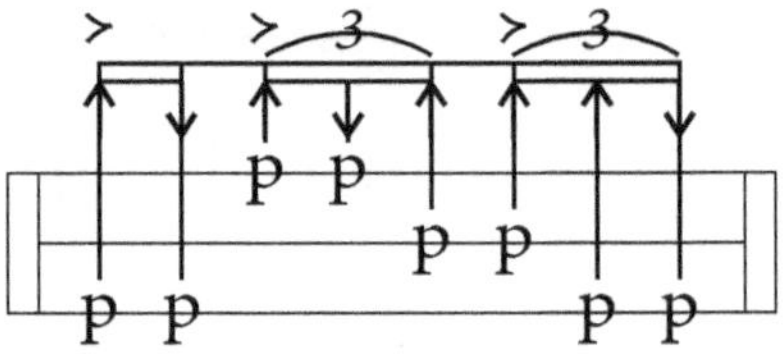

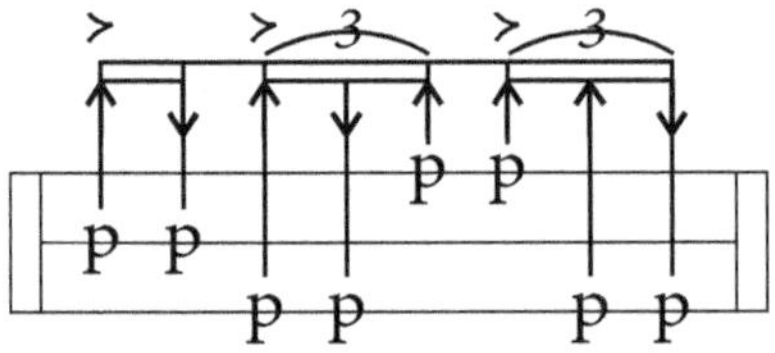

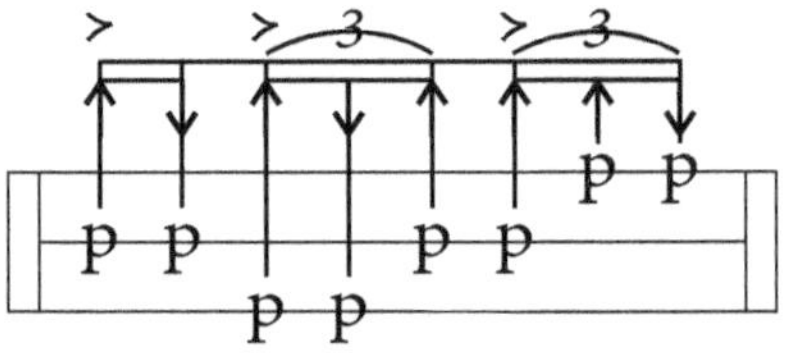

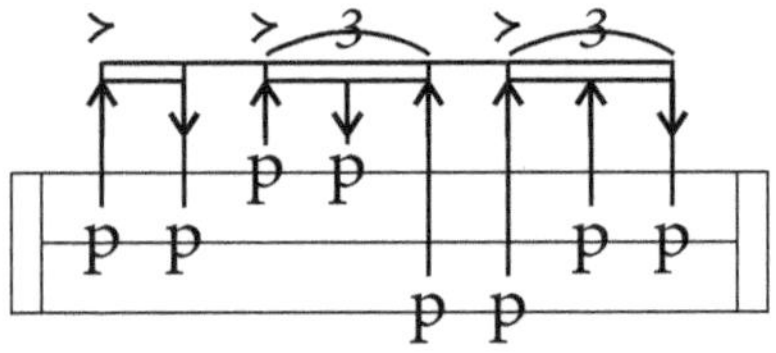

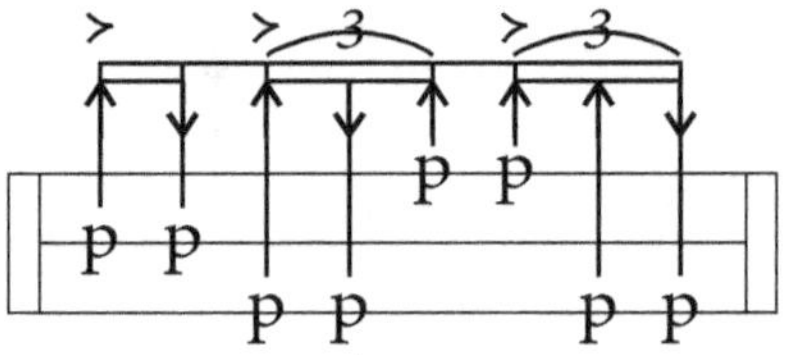

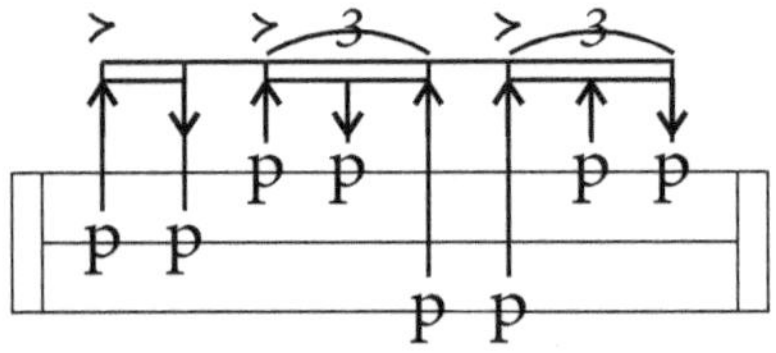

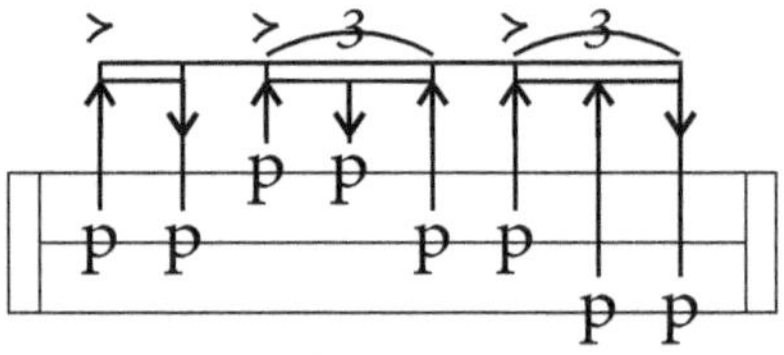

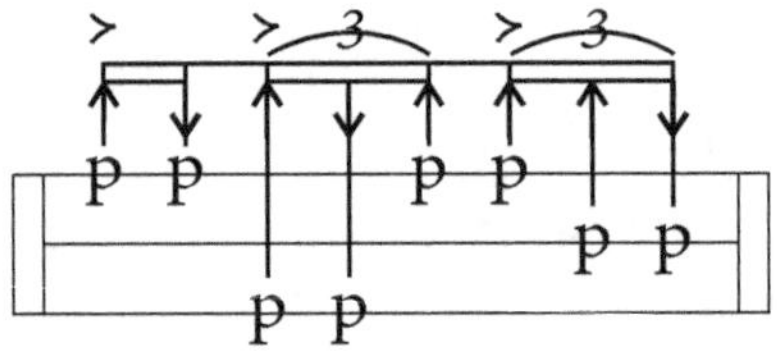

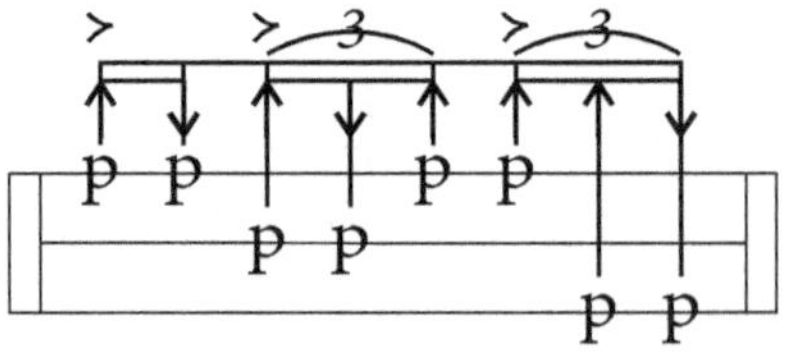

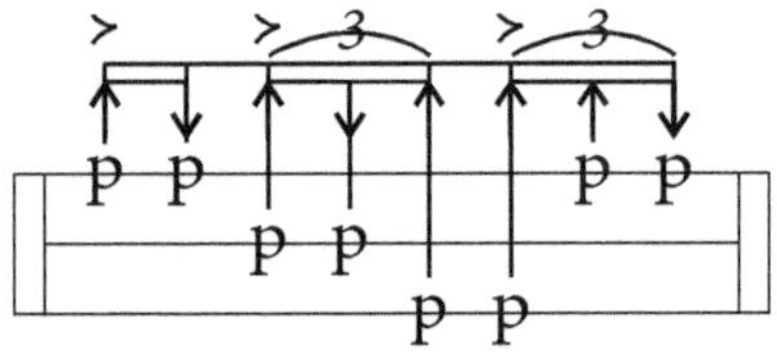

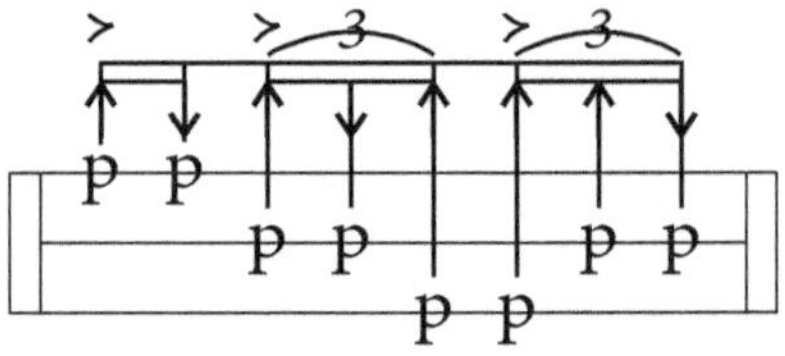

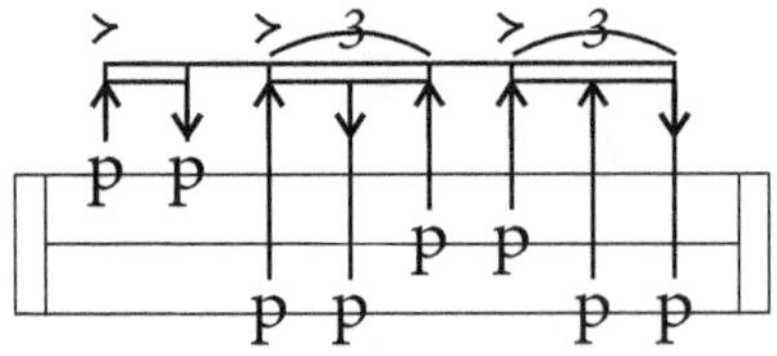

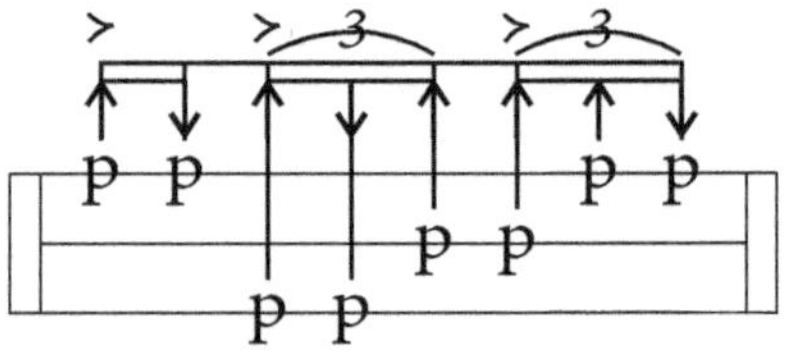

VARIATION II

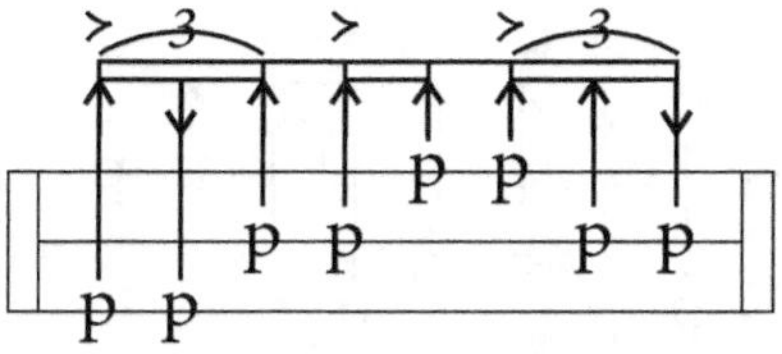

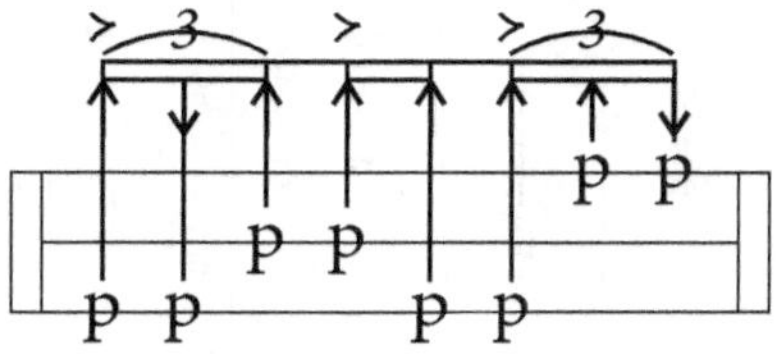

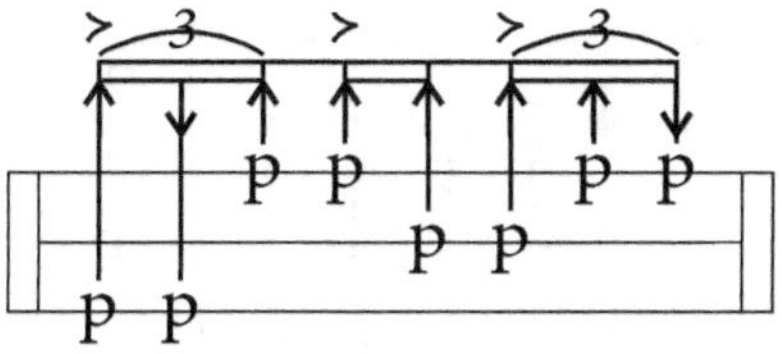

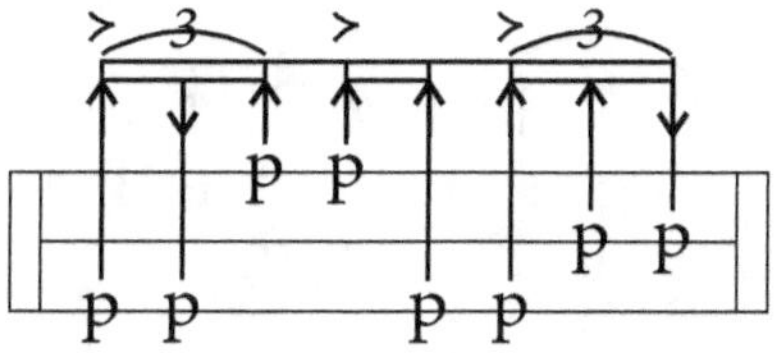

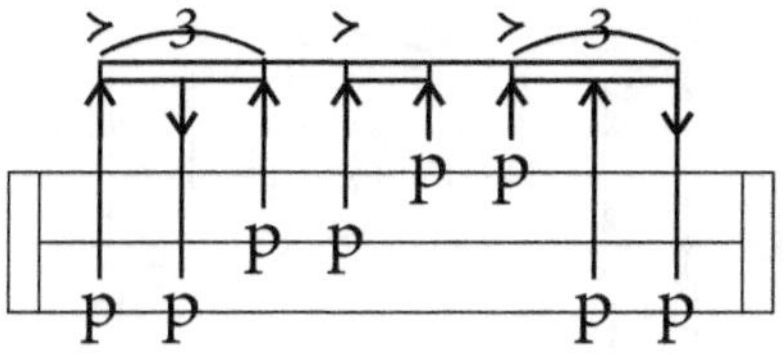

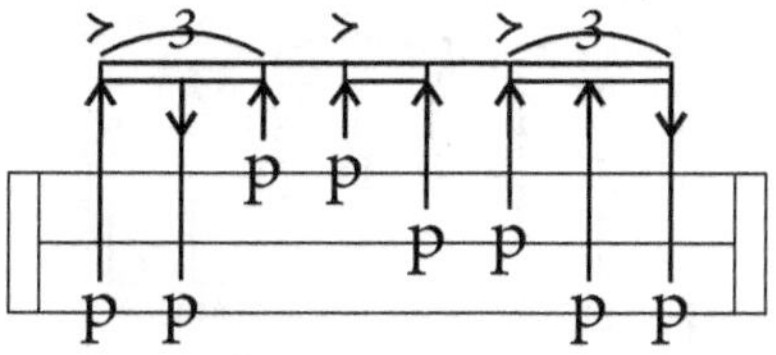

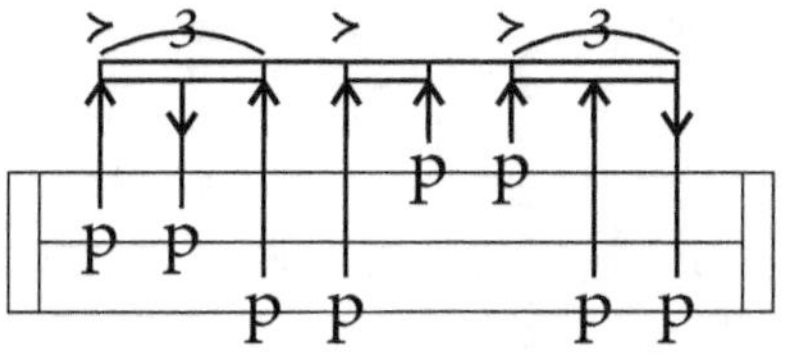

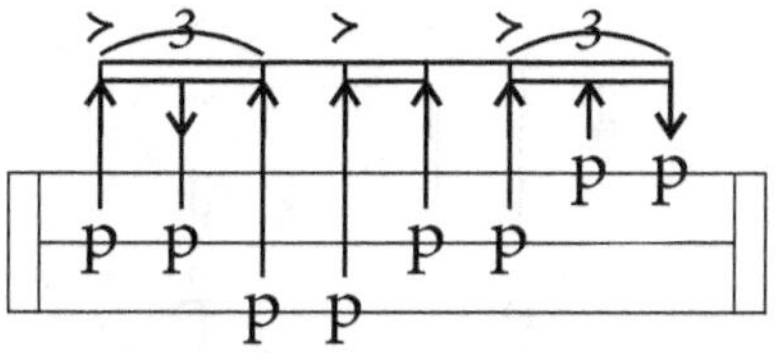

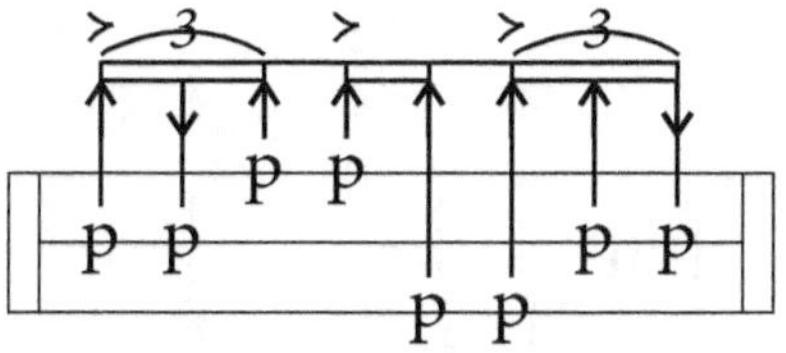

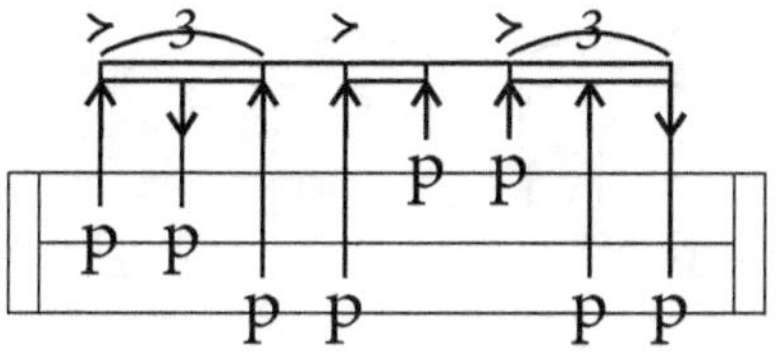

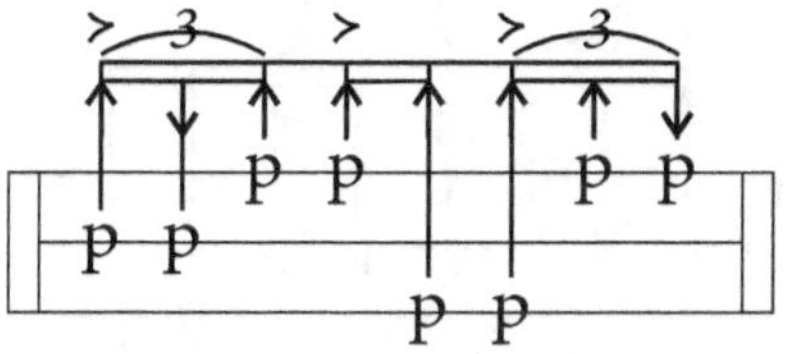

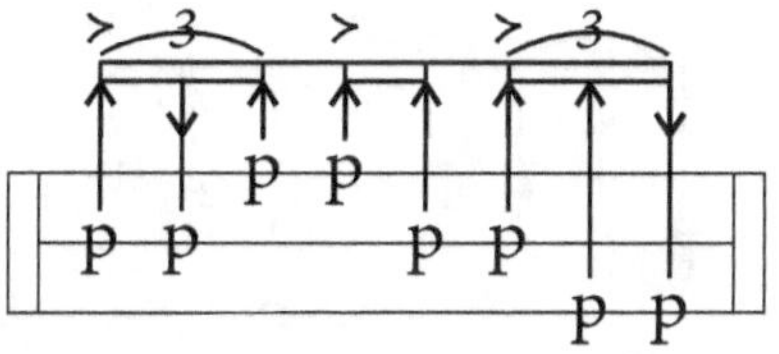

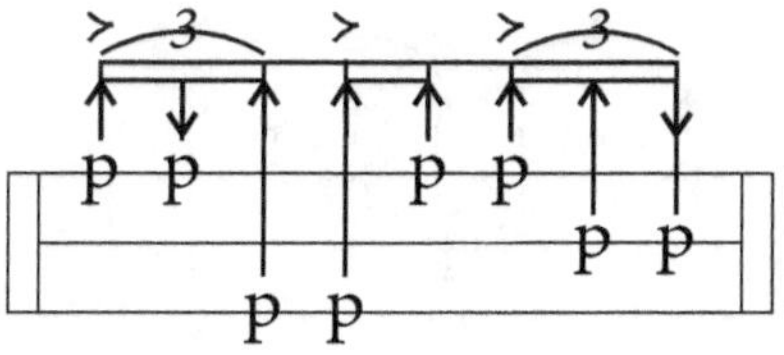

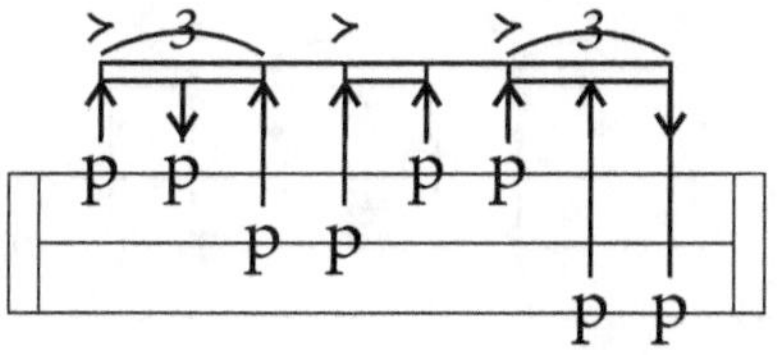

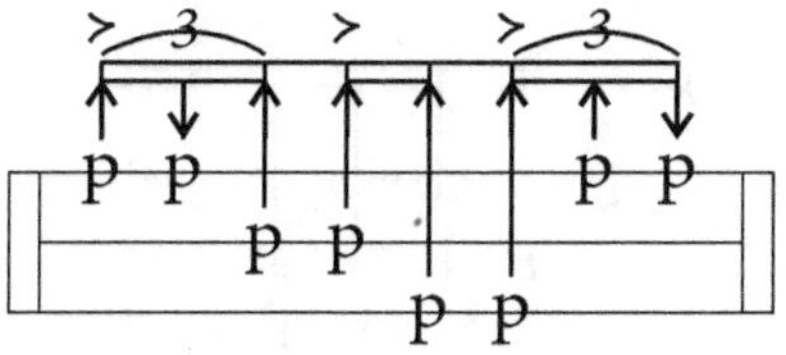

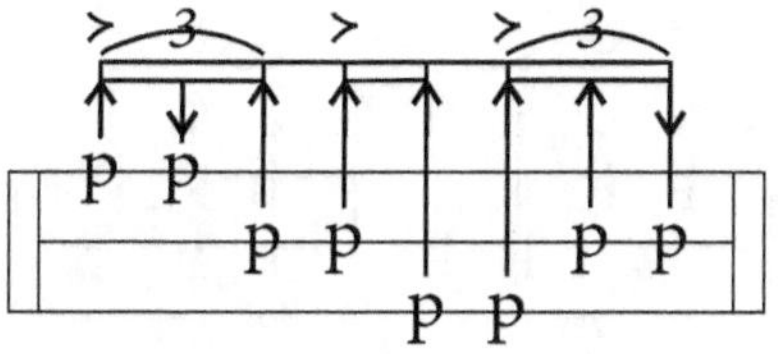

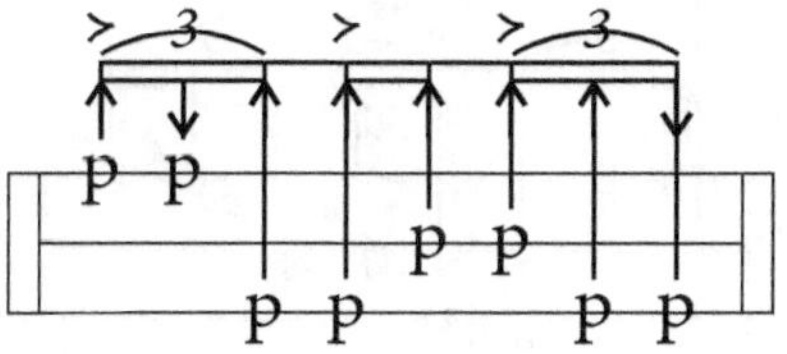

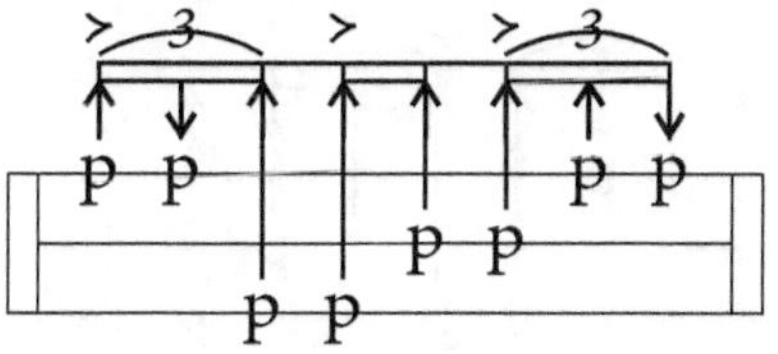

VARIATION III

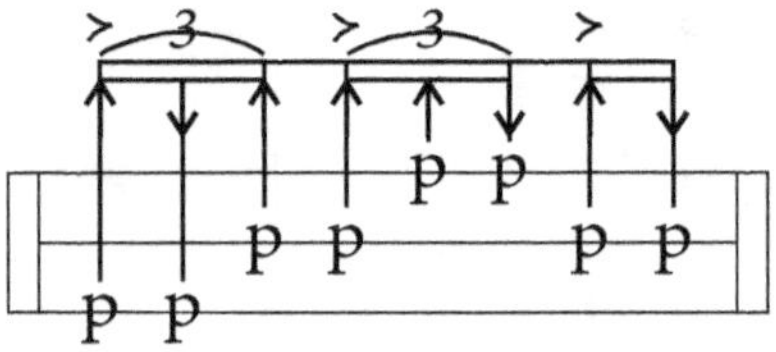

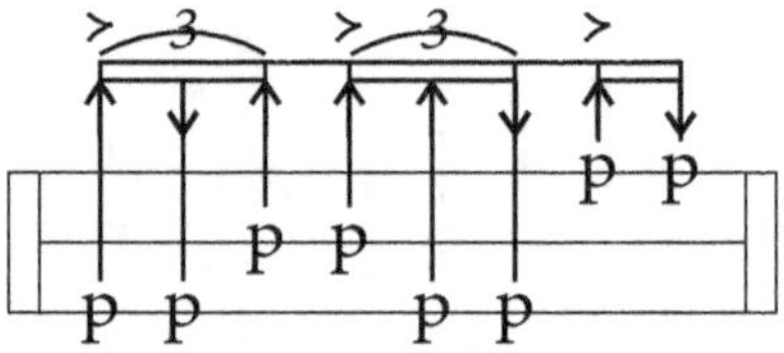

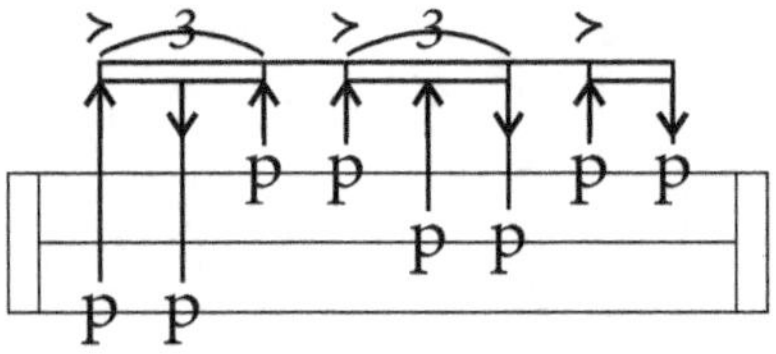

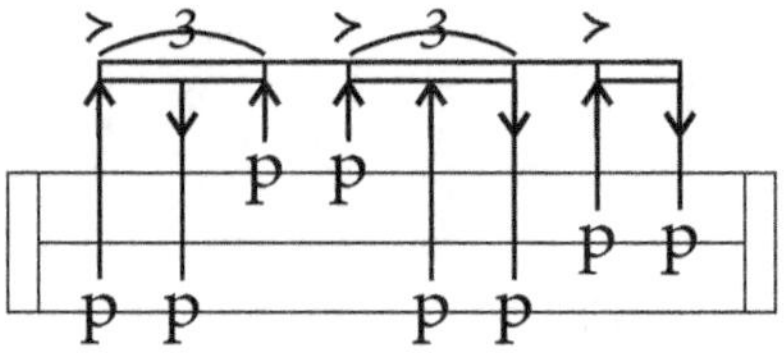

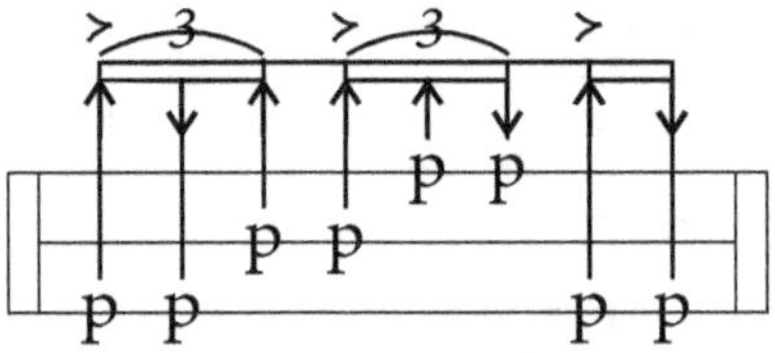

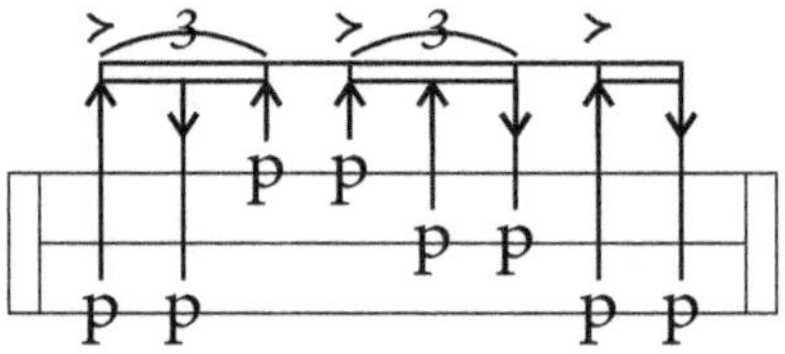

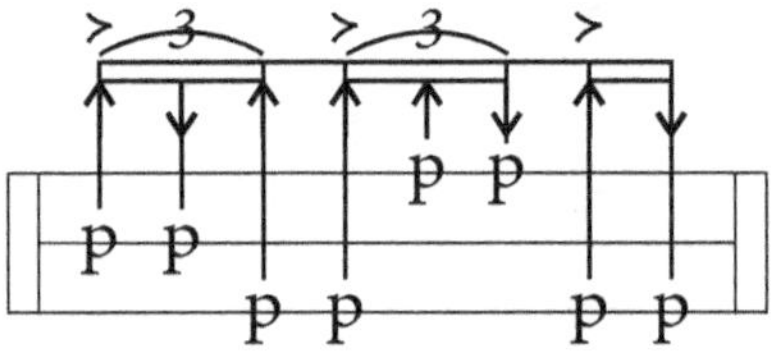

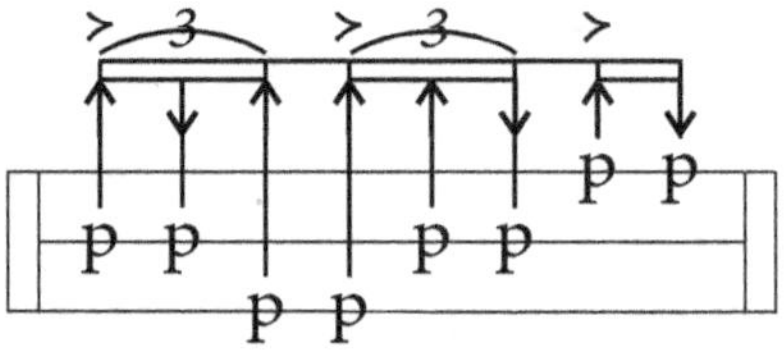

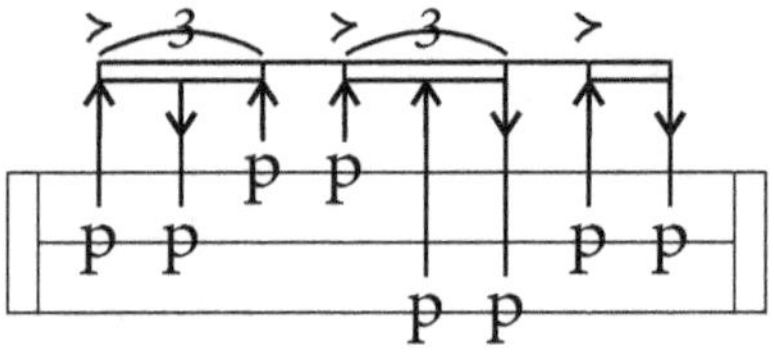

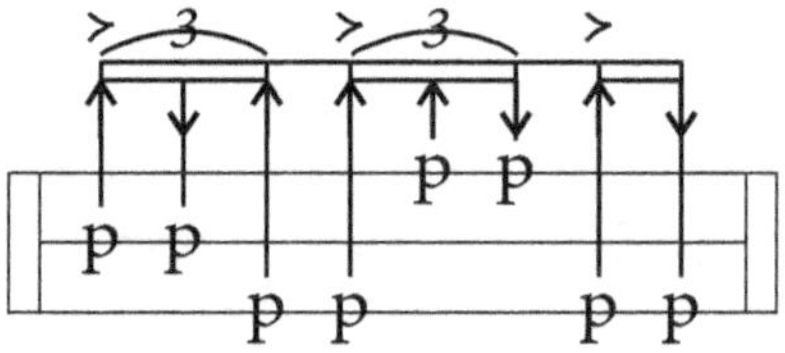

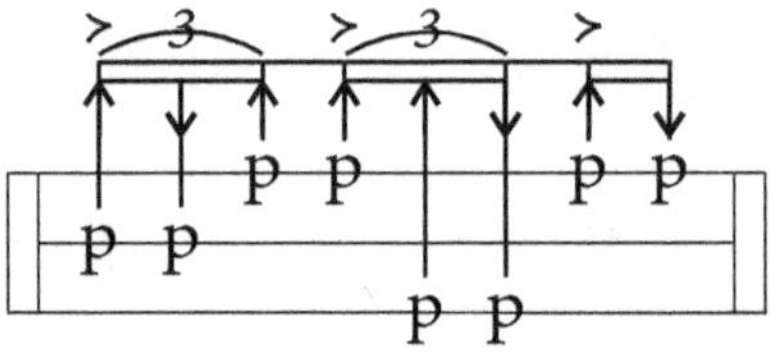

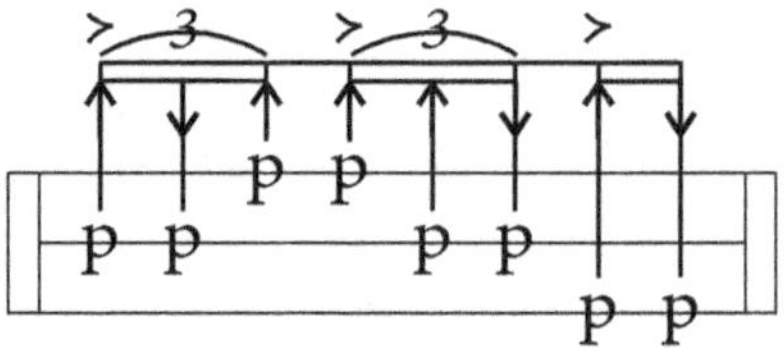

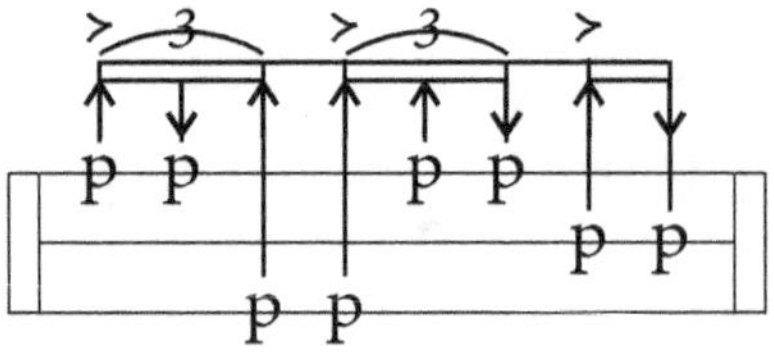

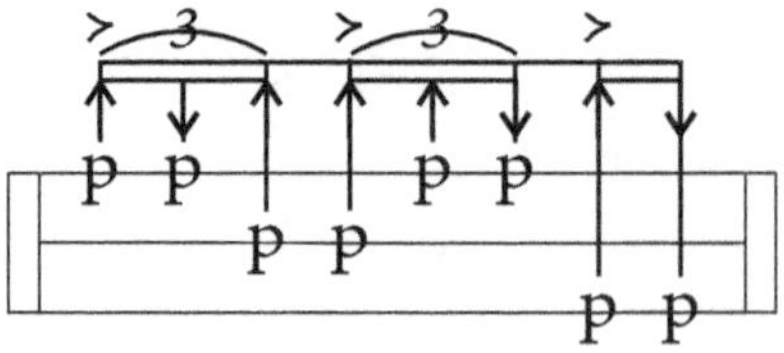

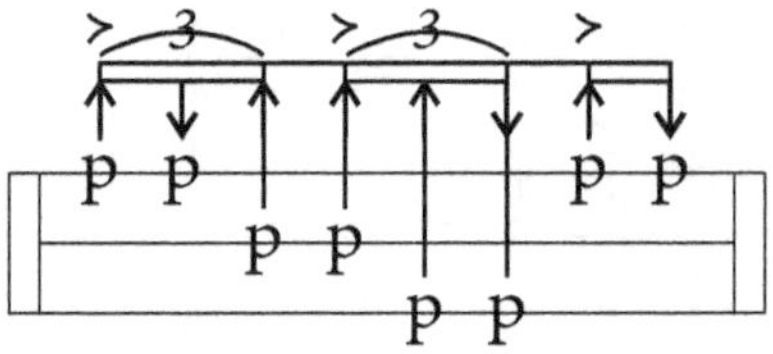

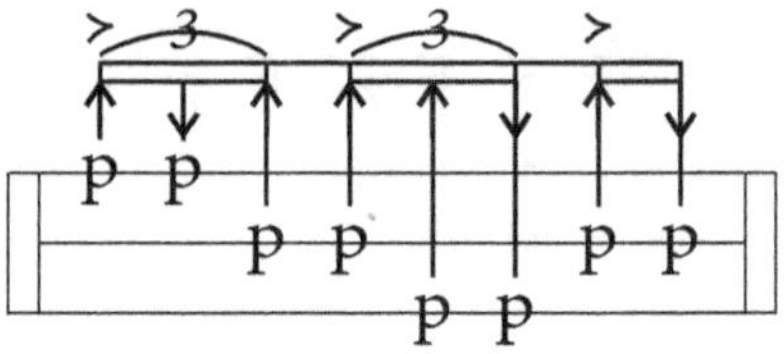

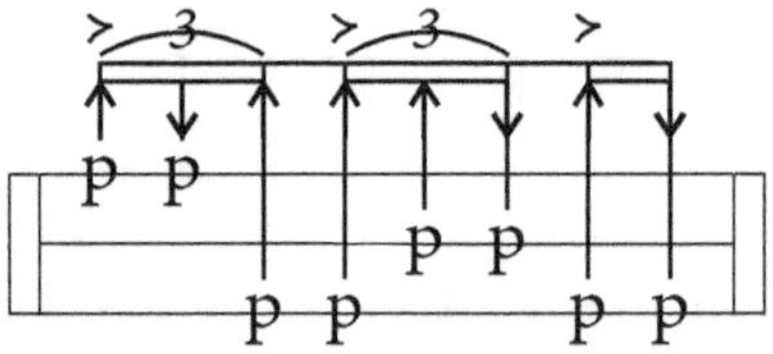

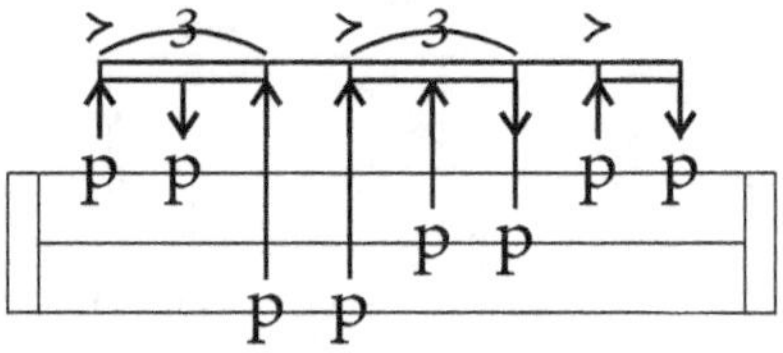

§ VIII

Exercise on pulgar on three adjacent strings with triple stroke (triplet). There are four triple (triplet) strokes within each Formula. The exercise contains 18 Formulas in total. Apart from the initial way in which the exercise is written, you can also practice in the following ways on the 18 Formulas.

1st mode (initial)

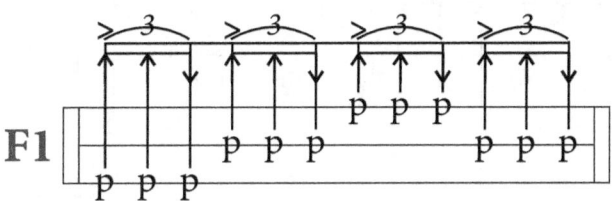

2nd mode

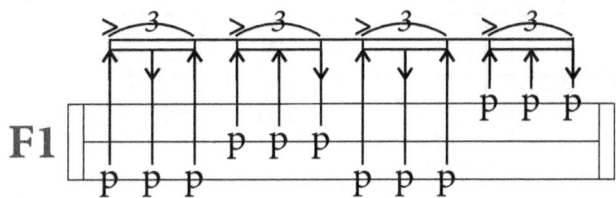

3rd mode

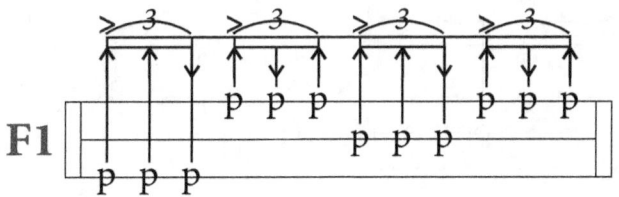

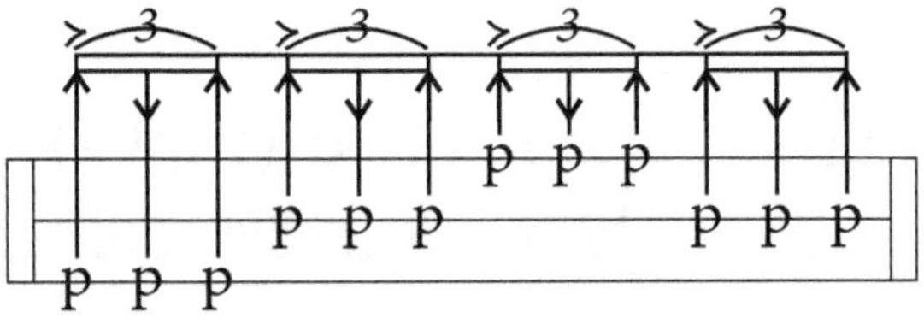

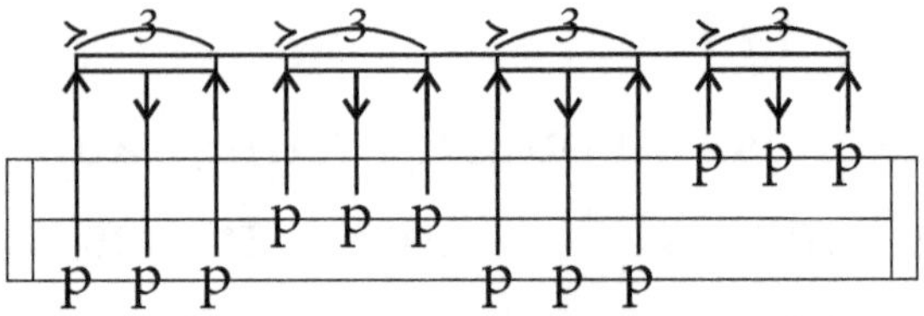

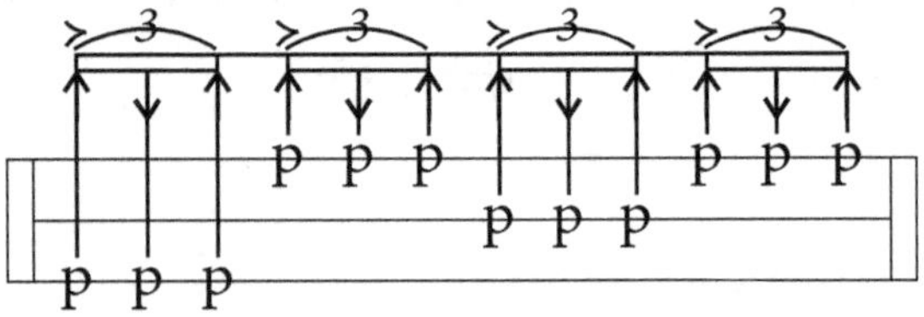

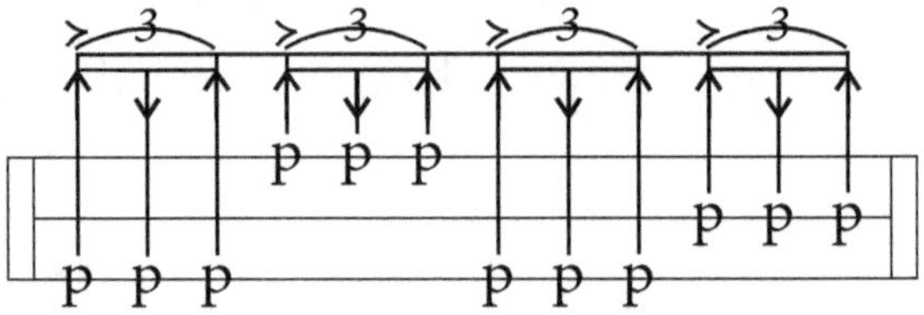

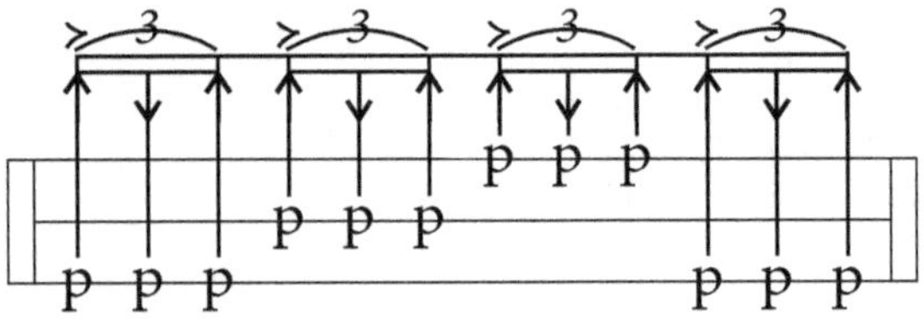

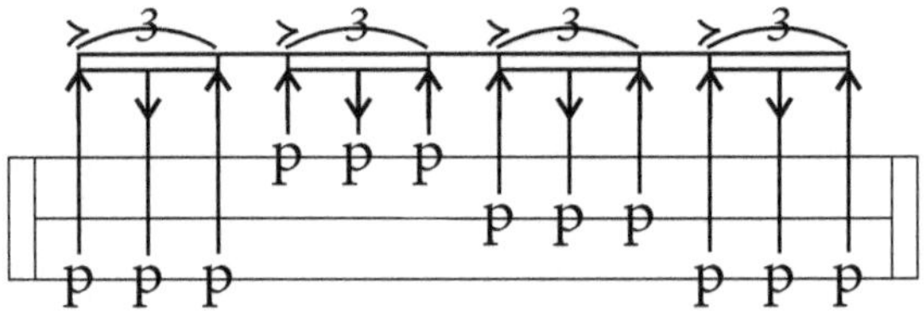

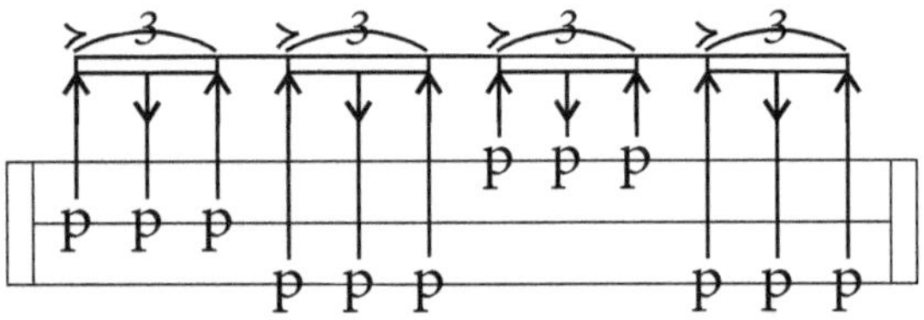

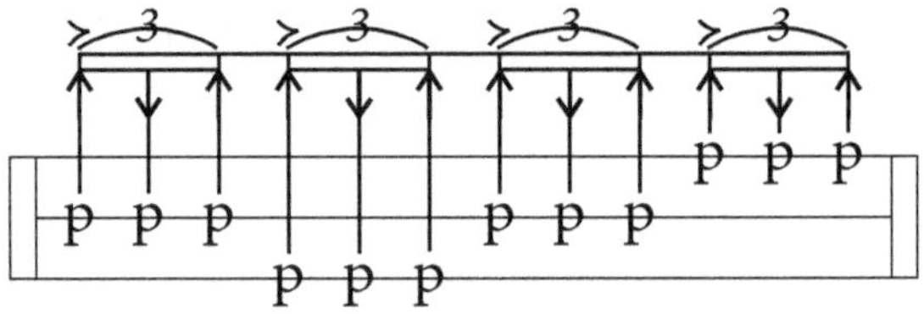

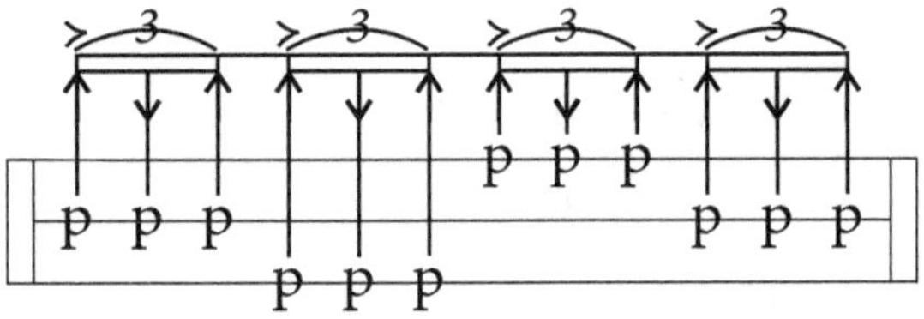

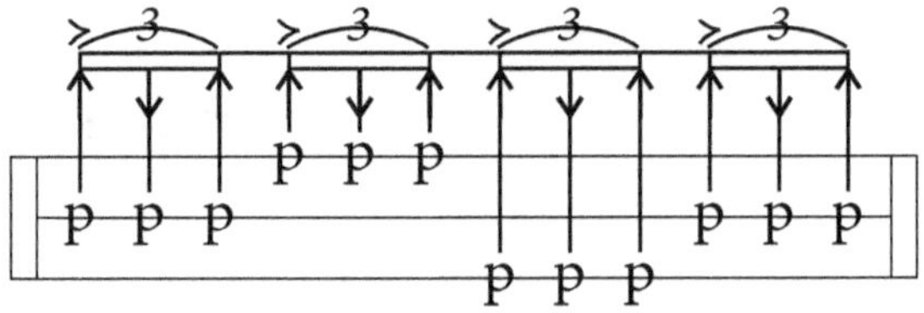

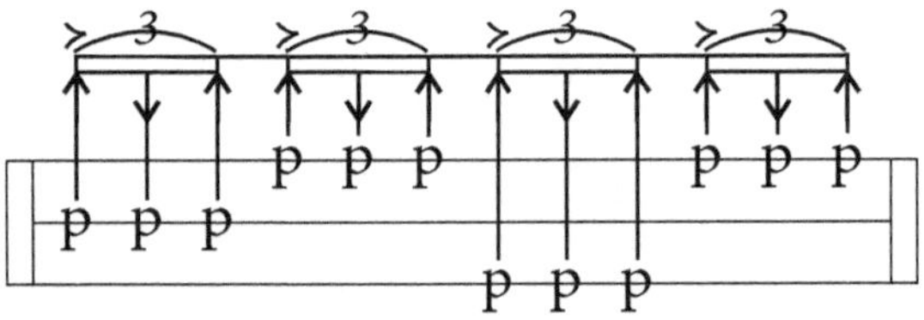

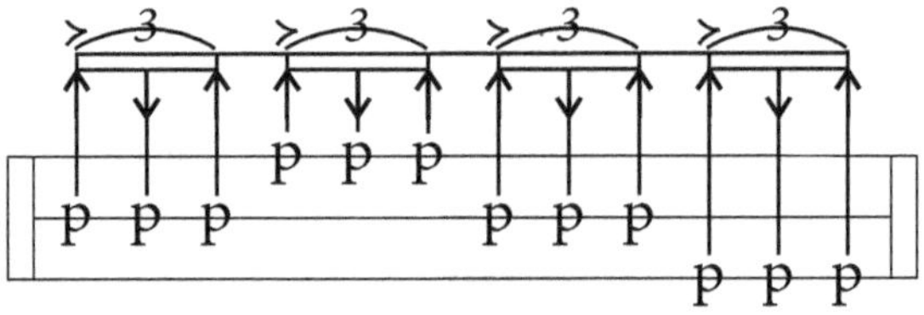

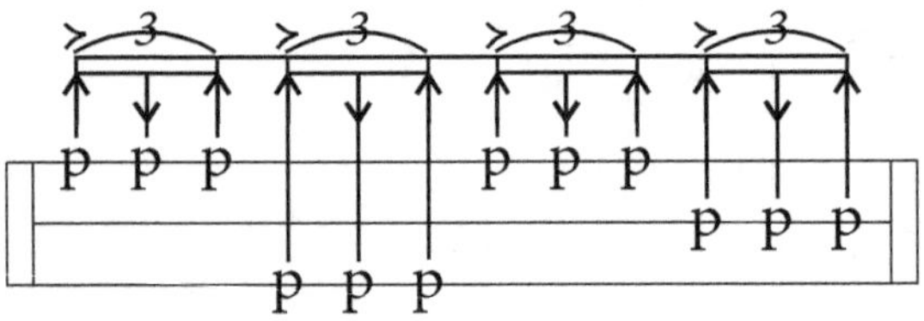

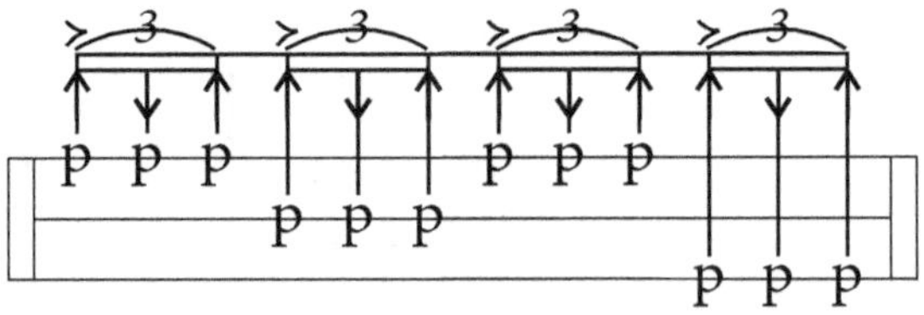

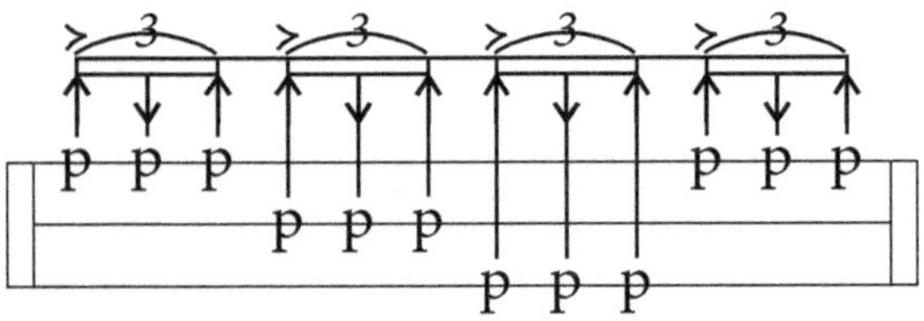

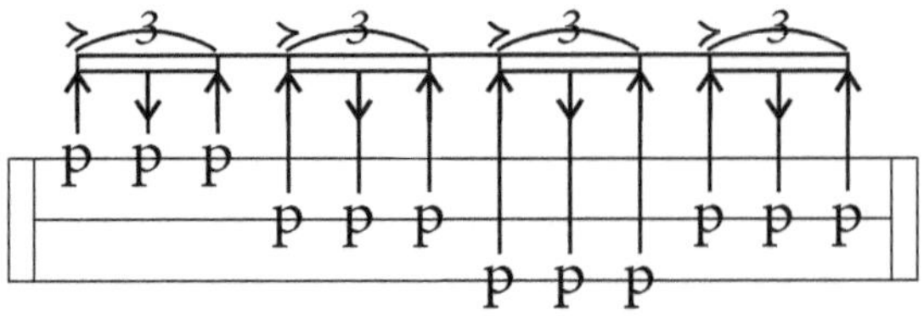

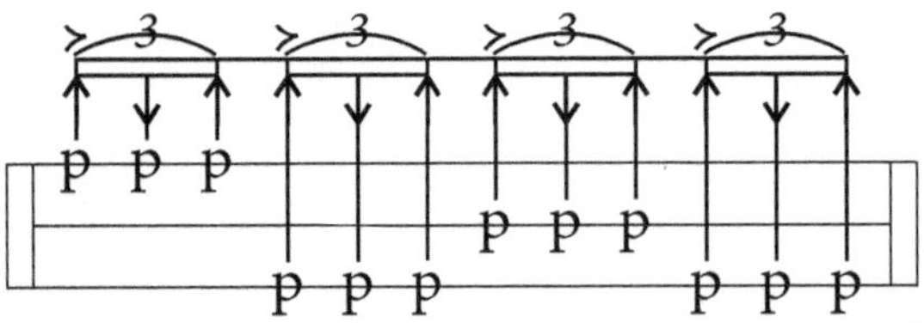

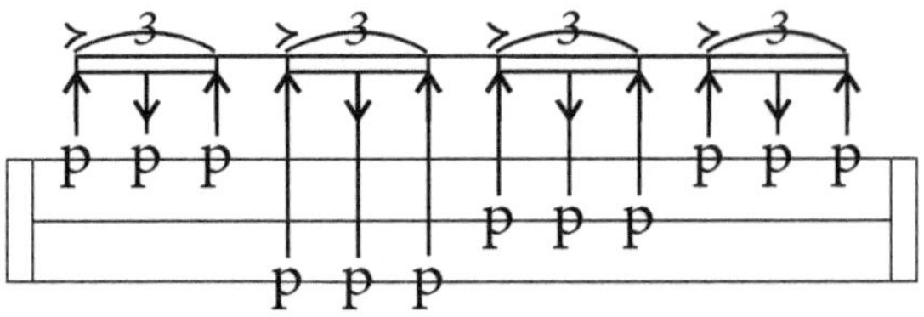

§ IX

Exercise on pulgar on three adjacent strings with quad stroke. There are four quad strokes in each Formula. The exercise contains 18 Formulas in total. Apart from the initial way in which the exercise is written, you can practice in the following ways on the 18 Formulas.

1st mode (initial)

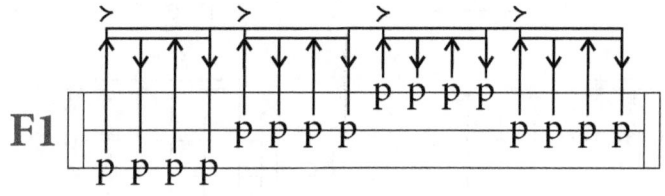

2nd mode

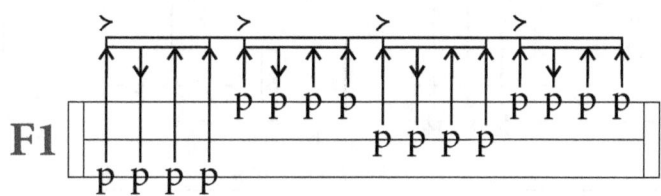

3rd mode

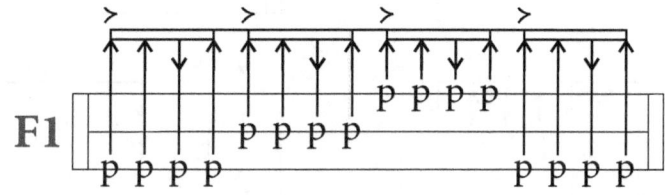

4th mode

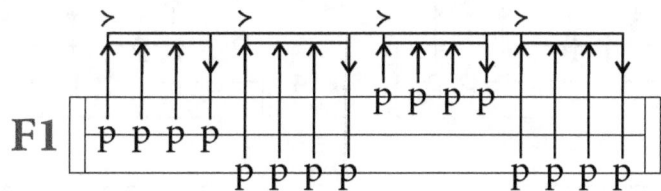

5th mode

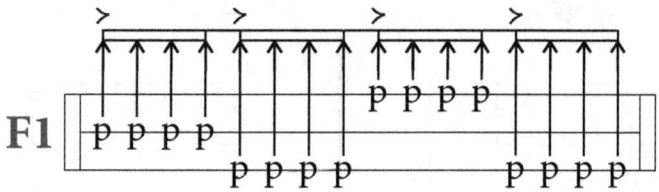

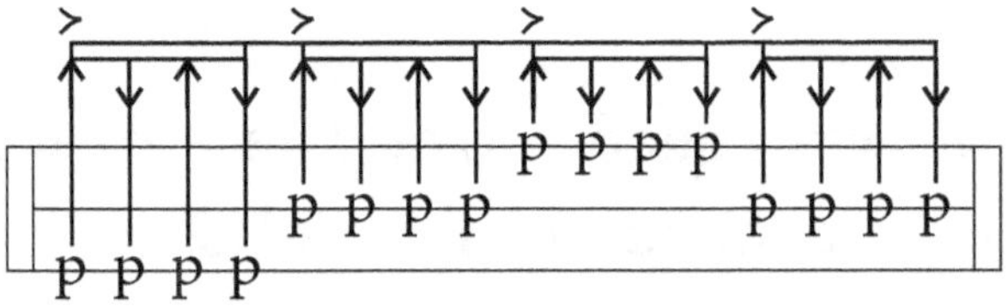

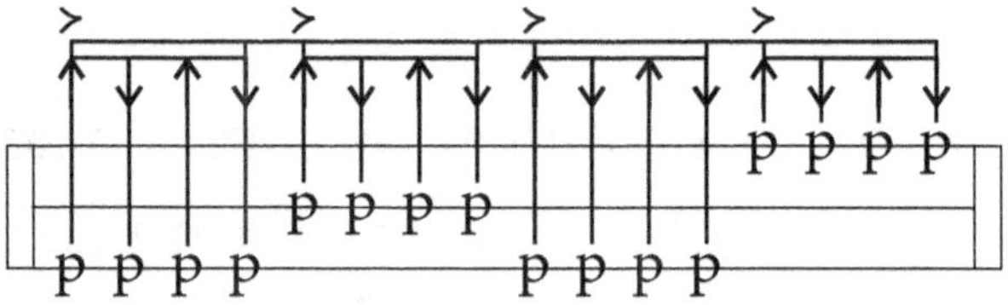

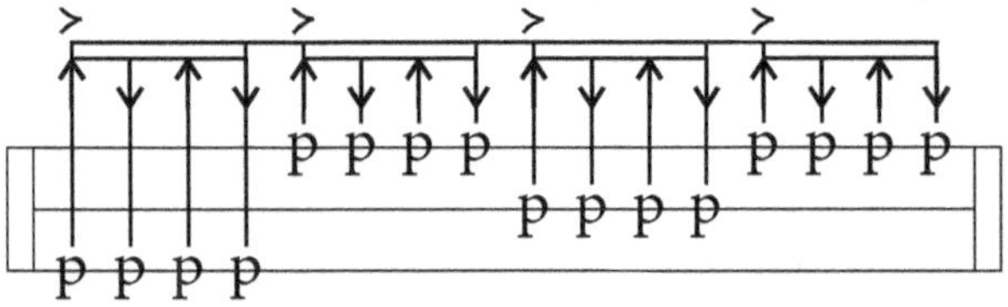

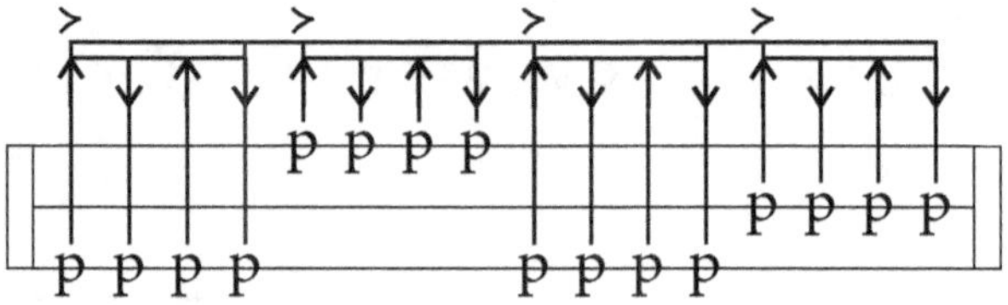

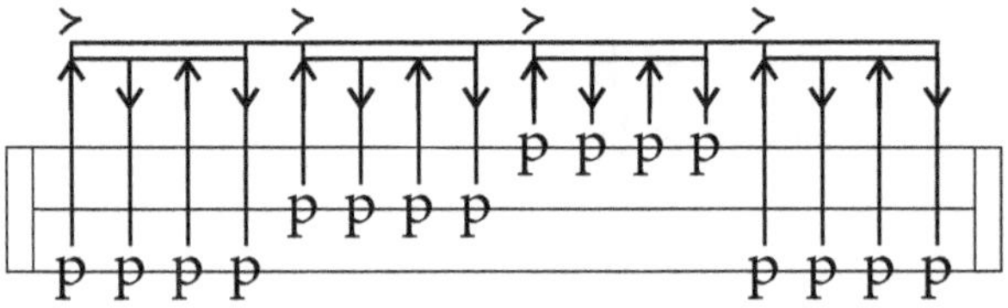

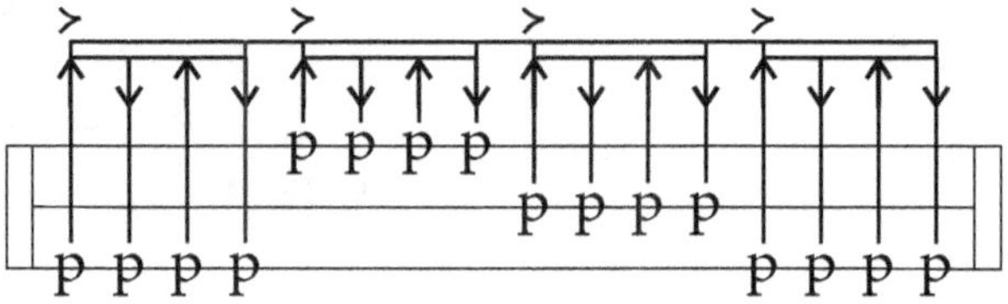

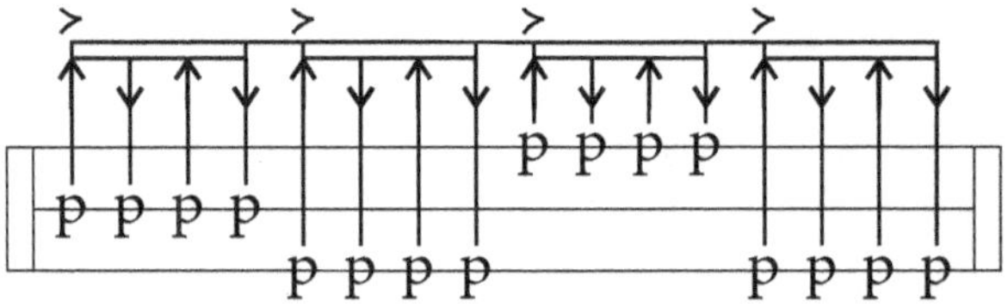

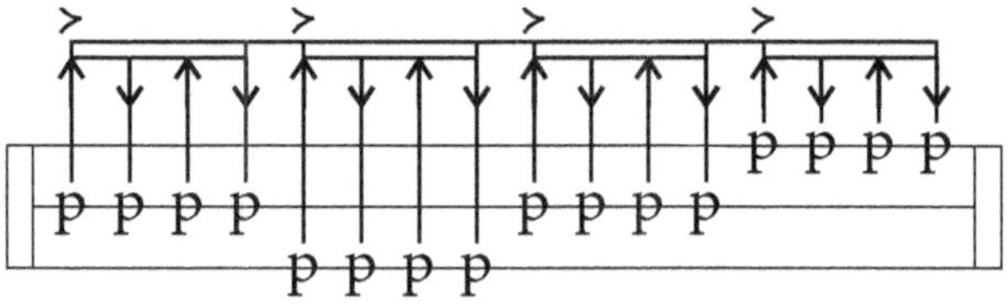

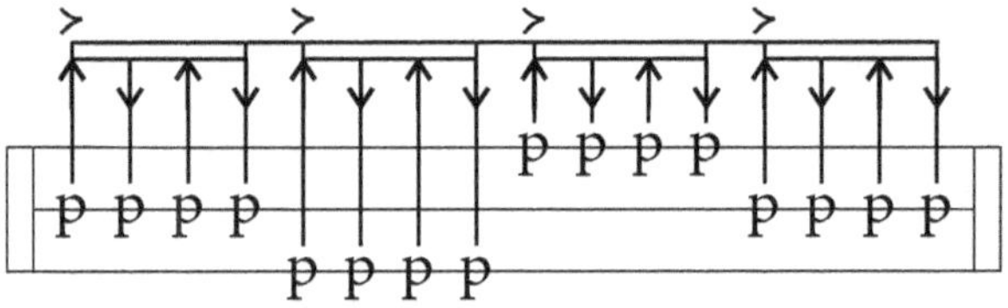

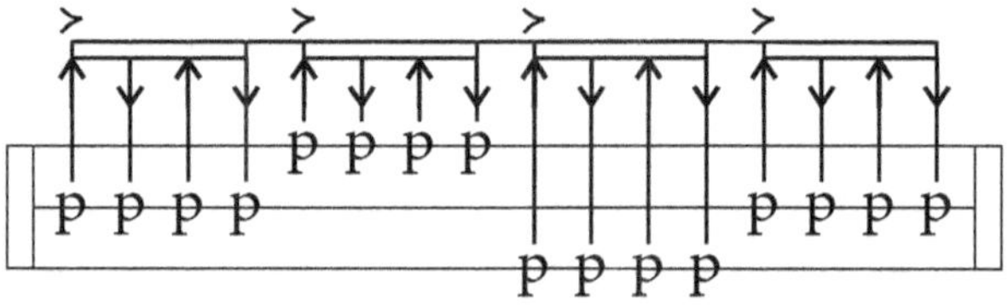

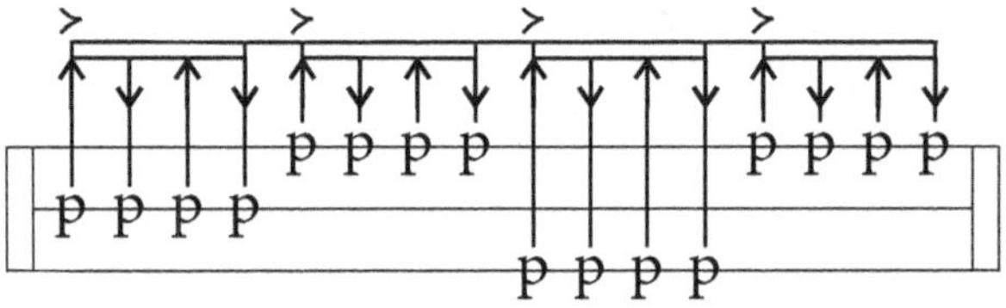

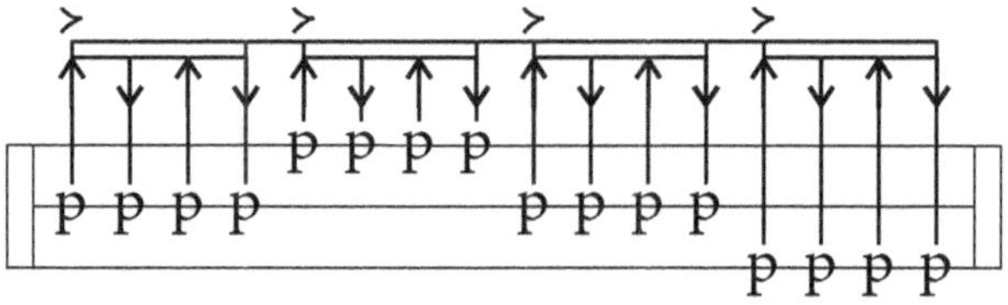

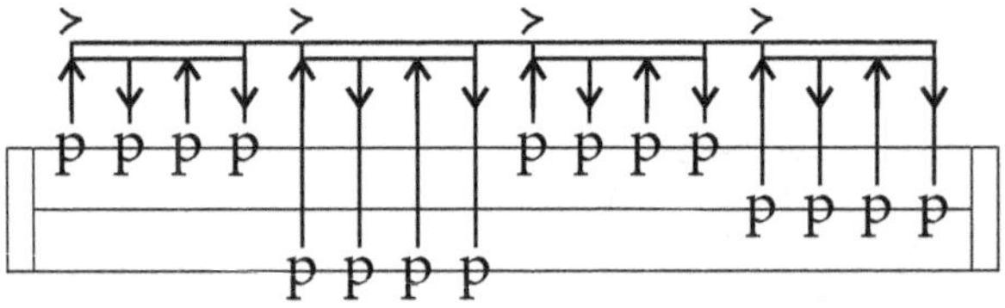

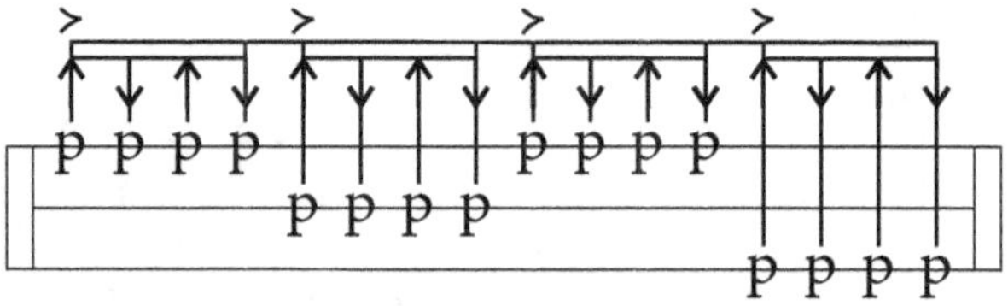

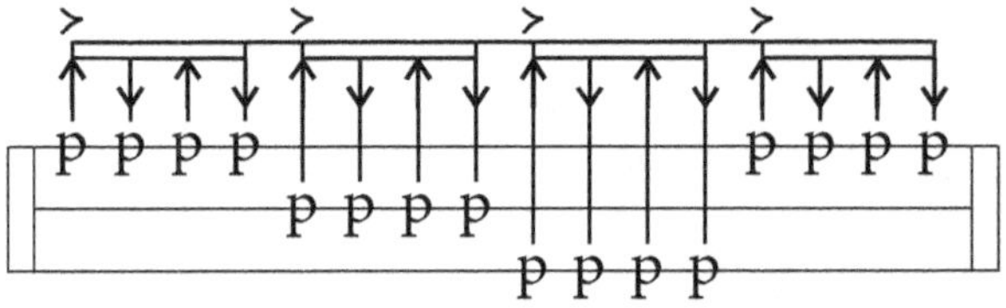

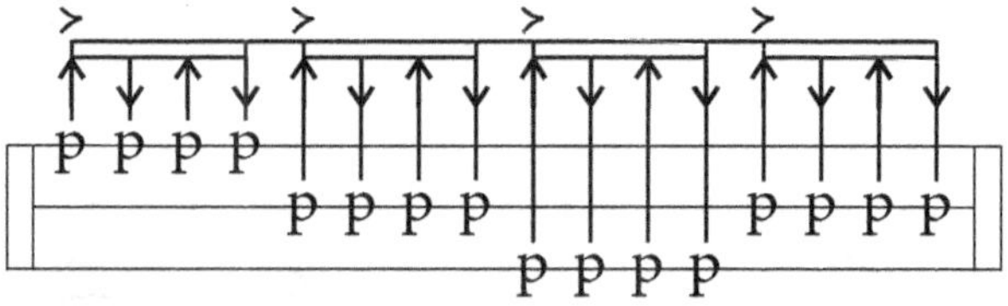

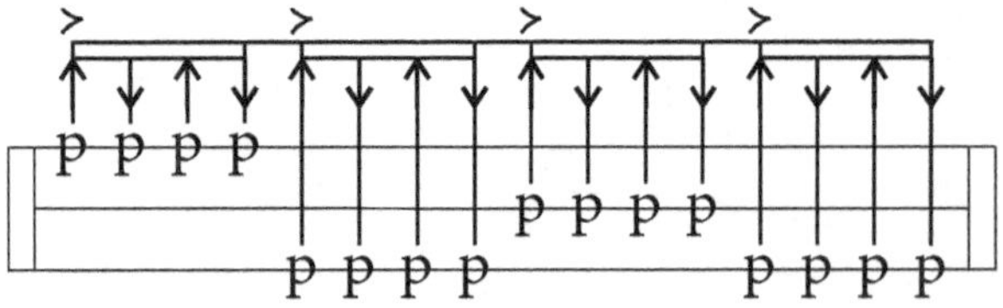

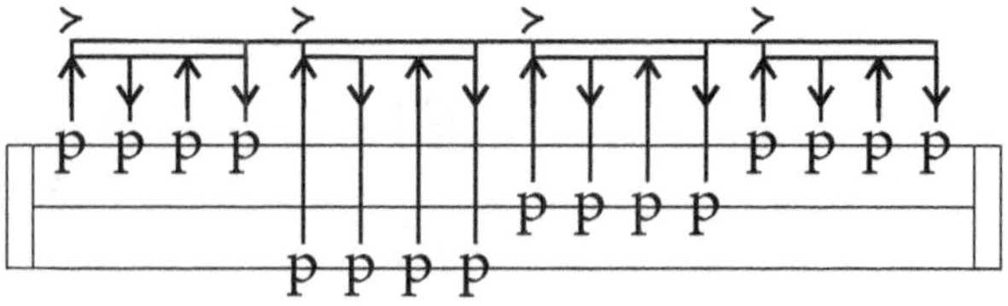

§ X

Exercise on pulgar on three adjacent strings with two double and two triple (triplets) strokes within each Formula. The exercise includes four variations with 18 Formulas in each. The direction of pulgar stroke is as follows:

↑ ↓ in the double stroke   ↑ ↓ ↑ in the triple stroke
p p   p p p

The first Formula of each variation is cited below. Isochronous playing of pulgar strokes double and triple.

VARIATION I

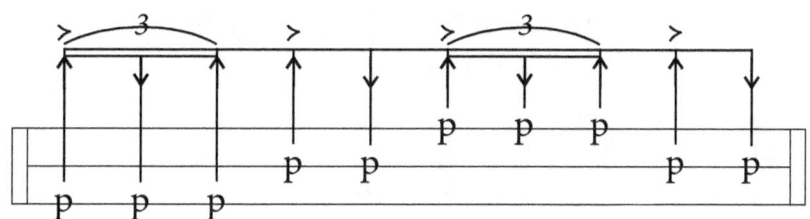

VARIATION II

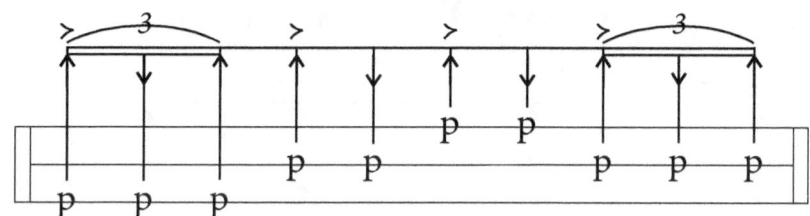

VARIATION III

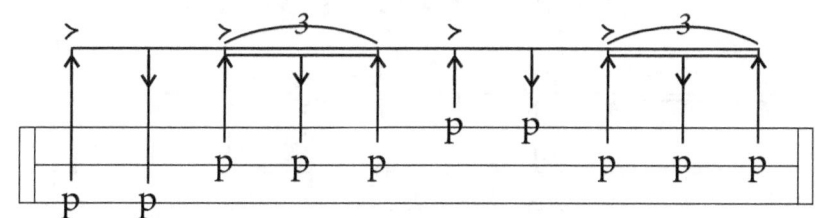

VARIATION IV

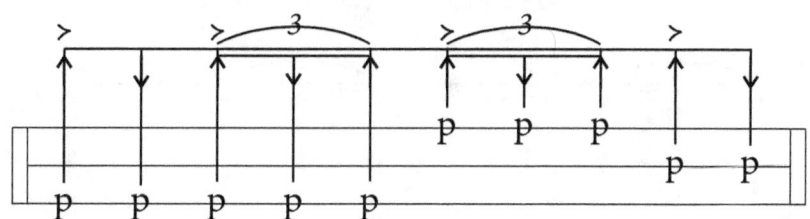

Apart from the original way in which the exercise is written you can practice in the following ways on all Formulas. The different modes of practice of the first Formula of variation I are cited below. You can find similar modes in the remaining variations too.

VARIATION I (1st mode)

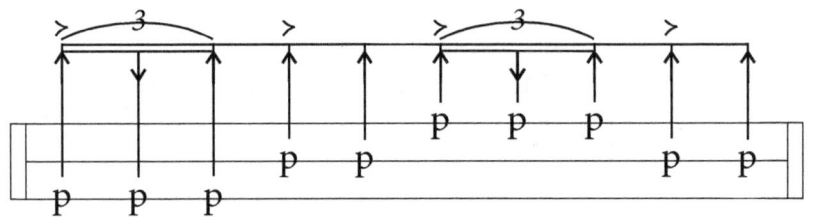

VARIATION I (2nd mode)

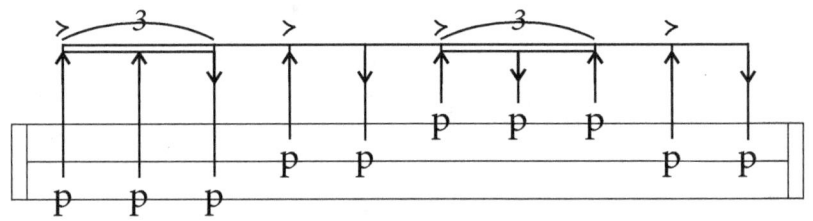

VARIATION I (3rd mode)

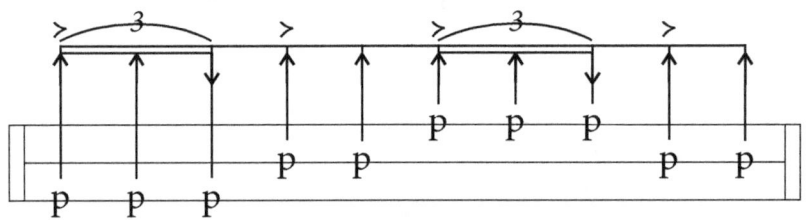

VARIATION I (4th mode)

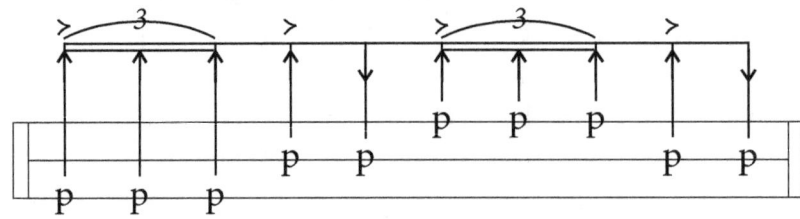

VARIATION I (5th mode)

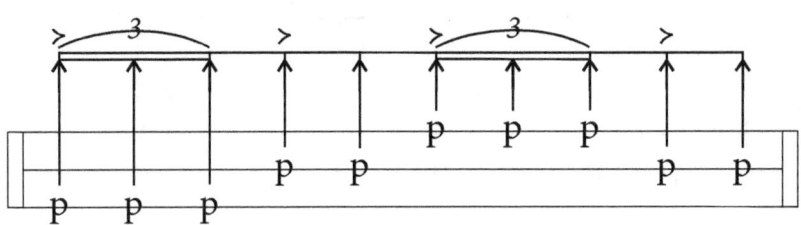

VARIATION I

F1
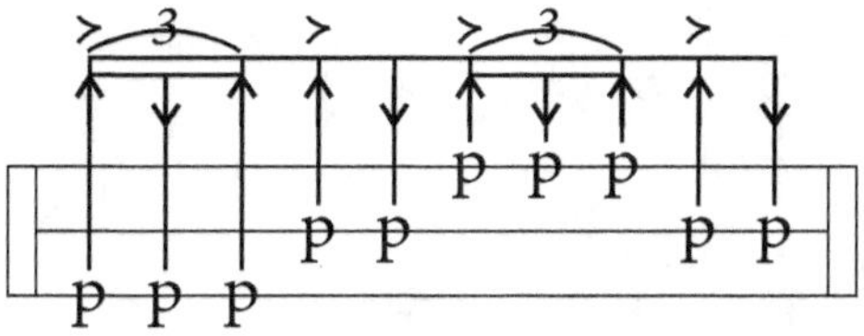

F2
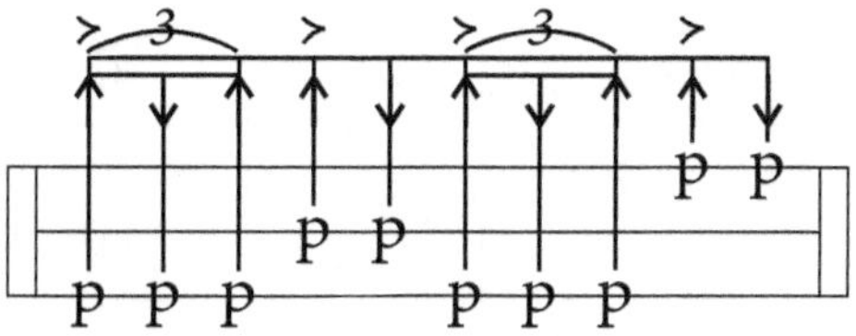

F3
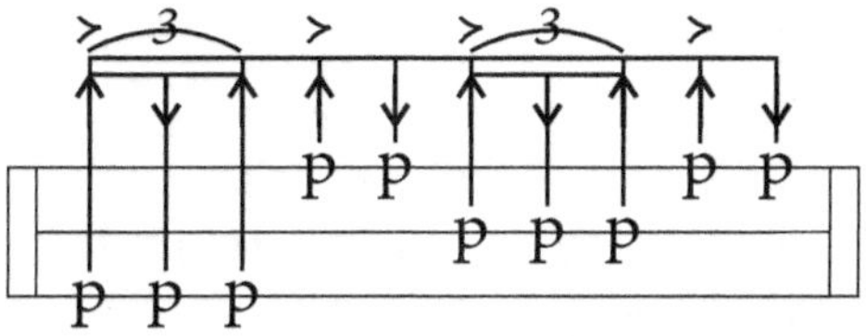

F4
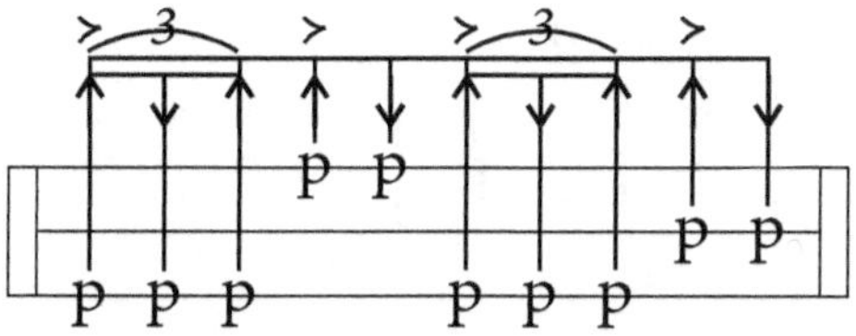

F5
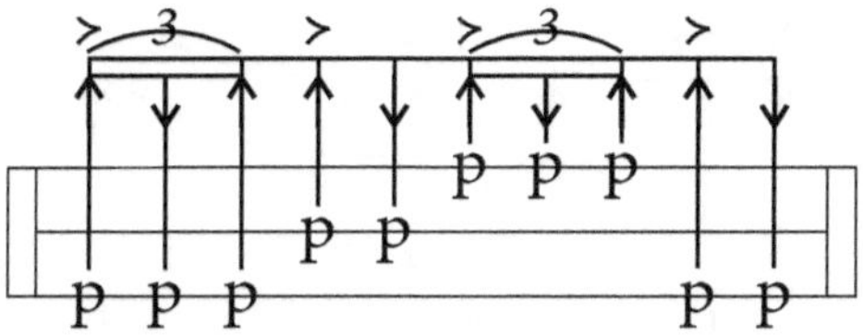

F6
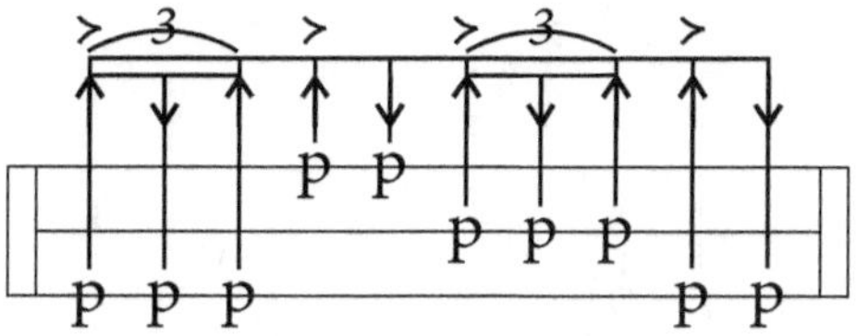

F7
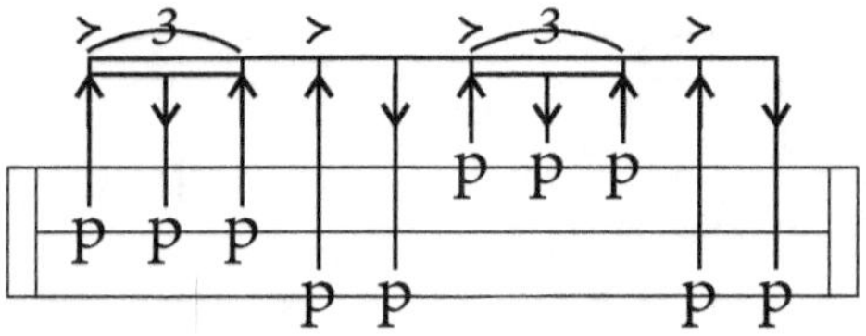

F8
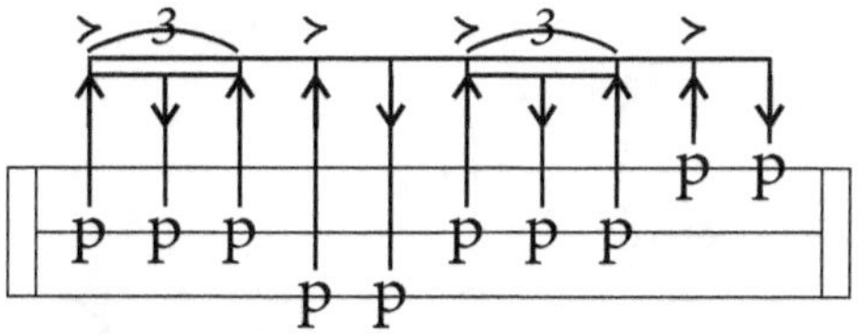

F9
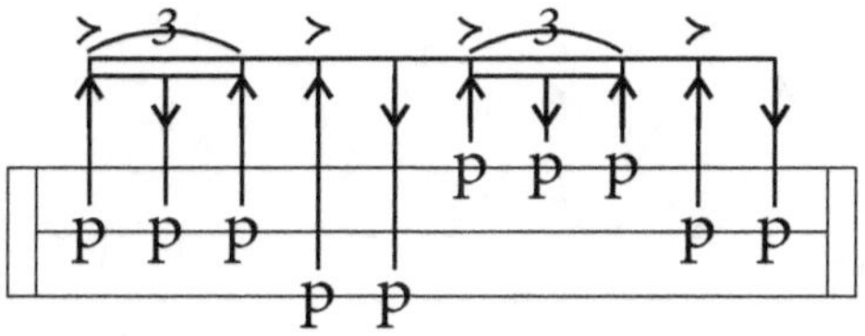

F10
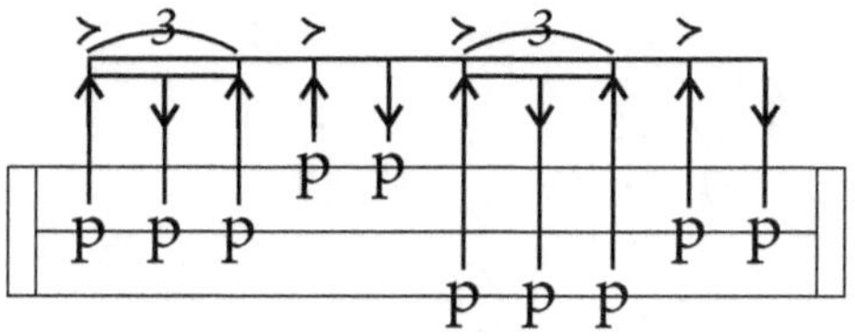

F11
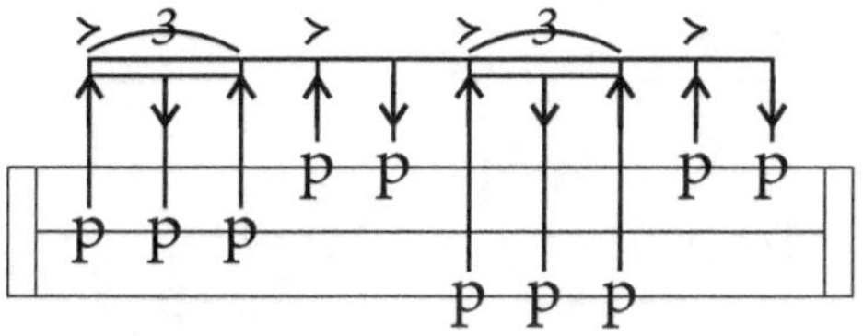

F12
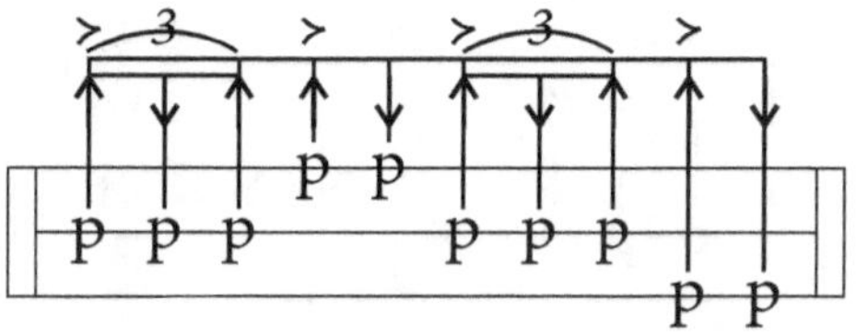

F13
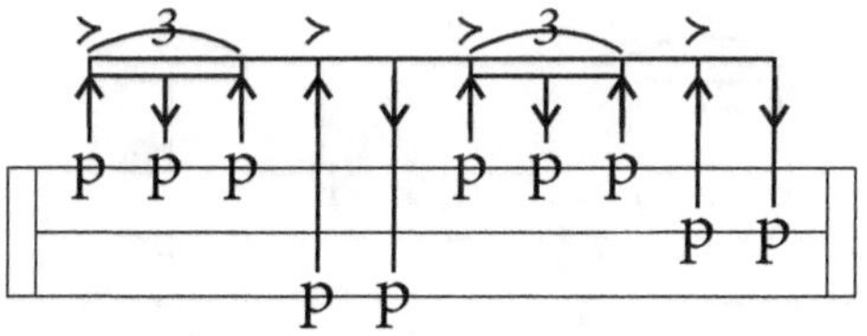

F14
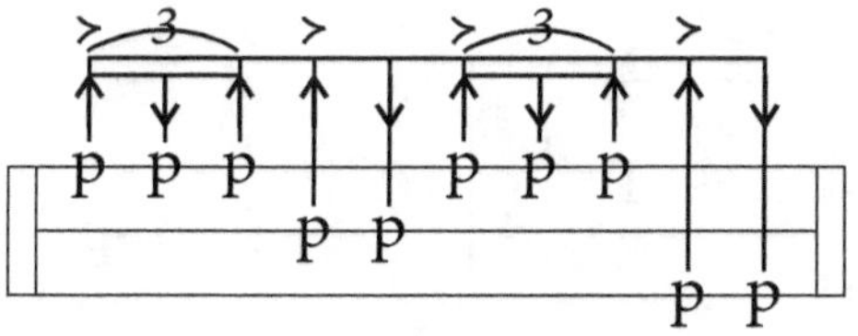

F15
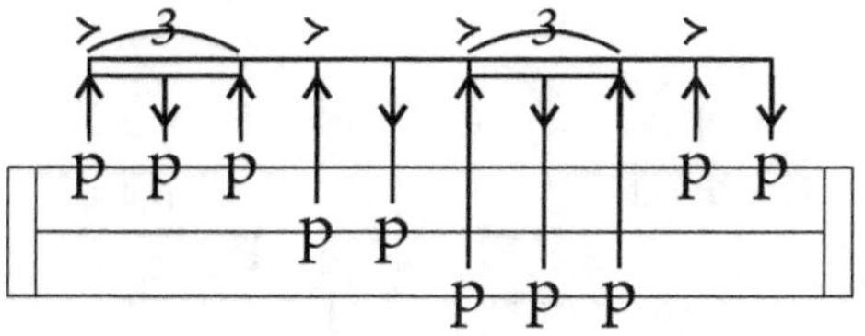

F16
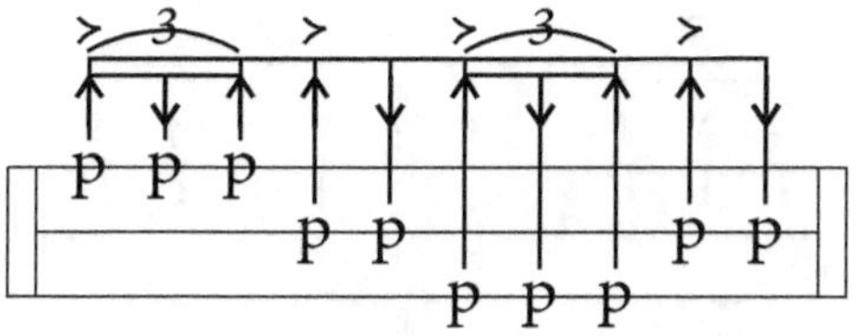

F17
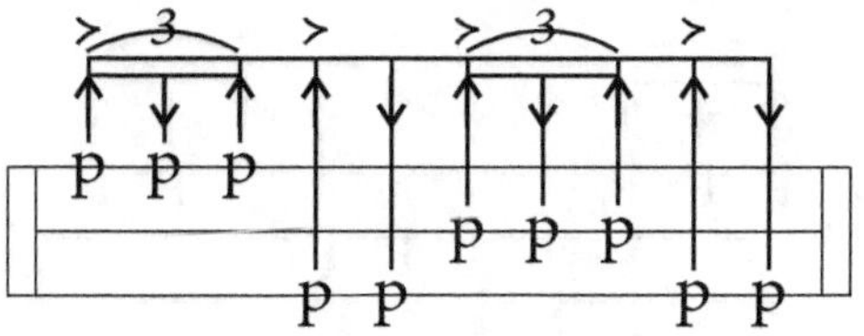

F18
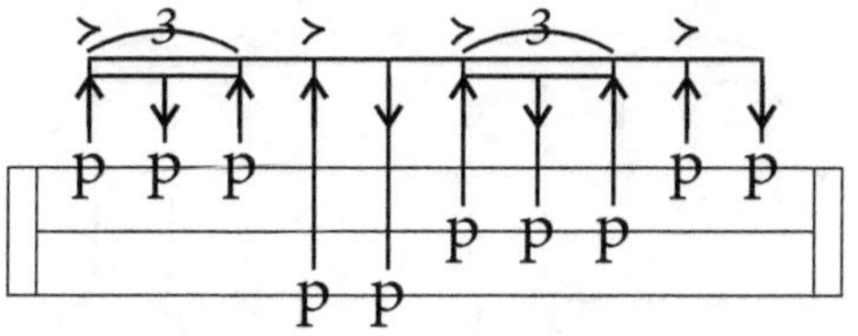

VARIATION II

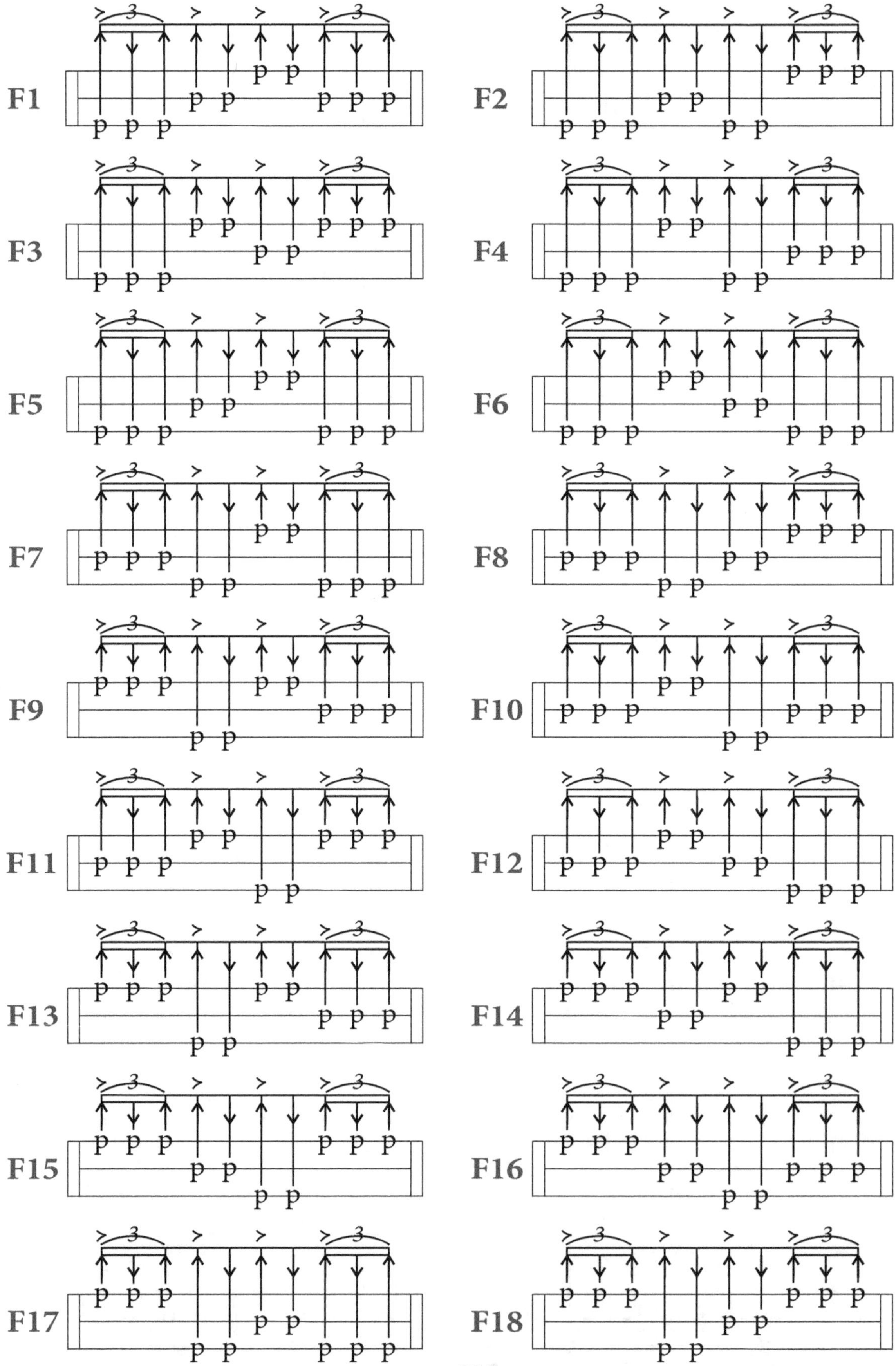

VARIATION III

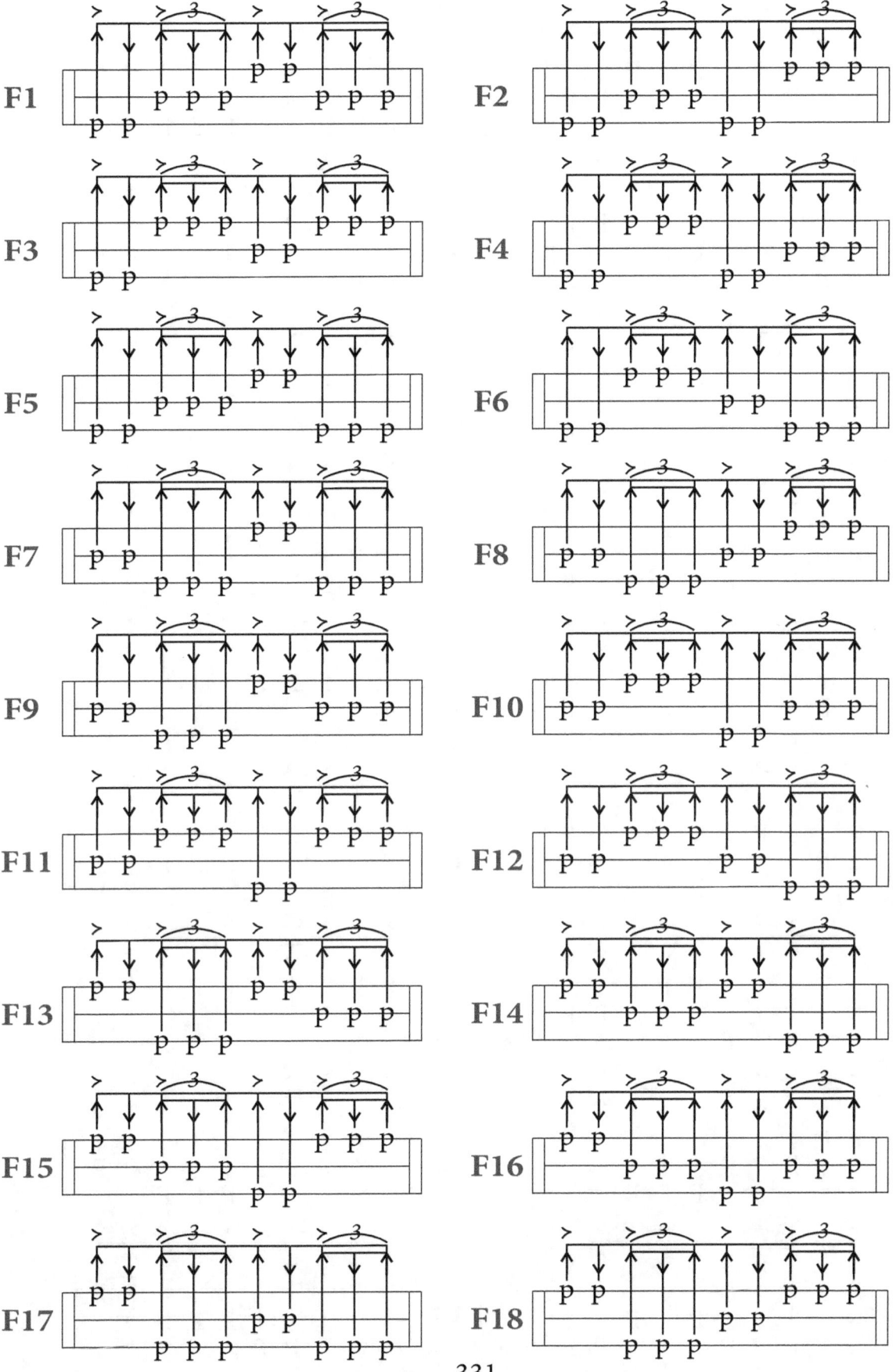

VARIATION IV

F1 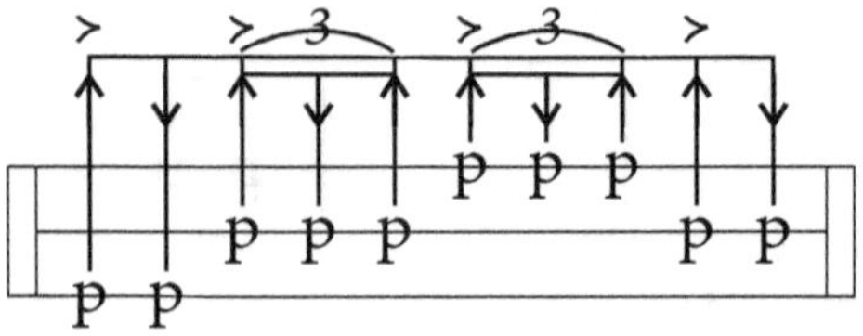

F2 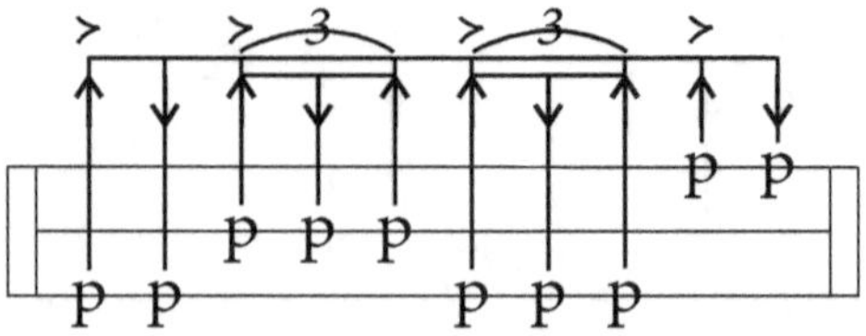

F3 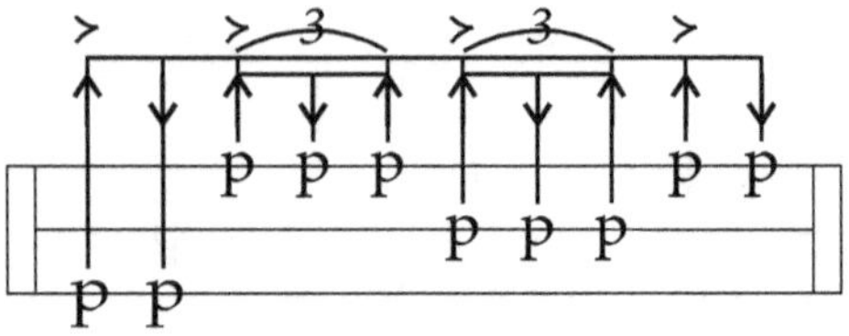

F4 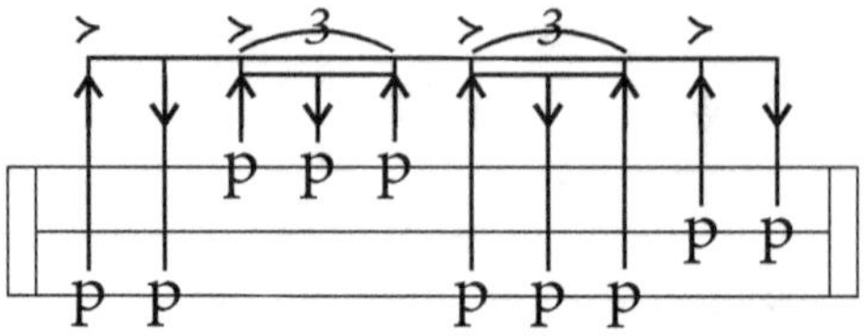

F5 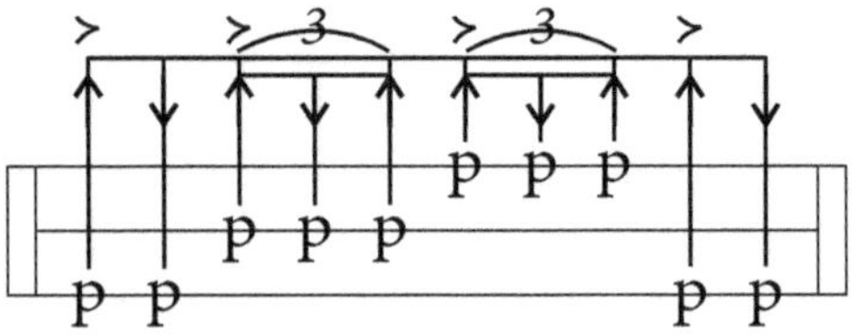

F6 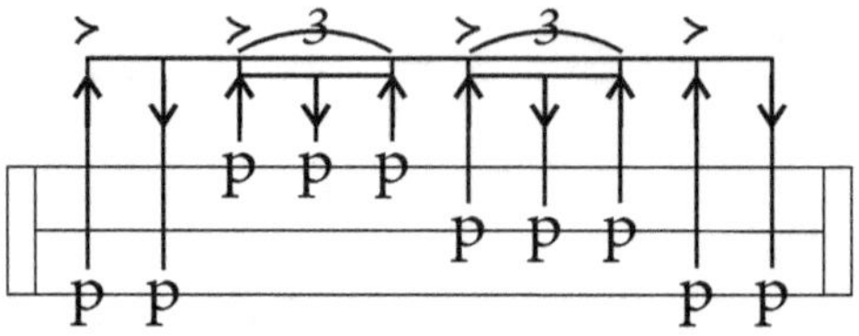

F7 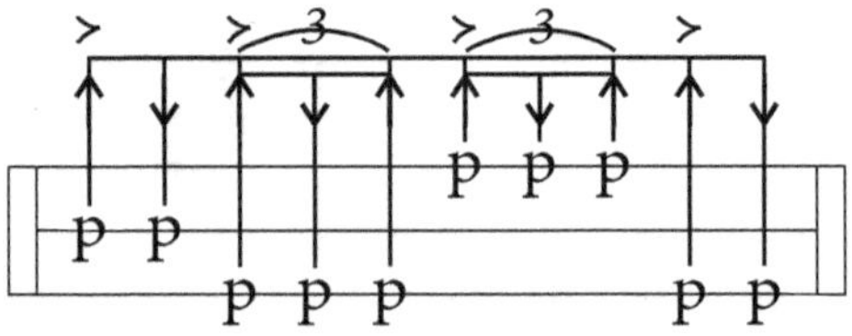

F8 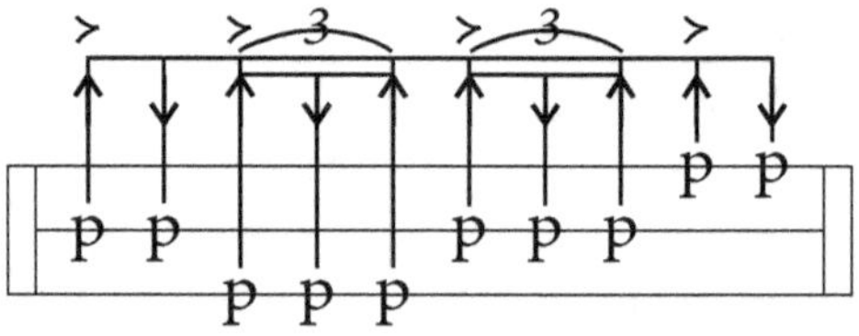

F9 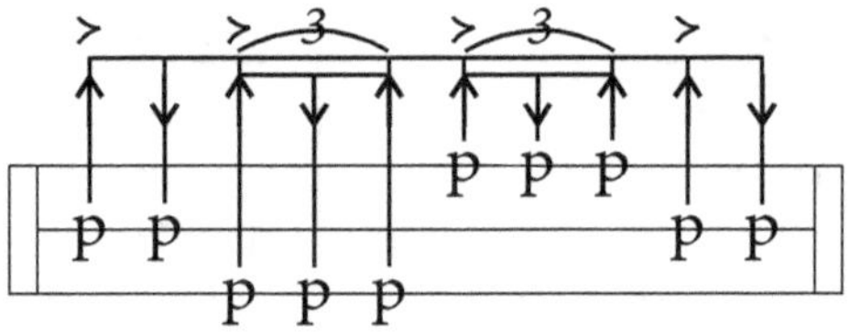

F10 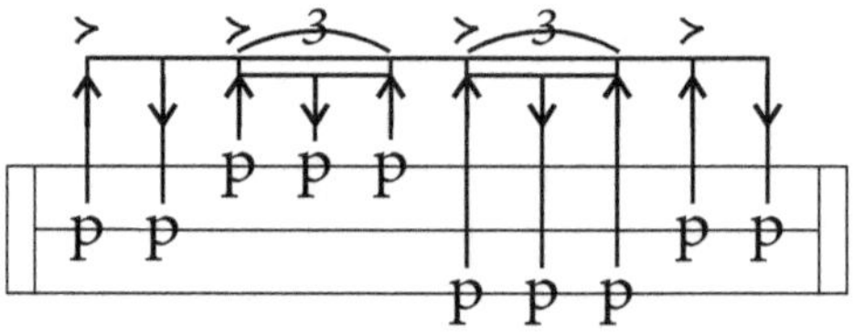

F11 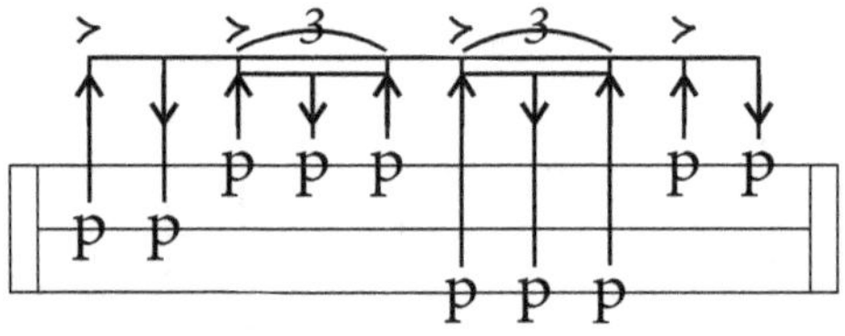

F12 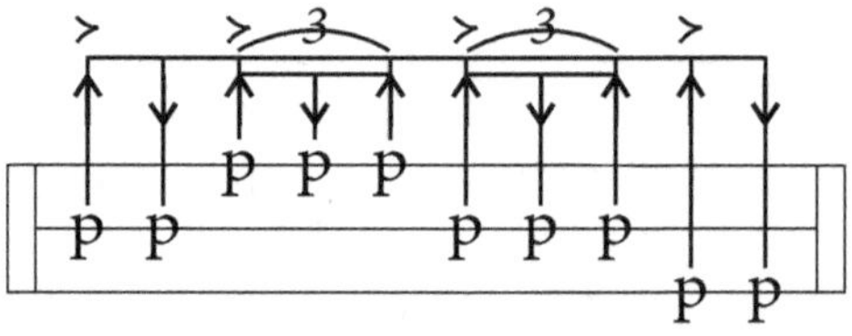

F13 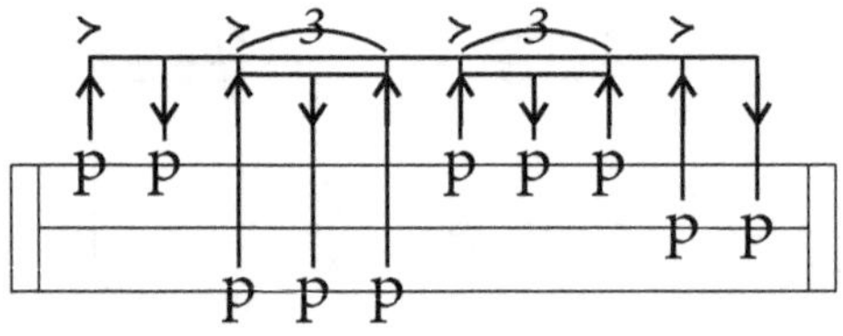

F14 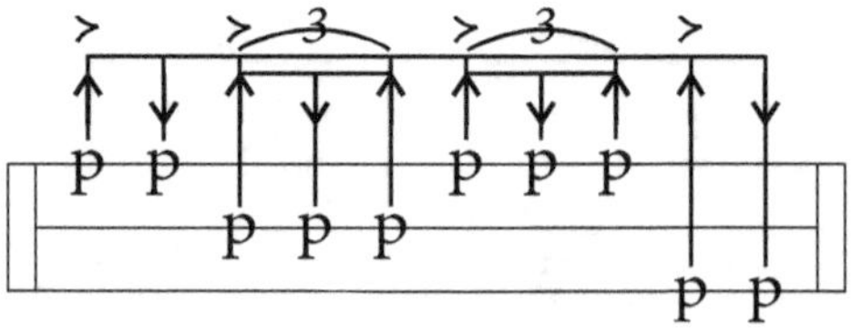

F15 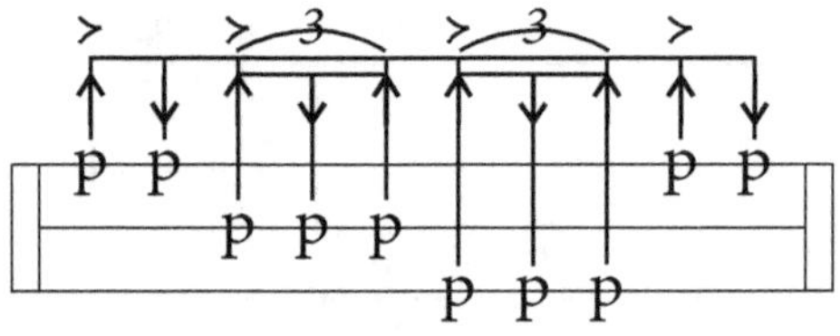

F16 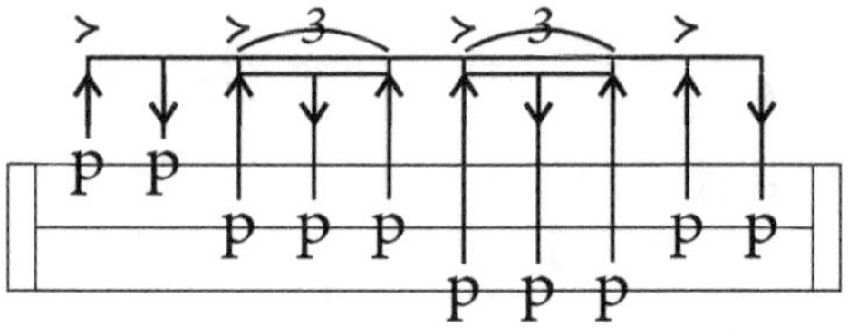

F17 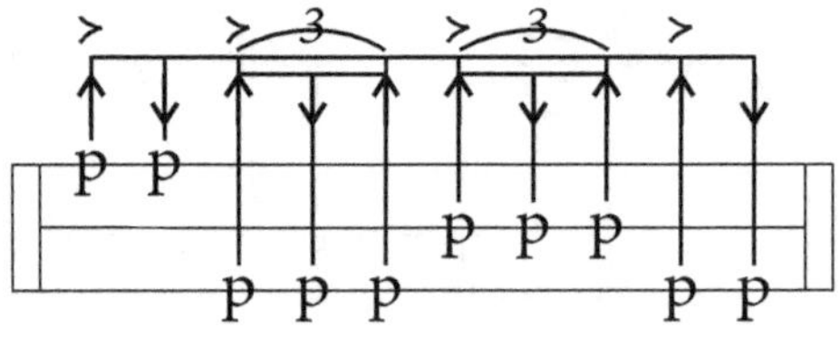

F18 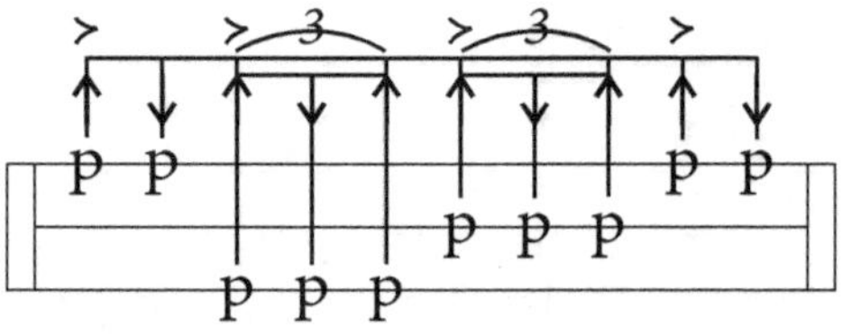

§ XI

Exercise on pulgar on three adjacent strings with two double and two quad strokes within each Formula. The exercise contains four variations with 18 Formulas in each. The direction of pulgar stroke is as follows:

↑ ↓ in the double stroke   ↑ ↓ ↑ ↓ in the quad stroke
p p   p p p p

The first Formula of each variation is cited below. Isochronous playing of pulgar strokes (double and quad).

VARIATION I

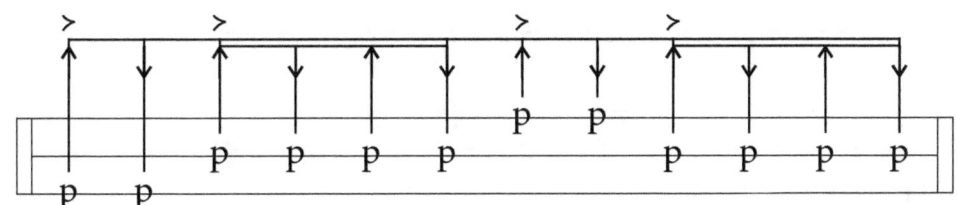

VARIATION II

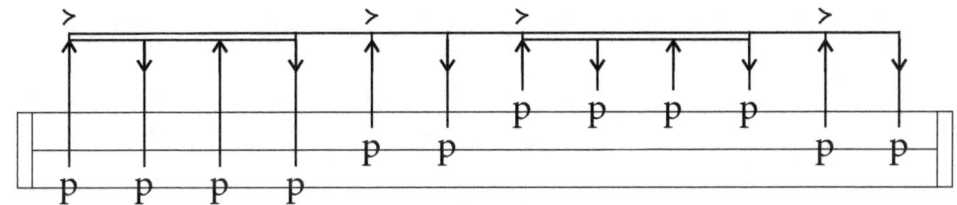

VARIATION III

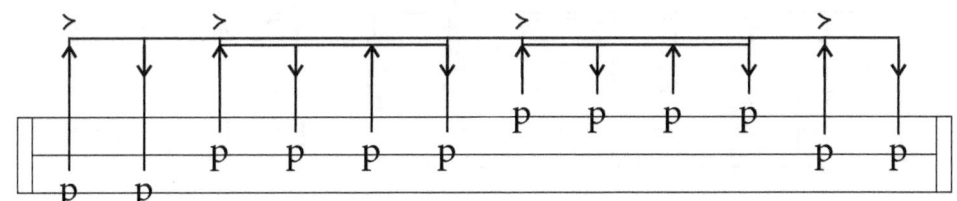

VARIATION IV

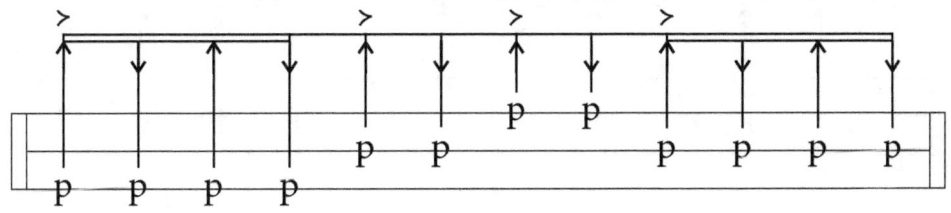

You can practice on all Formulas and all variations in various ways. 9 modes of practice of the first Formula from variation I are cited below:

VARIATION I (1st mode)

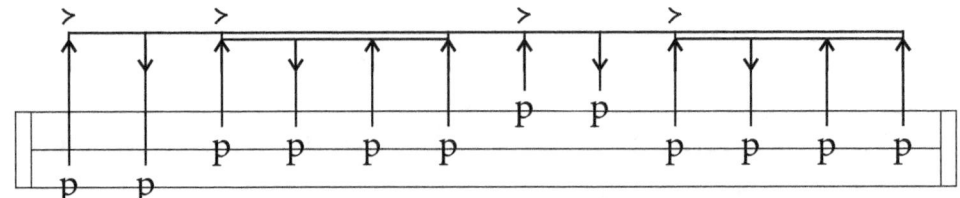

VARIATION I (2nd mode)

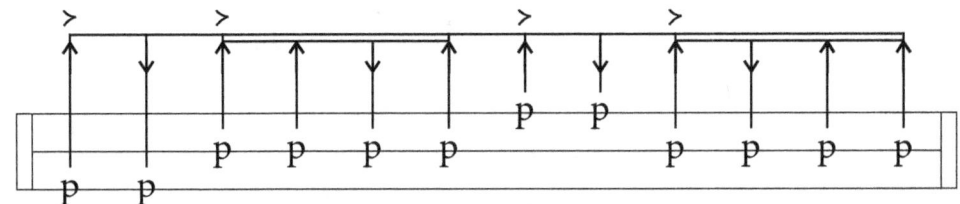

VARIATION I (3rd mode)

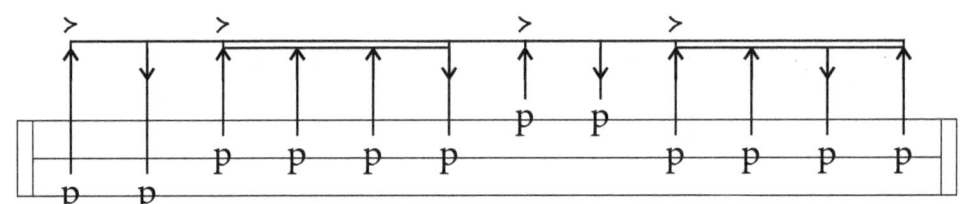

VARIATION I (4th mode)

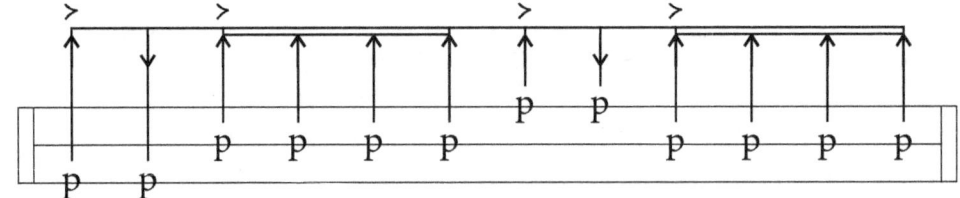

VARIATION I (5th mode)

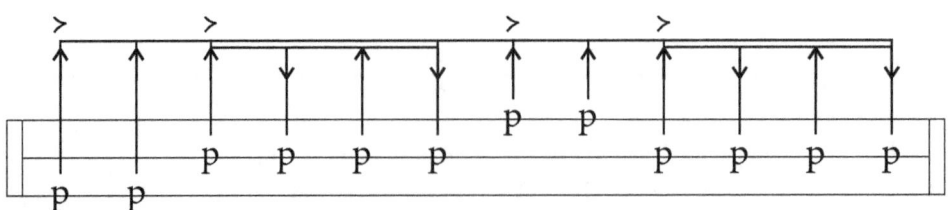

VARIATION I (6th mode)

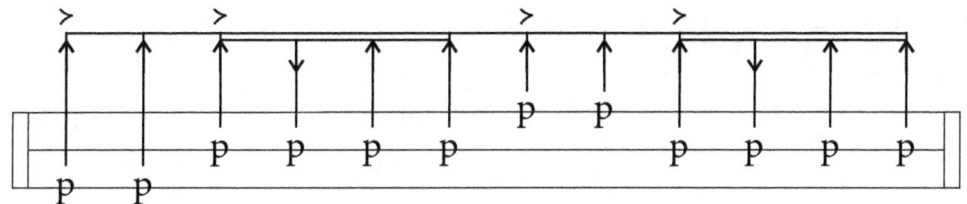

VARIATION I (7th mode)

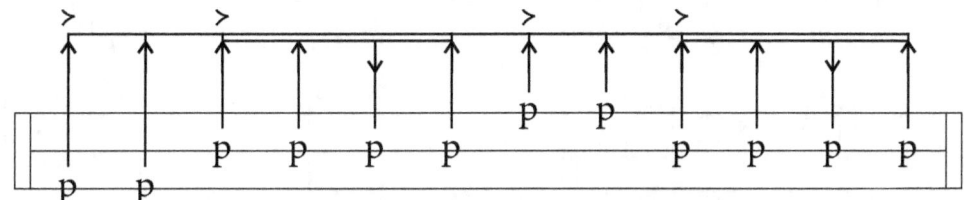

VARIATION I (8th mode)

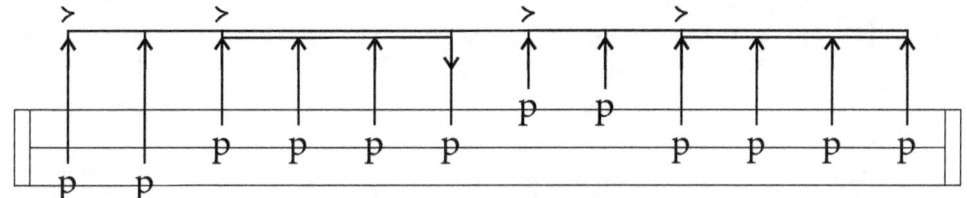

VARIATION I (9th mode)

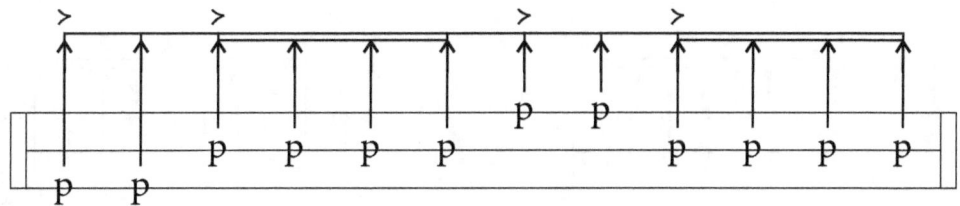

VARIATION I

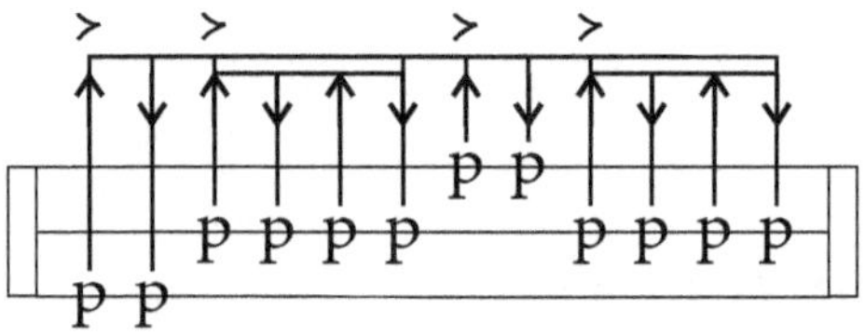

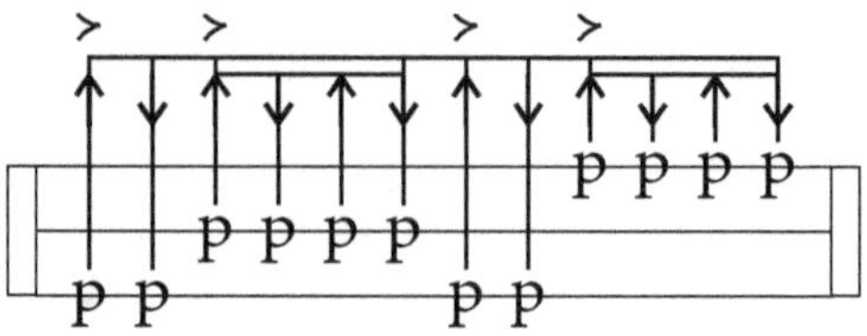

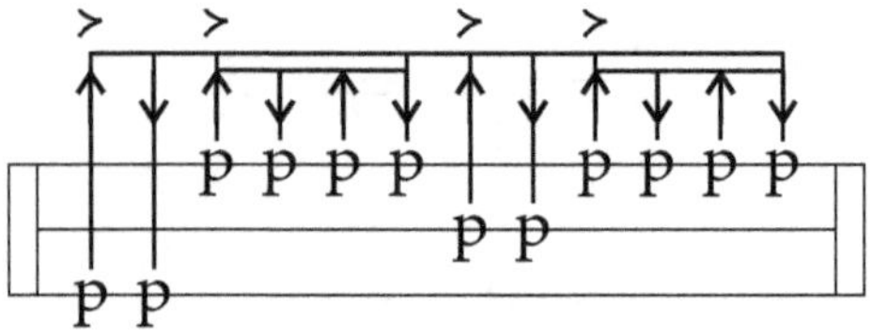

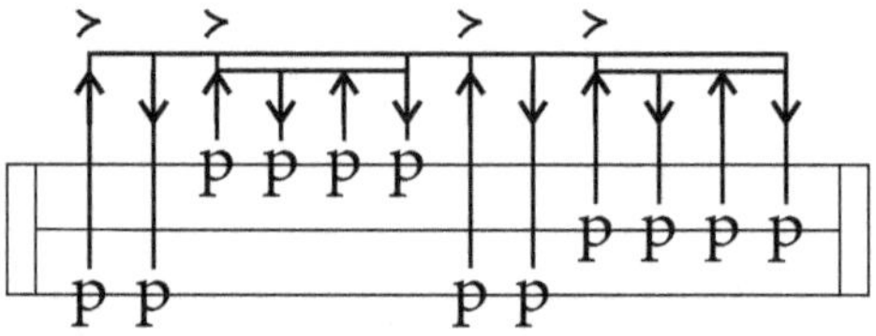

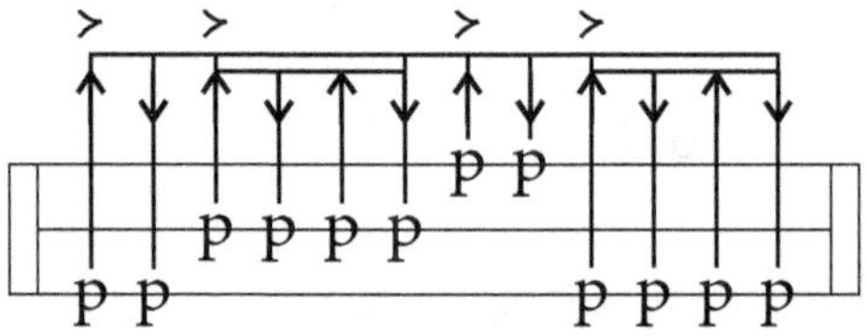

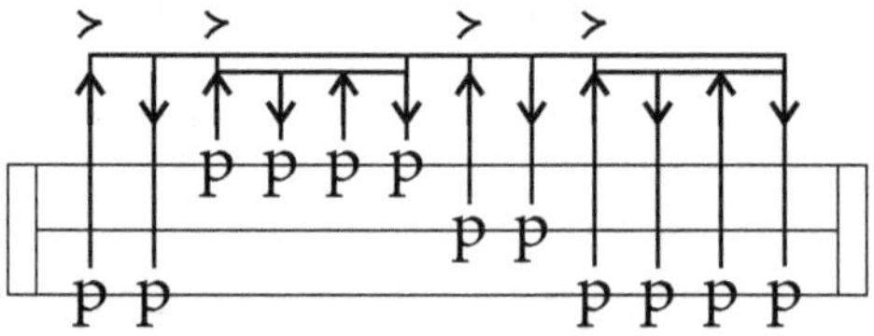

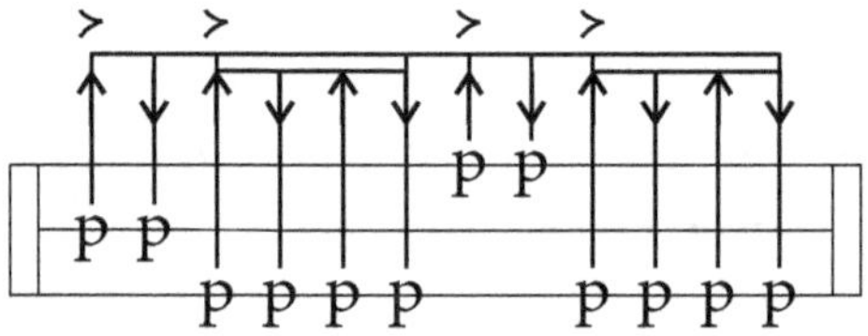

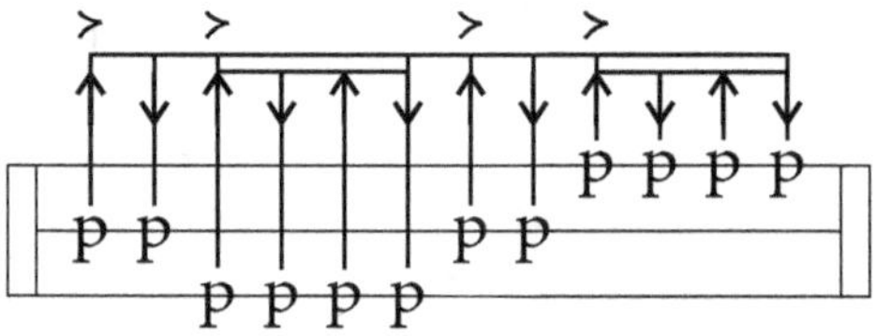

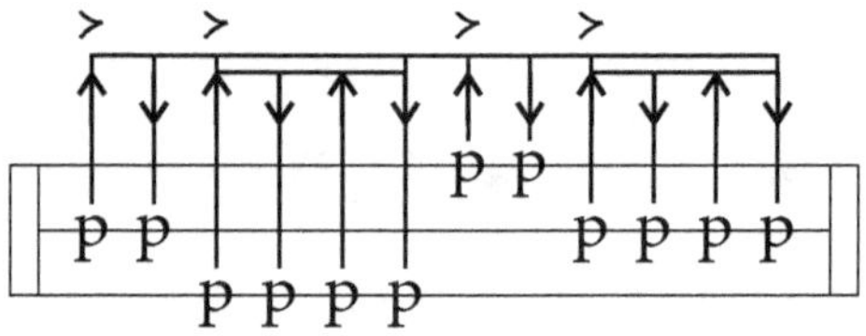

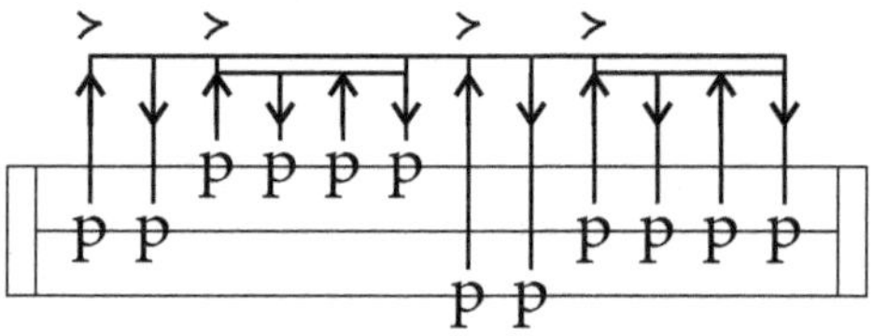

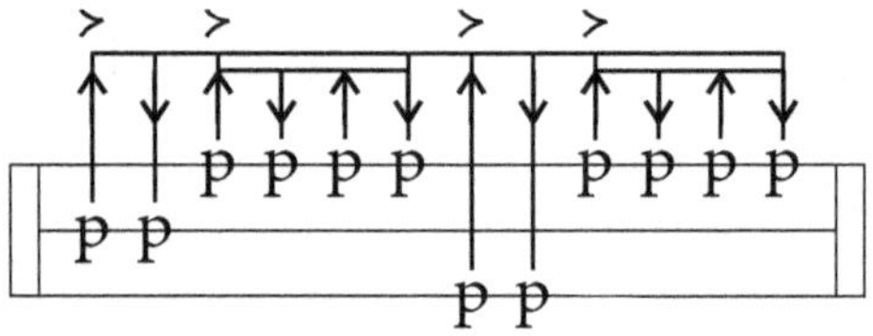

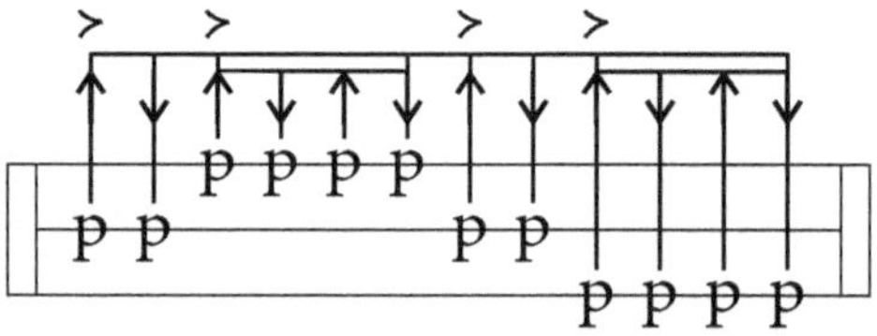

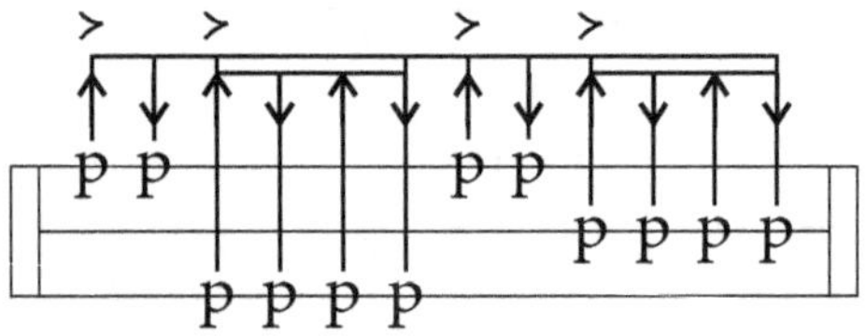

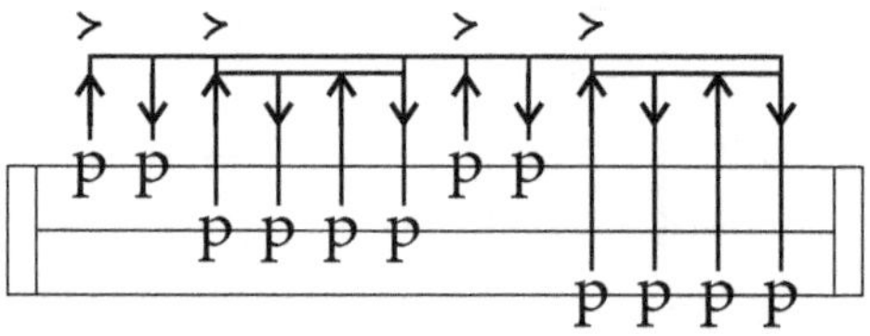

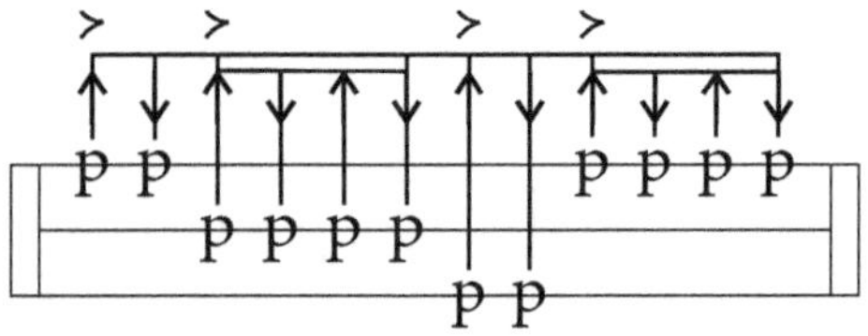

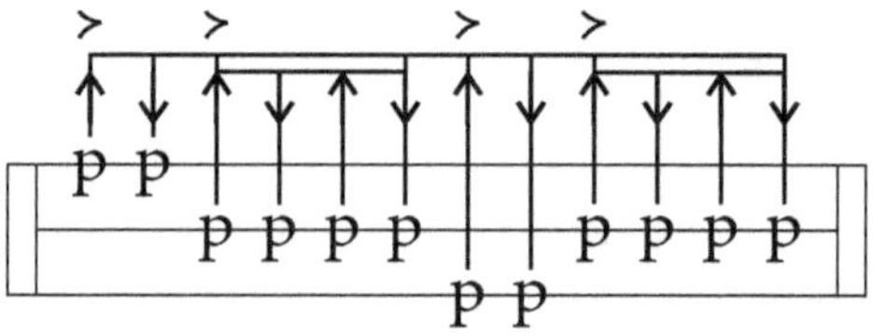

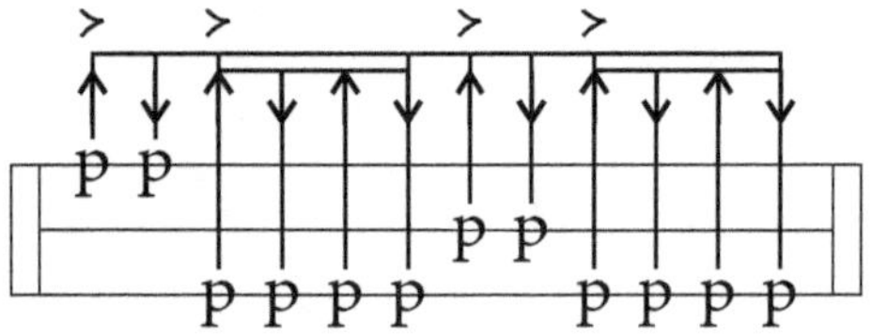

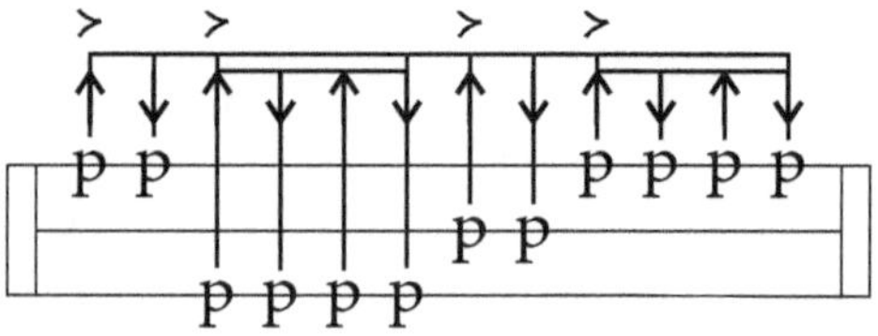

VARIATION II

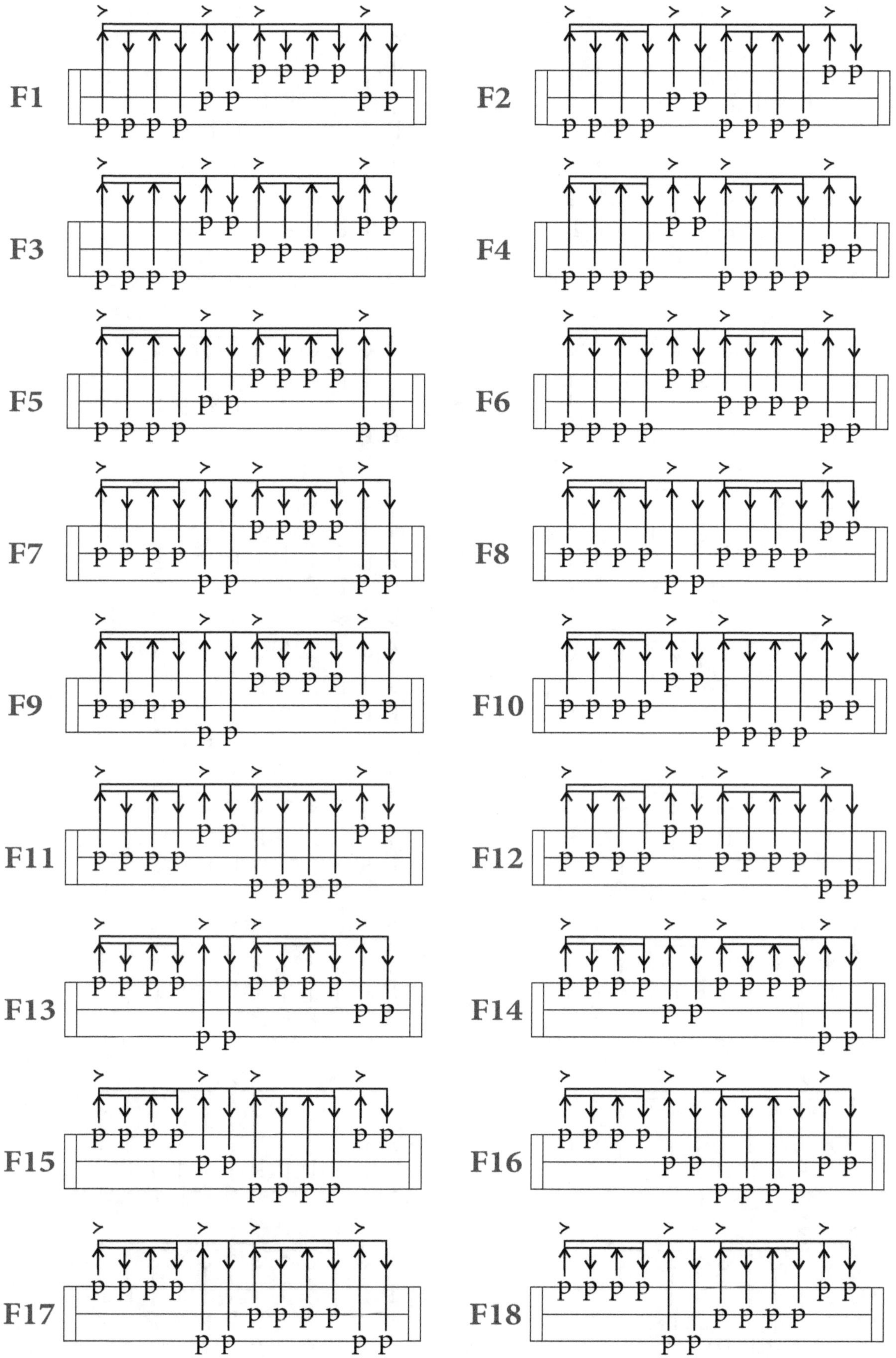

VARIATION III

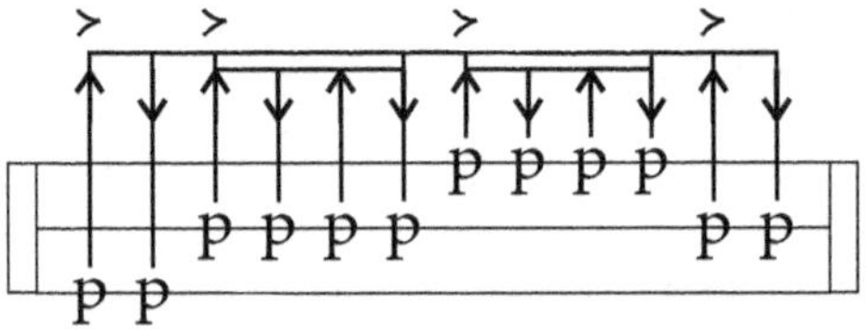

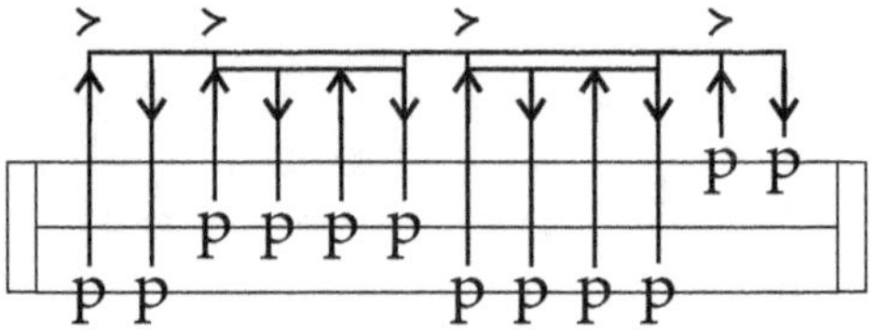

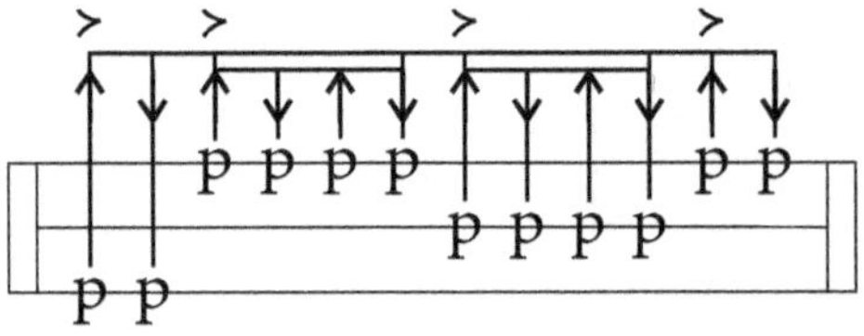

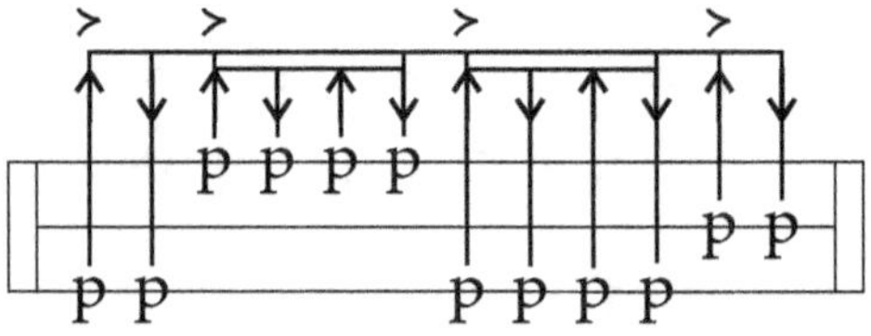

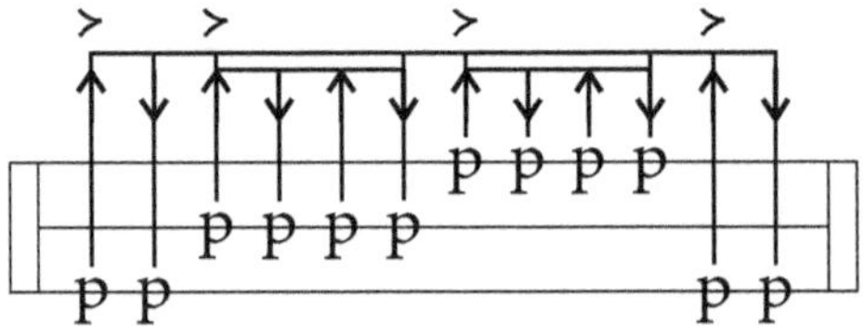

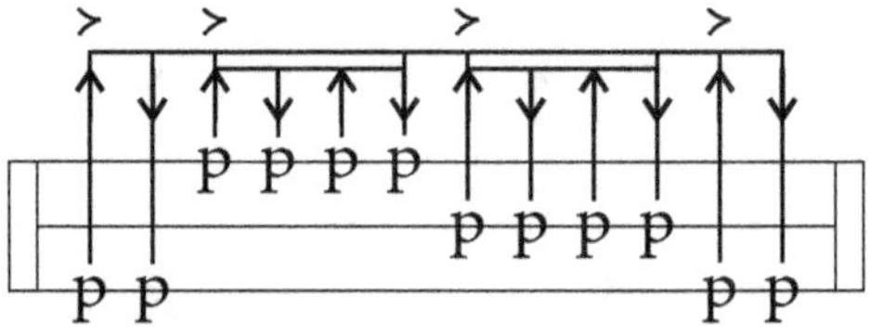

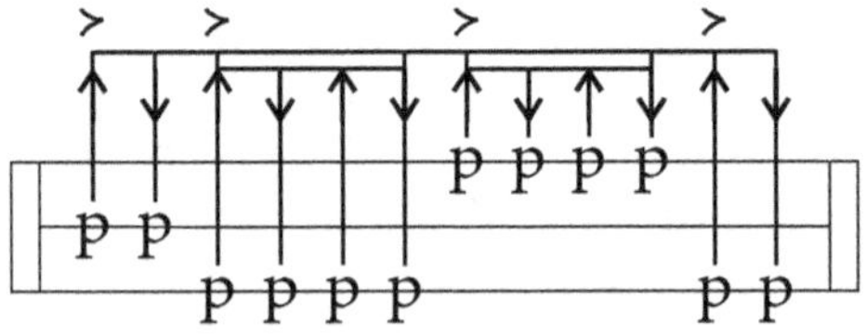

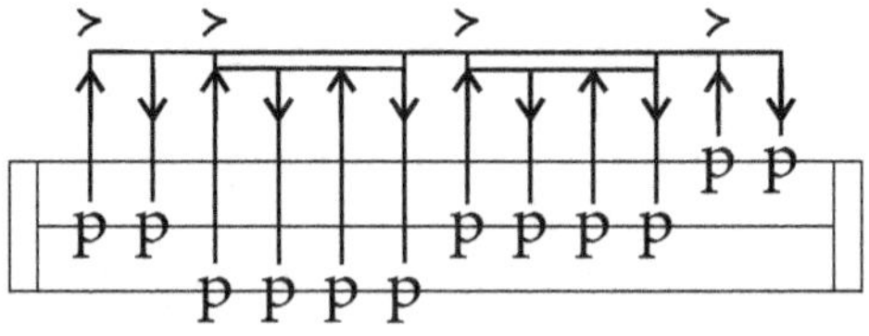

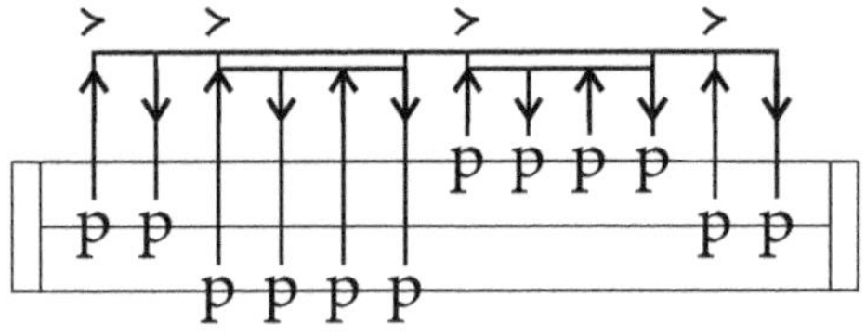

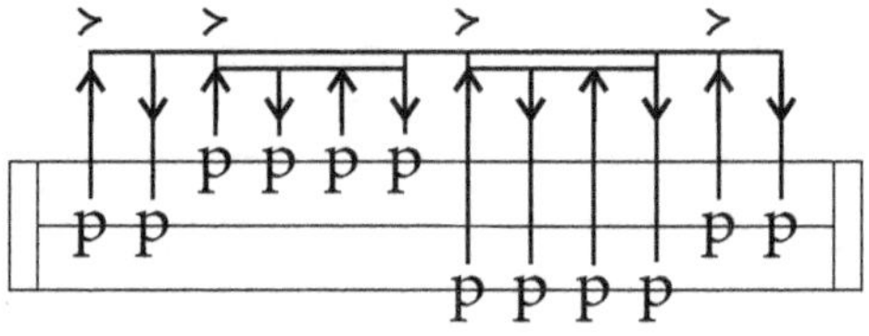

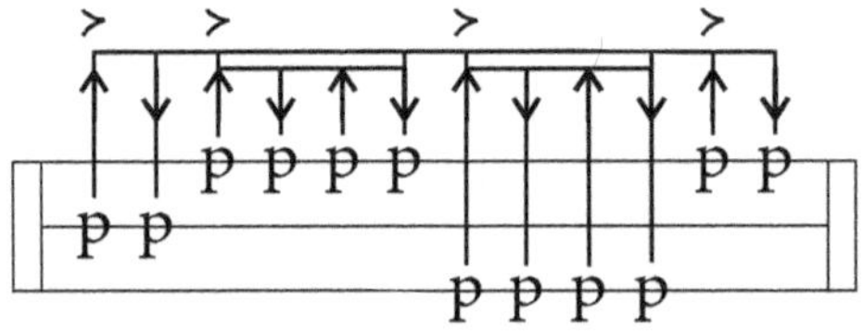

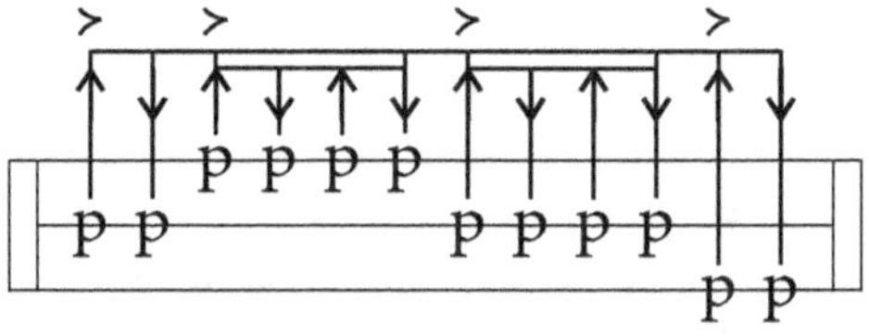

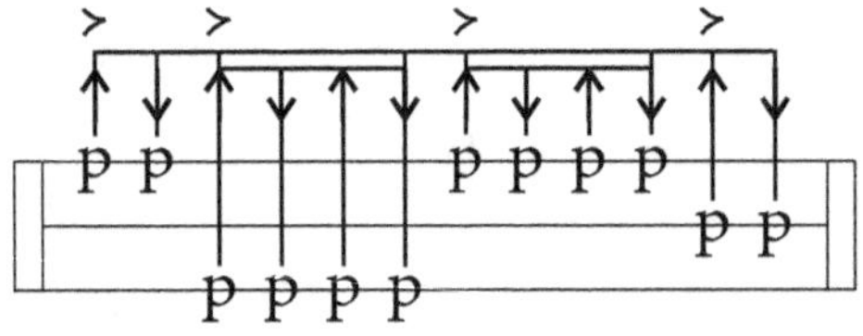

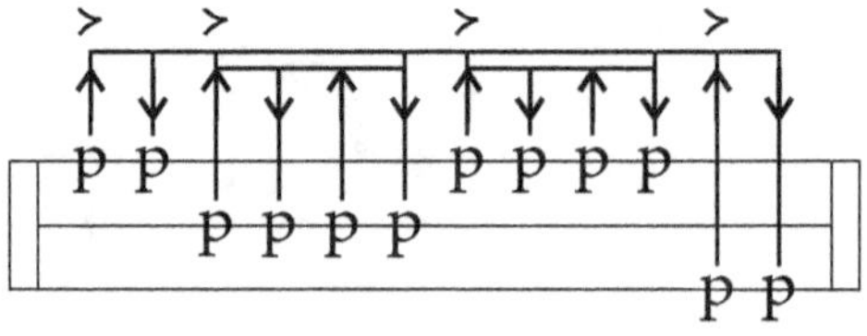

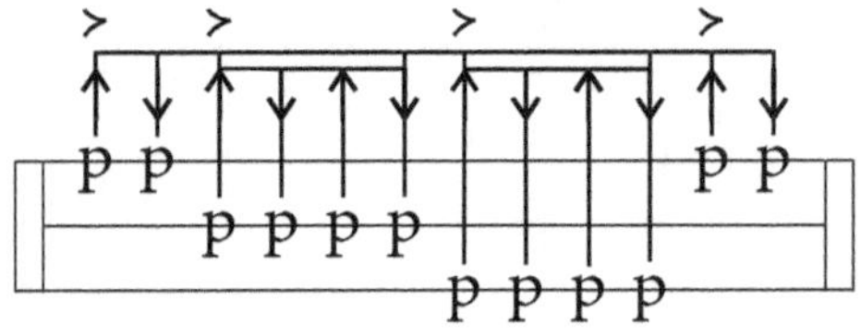

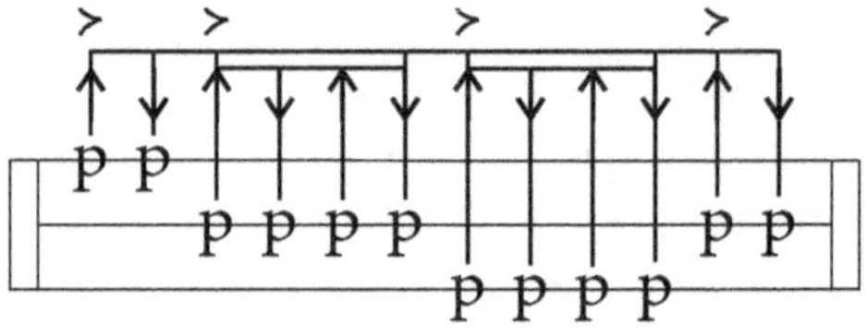

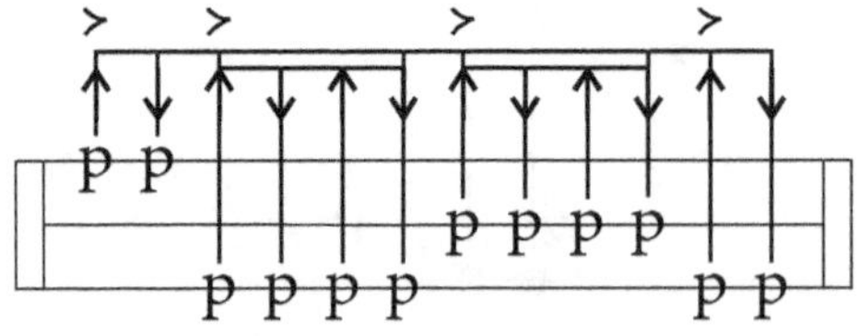

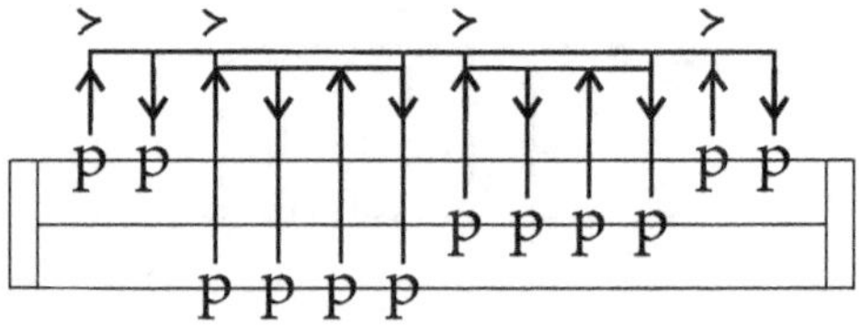

VARIATION IV

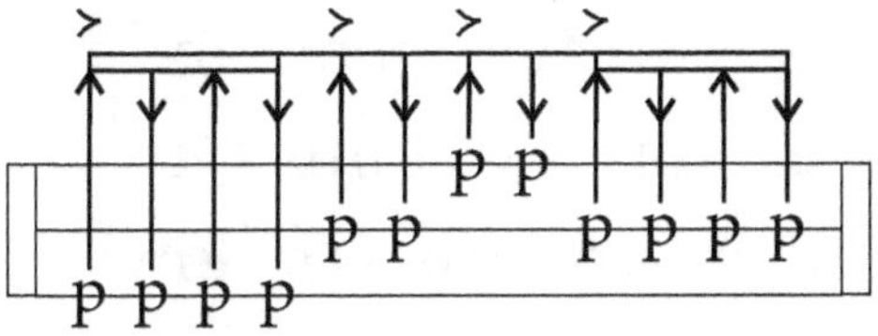

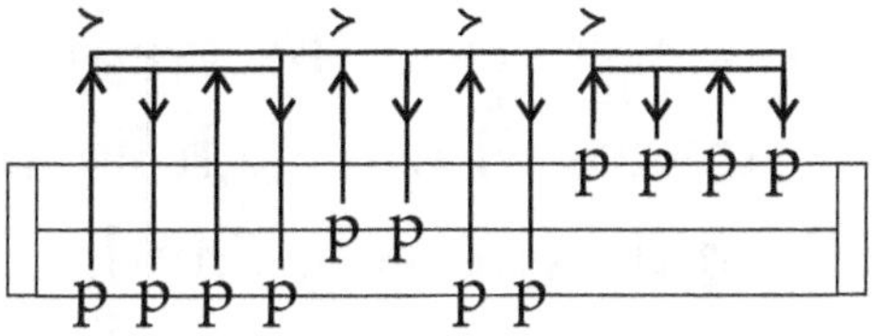

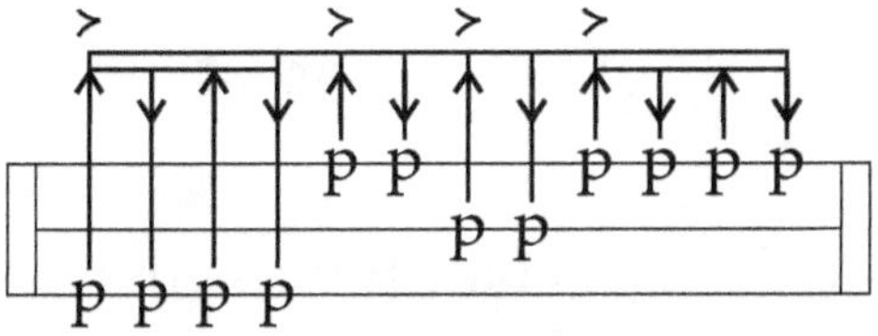

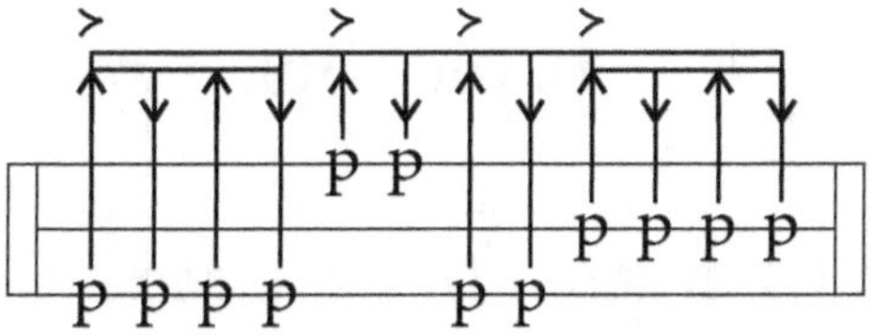

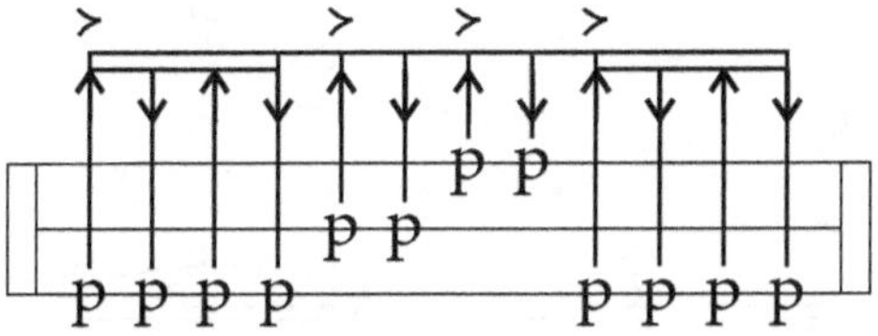

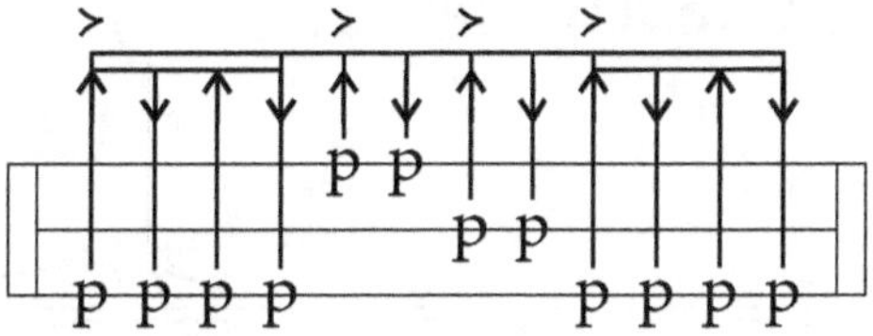

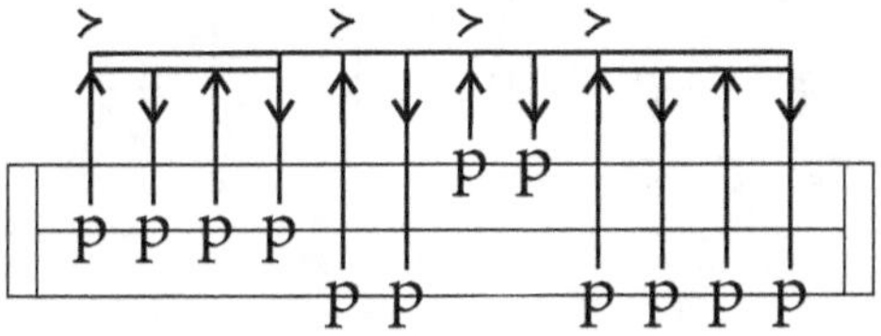

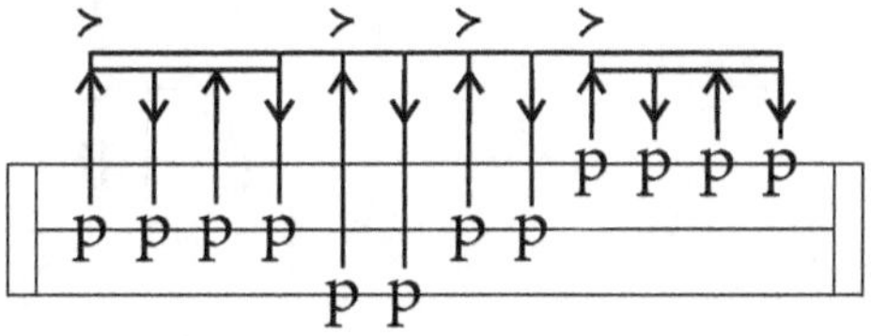

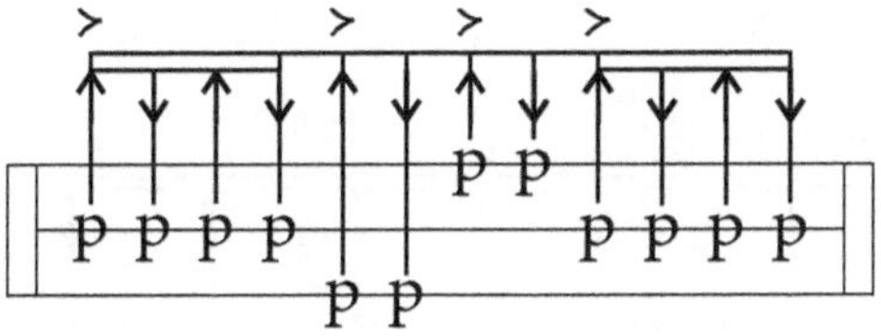

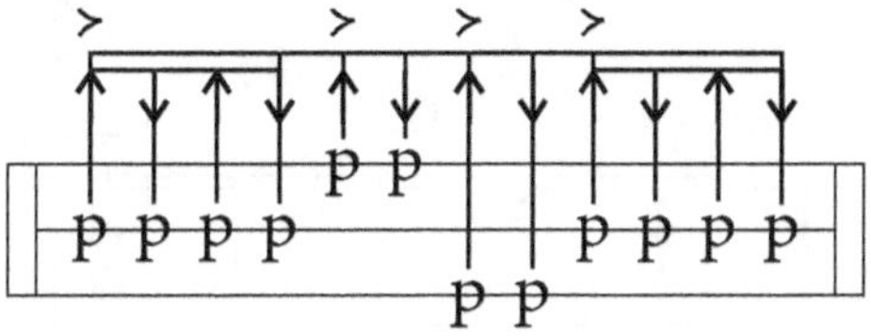

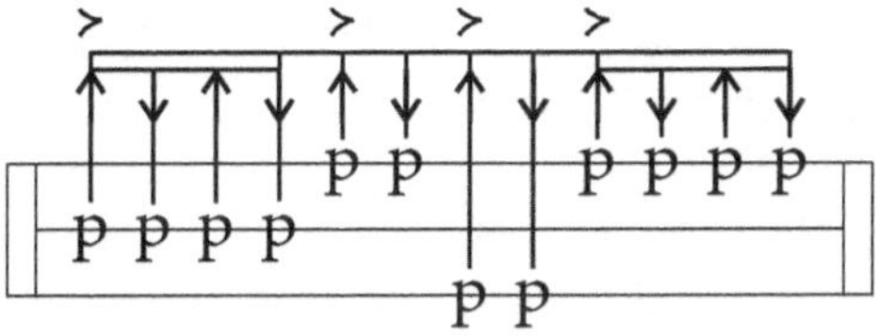

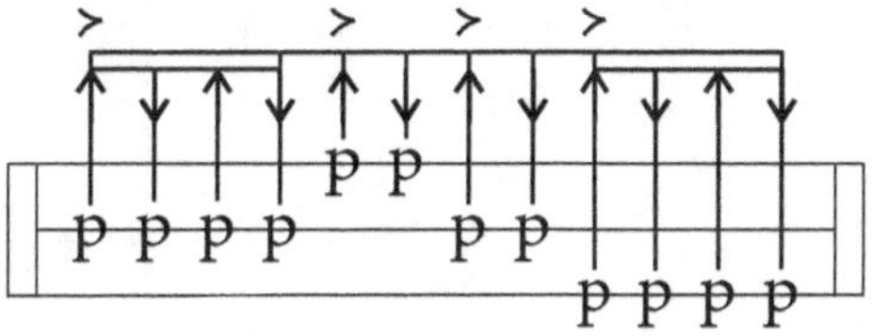

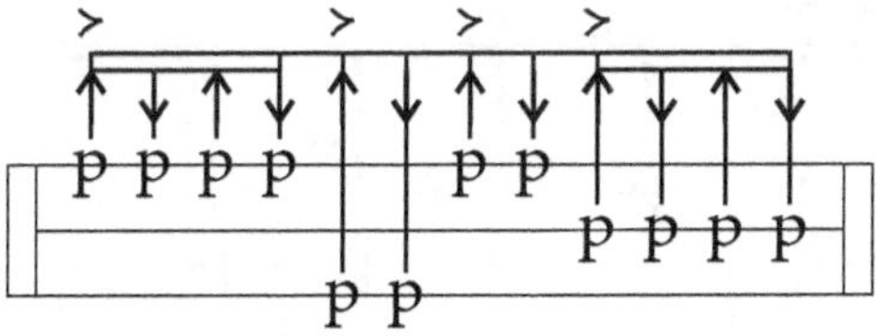

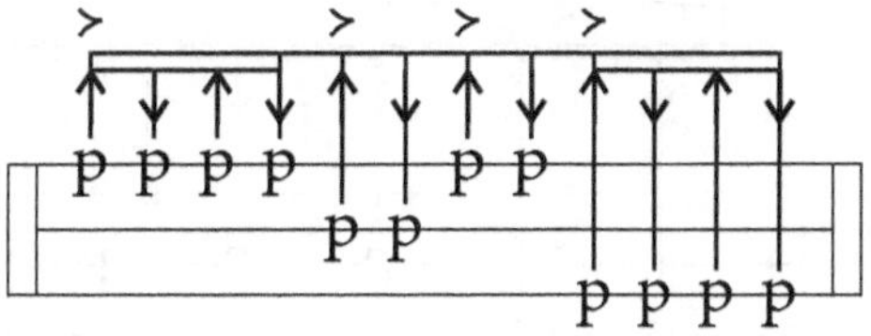

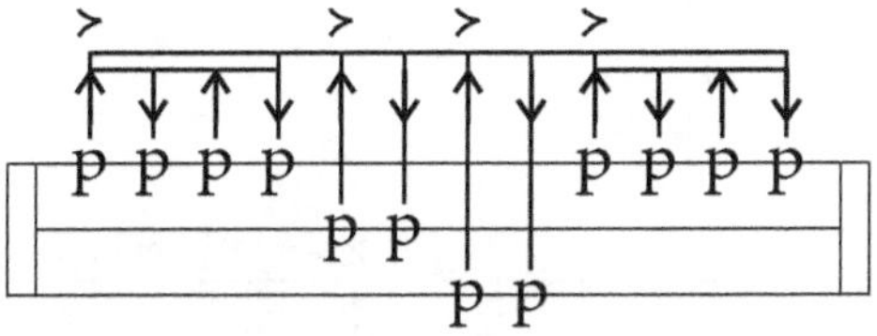

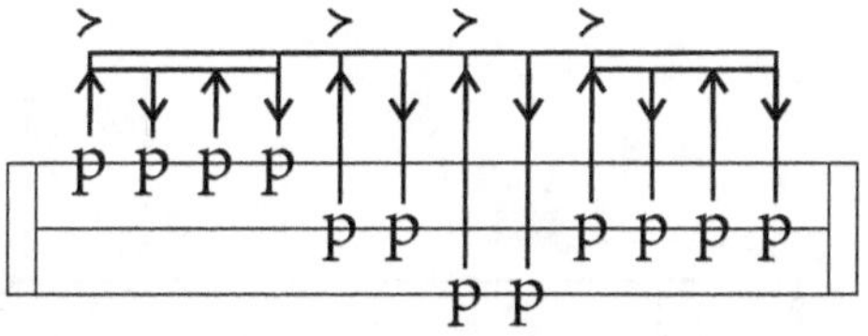

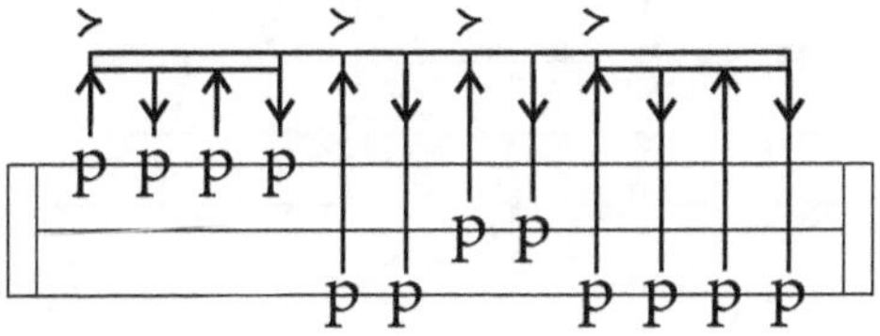

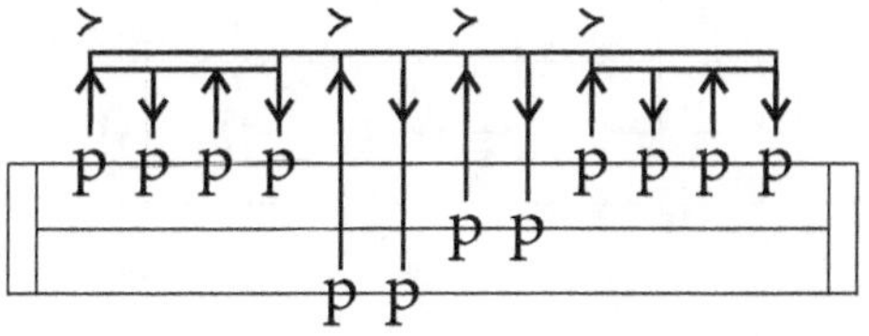

§ XII

Exercise on pulgar on three adjacent strings with two quad and two triple (triplets) strokes within each Formula. The exercise contains four variations with 18 Formulas in each. The direction of pulgar stroke is as follow:

↑↓↑ in the triple stroke   ↑↓↑↓ in the quad stroke
p p p   p p p p

The first Formula of each variation is cited below. Isochronous playing of pulgar strokes (triple and quad).

VARIATION I

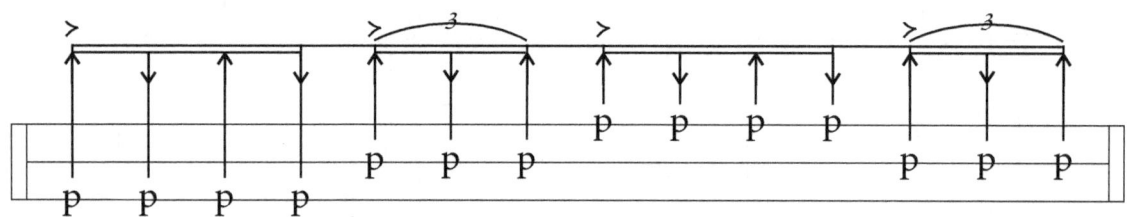

VARIATION II

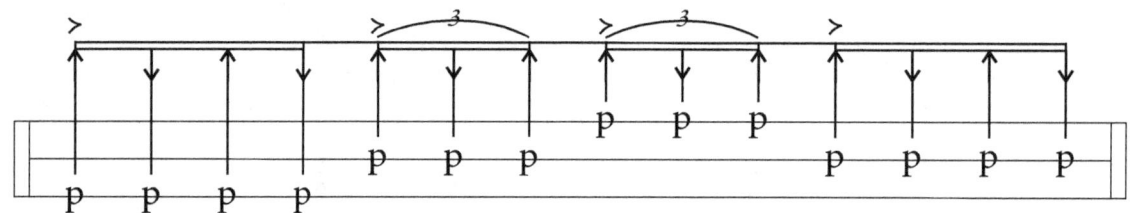

VARIATION III

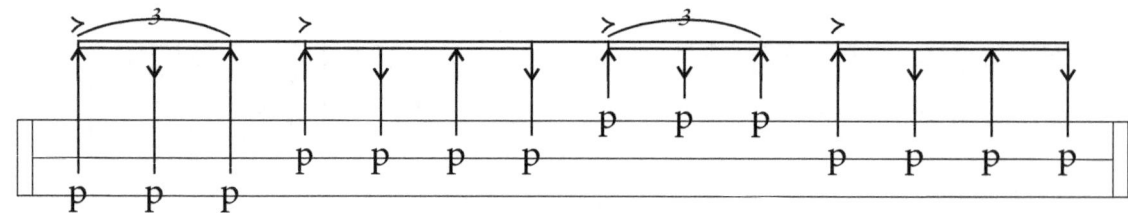

VARIATION IV

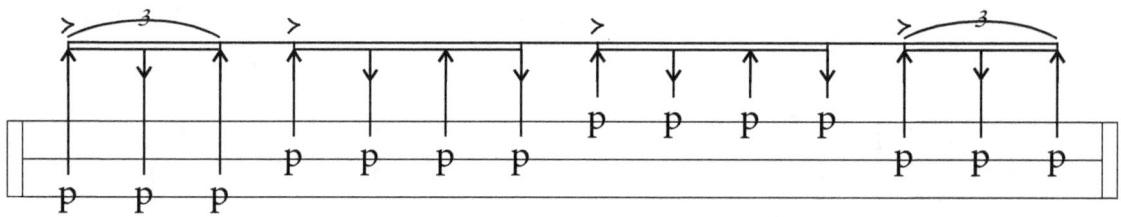

Other modes of practice with change in the direction of pulgar stroke.

VARIATION I (1st mode)

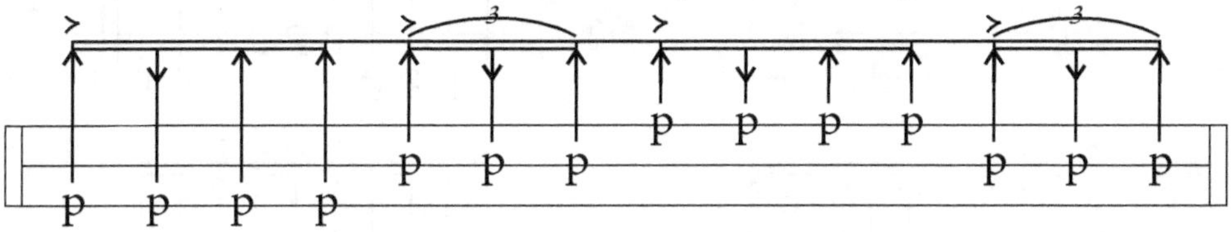

VARIATION I (2nd mode)

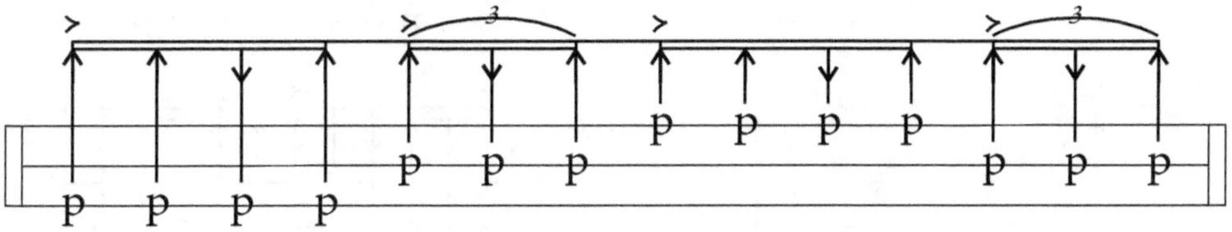

VARIATION I (3rd mode)

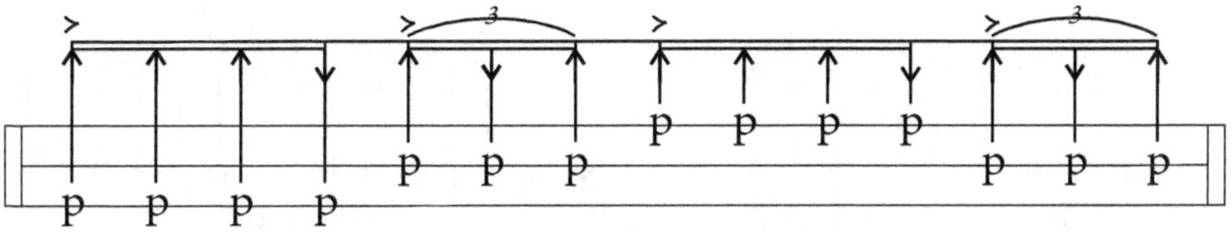

VARIATION I (4th mode)

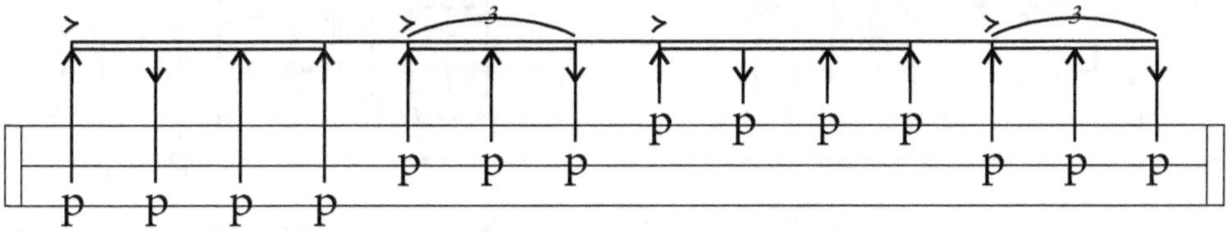

VARIATION I (5th mode)

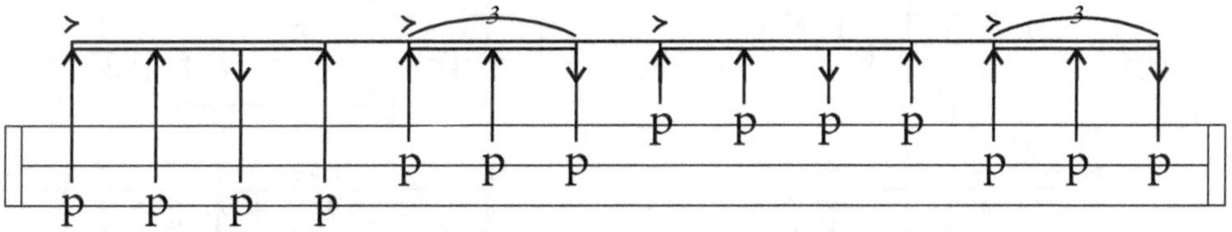

VARIATION I (6th mode)

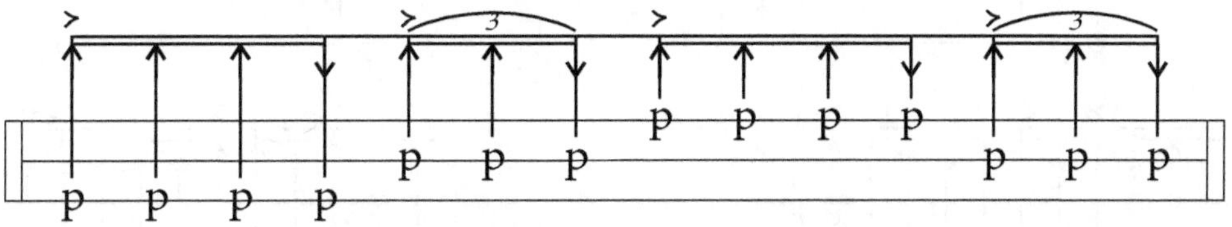

VARIATION I (7th mode)

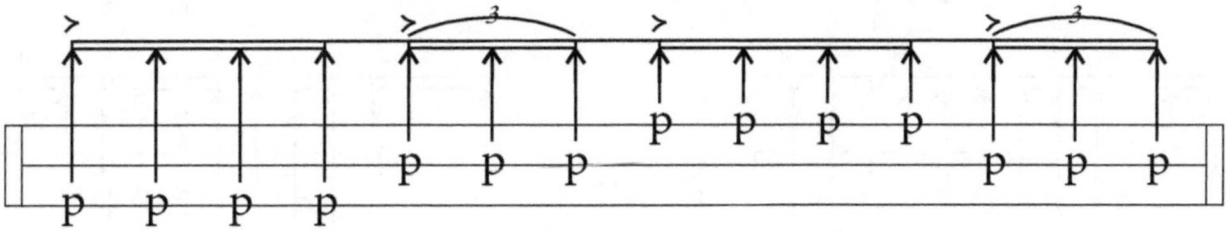

VARIATION I

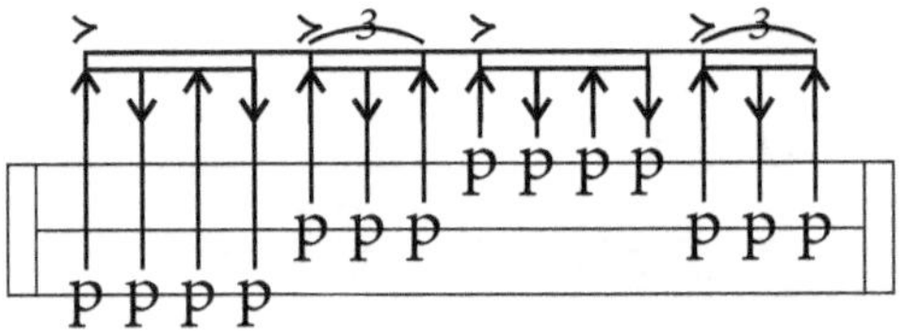

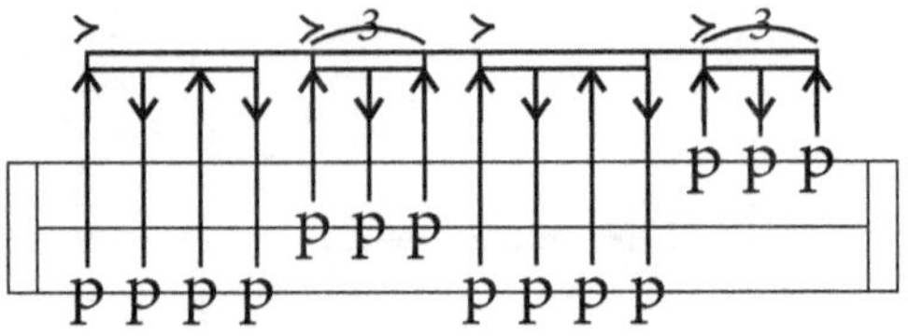

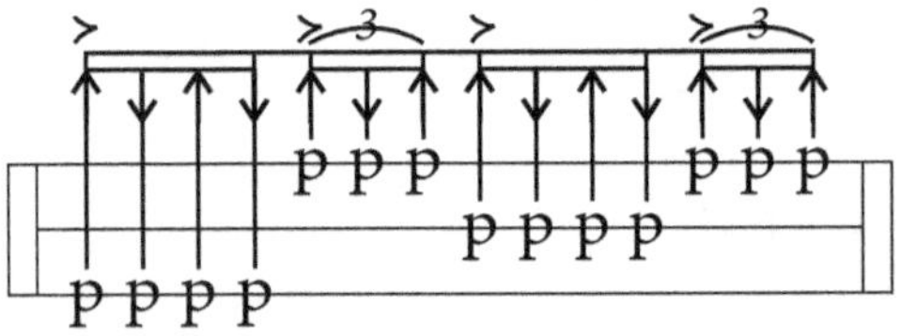

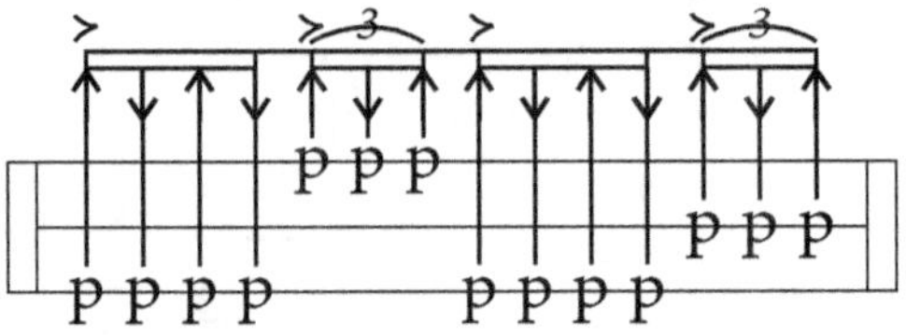

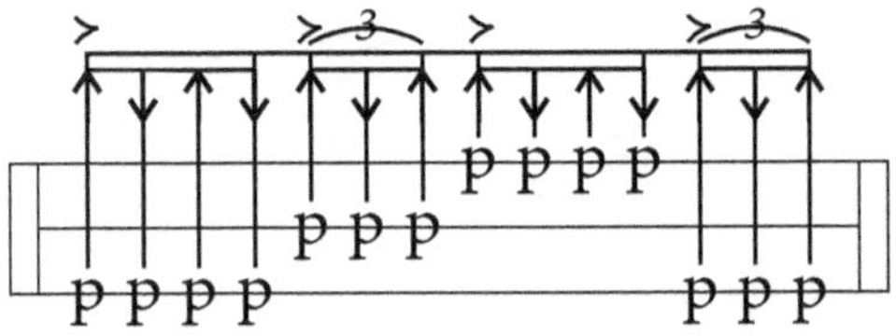

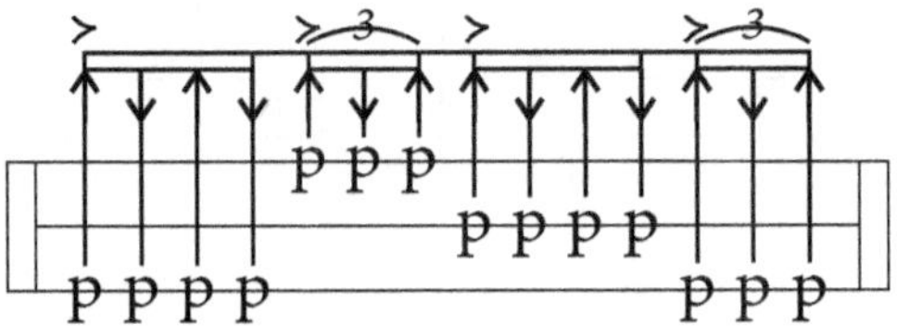

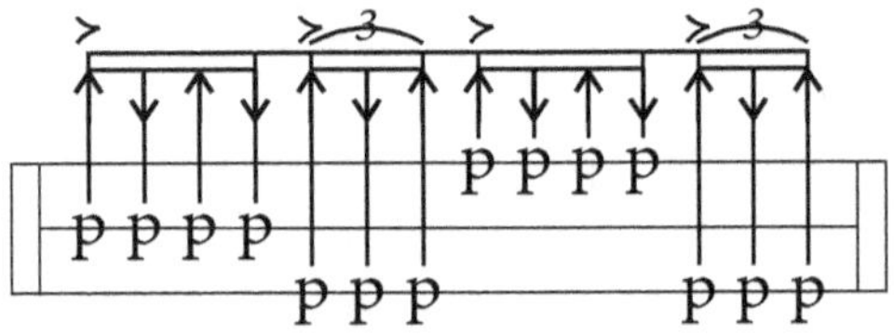

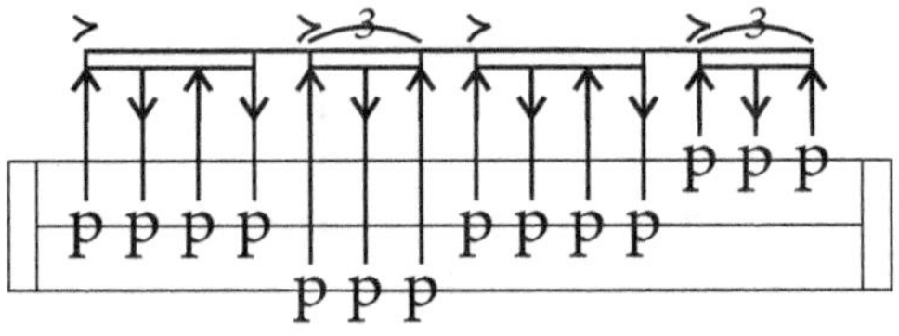

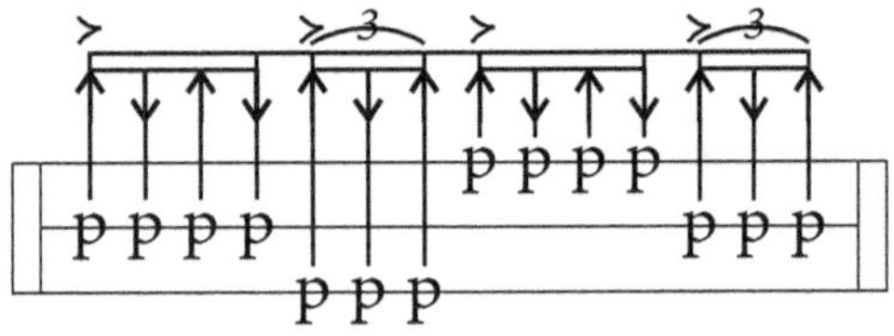

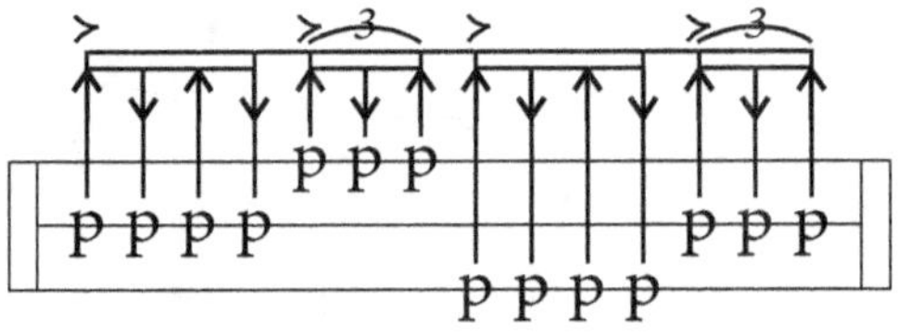

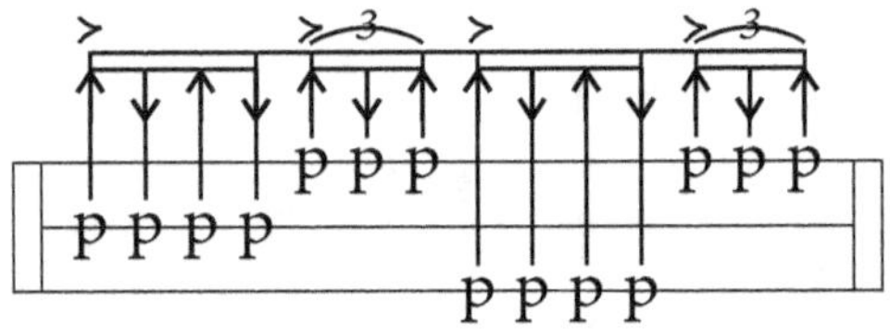

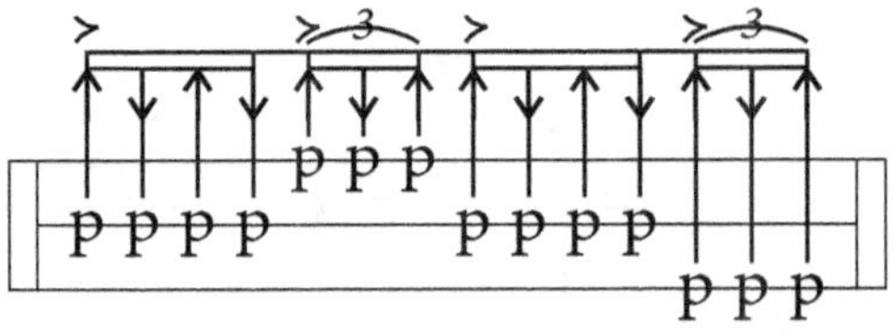

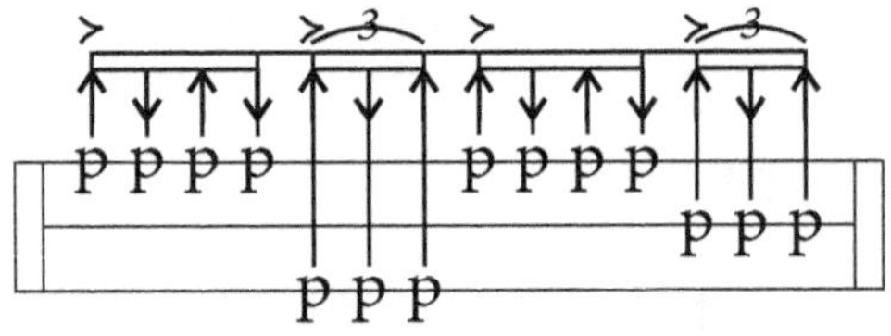

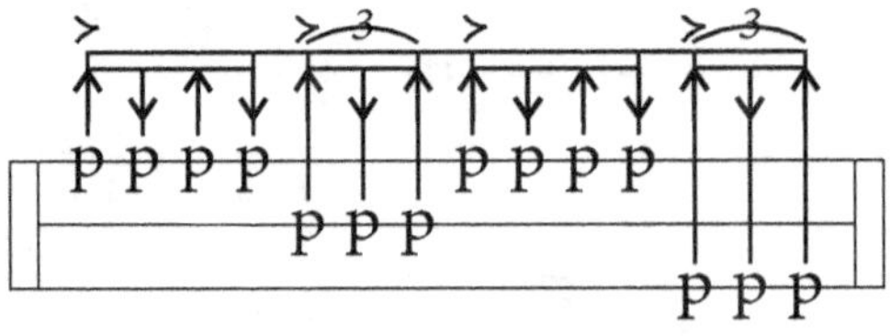

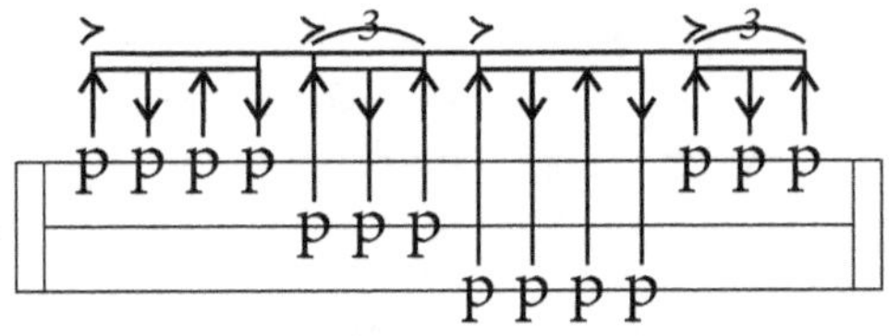

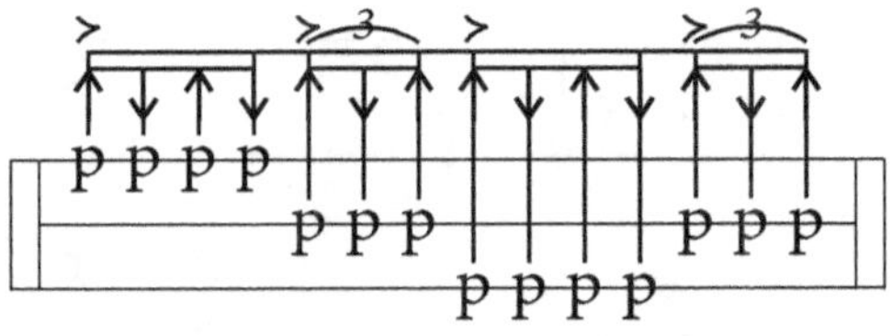

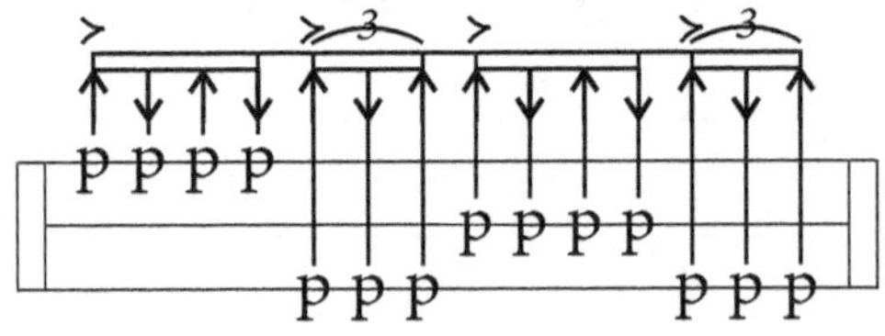

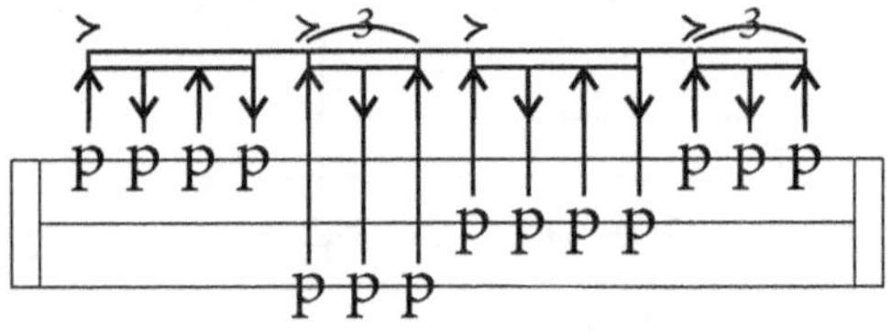

VARIATION II

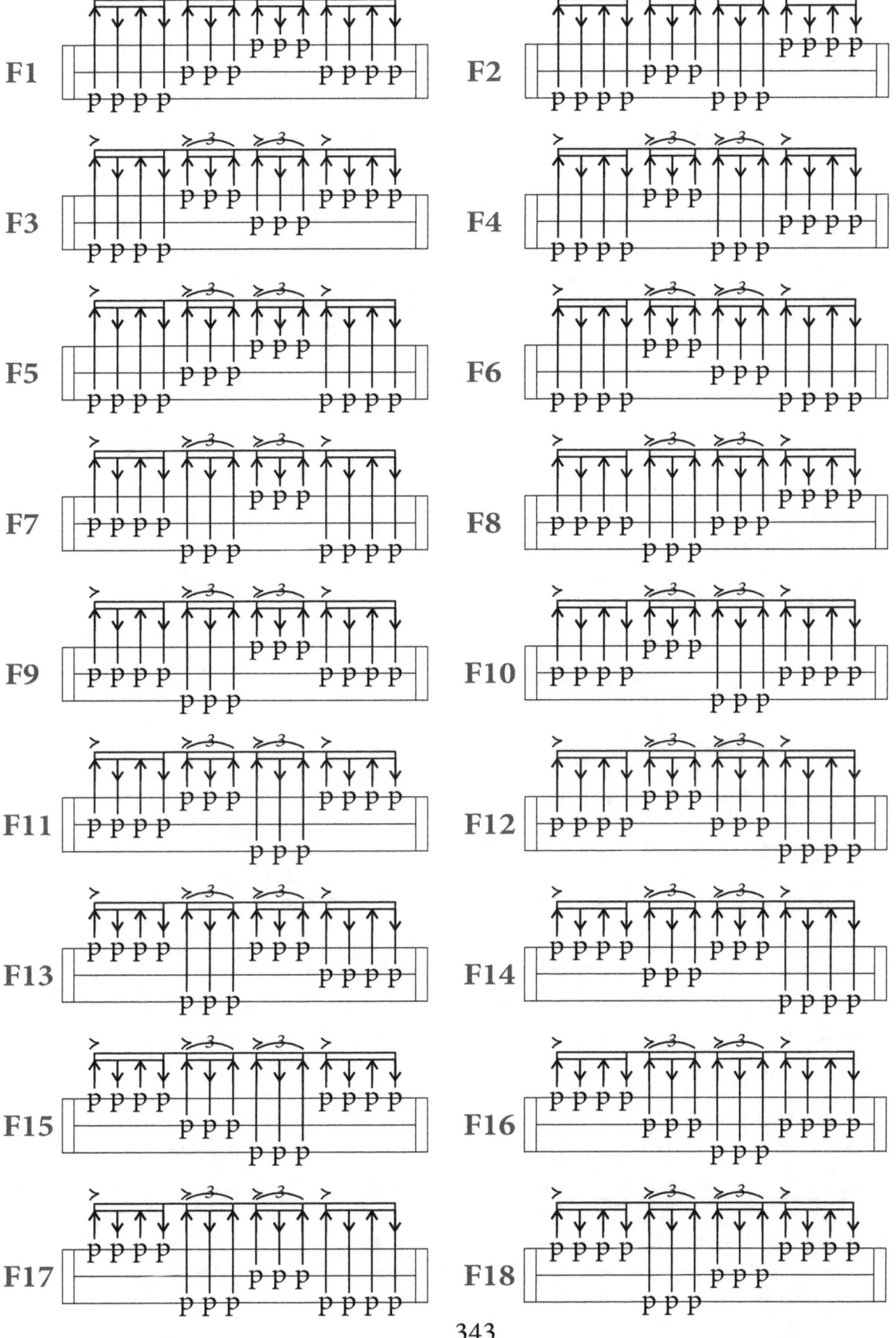

VARIATION III

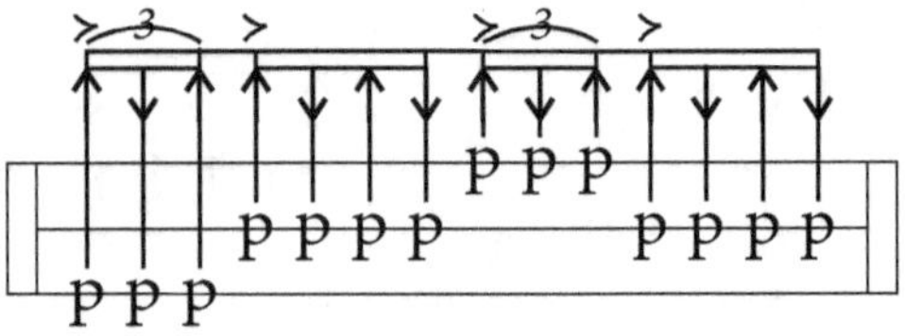

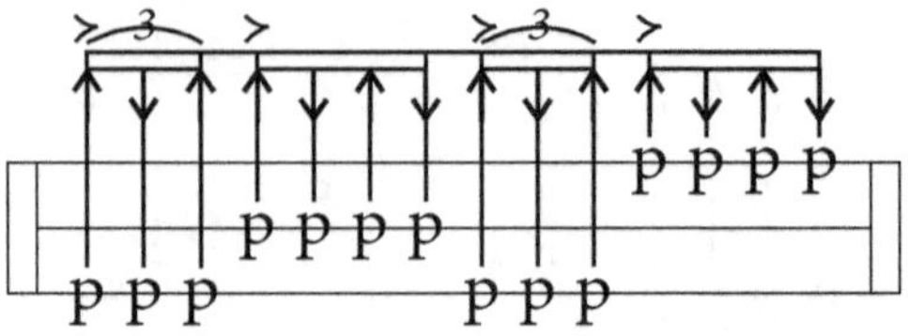

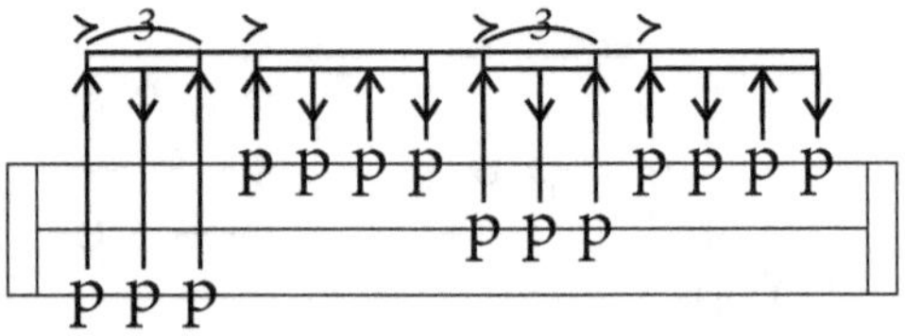

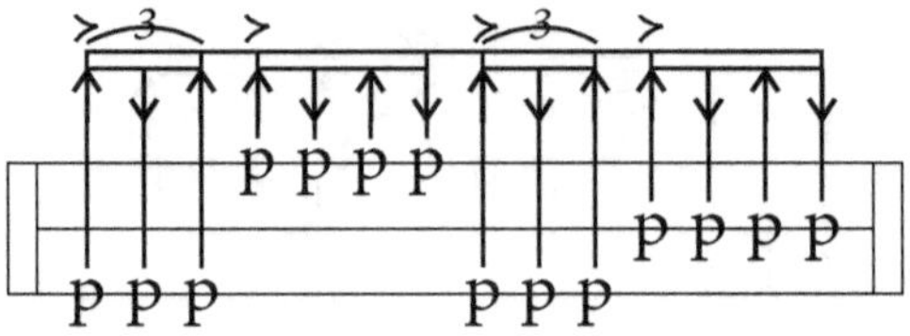

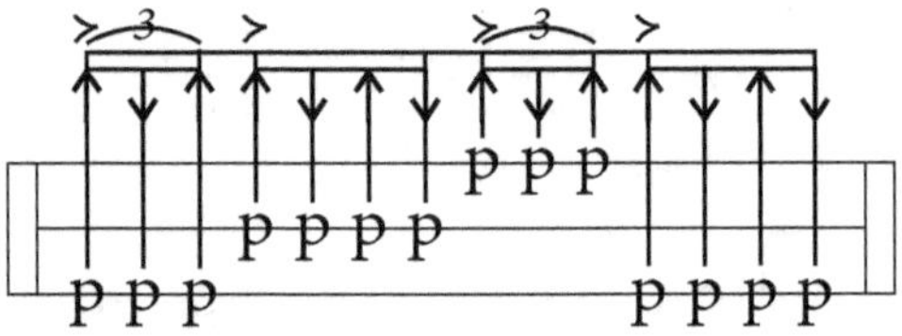

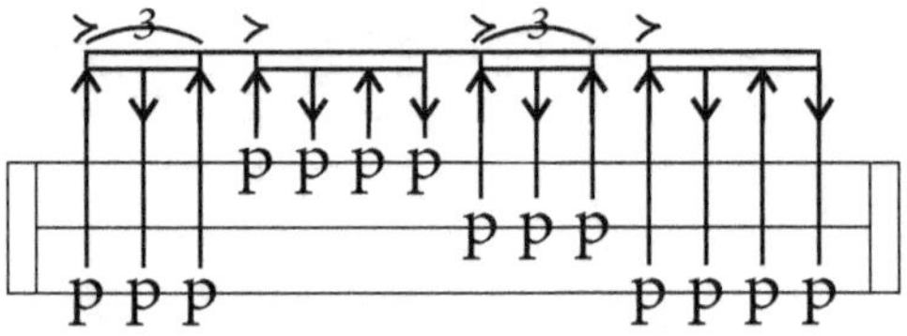

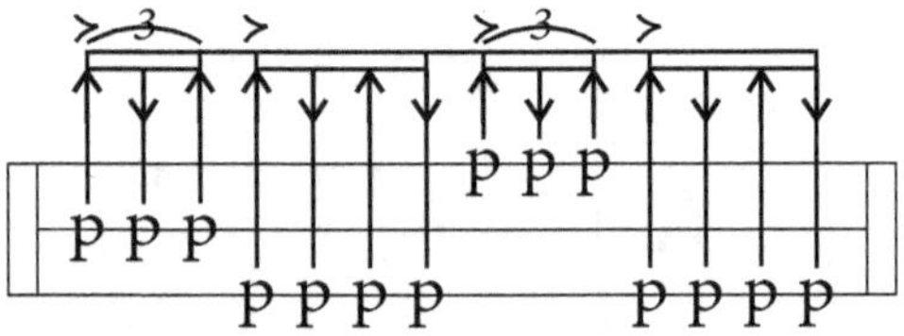

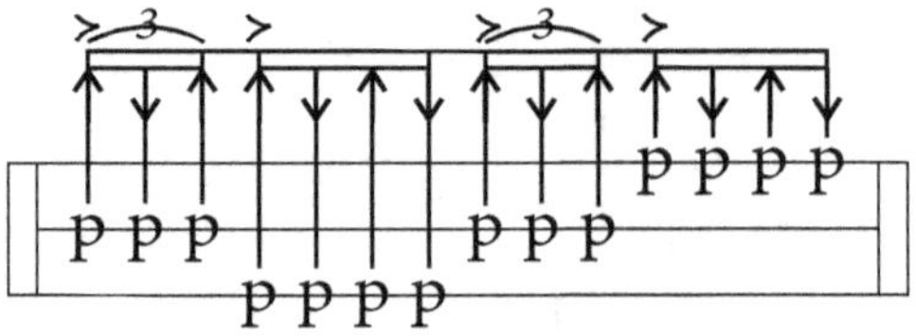

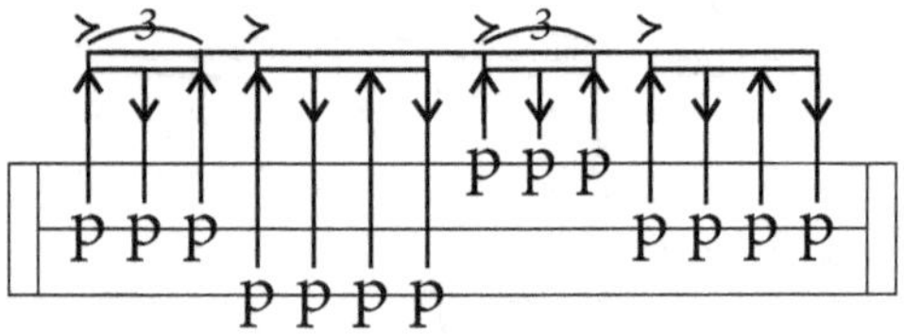

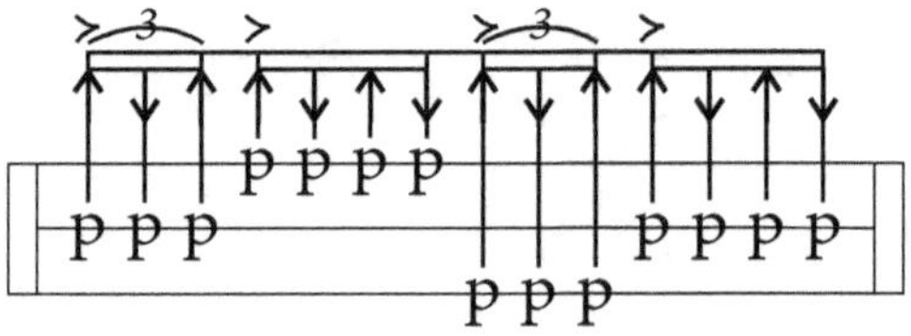

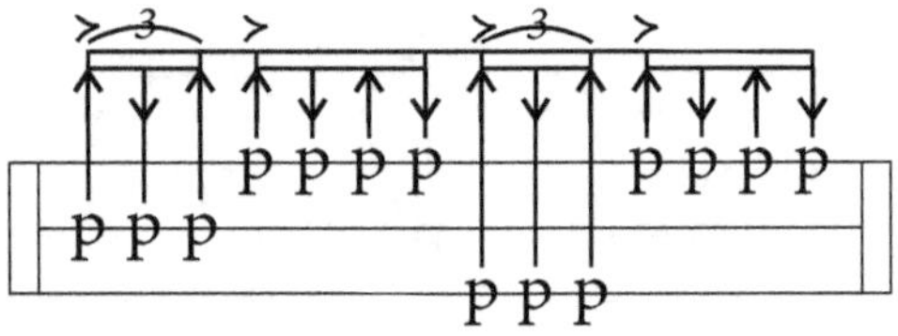

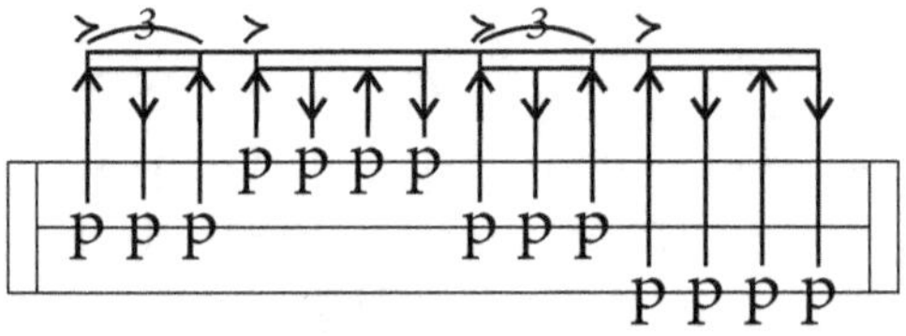

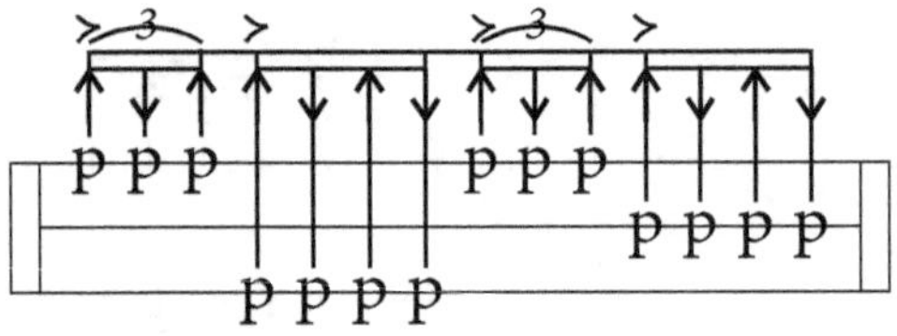

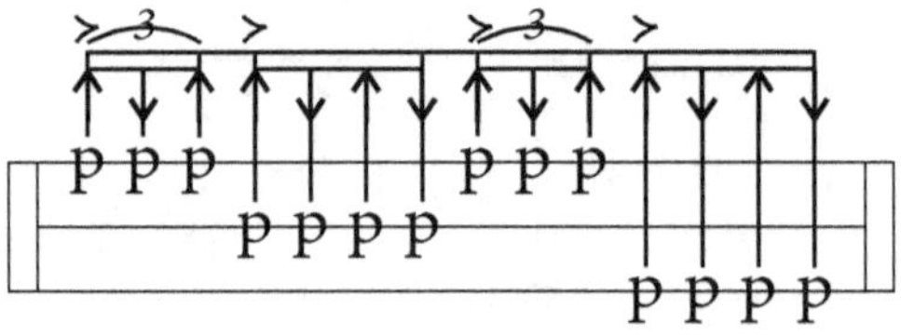

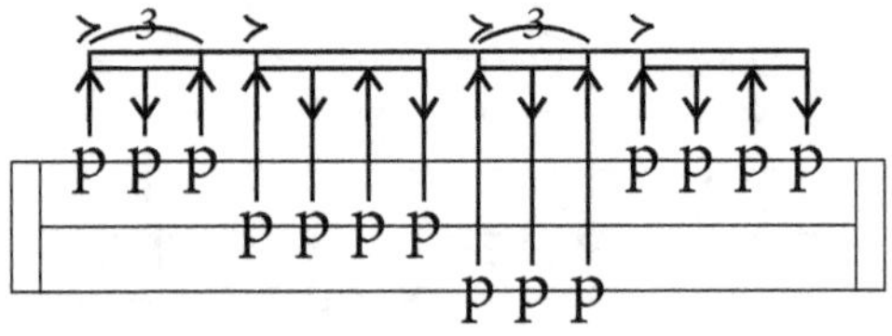

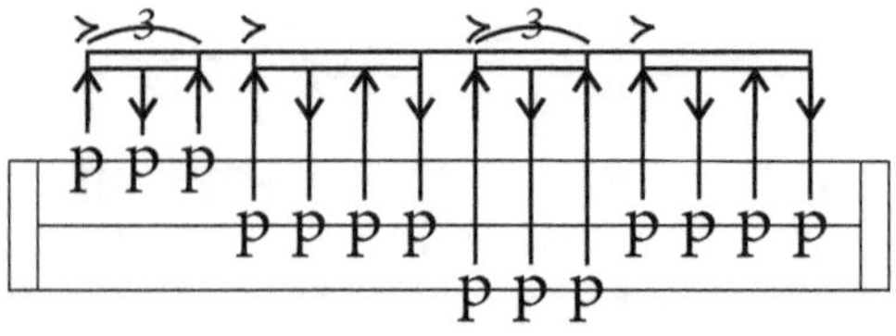

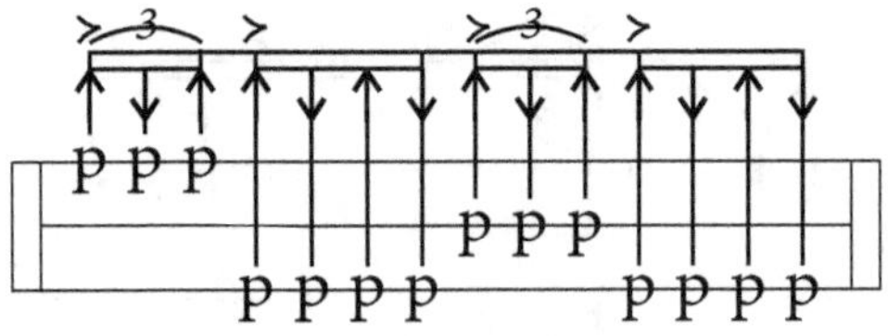

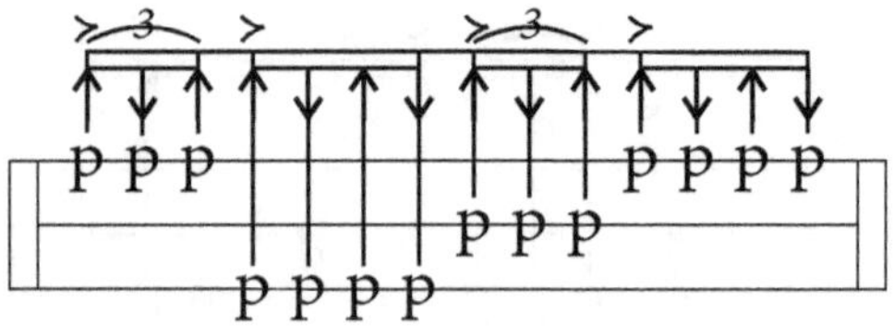

VARIATION IV

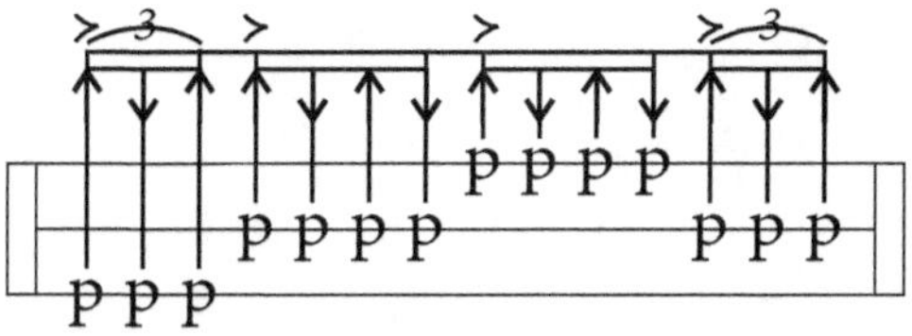

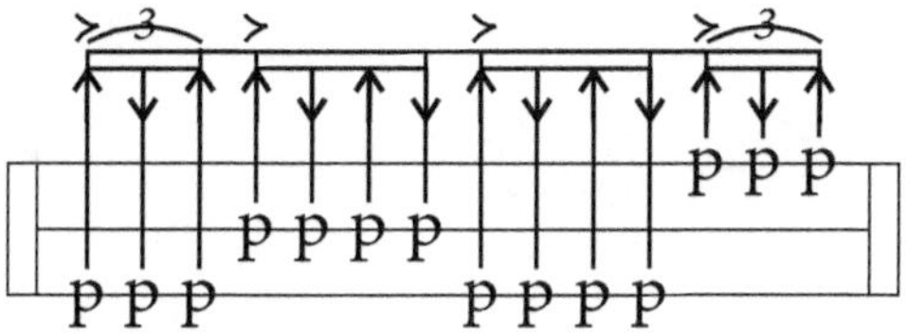

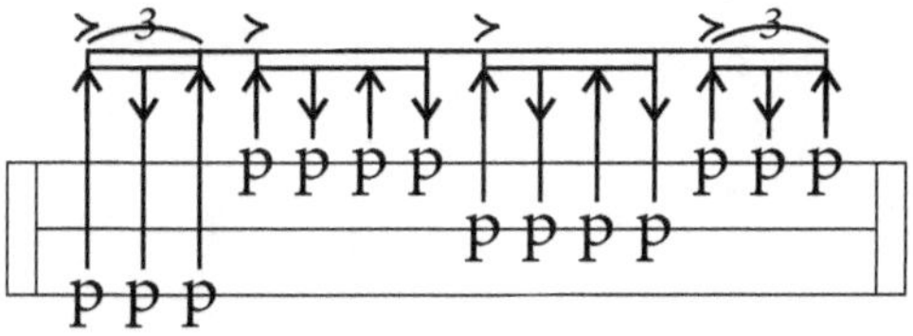

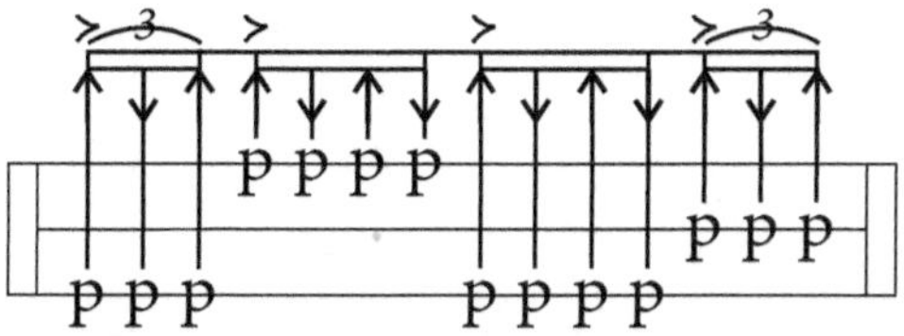

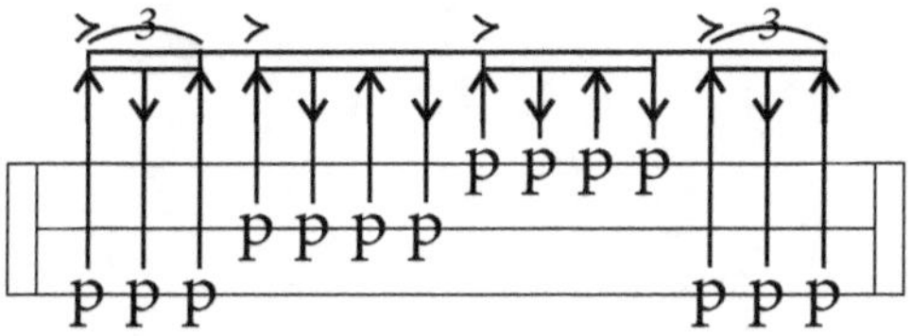

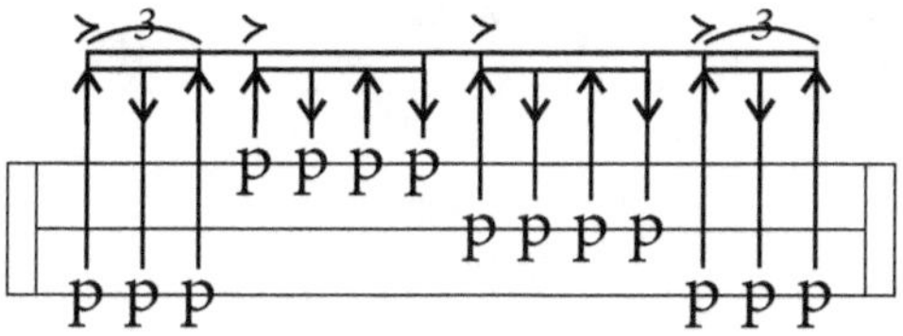

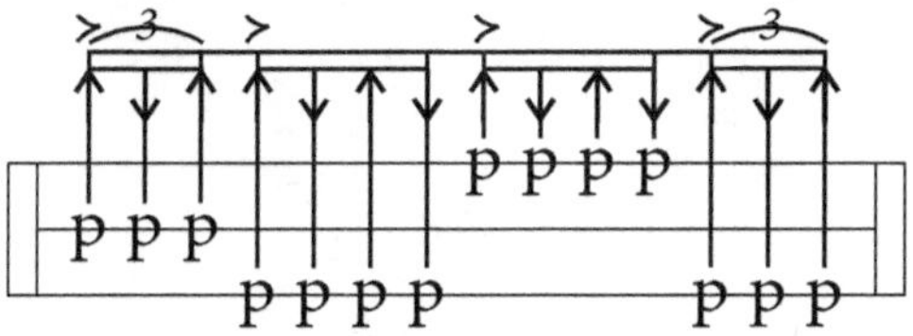

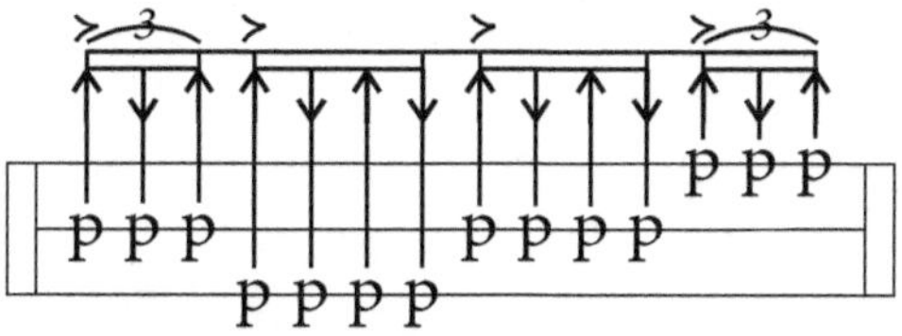

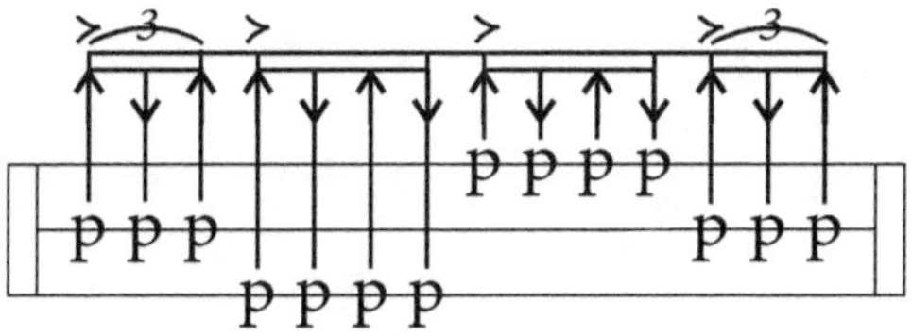

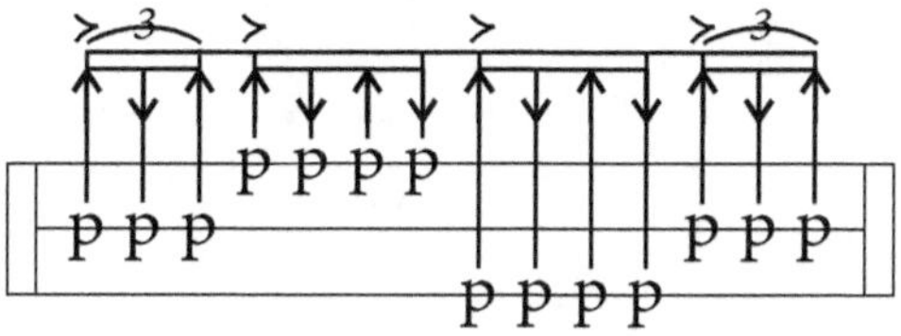

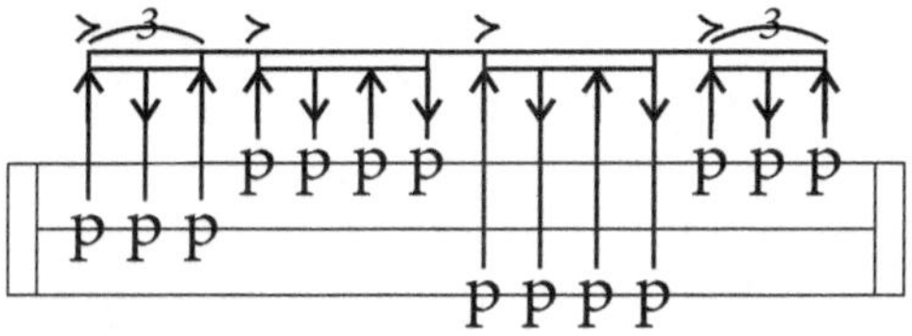

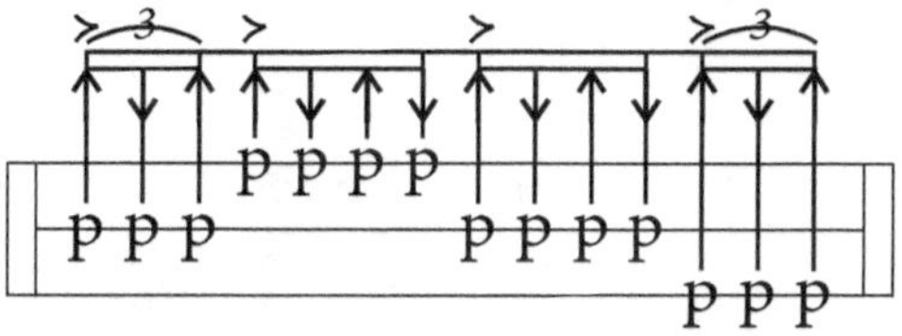

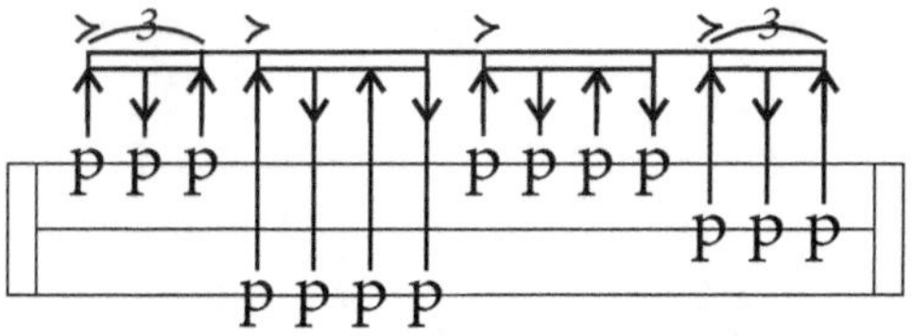

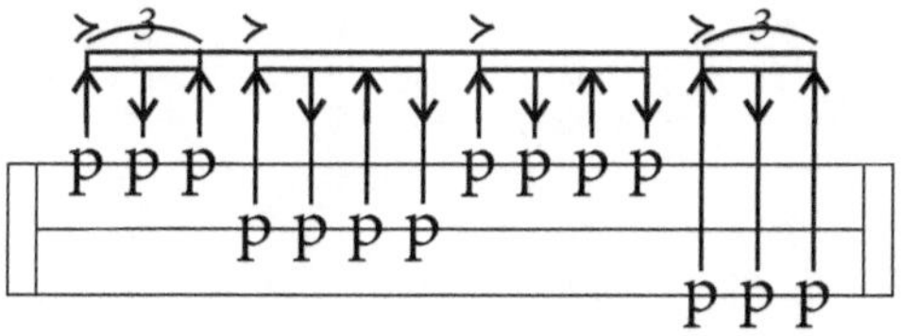

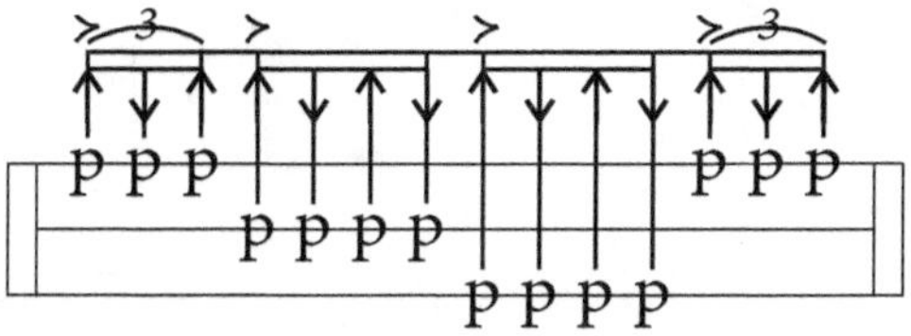

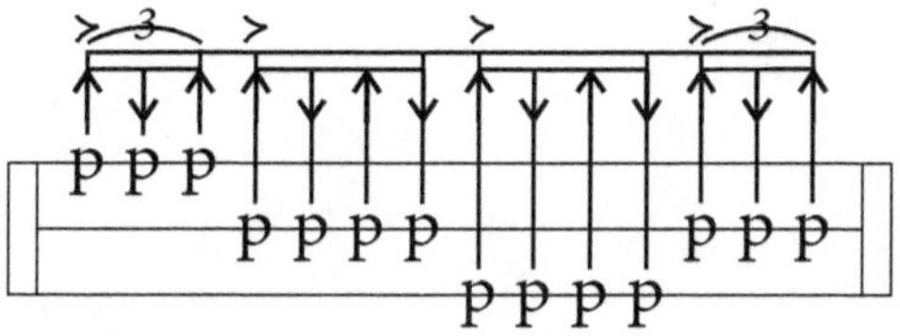

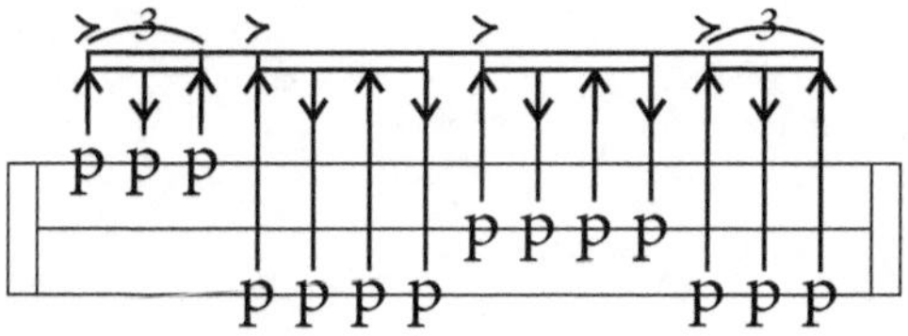

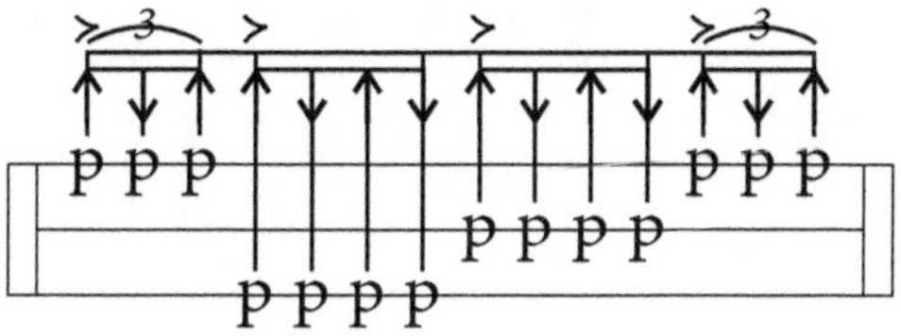

CHAPTER 3

SINGLE - DOUBLE - TRIPLE AND QUAD PULGAR STROKE
ON FOUR ADJACENT STRINGS
IN VARIOUS STROKE COMBINATIONS AND WITH CHANGES
IN THE DIRECTION OF THE PULGAR STROKE

Chapter 3 of this book contains exercises on pulgar on four adjacent strings with variations in the strokes, single, double, triple and quad strokes within each Formula.

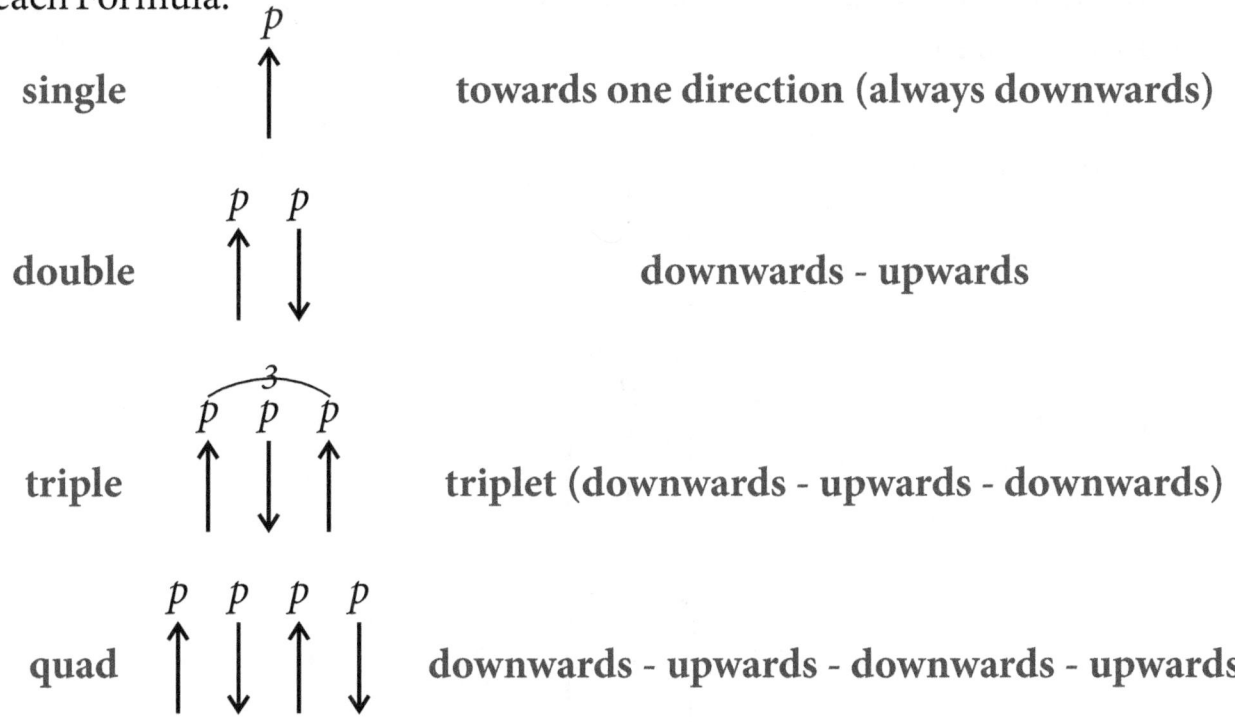

ATTENTION: within each Formula, the single, double, triple and quad pulgar strokes are isochronous.

Choose for the left hand a stable accord during the practice of each Formula. The accord way refer to the following strings:
A/ 6th, 5th 4th and 3rd strings
B/ 5th, 4th, 3rd and 2nd strings
C/ 4th, 3rd 2nd and 1st strings
An accord in position A, B, C is depicted below.

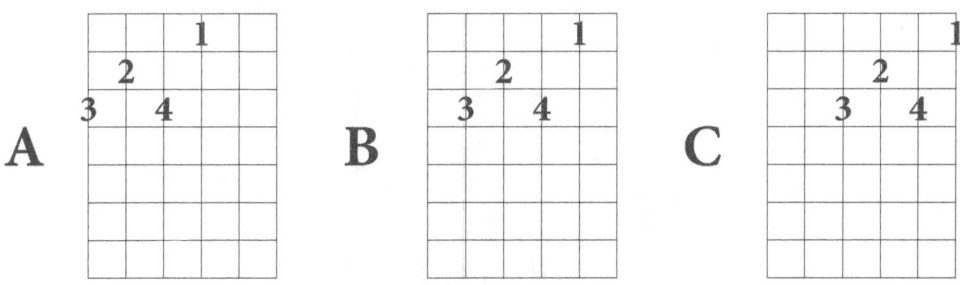

* the pulgar practice on four strings 4th, 3rd, 2nd and 1st exhibits greater degree of difficulty so it is preferable to start from position A and B.

ATTENTION:
All the exercises that follow can be carried out in various ways as far as the double, triple and quad pulgar strokes are concerned.
We propose alternatively:

for double stroke

        p p
        ↑ ↑

for triple stroke (triplet)

1. $\overset{3}{\frown}$
    p p p
    ↑ ↑ ↓

2. $\overset{3}{\frown}$
    p p p
    ↑ ↑ ↑

for quad stroke

1. p p p p
   ↑ ↓ ↑ ↑

2. p p p p
   ↑ ↑ ↓ ↑

3. p p p p
   ↑ ↑ ↑ ↓

4. p p p p
   ↑ ↑ ↑ ↑

§ I

Exercise on pulgar on four adjacent strings with four single strokes within each Formula. The pulgar strikes towards one direction. The exercise includes 24 Formulas.

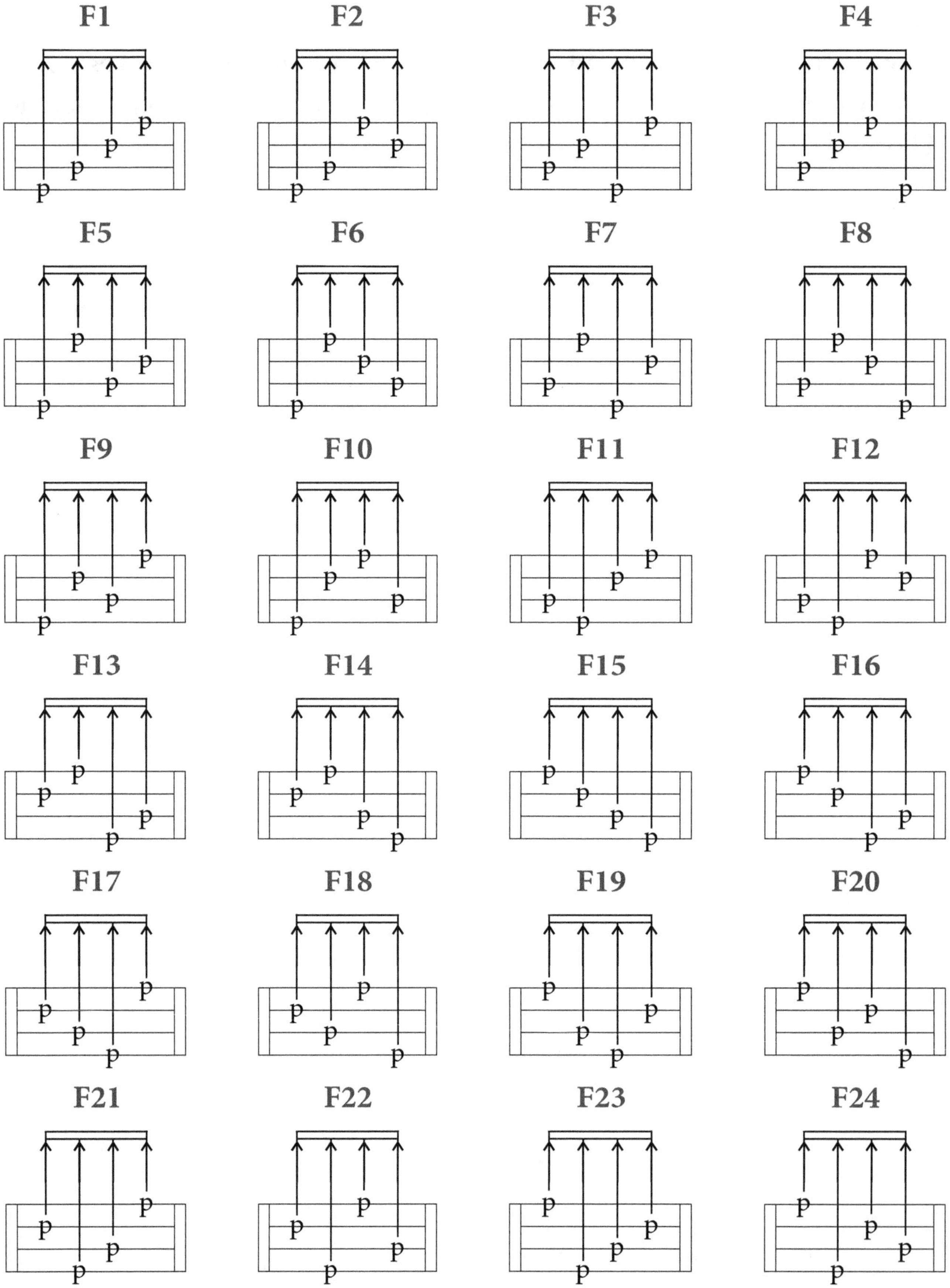

F1	F2	F3	F4
F5	F6	F7	F8
F9	F10	F11	F12
F13	F14	F15	F16
F17	F18	F19	F20
F21	F22	F23	F24

§ II

Exercise on pulgar on four adjacent strings with one double and three single strokes within each Formula. The exercise includes four variations with 24 Formulas in each one. The first Formula of each variation is cited below. Isochronous playing of pulgar strokes (single and double).

VARIATION I

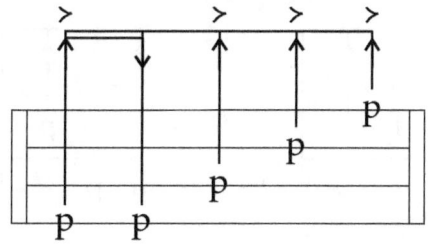

VARIATION II

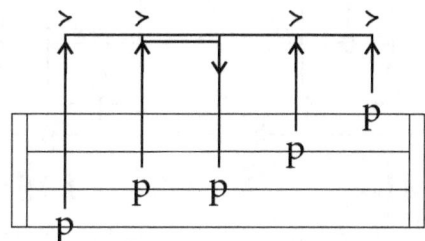

VARIATION III

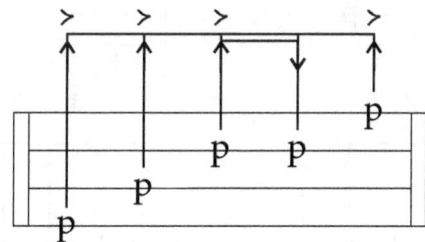

VARIATION IV

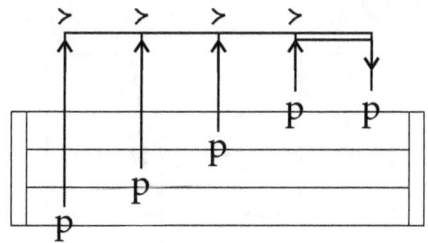

VARIATION I

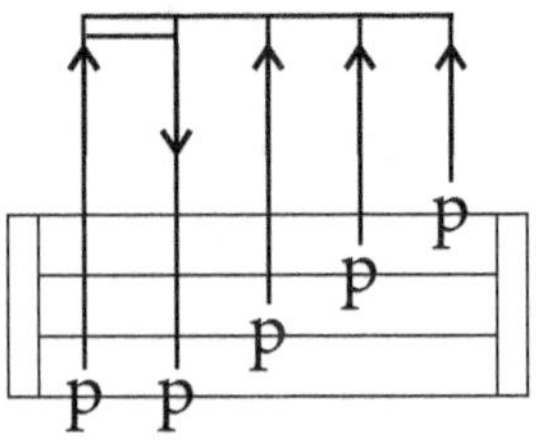

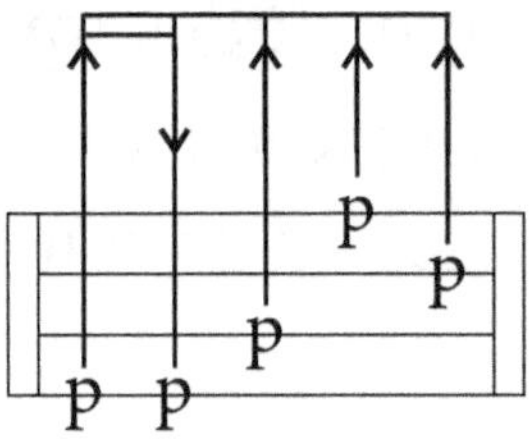

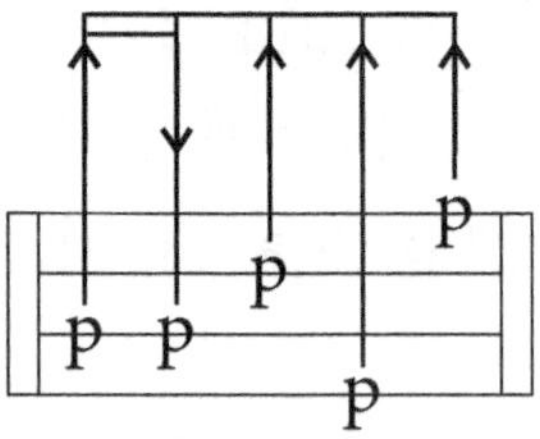

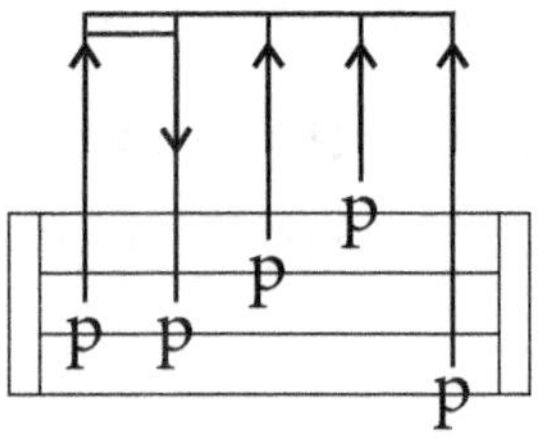

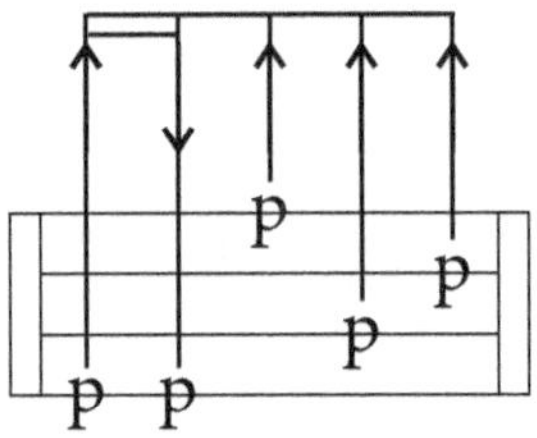

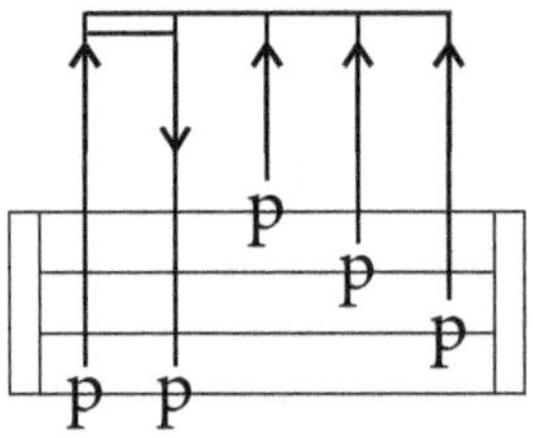

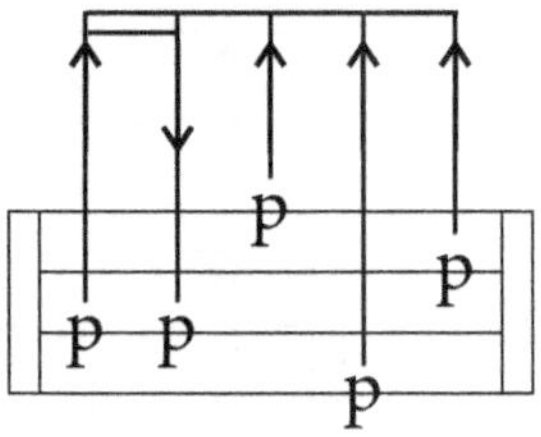

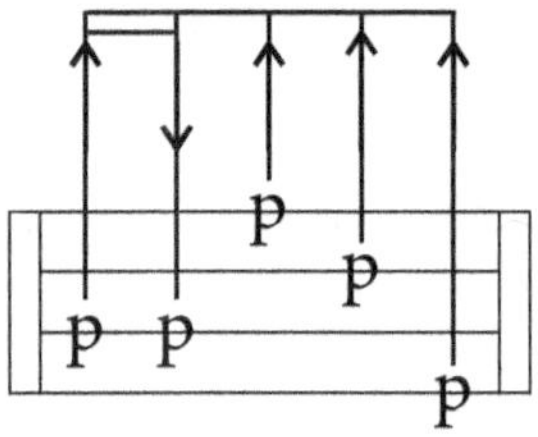

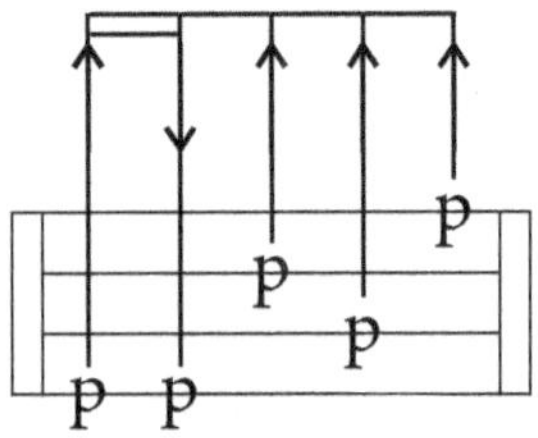

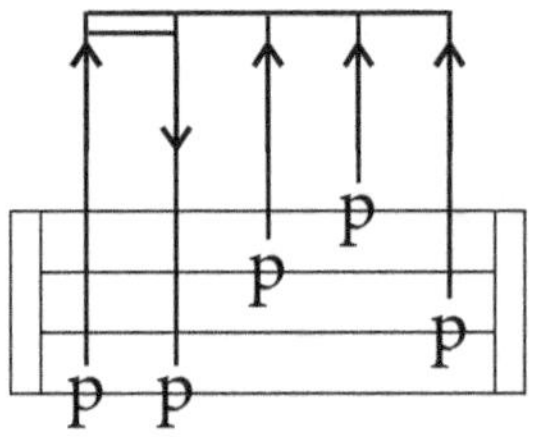

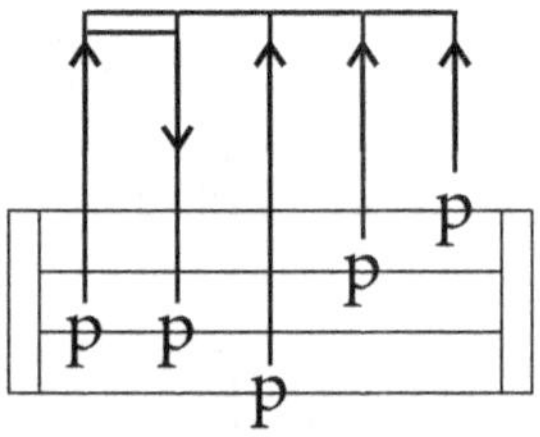

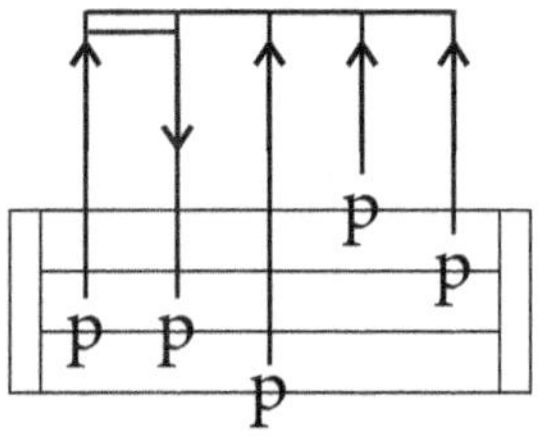

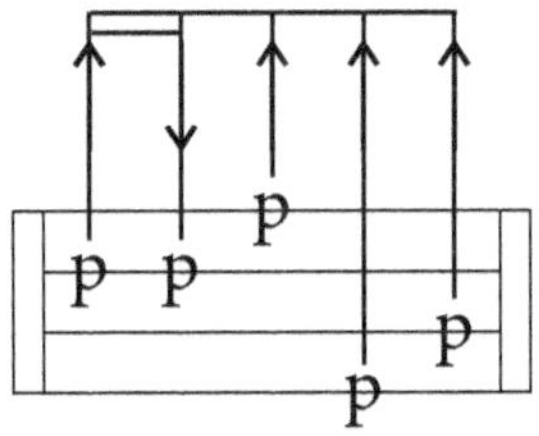

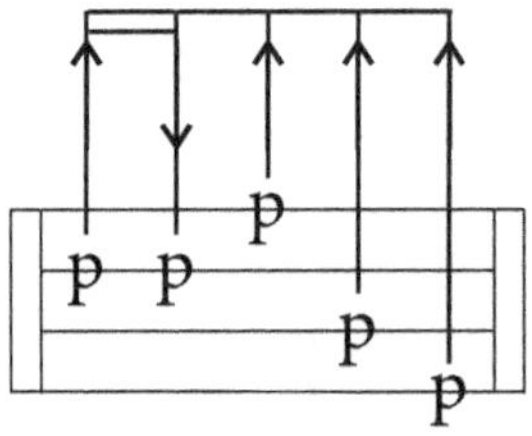

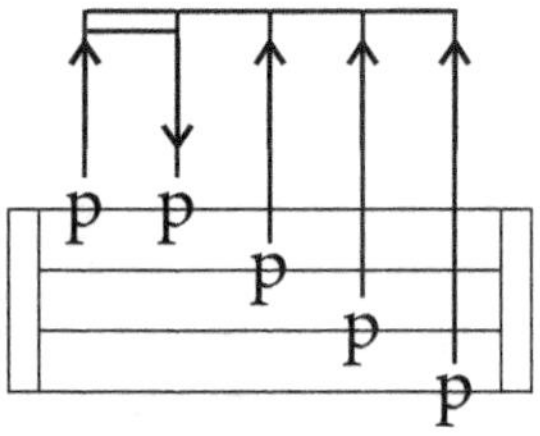

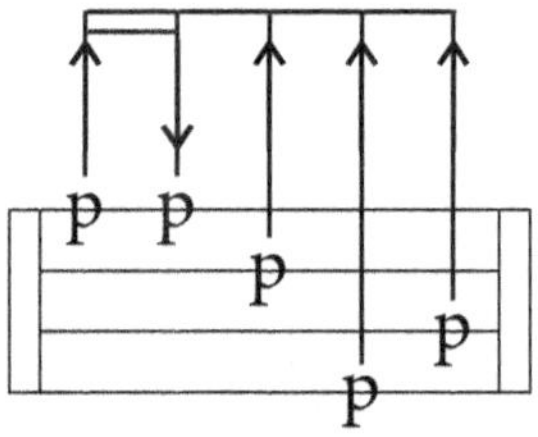

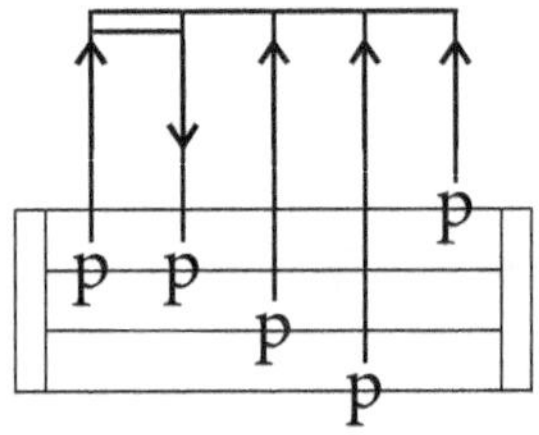

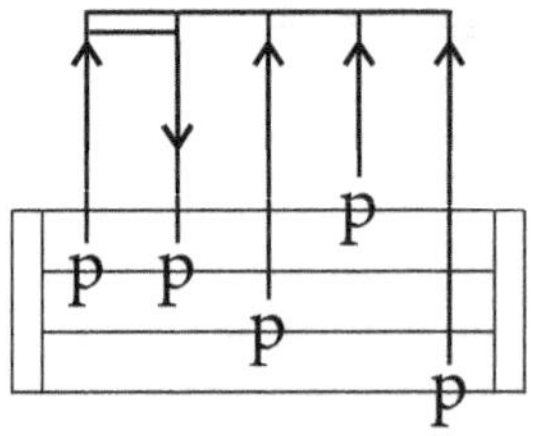

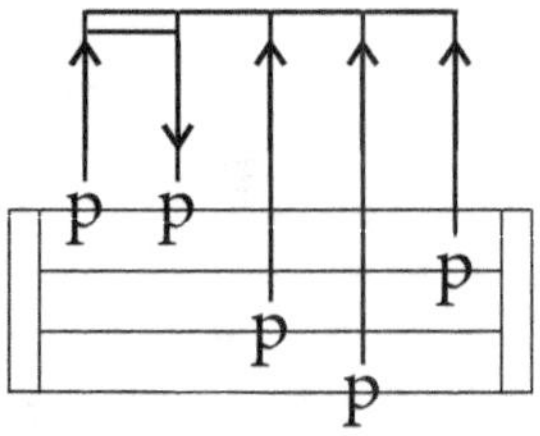

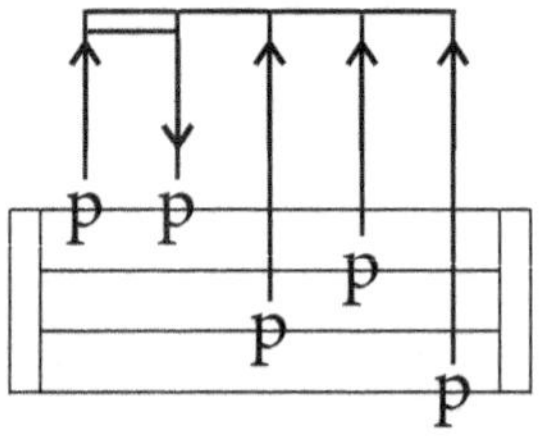

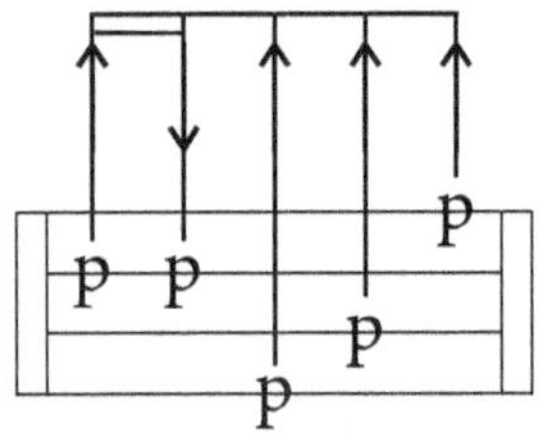

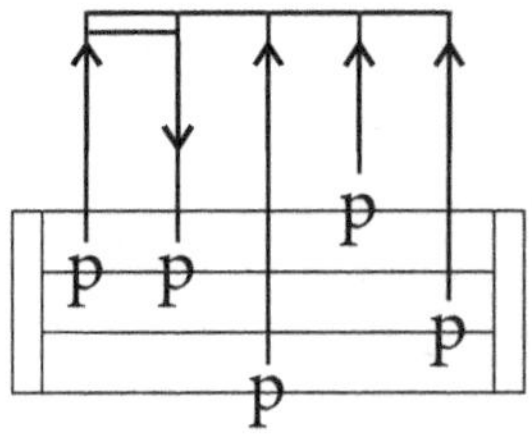

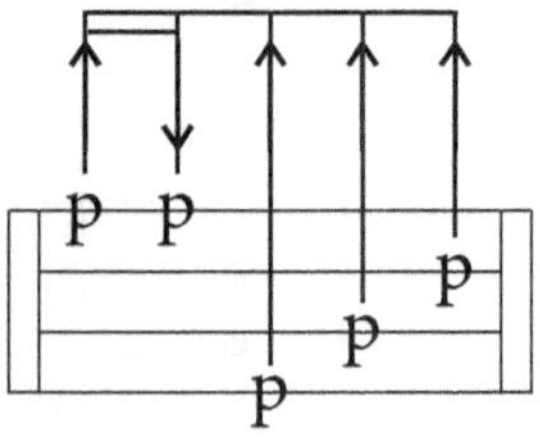

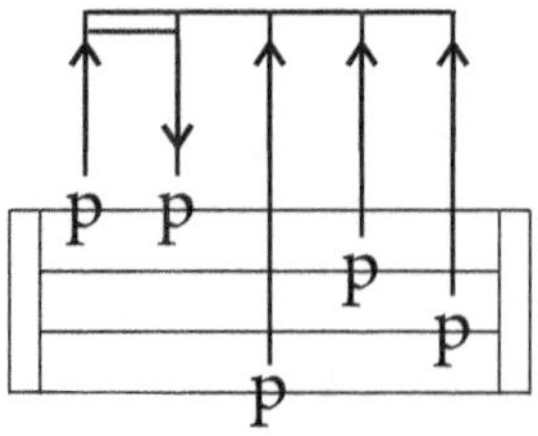

VARIATION II

F1 F2 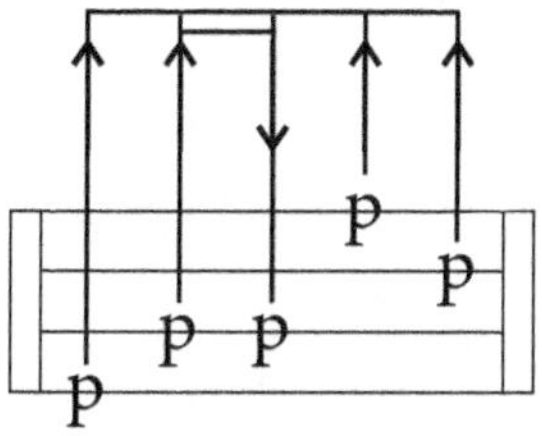 F3 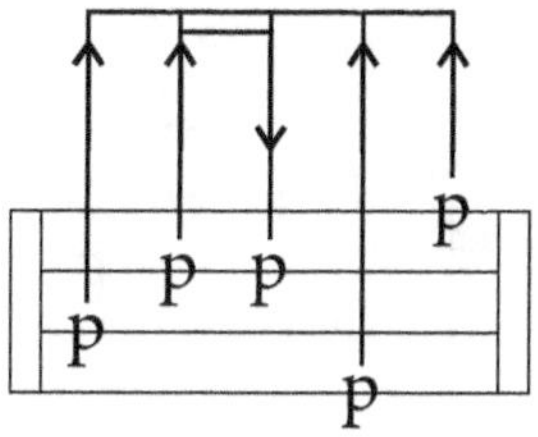 F4

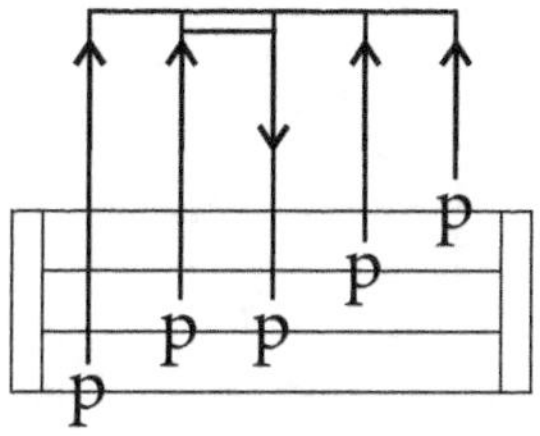

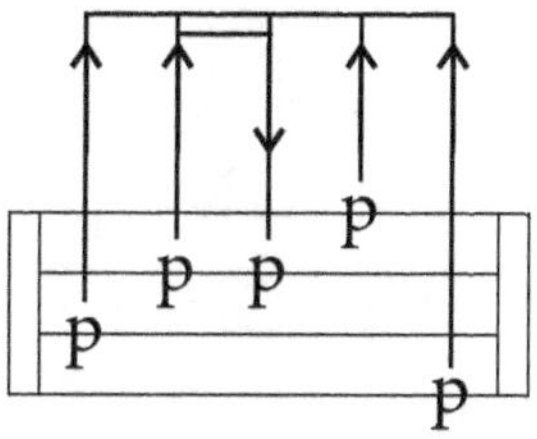

F5 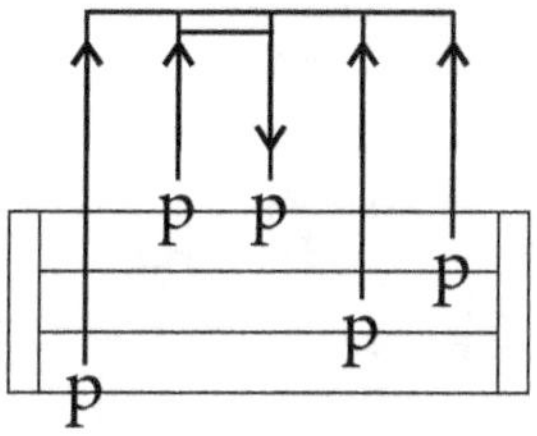 F6 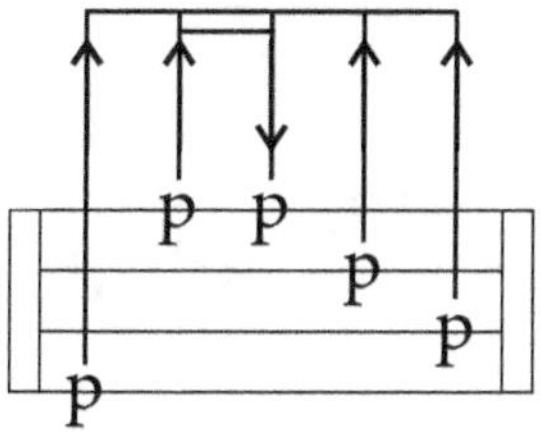 F7 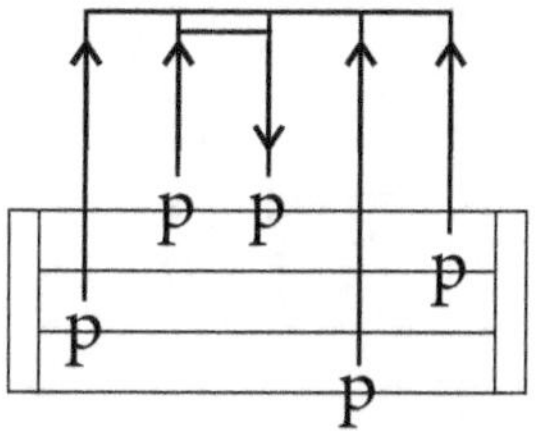 F8

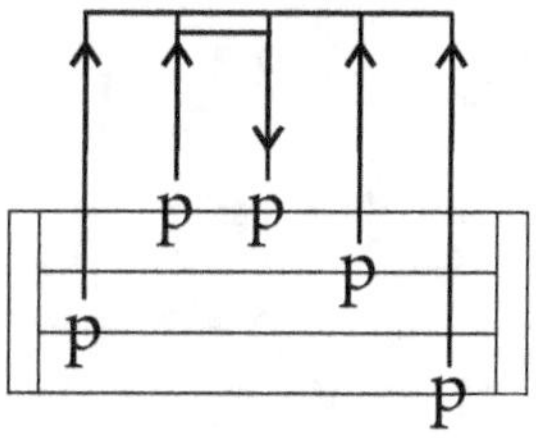

F9 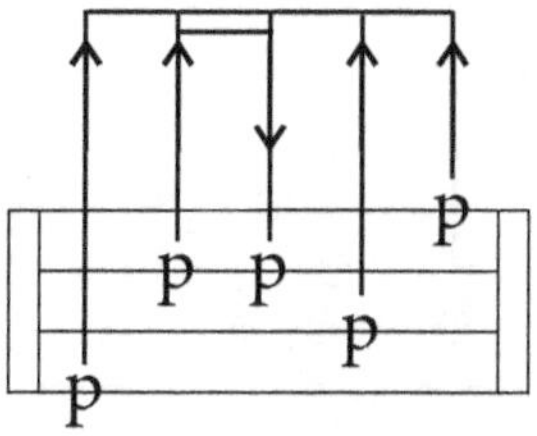 F10 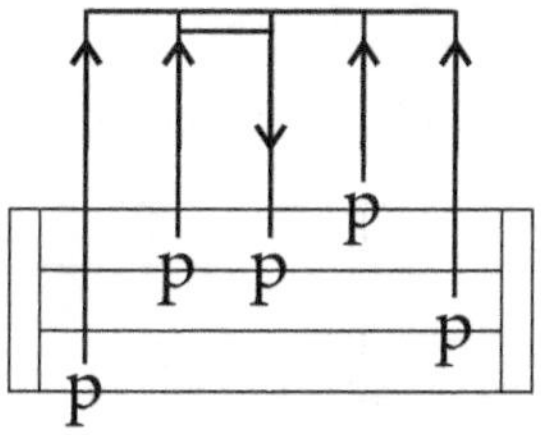 F11 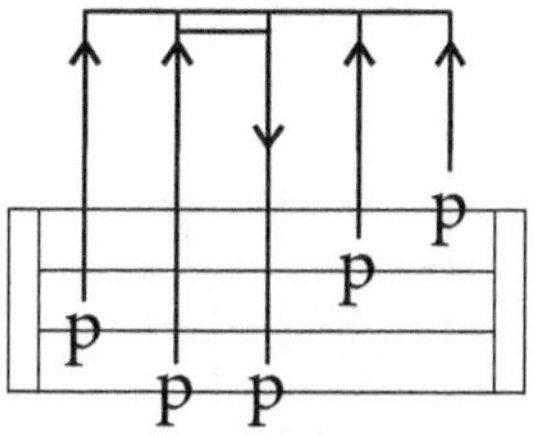 F12

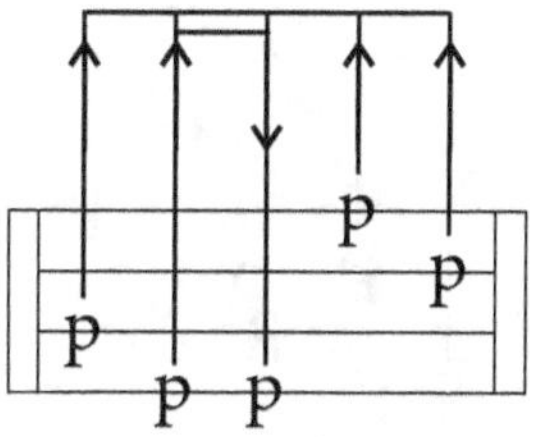

F13 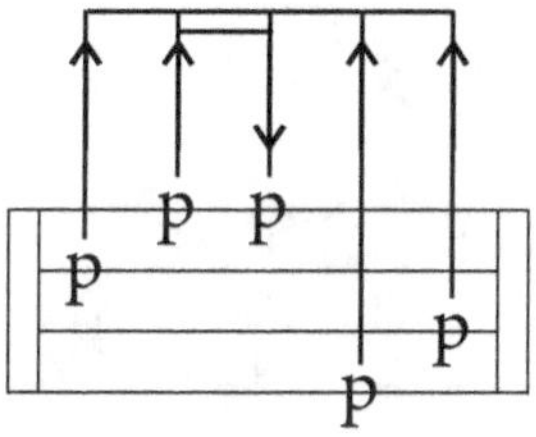 F14 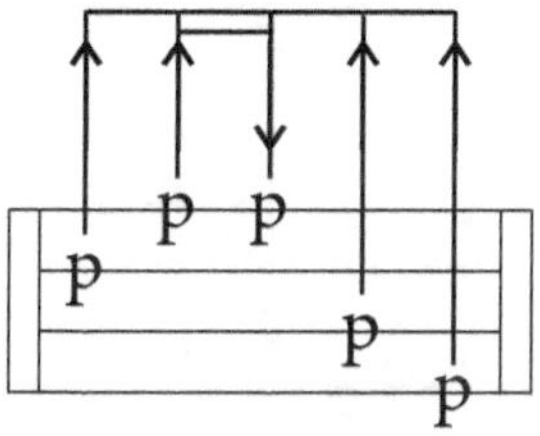 F15 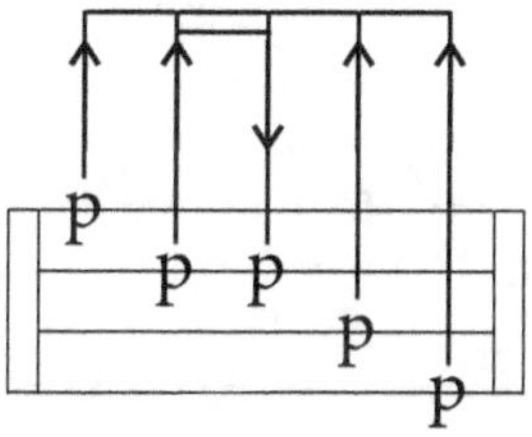 F16

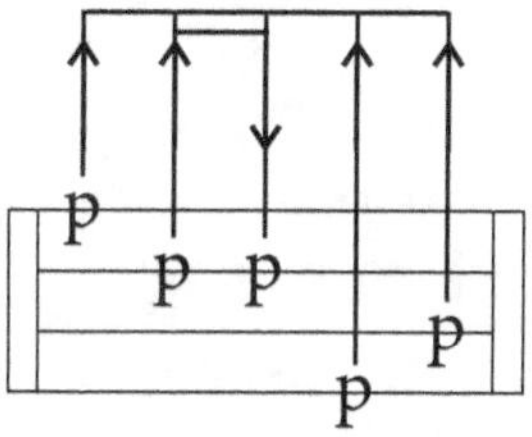

F17 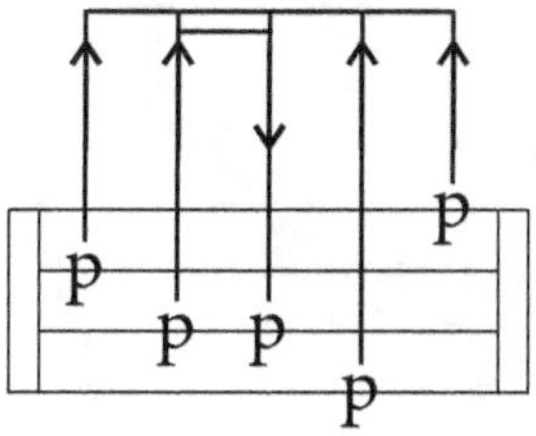 F18 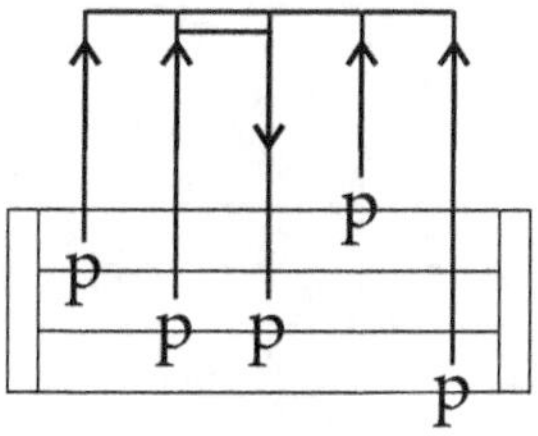 F19 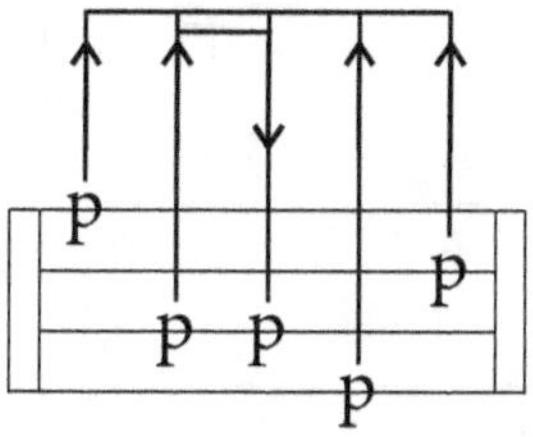 F20

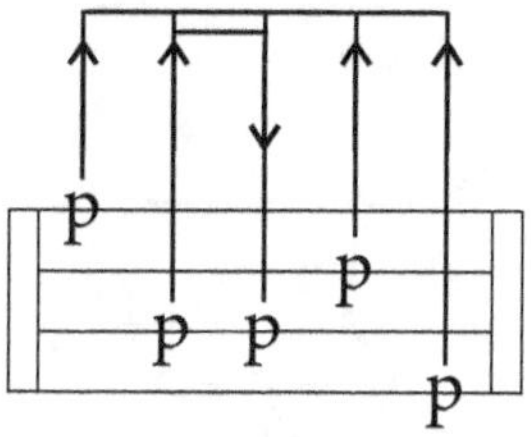

F21 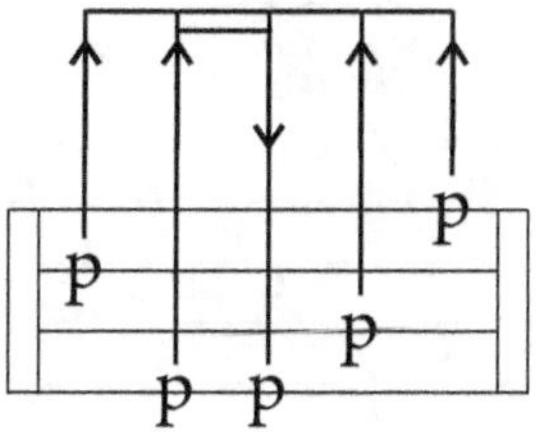 F22 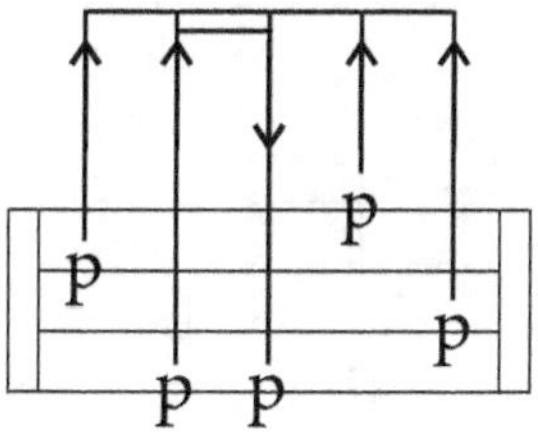 F23 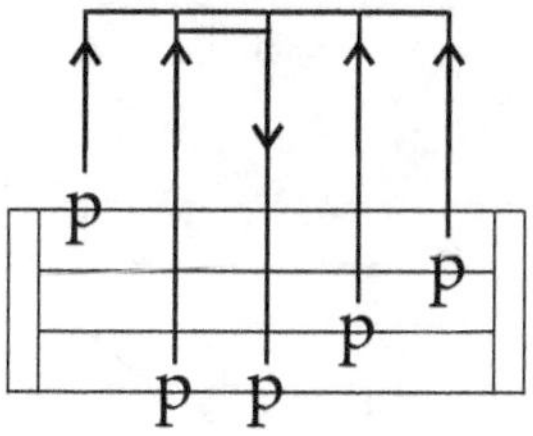 F24

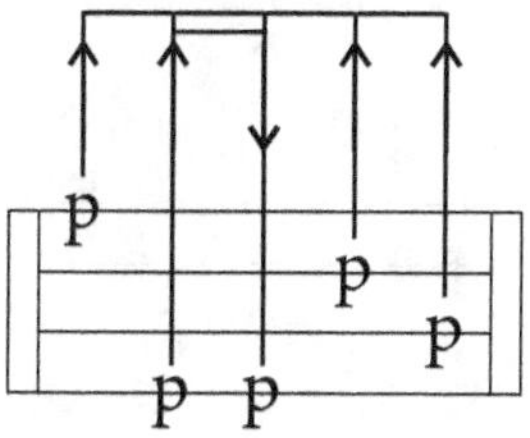

VARIATION III

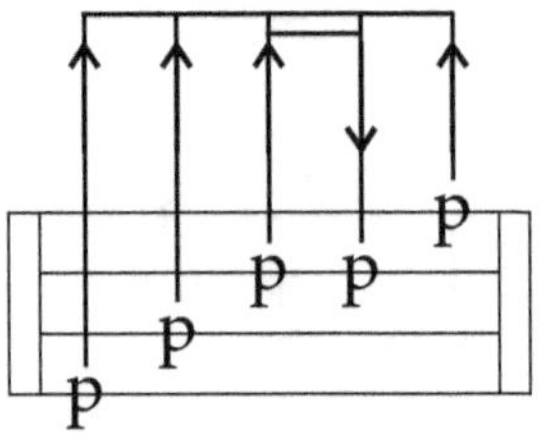

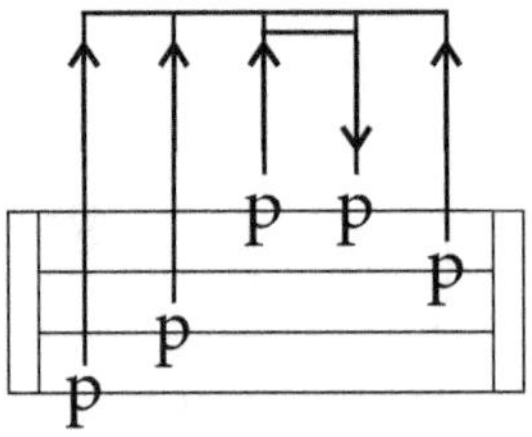

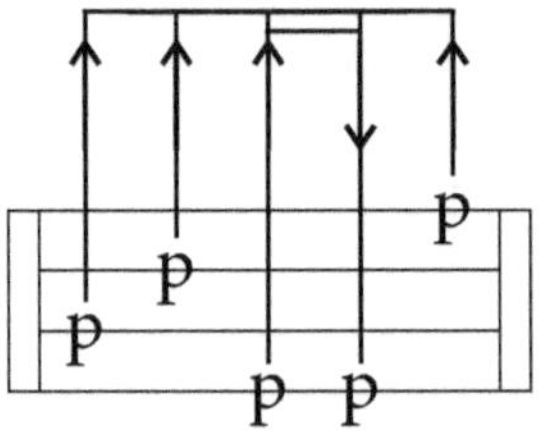

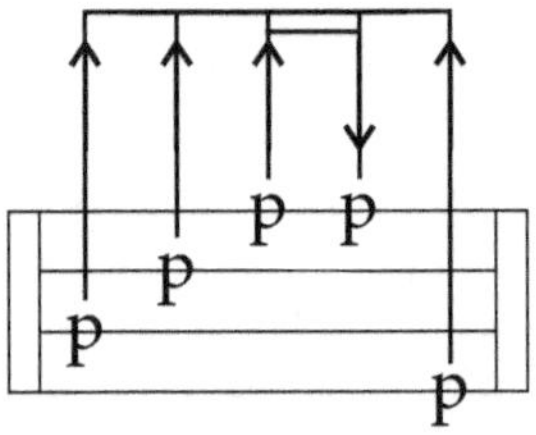

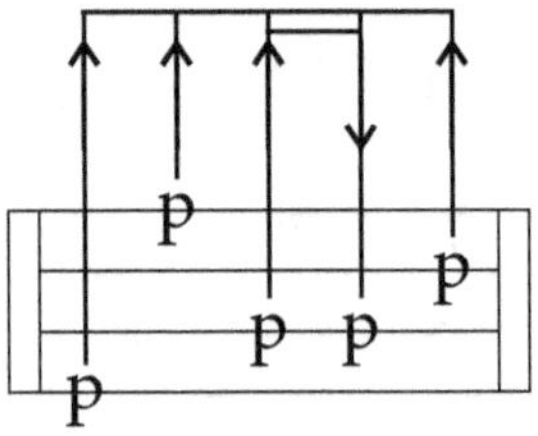

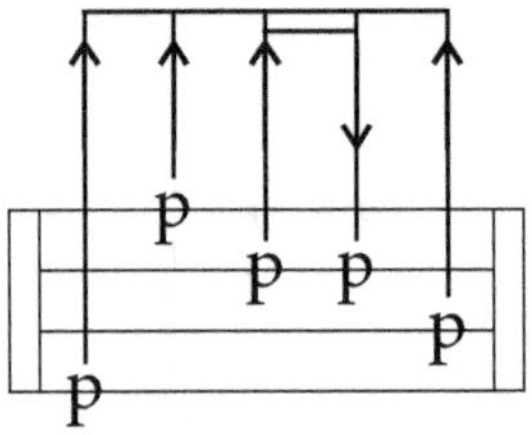

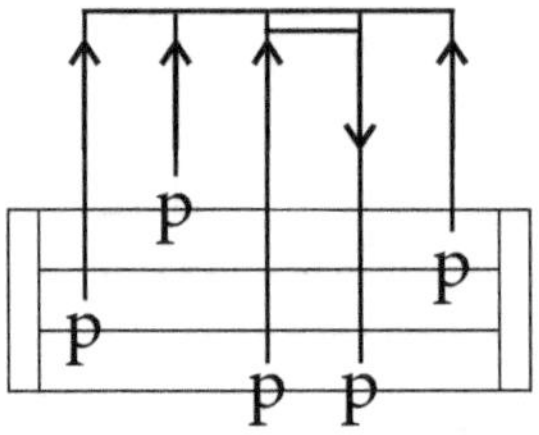

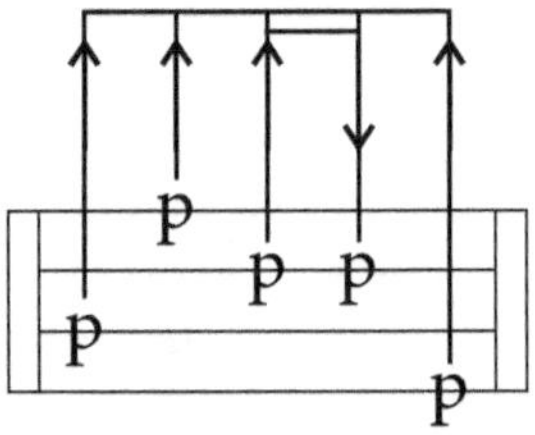

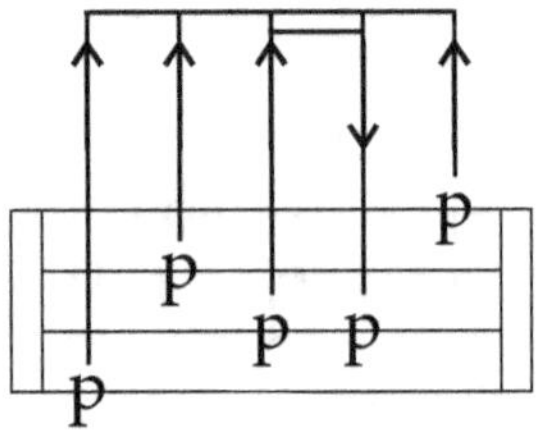

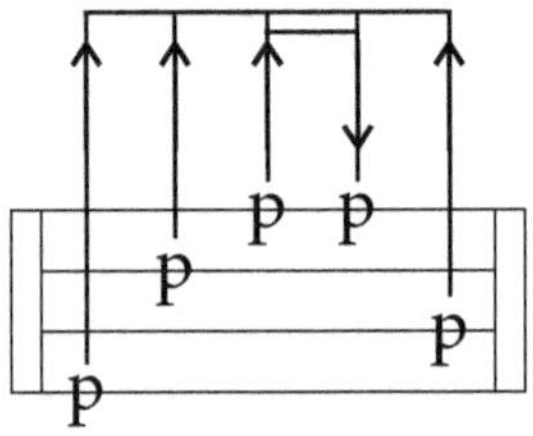

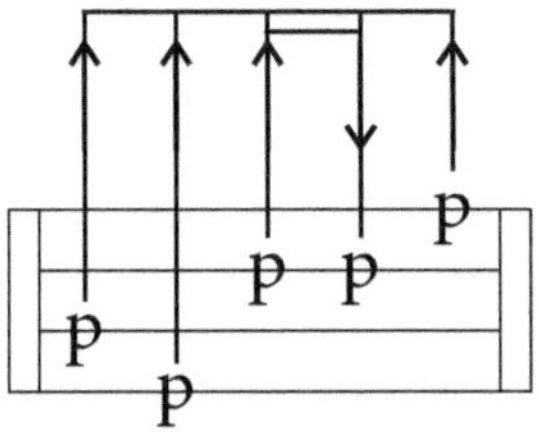

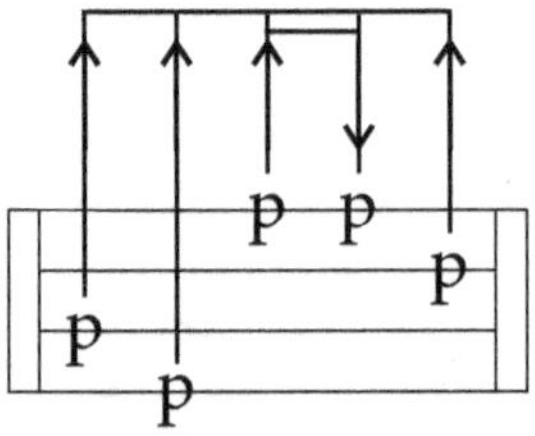

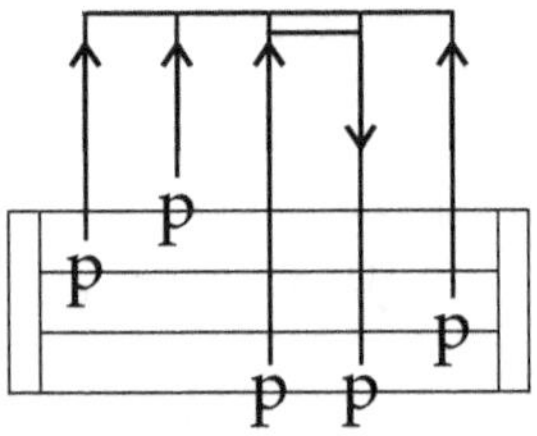

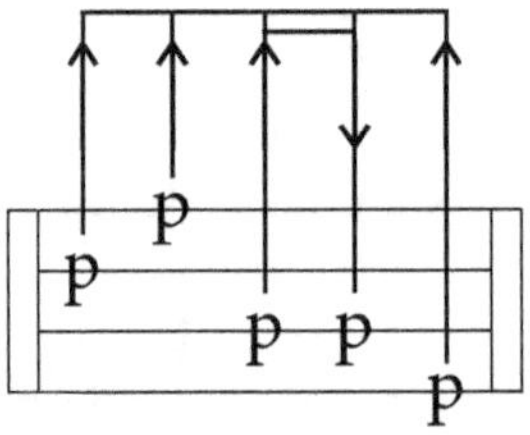

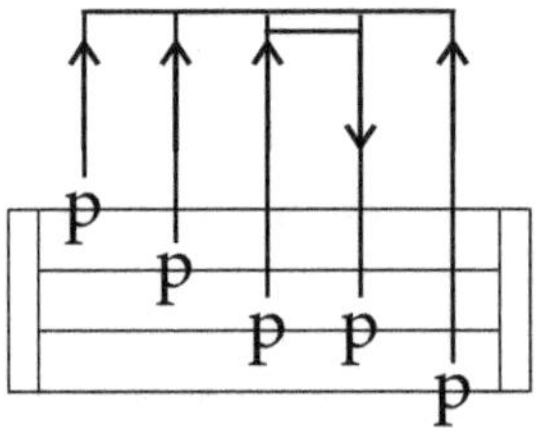

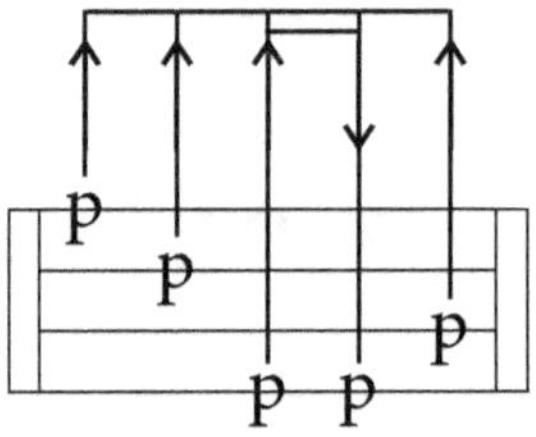

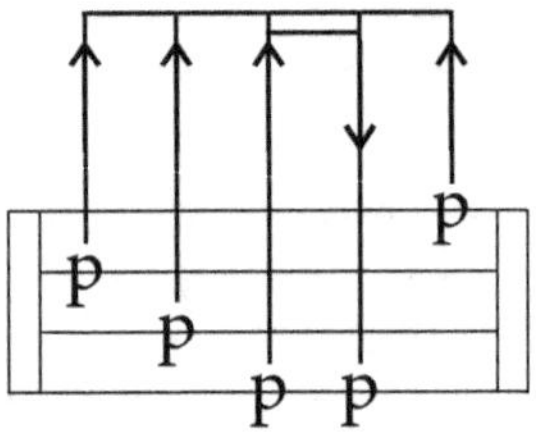

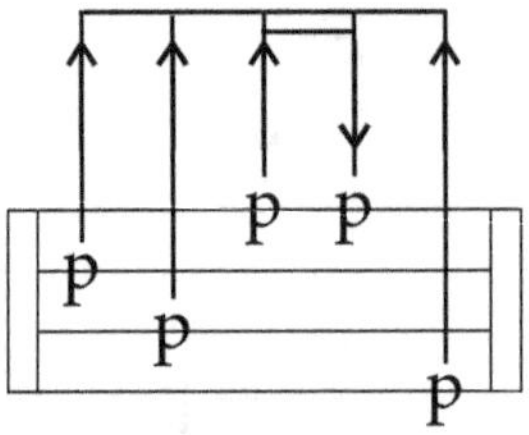

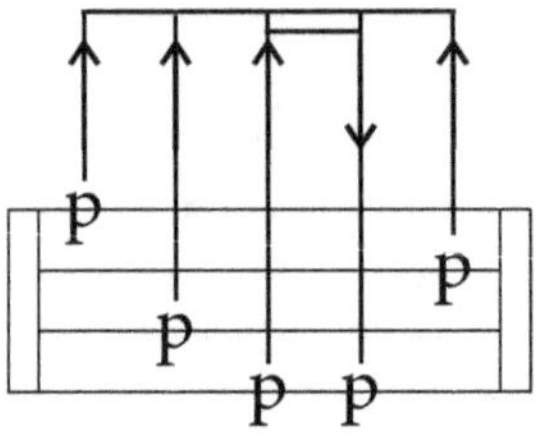

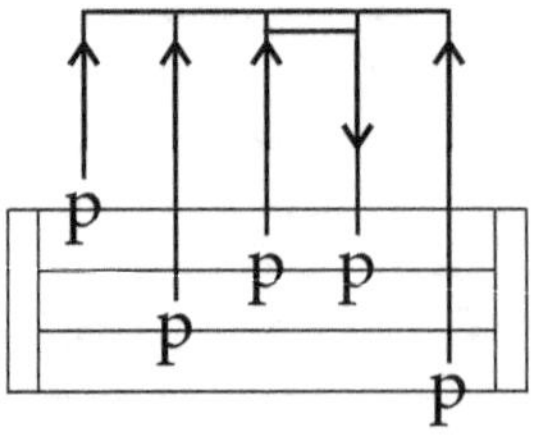

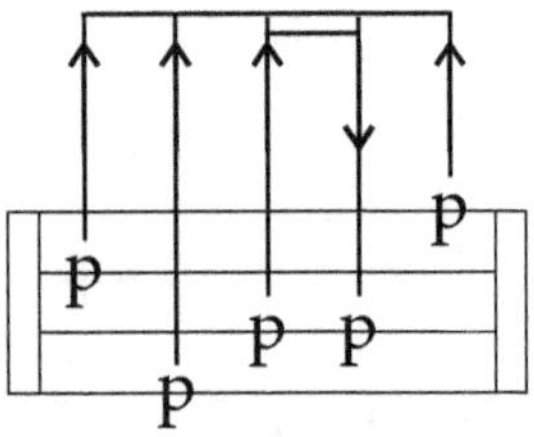

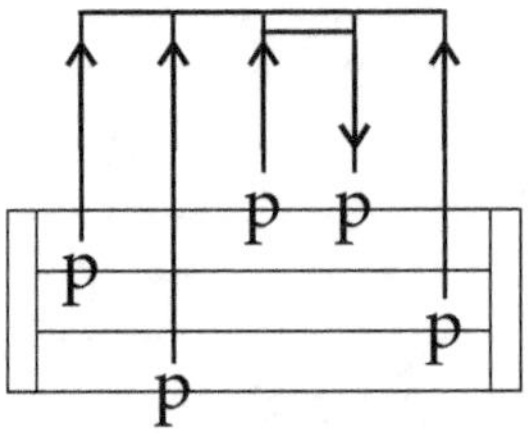

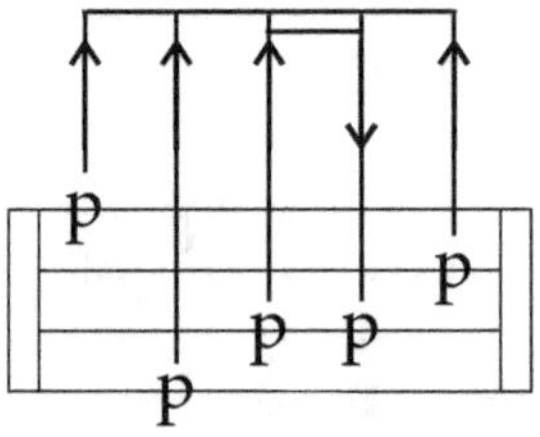

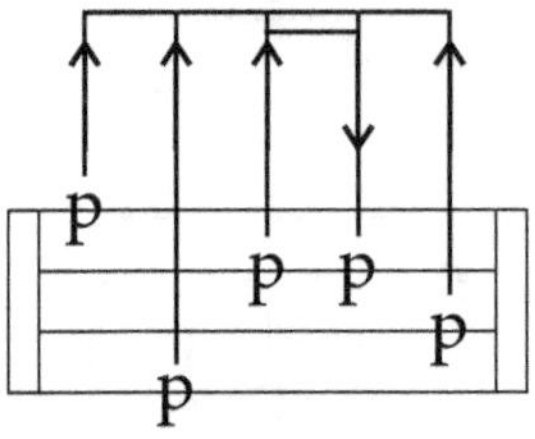

VARIATION IV

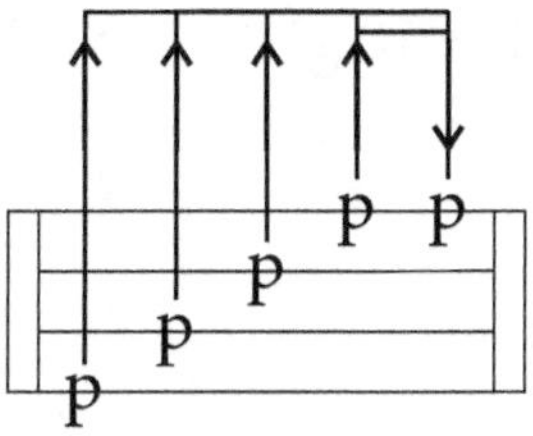

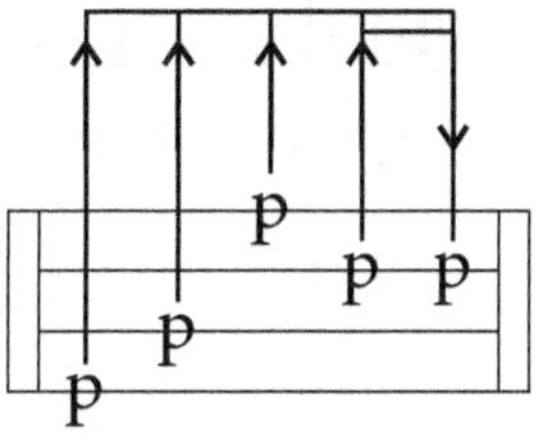

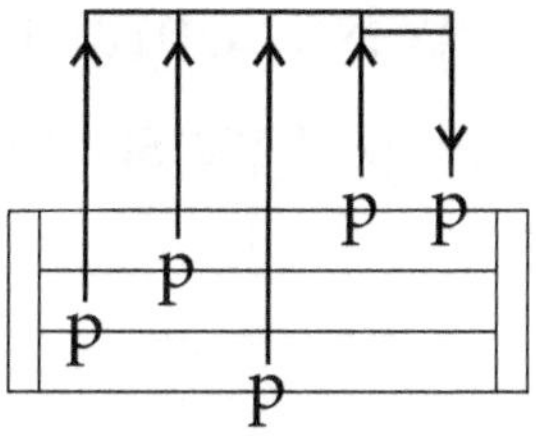

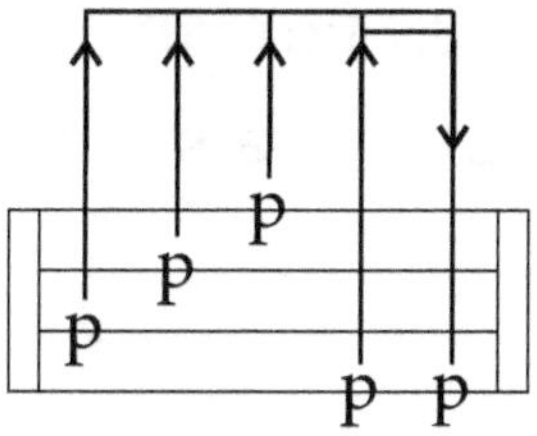

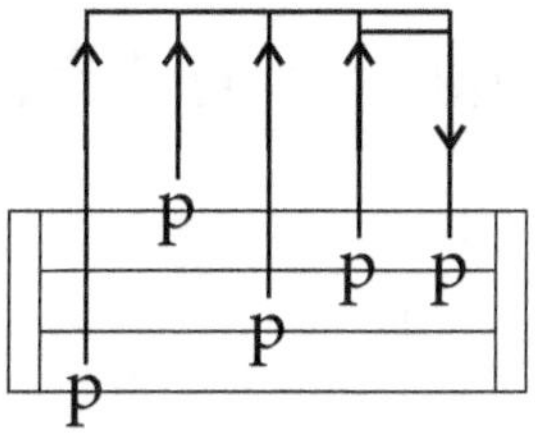

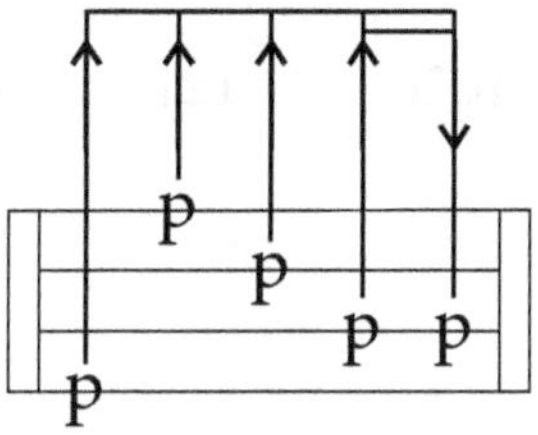

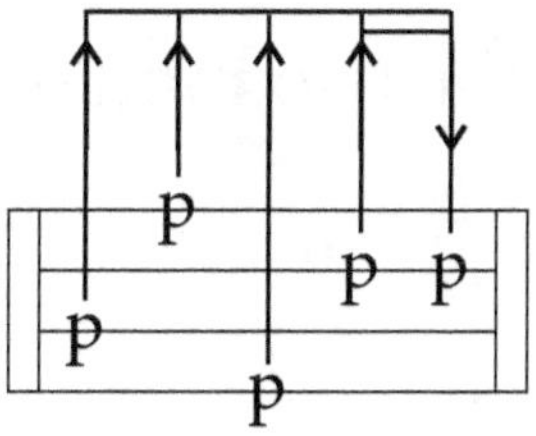

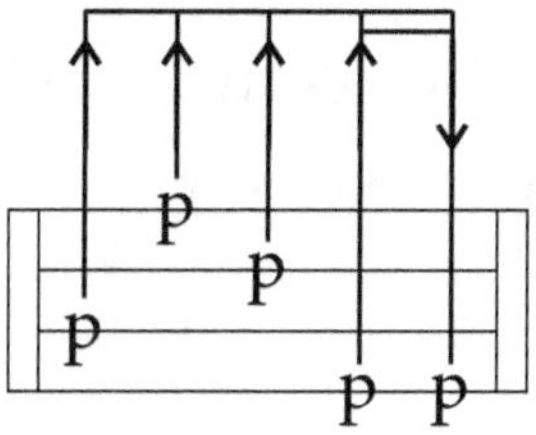

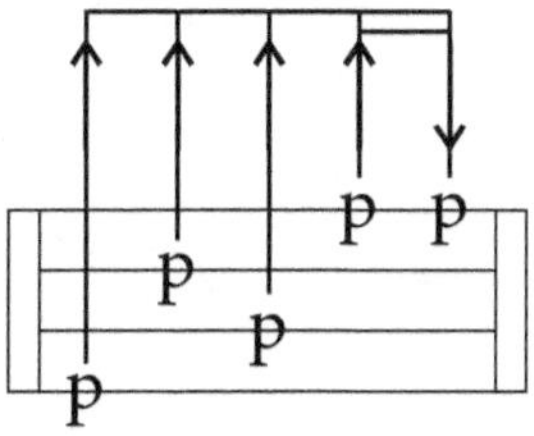

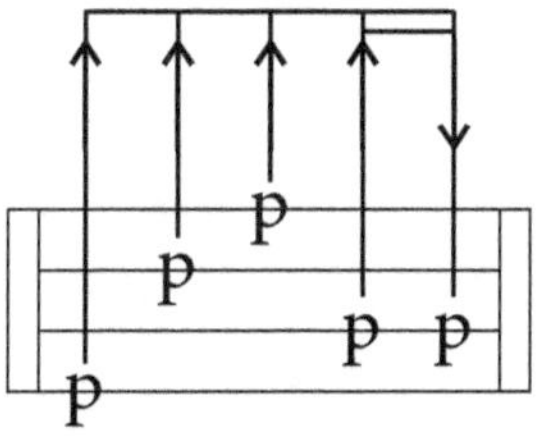

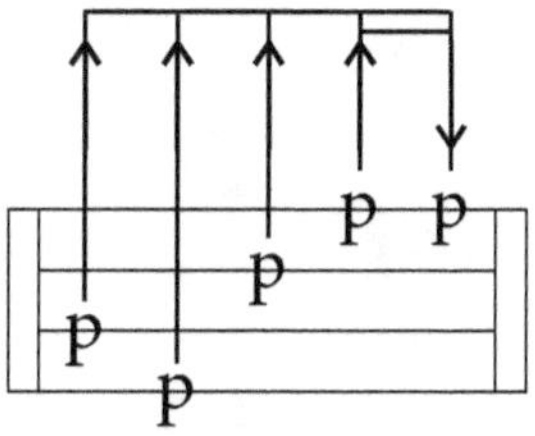

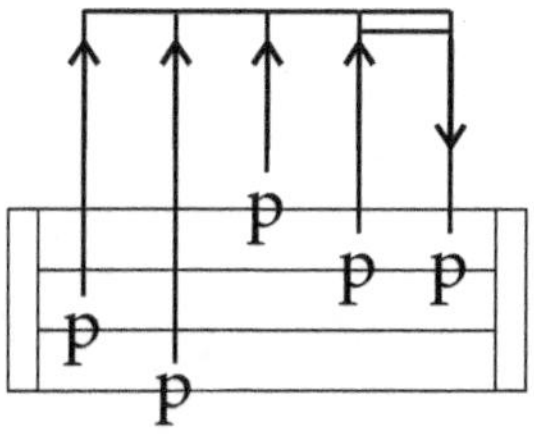

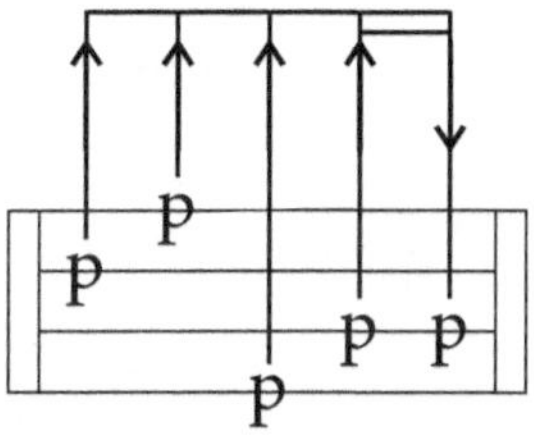

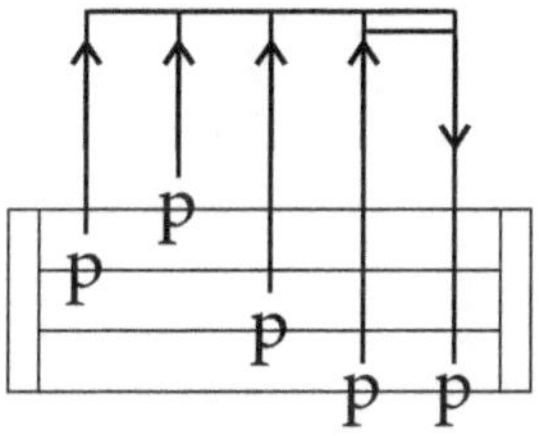

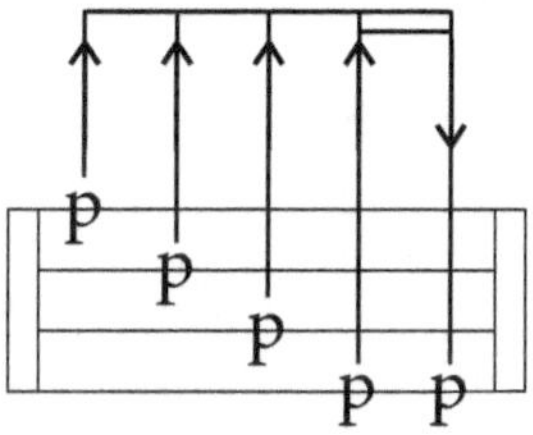

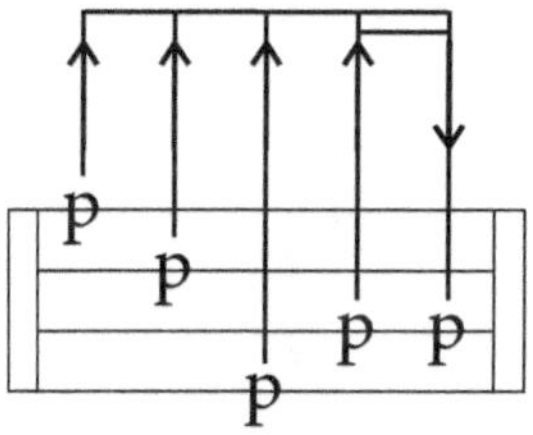

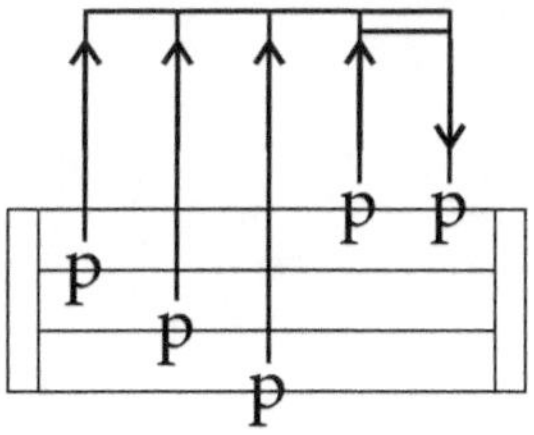

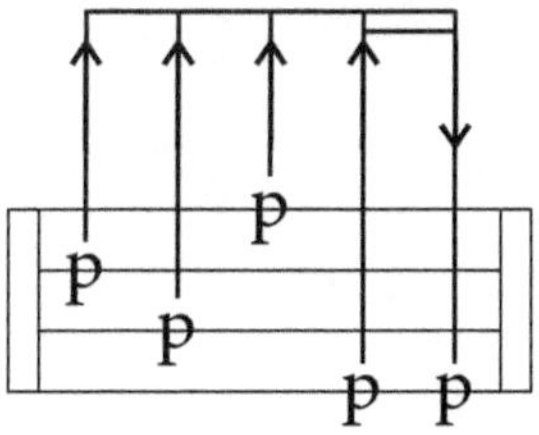

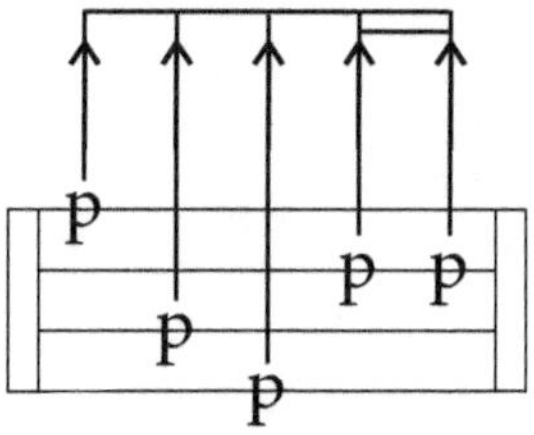

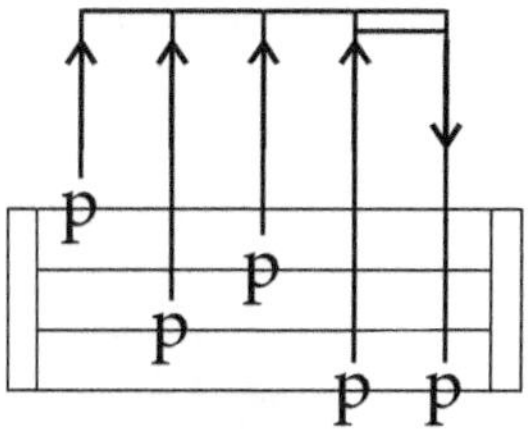

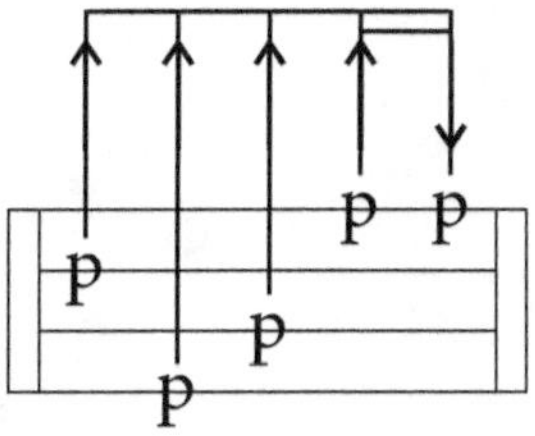

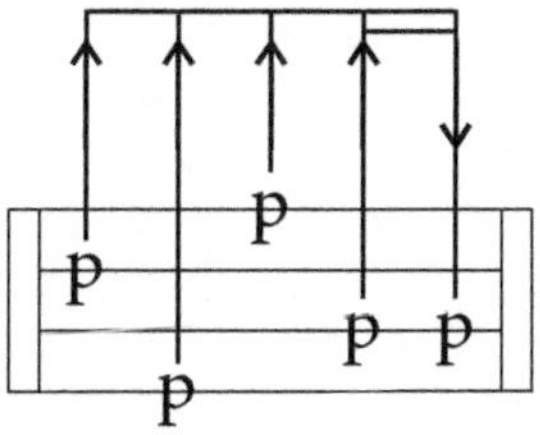

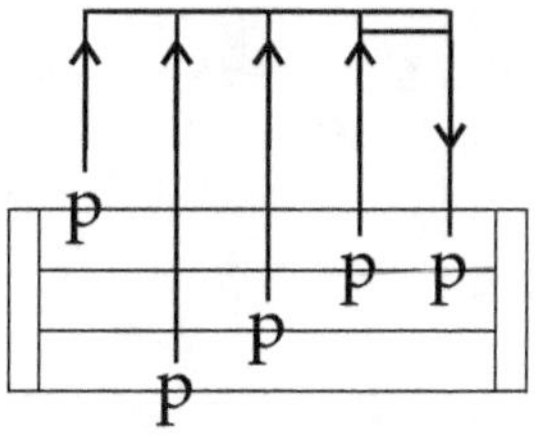

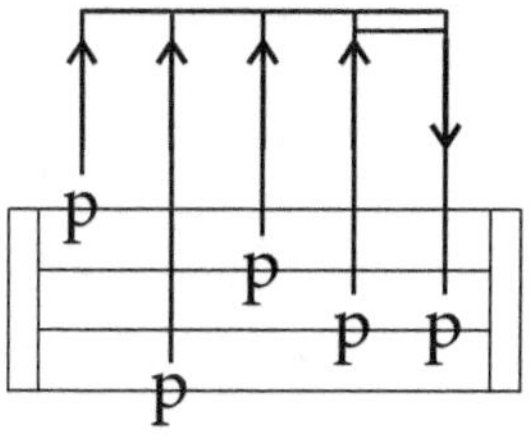

§ III

Exercise on pulgar on four adjacent strings with four double strokes within each Formula. The exercise contains 24 Formulas. Apart from the given way you can also practice the pulgar stroke towards one direction.

The combination of the two modes of practice offers additional material for the learner.

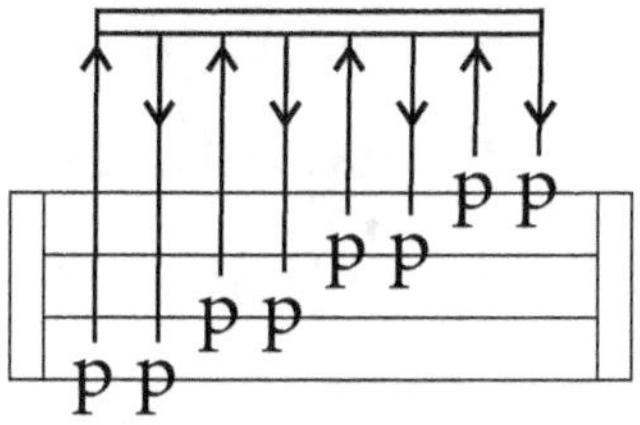

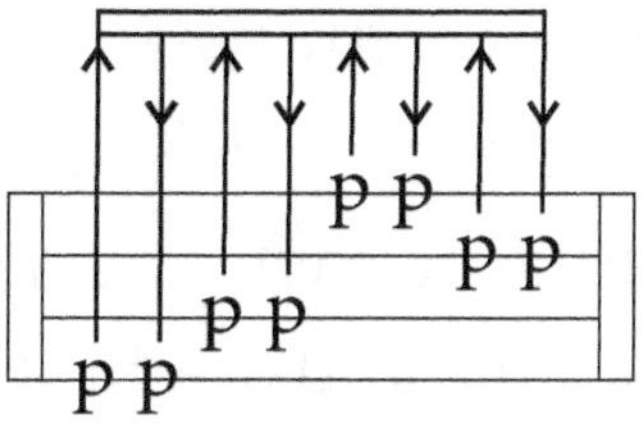

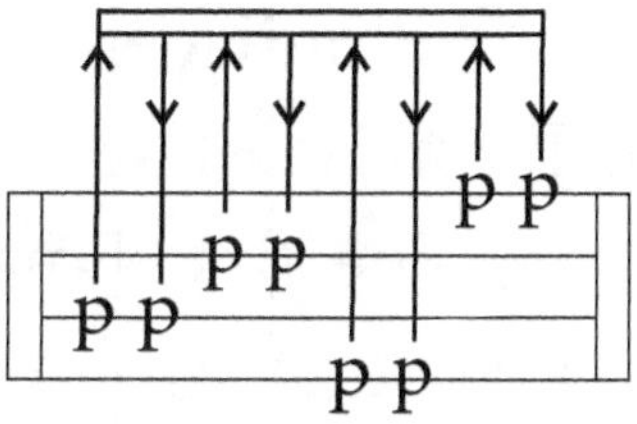

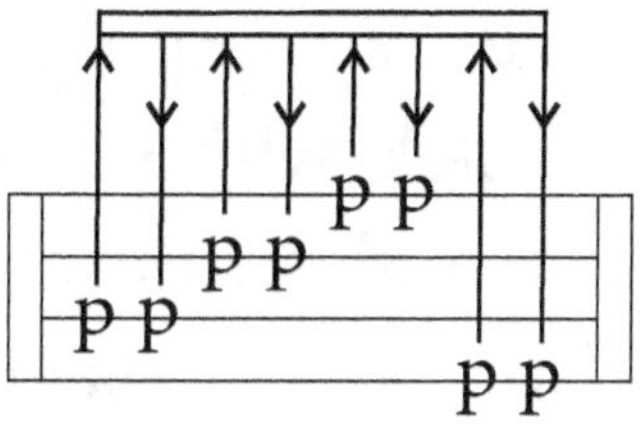

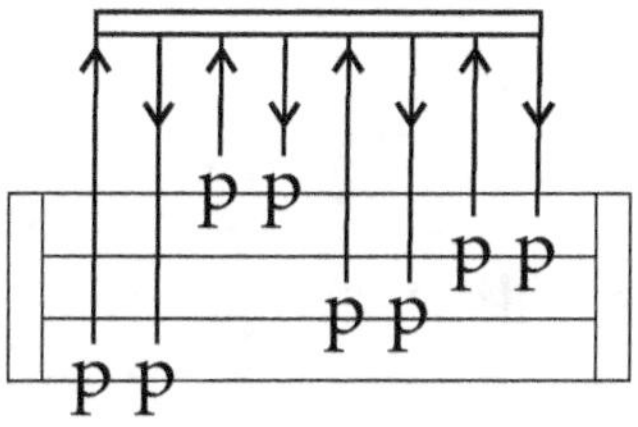

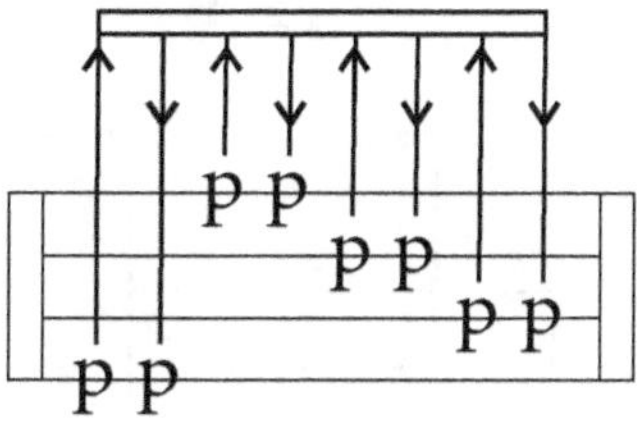

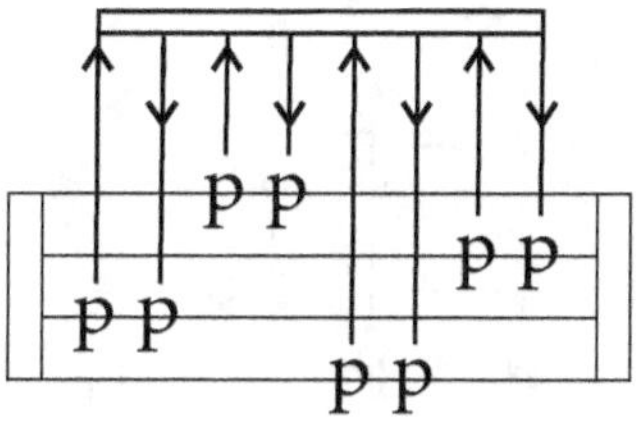

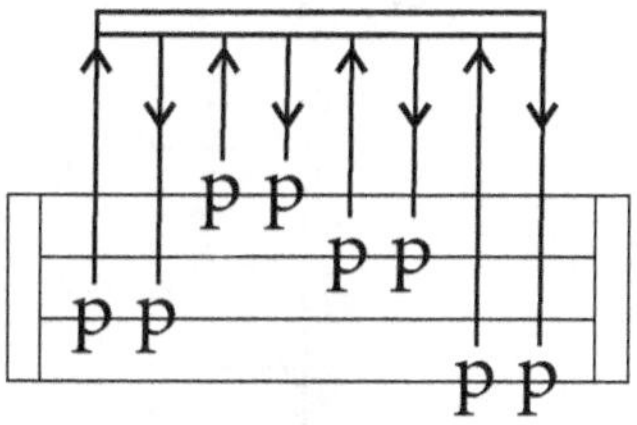

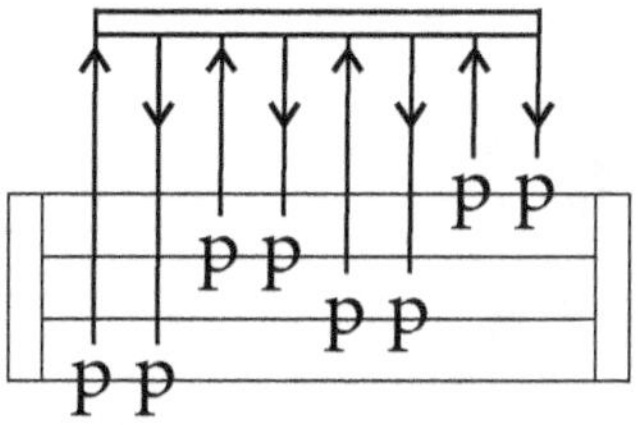

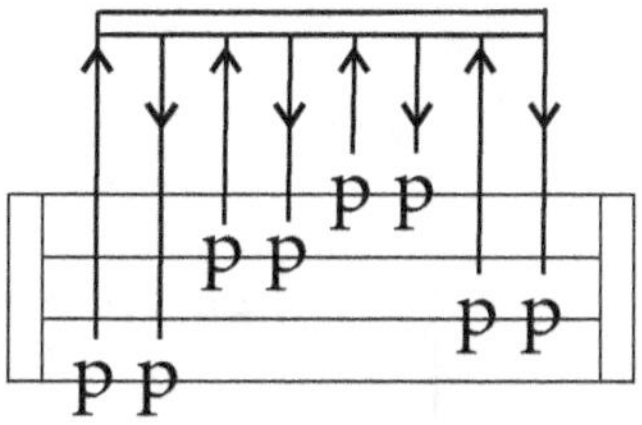

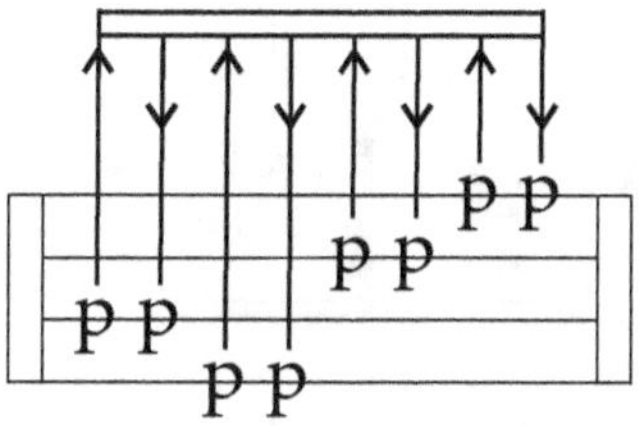

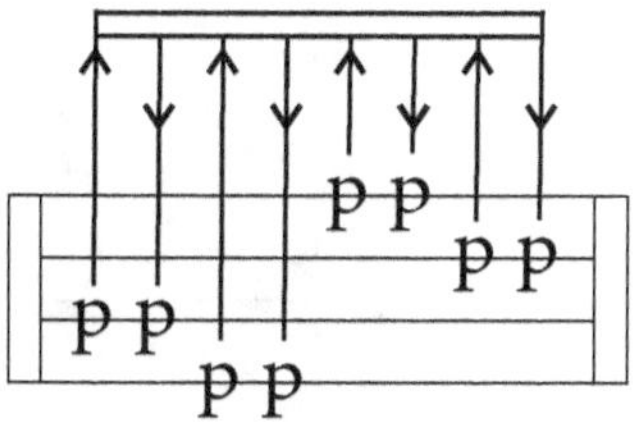

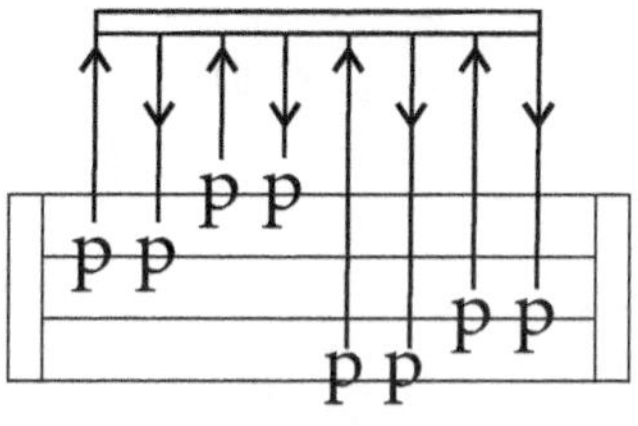

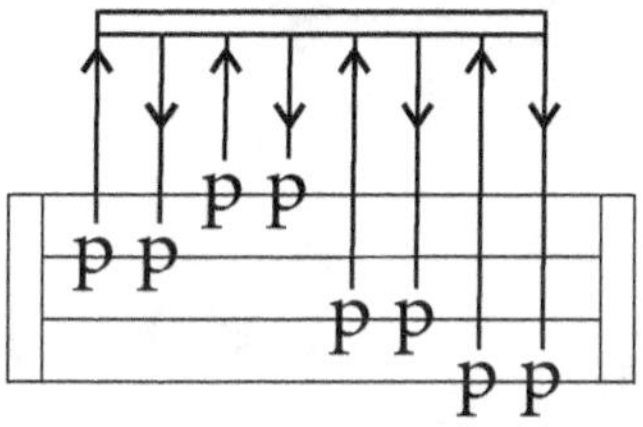

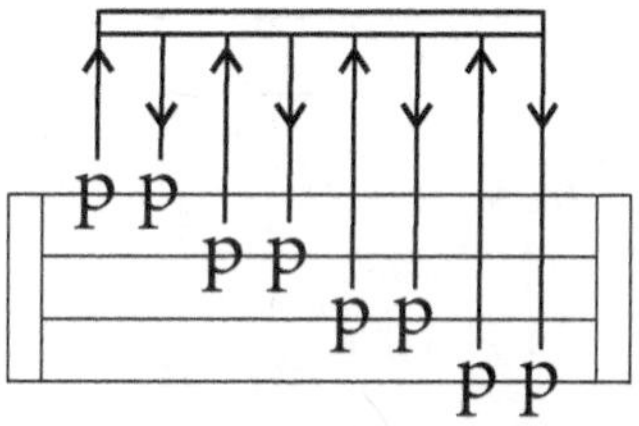

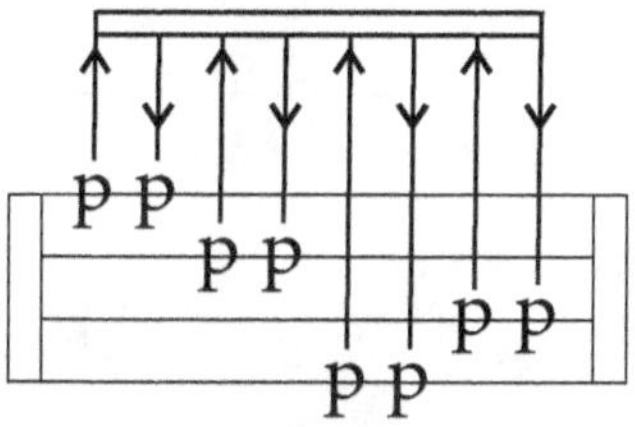

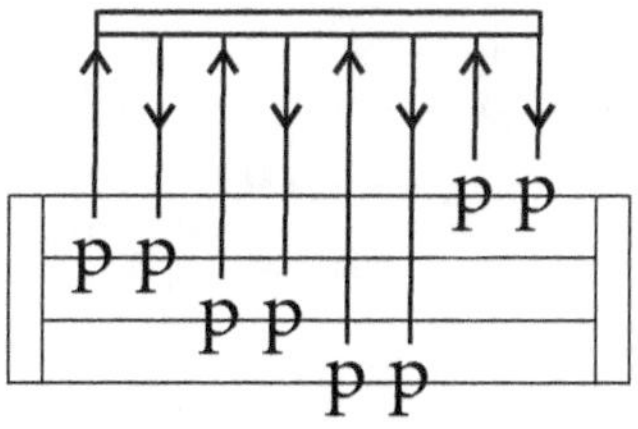

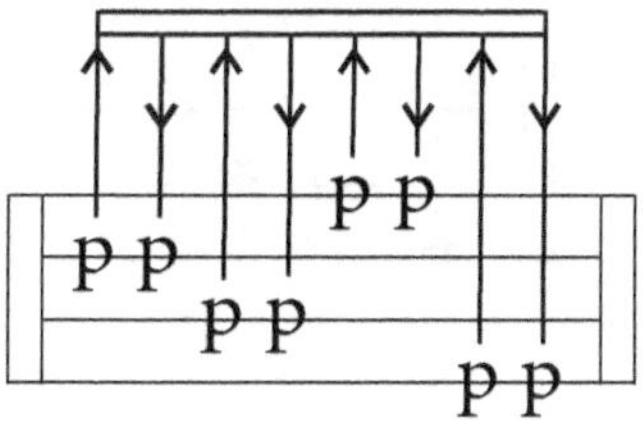

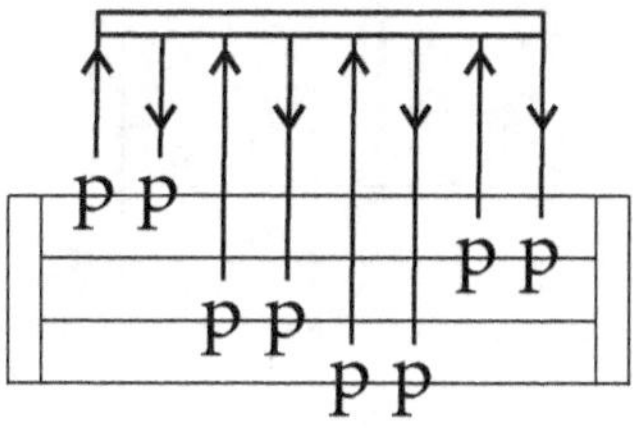

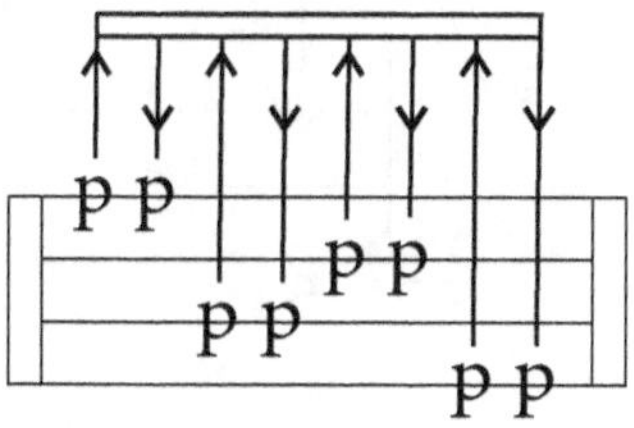

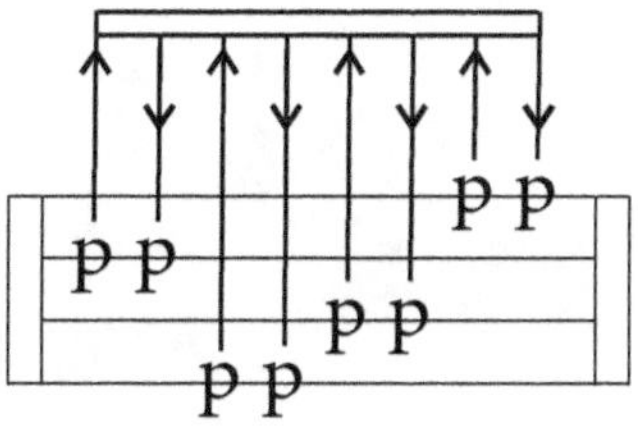

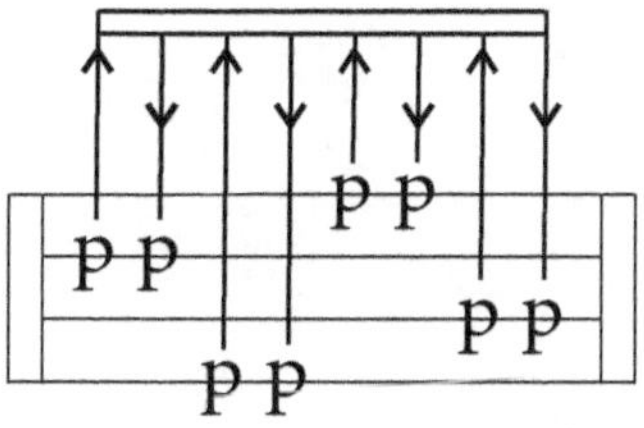

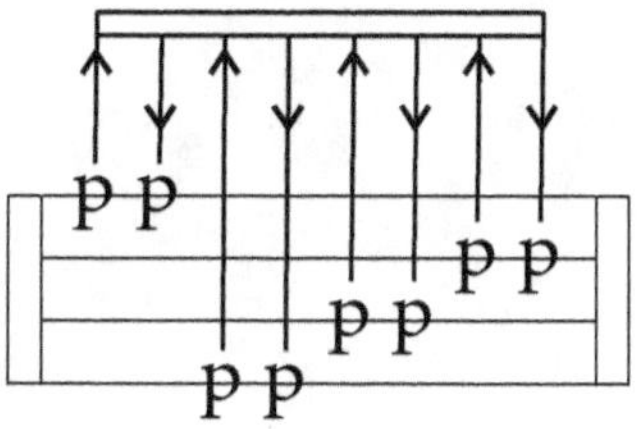

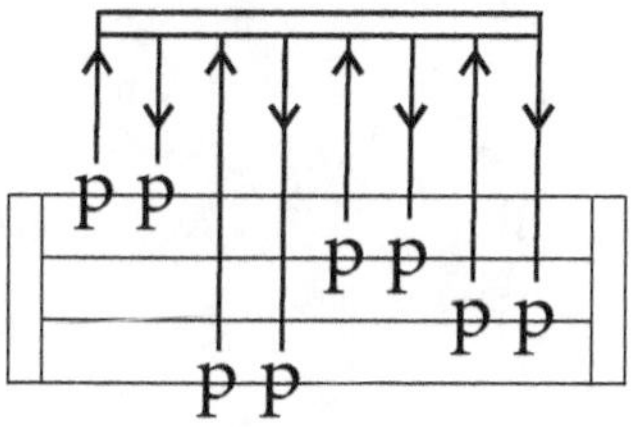

§ IV

Exercise on pulgar on four adjacent strings with two single and two double strokes within each Formula. The exercise contains six variations with 24 Formulas in each one. The first Formula of each variation is cited below. Isochronous playing on pulgar strokes (single and double).

VARIATION I
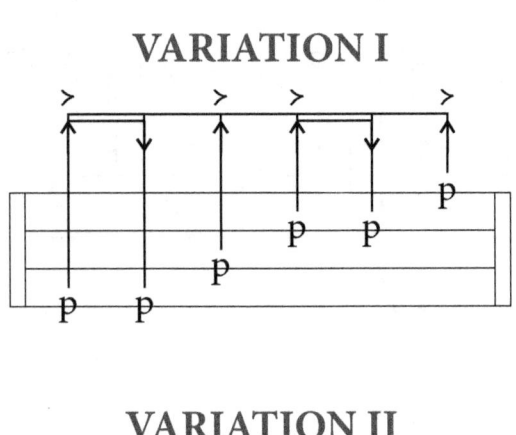

VARIATION IV
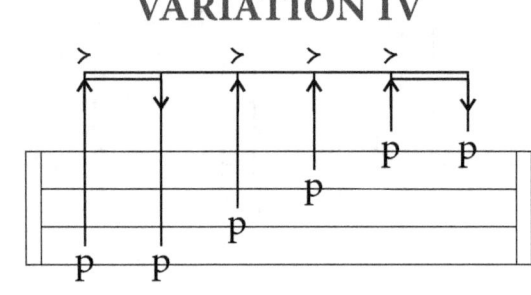

VARIATION II
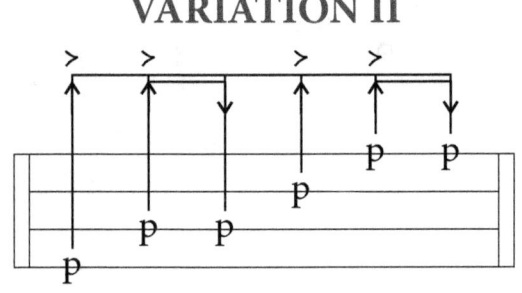

VARIATION V
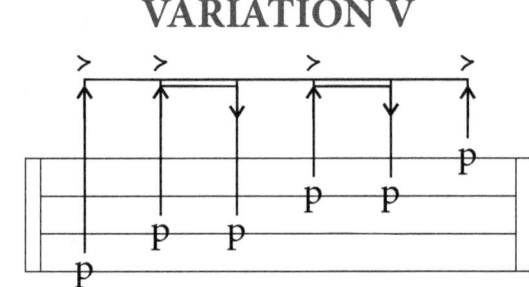

VARIATION III
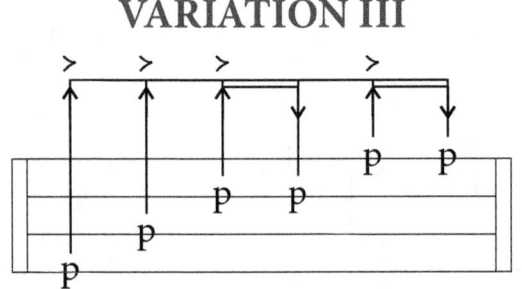

VARIATION VI
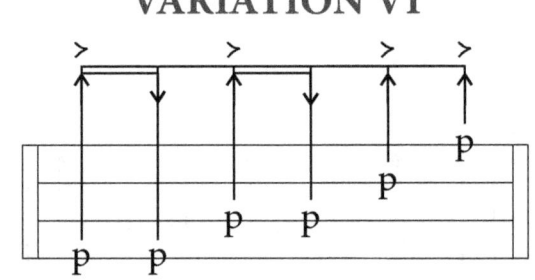

VARIATION I

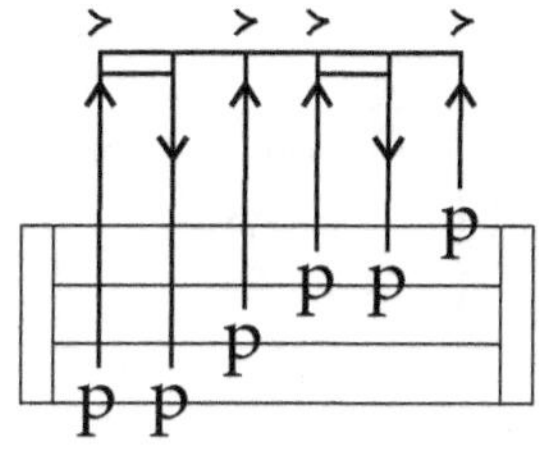

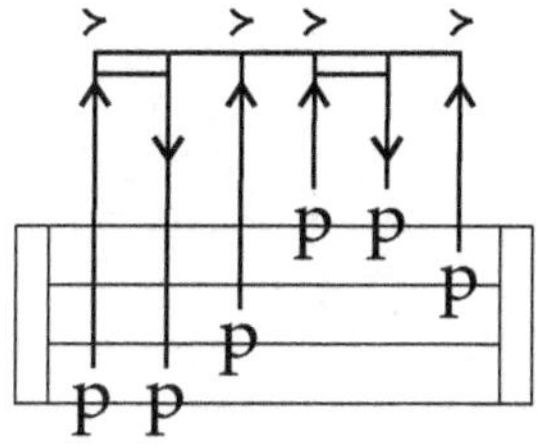

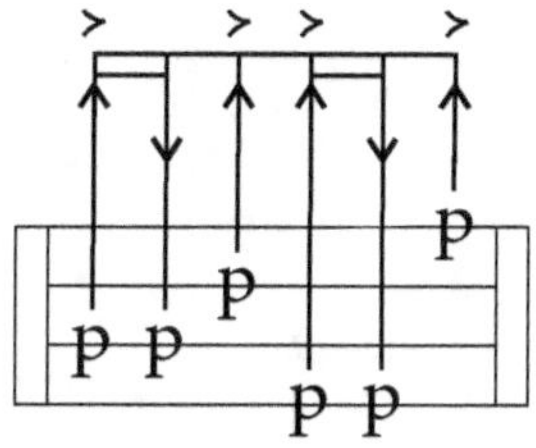

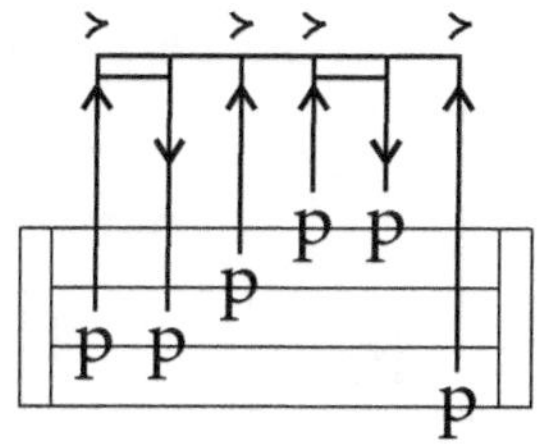

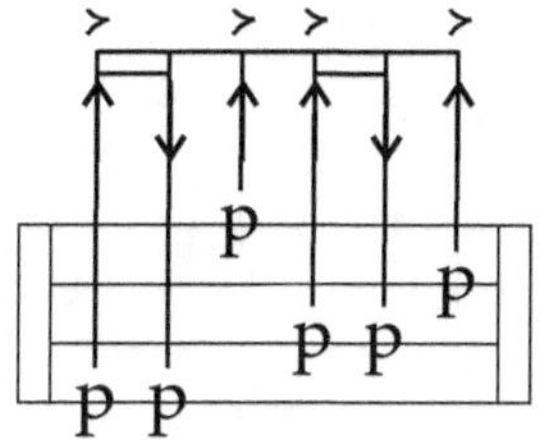

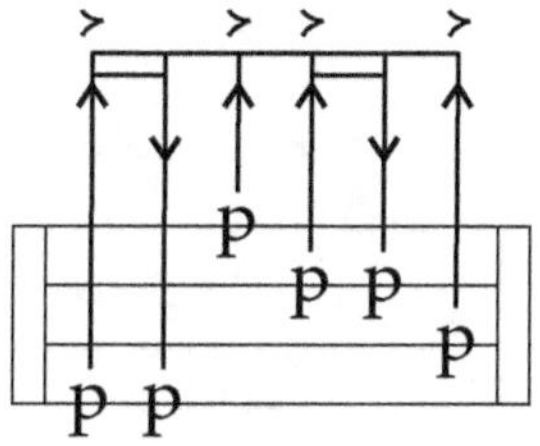

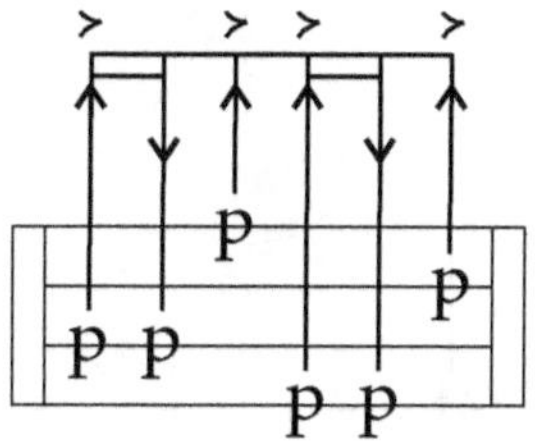

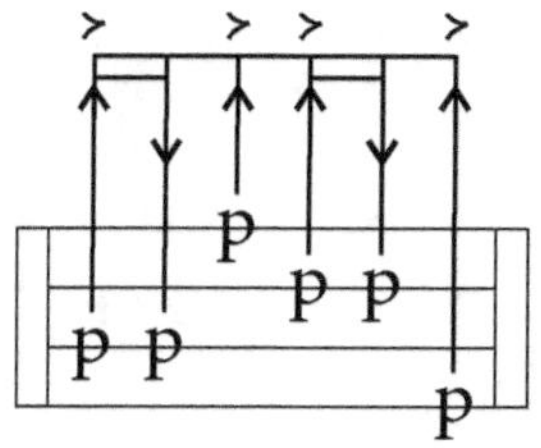

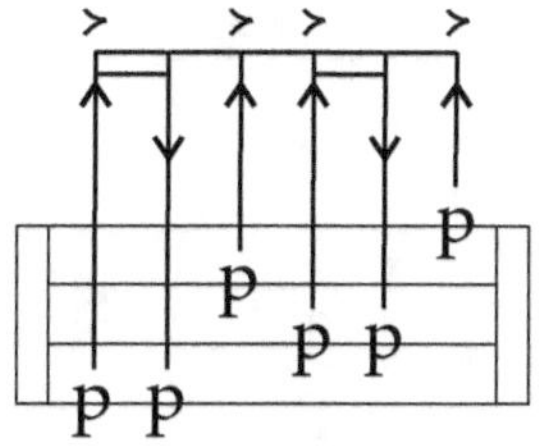

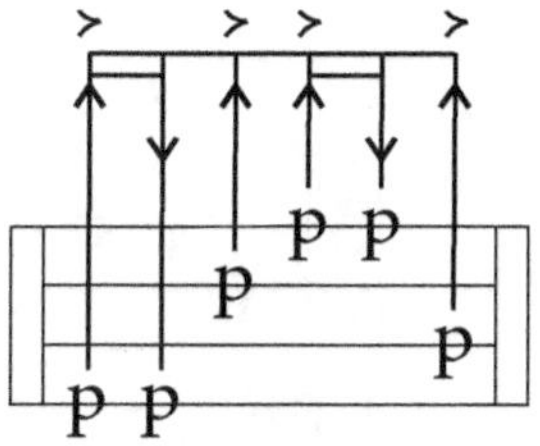

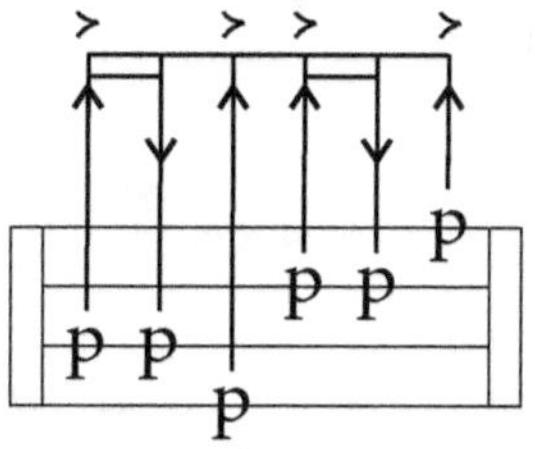

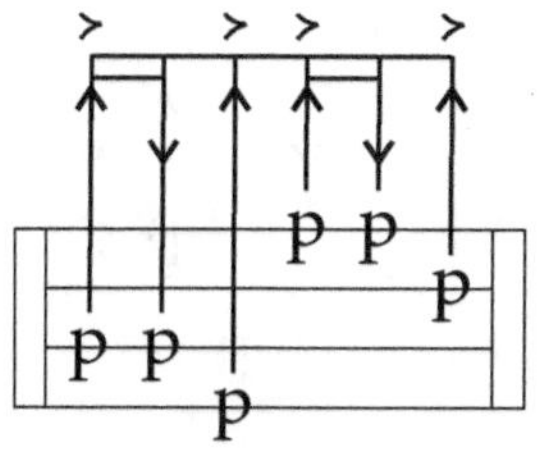

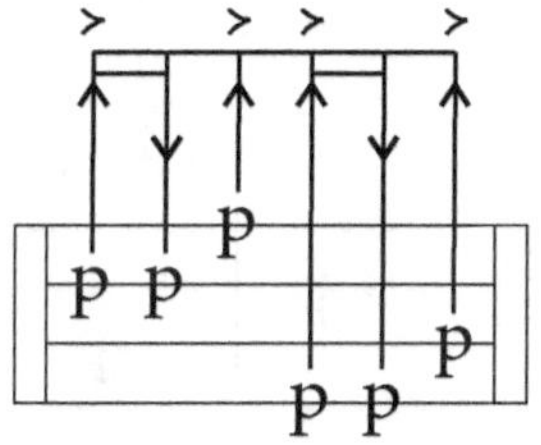

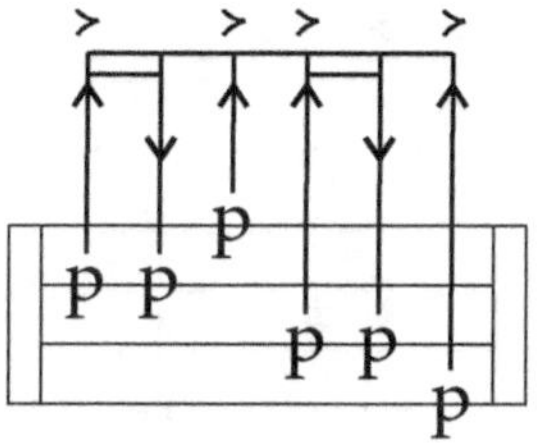

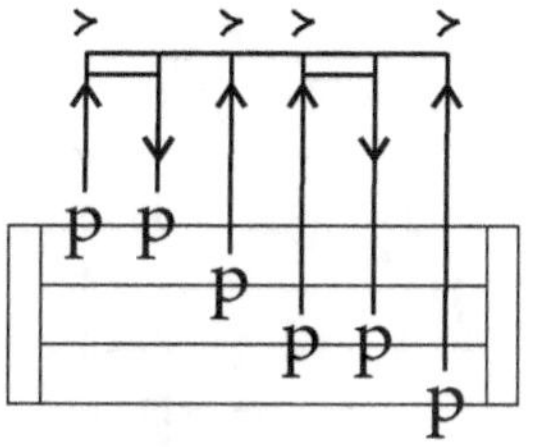

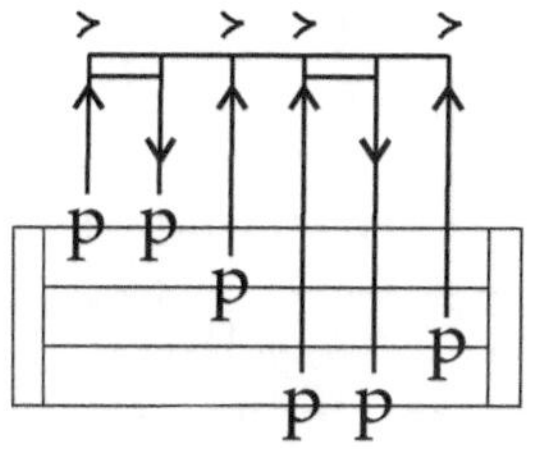

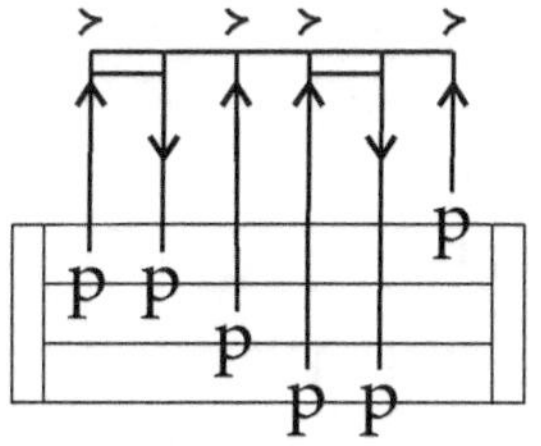

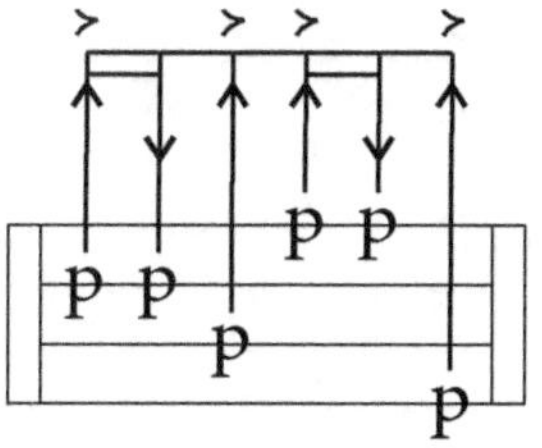

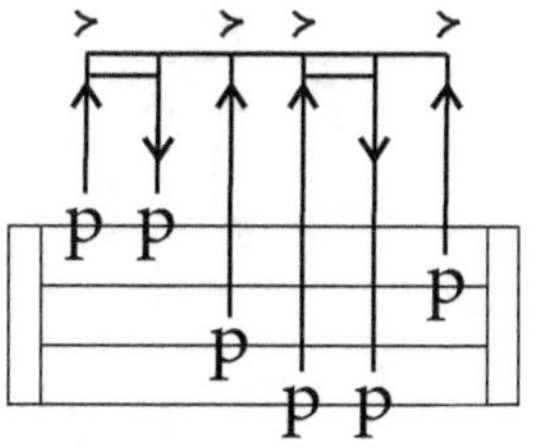

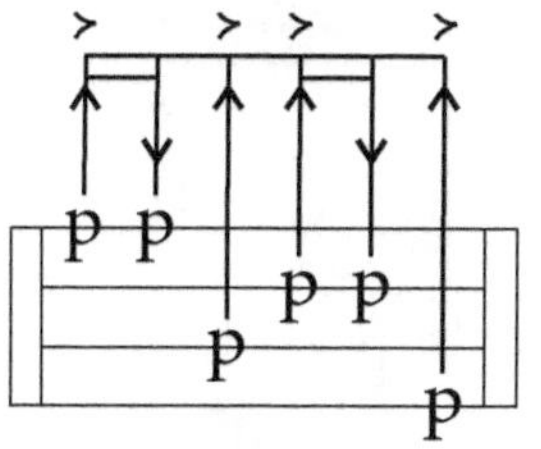

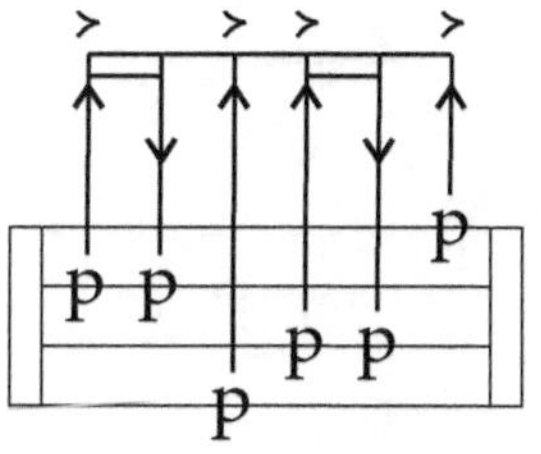

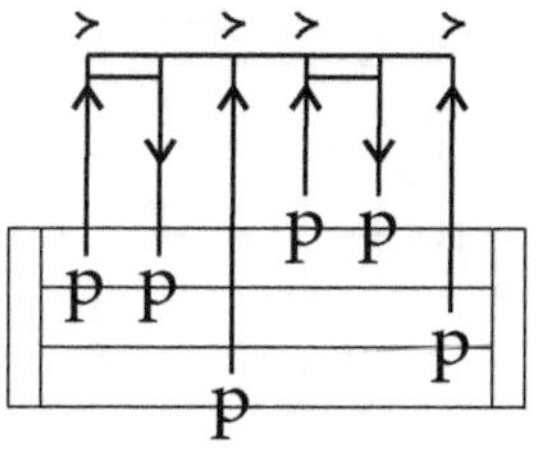

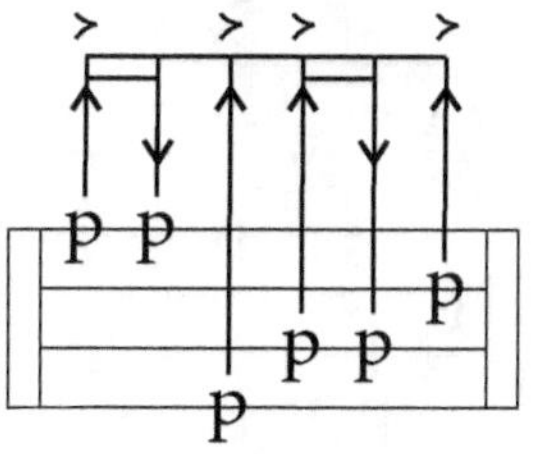

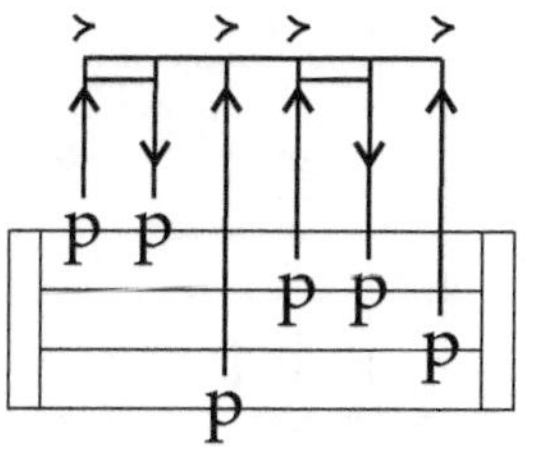

VARIATION II

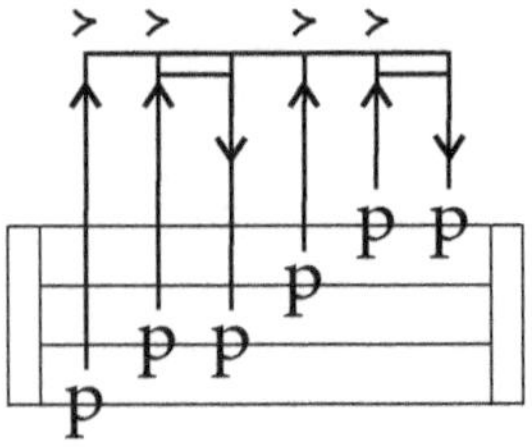

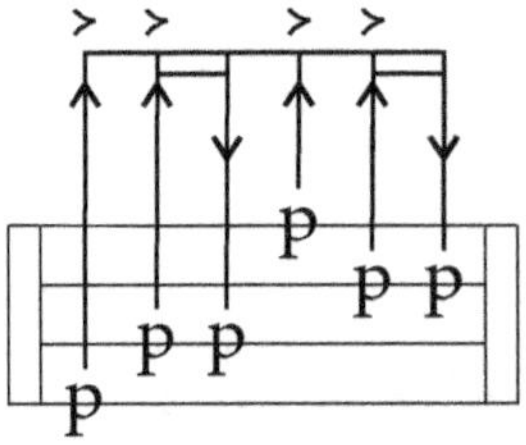

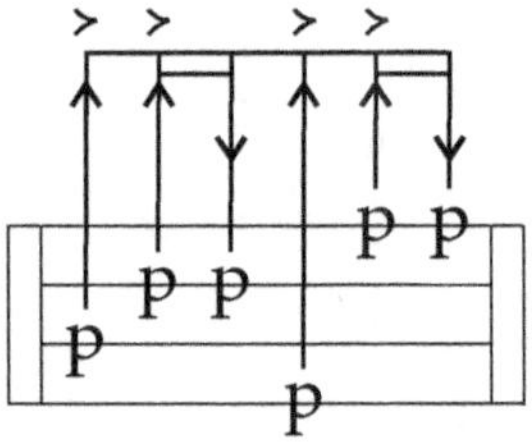

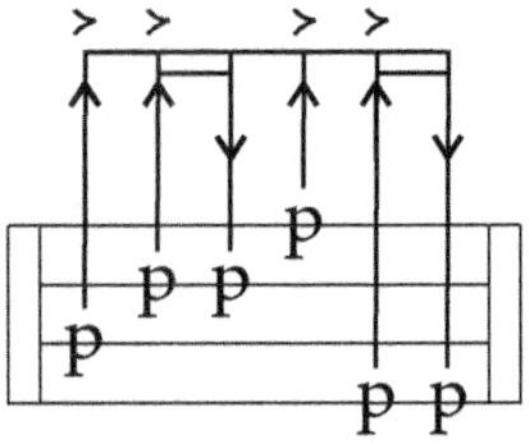

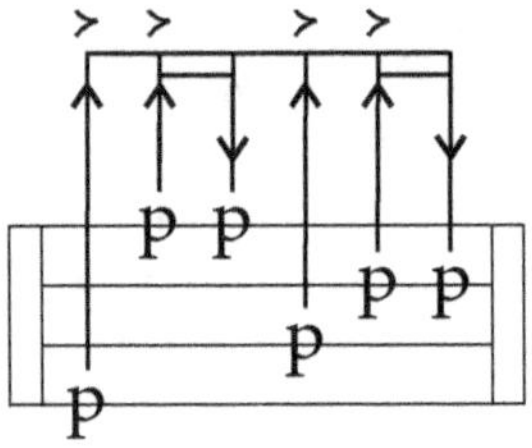

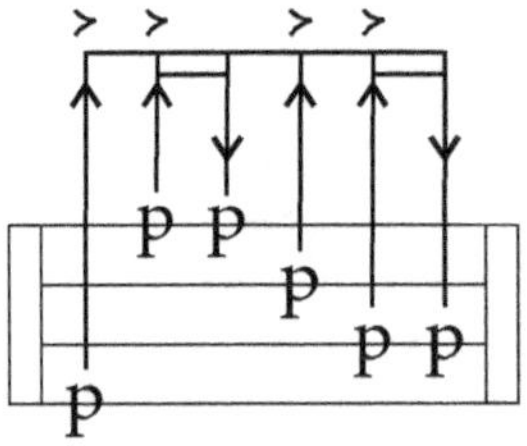

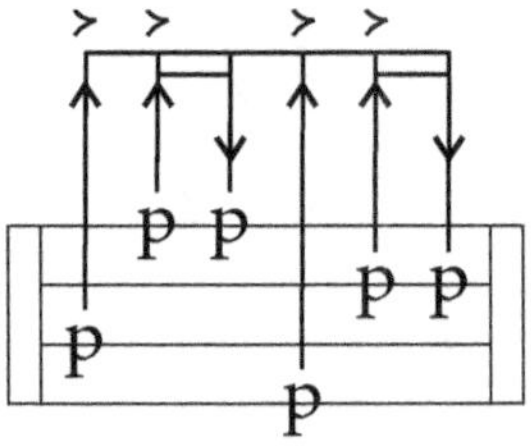

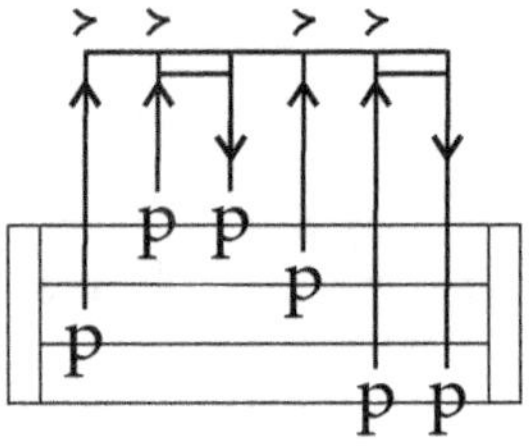

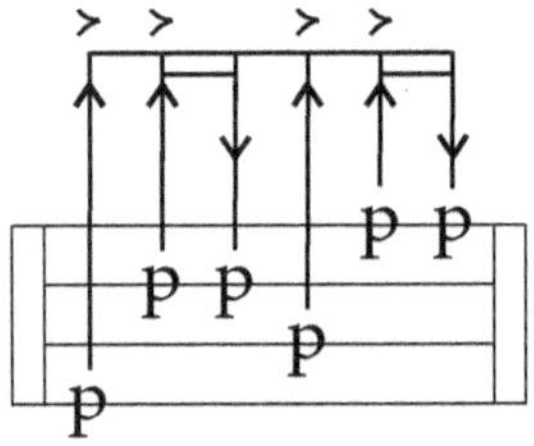

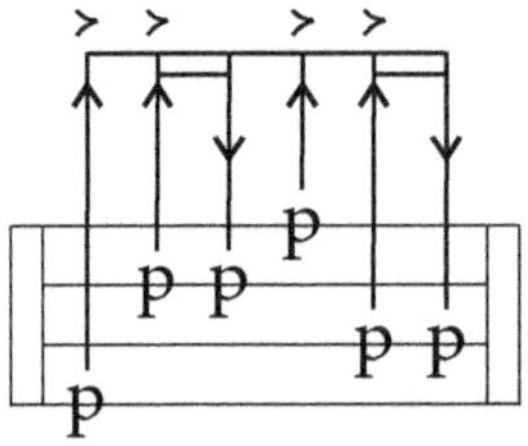

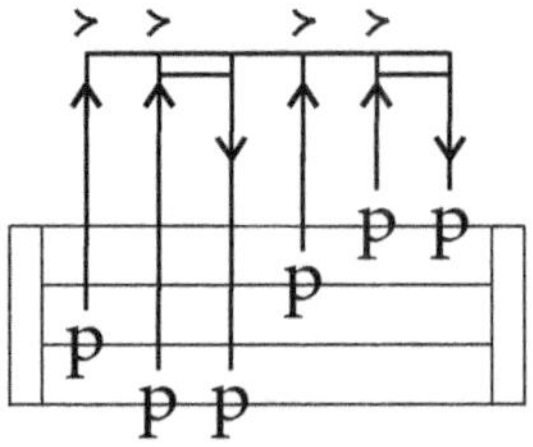

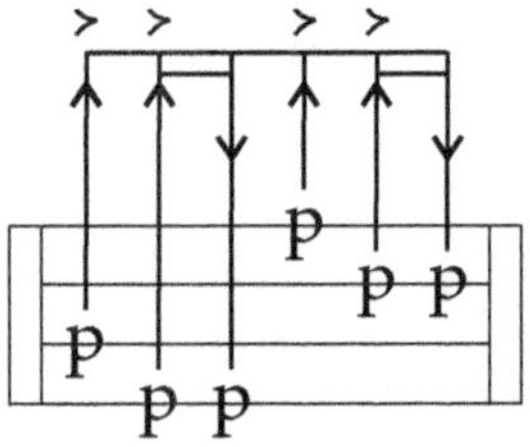

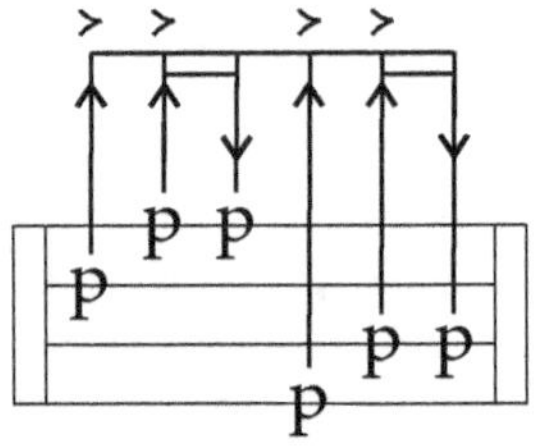

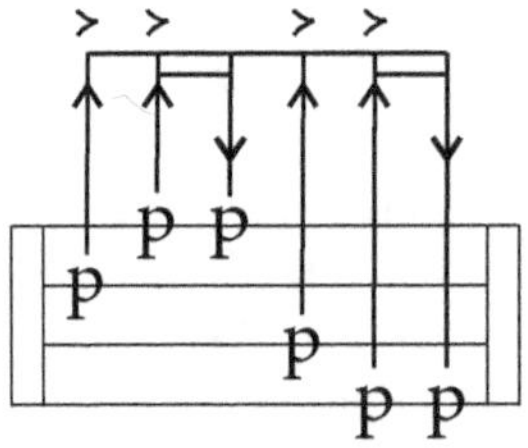

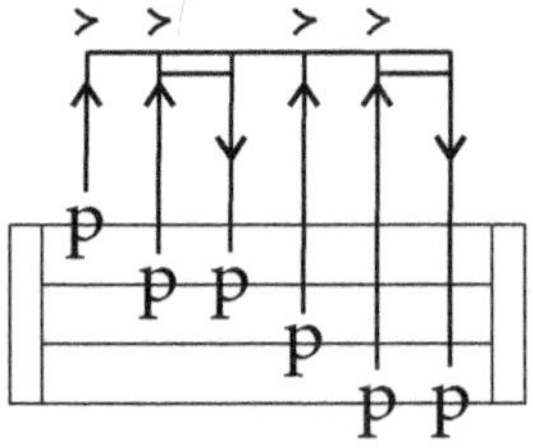

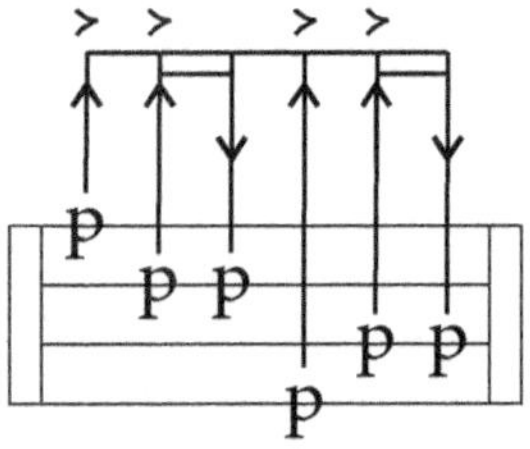

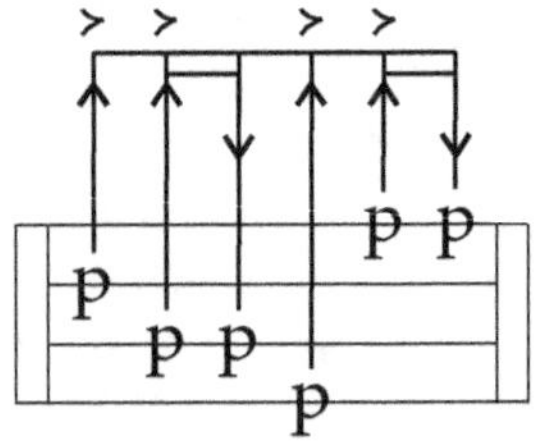

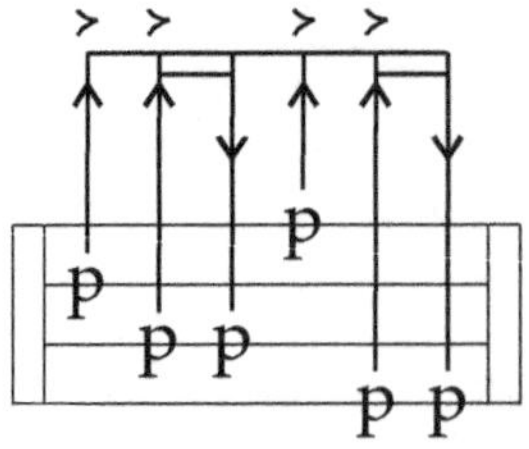

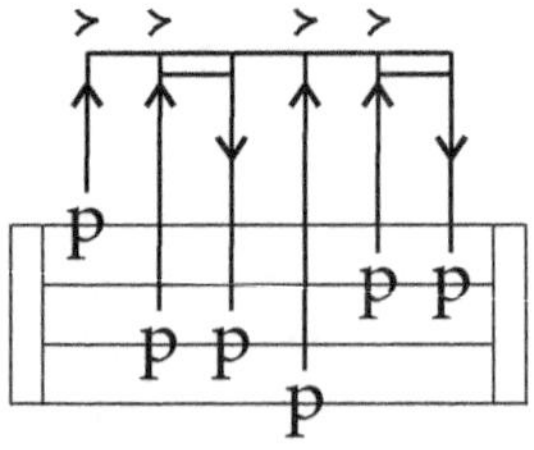

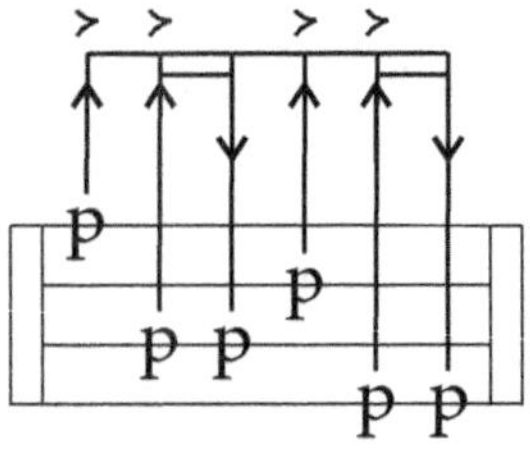

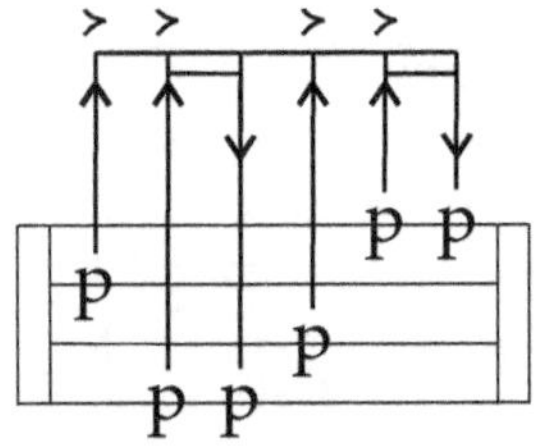

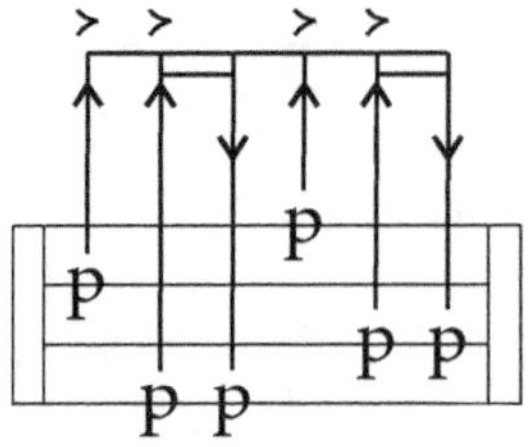

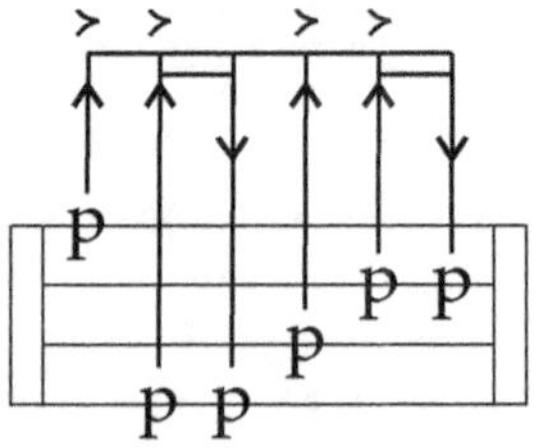

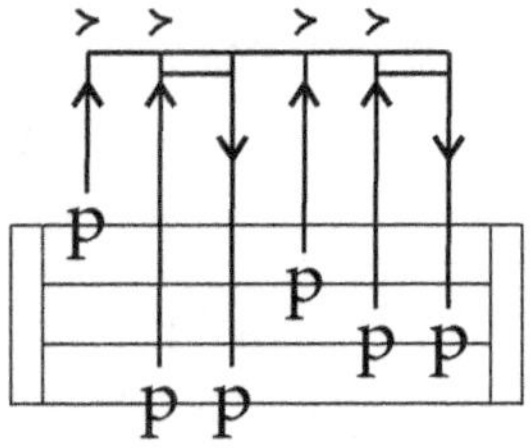

VARIATION III

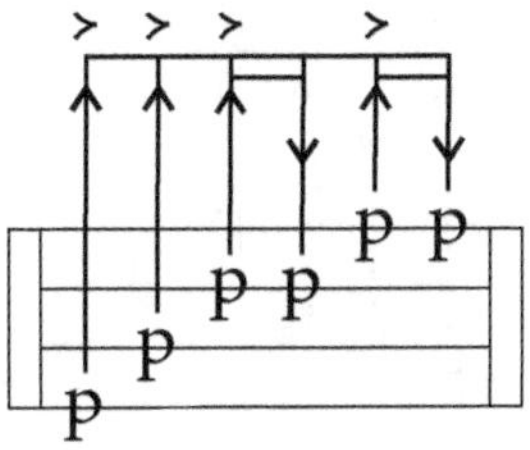

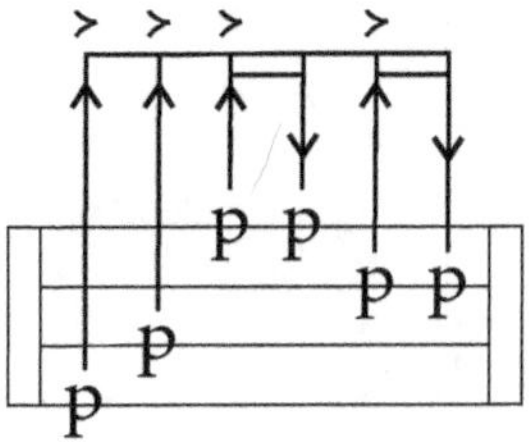

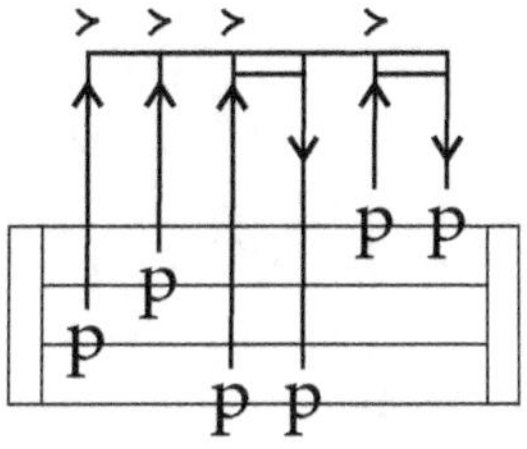

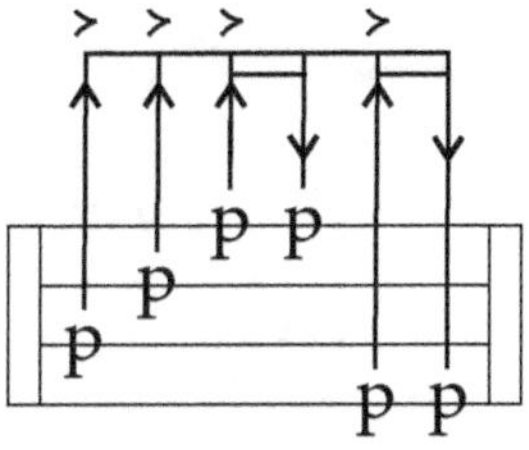

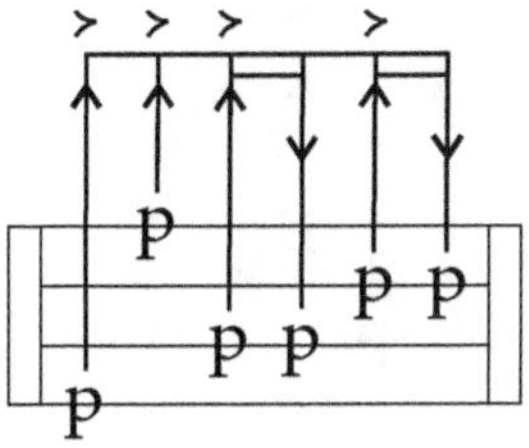

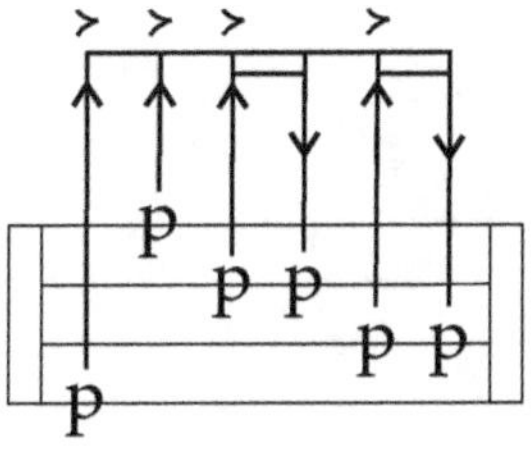

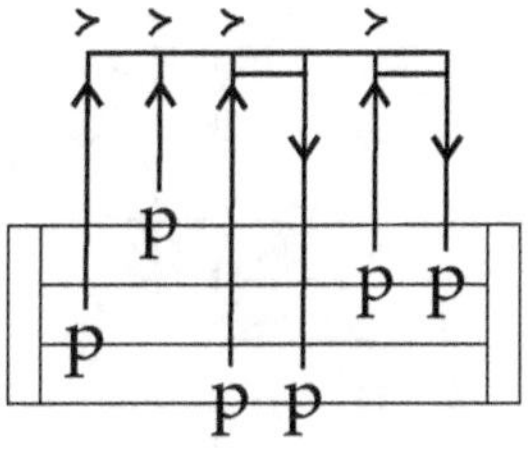

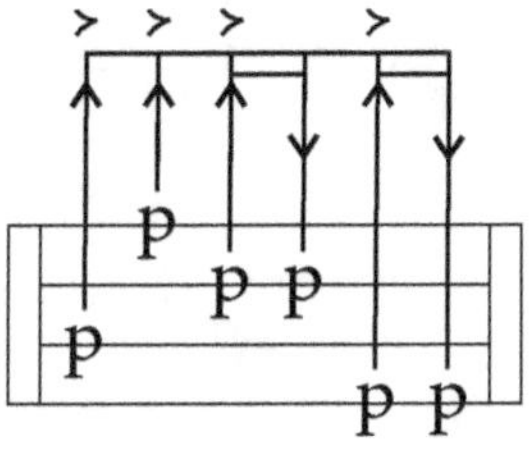

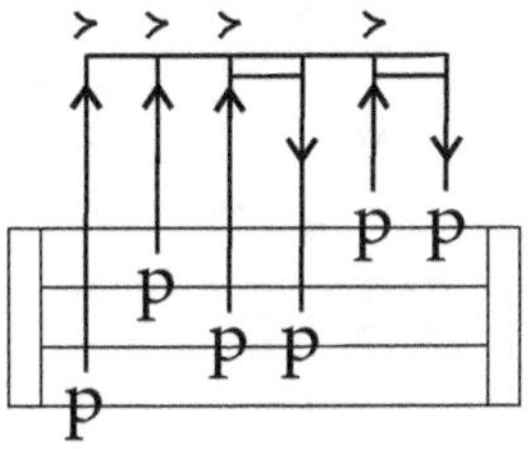

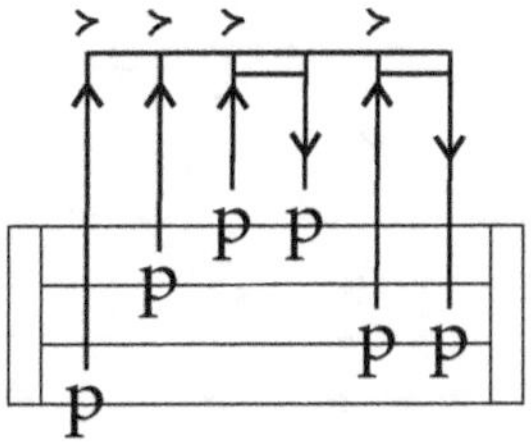

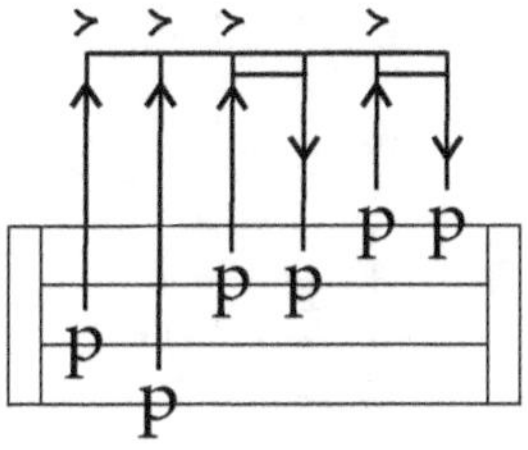

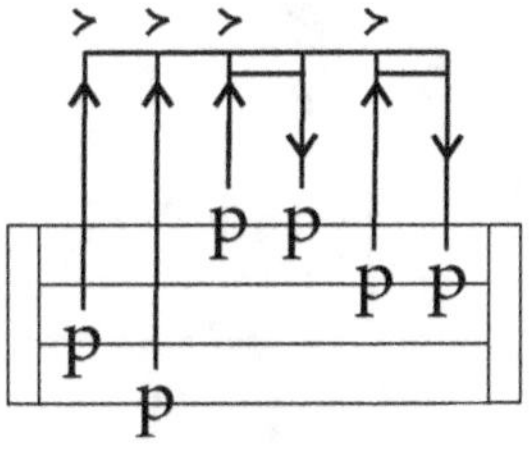

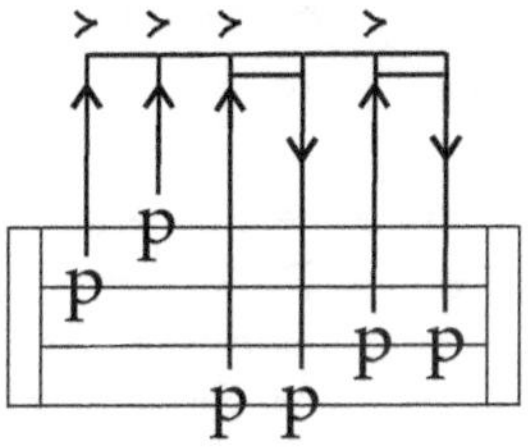

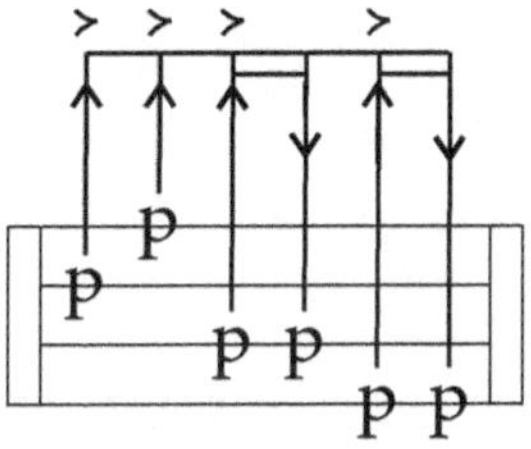

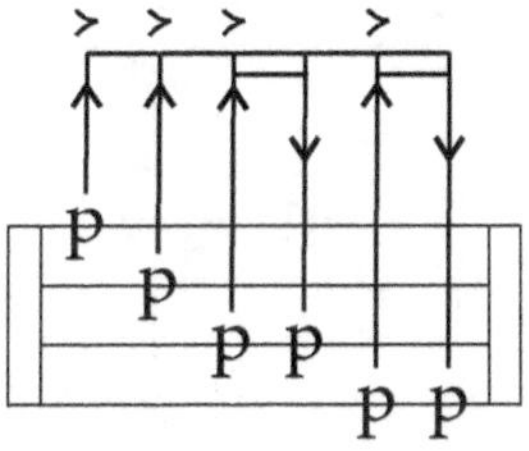

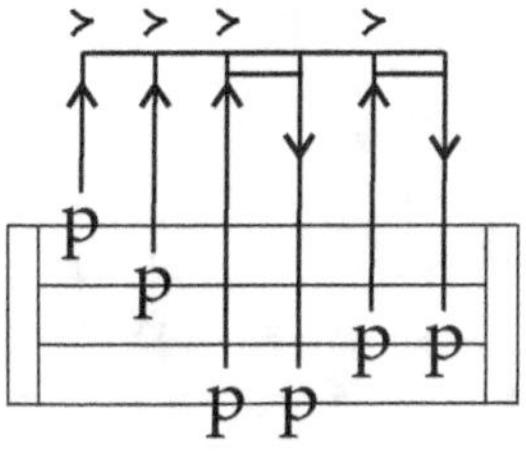

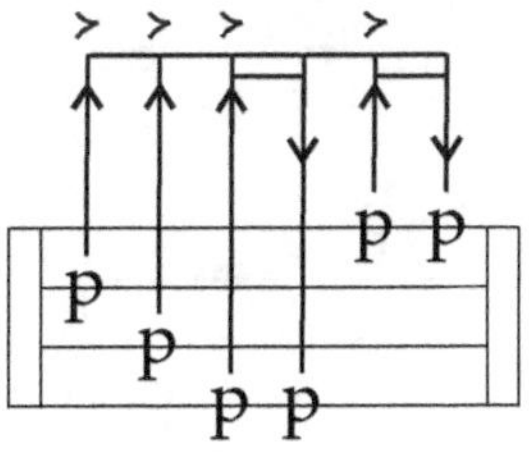

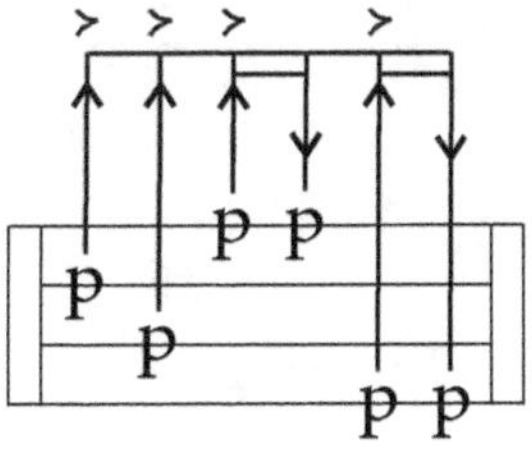

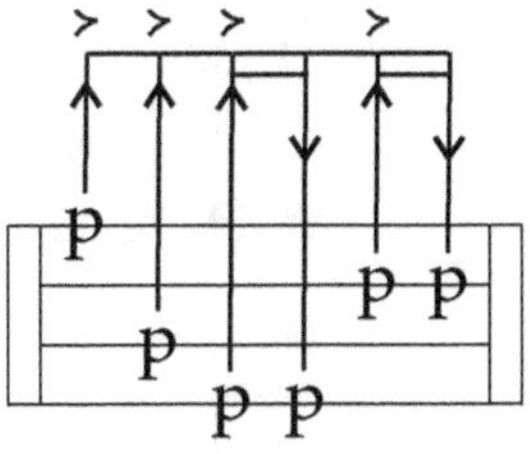

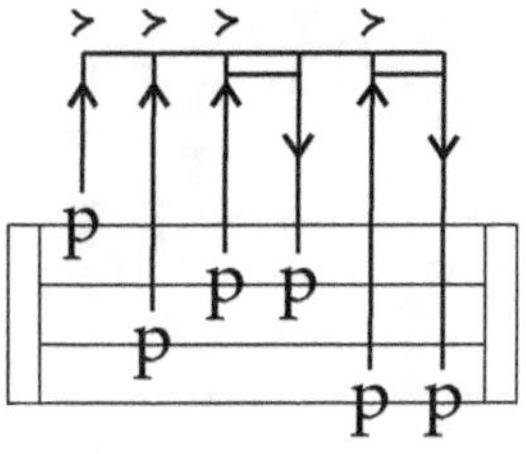

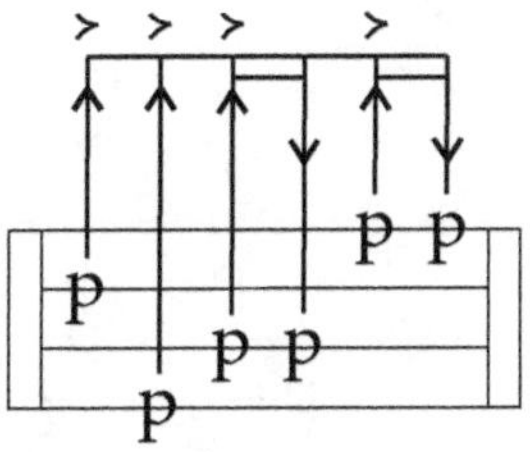

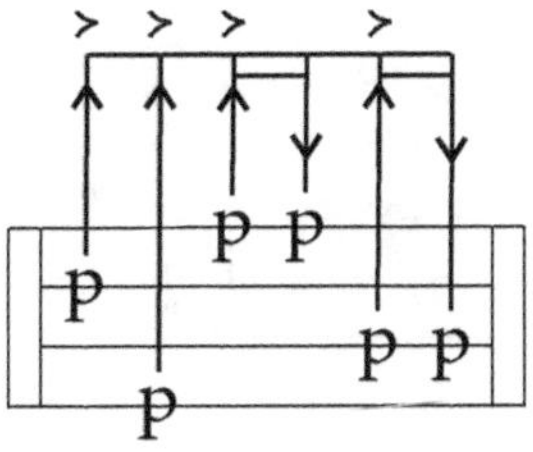

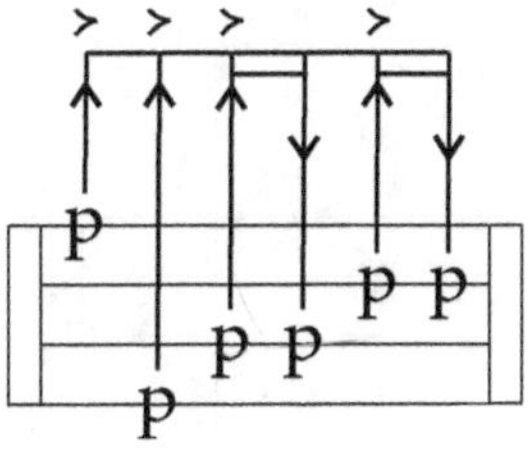

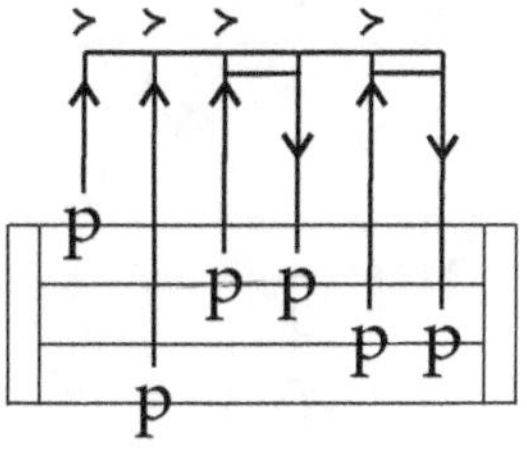

VARIATION IV

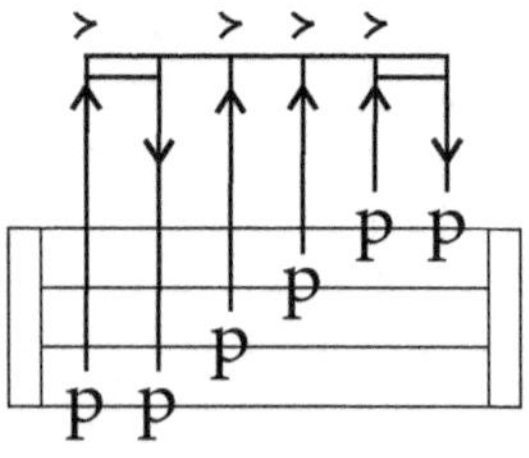

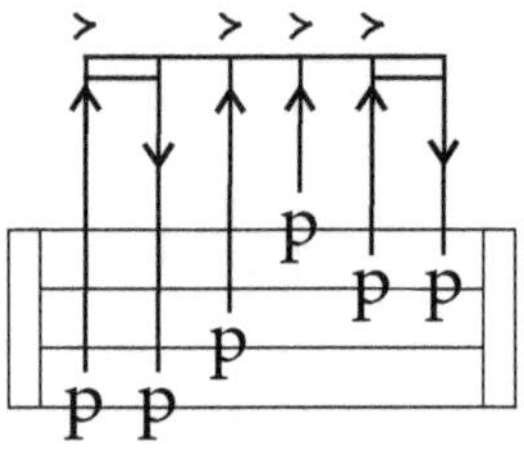

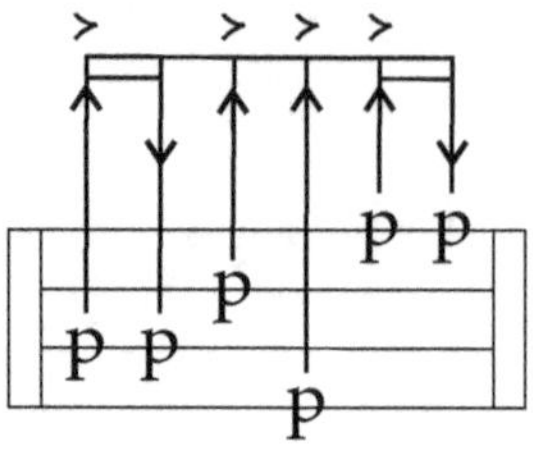

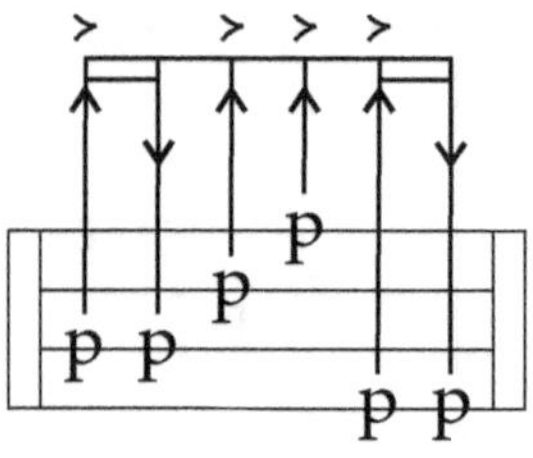

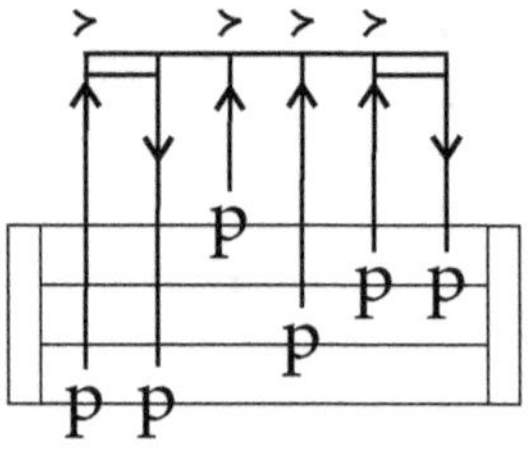

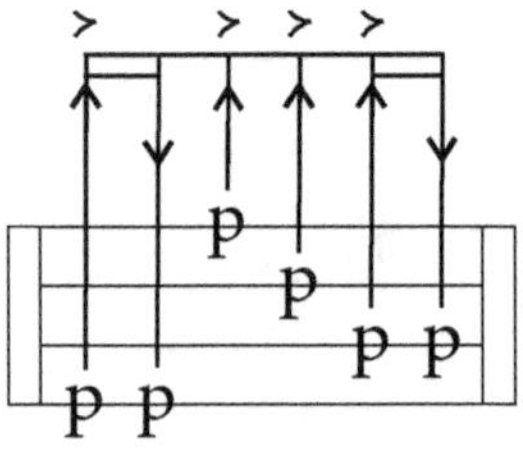

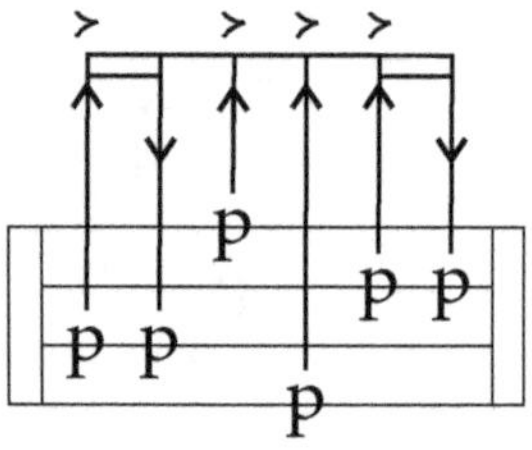

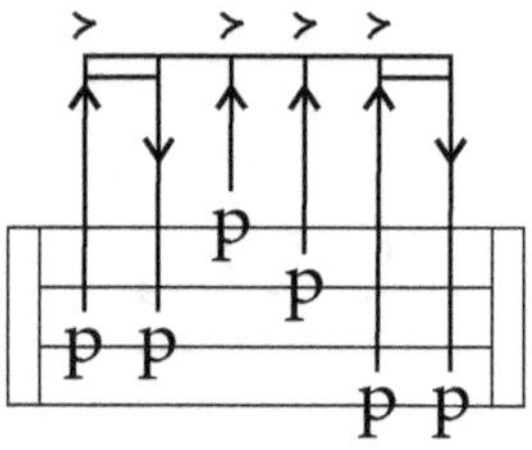

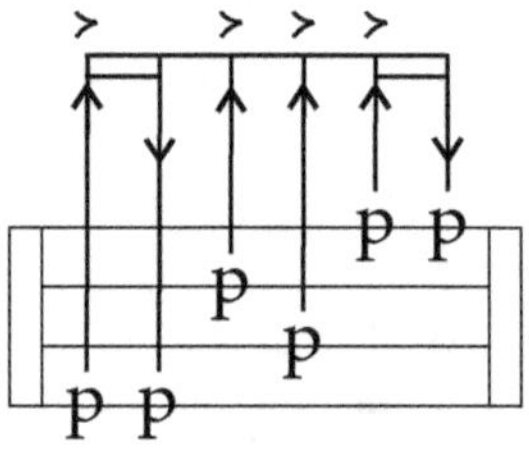

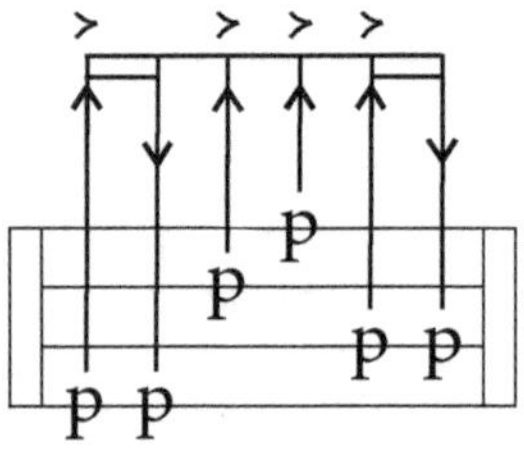

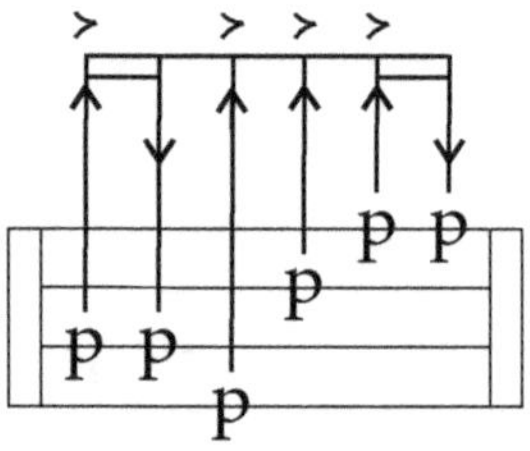

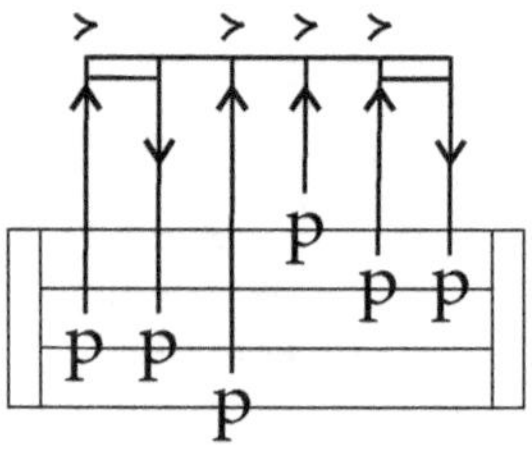

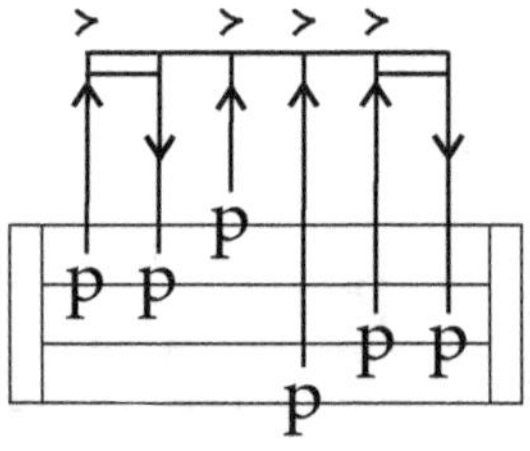

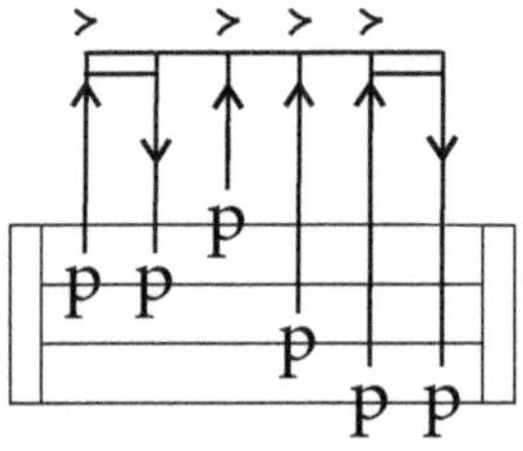

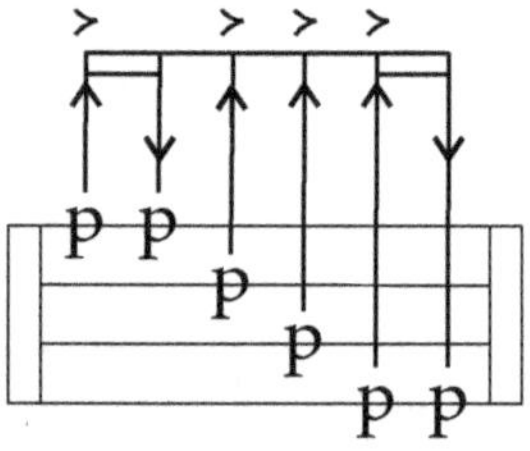

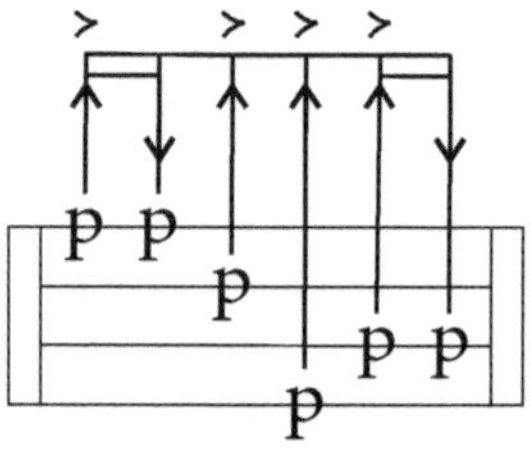

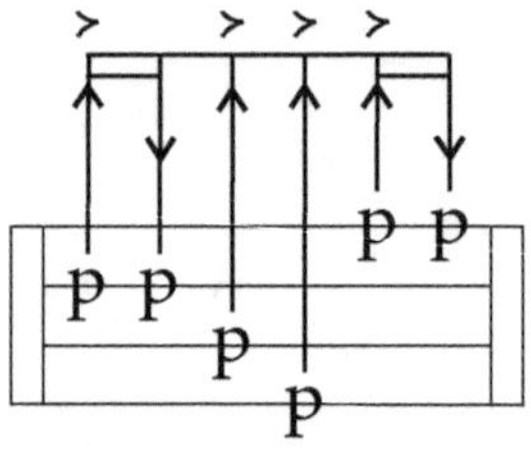

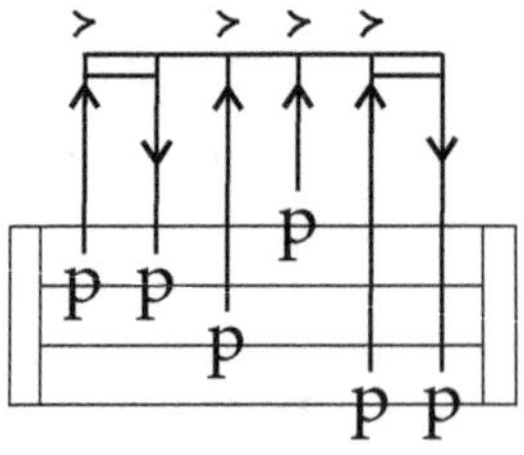

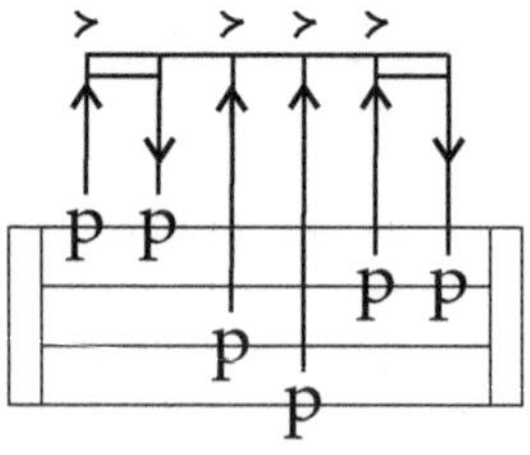

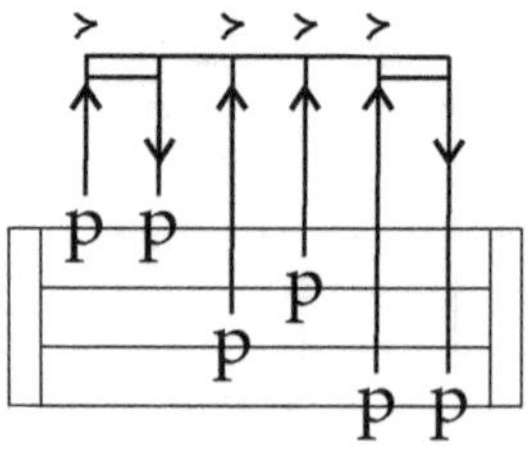

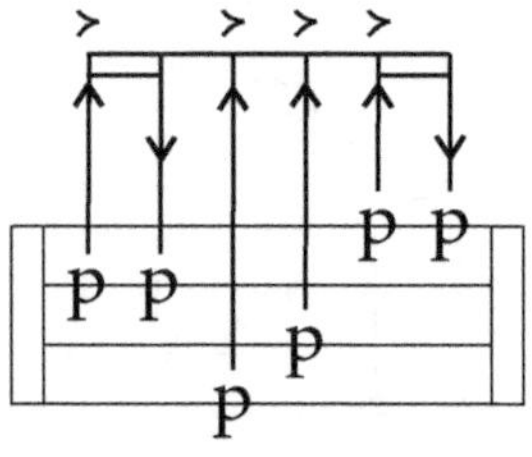

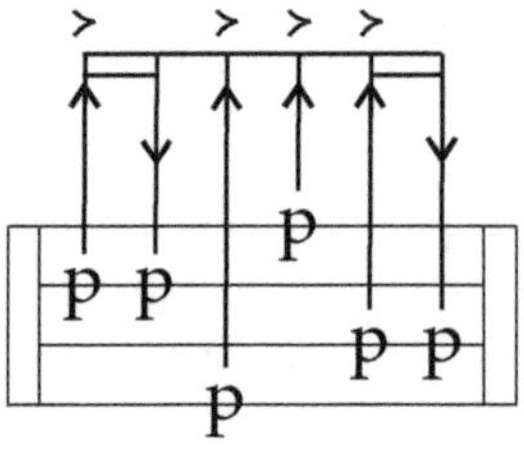

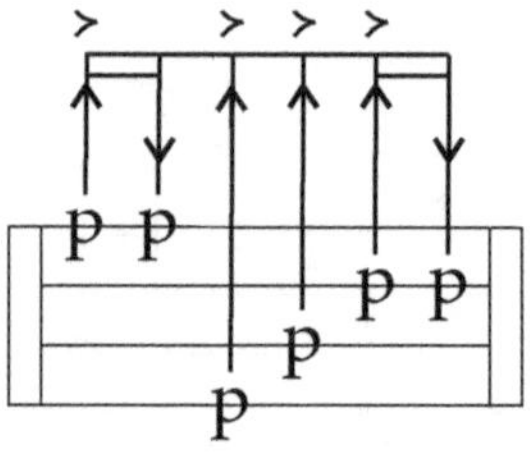

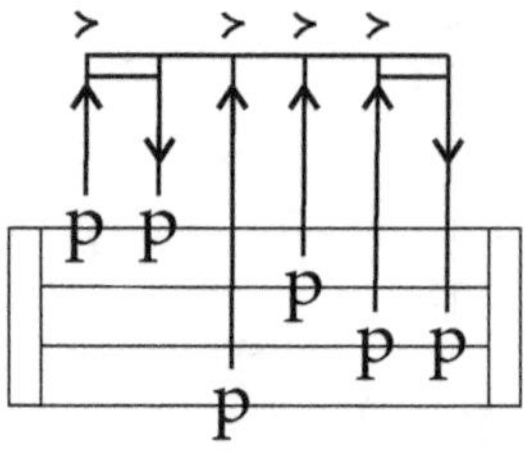

VARIATION V

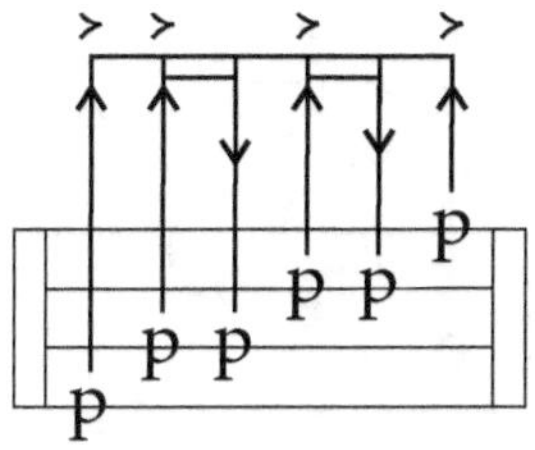

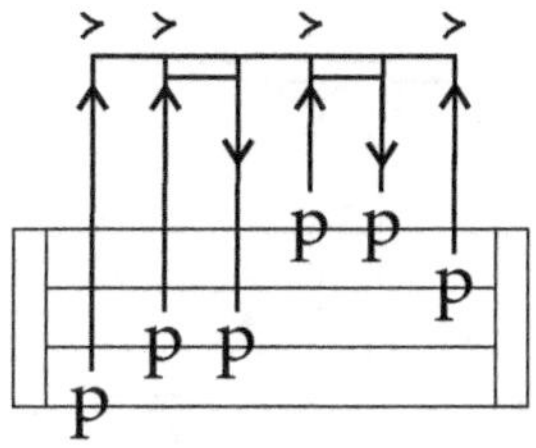

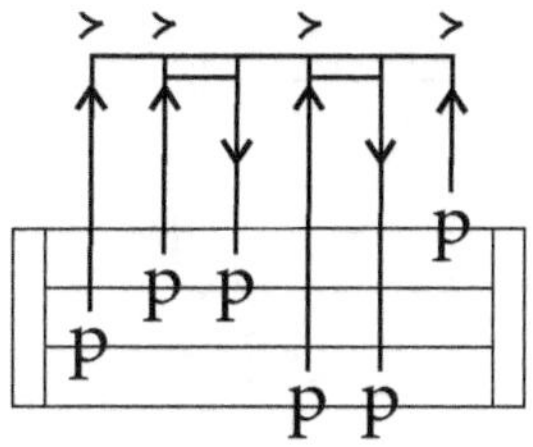

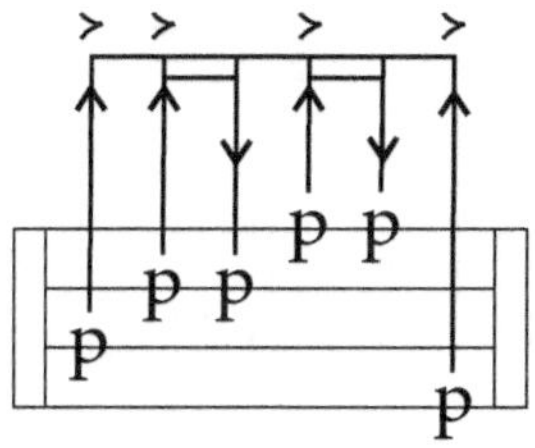

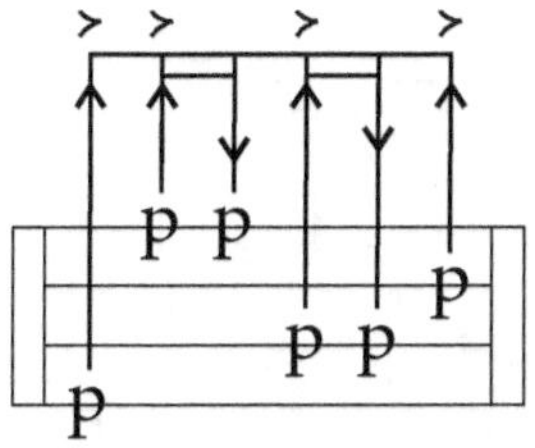

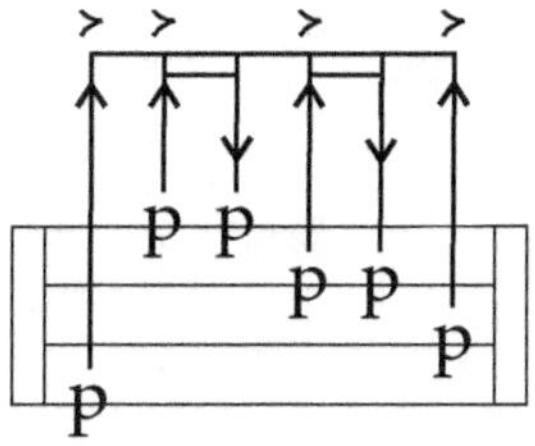

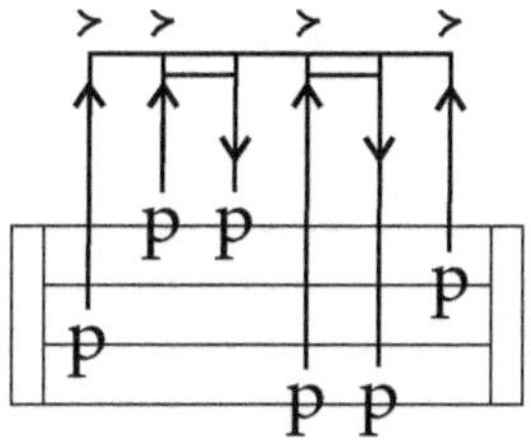

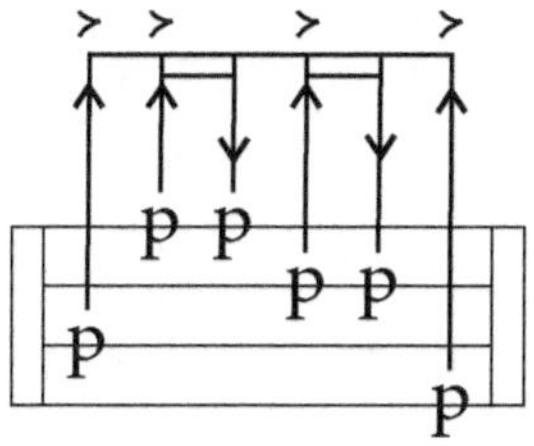

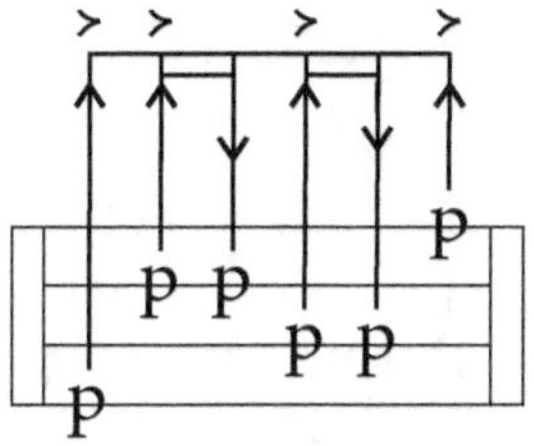

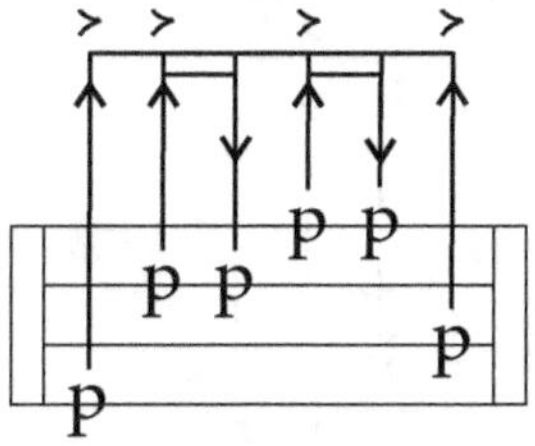

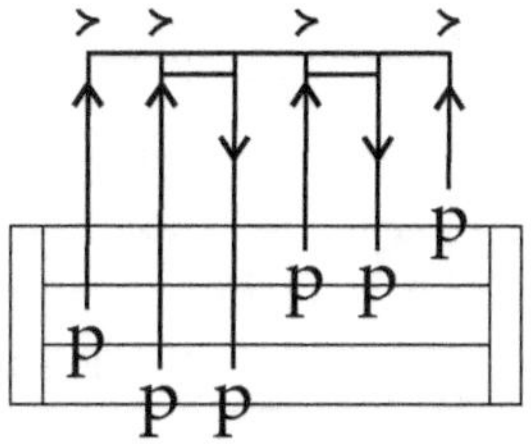

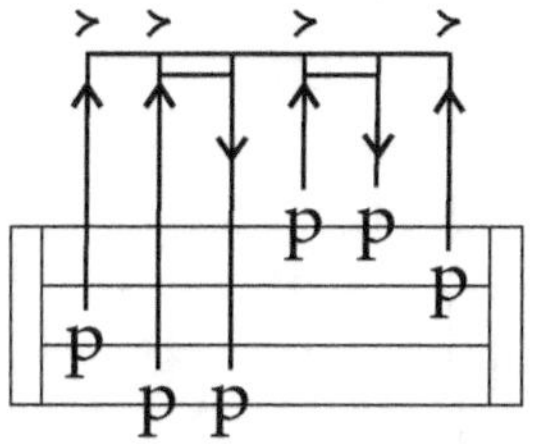

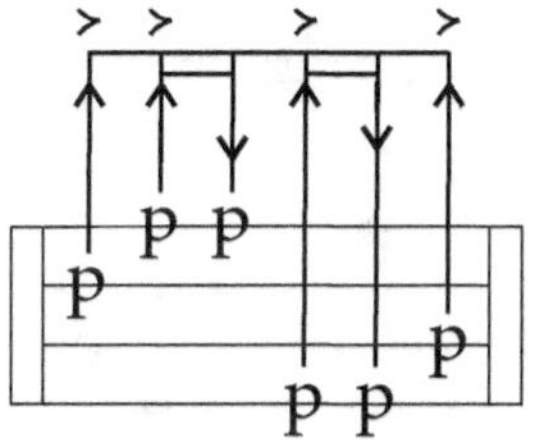

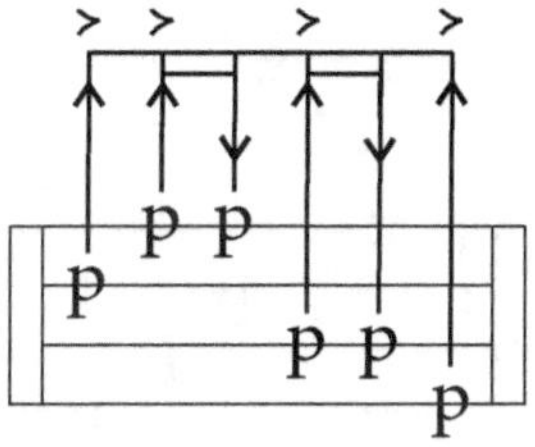

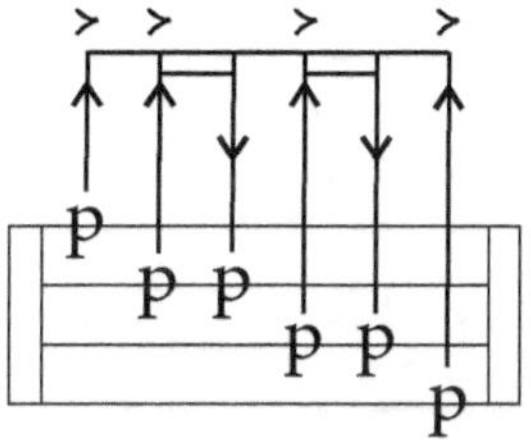

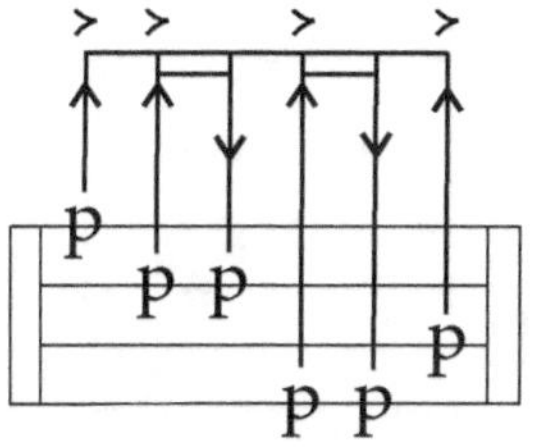

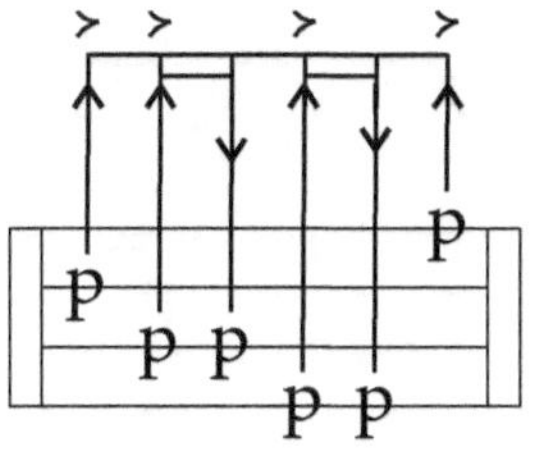

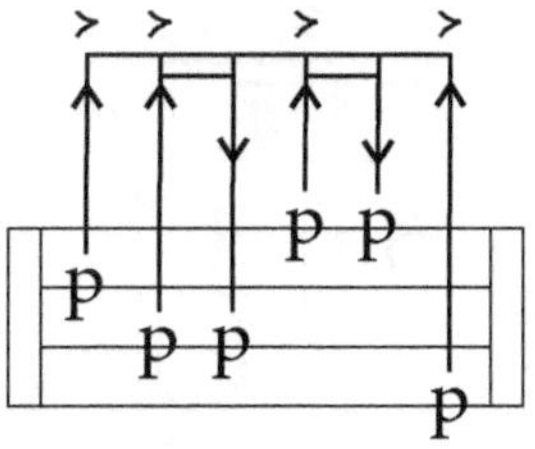

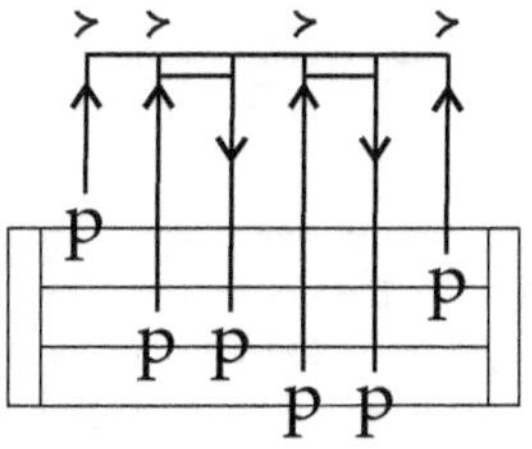

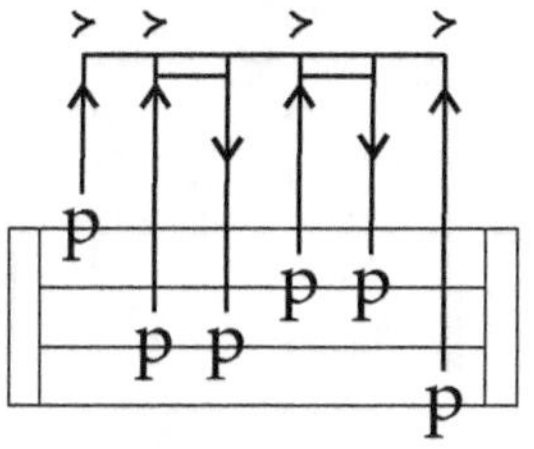

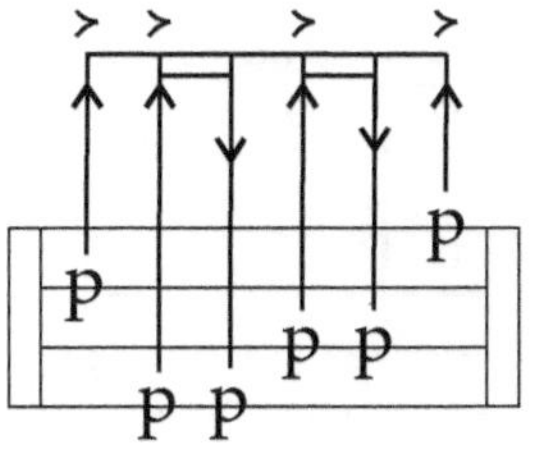

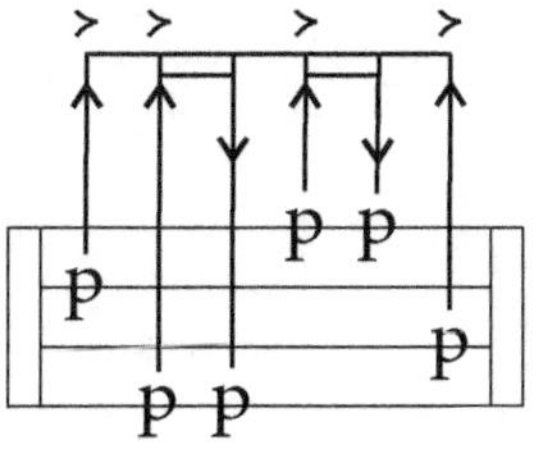

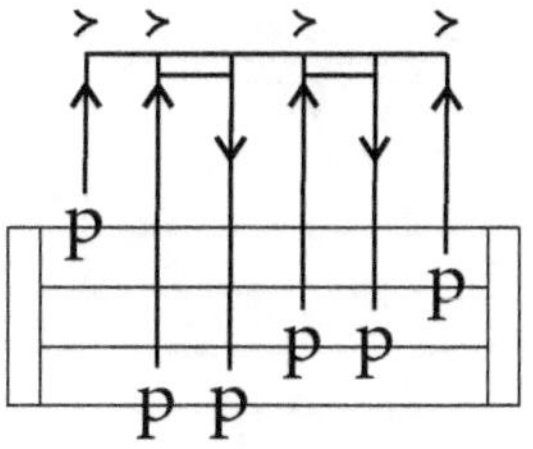

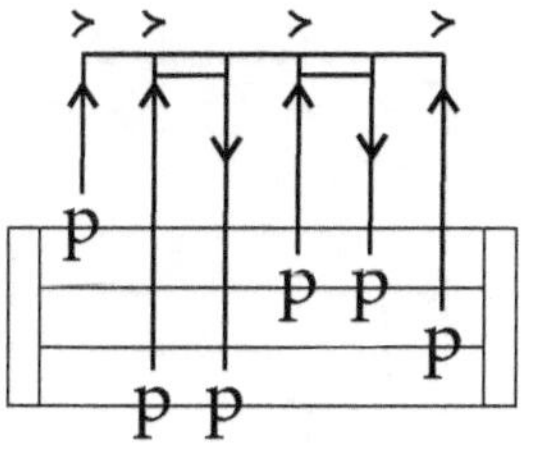

VARIATION VI

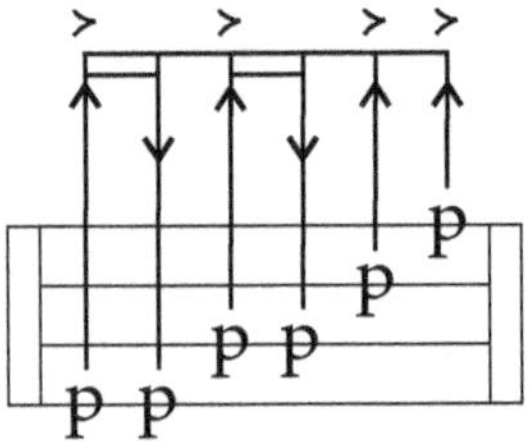

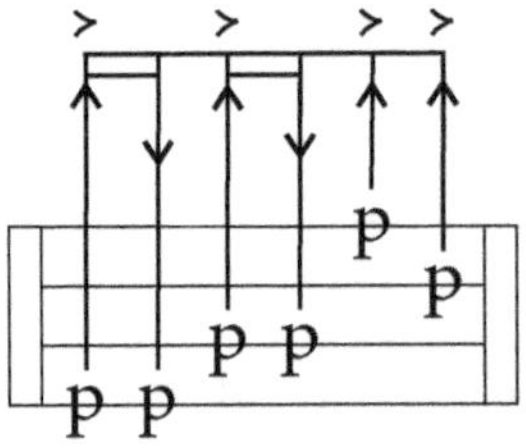

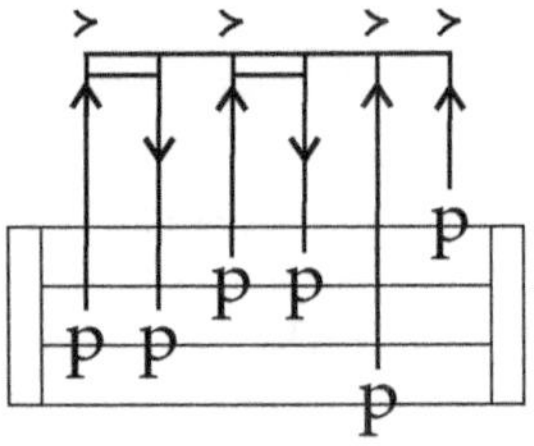

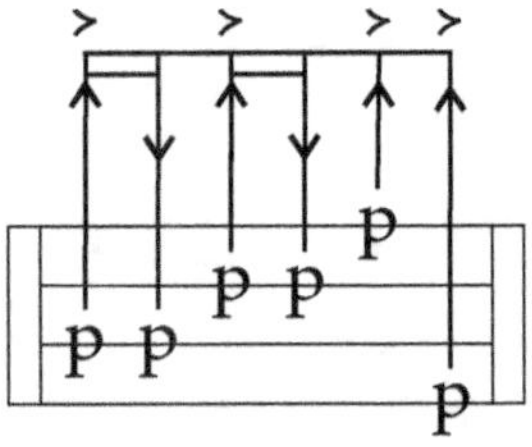

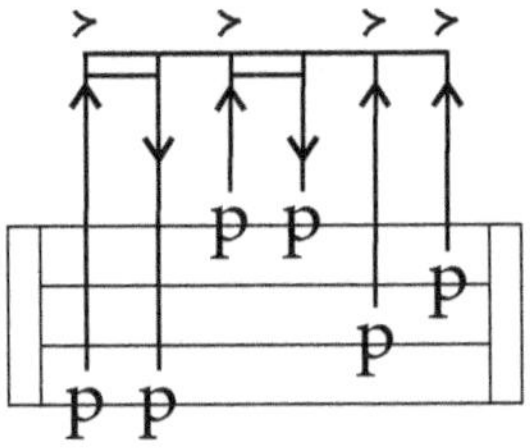

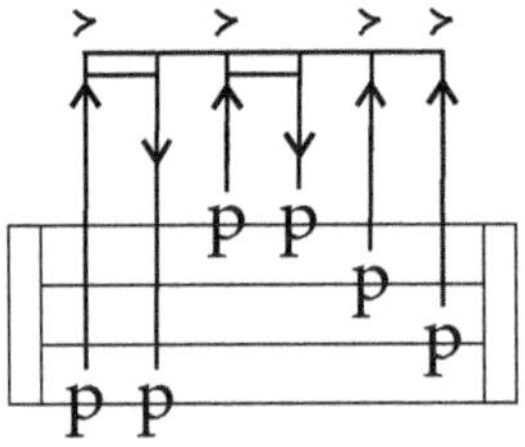

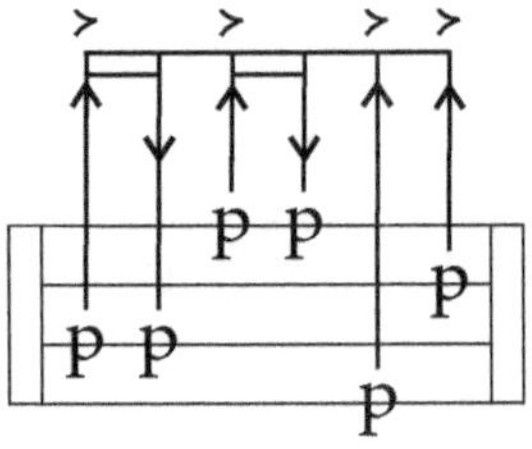

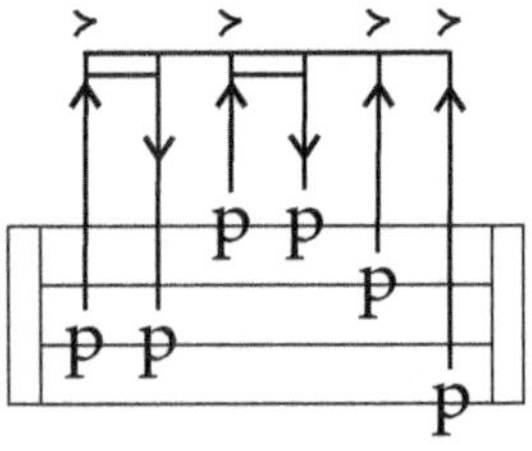

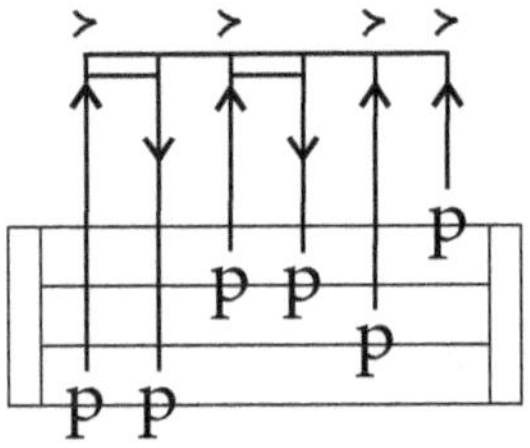

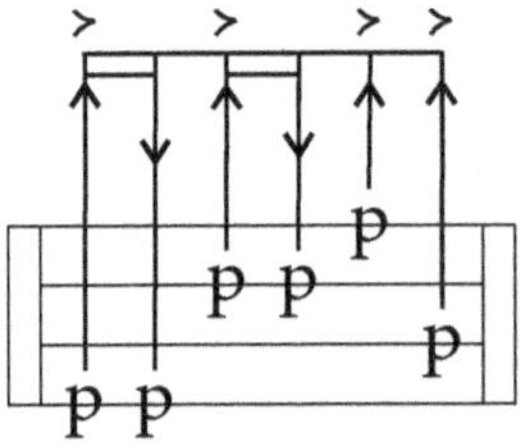

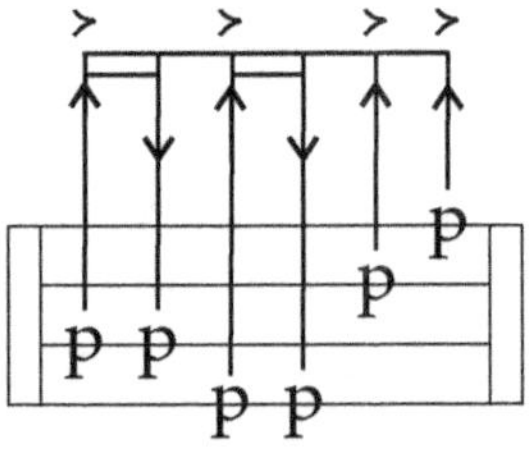

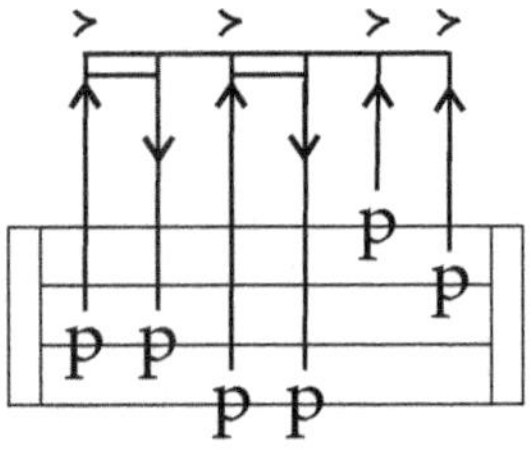

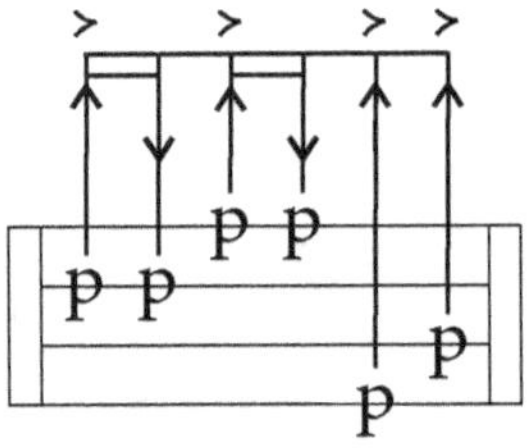

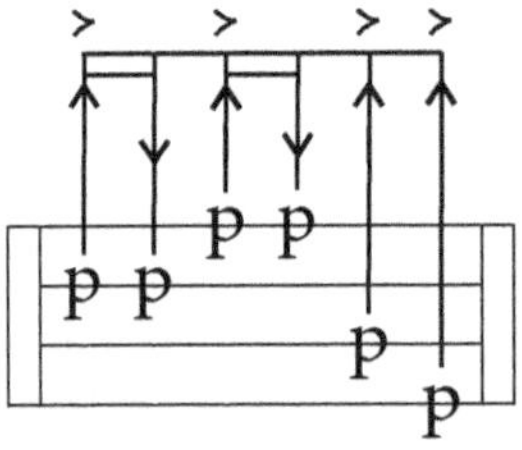

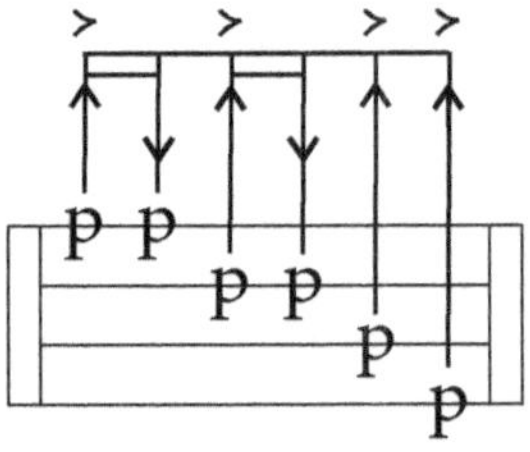

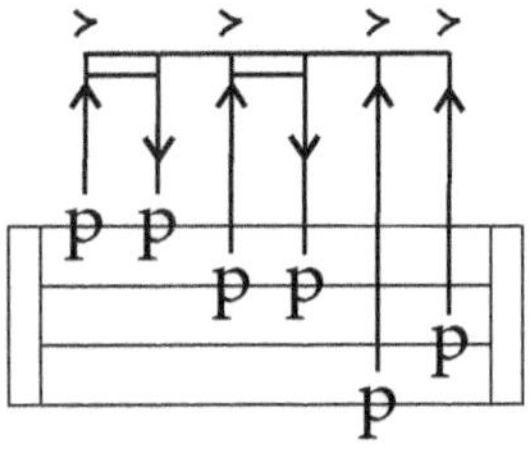

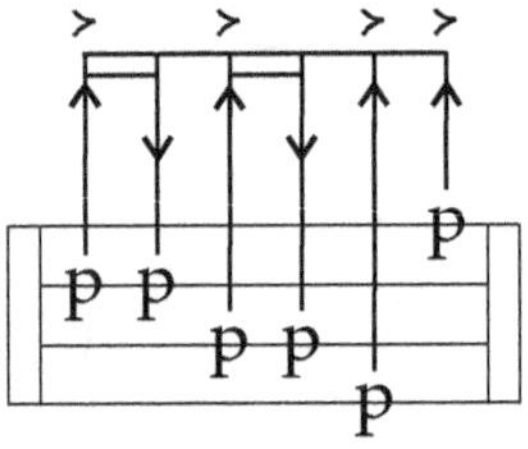

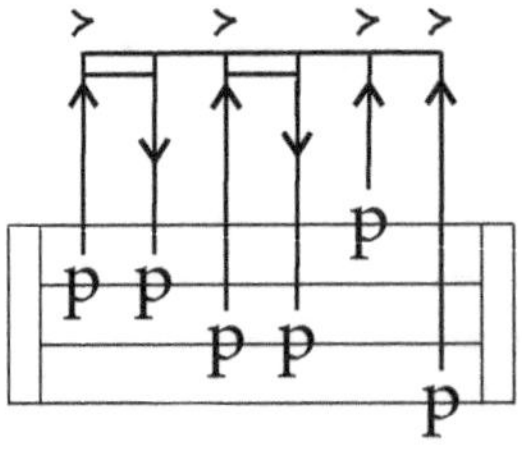

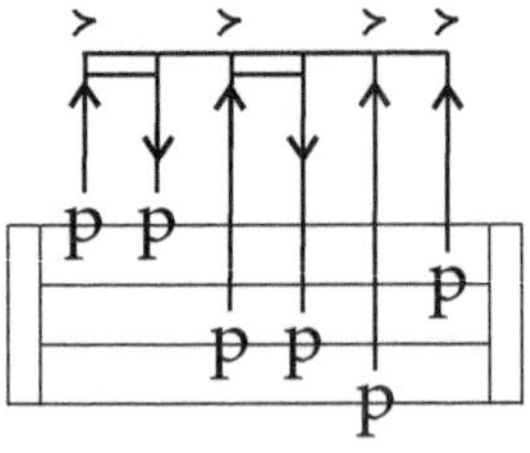

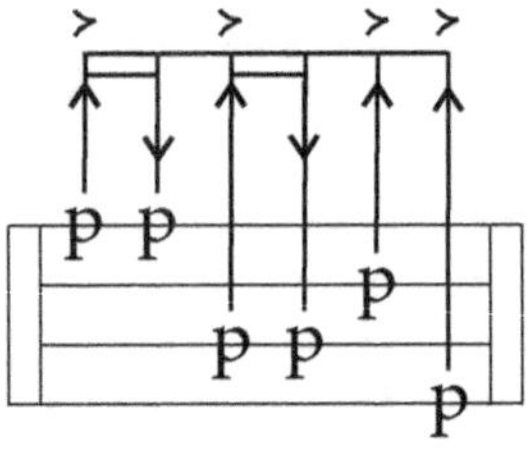

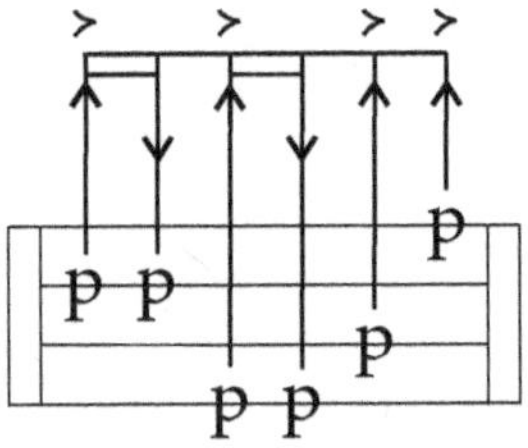

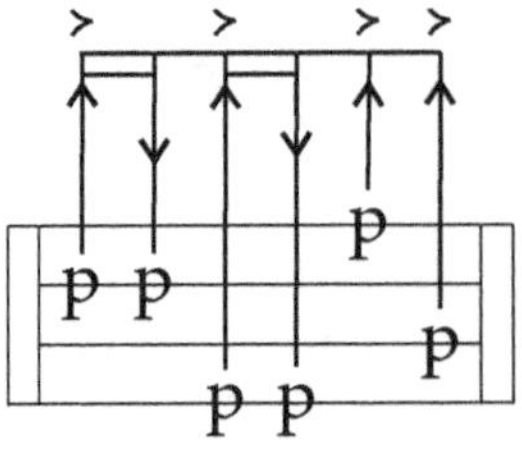

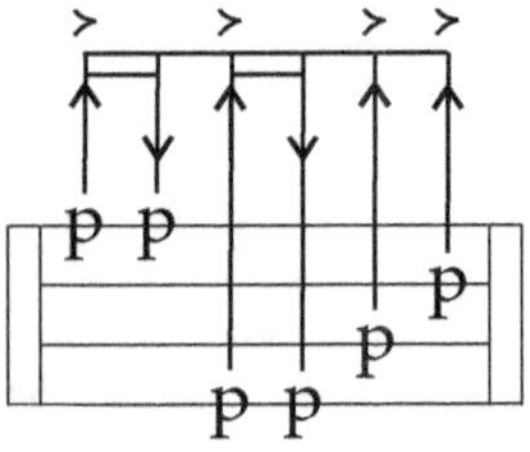

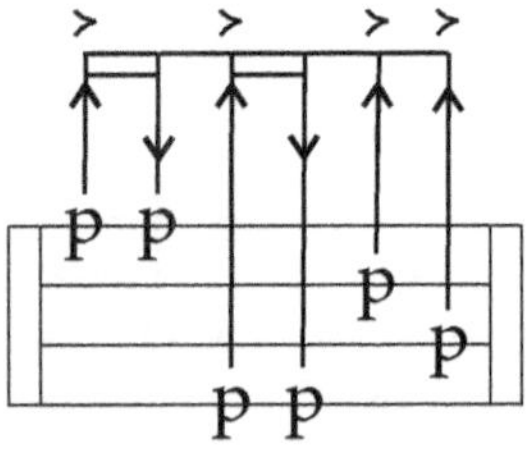

§ V

Exercise on pulgar on four adjacent strings with four triple strokes (triplets) within each Formula. You can alternatively practice on the 24 Formulas in the following way. The first Formula is cited below.

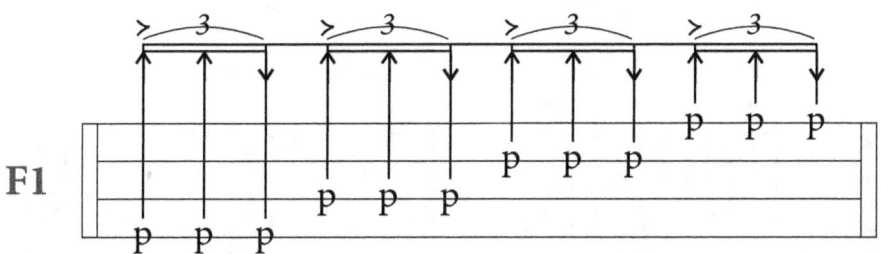

You can also apply successively the two performance modes within each Formula. For example:

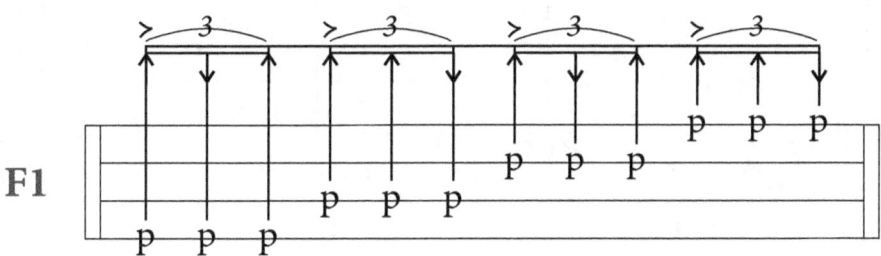

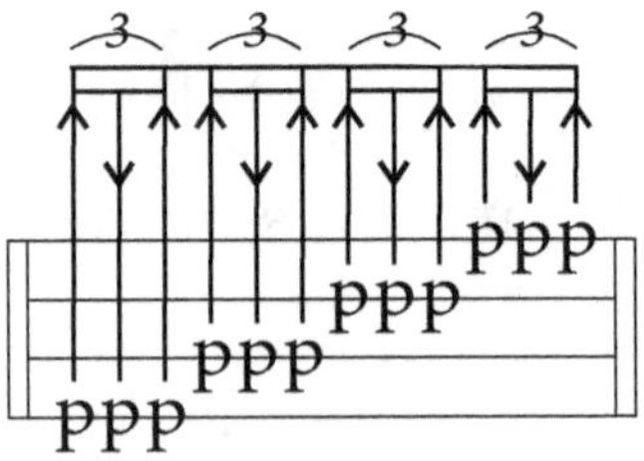

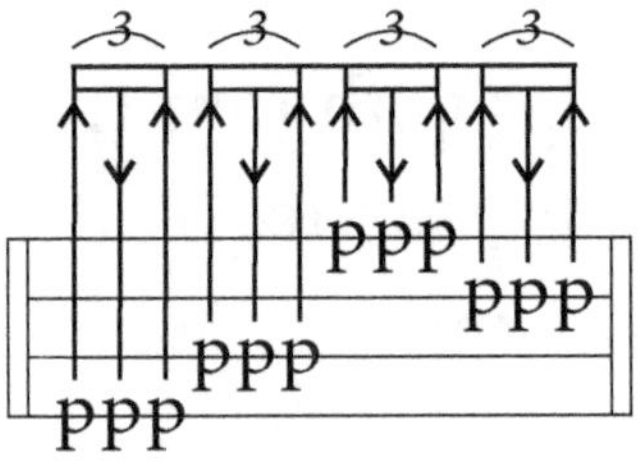

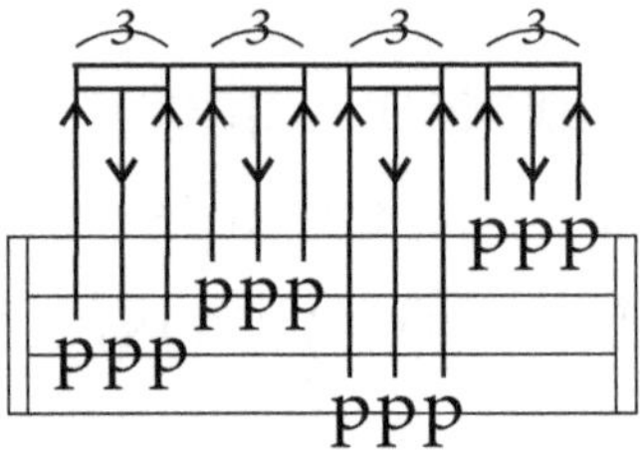

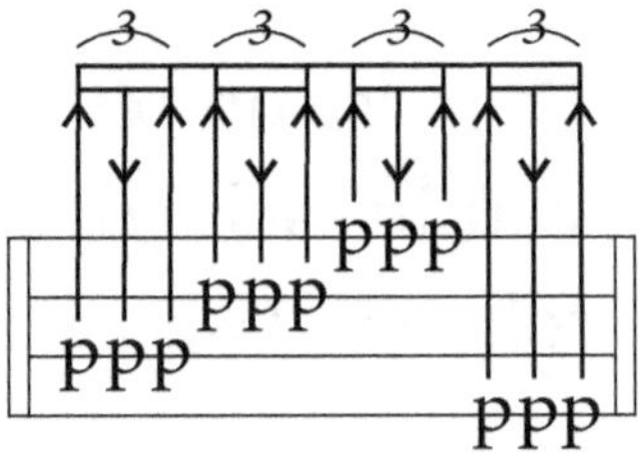

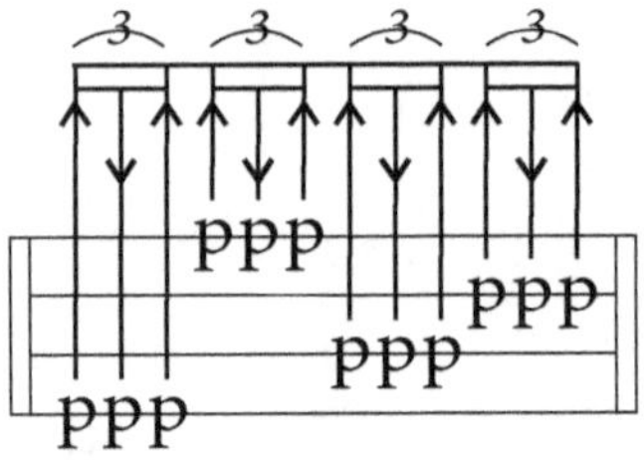

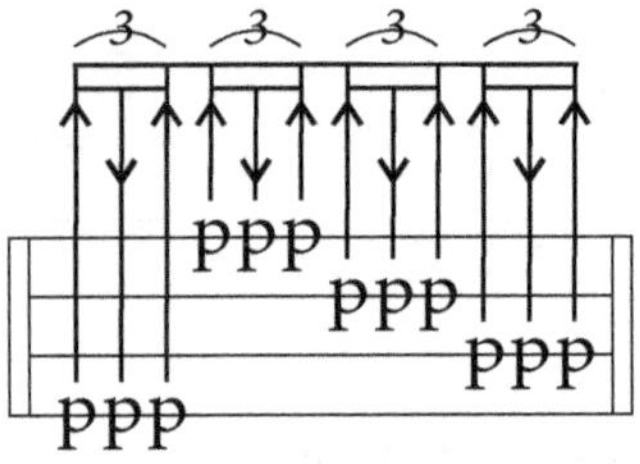

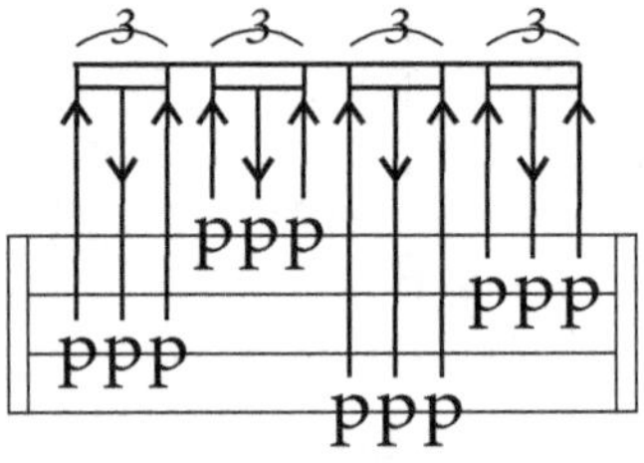

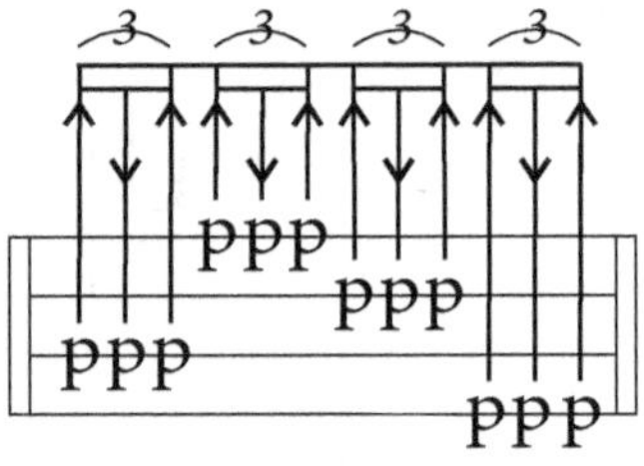

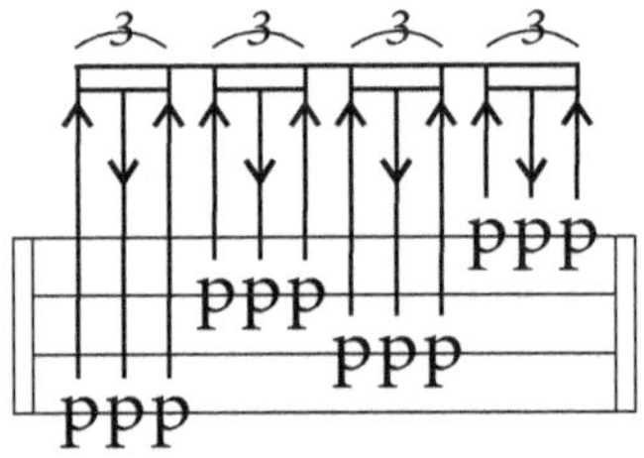

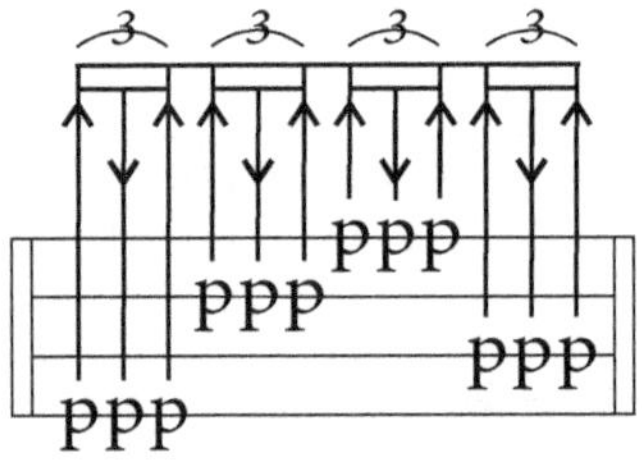

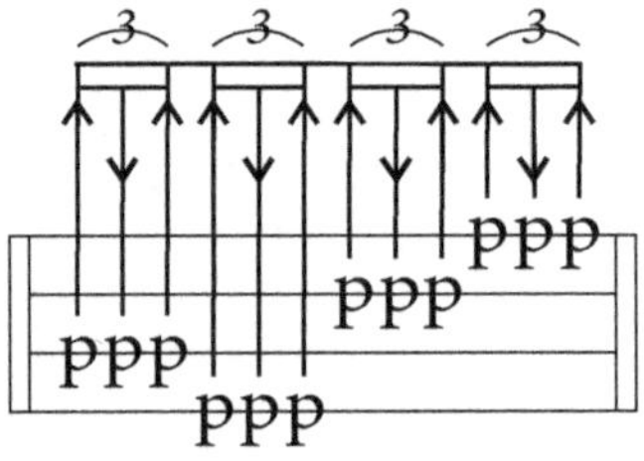

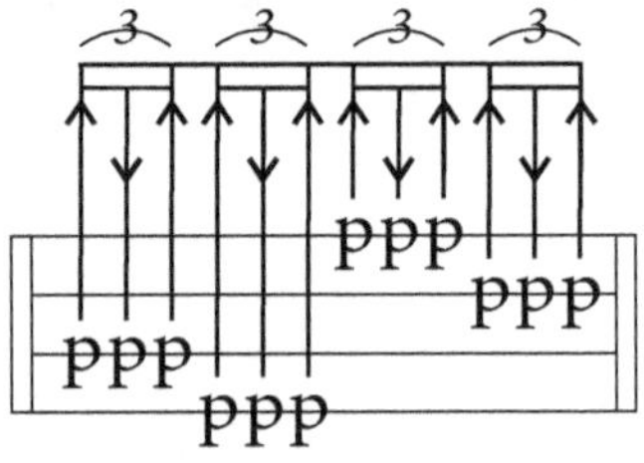

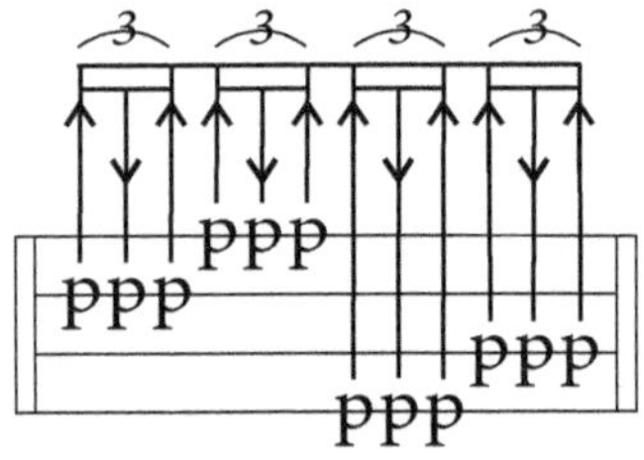

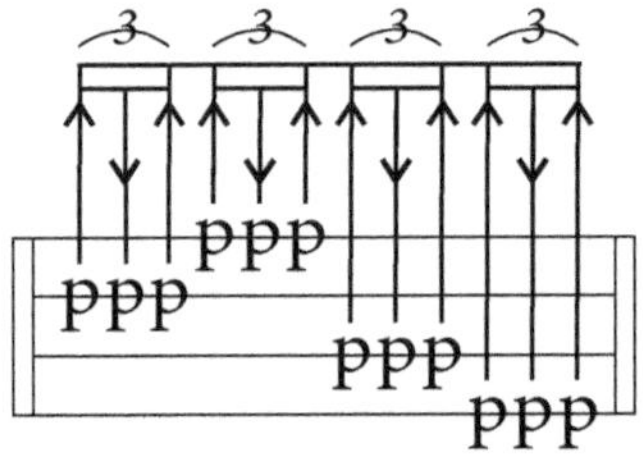

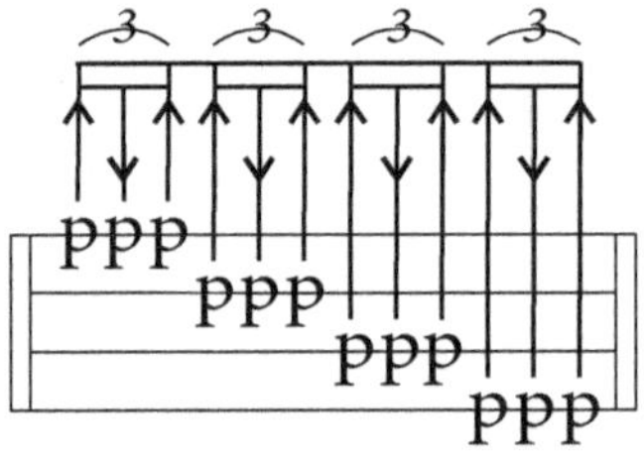

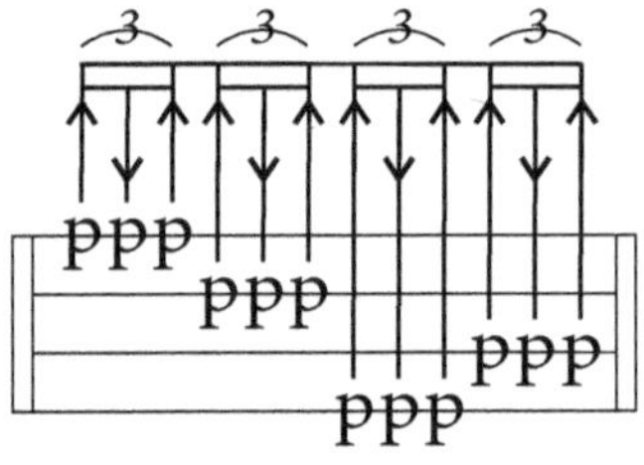

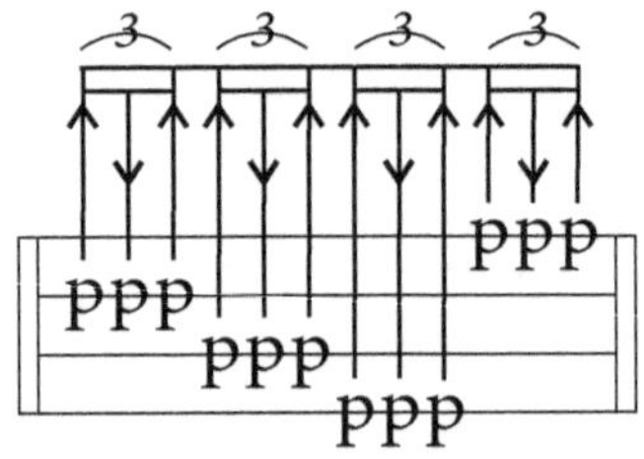

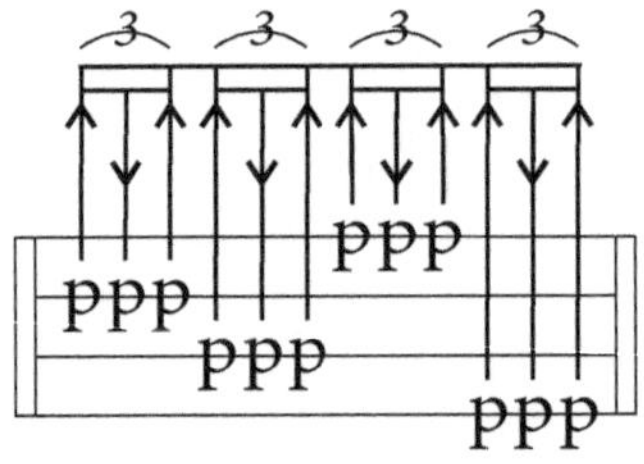

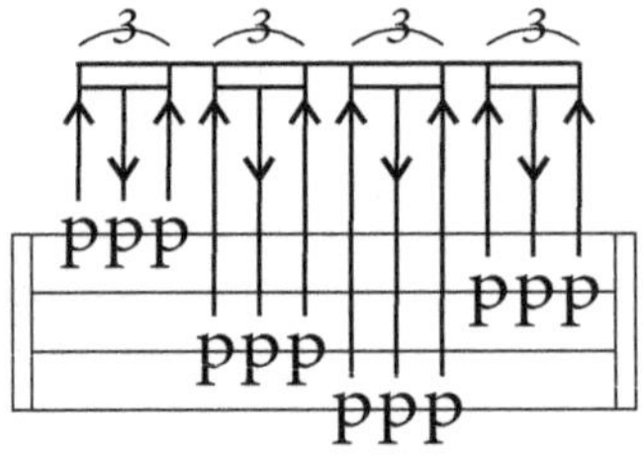

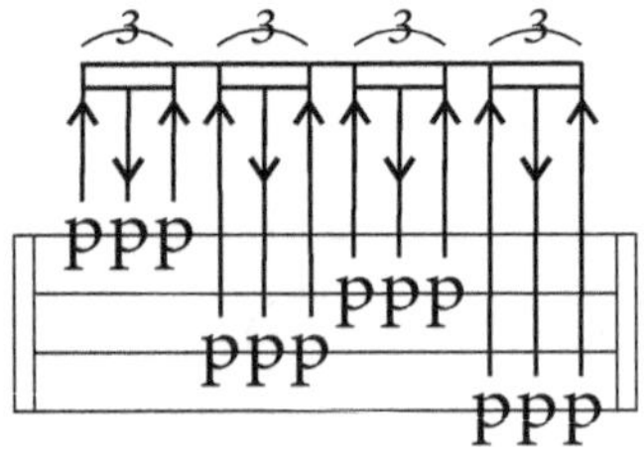

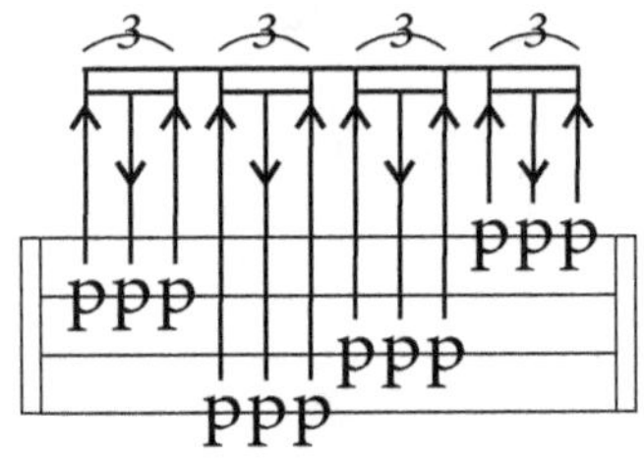

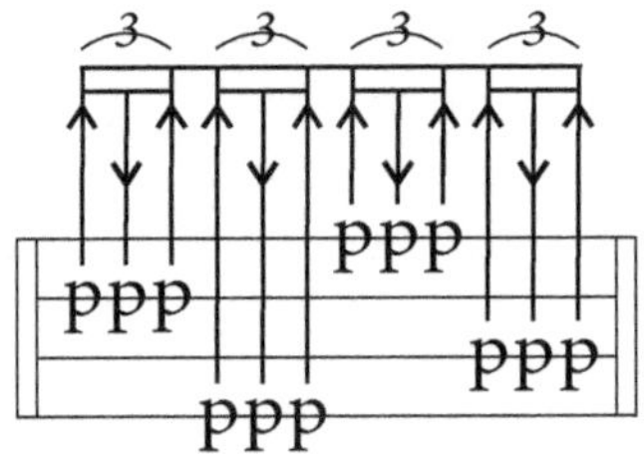

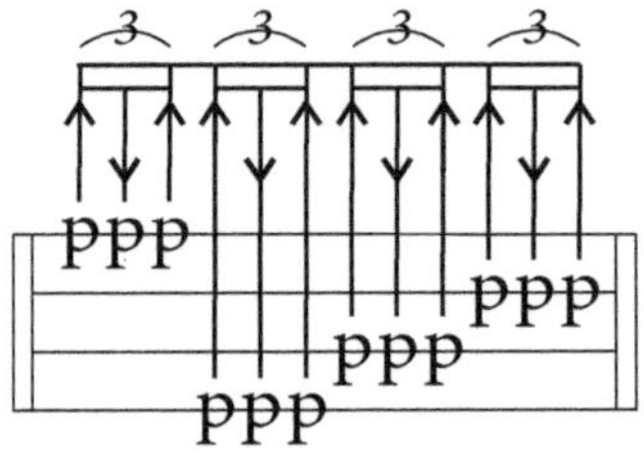

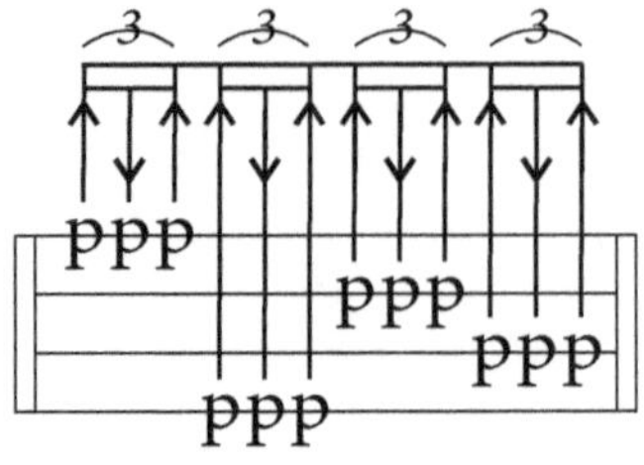

§ VI

Exercise on pulgar on four adjacent strings with two double and two triple (triplets) strokes within each Formula. The exercise contains six variations with 24 Formulas in each one. The first Formula of each variation is cited below. Isochronous playing of pulgar strokes (double and triple).

VARIATION I
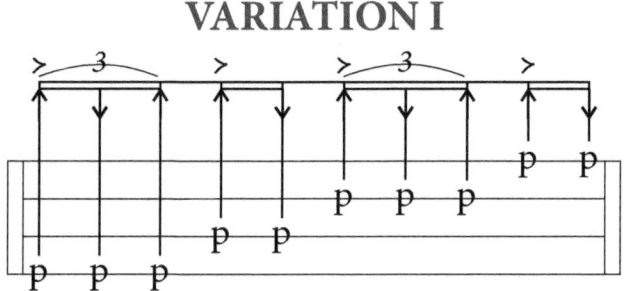

VARIATION IV
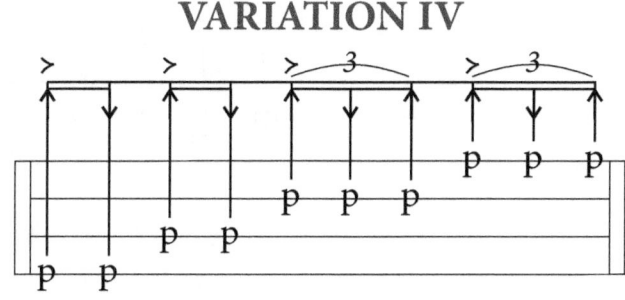

VARIATION II
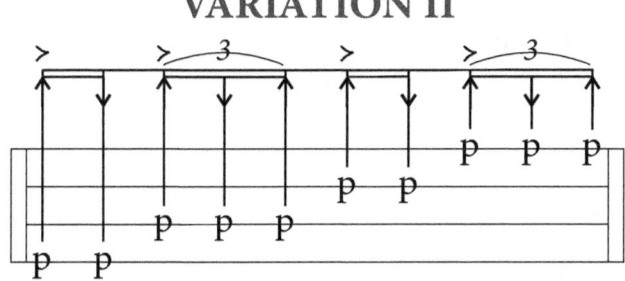

VARIATION V
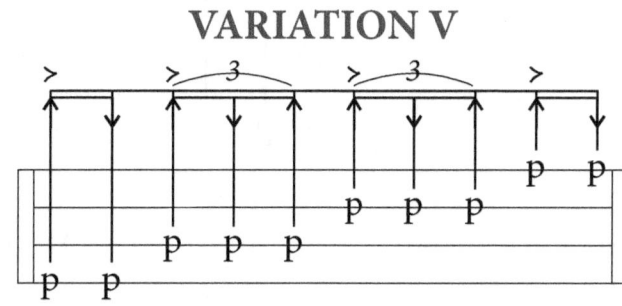

VARIATION III
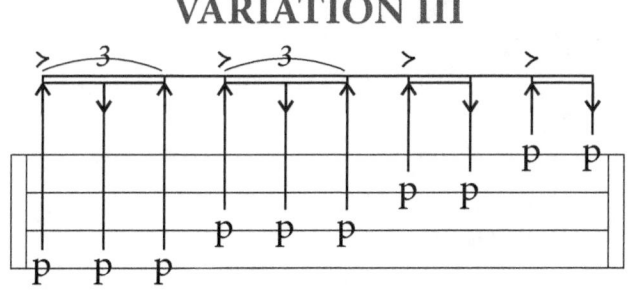

VARIATION VI
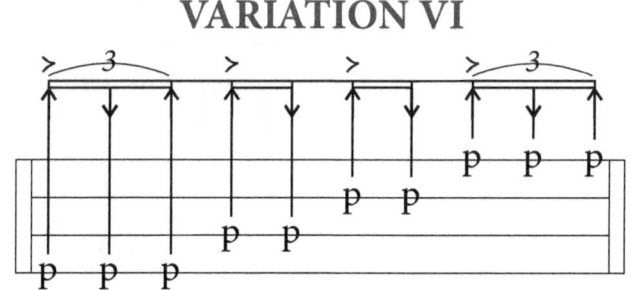

Practice in the following ways of pulgar stroke:

VARIATION I (1st mode)

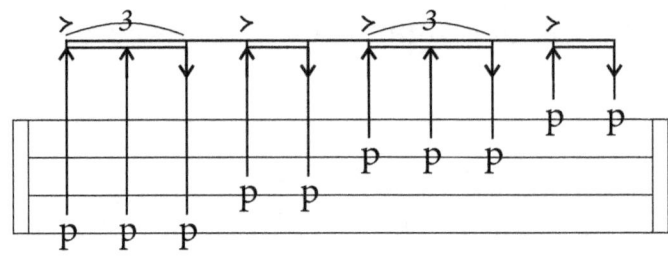

VARIATION I (2nd mode)

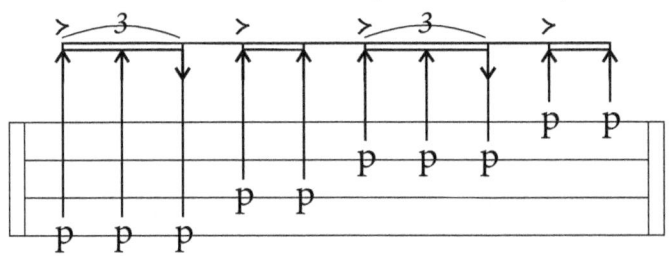

VARIATION I (3rd mode)

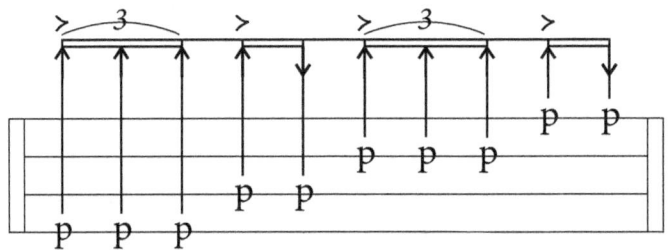

VARIATION I (4th mode)

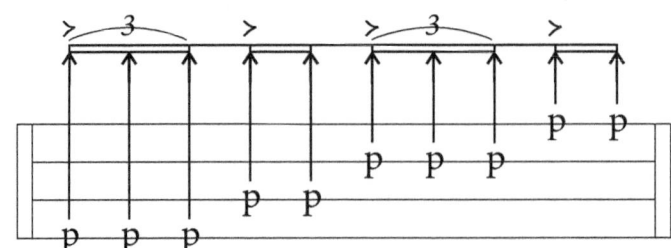

VARIATION I

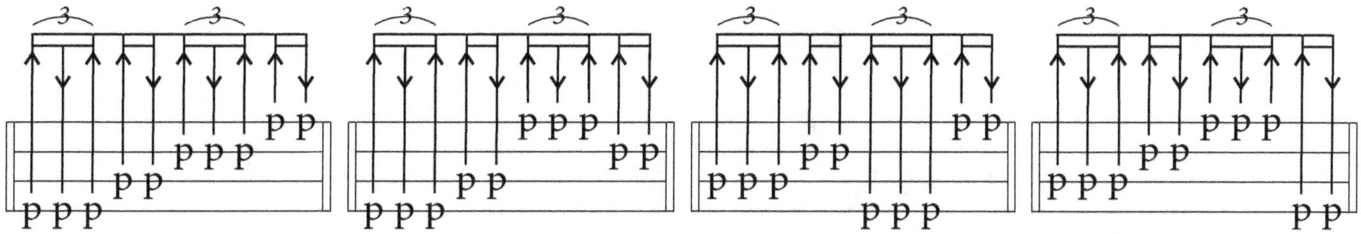

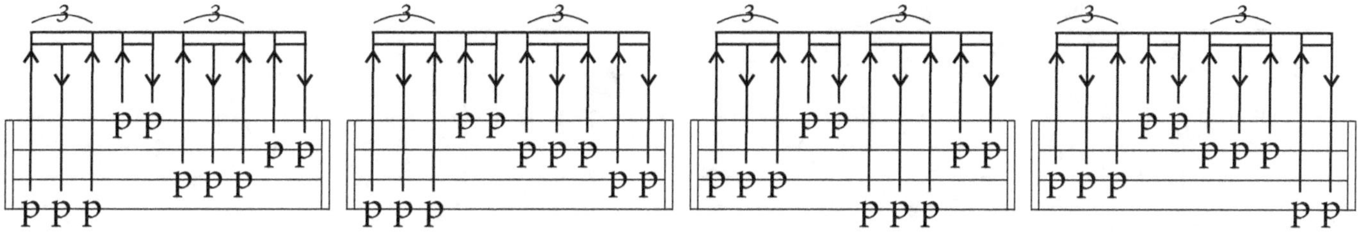

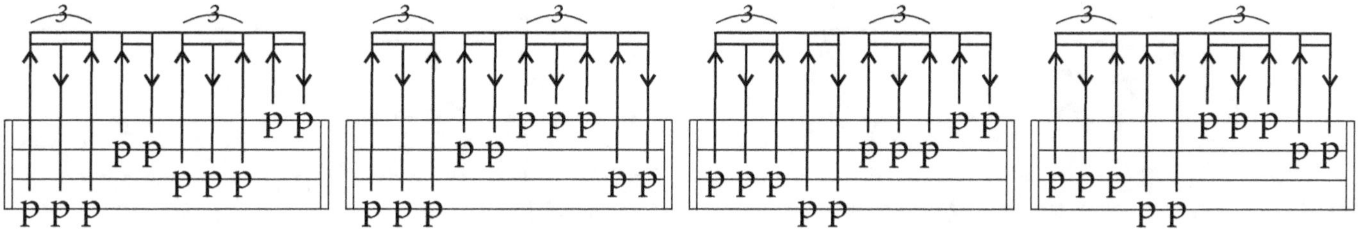

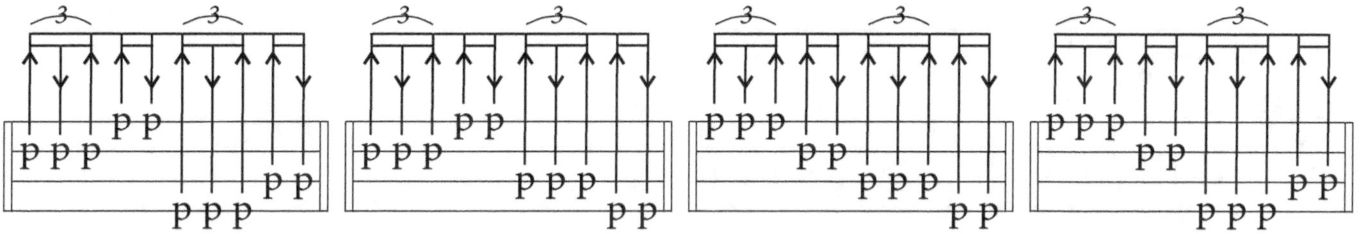

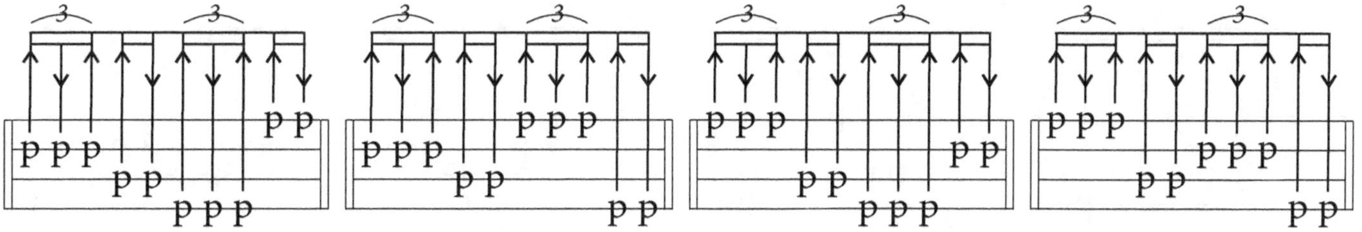

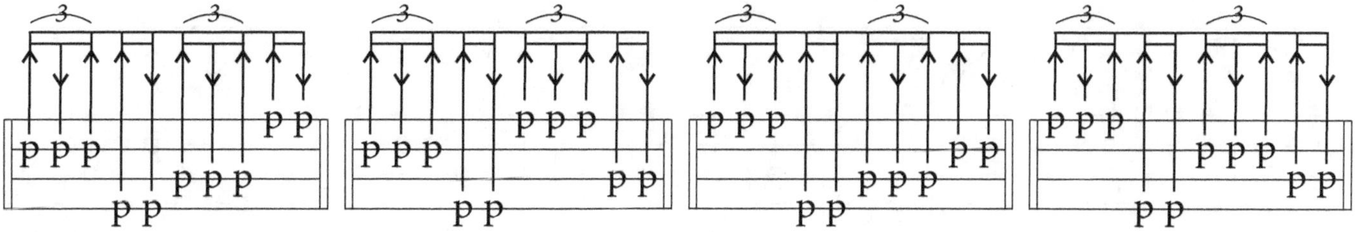

VARIATION II

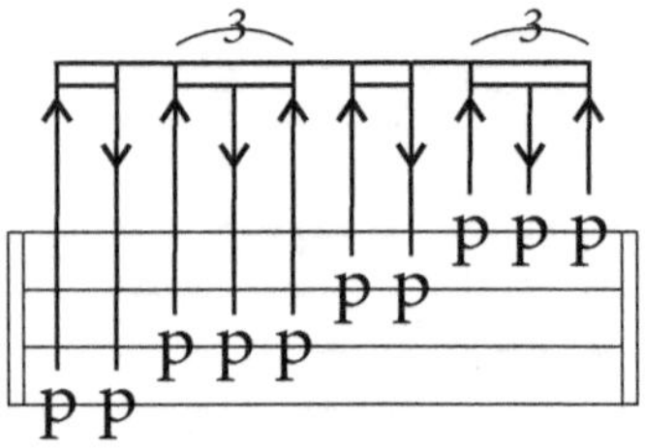

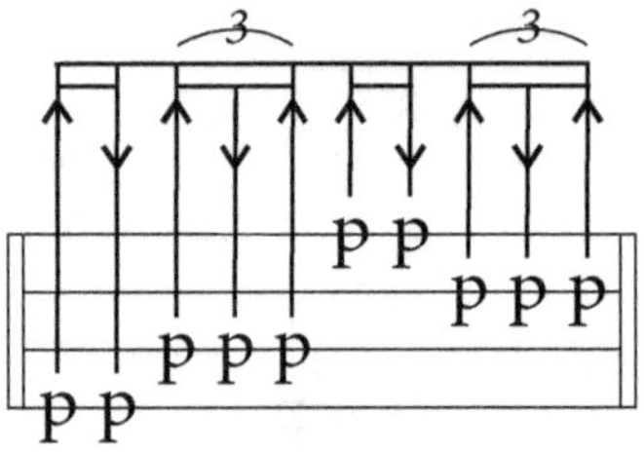

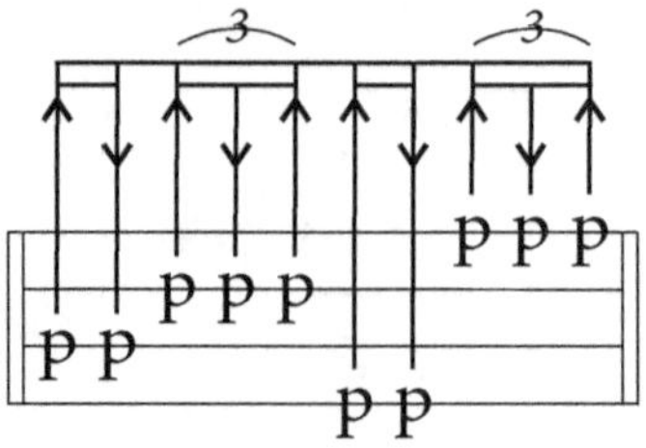

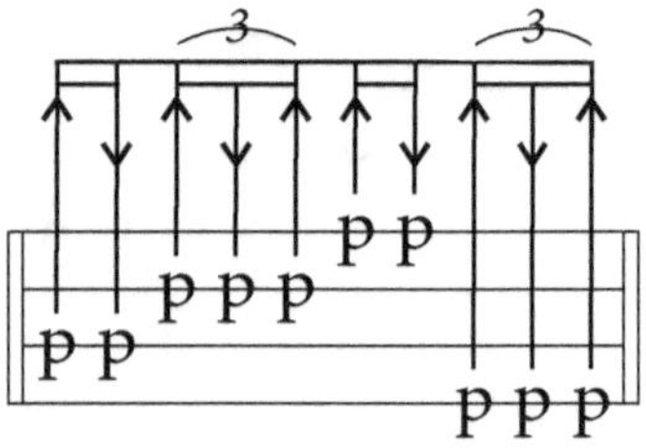

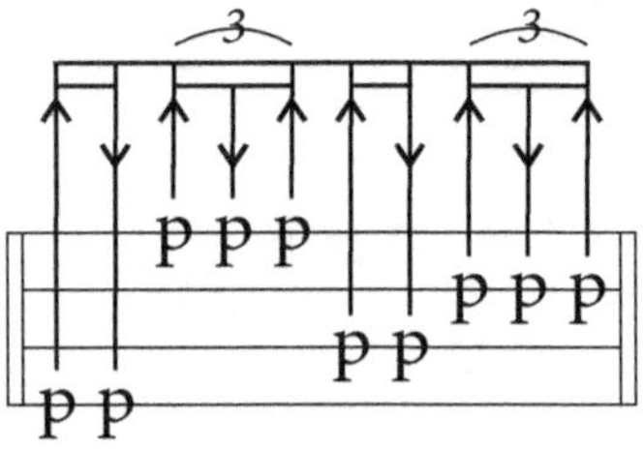

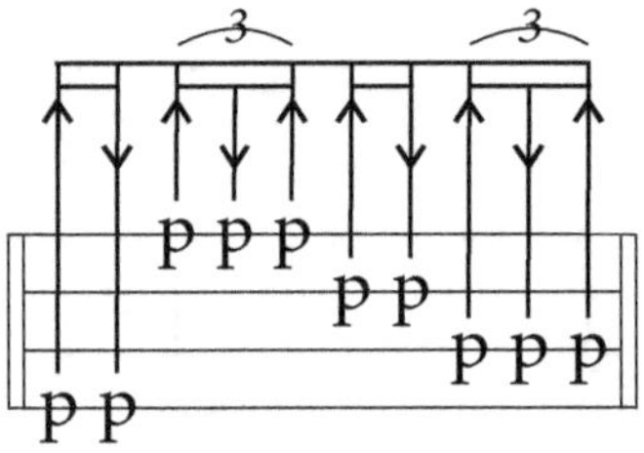

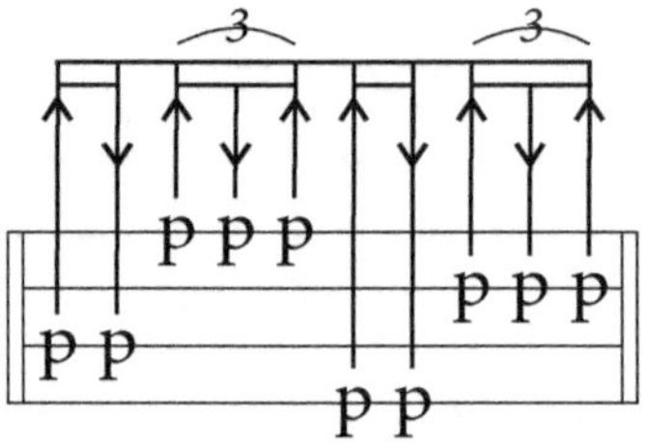

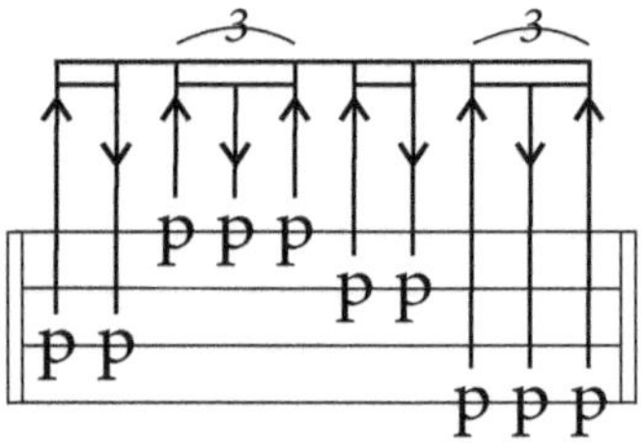

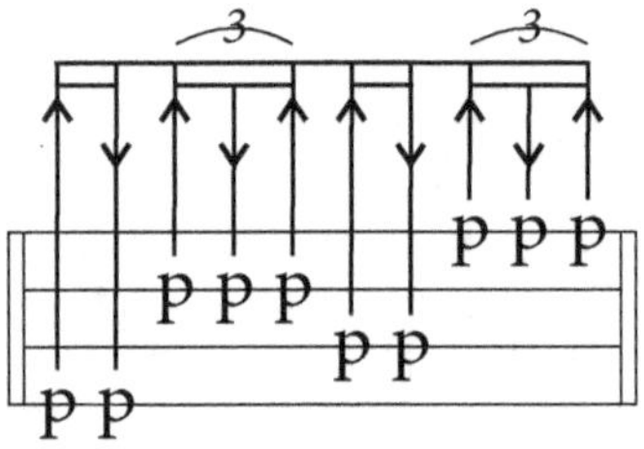

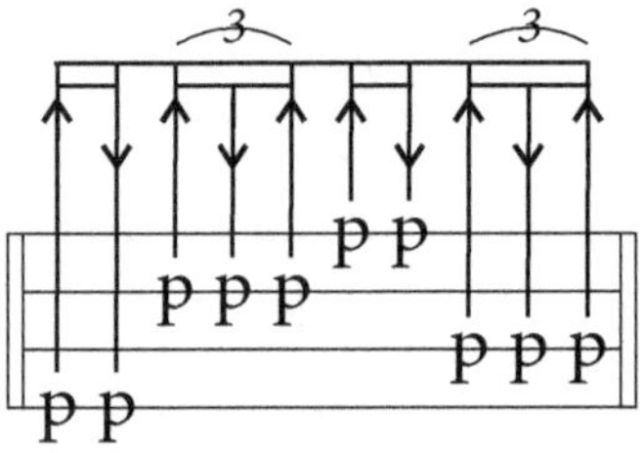

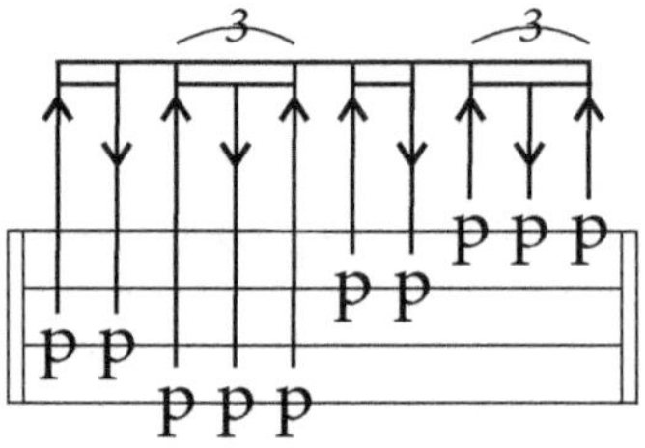

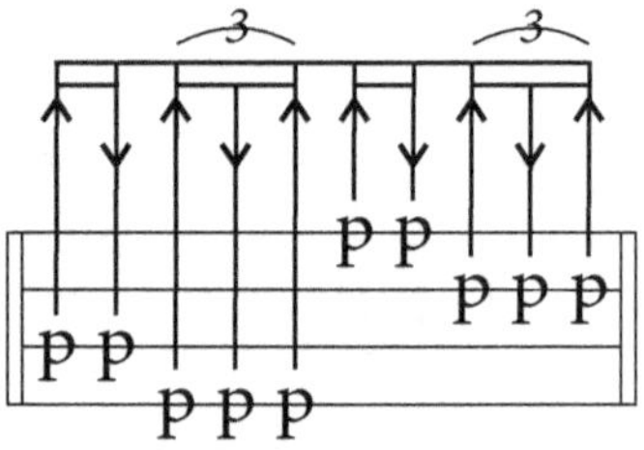

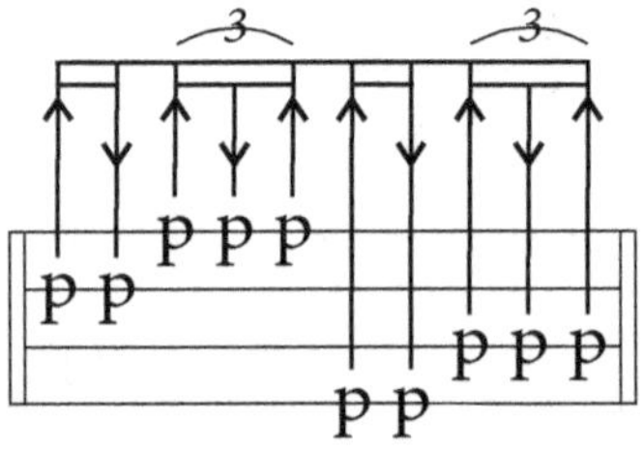

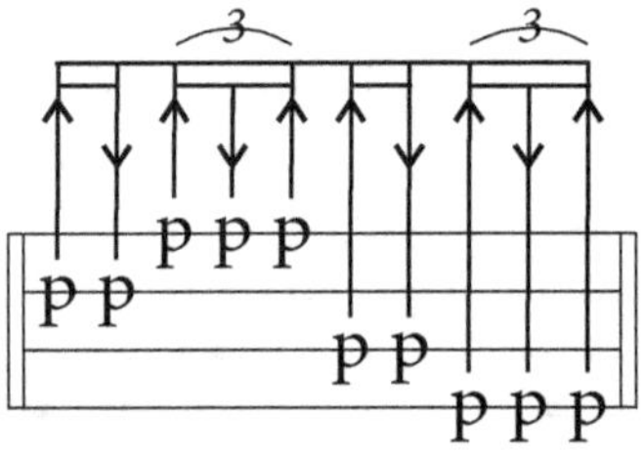

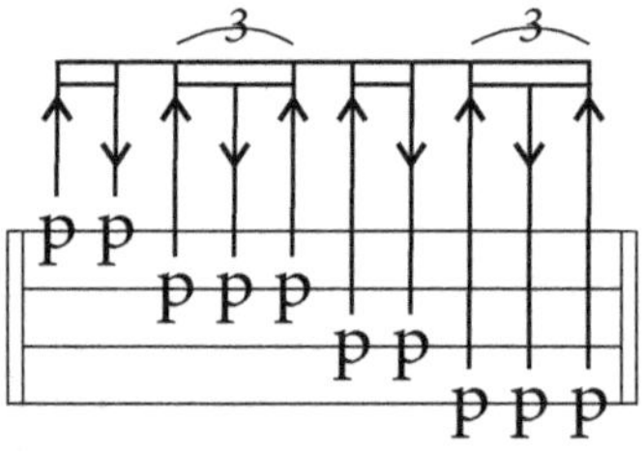

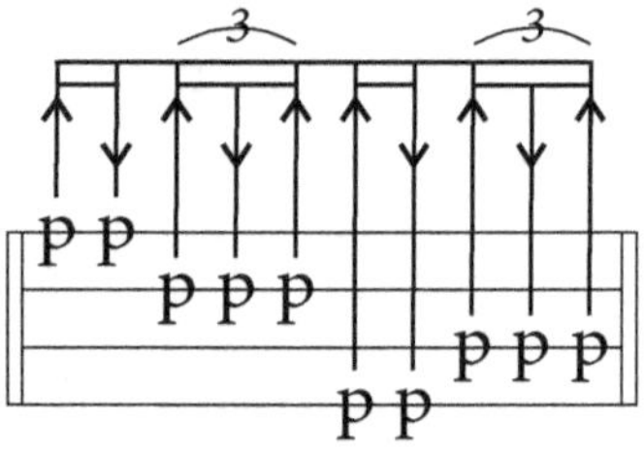

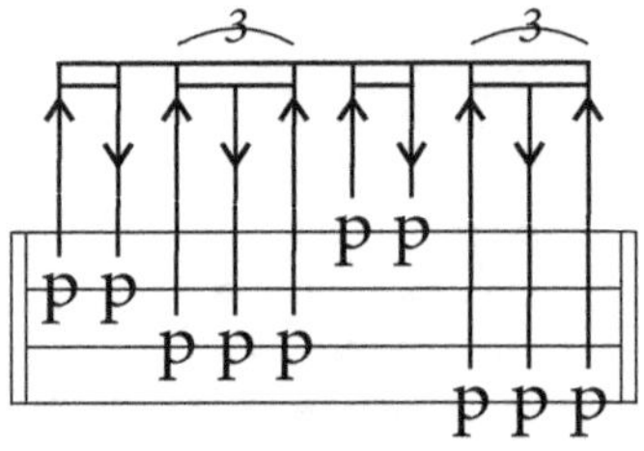

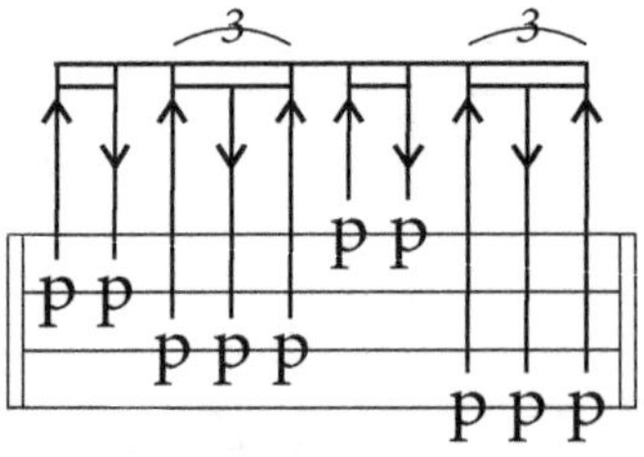

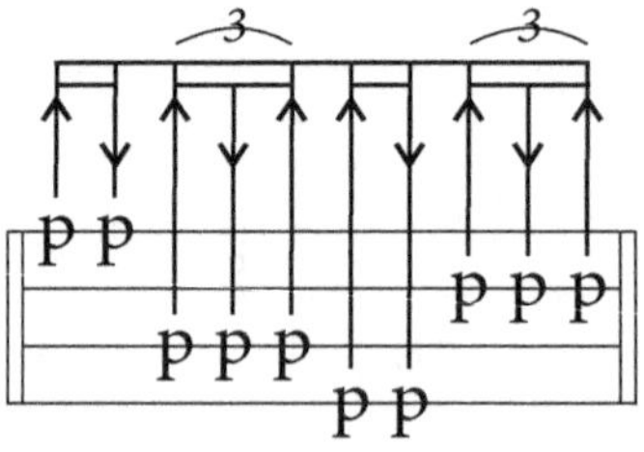

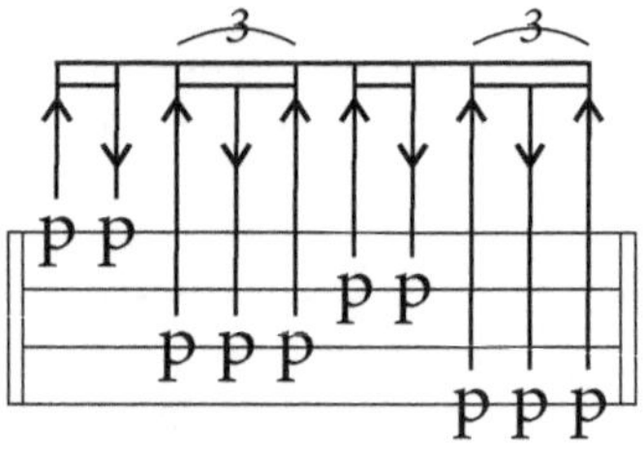

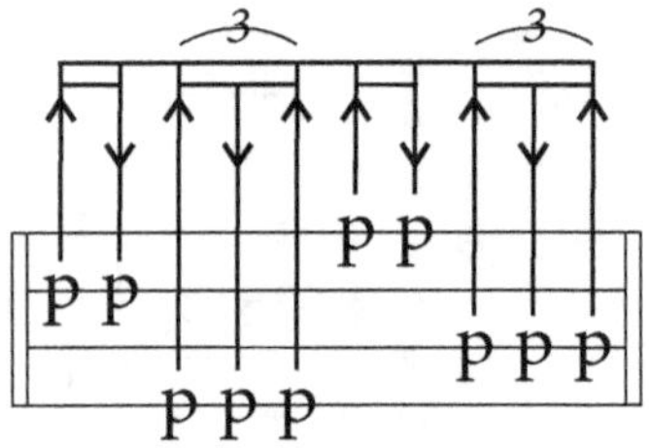

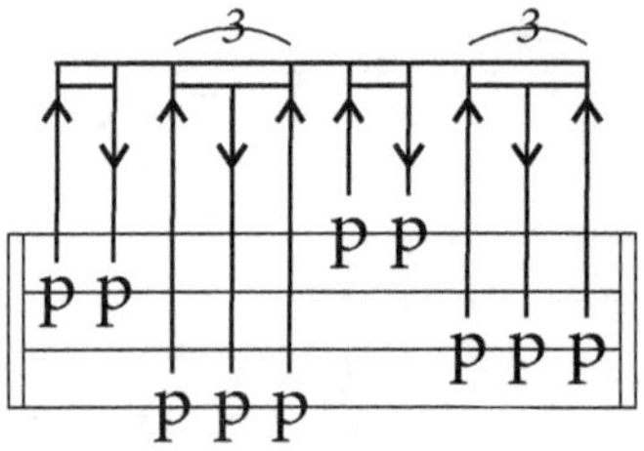

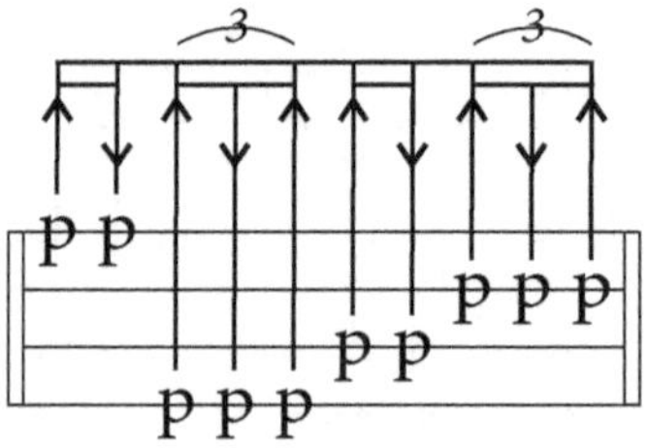

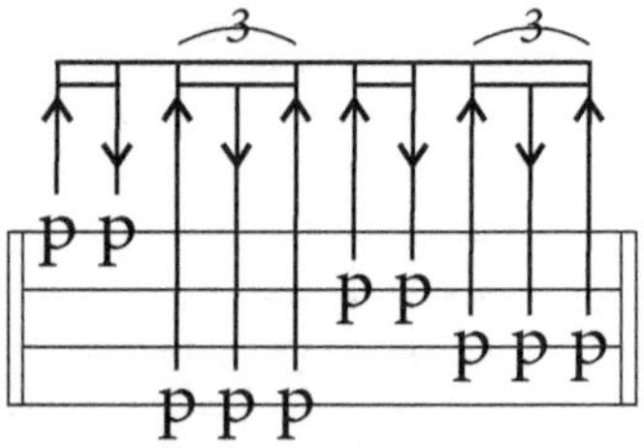

VARIATION III

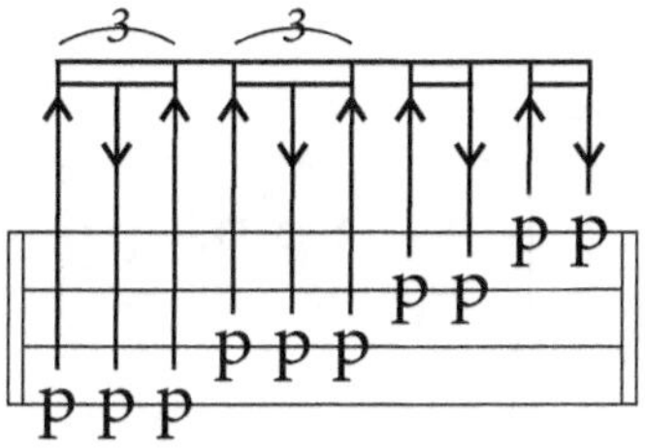

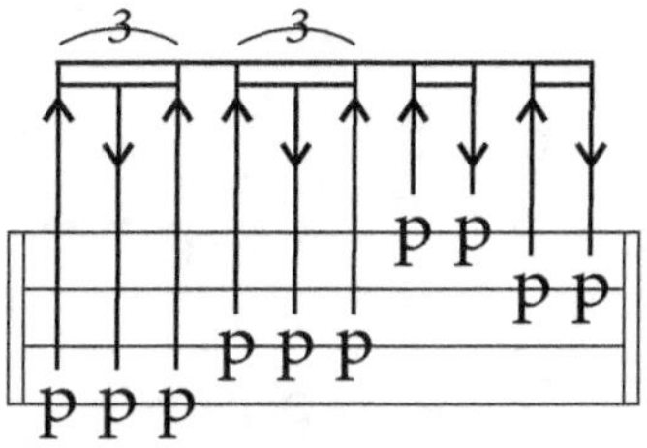

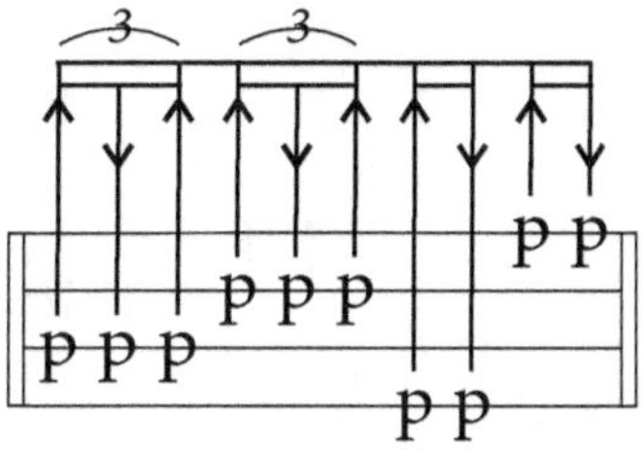

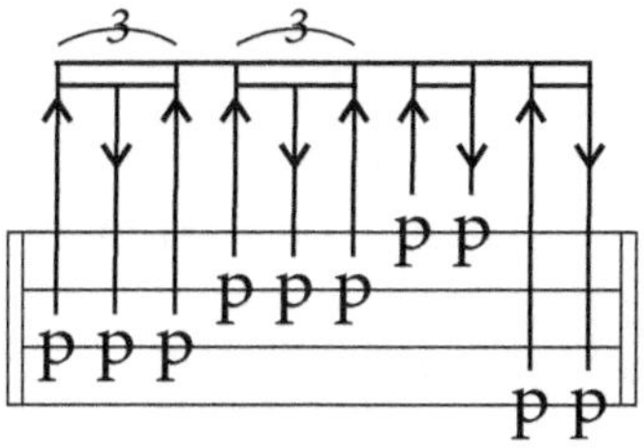

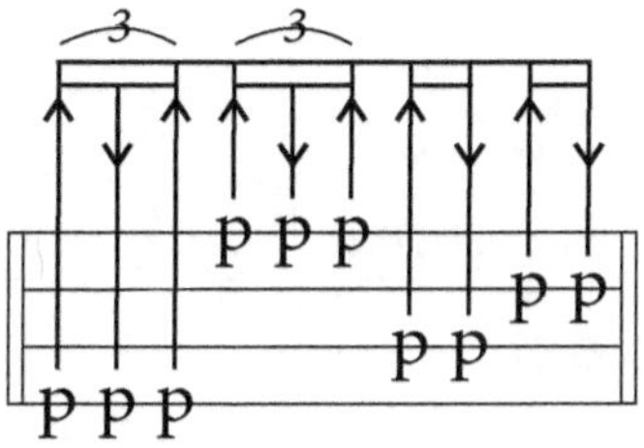

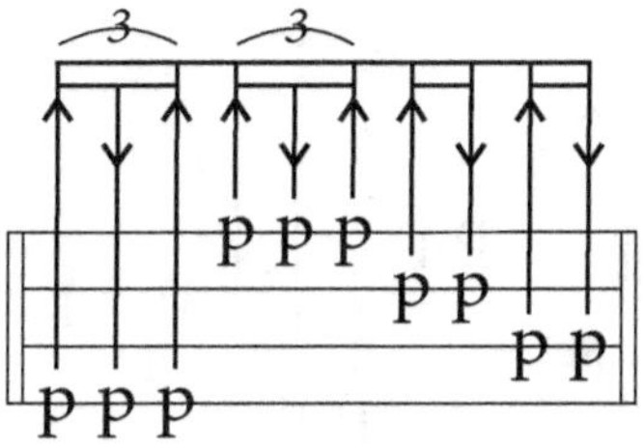

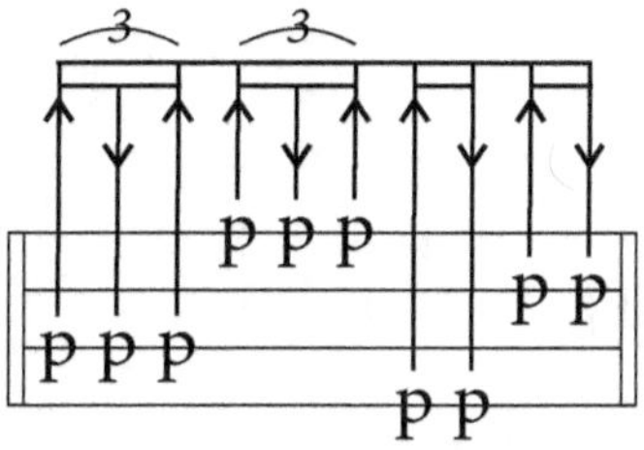

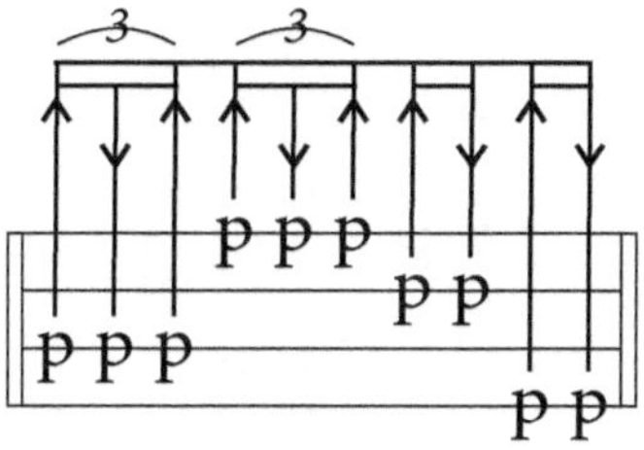

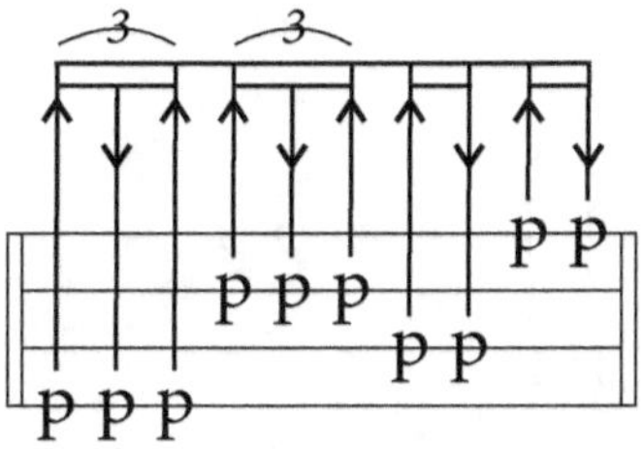

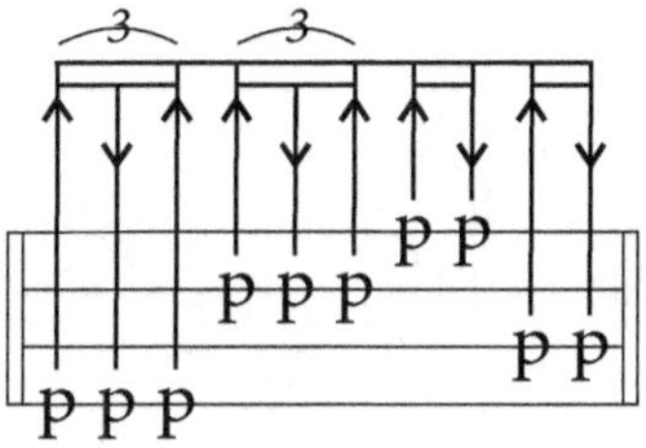

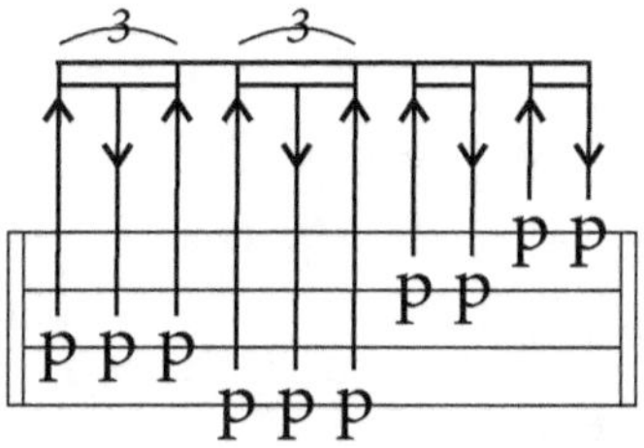

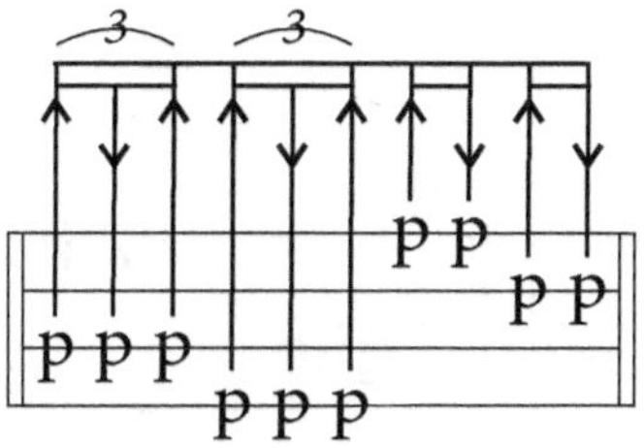

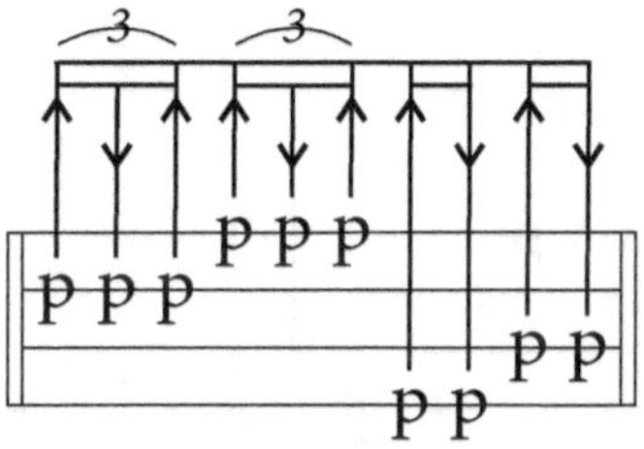

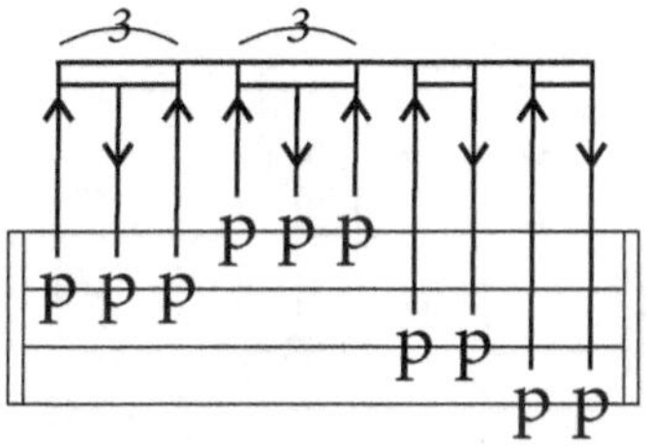

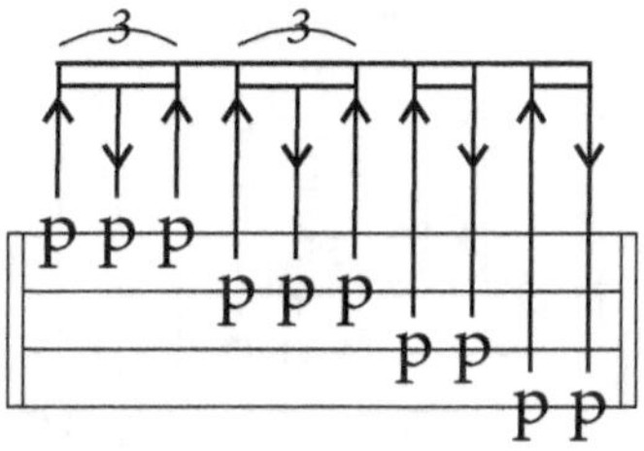

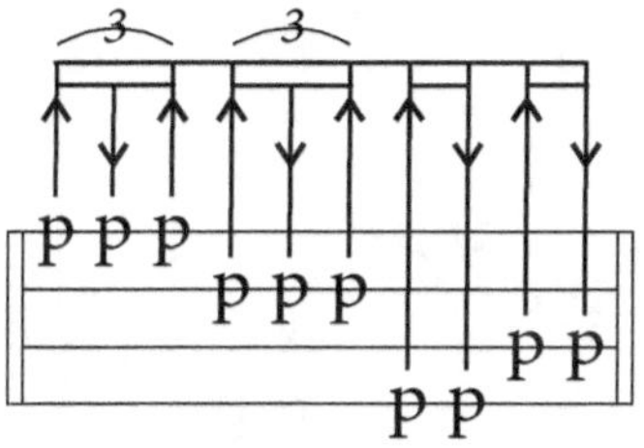

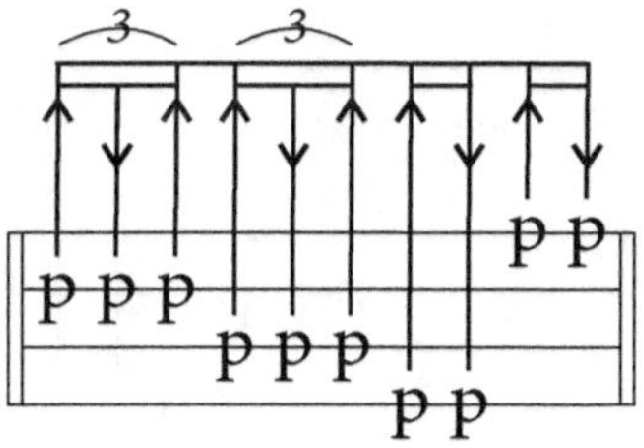

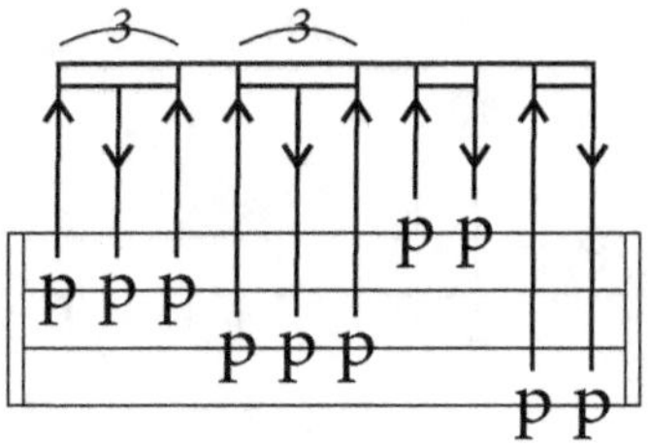

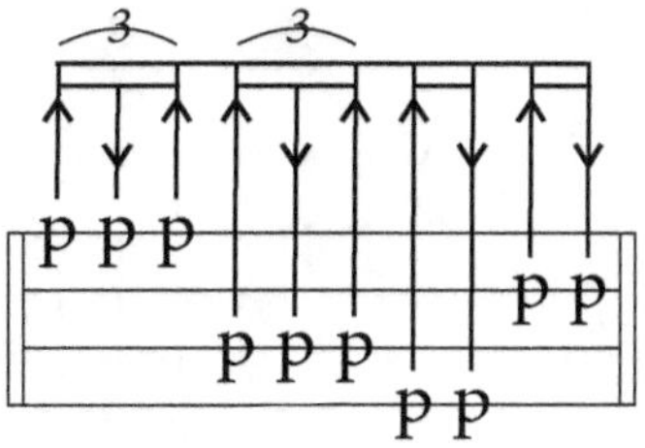

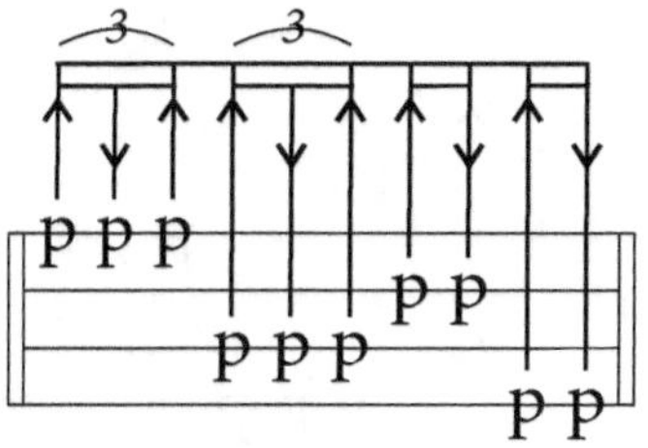

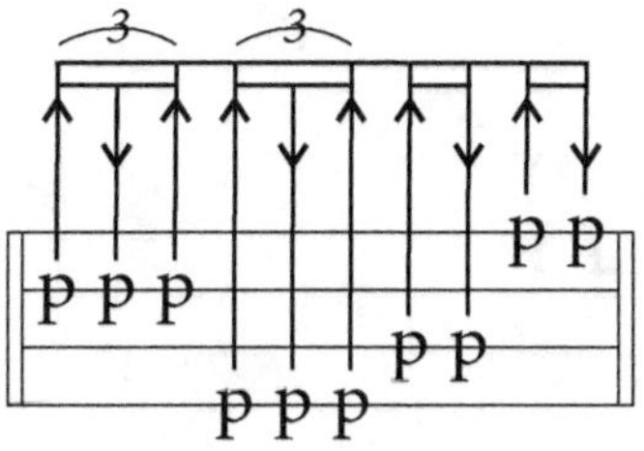

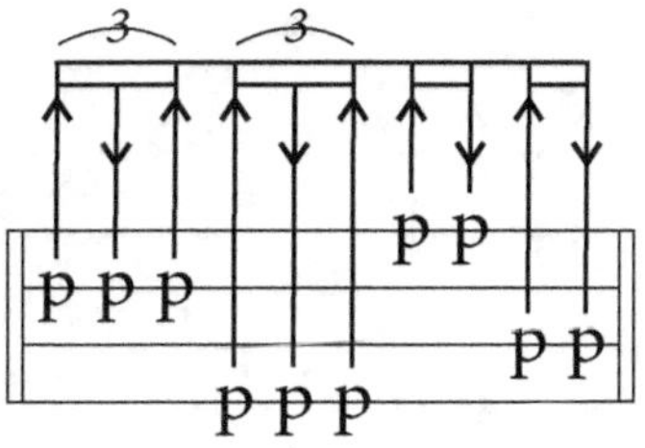

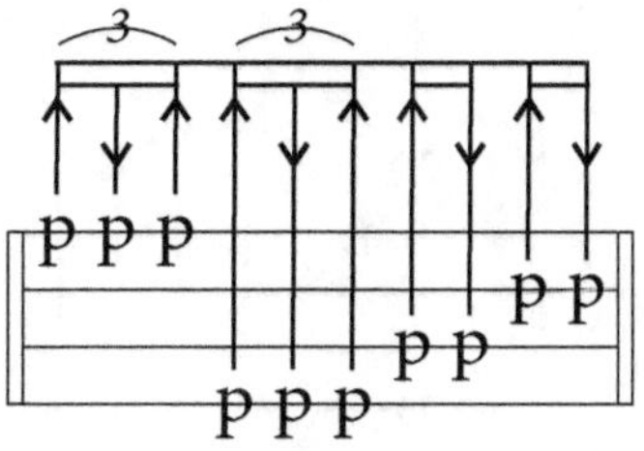

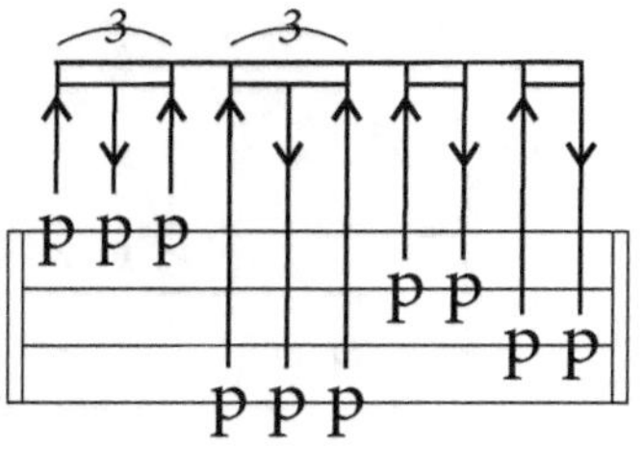

VARIATION IV

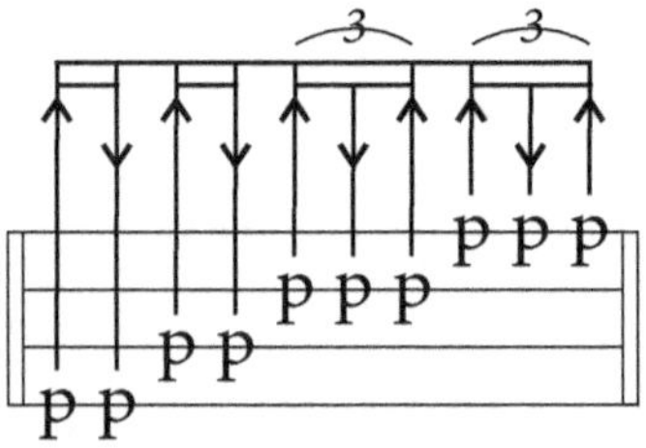

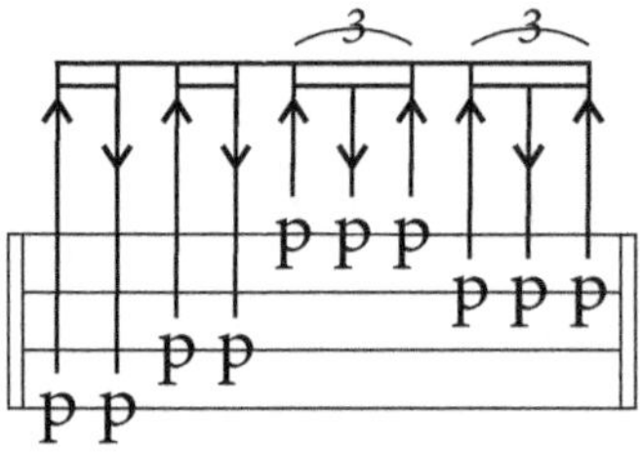

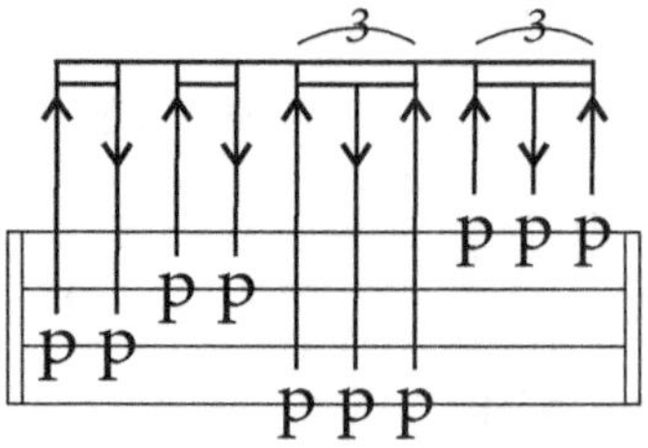

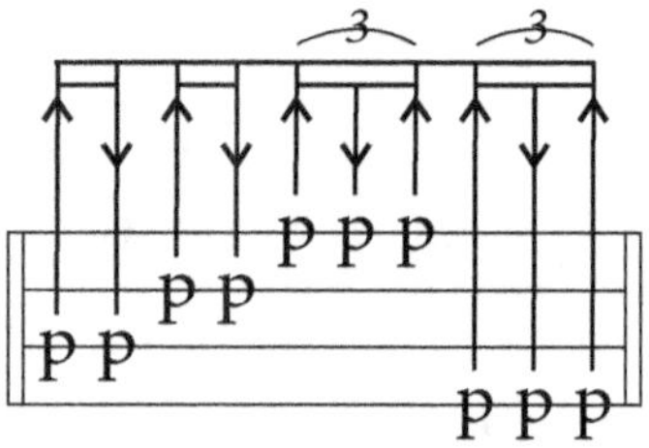

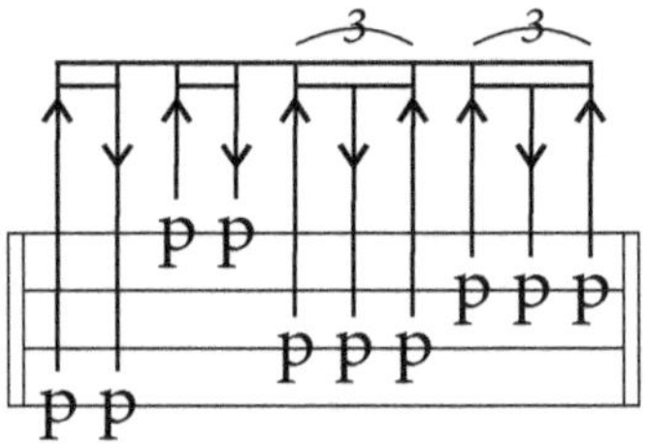

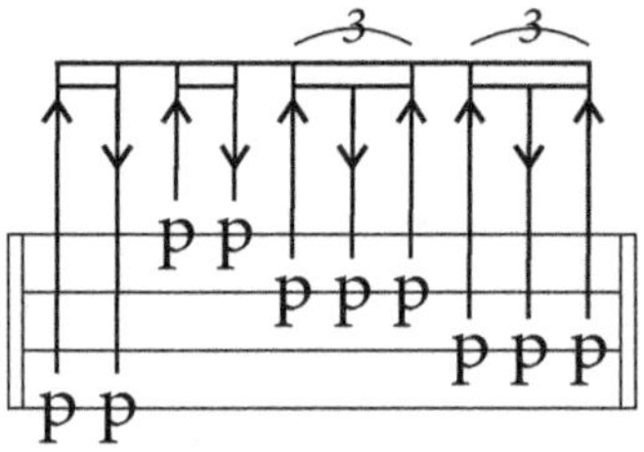

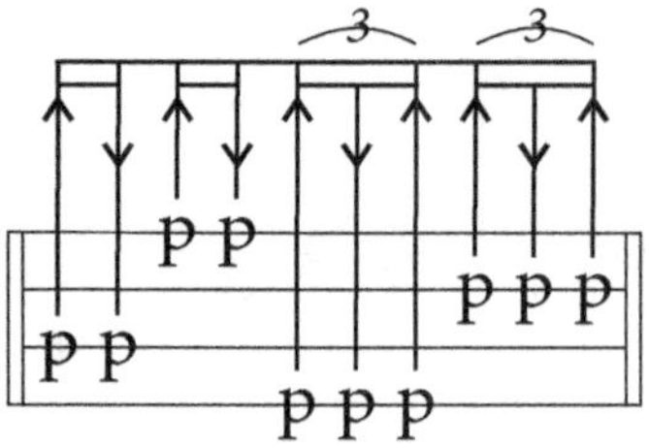

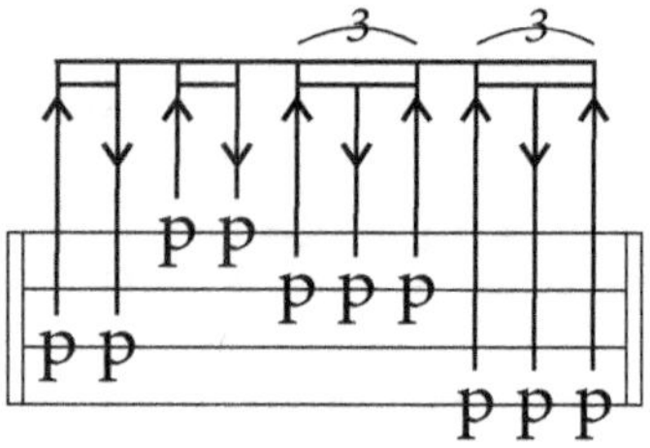

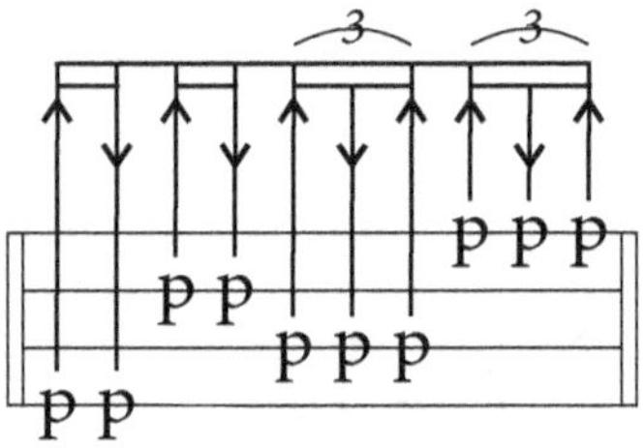

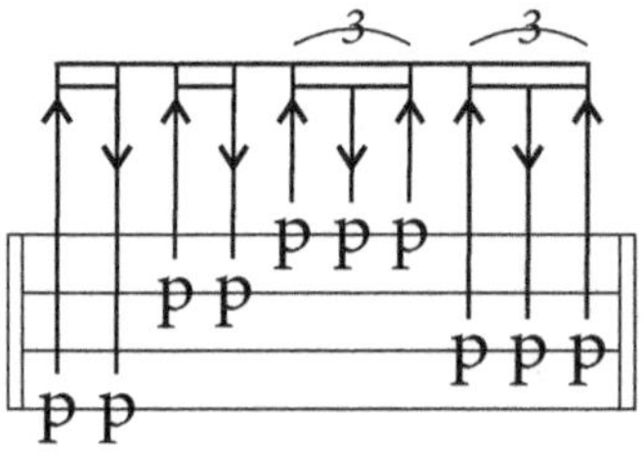

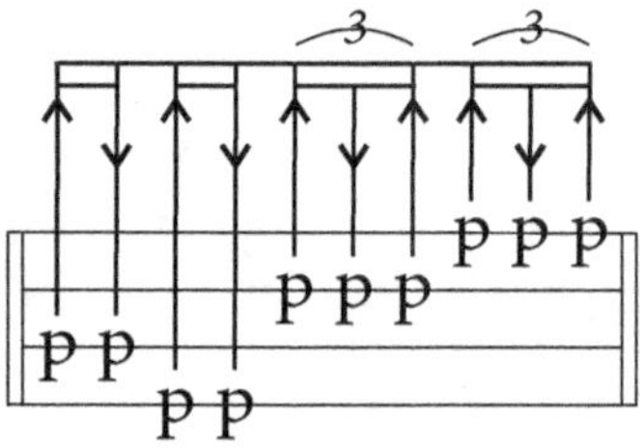

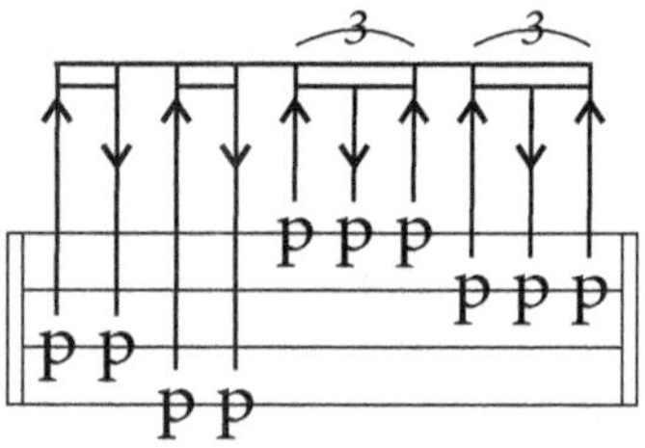

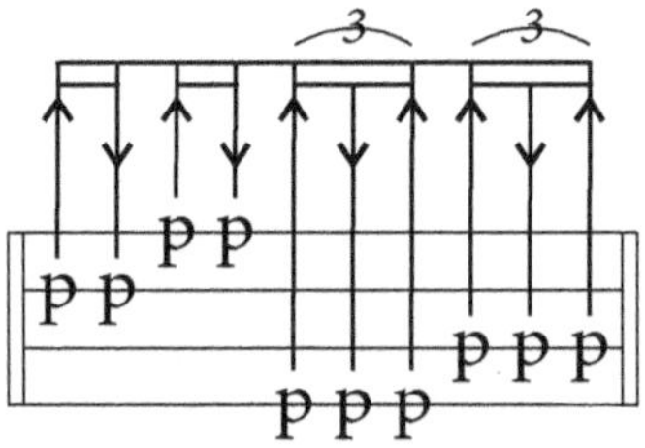

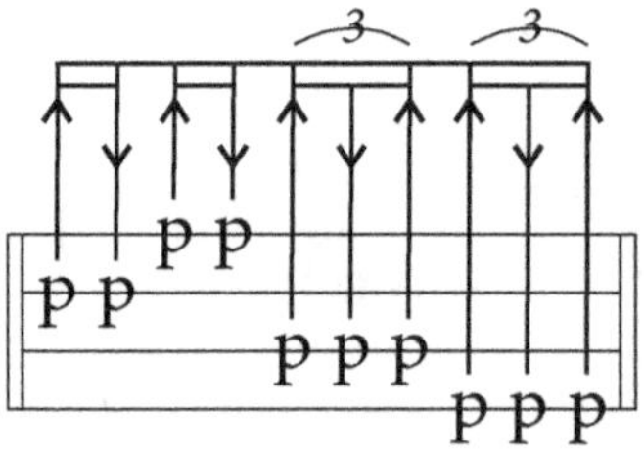

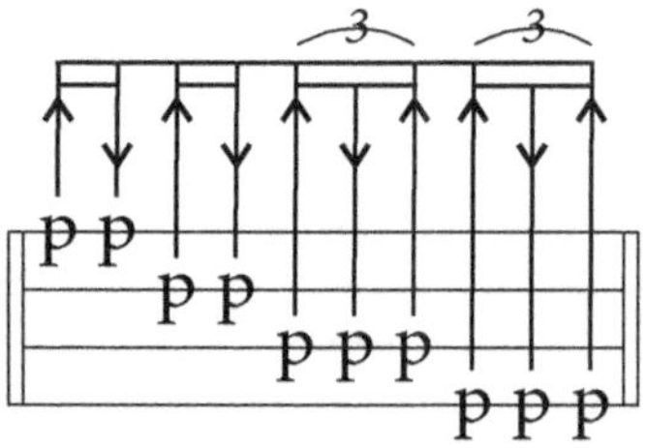

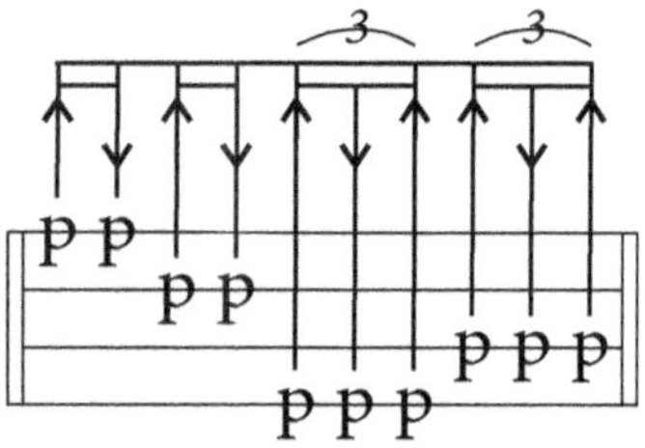

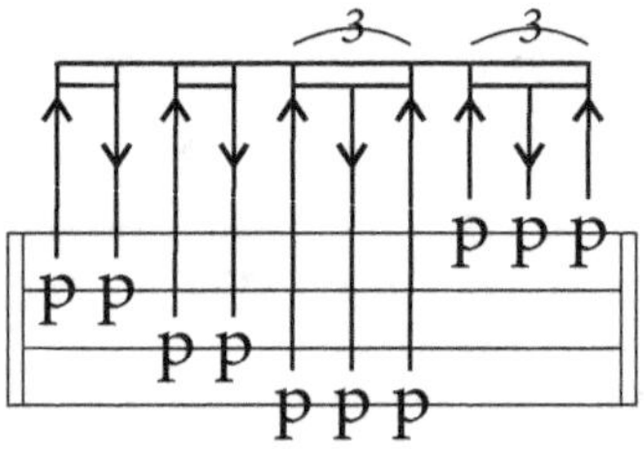

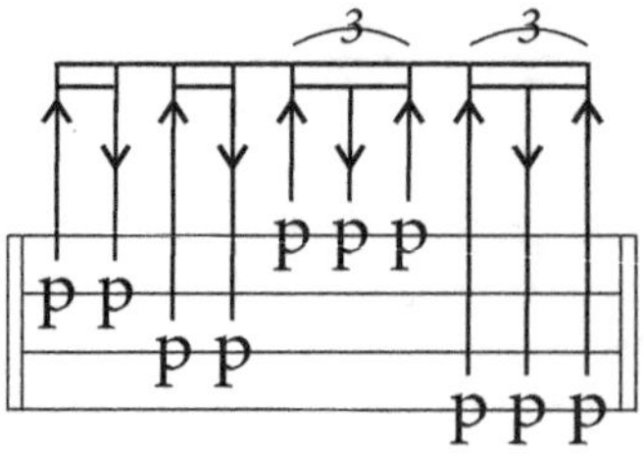

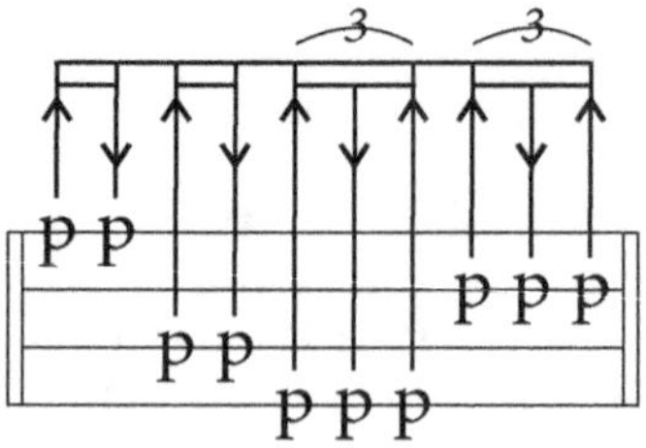

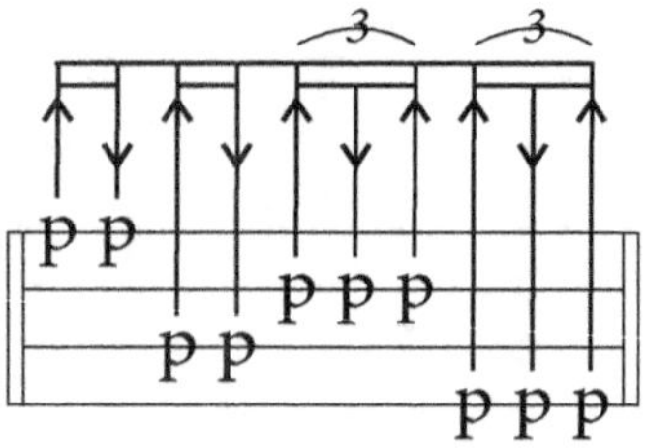

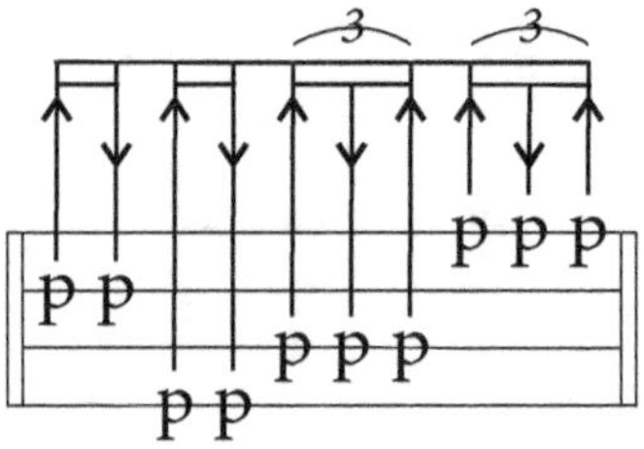

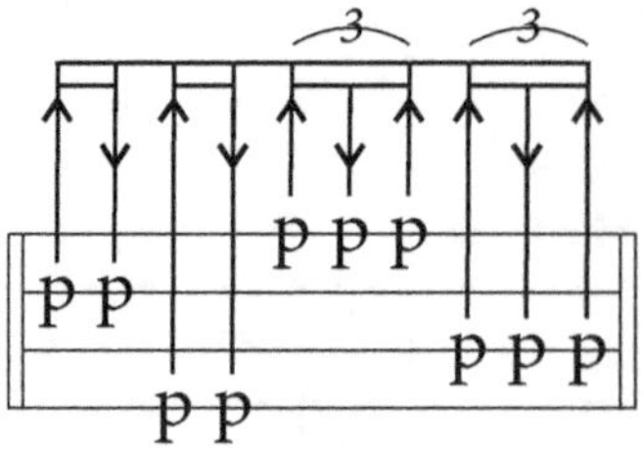

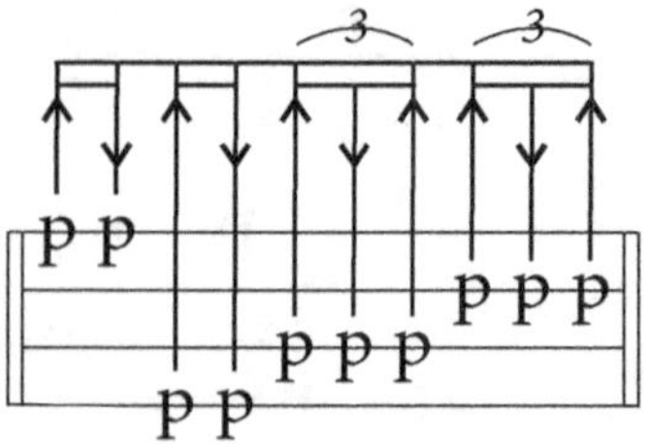

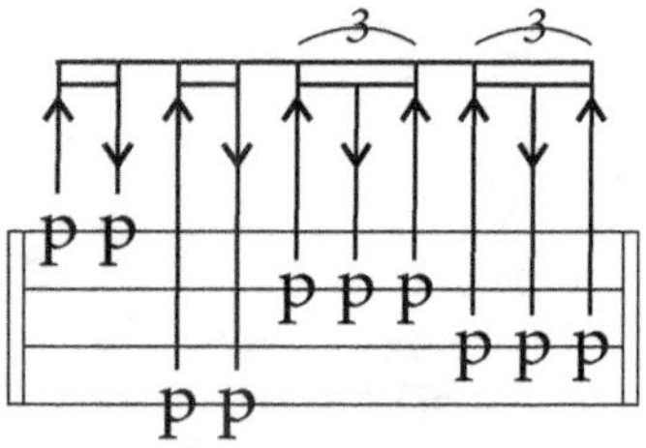

VARIATION V

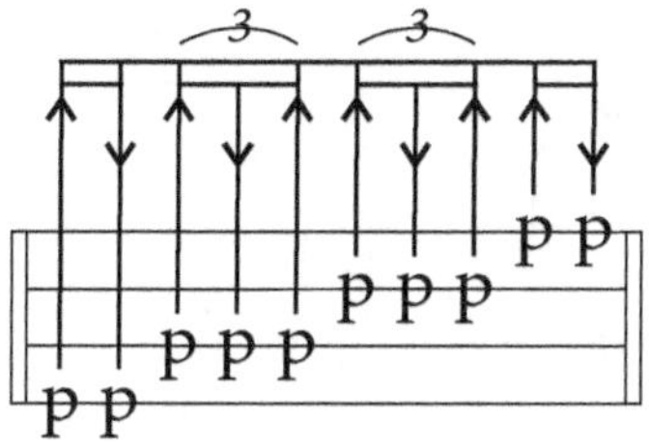

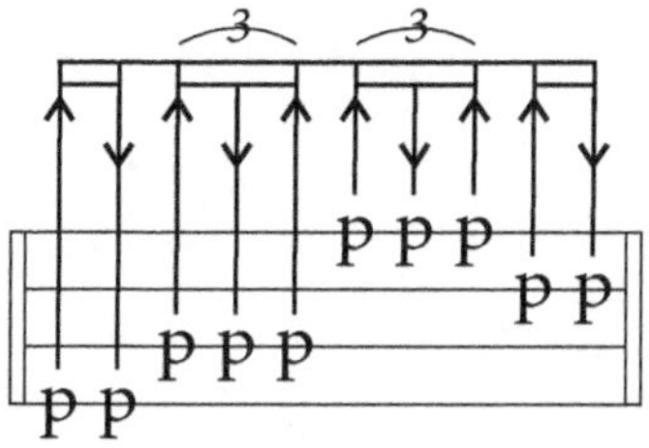

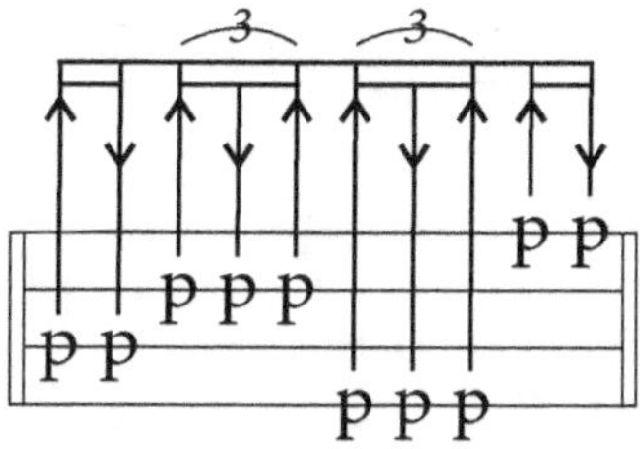

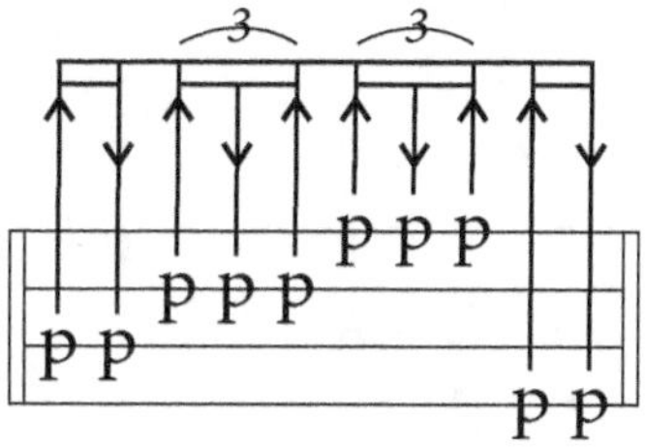

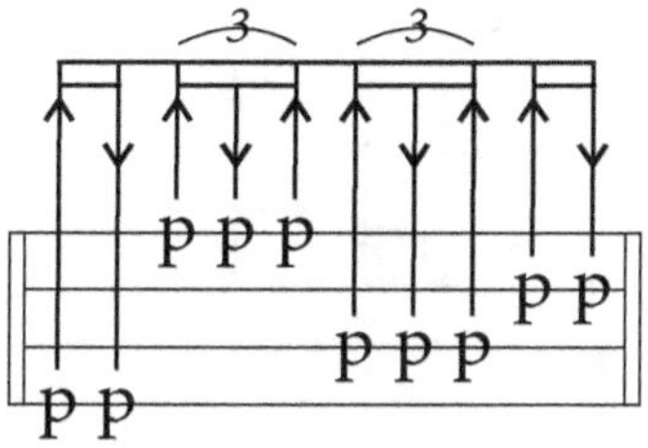

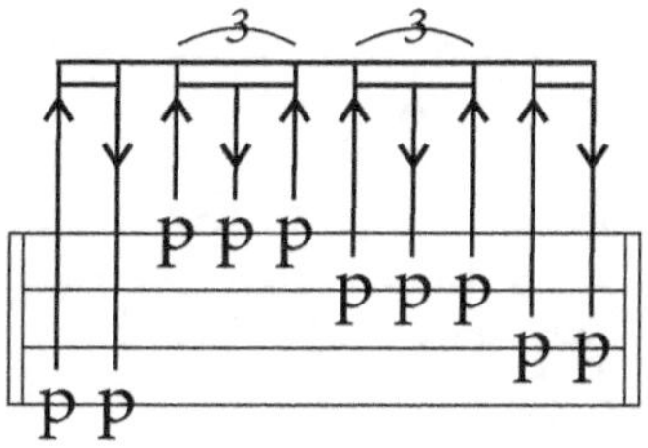

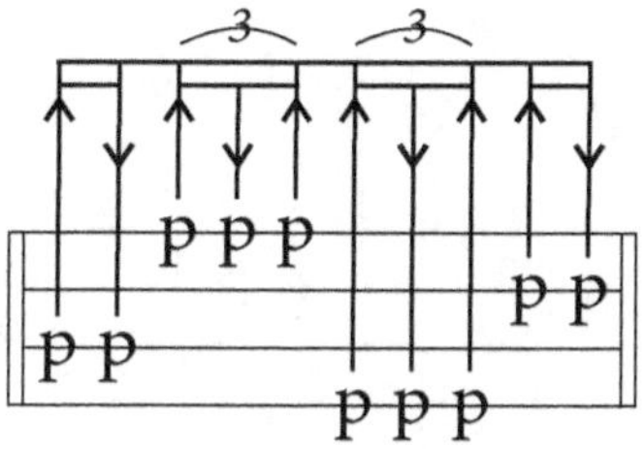

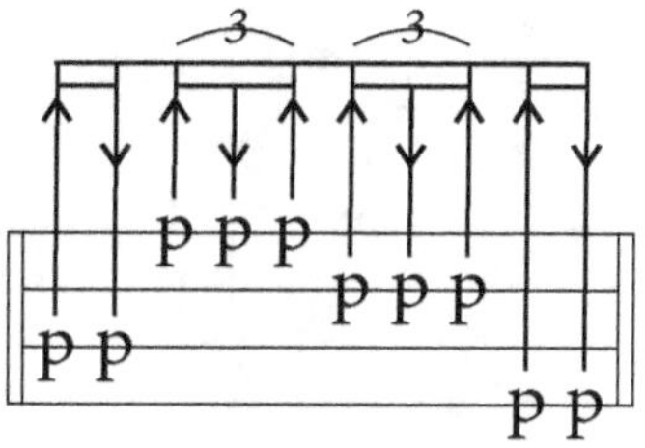

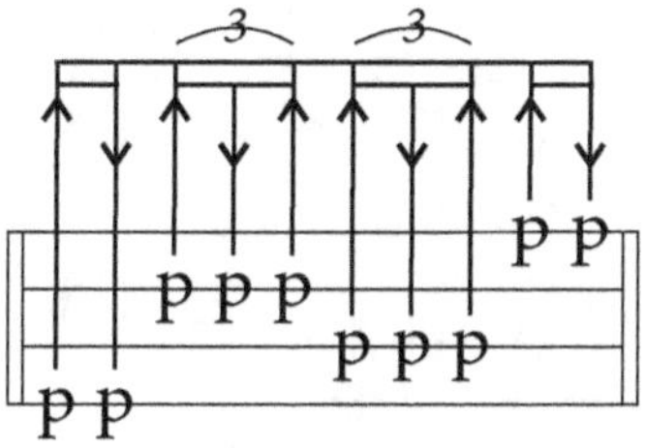

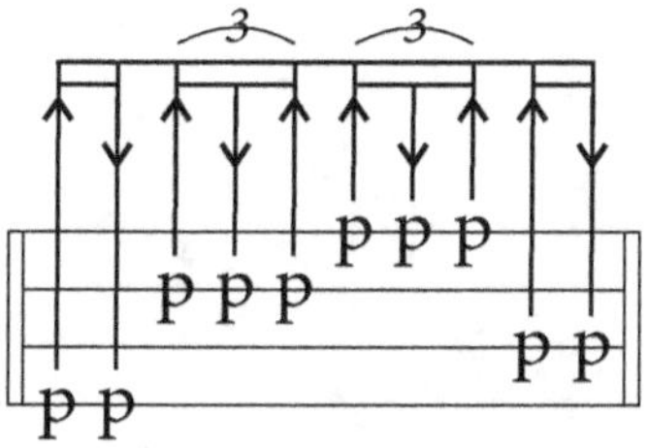

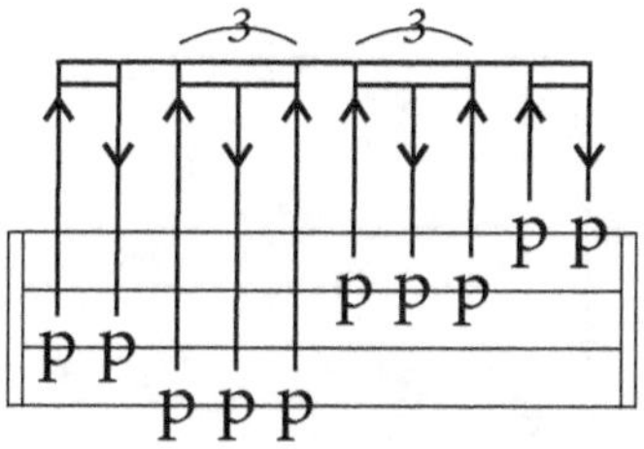

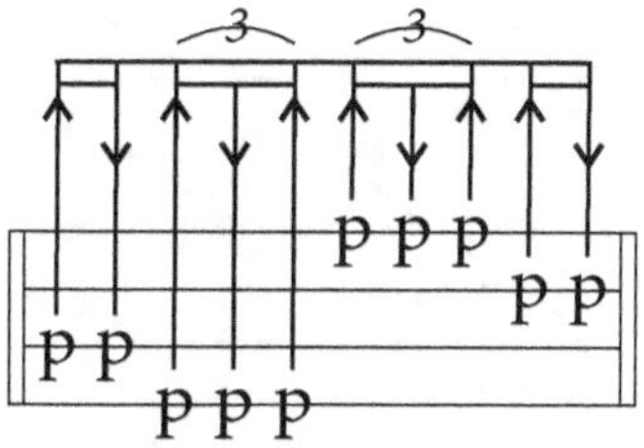

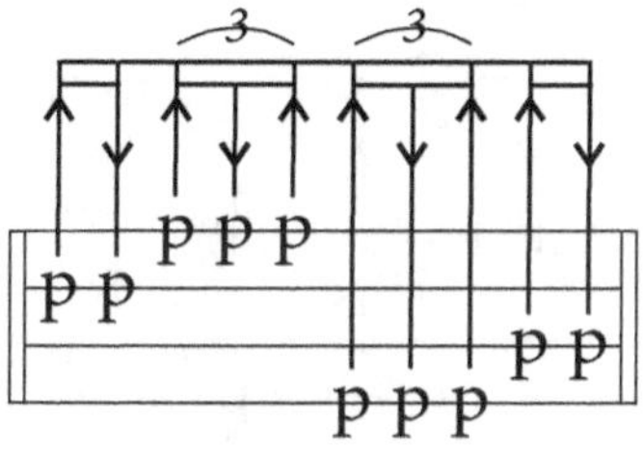

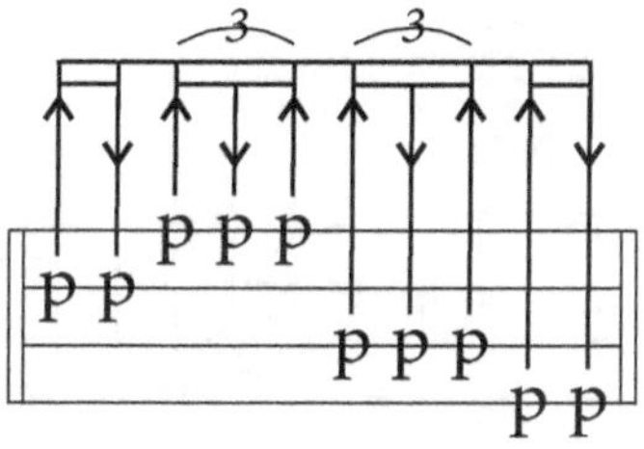

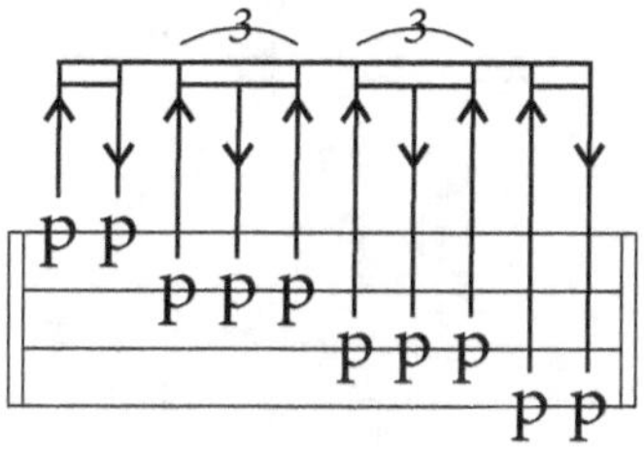

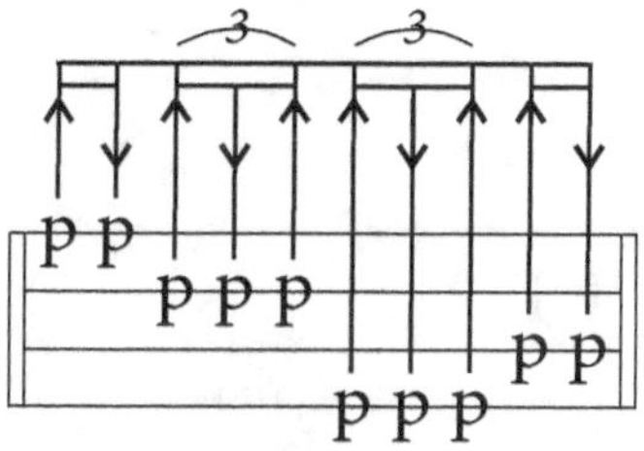

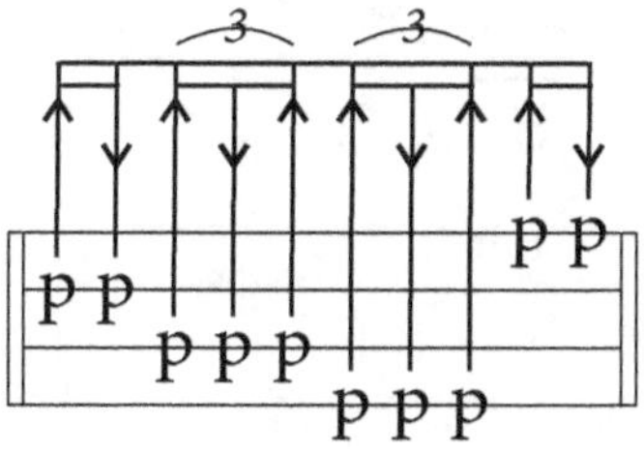

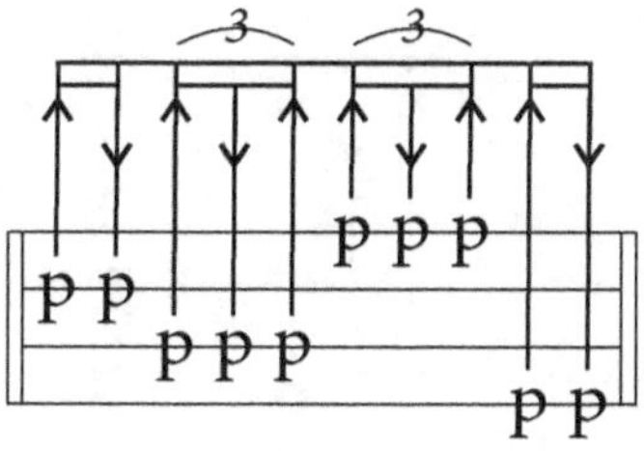

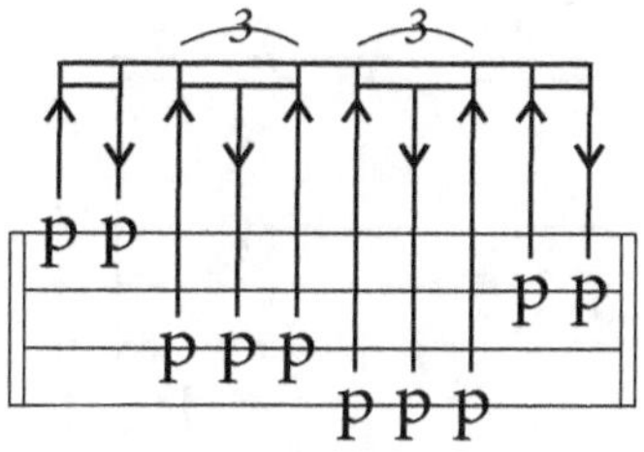

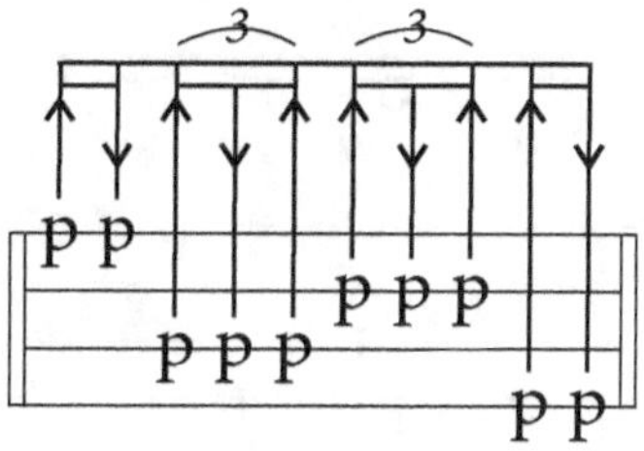

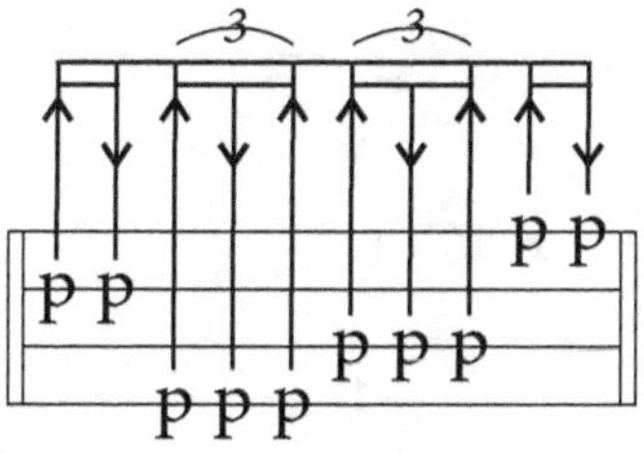

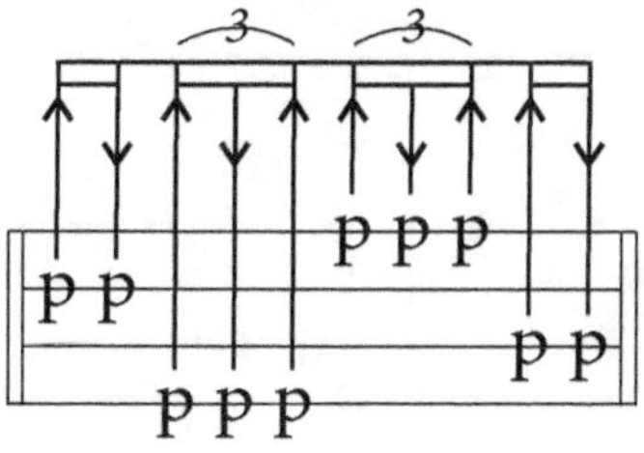

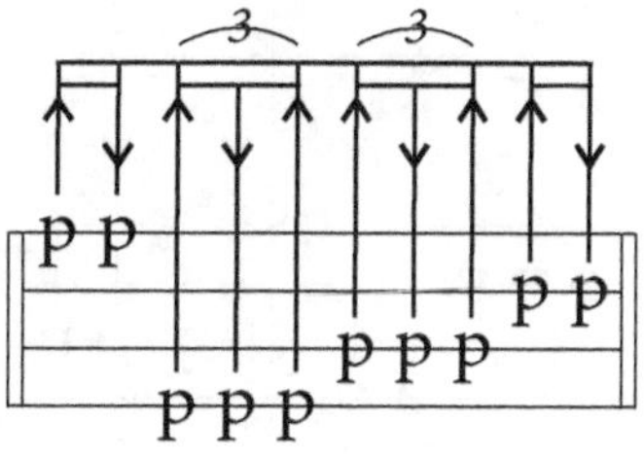

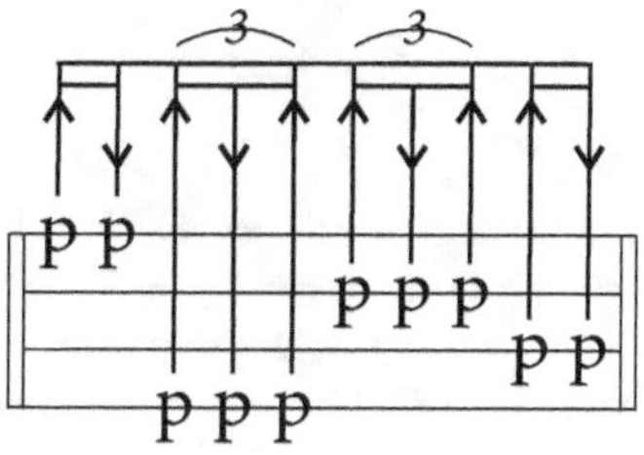

VARIATION VI

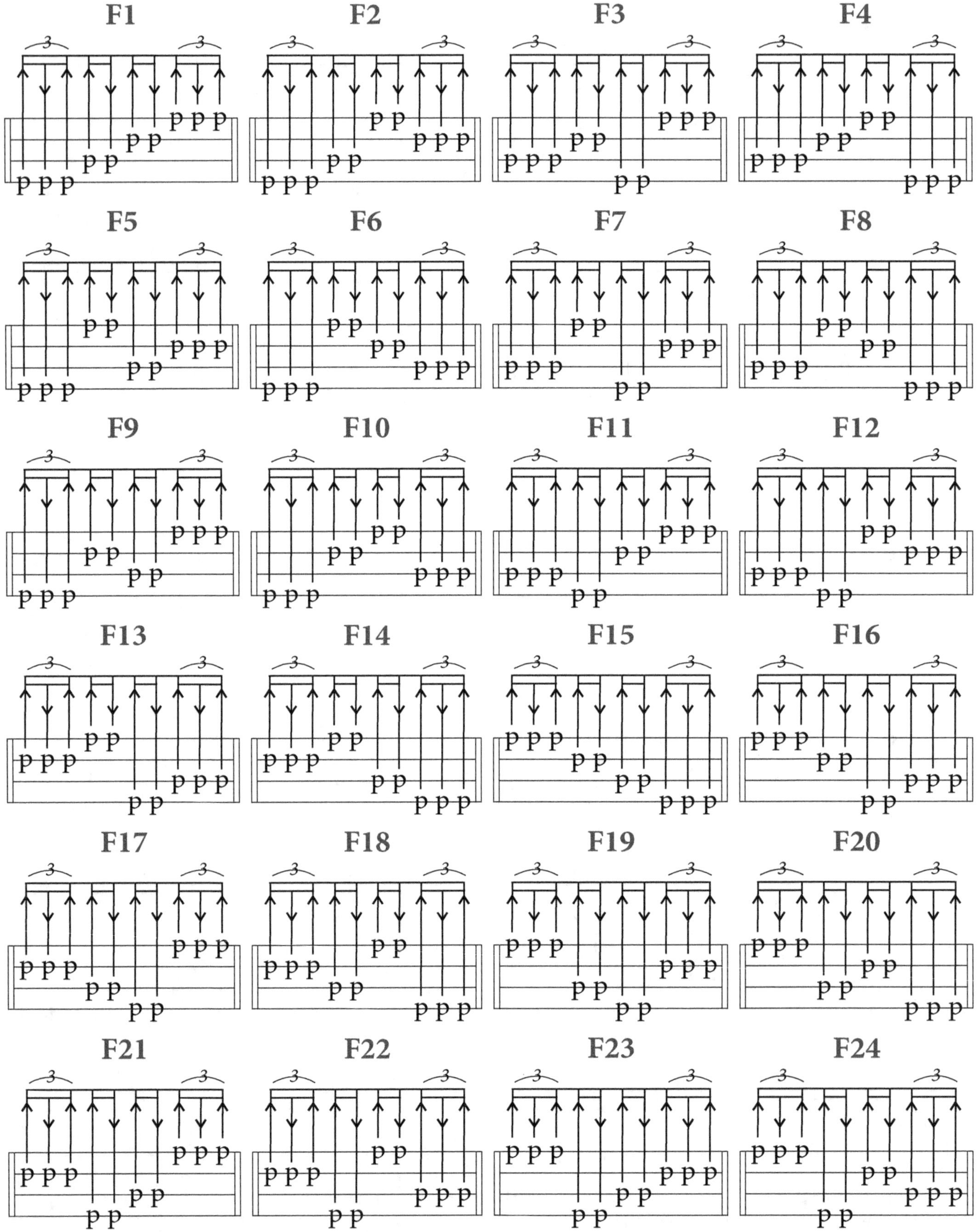

§ VII

Exercise on pulgar on four adjacent strings with four quad strokes within each Formula. In total there are 24 Formulas. The positions of the left hand are as described in previous pages. The striking of the pulgar (for the quad stroke) is as follows:

$$p\uparrow\downarrow \quad p\downarrow\downarrow \quad p\uparrow\downarrow \quad p\downarrow\downarrow$$

Alternatively you can practice by striking the pulgar as follows:

1.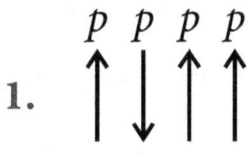

2.

3.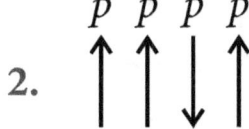

4.

Practice in the following ways of pulgar stroke:

F1 (1st mode)

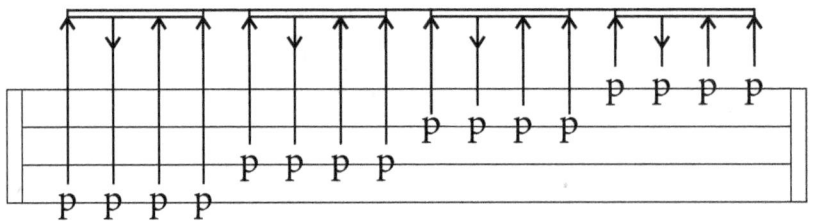

F1 (2nd mode)

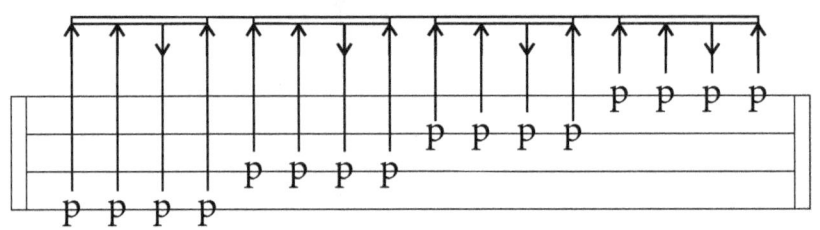

F1 (3rd mode)

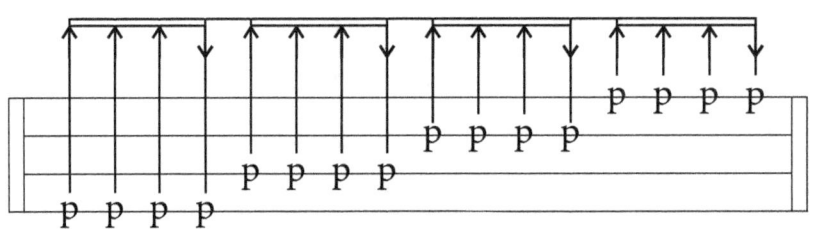

F1 (4th mode)

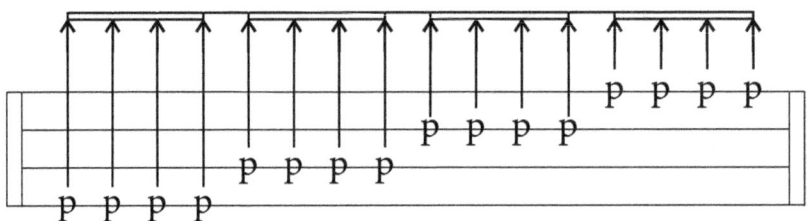

F1

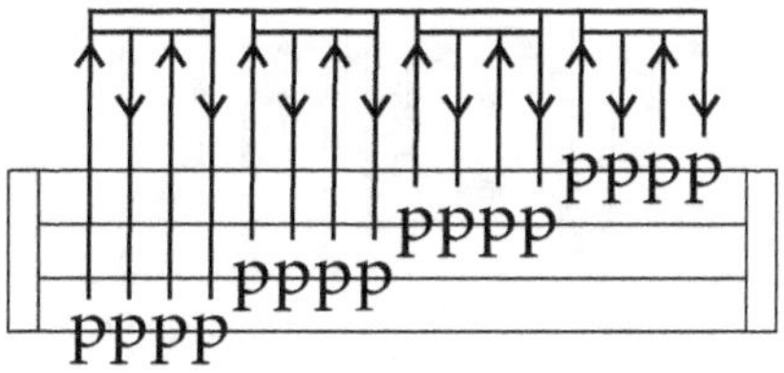

F2

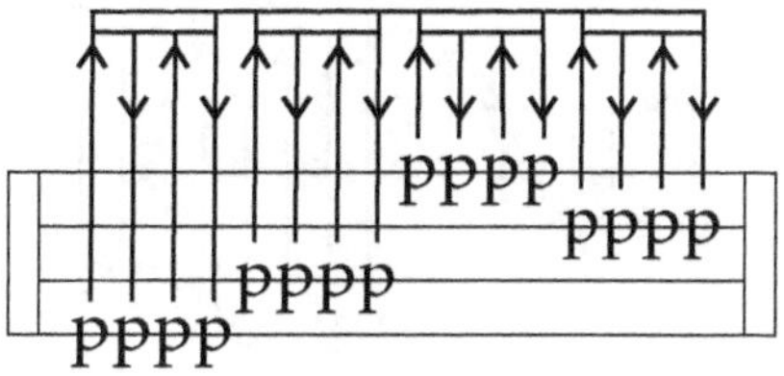

F3

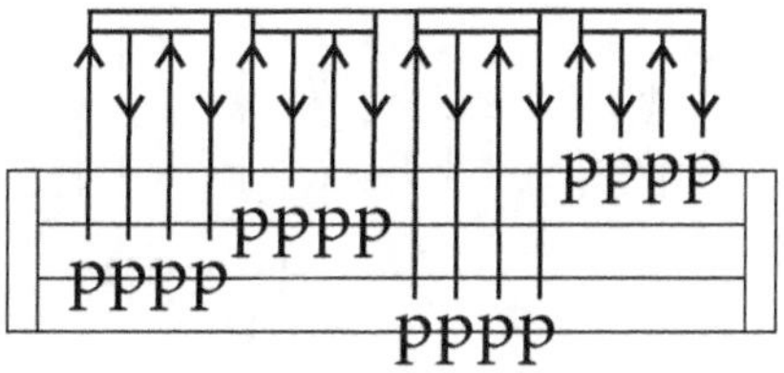

F4

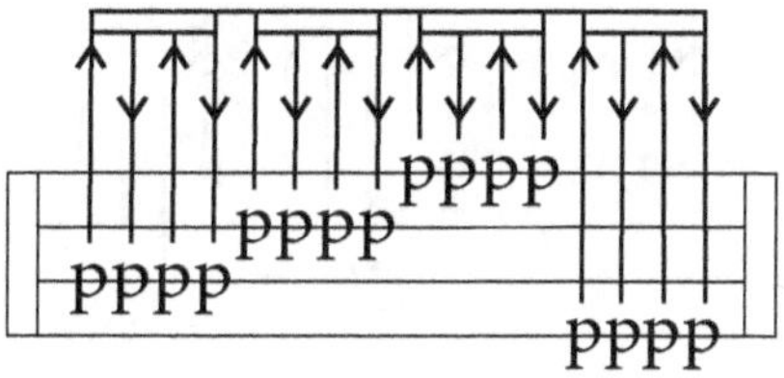

F5

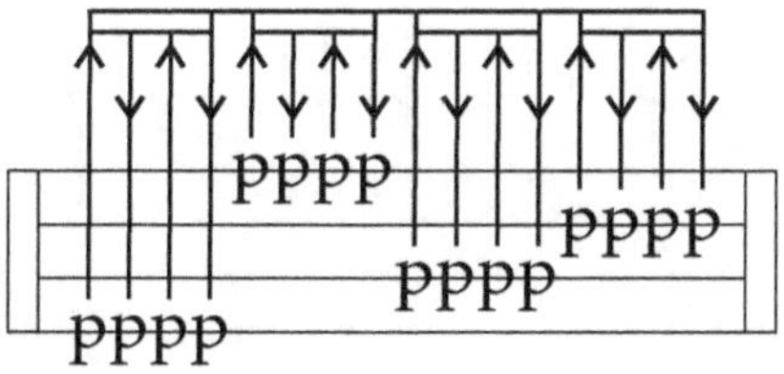

F6

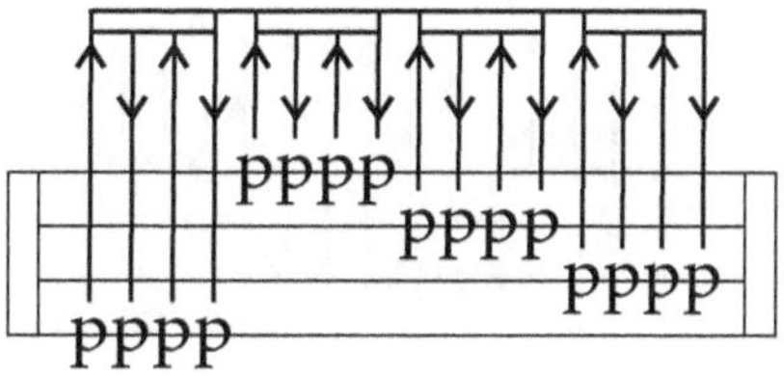

F7

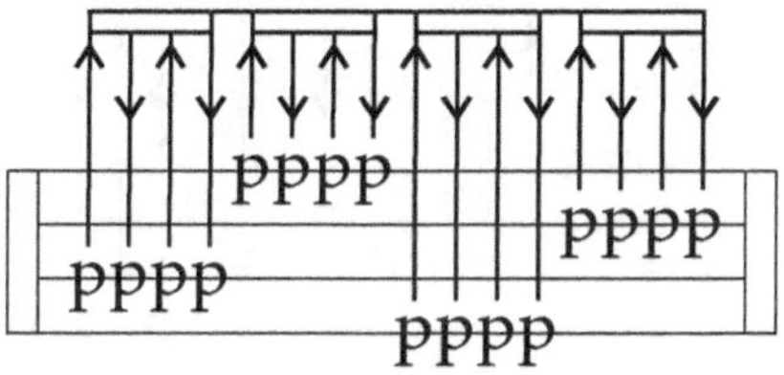

F8

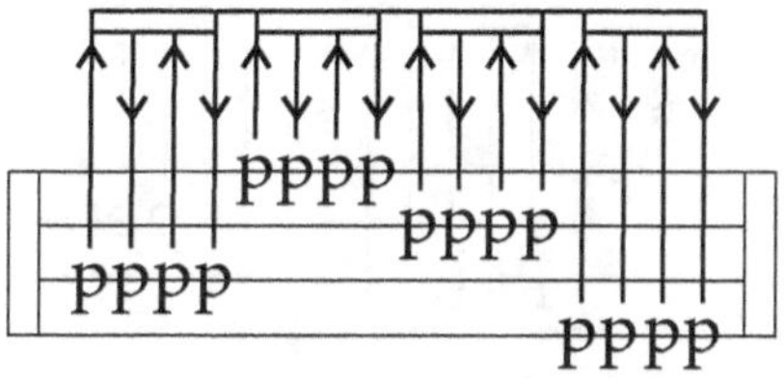

F9

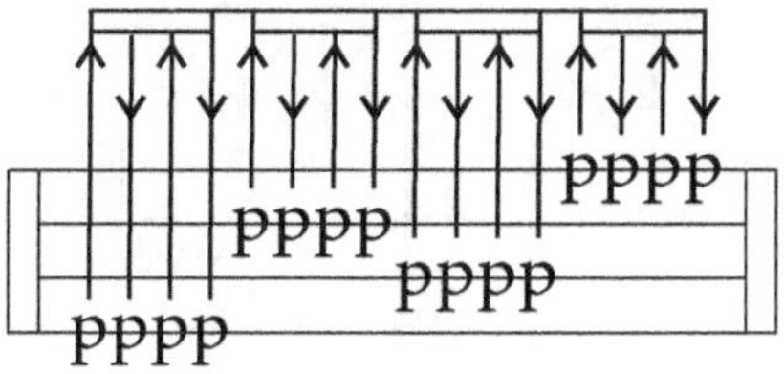

F10

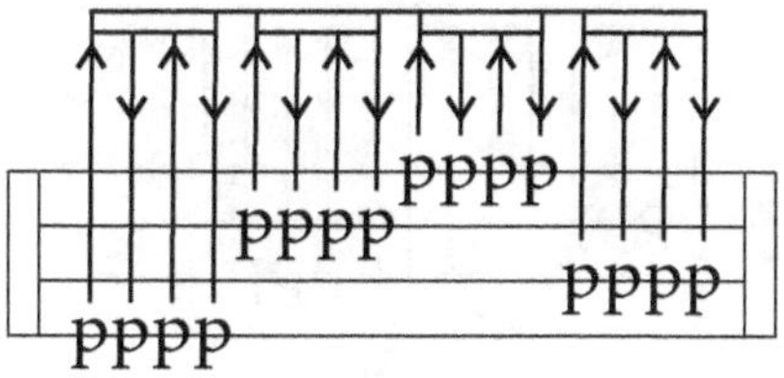

F11

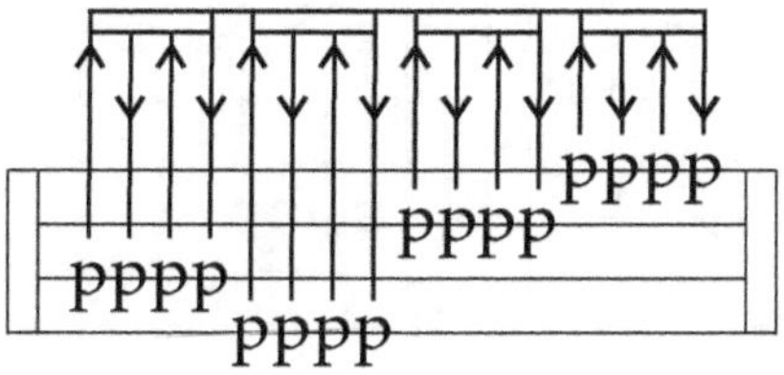

F12

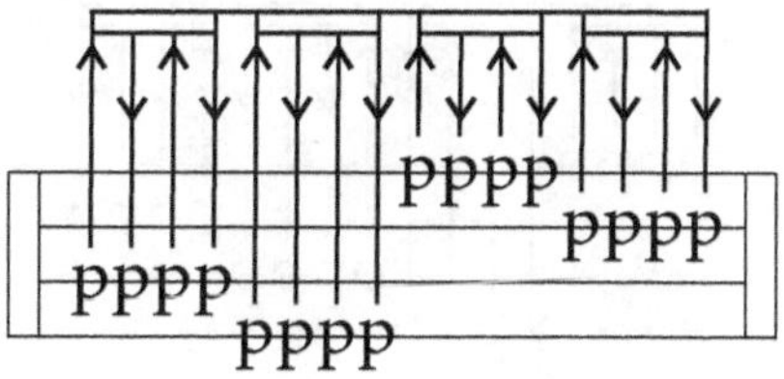

F13 F14

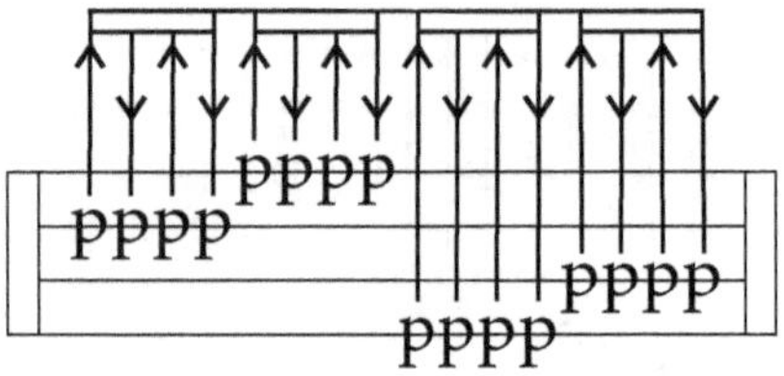

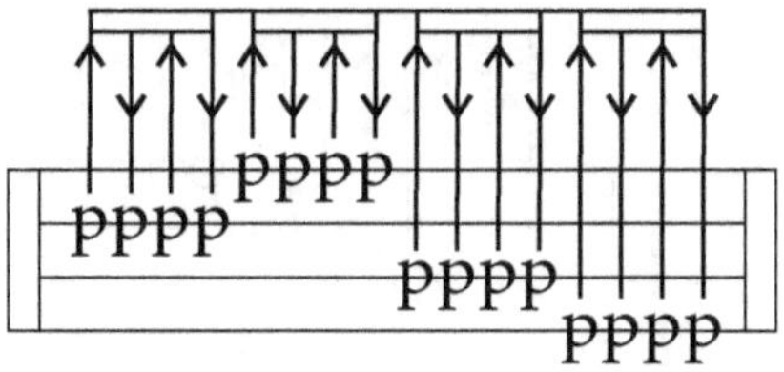

F15 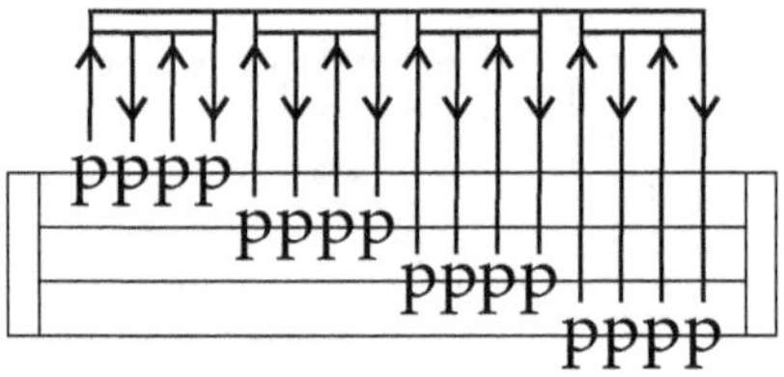 F16

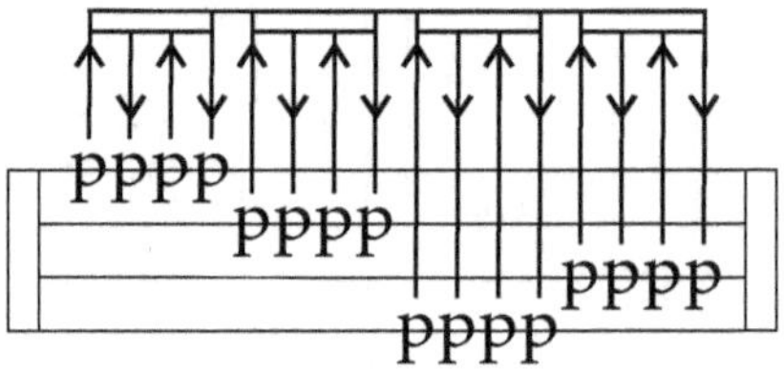

F17 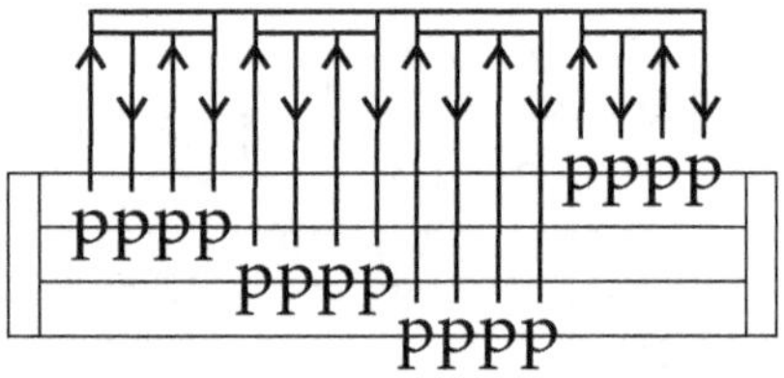 F18

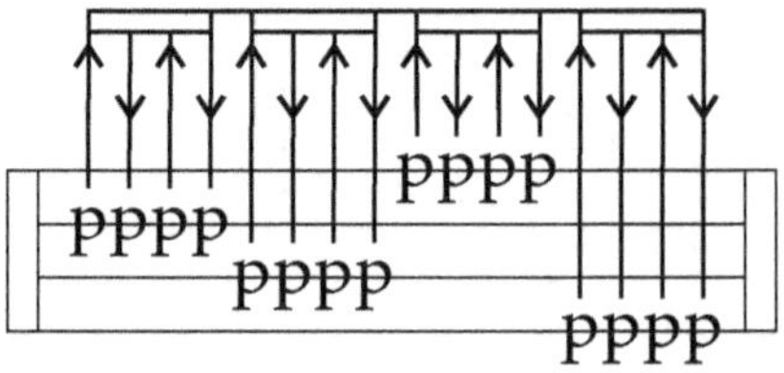

F19 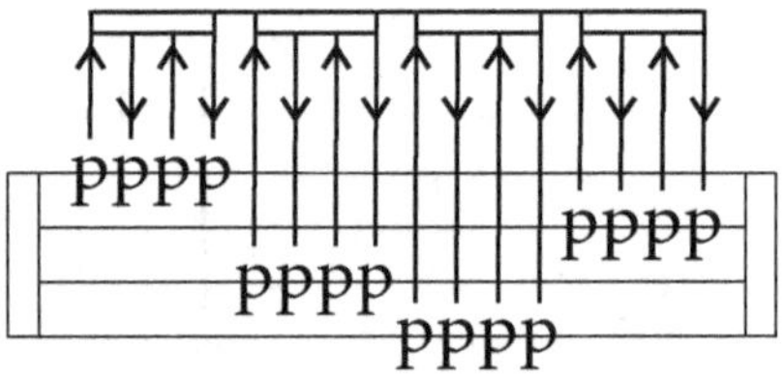 F20

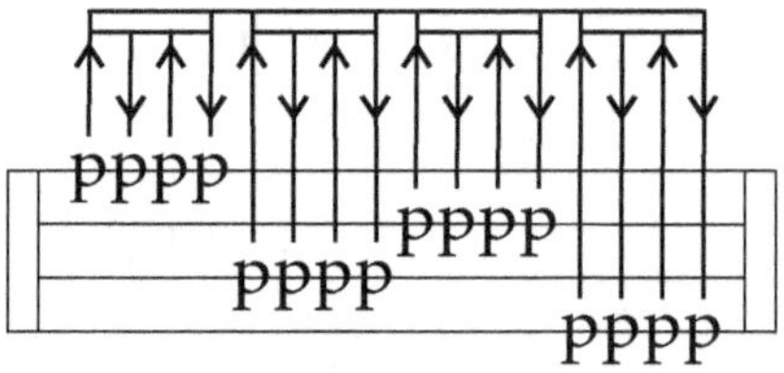

F21 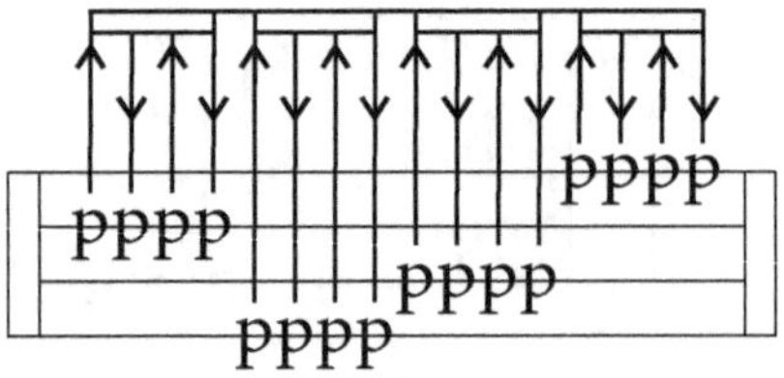 F22

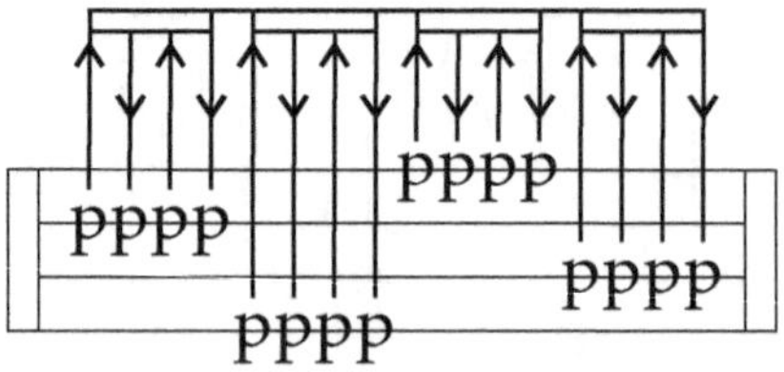

F23 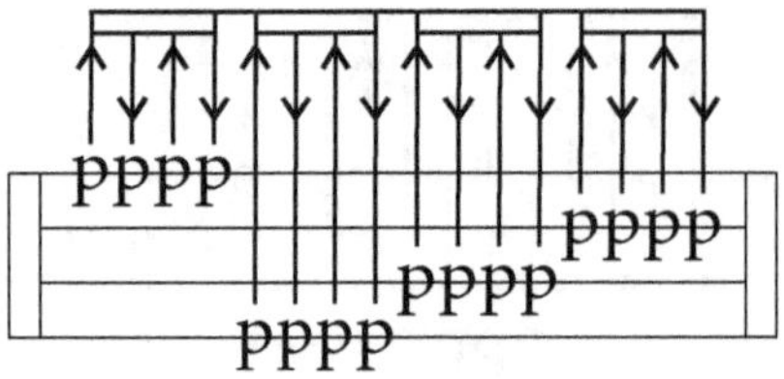 F24

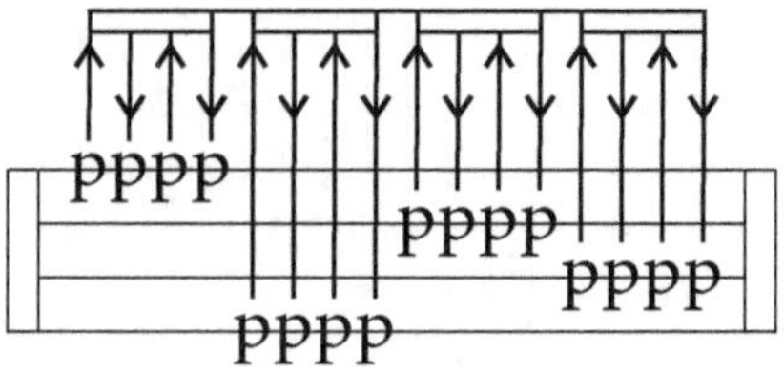

§ VIII

Exercise on pulgar on four adjacent strings with two double and two quad strokes within each Formula. The exercise contains six variations with 24 Formulas in each one. The first Formula of each variation is cited below. Isochronous playing of pulgar strokes (double and quad).

VARIATION I

VARIATION IV

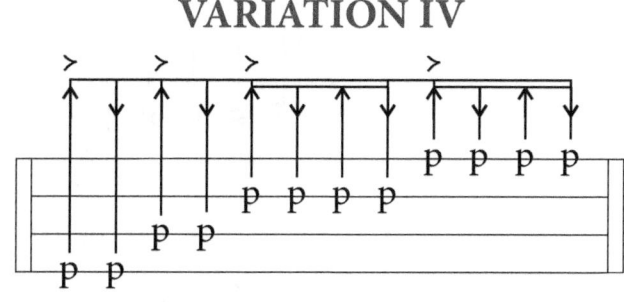

VARIATION II

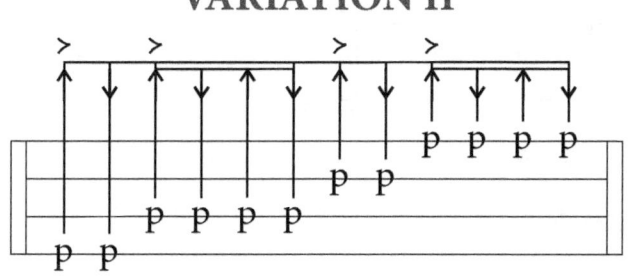

VARIATION V

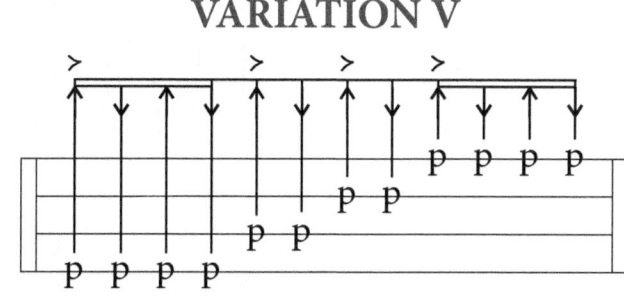

VARIATION III

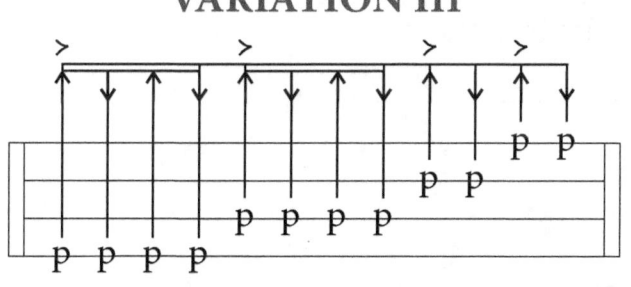

VARIATION VI

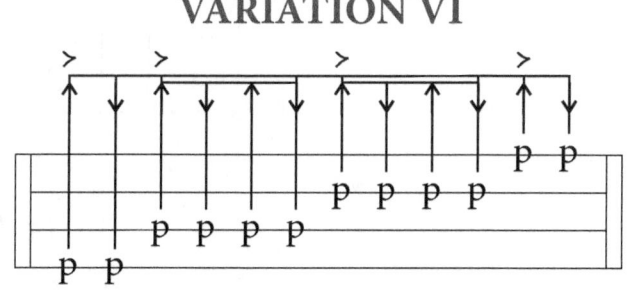

Practice in the following ways of pulgar stroke:

F1 (1st mode)

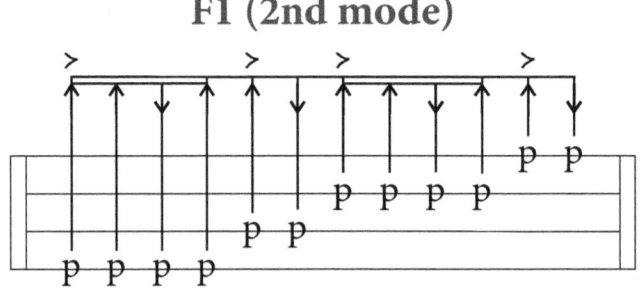

F1 (2nd mode)

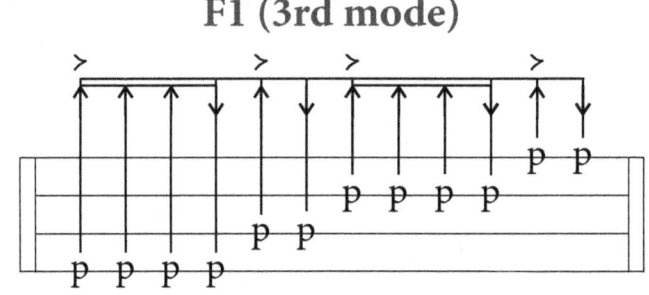

F1 (3rd mode)

F1 (4th mode)

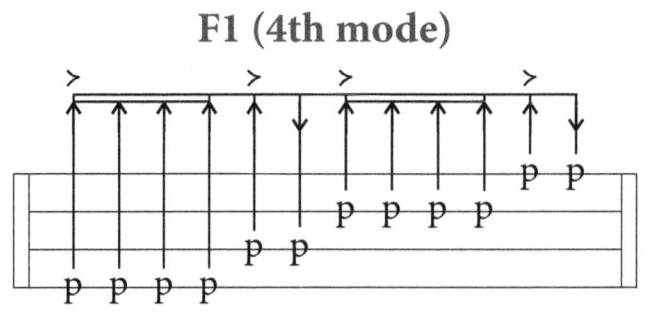

VARIATION I

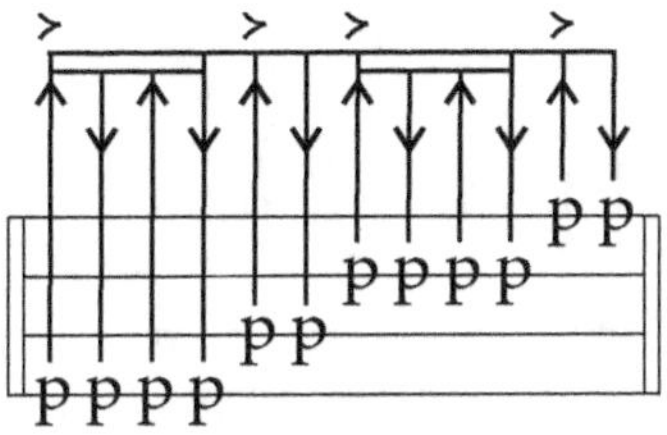

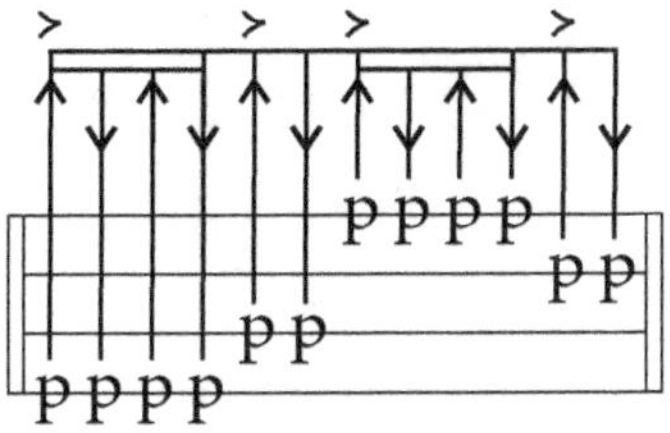

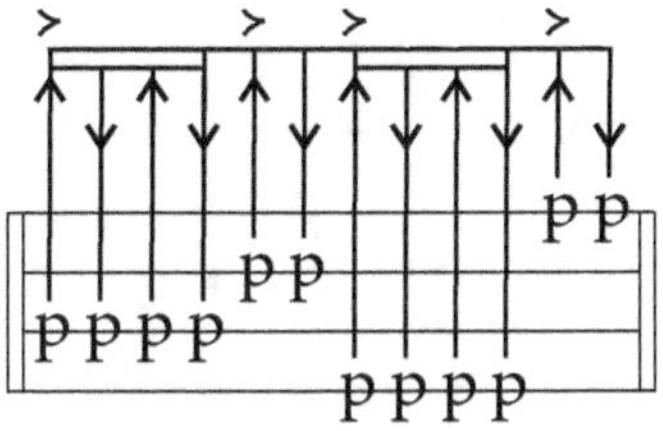

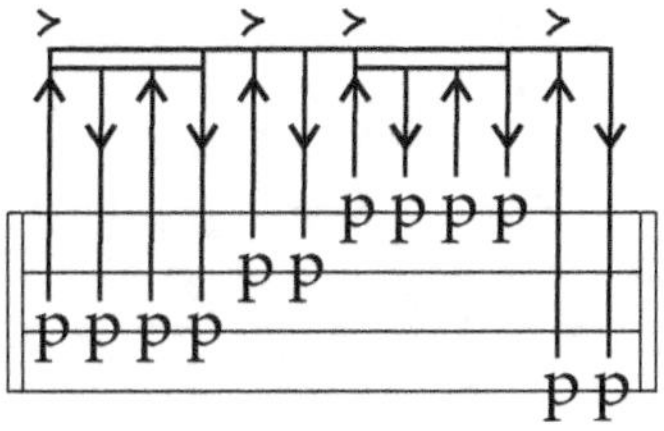

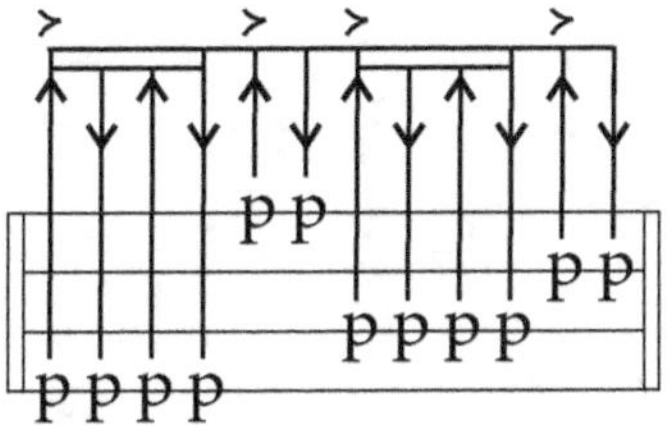

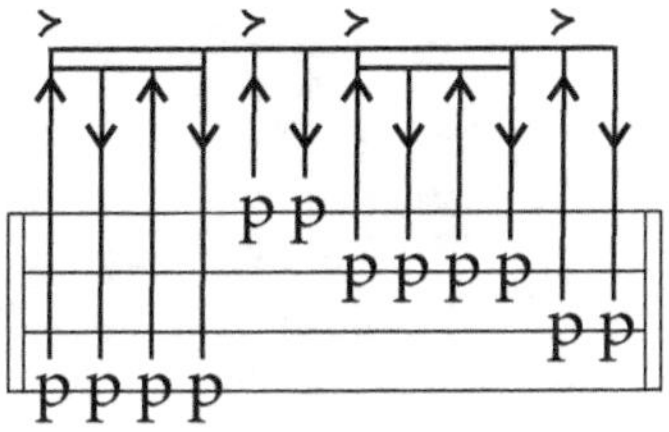

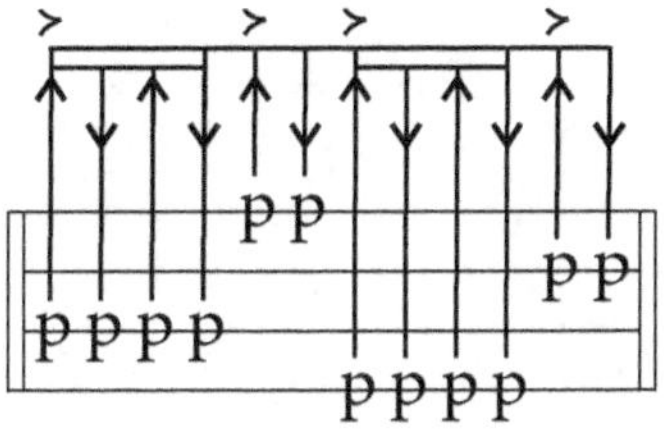

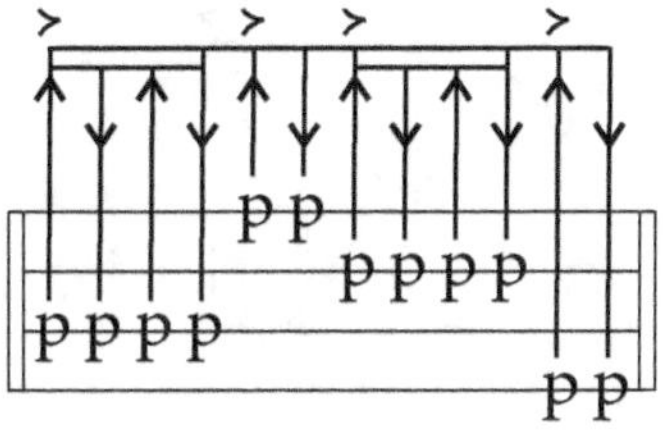

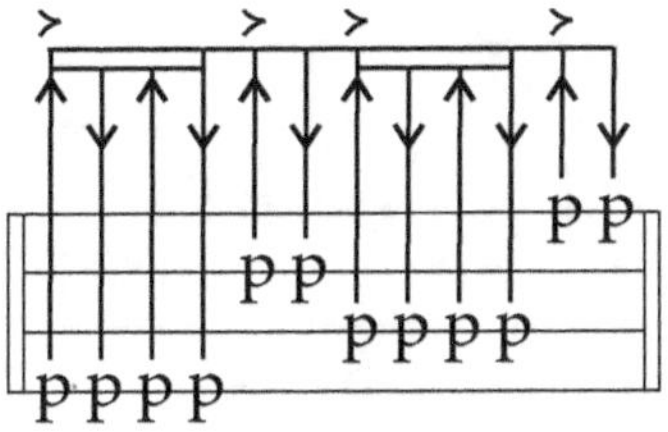

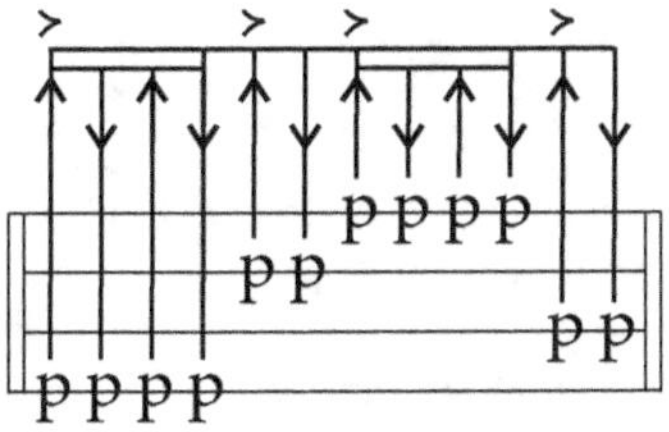

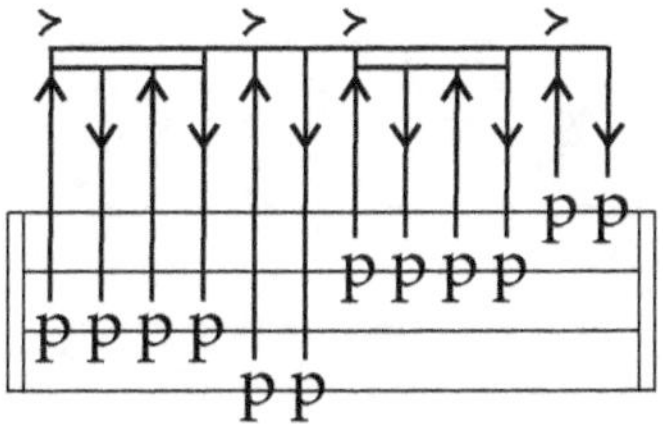

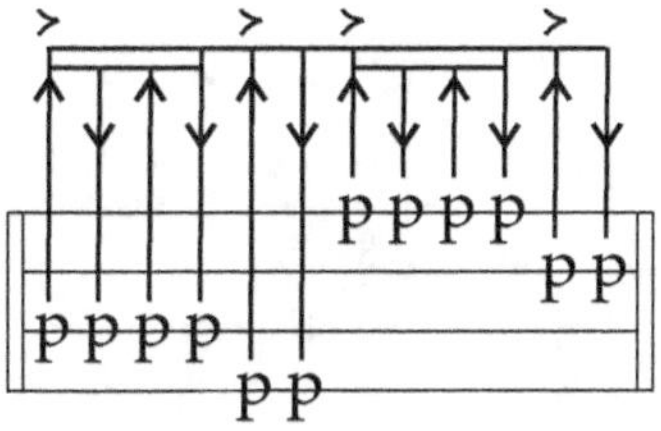

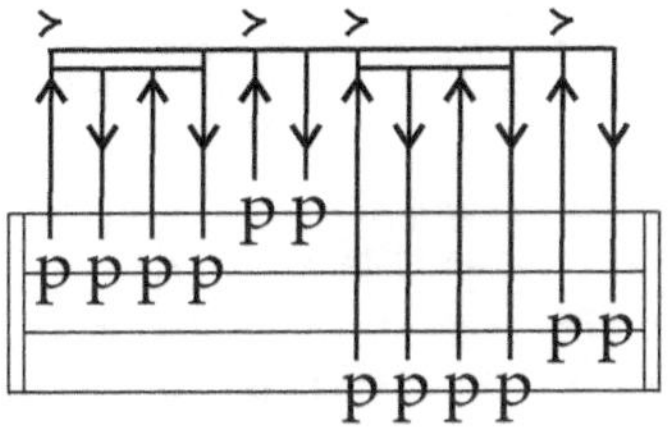

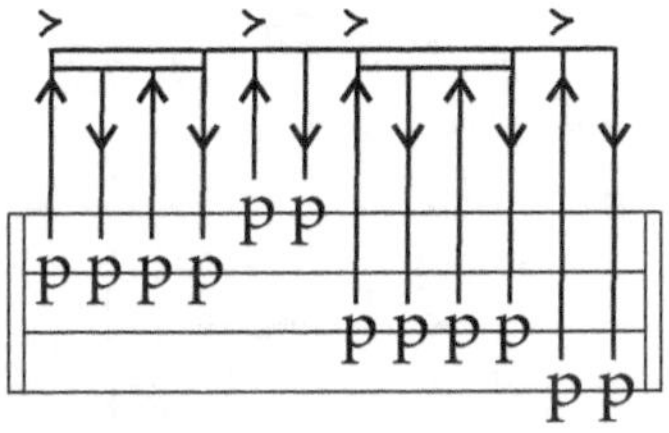

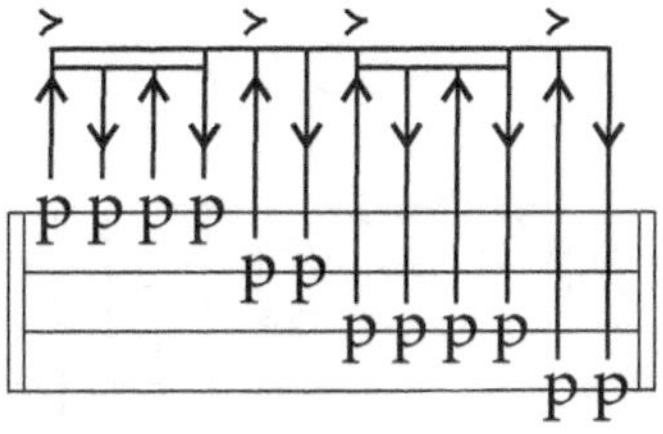

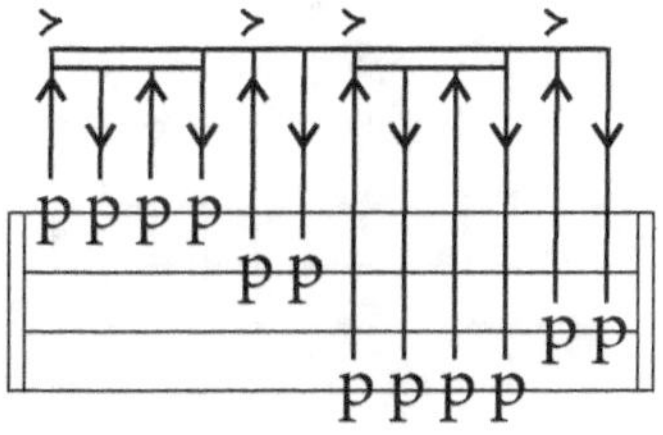

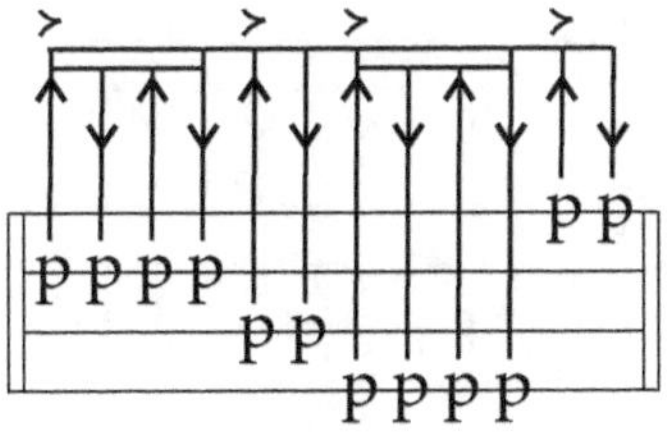

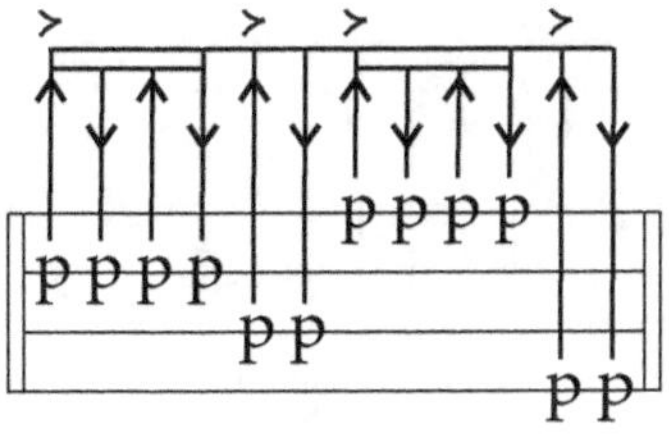

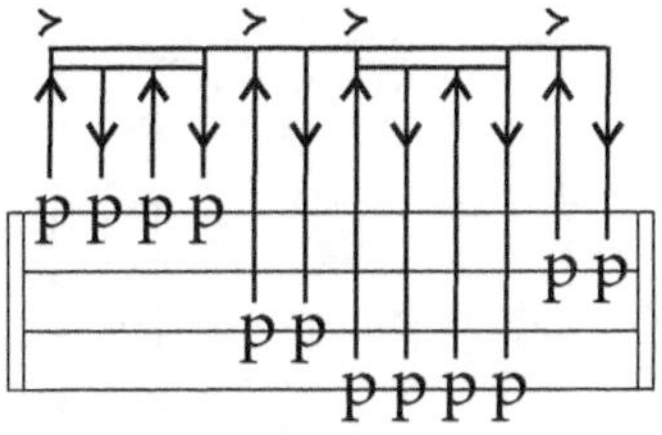

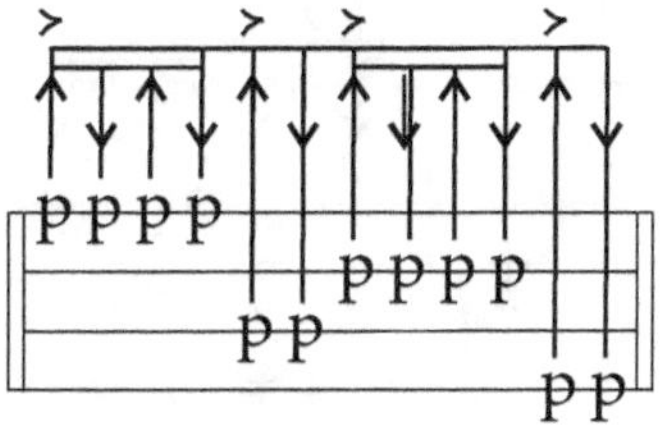

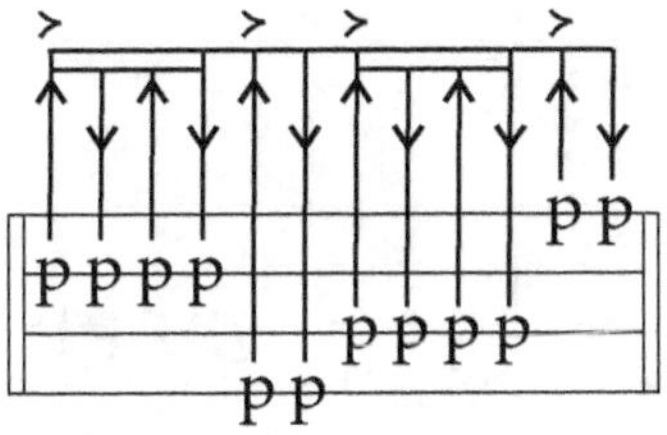

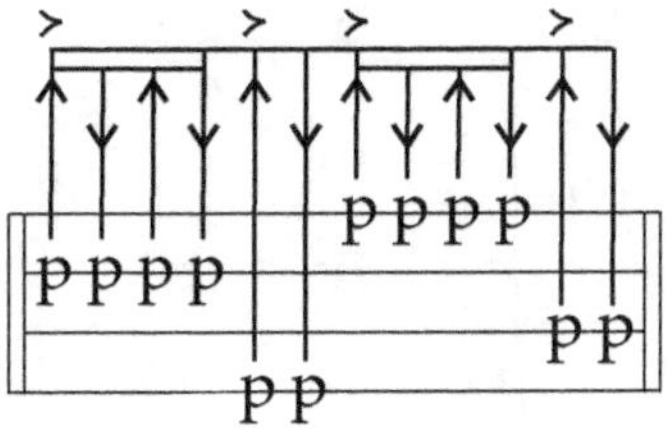

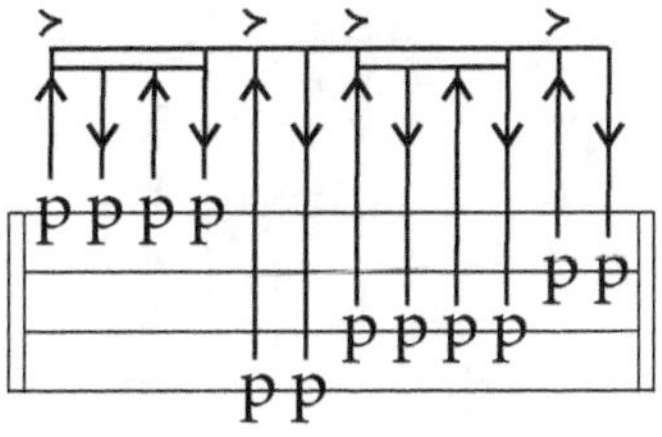

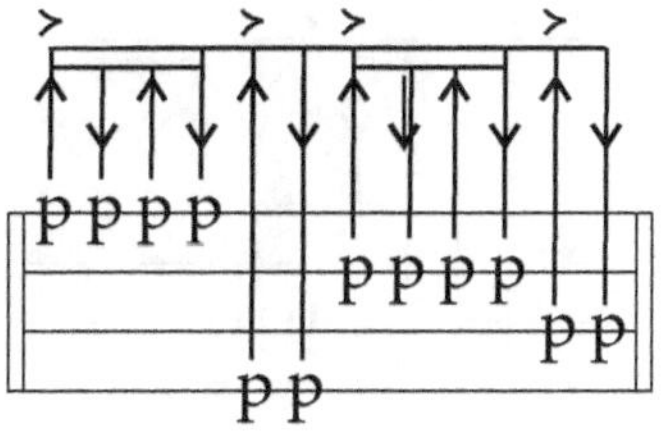

VARIATION II

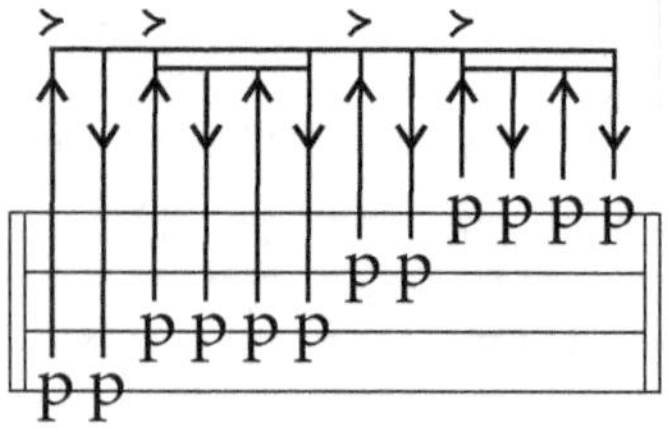

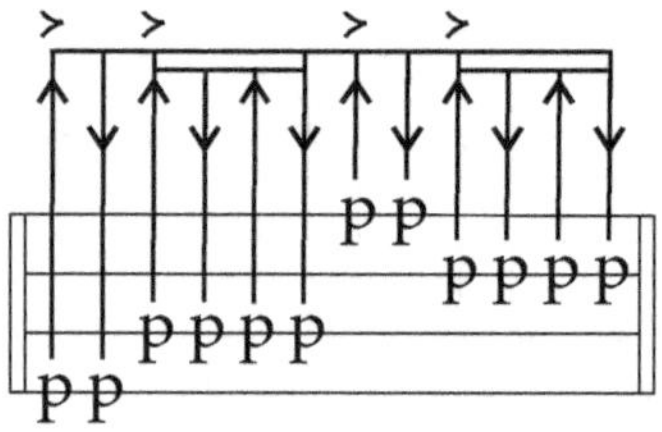

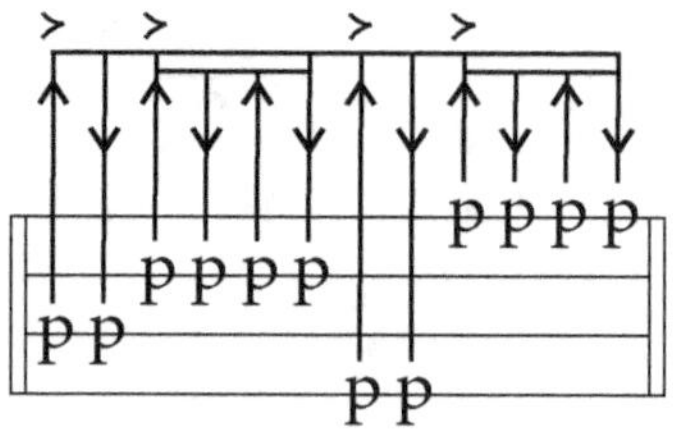

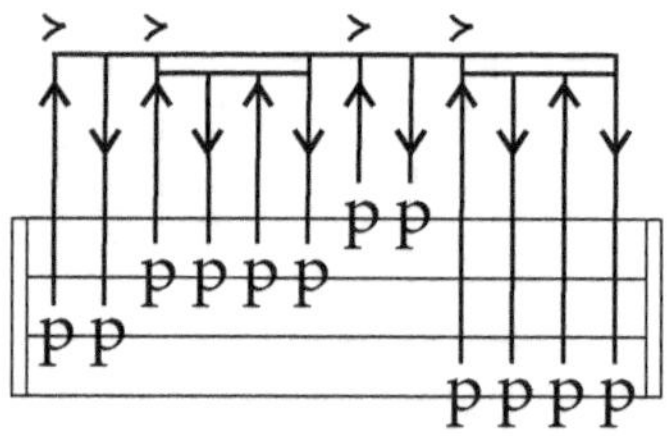

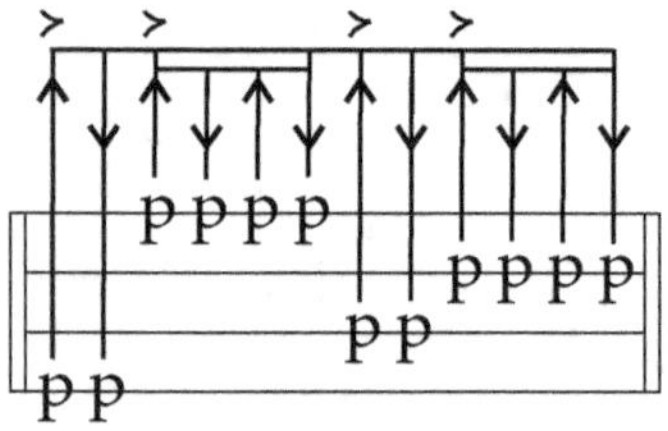

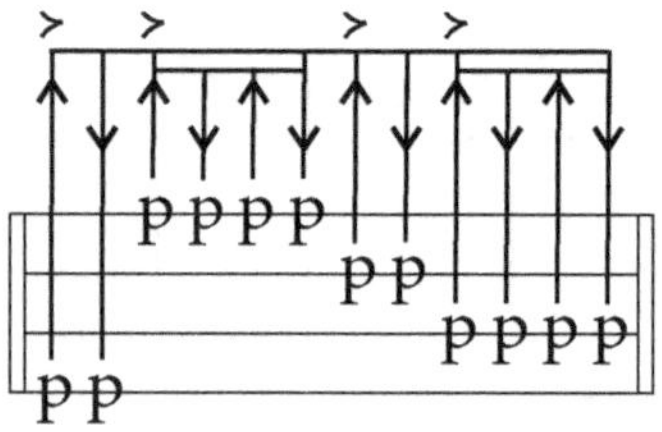

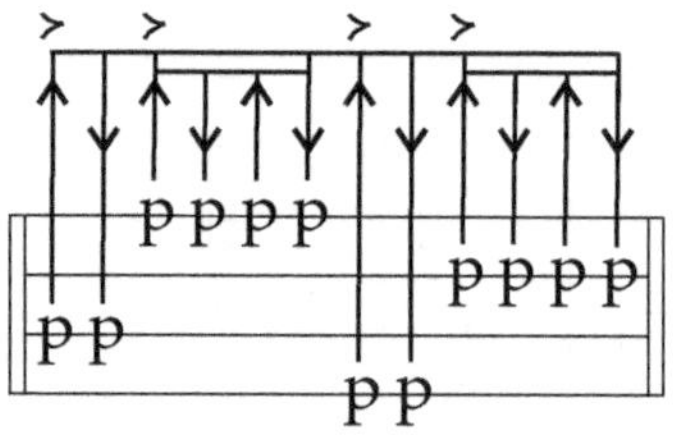

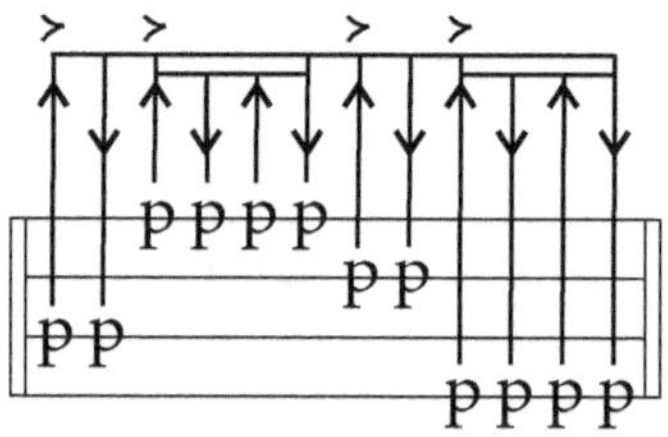

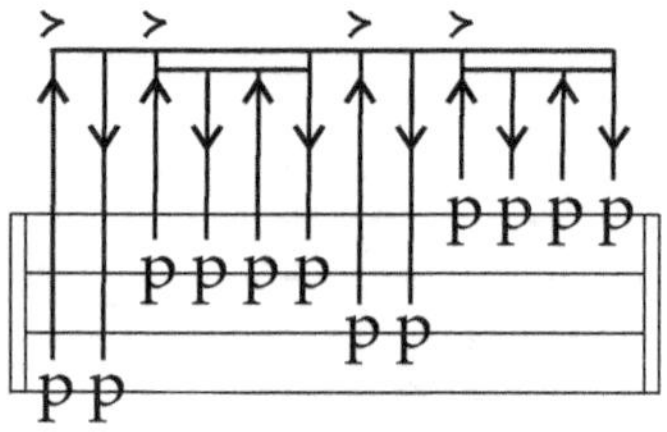

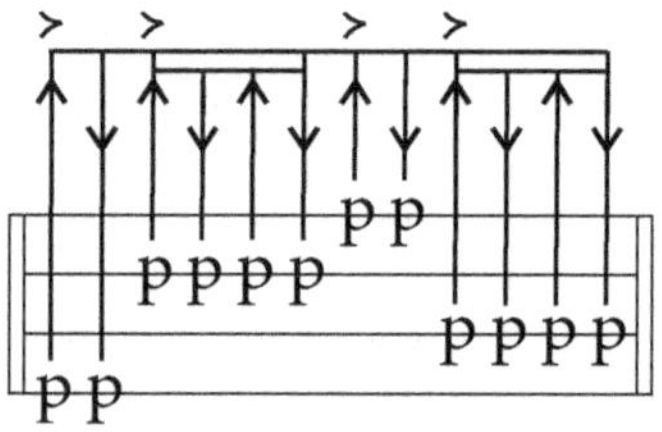

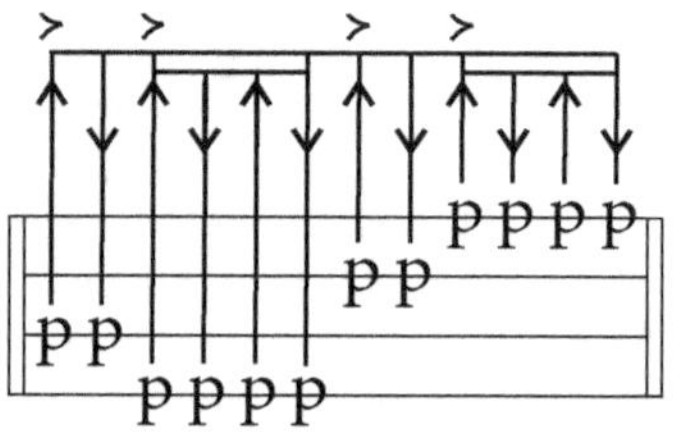

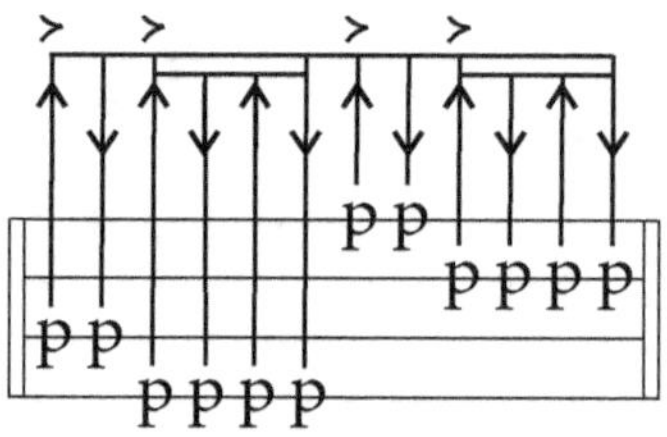

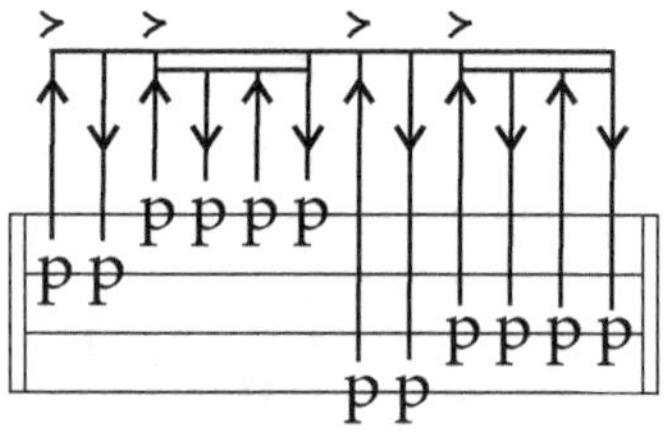

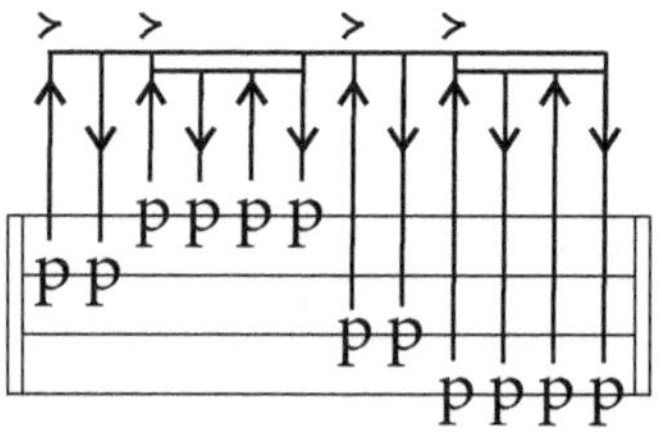

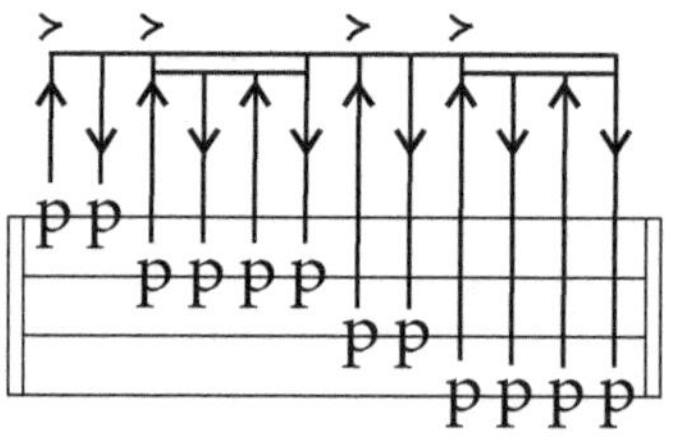

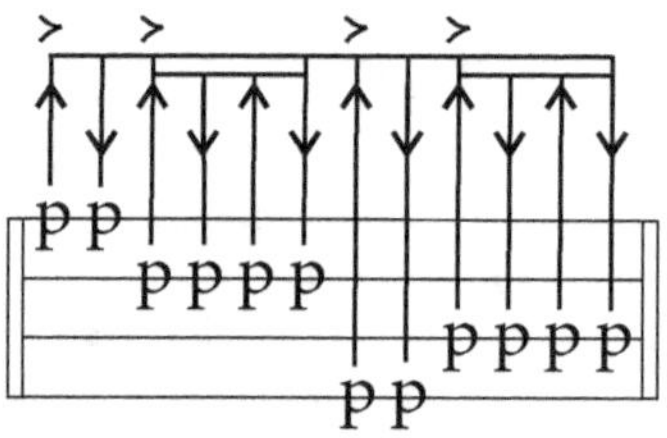

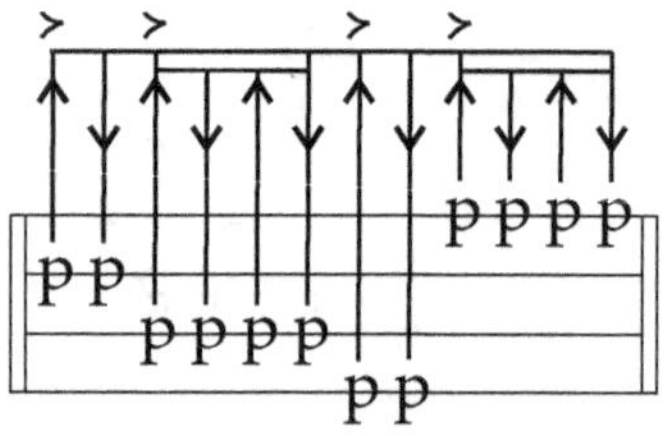

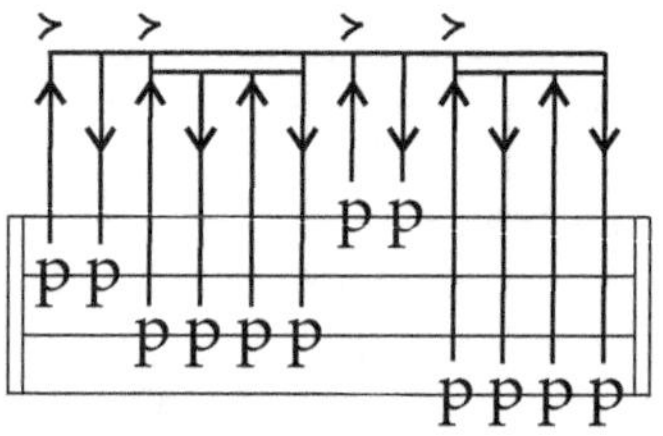

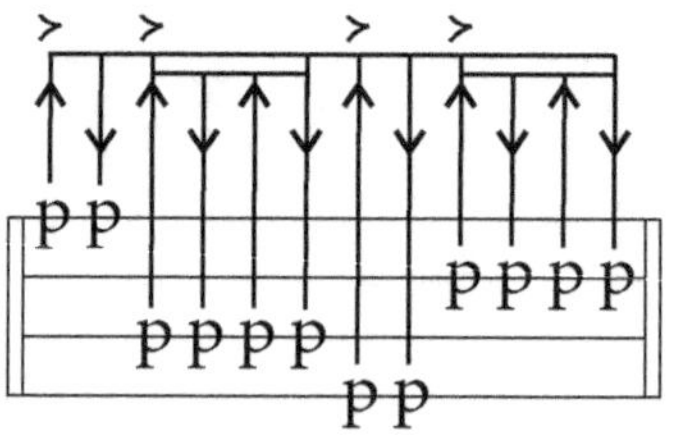

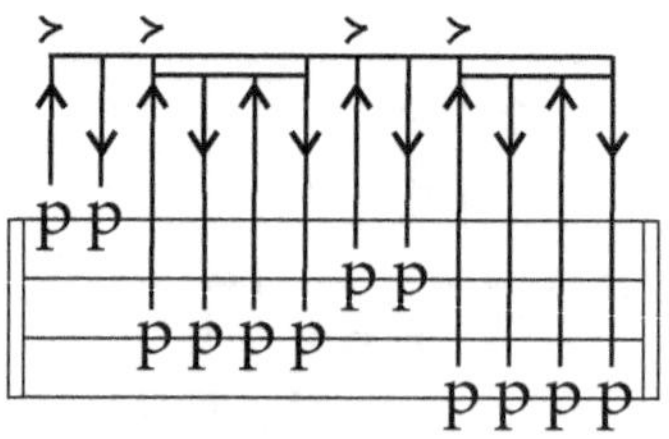

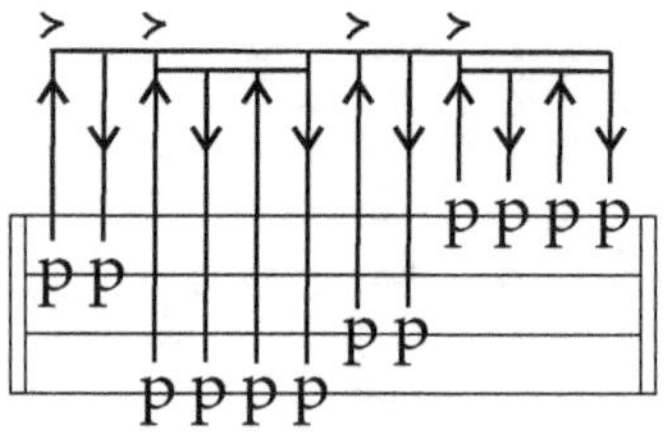

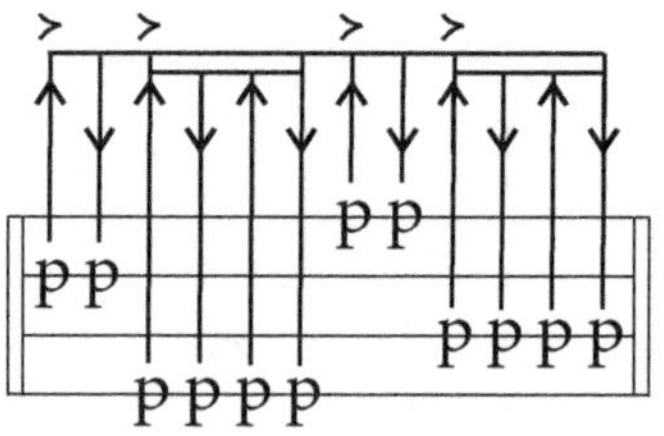

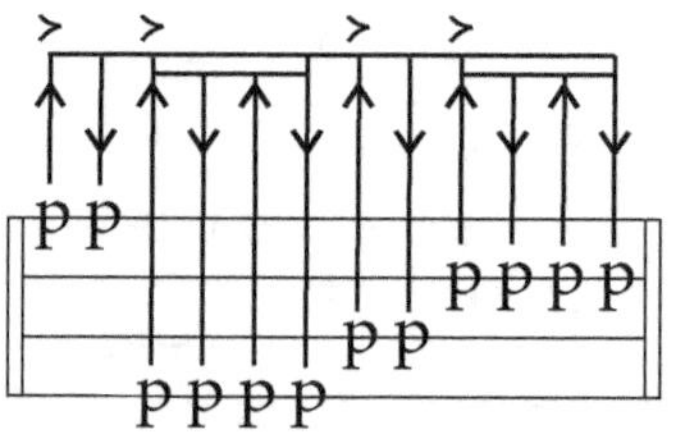

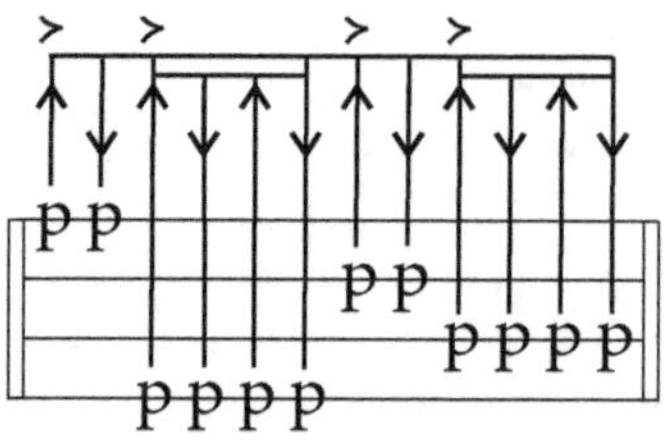

VARIATION III

F1 F2 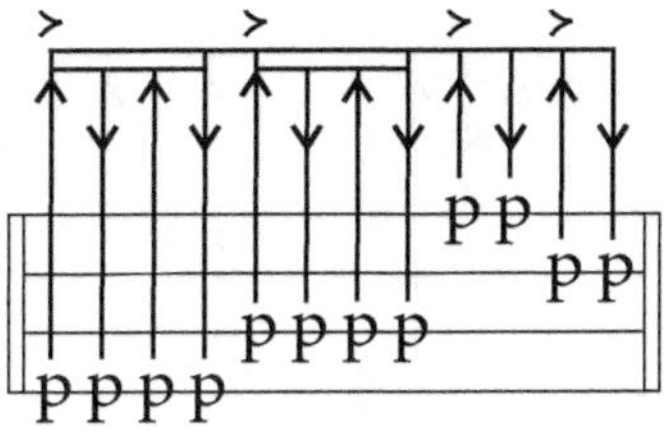 F3 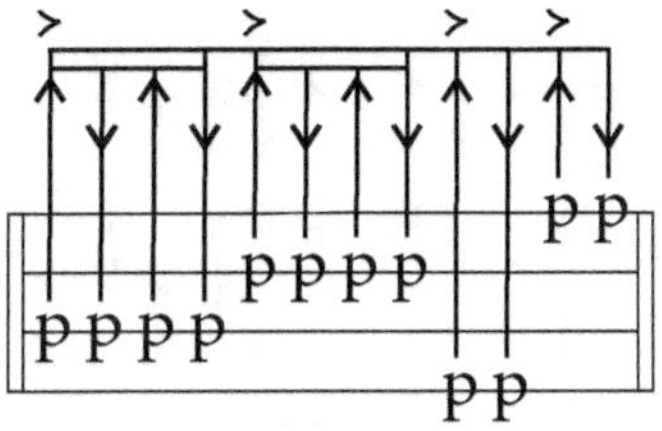 F4

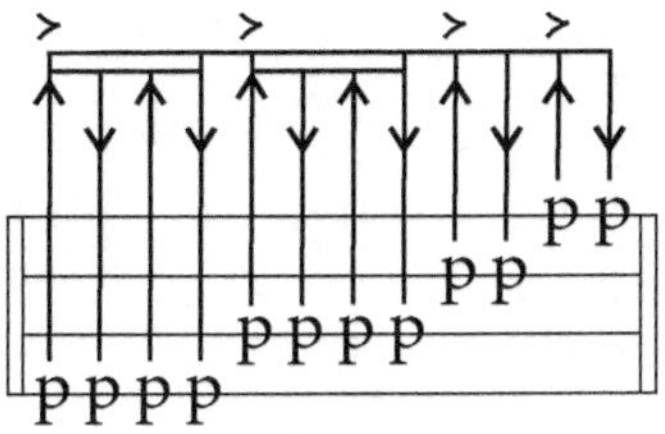

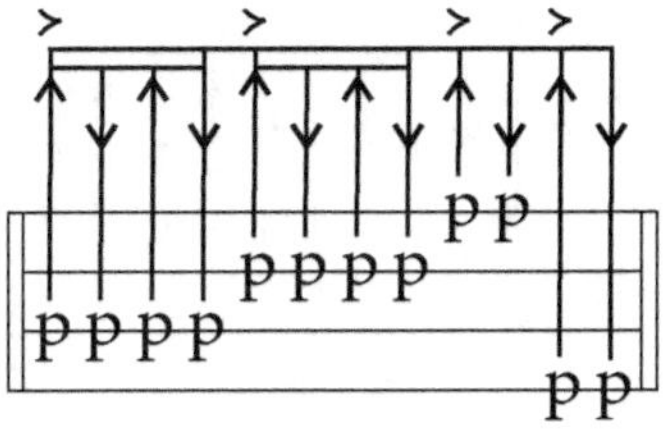

F5 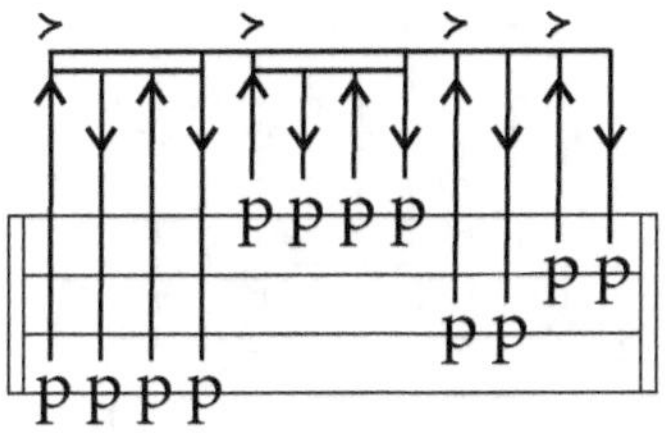 F6 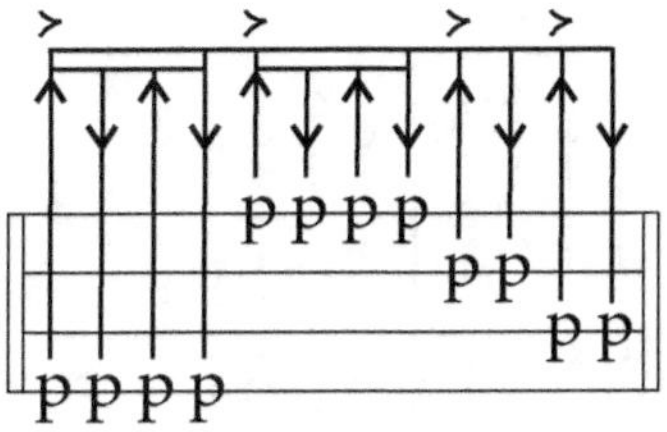 F7 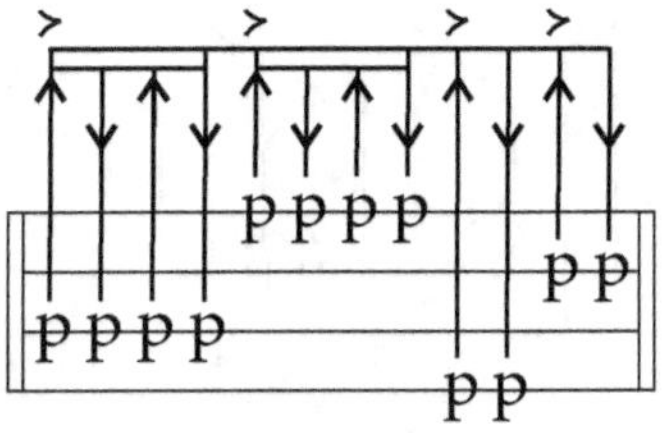 F8

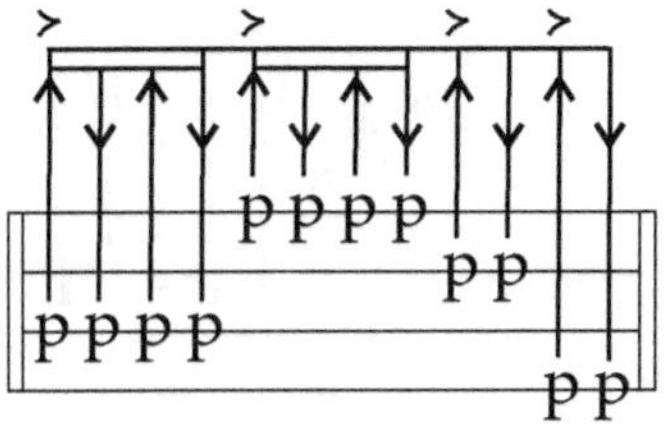

F9 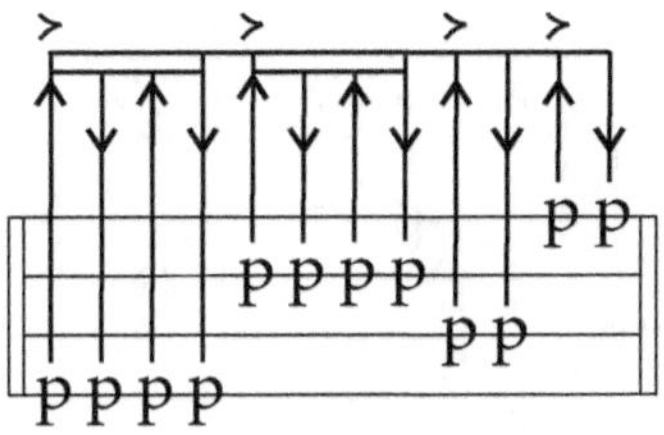 F10 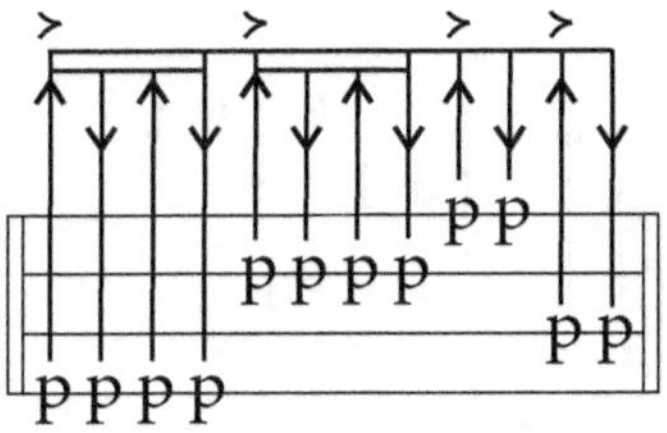 F11 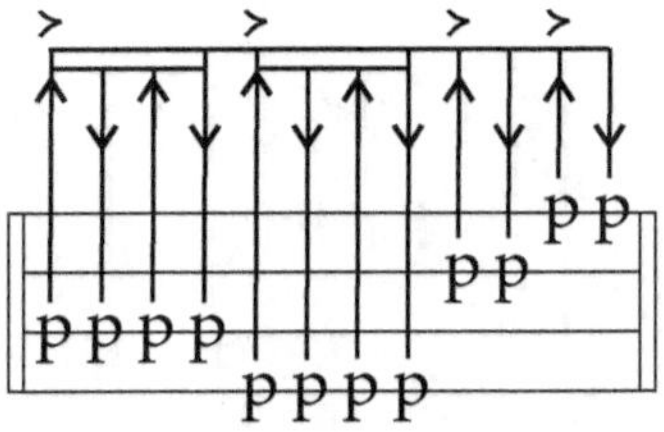 F12

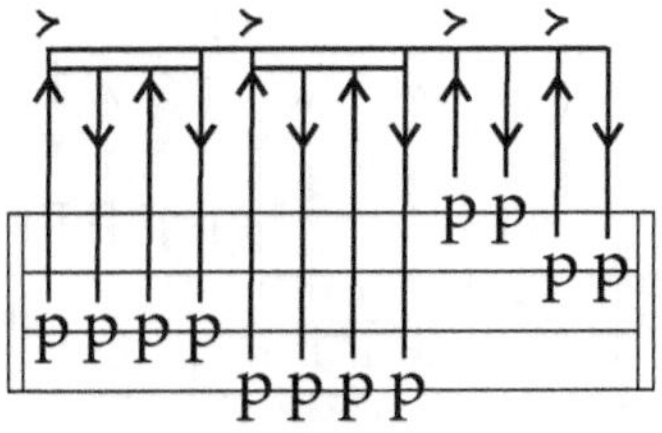

F13 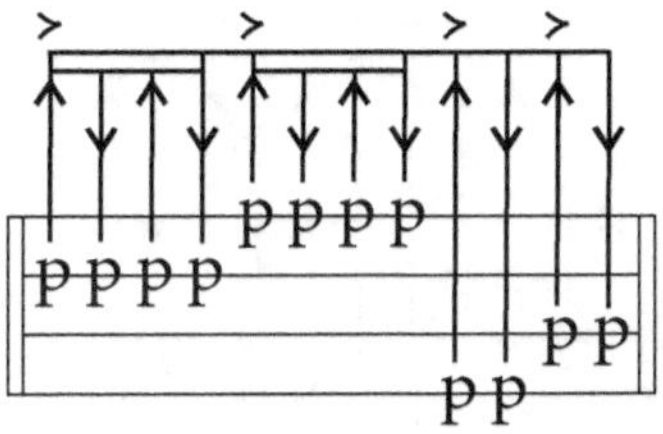 F14 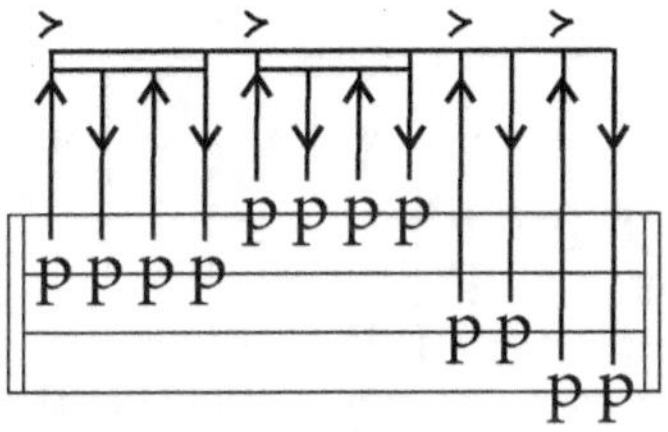 F15 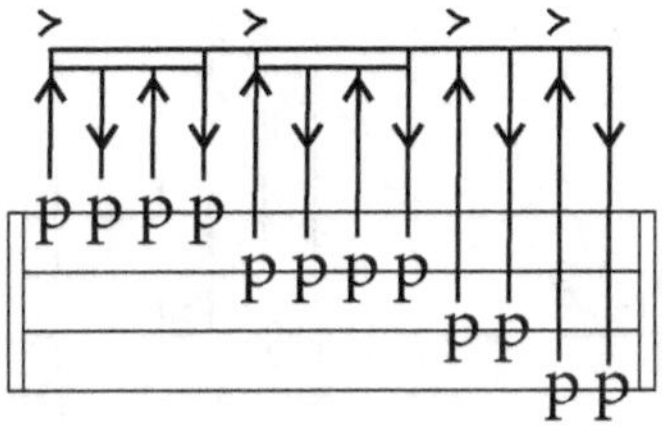 F16

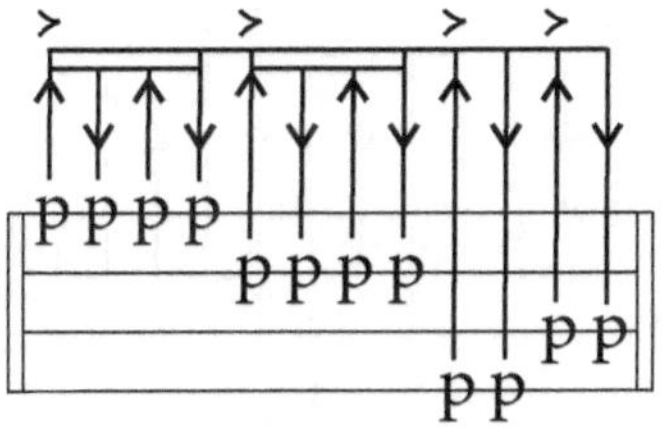

F17 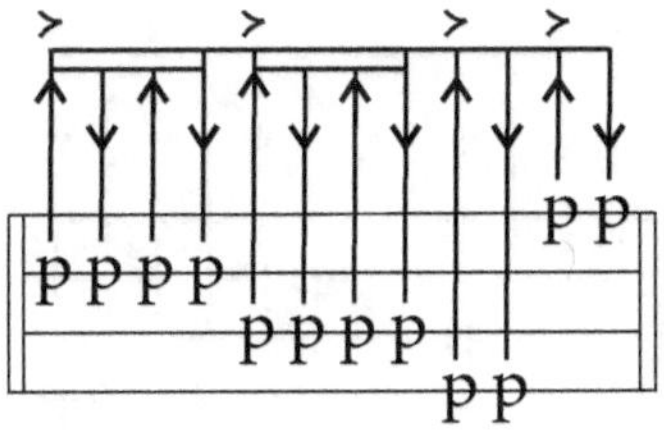 F18 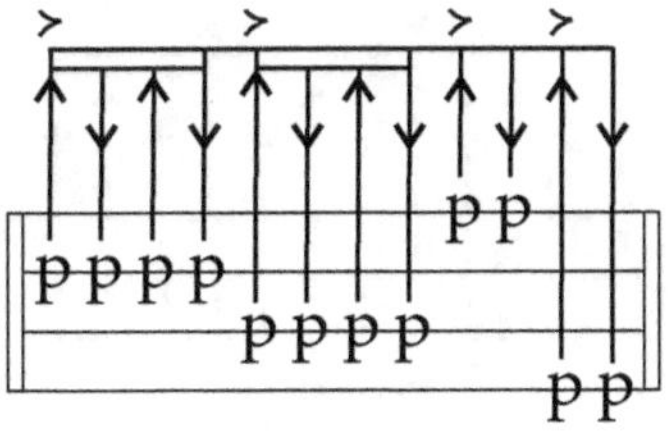 F19 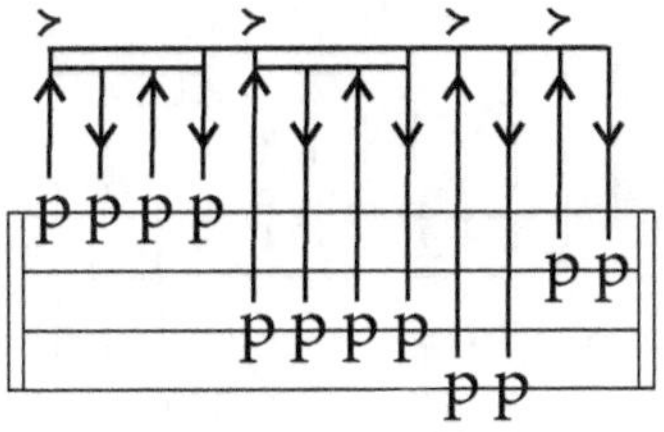 F20

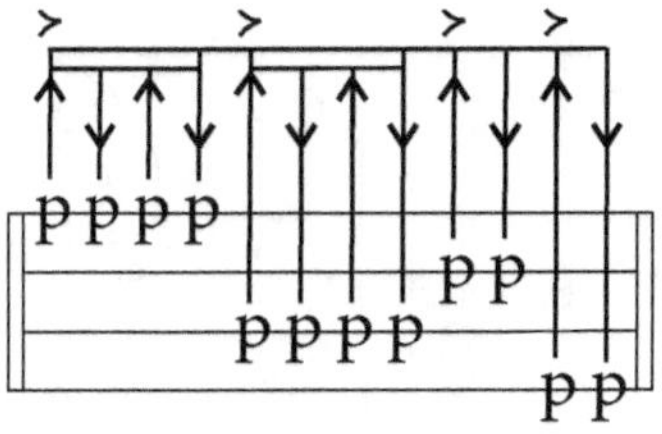

F21 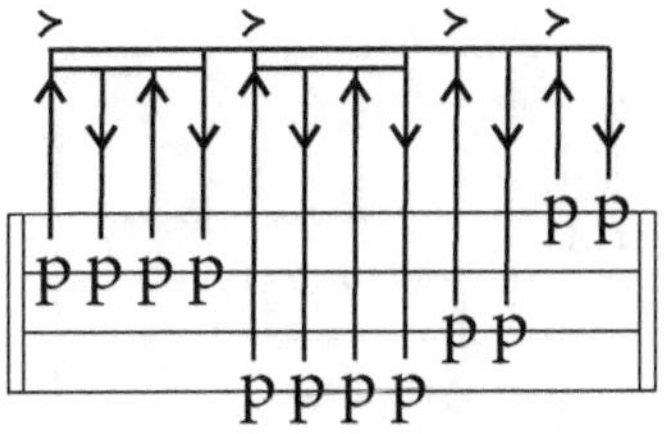 F22 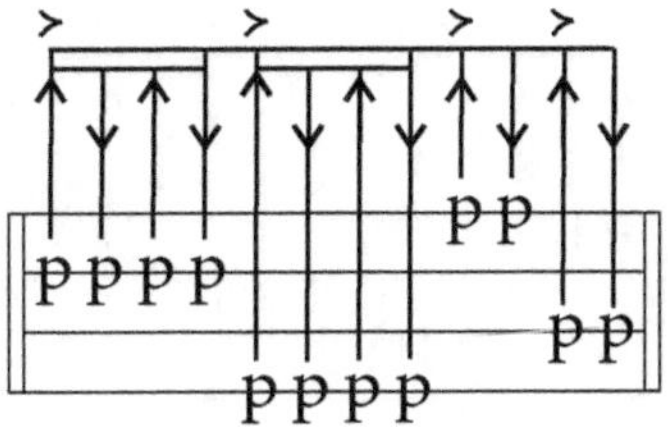 F23 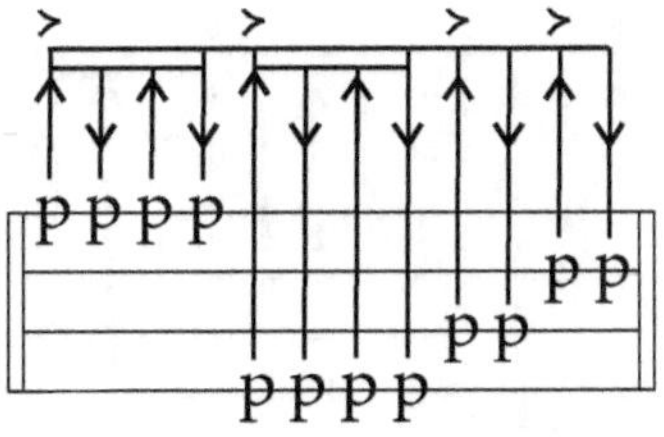 F24

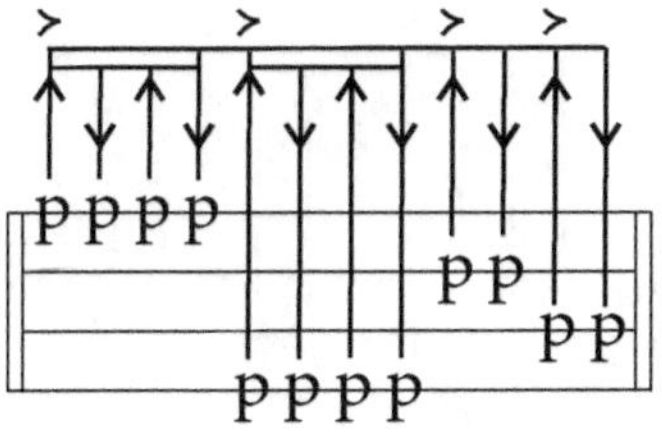

VARIATION IV

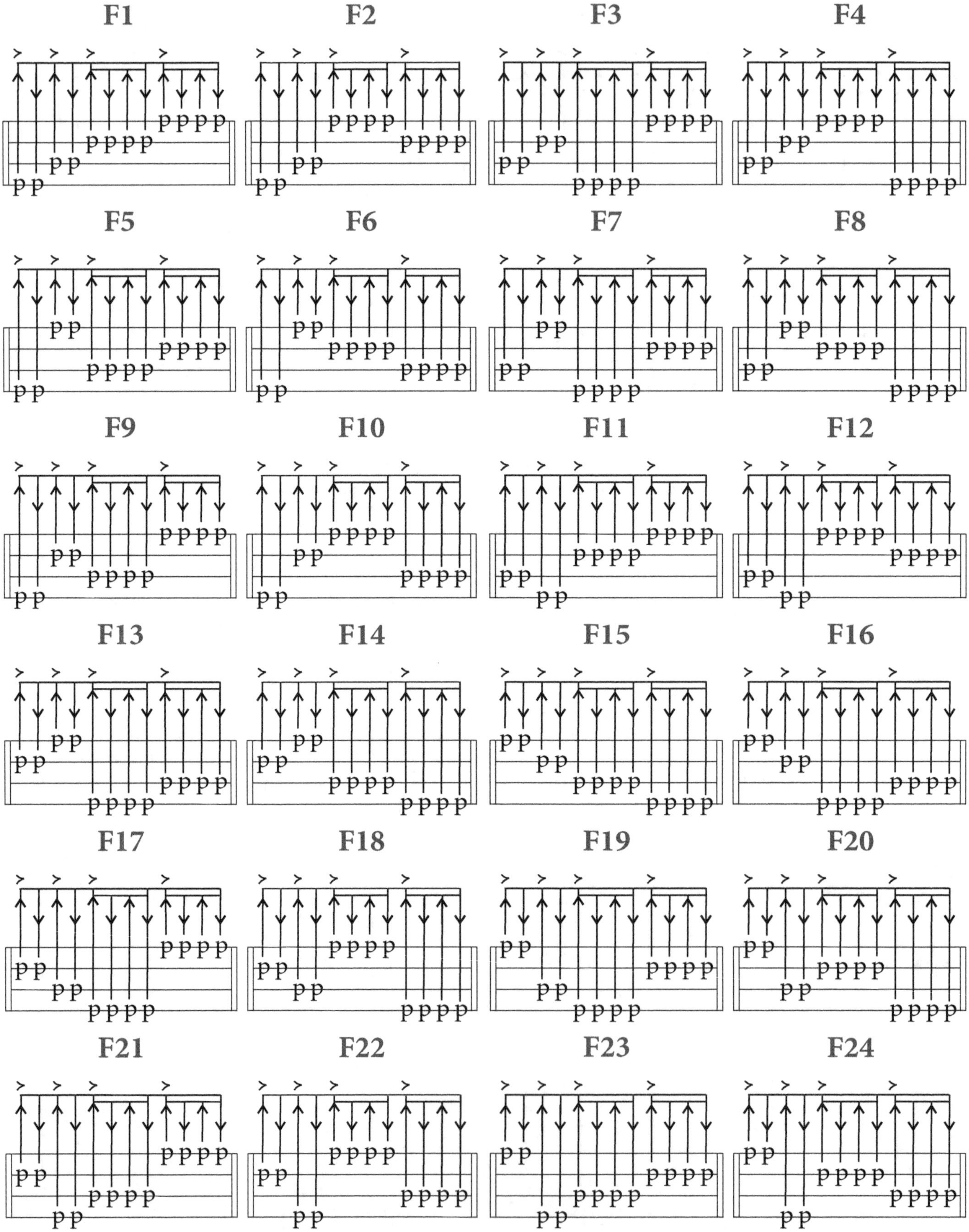

VARIATION V

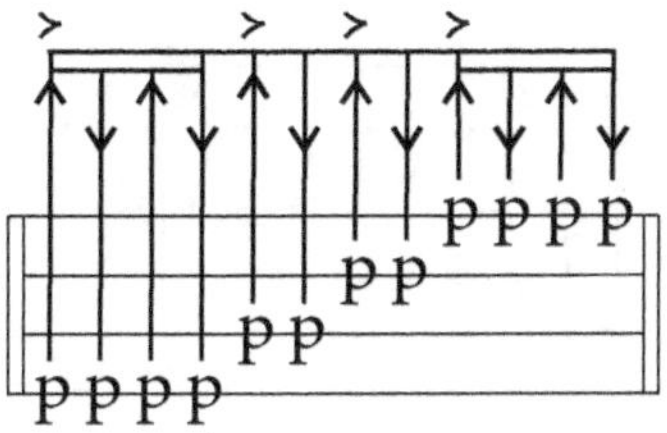

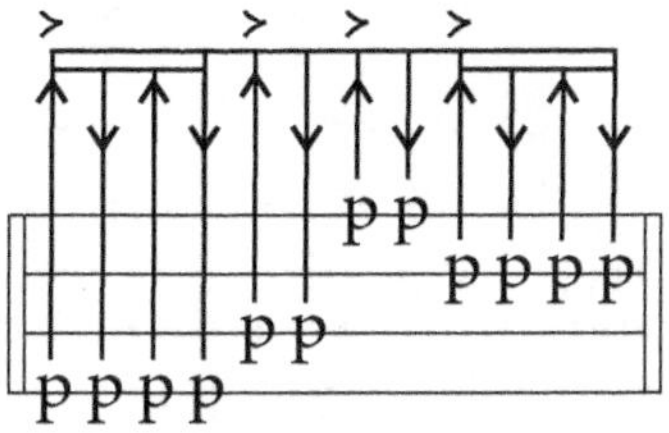

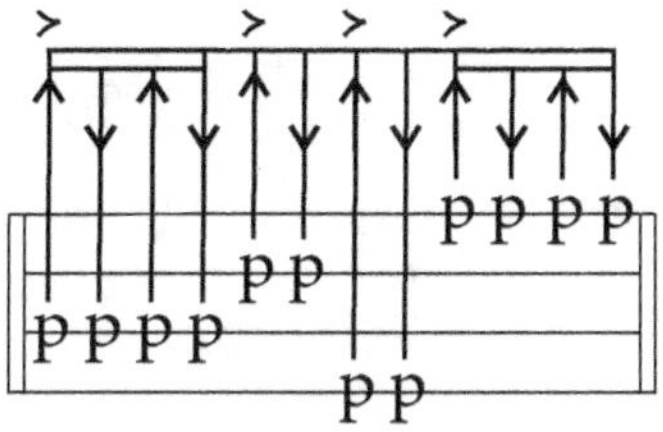

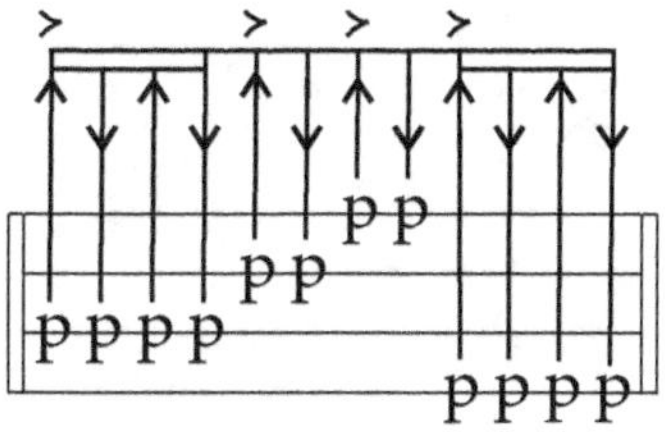

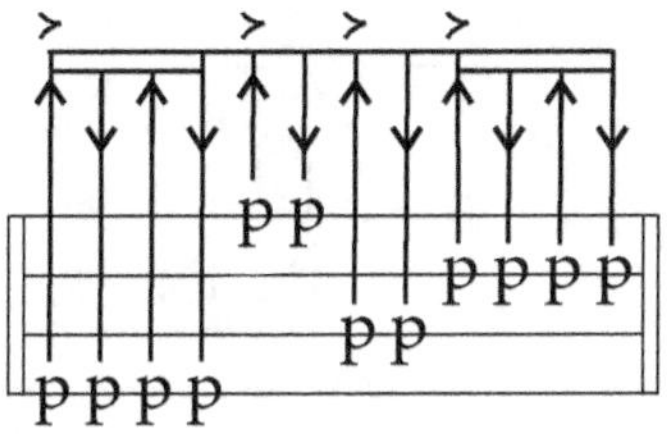

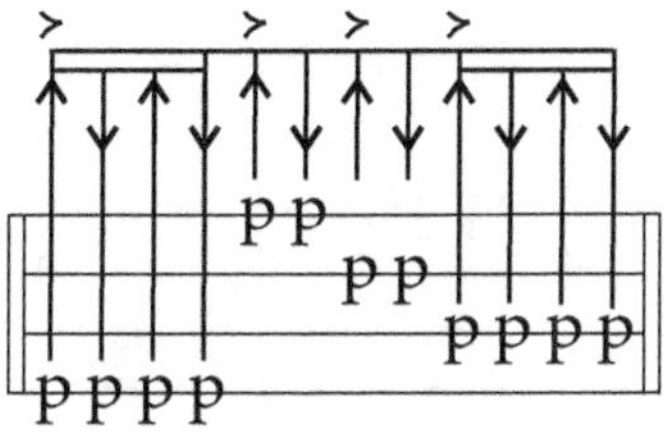

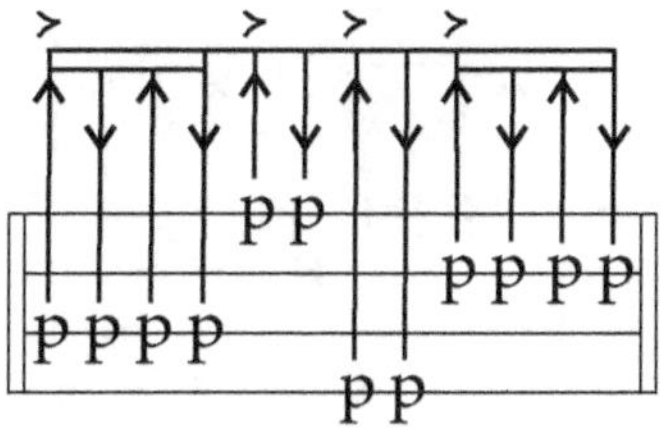

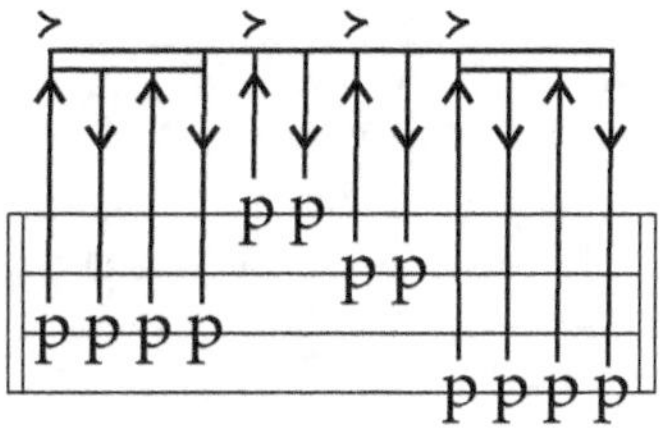

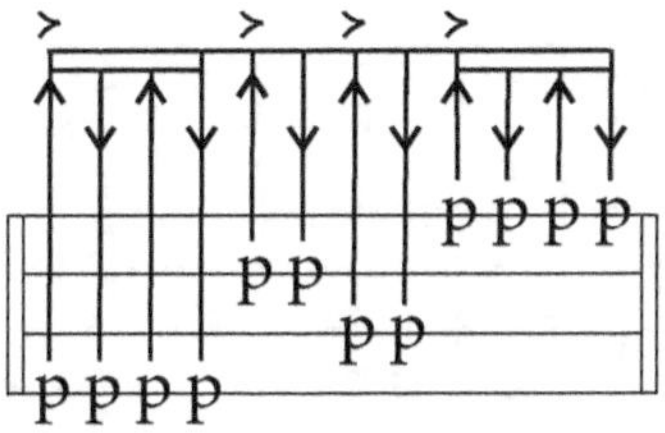

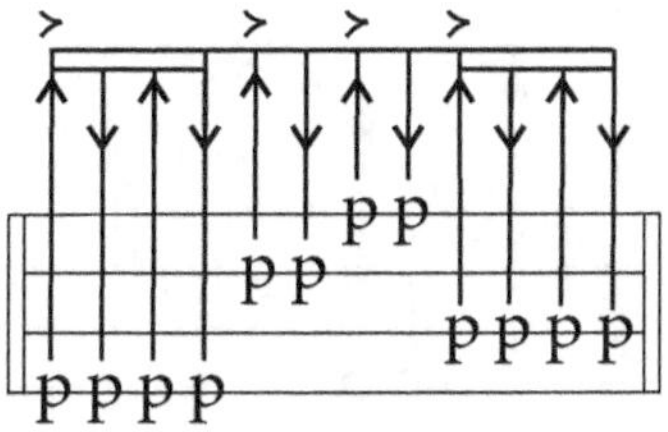

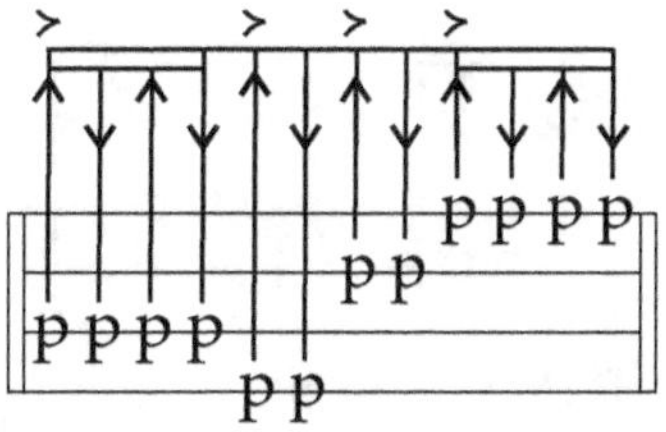

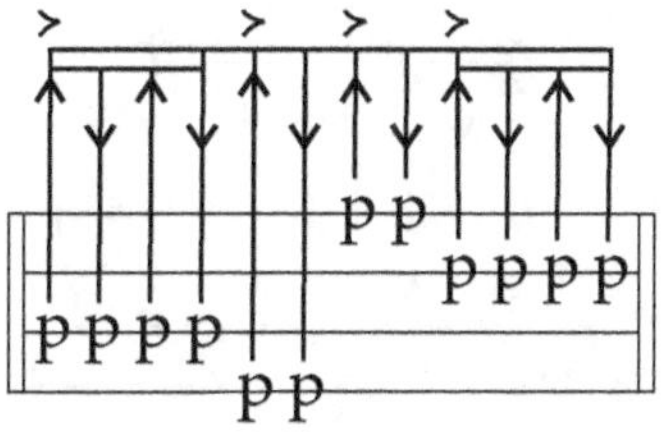

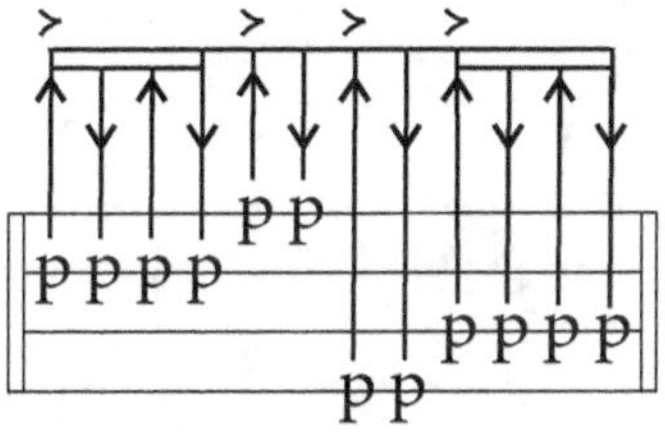

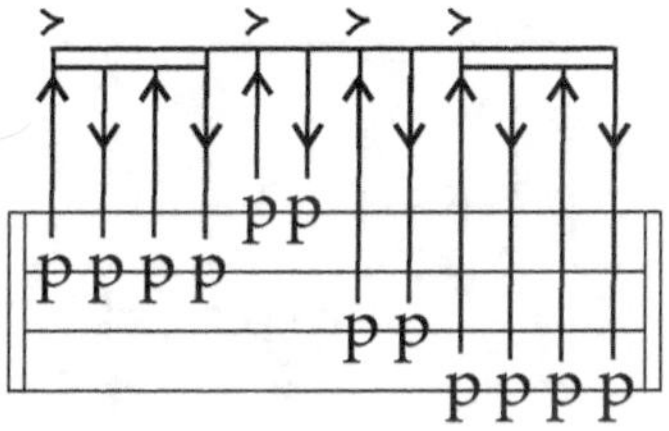

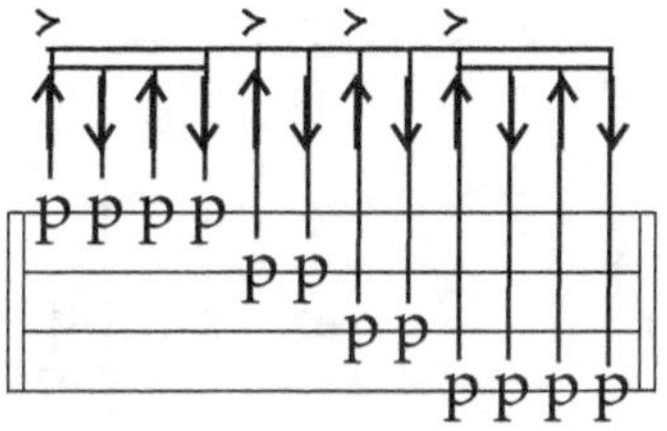

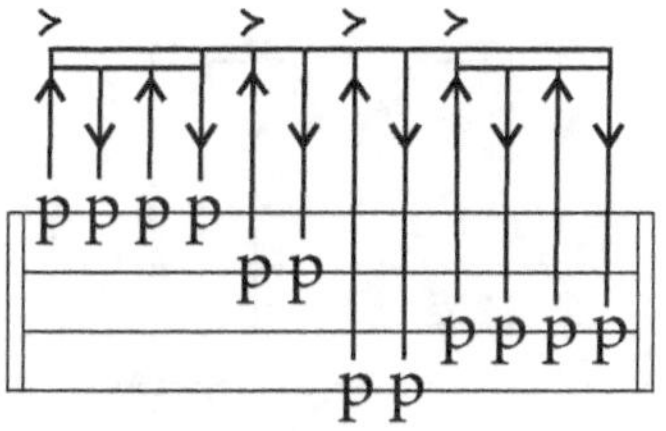

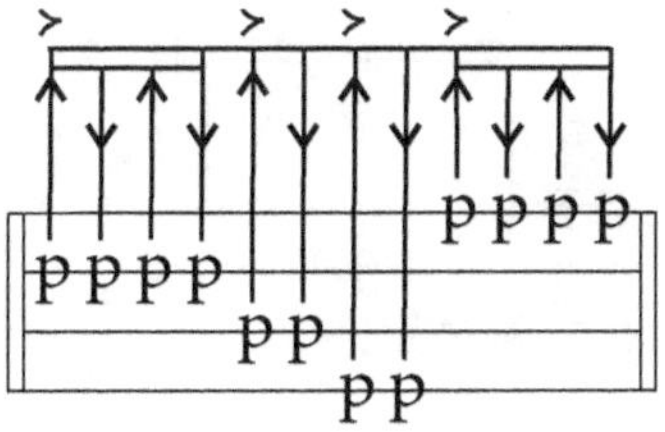

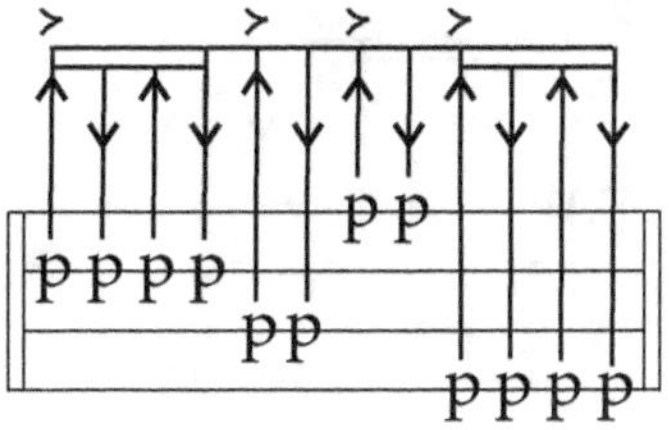

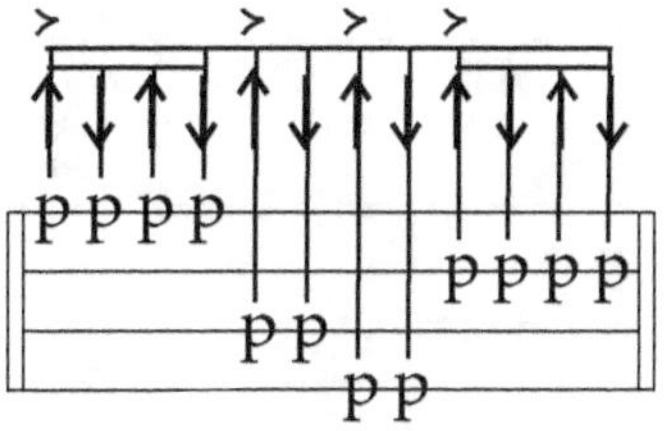

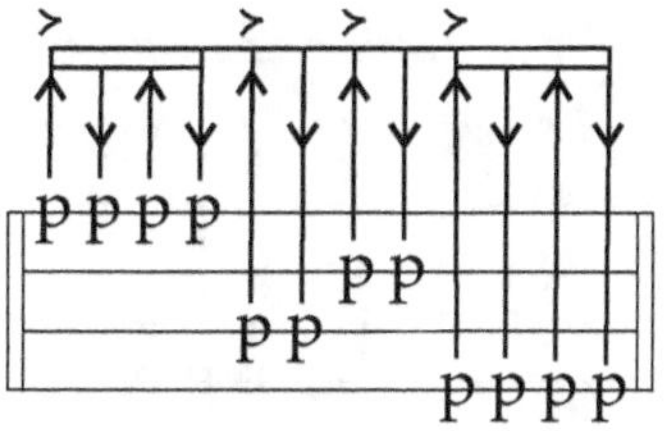

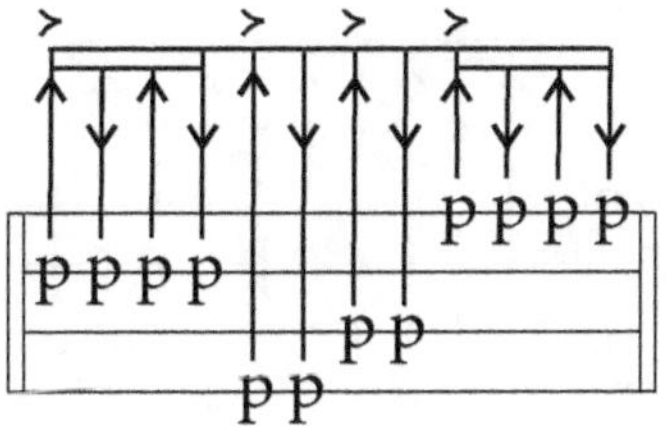

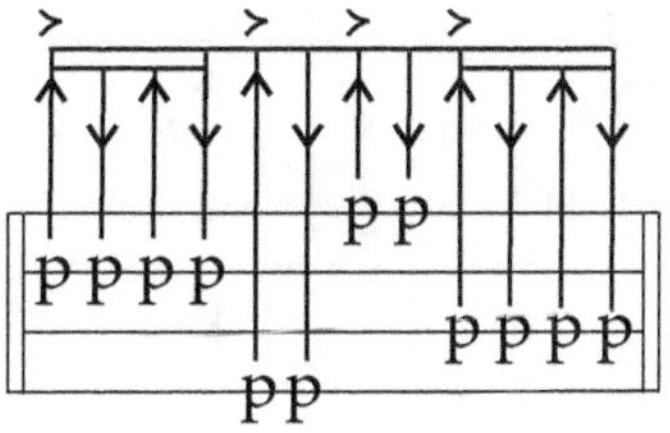

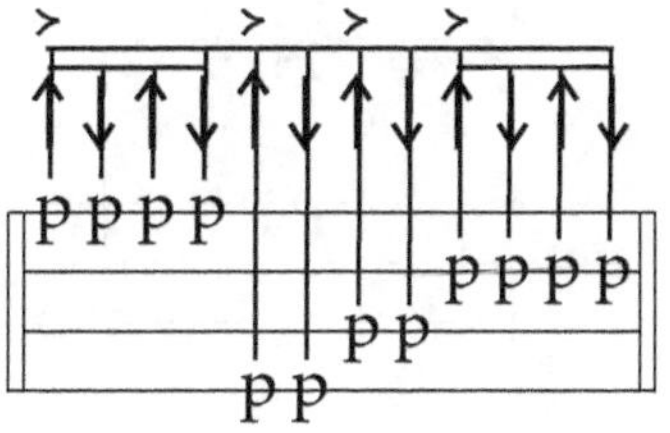

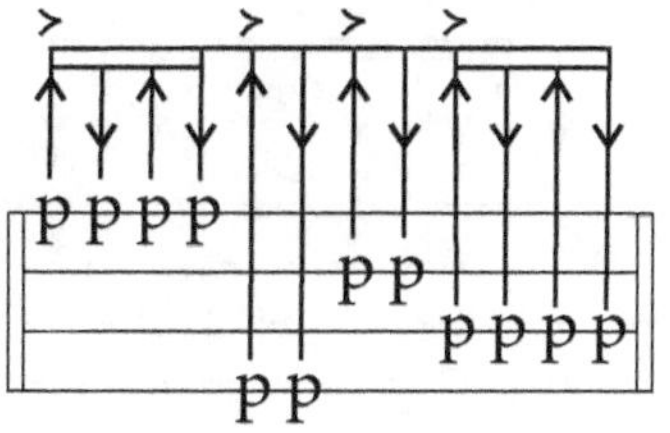

VARIATION VI

F1 F2 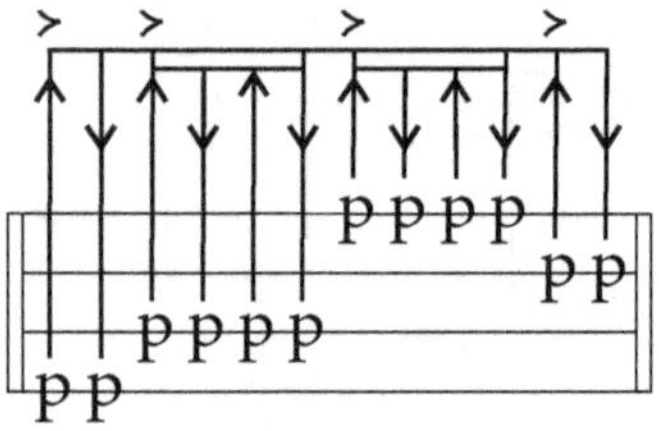 F3 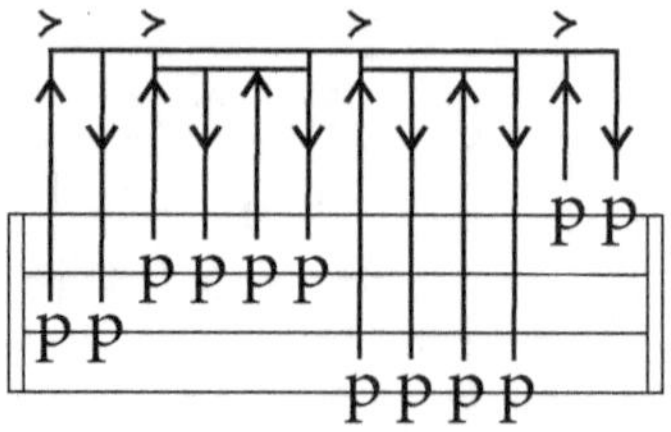 F4 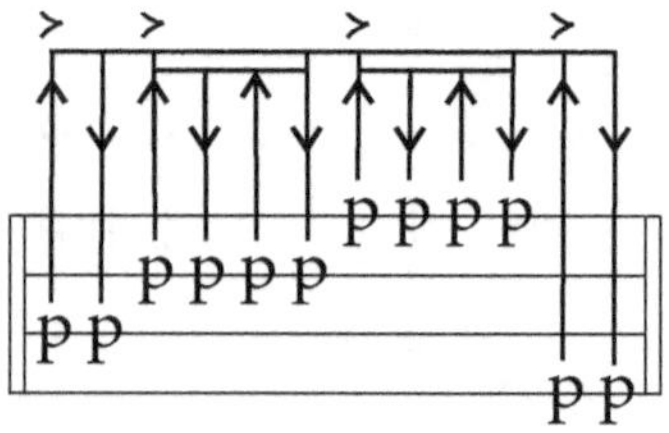
F5 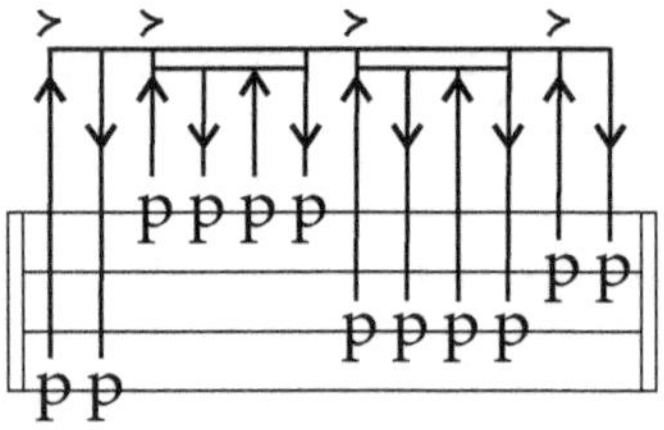 F6 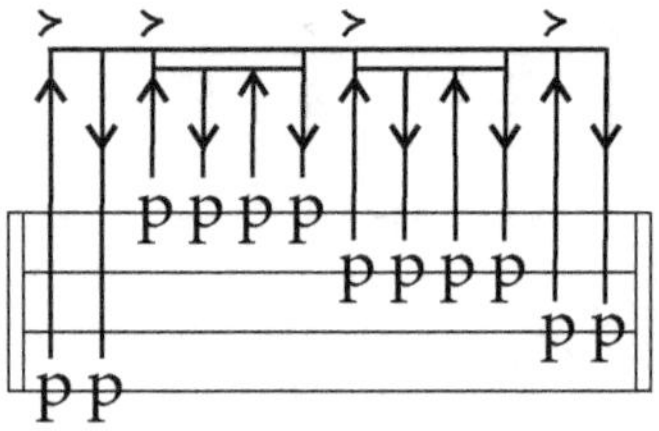 F7 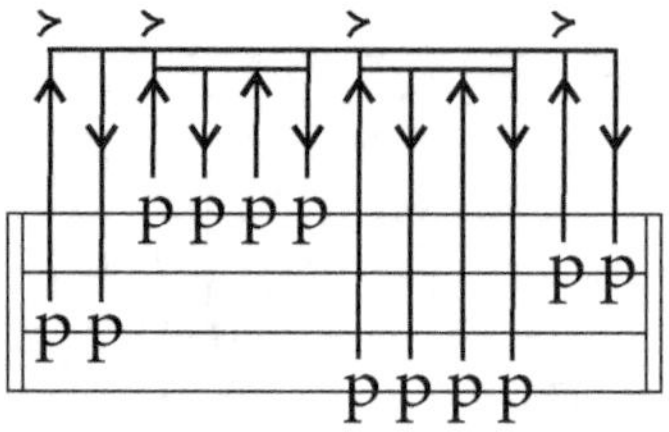 F8 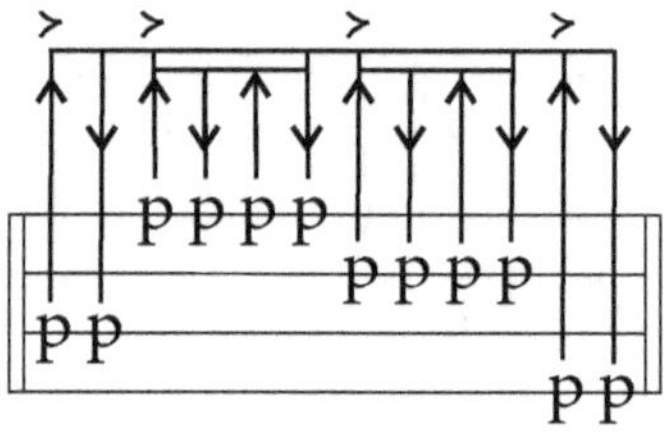
F9 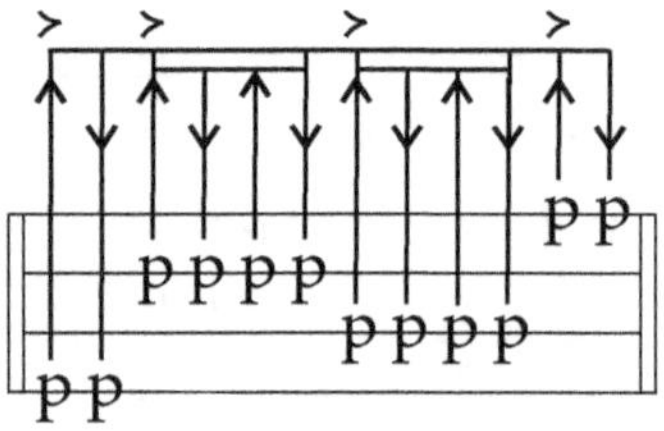 F10 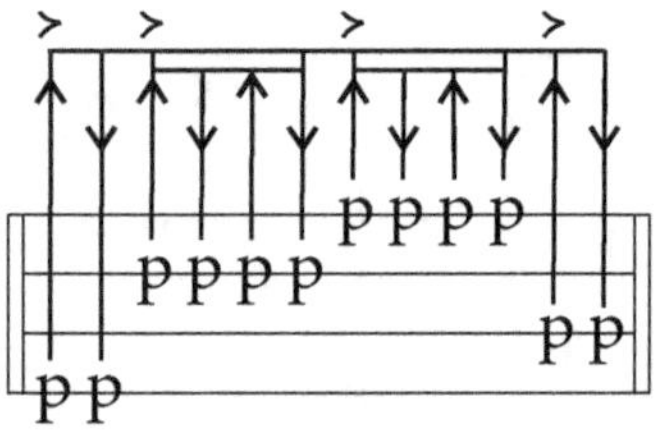 F11 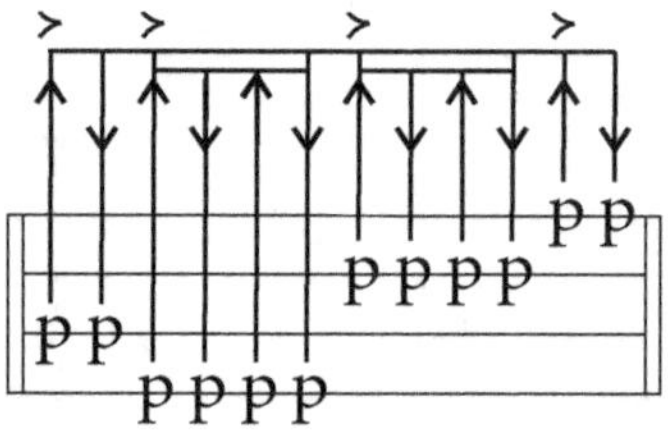 F12 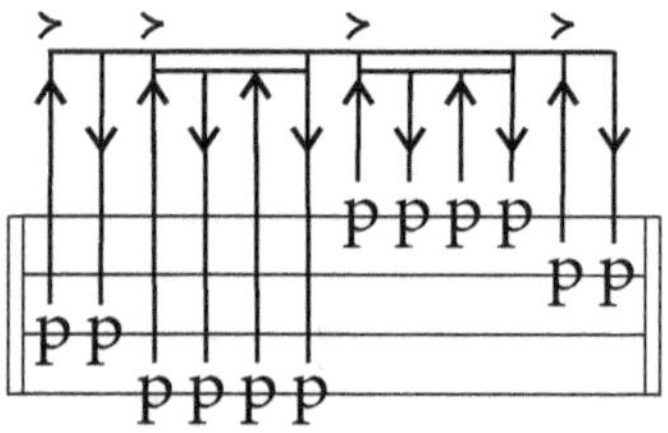
F13 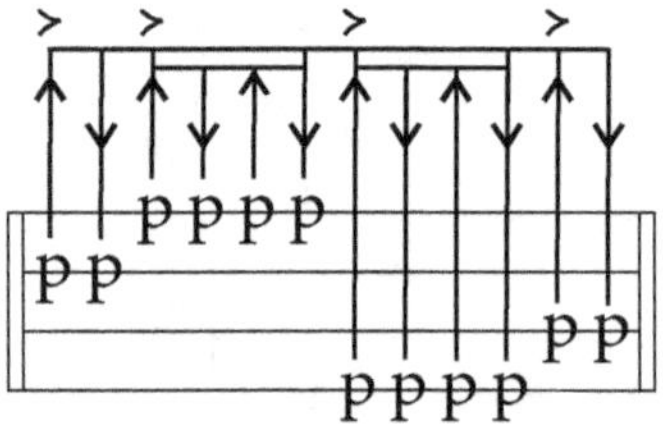 F14 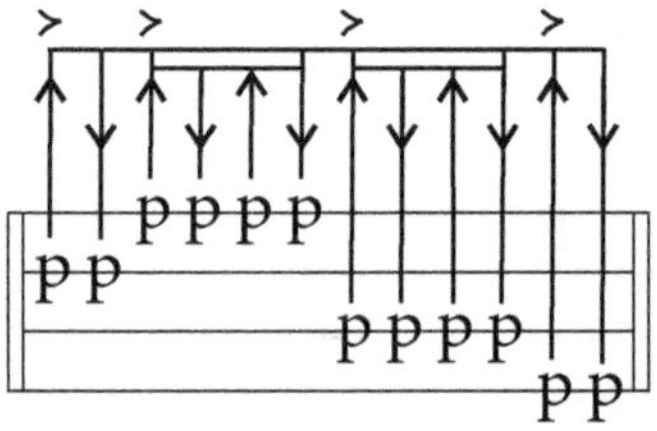 F15 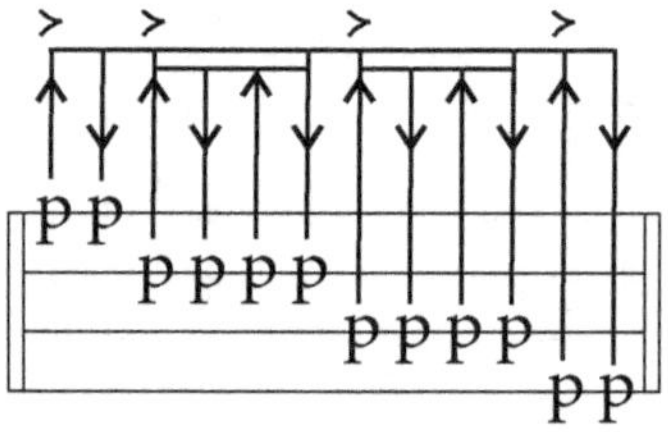 F16 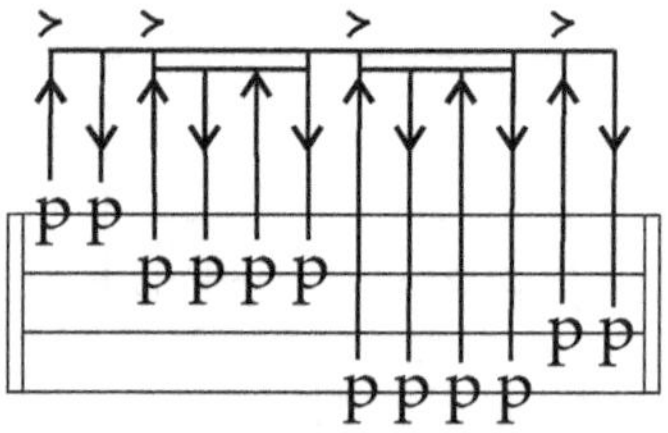
F17 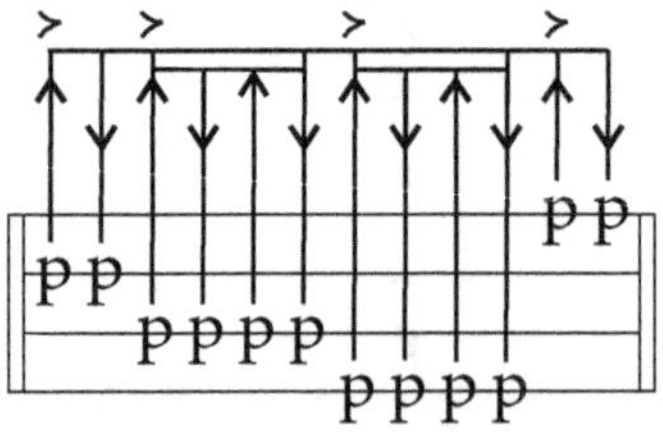 F18 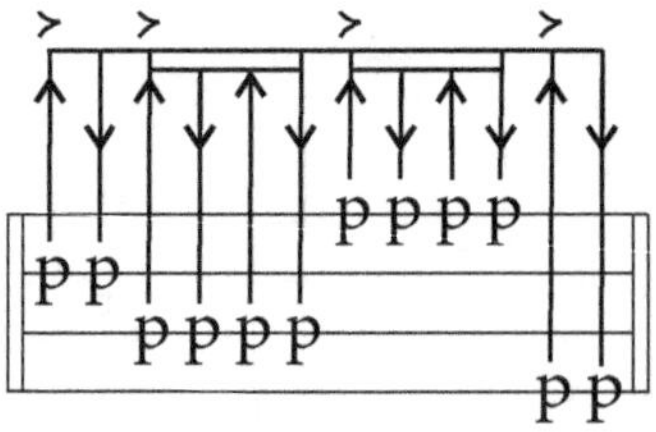 F19 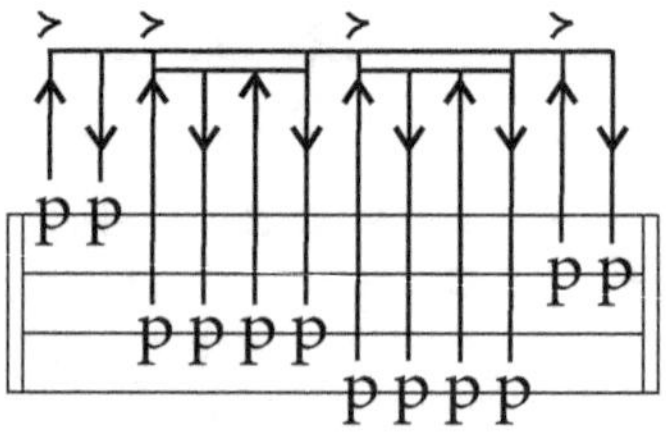 F20 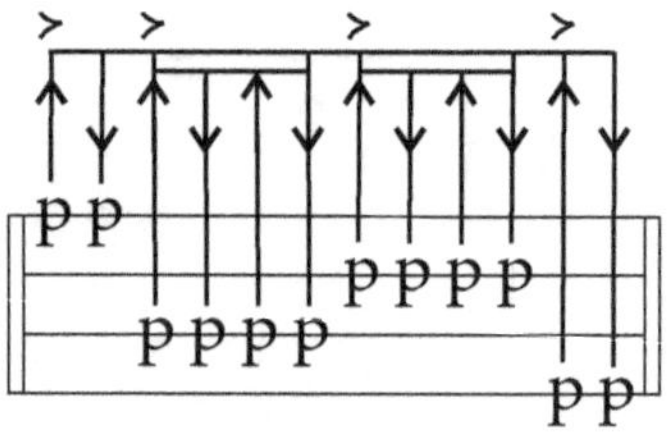
F21 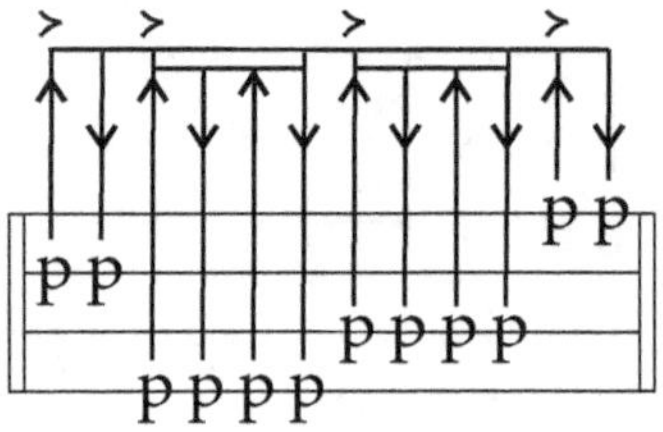 F22 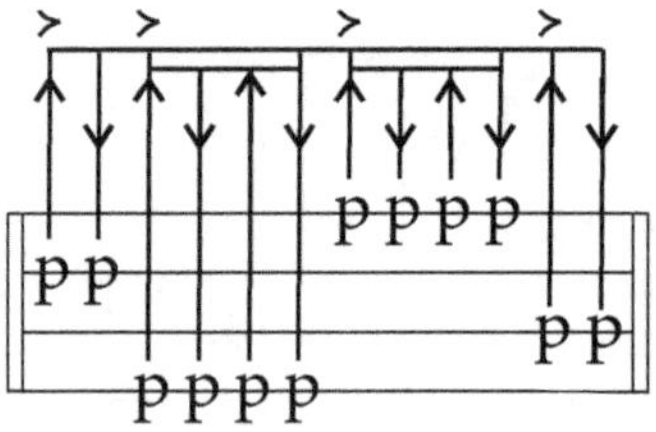 F23 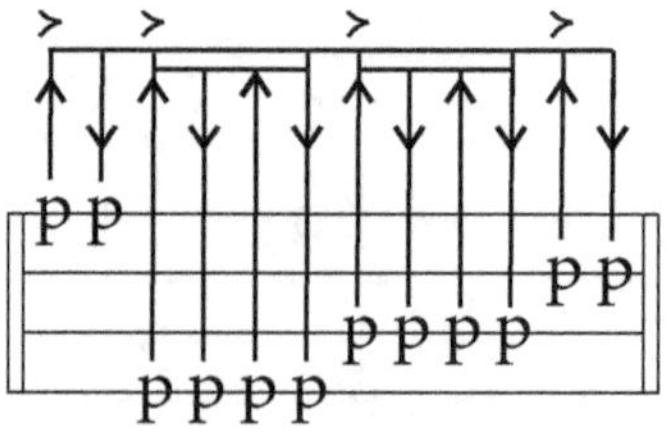 F24

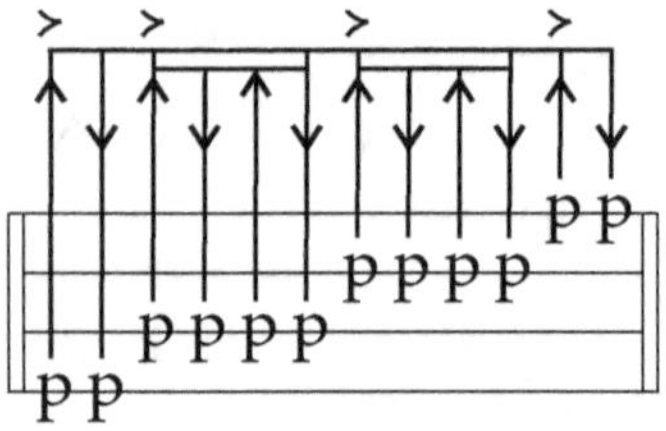

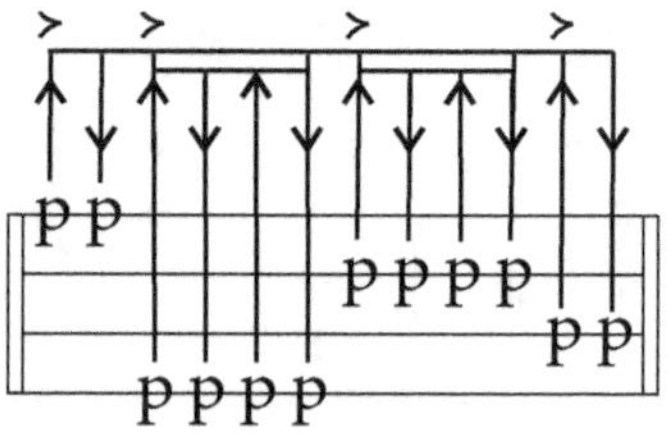

§ IX

Exercise on pulgar on four adjacent strings with two triple (triplets) and two quad strokes within each Formula. The exercise contains six variations with 24 Formulas in each one. The first Formula of each variation is cited below. Isochronous playing of pulgar strokes (triple and quad).

VARIATION I

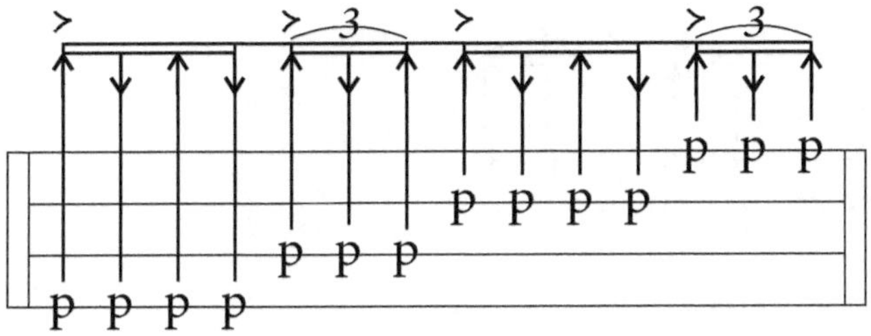

VARIATION II

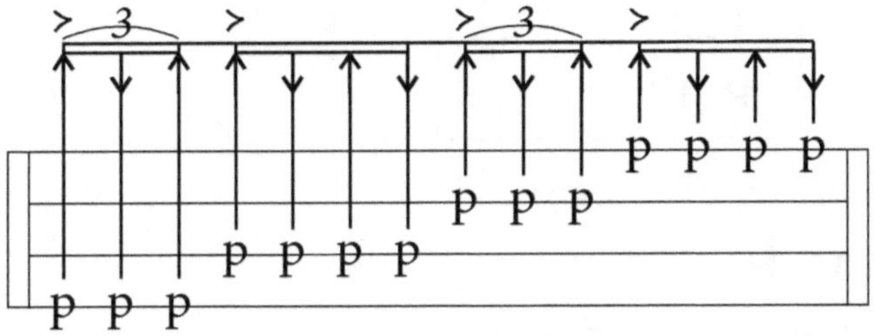

VARIATION III

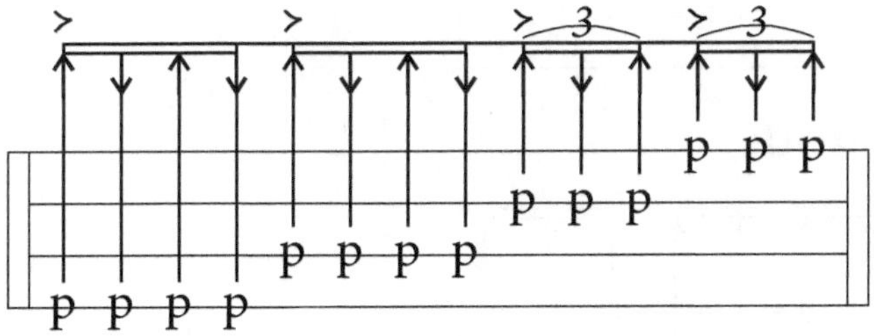

VARIATION IV

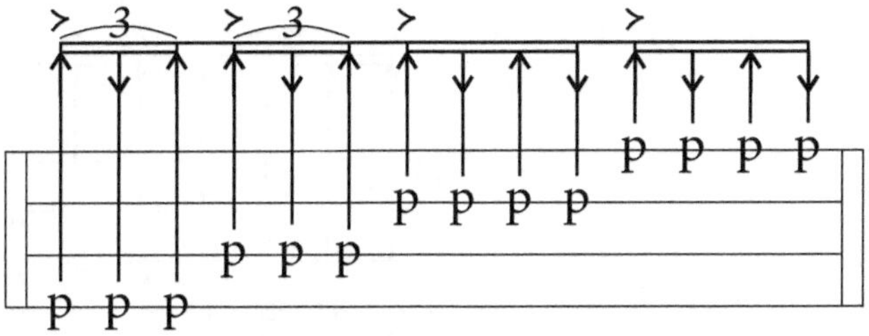

VARIATION V

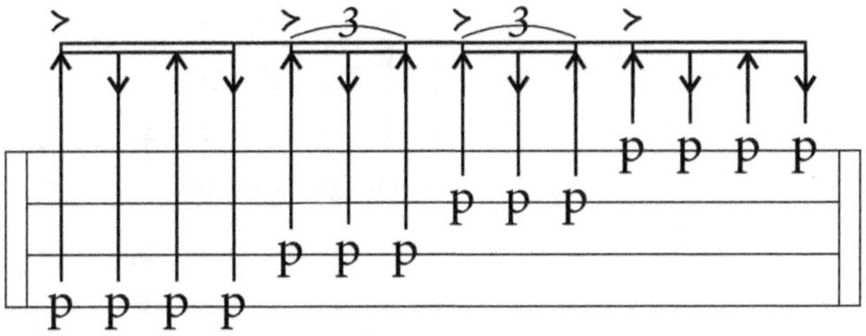

VARIATION VI

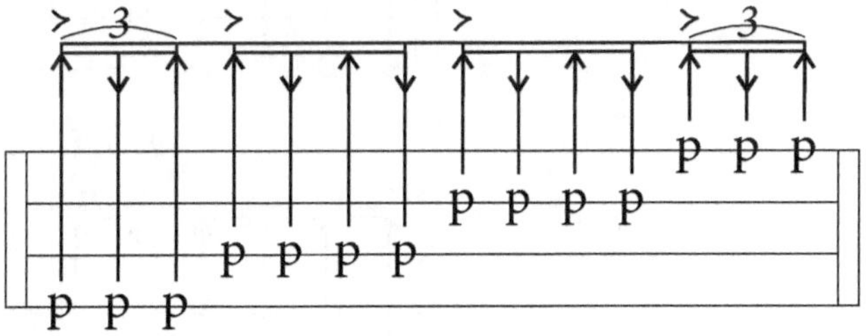

Practice in the following ways of pulgar stroke:

F1 (1st mode)

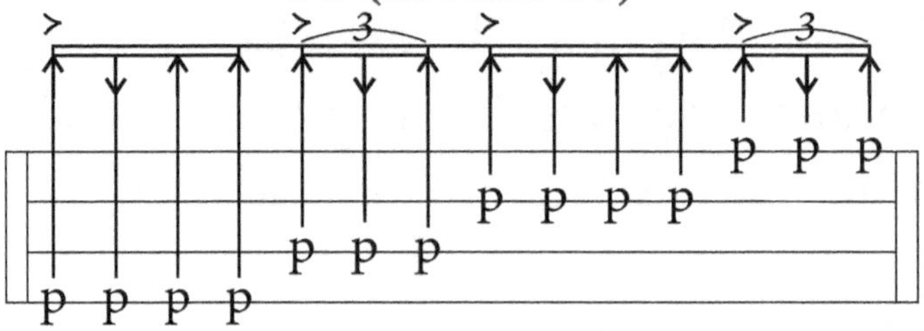

F1 (2nd mode)

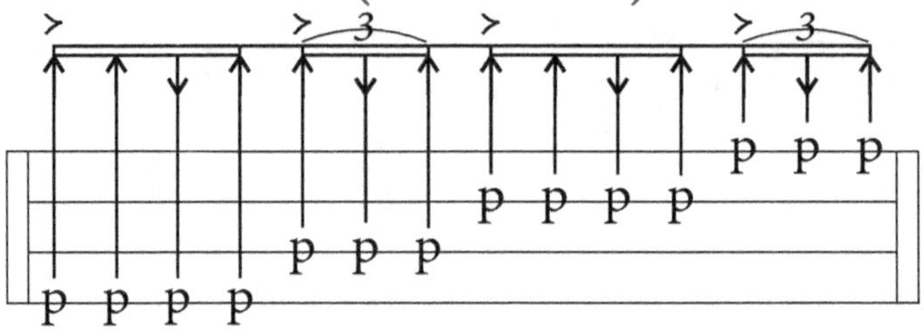

F1 (3rd mode)

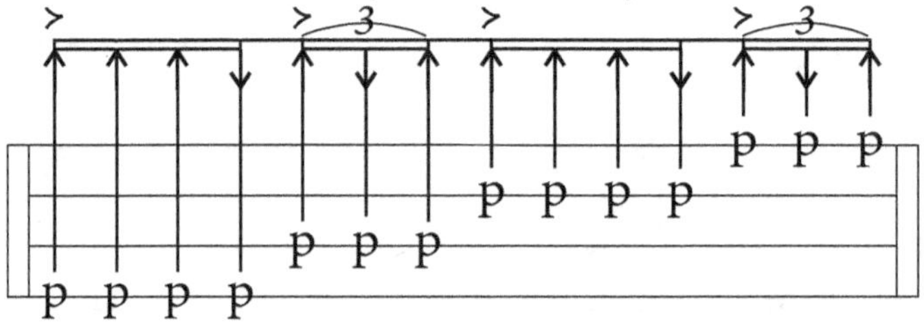

F1 (4th mode)

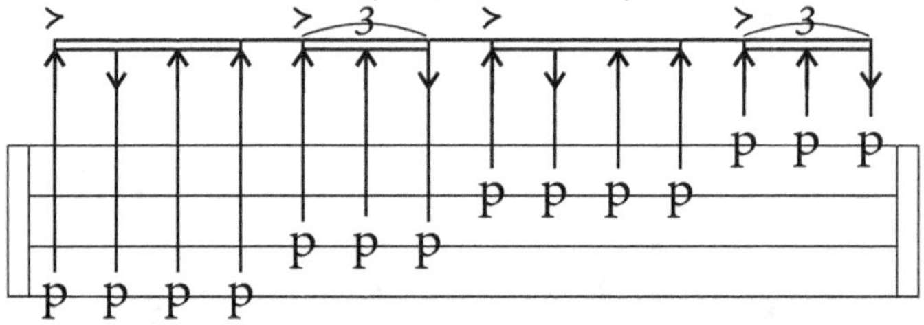

F1 (5th mode)

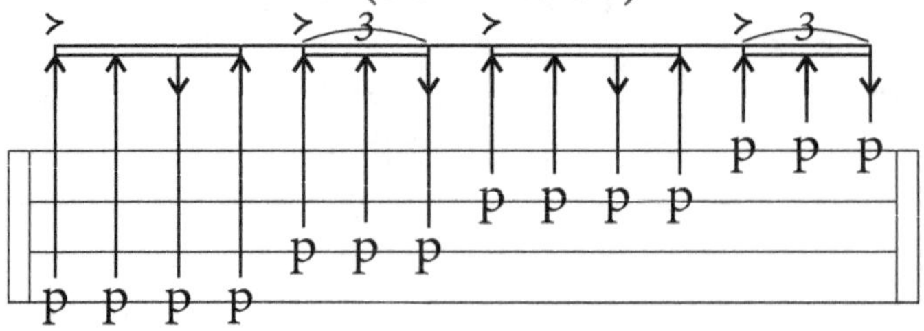

F1 (6th mode)

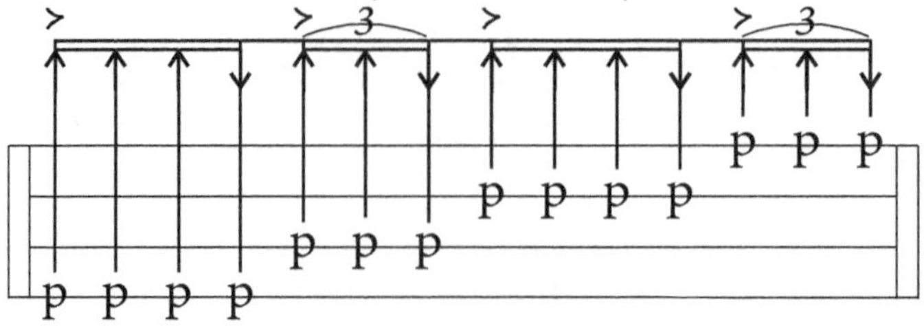

VARIATION I

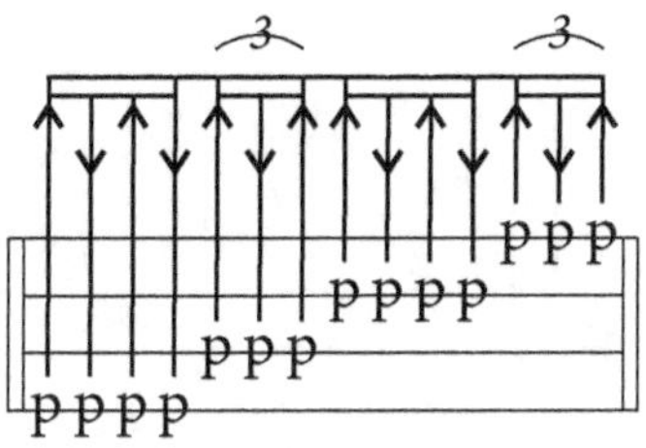

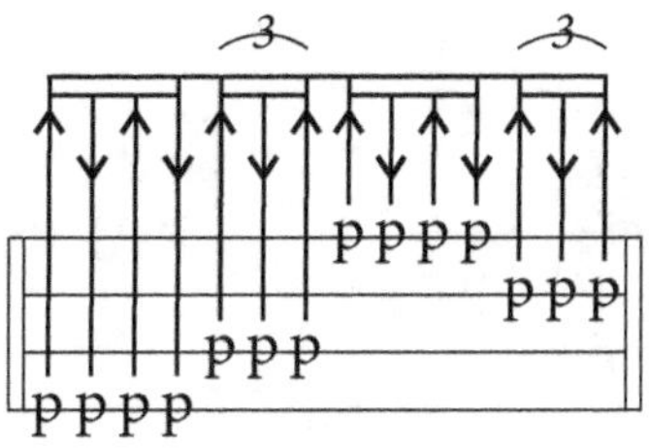

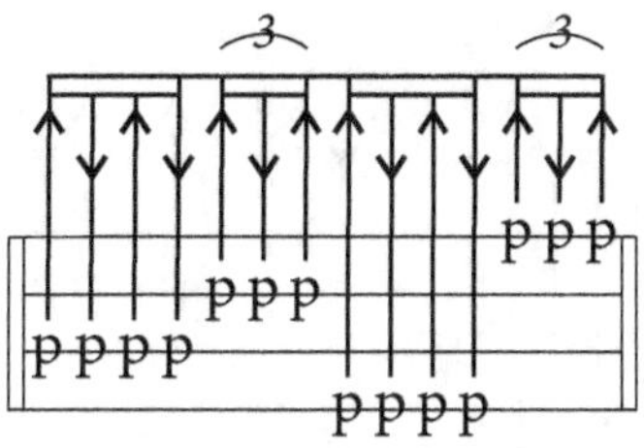

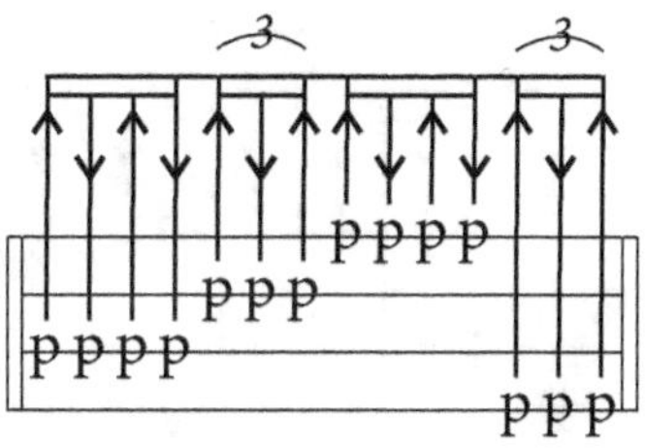

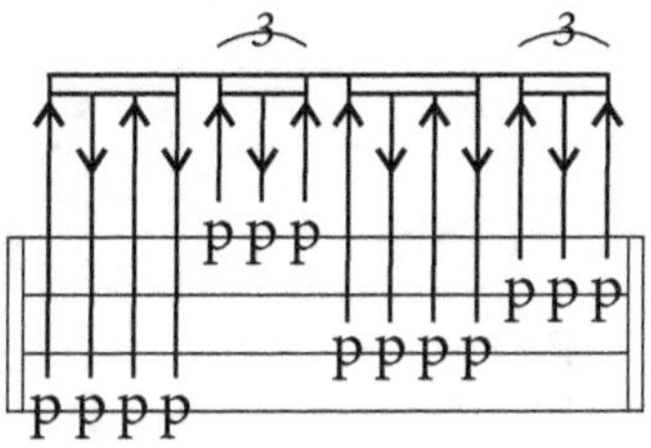

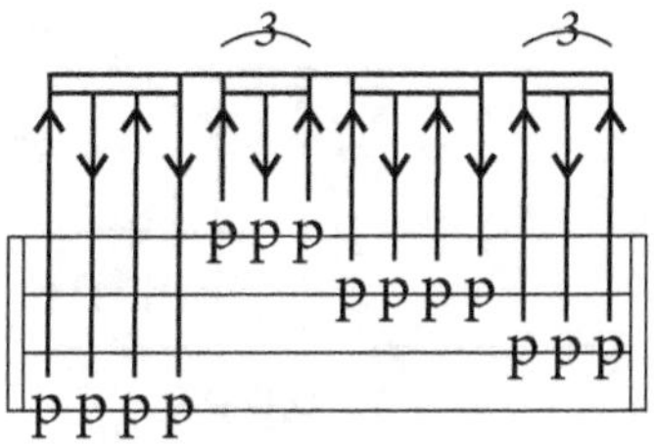

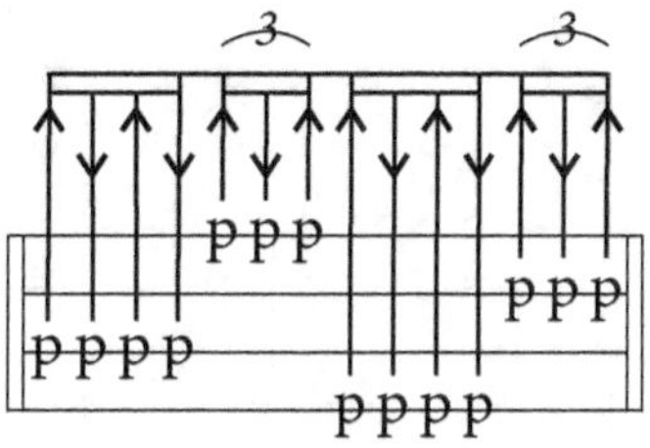

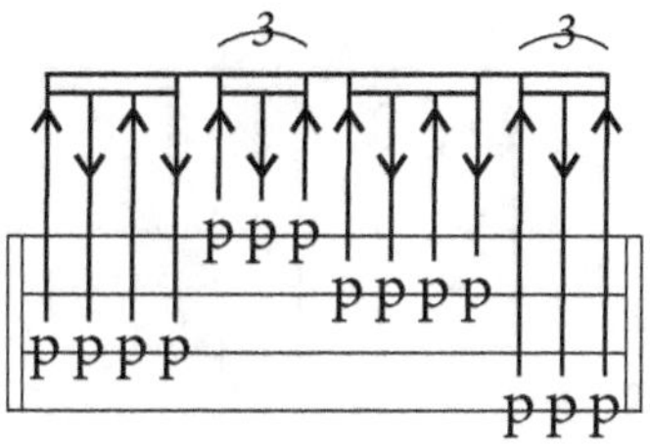

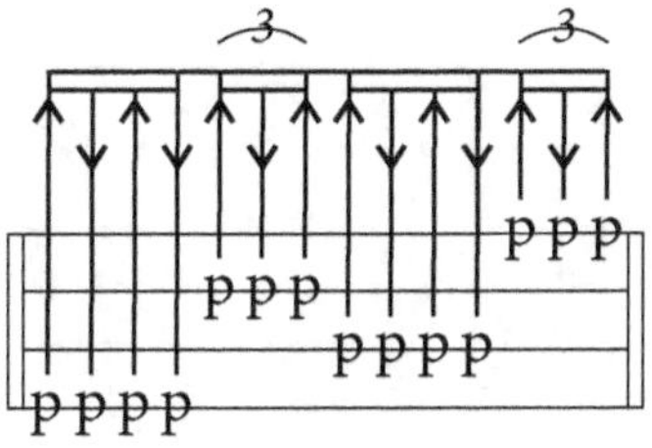

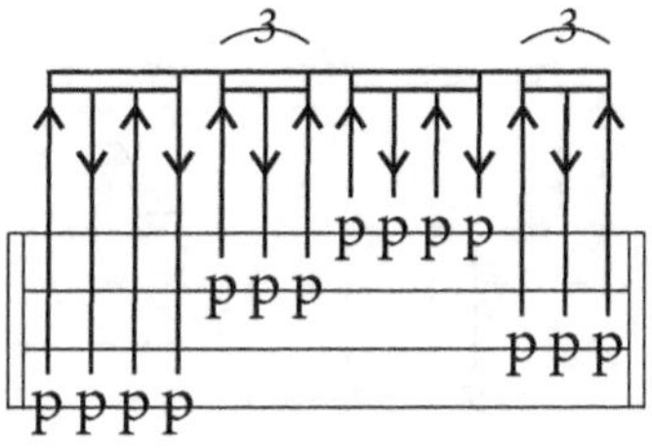

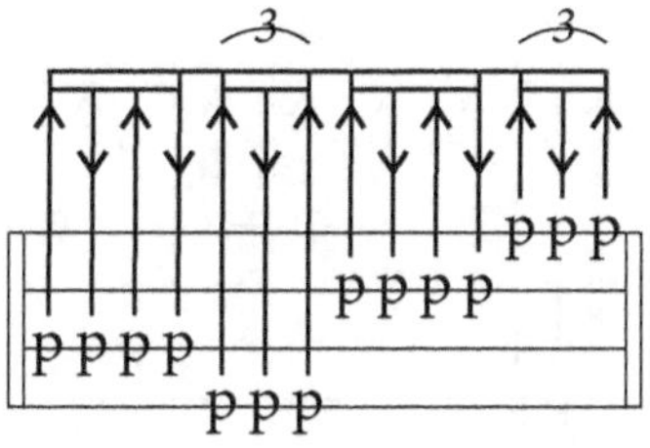

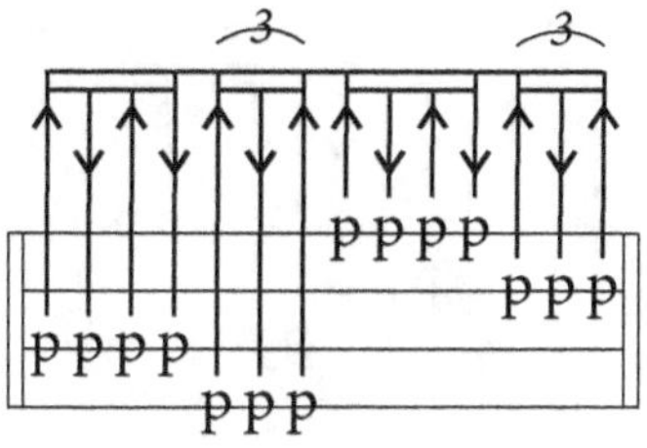

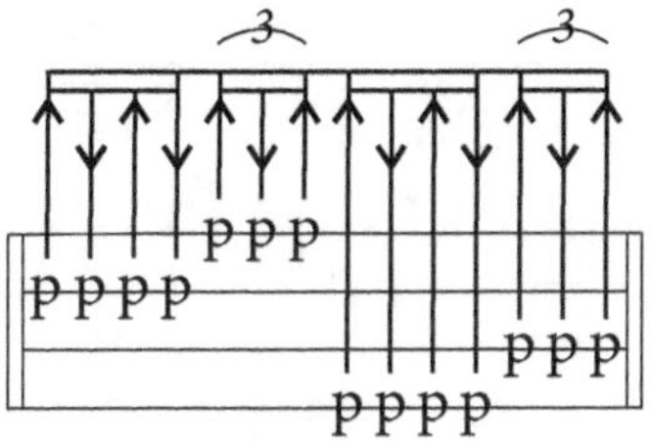

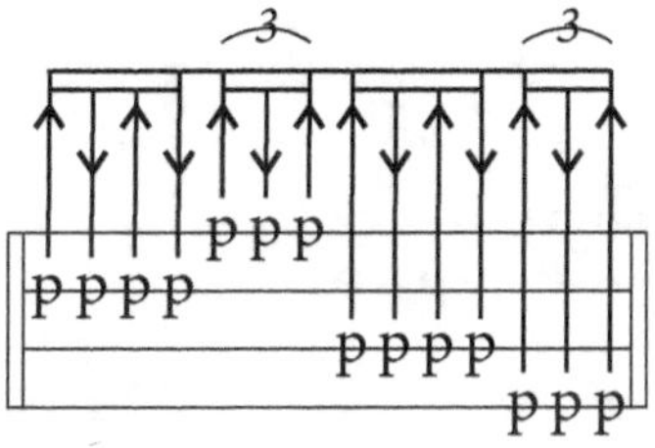

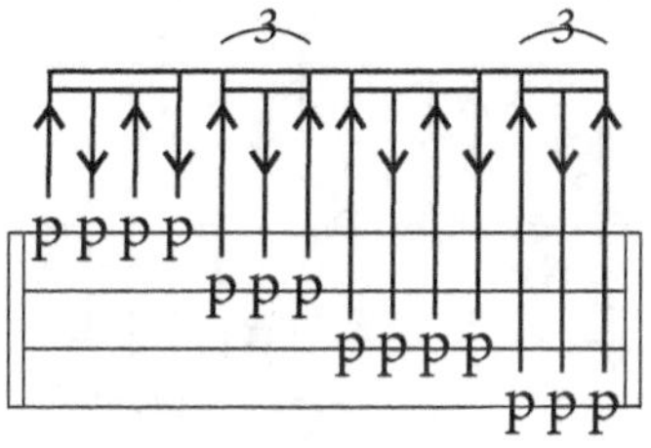

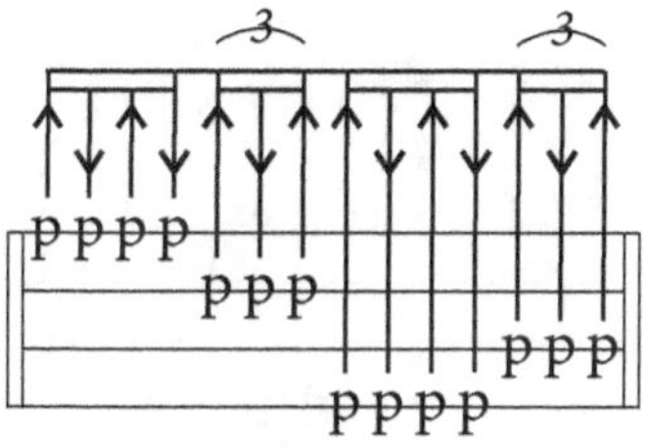

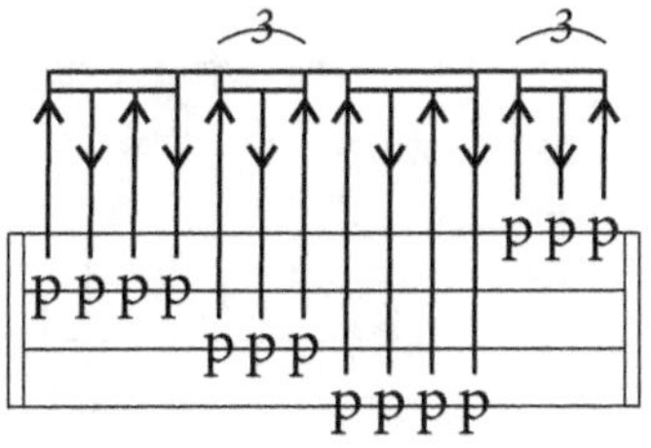

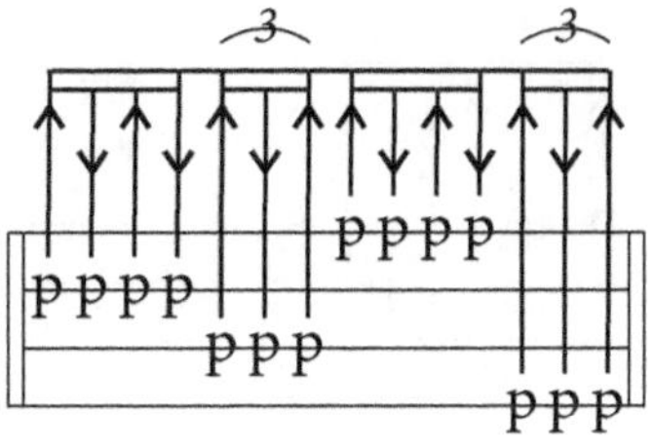

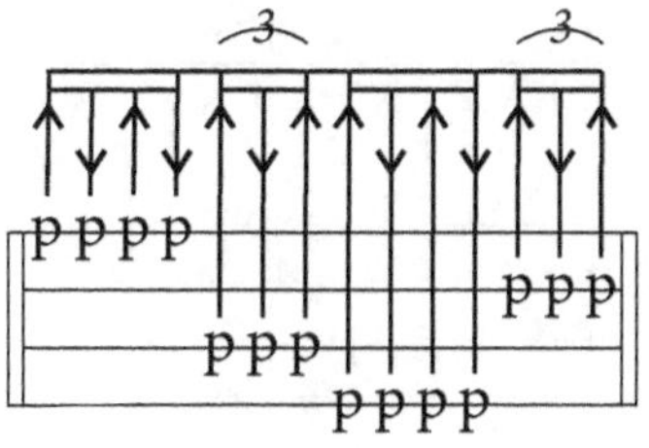

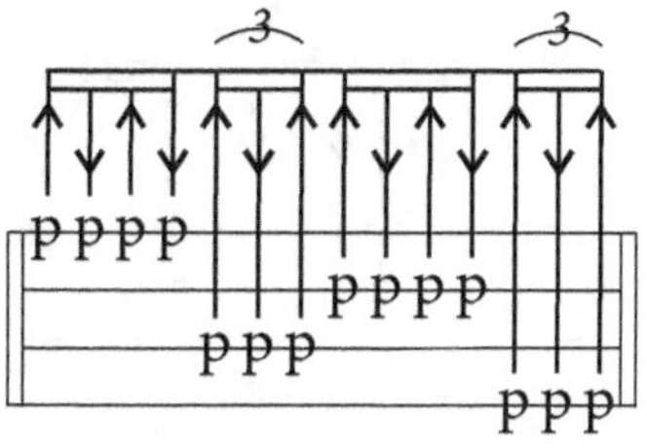

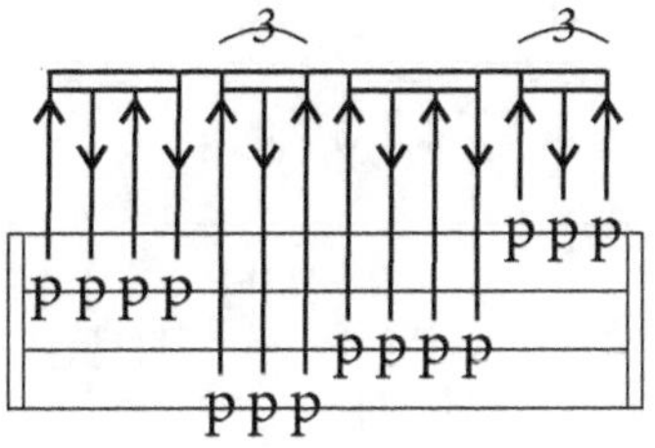

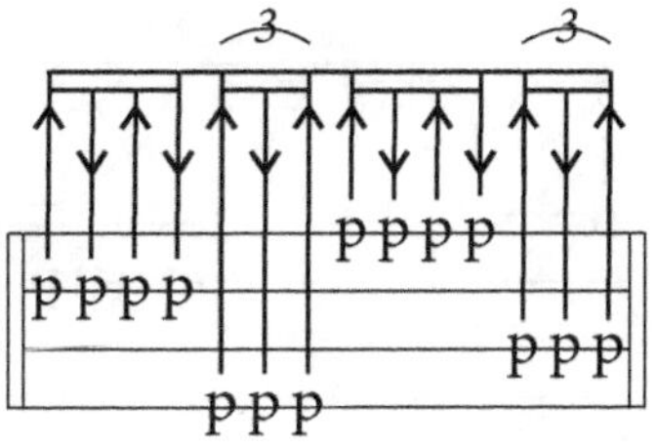

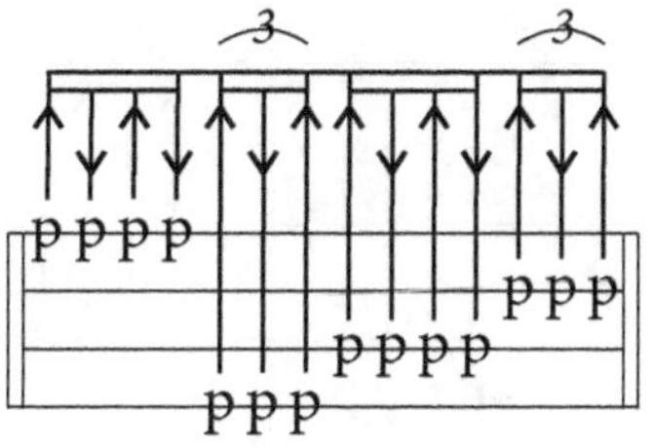

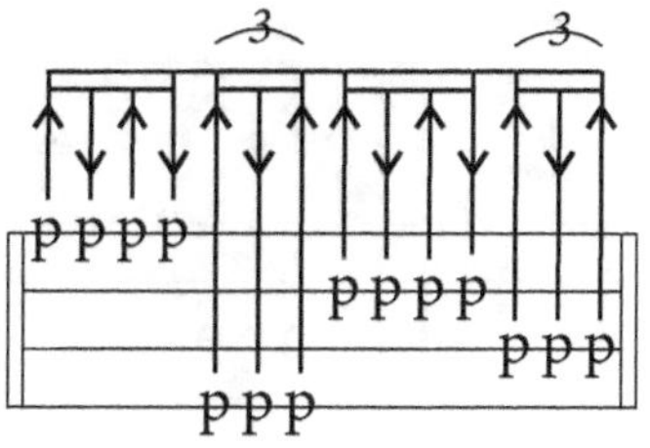

VARIATION II

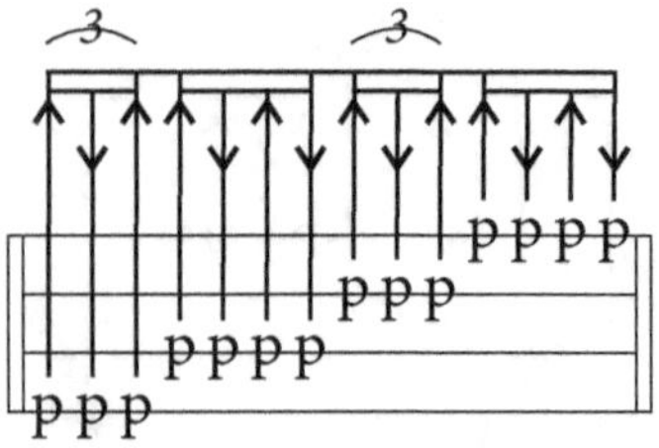

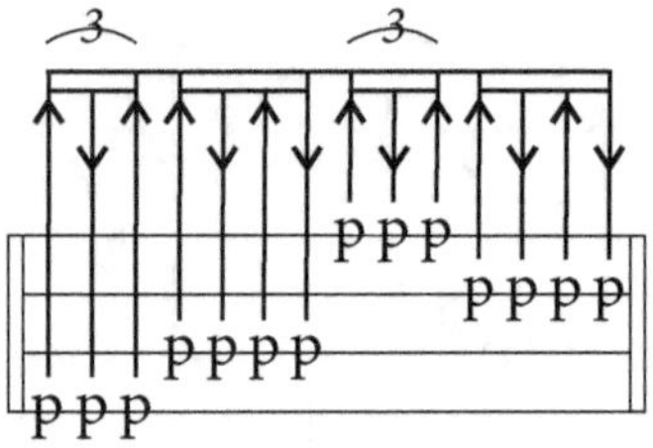

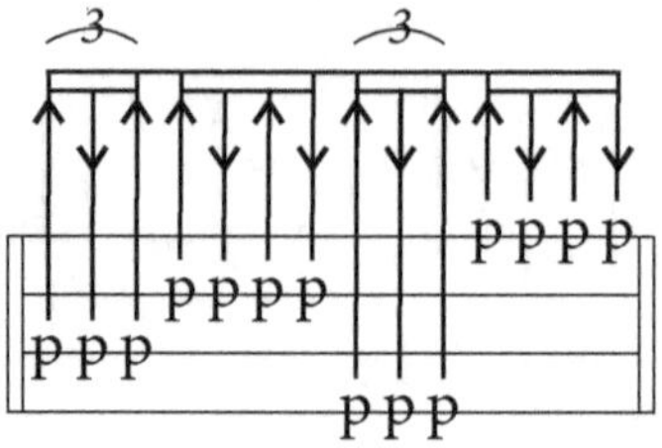

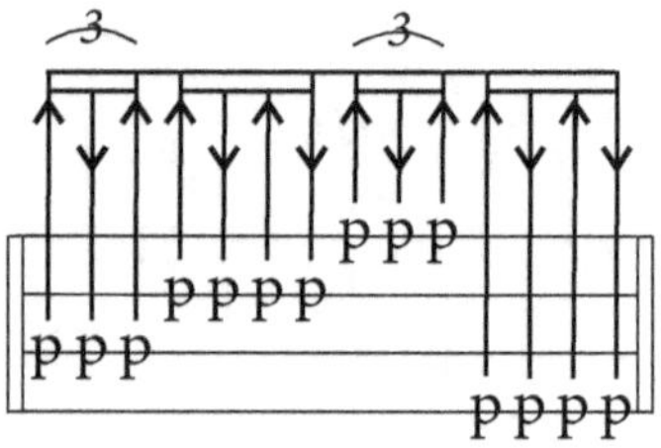

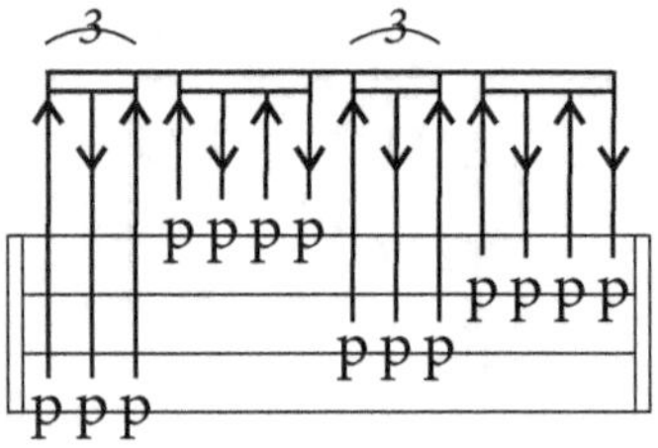

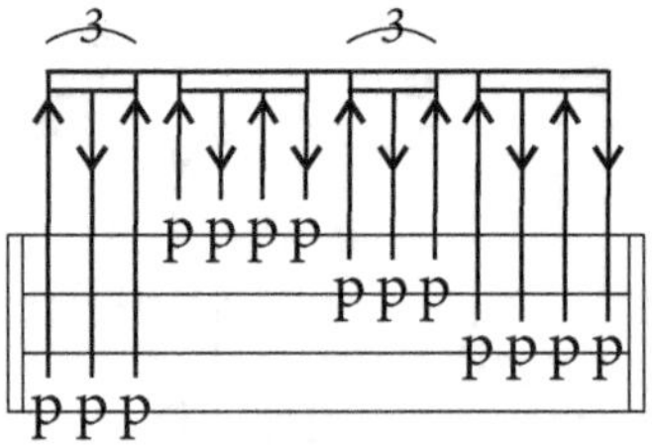

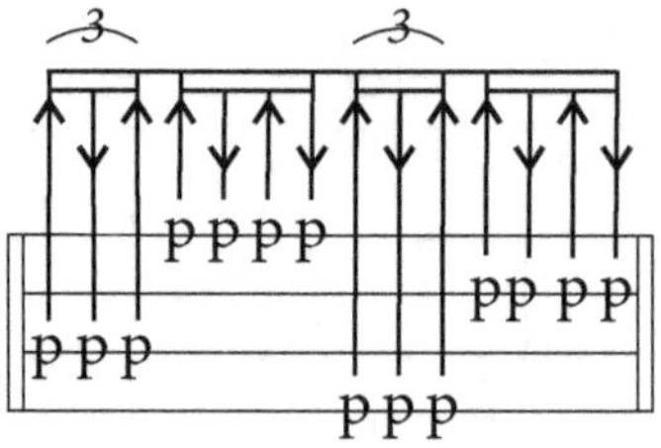

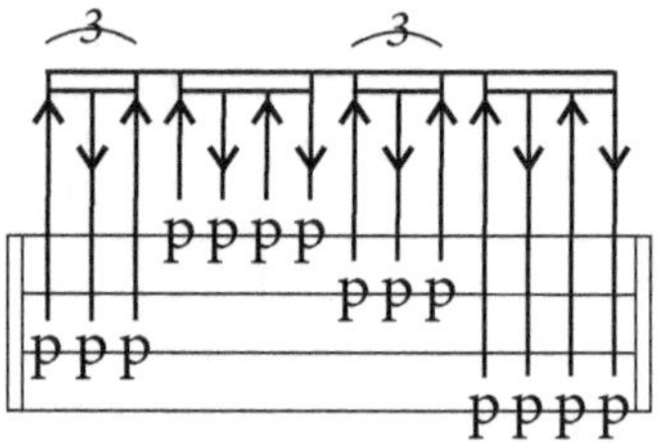

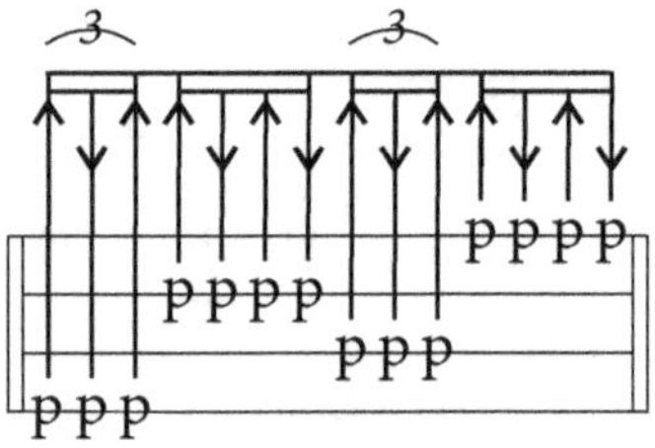

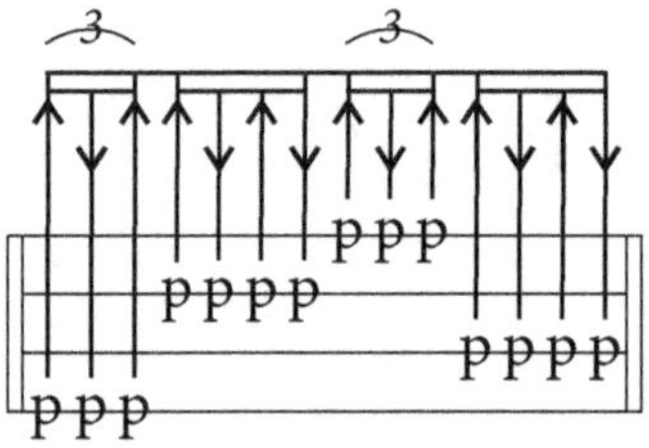

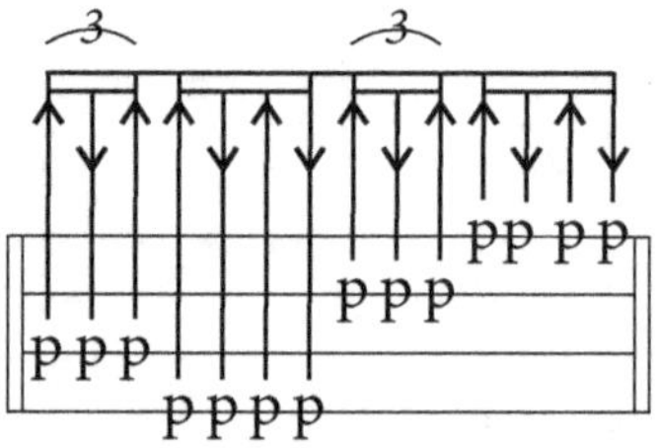

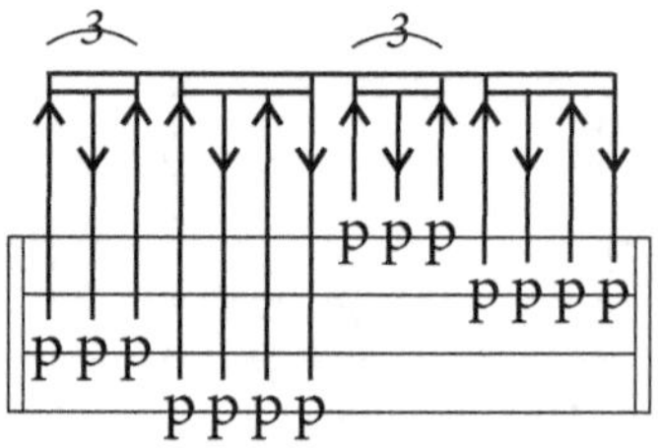

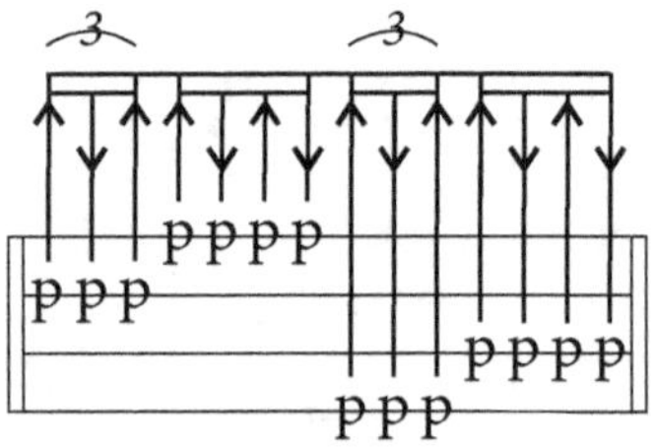

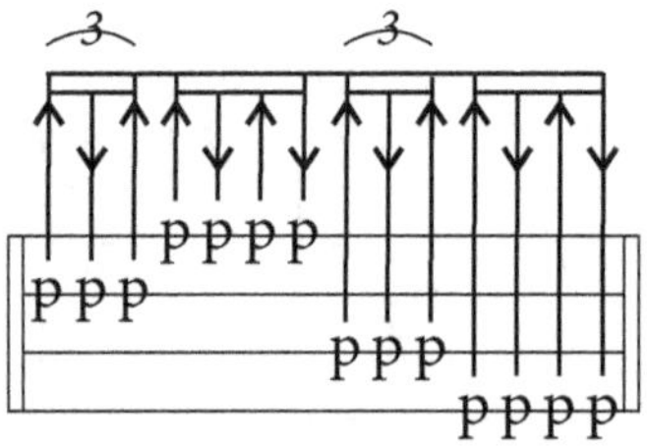

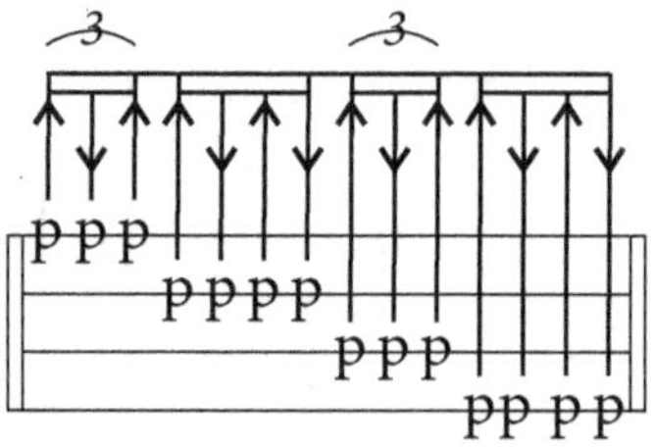

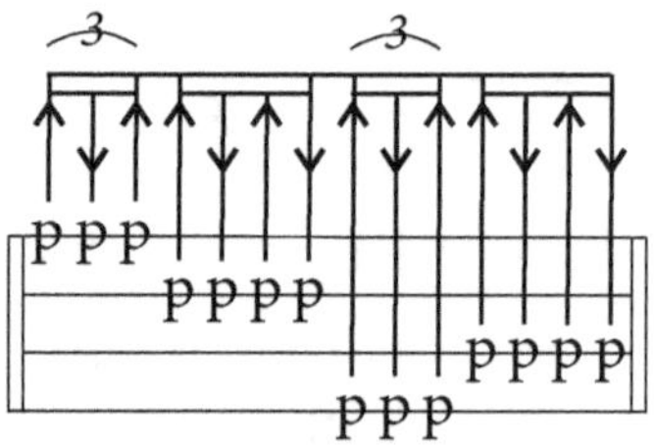

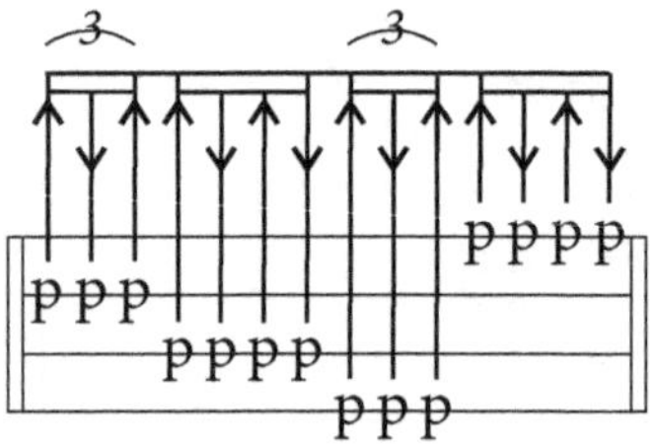

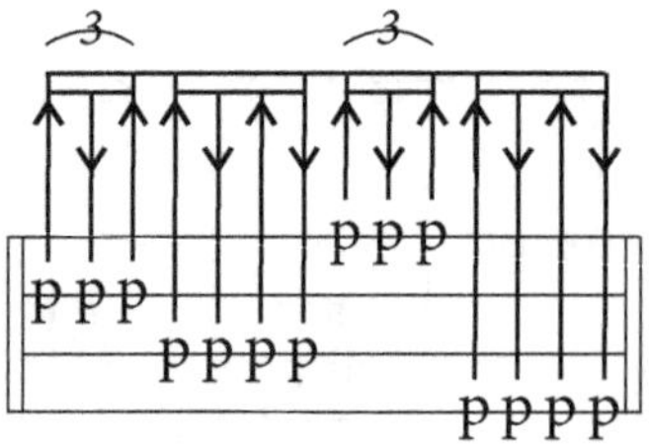

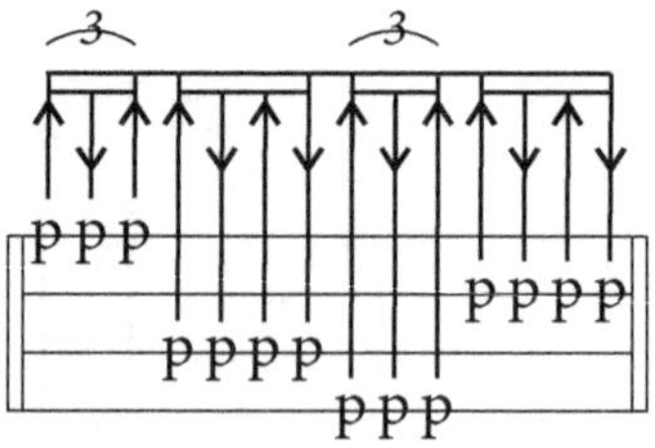

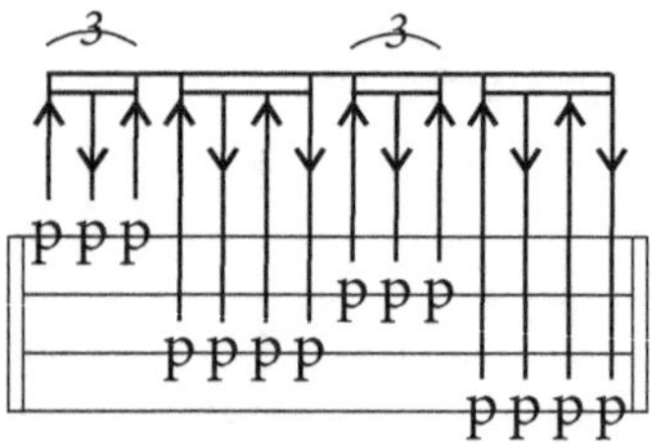

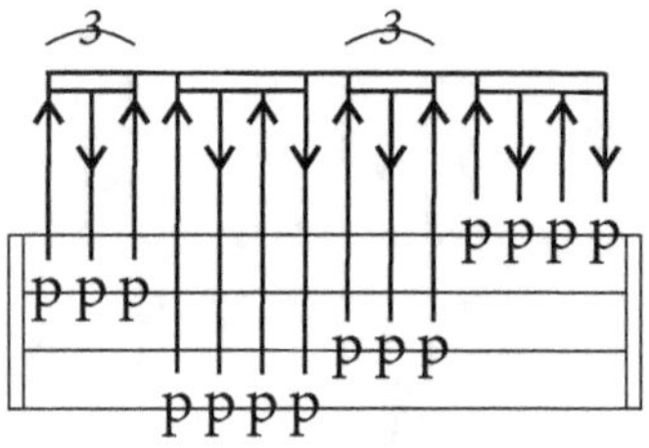

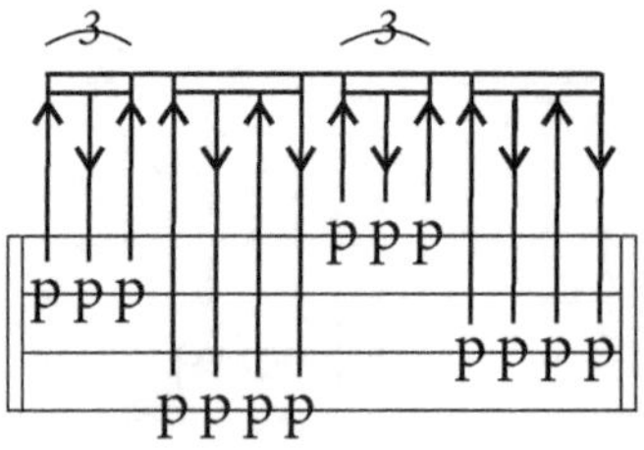

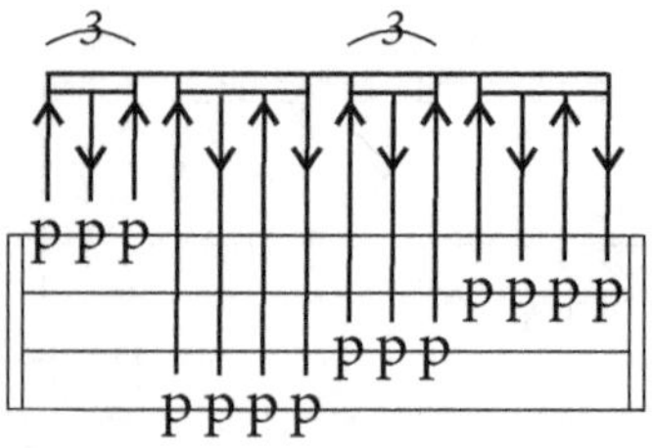

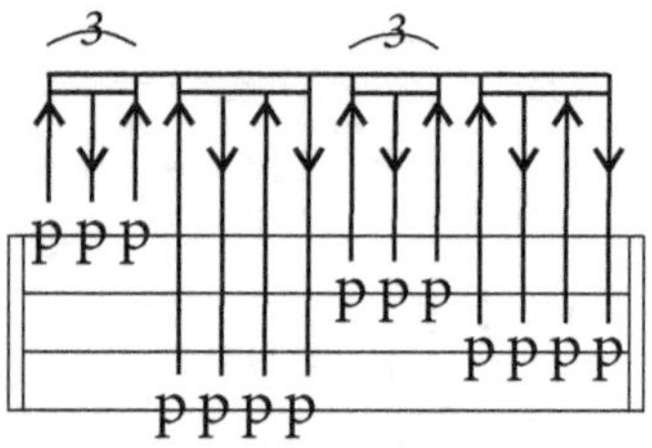

VARIATION III

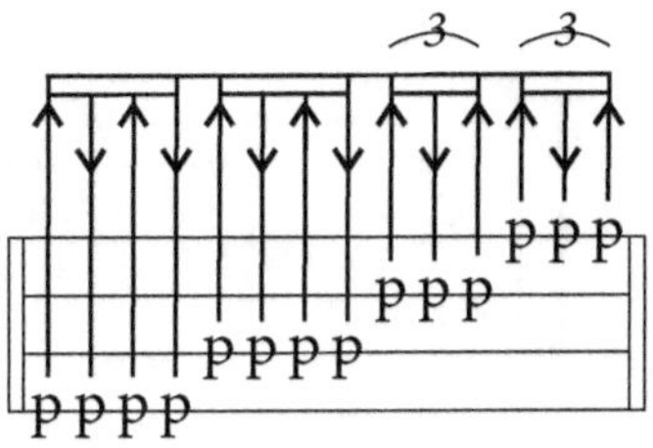

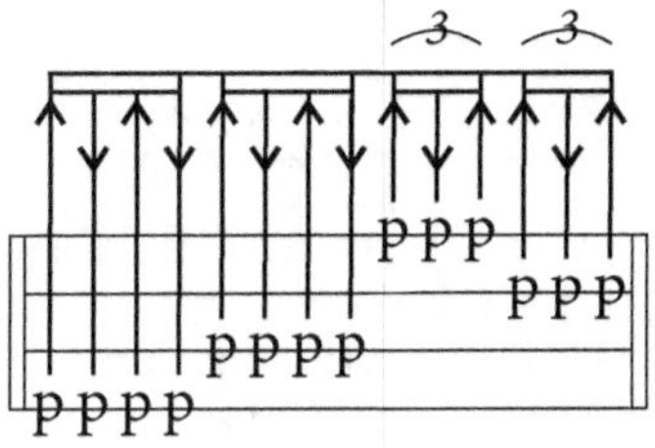

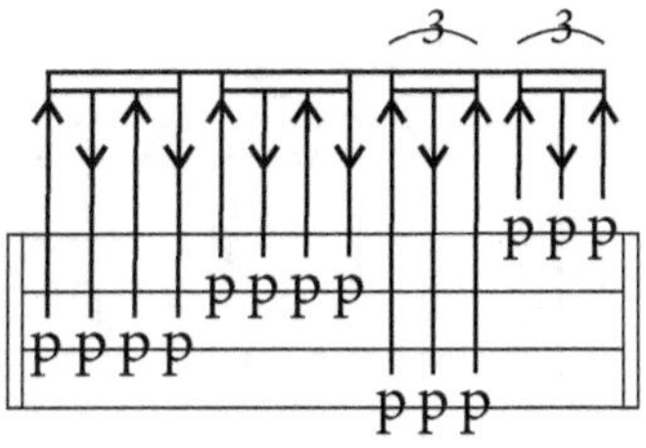

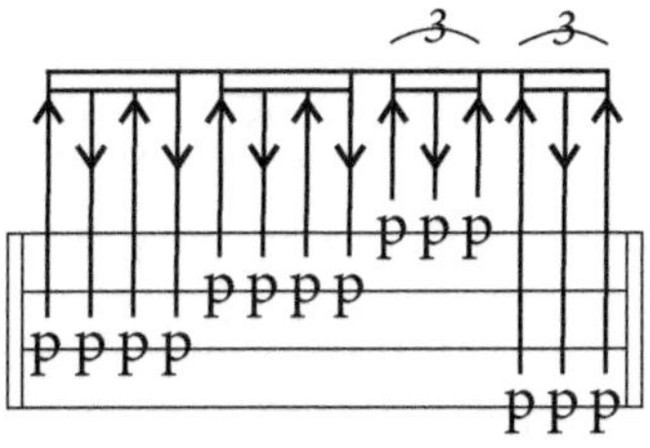

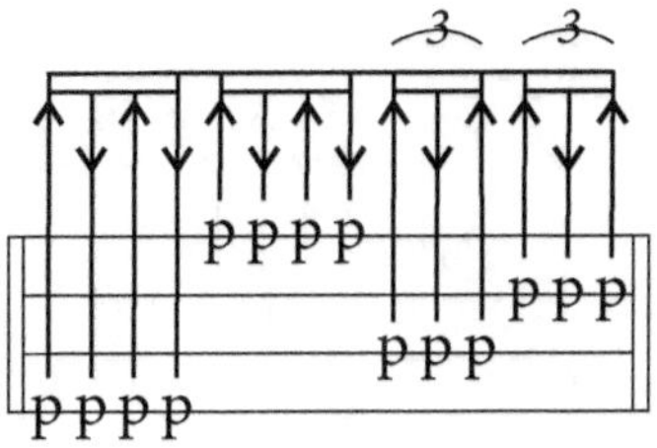

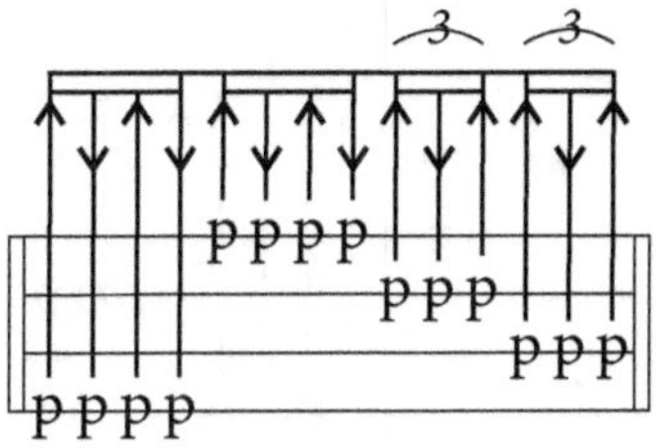

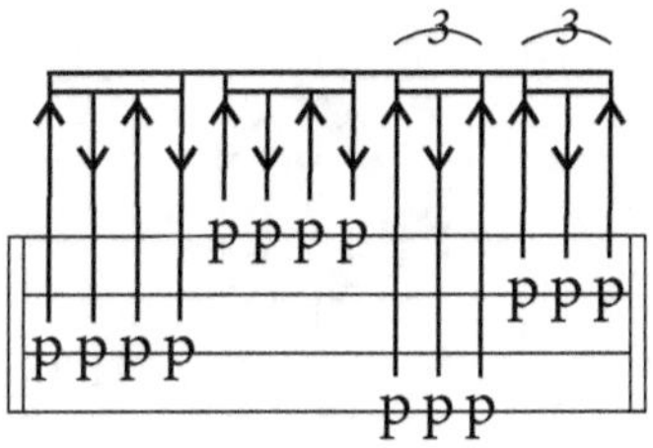

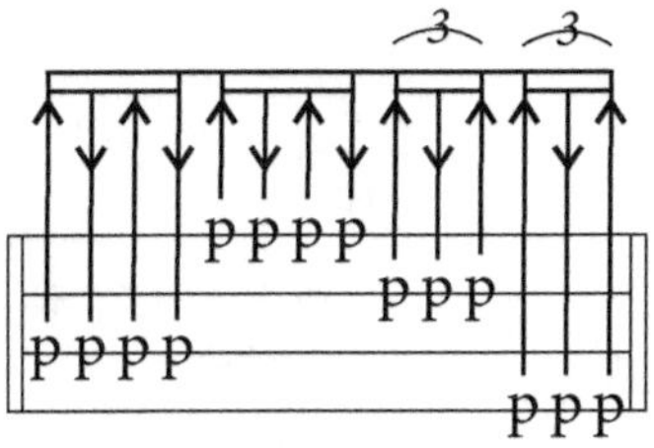

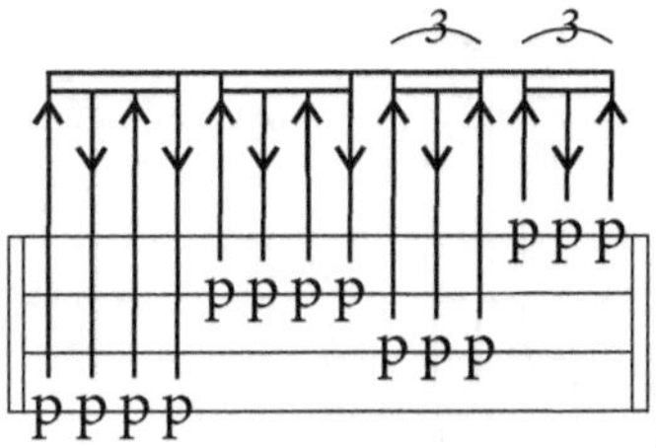

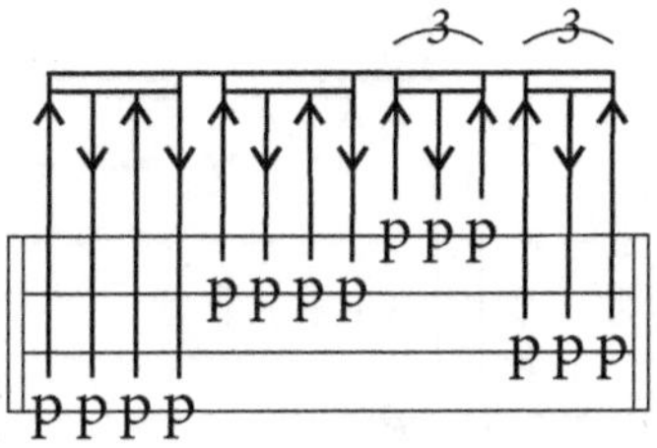

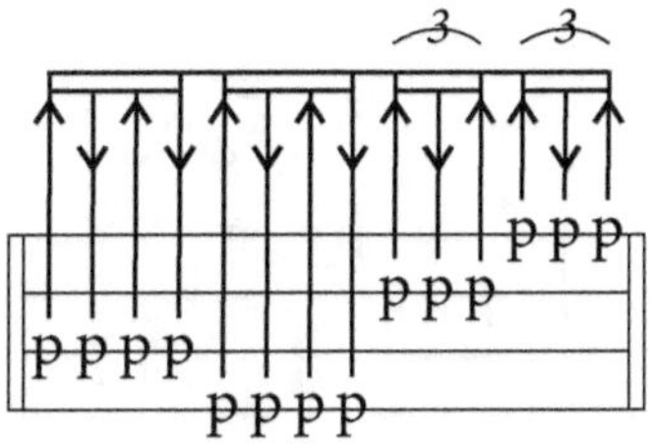

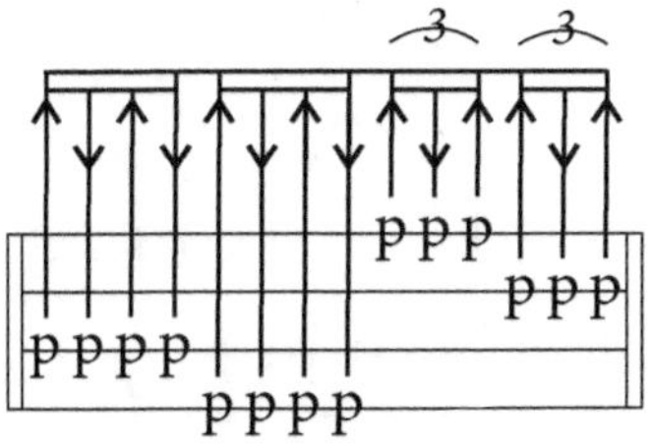

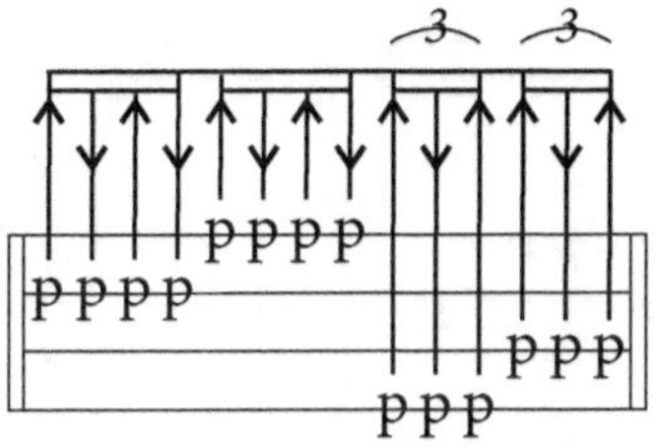

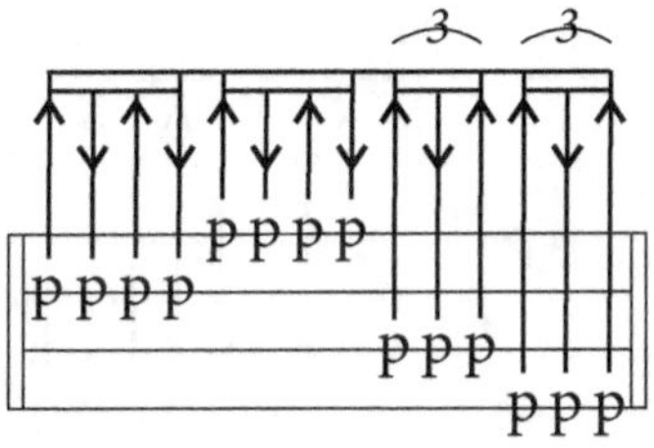

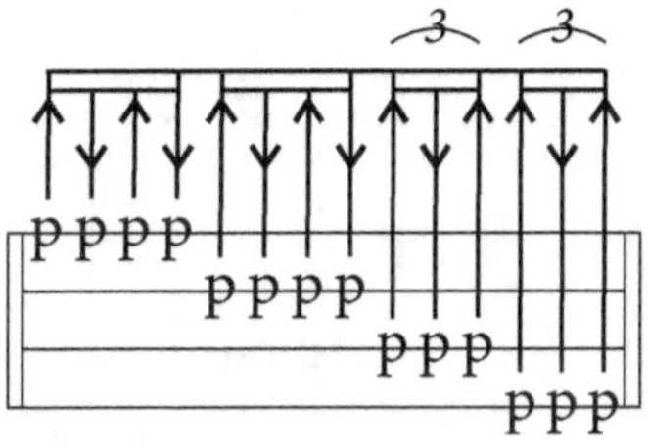

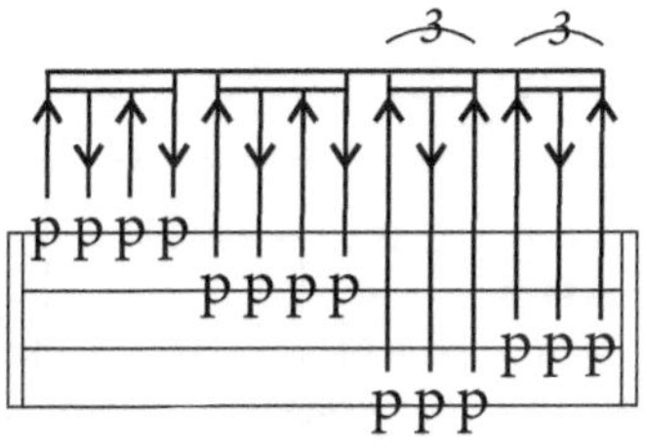

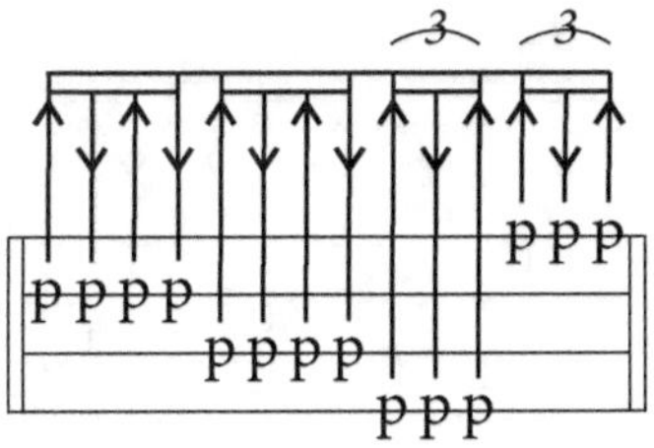

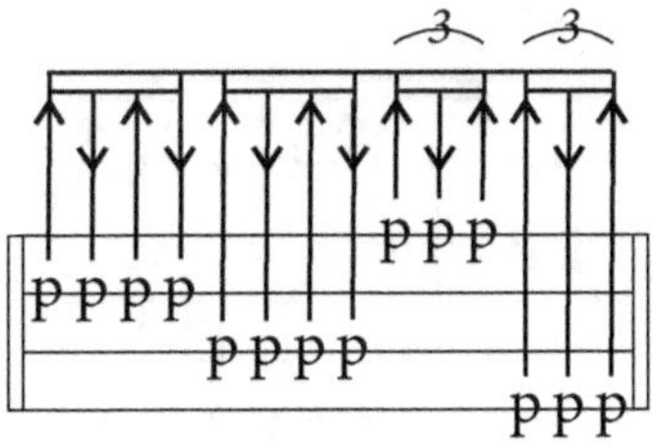

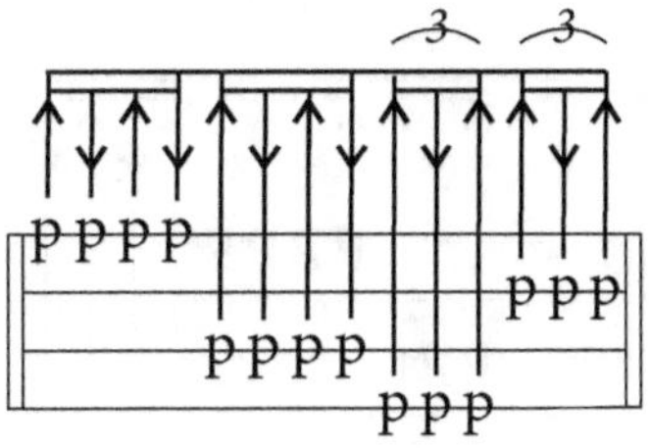

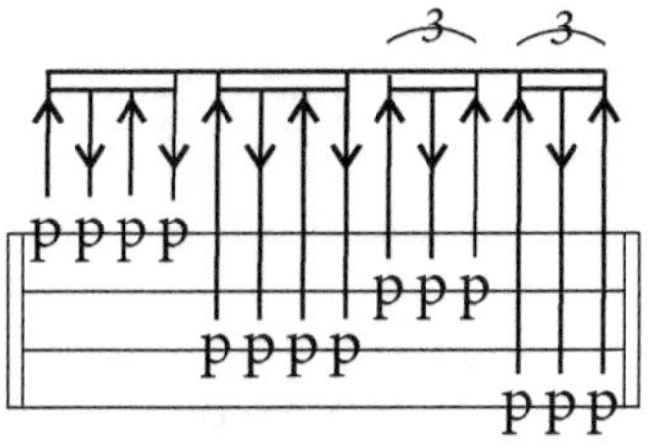

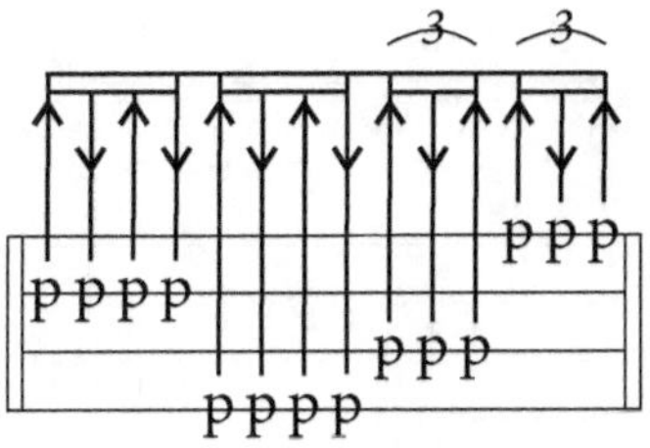

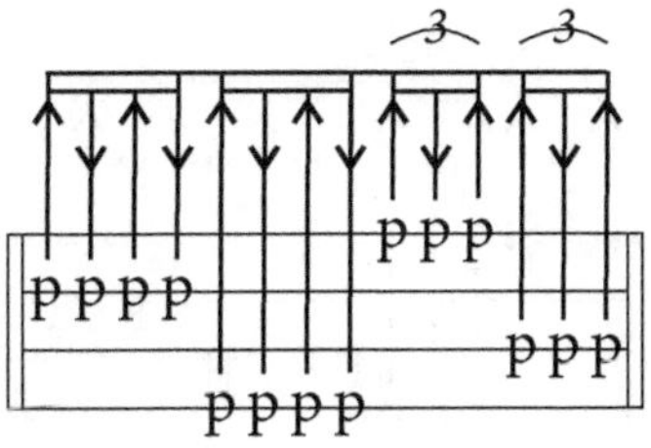

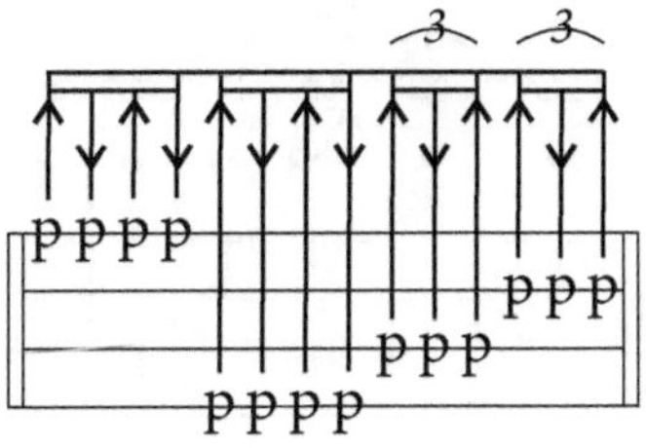

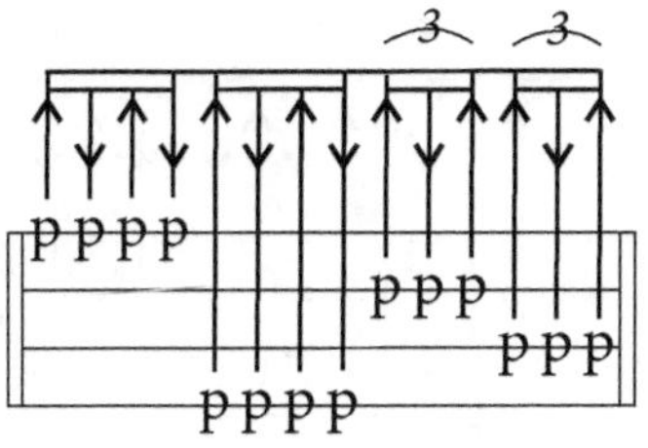

VARIATION IV

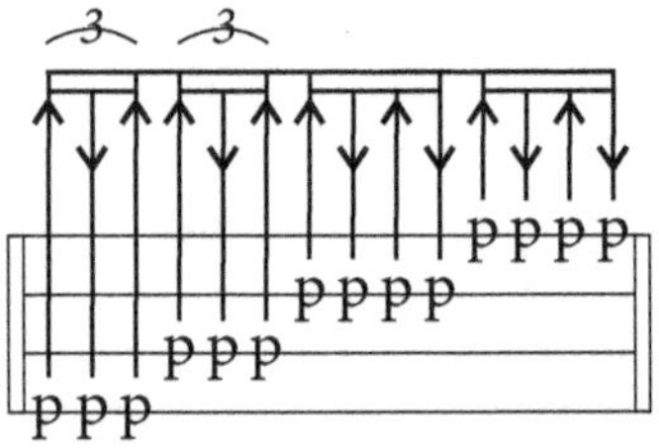

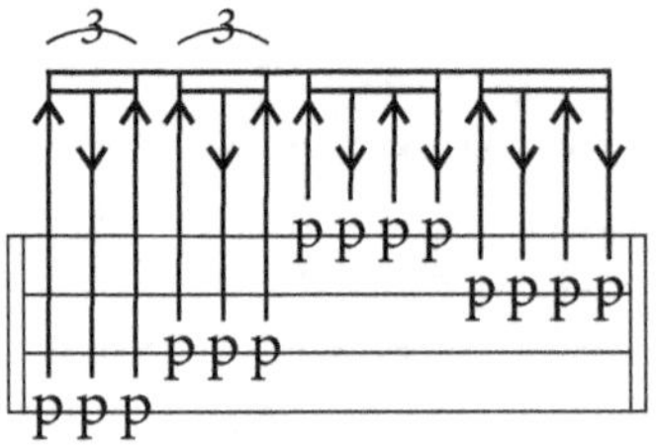

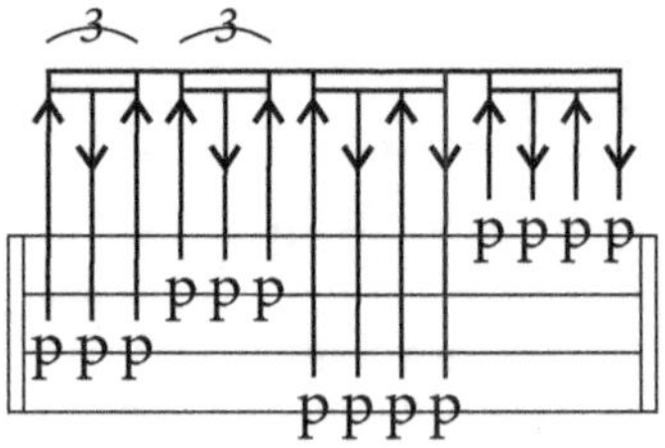

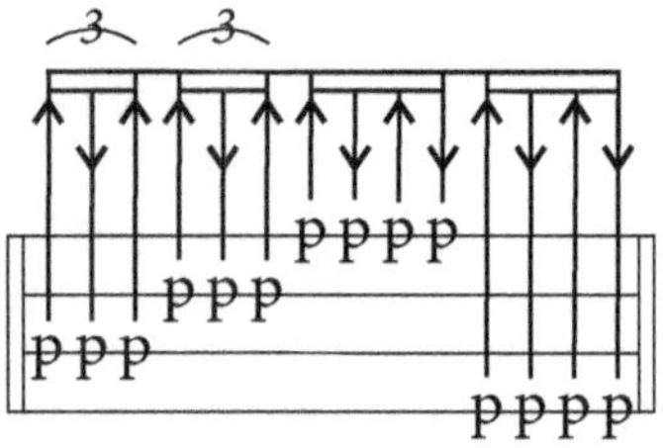

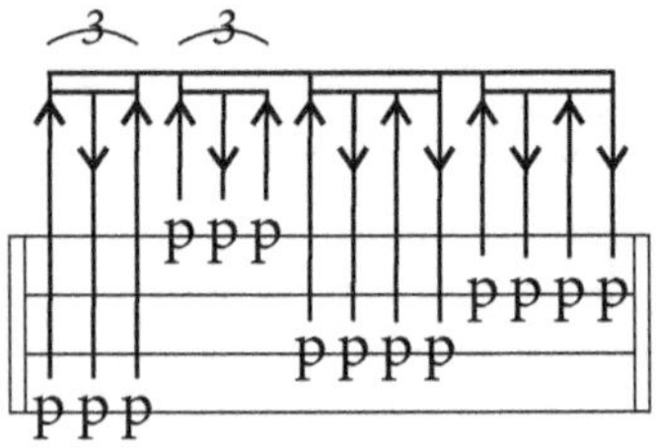

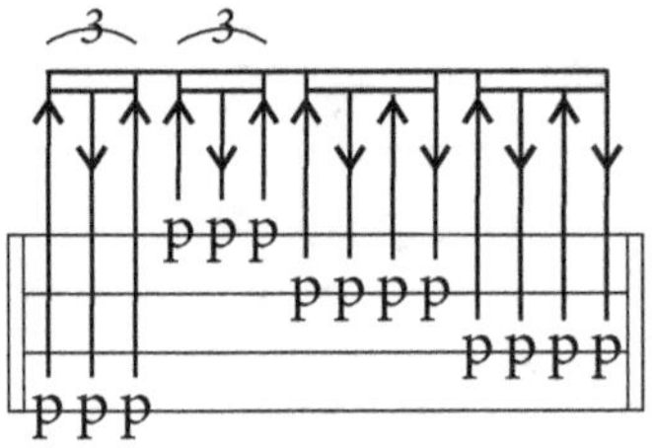

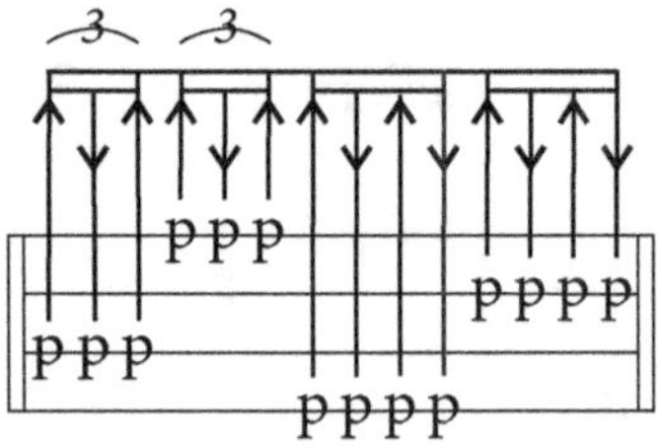

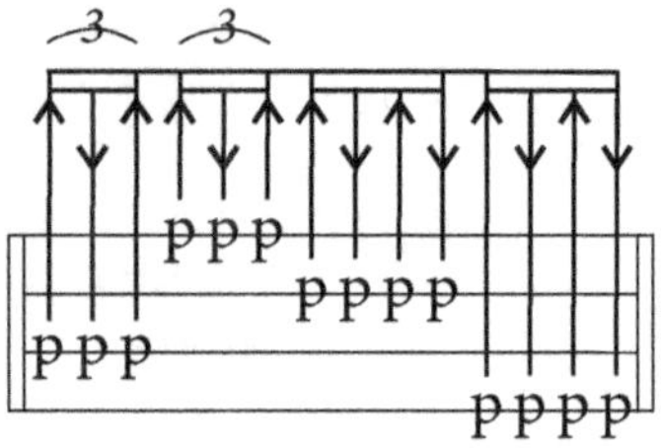

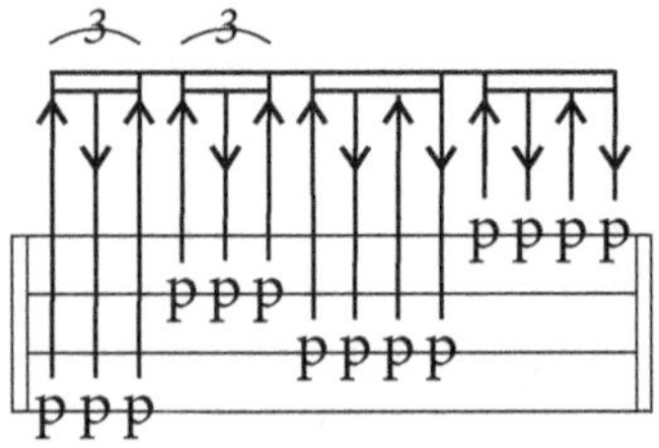

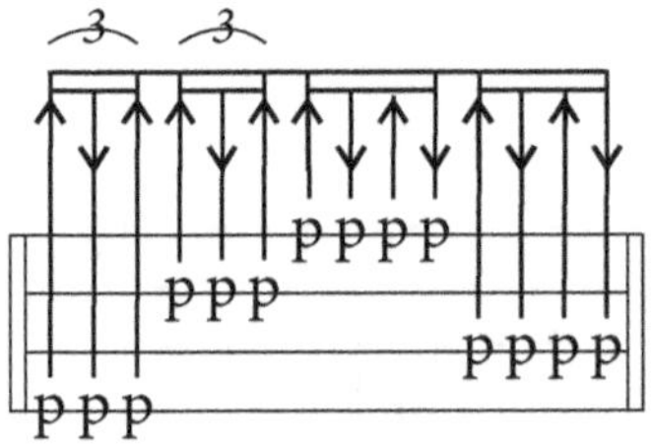

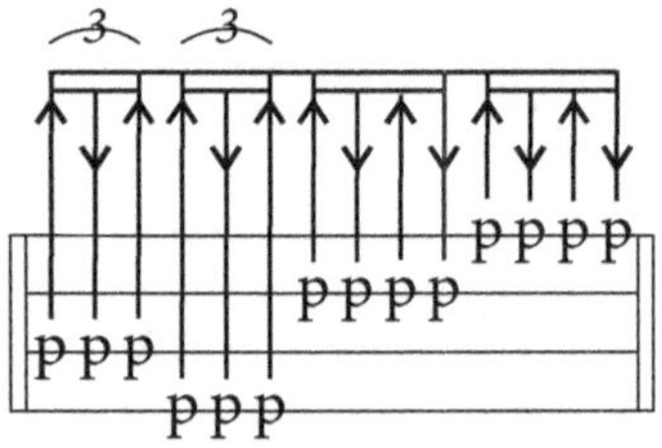

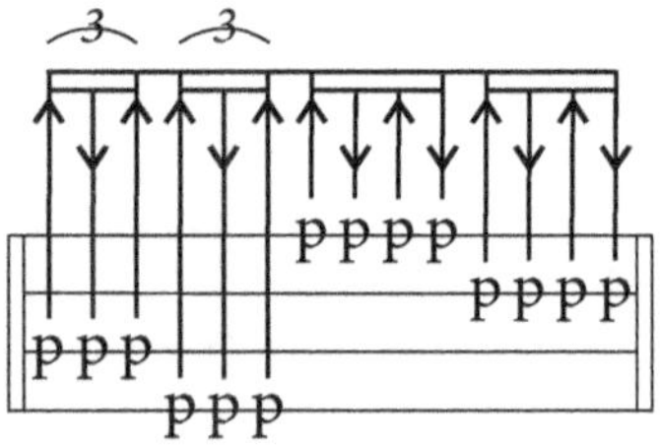

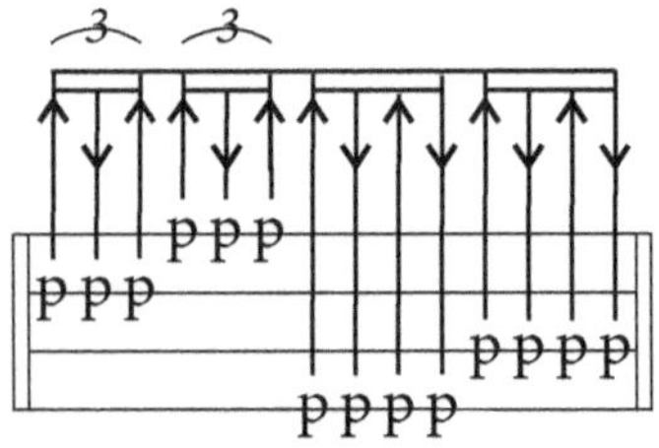

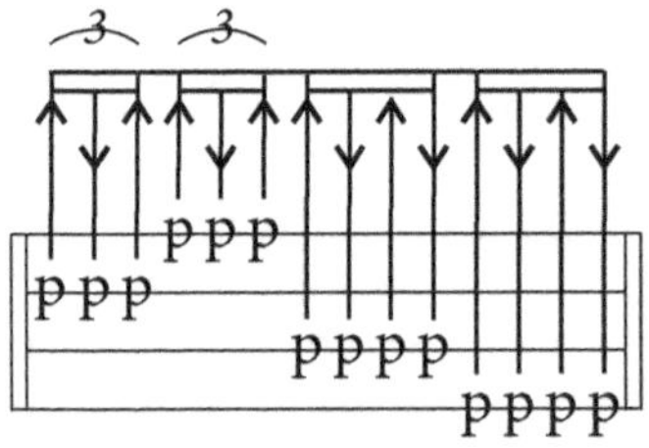

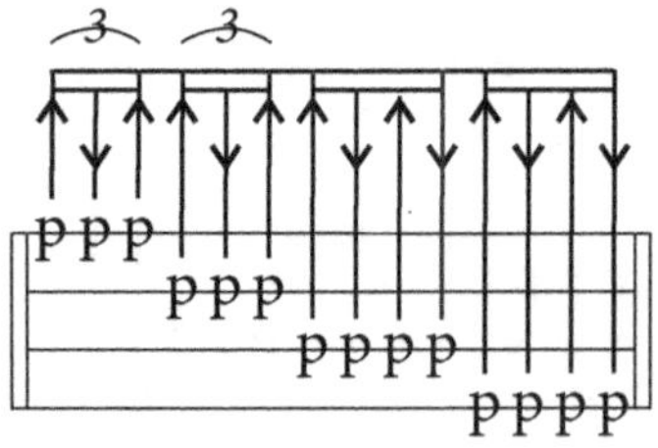

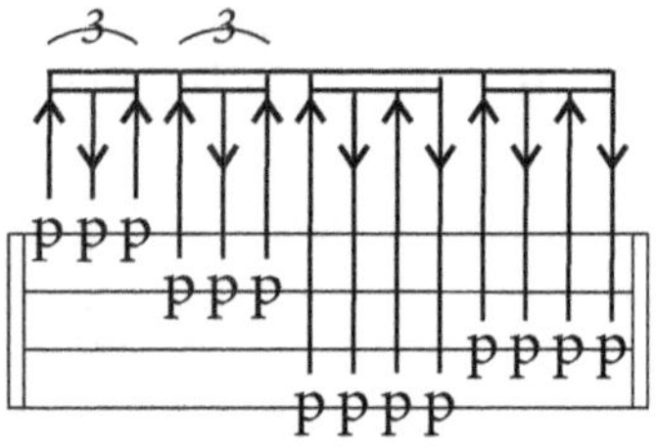

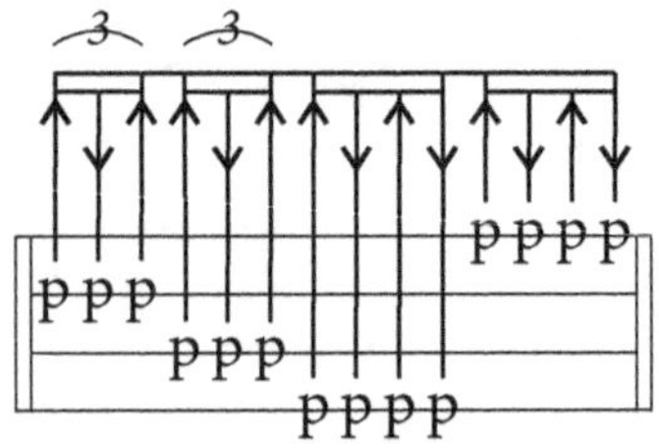

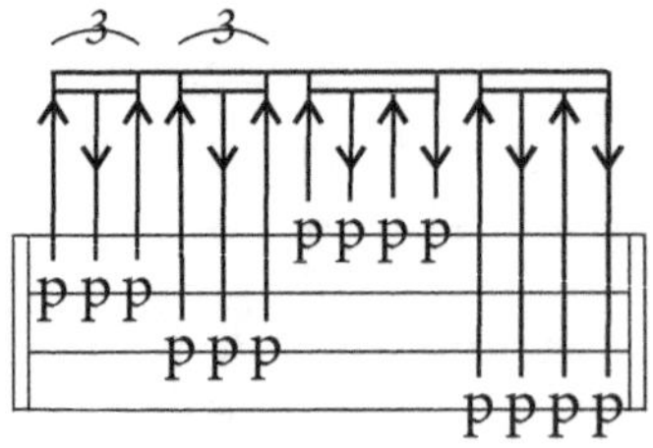

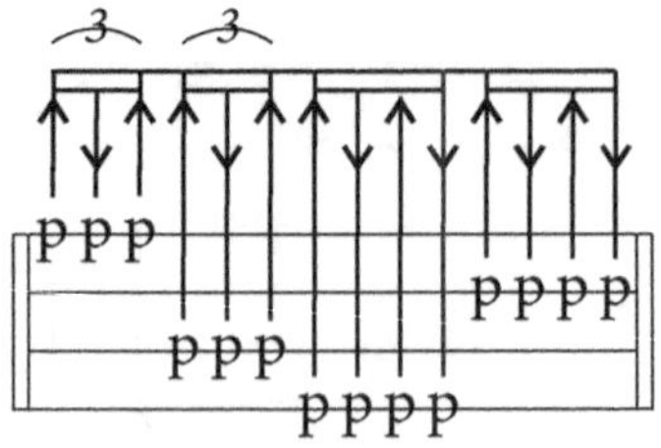

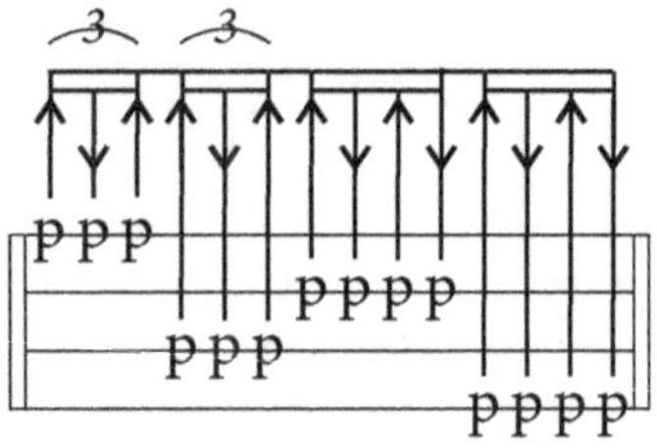

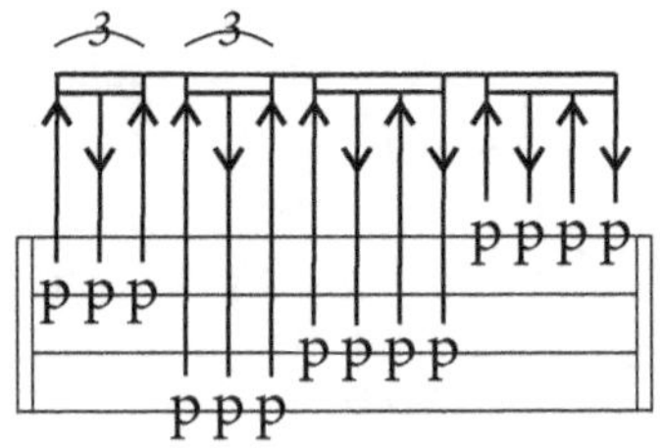

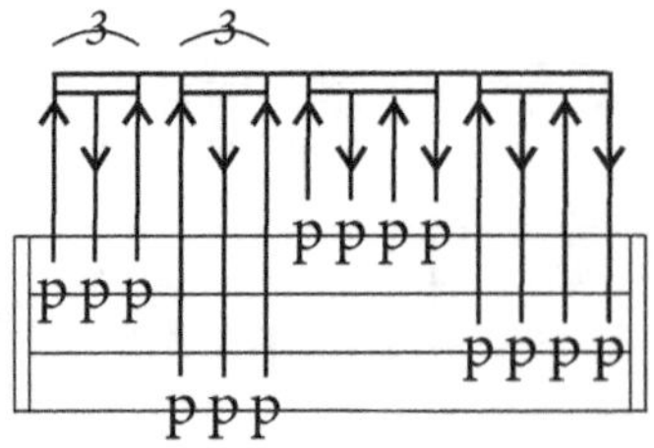

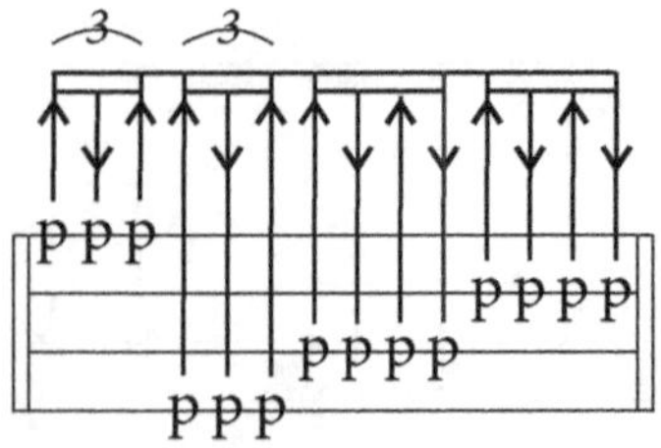

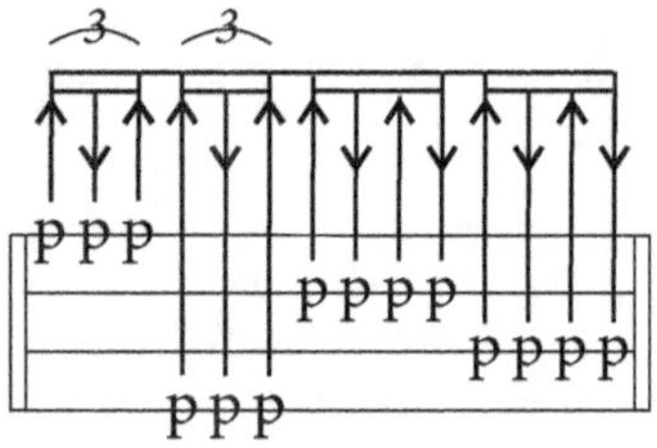

VARIATION V

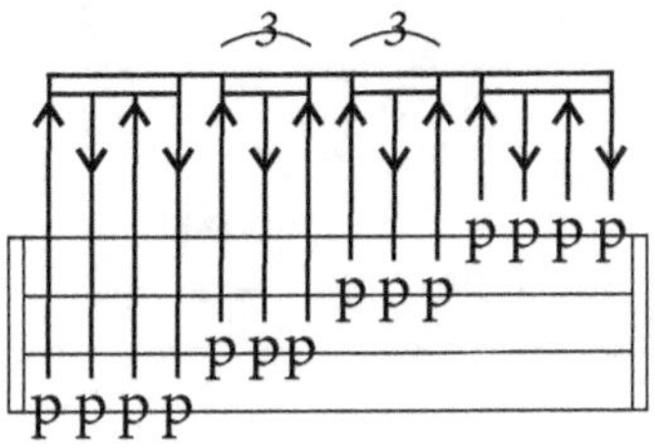

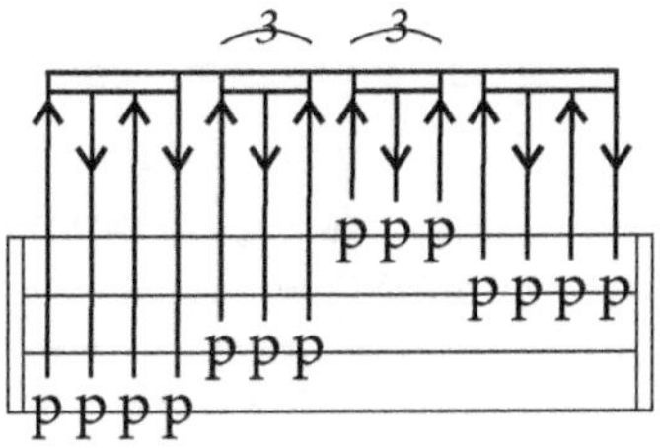

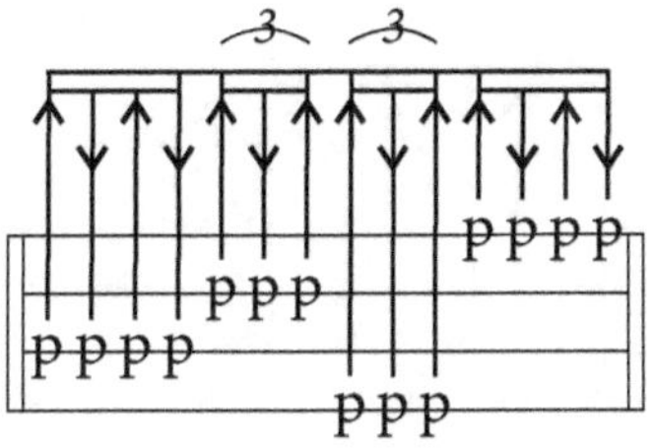

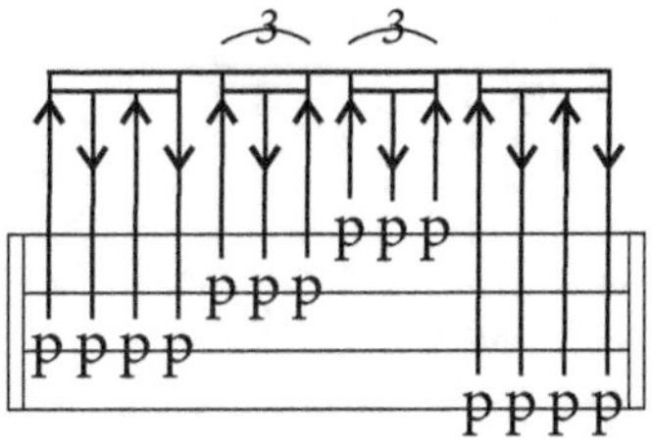

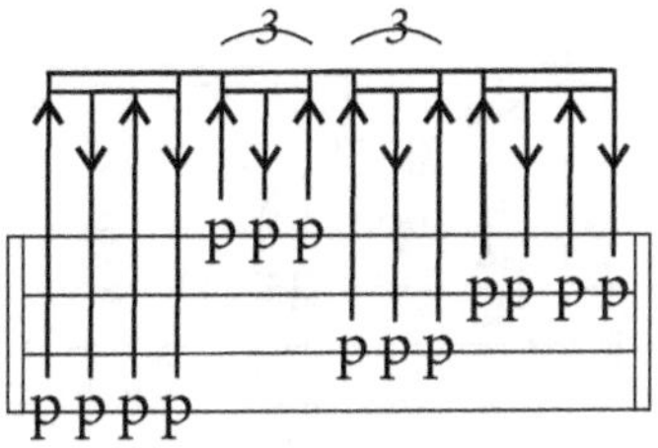

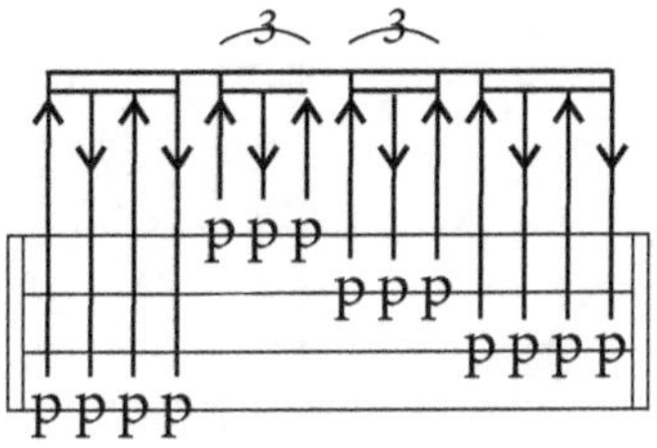

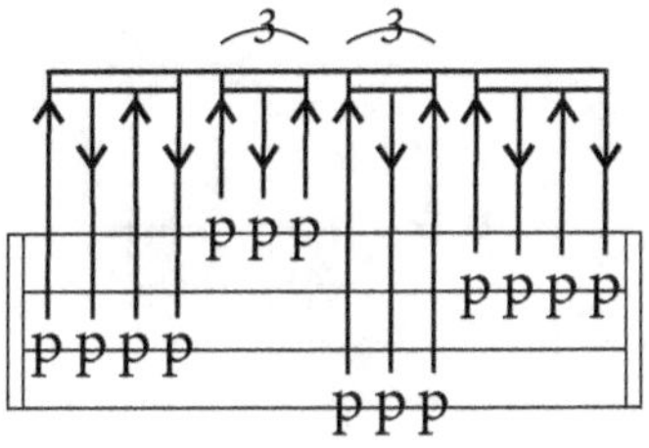

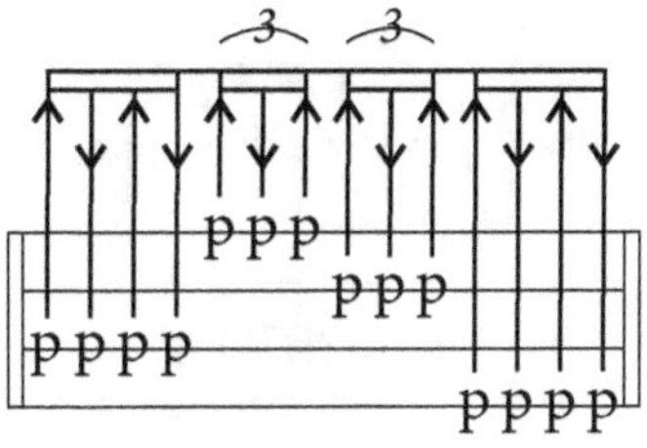

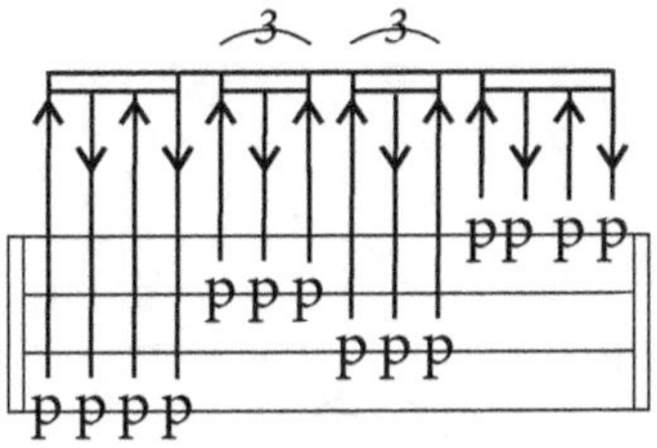

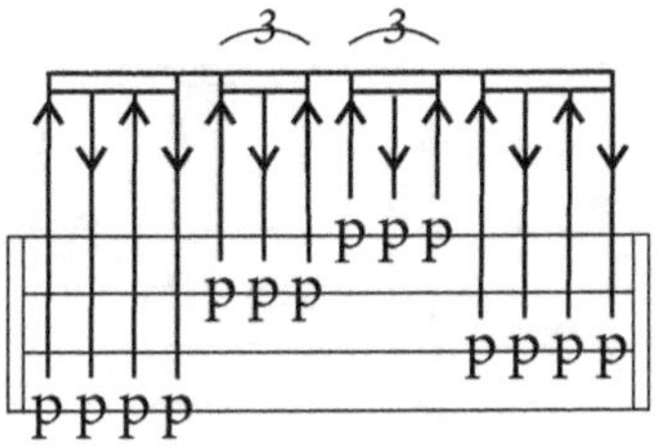

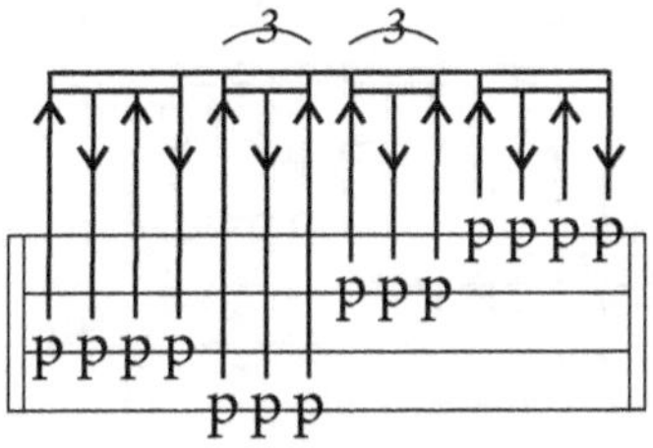

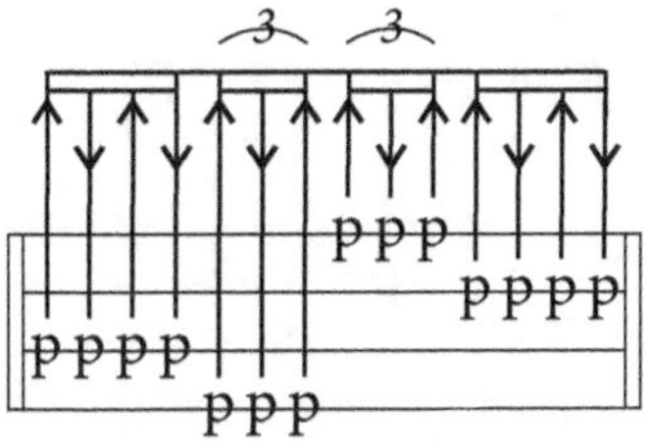

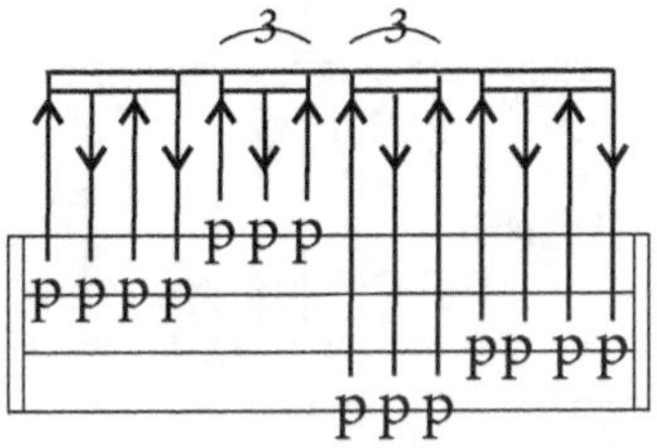

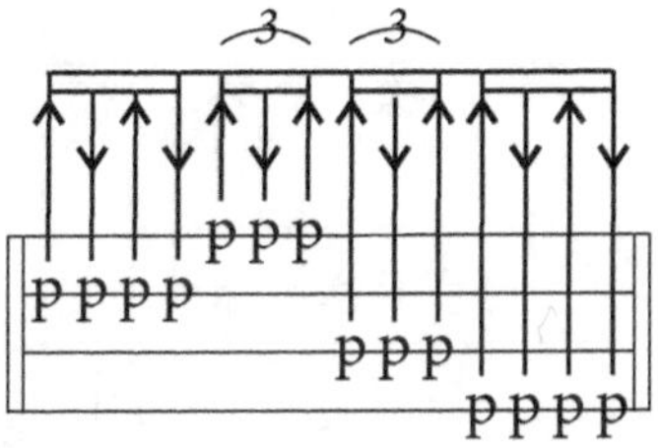

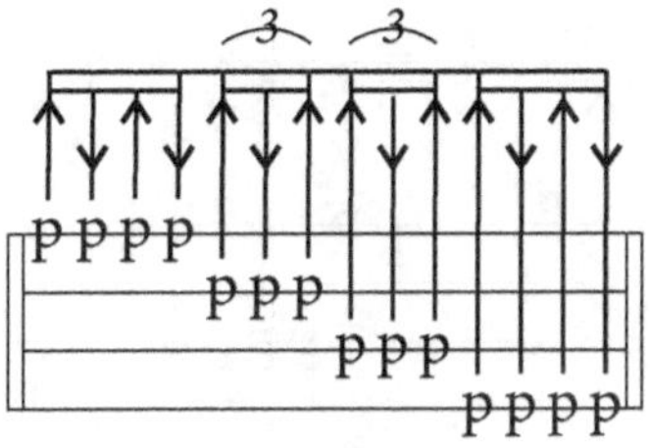

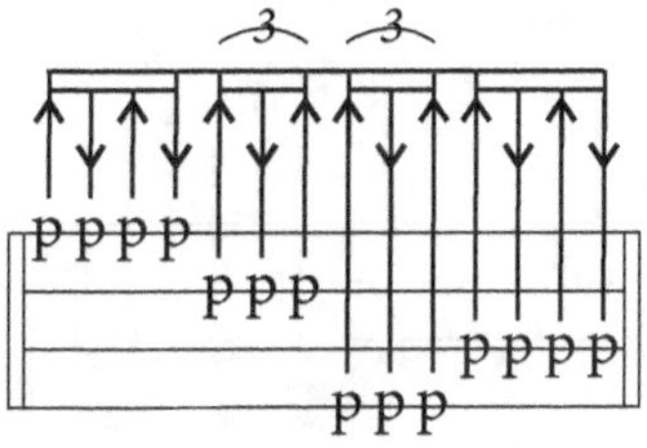

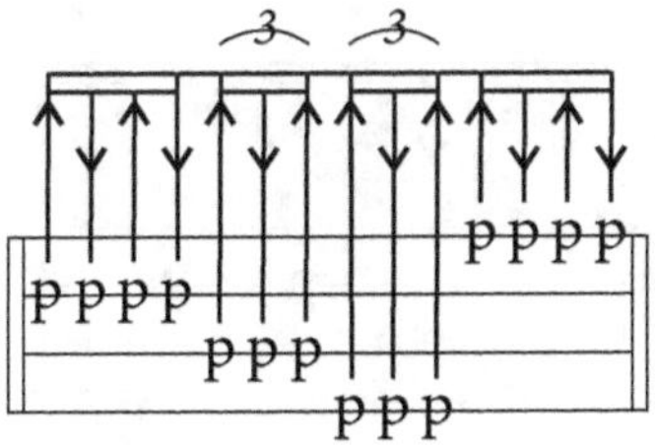

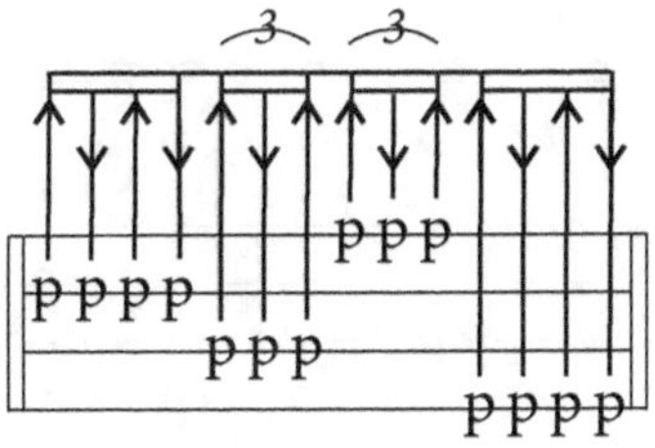

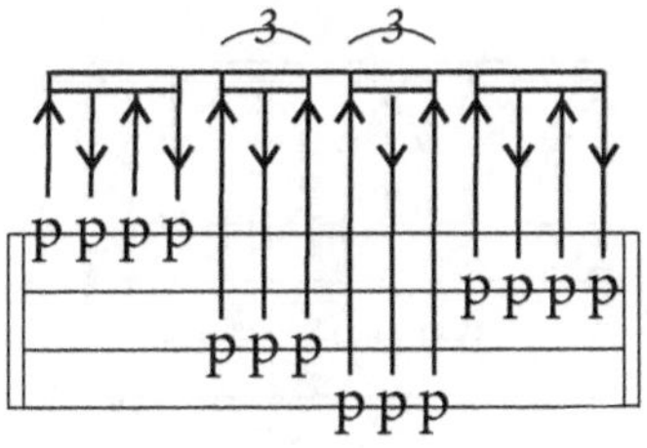

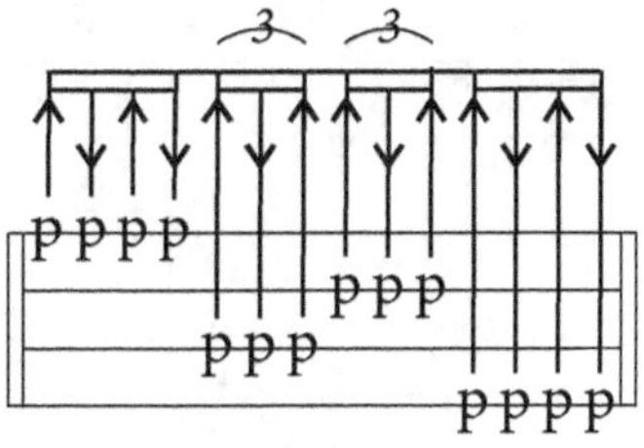

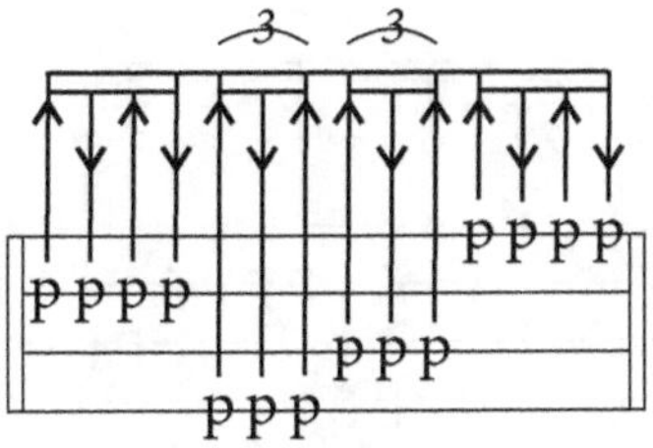

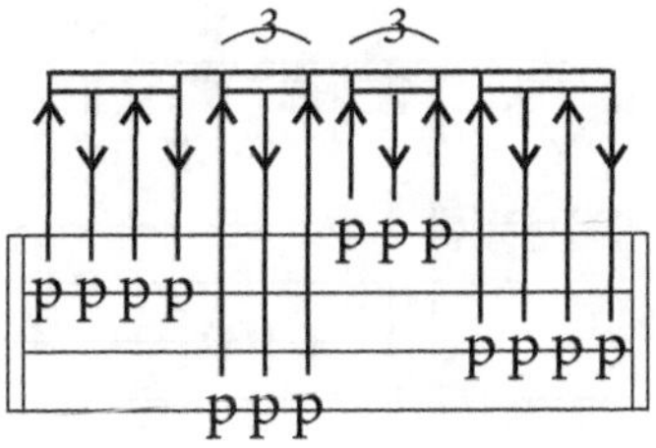

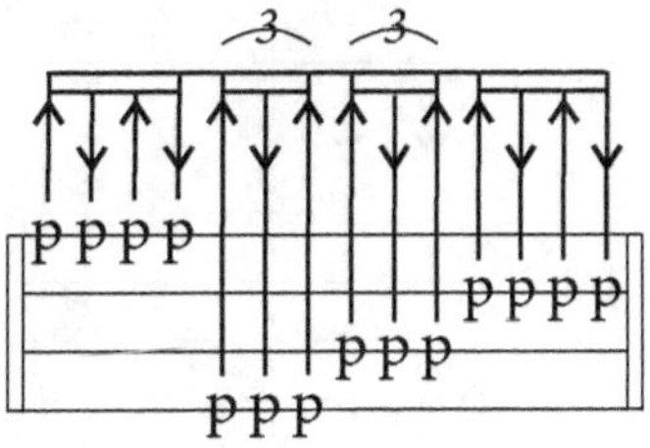

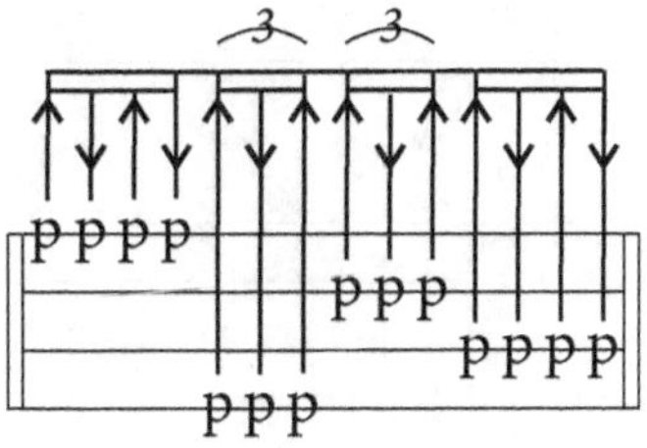

VARIATION VI

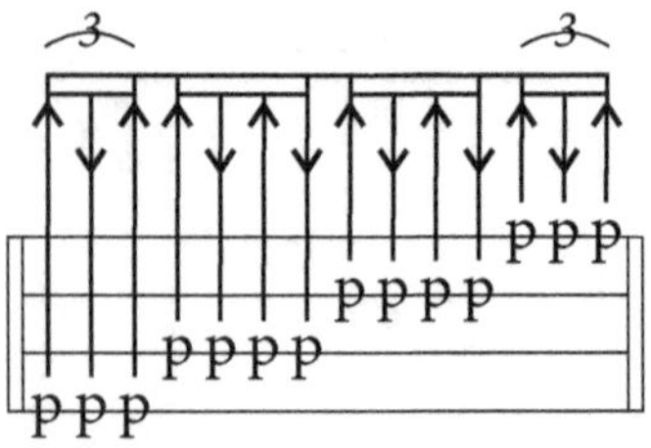

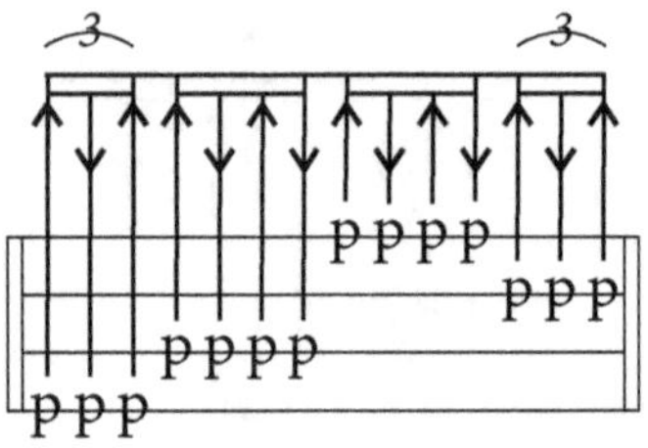

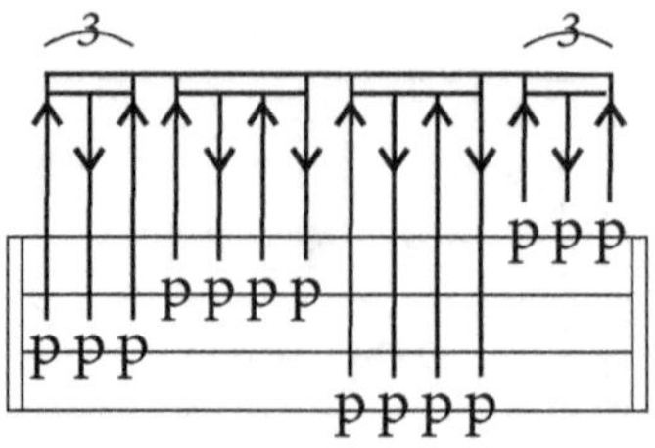

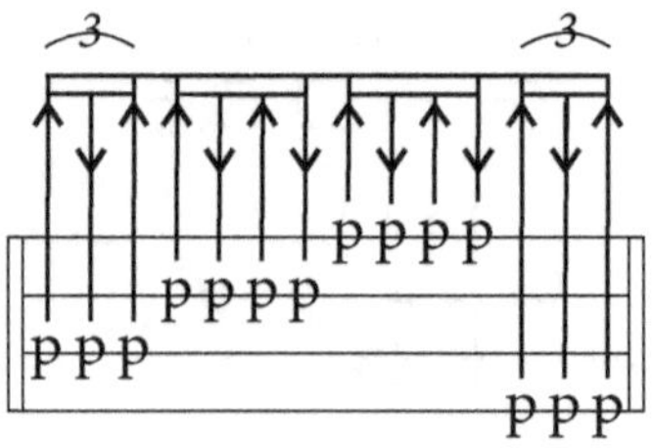

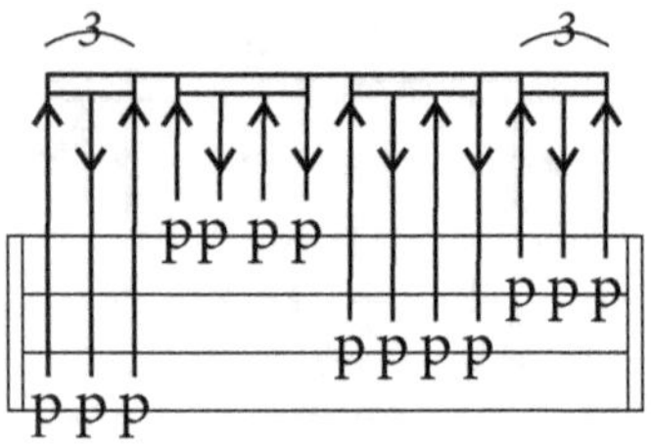

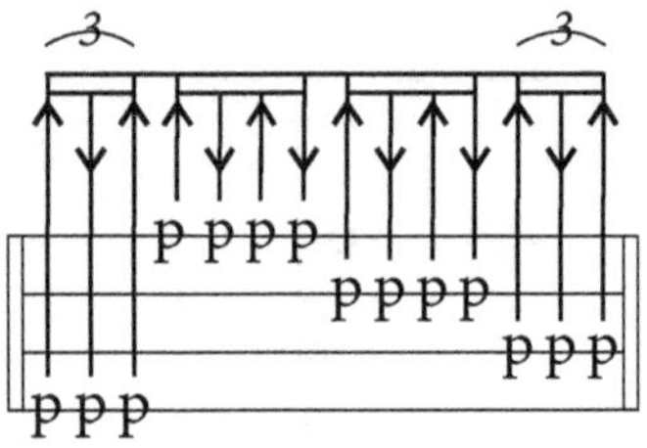

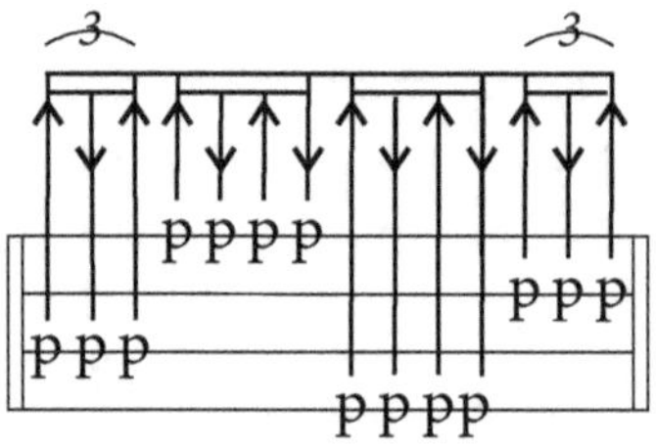

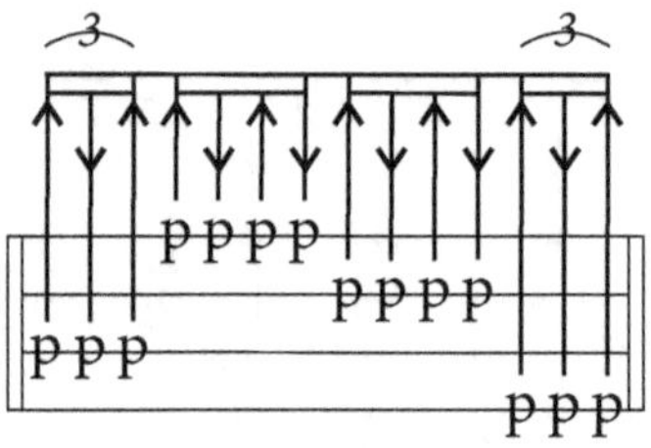

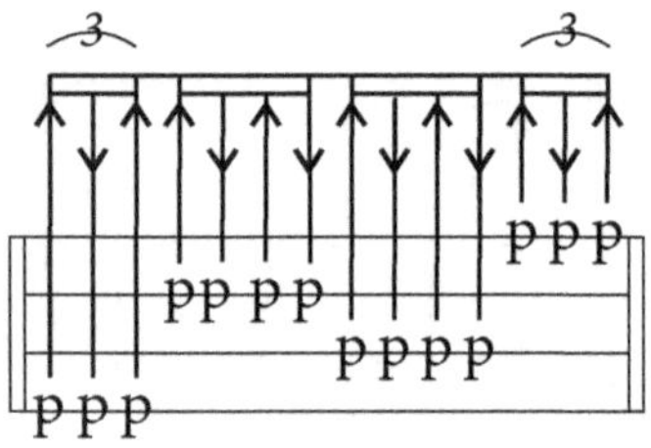

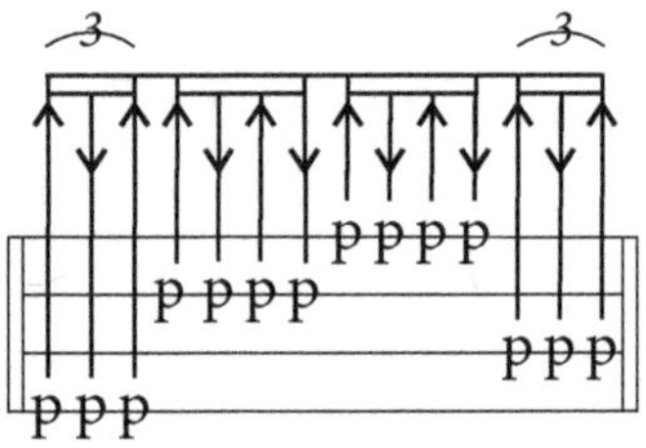

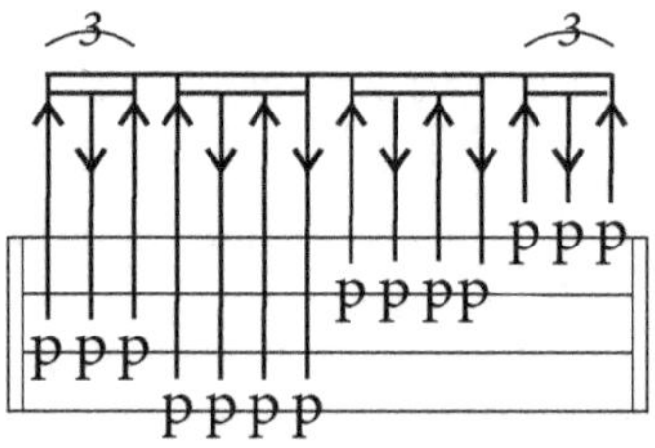

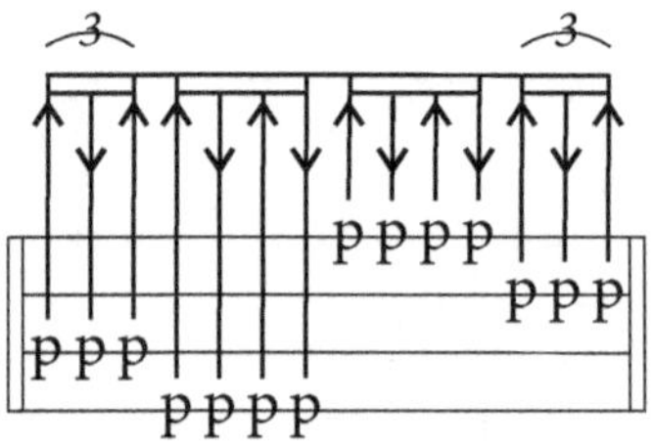

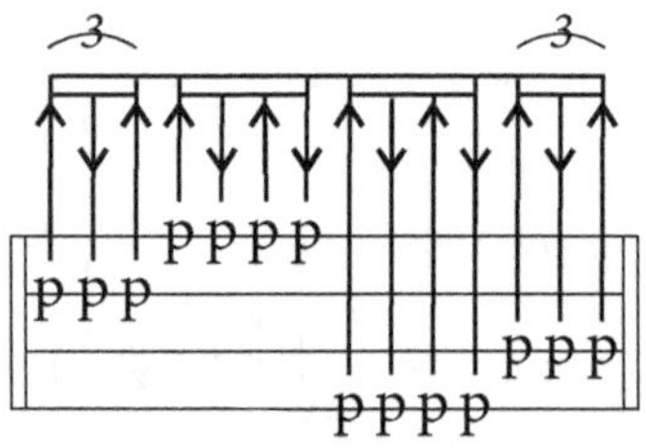

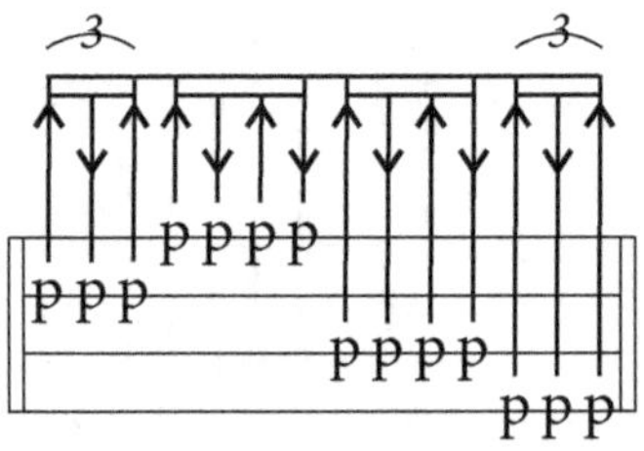

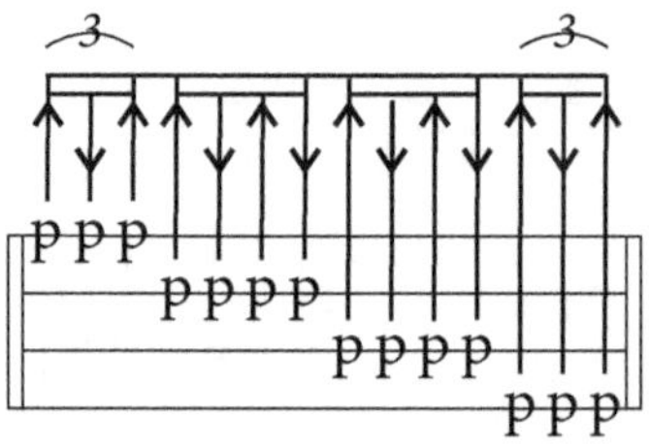

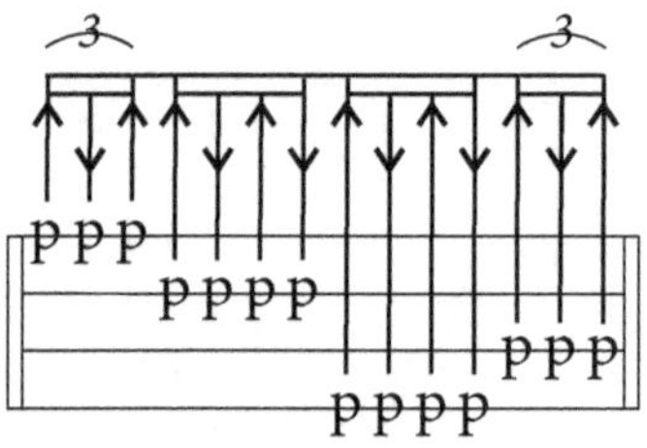

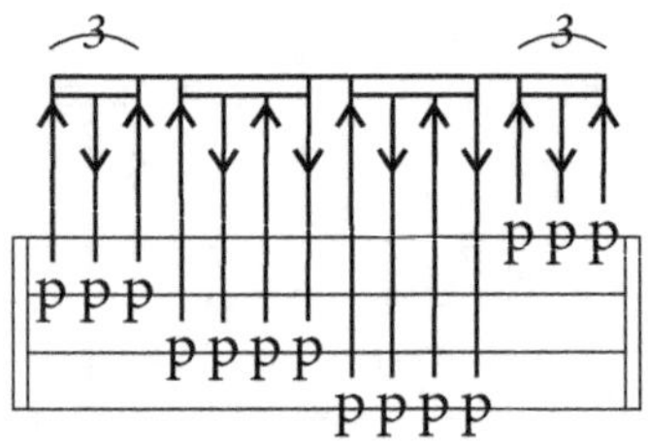

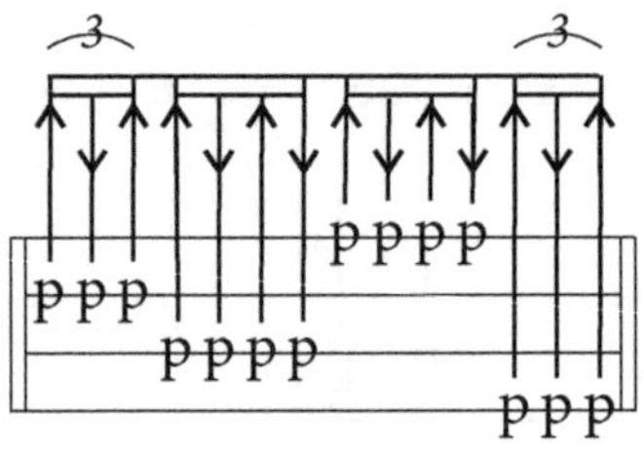

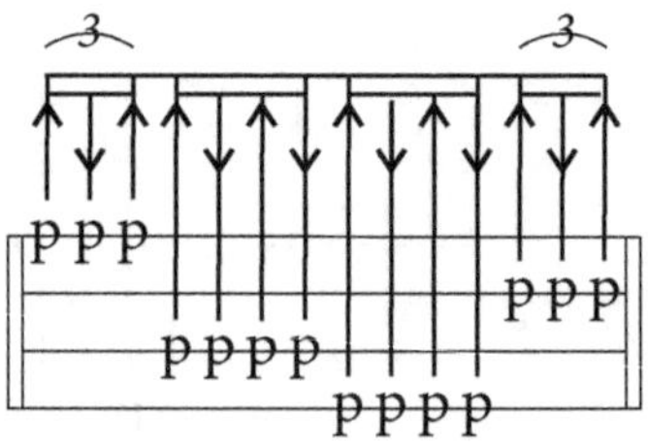

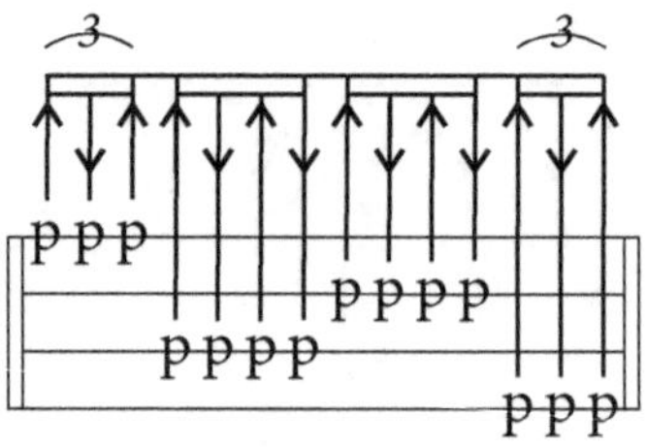

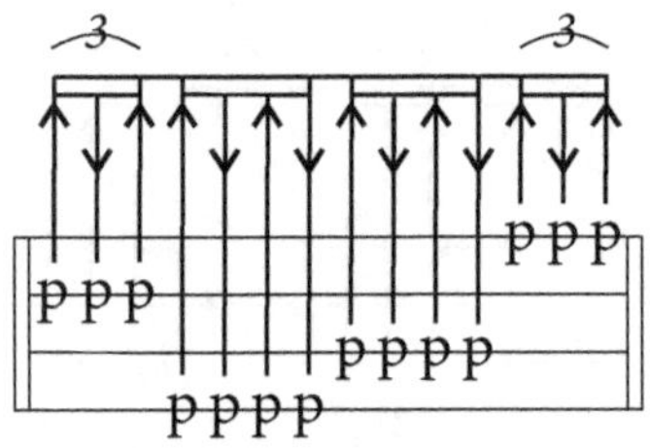

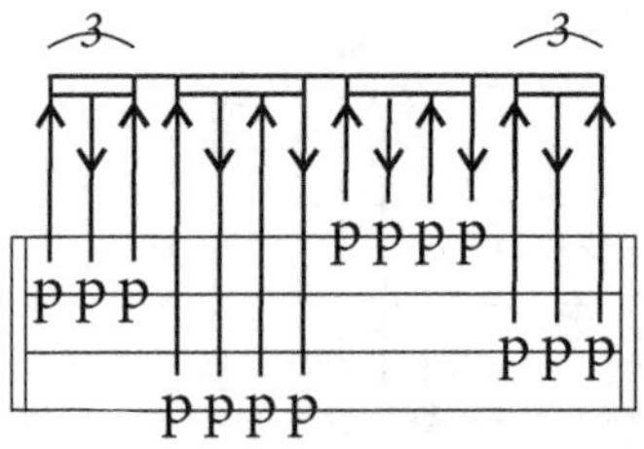

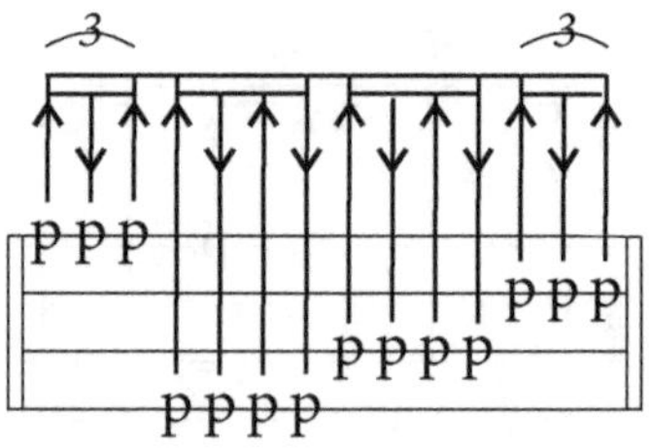

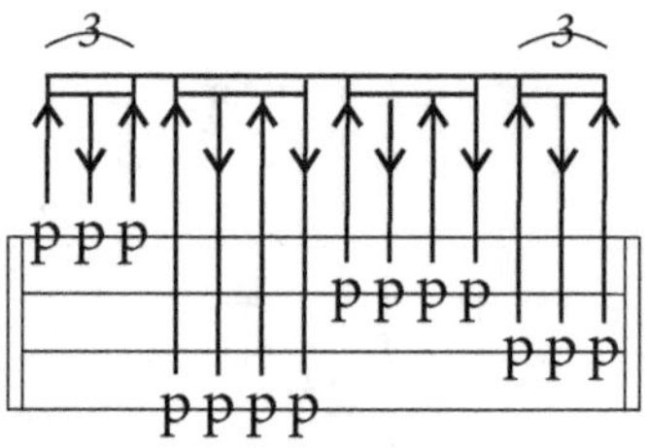

CHAPTER 4

SINGLE - DOUBLE - TRIPLE AND QUAD PULGAR STROKE
ON FOUR ADJACENT STRINGS WITHIN EACH FORMULA
MATCHING OF EACH FORMULA WITH ITS OPPOSITE

§ I

Exercise on pulgar on four adjacent strings with isochronous single, double, triple (triplet) and quad strokes. The Formulas of this chapter match their opposites and result in a different starting point for the single, double, triple and quad stroke on the strings. The positions of the left hand are the following:

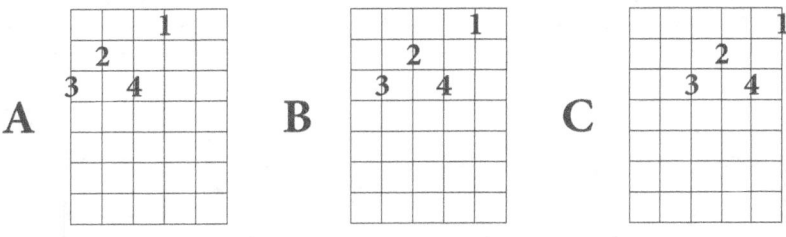

Since the exercise on pulgar in position C exhibits greater degree of difficulty, it is preferable for the learner to start practicing from positions A and B. Any other accord on four adjacent strings (accord of four notes) can be also used. The Formulas can be played both independently and in combination with their opposites.

The variations of this unit train the pulgar on striking different strings, adjacent or remote. The exercises contribute to the precision of pulgar strokes. You can modify these exercises by changing the direction of pulgar stroke:

1. For the double stroke apart from the already mentioned way (↑↓) you can also practise with stroke towards one direction (↑↑) leaving the rest unchanged.

2. For the triple stroke (triplet) apart from the already mention way, $\overset{\overset{3}{\frown}}{\underset{\uparrow\,\downarrow\,\uparrow}{p\ p\ p}}$ you can also practice with $\overset{\overset{3}{\frown}}{\underset{\uparrow\,\uparrow\,\downarrow}{p\ p\ p}}$ leaving the rest unchanged.

3. For the quad stroke apart from the already mentioned way, $\underset{\uparrow\,\downarrow\,\uparrow\,\downarrow}{p\ p\ p\ p}$ you can also practice on the following variations:

A) $\underset{\uparrow\,\downarrow\,\uparrow\,\uparrow}{p\ p\ p\ p}$ B) $\underset{\uparrow\,\uparrow\,\downarrow\,\uparrow}{p\ p\ p\ p}$ C) $\underset{\uparrow\,\uparrow\,\uparrow\,\downarrow}{p\ p\ p\ p}$ D) $\underset{\uparrow\,\uparrow\,\uparrow\,\uparrow}{p\ p\ p\ p}$

Modify the exercises as far as A, B, C and D are concerned leaving the rest unchanged. Of course there are plenty of combinations on which the learner can practice but that depends on the learner. The single, double, triple and quad strokes are isochronous.

§ I VARIATION I

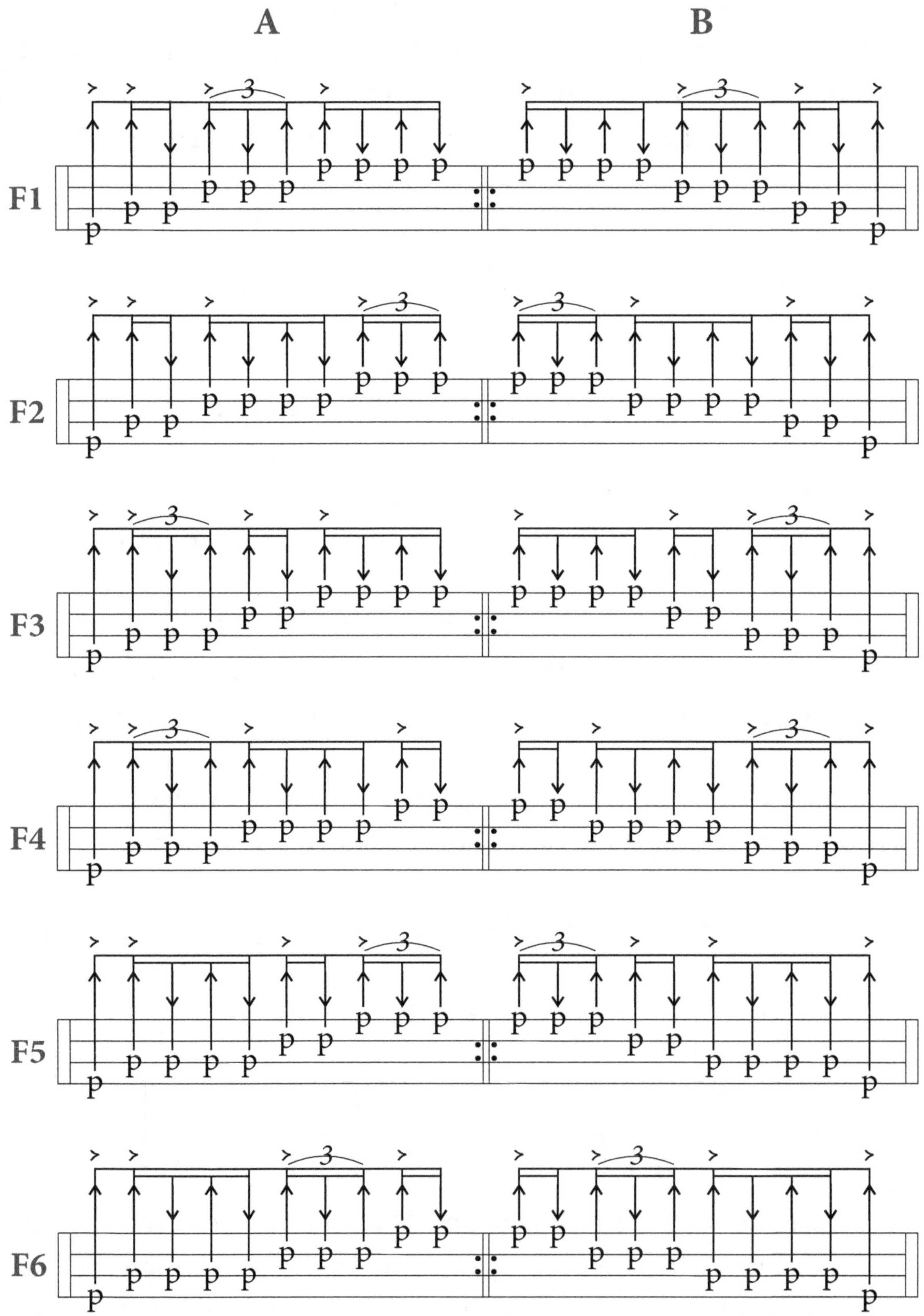

VARIATION II

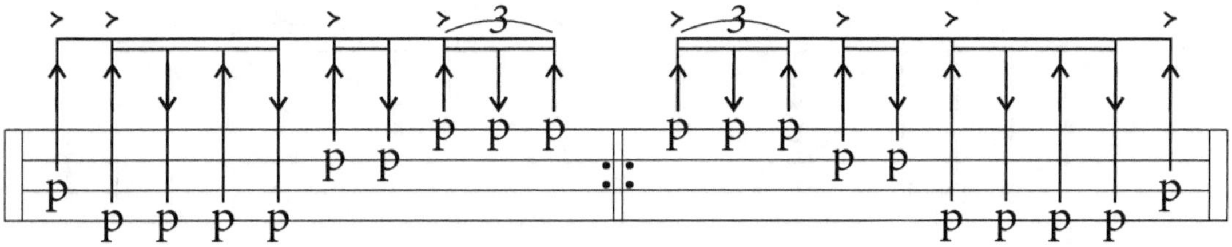

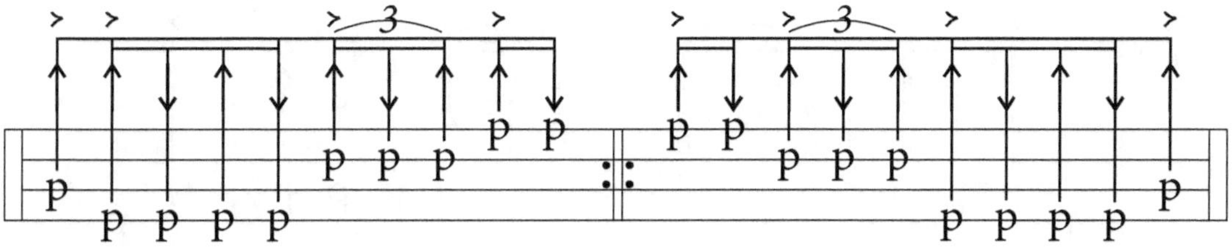

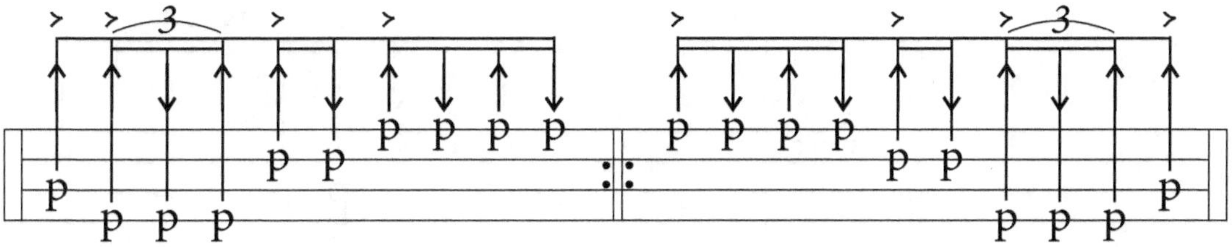

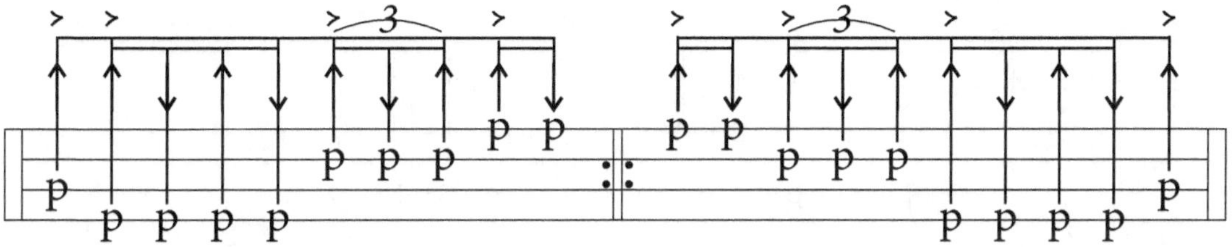

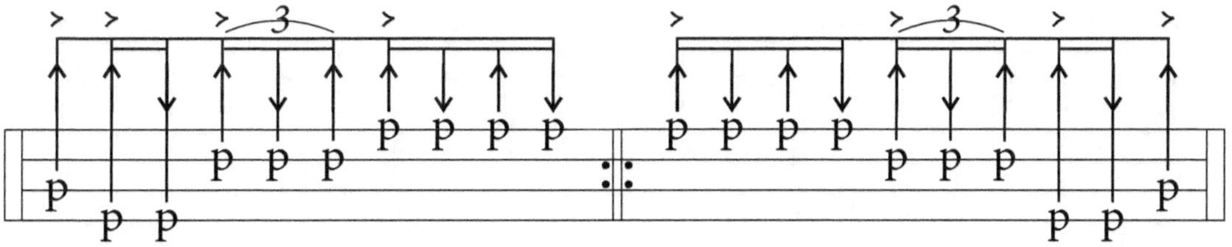

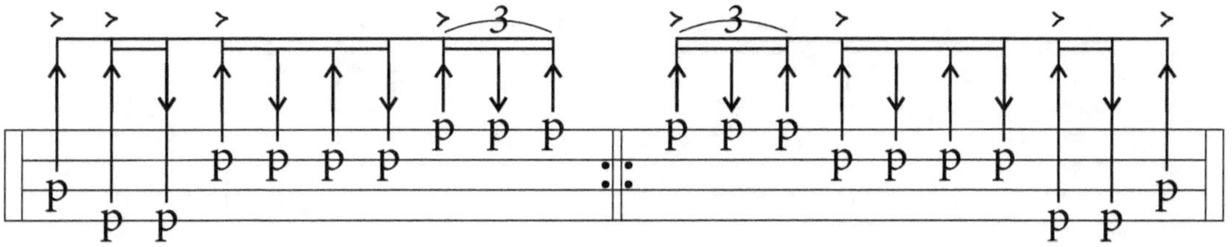

VARIATION III

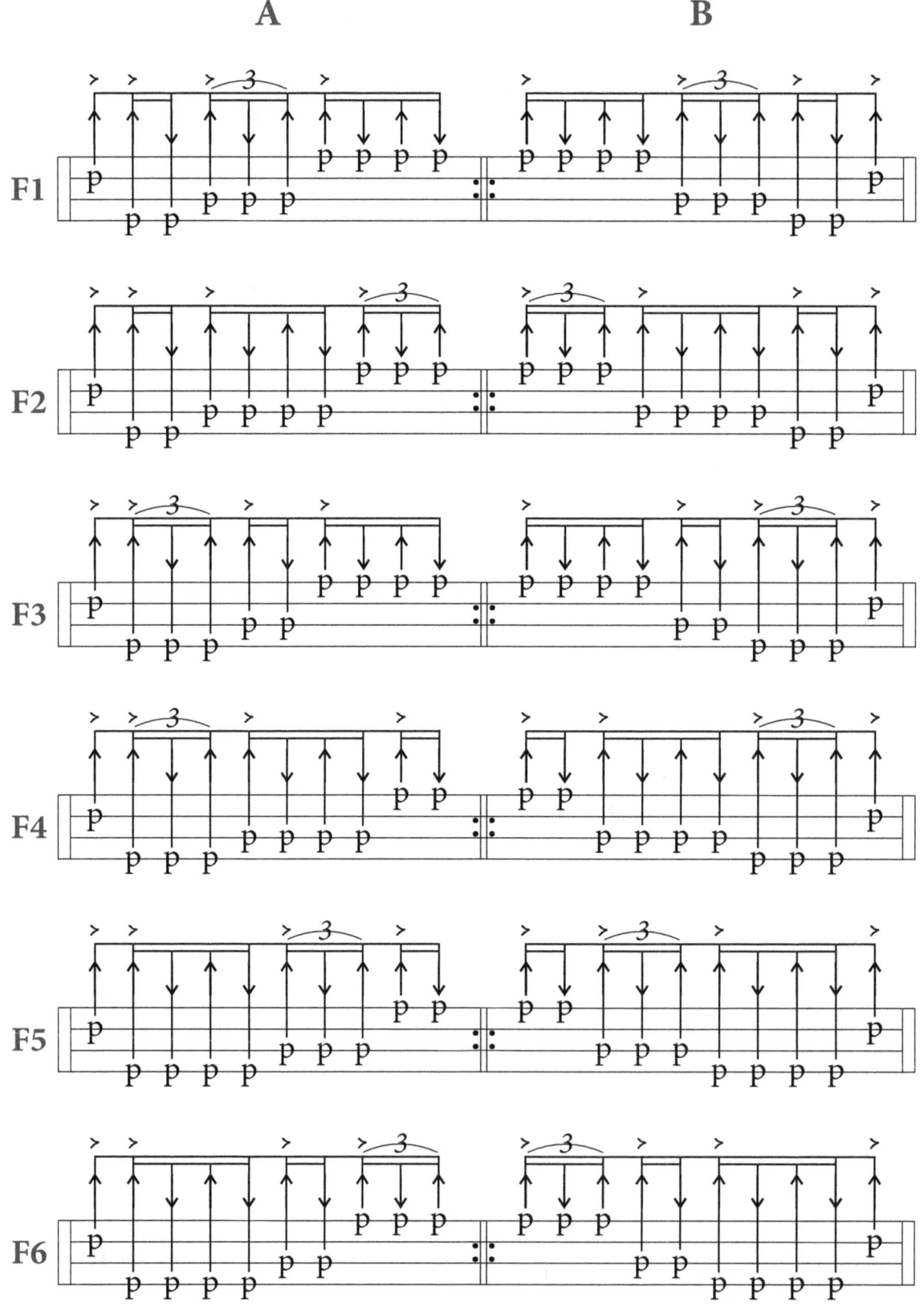

VARIATION IV

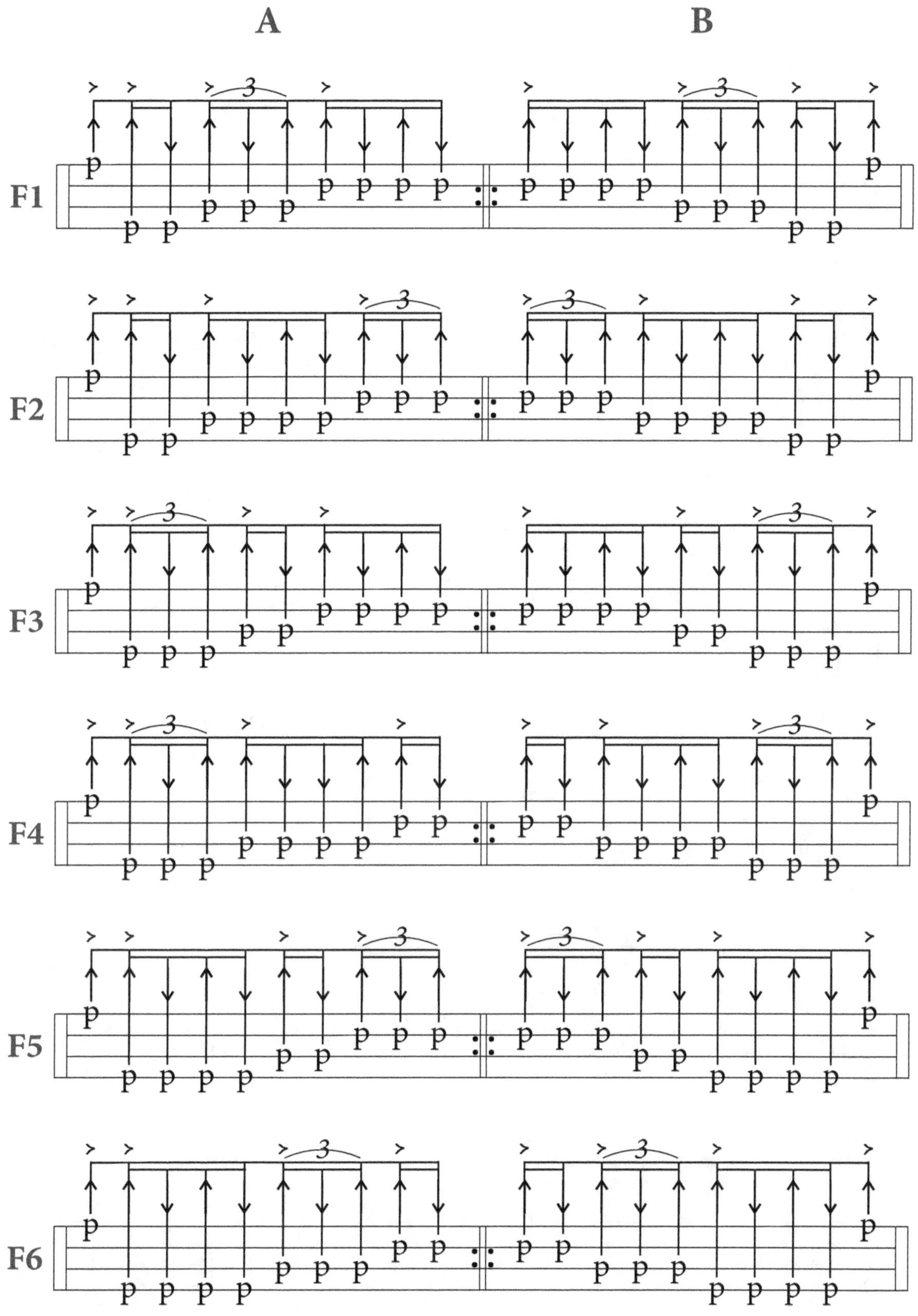

A B

§ II   **VARIATION I**

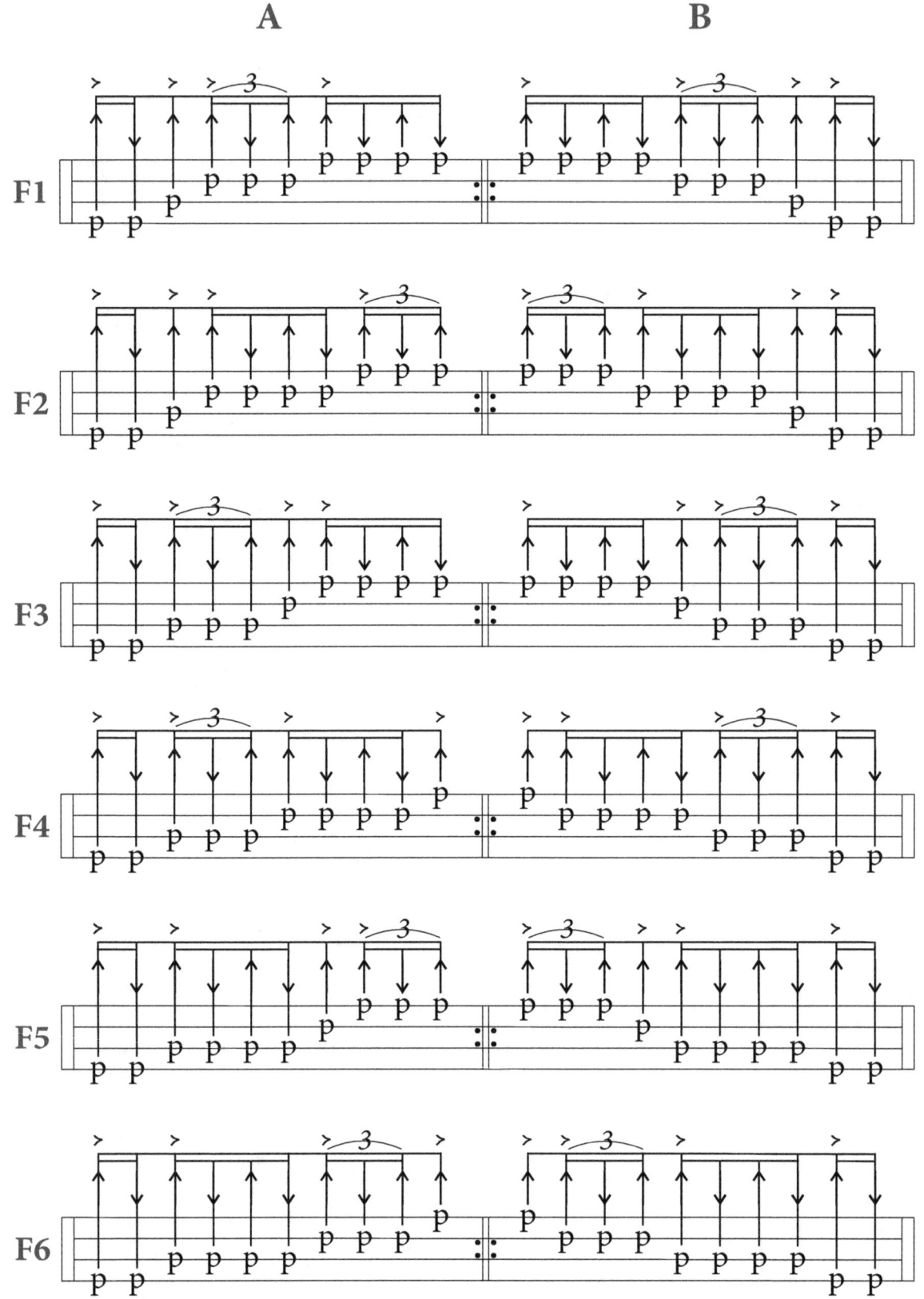

VARIATION II

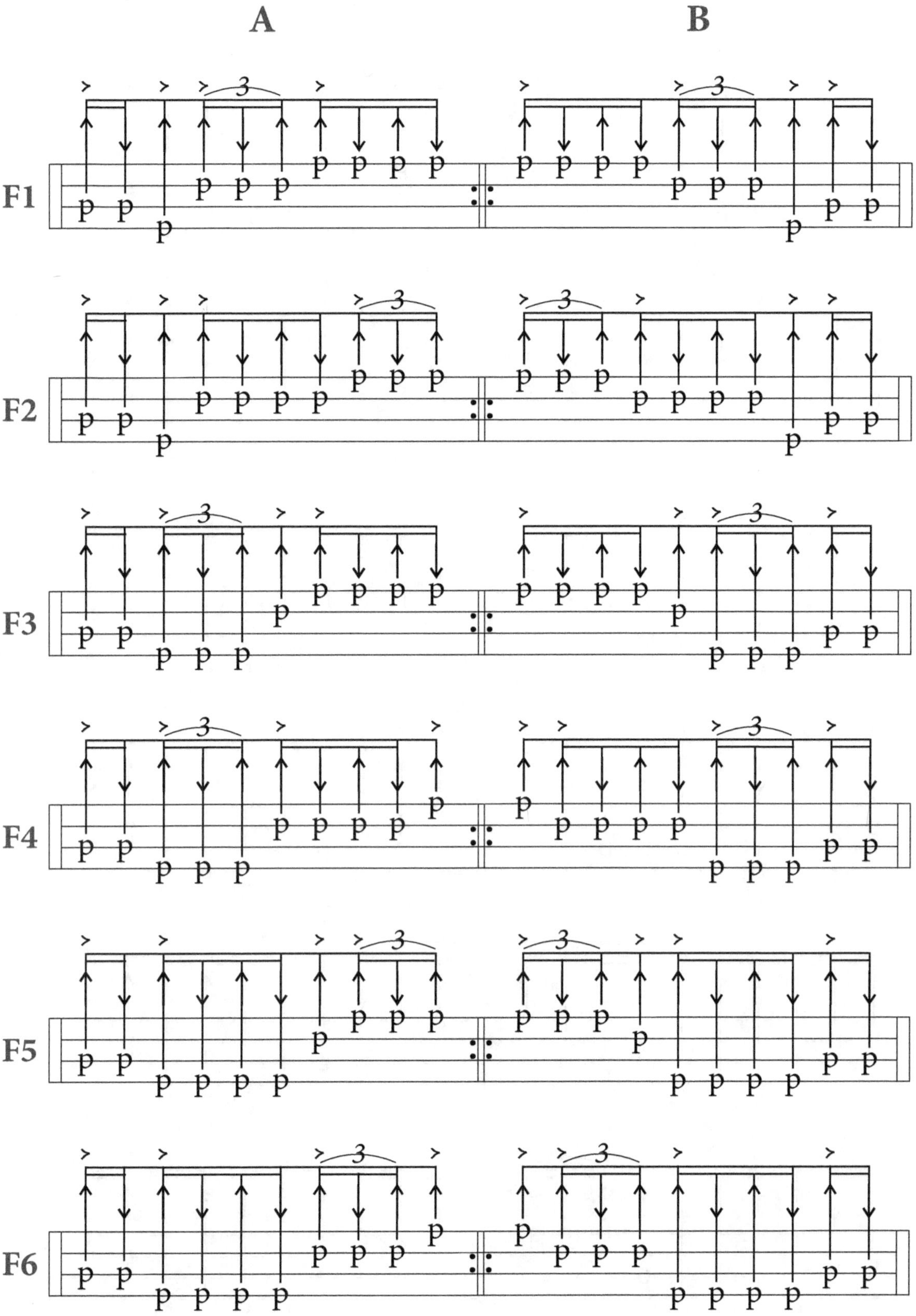

VARIATION III

A   B

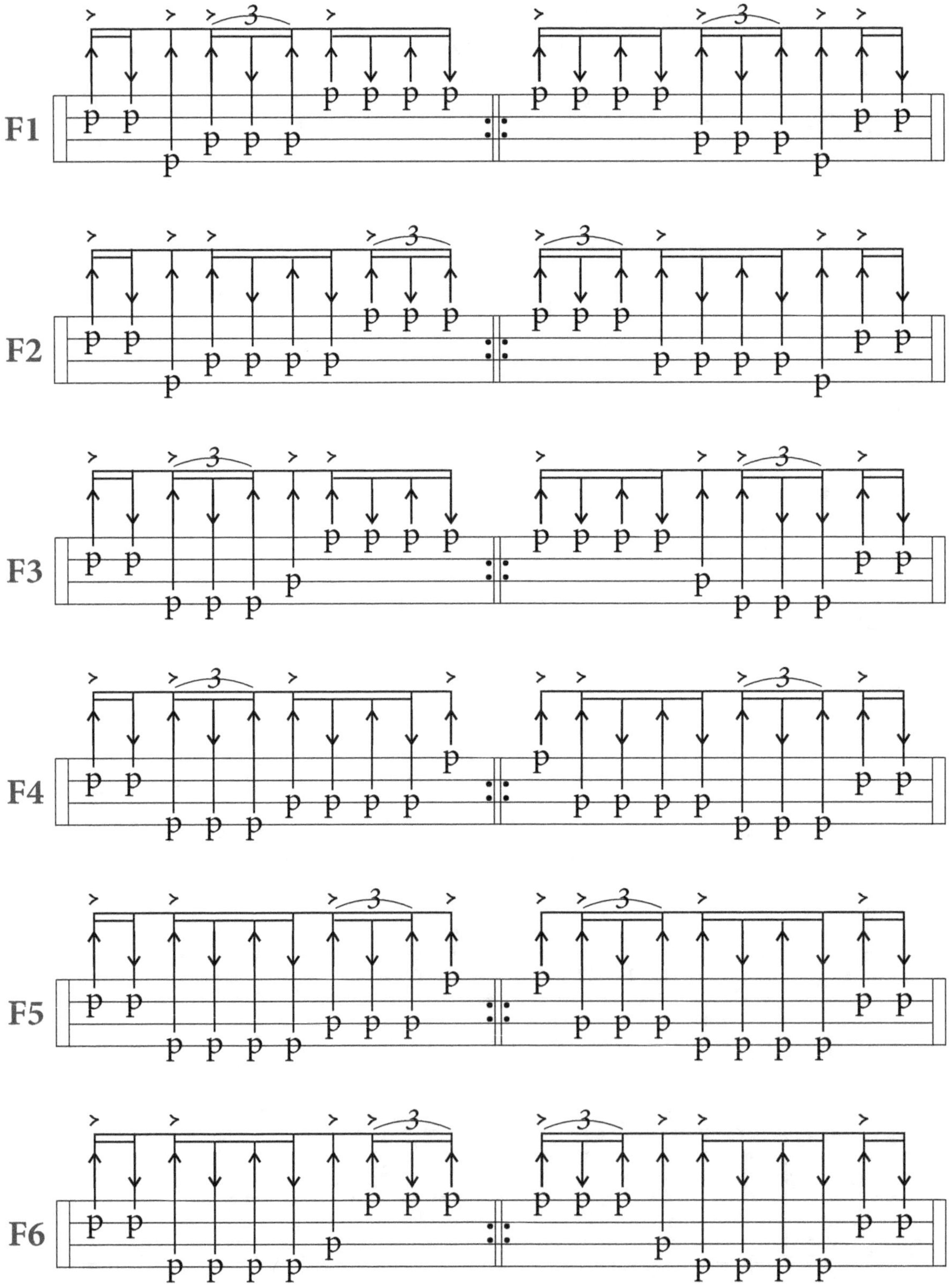

VARIATION IV

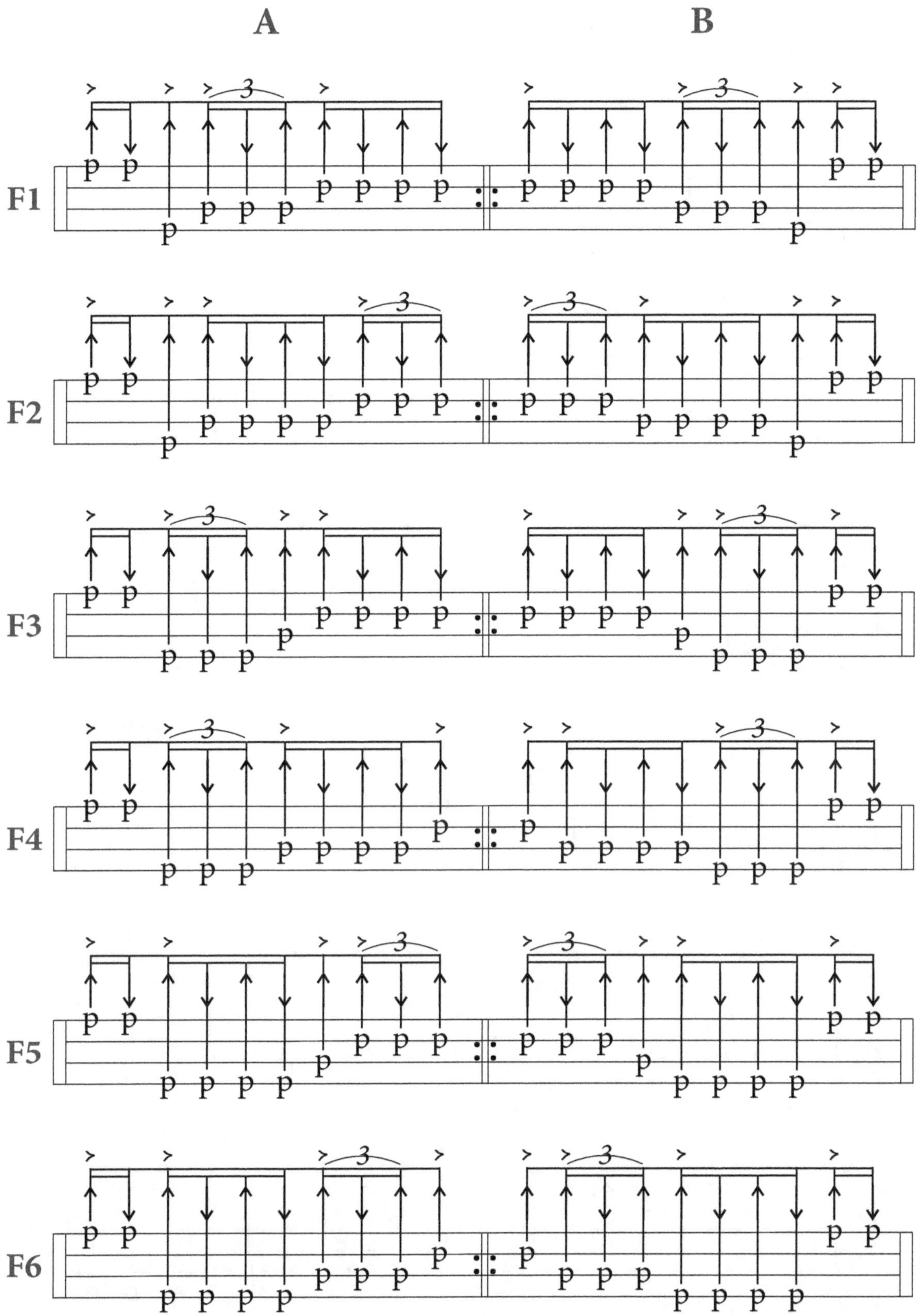

§ III VARIATION I

A B

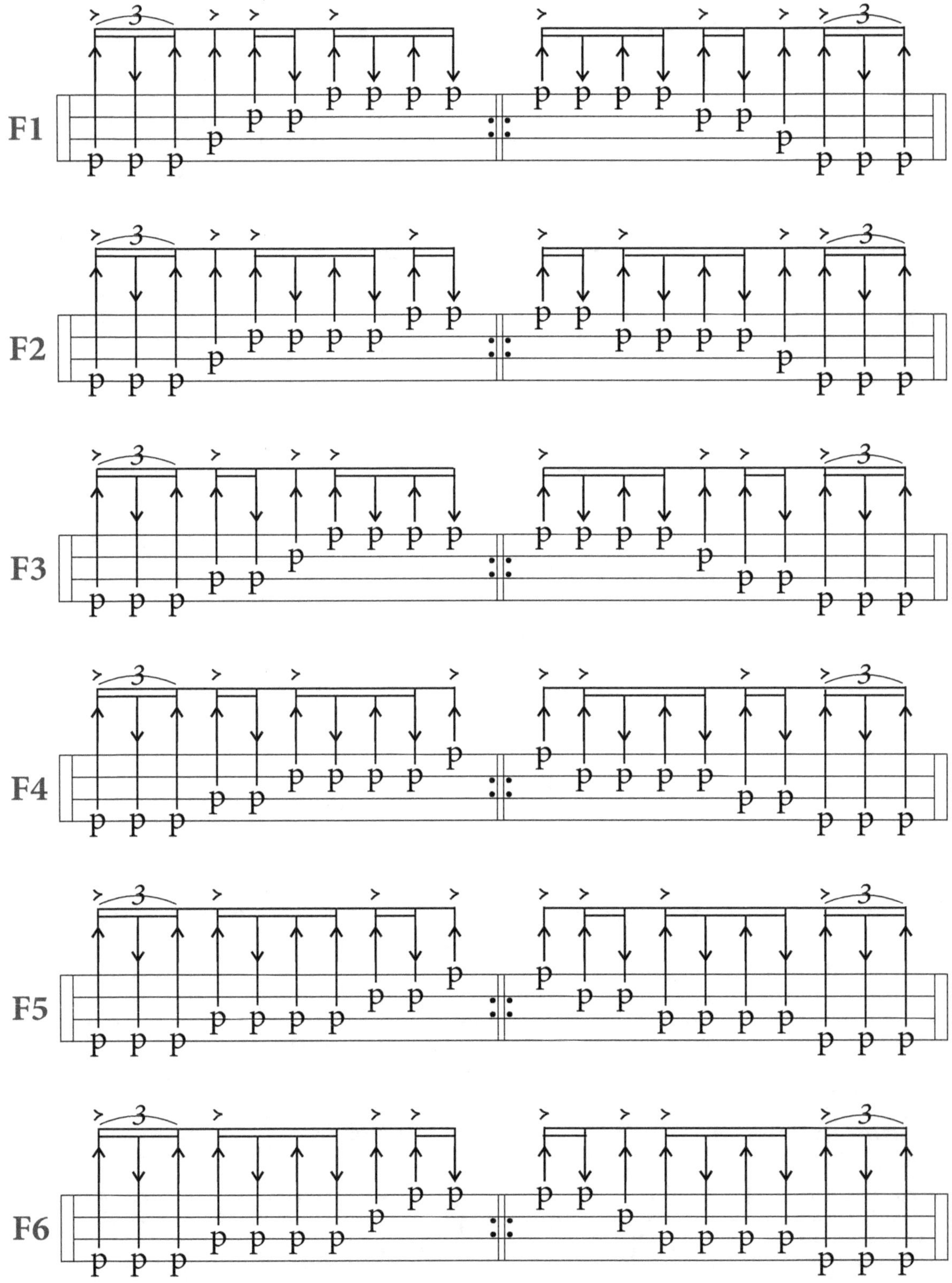

F1

F2

F3

F4

F5

F6

VARIATION II

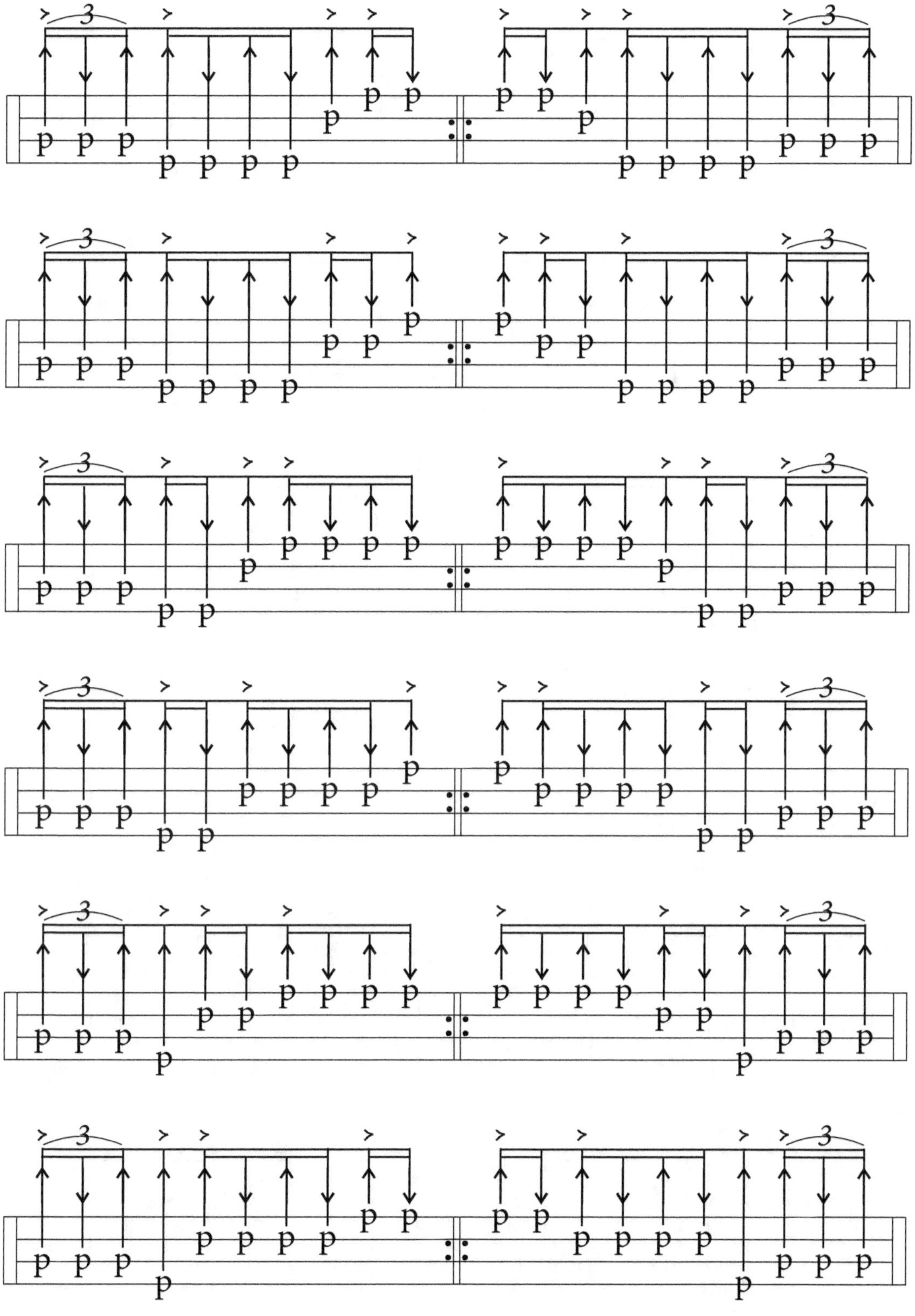

VARIATION III

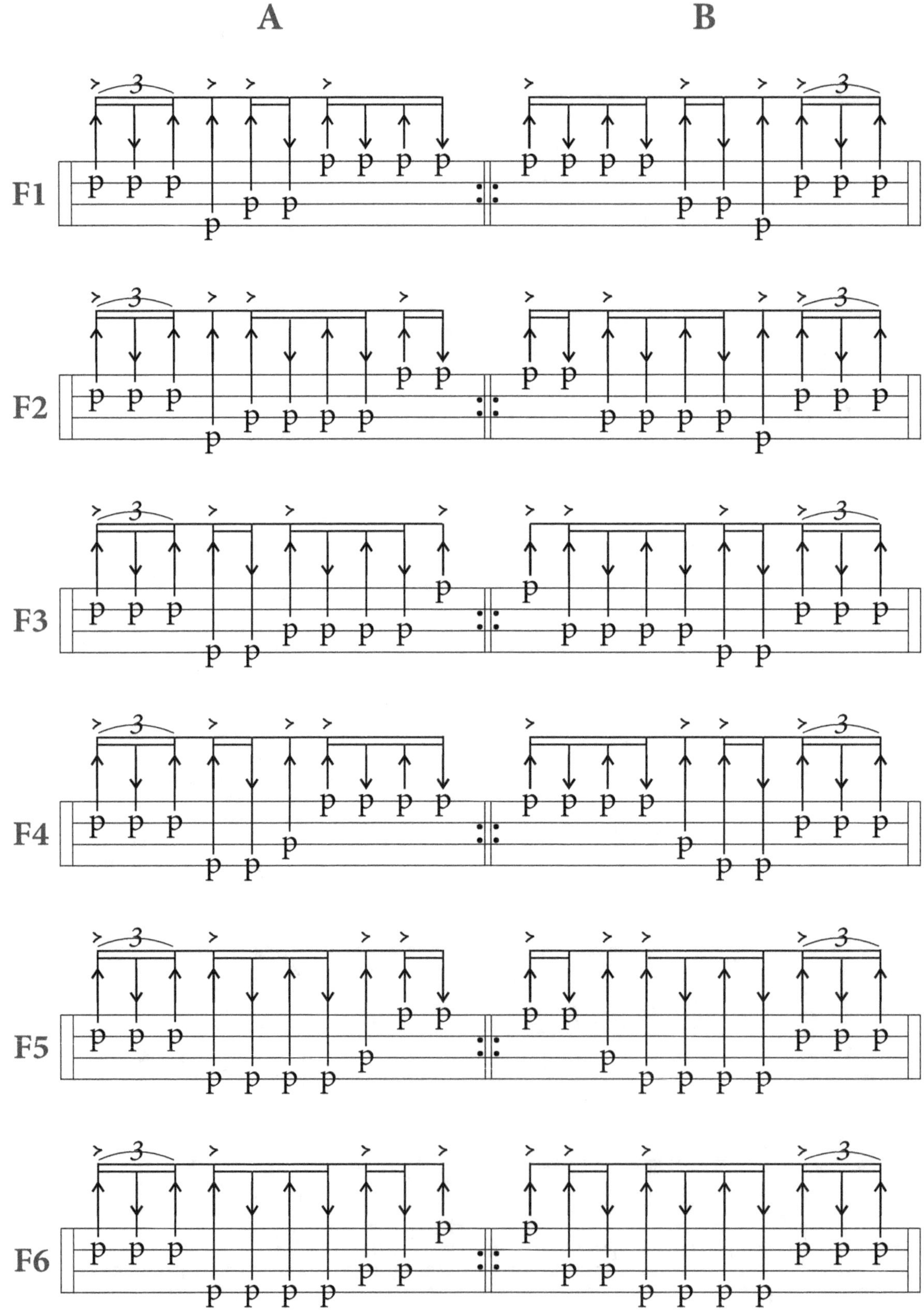

VARIATION IV

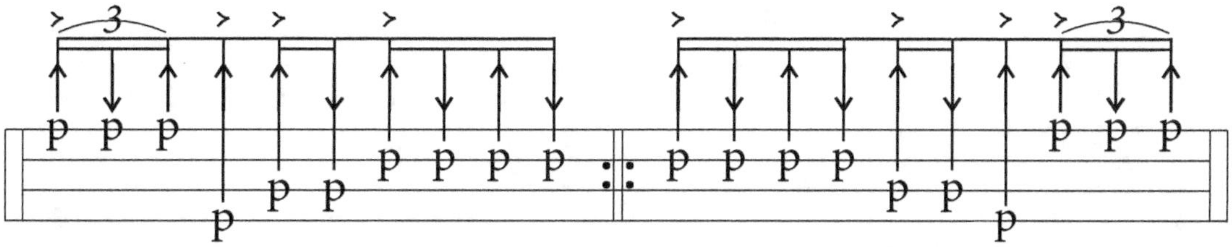

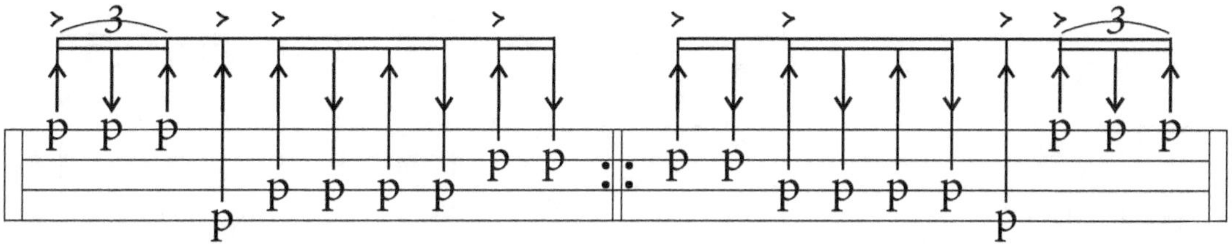

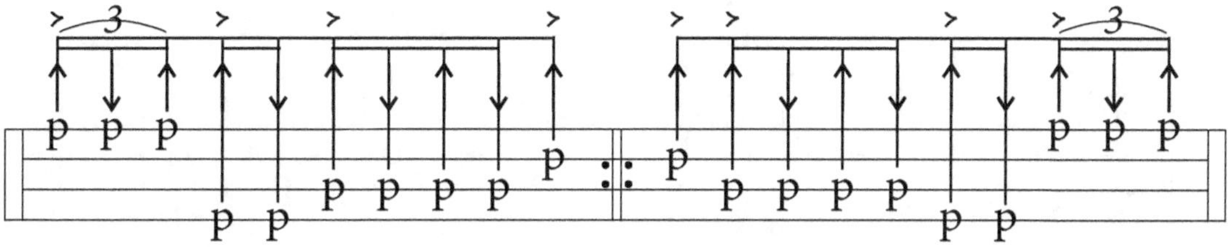

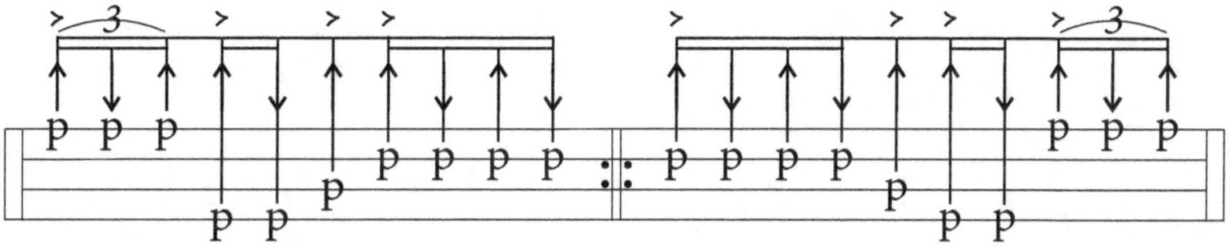

A B

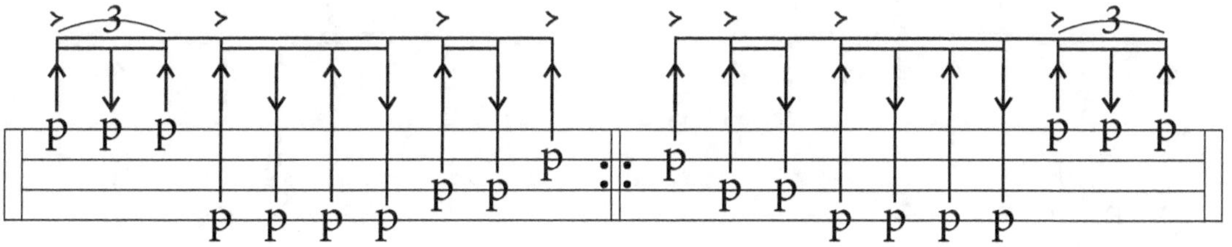

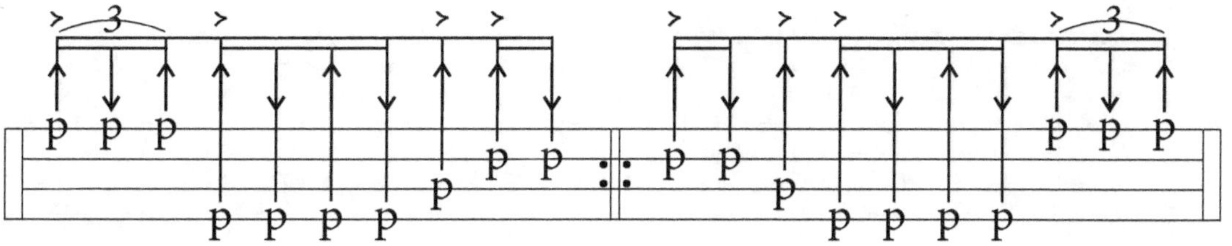

§ IV   VARIATION I

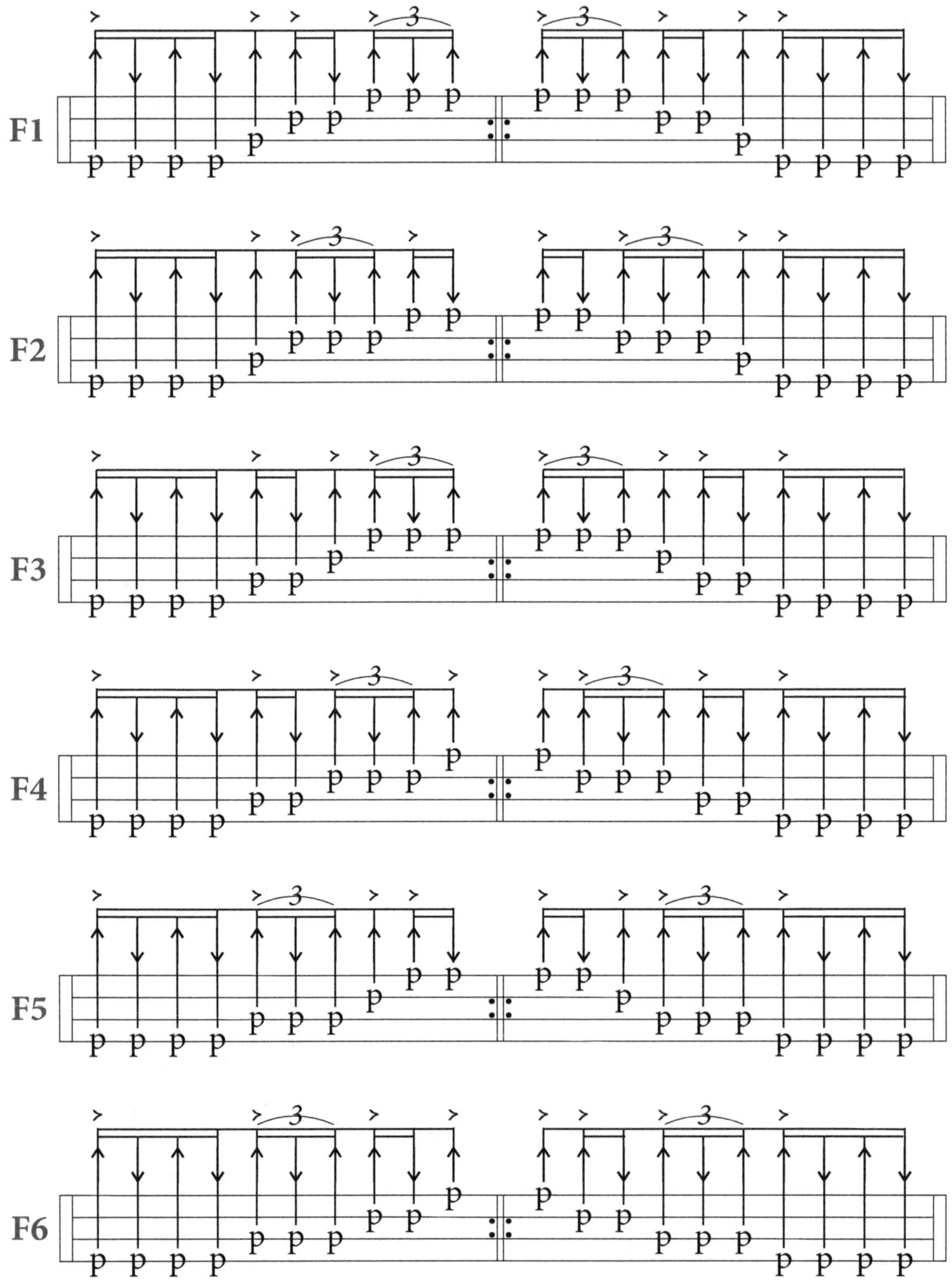

VARIATION II

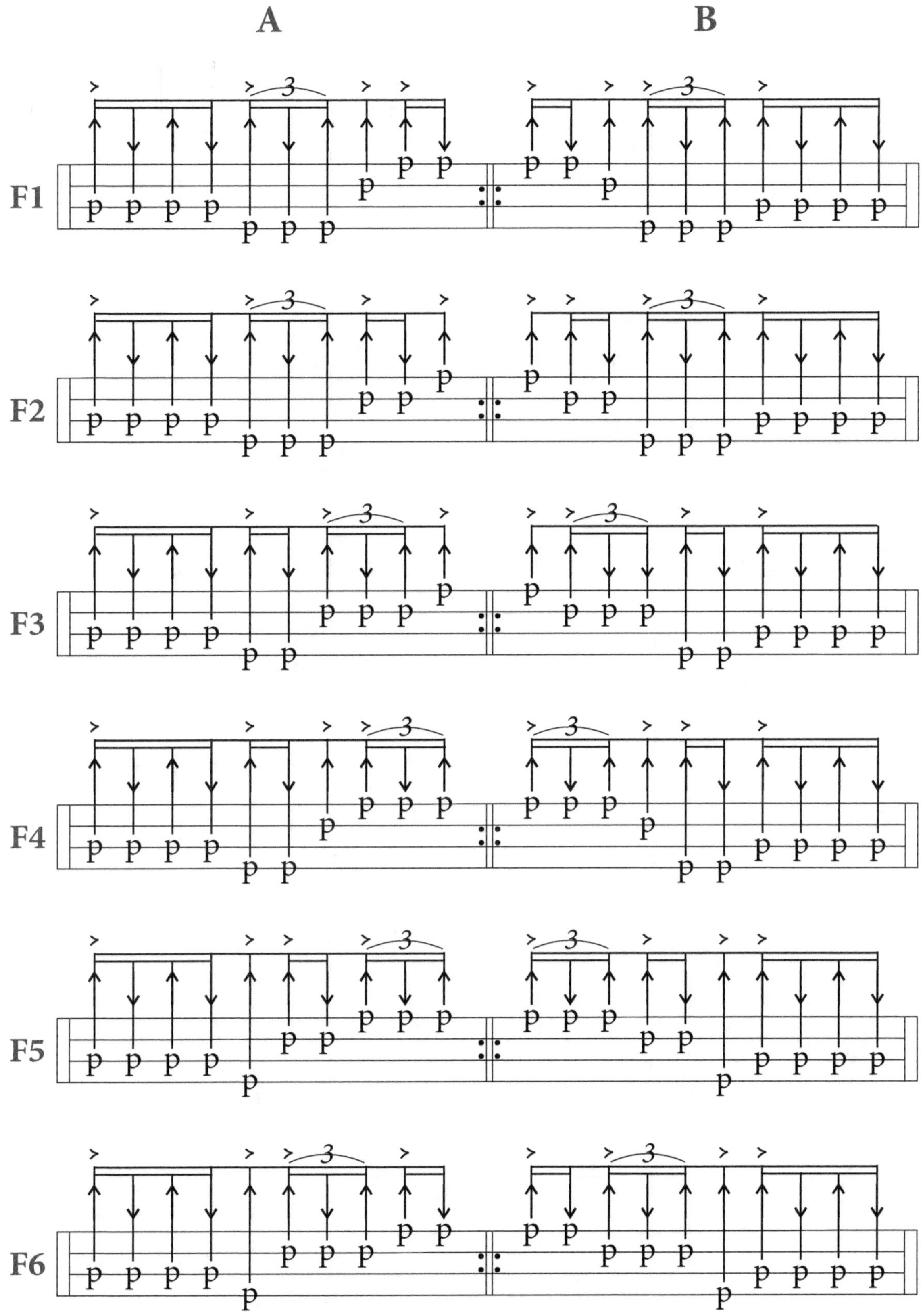

VARIATION III

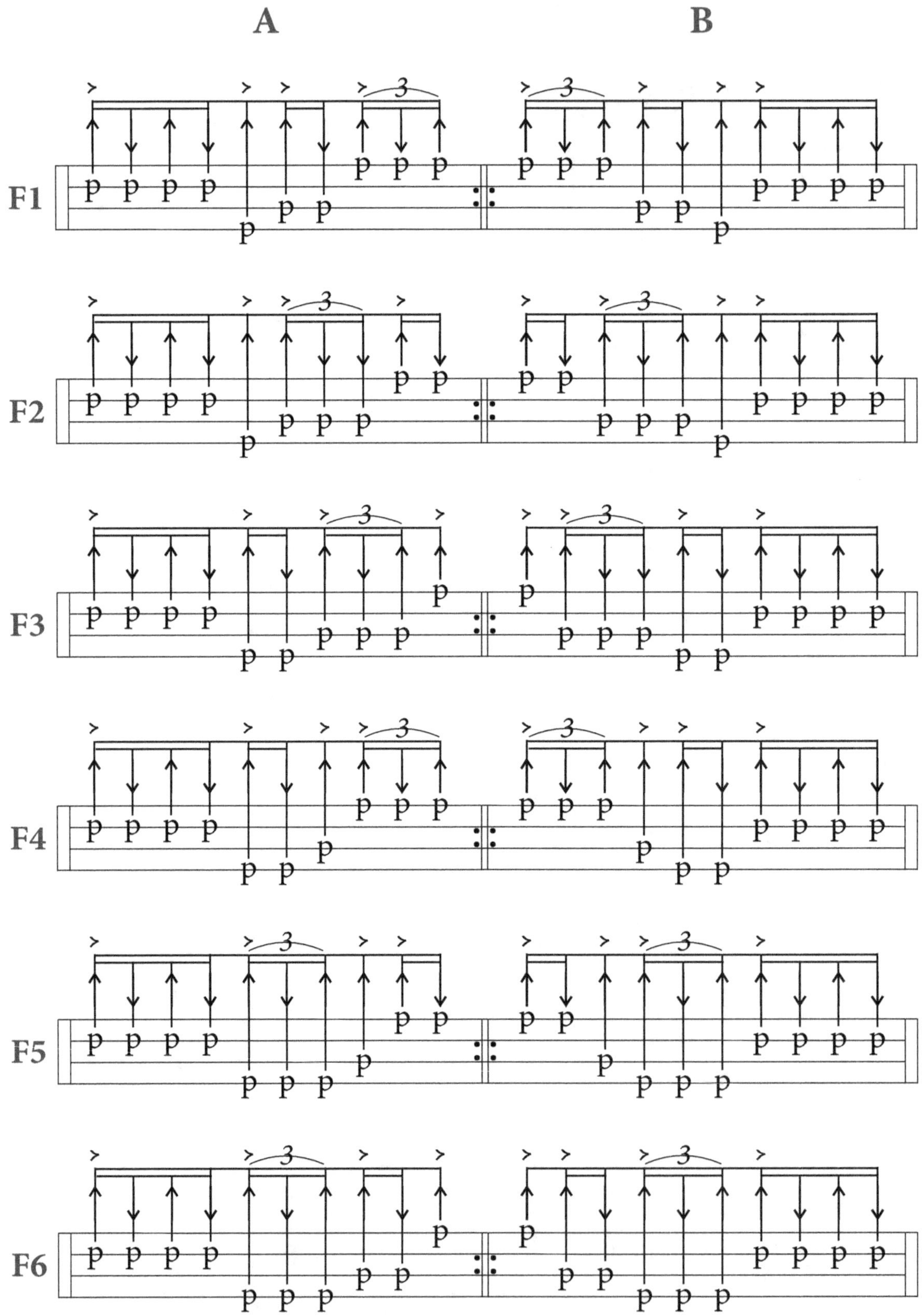

VARIATION IV

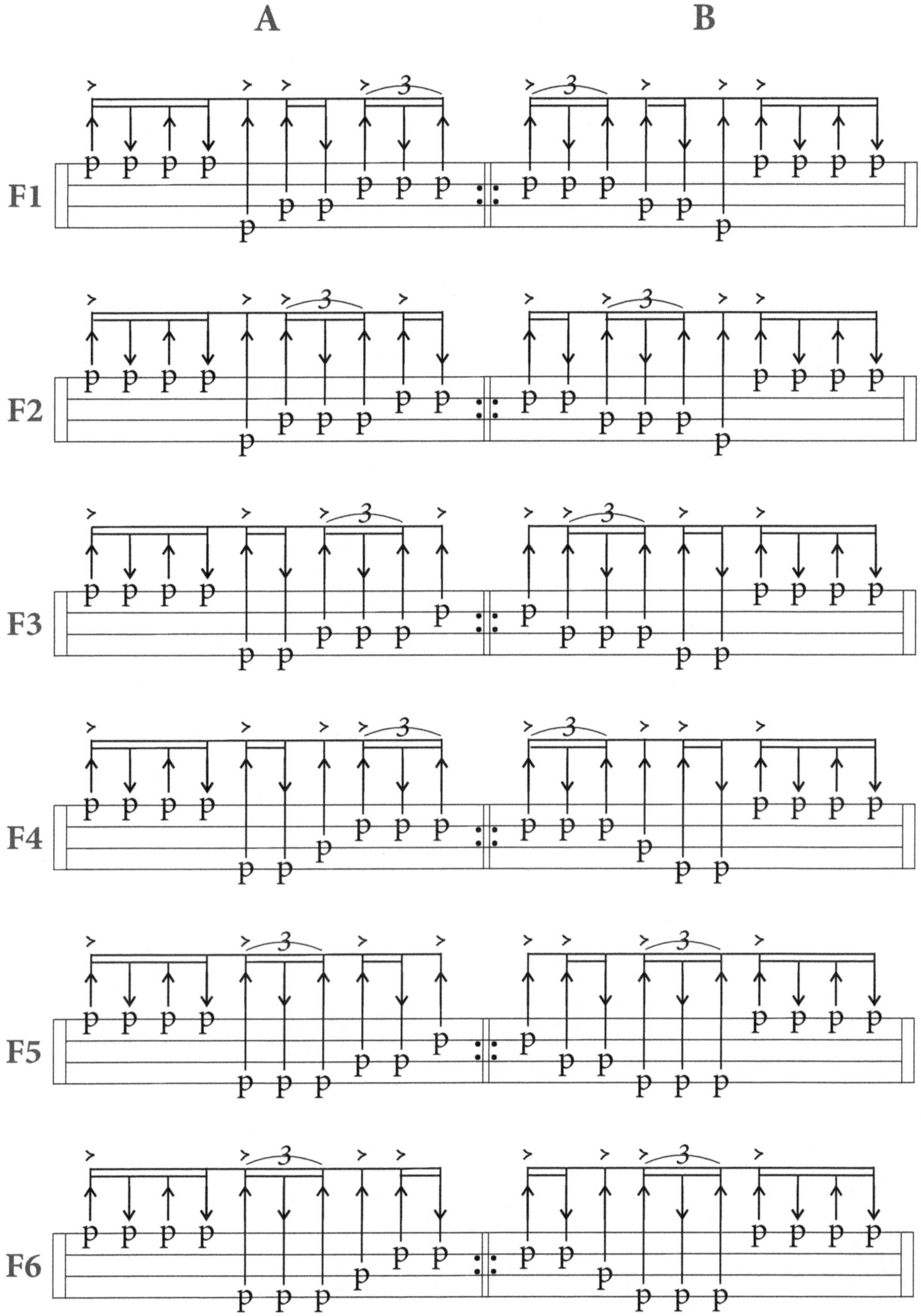

CHAPTER 5

EXERCISES FOR THE STRENGTHENING
OF THE PULGAR STROKE
EXERCISES THAT COMBINE THE STROKE OF ONE STRING
WITH TWO OR THREE STRINGS SIMULTANEOUSLY

This chapter contains exercises for the empowering and precision of pulgar strokes. Simultaneous pulgar stroke on one, two or three strings towards one direction: only downwards (↑) or downwards and upwards (↑ ↓).

Practice on any combination of three strings:
a/ 6th + 5th + 4th
b/ 5th + 4th + 3rd
c/ 4th + 3rd + 2nd
d/ 3rd + 2nd + 1st

The exercise on the first three strings (3rd + 2nd + 1st) exhibits greater degree of difficulty. Practice initially on the first (a) combination of strings: (6th + 5th + 4th)

The left hand holds steadily one chord of three notes pressing on three adjacent strings.
Example:

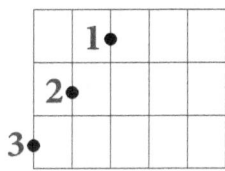

The descriptive expressions single - double - triple stroke indicate the striking of one, two or three strings simultaneously.

§ I

Simultaneous stroke of two strings by the pulgar. 14 Formulas in total. The first Formula is cited below.

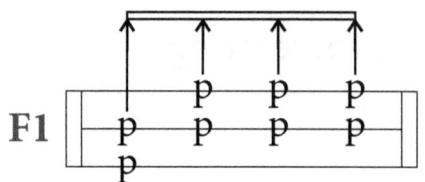

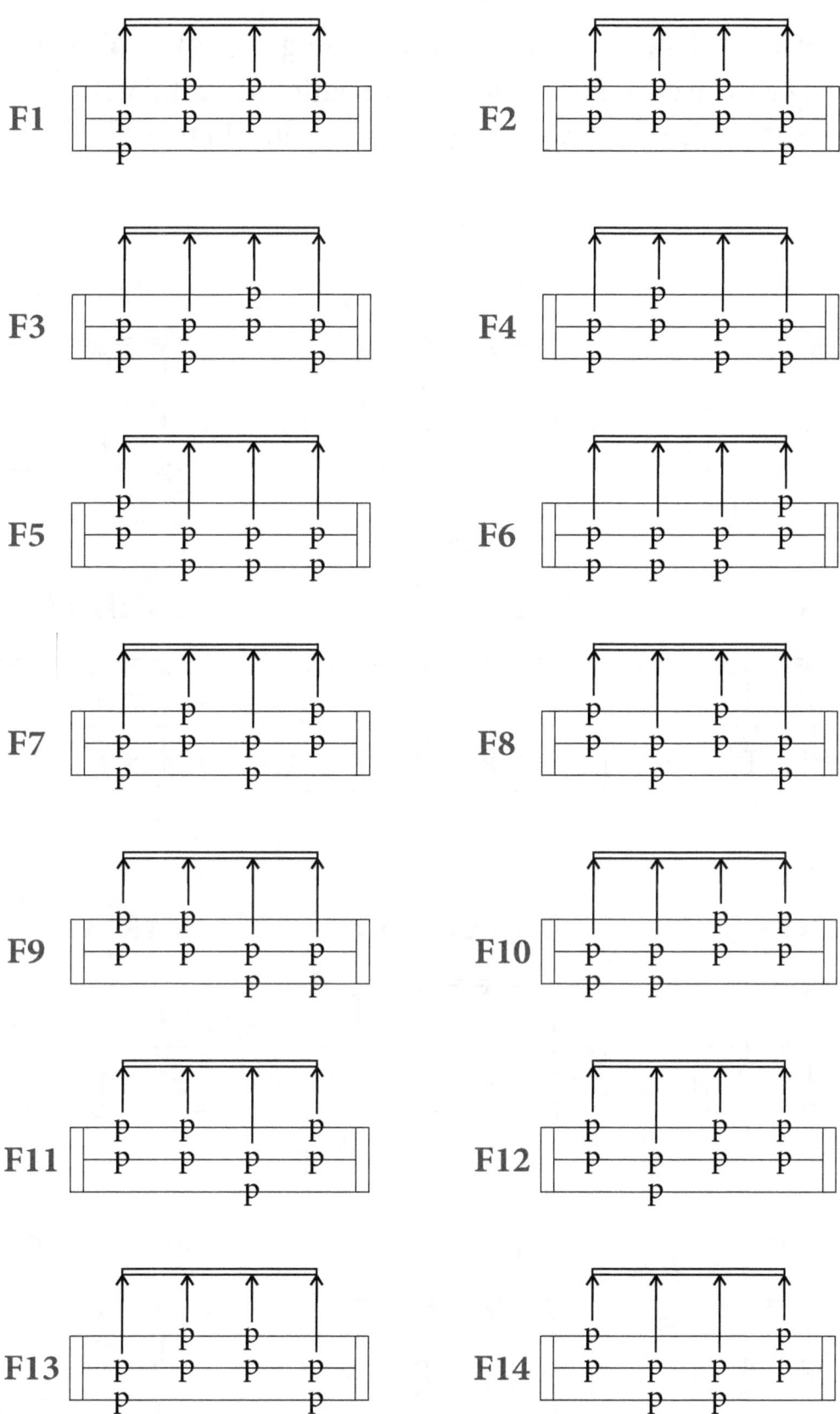

§ II

Two pulgar strokes of single strings and two pulgar strokes of three strings simultaneously within each Formula. Four variations in total with 6 Formulas in each one. The first Formula of each variation is cited below.

A

VARIATION I   **VARIATION II** 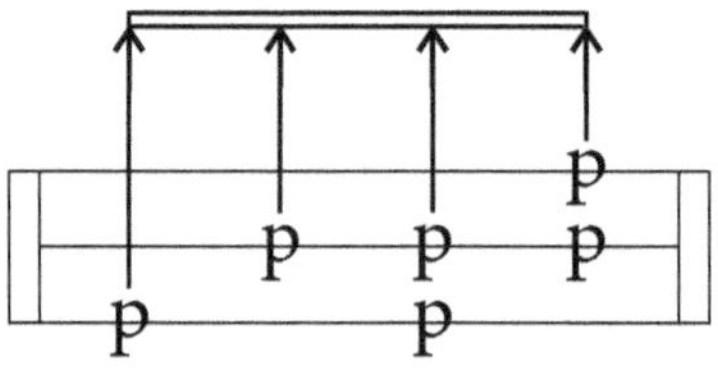   **VARIATION III**

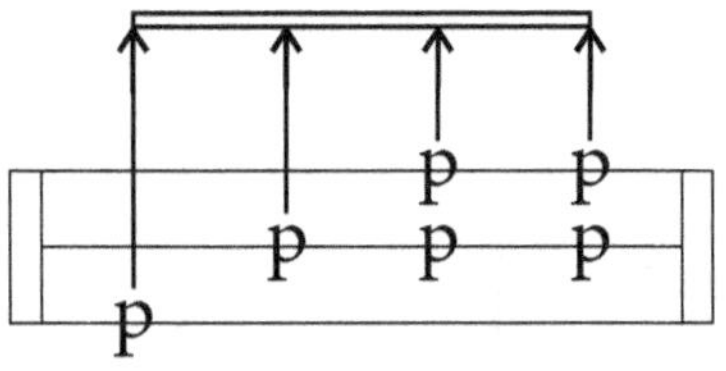

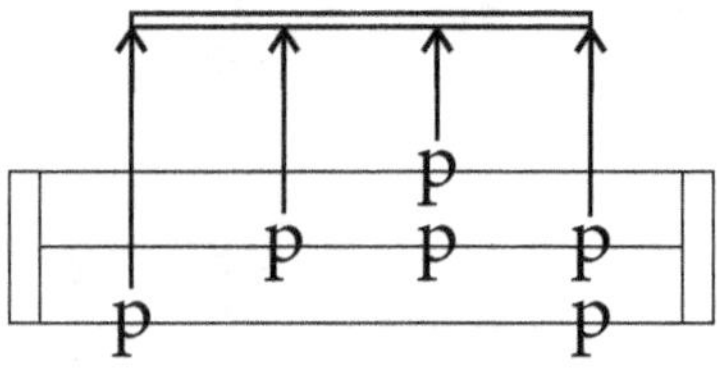

B

VARIATION I   **VARIATION II** 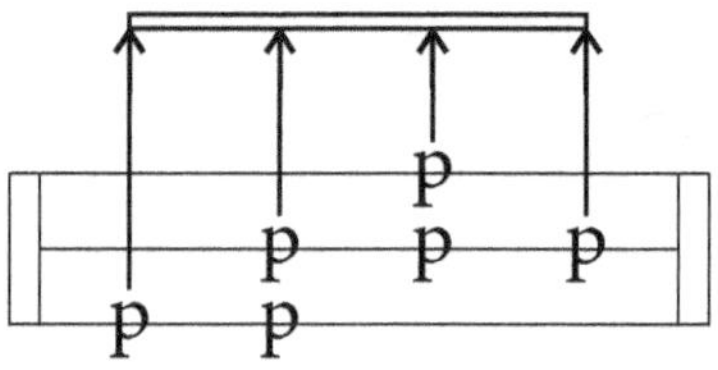   **VARIATION III**

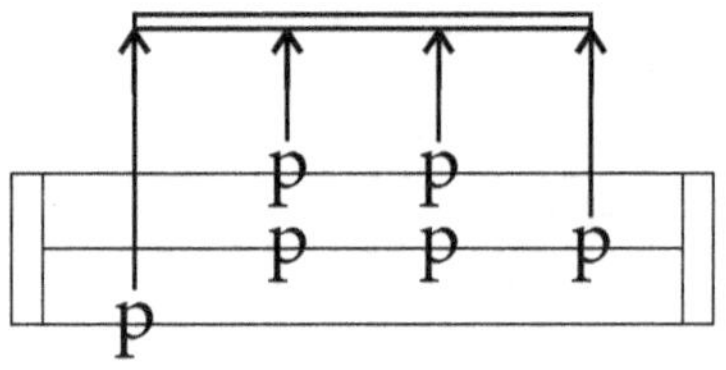

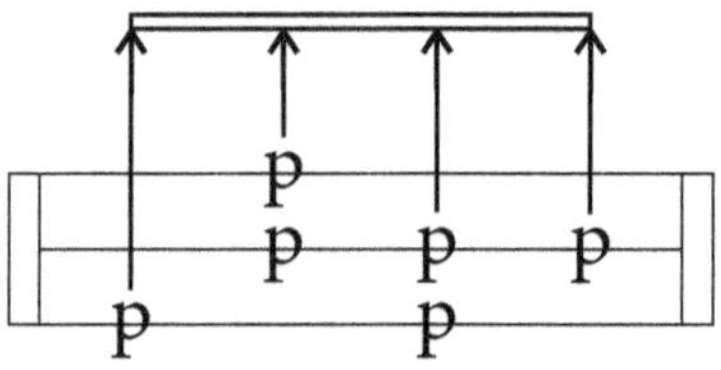

C

VARIATION I   **VARIATION II** 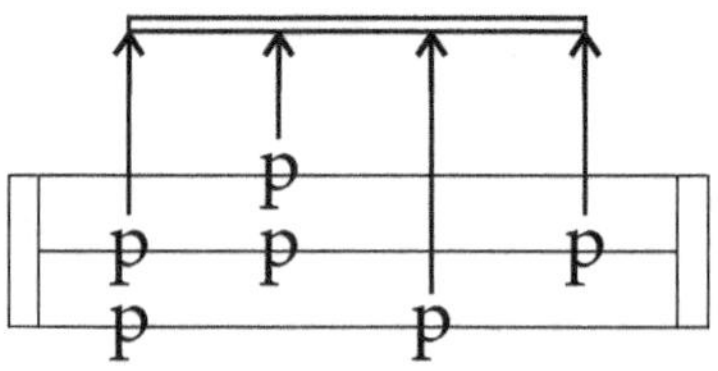   **VARIATION III**

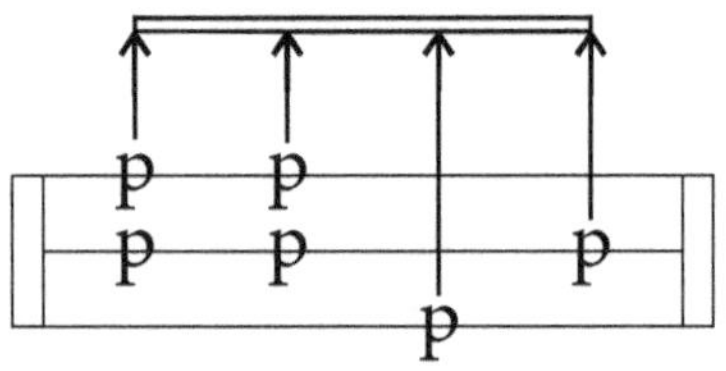

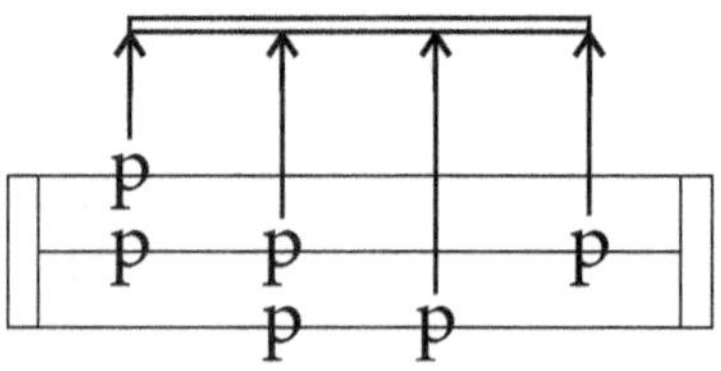

D

VARIATION I   **VARIATION II** 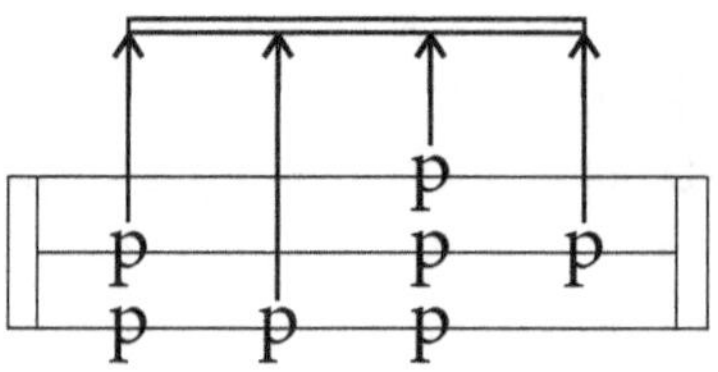   **VARIATION III**

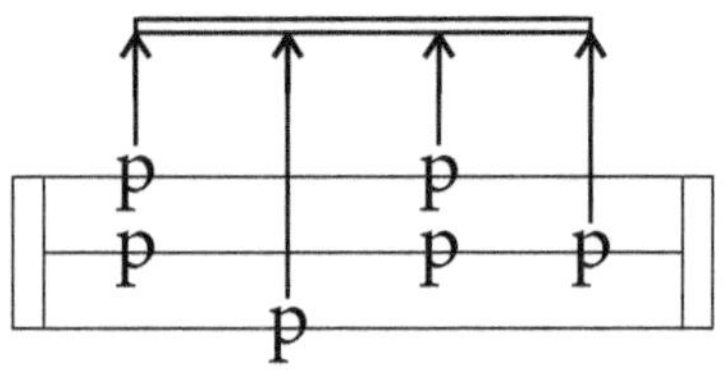

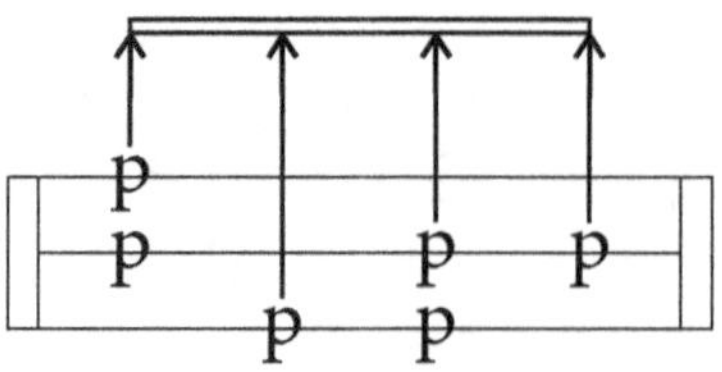

A

| VARIATION I | VARIATION II | VARIATION III |

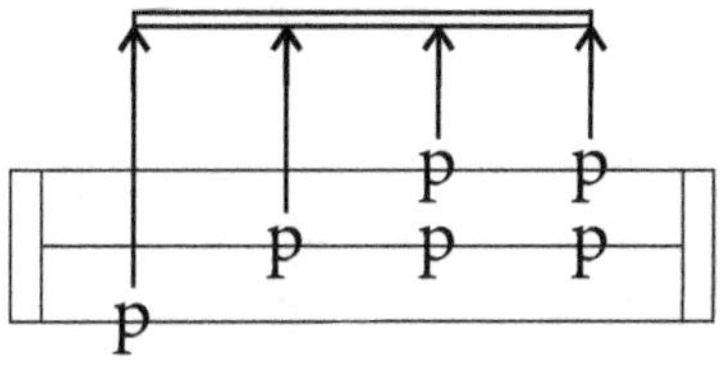

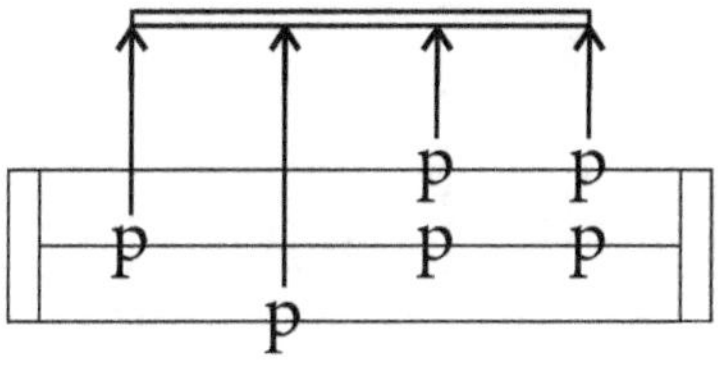

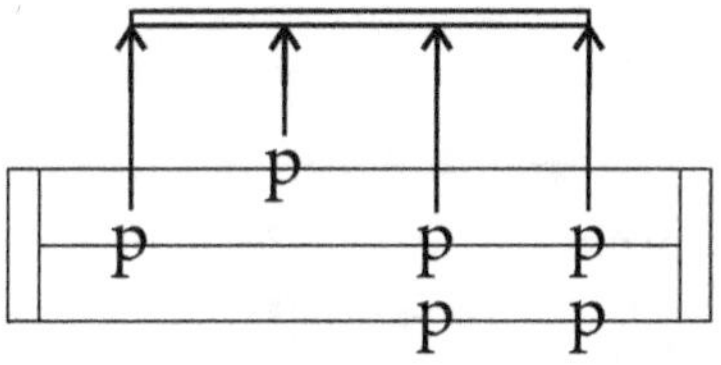

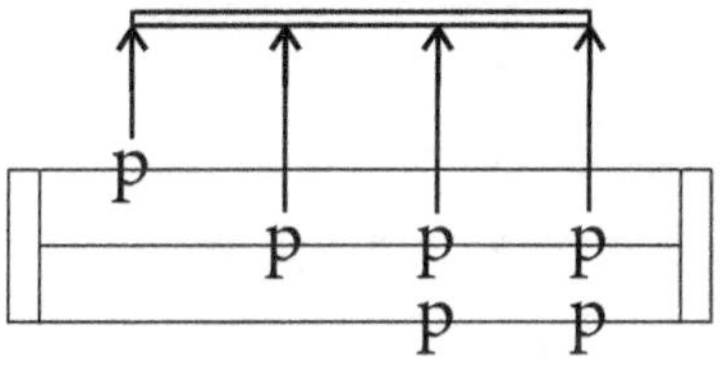

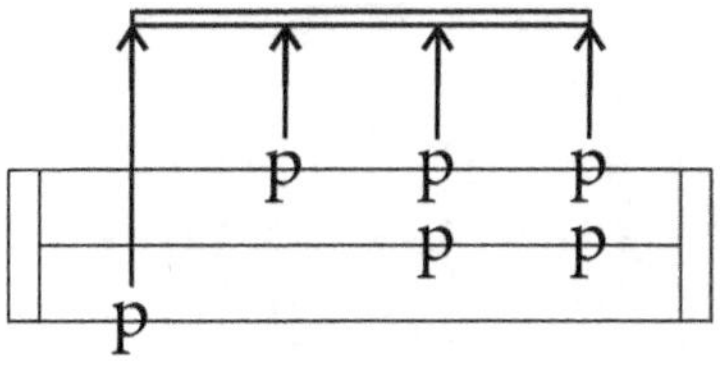

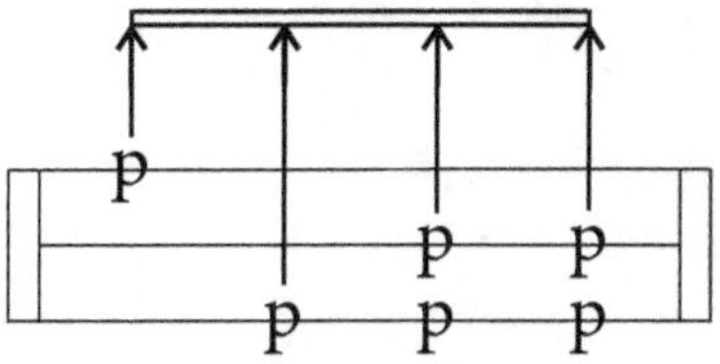

F1 — F1 — F1

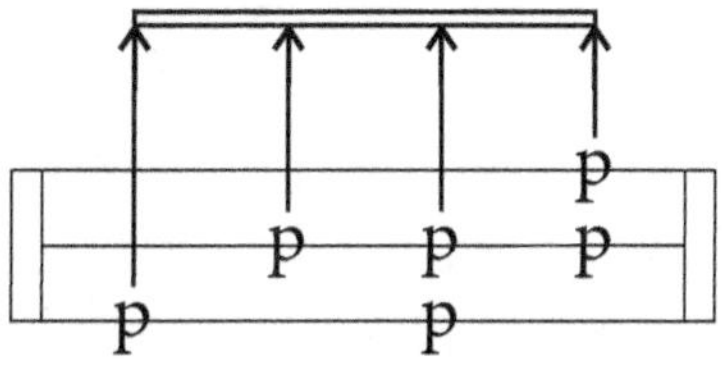

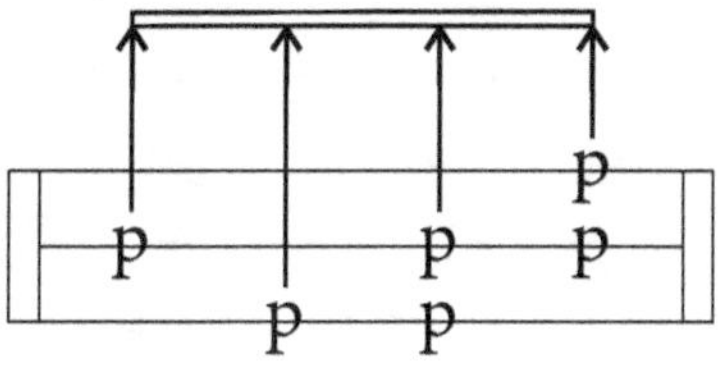

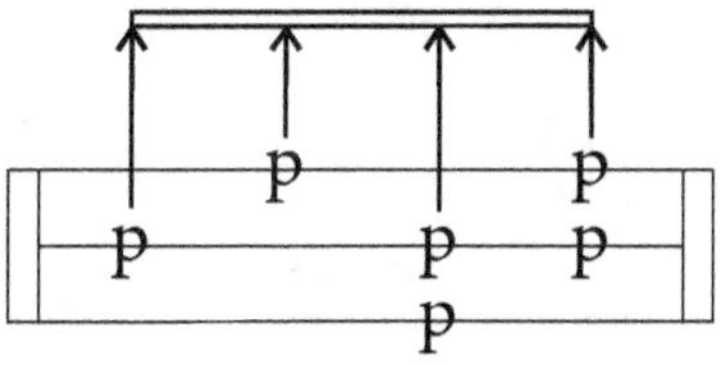

F2 — F2 — F2

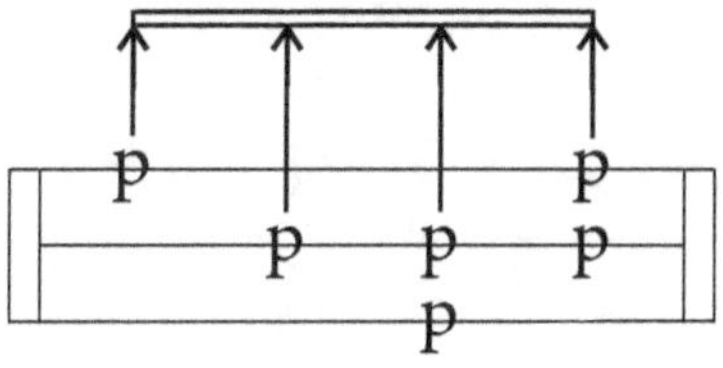

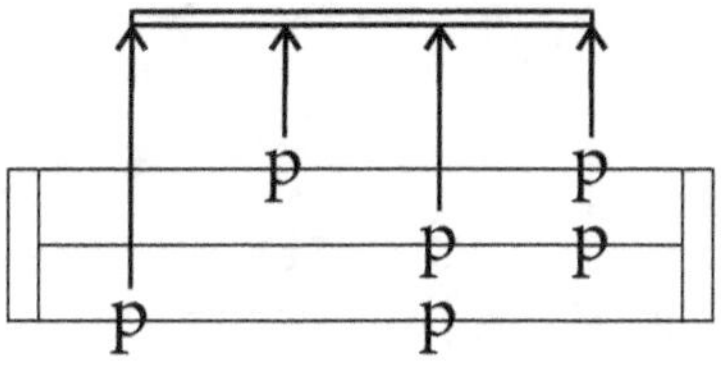

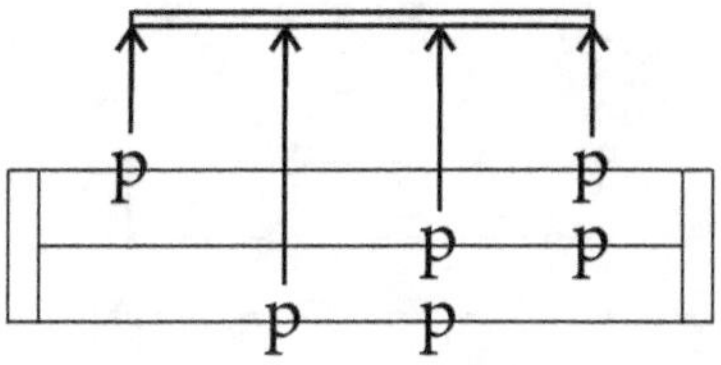

F3 — F3 — F3

F4 — F4 — F4

F5 — F5 — F5

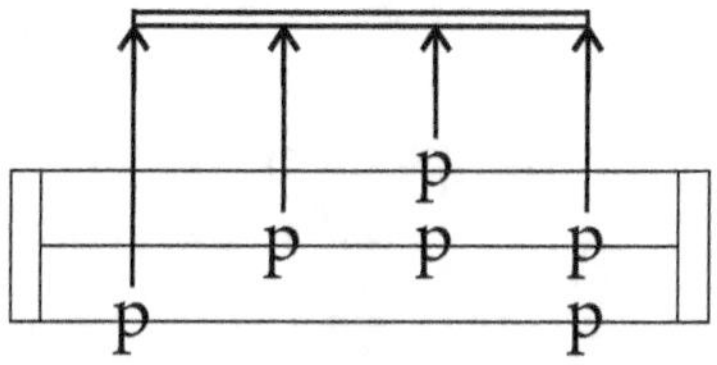

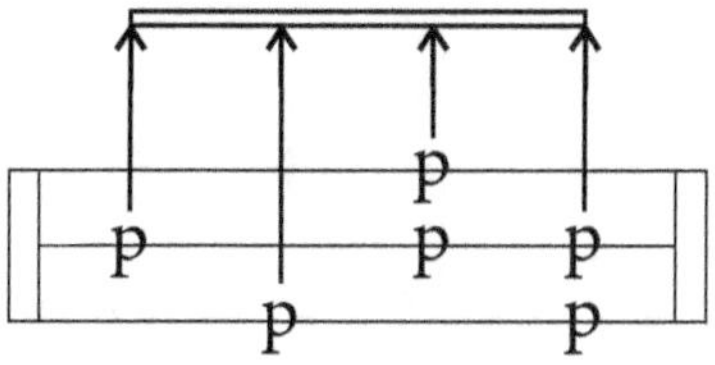

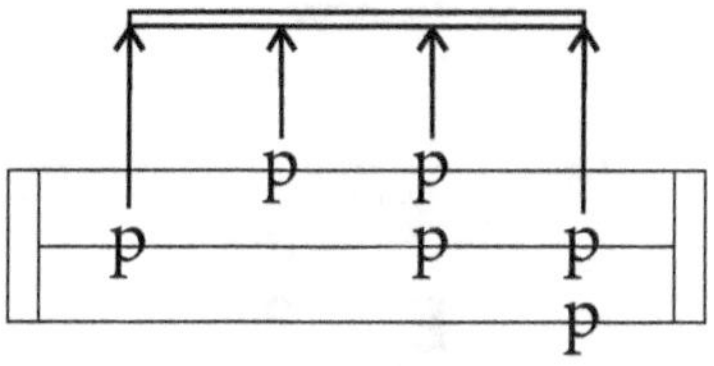

F6 — F6 — F6

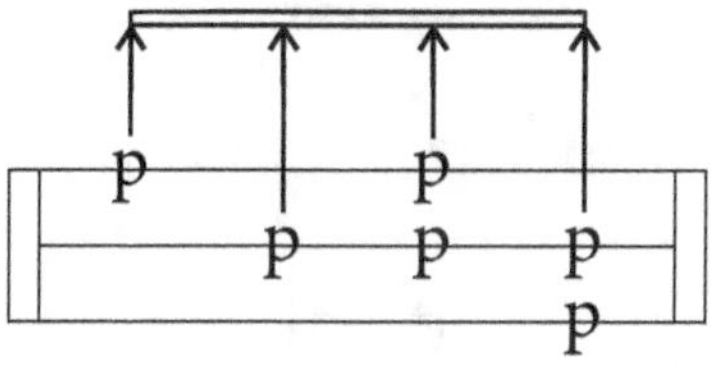

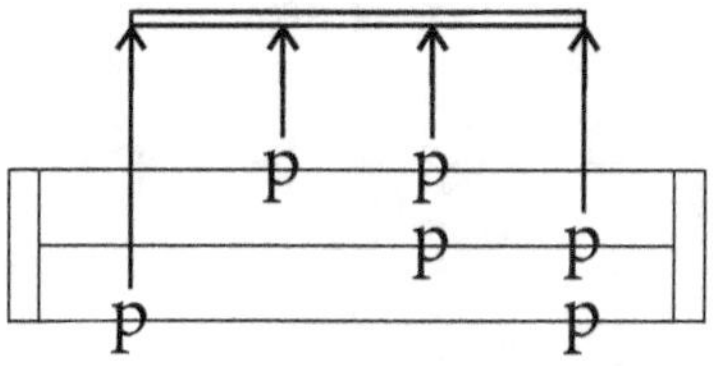

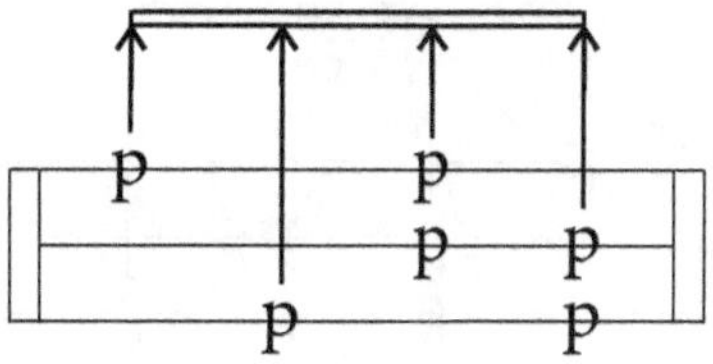

B

VARIATION I	VARIATION II	VARIATION III
F1	F1	F1
F2	F2	F2
F3	F3	F3
F4	F4	F4
F5	F5	F5
F6	F6	F6

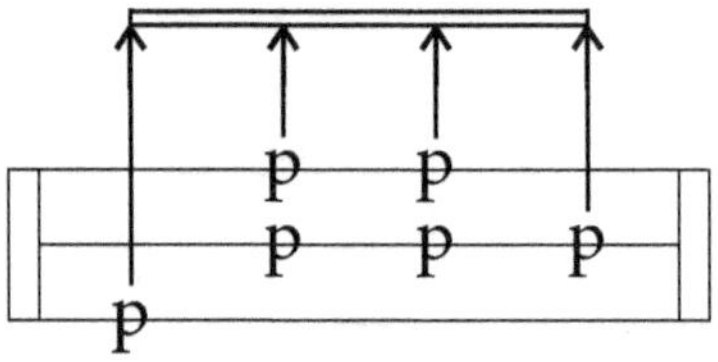

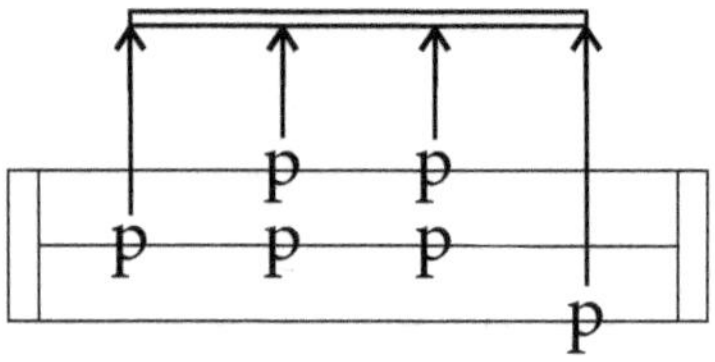

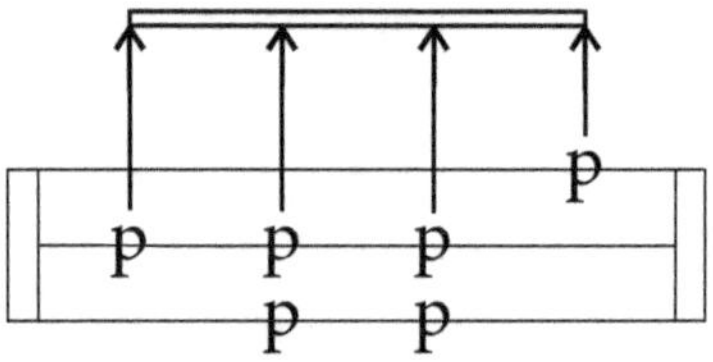

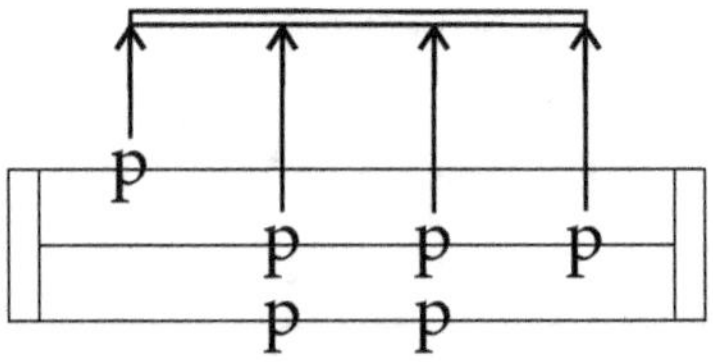

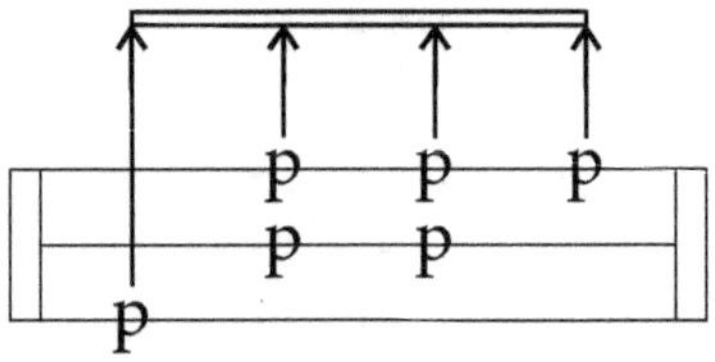

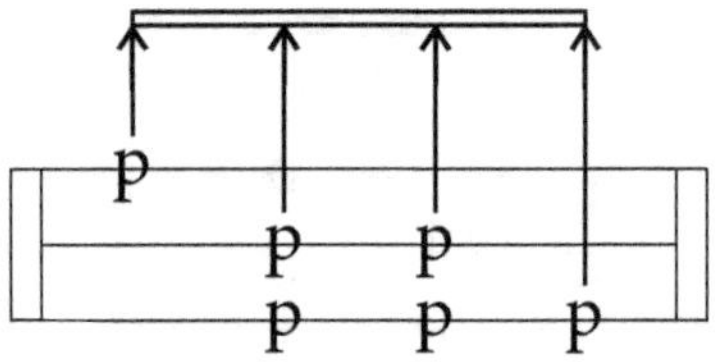

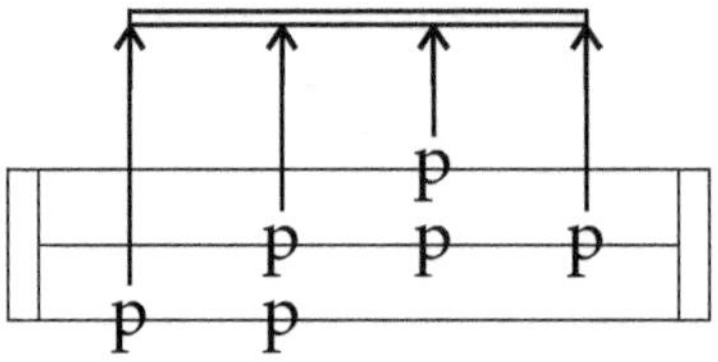

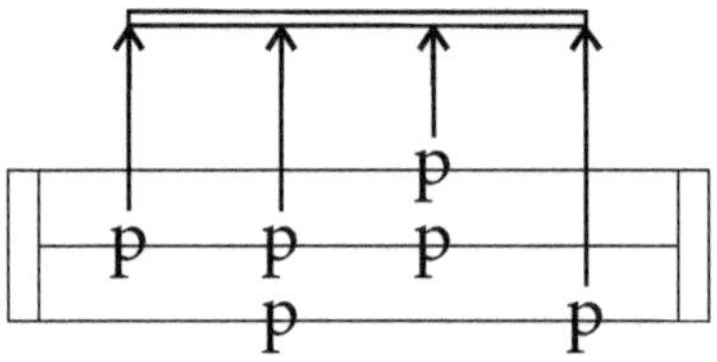

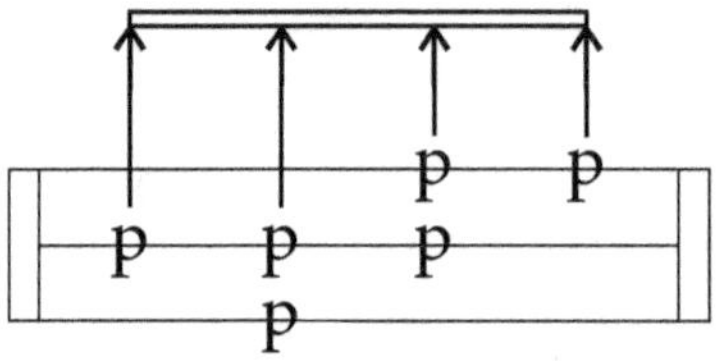

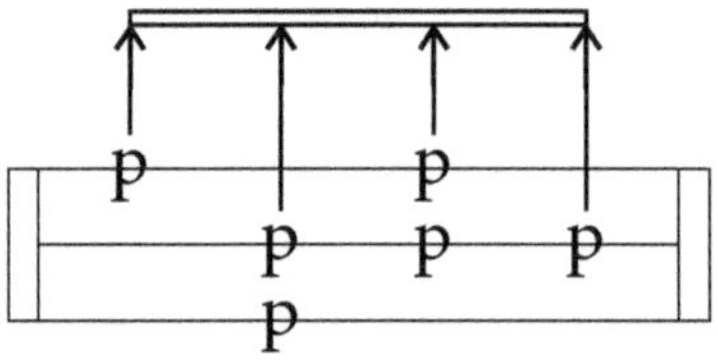

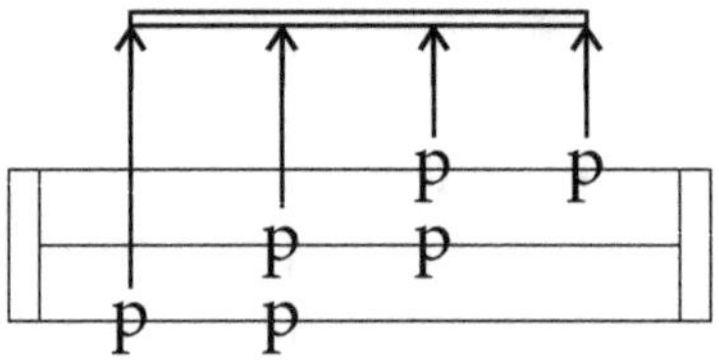

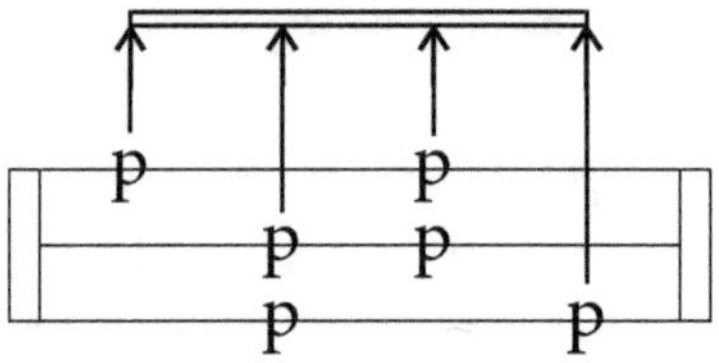

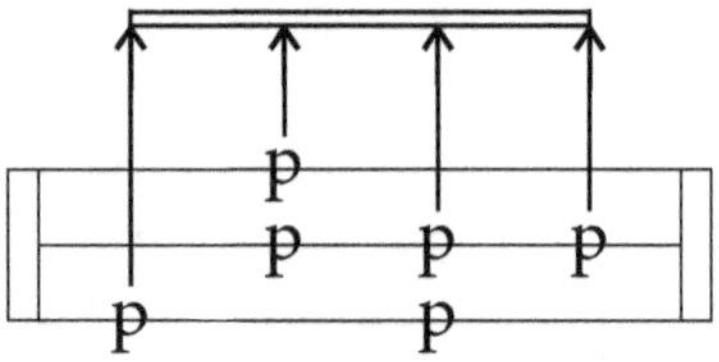

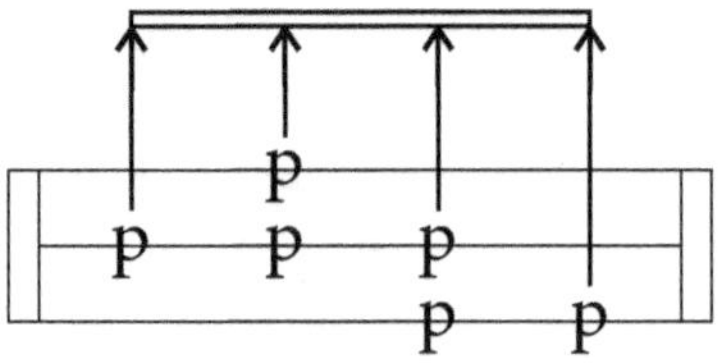

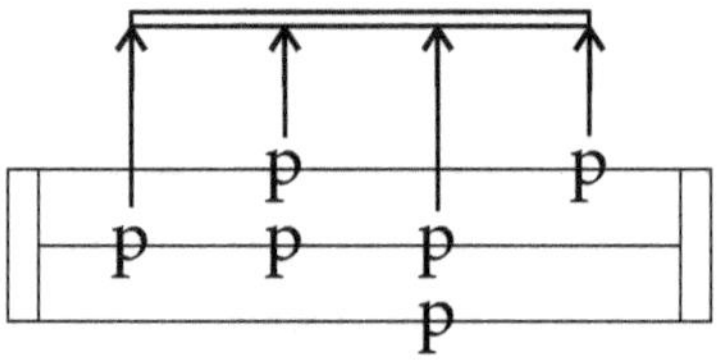

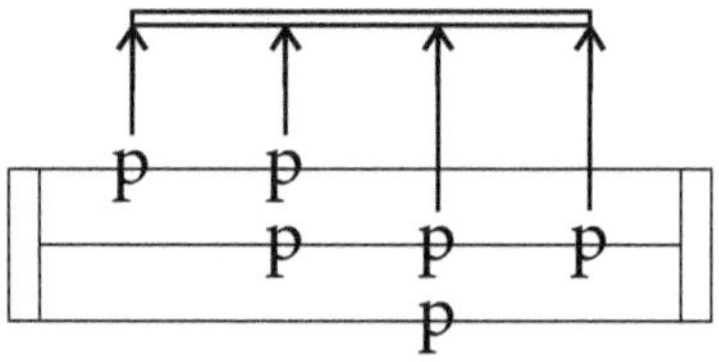

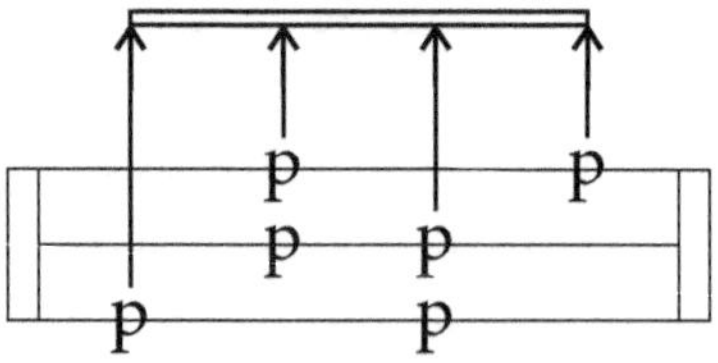

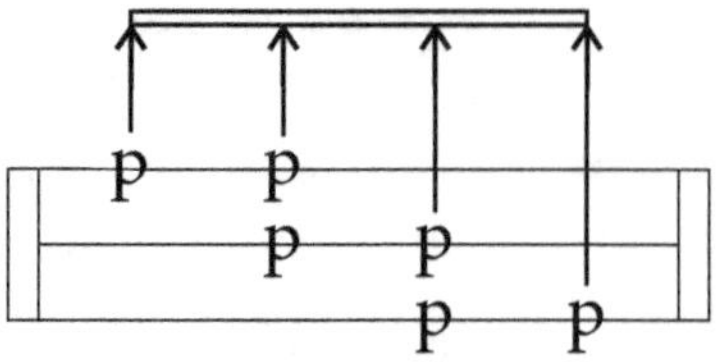

C

VARIATION I	VARIATION II	VARIATION III

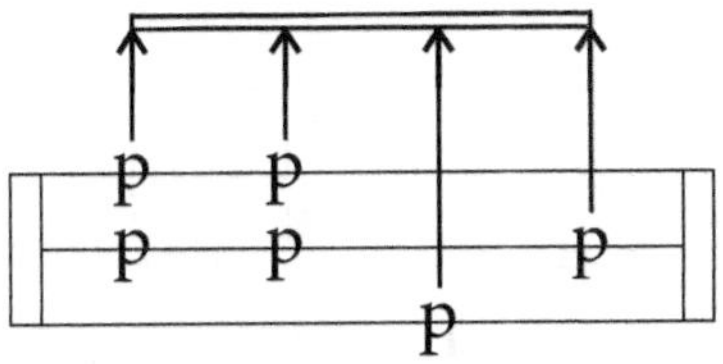

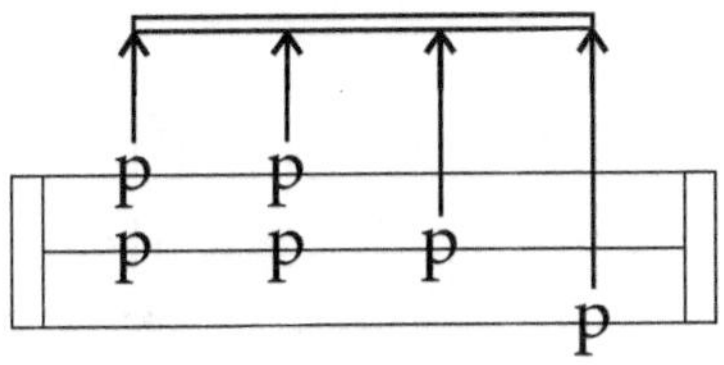

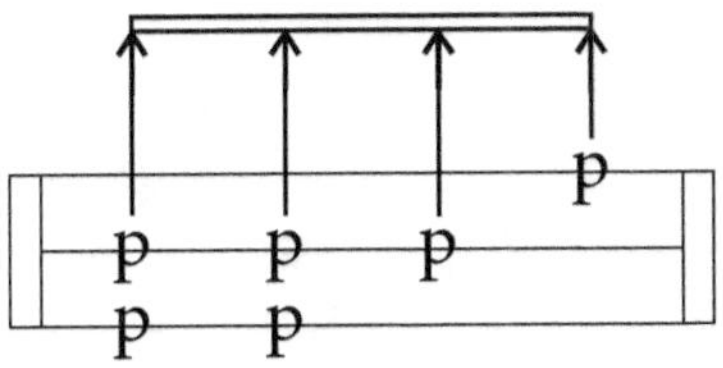

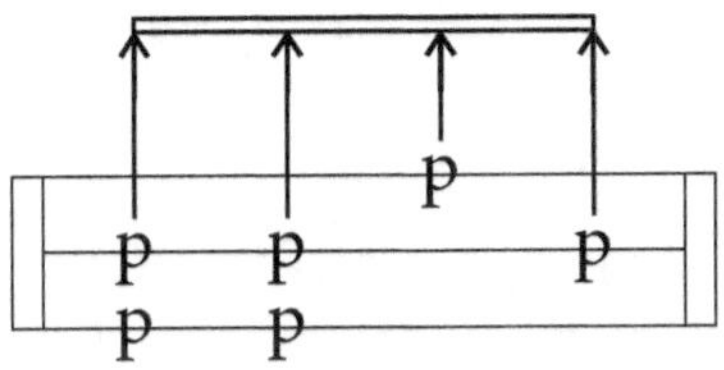

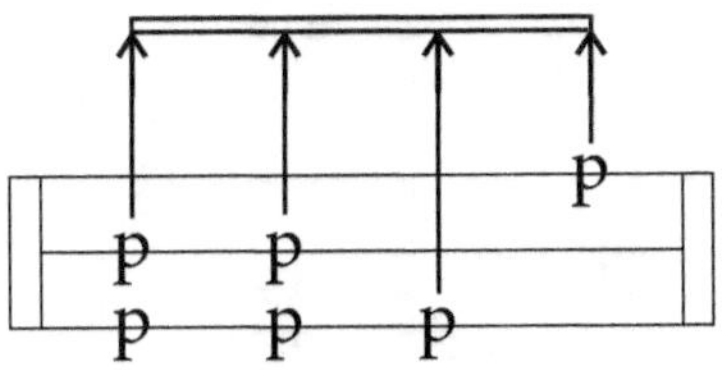

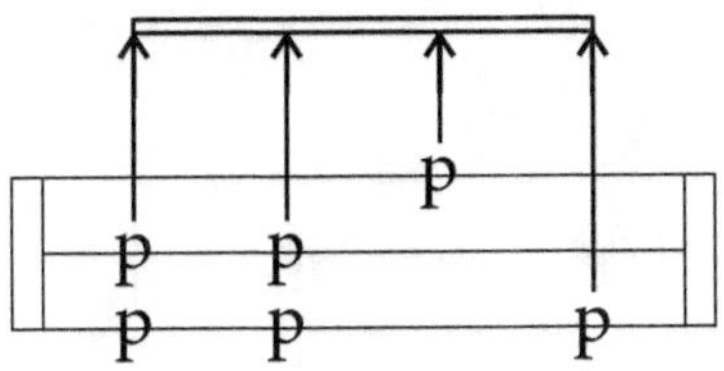

F1 F1 F1

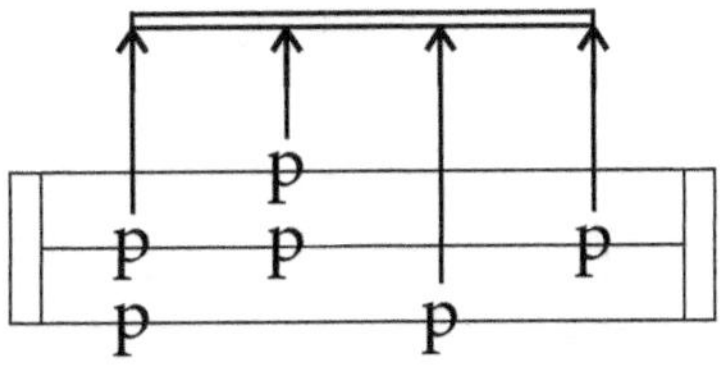

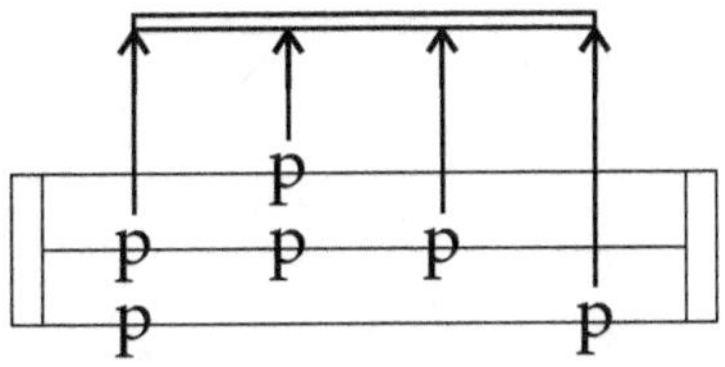

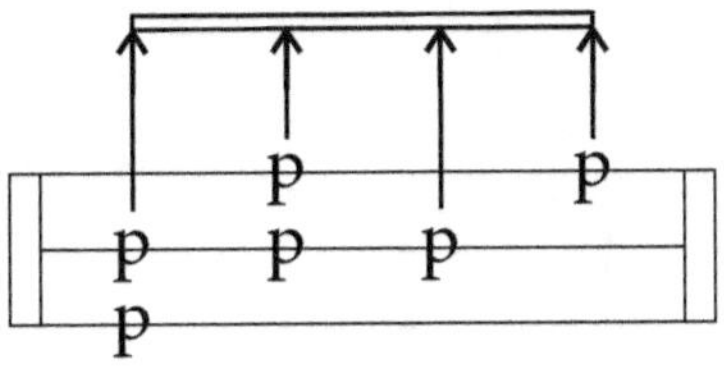

F2 F2 F2

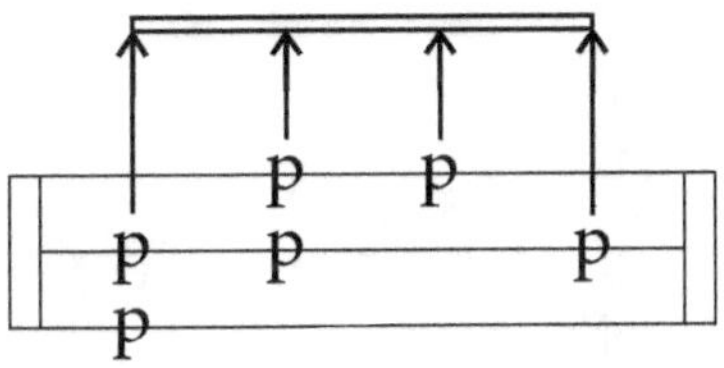

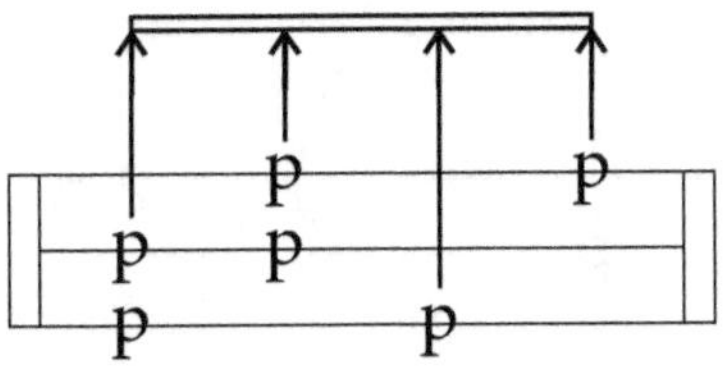

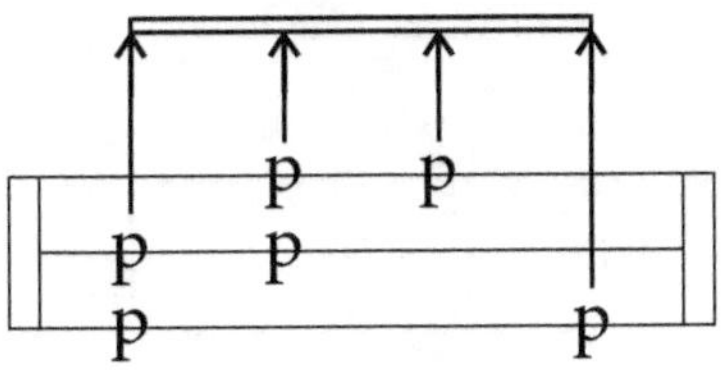

F3 F3 F3

F4 F4 F4

F5 F5 F5

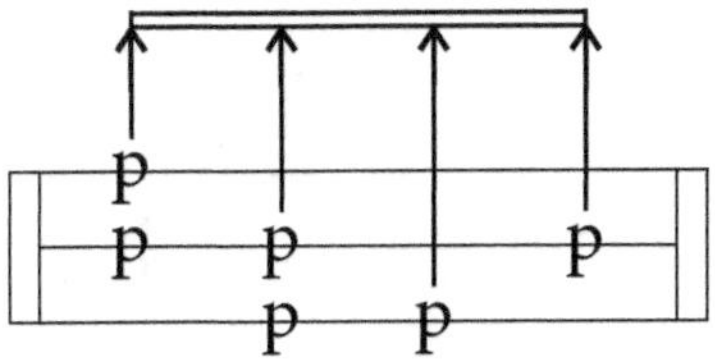

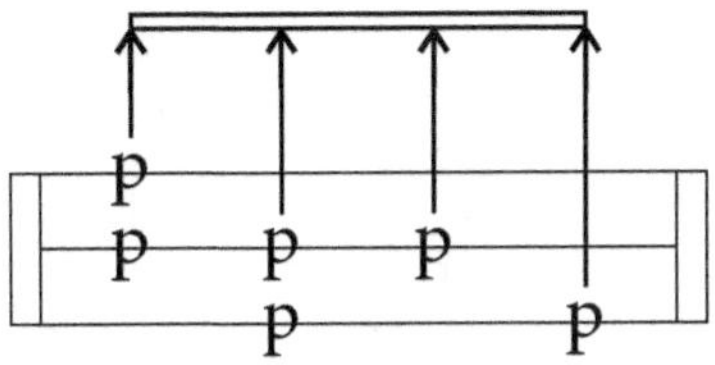

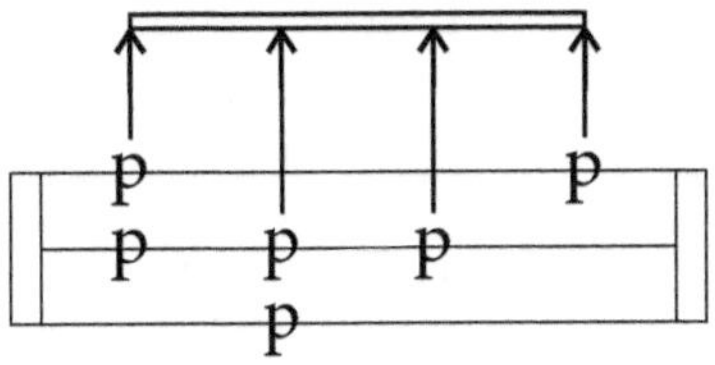

F6 F6 F6

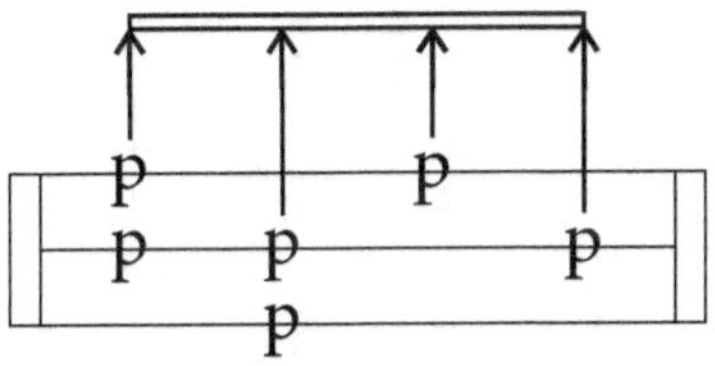

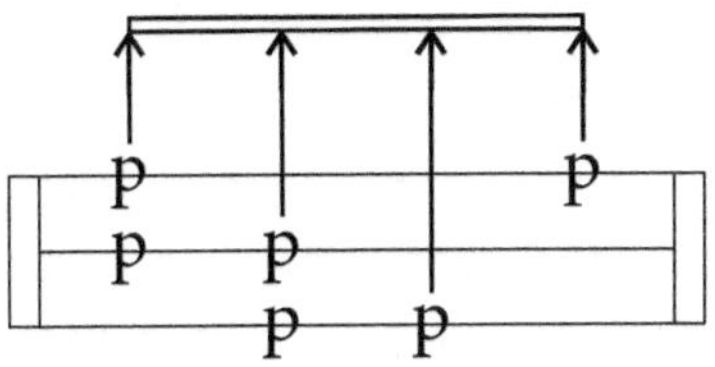

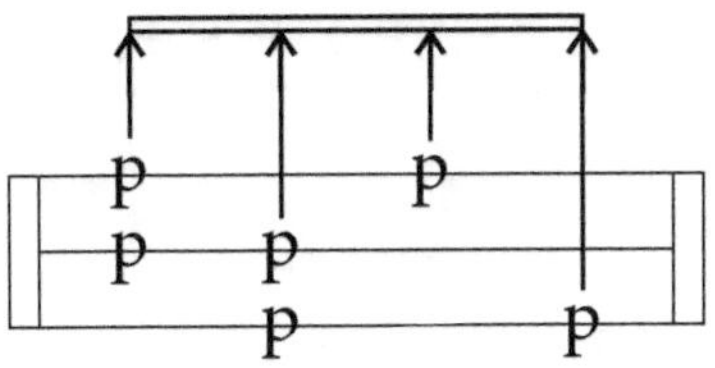

D

VARIATION I

F1

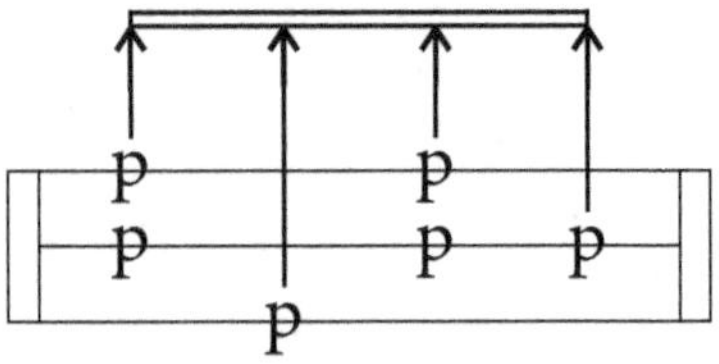

F2

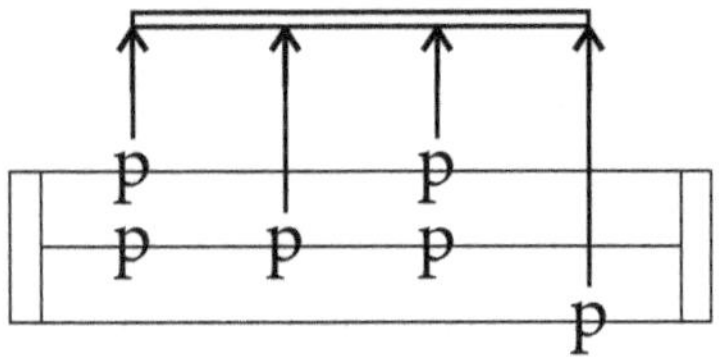

F3

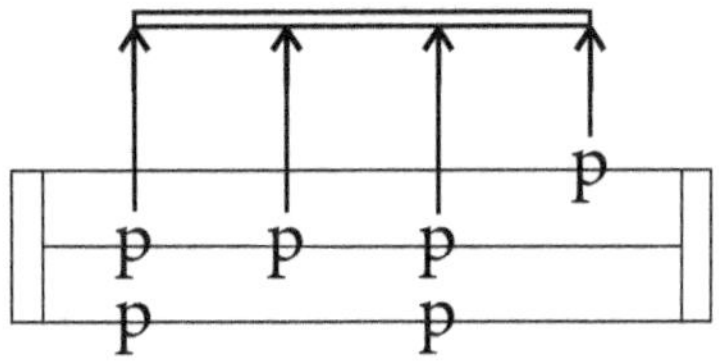

F4

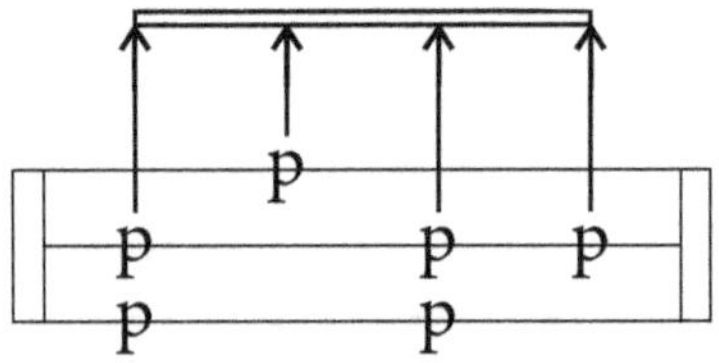

F5

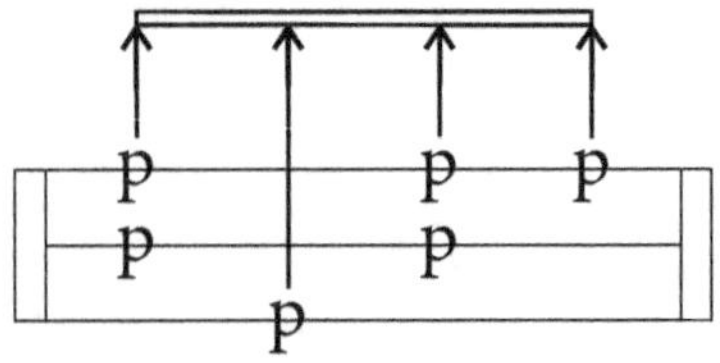

F6

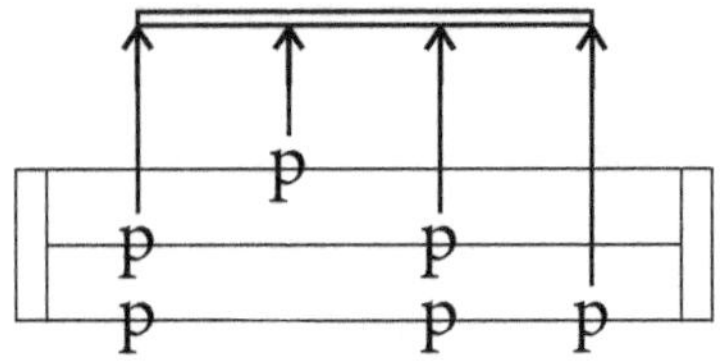

VARIATION II

F1

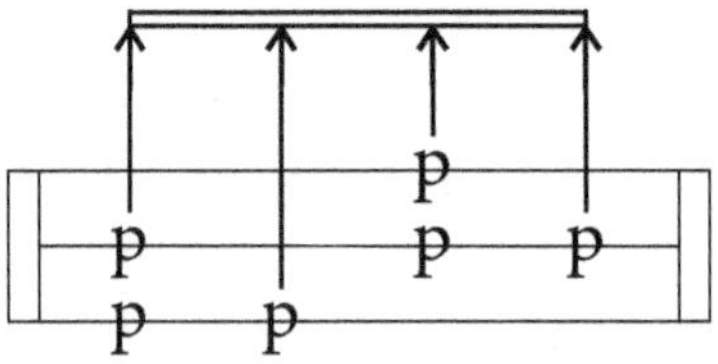

F2

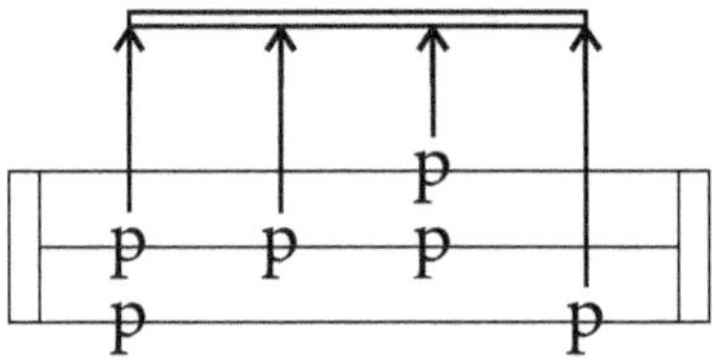

F3

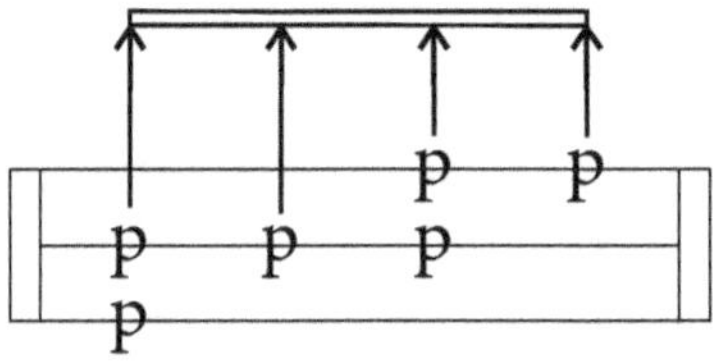

F4

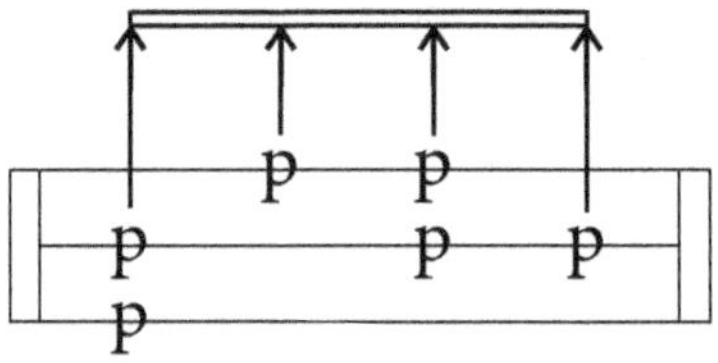

F5

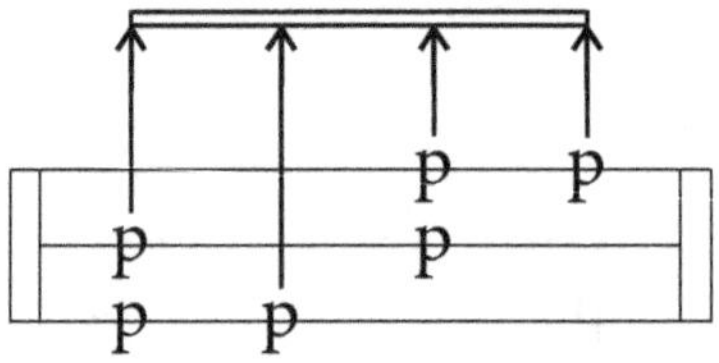

F6

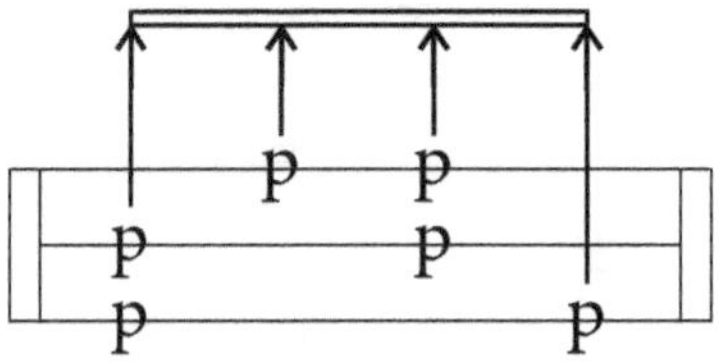

VARIATION III

F1

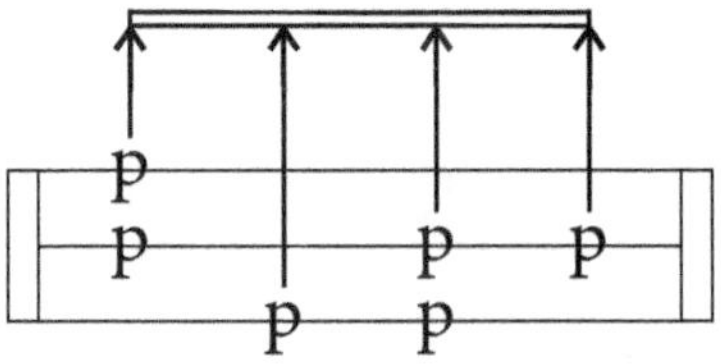

F2

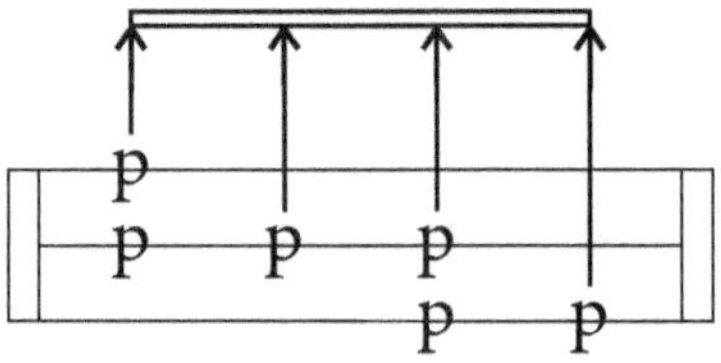

F3

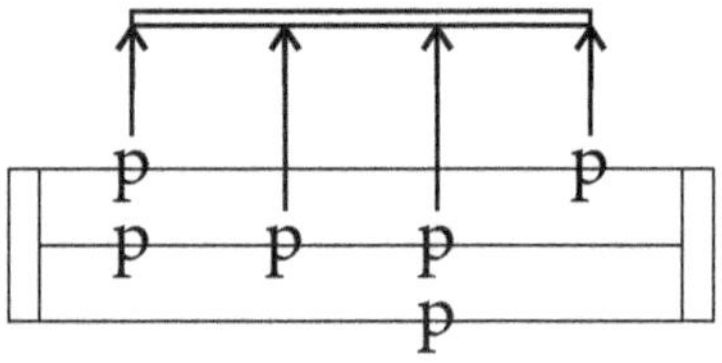

F4

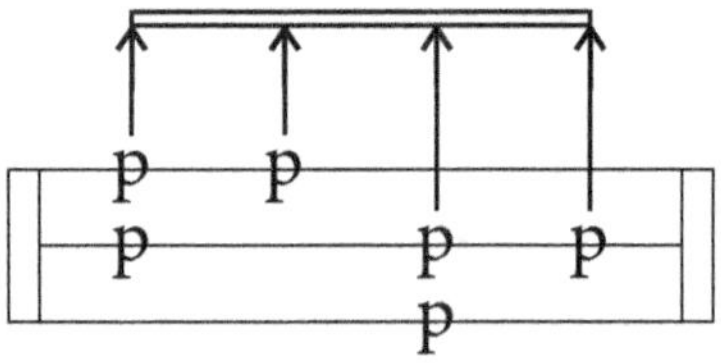

F5

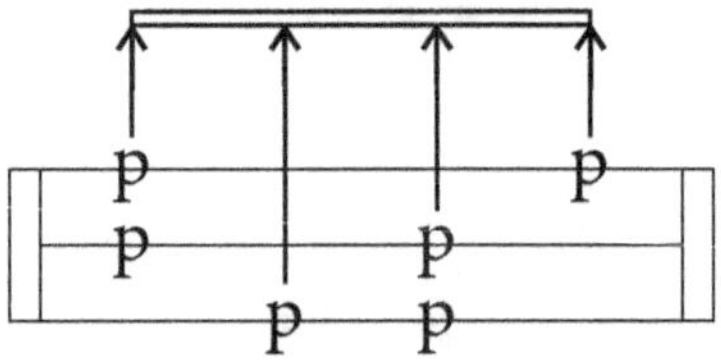

F6

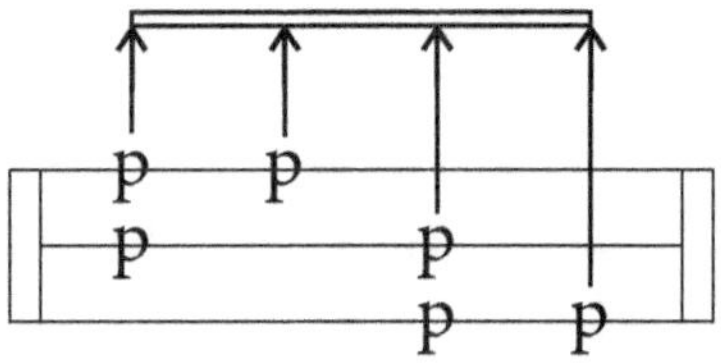

§ III

Two pulgar strokes of single strings and two pulgar strokes of three strings simultaneously within each Formula. Four variations in total with 6 Formulas in each one. The first Formula of each variation is cited below.

VARIATION I

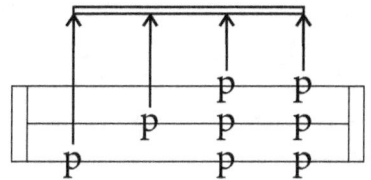

VARIATION II

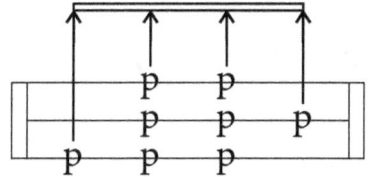

VARIATION III

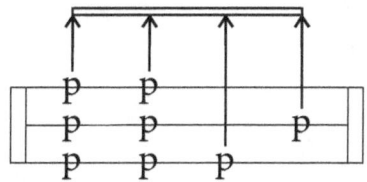

VARIATION IV

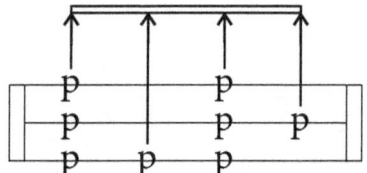

VARIATION I

F1
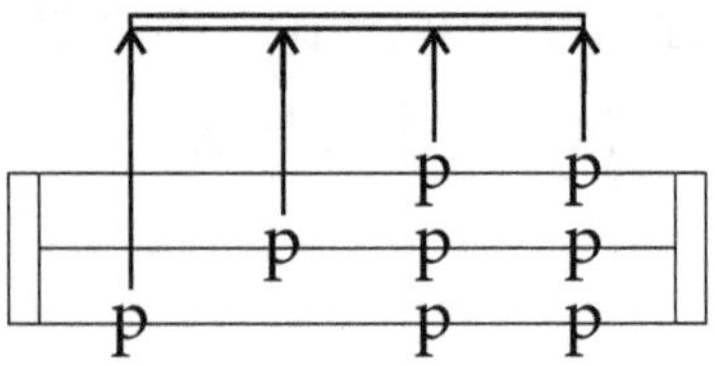

F2
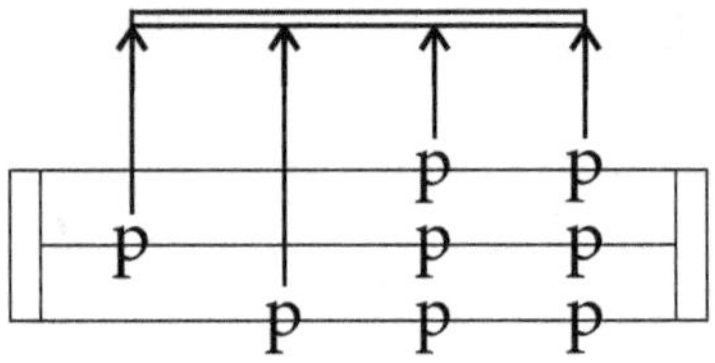

F3
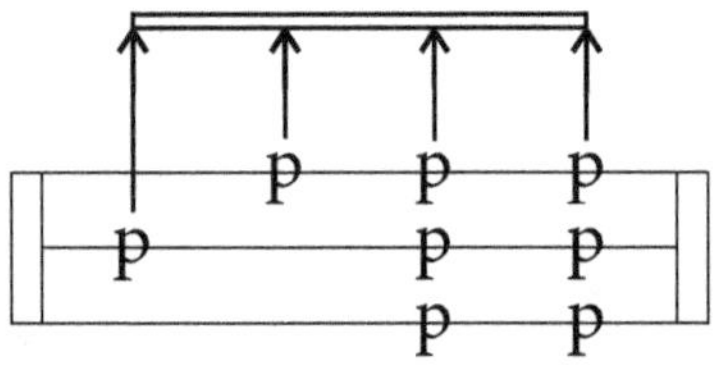

F4
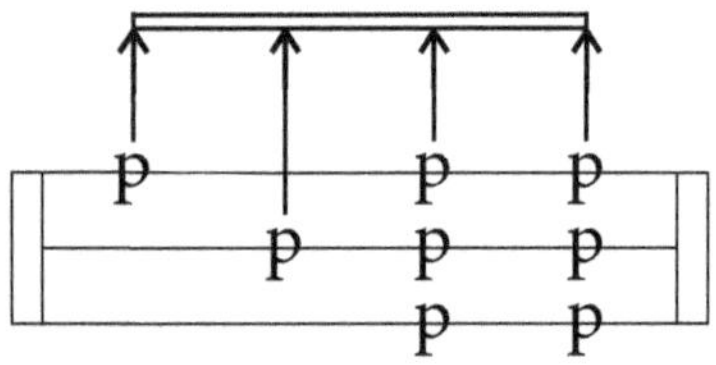

F5
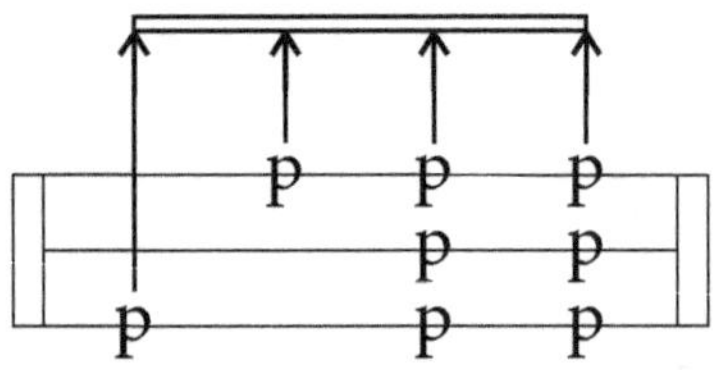

F6
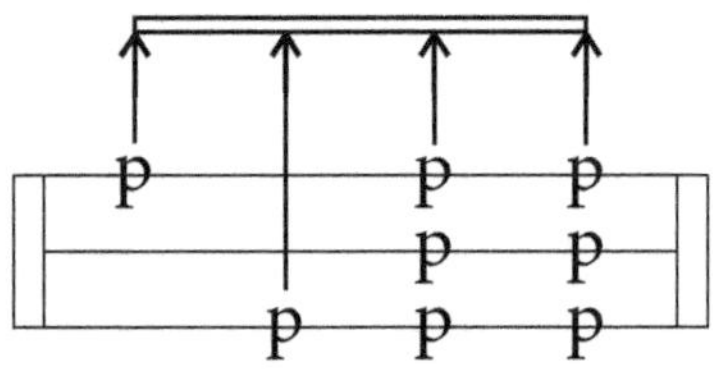

VARIATION II

F1
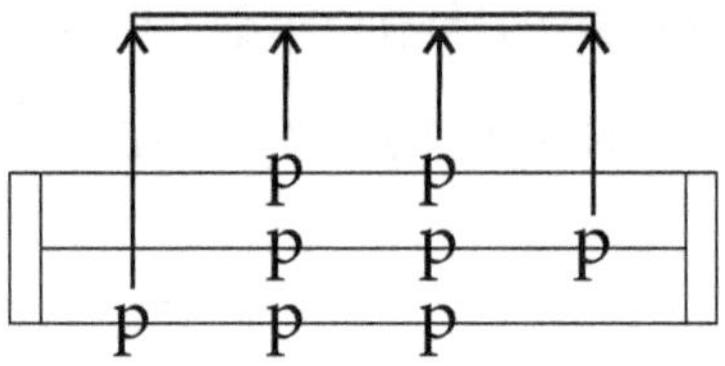

F2
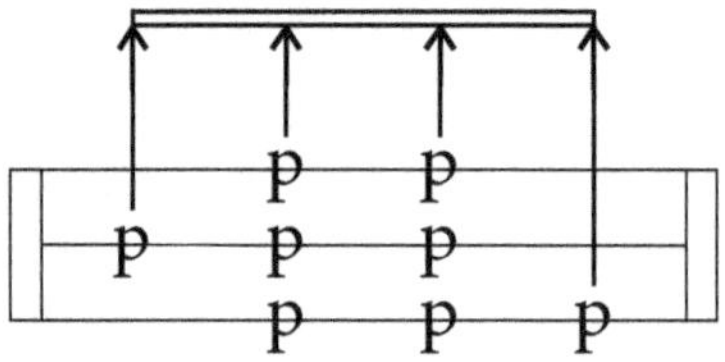

F3
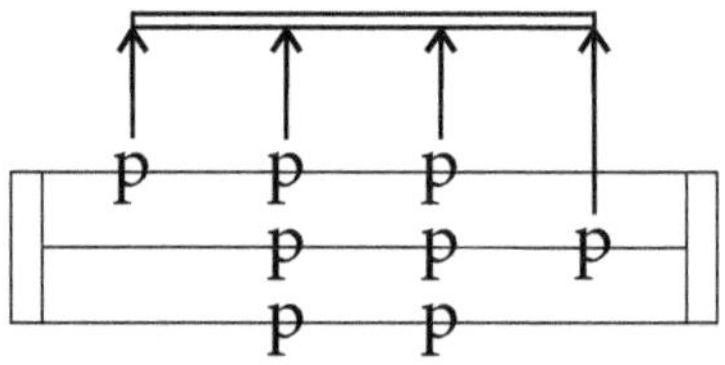

F4
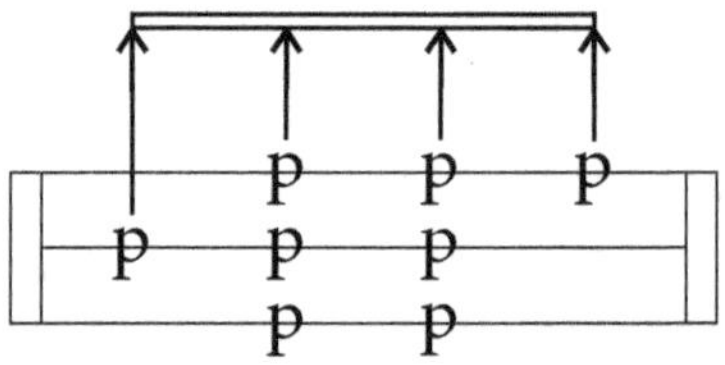

F5
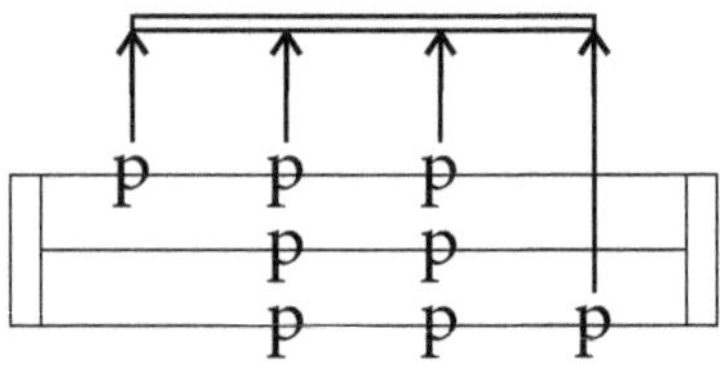

F6
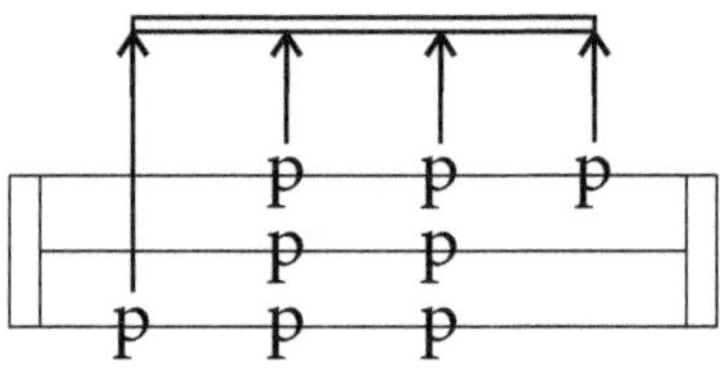

VARIATION III

F1
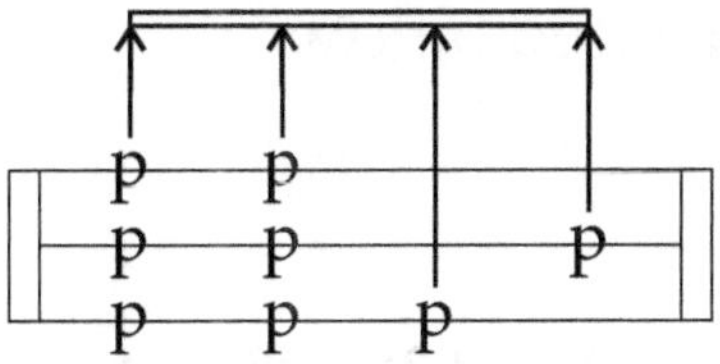

F2
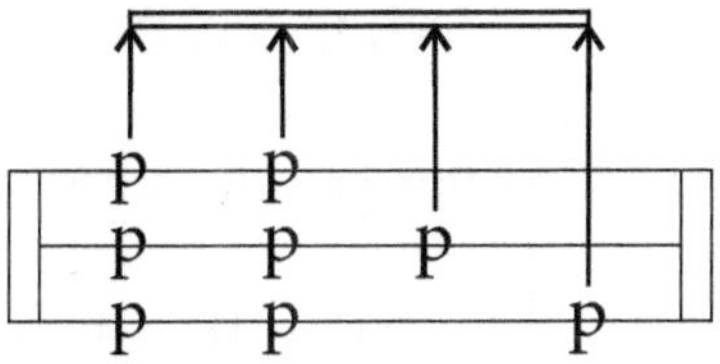

F3
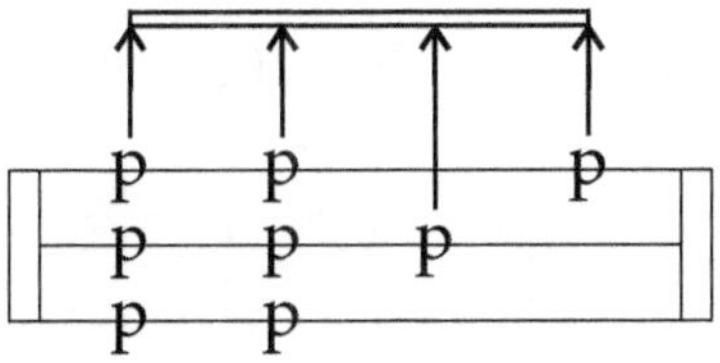

F4
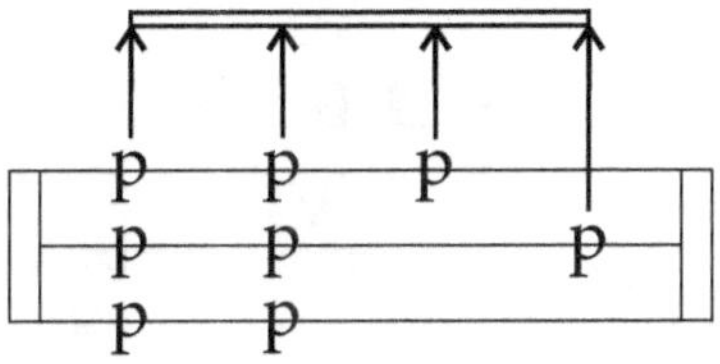

F5
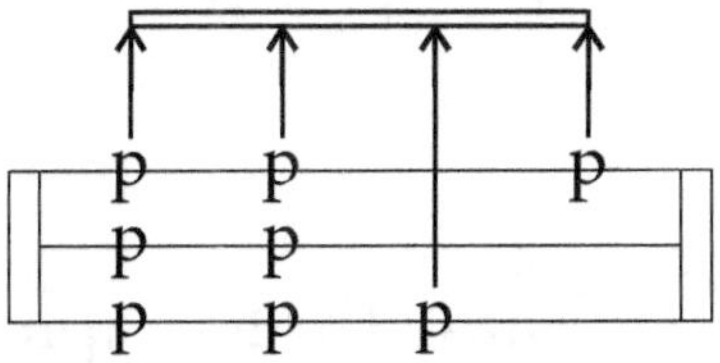

F6
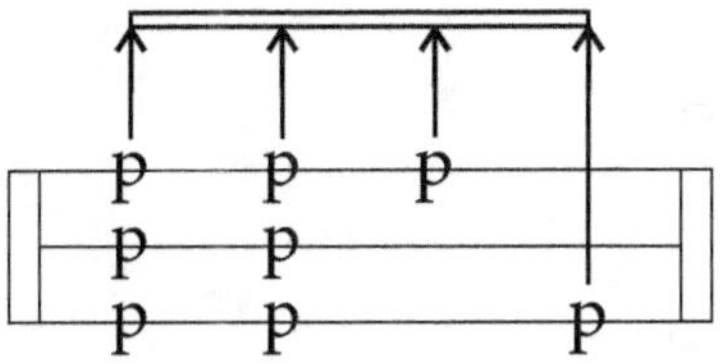

VARIATION IV

F1
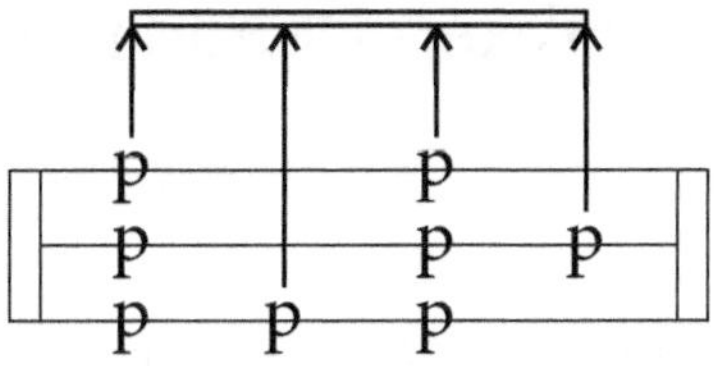

F2
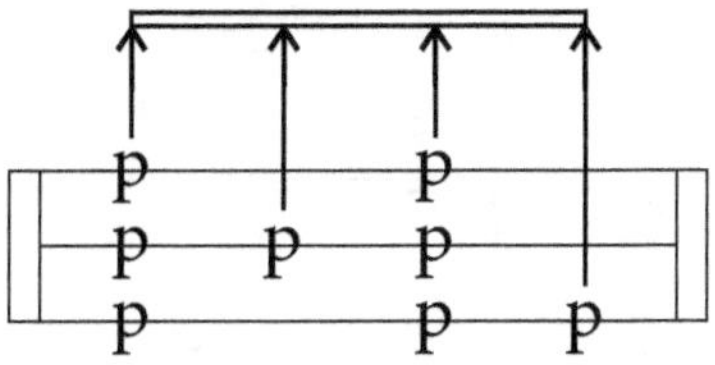

F3
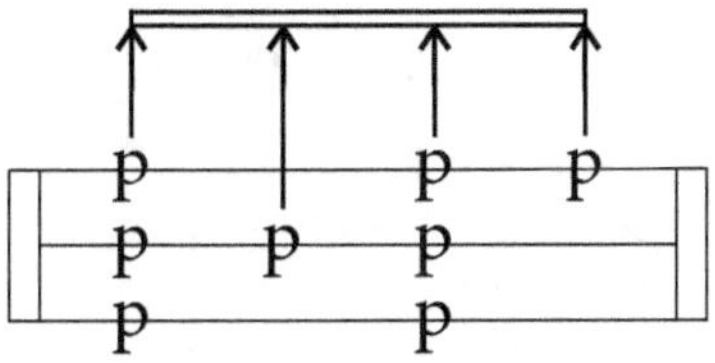

F4
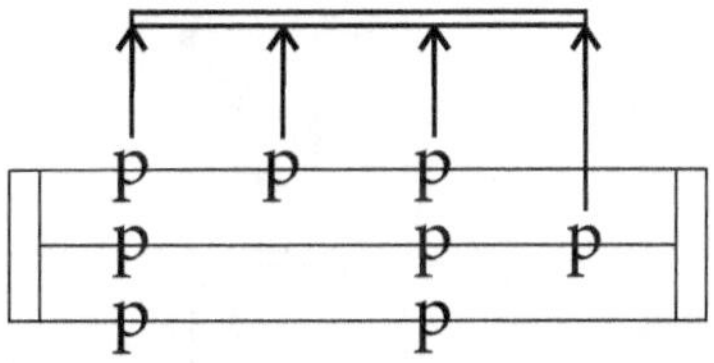

F5
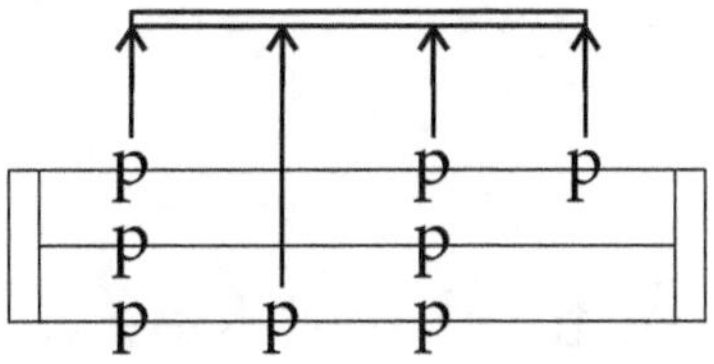

F6
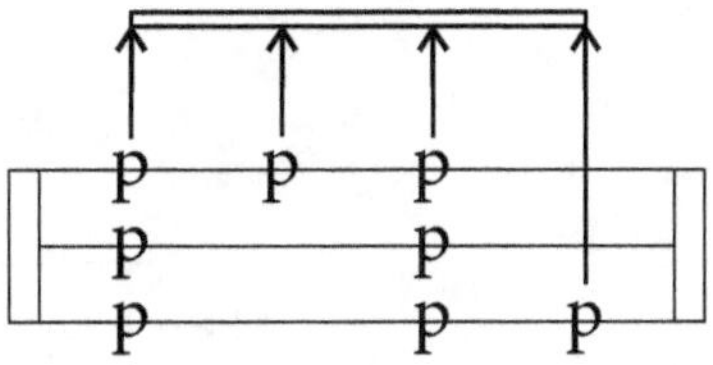

The following exercises are variations of pulgar exercises. The pulgar strikes one, two or three simultaneously and in various combinations. The first Formula of each exercise and its variations are cited below.

§ IV

Pulgar stroke of two strings and three strings simultaneously. Six variations in total with 4 Formulas in each variation.

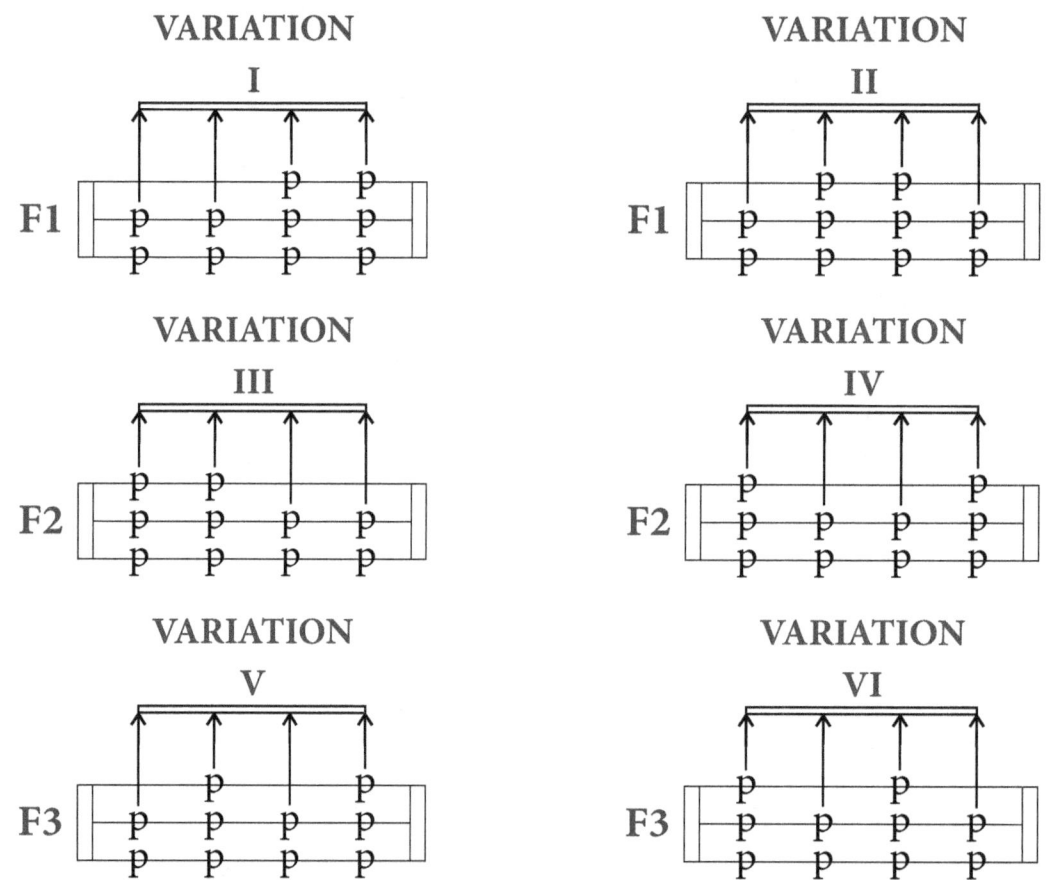

§ V

8 Formulas in total with one double (2 strings) and three triple (3 strings) pulgar strokes.

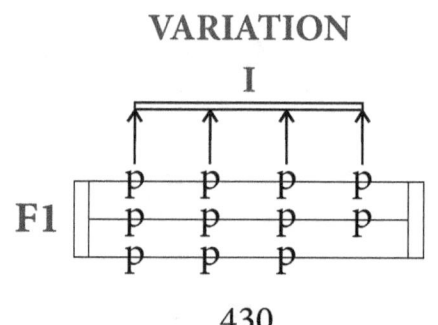

§ VI

Stroke of one, two and three strings simultaneously. Four variations with 6 Formulas in each variation.

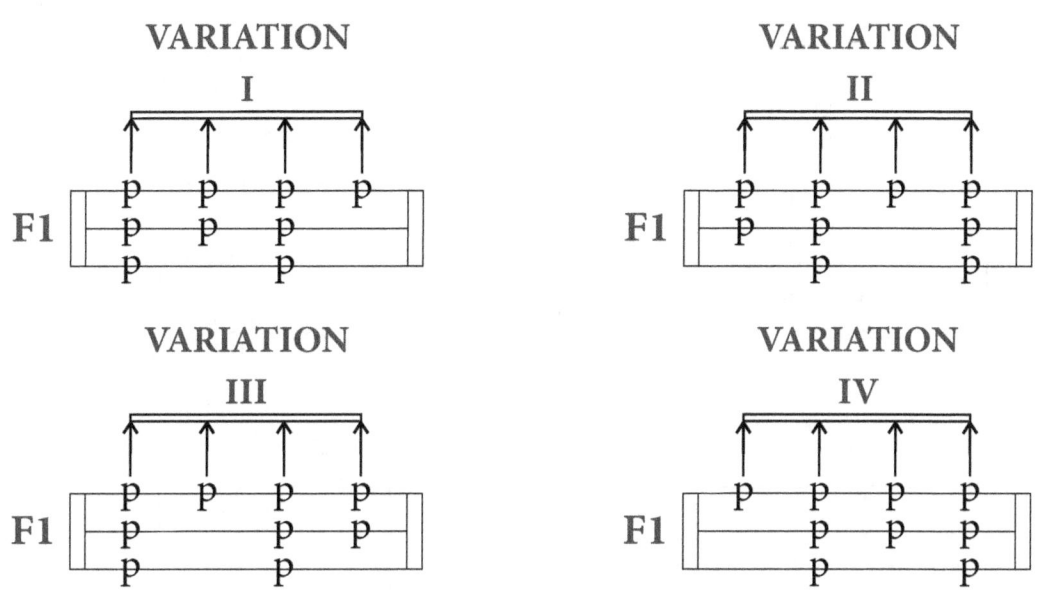

§ VII

Stroke of two single strings and three strings simultaneously (two times). Isochronous playing of single and triple pulgar strokes. 9 Formulas in total.

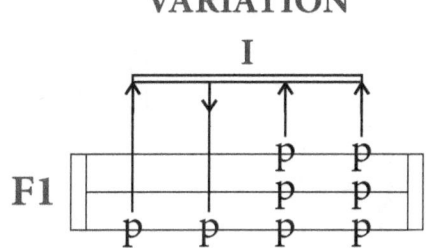

§ VIII

Stroke combination of one triplet and three strings simultaneously within each Formula. 6 Formulas in total. Isochronous playing of the triplet and the three simultaneously strings.

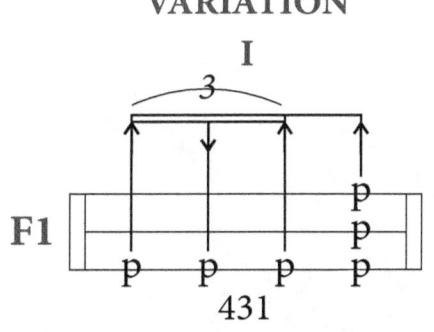

§ IV

VARIATION I

F1 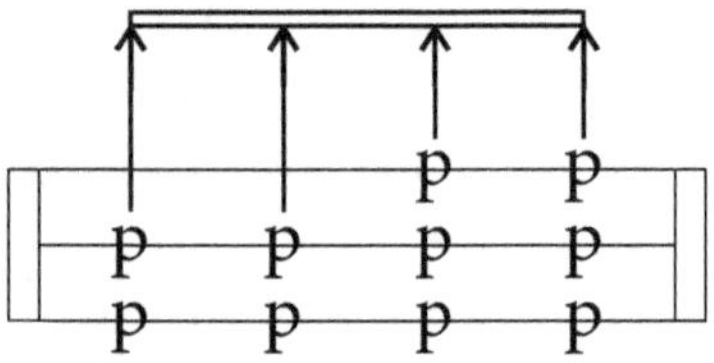

F2 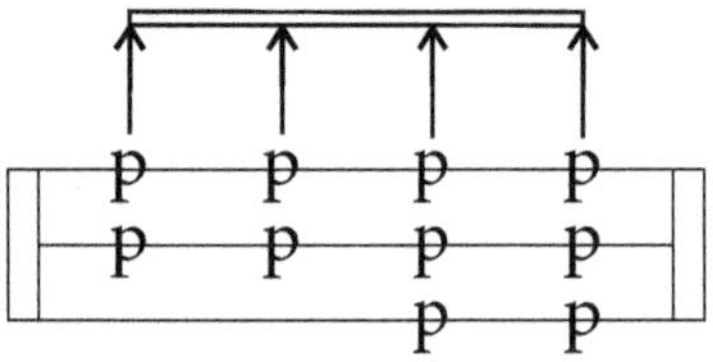

F3 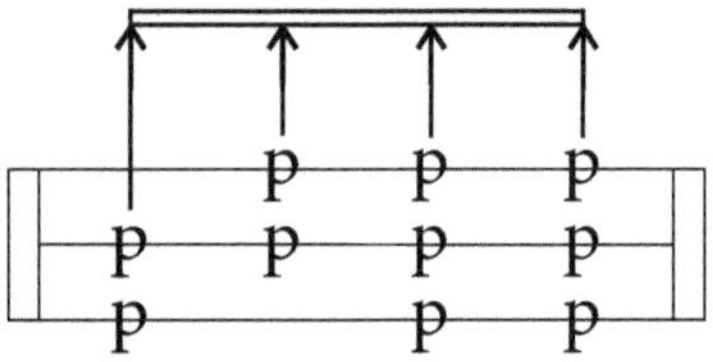

F4 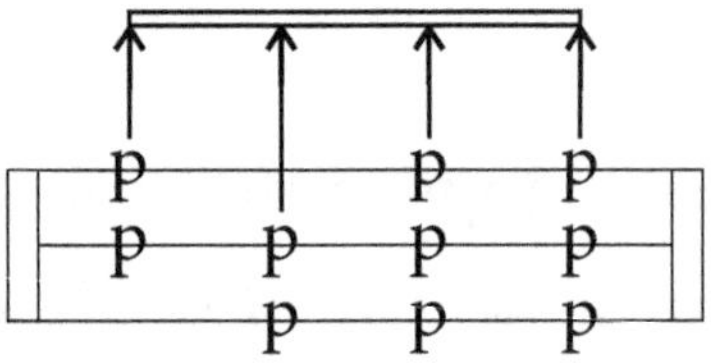

VARIATION II

F1 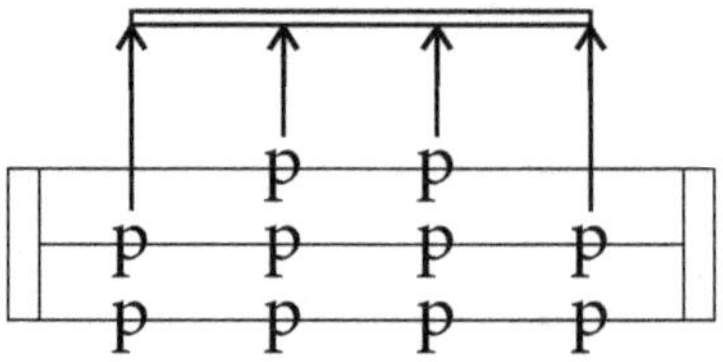

F2 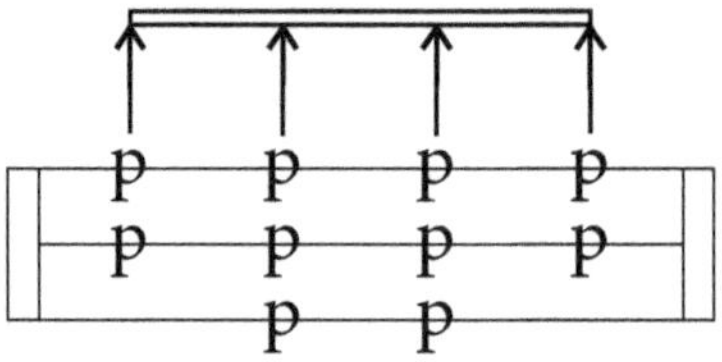

F3 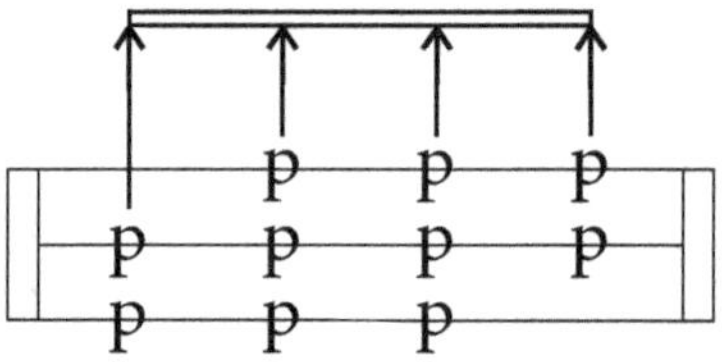

F4 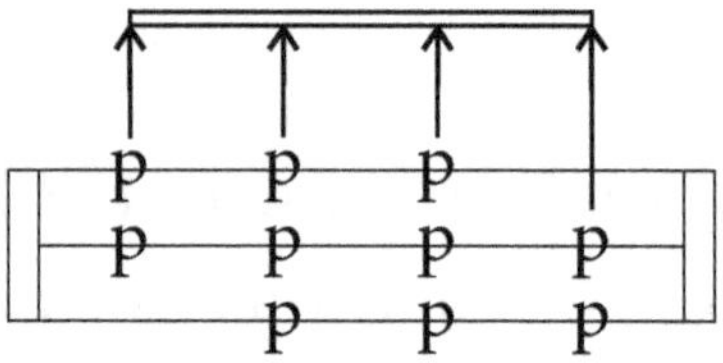

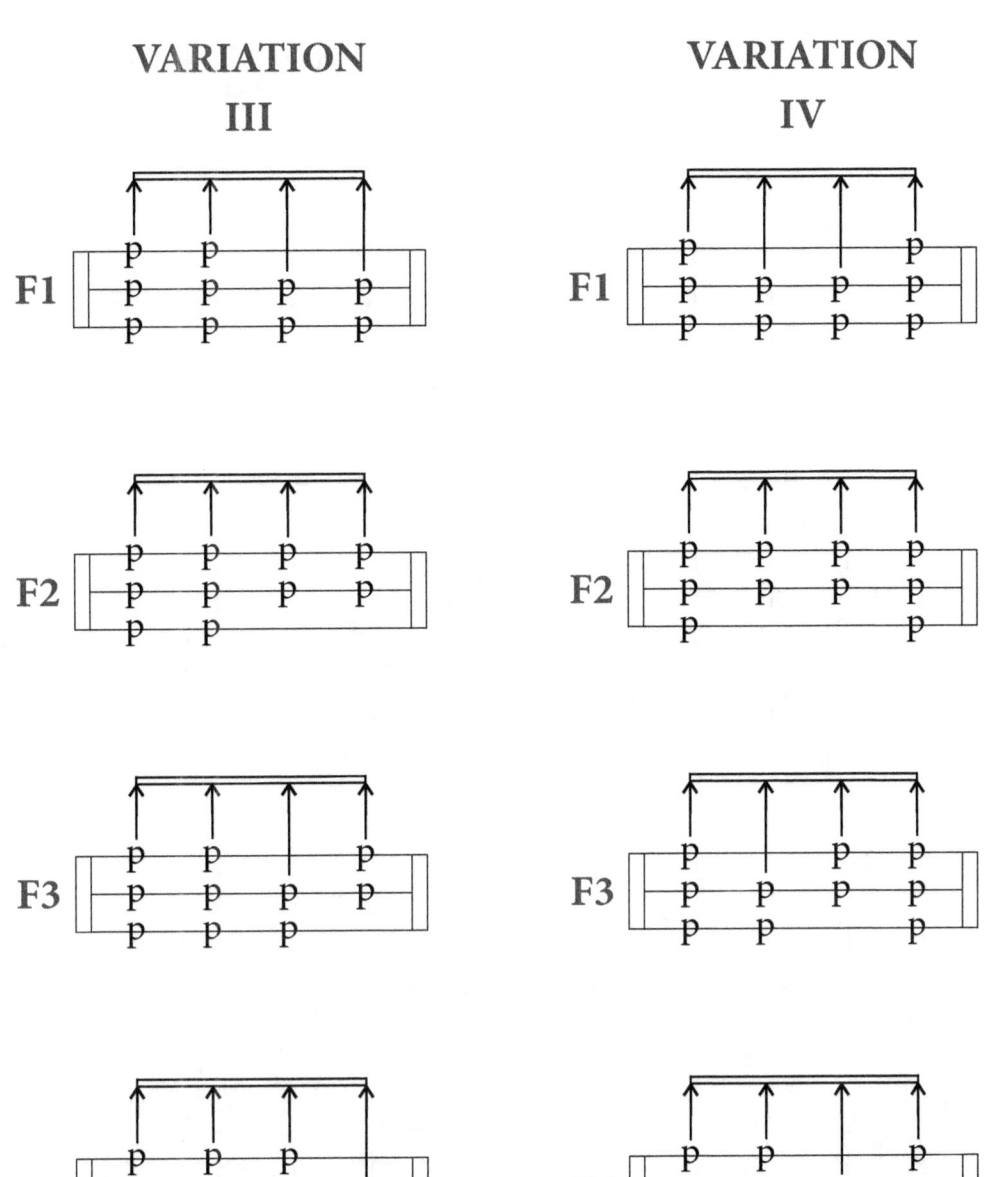

VARIATION V

F1

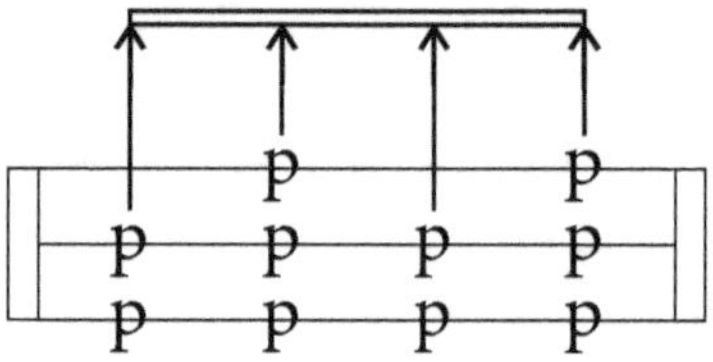

F2

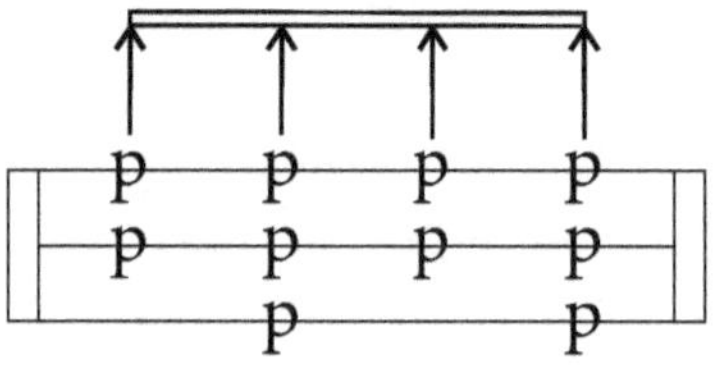

F3

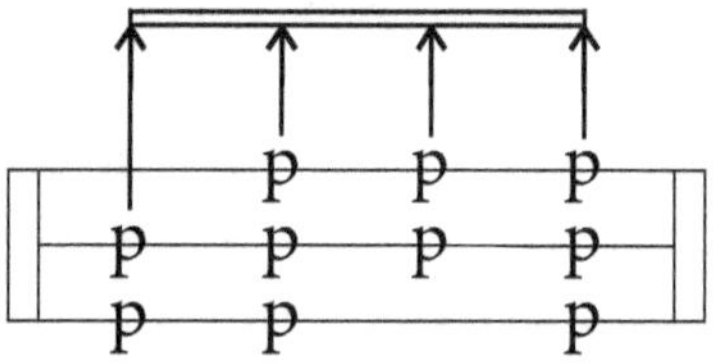

F4

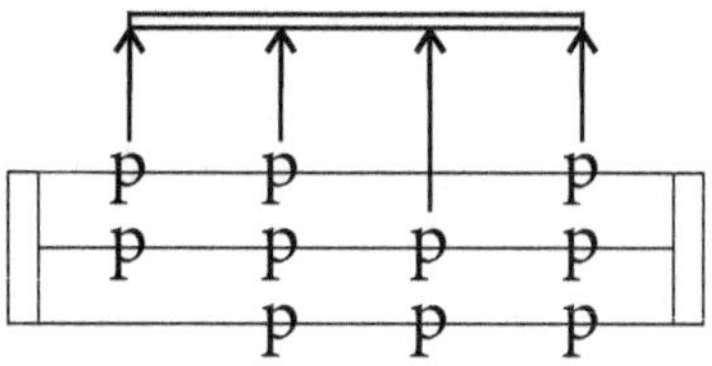

VARIATION VI

F1

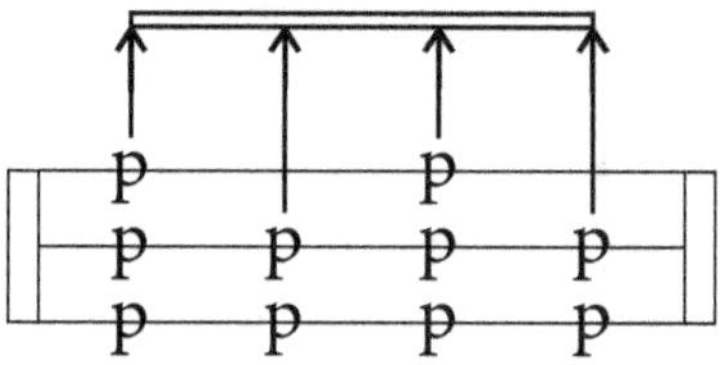

F2

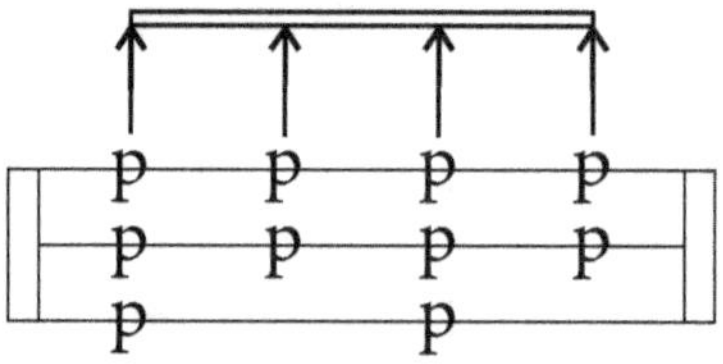

F3

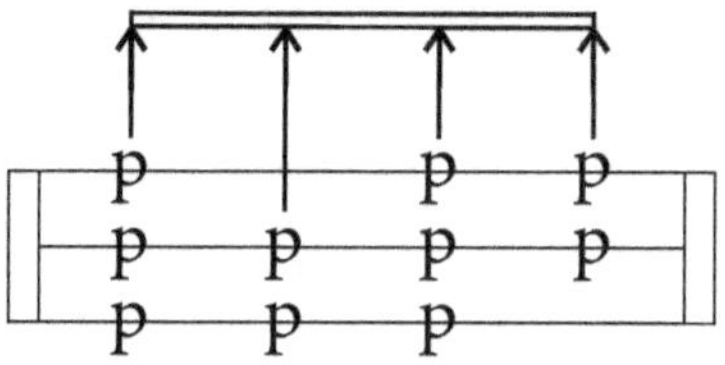

F4

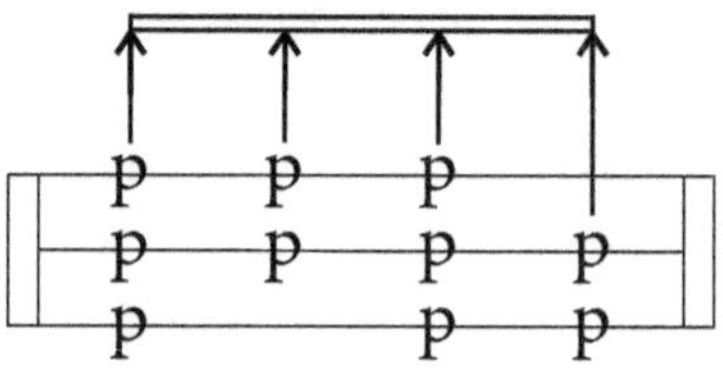

§ V

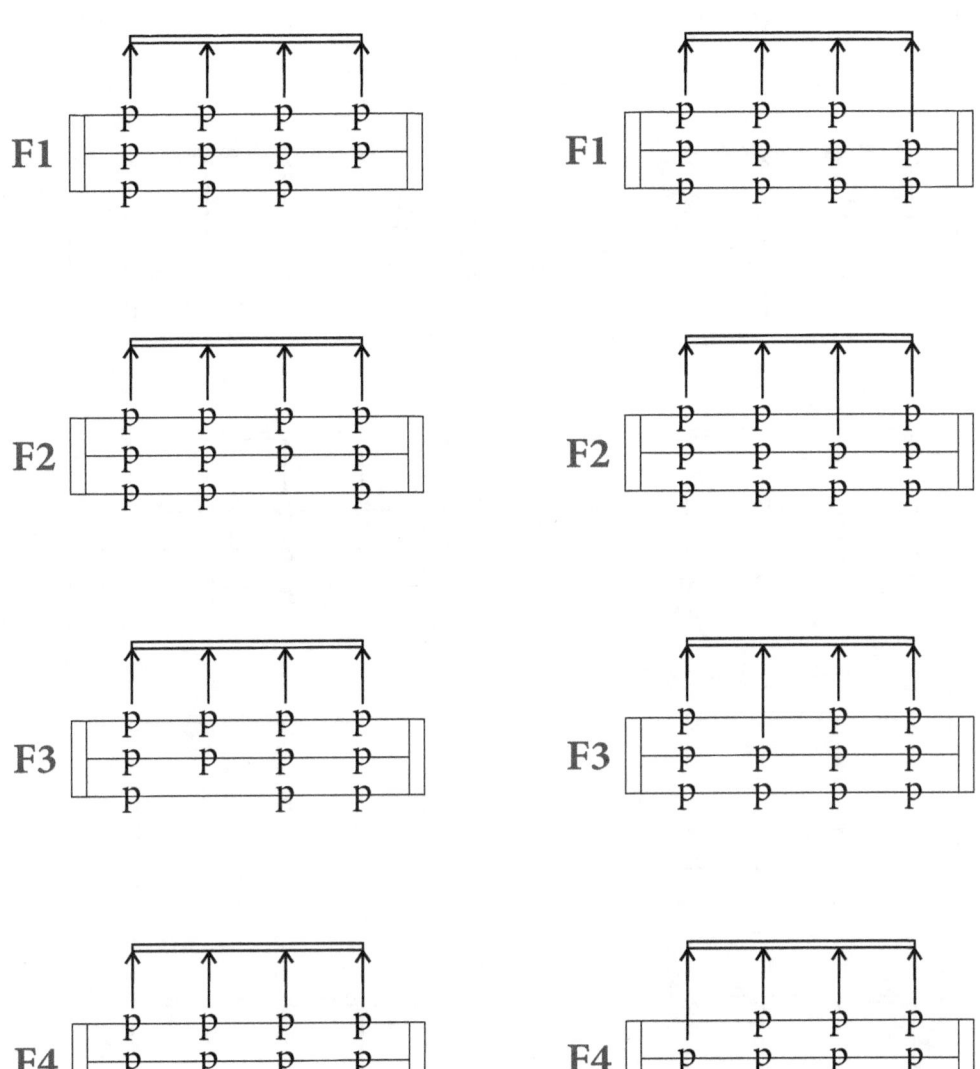

§ VI

VARIATION I

F1 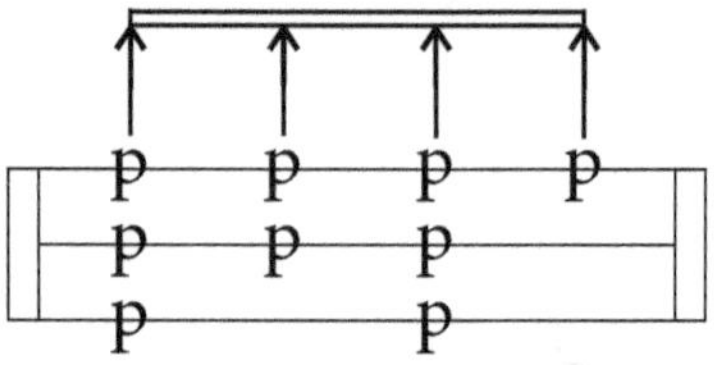

F2 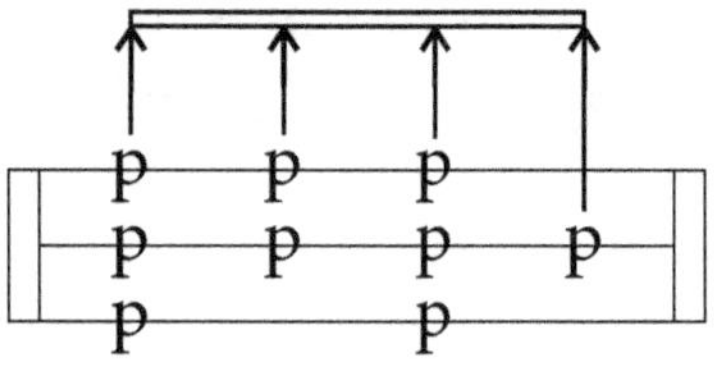

F3 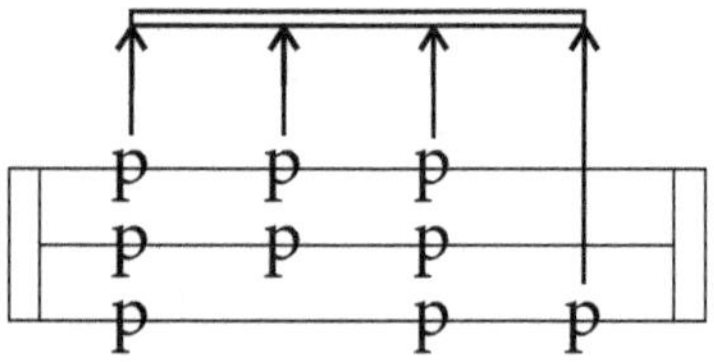

F4 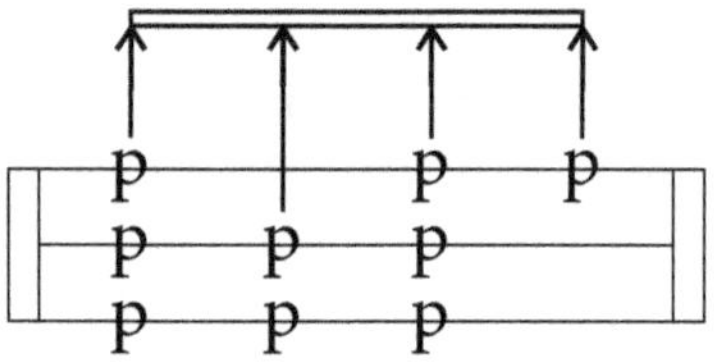

F5 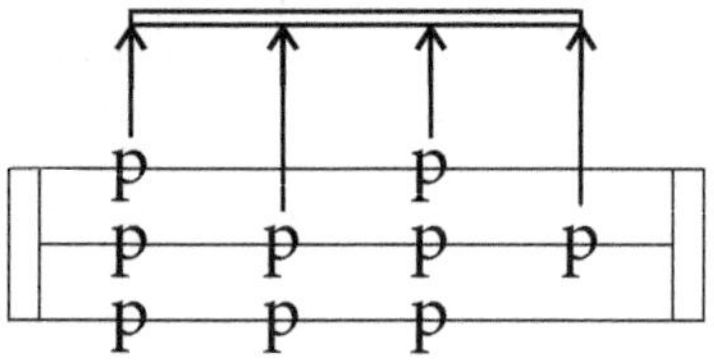

F6 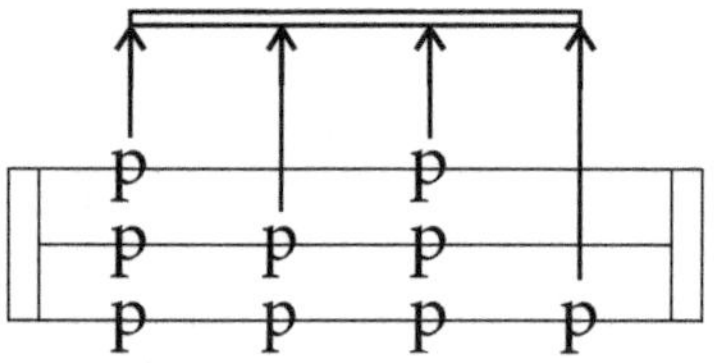

VARIATION II

F1 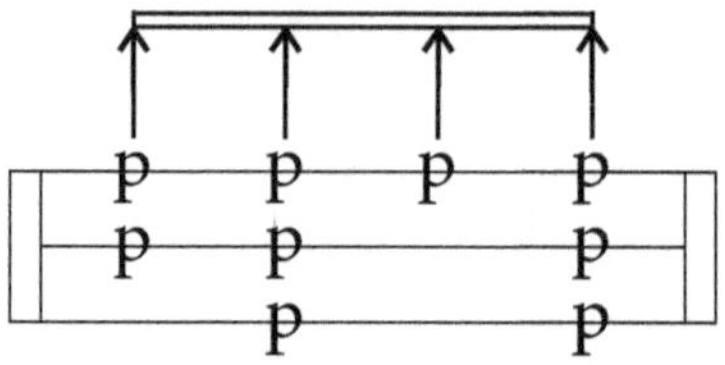

F2 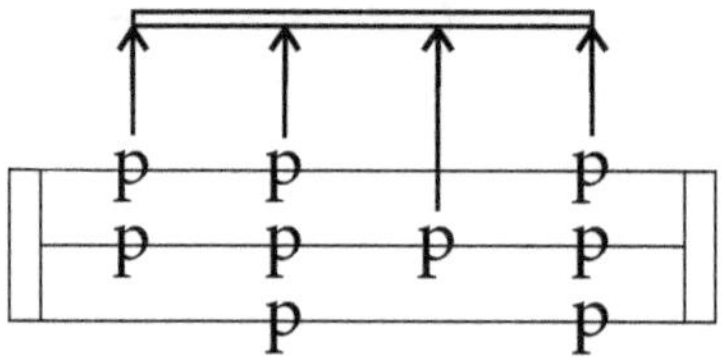

F3 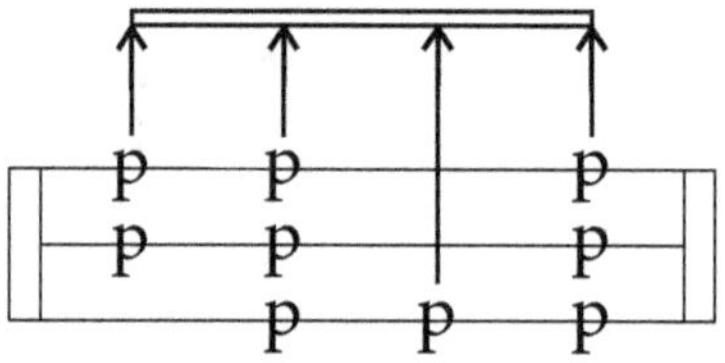

F4 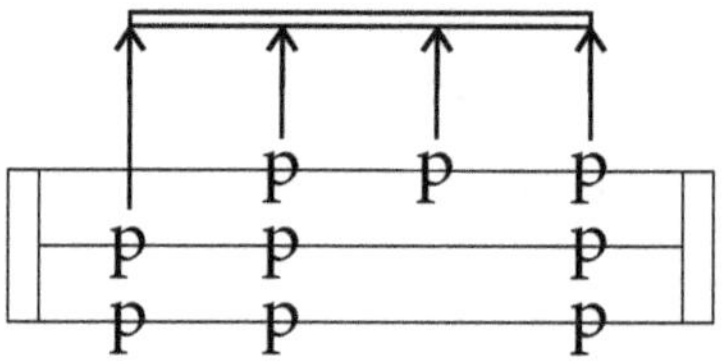

F5 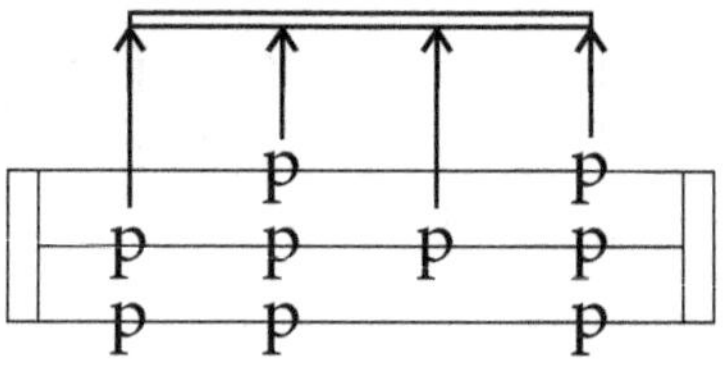

F6 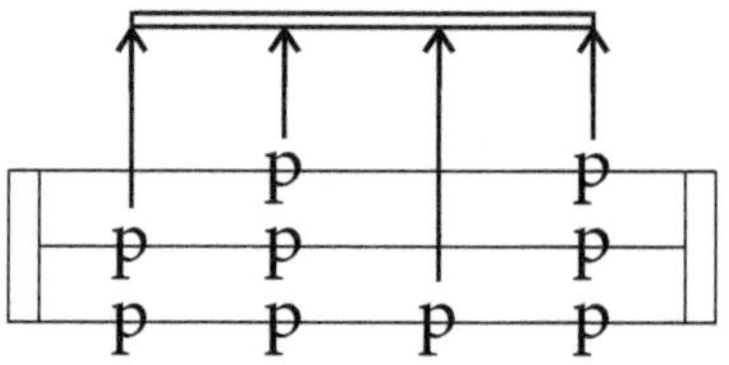

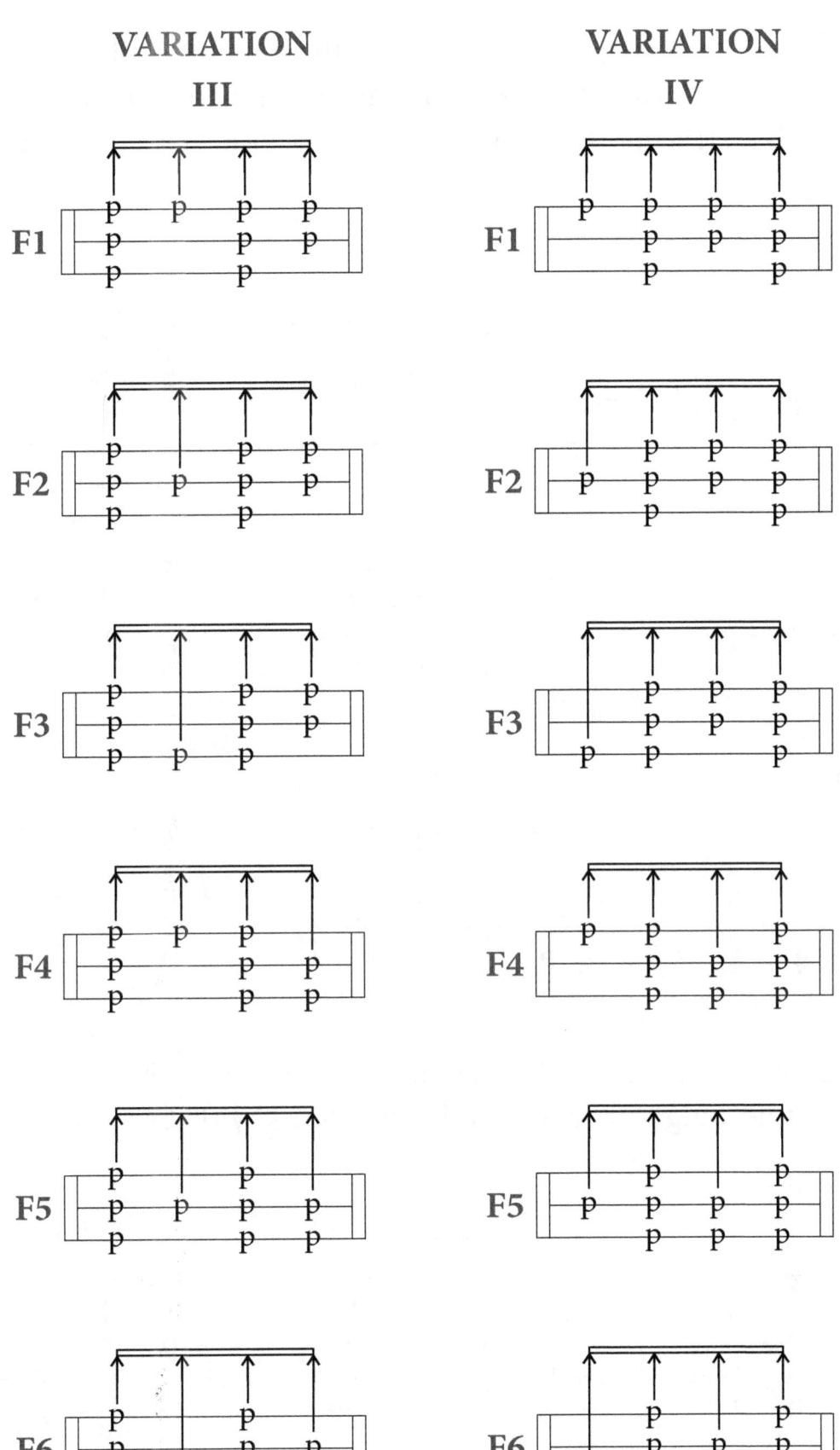

§ VII

Pulgar stroke of two single strings in sequence and of three strings simultaneously. Apart from the already mentioned performance way you can also practice by striking the pulgar towards one direction only (↑) downwards.

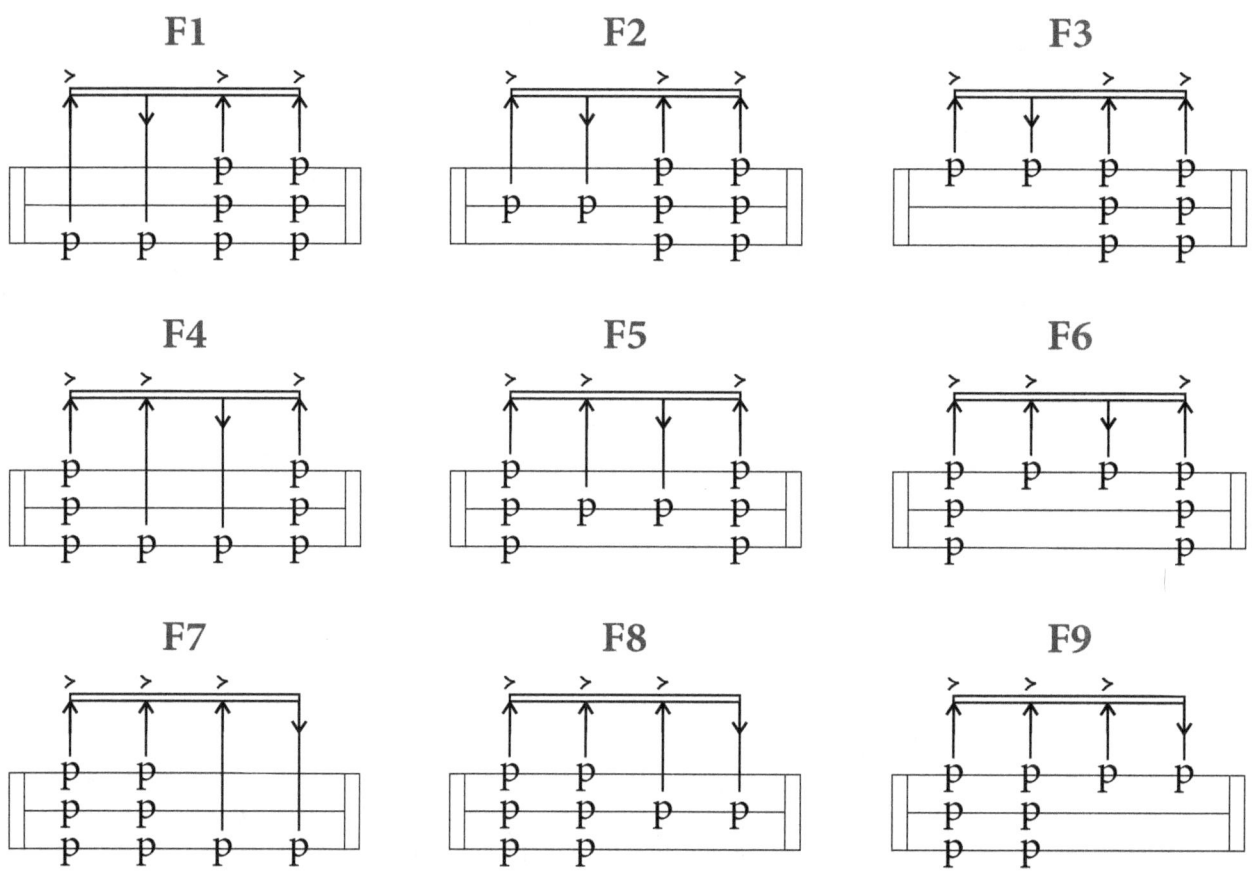

1. The strokes of one string and three strings are isochronous.
2. The two single pulgar strokes are isochronous with every three strings stroke.

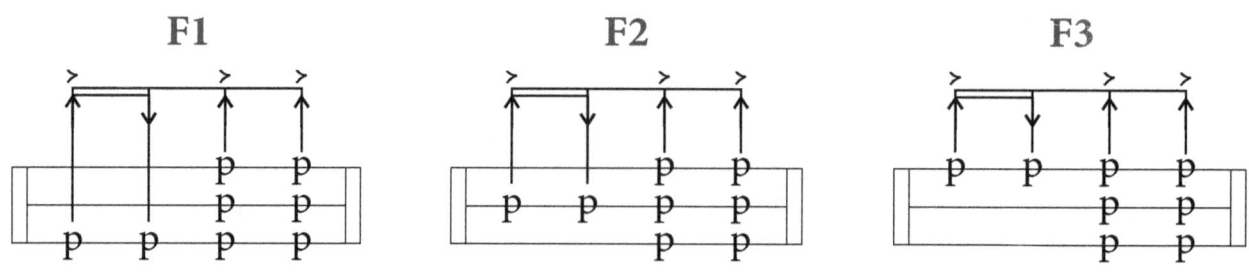

§ VIII

Combination of striking one triplet and three strings simultaneously within the Formula. Isochronous playing of the triplet and the three strings stroke. Depending on the direction of pulgar stroke, three variations of the exercise are formed.

VATIATION I

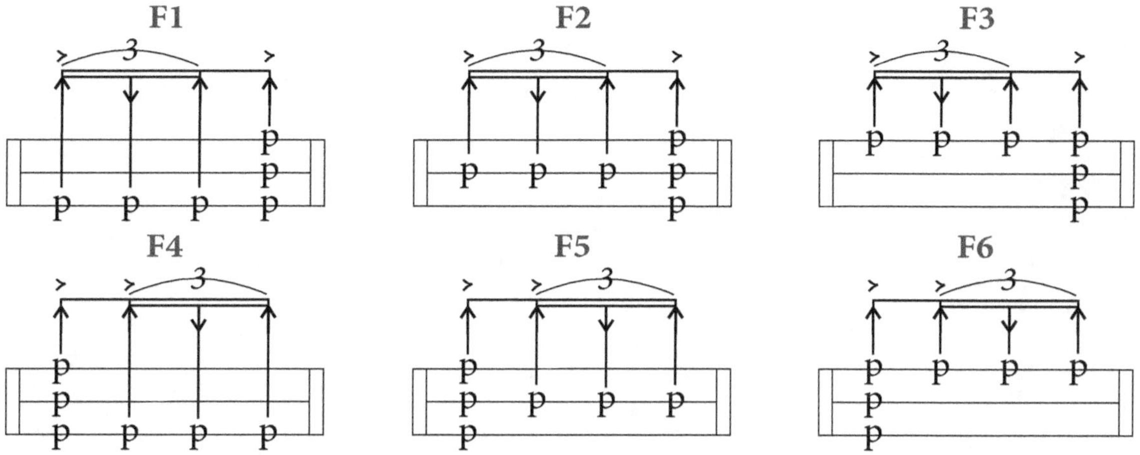

VARIATION II

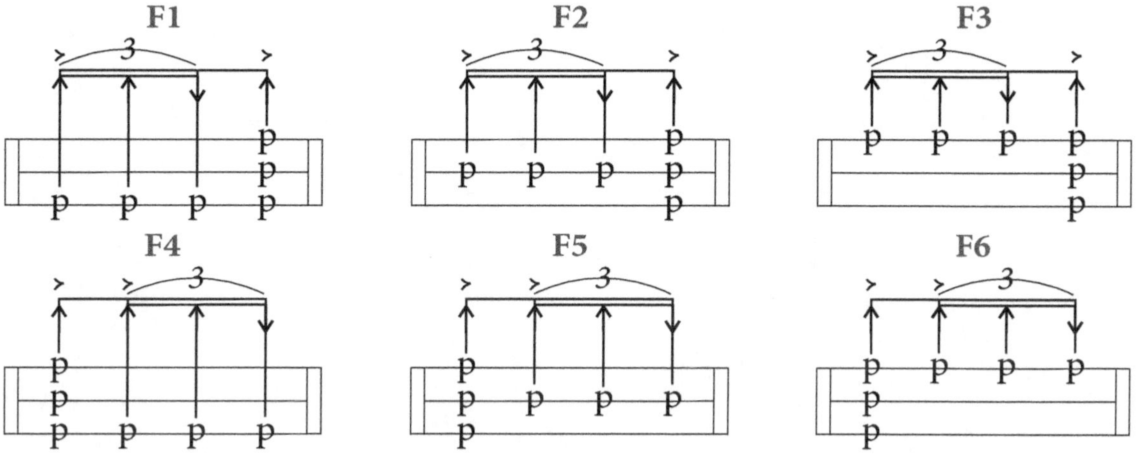

VARIATION III

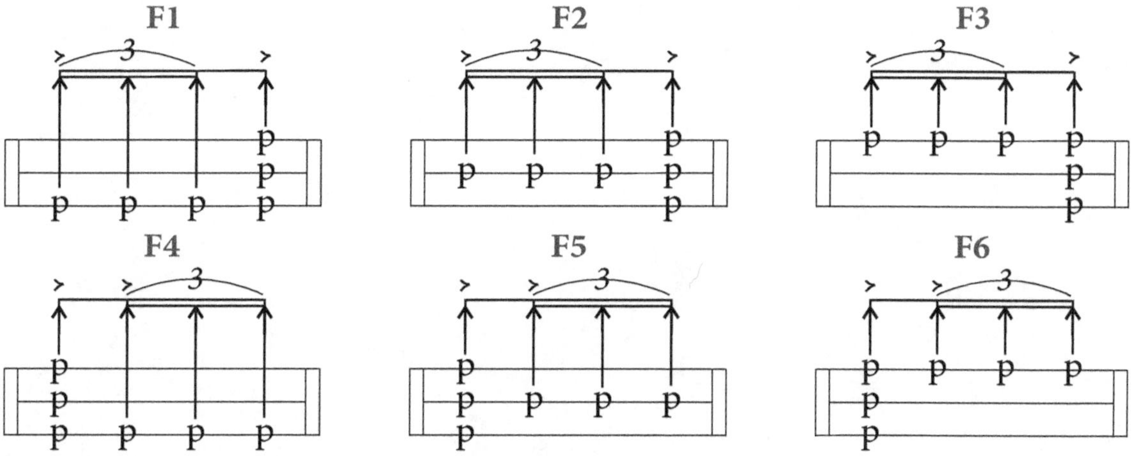

BOOK ON PULGAR

The book contains exercises either on the pulgar on its own or in combination with the fingers of the right hand of the index, middle or ring finger.

VOLUME I
PULGAR ONLY

VOLUME II
PULGAR ONLY

VOLUME III
Additional material on PULGAR
In combination with ARPEGGIOS

VOLUME IV
PULGAR in combination with
INDEX - MIDDLE - RING FINGER

About the Author

Angelo started his studies in 1971, at University Of Athens School Of Medicine in obstetrics and gynecology. Along his medical training and about the same time, he began formal studies in classical guitar at National Conservatory of Athens, Greece.

After successfully completing his medical and music studies, he began his career working as an obstetrician at Kalamata County Hospital, where he witnessed the delivery of hundreds of newborns. Later on, he successfully founded a privately owned medical clinic catered to the needs of the local community.

About 25 years ago Angelo's passion for music was rekindled when a family friend living in Spain, vacationing in Kalamata, introduced him to the unique rhythms and sounds of Flamenco.

Certainly, did not take long for him to completely fall head-over-heels with the music traditions of southern Spain communities of Andalusia, Extremadura and Murcia.

Early on, as a beginner, he struggled trying to locate teaching material and sources to augment his limited at that time knowledge of Flamenco guitar techniques and styles. He frantically searched to find books and lessons explaining these special techniques used in Rasgueados, Pulgar (Alzapua), Golpe and Tremolo. Nothing was available, nothing was organized.

Not be able to locate any Flamenco teaching material, Angelo started in the most amateur, coarse way to generate his own specific technique based exercises needed to develop skills and dexterity.

Decades-long research and effort went into this book and accompanied series in order to educate you in the most efficient, convenient and systematic way.

Organized and presented in current form, this material is guaranteed to satisfy the most demanding and widely possible Classical and Flamenco guitar audience committed in learning the most intricate details of these highly specialized guitar techniques.

Having faith that his work, book series and wearable devices will serve you well, Angelo looks forward in meeting and working with each of you, now and in the near future.

www.ingramcontent.com/pod-product-compliance
Lightning Source LLC
Chambersburg PA
CBHW080532300426
44111CB00017B/2690